Tolley's Capital Gains Tax 2000-01

by

David Smailes FCA
Kevin Walton BA (Hons)

Tolley Publishing

Published by Tolley
2 Addiscombe Road
Croydon CR9 5AF
England
Tel: 020–8686 9141

Typeset by
Interactive Sciences Ltd, Gloucester

Printed in Great Britain by The Bath Press, Bath

ISBN 0 75450 704–1

About This Book

This is the 23rd annual edition of Tolley's Capital Gains Tax, one of Tolley's principal Tax Reference Annuals. It includes the provisions of Finance Act 2000 as far as they concern capital gains tax and corporation tax on chargeable gains. It also includes all relevant case law, Revenue pronouncements and other information up to 1 July 2000. A summary of the relevant contents of *FA 2000* is included in Chapter 67.

The book includes the law and practice relating to capital gains tax and corporation tax on chargeable gains for at least six years (i.e. for 1994/95 onwards, and sometimes earlier) as well as the current year, and so provides comprehensive information for claims, late assessments etc. An index and tables of cases and statutes provide quick reference to the subject and to the legislation, and, in addition, the text is arranged into chapters alphabetically for ease of reference. Worked examples are included. Chapter 68 comprises a digest of relevant cases.

Comments and suggestions for improvement are always welcome.

TOLLEY PUBLISHING

Consolidation of Tax Enactments

With effect generally for 1992/93 and subsequent years of assessment (and for companies' accounting periods beginning after 5 April 1992) the *Taxes Acts* provisions relating to the taxation of chargeable gains are consolidated in the *Taxation of Chargeable Gains Act 1992 (TCGA 1992)*. The consolidation does not affect the application of the provisions concerned, but references to provisions which ceased to have effect before 6 April 1992 are omitted, as is the commencement date of the consolidated provisions (unless still relevant to the application of the current provisions).

Tolley's Capital Gains Tax 2000/01 continues, as in previous years, to set out the position for the six years prior to 2000/01, i.e. for 1994/95 to 1999/2000, but occasional references are still required to earlier years. In strictness, the legislation applicable to the years before 1992/93 etc. is that in force prior to the consolidation referred to above, and the Revenue (while acknowledging that 'on previous consolidation, inspectors, Commissioners and taxpayers alike got used to the new references in dealing with previous periods'), have indicated that claims etc. for those years should refer to the statute then applicable.

Accordingly, the approach which has been adopted to statutory references in this work is as follows.

(i) References to current legislation invariably quote the *TCGA 1992* reference in the familiar form, i.e. '*TCGA 1992, s XXX*' to identify a section thereof and '*TCGA 1992, Sch XX*' to identify a Schedule thereto. Remaining references to pre-consolidation legislation are in the same form. Where there has been no change in the legislation in the last six years, no statutory reference other than that for *TCGA 1992* is quoted.

(ii) Where the legislation has changed during the last six years, the earlier provisions continue to be described in the text, and the appropriate earlier statutory reference is quoted. Legislation current during those six years but now repealed is similarly dealt with. Where any part of the current legislation was introduced during those six years, the commencement date is quoted, but the statutory reference for that date is generally omitted.

(iii) Where a full pre-consolidation statutory reference is required, this may be obtained from Tolley's Capital Gains Tax 1991/92 or an earlier edition.

Contents

Contents

Notes

Sumption: Capital Gains Tax. Numerous references are made in the text to this looseleaf work published by Butterworth Tolley (enquiries 020–8662 2000, fax 020–8662 2012).

Years of Assessment run from 6 April. Thus '2000/01' or 'the year 2000/01' means the year from 6 April 2000 to 5 April 2001.

Inland Revenue explanatory publications may be obtained from local tax offices (except where otherwise stated, see list in Chapter 29) and are mostly free.

Retention of Tolley's. Subscribers should preserve each year's issue of 'Tolley's' because the necessity to include each year considerable new material involves the omission of some of the outdated matter.

Tolley's Income Tax 2000/01 is a comprehensive detailed guide to income tax and includes the provisions of the Finance Act 2000. £59.95.

Tolley's Corporation Tax 2000/01 is the companion publication to Tolley's Income Tax and is a comprehensive detailed guide to corporation tax and includes the provisions of the Finance Act 2000. £59.95.

Tolley's Inheritance Tax 2000/01 is a comprehensive detailed guide to inheritance tax and includes the provisions of the Finance Act 2000. £59.95.

Tolley's Tax Cases 2000 contains over 2,500 summaries of cases up to 1 January 2000 relevant to current legislation. £54.95.

Tolley's Tax Computations 2000/01 contains copious worked examples covering income tax, corporation tax, capital gains tax, inheritance tax and value added tax. £54.95.

Tolley's Income Tax, Corporation Tax and **Capital Gains Tax Workbooks 2000/01** contain comprehensive, clearly presented and up-to-date examples covering income tax, corporation tax and capital gains tax respectively. £21.95 each.

Butterworths Yellow Tax Handbook 2000/01 contains the text of the current legislation relating to income tax, corporation tax and capital gains tax, plus non-statutory material, and includes the Finance Act 2000. £POA.

Tolley's Practical Tax is a fortnightly newsletter, containing news, articles and items of practical use to all involved with UK tax. By subscription only.

Tolley's Roll-over, Hold-over and Retirement Reliefs (tenth edition) is a practical and comprehensive guide to the calculation and operation of some of the main capital gains tax reliefs, containing all the information required in one single reference work and including the provisions of the Finance Act 2000. £60.95.

Tolley's Tax Planning 2000/01 pinpoints clear, practical taxation strategies across the whole range of financial decision-making required of individuals, partnerships and corporate bodies. Two volumes £125.00.

Tolley's Estate Planning 2000/01 provides detailed guidance on how to formulate a plan for the provision, holding and transfer of personal and family resources at the lowest tax cost. £57.95.

Tolley's UK Taxation of Trusts (tenth edition) is written by specialists in the field to provide a detailed explanation of the impact of income tax, capital gains tax and inheritance tax on the various types of trusts, including chapters covering the UK taxation of offshore trusts, and including the provisions of the Finance Act 2000. £60.95.

Tolley's Self-Assessment 2000/01 (seventh edition) is the definitive work on self-assessment and the current year basis of assessment for businesses, and includes the provisions of the Finance Act 2000. £58.95.

Abbreviations and References

ABBREVIATIONS

A-G	Attorney-General.
BES	Business Expansion Scheme.
CA	Court of Appeal.
CAA	Capital Allowances Act.
CCA	Court of Criminal Appeal.
CCAB	Consultative Committee of Accountancy Bodies.
CES	Court of Exchequer (Scotland).
Cf.	compare.
CGT	Capital Gains Tax.
CGTA	Capital Gains Tax Act.
CJEC	Court of Justice of the European Communities.
Ch D	Chancery Division.
CIR	Commissioners of Inland Revenue ('the Board' or 'the Revenue').
Commrs	Commissioners of Income Tax (General or Special).
EC	European Community.
EIS	Enterprise Investment Scheme.
ESC	Inland Revenue Extra-Statutory Concession.
EU	European Union.
Ex D	Exchequer Division (now part of Chancery Division).
FA	Finance Act.
Fam D	Family Division (formerly Probate, Divorce and Admiralty Division).
HC	House of Commons.
HL	House of Lords.
I	Ireland.
ICAEW	Institute of Chartered Accountants in England and Wales.
ICTA	Income and Corporation Taxes Act.
IHT	Inheritance Tax.
IHTA	Inheritance Tax Act.
ISA	Individual Savings Account.
KB	King's Bench Division.
NI	Northern Ireland.
PC	Privy Council.
PDA	Probate, Divorce and Admiralty Division (now Family Division).
PEP	Personal Equity Plan.
QB	Queen's Bench Division.
R	Regina or Rex (i.e. The Crown).
Reg	Regulation.
RPI	Retail Prices Index.
s	Section.
SC(I)	Supreme Court (Ireland).
SCS	Scottish Court of Session.
Sch	Schedule.
SI	Statutory Instrument.
SP	Inland Revenue Statement of Practice.
Sp C	Special Commissioners.
TCGA	Taxation of Chargeable Gains Act.
TMA	Taxes Management Act.

Abbreviations and References

REFERENCES (*denotes a series accredited for citation in court).

All E R	All England Law Reports (Butterworths, Halsbury House, 35 Chancery Lane, London WC2A 1EL).
AC	*Law Reports, Appeal Cases (Incorporated Council of Law Reporting for England and Wales, 3 Stone Buildings, Lincoln's Inn, London, WC2A 3XN).
ATC	*Annotated Tax Cases (publication discontinued).
Ch	*Law Reports, Chancery Division.
CMLR	Common Market Law Reports.
Ex D	*Law Reports, Exchequer Division (1875–1880; see also below).
Fam D	*Law Reports, Family Division.
KB	*Law Reports, King's Bench Division (1900–1952).
IR	*Irish Reports (Law Reporting Council, Law Library, Four Courts, Dublin).
ITC	*Irish Tax Cases (Government Publications, 1 and 3 G.P.O. Arcade, Dublin 1).
LR Ex	*Law Reports, Exchequer Division (1865–1875; see also above).
NILR	Northern Ireland Law Reports.
[Year] QB	*Law Reports, Queen's Bench Division (1891–1901 and 1952 onwards).
QBD	Law Reports, Queen's Bench Division (1875–1890).
SLT	Scots Law Times.
Sp C	Special Commissioner's Decisions (Tax Tribunals, 15–19 Bedford Avenue, London, WC1B 3AS).
SSCD	Simon's Tax Cases—Special Commissioners' Decisions (Butterworths).
STC	Simon's Tax Cases (Butterworths).
STI	Simon's Tax Intelligence (Butterworths).
TC	*Official Reports of Tax Cases (The Stationery Office, P.O. Box 276, London, SW8 5DT).
TR	Taxation Reports (publication discontinued).
WLR	*Weekly Law Reports (Incorporated Council of Law Reporting above).

The first number in the citation refers to the volume, and the second to the page, so that *[1978] 2 WLR 10* means that the report is to be found on page ten of the second volume of the Weekly Law Reports for 1978. Where no volume number is given, only one volume was produced in that year. Some series have continuous volume numbers.

Where legal decisions are very recent and in the lower courts, it must be remembered that they may be reversed on appeal. However, references to the official Tax Cases ('*TC*'), and to the Appeal Cases ('*AC*') may be taken as final.

In English cases, Scottish and Northern Irish decisions (unless there is a difference of law between the countries) are generally followed but are not binding, and Republic of Ireland decisions are considered (and vice versa).

Acts of Parliament, Command Papers, 'Hansard' Parliamentary Reports and Statutory Instruments (SI) are obtainable from The Stationery Office, (bookshops at 49 High Holborn, London, WC1V 6HB and elsewhere; orders to P.O. Box 276, London, SW8 5DT). Fax orders should be made to 020–7873 8200. General enquiries should be made to 020–7873 0011. Telephone orders should be made to 020–7873 9090. **Hansard** (referred to as HC Official Report or H L Official Report) references are to daily issues and do not always correspond to the columns in the bound editions. **N.B.** Statements in the House, while useful as indicating the intention of enactments, have no legal authority except in the limited circumstances mentioned in 4.9 APPEALS.

1 Introduction

1.1 GENERAL

Capital gains tax (CGT) was introduced by the *Finance Act 1965* and commenced on 6 April 1965. It relates to chargeable gains in a 'year of assessment' accruing to individuals, personal representatives and trustees. '*Year of assessment*' is a year ending on 5 April. Thus '2000/01' indicates the year of assessment, otherwise known as the tax year, ending on 5 April 2001 (and so on). [*TCGA 1992, s 288(1)*]. For the position of companies (and other bodies), see 1.2 below.

The legislation was consolidated by the *Capital Gains Tax Act 1979* and subsequently by the *Taxation of Chargeable Gains Act 1992. TCGA 1992* has effect in relation to CGT for 1992/93 and subsequent years of assessment, to corporation tax for accounting periods beginning after 5 April 1992 and to certain other tax purposes after 5 April 1992. [*TCGA 1992, ss 289–291*].

An allowance, known as the indexation allowance (see 26 INDEXATION), was introduced by the *Finance Act 1982* with the intention of adjusting for the effects of inflation (but see below for changes made by *Finance Act 1998*). The provisions for it were substantially modified by the *Finance Act 1985* but such modifications were largely removed by the *Finance Act 1994*. Subject to this, a gain is computed by reference to the excess of the disposal (or deemed disposal) consideration over the acquisition (or deemed acquisition) consideration, received and given, for an asset (see 17 DISPOSAL).

Major changes in the scope of the tax were introduced by the *Finance Act 1988*. The original base date of 6 April 1965 was replaced by 31 March 1982 subject to the detailed provisions of 8 ASSETS HELD ON 31 MARCH 1982.

The *Finance Act 1988* also introduced rates of tax for 1988/89 and subsequent years that, in broad terms, are equivalent to the rates of income tax that would apply if gains were treated as the top slice of taxable income (but see below for changes made by *Finance Act 1999*). Before 1988/89, tax was charged at a rate of 30%. See 2 ANNUAL RATES AND EXEMPTIONS.

Self-assessment, introduced by *Finance Act 1994* and subsequent provisions of further Finance Acts, generally has effect for 1996/97 onwards (for CGT) and for company accounting periods ending on or after 1 July 1999 (for corporation tax), see 56 SELF-ASSESSMENT.

For CGT purposes, indexation allowance was frozen at its April 1998 level by *Finance Act 1998*. Assets acquired after 31 March 1998 do not attract indexation allowance at all. See 26 INDEXATION. For disposals after 5 April 1998, the allowance is replaced by a taper relief whereby a chargeable gain is progressively reduced according to the length of time the asset has been held, with more generous reductions for business assets (as defined) than for other assets (see 60 TAPER RELIEF). These changes do *not* apply for the purposes of corporation tax on chargeable gains.

A further change in the rates of CGT was made by *Finance Act 1999*. For 1999/2000, except to the extent that gains (if treated as the top slice of income) exceed the basic rate limit (in which case they are chargeable at a rate equivalent to the higher rate of income tax), CGT is charged at a rate equivalent to the lower rate of income tax. This continues for 2000/01 onwards, and in addition the 10% starting rate for income tax also applies for CGT where gains fall within the starting rate band. See 2.1 ANNUAL RATES AND EXEMPTIONS.

1.2 **THE CHARGE TO TAX**

Subject to exceptions and special provisions, a person is chargeable to capital gains tax in respect of chargeable gains accruing to him in a year of assessment during any part of which he is resident in the UK, or during which he is ordinarily resident in the UK. [*TCGA 1992, s 1, s 2(1)*].

Special rules apply to persons not resident or individuals not domiciled in the UK, to temporary visitors to the UK and to persons becoming temporarily non-UK resident. See 43 OFFSHORE SETTLEMENTS, 44 OVERSEAS MATTERS, 51 REMITTANCE BASIS and 52 RESIDENCE AND DOMICILE.

For 1990/91 and subsequent years, married persons are taxed independently. Transfers between spouses living together are made on a 'no gain, no loss' basis. See 41 MARRIED PERSONS.

Persons may be assessed in a representative capacity. See 5 ASSESSMENTS, 11 CHILDREN, 16 DEATH, 56 SELF-ASSESSMENT and 57 SETTLEMENTS.

There are special rules for UK resident or ordinarily resident shareholders of certain overseas resident companies. See 44.6 OVERSEAS MATTERS. See 43 OFFSHORE SETTLEMENTS for the provisions applying to trustees, settlors and beneficiaries of settlements which are or become overseas resident.

Companies and other corporate bodies within the scope of corporation tax are not chargeable to capital gains tax. The chargeable gains of such bodies are assessed to corporation tax. The computation of their gains is in accordance with the general principles applying for capital gains tax contained in *TCGA 1992* and subsequent legislation which is to be construed as one with it. In addition, *TCGA 1992* contains further provisions relating to corporation tax on chargeable gains. Previously these provisions had not been included within *CGTA 1979* but had been contained within the *Income and Corporation Taxes Acts 1970* and *1988*. Assessments on companies are made by reference to accounting periods instead of years of assessment. Although *TCGA 1992, s 2(1)* refers to a 'person' (i.e. including a company) and ordinary residence, the key factor in charging companies is residence in the UK. See 13 COMPANIES, 44.7 OVERSEAS MATTERS, and 52.6 RESIDENCE AND DOMICILE.

For unit and investment trusts and open-ended investment companies, see 64 UNIT TRUSTS ETC. For venture capital trusts, see 65.8 VENTURE CAPITAL TRUSTS.

See TOLLEY'S CORPORATION TAX under Friendly Societies and Life Insurance Companies for provisions of *TCGA 1992* (and related provisions) which are integral with the corporation tax regime applicable to life assurance business carried on by such entities.

TCGA 1992, ss 194–198, which deal with matters relating to oil exploration taxed under the *Oil Taxation Act 1975* and in practice apply mainly to companies, are not dealt with in this book.

2 Annual Rates and Exemptions

Cross-reference. See 13.3 COMPANIES as regards the rate of corporation tax in respect of chargeable gains.

2.1 RATES OF TAX — INDIVIDUALS

1999/2000 and subsequent years. Subject to the provisions below, the rate of capital gains tax applicable to an individual for 1999/2000 and subsequent years of assessment is equivalent to the lower rate of income tax for the year. [*TCGA 1992, s 4(1); FA 1999, s 26(2)(6)*]. For 1999/2000 and 2000/01, this rate is **20%**. [*ICTA 1988, s 1A(1B); FA 1999, s 22(7)(a)*].

For 1999/2000 only, the starting rate for income tax does not apply for capital gains tax purposes. For 2000/01 and subsequent years, the starting rate does so apply to the extent that taxable gains, if treated as though they were the top slice of taxable income, fall within the starting rate band. [*TCGA 1992, s 4(1AB)(1AC); FA 2000, s 37*]. For 2000/01 the starting rate is **10%** and the starting rate band applies to the first **£1,520** of taxable income and gains. [*ICTA 1988, s 1; FA 2000, s 31; SI 2000 No 806*].

If income tax is chargeable at the higher rate (or Schedule F upper rate) in respect of any part of an individual's income for a year of assessment, the rate of capital gains tax is equivalent to the higher rate. If no income tax is chargeable at the higher rate (or Schedule F upper rate) in respect of his income, but the amount on which he is chargeable to capital gains tax exceeds the unused part of his basic rate band, the rate of capital gains tax on the excess is equivalent to the higher rate of income tax for the year. The unused part of an individual's basic rate band is the amount by which the basic rate limit exceeds his total income (as reduced by any statutory deductions, e.g. the personal allowance). [*TCGA 1992, s 4(2)(3)(4); F(No 2)A 1997, Sch 4 para 24(2)(3)(6); FA 1999, s 26(5)(6)*]. For 1999/2000 and 2000/01, the higher rate of income tax is **40%**. [*FA 1999, s 23; FA 2000, s 31*]. For 2000/01 the basic rate limit is **£28,400**; for 1999/2000 it is £28,000. [*ICTA 1988, s 1; SI 1999 No 597; SI 2000 No 806*]. (The Schedule F upper rate is the special higher rate applicable to dividend income in excess of the basic rate limit — see TOLLEY'S INCOME TAX.)

Example

Emile, a single man under 65, owns an established business and has taxable profits of £22,500 for his accounting year ended 31 March 2001. In 2000/01, he receives building society interest of £3,200 (net of tax) and dividends of £4,500. He also has chargeable gains of £10,600 (after losses and taper relief but before deducting the annual exemption). His income tax and capital gains tax liabilities for 2000/01 are computed as follows.

	£	£
Income tax payable:		
Schedule D, Case I		22,500
Building society interest	3,200	
Tax deducted £3,200 x $\frac{20}{80}$	800	4,000
Carried forward		£26,500

		£	£
Brought forward			26,500
Dividends		4,500	
Tax credit $\frac{1}{9}$		500	5,000
Total income			31,500
Deduct Personal allowance			4,385
Taxable income			£27,115
	£	£	£
	1,520 @ 10% (starting rate)		152.00
	16,595 @ 22% (basic rate)		3,650.90
	4,000 @ 20% (savings rate)		800.00
	5,000 @ 10% (Schedule F rate)		500.00
	27,115		5,102.90
Deduct	Tax on savings income (20%)	800.00	
	Tax credit on dividend income (10%)	500.00	1,300.00
Net income tax liability			£3,802.90

Unused basic rate band = £1,285 (£28,400 – £27,115)

		£
Capital gains tax payable:		
Chargeable gains		10,600
Deduct Annual exemption (see 2.5 below)		7,200
Taxable gains		£3,400
	£	
	1,285 @ 20% (lower rate)	257.00
	2,115 @ 40% (higher rate)	846.00
	3,400	£1,103.00

Where for any year of assessment

(*a*) under *ICTA 1988, s 549(2)* (gains under life policy or life annuity contract), a deduction of an amount is made from a person's total income for the purposes of excess liability, or

(*b*) under *ICTA 1988, s 699(1)* (income accruing before death) the residuary income of an estate is treated as reduced so as to reduce a person's income by any amount for those purposes,

the ascertainment of the unused part of the basic rate band referred to above has effect as if his income for the year were reduced by that amount. [*TCGA 1992, s 6(2); FA 1995, Sch 29 Pt VIII(8)*].

Where under *ICTA 1988, s 547(1)(a)* (gains from insurance policies etc.) a person's total income for a year of assessment is deemed to include any amount(s),

(i) the ascertainment of the unused part of the basic rate band referred to above has effect as if his total income included not the whole of the amount(s) concerned but only the appropriate fraction within the meaning of *ICTA 1988, s 550(3)*, and

(ii) if relief is given under *ICTA 1988, s 550* and the calculation required by *section 550(2)(b)* does not involve the higher rate of tax, the ascertainment of the rate of tax applicable under *TCGA 1992, s 4* above is to have effect as if no income tax were chargeable at the higher rate (or the Schedule F upper rate) in respect of his income.

[*TCGA 1992, s 6(3); F(No 2)A 1997, Sch 4 para 25*].

Nothing in *TCGA 1992, s 6(2)(3)* above is to be taken to increase the amount of a deduction which a person is entitled to make from his total income under any provision of *ICTA 1988, Pt VII Ch I* (personal reliefs) which limits any allowance by reference to the level of total income. [*TCGA 1992, s 6(4)*].

See TOLLEY'S INCOME TAX for the income tax provisions mentioned above.

2.2 **1988/89 to 1998/99 inclusive.** Subject to the further provisions below, the rate of capital gains tax applicable to an individual for 1988/89 to 1998/99 inclusive is equivalent to the basic rate of income tax for the year. For 1997/98 and 1998/99, this rate is 23%. For 1988/89 to 1995/96 inclusive, this rate is 25% and for 1996/97 it is 24%. [*TCGA 1992, s 4(1); ICTA 1988, s 1; FA 1988, s 23; FA 1989, s 30(1); FA 1990, s 17(1); FA 1991, s 21(1); FA 1992, s 10(1)(b); FA 1993, s 51(1)(b); FA 1994, s 75(1)(b); FA 1995, s 35(1)(b); FA 1996, s 72(1)(b); FA 1997, s 54(1)(b); FA 1998, s 25*].

If income tax is chargeable at the higher rate in respect of any part of an individual's income for a year of assessment, the rate of capital gains tax is equivalent to the higher rate. [*TCGA 1992, s 4(2); F(No 2)A 1997, Sch 4 para 24(1)(2)(6)*]. If no income tax is chargeable at the higher rate in respect of his income, but the amount on which he is chargeable to capital gains tax exceeds 'the unused part of his basic rate band', the rate of capital gains tax on the excess is equivalent to the higher rate of income tax for the year. [*TCGA 1992, s 4(3); F(No 2)A 1997, Sch 4 para 24(1)(3)(6)*].

'*The unused part of an individual's basic rate band*' is the amount by which (ignoring any reduction made under *TCGA 1992, s 4(3B)(a)* below) the basic rate limit exceeds his total income (as reduced by any deductions made under the *Income Tax Acts*). [*TCGA 1992, s 4(4); FA 1993, s 79, Sch 6 para 22(2)*].

For 1988/89 to 1998/99 inclusive the higher rate of income tax is 40%.

For 1998/99 the basic rate limit is £27,100; for 1997/98 it is £26,100; for 1996/97 it is £25,500; for 1995/96 it is £24,300 and for 1991/92 to 1994/95 inclusive it is £23,700; for 1989/90 and 1990/91 it is £20,700; and for 1988/89 it is £19,300.

[*ICTA 1988, s 1; FA 1988, s 24(1)(2); SI 1989 No 167; FA 1989, s 30(2); FA 1990, s 17(1); FA 1991, s 21(1); FA 1992, s 10(1)(c), (2); FA 1993, s 51(1)(c), (2)(b); FA 1994, s 75(1)(c), (2)(b); SI 1994 No 3012; FA 1995, s 35(1)(c); FA 1996, s 72(1)(c), (2)(b); FA 1997, s 54(1)(c); SI 1998 No 755; FA 1998, s 25*].

For 1992/93 to 1998/99 inclusive, if an individual's income is such that there is an unused part (including the whole) of his lower rate band (i.e. the amount by which the lower rate limit exceeds his total income after this income has been reduced by any deductions made under the *Income Tax Acts*), then if the amount on which he is chargeable to capital gains tax exceeds the amount of that unused part, the rate of capital gains tax on that part of the amount chargeable to capital gains tax as corresponds to the amount of the unused part of the lower rate band is equivalent to the lower rate. Where there is no such excess, the rate of capital gains tax applying to all of the amount chargeable to capital gains tax is equivalent to the lower rate. [*TCGA 1992, s 4(1A)(1B); F(No 2)A 1992, s 23(1)(3); FA 1999, s 26(4)(6)*].

For 1992/93 to 1998/99 inclusive, the lower rate is 20%.

2.2 Annual Rates and Exemptions

For 1998/99 the lower rate limit is £4,300; for 1997/98 it is £4,100; for 1996/97 it is £3,900; for 1995/96 it is £3,200; for 1994/95 it is £3,000, for 1993/94 it is £2,500 and for 1992/93 it is £2,000.

[*ICTA 1988, s 1; FA 1992, s 9, s 10(1)(a); FA 1993, s 51(1)(a), (2)(a); FA 1994, s 75(1)(a), (2)(a); FA 1995, s 35(1)(a), (2); FA 1996, s 72(1)(a), (2)(a); FA 1997, s 54(1)(a); SI 1998 No 755; FA 1998, s 25*].

In effect, therefore, but with one exception applying for 1993/94 to 1998/99 inclusive, an individual's chargeable gains are taxed as if they constituted the top slice of taxable income. In addition, where an income tax relief is given by way of a reduction in income tax liability rather than by way of reduction of total income (e.g. for 1994/95 and subsequent years, married couple's allowance, certain interest payable (see further below for years before 1994/95), medical insurance premiums and enterprise investment scheme relief), the reduction in income tax liability has no effect on the marginal rate of capital gains tax.

The exception mentioned above relates to 1993/94 to 1998/99 inclusive when, in determining the amount of the individual's taxable gains to be charged at the lower rate under *TCGA 1992, s 4(1A)(1B)* above, certain specified income is disregarded in ascertaining the individual's total income for the year or whether he has any income. The same disregard applies even if the specified income is chargeable at the higher rate. [*TCGA 1992, s 4(3A); FA 1993, s 79, Sch 6 para 22(1); FA 1996, s 73, Sch 6 paras 27, 28; F(No 2)A 1997, Sch 4 para 24(1)(4)(6); FA 1999, s 26(4)(6)*].

For 1996/97 to 1998/99 inclusive, the income specified is that falling within *ICTA 1988, s 1A*. This refers broadly to certain income chargeable under Schedule D Case III, income chargeable under Schedule F and foreign income equivalent to Schedule D Case III and Schedule F income other than that taxed on the remittance basis. For 1993/94 to 1995/96 inclusive, the income specified was that falling within *ICTA 1988, s 207A*. This referred broadly to income chargeable under Schedule F and foreign income equivalent to Schedule F income other than that taxed on the remittance basis. In both cases the specified income is, with exceptions, treated as the highest part of the individual's income.

Any amount of gains chargeable at the lower rate only as a result of *TCGA 1992, s 4(3A)* is called '*the amount of the lower rate gains*'. The amount (if any) of income comprised in the individual's total income which is chargeable to income tax at the higher rate is determined, both for the purposes of the *Income Tax Acts* and *TCGA 1992, s 4*, as if the basic rate limit for the year were reduced in relation to the individual by the amount of the lower rate gains. [*TCGA 1992, s 4(3B)(a); FA 1993, s 79, Sch 6 para 22(1); F(No 2)A 1997, Sch 4 para 24(1)(5)(6); FA 1999, s 26(4)(6)*]. The amount (if any) on which the individual would otherwise be chargeable under *TCGA 1992, s 4(2)* above to capital gains tax at a rate equivalent to the higher rate is treated as reduced by the amount of the lower rate gains or, if the amount to be reduced is not more than the amount of those gains, to nil. [*TCGA 1992, s 4(3B)(b); FA 1993, s 79, Sch 6 para 22(1); FA 1999, s 26(4)(6)*].

The Revenue has acknowledged that, because of a subsequent reduction in the level of taxable income by reason of a claim for income tax relief, a capital gains tax assessment may charge gains at too high a rate. In such circumstances, *TMA 1970, s 31* (appeal against assessment to be made within thirty days of the date of notice) or the pre-self-assessment version of *TMA 1970, s 42(7)* (Revenue to give effect to claim by discharge or repayment of tax) can be invoked, as appropriate, by the individual (Revenue Tax Bulletin August 1993 p 87).

Example

In 1998/99 an individual receives income within *ICTA 1988, s 1A* of £23,900 (inclusive of tax credits and income tax deducted at source of £4,780). Her other income for that year is untaxed and, after all deductions under the *Income Tax Acts* (e.g. personal allowance under *ICTA 1988, s 257*), amounts to £2,800. There are no income tax reliefs which operate by way of reduction in income tax liability. After deduction of the annual exempt amount, losses etc., the amount on which she is chargeable to capital gains tax amounts to £4,000.

The lower rate limit for 1998/99 is £4,300 so, ignoring the income within *ICTA 1988, s 1A*, an amount of £1,500 of the lower rate band is unused. £1,500 'the amount of the lower rate gains' of the gains is therefore charged at a rate equivalent to the lower rate of 20%. The basic rate limit for that year is otherwise £27,100 but this is reduced to £25,600 (both for income tax purposes and capital gains tax purposes) after deduction of the amount of lower rate gains of £1,500. Total income amounts to £26,700, so £1,100 (all represented by income within *ICTA 1988, s 1A* as forming the top slice of income) is charged to income tax at the higher rate of 40%. The balance of the gains, £2,500 (£4,000 less £1,500), is charged to capital gains tax at a rate equivalent to the higher rate of 40% (*TCGA 1992, s 4(2)* applies because income tax is already chargeable at the higher rate).

Income tax payable:	£
£ 2,800 of other income at 20%	560
£22,800 of *income within ICTA 1988, s 1A* at 20%	4,560
£1,100 of *income within ICTA 1988, s 1A* at 40%	440
	5,560
Tax credits and income tax deducted £23,900 at 20%	(4,780)
Income tax payable	£780
Capital gains tax payable:	£
£1,500 at 20%	300
£2,500 at 40%	1,000
Capital gains tax payable	£1,300

For years before 1995/96 references in the above to income tax chargeable at the higher rate included references to tax chargeable under *ICTA 1988, s 683(1)* or *s 684(1)* (income arising under a settlement treated as income of settlor) in respect of excess liability.

Where for any year of assessment income is treated under either of those provisions as the income of the settlor for excess liability then, whether or not he is chargeable to tax otherwise than at the lower and basic rates, it is also treated as his income for the purposes of ascertaining the unused part of the lower and basic rate bands referred to above.

References in the above to income tax chargeable at the higher rate also included references to tax chargeable under *ICTA 1988, s 353(4)* or *s 369(3A)* (restriction to basic rate relief on interest paid before 6 April 1994 (whenever falling due) and relevant loan interest paid before 30 November 1993 (where due before 6 April 1994)) in respect of excess liability; and where for any year of assessment a deduction was denied by either of those provisions in computing total income for excess liability purposes then, whether or not he was chargeable to tax otherwise than at the lower and basic rates, that deduction was also denied for the purposes of ascertaining the unused part of the lower and basic rate bands.

References in the above to the lower rate apply for 1992/93 and subsequent years.

'*Excess liability*' for 1988/89 to 1991/92 (both years inclusive) is liability to income tax over what it would be if all income tax were charged at the basic rate to the exclusion of any higher rate; for 1992/93 it is liability to income tax over what it would be if all income tax not chargeable at the lower rate were charged at the basic rate to the exclusion of any higher rate; and for 1993/94 and subsequent years it is liability to income tax over what it would be if all income tax not chargeable at the lower rate under *ICTA 1988, s 1(2)(aa)* (lower rate of income tax in lower rate band) were charged at the basic rate, or (so far as applicable under *ICTA 1988, s 207A* above) the lower rate, to the exclusion of any higher rate. [*TCGA*

1992, s 6(1); F(No 2)A 1992, s 22(2)(3); FA 1993, s 79, Sch 6 para 24; FA 1994, Sch 26 Pt V; FA 1995, Sch 29 Pt VIII(8)].

Where for any year of assessment

(*a*) under *ICTA 1988, s 427(4)* (apportionment of close company income in relation to accounting periods ending before 1 April 1989) an amount is deemed not to form part of a person's income for the purposes of excess liability, or

(*b*) under *ICTA 1988, s 549(2)* (gains under life policy or life annuity contract) a deduction of an amount is made from a person's total income for those purposes, or

(*c*) for years before 1995/96 under *ICTA 1988, s 683(1)* or *s 684(1)* an amount of a person's income is treated as not being his income for those purposes, or

(*d*) under *ICTA 1988, s 699(1)* (income accruing before death) the residuary income of an estate is treated as reduced so as to reduce a person's income by any amount for those purposes,

the ascertainment of the unused part of the basic rate band referred to above has effect as if his income for the year were reduced by that amount. [*TCGA 1992, s 6(2); FA 1988, s 102(2)(a); FA 1989, Sch 17 Pt V; FA 1995, Sch 29 Pt VIII(8)*].

The provisions of *TCGA 1992, s 6(3)* apply as they do in 2.1 above, disregarding the reference to the Schedule F upper rate.

Nothing in *TCGA 1992, s 6(1)–(3)* is to be taken to reduce or increase (as the case may be), the amount of a deduction which a person is entitled to make from his total income under any provision of *ICTA 1988, Pt VI Ch I* (personal reliefs) which limits any allowance by reference to the level of his total income. [*TCGA 1992, s 6(4)*].

See TOLLEY'S INCOME TAX for the income tax provisions mentioned above.

2.3 **RATES OF TAX — PERSONAL REPRESENTATIVES ETC.**

Personal representatives. For 1998/99 and subsequent years, the rate of capital gains tax in respect of gains accruing to the personal representatives of a deceased person is equivalent to the 'rate applicable to trusts' in *ICTA 1988, s 686*. [*TCGA 1992, s 4(1AA); FA 1998, s 120; FA 1999, s 26(3)*]. For 1998/99 to 2000/01 inclusive, this is **34%**.

For 1988/89 to 1997/98 inclusive, the rate of capital gains tax for personal representatives was equivalent to the basic rate of income tax. [*TCGA 1992, s 4(1)*].

Settlements. Special provisions apply as regards the rate of tax for SETTLEMENTS (57.1) for 1988/89 and subsequent years.

2.4 **RATES OF TAX BEFORE 1988/89**

The principal rate of tax for all years of assessment from 1965/66 to 1987/88 (inclusive) was **30%**. [*CGTA 1979, s 3; FA 1988, Sch 14 Pt VII*]. Reduced rates applied for the years 1977/78 to 1979/80 inclusive where an individual's taxable gains for the year were less than £9,500. An alternative charge was available for all years up to 1977/78 inclusive, whereby half the gain was effectively taxed as the top slice of taxable income.

2.5 **ANNUAL EXEMPTION**

For 2000/01 an individual is exempt from capital gains tax on the first **£7,200** of his 'taxable amount' (see below for the figures for earlier years). For 1998/99 onwards, the '*taxable amount*' is the amount of chargeable gains for the year after deducting current year and brought-forward allowable losses and applying TAPER RELIEF (60). It also includes any of the following gains that might be attributed to the individual:

- gains treated under *TCGA 1992, s 77* as accruing to him as settlor from a UK resident settlement in which he has an interest (see 57.3 SETTLEMENTS);
- gains treated under *TCGA 1992, s 86* as accruing to him as settlor from a non-UK resident settlement in which he has an interest (see 43.4 OFFSHORE SETTLEMENTS);
- gains treated under *TCGA 1992, s 87* or *s 89(2)* as accruing to him as a beneficiary of a non-UK resident settlement (an offshore trust) (see 43.13 OFFSHORE SETTLEMENTS).

Where an individual's 'adjusted net gains' are equal to or less than the annual exempt amount, any allowable losses brought forward from a previous year or carried back from the year of death (see 16.5 DEATH) need not be deducted and are thus preserved for further carry-forward (or, if possible, carry-back). Where the 'adjusted net gains' exceed the annual exempt amount, such losses are deducted only to the extent necessary to wipe out the excess. The '*adjusted net gains*' are the chargeable gains for the year *before* TAPER RELIEF (60) *less* any current year allowable losses *plus* any gains attributed to the individual as above, except that the latter are added only to the extent that they do not exceed the annual exempt amount and will thus be covered by that amount (assuming it to be deductible against attributed gains in priority to other gains). See the examples below.

For 1997/98 and earlier years, the '*taxable amount*' was the amount of chargeable gains for the year less allowable losses. There was no taper relief and gains attributed as above were not considered separately from other gains. Losses brought forward (or carried back) were deducted from net chargeable gains for the year (i.e. chargeable gains less current year allowable losses) only to the extent necessary to reduce those net gains to the exempt amount.

These provisions also apply to personal representatives for the year of death and the following two years (see 16.7 DEATH).

The annual exempt amounts for earlier years were as follows:

1999/2000	£7,100
1998/99	£6,800
1997/98	£6,500
1996/97	£6,300
1995/96	£6,000
1994/95	£5,800
1993/94	£5,800
1992/93	£5,800
1991/92	£5,500
1990/91	£5,000
1989/90	£5,000
1988/89	£5,000
1987/88	£6,600
1986/87	£6,300
1985/86	£5,900
1984/85	£5,600

[*TCGA 1992, s 2(2), s 3(1)(2)(5)–(5C)(7); SI 1984 No 343; SI 1985 No 428; SI 1986 No 527; SI 1987 No 436; FA 1988, s 108; FA 1989, s 122; FA 1990, s 72; SI 1991 No 736; SI 1992 No 626; FA 1993, s 82; FA 1994, s 90; SI 1994 No 3008; SI 1995 No 3033; SI 1996 No 2957; SI 1998 No 757; FA 1998, s 121(3)(4), Sch 21 para 3; SI 1999 No 591; SI 2000 No 808*].

The exempt amount for the year (see above), unless Parliament determines otherwise, is the previous year's exempt amount as increased by a percentage which is the same as the percentage increase in the retail prices index for the September preceding the year of assessment over the index for the previous September. The resulting figure is rounded up to the nearest £100 and is announced before the relevant year of assessment in a Treasury statutory instrument (see list of references above). [*ICTA 1988, s 833(2); TCGA 1992, s 3(3)(4), s 288(2); FA 1993, s 83*].

See 57.4 and 57.5 SETTLEMENTS for further applications of the above rules.

The annual exemption is available regardless of the residence, ordinary residence or domicile status of the individual and is available separately to husband and wife.

Sumption: Capital Gains Tax. See A5.02.

Examples

For 2000/01, Paul has chargeable gains (after indexation but before taper relief) of £12,000 and allowable losses of £2,600. He also has allowable losses of £10,000 brought forward.

	£
Adjusted net gains (£12,000 – £2,600)	9,400
Losses brought forward (part)	2,200
	7,200
Annual exempt amount	7,200
Taxable gains	Nil
Losses brought forward	10,000
Less utilised in 2000/01	2,200
Losses carried forward	£7,800

Taper relief, if otherwise available, is effectively lost as the taxable gains are reduced to nil in any case.

For 2000/01, Mary has the same gains and losses (including brought-forward losses) as Paul above, but is also a beneficiary of an offshore trust. Trust gains of £7,400 are attributed to her for 2000/01 under *TCGA 1992, s 87*.

	£
Adjusted net gains (£12,000 – £2,600 + £7,200*)	16,600
Losses brought forward (part)	9,400
	7,200
Annual exempt amount	7,200
	Nil
Add: TCGA 1992, s 87 gains not brought in above	200
Taxable gains	£200
Losses brought forward	10,000
Less utilised in 2000/01	9,400
Losses carried forward	£600

* Attributed gains are included in adjusted net gains only to the extent that they do not exceed the annual exempt amount. Such gains cannot be covered by personal losses and will already have been reduced by any taper relief available to the trustees.

For 2000/01, Peter is in the same position as Mary except that his attributed gains are only £5,400.

	£
Adjusted net gains (£12,000 – £2,600 + £5,400)	14,800
Losses brought forward (part)	7,600
	7,200
Annual exempt amount	7,200
Taxable gains	Nil
Losses brought forward	10,000
Less utilised in 2000/01	7,600
Losses carried forward	£2,400

In Peter's case, £5,400 of the annual exempt amount is set against the attributed gains. Losses brought forward are used only to the extent necessary to reduce the personal gains to the balance of the annual exempt amount (£1,800).

3 Anti-Avoidance

Cross-references. See 14 CONNECTED PERSONS; 43 OFFSHORE SETTLEMENTS for provisions relating to overseas resident settlements; 44.7, 44.8 OVERSEAS MATTERS for interests in controlled foreign companies and in offshore funds respectively; 57.3 SETTLEMENTS for charge on settlors with interests in settlements; 57.9 SETTLEMENTS for restrictions on transfer of settlement losses to beneficiary becoming absolutely entitled to settled property; 57.12–57.15 SETTLEMENTS for further anti-avoidance provisions.

The headings in this chapter are as follows.

3.1 APPROACH OF THE COURTS

For the general approach of the Courts to transactions entered into solely to avoid or reduce tax liability, leading cases are *Duke of Westminster v CIR HL 1935, 19 TC 490; W T Ramsay Ltd v CIR; Eilbeck v Rawling HL 1981, 54 TC 101; CIR v Burmah Oil Co Ltd HL 1981, 54 TC 200; Furniss v Dawson (and related appeals) HL 1984, 55 TC 324.* See also *Coates v Arndale Properties Ltd HL 1984, 59 TC 516; Reed v Nova Securities Ltd HL 1985, 59 TC 516; Magnavox Electronics Co Ltd (in liquidation) v Hall CA 1986, 59 TC 610; Commissioner of Inland Revenue v Challenge Corporation Ltd PC, [1986] STC 548; Craven v White; CIR v Bowater Property Developments Ltd; Baylis v Gregory HL 1988, 62 TC 1; Dunstan v Young Austen Young Ltd CA 1988, 61 TC 448; Shepherd v Lyntress Ltd; News International plc v Shepherd Ch D 1989, 62 TC 495; Ensign Tankers (Leasing) Ltd v Stokes HL 1992, 64 TC 617; Moodie v CIR and another (and related appeals) HL 1993, 65 TC 610; Countess Fitzwilliam and others v CIR (and related appeals) HL 1993, 67 TC 614; Pigott v Staines Investments Co Ltd Ch D 1995, 68 TC 342.*

The classical interpretation of the constraints upon the Courts in deciding cases involving tax avoidance schemes is summed up in Lord Tomlin's statement in the *Duke of Westminster* case that 'every man is entitled if he can to order his affairs so that the tax attaching . . . is less than it otherwise would be'. The judgement was concerned with the tax consequences of a single transaction, but in *Ramsay*, and subsequently in *Furniss v Dawson*, the House of Lords has set bounds on the ambit within which this principle can be applied in relation to modern sophisticated and increasingly artificial arrangements to avoid tax. *Ramsay* concerned a complex 'circular' avoidance scheme at the end of which the financial position of the parties was little changed but it was claimed that a large capital gains tax loss had been created. It was held that where a preconceived series of transactions is entered into to avoid tax and with the clear intention to proceed through all stages to completion, once set in motion, the Duke of Westminster principle does not compel a consideration of the individual transactions and of the fiscal consequences of such transactions in isolation. The opinions of the House of Lords in *Furniss v Dawson* are of outstanding importance, and establish, *inter alia*, that the *Ramsay* principle is not confined to 'circular' devices, and that if a series of transactions is 'preordained', a particular transaction within the series, accepted as genuine, may nevertheless be ignored if it was entered into solely for fiscal reasons and without any commercial purpose other than tax avoidance, even if the series of transactions as a whole has a legitimate commercial purpose.

However, in *Craven v White* the House of Lords indicated that for the *Ramsay* principle to apply all the transactions in a series have to be preordained with such a degree of certainty that, at the time of the earlier transactions, there is no practical likelihood that the transactions would not take place. It is not sufficient that the ultimate transaction is simply of a kind that was envisaged at the time of the earlier transactions. In the unanimous decision of the House of Lords in *Ensign Tankers (Leasing) Ltd v Stokes*, the lead judgement drew a clear distinction between 'tax avoidance' and 'tax mitigation', it being said that the *Duke of Westminster* principle is accurate as far as the latter is concerned but does not apply to the former.

Fitzwilliam involved five transactions entered into over a short period of time to avoid capital transfer tax on appointments from a will trust, the last four transactions being determined by the Revenue to form a preordained series of transactions subject to the *Ramsay* principle but which the taxpayers claimed should be viewed separately with the result that by reason of a number of available reliefs no liability to capital transfer tax arose. The House of Lords stated that the correct approach to a consideration of steps 2 to 5 was to ask whether realistically they constituted a single and indivisible whole in which one or more of the steps was simply an element without independent effect and whether it was intellectually possible so to treat them. It was held that both questions should be answered in the negative. The case put by the Revenue did not depend on disregarding for fiscal purposes any one or more of steps 2 to 5 as having been introduced for fiscal purposes only and as having no independent effect, nor on treating the whole of steps 2 to 5 as having no such effect. Each of the four steps had a fiscal effect of giving rise to an income tax charge on two of the taxpayers for a period of time, and there was a potential capital transfer tax charge should either have died whilst in enjoyment of the income associated with the transactions. Although steps 2 to 5 were 'preordained', in the sense that they formed part of a pre-planned tax avoidance scheme and that there was no reasonable possibility that they would not all be carried out, the fact of preordainment in that sense was not sufficient in itself to negative the application of an exemption from liability to tax which the series of transactions was intended to create, unless the series was capable of being construed in a manner inconsistent with the application of the exemption. In the particular circumstances of the case, the series of transactions could not be so construed. Two or more transactions in the series could not be run together, as in *Furniss v Dawson*, nor could any one or more of them be disregarded. There was no rational basis on which the four separate steps could be treated as effective for the purposes of one provision which created a charge to tax on a termination of an interest in possession but ineffective for the purposes of two other provisions which gave exemptions from that charge where the interest was disposed of for a consideration and where the interest reverted to the settlor. Accordingly, the case was one to which the *Ramsay* principle, as extended by *Furniss v Dawson*, did not apply.

For an indication of Revenue practice as to the application of the principles established in decided cases up to and including *Furniss v Dawson* to certain types of transactions (e.g. 'bed and breakfasting' and transfers between spouses for retirement or rollover relief purposes), see ICAEW Guidance Note TR 588, 25 September 1985.

In *Hitch and Others v Stone Ch D, [1999] STC 431*, the Revenue mounted an unsuccessful challenge to a complex and artificial tax avoidance scheme on the grounds that agreements on which it was based were shams. It was noted that 'sham' meant acts done or documents executed by the parties thereto which were intended by them to give to third parties or to the court the appearance of creating between the parties legal rights and obligations different from the actual legal rights and obligations (if any) which the parties intended to create.

Sumption: Capital Gains Tax. See A2.05.

3.2 **LEGISLATION**

Anti-avoidance legislation is intended to counteract transactions designed to avoid taxation but bona fide transactions may sometimes be caught also. The provisions relating to capital gains tax and corporation tax on chargeable gains and dealt with in this chapter are as listed below, and see also the cross-references given at the beginning of the chapter.

3.3	UK domiciled and UK resident or ordinarily resident participator or shareholder in overseas resident company. [*TCGA 1992, s 13; FA 1996, s 174*]. See 44.6 OVERSEAS MATTERS for full coverage.
3.4	Value shifting. [*TCGA 1992, s 29*].
3.6–3.12	Value shifting to give tax-free benefit. [*TCGA 1992, ss 30–34*].
3.13	Connected persons. [*TCGA 1992, s 18*].
3.14	Assets disposed of in a series of transactions. [*TCGA 1992, ss 19, 20*].
3.15	Close company transferring asset at undervalue. [*TCGA 1992, s 125*].
3.16–3.17	Restrictions on company reconstructions and amalgamations. [*TCGA 1992, ss 137, 138*]. For schemes involving the transfer of a business owned by a company under *TCGA 1992, s 139*, see 13.7 COMPANIES for full coverage.
3.18	Groups of companies. See 3.6–3.12 , 3.19 and 3.20 below and 13.11–13.39 COMPANIES for full coverage.
3.19	Depreciatory transactions within groups of companies. [*TCGA 1992, s 176*].
3.20	Dividend stripping. [*TCGA 1992, s 177*].
3.21	Transactions in land. [*ICTA 1988, ss 776–778*]. See 36.4 LAND for full coverage.
3.22	Land sold and leased back. [*ICTA 1988, s 780*]. See 36.20 LAND for full coverage.
3.23	Provisions to deter abuse of concessions involving deferral of gains. [*TCGA 1992, ss 284A, 284B*].

For a detailed work on the subject, see Tolley's Anti-Avoidance Provisions.

3.3 **UK SHAREHOLDER IN OVERSEAS RESIDENT COMPANY** [*TCGA 1992, s 13; FA 1996, s 174*]

A participator in an overseas resident company which would be a close company if it were resident in the UK is assessable on a part of any chargeable gain made by the company provided that at the time the gain accrues the person is resident or ordinarily resident in the UK and, if an individual, is domiciled in the UK. For gains accruing before 28 November 1995 the gain could only arise if the person was a shareholder in the company and the charge could be avoided if the gain was distributed to shareholders within two years of its accruing.

See 44.6 OVERSEAS MATTERS.

3.4 **VALUE SHIFTING** [*TCGA 1992, s 29*]

Without prejudice to the generality of *TCGA 1992*, any of the following transactions are to be treated as giving rise to a disposal of an asset for capital gains tax purposes and, if made gratuitously or at an undervalue, the consideration (or additional consideration) for the disposal which could have been obtained in an arm's length transaction is treated as having been actually received. This also applies to the corresponding acquisition of an interest in the asset, the arm's length consideration being treated as the market value of what is acquired. [*TCGA 1992, s 29(1)*].

(*a*) If a person having control of a company exercises his control so that value passes out of shares in the company owned by him (or by CONNECTED PERSONS (14)) or out of rights over the company exercisable by him (or by connected persons) and passes into other shares in or rights over the company, a disposal is deemed to have been made out of those shares or rights. Losses arising from such a deemed disposal are not allowable. [*TCGA 1992, s 29(2)(3)*]. An omission to act may be treated as an exercise of control and 'person' includes the plural i.e. the provisions apply where two or more persons have control (*Floor v Davis HL 1979, 52 TC 609*).

(*b*) Where an owner of property enters into a transaction whereby he becomes the lessee of that property (e.g. a sale and lease-back) and there is a subsequent adjustment of the rights and liabilities under the lease (whether or not including the grant of a new lease) which is as a whole favourable to the lessor, such an adjustment is a disposal by the lessee of an interest in the property. [*TCGA 1992, s 29(4)*].

(*c*) If an asset is subject to any right or restriction, the extinction or abrogation, in whole or part, of that right, etc. by the person entitled to enforce it is treated as a disposal thereof. [*TCGA 1992, s 29(5)*].

3.5 *Example*

J owns all the 1,000 £1 ordinary shares of K Ltd. The shares were acquired on subscription in 1972 for £1,000 and had a value of £99,000 on 31 March 1982. In December 2000, the trustees of J's family settlement subscribed at par for 3,000 £1 ordinary shares in K Ltd, thereby acquiring 75% of the voting power in the company. It is agreed that the price an unconnected party would have paid for 75% of the equity in a transaction at arm's length is £150,000. J's remaining 25% holding is valued at £15,000.

J will have a capital gain for 2000/01 as follows (subject to indexation allowance to April 1998 and TAPER RELIEF (60))

	£
Proceeds of deemed disposal	150,000
Allowable cost $\dfrac{150{,}000}{150{,}000 + 15{,}000} \times £99{,}000$	90,000
Unindexed gain	£60,000

Sumption: Capital Gains Tax. See A2.04.

3.6 **VALUE SHIFTING TO GIVE TAX-FREE BENEFIT** [*TCGA 1992, ss 30–34*]

These provisions apply to the disposal of an asset (the *section 30* disposal) if a scheme has been effected or arrangements have been made (whether before or after the disposal) whereby the value of the asset or a 'relevant asset' has been materially reduced and a 'tax-free benefit' is conferred at any time on

(*a*) the person making the disposal or a person connected with him (see 14 CONNECTED PERSONS), or (*b*) any other person, except in a case where tax avoidance was not a main purpose of the scheme or arrangements.

Where the disposal of an asset precedes its acquisition, references to a reduction include references to an increase.

Any allowable loss or chargeable gain accruing on the *section 30* disposal is to be calculated as if the consideration were increased by such amount as is 'just and reasonable' having regard to the scheme or arrangements and the tax-free benefit. Where such an increase of consideration has been made for one asset and the tax-free benefit was an increase in value of another asset, the consideration for the first subsequent disposal of that other asset is to be reduced by such amount as is 'just and reasonable' in the circumstances. (There is no provision for the acquirer's cost of the asset to be correspondingly increased or reduced.)

These provisions do not apply to disposals by personal representatives to legatees (see 16.9 DEATH), or between spouses living together (see 41.3 MARRIED PERSONS) or between companies in a group (see 13.12 COMPANIES).

[*TCGA 1992, s 30(1)(4)–(7)(9); FA 1996, Sch 20 paras 46, 47(a)*].

An asset ('the second asset') is a '*relevant asset*' if

(1) the disposal of an asset (here called 'the first asset') is made by a company ('the disposing company'),

(2) the first asset comprises shares in, or securities (within *TCGA 1992, s 132* as in 21.5 EXEMPTIONS AND RELIEFS) of, a company, and

(3) the second asset is owned at the time of disposal of the first asset by a company 'associated' (see 3.11 below) with the disposing company.

A reduction in value of a relevant asset is not taken into account except in a case where

(A) during the period from the reduction in value to the time immediately before the disposal of the first asset there is no disposal of it other than one within *TCGA 1992, s 171* (intra-group transfers at no gain/no loss price as in 13.12 COMPANIES),

(B) no disposal of that asset is treated as occurring during that period under *TCGA 1992, s 179* (company ceasing to be member of group as in 13.19 COMPANIES), and

(C) if the reduction had not occurred, but any consideration given for the relevant asset and any other material circumstances (including any consideration given before the disposal for the first asset disposed of) were unchanged, the value of the first asset would have been materially greater at the time of its disposal.

Where the disposal of an asset precedes its acquisition, references to a reduction include references to an increase.

[*TCGA 1992, s 30(2)(9); FA 2000, Sch 40 Pt II(12)*].

A '*tax-free benefit*' arises to a person if he becomes entitled to money or money's worth or his interest in the value of any asset is increased or he is wholly or partly relieved from any liability to which he is subject *and* none of the foregoing benefits when conferred is otherwise liable to income tax, capital gains tax or corporation tax. [*TCGA 1992, s 30(3)*].

The Revenue do not regard ordinary commercial group relief transactions (e.g. the purchase of group relief) as falling within *TCGA 1992, s 30*.

A lease of a farm at a rack-rent by a retiring farmer to his son, followed by a sale of the reversion at market value to an outside investor, would likewise be outside it (Revenue Pamphlet IR 131, SP D18).

Where a disposal within *TCGA 1992, s 30* would otherwise form the basis for a claim for loss relief against income under *ICTA 1988, s 573* or *s 574* these provisions apply if *any* benefit is conferred, whether tax-free or not. [*ICTA 1988, s 576(2)*]. See also 39.13 and 39.15 LOSSES.

The Revenue has confirmed that where a person was caught by the value-shifting provisions, the deemed gain could be held over under *FA 1980, s 79* (when extant after 5 April 1980 and before 14 March 1989 and provided that the other conditions were satisfied). This may also apply to the other reliefs mentioned in 25 HOLD-OVER RELIEFS which are still current.

3.7 **Certain disposals of shares by companies.** The provisions at 3.8–3.10 below apply where a disposal within 3.6 above ('the *section 30* disposal') occurs and is of shares ('the principal asset') which are owned by a company ('the first company') in another company ('the second company'). [*TCGA 1992, s 30(8)*].

3.8 **Distributions within a group followed by a disposal of shares.** If a reduction in the value of an asset is attributable to the payment of a dividend by the second company while the two companies are 'associated' (see 3.11 below), it is not treated as a reduction for the purposes of 3.6 above except to the extent (if any) that the dividend is attributable (see below) to 'chargeable profits' of the second company; and, in such a case, the tax-free benefit is ascertained without regard to any part of the dividend that is not attributable to such profits.

'*Chargeable profits*' are

(*a*) the 'distributable profits' of a company, to the extent that they arise from a 'transaction caught by this *section*', and

(*b*) the distributable profits of a company, to the extent that they represent so much of a distribution received from another company as was attributable to chargeable profits of that company (including ones similarly representing a distribution).

'*Distributable profits*' are such profits computed on a commercial basis as, after allowance for any provision properly made for tax, the company is empowered, assuming sufficient funds, to distribute to persons entitled to participate in its profits. So far as possible in ascertaining distributable profits, losses and other amounts to be set against profits must be set against profits other than ones which could be chargeable profits.

Profits arising on a '*transaction caught by this section*' are profits of a company (here called 'company X') where the three conditions in (1)–(3) below are met but the three exceptions to them (see (A)–(C) below) do not apply.

(1) The transaction is

- (i) a no gain/no loss disposal by company X to another group company within *TCGA 1992, s 171(1)* (see 13.12 COMPANIES), or
- (ii) an exchange, or a transaction treated as an exchange for *TCGA 1992, s 135(2)(3)* (see 58.10 SHARES AND SECURITIES), of shares in or debentures of a company held by company X for shares in or debentures of another company which immediately after the transaction is associated with company X, and which is treated as a reorganisation by *TCGA 1992, s 135(3)*, or
- (iii) a revaluation of an asset in the accounting records of company X.

(2) No disposal of the 'asset with enhanced value'

(i) occurs, other than one within *TCGA 1992, s 171(1)*, during the period beginning with the transaction within (1) above and ending immediately before the *section 30* disposal, or

(ii) is treated as having occurred during that period by virtue of *TCGA 1992, s 179* (company ceasing to be member of group as in 13.19 COMPANIES).

(3) Immediately after the *section 30* disposal the asset with enhanced value is owned by a person other than the disposing company or a company associated with it (see 3.11 below).

'*Asset with enhanced value*' is defined as follows, according to which transaction within (1)(i), (1)(ii) or (1)(iii) above occurs respectively: the asset acquired from company X; the shares or debentures acquired by company X as a result of the exchange; and the revalued asset.

The three exceptions to the foregoing three conditions are as follows.

(A) At the time of the transaction within (1) above, company X carries on a trade, and a profit on a disposal of the asset with enhanced value would form part of the trading profits.

(B) By reason of the nature of the asset with enhanced value, there could be no chargeable gain or allowable loss on its disposal.

(C) Immediately before the *section 30* disposal, the company owning the asset with enhanced value carries on a trade, and a profit on disposal would form part of the trading profits.

Attribution of profits to a distribution is made by determining the total distributable profits and chargeable profits which remain at the time of distribution, after allowing for all earlier distributions and distributions to be made then or subsequently in respect of other classes of shares etc. and so far as possible by attributing distributable profits other than chargeable profits.

Chargeable profits are treated as arising to shareholders, etc. proportionately to their holdings of shares, etc.

[*TCGA 1992, s 31; FA 2000, Sch 40 Pt II(12)*].

3.9 **Asset-holding company leaving the group.** Where the *section 30* disposal (see 3.6 above) occurred before 9 March 1999, the provisions at 3.8 above were not triggered if that disposal was to a non-UK resident subsidiary such that the asset with enhanced value (see 3.8 above) continues to be owned within the capital gains group of which the company making the disposal is a member. This is because the condition at 3.8(3) above is not then satisfied. That asset could subsequently be sold by the non-resident subsidiary to a third party with impunity from the value shifting provisions. The provisions described below were introduced to counteract this avoidance device as regards any disposal of an asset on or after 9 March 1999. They apply wherever profits of a company would be profits on a transaction caught by *TCGA 1992, s 31* (see 3.8 above) but for the fact that condition 3.8(3) above is not satisfied.

Where the above-mentioned provisions apply, the said profits are treated as profits arising on a transaction caught by *section 31* (with the result that *TCGA 1992, s 30* at 3.6 above has effect with the consequences described below) if either:

(*a*) at any time during the period of six years beginning with the date of the *section 30* disposal, an event occurs which consists of the 'asset-holding company' ceasing to be a member of the 'disposal group' (otherwise than by virtue of the principal company of the group becoming a member of another group, i.e. the group being taken over); or (*b*) at any time during the said six-year period, the asset-holding company ceases to be a member of the disposal group by virtue only of the principal company of the group becoming a member of another group *and* at any time in that period an event occurs as a result of which

- there is no member of the disposal group of which the asset-holding company is a 75% subsidiary, or
- there is no member of the disposal group of which the asset-holding company is an effective 51% subsidiary (see 13.11 COMPANIES).

However, these provisions do not apply (and there is thus no double charge) if, during the said six-year period but prior to the occurrence of an event within (*a*) or (*b*) above, a disposal of the asset with enhanced value has been treated as having occurred by virtue of *TCGA 1992, s 179* (company leaving a group after acquiring an asset intra-group — see 13.19 COMPANIES).

In relation to any particular time, the '*asset-holding company*' is the company holding the asset with enhanced value at that time. The '*disposal group*' is the group of which the company which made the *section 30* disposal was a member at the time of that disposal (or a group regarded as being the same as that group under *TCGA 1992, s 170(10)* — see 13.11 COMPANIES).

Where *section 30* has effect by virtue of the above, the consideration for the *section 30* disposal is not adjusted but a chargeable gain is treated as accruing to the 'chargeable company' immediately before the event within (*a*) or (*b*) above. The '*chargeable company*' is normally the company which made the disposal but if that company is at that time no longer a member of the disposal group, the chargeable company is

- (for disposals on or after 1 April 2000) any other company which is at that time a member of that group and which is designated as the chargeable company by Revenue notice; or
- (for disposals before 1 April 2000) the principal company of that group.

The amount of the gain is the shortfall between the allowable loss or chargeable gain which accrued on the *section 30* disposal and the allowable loss or chargeable gain which would have accrued on that disposal if the consideration had been notionally increased as in 3.6 above.

If an allowable loss arose on the *section 30* disposal and has not been otherwise utilised, it may be set against the notional gain arising above, notwithstanding the connected persons rule in *TCGA 1992, s 18(3)* (see 39.5 LOSSES).

[*TCGA 1992, s 31A; FA 1999, s 74, Sch 9 paras 2, 5; FA 2000,Sch 29 para 17*].

3.10 **Disposals within a group followed by a disposal of shares.** A reduction in the value of an asset is not treated as a reduction for the purposes of 3.6 above if it is attributable to the disposal of any asset ('the underlying asset') by the second company while the two companies are 'associated' (see 3.11 below) and the disposal is within *TCGA 1992, s 171(1)* (no gain/no loss disposals in a group as in 13.12 COMPANIES), unless

(*a*) the actual consideration for the disposal of the underlying asset is less than both its market value and its 'cost',

(*b*) the disposal is not effected for bona fide commercial reasons and forms part of a scheme or arrangements of which the main purpose, or one of the main purposes, is the avoidance of a corporation tax liability, and

(*c*) the first company is not treated as disposing of an interest in the principal asset by virtue of a distribution in a dissolution or winding up of the second company.

For the purpose of (*a*) above, the '*cost*' of an asset is the aggregate of any capital expenditure incurred by the company in acquiring or providing it, or in respect of it while owned after its acquisition.

In the case of a part disposal of an underlying asset,

(A) the market value in (*a*) above is the market value of the asset acquired by the transferee, and

(B) the amounts attributed to the cost of the underlying asset are reduced to the '*appropriate proportion*' thereof; i.e.,

 (i) the proportion of capital expenditure properly attributed in the company's accounting records to the asset acquired by the transferee; or

 (ii) if (i) does not apply, such proportion as is 'just and reasonable'.

[*TCGA 1992, s 32; FA 1996, Sch 20 para 47(b)*].

3.11 **Interpretation of the value shifting provisions.** The following interpretational provisions apply to the value shifting provisions described at 3.6–3.10 above.

As regards any asset ('the original asset'), the provisions in (1)–(5) below apply in relation to the enactments mentioned in (*a*) and (*b*) below.

(*a*) The enactments concerning relevant assets in *TCGA 1992, s 30(2)*: namely, in 3.6 above, (1)–(3) and (A)–(C).

(*b*) The enactments concerning distributions within a group followed by a disposal of shares in *TCGA 1992, s 31(7)–(9)*: namely, in 3.8 above, the second and third conditions ((2) and (3)) and the three exceptions ((A)–(C)) to the three conditions.

The provisions in (1)–(5) below also apply in connection with *TCGA 1992, s 31A* (see 3.9 above) for the purposes of determining any question in relation to the asset with enhanced value.

(1) In (A) and (B) in 3.6 above and in condition (2) in 3.8 above, references to the disposal of an asset do not include a part disposal. The same applies as regards the reference in 3.9 above to a disposal occurring by virtue of *TCGA 1992, s 179.*

(2) For the purposes of the enactments mentioned in (*a*) and (*b*) above, references to an asset are to the original asset; except that if subsequently one or more assets are treated under (4) or (5) below as the same as the original asset,

 (i) if there has been no disposal falling within (A) or (B) in 3.6 above or (2) in 3.8 above, the references are to the asset(s) so treated; and

 (ii) in any other case, the references are to the asset(s) representing that part of the value of the original asset remaining after allowing for earlier disposals within the relevant provision.

 For the above purposes a disposal includes a part disposal which would have been within (A) or (B) in 3.6 above or (2) in 3.8 above if it had not been excluded by (1) above.

 For the purposes of *TCGA 1992, s 31A* at 3.9 above, the following apply where one or more assets are treated under (4) or (5) below as the same as the asset with enhanced value.

 (I) If in the period beginning with the transaction in 3.8(1) and ending with the event in 3.9(*a*) or (*b*),

- there is no disposal of the asset with enhanced value to any person other than a no gain/no loss intra-group disposal within *TCGA 1992, s 171(1)* (see 13.12 COMPANIES), and
- no disposal of that asset is treated as having occurred by virtue of *TCGA 1992, s 179* (company leaving a group after acquiring an asset intra-group — see 13.19 COMPANIES),

references to the asset with enhanced value are to the asset(s) treated under (4) or (5) below as the same as that asset.

(II) In any other case, references to the asset with enhanced value are to the asset(s) representing that part of the value of the asset with enhanced value remaining after allowing for disposals of either kind mentioned in (I) above.

(3) If, by virtue of (2) above, a reference to an asset is treated as a reference to two or more assets,

(i) the assets are treated as a single asset,

(ii) a disposal of any of them is a part disposal, and

(iii) the reference to the second asset in (3) in 3.6 above, to the asset in condition (3) in 3.8 above and to the asset in the definition of 'asset-holding company' in 3.9 above is in each case a reference to all or any of those two or more assets.

(4) If there is a part disposal of an asset, that asset and the asset acquired by the transferee are treated as the same.

(5) Where

(i) the value of an asset is derived from another asset owned by the same or an 'associated company' (see below), and

(ii) assets have been merged or divided or have changed their nature, or rights or interests in or over assets have been created or extinguished,

the two assets are treated as the same.

Where a reduction in the value of a relevant asset is to be taken into account under *TCGA 1992, s 30(2)* (see (1)–(3) and (A)–(C) in 3.6 above) and at the time of the disposal of the first asset in 3.6(1) by the disposing company

(A) references to the relevant asset are treated under (1)–(5) above as references to two or more assets treated as a single asset, and

(B) one or more, but not all, of those assets is owned by a company 'associated' (see below) with the disposing company,

the amount of the reduction in the value of the relevant asset to be taken into account is reduced to such amount as is 'just and reasonable'.

For the purposes of the provisions in TCGA 1992, s 31 concerning distributions within a group followed by a disposal of shares (see 3.8 above), the reduction in value of the principal asset (see 3.7 above) is to be reduced to such amount as is 'just and reasonable' if

(*aa*) a dividend paid by the second company is attributable to that company's chargeable profits, and

(*bb*) the criterion in (2), (3) or (C) in 3.8 above is satisfied by reference to an asset, or assets treated as a single asset, treated under (2)(ii) above as the same as the asset with enhanced value.

Where *TCGA 1992, s 31A* (see 3.9 above) treats profits as arising on a transaction caught by *section 31* (see 3.8 above) and either condition (2) in 3.8 above or a condition in 3.9 above is satisfied by reference to an asset (or assets treated as a single asset) treated by virtue of (2)(II) above as the same as the asset with enhanced value, the reduction in value of the principal asset (see 3.7 above) is to be reduced to such amount as is 'just and reasonable'.

The definitions relating to groups of companies in *TCGA 1992, s 170(2)–(11)* apply as in 13.11 COMPANIES; and companies are *'associated'* if they are members of the same group. The change in the residence requirement as regards groups of companies (see 13.11 COMPANIES) has effect for the purposes of the value shifting provisions, including those at 3.12 below, in relation to disposals on or after 1 April 2000.

[*TCGA 1992, s 33; FA 1996, Sch 20 para 47(c); FA 1999, s 74, Sch 9 paras 3, 5; FA 2000, Sch 29 para 17(4)*].

The provisions of *TCGA 1992, ss 30–33* are considered by the Revenue at Revenue Capital Gains Manual CG 46800–46922.

3.12 **Transactions treated as a reorganisation of share capital.** If the following conditions apply, a 'disposing company' is treated as receiving the amount specified in (*b*) below on a part disposal within *TCGA 1992, s 128(3)* (see 58.5 SHARES AND SECURITIES) of the 'original holding'.

(*a*) But for the rules whereby shares etc. held after a reorganisation, reconstruction etc. are treated as the same as those held beforehand (see 58.5, 58.8 SHARES AND SECURITIES), *TCGA 1992, s 30* in 3.6 above would apply on an exchange by a company (the 'disposing company') of shares, etc. in another company (the 'original holding') for shares etc. in a further company which immediately afterwards is not in the same 'group' (see the note on definitions in 3.11 above) as the disposing company.

(*b*) If *section 30* had applied, and the reduction in value causing them to apply had occurred after 13 March 1989, any allowable loss or chargeable gain on the disposal would have been calculated as if the consideration had been increased by an amount.

Similarly, if, but for the rules mentioned in (*a*) above, *section 30* would have applied by virtue of *TCGA 1992, s 31A* (asset-holding company leaving the group — see 3.9 above) on an exchange of the kind mentioned in (*a*) above, *section 31A* is applied (with appropriate modification) as if the said rules did not apply. In the computation of the shortfall mentioned in 3.9 above, an allowable loss is in this case regarded as a chargeable gain of nil.

These provisions are interpreted as if *TCGA 1992, s 136* (see 58.10 SHARES AND SECURITIES) had effect generally for the capital gains tax legislation.

[*TCGA 1992, s 34; FA 1999, s 74, Sch 9 paras 4, 5*].

3.13 **CONNECTED PERSONS** [*TCGA 1992, s 18*]

Sumption: Capital Gains Tax. See A2.02.

A transaction between CONNECTED PERSONS (14) is treated as having been made by way of a non-arm's length bargain so that acquisition and disposal are treated as being made at market value in most cases (see 40.1 MARKET VALUE). [*TCGA 1992, s 18(1)(2)*]. There are restrictions on losses in such circumstances. See 39.5 LOSSES.

Where the asset disposed of is subject to a right or restriction enforceable by the person making the disposal or a person connected with him, then if the acquisition consideration is treated as being the market value of the asset, that value is ascertained by deducting from the market value of the unencumbered asset either the market value of the right or restriction or, if less, the amount by which its extinction would enhance the value of the asset to its owner. Rights or restrictions the enforcement of which might effectively destroy or substantially impair the value of the asset without bringing any countervailing advantage either to the person making the disposal or to a person connected with him are disregarded, e.g. rights to extinguish incorporeal assets by way of forfeiture or merger (but see below). Options and other rights to acquire assets are also disregarded.

The valuation provisions outlined above do not apply to rights of forfeiture etc. exercisable on the breach of a covenant in a lease, nor to any right or restriction under a mortgage or other charge. [*TCGA 1992, s 18(6)–(8)*].

3.14 ASSETS DISPOSED OF IN A SERIES OF TRANSACTIONS [*TCGA 1992, ss 19, 20*]

Sumption: Capital Gains Tax. See A23.05.

Position after 19 March 1985. Where by way of two or more 'material transactions' which are linked (a '*series of linked transactions*')

(*a*) a person disposes of assets to another person with whom he is connected (or to two or more other persons with each of whom he is connected) (see 14 CONNECTED PERSONS); and

(*b*) the 'original market value' of the assets disposed of by any of the transactions in the series is less than the appropriate portion of the 'aggregate market value' of the assets disposed of by all the transactions in the series,

the disposal effected by the linked transaction in (*b*) is deemed to be for a consideration equal to the appropriate portion referred to in that paragraph. The above is not, however, to affect the consideration for any disposals between MARRIED PERSONS (41) living together.

A '*material transaction*' is a transaction taking place after 19 March 1985, and two or more such transactions are linked if they occur within the period of six years ending on the date of the last of them.

The provisions apply *both* when a second material transaction causes a series of linked transactions to come into being *and* when an existing series is extended by a further material transaction (whether or not an earlier transaction ceases to form part of the series). Assessments and adjustments are made accordingly.

In consequence of the provisions above applying after 19 March 1985, previous provisions for assets disposed of in a series of transactions (see below) were repealed for transactions after 19 March 1985. If any transaction(s) occurred before 20 March 1985, and any after 19 March 1985, such of the former as occurred not more than two years before the first of the latter will be treated as material transactions within the provisions applying after 19 March 1985 if all the transactions would have been within the previous provisions if they had not been repealed and all the transactions would have been within the provisions applying after 19 March 1985 if they had all occurred after that date. See also below for the Revenue attitude to the making of elections for 6 April 1965 value out of time which presumably still applies under provisions applying after 19 March 1985. The Revenue's practice might also apply to 31 March 1982 re-basing elections.

'*Original market value*'. If a transaction is the most recent in the series, the original market value of the assets disposed of by it is the market value which would otherwise be deemed to be the consideration for it under the general capital gains tax rules (e.g. 40 MARKET VALUE). In the case of any other transaction in the series, the original market value of the assets disposed of by it is the value which, prior to the occurrence of the most recent transaction in the series, was or would have been deemed to be the consideration, whether under the general capital gains tax rules or by the previous operation of the provisions applying after 19 March 1985.

'*Aggregate market value*'. Subject to further provisions below, aggregate market value is the amount which would have been the market value of all the transactions in the series under the general capital gains tax rules if, 'considering all the assets together', they had been disposed of by one disposal occurring at the time of the transaction concerned. The appropriate portion of the aggregate market value is that portion which it is reasonable to apportion to those of the assets which were actually disposed of by the transaction concerned.

'*Considering all the assets together*' is to include not only to considering them as a group or holding or collection of assets retaining their separate identities but also (if it gives a higher market value) to considering them as brought together, physically or in law, so as to constitute either a single asset or a number of assets which are distinct from those which were comprised in each of the transactions concerned.

Groups of companies. Intra-group transfers of assets which are treated as taking place on a no gain, no loss basis (see 13.12 COMPANIES and called here an 'intra-group transfer') are not material transactions. In a case where

(*a*) a company ('company A') disposes of an asset by way of a material transaction; and

(*b*) company A acquired the asset after 19 March 1985 by way of an intra-group transfer; and

(*c*) the disposal by company A is to a person who is connected with another company ('company B') which at some time after 19 March 1985 disposed of the asset by way of an intra-group transfer; and

(*d*) either the disposal by way of intra-group transfer which is referred to in (*c*) above was the occasion of the acquisition in (*b*) above or, between that disposal and acquisition, there has been no disposal of the asset which was not an intra-group transfer,

then, in determining whether the new provisions apply in relation to a series of linked transactions, the disposal by company A is treated as having been made by company B; but any increase in the consideration for that disposal resulting from the application of the new provisions has effect with respect to company A.

Disposal preceding acquisition. If any of the assets disposed of by all the transactions in a series of linked transactions were acquired after the time of the first of those transactions, then, in considering aggregate market value in relation to each of the transactions in the series, no account is taken of any assets which were acquired after the time of that transaction (unless they were acquired by way of an intra-group transfer). Further, the number of assets taken into account is limited to the maximum number held at any time in the period beginning immediately before the first transaction and ending immediately before the last; and in arriving at this figure any intra-group transfers prior to the first transaction are treated as taking place after that transaction. For identification purposes fungible assets are treated as disposed of on a 'first in, first out' basis. [*TCGA 1992, ss 19, 20, Sch 11 para 1, para 2(1)(2)(4)*].

Example

L purchased a set of 6 antique chairs in June 1989 at a cost of £12,000. He gave 2 chairs to his daughter in February 1995, another pair to his son in November 1998, and sold the final pair to his brother for their market value in August 2000.

The market value of the chairs at the relevant dates were

	2 chairs	4 chairs	6 chairs
	£	£	£
February 1995	6,000	14,000	26,000
November 1998	7,800	18,000	34,200
August 2000	10,400	24,000	46,200

Indexation factors are

June 1989 – February 1995	0.273
June 1989 – April 1998	0.409

The capital gains tax computations are as follows

February 1995
Disposal to daughter

Deemed consideration	£6,000

As the consideration does not exceed £6,000, the disposal is covered by the chattel exemption (see note (1)).

November 1998
(i) *1994/95 disposal to daughter recomputed*

Original market value (deemed disposal consideration at February 1995)	£6,000
Reasonable proportion of aggregate market value as at February 1995 of all assets disposed of to date £14,000 × $\frac{2}{4}$	£7,000
	£
Deemed consideration (greater of £6,000 and £7,000)	7,000
Cost $\frac{7{,}000}{7{,}000 + 14{,}000} \times$ £12,000	4,000
Unindexed gain	3,000
Indexation allowance £4,000 × 0.273	1,092
Chargeable gain 1994/95	£1,908

(ii) *1998/99 disposal to son*

Original market value (deemed disposal consideration)	£7,800
Reasonable proportion of aggregate market value as at November 1998 of all assets disposed of to date £18,000 × $\frac{2}{4}$	£9,000
	£
Deemed consideration (greater of £7,800 and £9,000)	9,000
Cost $\frac{9{,}000}{9{,}000 + 7{,}800} \times$ (£12,000 – £4,000)	4,286
Unindexed gain	4,714
Indexation allowance £4,286 × 0.409	1,753
Chargeable gain 1998/99	£2,961

3.14 Anti-Avoidance

August 2000

(i) *Gain on 1994/95 disposal to daughter recomputed*

Original market value (deemed consideration in recomputation at November 1998)	£7,000
Reasonable proportion of aggregate market value as at February 1995 of all assets disposed of to date £26,000 × $\frac{2}{6}$	£8,667
	£
Deemed consideration (greater of £7,000 and £8,667)	8,667
Cost $\frac{8,667}{8,667 + 14,000} \times$ £12,000	4,588
Unindexed gain	4,079
Indexation allowance £4,588 × 0.273	1,253
Revised chargeable gain 1994/95	£2,826

(ii) *Gain on 1998/99 disposal to son recomputed*

Original market value (deemed consideration in computation at November 1998)	£9,000
Reasonable proportion of aggregate market value as at November 1998 of all assets disposed of to date £34,200 × $\frac{2}{6}$	£11,400
	£
Deemed consideration (greater of £9,000 and £11,400)	11,400
Cost $\frac{11,400}{11,400 + 7,800} \times (12,000 - 4,588)$	4,401
Unindexed gain	6,999
Indexation allowance £4,401 × 0.409	1,800
Revised chargeable gain 1998/99	£5,199

(iii) *Gain on 2000/01 disposal to brother*

Original market value (actual consideration)	£10,400
Reasonable proportion of aggregate market value as at August 2000 of all assets disposed of to date £46,200 × $\frac{2}{6}$	£15,400
	£
Deemed consideration (greater of £10,400 and £15,400)	15,400
Cost (£12,000 – £4,588 – £4,401)	3,011
Unindexed gain	12,389
Indexation allowance £3,011 × 0.409	1,231
Chargeable gain 2000/01 (subject to TAPER RELIEF (60))	£11,158

Notes to the example

(1) The disposal in February 1995 is at first covered by the chattel exemption (£6,000). As the second disposal in November 1998 is to a person connected with the recipient of the first disposal, the two must then be looked at together for the purposes of the chattel exemption, and, as the combined proceeds exceed the chattel exemption limit, the exemption is not available. [*TCGA 1992, s 262*].

(2) The three disposals are linked transactions within *TCGA 1992, s 19* as they are made by the same transferor to persons with whom he is connected, and take place within a six-year period.

(3) It is assumed in the above example that it is 'reasonable' to apportion the aggregate market value in proportion to the number of items. In other instances a different basis may be needed to give the 'reasonable' apportionment required by *TCGA 1992, s 20(4)*.

Position before 20 March 1985. If a person 'is given or acquires' from one or more persons with whom he is connected by way of more than one transaction, assets of which the aggregate of their market values is less than their total market value when considered together, the market value of each shall be the appropriate portion of their total value. [*TCGA 1992, Sch 11 para 2(1)(3)*].

Prior to 27 December 1984 the Revenue took the view that connected transactions could be taken into consideration without time limit (even before 6 April 1965) (CCAB Statement June 1968). But in a Revenue Press Release of 27 December 1984 it was declared (without reasons being given) that the legislation applied only to those transactions which occurred within the two-year period preceding the latest transaction in the series and that this practice would be followed henceforth. Subject to this the values attributed to assets at the time of any previous acquisition (or acquisitions) since 6 April 1965 and (subject to the BACK DUTY (9) provisions) within the normal time limits for making assessments, were reconsidered on the footing that the value of the assets acquired on each such occasion was a proportionate part of the value of the total asset acquired up to the time of the last acquisition. Insofar as this reconsideration produced a larger value for the acquisition, a recomputation of the liability on the corresponding disposal had to be made. The Revenue regarded the making of additional assessments under these provisions as sufficient reason for allowing an election to be made for valuation at 6 April 1965 outside the normal time limits. Where, however, an election had already been made, it could not be withdrawn (CCAB Statement June 1968).

3.15 CLOSE COMPANY TRANSFERRING ASSET AT UNDERVALUE [*TCGA 1992, s 125*]

Where a close company (as defined by *ICTA 1988, ss 414, 415*) transfers (other than within a group of companies under *TCGA 1992, s 171(1)*, see 13.12 COMPANIES) an asset to any person otherwise than at arm's length and for a consideration of an amount or value less than the market value of the asset, an amount equal to the difference is apportioned among the issued shares of the company. On a disposal of the shares by the person who owned them at the date of transfer, an amount equal to the amount so apportioned is not treated as allowable expenditure. Where the owner of such shares is itself a close company, an amount equal to the amount apportioned to those shares is apportioned among the issued shares of that close company, the owners thereof being treated as above, and so on through any number of close companies.

Where re-basing at 31 March 1982 applies to disposals after 5 April 1988, only transfers after 31 March 1982 (rather than 6 April 1965) are taken into account for the purposes of the above.

Where the asset is transferred to a settlement for the benefit of employees, etc. (see 21.79 EXEMPTIONS AND RELIEFS), the amount apportioned is the difference between the market value of the asset or the amount of the allowable expenditure attributable to the asset, whichever is the less, and the consideration. [*TCGA 1992, s 239(3)*].

By concession, *TCGA 1992, s 125* is not applied in two sets of circumstances. The first is where the transferee is a participator or an associate of a participator in the company and the transfer is treated as an income distribution within *ICTA 1988, s 209(2)(b)* or *(4)* or the transfer is treated as a capital distribution within *TCGA 1992, s 122* (see 58.14 SHARES AND SECURITIES). The second is where the transferee is an employee of the company who is assessed to income tax under Schedule E on the excess of the market value of the asset over the price paid for it (Revenue Pamphlet IR 1, D51).

3.16 **RESTRICTIONS ON COMPANY RECONSTRUCTIONS AND AMALGAMATIONS** [*TCGA 1992, ss 137, 138*]

TCGA 1992, s 135 applies to the takeover of one company by another wholly or partly for shares or debentures and provides that the original holding and the new holding are to be treated as the same asset. See 58.8 SHARES AND SECURITIES. *TCGA 1992, s 136* deals with company reconstructions where a company issues shares or debentures to another company's shareholders whose original holdings are either retained or cancelled. The original and new holdings are likewise treated as the same asset. See 58.10 SHARES AND SECURITIES. Neither of these provisions applies, however, unless the exchange, reconstruction, or amalgamation is for 'bona fide commercial reasons', and not part of a scheme or arrangement for the main or only purpose of avoiding capital gains tax or corporation tax. This restriction does not apply where a recipient of the shares, etc. holds 5% or less of, or of any class of, the relevant shares, etc. (including holdings by connected persons) in the company being acquired etc., or where the Board, on written application by either company, has indicated its satisfaction with the transfer before it is made. Such application must contain particulars of operations contemplated and the Board may, within thirty days of receipt, call for further particulars (to be supplied within thirty days, or longer if the Board allows). If the particulars are not supplied, the application lapses. Subject to this, the Board must indicate its decision within a further thirty days. If not so notified, or if dissatisfied with the decision, the applicants may within a further thirty days require the Board to refer the particulars to the Special Commissioners for their decision. All material facts and considerations must be disclosed, otherwise any decision is void. Applications should be made to Inland Revenue, Capital and Valuation Division (CGT), Sapphire House, 550 Streetsbrook Road, Solihull, West Midlands, B91 1QU. Tel. 0121-713 4600.

The above provisions also apply to interests in a company without share capital and certain quoted options.

Tax assessed on the chargeable person and not paid within six months of the date when it is payable may be recovered, in whole or in part, from certain third parties, in the name of the chargeable person, within two years of that date. There is a right of recourse to the chargeable person for the tax so paid. The third parties are restricted to persons holding the shares, etc. issued to the chargeable person who acquired them as a result of one or more disposals within *TCGA 1992, s 58(1)* (spouses living together) or *s 171(1)* (companies within same group) without any intervening disposals not within those provisions. In the case of a chargeable person who is a company, the rights of recovery and recourse are suitably adapted for accounting periods ending after 30 September 1993 (Pay and File) so that, in particular, the right of recourse also extends to any interest on unpaid tax which the third party has paid in respect of the outstanding tax.

Seeking to retain family control of a company may be a 'bona fide commercial reason', see *CIR v Brebner HL 1967, 43 TC 705; Clark v CIR Ch D 1978, 52 TC 482* and *CIR v*

Goodwin HL 1976, 50 TC 583, which deal with the similar phrase in *ICTA 1988, s 703(1)*.

Strictly speaking, the reconstructed company or amalgamated companies should carry on substantially the same business and have substantially the same members as the original company or companies, but in practice the latter requirement may be waived if the scheme was carried out for bona fide commercial reasons. Where new companies are formed to take over separate parts of the original company's business, this provision may be applied even if the new companies have no common shareholder, provided that there is an actual segregation of trades or businesses which can be carried on in their own right, and not merely a segregation of assets (Revenue Pamphlet IR 131, SP 5/85).

For the Revenue's response to a number of concerns regarding aspects of clearances under *TCGA 1992, s 138*, see ICAEW Guidance Note TR 657, 10 April 1987. For the possibility of the Revenue expediting a reply by such means as facsimile transmission, see Law Society's Gazette 27 March 1991 practice note (reproduced at 1991 STI 389).

3.17 **Schemes involving the transfer of a business owned by companies.** [*TCGA 1992, s 139*]. See 13.7 COMPANIES where a scheme of reconstruction involves the transfer of a UK resident company's business to another UK resident company for no consideration other than the assumption of liabilities of the business.

3.18 GROUPS OF COMPANIES

There are a number of anti-avoidance provisions relating to groups of companies generally. See 13.11–13.39 COMPANIES and in particular 13.19 for a company ceasing to be a member of a group. In addition, see 3.6–3.12 above for value shifting to give a tax-free benefit which may involve groups, 3.19 below for depreciatory transactions within groups of companies and 3.20 for dividend stripping treated as a depreciatory transaction.

3.19 DEPRECIATORY TRANSACTIONS WITHIN GROUPS OF COMPANIES

[*TCGA 1992, s 176; FA 1996, Sch 20 para 57; FA 2000, Sch 29 para 24*]

Sumption: Capital Gains Tax. See A10.13.

Where (after 5 April 1965 or, where re-basing at 31 March 1982 takes effect in relation to disposals after 5 April 1988, after 30 March 1982) two or more members of a group of companies are parties to a 'disposal of assets' at other than market value which has the effect of materially reducing the value of the shares or 'securities' of one of those companies ('a depreciatory transaction'), any loss arising on the ultimate disposal of those shares or securities by a member or a former member of the group (having been a member when the transaction took place) is to be allowable only so far as is 'just and reasonable'. For disposals before 30 November 1993 when indexation allowance could normally create or increase an allowable loss, the *section 176* restriction had to be applied to the otherwise allowable loss after indexation rather than to the unindexed loss (*Tesco plc v Crimmin Ch D 1997, 69 TC 510*). Account must be taken of any other transaction (after 5 April 1965 or, where re-basing at 31 March 1982 takes effect as above, after 30 March 1982) which may have

(i) enhanced the value of the assets of the company the shares in which are being disposed of, and

(ii) depreciated the assets of any other group member.

Where such a loss has been wholly or partly disallowed, any chargeable gain accruing within six years of the depreciatory transaction on the disposal of shares or securities of another company which was a party to it is reduced as is just and reasonable (but not so as to exceed the reduction in the allowable loss). Regard is to be had to the effect of the depreciatory

transaction on the value of the shares at the date of disposal. All adjustments, by discharge or repayment of tax, or otherwise, as are required to give effect to these provisions may be made at any time.
Under self-assessment the Revenue has general powers within *TMA 1970* to enquire into any return, claim or election (see SELF-ASSESSMENT (56)).

A '*depreciatory transaction*' also includes any other transaction where

(*a*) the company, the shares or securities in which are the subject of the ultimate disposal, or any 75% subsidiary of that company, was party to that transaction; and

(*b*) the parties to the transaction were, or included, two or more companies which, when the transaction occurred, were in the same group.

A transaction is not depreciatory to the extent that it is a payment which is required to be, or has been, brought into account in computing a chargeable gain or allowable loss of the company making the ultimate disposal. Cancellation within *Companies Act 1985, s 135* of shares or securities of one member of a group which are owned by another is deemed to be a depreciatory transaction unless it falls within this exemption. The deemed disposal arising under a claim that shares or securities have become of negligible value under *TCGA 1992, s 24(2)* (see 39.9 LOSSES) may constitute a depreciatory transaction.

References to '*disposal of assets*' include appropriation by one member of a group of the goodwill of another member.

'*Securities*' includes loan stock or similar securities whether secured or unsecured.

A group of companies, and related expressions, are construed for these purposes in accordance with 13.11 COMPANIES, except that a group could include non-UK resident companies even before the change in the residence requirement there mentioned.

Where a subsidiary company pays dividends to its parent out of post-acquisition profits, the Revenue do not regard the payment as being a depreciatory transaction (ICAEW Guidance Note TR 588, 25 September 1985).

For consideration of these provisions, see Revenue Capital Gains Manual CG 46500–46683.

3.20 **DIVIDEND STRIPPING** [*TCGA 1992, s 177; F(No 2)A 1992, s 46(1)(6); FA 2000, Sch 29 para 25*]

Sumption: Capital Gains Tax. See A10.13.

Where a company (the 'first company') holds 10% or more of a class of shares in another company (the 'second company') otherwise than as a dealing company, and a distribution is or has been made to the first company which materially reduces or has reduced the value of the holding, the distribution is to be treated as a depreciatory transaction under *TCGA 1992, s 176* (see 3.19 above) in relation to any disposal of the shares. This applies whether the disposal is by the first company or any other company to which the holding has been transferred under the provisions of *TCGA 1992, s 140A* (transfer of UK trade between companies in different EC member States, see 44.10 OVERSEAS MATTERS), *s 171* (transfers within a group, see 13.12 COMPANIES) or *s 172* (now repealed — see 44.3 OVERSEAS MATTERS). If the first and second companies are not members of the same group, they are deemed to be so.

For these purposes, a company's holding of different classes in another company are treated as separate holdings and holdings of the same class which differ in the entitlements or obligations they confer are treated as holdings of different classes. Subject to this, all of a company's holdings of the same class in another company must be treated as a single holding and other holdings of the same class held by connected persons are aggregated in determining whether the 10% test is satisfied. For the meaning of connected persons, see 14 CONNECTED PERSONS. For the above provisions only, the persons mentioned in 14.6 specifically include persons acting together to secure or acquire a holding in a company (and not just control).

A distribution need not be treated as a depreciatory transaction under these provisions to the extent that it consists of a payment which is required to be, or has been, brought into account in calculating a chargeable gain or allowable loss by the person making the ultimate disposal.

3.21 **TRANSACTIONS IN LAND** [*ICTA 1988, ss 776–778*]

Where land in the UK is acquired or developed with the sole or main object of realising a gain from disposing of it or is held as trading stock, any capital gain from 'disposal' of the land is, subject to certain exemptions, treated as *income* of the person realising the gain (or the person who transmitted to him the opportunity of making that gain). See 36.4 LAND.

3.22 **LAND SOLD AND LEASED BACK** [*ICTA 1988, s 780*]

As regards certain arrangements within *ICTA 1988, s 779*, part of the consideration received by the lessee for giving up the original lease (or undertaking to pay an increased rent) is treated as an income receipt and not a capital one. See 36.20 LAND.

3.23 **ABUSE OF CONCESSIONS**

Prior to 9 March 1999, there was no statutory authority for a charge to tax arising by virtue of a concession under the terms of which a gain was initially deferred with the intention that it be brought back into charge (whether directly or indirectly) on the occasion of a subsequent event in a later chargeable period. As a result it was impossible for the Revenue to enforce payment of the tax. A statutory charge was therefore introduced by *Finance Act 1999* to have effect where the deferred gain is to be brought back into charge under the terms of the concession and that gain is not returned (i.e. included in a tax return).

The statutory charge applies where a person (the '*original taxpayer*') has at any time obtained the benefit of a capital gains relief in reliance on a 'concession' and circumstances arise in a subsequent chargeable period and on or after 9 March 1999, which, if that benefit had been obtained under a statutory relief, would have resulted in the whole (or part) of the benefit falling to be recouped from any person (whether or not the original taxpayer). A chargeable gain equal to the amount (or part) of that benefit is deemed to accrue to the latter person for the chargeable period in which the circumstances arise. The chargeable gain is not eligible for TAPER RELIEF (60).

The above provision does not, however, apply where the person to whom the deemed chargeable gain would otherwise accrue indicates in writing to the Board that he accepts that the benefit obtained by the original taxpayer may be recouped from him. Such acceptance may be indicated simply by the making or amending of a self-assessment to include the deferred gain. Where, *following* an assessment under this provision,

- such indication of acceptance is given on or before the latest of the deadlines listed below, or
- it transpires that the original taxpayer did not, or was not entitled to, rely on the concession and *his* tax position for the earlier period is finally determined on that basis,

such adjustments are to be made to ensure that the chargeable person's liability is no greater than would have been the case had such an event occurred earlier such that no assessment would have been necessary. The above-mentioned deadlines are:

- twelve months after an assessment is made under the above provision;
- the latest date for amending the self-assessment tax return or company tax return for the period in which the gain accrues (see 54.7, 54.11 RETURNS); and,
- where a claim for further relief is possible against the gain and is made, the latest possible date for making that claim.

For the purpose of the above provision, '*concession*' means any concession which

- was first published by the Board before 9 March 1999 or replaces a concession so published and having similar effect;
- was available generally to any person falling within its terms at the time it was relied upon by the original taxpayer;

and which has the effect of

- applying (with or without modifications) the provisions of any enactment to a case to which they would not otherwise have applied; or
- treating, without applying a specific enactment,
  - (i) any asset as the same as any other asset and acquired as the other asset was acquired;
  - (ii) any two or more assets as a single asset; or
  - (iii) any disposal as having been a disposal on which neither a gain nor a loss accrued.

For these purposes, the term 'concession' is not restricted to those listed as EXTRA-STATUTORY CONCESSIONS (30) but includes any practice, interpretation or other statement in the nature of a concession and within the above definition.

[*TCGA 1992, ss 284A, 284B; FA 1999, s 76*].

The following extra-statutory concessions are *examples* of concessions at which the above provisions are aimed.

- D15 (which extends rollover relief on business assets to cover gains on assets of a company which is 90% owned by an unincorporated association — see 55.5 ROLLOVER RELIEF).
- D16 (which extends rollover relief on business assets where the proceeds from the disposal of an asset are reinvested in the repurchase of the same asset — see 55.3 ROLLOVER RELIEF).
- D22 (which extends rollover relief on business assets where the proceeds from the disposal of an asset are used to enhance the value of another asset — see 55.3 ROLLOVER RELIEF).
- D39 (which treats a lease of property which is surrendered before its expiry date as the same asset as a new lease to replace it — see 36.14 LAND).

(Treasury Explanatory Notes to the Finance Bill 1999).

4 Appeals

Cross-references. See 5 ASSESSMENTS; 9.8 BACK DUTY for investigatory powers of the Revenue; 12.6 CLAIMS for appeals in respect of claims; 35 INTEREST AND SURCHARGES ON UNPAID TAX; 46 PAYMENT OF TAX; 47.8 and 47.9 PENALTIES; 52.8 RESIDENCE AND DOMICILE. See 56.28 for the appeals procedure under SELF-ASSESSMENT effective from 1996/97 onwards.

Simon's Direct Tax Service. See A3.5, A3.7.

4.1 The majority of appeals are against assessments, the right of appeal being conferred by *TMA 1970, s 31,* but, with unimportant exceptions, the taxpayer may appeal against any formal decision by the inspector or the Board. In particular a decision on CLAIMS (12) may be appealed. [*TMA 1970, s 42*]. An appeal against an assessment to corporation tax is an appeal against the total amount of profits charged to tax in the assessment (*Owton Fens Properties Ltd v Redden Ch D 1984, 58 TC 218*).

4.2 SPECIAL REGULATIONS

These regulations make certain provisions in relation to capital gains tax appeals which are not covered by the general statutory provisions on appeals (see 4.3 *et seq.* below). In particular, they lay down procedures under which a question of market value or apportionment which affects the liability of two or more persons (e.g. a donor and donee, or a vendor and purchaser in a transaction not at arm's length) can be settled. The regulations, authorised by *TMA 1970, s 57,* are contained in *The Capital Gains Tax Regulations 1967 (SI 1967 No 149)*. Following the introduction of regulations governing the jurisdiction of the General and Special Commissioners and the procedure for proceedings before them with effect from 1 September 1994 (see 4.8 below), the regulations relating to capital gains tax appeals were consequentially amended, and are summarised below in their amended form.

(*a*) **Joinder of third parties in appeals.** Where the market value of an asset on a particular date or the apportionment of any amount or value is a material question in an appeal, any person whose liability to capital gains tax for any period may be affected by that market value may apply to be joined in the appeal. Application is in writing to the inspector and should state, *inter alia*, how the applicant's liability may be affected and his contention in relation to the matters under appeal. A copy of the application is sent by the inspector to the appellant and any other party to the appeal. If the application is received more than thirty days before the date of the appeal hearing, or before that date is set, then if the inspector is satisfied with the propriety of the applicant's case, the applicant will be joined as a third party and appropriate notice given to the other parties. Otherwise, the inspector will refer the application to the Commissioners who may allow or refuse the application at their discretion. Insofar as his interest is being considered, the third party has the same rights as the appellant. [*SI 1967 No 149, Reg 8*].

(*b*) **Applications for determination of market value.** Where the market value of an asset or the apportionment of any amount or value may affect the liability to capital gains tax of two or more persons, either or any of them may apply to the Commissioners (General or Special) for a ruling if the point is not, nor has been, a material question in an appeal brought by any of them. The inspector is a party to such proceedings. [*SI 1967 No 149, Reg 9*].

(*c*) **Conclusive effect of determination on appeal.** The values as determined are conclusive between the Revenue, the parties to the appeal and any third party who was given notice of the appeal in reasonable time unless that person's application (made without undue delay) to be joined as a party to the appeal was refused. [*SI 1967 No 149, Reg 11*].

(*d*) **Agreements in writing.** There can be no binding agreement on the value of an asset between the Revenue and the taxpayer unless the agreement is joined by any proper third party to the appeal. A written agreement will be effective against the taxpayer's personal representatives, trustee in bankruptcy, etc. An agreement conclusive against trustees of a settlement will be effective against any person becoming absolutely entitled to the settled property. [*SI 1967 No 149, Regs 12, 13*].

4.3 GENERAL RIGHT OF APPEAL

Unless otherwise stated or required by the context, the paragraphs 4.4–4.11 below apply to all appeals and matters treated as appeals, and not only to appeals against assessments.

An appeal once made cannot be withdrawn unilaterally (see *R v Special Commissioners (ex p. Elmhirst) CA 1935, 20 TC 381* and *Beach v Willesden General Commissioners Ch D 1981, 55 TC 663*) but see 4.6 below for the withdrawal of appeals by agreement and 4.9 below regarding appeals to the High Court.

4.4 TIME LIMIT FOR APPEALS ETC.

An appeal *against an assessment* must be made within 30 days of the date of *issue* of the notice of assessment or of the making of the disputed decision and state the grounds of appeal, but grounds not stated may be advanced at any hearing of the appeal if the Commissioners so allow. [*TMA 1970, s 31(1)(5); F(No 2)A 1975, s 67(1)*]. An appeal *against a decision on a claim* must be made within 30 days of *receipt* of written notice of the decision, except for matters relating to residence, ordinary residence and domicile (see 52.8 RESIDENCE AND DOMICILE). [*TMA 1970, s 42(3)*].

A late appeal may be accepted by the inspector if there is reasonable excuse for the delay and, if he does not accept it, he must refer the application to the Commissioners for their decision. [*TMA 1970, s 49*]. If they refuse, their decision is not subject to appeal by way of stated case (*R v Special Commrs (ex p. Magill) QB (NI) 1979, 53 TC 135*, but is subject to judicial review (see *R v Hastings and Bexhill General Commrs and CIR (ex p. Goodacre) QB 1994, 67 TC 126*, in which a refusal was quashed and the matter remitted to a different body of Commissioners).

4.5 JURISDICTION OF APPEAL COMMISSIONERS

An appeal is made to the General or Special Commissioners. Notice of the appeal is given in writing to the appropriate inspector or officer of the Board. If not settled by agreement (4.6 below) it is heard by the Commissioners. Except in the circumstances outlined below regarding unquoted shares and land in the UK, the appeal is to the General Commissioners, unless the taxpayer elects for the Special Commissioners, either when the appeal is made or separately but within the time limit for making the appeal. See also 12.6 CLAIMS. After 31 December 1984, such an election is, however, disregarded if the appellant and the inspector so agree in writing before the appeal is determined, or if before the appeal is determined the inspector refers the election to the General Commissioners (after notifying the appellant) and they so direct. They must give such a direction unless satisfied that the appellant has arguments to present or evidence to adduce on the merits of the appeal. Such a direction may be revoked at any time before determination of the appeal if that condition is subsequently satisfied. The decision to give or revoke a direction is final. [*TMA 1970, s 31(5A)–(5E), s 46(1), Sch 2 paras 1A–1E; FA 1984, s 127, Sch 22 para 3; SI 1984 No 1836*]. In deciding when the appeal should be listed for hearing, inspectors of taxes are to treat appeals to the Special Commissioners no differently from appeals to the General Commissioners. Inspectors are only to ask taxpayers to agree that an election for hearing by the Special Commissioners should be disregarded when a decision is needed to arrange the listing, and then only where the inspector is satisfied that it is a delay appeal as opposed to a contentious appeal. A contentious appeal does not become a delay appeal by reason of the fact that the inspector may still be seeking further information (Revenue Press Release 26 February 1990).

Appeals to the General Commissioners may, if the parties so apply and the Commissioners consent, be transferred to the Special Commissioners (and vice versa) despite the expiry of the time limit for election as above or the making of such an election. [*TMA 1970, s 44(3)*]. In addition, after 31 December 1984, the General Commissioners may arrange that an appeal brought before them be transferred to the Special Commissioners, with the Special Commissioners' consent, if, after considering any representations made to them by the parties to the appeal, the General Commissioners consider that, because of the complexity of, or likely time required to hear, the appeal, it should be so transferred. [*TMA 1970, s 44(3A); FA 1984, s 127, Sch 22 para 5; SI 1984 No 1836*].

Where the General Commissioners have jurisdiction, rules for prescribing the appropriate Division are in *TMA 1970, Sch 3* as amended, although the parties may come to an agreement that the proceedings be brought before any body of General Commissioners specified in the agreement. [*TMA 1970, s 44(1)(2); FA 1988, s 133(2)*]. In general, inspectors will agree to transfer jurisdiction for an appeal to be heard in a Division more convenient for the taxpayer (Revenue Tax Bulletin May 1993 p 70; comments made there about Schedule E appeals are understood to apply also to capital gains tax appeals).

In relation to proceedings instituted after 31 December 1988, the Board may, however, direct that specified proceedings be brought before the General Commissioners for a specified division, provided that the inspector notifies the other party of the effect of that direction, unless

(A) the other party objects to the direction within 30 days of the service of the inspector's notice, or, in the case of an appeal, has elected for a hearing in the place where he ordinarily resides (see below), or

(B) the proceedings are subject to the special rules applicable where more than one taxpayer may be a party to the proceedings.

Any such direction may be superseded by an agreement between the parties (as above). [*TMA 1970, s 44(1A)(1B); FA 1988, s 133(1)*]. The power to make a direction is used broadly where the inspector has no expectation that the taxpayer will appear at the hearing of the appeal, but as a direction is made well in advance the inspector will withdraw it if the taxpayer objects because of an inconvenient journey (Revenue Tax Bulletin May 1993 p 70; comments made there about Schedule E appeals are understood to apply to capital gains tax appeals, and for both such types of appeal, even though the taxpayer's objection is made outside the 30-day time limit (provided it is made before the case is set down for hearing in the Division directed by the inspector)).

For appeals against *assessments* the broad effect of *TMA 1970, Sch 3* is to designate the Division in which the appellant's trade etc. is carried on, or if he has no trade etc., the Division in which he is employed, *or (in either case) at his election by notice in writing given not later than the notice of appeal*, the Division in which he ordinarily resides. If he has no trade etc. or employment, the Division of ordinary residence applies. Although the election for a hearing in the Division of the ordinary place of residence should be given not later than the notice of appeal, in practice inspectors will accept such an election at any time before the case is set down for hearing in the Division determined as above (Revenue Tax Bulletin May 1993 p 70; comments there made about Schedule E appeals are understood to apply also to capital gains tax appeals).

4.6 Appeals

Corporation tax appeals are heard in the Division in which the company carries on its trade or where its head office is situate.

The above rules are, however, directory and not mandatory (*CIR v Adams CA 1971, 48 TC 67; Murphy v Elders Ch D 1973, 49 TC 135*) and a decision of the Commissioners cannot be invalidated for want of jurisdiction if there was no objection to jurisdiction before the decision. [*TMA 1970, s 44(4)*]. See also *R v Kingston & Elmbridge Commrs (ex p. Adams) QB 1972, 48 TC 75; R v St Pancras Commrs (ex p. Church of Scientology of California) QB 1973, 50 TC 365; Parikh v Birmingham North Commrs CA, [1976] STC 365.*

The Special Commissioners go on circuit to the chief provincial towns, but appeals to them may generally by arrangement be heard in London, which is usually more convenient if it is intended to engage counsel.

Certain specified questions in dispute on an appeal must be determined by the Special Commissioners. These include any question as to the value of unquoted shares or securities of a UK-resident company which arises in relation to the taxation of chargeable gains. [*TMA 1970, s 46B; FA 1996, Sch 22 para 7; FA 1998, Sch 19 para 24*]. Insofar as an appeal involves the question of the value of any land, or of a lease of land, and it arises in relation to the taxation of chargeable gains, that question is to be determined by the Lands Tribunal (in England and Wales, Scotland or Northern Ireland depending on where the land is situate). [*TMA 1970, s 46D; FA 1996, Sch 22 para 7; FA 1998, Sch 19 para 26*]. Before self-assessment, provisions similar to those of *TMA 1970, s 46B* and *s 46D* were contained in *TMA 1970, s 47*.

The Lord Chancellor has powers, by regulation, to provide for the transfer of appeals between the General and Special Commissioners or between General Commissioners for different divisions, and for varying the number of General or Special Commissioners required or permitted to hear appeals. Different provision may be made for different cases and different circumstances. [*TMA 1970, s 46A; F(No 2)A 1992, Sch 16 para 3*]. See now *SI 1994 Nos 1811–1813* and 4.8 below.

4.6 **SETTLEMENT OF APPEALS BY AGREEMENT**

Where agreement, written or otherwise, has been reached at any time between the Revenue and the appellant or his agent on any appeal to the Commissioners against any assessment or decision, the assessment or decision as upheld, varied, discharged, or cancelled by that agreement, is treated as if it had been determined on appeal, provided that

(*a*) the taxpayer may withdraw from the agreement by giving written notice within 30 days of making it, and

(*b*) oral agreements are ineffective unless confirmed in writing by either side (the date of such confirmation then being the effective date of agreement).

[*TMA 1970, s 54*].

The agreement must specify the figure for assessment or a precise formula for ascertaining it (*Delbourgo v Field CA 1978, 52 TC 225*). The inspector has no power unilaterally to withdraw ('vacate') an assessment (*Baylis v Gregory HL 1988, 62 TC 1*). See *Gibson v General Commissioners for Stroud Ch D 1989, 61 TC 645* for a case where there was held not to have been a determination and *R v Inspector of Taxes, ex p. Bass Holdings Ltd; Richart v Bass Holdings Ltd QB 1992, 65 TC 495* for one where rectification of an agreement was ordered where a relief had been deducted twice contrary to the intention of Revenue and taxpayer. An agreement based on a mutual mistake of fact was thereby vitiated, so that the taxpayer could proceed with his appeal (*Fox v Rothwell (Sp C 50), [1995] SSCD 336*). See *CIR v West CA 1991, 64 TC 196* for a case where the taxpayer was unsuccessful in seeking leave to defend a Crown action for payment of tax on the ground that the accountant who had entered into an agreement had no authority to do so given him by the taxpayer. For the extent to which further assessments or error or mistake claims are permissible if an appeal has been determined by agreement, see 5.2 ASSESSMENTS.

The issue of an amended notice of assessment cannot in itself constitute an offer for the purposes of a *section 54* agreement; nor can a lack of response by the taxpayer constitute acceptance of an offer (*Schuldenfrei v Hilton CA, [1999] STC 821*).

A taxpayer cannot withdraw an appeal made to the Commissioners (see 4.3 above), but if, having appealed, he or his agent gives the inspector oral or written notice of his desire not to proceed, then unless the inspector gives written notice of objection within 30 days thereof, the appeal is treated as if settled by agreement, as above. Agreement is effective from the date of the taxpayer's notification that the assessment, etc. be upheld without variation. [*TMA 1970, s 54(4)*].

In *Tod v South Essex Motors (Basildon) Ltd Ch D 1987, 60 TC 598*, the taxpayer company's agent and the inspector agreed in 1974 that a disposal by the company in 1968 (details of which had been fully disclosed) had resulted in an allowable loss available for carry forward. However, neither party had appreciated that a correct application of the law would have resulted in the disposal being treated as giving rise to neither a gain nor a loss. In 1977 a new inspector and new agent agreed that part of the previously agreed loss should be allowed against gains arising in 1975. In 1981 the company made a substantial gain against which it claimed to set the balance of the loss but the then inspector's refusal to allow the claim was upheld. The binding effect of an agreement under *TMA 1970, s 54(1)* could be no wider than the binding effect of a determination by Commissioners or by a court on appeal. There was nothing to prevent the parties agreeing under *TMA 1970, s 54* to correct a previous agreement (as was done here); the corrected agreement became operative both for the ordinary law of contract as well as this taxing statute. Provided that full disclosure had been made, the fact that the correction proceeded upon an erroneous view of fact or law made no difference. See also Revenue Capital Gains Manual CG 40234. (For 1996/97 onwards, capital losses are subject to a formal notification procedure — see 39.3 LOSSES).

4.7 THE HANDLING OF TAXPAYERS' APPEALS

Appeal meetings must be notified to the appellant and the inspector (or other Revenue party) (see 4.8 below). In practice the inspector normally gives details of appeals ready for hearing to the Clerk who, after consulting the inspector and, in important appeals, the taxpayer or his agent as appropriate, makes the necessary arrangements, notifies the inspector and issues notices of the hearing to the appellant. In some Divisions he may, by arrangement, also notify the appellant's agent.

4.8 APPEALS HEARD BY APPEAL COMMISSIONERS

The Lord Chancellor has wide regulatory powers in relation to the practice and procedure to be followed in connection with appeals, including the power to make different provision for different cases and different circumstances. [*TMA 1970, ss 56B–56D; F(No 2)A 1992, Sch 16 para 4; FA 1994, s 254*]. With effect from 1 September 1994, regulations were brought in governing the jurisdiction of the General Commissioners and the procedure for proceedings before them. [*SI 1994 No 1812*]. Similar regulations apply in relation to the Special Commissioners [*SI 1994 No 1811*], and *SI 1994 No 1813* makes consequential and complementary amendments to other enactments.

In relation to the General Commissioners, these regulations do not apply to any proceedings set down (or first set down) for hearing by notice given before 1 September 1994 if any party to those proceedings so elects (by notice to the Clerk to the

Commissioners) prior to commencement of the hearing (or to the recommencement of adjourned proceedings which were commenced before 1 September 1994). They also do not apply to any proceedings under *TMA 1970, s 100C* (see 47.10 PENALTIES) in respect of which a summons was issued prior to 1 September 1994 to the defendant to appear before them at a time and place stated in the summons. Where these regulations *do* apply to proceedings set down (or first set down) for hearing by notice given before 1 September 1994, anything done in relation to those proceedings before that date which, if the proceedings had commenced on or after that date, could have been done pursuant to these regulations, is to have effect as if done pursuant to these regulations. [*SI 1994 No 1812, Reg 1*].

In relation to the Special Commissioners, these regulations do not apply to any proceedings set down for hearing by notice given before 1 September 1994, or in respect of which a summons was issued before that date. [*SI 1994 No 1811, Reg 1*].

The earlier jurisdictional and procedural rules were broadly similar, the most significant difference being the absence of the powers of the Special Commissioners to hear cases in public, to publish their decisions and to award costs in certain cases.

The remainder of this section deals with the rules applicable from 1 September 1994, and with the general and case law which is of continuing application.

(*a*) **General Commissioners.**

Constitution of Tribunal. Two or more, but not more than five, General Commissioners for a division may hear any proceedings. [*SI 1994 No 1812, Reg 2*]. They will themselves decide which one of them will preside at the hearing. Where possible at least three will sit, and, with the consent of all the parties, proceedings may be continued by any one or more of them. [*SI 1994 No 1812, Reg 11*]. For the effect of personal business connection between a Commissioner and a party to proceedings, see *R v Holyhead Commrs (ex p Roberts) QB 1982, 56 TC 127.*

The Clerk to the Commissioners, who is frequently a local solicitor, normally attends the meeting to take minutes and to advise them as required, but a meeting without the Clerk would not be invalid (*Venn v Franks CA 1958, 38 TC 175*).

Preparation for hearing. *Listing and notice of hearing.* Except in relation to proceedings under *TMA 1970, s 100C* (see 47.10 PENALTIES), any party to the proceedings may serve notice on the Clerk to the Commissioners that he wishes a date for the hearing to be fixed, on receipt of which the Clerk must send notice to each party of the place, date and time of the hearing. Unless the parties otherwise agree, or the Commissioners otherwise direct, the date must not be earlier than 28 days after the date of the Clerk's notice. [*SI 1994 No 1812, Reg 3*].

Witnesses. A General Commissioner, on the application of any party to the proceedings, may issue a witness summons (in Scotland, a witness citation) requiring any person in the UK either to attend the hearing of those proceedings to give evidence or to produce any relevant document in his possession, custody or power. The party applying for issue of the summons is responsible for its service (for which see *Reg 4(3)*), and attendance may not be required within seven days of service unless the witness informs the Clerk that he accepts shorter notice. That party must also agree to meet the witness's reasonable travelling expenses. The witness may apply, by notice served on the Clerk, for the Commissioner to set aside the summons (in whole or part), on which application the party on whose application the summons was issued is entitled to be heard.

Except in Scotland, a witness so summoned to give evidence may only be cross-examined by the party on whose application the summons was issued if the Commissioners decide that the witness is a hostile witness and give leave.

A witness cannot be compelled to give evidence or produce documents which he could not be compelled to give or produce in an action in a court of law. An auditor or tax adviser (within *TMA 1970, s 20B(10)*) cannot be compelled to produce any document which he would not be obliged to deliver or make available by notice under *TMA 1970, s 20(3)* or *(8A)* (having regard to *TMA 1970, s 20B(9)–(13)*), and copies of, or of parts of, documents may similarly be produced in certain cases (see 9.8 BACK DUTY).

In the event of failure by a witness to attend in obedience to the summons, or refusal to be sworn or to affirm, or refusal to answer any lawful question or to produce a document he is required to produce by the summons, the Commissioners may summarily determine a penalty not exceeding £1,000, to be treated as tax charged by an assessment and due and payable.

[*SI 1994 No 1812, Reg 4*].

Joint hearings. The Commissioners have powers to direct that two or more proceedings, in one or more divisions, with common issues be heard at the same time or consecutively within one division, either of their own motion or on an application by any of the parties to any of those proceedings. All the parties must be notified, and are entitled to be heard before such a direction is given. On the giving of a direction, the Clerk must send notice of its date and terms to all parties. [*SI 1994 No 1812, Reg 6*]. The Commissioners have an inherent power to deal with two or more appeals simultaneously where the appellants' affairs are so intermingled as to be incapable of separation, and where they are satisfied that it would result in no injustice to either party (*Johnson v Walden; King v Walden CA 1995, 68 TC 387*).

Postponements and adjournments. The Commissioners may postpone or adjourn the hearing of any proceedings, the Clerk being responsible for notifying all parties of the place, date and time of the postponed or adjourned hearing (unless announced before an adjournment in the presence of all parties). Where a hearing is adjourned for the obtaining of further information or evidence, the Commissioners may direct the parties regarding the disclosure of such information or evidence prior to resumption. [*SI 1994 No 1812, Reg 8*]. In *Packe v Johnson Ch D 1991, 63 TC 507*, a determination was quashed because of the Commissioners' refusal to consider all relevant information in deciding to refuse an adjournment at a second hearing.

Other matters in preparation for hearing. There are also regulations dealing with the agreement of documents [*Reg 5*], the joinder of additional parties to the proceedings [*Reg 7*] and the admission of expert evidence [*Reg 9*].

Hearing and determination of proceedings. Hearings are in private, except that certain persons with official responsibilities may be present, and may remain present during, but not take part in, the Commissioners' deliberations. With the consent of the parties, the Commissioners may permit any other person to attend the hearing. [*SI 1994 No 1812, Reg 13*].

Preliminary points will be considered prior to the hearing of the substantive appeal only in cases where the facts are complicated and the legal issue is short and easily decided (*Investment Trust v CIR (Sp C 173), [1998] SSCD 287*).

Power to obtain information. The Commissioners may, at any time before final determination of the proceedings, serve on any party to the proceedings (other than the Revenue) notice requiring that party, within a specified time,

(i) to deliver such particulars as may be required to determine any issue of the proceedings, and

(ii) to make available for inspection by the Commissioners or by an officer of the Board such specified or described books, accounts, etc. in his possession or power as may, in their opinion, contain information relevant to the proceedings.

The Commissioners may summarily determine a penalty (to be treated as tax charged in an assessment and due and payable) of up to £300 for failure to comply with such a notice, plus up to £60 per day for continuing failure after such a penalty is determined. Any officer of the Board (and the Commissioners in the case of (ii)) may, at all reasonable times, take copies of, or extracts from, any such particulars, books, etc.. [*SI 1994 No 1812, Reg 10*].

Representation at hearing. A party to the proceedings may be represented by any person, except that the Commissioners may, if satisfied that there are good and sufficient reasons for doing so, refuse to permit a party to be represented by a particular person, not being a legally qualified person or a person who is currently (see *Cassell v Crutchfield (No 1) Ch D 1995, 69 TC 253*) a member of an incorporated society of accountants. In practice, most bodies of Commissioners permit the taxpayer to be represented by any person who they are satisfied is competent to present the appellant's case. The Revenue may be represented by a barrister, advocate, solicitor or any officer of the Board. [*SI 1994 No 1812, Reg 12*]. The Revenue representative is normally an inspector. The secretary or 'other proper officer' represents a company (the liquidator if in liquidation). [*TMA 1970, s 108*].

Failure to attend hearing. Where a party fails to attend or be represented at a hearing of which he has been duly notified, the Commissioners may postpone or adjourn a hearing or (unless satisfied that there is good and sufficient reason for such failure, and after considering any written or other representations) hear and determine the proceedings. [*SI 1994 No 1812, Reg 14*]. Determinations in the absence of the taxpayer or his agent have been upheld where notice of the meeting was received by the appellant (*R v Tavistock Commrs (ex p Adams) (No 1) QB 1969, 46 TC 154; R v Special Commr (ex p Moschi) CA, [1981] STC 465* and see *Fletcher & Fletcher v Harvey CA 1990, 63 TC 539*), but Commissioners were held to have acted unreasonably in refusing to re-open proceedings when the taxpayer's agent was temporarily absent when the appeal was called (*R & D McKerron Ltd CS 1979, 52 TC 28*). Where the taxpayer was absent through illness, a determination was quashed because the Commissioners, in refusing an adjournment, had failed to consider whether injustice would thereby arise to the taxpayer (*R v Sevenoaks Commrs (ex p Thorne) QB 1989, 62 TC 341* and see *Rose v Humbles CA 1971, 48 TC 103*). See also *R v O'Brien (ex p Lissner) QB, [1984] STI 710* where the determination was quashed when the appellant had been informed by the inspector that the hearing was to be adjourned.

Procedure and evidence at hearing. The Commissioners have wide discretion as to the manner in which the proceedings are conducted, and should seek to avoid inappropriate formality. They may require any witness to give evidence on oath or affirmation, and may admit evidence which would be inadmissible in a court of law. Evidence may be given orally or, if they so direct, by affidavit or statement recorded in a document (and they may, on their own motion or on the application of any party, at any stage require the personal attendance as a witness of the maker of such a statement or affidavit or the person who recorded the statement). They may take account of the nature and source of any evidence, and the manner in which it is given, in assessing its truth and weight. The parties may be heard in any order, but are entitled to give evidence, to call witnesses, to question witnesses (including other parties who give evidence), and to address the Commissioners both on the evidence and on the subject matter of the proceedings. [*SI 1994 No 1812, Reg 15*]. A party to the proceedings cannot insist on being examined on oath (*R v Special Commrs (in re*

Fletcher) CA 1894, 3 TC 289). False evidence under oath would be perjury under criminal law (*R v Hood Barrs CA, [1943] 1 All ER 665*). A taxpayer was held to be bound by an affidavit he had made in other proceedings (*Wicker v Fraser Ch D 1982, 55 TC 641*). A remission to Commissioners to hear evidence directed at the credit of a witness was refused in *Potts v CIR Ch D 1982, 56 TC 25*. Rules of the Supreme Court under which evidence can be obtained from a witness abroad cannot be used in proceedings before the Commissioners (*In re Leiserach CA 1963, 42 TC 1*). As to hearsay evidence under *Civil Evidence Act 1968*, see *Forth Investments Ltd Ch D 1976, 50 TC 617* and *Khan v Edwards Ch D 1977, 53 TC 597*.

The Commissioners are under no obligation to adjourn an appeal for the production of further evidence (*Hamilton v CIR CS 1930, 16 TC 28; Noble v Wilkinson Ch D 1958, 38 TC 135*), and were held not to have erred in law in determining assessments in the absence abroad of the taxpayer (*Hawkins v Fuller Ch D 1982, 56 TC 49*).

The taxpayer has no general right to conduct his appeal in writing without attending the hearing (*Banin v Mackinlay CA 1984, 58 TC 398*), although written pleadings may, at the Commissioners' discretion, be taken into account (*Caldicott v Varty Ch D 1976, 51 TC 403*).

In reaching their decision, the Commissioners may not take into account matters appropriate for application for judicial review (*Aspin v Estill CA 1987, 60 TC 549*). They do not generally have the power to review on appeal the exercise of a discretion conferred on the Revenue by statute (see *Slater v Richardson & Bottoms Ltd Ch D 1979, 53 TC 155; Kelsall v Investment Chartwork Ltd Ch D 1993, 65 TC 750*).

For the extent to which Commissioners may use their local knowledge, see *Forest Side Properties (Chingford) Ltd v Pearce CA 1961, 39 TC 665*.

Onus of proof. The onus is on the appellant to displace an assessment (but see 9.2 BACK DUTY for onus on Crown to prove fraud or wilful default to support extended time limit assessments). See *Brady v Group Lotus Car Companies plc CA 1987, 60 TC 359* where the onus of proof remained with the taxpayer where the amount of normal time limit assessment indicated contention of fraud. The general principle emerges in appeals against estimated assessments in 'delay cases' (see 4.7 above) which are the bulk of appeals heard by the General Commissioners. For examples of cases in which the Commissioners have confirmed estimated assessments in the absence of evidence that they were excessive, see *T Haythornthwaite & Sons Ltd v Kelly CA 1927, 11 TC 657; Stoneleigh Products Ltd v Dodd CA 1948, 30 TC 1; Rosette Franks (King St) Ltd v Dick Ch D 1955, 36 TC 100; Pierson v Belcher Ch D 1959, 38 TC 387*. In a number of cases, the Courts have supported the Commissioners' action in rejecting unsatisfactory accounts (e.g. *Cain v Schofield Ch D 1953, 34 TC 362; Moll v CIR CS 1955, 36 TC 384; Cutmore v Leach Ch D 1981, 55 TC 602; Coy v Kime Ch D 1986, 59 TC 447*) or calling for certified accounts (e.g. *Stephenson v Waller KB 1927, 13 TC 318; Hunt & Co v Joly KB 1928, 14 TC 165; Wall v Cooper CA 1929, 14 TC 552*). In *Anderson v CIR CS 1933, 18 TC 320*, the case was remitted where there was no evidence to support the figure arrived at by the Commissioners (which was between the accounts figure and the estimated figure assessed), but contrast *Bookey v Edwards Ch D 1981, 55 TC 486*. The Commissioners are entitled to look at each year separately, accepting the appellant's figures for some years but not all (*Donnelly v Platten CA(NI) 1980, [1981] STC 504*). Similarly, the onus is on the taxpayer to substantiate his claims to relief (see *Eke v Knight CA 1977, 51 TC 121; Talib v Waterson Ch D, [1980] STC 563*).

For the standard of proof required in evidence, see *Les Croupiers Casino Club v Pattinson CA 1987, 60 TC 196*.

The Commissioners' decision. The Revenue representative must not be present while the Commissioners are deliberating their decision unless the other party or parties (or their representative(s)) are also present (*R v Brixton Commrs KB 1912, 6 TC 195*). The Commissioners' determination was quashed where the Clerk had discussed the case with Revenue representatives between hearing and announcement of determination (*R v Wokingham Commrs (ex p Heron) QB 1984, [1984] STI 710*).

If it appears to the Commissioners that the appellant has been over- or under-charged by any assessment under appeal, they must reduce or increase that assessment accordingly, but otherwise the assessment stands good. A determination of gains assessable determines the appeal; if the Commissioners alter the assessment, they are not obliged to determine the revised tax payable. [*TMA 1970, s 50(6)–(8); SI 1994 No 1813*]. Only the assessment by which the taxpayer was overcharged may be reduced under *TMA 1970, s 50(6)*. Any decision is by a majority of the Commissioners hearing the proceedings, with the presiding Commissioner having a casting vote where necessary. The final determination may be announced orally at the end of the hearing or may be reserved. In either case, the Clerk to the Commissioners must send to each party a notice (including details of the procedure for appeals from the General Commissioners) setting out the determination, and unless the determination was given at the hearing, the date of such notice is the date of the determination. [*SI 1994 No 1812, Reg 16; SI 1999 No 3293, Reg 3*]. Where the Clerk announced the decision wrongly, it was held that the correct decision stood good (*R v Morleston & Litchurch Commrs KB 1951, 32 TC 335*) (and see below under *Miscellaneous: Irregularities*).

Where Commissioners determined appeals in principle and held a further hearing to adjust assessments, their action in refusing to admit further evidence for the taxpayer at the later hearing was upheld (*R v St Marylebone Commrs (ex p Hay) CA 1983, 57 TC 59*). They are entitled, however, to alter their decision in principle at a later hearing (*Larner v Warrington Ch D 1985, 58 TC 557*). See also *Gibson v Stroud Commrs Ch D 1989, 61 TC 645*.

A decision of the Commissioners is not legally binding on them or any other Commissioners in any other proceedings, even on appeal by the same taxpayer against a similar assessment for another year (*CIR v Sneath CA 1932, 17 TC 149* and cf. *Edwards v 'Old Bushmills' Distillery HL 1926, 10 TC 285; Abdul Caffoor Trustees PC 1961, 40 ATC 93*).

Review of the Commissioners' final determination. A decision of the Commissioners is generally final and conclusive [*TMA 1970, s 46(2)*], but the Commissioners may review and set aside or vary their final determination on the application of any party or of their own motion where they are satisfied that either

(1) it was wrongly made as a result of administrative error, or

(2) a party entitled to be heard failed to appear or be represented for good and sufficient reason, or

(3) relevant information had been supplied to the Clerk or to the appropriate inspector or other Revenue officer prior to the hearing but was not received by the Commissioners until after the hearing.

A written application for such a review must be made to the Commissioners not later than 14 days after the date of the notice of the determination (or by such later time as the Commissioners may allow), stating the grounds in full. Where the Commissioners propose of their own motion to review a determination, they must serve notice on the parties not later than 14 days after the date of the notice of the determination.

The parties are entitled to be heard on any such review or proposed review. If practicable, the review is to be determined by the Commissioners who decided the case, and if they set aside the determination, they may substitute a different determination or order a rehearing before the same or different Commissioners. A decision to vary or substitute a final determination is to be notified in the same way as the original determination (see above).

[*SI 1994 No 1812, Reg 17*].

See 4.10 below as regards application for judicial review where the Commissioners have acted unfairly or improperly.

Special procedure. *Proceedings relating to tax on chargeable gains.* Where material, the market value of an asset or the apportionment of an amount or value is, if so required by any party, to be recorded in the final determination. They may be proved in any proceedings relating to tax on chargeable gains by a certificate signed by the Clerk to the Commissioners (in certain cases the clerk or registrar of another tribunal), or by the inspector where the appeal was settled by agreement, stating the material particulars. [*SI 1994 No 1812, Reg 18; SI 1999 No 3293, Reg 4*].

Reference to other tribunals. Certain questions relating to the value of land or of a lease of land must be referred to the appropriate Lands Tribunal, and similarly in relation to unquoted shares to the Special Commissioners (see *TMA 1970, ss 46B, 46D* at 4.5 above). The instant proceedings are to be determined without awaiting the outcome of such referral. [*SI 1994 No 1812, Reg 19; SI 1999 No 3293, Reg 5*].

Miscellaneous. *Irregularities.* Any irregularity resulting from failure to comply with regulations or with any Commissioners' direction given before a final determination is reached, shall not, of itself, render the proceedings void, and before reaching that determination the Commissioners may, and if they consider that any person has been prejudiced by the irregularity must, give such direction as they think just to cure or waive any irregularity which comes to their attention. Clerical errors in any document recording a direction or decision of the Commissioners may be corrected by any of the Commissioners concerned (or by the Clerk if all the Commissioners have died or ceased to be Commissioners) by certificate under his hand. [*SI 1994 No 1812, Reg 24*].

Notices must be in writing unless the Commissioners authorise them to be given orally. [*SI 1994 No 1812, Reg 25*].

Service of any notice or document (other than a witness summons, see above) may be by post, by (legible) facsimile transmission etc. or by delivery at the proper address. [*SI 1994 No 1812, Reg 26(1)*]. The persons and addresses to whom and which a document may be sent or delivered are set out in *Reg 26(2)(3)*, and the provisions for substituted or waived service in certain cases in *Reg 27*.

Penalties. Any appeal against summary penalties determined under regulations as above lies to the High Court (in Scotland, the Court of Session). [*TMA 1970, s 53; SI 1994 No 1813*].

Guidance notes on Appeals to the General Commissioners (TAXGUIDE 4/00) were published in June 2000 by the Tax Faculty of the ICAEW.

(*b*) **Special Commissioners**

The provisions applicable to the General Commissioners (see (*a*) above) apply equally to the Special Commissioners, with the following variations.

4.8 Appeals

Constitution of Tribunal. Any one, two or three of the Special Commissioners may hear any proceedings. If two or three Commissioners are sitting, the Presiding Special Commissioner, or, if he is not sitting, the Commissioner nominated by him, shall preside at the hearing. With the consent of all parties, proceedings may be continued by any one or two of the Commissioners unless the Presiding Special Commissioner otherwise directs. [*SI 1994 No 1811, Regs 2, 13*].

Preparation for hearing. *Listing and notice of hearing.* Before notifying the parties of the place, date and time of a hearing, the Clerk to the Commissioners must satisfy himself that the Special Commissioners have jurisdiction over the proceedings and that he has sufficient particulars for determination. The Presiding Special Commissioner may direct that such notifications are not to be sent. [*SI 1994 No 1811, Reg 3*].

General power to give directions. The Commissioner(s) have wide direction-giving powers, on the application of any of the parties to proceedings or of their own motion. Applications by the parties (otherwise than during the hearing) must be in writing to the Clerk, and if not made with the consent of all the parties, must be served by the Clerk on any affected party, who may object. [*SI 1994 No 1811, Reg 4*].

Witnesses. The maximum penalty which the Commissioner(s) may summarily determine for failure to attend or refusal to be sworn or affirm, to answer any lawful question or to produce documents as required is £10,000. [*SI 1994 No 1811, Regs 5, 24(2)*].

Preliminary hearing. Where it appears to a Special Commissioner that any proceedings would be facilitated by holding a preliminary hearing, he may, on the application of a party or of his own motion, give directions for such a hearing to be held. The Clerk to the Special Commissioners must give to all the parties 14 days' notice (or such shorter time as the parties agree or the Commissioner sees fit to impose) of the time and place of the hearing. On a preliminary hearing, the Commissioner has wide direction-giving powers, and may, if the parties so agree, determine the proceedings without any further hearing. [*SI 1994 No 1811, Reg 9*]. See below as regards powers of Commissioner to obtain information on preliminary hearing of any proceedings.

Hearing and determination of proceedings. *Hearings in public or private.* Hearings before the Special Commissioner(s) are in public, unless any party applies by notice to the Clerk for the hearing (or any part) to be in private. A Revenue application for a private hearing requires in addition a direction by a Special Commissioner. The rules for attendance at a private hearing follow those before the General Commissioners (as above). [*SI 1994 No 1811, Reg 15*].

Power to obtain information. The powers of General Commissioners to obtain information apply to both a preliminary hearing before a Special Commissioner and to the hearing of the proceedings, except that the specific penalty provisions for failure to comply with a notice do not apply (although the general penalty for failure to comply with Commissioner's direction, see below, *does* apply). [*SI 1994 No 1811, Regs 10, 24(1)*].

The Commissioners' decision. The recording of the Commissioner(s)' decision must contain a statement of the facts found and the reasons for the determination. After reserving the final determination, the Commissioner(s) may give a written decision in principle on one or more of the issues arising, and adjourn the making of the final determination until after that decision has been issued and any further questions arising from it have been agreed by the parties or decided by the Commissioner(s) after hearing the parties. A decision in principle must contain a statement of the facts and the reasons for the decision, and these need not be repeated in the document recording the final determination. [*SI 1994 No 1811, Reg 18; SI 1999 No 3292, Reg 4*].

Review of the Commissioners' decision in principle may proceed in the same way as a review of a final determination. [*SI 1994 No 1811, Reg 19*].

Publication of decisions in principle or final determinations. The Presiding Special Commissioner may arrange for the publication of such reports of decisions in principle and final determinations as he considers appropriate. If the proceedings (or any part) were held in private, he must ensure that the report is in a form which, so far as possible, prevents the identification of any person whose affairs are dealt with. [*SI 1994 No 1811, Reg 20*]. A substantial number of cases (amounting to well over 50 in the first year from early 1995) is now reported, and these are referred to in the text of this publication where relevant. The Special Commissioners expect to have their attention drawn in appropriate cases to any of their previous published decisions which is relevant, unless superseded by a higher court decision. The Revenue considers that, whilst not creating any binding legal precedent, these decisions may be relevant in other cases, particularly if not appealed against, but that it would be inappropriate to enter into any discussion of a case which is, or may be, the subject of appeal to the High Court etc. (Revenue Tax Bulletin October 1995 pp 258, 259).

Orders for costs. The Commissioner(s) may make an order awarding costs (in Scotland expenses) of, or incidental to, the hearing of any proceedings against any party who has, in their opinion, acted wholly unreasonably in connection with the hearing, but not without giving that party the opportunity of making representations against the award. The award may be of all or part of the costs of the other party or parties, such costs to be taxed in the county court (in Scotland the sheriff court) if not agreed. In Northern Ireland, the Commissioners may determine the costs. [*SI 1994 No 1811, Reg 21*]. For this purpose an act 'in connection with the hearing' includes any action taken once the appeal has been consigned by one or both parties to the Special Commissioners (*Carter v Hunt 1999 (Sp C 220), [2000] SSCD 17*). Failure by the taxpayer to attend or be represented at the hearing without giving prior notification may be a contributory factor in an award of costs, as may a failure to comply with a Commissioners' direction (*Phillips v Burrows 1998 (Sp C 229, 229A), [2000] SSCD 107, 112*).

For a case in which costs were awarded against the Revenue, see *Scott and another (trading as Farthings Steak House) v McDonald (Sp C 91), [1996] SSCD 381*. In *Salt v Young (Sp C 205), [1999] SSCD 249*, the Revenue were refused costs on the grounds that although the taxpayer had, on an objective test, behaved unreasonably, he had not been *wholly* unreasonable, and his unreasonableness was connected with the hearing only to a very minor extent. Only in 'a very rare case' would the Court interfere with the Commissioners' decision as regards costs (see *Gamble v Rowe Ch D 1998, 71 TC 190* in which a refusal of costs was upheld).

Dismissal of appeal without full hearing. An appeal may be dismissed without a full hearing if there is no longer any live issue between the parties and it would not be in the public interest to proceed (*Self-assessed v Inspector of Taxes (No 2) 1999 (Sp C 224), [2000] SSCD 47*).

Penalty for failure to comply with Commissioner(s)' direction. The Commissioner(s) may summarily determine a penalty of up to £10,000 for any such failure, to be treated as if it were tax charged in an assessment and due and payable. [*SI 1994 No 1811, Reg 24(1)(3)*].

4.9 **APPEALS TO THE HIGH COURT**

Prior to the determination of an appeal by the Commissioners, the Court may be prepared to consider an application seeking a determination as to whether the Revenue may make use of certain 'tax-altering' provisions in relation to the assessments under appeal (*Balen v CIR Ch D 1976, 52 TC 406; Beecham Group plc v CIR Ch D 1992, 65 TC 219*).

Case stated procedure — General Commissioners. Within 30 days of the date of final determination of an appeal (or of the variation or substitution of such a determination, see above) any party dissatisfied with the determination as being erroneous in point of law (for which see e.g. *Billows v Robinson CA 1991, 64 TC 17*) may serve notice on the Clerk requiring the Commissioners to state and sign a case for the opinion of the High Court (in Scotland the Court of Session, in Northern Ireland the Court of Appeal (NI)), setting forth the facts and final determination of the Commissioners. See *Grainger v Singer KB 1927, 11 TC 704* as regards receipt of the case. The 30-day time limit for requesting a case does not apply to the payment of the fee (*Anson v Hill CA 1968, 47 ATC 143*). The Commissioners may serve notice on the person who required the stated case requiring him, within a specified period of not less than 28 days, to identify the question of law on which he requires the case to be stated. They may refuse to state a case until such notice is complied with, or if they are not satisfied that a question of law is involved, or if the requisite fee (see below) has not been paid. A requirement for a case to be stated becomes invalid if the determination to which it relates is set aside or varied. After 31 December 1999, the case stated procedure does not apply to a final determination by the General Commissioners of an appeal in which a question has been referred to another tribunal (the Lands Tribunal or the Special Commissioners — see *TMA 1970, ss 46B, 46D* at 4.5 above) and all appeal rights have been exhausted. [*SI 1994 No 1812, Regs 20, 23; SI 1999 No 3293, Reg 6*].

A fee of £25 is payable to the Clerk by the person requiring the case before he is entitled to have it stated. [*TMA 1970, s 56(3); SI 1994 No 1813*]. A single case may have effect as regards each of a number of appeals heard together (*Getty Oil Co v Steele and related appeals Ch D 1990, 63 TC 376*).

If the taxpayer dies, his personal representatives stand in his shoes (*Smith v Williams KB 1921, 8 TC 321*).

Although the case stated procedure envisages the determination of the proceedings before the Commissioners, where an appeal has been decided in principle but there may be considerable delay in reaching figures for the formal determination, the Court will accept a case stated in principle (see e.g. *Rank Xerox Ltd v Lane HL 1979, 53 TC 185*).

The case stated procedure is not open to a successful party to an appeal (*Sharpey-Schafer v Venn Ch D 1955, 34 ATC 141*), but where another party requires a case, the successful party may invite the Commissioners to include in the case an additional question relating to another ground on which the Commissioners had found against it (*Gordon v CIR CS 1991, 64 TC 173*). In the case of a partnership, the procedure is available to any one of the partners, with or without the consent of the others (*Sutherland & Partners v Barnes and Another CA 1994, 66 TC 663*).

Consideration of draft case. Within 56 days of receipt of a notice requiring a stated case (or of the Commissioners being satisfied as to the question of law involved), the Clerk must send a draft of the case to all the parties. Written representations thereon may be made to the Clerk by any party within 56 days after the draft case is sent out, with copies to all the other parties, and within a further 28 days further representations may similarly be made in response. Any party to whom copies of representations are not sent may apply to the Clerk for a copy. The validity of a case after it has been stated and signed (see below), and of any subsequent proceedings, is not affected by a failure to meet these time limits or by a failure to send copies of representations to all parties. [*SI 1994 No 1812, Reg 21*].

An application for the taxpayer's name to be withheld was refused (*In re H Ch D 1964, 42 TC 14*) as was an application for the deletion of a passage possibly damaging the taxpayer (*Treharne v Guinness Exports Ltd Ch D 1967, 44 TC 161*). An application for judicial review on the ground that the case did not cover all matters in dispute was refused in *R v Special Commrs (ex p Napier) CA 1988, 61 TC 206*. In *Danquah v CIR Ch D 1990, 63 TC 526*, an application for the statement of a further case was refused where the case did not set out all the questions raised by the taxpayer in the originating motion by which he had sought an order directing the Commissioners to state a case. The proper course was for the taxpayer to apply for remission of the case for amendment under *TMA 1970, s 56(7)*. See also *Consolidated Goldfields plc v CIR Ch D 1990, 63 TC 333* (dealt with further below) in which a request to remit a case to the Commissioners for further findings of fact was refused.

Preparation and submission of final case. As soon as may be after the final date for representations (see above), the Commissioners, after taking into account any representations, must state and sign the case. In the event of the death of a Commissioner, or of his ceasing to be a Commissioner, the case is to be signed by the remaining Commissioner(s) or, if there are none, by the Clerk. The case is then sent by the Clerk to the person who required it to be stated, and the other parties notified accordingly.

In England, Wales and Scotland, the party requiring the case must transmit it to the High Court (in Scotland, the Court of Session) within 30 days of receiving it, and at or before the time he does so must notify each of the other parties that the case has been stated on his application and send them a copy of the case. The 30 day time limit (under the similar earlier provisions of *TMA 1970, s 56(4)*) is mandatory (*Valleybright Ltd (in liquidation) v Richardson Ch D 1984, 58 TC 290; Petch v Gurney CA 1994, 66 TC 473*), and may run from the date the case is received by the taxpayer's authorised agent (*Brassington v Guthrie Ch D 1991, 64 TC 435*). The notification (and copy) to the other parties is required only to give 'adequate notice' of the appeal and not to be 'too long delayed' (*Hughes v Viner Ch D 1985, 58 TC 437*). In Northern Ireland, slightly different rules apply (and see *CIR v McGuckian CA(NI) 1994, 69 TC 1*).

[*SI 1994 No 1812, Regs 22, 23*].

The High Court (or Court of Session or Court of Appeal (NI)) hears and determines any question(s) of law arising on the case, and may reverse, affirm or amend the determination of the Commissioners, or may remit the matter to the Commissioners with the opinion of the Court thereon, or may make such other order as seems to it fit. It may also cause the case to be sent back for amendment. An appeal from the decision of the High Court lies (in England and Wales) to the Court of Appeal and thence (with leave) to the House of Lords. In certain cases, 'leap-frog' appeals direct from the High Court to the House of Lords may be permitted under *Administration of Justice Act 1969, s 12* (see e.g. *Fitzleet Estates Ltd v Cherry HL 1977, 51 TC 708*). In the case of an appeal against a decision on an appeal against an assessment, tax must be paid in accordance with the Commissioners' decision. Following the decision on appeal, any tax overpaid is refunded with such interest as the Court may allow, and any amount undercharged is due and payable 30 days after the inspector issues a notice of the amount due. [*TMA 1970, s 56(6)–(9)*].

Once set down for hearing, a case cannot be declared a nullity (*Way v Underdown CA 1974, 49 TC 215*) or struck out under *Order 18, Rule 19 of the Rules of the Supreme Court* (*Petch v Gurney CA, [1994] STC 689*), but the appellant may withdraw (*Hood Barrs v CIR (No 3) CA 1960, 39 TC 209*, but see *Bradshaw v Blunden (No 2) Ch D 1960, 39 TC 73*). Where the appellant was the inspector and the taxpayer did not wish to proceed, the Court refused to make an order on terms agreed between the parties (*Slaney v Kean Ch D 1969, 45 TC 415*).

The Court may, however, return a case for amendment. [*TMA 1970, s 56(7)*]. In *Consolidated Goldfields plc v CIR Ch D 1990, 63 TC 333*, the taxpayer company's request that the High Court remit a case to the Commissioners for further findings of fact was refused. Although the remedy was properly sought, it would only be granted if it could be shown that the desired findings were (*a*) material to some tenable argument, (*b*) reasonably open on the evidence adduced, and (*c*) not inconsistent with the findings already made. However, in *Fitzpatrick v CIR CS 1990, [1991] STC 34*, a case was remitted where the facts found proved or admitted, and the contentions of the parties, were not clearly set out, despite the taxpayer's request for various amendments and insertions to the case, and in *Whittles v Uniholdings Ltd (No 1) Ch D, [1993] STC 671*, remission was appropriate in view of the widely differing interpretations which the parties sought to place on the Commissioners' decision (and the case was remitted a second time (see *[1993] STC 767*) to resolve misunderstandings as to the nature of a concession made by the Crown at the original hearing and apparent inconsistencies in the Commissioners' findings of fact). If a case is remitted, the taxpayer has the right to attend any further hearing by the Commissioners (*Lack v Doggett CA 1970, 46 TC 497*) but the Commissioners may not, in the absence of special circumstances, admit further evidence (*Archer-Shee v Baker CA 1928, 15 TC 1; Watson v Samson Bros Ch D 1959, 38 TC 346; Bradshaw v Blunden (No 2) Ch D 1960, 39 TC 73*), but see *Brady v Group Lotus Car Companies plc CA 1987, 60 TC 359* where the Court directed the Commissioners to admit further evidence where new facts had come to light suggesting the taxpayers had deliberately misled the Commissioners. Errors of fact in the case may be amended by agreement of the parties prior to hearing of the case (*Moore v Austin Ch D 1985, 59 TC 110*). See *Jeffries v Stevens Ch D 1982, 56 TC 134* as regards delay between statement of case and motion for remission.

A new question of law may be raised in the Courts on giving due notice to the other parties (*Muir v CIR CA 1966, 43 TC 367*) but the Courts will neither admit evidence not in the stated case (*Watson v Samson Bros Ch D 1959, 38 TC 346; Cannon Industries Ltd v Edwards Ch D 1965, 42 TC 625; Frowd v Whalley Ch D 1965, 42 TC 599*, and see *R v Great Yarmouth Commrs (ex p Amis) QB 1960, 39 TC 143*) nor consider contentions of which evidence in support was not produced before the Commissioners (*Denekamp v Pearce Ch D 1998, 71 TC 213*).

Following the decision in *Pepper v Hart HL 1992, 65 TC 421*, the Courts are prepared to consider the parliamentary history of legislation, or the official reports of debates in Hansard, where all of the following conditions are met.

(*a*) Legislation is ambiguous or obscure, or leads to an absurdity.

(*b*) The material relied upon consists of one or more statements by a Minister or other promoter of the Bill together if necessary with such other parliamentary material as is necessary to understand such statements and their effect.

(*c*) The statements relied upon are clear.

Any party intending to refer to an extract from Hansard in support of any argument must, unless otherwise directed, serve copies of the extract and a brief summary of the argument intended to be based upon the extract upon all parties and the court not less than five clear working days before the first day of the hearing (Supreme Court Practice Note, 20 December 1994) (1995 STI 98).

Many Court decisions turn on whether the Commissioners' decision was one of fact supported by the evidence, and hence final. The Courts will not disturb a finding of fact if there was reasonable evidence for it, notwithstanding that the evidence might support a different conclusion of fact. The leading case is *Edwards v Bairstow & Harrison HL 1955, 36 TC 207*, in which the issue was whether there had been an adventure in the nature of trade. The Commissioners' decision was reversed on the ground that the *only* reasonable conclusion from the evidence was that there had been such an adventure. For a recent discussion of the application of this principle, see *Milnes v J Beam Group Ltd Ch D 1975, 50 TC 675.*

A Court decision is a binding precedent for itself or an inferior Court except that the House of Lords, while treating its former decisions as normally binding, may depart from a previous decision should it appear right to do so. For this see *Fitzleet Estates Ltd v Cherry HL 1977, 51 TC 708*. Scottish decisions are not binding on the High Court but are normally followed. Decisions of the Privy Council and of the Irish Courts turning on comparable legislation are treated with respect. A Court decision does not affect other assessments already final and conclusive (see 5.4 ASSESSMENTS) but may be followed, if relevant, in the determination of any open appeals against assessments and in assessments made subsequently irrespective of the years of assessment or taxpayers concerned (*Re Waring decd Ch D, [1948] 1 All ER 257; Gwyther v Boslymon Quarries Ltd KB 1950, 29 ATC 1; Bolands Ltd v CIR SC(I) 1925, 4 ATC 526*). Further, a Court decision does not estop the Crown from proceeding on a different basis for other years (*Hood Barrs v CIR (No 3) CA 1960, 39 TC 209*). A general change of practice consequent on a Court decision may affect error or mistake relief (see 12.7 CLAIMS).

For joinder of CIR in non-tax disputes, see *In re Vandervell's Trusts HL 1970, 46 TC 341.*

Special Commissioners. In the case of an appeal to the Special Commissioners, if the appellant or the Revenue is dissatisfied in point of law with a decision (whether in principle or on final determination) or with a decision varying or substituting such a decision, appeal may be made to the High Court. (This does not apply after 31 December 1999 in the case of a final determination by the Special Commissioners of an appeal in which a question has been referred to the Lands Tribunal and all appeal rights have been exhausted.) Further appeal may be made to the Court of Appeal and thence (with leave) to the House of Lords. A 'leap-frog' appeal to the Court of Appeal may be made if all the parties agree, the Commissioners certify that a point of law is involved relating wholly or mainly to the construction of an enactment which was fully argued and considered before them, and the leave of the Court of Appeal has been obtained. In Scotland appeals are to the Court of Session, in Northern Ireland to the Court of Appeal (NI), and thence in either case to the House of Lords. When a decision against which an appeal has been made is set aside or varied (see above), the appeal is treated as withdrawn.

In the case of an appeal against a decision on an appeal against an assessment, tax must be paid in accordance with the Commissioners' decision. Following the decision on appeal, any tax overpaid is refunded with such interest as the Court may allow, and any amount undercharged is due and payable 30 days after the inspector issues a notice of the amount due.

[*TMA 1970, ss 56A, 58; SI 1994 No 1813; SI 1999 No 3294*].

For the general statutory provisions and case law applicable equally to Special Commissioners, see above in relation to General Commissioners.

4.10 JUDICIAL REVIEW (PREROGATIVE ORDERS)

A taxpayer who is dissatisfied with the exercise of administrative powers may in certain circumstances (e.g. where the Revenue has exceeded or abused its powers or acted contrary to the rules of natural justice, or where the Appeal Commissioners have acted unfairly or improperly) seek a remedy in one of the prerogative orders of mandamus, prohibition and certiorari. This is now done by way of application for judicial review under *Supreme Court Act 1981, s 31* and *Order 53* of the *Rules of the Supreme Court.*

The issue on an application for leave to apply for judicial review is whether there is an arguable case (*R v CIR (ex p. Howmet Corporation and another) QB, [1994] STC 413*). The procedure is generally used where no other, adequate, remedy, such as a right of appeal, is available. See *R v Special Commr (ex p. Stipplechoice Ltd) (No 1) CA, [1985] STC 248 and (No 3) QB 1988, 61 TC 391*, *R v HMIT (ex p. Kissane and Another) QB, [1986] STC 152*, *R v CIR (ex p. Goldberg) QB 1988, 61 TC 403* and *Re McGuckian CA(NI) 1999, [2000] STC 65*.

There is a very long line of cases in which the courts have consistently refused applications where a matter should have been pursued through the ordinary channels as described above. See, for example, *R v Special Commrs (ex p. Morey) CA 1972, 49 TC 71; R v Special Commrs (ex p. Emery) QB 1980, 53 TC 555; R v Walton General Commrs (ex p. Wilson) CA, [1983] STC 464; R v Special Commrs (ex p. Esslemont) CA, 1984 STI 312; R v Brentford General Commrs (ex p. Chan and Others) QB 1985, 57 TC 651; R v Special Commr (ex p. Napier) CA 1988, 61 TC 206; R v North London General Commrs (ex p. Nii-Amaa) QB, [1999] STC 644*. See, however, *R v HMIT and Others (ex p. Lansing Bagnall Ltd) CA 1986, 61 TC 112* for a successful application where the inspector issued a notice under a discretionary power on the footing that there was an obligation to do so, and *R v CIR (ex p. J Rothschild Holdings plc) CA 1987, 61 TC 178* where the Revenue were required to produce internal documents of a general character relating to their practice in applying a statutory provision. See also *R v CIR (ex p. Taylor) (No 1) CA 1988, 62 TC 562* where an application for discovery of a document was held to be premature, and *R v Inspector of Taxes, Hull, ex p. Brumfield and others QB 1988, 61 TC 589*, where the court was held to have jurisdiction to entertain an application for judicial review of a failure by the Revenue to apply an established practice not embodied in an extra-statutory concession (cf. *R v CIR (ex p. Fulford-Dobson) QB 1987, 60 TC 168* at 27.4 INLAND REVENUE: ADMINISTRATION, which see for 'care and management' powers of the Revenue). It was held that there had been no unfairness by the Revenue when it refused to assess on the basis of transactions that would have been entered into by the applicants had a Revenue Statement of Practice been published earlier (*R v CIR, ex p. Kaye QB 1992, 65 TC 82*). A similar view was taken in *R v CIR (ex p. S G Warburg & Co Ltd) QB 1994, 68 TC 300* where the Revenue declined to apply a previously published practice because not only was it not clear that the taxpayer's circumstances fell within its terms but also the normal appeal procedures were available.

The first step is to obtain leave to apply for judicial review from the High Court. Application for leave is made ex parte to a single judge who will usually determine the application without a hearing. The Court will not grant leave unless the applicant has a sufficient interest in the matter to which the application relates. See *CIR v National Federation of Self-Employed and Small Businesses Ltd HL 1981, 55 TC 133* for what is meant by 'sufficient interest' and for discussion of availability of judicial review generally.

Time limit. Applications must be made **within three months** of the date when the grounds for application arose. The Court has discretion to extend this time limit where there is good reason, subject to conditions, but is generally very reluctant to do so. Grant of leave for review does not amount to a ruling that application is made in good time (*R v Tavistock Commrs (ex p. Worth) QB 1985, 59 TC 116*).

4.11 COSTS

Costs may be awarded by the Courts in the usual way. In suitable cases, e.g. 'test cases', the Revenue may undertake to pay the taxpayer's costs. There is no provision for the award of costs of appearing before General Commissioners or, for hearings notified before 1 September 1994, Special Commissioners. Costs awarded by the Courts may include expenses connected with the drafting of the Stated Case (*Manchester Corporation v Sugden CA 1903, 4 TC 595*). Costs of a discontinued application for judicial review were refused where the Revenue were not informed of the application (*R v CIR (ex p. Opman International UK) QB 1985, 59 TC 352)*. Law costs of appeals are not allowable for tax purposes generally (*Allen v Farquharson KB 1932, 17 TC 59; Smith's Potato Estates Ltd v Bolland HL 1948, 30 TC 267; Rushden Heel Co v Keene HL 1948, 30 TC 298; Spofforth & Prince v Golder KB 1945, 26 TC 310*) but see 17.3 DISPOSAL.

See 4.8 above as regards costs of Special Commissioners' hearings.

5 Assessments

Cross-references. See 4 APPEALS; 9 BACK DUTY; 11 CHILDREN; 44.3 OVERSEAS MATTERS; 45.4 PARTNERSHIPS; 56 SELF-ASSESSMENT for changes broadly from 1996/97; 63 UNDERWRITERS AT LLOYD'S. See 56.27 for assessment procedures under SELF-ASSESSMENT effective from 1996/97 onwards.

5.1 ASSESSMENTS

These are made by inspectors, or their delegates [*TMA 1970, s 113(1A)(1B)*] on the chargeable gains (less allowable losses) realised by the taxpayer in the year of assessment. Companies are assessed by reference to accounting periods as in 13.1 COMPANIES. Notices of assessment are served which must also state the date of issue and the time limit for making APPEALS (4). [*TMA 1970, s 29(1)(2)(5); F(No 2)A 1975, s 44(5)*]. The assessment must include a statement of the tax actually payable (*Hallamshire Industrial Finance Trust Ltd v CIR Ch D 1978, 53 TC 631*). A taxpayer may request the inspector (on form 64-8) to provide a copy of any assessment to any agent. As the inspector will calculate the amount of the assessment from the return forms, and the assessment becomes binding if not appealed against within 30 days after the date of the notice of assessment [*TMA 1970, s 31; F(No 2) A 1975, s 67(1)*], it is most important that the taxpayer should make accurate RETURNS (54) and at once check any assessment received. If assessments are not dealt with promptly, interest on unpaid tax may arise and APPEALS (4.4) may be out of time. The inspector's power of assessment is not limited to persons (or sources of income) within the area of his tax office (*R v Tavistock Commrs (ex p. Adams) (No 2) CA 1971, 48 TC 56*). See 4.5 APPEALS for jurisdiction of Commissioners on appeal.

In the absence of a satisfactory return the inspector may make an assessment to the best of his judgement. [*TMA 1970, s 29(1)(b)*]. As to this see *Blackpool Marton Rotary Club v Martin CA 1989, 62 TC 686, Phillimore v Heaton Ch D 1989, 61 TC 584* and *Van Boeckel v Customs & Excise Commissioners QB 1980, [1981] STC 290* (which related to the comparable value added tax provision of what is now *VATA 1994, s 73(1)*).

An assessment defective in form or containing errors may be validated by *TMA 1970, s 114(1)* but this provision does not extend to integral fundamental parts of the assessment such as the year of assessment for which it is made (*Baylis v Gregory HL 1988, 62 TC 1*). The courts may amend an assessment on appeal under *TMA 1970, s 56(6)* (*Pickles v Foulsham HL 1925, 9 TC 261; Bath & West Counties Property Trust Ltd v Thomas Ch D 1977, 52 TC 20*). For cases where it is sought to make an assessment out of time (see 5.5 below) by virtue of the taxpayer's fraudulent or negligent conduct etc., see 9.4 BACK DUTY.

Following the introduction of the 'Pay and File' system of corporation tax returns and payments (see TOLLEY'S CORPORATION TAX under Returns for a synopsis) for accounting periods ending after 30 September 1993, corporation tax assessments (including those charging corporation tax on chargeable gains) will in general be issued in agreed figures, as they will still be needed to finalise the position (unless no liability arises). Subject to this, the power of the inspector to make an assessment (e.g. where there is no return made by a company or he is dissatisfied with its return, there is a dispute which he or the company wishes to take to appeal or he makes a 'discovery' as in 5.2 below) is broadly unaffected save that revised assessing procedures apply in relation to determinations of claims for trading losses, capital allowances and group relief. See TOLLEY'S CORPORATION TAX under Capital Allowances, Groups of Companies and Losses. For accounting periods ending on or after 1 July 1999, the above is superseded by corporation tax self-assessment.

See 56.27 for assessment procedures under SELF-ASSESSMENT.

5.2 **DISCOVERY**

Self-assessment. If, as regards 1996/97 and subsequent years of assessment or company accounting periods ending on or after 1 July 1999 (see 13.2 COMPANIES), the Revenue 'discover', as regards any person (the taxpayer) and a chargeable period (i.e. for income tax and capital gains tax purposes, a year of assessment or for corporation tax, an accounting period), that

(*a*) any profits (i.e. income or chargeable gains) which ought to have been assessed to tax have not been assessed, or

(*b*) an assessment is or has become insufficient, or

(*c*) any relief given is or has become excessive,

then with the exceptions below, an assessment (a discovery assessment) may be made to make good to the Crown the apparent loss of tax.

No discovery assessment may be made in respect of a chargeable period, where a return under *TMA 1970, s 8* or *s 8A* (see 54.3 RETURNS) or a company tax return (see 54.11 RETURNS) has been delivered in respect of that period,

(1) if it would be attributable to an error or mistake in the return as to the basis on which the liability ought to have been computed and the return was, in fact, made on the basis, or in accordance with the practice, generally prevailing at the time when it was made; or

(2) unless either

  (i) the loss of tax is attributable to fraudulent or negligent conduct by the taxpayer or a person acting on his behalf, or

  (ii) at the time when the Revenue either ceased to be entitled to enquire (see 56.11 SELF-ASSESSMENT) into the return or completed their enquiries, they could not have been reasonably expected, on the basis of the information so far made available to them (see below), to be aware of the loss of tax.

For the purposes of (2)(ii) above, information is regarded as having been made available to the officer if it has been included in

(A) the return (or accompanying accounts, statements or documents) for the chargeable period concerned or for either of the two immediately preceding it, or

(B) a partnership return (see 54.14 RETURNS), where applicable, in respect of the chargeable period concerned or either of the two immediately preceding it, or

(C) any claim for the chargeable period concerned, or

(D) documents, etc. produced for the purposes of any enquiries into such a return or claim,

or is information the existence and relevance of which could reasonably be expected to be inferred from the above-mentioned information or are notified in writing to the Revenue. See also below.

An objection to a discovery assessment on the grounds that neither (i) nor (ii) in (2) above applies can be made only on an appeal against the assessment. (See 56.28 SELF-ASSESSMENT for right of appeal.)

[*TMA 1970, s 29; FA 1994, s 191(1), s 199(2)(3); FA 1998, s 117, Sch 18 paras 41–46, Sch 19 para 12*].

See 46.1 PAYMENT OF TAX as regards due date of payment of income tax and capital gains tax under these provisions.

A change of Revenue opinion on information previously made available to them is not grounds for a discovery assessment.

Particularly in large or complex cases, the standard accounts information details and other information included in the personal tax return (see 56.5 SELF-ASSESSMENT) may not provide a means of disclosure adequate to avoid falling within (2)(ii) above. The submission of further information, including perhaps accounts, may be considered appropriate but will not necessarily provide protection against a discovery assessment beyond that arising from submission of the return alone. The reasonable expectation test (see (2)(ii) above) must be satisfied. Where voluminous information beyond the accounts and computations is sent with the return, the Revenue recommend that there should be a brief indication of the relevance of the material. The Revenue will accept that for *TMA 1970, s 29* purposes documents submitted within a month of the return 'accompany' it (see (A) above) provided the return indicates that such documents have been or will be submitted. They will consider sympathetically a request that this condition be treated as satisfied where the time lag is longer than a month. (Revenue Press Release 31 May 1996 and Tax Bulletin June 1996 pp 313–315).

In *Hancock v CIR (Sp C 213), [1999] SSCD 287*, it was held that a taxpayer who had made errors in his tax return had exhibited standards of competence below those to be reasonably expected, that his conduct thus amounted to negligence (see (2)(ii) above), and that the Revenue did therefore have the power to make a discovery assessment.

Amendment of partnership statement where loss of tax discovered. Provisions broadly similar to those apply as regards an understatement of profits or excessive claim for relief or allowance in a partnership statement (see 56.9 SELF-ASSESSMENT), although the Revenue's remedy in this case is to amend the partnership statement, with consequent amendment of partners' self-assessments. [*TMA 1970, s 30B; FA 1994, s 196, s 199(2)(3), Sch 19 para 6; FA 1995, s 103(7), s 115(5)*].

Pre-self-assessment. The following provisions applied in respect of years of assessment before 1996/97 and company accounting periods ended before 1 July 1999. As regards partnership businesses commenced (or deemed to commence) before 6 April 1994, they continued to apply for all years of assessment before 1997/98. [*FA 1994, s 191(2)*].

If an inspector or the Board 'discovers' that insufficient gains have been assessed, insufficient tax assessed or excessive relief has been given, a corrective assessment can be made. [*TMA 1970, s 29(3)*]. The existence of an assessment under appeal capable of being increased and determined in the correct amount does not preclude the making of a further assessment and the consequent determination of both the original and further assessment (*Duchy Maternity Ltd v Hodgson Ch D 1985, 59 TC 85*). 'Discovery' has been given a very wide meaning by the courts. There is a discovery by the inspector if he comes to the honest conclusion that there has been under-assessment (*R v St Giles & St George Commrs (ex p. Hooper) KB 1915, 7 TC 59*). It has been established in a number of cases that a change of opinion or rectification of an error by the Revenue, including an arithmetical error in calculating the tax, without the ascertainment of any new fact amounts to discovery and this is so notwithstanding that the taxpayer had been notified of the former opinion. However, *if in the determination of an appeal (including a determination by agreement under TMA 1970, s 54)* (see 4.6 APPEALS) a specific matter has been adjudicated upon or agreed, the Revenue cannot re-open the matter by making a further assessment (*Cenlon Finance Co Ltd v Ellwood HL 1962, 40 TC 176*). The matter must have been dealt with specifically or clearly have been raised by implication, so that an inspector of average experience must have appreciated it was being raised (*Scorer v Olin Energy Systems Ltd HL 1985, 58 TC 592*). A further assessment may be made on incomplete information supplied on behalf of the taxpayer (*Gray v Matheson Ch D 1993, 65 TC 577*) and successive further assessments are permissible.

Similar considerations apply in determining whether an agreement under *TMA 1970, s 54* prevents a taxpayer making an error or mistake claim under *TMA 1970, s 33* (see 12.7 CLAIMS) (and see *Eagerpath Ltd v Edwards Ch D, [1999] STC 771*).

For other cases concerning discovery, see TOLLEY'S INCOME TAX and/or TOLLEY'S TAX CASES.

The Revenue has set out its view of the application in practice of the case law outlined above. The following are listed as circumstances in which there are clearly no grounds for *not* making discovery assessments:

(*a*) profits, gains or income have not earlier been charged to tax because of any form of fraudulent or negligent conduct;

(*b*) the inspector has been misled or misinformed in any way about the particular matter at issue;

(*c*) there is an arithmetical error in a computation which had not been spotted at the time agreement was reached, and which can be corrected by the making of an in date discovery assessment;

(*d*) an error is made in accounts and computations which it cannot be reasonably alleged was correct or intended, e.g. the double deduction from a capital gains tax computation of a particular item (say, retirement relief).

The Revenue also makes it clear that, by concession, the principles determining the making of a further assessment following settlement of an appeal by agreement will also be applied where agreement is reached prior to the issue of an assessment. Also by concession, whether or not there has been an appeal, a discovery assessment will not be made where, although the matter in question may not have been the subject of a specific agreement within the case law principles outlined above, the inspector's decision was based on full and accurate disclosure and was a tenable view, so that the taxpayer could have reasonably believed the inspector's decision to be correct (Revenue Pamphlet IR 131, SP 8/91).

See 12.5 CLAIMS for extended time limits for claims where fraudulent or negligent conduct is not involved.

Sumption: Capital Gains Tax. See A24.05.

5.3 DOUBLE ASSESSMENT

Where there has been 'double assessment' for the same cause and for the same chargeable period, a claim may be made to the Board for the assessment reflecting the overcharge to be vacated. An appeal on a claim may be made to the Commissioners having jurisdiction to hear an appeal against the assessment, or the later of the assessments, to which the claim relates. [*TMA 1970, s 32*]. See 12.7 CLAIMS for error or mistake relief and 33.1 INTERACTION WITH OTHER TAXES as regards alternative income tax and capital gains tax assessments.

5.4 FINALITY OF ASSESSMENTS

An assessment cannot be altered after the notice has been served except in accordance with the express provisions of the *Taxes Acts* [*TMA 1970, s 29(6)*], e.g. where the taxpayer appeals (see 4 APPEALS). Where over-assessment results from an *error or mistake* in a return, see 12.7 CLAIMS. An assessment as determined on appeal or not appealed against is final and conclusive (but see 46.13 PAYMENT OF TAX for Revenue 'equitable liability' treatment).

5.5 TIME LIMITS

For time limits under SELF-ASSESSMENT effective from 1996/97 onwards see 56.27 SELF-ASSESSMENT.

In cases other than SELF-ASSESSMENT assessment or additional assessment cannot be made later than six years from the end of the tax year to which it relates (or accounting period in the case of a company) [*TMA 1970, s 34*] except in cases of fraudulent or negligent conduct (for 1982/83 and earlier years, cases of fraud, wilful default, or neglect) or where there is specific statutory provision for later assessment. Assessments on personal representatives in respect of the deceased's chargeable gains before death must be made within three years after the end of the tax year in which death occurred and those arising from the fraudulent or negligent conduct (or fraud, wilful default, or neglect) of the deceased are restricted to years of assessment ending not earlier than six years before the death. [*TMA 1970, s 40; FA 1989, s 149(4)*]. In certain cases, specific provisions extend these time limits. See also 9.4, 9.5 BACK DUTY; 46.10, 46.12 PAYMENT OF TAX; 61 TIME LIMITS—FIXED DATES; 62 TIME LIMITS—MISCELLANEOUS and 63.1, 63.5 UNDERWRITERS AT LLOYD'S.

An assessment is made on the date on which the inspector authorised to make it signs a certificate in the appropriate assessments volume that he made certain assessments including the assessment in question (*Honig v Sarsfield CA 1986, 59 TC 337*).

5.6 TRUSTEES AND PERSONAL REPRESENTATIVES

For 1996/97 and subsequent years, CGT due from trustees or personal representatives may be assessed and charged on and in the name of any one or more of the 'relevant trustees' or, as the case may be, 'relevant personal representatives'. In relation to chargeable gains, the '*relevant trustees*' means the trustees in the tax year in which the gains accrue and any subsequent trustees of the settlement, and '*relevant personal representatives*' has a corresponding meaning. See 43.2 OFFSHORE SETTLEMENTS for the modification of this rule in relation to the 'exit charge' under *TCGA 1992, s 80* on trustees ceasing to be resident in the UK.

For 1995/96 and earlier years, trustees and personal representatives are assessed and charged in the name of any one or more of them in respect of disposals etc. made by them, but if an assessment is raised otherwise than on all of them, any person who is not resident or ordinarily resident in the UK may not be included.

Unless the assets are held by the trustees or personal representatives as nominees or bare trustees for another person absolutely (see 57.2 SETTLEMENTS), chargeable gains accruing to, and capital gains tax chargeable on, the trustees or personal representatives are not to be regarded as accruing to, or chargeable on, any other person. No trustee or personal representative is to be regarded as an individual for the purposes of the capital gains tax legislation.

[*TCGA 1992, s 65(1)(2)(4); FA 1995, s 103(7), s 114*].

See also 57.3 SETTLEMENTS.

5.7 NON-CORPORATE BODIES, PERSONAL REPRESENTATIVES AND RECEIVERS

Assessments may be made on the treasurer etc. of bodies which are not corporations; on personal representatives in respect of disposals made *by the deceased person* (cf. 5.6 above); and receivers appointed by a court. [*TMA 1970, ss 71, 74, 75, 77*].

Sumption: Capital Gains Tax. See A24.03.

6 Assets

Cross-references. See 7 ASSETS HELD ON 6 APRIL 1965; 8 ASSETS HELD ON 31 MARCH 1982; 21 EXEMPTIONS AND RELIEFS for assets exempt from capital gains tax; 22 FURNISHED HOLIDAY ACCOMMODATION; 24 GOVERNMENT SECURITIES; 36 LAND; 39.9 LOSSES for assets of negligible value; 42 MINERAL ROYALTIES; 48 PRIVATE RESIDENCES; 49 QUALIFYING CORPORATE BONDS; 58 SHARES AND SECURITIES; 64 UNIT TRUSTS ETC.; 65 VENTURE CAPITAL TRUSTS; 66 WASTING ASSETS.

6.1 Capital gains tax is charged in respect of chargeable gains accruing to a person on the disposal of 'assets'. [*TCGA 1992, s 1(1)*].

'*Assets*' comprise all forms of property, wherever situated, including incorporeal property (goodwill, options, debts, etc.), currency other than sterling, and any form of property created by the disposer, or otherwise coming to be owned without being acquired. [*TCGA 1992, s 21(1)*]. Sovereigns minted after 1837 are still sterling currency and as such are not within this definition.

The restating in euros of a holding of a participating EU currency on or after 1 January 1999 is not treated as involving the disposal of the original currency or the acquisition of a new holding of euros. The original currency and the new holding are treated as the same asset, acquired as the original currency was acquired. [*SI 1998 No 3177, Reg 36*].

For the treatment of currency other than sterling when disposed of by a 'qualifying company' in certain circumstances, see 21.5 and 21.8 EXEMPTIONS AND RELIEFS.

There is no general principle that assets must have a market value or that they must be transferable or assignable (*O'Brien v Benson's Hosiery (Holdings) Ltd HL 1979, 53 TC 241*). A right to share in a statutory fund for compensation to owners of expropriated foreign property is a form of property and therefore an asset (*Davenport v Chilver Ch D 1983, 57 TC 661*). (To a great extent this decision was superseded by ESC D50 announced in Revenue Press Release 19 December 1994 (see 17.7 DISPOSAL)). Tax is only chargeable in relation to an asset which existed at the time of disposal and not to an asset coming into existence only on a disposal which created it. 'Property' has the meaning of that which is capable of being owned in a normal legal sense and thus does not extend to include the right of freedom to trade and compete in the market place, but such a right must be distinguished from the goodwill in respect of the trade in question and which is an asset for capital gains tax purposes (*Kirby v Thorn EMI plc CA 1987, 60 TC 519*). The right to unquantified and contingent future consideration on the disposal of an asset is itself an asset (*Marren v Ingles HL 1980, 54 TC 76*).

The right to bring an action to enforce a bona fide claim, and which can be turned to account by negotiating a compromise yielding a capital sum, constitutes an asset. Such a right is acquired otherwise than by way of a bargain made at arm's length and at the time when the cause of action arises. Any capital sum received derives only from the right and not from other assets which may have been associated with the existence of the right (*Zim Properties Ltd v Proctor Ch D 1984, 58 TC 371*). However, in similar cases not involving contractual or statutory rights of action (see Revenue Capital Gains Manual CG 13010) by concession the Revenue now treat damages and compensation payments as derived from any underlying asset (and therefore exempt or taxable like that asset), and as exempt if there is no underlying asset. Entitlement to other reliefs is also determined on this basis, and the Revenue are prepared to consider extending time limits for claims where there has been a delay in obtaining compensation (Revenue Pamphlet IR 1, D33).

See also 17.7 DISPOSAL regarding capital sums derived from assets.

6.2 LOCATION OF ASSETS ('SITUS')

Where liability depends on where the assets are actually situated (e.g. a non-resident trading in the UK or individuals not domiciled here, see 44 OVERSEAS MATTERS) the following provisions apply to determine the location of assets.

(*a*) The situation of rights or interests (otherwise than by way of security) in or over *immovable property* is that of the immovable property.

(*b*) Subject to the following provisions, the situation of rights or interests (otherwise than by way of security) in or over *tangible movable property* is that of the tangible movable property.

(*c*) Subject to the following provisions, *a debt*, secured or unsecured, is situated in the UK if, and only if, the creditor is resident in the UK.

(*d*) *Shares or securities issued by any municipal or governmental authority*, or by any body created by such an authority, are situated in the country of that authority.

(*e*) Subject to paragraph (*d*) above, *registered shares or securities* are situated where they are registered and, if registered in more than one register, where the principal register is situated. A depositary receipt (see 58.21 SHARES AND SECURITIES) issued outside the UK for shares registered in the UK does not alter the location of the underlying shares, to which any consideration on disposal of the receipt will be largely, if not totally, attributable (Revenue Capital Gains Manual CG 50243).

(*f*) A *ship or aircraft* is situated in the UK if, and only if, the owner is then resident in the UK, and an interest or right in or over a ship or aircraft is situated in the UK if, and only if, the person entitled to the interest or right is resident in the UK.

(*g*) The situation of *goodwill* as a trade, business or professional asset is at the place where the trade, business or profession is carried on.

(*h*) *Patents, trade-marks and registered designs* are situated where they are registered, and if registered in more than one register, where each register is situated, and rights and licences to use a patent, trade-mark or registered design are situated in the UK if they, or any rights derived from them, are exercisable in the UK.

(*j*) *Copyright, design right and franchises*, and rights or licences to use any copyright work or design in which design right subsists, are situated in the UK if they or any right derived from them are exercisable in the UK.

(*k*) A *judgement debt* is situated where the judgement is recorded.

(*l*) A *non-sterling debt owed by a bank* and represented by a sum standing to the credit of an individual not domiciled in the UK is situated in the UK if, and only if, that individual is resident in the UK and the branch or other place of business of the bank where the account is maintained is itself situated in the UK.

[*TCGA 1992, s 275; Trade Marks Act 1994, Sch 5*].

Under the general law, *bearer shares and securities* transferable by delivery are situated where the certificate, etc. is kept (*Winans v A-G (No 2) HL, [1910] AC 27*).

See also *Standard Chartered Bank Ltd v CIR Ch D, [1978] STC 272* where share certificates lodged in the UK by a person who was resident and domiciled abroad were held to be situated abroad, being registered in South Africa and effectively transferable only in that country. Renounceable letters of allotment of registered shares in a company are documents evidencing rights against the company and are only enforceable (and thus situated) where the register is kept (*Young and Another v Phillips Ch D 1984, 58 TC 232*).

Securities issued by designated European Communities or international organisations (e.g. The Asian Development Bank, The African Development Bank and The European and

International Banks for Reconstruction and Development) or the European Investment Bank are taken for the purposes of capital gains tax to be situated outside the UK. Organisations are designated by Treasury order. [*TCGA 1992, s 265*]. A similar treatment applies to securities issued by the Inter-American Development Bank [*TCGA 1992, s 266*] and by the OECD Support Fund [*OECD Support Fund Act 1975, s 4*].

Sumption: Capital Gains Tax. See A3.31.

6.3 APPROPRIATIONS TO AND FROM TRADING STOCK

Where an asset acquired by a person otherwise than as trading stock is appropriated by him for the purposes of his trade as trading stock (whether on the commencement of the trade or otherwise) and a chargeable gain or allowable loss would have accrued to him if he had then sold the asset for its market value, he is treated as having then disposed of the asset at its then market value. Where the asset is appropriated for the purposes of a trade chargeable to income tax under Schedule D, Case I, the person may alternatively elect (under *TCGA 1992, s 161(3)*) that, in computing the assessable profits of the trade, the market value of the asset is reduced by the amount of the chargeable gain or increased by the allowable loss that would otherwise arise (i.e. he may treat the gain or loss as subject to income tax rather than capital gains tax). A partner must have the agreement of all his co-partners to make the election effective.

It used to be the case that no time limit was specified for making the above-mentioned election, and so a six-year time limit operated by virtue of *TMA 1970, s 43(1)* (see 12.5 CLAIMS). For 1996/97 onwards for CGT purposes and for company accounting periods ending on or after 1 July 1999 (the appointed day for corporation tax self-assessment — see 13.2 COMPANIES), less generous time limits have been specified. For CGT purposes, the election must be made on or before the first anniversary of 31 January following the tax year in which ends the period of account in which the asset is appropriated. For corporation tax purposes, it must be made within two years after the end of the accounting period in which the asset is appropriated.

[*TCGA 1992, s 161(1)(3)(3A)(4); FA 1996, Sch 21 para 36*].

Where an asset forming part of a person's trading stock is

(*a*) appropriated by him for any other purpose, or

(*b*) retained by him on his ceasing to carry on the trade,

he is treated as having acquired it at the time for a consideration equal to the amount brought into the accounts of the trade for tax purposes. [*TCGA 1992, s 161(2)*]. For the valuation of trading stock in such circumstances, see TOLLEY'S INCOME TAX under Schedule D, Cases I and II.

See 13.10 COMPANIES for appropriations of gilt-edged securities and qualifying corporate bonds and see also 13.14 COMPANIES for intra-group transfers of assets which are trading stock of one of the companies but not of the other and for acquisition 'as trading stock' generally.

See 36.4 LAND for deemed appropriation as trading stock where transactions in land are within *ICTA 1988, s 776(2)(c)*.

See 26.2 INDEXATION for transitional relief for 1993/94 and 1994/95 in respect of 'indexation losses' referable to appropriations to trading stock in the case of individuals and trustees of settlements made before 30 November 1993.

6.4 **KNOW-HOW**

Consideration for a disposal of know-how used in a trade which continues to be carried on by the disposer after the disposal is treated, for all purposes, as a trading receipt unless

(i) the consideration is otherwise chargeable as a revenue or income receipt; or

(ii) the buyer is a body of persons (this term, here and in (iii) and (iv) below, includes a partnership), exercising control over the seller; or

(iii) the seller is a body of persons exercising control over the buyer; or

(iv) the buyer and seller are bodies of persons together controlled by a third person.

Where a person disposes of know-how in connection with the disposal of part or the whole of the trade in which it was used, any consideration for the know-how is treated as a payment for goodwill. These provisions do not apply to

(*a*) both parties where a written joint election is made within two years of the disposal; or

(*b*) the acquirer only where the trade concerned was, before the acquisition, carried on wholly outside the UK.

If the consideration is, under (*a*) or (*b*), not regarded as a payment for goodwill, the acquirer is treated, for the purpose of claiming writing-down allowances, as if he had acquired the know-how for use in a trade previously carried on by him. However, the exclusion at (*a*) or (*b*) does not apply where any of (ii)–(iv) above applies.

Where consideration for the disposal of know-how is not taxed as a deemed trading receipt, or otherwise as an income or revenue receipt, or as a payment for goodwill, it is taxed under Schedule D, Case VI unless any one of (ii)-(iv) above applies. The consideration received is subject to the deduction of expenditure wholly and exclusively incurred in the acquisition or disposal of the know-how concerned. [*ICTA 1988, ss 530, 531*].

6.5 **PATENTS**

Capital sums received from the sale of patent rights are specifically taxable as income under Schedule D, Case VI. See TOLLEY'S INCOME TAX under Patents. [*ICTA 1988, s 524*].

6.6 **MILK QUOTA**

The milk quota system was introduced by the European Community in 1984 in order to regulate overall milk production (EC Council Regulation 856/84). Under the scheme, each member state was allocated a production quota. The national quota was then divided between all of the country's milk producers. If total UK production for any year exceeds the national quota then a levy is payable to the European Union by the Intervention Board (previously the Milk Marketing Board). This levy is then charged on to individual producers who have exceeded their own quota.

Quota was originally allocated to milk producers in the UK by reference to levels of production for 1983 and was attached both to the producer and to the producer's land in use for milk production at 1 April 1984 (his 'holding'). Originally it was only possible to transfer milk quota permanently to another producer as part of a disposal of all or part of the holding to which it was attached *(SI 1984 No 1047)*. This could be by outright sale of the land or by use of a scheme by which a permanent transfer of the quota is achieved by granting a short lease of the land. From 1 April 1994, it is possible in limited circumstances to sell milk quota without selling the land (*SI 1994 No 160*).

The Revenue consider that milk quota is an asset separate from the land to which it is attached, and does not constitute an interest in or right over land. The decision in

Cottle v Coldicott (Sp C 40), [1995] SSCD 239 supports this view. The taxpayer sold part of his quota using the scheme involving a short lease of land referred to above. The Special Commissioners held that the sale of milk quota amounted to the disposal of a separate asset. It was not a part disposal of the taxpayer's land, as he had contended, and neither were the proceeds a capital sum derived from the land within *TCGA 1992, s 22(1)* (see 17.7 DISPOSAL). Since the quota was a separate asset which had been allocated without cost in 1984, it followed that the allowable cost of acquisition was nil.

For the Revenue's view of the treatment of milk quota as a separate asset, see Revenue Capital Gains Manual CG 77820–77860. See also Revenue Tax Bulletin February 1993 pp 49–51 and December 1995 p 265.

Where land and milk quota were acquired in a single transaction and the consideration has not been allocated separately to each, an apportionment will be required on a just and reasonable basis under *TCGA 1992, s 52(4)*. Where some of a producer's quota was allocated without cost in 1984 and some was subsequently purchased, the Revenue consider that the acquisition cost should be apportioned under *section 52(4)* by reference to the total holding of quota. (Revenue Capital Gains Manual CG 77887b, 77887c). However, the Revenue are also believed to take the not unreasonable view that milk quota are fungible assets and that therefore, under *TCGA 1992, s 104(3)*, the same identification rules should apply as for shares and securities (see 59.2 SHARES AND SECURITIES—IDENTIFICATION RULES). Whilst for disposals before 6 April 1998, the share pooling rules may be said to be analogous with the above apportionment rule, disposals on or after that date should be identified with acquisitions as summarised at 59.1 SHARES AND SECURITIES—IDENTIFICATION RULES.

Tenant farmers. On the termination of a tenancy, the milk quota reverts to the landlord. The tenant and the landlord may agree compensation for the tenant's loss of milk quota. If not, the tenant is entitled to statutory compensation under *Agriculture Act 1986, s 13*. Where the compensation is paid under a contract, the time of the disposal is the time the contract is made. If the contract is conditional, it is the time the condition is satisfied. Where the compensation is statutory or is paid under a contractual agreement which does not provide for the reversion of the quota, the date of the disposal is the date of receipt of the compensation.

Tenant farmers require the consent of the landlord before selling milk quota. If the tenant makes a payment to the landlord in consideration of such consent the expenditure qualifies as a deduction in computing the chargeable gain on disposal of the milk quota. The landlord will have received a capital sum derived from an asset, taxable under *TCGA 1992, s 22(1)* (see 17.7 DISPOSAL).

(Revenue Capital Gains Manual CG 77885, 77942–77946).

Compensation payments.

(1) '*Outgoers Schemes*'. On the introduction of the scheme, existing milk producers not wishing to receive quota and preferring to cease production were paid compensation under the Milk Supplementary Levy (Outgoers) Scheme 1984. Any farmer claiming payment under that scheme had the option to apply either for compensation for loss of profits in the five years immediately after ceasing to produce milk, or for compensation for the surrender of his milk quota. Payments in respect of loss of profits were treated as receipts of the farming business and therefore liable to tax as income. Payments in respect of surrender of quota were treated as capital and liable to capital gains tax (Hansard 18 July 1984, col 218 and 15 April 1985, col 27). Similar comments apply to the Milk (Community Outgoers) and Milk (Partial Cessation of Production) Schemes (Hansard 13 February 1987, col 384). Where compensation is so chargeable to CGT, it is chargeable for the year in which the producer was accepted into the scheme, although deferral of tax may be due under *TCGA*

1992, s 280 (consideration receivable in instalments — see 46.6 PAYMENT OF TAX) (Revenue Capital Gains Manual CG 77867).

(2) Compensation was paid to certain producers, (known as 'SLOM' producers), who were initially not allocated quota because of their participation in another scheme for temporary non-production of milk at the time the milk quota scheme was introduced. These producers were later allocated quota and were able to claim compensation for the loss of income arising from their temporary exclusion from the scheme. Claims had to be made by 30 September 1993. The compensation is for loss of profits and is treated as a receipt of the farming business, liable to tax as income. See Revenue Tax Bulletin May 1994 pp 127, 128.

(3) Compensation in respect of the temporary suspension of a proportion of quota is treated as a receipt of the farming trade, taxable as income. Such compensation was paid for 1987/88 and 1988/89. (Revenue Capital Gains Manual CG 77921).

(4) Compensation paid for a permanent reduction in milk quota is a capital sum derived from an asset, chargeable to capital gains tax under *TCGA 1992, s 22(1)* (see 17.7 DISPOSAL). Compensation for cuts announced between 1987 and 1990 was chargeable in the year in which the first instalment was received, but with deferral due under *TCGA 1992, s 280* as in (1) above. A further cut was announced in 1991 and the compensation was paid in five annual instalments starting in June 1992. A further instalment for UK producers, arising as a result of changes in rules which affected the conversion of the compensation into sterling, was announced in January 1997 and paid in 1996/97 or, in a few cases, 1997/98. Each of these instalments is chargeable in the year of receipt. The last-mentioned instalment included an element described as 'compensation in lieu of interest'; this is not chargeable to CGT but is instead taxable as income under Schedule D, Case III. (Revenue Capital Gains Manual CG 77922–77924 and Revenue Tax Bulletins May 1994 p 128, October 1997 p 474).

Rollover relief etc. Milk quota is a qualifying asset for rollover relief purposes (see 55.3 ROLLOVER RELIEF). It is not regarded as a WASTING ASSET (66) (Revenue Capital Gains Manual CG 77940). The concessionary rollover relief available for the exchange of joint interests in land also includes the parallel exchange of joint interests in milk quota (see 36.12 LAND).

6.7 **Bonus issue of Milk Marque shares to dairy farmers.** In October 1998, milk producers who supplied Milk Marque Ltd in the year to 31 March 1998 were awarded a bonus consisting of preference shares (or in some cases loan stock) in the company. The Revenue consider that the cost of acquisition of the shares or loan stock for capital gains tax purposes is equal to their nominal value. Such value should also be included in the producer's accounts as a trading receipt. (Revenue Tax Bulletin August 1999 p 685).

6.8 BOOKMAKERS' PITCHES

A bookmaker's pitch is a specified position at a racecourse on which the bookmaker may erect a stand and take bets. The Revenue take the view that the right to occupy a particular pitch at a particular racecourse is an asset for capital gains tax purposes. A disposal of such a right by way of auction, which is permitted with effect from 8 October 1998, is therefore a disposal of a chargeable asset. The date of disposal is the date on which the purchaser's bid is accepted. Where a pitch has not previously changed hands by way of auction, it will normally have no acquisition cost and no 31 March 1982 value. The exception is where the pitch was acquired by inheritance on or after 8 October 1998, in which case its acquisition cost to the legatee will be its market value at date of death, under the general rule at 16.1 DEATH.

A pitch qualifies as a business asset for the purposes of TAPER RELIEF (60). It does not fall within any of the classes of asset qualifying for ROLLOVER RELIEF (55.3).

(Revenue Tax Bulletin October 1999 pp 699, 700).

7 Assets held on 6 April 1965

Cross-reference. See 8 ASSETS HELD ON 31 MARCH 1982 for the restricted circumstances in which disposals after 5 April 1988 of such assets will be assessed by reference to the provisions of this chapter.

Sumption: Capital Gains Tax. See A4A.06.

7.1 Assets held on 6 April 1965 (the original base date for the purposes of capital gains tax) are still subject to special provisions contained in *TCGA 1992, s 35(9), Sch 2* and for this purpose may be divided into three categories.

(i) Quoted securities (see 7.2–7.7 below).

(ii) Land subsequently disposed of at a price including development value (see 7.8 below).

(iii) Other assets and miscellaneous aspects (see 7.9–7.14 below).

Married persons. The provisions relating to assets held on 6 April 1965 apply in relation to the disposal of an asset by one spouse, and who acquired it from the other spouse in a year of assessment when they were living together, as if the other's acquisition or provision of the asset had been the acquisition etc. of the asset by the spouse making the disposal. [*TCGA 1992, Sch 2 para 22*].

Groups of companies. The provisions relating to assets held on 6 April 1965 apply in relation to the disposal of an asset by a company which is or has been a member of a group of companies (within 13.11 COMPANIES), and which acquired the asset from another member of the group at the time when both were members of the group, as if all members of the group for the time being were the same person, and as if the acquisition or provision of the asset by the group, taken as a single person, had been the acquisition or provision of it by the member disposing of it. *After 31 March 1980*, this does not apply where the disposing company is an investment trust or acquired the asset after that date from an investment trust. [*TCGA 1992, s 174(4)(5)*].

7.2 **QUOTED SECURITIES: GENERAL RULES**

The provisions apply to 'quoted securities', namely

(i) Shares and securities which on 6 April 1965, or at any time within six years prior to that date, had quoted market values on a 'recognised stock exchange' in the UK or elsewhere.

(ii) Interests in unit trusts (see 64 UNIT TRUSTS ETC.), the prices of which are published regularly by the scheme's managers.

Shares or securities issued to an employee on terms restricting his right to dispose of them are excluded. [*TCGA 1992, Sch 2 para 1*].

'*Recognised stock exchange*' has its natural meaning. So far as the UK is concerned, it is understood that the Board accept that all the stock exchanges in the UK during the six years ended on 6 April 1965 were within this meaning but that the Provincial Brokers Exchange was outside it.

Subject to the election in 7.3 below, on a disposal of such assets after 5 April 1965, computation of the gain or loss accruing is made

(*a*) by reference to allowable expenditure computed according to the normal rules (i.e. cost/value at the *actual* date of acquisition and other allowable expenditure) (see 17.3 DISPOSAL), *and* (*b*) by reference to allowable expenditure, etc. calculated according to identical rules, except that market value at 6 April 1965 is treated as the acquisition cost. Market value at 6 April 1965 (except where special circumstances may affect the value, see *Hinchcliffe v Crabtree HL 1971, 47 TC 419*) is the greater of

   (i) a price half-way between the prices quoted in The Stock Exchange Daily Official List (or, for unit trusts, those published by the managers) and

   (ii) for shares and securities, the average of the highest and lowest prices for normal bargains, if any, on that day.

Of the computations under (*a*) and (*b*), the one which prevails is that which produces (after, if available, any indexation allowance) the smaller gain or the smaller loss. But if one computation produces a gain and the other a loss, the disposal is treated as giving rise to neither a chargeable gain nor an allowable loss. [*TCGA 1992, Sch 2 para 2(1), Sch 11 para 6*].

Where the original cost of the shares is not known and no election (see 7.3 below) has been made, it is the Revenue's practice to compute gains by reference to the value of the shares at 6 April 1965 and to disallow losses (computed on the same basis) altogether.

7.3 **Elections.** The taxpayer (or his personal representatives) may, however, elect (under *TCGA 1992, Sch 2 para 4*) that in respect of *all* disposals after 19 March 1968 (including those made before the election) of

(*a*) fixed interest securities and preference shares, or

(*b*) other quoted securities etc., or

(*c*) both kinds of securities etc. under (*a*) and (*b*),

their actual cost be ignored and computations made by reference to their market value at 6 April 1965 only. The election, which is irrevocable, must be made, by notice in writing to an officer of the Board. An election for pooling may be made for the purposes of capital gains tax on or before the first anniversary of the 31st January next following the year of assessment in which the first relevant disposal is made. In the case of an election for the purposes of corporation tax not later than two years after the end of the accounting period in which the first relevant disposal is made. In either case, the Board may allow an extension.

Prior to the introduction of self-assessment an election had to be made within two years after the end of the year of assessment or accounting period in which the first post-19 March 1968 disposal (the 'first relevant disposal') is made of shares or securities of the kind covered by the election or within such further time as the Board allow. [*TCGA 1992, Sch 2 para 11; FA 1996, Sch 21 para 42(2)*].

After 5 April 1985 (31 March 1985 for companies), another opportunity is available for an election to be made where the time limit given above has expired by reference to the first relevant disposal after 19 March 1968. The time limit is extended so as to apply by reference to the first relevant disposal after 5 April 1985 (31 March 1985 for companies).

'Fixed interest security' is as defined in 58.11 SHARES AND SECURITIES.

'Preference share' means any share the holder of which has a right to a dividend at a fixed rate but no other right to share in the profits of the company. Fixed rate dividends include those payable before 6 April 1973 and which varied at a rate fluctuating in accordance with the standard rate of income tax.

Married persons. An election does not cover quoted securities which the holder acquired from his spouse on a disposal after 19 March 1968 (or, again, after 31 March 1985) but such securities continue to be covered by an election which the transferor may have made. Where it is necessary to identify securities disposed of, earliest acquisitions are deemed to be disposed of first.

Example

H acquired 3,000 U plc ordinary shares in 1962 for £15,000. Their market value was £10 per share on 6 April 1965 and £12 per share on 31 March 1982. In September 2000, H sells 2,000 of the shares for £30 per share. The indexation factor for March 1982 to April 1998 is 1.047.

	£	£	£
Sale proceeds	60,000	60,000	60,000
Cost	10,000		
6 April 1965 value		20,000	
31 March 1982 value			24,000
Unindexed gain	50,000	40,000	36,000
Indexation allowance			
£24,000 × 1.047	25,128	25,128	25,128
Indexed gain	£24,872	£14,872	£10,872
Chargeable gain (subject to TAPER RELIEF (60))			£10,872

Notes to the example

(1) The comparison is firstly between the gain arrived at by deducting cost and that arrived at by deducting 6 April 1965 value. The smaller of the two gains is taken. If, however, an election had been made under either *TCGA 1992, Sch 2 para 4* or *TCGA 1992, s 109(4)* for 6 April 1965 value to be used in computing all gains and losses on quoted shares held at that date, this comparison need not be made and the taxable gain, subject to (*b*) below, would be £14,872.

(2) The second comparison is between the figure arrived at in (*a*) above and the gain using 31 March 1982 value. As the latter is smaller, it is substituted for the figure in (*a*) above by virtue of *TCGA 1992, s 35(2)*. If, however, an election had been made under *TCGA 1992, s 35(5)* for 31 March 1982 value to be used in computing all gains and losses on assets held at that date, neither this comparison nor that in (*a*) above need be made and the taxable gain would still be £10,872.

(3) Indexation is based on 31 March 1982 value in all three calculations as this gives the greater allowance.

(4) All comparisons are between gains *after* indexation and *before* taper relief.

Groups of companies. An election does not cover quoted securities which a company acquired from another group company (see 13.11 COMPANIES and note that the change in the residence requirement therein mentioned has effect for this purpose after 31 March 2000) on a disposal after 19 March 1968 (or, again, after 31 March 1985) but such securities continue to be covered by an election which the transferor company may have made. Where it is necessary to identify securities disposed of, earliest acquisitions are deemed to be disposed of first. An election by a company which is at the 'relevant time' the principal company of the group has effect as an election by any other company which at that time is a member of the group. No election may be made by any other company which is a member of the group at that time. The '*relevant time*' is the first occasion after 19 March 1968 (or, again, after 31 March 1985) when any company which is then a member of the group disposes of quoted securities of a kind covered by the election. These provisions apply notwithstanding that a company ceases to be a member of the group at any time after the relevant time. They do not apply to securities owned by a company which, after 19 March 1968 (or, again, after 31 March 1985) and before the relevant time, was not a member of the group and in relation to which either an election was made or no election was made within the time limit following a disposal.

[*TCGA 1992, s 109(4)(5), Sch 2 para 3, para 4(1)(2)(8)–(13), paras 5, 8; FA 2000, Sch 29 para 37*].

For the position as regards *partnerships*, see 45.13 PARTNERSHIPS.

7.4 QUOTED SECURITIES: IDENTIFICATION RULES

Where quoted securities of the same class are held on 6 April 1965, the identification rules for matching acquisitions with disposals depend on whether an election for 6 April 1965 market values under 7.3 above has been made or not. In addition, the rules are further governed by the general identification rules for securities etc. at 59 SHARES AND SECURITIES—IDENTIFICATION RULES. Consequently this paragraph (dealing with the situation on or after the '1985 date') and 7.5 below (covering the period before the '1985 date' but on or after the '1982 date') should be read with those general rules. The position before the '1982 date' is dealt with at 7.6 below. For the position where there has been a reorganisation or exchange etc. of quoted securities following an election under 7.3(*a*) or (*b*) but not both, see 7.7 below.

After the '1985 date', the identification rules given in (*a*) or (*b*) below apply to quoted securities held on 6 April 1965 excluding any 'relevant securities' so held. Note that for disposals after 5 April 1998, 'relevant securities' are no longer excluded from the general identification rules for capital gains tax purposes as opposed to those of corporation tax on chargeable gains. The full definition of 'relevant securities' is given at 59.6 SHARES AND SECURITIES—IDENTIFICATION RULES as are the identification rules. So far as concerns quoted securities held on 6 April 1965, this definition is only relevant to securities within the accrued income provisions (bondwashing) of *ICTA 1988, ss 710–728* (broadly any government, public authority, or company loan stock). Government securities retain their own identification rules for disposals before 2 July 1986, being exempt from capital gains tax for disposals on or after that date.

(*a*) Where *no* election has been made, pre-7 April 1965 acquisitions are treated as disposed of on a 'last-in, first-out' basis and only identified with disposals after all post-6 April 1965 acquisitions have been identified under the general identification rules. See 59.2–59.5 SHARES AND SECURITIES—IDENTIFICATION RULES.

(*b*) Where an election *is* made, pre-7 April 1965 acquisitions (at 6 April 1965 market values) form part, or the whole, of the '1982 holding' which is treated as a single asset (but one which cannot grow by further acquisitions). See 59.5 SHARES AND SECURITIES—IDENTIFICATION RULES. Disposals are only identified with the '1982 holding' after any subsequent acquisitions have been identified.

The '*1985 date*' is 6 April 1985 (1 April 1985 for companies). Similarly the '*1982 date*' should be read as 6 April 1982 (1 April 1982 for companies) although the legislation does not specifically use the latter definition.

7.5 Assets held on 6 April 1965

[*TCGA 1992, s 104(3), ss 105, 106A, 107, 108, Sch 2 para 2(2), para 3, para 4(3)–(7); FA 1998, s 123(3), s 124*].

7.5 **Position on or after the 1982 date but before the 1985 date.** The identification rules given in (*a*) or (*b*) below applied to quoted securities held on 6 April 1965 (but not government securities) and are subject to the general rules at 59.7–59.10 SHARES AND SECURITIES—IDENTIFICATION RULES.

(*a*) Where *no* election had been made, pre-7 April 1965 acquisitions were treated as disposed of on a 'last-in, first-out' basis and were only identified with disposals after all post-6 April 1965 acquisitions had been identified. Such post-6 April 1965 acquisitions forming a holding in existence immediately before the '1982 date' (see 7.4 above), subject to transitional provisions, continued to be treated as a single asset (but one which could not grow by further acquisitions). In general, disposals were identified, on a 'first-in, first-out' basis, with acquisitions within the twelve months preceding the disposal. Otherwise, disposals were to be identified on a 'last-in, first-out' basis.

(*b*) Where an election *was* made, pre-7 April 1965 acquisitions (at 6 April 1965 values) and any acquisitions post-6 April 1965 *and* before the '1982 date' and which together formed a holding in existence before the '1982 date', subject to transitional provisions, continued to be treated as a single asset (but one which could not grow by further acquisitions). Otherwise, disposals were identified as under the general rules in (*a*) above.

[*TCGA 1992, s 104(3), s 105, Sch 2 para 2(2), para 3, para 4(3)–(7); FA 1982, ss 88, 89, Sch 13 Pt II*].

7.6 **Position before the 1982 date.** The identification rules given in (*a*) or (*b*) below applied to quoted securities held on 6 April 1965 (but not government securities).

(*a*) Where *no* election had been made, pre-7 April 1965 acquisitions were treated as disposed of on a 'first-in, first-out' basis and post-6 April 1965 acquisitions formed a 'holding' which was treated as a single asset. Disposals were treated as made out of pre-7 April 1965 acquisitions before those in the holding. This rule also applied to determine how securities held on 6 April 1965 were to be identified with previous acquisitions where there had been disposals pre-7 April 1965. Disposals out of the holding were identified on a 'pool' basis, see 59.12 SHARES AND SECURITIES—IDENTIFICATION RULES.

(*b*) Where an election had been made, pre-7 April 1965 acquisitions and any acquisitions post-6 April 1965 together formed a 'holding' which was treated as a single asset.

[*TCGA 1992, s 104(3), s 105, Sch 2 para 1(2), para 3, para 4(3)–(7)*].

7.7 **Reorganisation, exchange etc. following partial election.** Where an election has been made under 7.3(*a*) *or* under 7.3(*b*) above *but not both* and there is a disposal out of a 'new holding' (see definition below) following a reorganisation or exchange etc. of quoted securities held on 6 April 1965, the election applies according to the nature of the securities in the new holding, notwithstanding that it is to be treated as one with the 'original holding' and that the election would have applied differently to the original holding. Where the election does cover the disposal out of the new holding, but does not cover quoted securities of the kind comprised in the original holding, the question of how much of the new holding derives from securities held on 6 April 1965, and how much derives from other quoted securities is decided by the rules in 7.4(*a*), 7.5(*a*) and 7.6(*a*) above as appropriate.

Where the election does not cover a disposal out of the new holding, but does cover quoted securities of the kind comprised in the original holding, then, in computing the gain accruing on the disposal out of the new holding, the question of what remained undisposed of on any disposal out of the original holding is to be decided by the rules given in 7.4(*a*), 7.5(*a*) and 7.6(*a*) above, notwithstanding the fact that following an election the rules given in 7.4(*b*), 7.5(*b*) and 7.6(*b*) applied on a disposal out of the original holding. [*TCGA 1992, Sch 2 para 6*].

'Original holding' means securities held before and concerned in the reorganisation etc. and *'new holding'* means, in relation to any original holding, the shares in and debentures of the company which, following the reorganisation etc., represent the original holding, together with any remaining original holding. [*TCGA 1992, ss 126, 127*]. See 58.5 SHARES AND SECURITIES for full coverage of reorganisations etc. generally.

Note. Where (i) disposals are made on or after the '1982 date' (see 7.4 above) out of the new holding and (ii) there were disposals out of the original holding before the '1982 date', the legislation does not make clear whether the 'last-in, first-out' basis applying on or after the '1982 date' in respect of original shares held on 6 April 1965 (as under 7.4(*a*) and 7.5(*a*) above) is the appropriate identification procedure for disposals in (ii) or if it is the 'first-in, first-out' basis applying before the 1982 date as under 7.6(*a*) above. In addition it should be noted that there is no provision to adjust the original *computation* of any gain arising on a disposal out of the original shares.

7.8 LAND REFLECTING DEVELOPMENT VALUE

If land in the UK held on 6 April 1965 is disposed of after 17 December 1973 either

(i) at a price exceeding 'current use value' (as defined and see *Morgan v Gibson Ch D 1989, 61 TC 654*) at the time of the disposal, or

(ii) if any 'material development' (as defined) has been carried out after 17 December 1973 by the disposer,

on the disposal, computations of the gain or loss accruing are made

(*a*) by reference to the original cost, or market value when acquired if appropriate—see 40 MARKET VALUE, and

(*b*) by reference to market value on 6 April 1965.

Of these two computations, the one which produces the smaller gain or the smaller loss prevails, but if one computation produces a gain and the other a loss, the result is treated as giving rise to neither gain nor loss. The provisions apply only if before 6 April 1965, expenditure was *incurred* which would otherwise have been deductible in computing the gain on the disposal. A deemed acquisition cost by virtue of *TCGA 1992, s 17* (or similar previous legislation) is 'expenditure incurred' for this purpose. See *Mashiter v Pearmain CA 1984, 58 TC 334*. [*TCGA 1992, Sch 2 paras 9–15*].

Example

K sells a building plot, on which planning permission has just been obtained, in November 2000 for £200,000. He acquired the plot by gift from his father in 1956 when its value was £2,000. The market value was £5,000 at 6 April 1965 and £10,000 at 31 March 1982, and the current use value in November 2000 is £15,000. The indexation factor for March 1982 to April 1998 is 1.047.

	£	£	£
Sale proceeds	200,000	200,000	200,000
Cost	2,000		
Market value 6.4.65		5,000	
Market value 31.3.82			10,000
Unindexed gain	198,000	195,000	190,000
Indexation allowance			
£10,000 × 1.047	10,470	10,470	10,470
Gain after indexation	£187,530	£184,530	£179,530
Chargeable gain (subject to TAPER RELIEF (60))			£179,530

Notes to the example

(1) Time apportionment would have substantially reduced the gain of £179,530, using cost, such that re-basing to 31 March 1982 would have given a greater gain than that based on cost and would not therefore have applied. However, as the plot has been sold for a price in excess of its current use value, no time apportionment can be claimed.

(2) Gains are compared after applying the indexation allowance, which is based on 31 March 1982 value, this being greater than either cost or 6 April 1965 value. The comparison is made before applying taper relief.

(3) In this case, the gain is computed in accordance with the rules in 8 ASSETS HELD ON 31 MARCH 1982 as the gain by reference to 31 March 1982 value is lower than the lowest of the alternatives at (*a*) and (*b*) above.

See 36.7 LAND for part disposals with development value of an estate of land acquired before 6 April 1965.

7.9 **OTHER ASSETS AND MISCELLANEOUS ASPECTS**

Special provisions apply to other assets not falling within 7.2–7.8 above (including unquoted shares and land not covered by 7.8 above) held on 6 April 1965.

Subject to 7.10 below, gains on disposals of such assets which are held on 6 April 1965 are apportioned (on the basis of relative costs) between the original asset and any additions to it, and are deemed to have arisen evenly over the period from acquisition (or addition), or from 6 April 1945 if later, to the date of disposal. Only the part of the gain or loss attributable, on this basis, to the period from 6 April 1965 to disposal is taxable or allowable. [*TCGA 1992, Sch 2 para 16*]. This basis is known as **time apportionment**. According to Revenue Pamphlet IR 131, SP 3/82, indexation allowance, where available, is calculated and deducted before applying such apportionment, and the case of *Smith v Schofield HL 1993, 65 TC 669* subsequently confirmed this practice.

Example

On 6 April 1951, A acquired 5,000 shares in C Ltd, an unquoted company, for £15,201. He sells these shares (his entire holding in the company) on 6 April 2000 for £75,000. The retail prices index for March 1982 is 79.44 and for April 1998 it is 162.6. No election for universal 31 March 1982 re-basing is made but the market value of the holding on that date is agreed at £17,000.

The chargeable gain is computed thus

Total period of ownership	49 years
Period after 6 April 1965	35 years
Unindexed gain	
£(75,000 – 15,201)	£59,799
Indexation allowance	
$\dfrac{1.62.6 - 79.44}{79.44} \times$ £17,000	£17,799 (indexation factor 1.047)
Overall gain £(59,799 – 17,799)	£42,000

Chargeable gain (subject to TAPER RELIEF (60)) £42,000 × $\frac{35}{49}$ = £30,000
The gain by reference to 31 March 1982 value is
£(75,000 – 17,000 – 17,799) £40,201

31 March 1982 re–basing does not apply as a higher gain would thereby result. See also 7.10 below re election for 6 April 1965 value (not illustrated above).

Assume, however, that in April 1960, A, having discovered a defect in his title to the shares, incurred legal costs of £3,000 in order to correct it.

The gain would then be computed as follows

Overall gain (as revised)
£75,000 – £(15,201 + 3,000 + 17,799) £39,000

Proportion of gain attributable to original expenditure (E(0)) $\dfrac{£15{,}201}{£18{,}201} \times £39{,}000 = £32{,}572$

Proportion of gain attributable to enhancement expenditure (E(1)) $\dfrac{£3{,}000}{£18{,}201} \times £39{,}000 = £6{,}428$

$$\frac{\text{Period of ownership since 6 April 1965}}{\text{Total period of ownership}} \times E(0)$$

$= \frac{35}{49} \times £32{,}572 = £23{,}266$

$$\frac{\text{Period of ownership since 6 April 1965}}{\text{Total period of ownership since enhancement}} \times E(1)$$

$= \frac{35}{40} \times £6{,}428 = £5{,}624$

Total chargeable gain £23,266 + £5,624 = £28,890

The gain by reference to 31 March 1982 value is again £40,201 so re-basing at that date does not apply.

The formulae for apportionment of gains are contained in *TCGA 1992, Sch 2 para 16* (whence the designations 'E(0)' and 'E(1)' are taken).

Where the original expenditure (compared with the enhancement expenditure) is disproportionately small having regard to the value of the asset immediately before the enhancement expenditure was incurred (or where there is no original expenditure) the *actual gain* attributable to the enhancement expenditure is substituted for the figure arrived at under the formula, and the balance is treated as attributable to original expenditure. This is done in practice by establishing as a fact what the proceeds for the asset would have been without any of the enhancement expenditure in question.

The Revenue are prepared to accept a period of tenancy prior to a period of ownership as part of the time apportionment denominator e.g. where farm land was gifted by a father to his son in 1956 and subsequently sold by the son in 1980, if the son had been a tenant since 1945 a time apportionment factor of 15/(20+15) would apply rather than 15/(15+9). The existence of an ordinary tenancy is sufficient to allow the extended time apportionment formulae to apply even though no formal lease or tenancy agreement was in existence, provided sufficient rent was paid. Any sale of land, including buildings, follows the same pattern but any 'wasted cost' of a lease has to be added to the cost of the 'freehold reversion'. (CCAB Statement TR 500, 10 March 1983).

For the circumstances in which the Inland Revenue will require a valuation of the asset transferred where a claim for hold-over relief is made, see 25.1 HOLD-OVER RELIEFS.

7.10 **Election.** Alternatively (except in the case of an asset which has been the subject of a previous part disposal after 5 April 1965; see 17.6 DISPOSAL) the taxpayer may elect, by notice in writing that the gain should be computed by reference to the market value at 6 April 1965 of the asset disposed of. An election for the purposes of capital gains tax must be made on or before the first anniversary of 31st January following the year of assessment in which the disposal is made. In the case of corporation tax, it must be made within two years after the end of the accounting period in which the disposal is made. Prior to self-assessment the election had to be made within two years from the end of the year of assessment, or accounting period of a company, in which the disposal was made.

The Board has discretion to extend the time limit for instances of which see *Whitaker v Cameron Ch D 1982, 56 TC 97*, 3.14 ANTI-AVOIDANCE and 13.19 COMPANIES. The election is irrevocable, and the Revenue will not normally discuss a valuation before an election is made. On a part disposal, an election will affect all later such disposals, or the ultimate disposal, made by the same person. [*TCGA 1992, Sch 2 para 17(1)(3)–(5); FA 1996, Sch 21 para 42(3)*].

If the election to use 6 April 1965 value results in a gain, it is valid irrespective of all other figures (and the election will thus be to the detriment of the taxpayer if the time apportionment basis would have produced a smaller gain or a loss). If the election results in a loss, that loss is allowable, unless

(i) there is a smaller loss by reference to cost in which case that smaller loss is taken (and this means that the full loss by reference to cost is taken instead of the time apportionment loss, so that the election has been beneficial to the taxpayer), or

(ii) there is a gain by reference to cost, in which case the disposal will be treated as producing neither a gain nor a loss.

[*TCGA 1992, Sch 2 para 17(2)*].

Part disposals out of an estate of land may be able to be treated as disposals of separate assets and thus allow 6 April 1965 value to be used in relation only to parts. See 36.7 LAND.

7.11 **Identification rules for unquoted securities, commodities etc. where no election under 7.10 above.** *After 5 April 1982 (31 March 1982 for companies)* on the realisation of part of an unquoted shareholding or other fungible assets, any shares held on 6 April 1965 are not pooled but are identified with shares disposed of on a last-in, first-out basis. *Before 6 April 1982 (1 April 1982 for companies)* the part sold was identified on a first-in, first-out basis with shares held on 6 April 1965 which again were not pooled. [*TCGA 1992, Sch 2 para 18; CGTA 1979, Sch 5 para 13*].

Post-6 April 1965 acquisitions are treated as in 59 SHARES AND SECURITIES—IDENTIFICATION RULES.

7.12 **Time apportionment restrictions.** Where, after the date of acquisition and before 6 April 1965,

(*a*) there was a *reorganisation* of a company's share capital (see 58.5 SHARES AND SECURITIES), time apportionment is not available. In such a case, 6 April 1965 value must be used. [*TCGA 1992, Sch 2 para 19(1)*], or

(*b*) a *part disposal* was made, time apportionment is calculated from the date of that part disposal by reference to market value at that time. [*TCGA 1992, Sch 2 para 16(7)*].

Where, after 5 April 1965,

(i) there is a *reorganisation* of a company's share capital, the new holding is treated as having been sold and immediately re-acquired at that time by the owner at the then market value. The amount of any gain on the disposal of the new holding, or part thereof, is computed by time apportioning any gain or loss over the period ending at that time and bringing into account the full gain or loss from that time to the date of disposal, computed by reference to the ultimate disposal value and the aforesaid market value. [*TCGA 1992, Sch 2 para 19(2)*], or

(ii) there is a *part disposal*, the asset is treated as having been sold and immediately re-acquired at that time by the owner at the then market value. The amount of any gain on the disposal is calculated as under (i) above. [*TCGA 1992, Sch 2 para 16(8)*].

The provisions under (*a*) and (i) above do not apply (i.e. normal time apportionment applies) in relation to a reorganisation of a company's share capital if the new holding differs only from the original shares in being a different number of shares of the same class as the original shares. [*TCGA 1992, Sch 2 para 19(3)*]. Following the decision in *CIR v Beveridge CS 1979, 53 TC 178*, in all cases where liability is finalised after 19 July 1979, the Revenue do not consider this provision to apply where the shares comprised in the new holding are in a different company from the old shares. Previously, the practice of the Revenue had been to apply the wording to such a reorganisation (Revenue Pamphlet IR 131, SP 14/79).

Where (*a*) or (i) above has applied, gains chargeable on the disposal of the entire new holding are limited to the actual gains realised. Separate transactions in the year or accounting period are treated as a single disposal provided the entire holding is so disposed of (Revenue Pamphlet IR 1, D10).

Where the provisions in (ii) above would normally apply to unquoted shares in a winding-up, the time apportionment fraction determined at the date of the first distribution may be able to be used to calculate the gain on each additional distribution without further adjustment (Revenue Pamphlet IR 131, SP D3). See also 58.15 SHARES AND SECURITIES.

Part disposals out of an estate of land may be able to be treated as disposals of separate assets and so prevent the operation of (*b*) and (ii) above. See 36.7 LAND.

7.13 **Capital allowances.** Where the gain on the disposal of an asset is calculated by reference to its value on 6 April 1965, the restriction of relief given for losses accruing on assets which have qualified for capital allowances (*TCGA 1992, s 41*, see 17.5(*j*) DISPOSAL) and the provisions relating to wasting assets qualifying for capital allowances (*TCGA 1992, s 47*, see 66.1 WASTING ASSETS) apply as if the capital allowances for 1965/66 and subsequent years were allowances in respect of expenditure incurred on the asset on 6 April 1965. [*TCGA 1992, Sch 2 para 20*].

7.14 **Assets transferred to close companies.** Where, at any time, a person who has 'control' of a 'close company', or a person 'connected' with him, transfers an asset to the company, and subsequently the first person (or any person with a 'substantial holding' of shares in the company) disposes of shares in circumstances such that the chargeable gain is to be determined by time apportionment, to the extent that the gain accruing on the disposal is attributable to a profit on the asset transferred, the shares are deemed to have been acquired at the date when the asset was transferred. The provisions do not apply where a loss accrues on the disposal. [*TCGA 1992, Sch 2 para 21*].

'*Control*' is as given by *ICTA 1988, s 416*. '*Close company*' has the meaning given by *ICTA 1988, ss 414, 415*. '*Connected*' is as given at CONNECTED PERSONS (14). '*Substantial holding*' is not defined.

8 Assets held on 31 March 1982

Cross-references. See 59.5 and 59.10 SHARES AND SECURITIES—IDENTIFICATION RULES for identification of certain share pools held by companies at 31 March 1982 and by others at 5 April 1982; 45.5, 45.13 PARTNERSHIPS for partnership transactions involving assets held on 31 March 1982.

Sumption: Capital Gains Tax. See A4A.01.

8.1 RE-BASING TO 31 MARCH 1982

Subject to certain exceptions, disposals after 5 April 1988 of assets which were held on 31 March 1982 by the person making the disposal are re-based by reference to the market value of the assets on the last-mentioned date; see 8.2 below. However, the taxpayer may irrevocably (with one exception mentioned in 8.3 below), subject to the modification in 8.2 below concerning certain disposals of 'oil industry assets', elect for such re-basing to apply to all assets held on 31 March 1982 regardless of the exceptions; see 8.3 below. Subject to certain exceptions and such election, re-basing applies to both the unindexed gain and the indexation allowance.

A 50% reduction is made in taxing certain deferred gains (except, in certain cases, where the deferred gain is never deemed to accrue at all) which arise after 5 April 1988 where such gains are wholly or partly attributable to an increase in value of an asset before 31 March 1982; see 8.12 below.

In addition, disposals after 5 April 1985 (31 March 1985 for companies) and before 6 April 1988 of assets held on 31 March 1982 could, on a claim, be the subject of a similar re-basing treatment as regards indexation allowance only; see 8.13 below.

8.2 GENERAL RE-BASING RULE

The general re-basing rule is that on a disposal after 5 April 1988 of an asset held on 31 March 1982 it is to be assumed that the asset was sold on the last-mentioned date by the person making the disposal and immediately reacquired by him at its market value on that date. [*TCGA 1992, s 35(1)(2)*].

Subject to the irrevocable (with one exception mentioned in 8.3 below) election in 8.3 below and subject to the modification below concerning certain disposals of 'oil industry assets', the general re-basing rule is not applied to a disposal where

(*a*) a gain would accrue on the disposal if the general rule applied, and either a smaller gain or a loss would accrue if it did not, or

(*b*) a loss would accrue if the general rule applied, and either a smaller loss or a gain would accrue if it did not, or

(*c*) either on the facts of the case or by virtue of the provisions for ASSETS HELD ON 6 APRIL 1965 (7) in *TCGA 1992, Sch 2*, neither a gain nor a loss would accrue if the general rule did not apply, or

(*d*) the disposal is a 'no gain/no loss disposal' as in 8.7 below.

[*TCGA 1992, s 35(3)*].

Where the effect of the general re-basing rule would be to substitute a loss for a gain or a gain for a loss, but under (*a*)–(*d*) the application of that rule is excluded, it is to be assumed in relation to the disposal that the asset was acquired for a consideration such that, on the disposal, neither a gain nor a loss accrues. [*TCGA 1992, s 35(4)*].

Indexation allowance on the disposal after 5 April 1988 of an asset held on 31 March 1982 is calculated, without need for a claim, on the assumption that the asset was sold on the last-mentioned date by the person making the disposal and immediately reacquired by him at its market value on that date. [*TCGA 1992, s 55(1)*]. Except where an irrevocable (with one exception mentioned in 8.3 below) election as in 8.3 below has effect and subject to the modification below concerning certain disposals of 'oil industry assets', neither this provision nor the general re-basing rule of *TCGA 1992, s 35(1)(2)* above is to apply for the purposes of calculating indexation allowance in a case where that allowance would be greater if they did not apply. [*TCGA 1992, s 55(2)*].

Modifications apply to the above provisions in respect of certain disposals after 21 January 1990 and before 30 November 1993 of 'oil industry assets'. These apply where the person making the disposal held the asset on 31 March 1982 (or is deemed to have done so because of previous no gain/no loss disposals as in 8.7 below), a loss would accrue on the disposal (disregarding the modifications below), and the general re-basing rule of *TCGA 1992, s 35(1)(2)* is disapplied by (*b*) above, i.e. because a smaller loss accrues if re-basing is not applied. For the purpose of the modifications, the loss or gain on the disposal (to be known as the '*non-rebased loss*' or '*non-rebased gain*') is calculated on the assumption that neither the general re-basing rule of *TCGA 1992, s 35(1)(2)* nor the equivalent rule for indexation allowance of *TCGA 1992, s 55(1)* applies. The non-rebased loss or gain is then compared with the loss arising but for the modifications below, i.e. the loss computed on the basis that the general re-basing rule of *TCGA 1992, s 35(1)(2)* does not apply but that the equivalent rule of *TCGA 1992, s 55(1)* does apply. If there is a non-rebased loss which is less than the loss arising but for the modifications below, the allowable loss is modified so as to be restricted to the non-rebased loss. If there is a non-rebased gain, or if there is neither a non-rebased gain nor a non-rebased loss, the modification is that it is to be assumed that the person making the disposal acquired the asset for a consideration such that neither a gain nor a loss accrues on the disposal. For the purposes of these provisions, the following are '*oil industry assets*': a licence under *Petroleum (Production) Act 1934* or *Petroleum (Production) Act (Northern Ireland) 1964*; shares of the kind excluded under 8.4 below from global re-basing elections under *TCGA 1992, s 35(5)*; 'oil exploration or exploitation assets' as mentioned in 8.4 but with suitable modifications; and any interest in an asset falling within these categories. These modifications do not apply to disposals on or after 30 November 1993. [*TCGA 1992, s 200; FA 1994, s 93(7)(11), Sch 26 Pt V*].

Valuations. Where, for the purposes of the re-basing provisions in *TCGA 1992, s 35* and the indexation provisions in *TCGA 1992, s 55*, it is necessary to determine the market value of shares or securities of the same class in any company on 31 March 1982, all the shares or securities held at that date will be valued as a single holding whether they were acquired on or before 6 April 1965 or after that date. If the shares or securities in the relevant disposal represent some but not all of those valued at 31 March 1982 then the allowable cost or indexation allowance as appropriate will be based on the proportion that the shares or securities disposed of bears to the total holding at 31 March 1982 (Revenue Pamphlet IR 1, D34). See also 8.7 below for the Revenue's practice as to the valuation of shares deemed held on 31 March 1982 by reason of 'no gain/no loss disposals' since that date.

Where a valuation at 31 March 1982 of unquoted shares is required for a number of shareholders, all of whom agree to be bound by the valuation, the Inland Revenue's Shares Valuation Division may initiate valuation procedures before receiving a formal request to do so from the inspector, provided that a full list of the company's shareholders and the size of their holdings, both at 31 March 1982 and at the date of disposal, is supplied, together with details of the tax offices involved, if available. It should be noted that entering into negotiations with Shares Valuation Division does not constitute a return for taxation purposes (Revenue Press Release 18 November 1991).

After 20 March 2000, for a trial period expected to last two years, companies and groups of companies may ask the Revenue to agree the value of land and buildings held by them at 31 March 1982. The request must extend to the entire property portfolio of the company or group. The service is available only if the company or group have at least 30 properties held since 31 March 1982 or fewer such properties but with an aggregate current value greater than £30 million. Companies must provide values for checking, and these must be supported by professional valuations. Companies may obtain further information on this service from Inland Revenue, Capital and Savings Division, Room 133, Sapphire House, 550 Streetsbrook Road, Solihull, West Midlands, B91 1QU. (Revenue News Release BN2G, 21 March 2000).

Example 1

An asset (which is neither tangible movable property nor otherwise exempt) was acquired for £900 in 1980 and, after having been held continuously by the same owner, is disposed of in 2000/01. The indexation factor is taken to be 80%. The disposal proceeds are £1,900. The capital gains tax consequences, for differing 31 March 1982 values, are as follows. 'N/A' means that indexation allowance is not applicable and 'NGNL' means that the disposal is treated as giving rise to neither a gain nor a loss. Amounts shown as chargeable gains are subject to TAPER RELIEF (60) (assuming the owner not to be a company).

Example 1A

	(1)	(2)
	£	£
Sale proceeds	1,900	1,900
(1) Cost; (2) 31.3.1982 value	900	1,000
Unindexed gain	1,000	900
Indexation allowance at 80% of higher of (1) and (2)	800	800
Gain arising	£200	£100
Chargeable gain		£100

Example 1B

	(1)	(2)
	£	£
Sale proceeds	1,900	1,900
(1) Cost; (2) 31.3.1982 value	900	1,200
Unindexed gain	1,000	700
Indexation allowance at 80% of higher of (1) and (2)	960	N/A
Gain/NGNL arising	£40	£NGNL

The disposal is treated as giving rise to neither a gain nor a loss. The corresponding acquisition is unaffected by this treatment.

Example 1C

	(1)	(2)
	£	£
Sale proceeds	1,900	1,900
(1) Cost; (2) 31.3.1982 value	900	800
Unindexed gain	1,000	1,100
Indexation allowance at 80% of higher of (1) and (2)	720	720
Gain arising	£280	£380
Chargeable gain	£280	

Example 1D

	(1)	(2)
	£	£
Sale proceeds	1,900	1,900
(1) Cost; (2) 31.3.1982 value	900	3,000
Unindexed gain/(Loss)	1,000	(1,100)
Indexation allowance at 80% of higher of (1) and (2)	N/A	N/A
NGNL/(Loss) arising	NGNL	£(1,100)

The disposal is treated as giving rise to neither a gain nor a loss. The corresponding acquisition is unaffected by this treatment.

Example 2

An asset (which is neither tangible movable property, land with development value, quoted securities nor otherwise exempt) was acquired in 1960 for £500. After having been held continuously by the same owner, the asset is completely destroyed in 2000/01. The indexation factor is taken to be 80%. The asset was under-insured and, later in the month of disposal, £1,900 only was recovered from the insurers. The owner elects for valuation at 6 April 1965, which value is later agreed with the Revenue to be £2,000. The value at 31 March 1982 was similarly agreed at £1,700.

	(1)	(2)
	£	£
Insurance proceeds	1,900	1,900
(1) Cost; (2) 6.4.1965 value	500	2,000
	1,400	(100)
Indexation allowance at 80% of 31.3.1982 value (£1,700) for (1) only	1,360	N/A
Gain/(Loss) arising	£40	£(100)

Re-basing at 31 March 1982 does not apply since, under *TCGA 1992, Sch 2 para 17(2)* (see 7.10 ASSETS HELD ON 6 APRIL 1965), the disposal is deemed to have given rise to neither a gain nor a loss. The corresponding acquisition is unaffected by this treatment.

8.3 **ELECTION FOR UNIVERSAL RE-BASING AT 31 MARCH 1982**

If a person so elects (under *TCGA 1992, s 35(5)*), disposals made by him (including any made by him before the election) after 5 April 1988 of assets which he held on 31 March

1982 will all have the general re-basing rule of *TCGA 1992, s 35(1)(2)* in 8.2 above applied to them regardless of the exclusion of that rule that might otherwise apply under *TCGA 1992, s 35(3)*. Similarly in such a case, indexation allowance will always be calculated under the equivalent provision of *TCGA 1992, s 55(1)* as in 8.2 above regardless of the exclusion of that provision that might otherwise apply under *TCGA 1992, s 55(2)*. [*TCGA 1992, s 35(5), s 55(2)*].

An election is, with one exception as below, irrevocable and must be made by notice in writing to an officer of the Board at any time before 6 April 1990 or at any time during the period beginning with the time of the first disposal after 5 April 1988 of an asset held on 31 March 1982 or treated (see 8.7 below) as so held ('*the first relevant disposal*') and ending in the case of an election for capital gains tax by the first anniversary of 31 January next following the year of assessment in which the disposal is made, and in the case of an election for corporation tax within two years after the end of the accounting period in which the disposal is made and in either case such later period as the Board may allow.

Prior to the introduction of self-assessment an election had to be made by two years (or such longer period as may be allowed by the Board) after the end of the year of assessment or accounting period in which that disposal is made. An election made by a person in one capacity does not cover disposals made by him in another capacity. Adjustments as required may be made, whether by way of discharge or repayment of tax, the making of assessments or otherwise, to give effect to an election. [*TCGA 1992, s 35(6)–(8); FA 1996, Sch 21 para 35*].

The Revenue will always exercise their discretion to extend the time limit for an election to at least the date on which the statutory time limit would expire if certain disposals did not count as a first relevant disposal. There are three such kinds of disposal, as follows.

(1) Disposals on which the gain would not be chargeable by virtue of a particular statutory provision. The main examples of these provisions are as follows.

  (*a*) Private cars (see 21.11 EXEMPTIONS AND RELIEFS).

  (*b*) Chattels, except commodity futures and foreign currency, worth less than the chattel exemption (see 21.4 EXEMPTIONS AND RELIEFS).

  (*c*) Chattels which are wasting assets, except plant and machinery used in business and commodity futures (see 21.4 EXEMPTIONS AND RELIEFS).

  (*d*) Non-marketable government securities (see 21.13 EXEMPTIONS AND RELIEFS).

  (*e*) Gilt-edged securities and qualifying corporate bonds, except ones received in exchange for shares or other securities (see 24 GOVERNMENT SECURITIES and 49 QUALIFYING CORPORATE BONDS).

  (*f*) Life assurance policies and deferred annuity contracts, unless purchased from a third party (see 37.1 LIFE ASSURANCE POLICIES AND DEFERRED ANNUITIES).

  (*g*) Foreign currency acquired for personal or family expenditure abroad (see 21.8 EXEMPTIONS AND RELIEFS).

  (*h*) Rights of compensation for a wrong or injury suffered by an individual in his person, profession or vocation (see 21.21 EXEMPTIONS AND RELIEFS).

  (*j*) Debts, not on a security, held by the original creditor, his personal representative or his legatee (see 21.5 EXEMPTIONS AND RELIEFS).

  (*k*) Business expansion scheme shares issued after 18 March 1986 for which relief has been given and not withdrawn (see 20.15 ENTERPRISE INVESTMENT SCHEME (AND BES)).

(*l*) Personal equity plan shareholdings (see 58.22 SHARES AND SECURITIES).

(*m*) Gifts of eligible property, including works of art, for the benefit of the public (see 21.26, 21.33 EXEMPTIONS AND RELIEFS).

(*n*) Decorations for valour or gallantry (see 21.6 EXEMPTIONS AND RELIEFS).

(*o*) Betting winnings (see 21.18 EXEMPTIONS AND RELIEFS).

(*p*) A right to or to any part of an allowance, annuity or capital sum from a superannuation fund or any other annuity (but not under a deferred annuity policy) or annual payments received under a covenant which is not secured on property (see 21.3 EXEMPTIONS AND RELIEFS).

(2) Disposals which, in practice, do not give rise to a chargeable gain or allowable loss. The main examples of these disposals are as follows.

(*a*) Withdrawals from building society accounts.

(*b*) The disposal of an individual's private residence where the whole of the gain is exempt under *TCGA 1992, s 223(1)* (see 48.1 PRIVATE RESIDENCES).

(*c*) Disposals which give rise to neither a chargeable gain nor an allowable loss by virtue of the statutory 'no gain/no loss' provisions listed at *TCGA 1992, s 35(3)(d)* (see 8.7 below).

(3) Excluded disposals (see 8.4 below).

As sterling is not an asset for capital gains tax purposes (see 6.1 ASSETS), a disposal of it cannot be a first relevant disposal.

Where a person holds assets in more than one capacity (for example, as an individual, trustee, partner or member of a European Economic Interest Grouping), there will be a first relevant disposal and a separate time limit for each group of assets which the person holds in a different capacity. An individual who holds assets in different capacities should indicate at the time an election under *TCGA 1992, s 35(5)* is made in what capacity it should be regarded as applying. See also 45.13 PARTNERSHIPS.

Where a person who is non-UK resident on 6 April 1988 makes a disposal which would otherwise count as a first relevant disposal between that date and the date on which they first become UK resident, the Revenue will give sympathetic consideration to extending the time limit to the end of the second year of assessment (for companies, the second accounting period) after the year in which the first disposal is made subsequent to becoming UK resident. In other words, the disposal made while non-resident may be disregarded at the discretion of the Board. The extension will not be available where the assets are within *TCGA 1992, s 10* (non-resident with UK branch or agency: see 44.3 OVERSEAS MATTERS).

Where, after 5 April 1988, an individual who is resident but not domiciled in the UK disposes of an asset situated outside the UK, the date of the first relevant disposal will be the date on which the proceeds of an overseas gain are remitted to the UK or the date of the first disposal of a UK asset, whichever is earlier.

Where an individual who was resident in the UK on 6 April 1988 has a period of non-residence before resuming UK residence, the first relevant disposal will be the first disposal made after 5 April 1988 on which the individual is chargeable to UK capital gains tax.

There are a variety of other circumstances where, having regard to the facts of each case, the Inland Revenue will or may exercise their discretion to extend the statutory time limit. (Revenue Pamphlet IR 131, SP 4/92). In circumstances other than those covered by SP 4/92, a late election may be accepted if the delay in making it is less than twelve months from the statutory time limit and resulted from events outside the taxpayer's control or any other reasonable cause (Revenue Capital Gains Manual CG 16821 and 46374).

The Revenue point out that in special cases elections need to be made by a person other than the person assessed. In the case of an assessment under *TCGA 1992, s 13* (charge on UK resident shareholder of an overseas resident company; see 44.6 OVERSEAS MATTERS), the election needs to be made by the company concerned. Similarly, the trustees concerned should make an election where the gains of a settlement are assessed under *TCGA 1992, s 77* (charge on settlor of UK resident; see 57.3 SETTLEMENTS), *s 86* (charge on UK resident settlor of overseas resident settlement; see 43.4 OFFSHORE SETTLEMENTS) or *s 87* (charge on UK resident beneficiary of overseas resident settlement; see 43.13 OFFSHORE SETTLEMENTS) (Revenue Capital Gains Manual CG 16762–16764).

8.4 **Excluded disposals.** An election does not cover a disposal of (or of an interest in): plant or machinery; an asset which the person making the disposal held at any time for the purposes of or in connection with a trade or part of a trade involving the working of a 'source of mineral deposits' (within *CAA 1990, s 121*); a licence under *Petroleum Act 1998, Pt I* (or earlier corresponding legislation) or *Petroleum (Production) Act (Northern Ireland) 1964*; or, for disposals after 21 January 1990, 'shares' which, on 31 March 1982, were 'unquoted' and derived their value, or the greater part thereof, directly or indirectly from 'oil exploration or exploitation assets' situated in the UK or a 'designated area' or from such assets and 'oil exploration or exploitation rights' taken together (the quoted terms having the meanings given by the legislation). However, disposals within the first two of these four categories are not excluded unless a capital allowance in respect of any expenditure attributable to the asset has been made to the person making the disposal or would have been made to him had he made a claim. Where that person acquired the asset on a 'no gain/no loss disposal' (see 8.7 below), references in the foregoing to the person making the disposal are references to that person, the person who last acquired the asset other than on a no gain/no loss disposal or any person who subsequently acquired the asset on such a disposal. [*TCGA 1992, Sch 3 para 7; Petroleum Act 1998, Sch 4 para 32*].

8.5 **Married persons.** Where a spouse disposes of an asset acquired by him from the other spouse after 5 April 1988 and the no gain/no loss basis of *TCGA 1992, s 58* applied to the acquisition (see 41.3 MARRIED PERSONS and 8.7 below), an election made by the transferee spouse does not apply to the disposal, and, whether or not an election is made by that spouse, the making of such an election by the transferor spouse applies to the ultimate disposal made by the transferee spouse. Where the transferor spouse also acquired the asset after 5 April 1988 and *TCGA 1992, s 58* applied to that acquisition, an election made by him does not have effect on the ultimate disposal, but an election made by the last person by whom the asset was acquired after 5 April 1988 otherwise than on an acquisition to which *TCGA 1992, s 58* applied or, if there is no such person, the person who held the asset on 5 April 1988, does have effect on the ultimate disposal. [*TCGA 1992, Sch 3 para 2*].

8.6 **Groups of companies.** Where a member of a group of companies disposes of an asset acquired by it from another group member after 5 April 1988 and the no gain/no loss basis of *TCGA 1992, s 171* applied to the acquisition (see 13.12 COMPANIES and 8.7 below), an election made by the transferee company does not apply to the disposal, and, whether or not an election is made by that company, the making of such an election by the transferor company applies to the ultimate disposal made by the transferee company. Where the transferor company also acquired the asset after 5 April 1988 and *TCGA 1992, s 171* applied to that acquisition, an election made by it does not have effect on the ultimate disposal, but an election made by the last company by which the asset was acquired after 5 April 1988 otherwise than on an acquisition to which *TCGA 1992, s 171* applied or, if there is no such company, the company which held the asset on 5 April 1988, does have effect on the ultimate disposal. [*TCGA 1992, Sch 3 para 2*].

Election by principal company. Only a company which is the 'principal company' of a 'group' (for both of which see 13.11 COMPANIES and note that the change in the residence requirement therein mentioned has effect for this purpose after 31 March 2000) may make an election unless the company did not become a group member until after the 'relevant time'. For this purpose the time limit for the making of an election (see 8.3 above) applies with the modification that a reference to 'the first relevant disposal' is a reference to the first disposal after 5 April 1988 of an asset held on 31 March 1982 by a company which is *either* a group member but not an 'outgoing company' in relation to the group *or* an 'incoming company' in relation to the group. An election made by the principal company also has effect as one made by any other company which is a group member at the relevant time; but this treatment does not extend to a company which, in some period after 5 April 1988 and before the relevant time, is not a member of the group if during that period the company makes a disposal of an asset which it held on 31 March 1982 and the time limit for the making of an election expires without an election having been made. However, the effect of an election continues to extend to a company notwithstanding that it ceases to be a group member after the relevant time except where it is an outgoing company in relation to the group and the election relating to the group is made after it ceases to be a group member. [*TCGA 1992, Sch 3 para 8, para 9(3); FA 2000, Sch 29 para 38*].

'*The relevant time*', in relation to a group, is the earliest of: the first time when any company which is then a group member, and is not an outgoing member in relation to the group, makes a disposal after 5 April 1988 of an asset which it held on 31 March 1982; the time immediately following the first occasion when a company which is an incoming company in relation to the group becomes a group member; and the time when an election is made by the principal company. [*TCGA 1992, Sch 3 para 9(1)*].

'*Incoming company*', in relation to a group, means a company which makes its first disposal after 5 April 1988 of an asset which it held on 31 March 1982 at a time when it is not a group member, and which becomes a group member before the expiry of the time limit for the making of an election which would apply to it and at a time when no such election has been made.

'*Outgoing company*', in relation to a group, means a company which ceases to be a group member before the expiry of the time limit for the making of an election which would apply to it and at a time when no such election has been made. [*TCGA 1992, Sch 3 para 9(2)*].

See Revenue Capital Gains Manual CG 46330–46395 for consideration of the above provisions (including extension of time limits in certain cases).

8.7 **SUPPLEMENTARY PROVISIONS FOR RE-BASING AT 31 MARCH 1982**

Previous no gain/no loss disposals. Where

(*a*) a person makes a disposal, other than a 'no gain/no loss disposal', after 5 April 1988 of an asset which he acquired after 31 March 1982, and

(*b*) the disposal by which he acquired the asset and any previous disposal of the asset after 31 March 1982 was a no gain/no loss disposal,

he is treated for the purposes of the re-basing provisions of *TCGA 1992, s 35* and the equivalent provisions for indexation allowance of *TCGA 1992, s 55(1)* in 8.2 and 8.3 above as having held the asset on 31 March 1982. The Inland Revenue has confirmed that where a person is treated as having held an asset on 31 March 1982 under these provisions, enhancement expenditure on the asset incurred after 31 March 1982 by a previous owner may be taken into account for indexation and re-basing purposes on a disposal by the current owner (Revenue Tax Bulletin, August 1992, p.32).

A '*no gain/no loss disposal*' is one under the following enactments (being enactments by virtue of which neither a gain nor a loss accrues).

(i) *TCGA 1992, s 58* (transfers between spouses living together, see 41.3 MARRIED PERSONS), *s 73* (reversion of settled property to settlor on death of person entitled to life interest, see 57.11 SETTLEMENTS), *s 139* (company reconstruction or amalgamation, see 13.7 COMPANIES), *s 140A* (transfer of UK trade between companies in different EC member States, see 44.10 OVERSEAS MATTERS), *s 171* (intra-group disposals of assets, see 13.12 COMPANIES), *s 172* (transfer of UK branch or agency before 1 April 2000, see 44.3 OVERSEAS MATTERS), *s 215* (amalgamation of building societies, see 13.7 COMPANIES), *s 216* (transfer of building society's business to company, see 13.7 COMPANIES), *s 217A* (transfer of assets on incorporation of registered friendly society, see 21.42 EXEMPTIONS AND RELIEFS), *ss 218–220* (housing associations, see 21.44 EXEMPTIONS AND RELIEFS), *s 221* (harbour authorities, see 21.67 EXEMPTIONS AND RELIEFS), *s 257(2)* (gifts to charities etc., see 10.5 CHARITIES), *s 257(3)* (gifts to charities etc. out of settlements, see 10.6 CHARITIES), *s 258(4)* (gifts of national heritage property, see 21.74 EXEMPTIONS AND RELIEFS), *s 259(2)* (gifts to housing associations, see 21.44 EXEMPTIONS AND RELIEFS), *s 264* (transfers between constituency associations, see 21.61 EXEMPTIONS AND RELIEFS) and *s 267(2)* (sharing of transmission facilities, see 13.7 COMPANIES);

(ii) *CGTA 1979, s 148* (assets transferred to maintenance funds for historic buildings, see 21.72 EXEMPTIONS AND RELIEFS);

(iii) *FA 1982, s 148* (transfers by Hops Marketing Board, see 21.69 EXEMPTIONS AND RELIEFS);

(iv) *Trustee Savings Banks Act 1985, Sch 2 para 2* (see 13.7 COMPANIES);

(v) *Transport Act 1985, s 130(3)* (see 13.7 COMPANIES);

(vi) *ICTA 1988, s 486(8)* (amalgamation of industrial and provident societies, see 13.7 COMPANIES);

(vii) *FA 1990, Sch 12 para 2(1)* (broadcasting undertakings, see 13.7 COMPANIES);

(viii) *F(No 2)A 1992, Sch 17 para 5(3)* (privatisation of Northern Ireland Electricity, see 13.7 COMPANIES);

(ix) *FA 1994, Sch 24 para 2(1), para 7(2), para 11(3)(4), para 25(2)* (provisions relating to *Railways Act 1993*, see 13.7 COMPANIES); and

(x) *FA 1994, Sch 25 para 4(2)* (Northern Ireland Airports Ltd, see 13.7 COMPANIES).

[*TCGA 1992, s 35(3)(d)(10), s 55(5)(6)(a), Sch 3 para 1; F(No 2)A 1992, s 46(1)(2), ss 56, 77, Sch 9 para 21(1)(2), Sch 17 para 5(9); FA 1994, ss 252, 253, Sch 24 para 2(2), Sch 25 para 4(3); FA 2000, Sch 40 Pt II(12)*].

(*Note.* Neither *TCGA 1992, s 257(2)* nor *s 259(2)* is in strictness included as no gain/no loss provisions for the purposes of re-basing under *TCGA 1992, s 35* although they are for the equivalent provisions for indexation allowance under *TCGA 1992, s 55(1)*. However, both provisions deem (for the purposes of *TCGA 1992*) the original acquisition by the transferor making the disposal to which the provision concerned applies to be the acquisition of the transferee on the occasion of the transferee making a subsequent disposal.

Consequently it seems that in practice both provisions are no gain/no loss provisions for the purposes of re-basing under *TCGA 1992, s 35*. It appears that the reason that both provisions have to be specifically included as no gain/no loss provisions for the purposes of *TCGA 1992, s 55(1)* is because of the effect of *TCGA 1992, s 56(2)* (see further below).)

Certain disposals of a share in partnership assets may be treated as if they were no gain/no loss disposals. See 45.5 PARTNERSHIPS.

Where (*a*) and (*b*) above apply on the disposal of an asset so that, as stated above, the person making the disposal is treated for the purposes of computing the indexation allowance on the disposal as having held the asset on 31 March 1982 [*TCGA 1992, s 55(6)(a)*], then for the purpose of determining any gain or loss on the disposal, the consideration which otherwise that person would be treated as having given for the asset is reduced by the amount of indexation allowance brought into account under *TCGA 1992, s 56(2)* (consideration on disposal treated as giving rise to neither a gain nor a loss to be computed on assumption that on the disposal an unindexed gain accrues equal to the indexation allowance on the disposal; see 26.4 INDEXATION) on any disposal falling within (*b*) above. [*TCGA 1992, s 55(6)(b)*].

Further rules as below apply (after the application of the computation of any indexation allowance under *TCGA 1992, s 53* (see 26.1 INDEXATION) but before the application of the provisions of *TCGA 1992, s 35(3)* or *(4)* (which disapply or amend the general re-basing rule of *TCGA 1992, s 35(1)(2)* in certain cases; see 8.2 above) in relation to disposals on or after 30 November 1993. The rules apply where (*a*) and (*b*) above apply to the disposal ('*the disposal in question*') of an asset by any person ('*the transferor*') and, but for *TCGA 1992, s 55(6)(b)* above, the consideration the transferor would be treated as having given for the asset would include an amount or amounts of indexation allowance brought into account under *TCGA 1992, s 56(2)* on any disposal made before 30 November 1993. [*TCGA 1992, s 55(7); FA 1994, s 93(4)(11)*]. The rules are that

(A) where otherwise there would be a loss, an amount equal to the 'rolled-up indexation' is added to it so as to increase it,

(B) where otherwise the unindexed gain or loss would be nil, a loss is deemed to accrue equal to the rolled-up indexation, and

(C) where otherwise there would be an unindexed gain and the gain or loss would be nil but the amount of the indexation allowance used to extinguish the gain would be less than the rolled-up indexation, the difference is deemed to constitute a loss.

[*TCGA 1992, s 55(8); FA 1994, s 93(4)(11)*].

For the purposes of the above, the '*rolled-up indexation*' means, subject to *TCGA 1992, s 55(10)* and *(11)* below (which provisions, as well as applying on the disposal in question, are also treated as having applied on any previous part disposal by the transferor), the amount or, as the case may be, the aggregate of the amounts of indexation allowance which, but for *TCGA 1992, s 55(6)(b)* above, would be brought into account under *TCGA 1992, s 56(2)* on any disposal made before 30 November 1993. [*TCGA 1992, s 55(9); FA 1994, s 93(4)(11)*].

Where, for the purposes of any disposal of the asset made by the transferor on or after 30 November 1993, any amount, amounts or combination of amounts within *TCGA 1992, s 38(1)(a)–(c)* (acquisition consideration etc., enhancement expenditure etc. and incidental disposal costs respectively; see 17.3 DISPOSAL) is required to be excluded, reduced or written down, the amount or amounts constituting the rolled-up indexation (or so much of it as remains after the application of this provision and *TCGA 1992, s 55(11)* below on a previous part disposal) are reduced in proportion to any reduction made in the amount falling within one or any combination of *TCGA 1992, s 38(1)(a)–(c)*. [*TCGA 1992, s 55(10); FA 1994, s 93(4)(11)*].

Where the transferor makes a part disposal of the asset at any time on or after 30 November 1993, then, for the purposes of that and any subsequent part disposal, the amount or amounts constituting the rolled-up indexation (or so much of it as remains after the application of this provision and *TCGA 1992, s 55(10)* above on a previous part disposal by him or after the application of *TCGA 1992, s 55(10)* on the part disposal) is apportioned between the property disposed of and the property which remains in the same proportions as the amounts within *TCGA 1992, s 38(1)(a)* and *(b)*. [*TCGA 1992, s 55(11); FA 1994, s 93(4)(11)*].

Example

X Ltd, Y Ltd and Z Ltd are all members of the same group within *TCGA 1992, s 170* (see 13.11 COMPANIES), all three companies having joined the group before 1 April 1987 (see 13.24 COMPANIES) and making up annual accounts for calendar years. No election under *TCGA 1992, s 35(5)* (universal re-basing; see 8.3 and 8.6 above) is in force. An asset was acquired by X Ltd from outside the group for £90,000 in 1980 and at 31 March 1982 the value of the asset is £100,000. The asset was transferred to Y Ltd in October 1985 such that the no gain/no loss basis of *TCGA 1992, s 171* (see 13.12 COMPANIES) applied. X Ltd made the appropriate election under *FA 1985, s 68(4)(5)* (indexation allowance to be calculated by reference to value at 31 March 1982 rather than original cost; see 8.13 and 8.14 below). In January 1995 Y Ltd transferred the asset to Z Ltd such that *TCGA 1992, s 171* again applied. Z Ltd sells the asset outside the group in March 2001 for £80,000. The relevant retail prices indices are

March 1982	79.44	January 1995	146.0
October 1985	95.59		

	£
Original cost of asset to X Ltd in 1980	90,000
Indexation allowance: March 1982 – October 1985 on 31 March 1982 value under *FA 1985, s 68(4)(5)*	
$\frac{95.59 - 79.44}{79.44}$ × £100,000 (indexation factor 0.203)	20,300
Deemed consideration under *TCGA 1992, s 56(2)*	£110,300

	£
Deemed cost of asset to Y Ltd in October 1985	110,300
Indexation allowance: October 1985–January 1995	
$\frac{146.0 - 95.59}{95.59}$ × £110,300 (indexation factor 0.527)	58,128
Deemed consideration under *TCGA 1992, s 56(2)*	£168,428

Under *TCGA 1992, s 35(10), s 55(6)(a), Sch 3 para 1*, Z Ltd is treated as having held the asset on 31 March 1982 for the purposes of re-basing under *TCGA 1992, s 35* and calculating indexation allowance.

	Cost	Re–base
	£	£
Proceeds received by Z Ltd	80,000	80,000
Deemed consideration under *TCGA 1992, s 55(6)(b)* (£168,428 – £58,128 – £20,300)	90,000	
Market value at 31 March 1982		100,000
Loss before *TCGA 1992, s 55(8)* adjustment	10,000	20,000
Rolled-up indexation under *TCGA 1992, s 55(9)*	20,300	20,300
Loss after *TCGA 1992, s 55(8)* adjustment	£30,300	£40,300

TCGA 1992, s 35(3) applies, so the allowable loss arising is £30,300.

Note to the example

(1) It should be noted that the effect of the legislation in force for disposals before 30 November 1993 meant that Z Ltd would not have been prejudiced on the ultimate disposal outside the group if X Ltd had not made a valid claim under *FA 1985, s 68(4)(5)* within the time limit in respect of the transfer of the asset to Y Ltd in October 1985. However, the legislation in force for disposals on or after 30 November 1993 means that, in the absence of such an election in respect of that disposal, the rolled-up indexation in the above example would have to be computed by reference to the original cost to X Ltd (i.e. 0.203 × £90,000 = £18,270). The allowable loss would then be £28,270 (i.e. £18,270 + £10,000). It is not known whether the Revenue would use the discretion it had in similarly affected cases to extend the time limit of two years after the end of the year of assessment or accounting period in which the disposal fell.

Shares or securities of the same class in any company which are *treated* as above as held on 31 March 1982 by a person will be treated as a single holding with any shares or securities of the same class in the same company *actually* held by that person in determining the market value for re-basing purposes of the shares or securities. If the shares or securities in the relevant disposal represent some but not all of those valued at 31 March 1982 then the allowable cost or indexation allowance as appropriate will be based on the proportion that the shares or securities disposed of bears to the total holding (Revenue Pamphlet IR 131, SP 5/89). See also 8.2 above regarding the concessional valuation of a holding of shares or securities at 31 March 1982 where part of the holding was held on 6 April 1965.

Where SP 5/89 above applies, the Revenue will also apply the following concessional valuation treatment where shares or securities of the same class are acquired by way of no gain/no loss transfer under *TCGA 1992, s 58* (spouses living together) or *s 171* (intra-group disposals). The concessional treatment applies to disposals within the scope of SP 5/89 made before 16 March 1993 in relation to which a claim is made before liabilities are finally determined, and all such disposals made after 15 March 1993 provided that a claim is made within two years (or such further time as the Board may allow) of the end of the year of assessment or accounting period in which the disposal is made. Under the concessional valuation treatment the value of a single holding may be regarded as the appropriate proportion of the value of any larger holding of shares or securities of the same class which were held by a spouse or another company at 31 March 1982 and from which part or all of the single holding was derived by one or more transfers within *TCGA 1992, s 58* or *s 171* respectively (Revenue Pamphlet IR 1, D44).

8.8 **Capital allowances.** If, under either the re-basing provisions of *TCGA 1992, s 35* or the equivalent provisions for indexation allowance of *TCGA 1992, s 55(1)* (see 8.2 and 8.3 above), it is to be assumed that any asset was on 31 March 1982 sold by the person making the disposal and immediately reacquired by him, *TCGA 1992, s 41* (restriction of losses by reference to capital allowances, see 17.5(*j*) DISPOSAL) and *s 47* (wasting assets qualifying for capital allowances, see 66.1 WASTING ASSETS) apply with suitable modifications on the assumed reacquisition at 31 March 1982. [*TCGA 1992, s 55(3), Sch 3 para 3*].

8.9 **Part disposals etc.** Where, on a disposal to which the general re-basing rule of *TCGA 1992, s 35(1)(2)* in 8.2 above applies, *TCGA 1992, s 42* (allowable expenditure on a part disposal, see 17.6 DISPOSAL) has effect by reason of an earlier disposal made after 31 March 1982 and before 6 April 1988, the sums to be apportioned under that provision on the later disposal are to take the general re-basing rule into account. [*TCGA 1992, Sch 3 para 4(1)*].

If in relation to disposals after 5 April 1989 the general re-basing rule of *TCGA 1992, s 35(1)(2)* applies, and if that rule did not apply expenditure would under specified enactments not be allowable in computing a gain arising on the disposal, and the disallowance would be attributable to the reduction of the amount of the consideration for a disposal made after 31 March 1982 but before 6 April 1988, the amount otherwise allowable as a deduction on the disposal is reduced by the amount of the disallowance that would have been made if the general re-basing rule had not applied. The enactments specified are

(i) *TCGA 1992, s 23(2)* (disallowance of allowable expenditure where allowance already given against receipts of compensation or insurance money, see 17.8 DISPOSAL);

(ii) *TCGA 1992, s 122(4)* (disallowance where allowance already given against capital distribution, see 58.14 SHARES AND SECURITIES);

(iii) *TCGA 1992, s 133(4)* (disallowance where allowance already given against premium on conversion of securities, see 58.11 SHARES AND SECURITIES); and

(iv) *TCGA 1992, s 244* (disallowance where allowance already given against gain from small part disposal of land, see 36.8 and 36.10 LAND).

[*TCGA 1992, Sch 3 para 4(2)*].

8.10 **Assets derived from other assets.** The re-basing provisions of *TCGA 1992, s 35* in 8.2 and 8.3 above apply with the necessary modifications in relation to a disposal of an asset which was not held on 31 March 1982, if its value is derived from another asset which is taken into account under *TCGA 1992, s 43* (assets derived from other assets, see 17.6 DISPOSAL). [*TCGA 1992, Sch 3 para 5*]. For indexation allowance purposes, where, after 31 March 1982, an asset which was held on that date has been merged or divided or has changed its nature or rights in or over the asset have been created, then *TCGA 1992, s 55(1)(2)* (re-basing for indexation allowance purposes) in 8.2 above has effect to determine for the purposes of *TCGA 1992, s 43* the amount of the consideration for the acquisition of the asset which was so held. [*TCGA 1992, s 55(4)*].

8.11 **Time apportionment of pre-6 April 1965 gains and losses.** If *TCGA 1992, Sch 2 para 16* (time apportionment of gains and losses accruing on ASSETS HELD ON 6 APRIL 1965; see 7.9) applies so that only part of a gain or loss is a chargeable gain or an allowable loss, the exclusion of the general re-basing rule of *TCGA 1992, s 35(1)(2)* under 8.2(*a*) and (*b*) above has effect as if the amount of the gain or loss that would accrue if the general re-basing rule did not apply were equal to that part. [*TCGA 1992, Sch 3 para 6*].

8.12 DEFERRED CHARGES ON GAINS BEFORE 31 MARCH 1982

Where, before 6 April 1988, a gain was deferred in respect of one or more disposals which related in whole or in part to an asset acquired before 31 March 1982, and the deferred gain is brought into charge on a disposal or other occasion after 5 April 1988, the deferred gain will, subject to conditions and on a claim, be halved (except, in certain cases, where the deferred gain is never deemed to accrue at all) when the charge to tax is computed in respect of it.

The provisions under which a gain can be deferred effectively fall into two groups for this purpose. In the first group (*TCGA 1992, Sch 4 para 2*), which includes the hold-over provisions for gifts made before 14 March 1989 and rollover relief on the replacement of business assets, the deferred gain is deducted from the expenditure allowable in computing the gain on a later disposal. In the second group (*TCGA 1992, Sch 4 paras 3, 4*), the deferred gain is brought into charge on the occurrence of a subsequent event. For both groups, the deferred gain will be half of what it would otherwise be. [*TCGA 1992, s 36, Sch 4 para 1*].

As regards the first group of provisions, both of the following circumstances must be fulfilled in order to bring about the halving of the deferred gain.

(*a*) There is a disposal, other than a 'no gain/no loss disposal' (see 8.7 above), after 5 April 1988 of an asset acquired after 31 March 1982 by the person making the disposal.

(*b*) A deduction from allowable expenditure falls to be made under any of the first group of provisions in computing the gain on that disposal and is attributable directly or indirectly, in whole or in part, to a chargeable gain accruing on the disposal before 6 April 1988 of an asset acquired before 31 March 1982 by the person making that disposal.

No relief is given under *TCGA 1992, Sch 4* where, by reason of the previous operation of it, the amount of the deduction in (*b*) is less than it otherwise would be. Where the disposal takes place after 18 March 1991, no relief under *TCGA 1992, Sch 4* is available if the amount of the deduction would have been less had relief by virtue of a previous application of it been duly claimed. (In effect, for disposals after 18 March 1991, the relief for the first group of provisions (*TCGA 1992, Sch 4 para 2*) cannot be claimed twice for the same gain and must be claimed in respect of the earliest possible occasion. For disposals after 5 April 1988 and before 19 March 1991, it was possible to claim other than on the earliest possible occasion. See below as regards time limits for claims affected by this change.) [*TCGA 1992, Sch 4 para 2(1)–(3)*].

Where the asset was acquired after 18 March 1991, the deduction is partly attributable to a claim under *TCGA 1992, s 154(4)* (rollover into non-depreciating asset instead of into depreciating asset, see 55.7 ROLLOVER RELIEF), and the claim applies to the asset, no relief under *TCGA 1992, Sch 4* is available by virtue of its application in respect of the first group of provisions below (*TCGA 1992, Sch 4 para 2*) (but see below as regards the relief available in respect of the second group of provisions). [*TCGA 1992, Sch 4 para 2(4)*].

In the case of rollover relief on the replacement of business assets and subject to the usual time limits, the disposal of the old asset may be before 31 March 1982, and the replacement asset may be acquired afterwards (Revenue Press Release 8 July 1988).

For the circumstances in which the Inland Revenue will require a valuation of the asset transferred where a hold-over relief claim is made, see 25.1 HOLD-OVER RELIEFS.

The first group of provisions mentioned above is as follows.

(i) *TCGA 1992, s 23(4)(5)* (rollover where replacement asset acquired after receipt of compensation or insurance money, see 17.9 DISPOSAL);

(ii) *TCGA 1992, s 152* (rollover where replacement asset acquired on disposal of business asset, see 55 ROLLOVER RELIEF);

(iii) *TCGA 1992, s 162* (hold-over where shares acquired on disposal of business to company, see 25.10 HOLD-OVER RELIEFS);

(iv) *TCGA 1992, s 165* (hold-over where business asset acquired by gift, see 25.1–25.6 HOLD-OVER RELIEFS);

(v) *TCGA 1992, s 247* (rollover where replacement land acquired on compulsory acquisition of other land, see 36.11 LAND);

(vi) *FA 1980, s 79* (hold-over where asset acquired by gift after 5 April 1980 and before 14 March 1989, see 25.9 HOLD-OVER RELIEFS).

[*TCGA 1992, Sch 4 para 2(5)*].

As regards the second group of provisions and subject to the exception below, both of the following circumstances must be fulfilled in order to bring about the halving of the deferred gain.

(A) Under any of the second group of provisions a gain is treated as accruing in consequence of an event occurring after 5 April 1988.

(B) The gain is attributable directly or indirectly, in whole or in part, to the disposal before 6 April 1988 of an asset acquired before 31 March 1982 by the person making that disposal.

[*TCGA 1992, Sch 4 para 4(1)*].

Where a gain is treated as accruing in consequence of an event after 18 March 1991, relief under *TCGA 1992, Sch 4* does not apply if the gain is attributable directly or indirectly, in whole or in part, to the disposal of an asset after 5 April 1988, or the amount of the gain would have been less had relief by virtue of a previous application of *TCGA 1992, Sch 4* been duly claimed. [*TCGA 1992, Sch 4 para 4(4)*]. (In effect, for events after 18 March 1991, the relief for the second group of provisions (*TCGA 1992, Sch 4 paras 3, 4*, and see below as regards *TCGA 1992, Sch 4 para 3*) cannot be claimed twice for the same gain and must be claimed in respect of the earliest possible occasion. For events after 5 April 1988 and before 19 March 1991, it was possible to claim other than on the earliest possible occasion and more than once. See below as regards time limits for claims affected by this change.)

The second group of provisions mentioned above is as follows (and see also below).

(I) *TCGA 1992, s 116(10)(11)* (postponement of charge on reorganisation etc. involving acquisition of qualifying corporate bonds, see 49.3 QUALIFYING CORPORATE BONDS).

(II) *TCGA 1992, s 134* (postponement of charge where gilts acquired on compulsory acquisition of shares, see 58.11 SHARES AND SECURITIES);

(III) *TCGA 1992, s 140* (postponement of charge where securities acquired in exchange for business acquired by overseas resident company until transferor company disposes of securities as mentioned in *s 140(4)* or transferee company within six years of exchange disposes of assets acquired on exchange as mentioned in *s 140(5)*, see 44.9 OVERSEAS MATTERS);

(IV) *TCGA 1992, s 154(2)* (postponement of charge where depreciating asset acquired as replacement for business asset, see 55.7 ROLLOVER RELIEF) (and see below as regards *TCGA 1992, Sch 4 para 3*);

(V) *TCGA 1992, s 168* (as modified by *TCGA 1992, s 67(6)*) (activation of charge held over under *FA 1980, s 79* on emigration of donee in relation to a gift after 5 April 1981 and before 14 March 1989, see 25.9 HOLD-OVER RELIEFS);

(VI) *TCGA 1992, s 179(3)* (or earlier equivalent) (charge on company leaving group of companies in respect of asset acquired from another member of same group within previous six years, see 13.19 COMPANIES, but only if the asset was acquired by the chargeable company before 6 April 1988, so no longer relevant);

(VII) *TCGA 1992, s 248(3)* (postponement of charge where depreciating asset acquired on compulsory acquisition of land, see 36.11 LAND);

[*TCGA 1992, Sch 4 para 4(2)(3); FA 2000, Sch 40 Pt II(12)*].

Where relief under *TCGA 1992, Sch 4* would have applied on a disposal but for the effect of *TCGA 1992, Sch 4 para 2(4)* (exclusion of relief under *TCGA 1992, Sch 4 para 2* where deduction partly attributable to claim under *TCGA 1992, s 154(4)*) above, then such relief (on the same lines as for the second group of provisions above) is available (under *TCGA 1992, Sch 4 para 3*) if the relief for the second group of provisions (*TCGA 1992, Sch 4 para 4*) would have applied had *TCGA 1992, s 154(2)* (see (IV) above) continued to apply to the gain carried forward as a result of the claim under *TCGA 1992, s 154(4)*, and the time of disposal been the time when that gain was treated as accruing by virtue of *TCGA 1992, s 154(2)*. [*TCGA 1992, Sch 4 para 3*].

There is an exception to the bringing about of the halving of the deferred gain in respect of certain provisions contained in the second group. Neither *TCGA 1992, s 134, s 140(4), s 154(2)* nor *s 248(3)* (see (II)–(IV) and (VII) above) is to apply in consequence of an event occurring after 5 April 1988 if its application would be *directly* attributable to the disposal of an asset before 1 April 1982. [*TCGA 1992, Sch 4 para 4(5)*]. In effect the deferred gain is in such circumstances never deemed to accrue. See also below regarding views expressed by the Revenue.

Relief is available as regards both groups of provisions where a person makes a disposal of an asset which he acquired after 30 March 1982 where the disposal by which he acquired it and any previous disposal of it after that date was a 'no gain/no loss disposal' (see 8.7 above). In such a case, the person is treated for the purposes of (*b*) and (B) above as having acquired the asset before 31 March 1982. [*TCGA 1992, Sch 4 paras 5, 7*].

Where deferral has been claimed under one of the first group of provisions and there is a subsequent no gain/no loss disposal (or continuous series of such disposals) as in 8.7 above, relief is available (subject to the conditions in (*a*) and (*b*) above) in computing the gain on the first later disposal which is not a no gain/no loss disposal. [*TCGA 1992, Sch 4 paras 6, 7*].

Relief is available as regards both groups of provisions for an asset which was not acquired before 31 March 1982 if its value was derived from another asset which was so acquired and which is taken into account under *TCGA 1992, s 43* (see 17.6 DISPOSAL). [*TCGA 1992, Sch 4 para 8*].

No relief is available under *TCGA 1992, Sch 4* unless a claim is made

(*a*) in respect of gains accruing to a person chargeable to corporation tax within two years of the end of the accounting period, and

(*b*) in respect of gains accruing to a person chargeable to capital gains tax, on or before the first anniversary of the 31st January next following the year of assessment in which the disposal is made or the gain in question is treated as accruing,

(*c*) on or before such later date as the board may allow,

in which, for the first group of provisions, the disposal to which the claim relates is made, or for the second group of provisions, the deferred gain is treated as accruing (except where (VI) above applied where the claim had to be made within two years of the end of the accounting period in which the chargeable company ceased to be a member of the group). A claim must be supported by any particulars the inspector may require for establishing the validity and quantum of any relief. [*TCGA 1992, Sch 4 para 9; FA 1996, Sch 21 para 43; FA 2000, Sch 40 Pt II(12)*]. A late claim may be accepted if the delay in making it is less than twelve months and resulted from events outside the taxpayer's control or any other reasonable cause (Revenue Capital Gains Manual CG 16821, 17012).

It is understood that the Revenue accept that the crystallisation under *TCGA 1992, s 67(4)(5)* of a gain deferred by *FA 1980, s 79* (as extended by *FA 1981, s 78* and *FA 1982, s 82*) (clawback of deferred gain on death of life tenant, see 25.5 and 25.9 HOLD-OVER RELIEFS) can by concession be treated as if it were amongst the second group of provisions in (I)–(VII) above. In addition, a gain deferred on a transfer into settlement occurring before 1 April 1982 and which would otherwise crystallise on the death after 5 April 1988 of a life tenant will by concession be deemed never to accrue (and so treated in the same way as for the exception given by *TCGA 1992, Sch 4 para 4(5)* above).

Example

1980 A acquires an asset for £10,000

1983 The asset is gifted to B with a hold-over election under *FA 1980, s 79* when worth £12,000. Indexation allowance is taken to be £500 (for illustration purposes only).

Gain held over £12,000 – £10,000 – £500 = £1,500

B's cost of the asset £12,000 – £1,500 = £10,500

1985 B sells the asset for £15,000 and replaces it by one costing £17,000 at the same time. Indexation allowance is taken to be £750 by reference to the reduced base cost of £10,500. Full rollover under *TCGA 1992, s 152* (formerly *CGTA 1979, s 115*) is available and claimed.

Gain rolled over £15,000 – £10,500 – £750 = £3,750

Base cost of second asset £17,000 – £3,750 = £13,250

1987 B sells the replacement asset for £20,000 replacing it by one costing £22,000 at the same time. Indexation allowance is taken to be £1,250 by reference to the reduced base cost of £13,250. Full rollover as in 1985 is claimed.

Gain rolled over £20,000 – £13,250 – £1,250 = £5,500

Base cost of third asset £22,000 – £5,500 = £16,500 (but see below)

2000 B sells the third asset for £35,000 and does not replace it. The increase in the retail prices index between the month of acquisition in 1987 and April 1998 is taken to be 60%.

On a claim the deduction (£5,500) otherwise taken into account in arriving at the base cost of the third asset is reduced by half because it is partly attributable to the gain arising in 1983 in respect of the asset acquired in 1980.

Revised base cost of third asset £22,000 – £2,750 = £19,250

Chargeable gain (subject to TAPER RELIEF (60))
£35,000 – £19,250 – (60% × £19,250) = £4,200

8.13 Assets held on 31 March 1982

8.13 **INDEXATION ALLOWANCE: CLAIM BEFORE 6 APRIL 1988 FOR RE-BASING AT 31 MARCH 1982**

For disposals on or after the '1985 date' (1 April 1985 for companies and 6 April 1985 for others) and before 6 April 1988, a claim could be made for the indexation allowance (but not the unindexed gain or loss) arising on a disposal of an asset held on 31 March 1982 by the person making the disposal to be calculated on the assumption that on that date the asset was sold by the person concerned and immediately reacquired by him at its market value on that date. Such a claim had to be made within two years of the end of the year of assessment or accounting period in which the disposal occurred or within such longer period as the Board by notice in writing allowed. [*FA 1985, s 68(4)(5) (as originally enacted)*].

Although allowable expenditure relating to an asset held on 31 March 1982 may have been reduced (e.g. by rollover relief), there was no corresponding restriction applied to the market value on that date for the purposes of any deemed reacquisition on that date.

The Revenue in practice allowed a claim to be withdrawn within the time limit for making the claim provided the relevant assessment had not become final and conclusive (Tolley's Practical Tax 1986 pp 33, 88).

8.14 **Previous no gain/no loss disposals.** Where

(*a*) a person made a disposal, other than a 'no gain/no loss disposal', of an asset which he acquired after 31 March 1982, and

(*b*) the disposal by which he acquired the asset and any previous disposal of the asset after 31 March 1982 was a no gain/no loss disposal,

he was treated for the purposes of the re-basing provisions of *FA 1985, s 68(4)(5)* in 8.13 above as having held the asset on 31 March 1982.

A '*no gain/no loss disposal*' was one under the following enactments (being enactments by virtue of which neither a gain nor a loss accrues): *TCGA 1992, ss 58, 139, 171* and *264*; and *FA 1982, s 148*. See 8.7 above for details of these enactments and note the wider definition given there to a no gain/no loss disposal.

In computing the gain or loss on a person's disposal (not being a no gain/no loss disposal) of an asset which he was treated as having held on 31 March 1982, the no gain/no loss acquisition value which otherwise would have been deductible as allowable expenditure (see 26.4 INDEXATION) was reduced by any indexation allowance given on the disposal to him or any previous no gain/no loss disposal. [*FA 1985, s 68(7)(8) (as originally enacted)*].

8.15 **Assets derived from other assets.** For indexation allowance purposes, where, after 31 March 1982, an asset which was held on that date was merged or divided or changed its nature or rights in or over the asset were created, then the re-basing provisions of *FA 1985, s 68(4)(5)* in 8.13 above had effect to determine for the purposes of *TCGA 1992, s 43* (assets derived from other assets, see 17.6 DISPOSAL) the amount of the consideration for the acquisition of the asset which was so held. [*FA 1985, s 68(6)*].

9 Back Duty

Cross-references. See 5 ASSESSMENTS; 12 CLAIMS; 35 INTEREST AND SURCHARGES ON UNPAID TAX; 46 PAYMENT OF TAX; 47 PENALTIES; 56 SELF-ASSESSMENT for changes broadly from 1996/97.

9.1 BACK DUTY CLAIMS

These are made by the Revenue where they consider tax to have been lost by a taxpayer's fraudulent or negligent conduct (or by his fraud, wilful default or neglect). In such cases, the normal time limits for assessments are extended (see 9.4 below) and INTEREST AND SURCHARGES ON UNPAID TAX (35.6) and (35.8) and PENALTIES (47) are incurred, which the Board may mitigate in appropriate circumstances. For cases relating to back duty, see TOLLEY'S TAX CASES.

9.2 FRAUD OR WILFUL DEFAULT

See 9.4 below as regards the replacement of 'fraud, wilful default or neglect' assessments by 'fraudulent or negligent conduct' assessments. The later expression is not defined, and the following cases may be of continued assistance in this respect.

The onus of proving fraud or wilful default is on the Crown but the onus then shifts to the taxpayer to prove the revised assessments incorrect if he wishes to do so (*Johnson v Scott CA 1978, 52 TC 383; Jonas v Bamford Ch D 1973, 51 TC 1; Hurley v Taylor CA 1998, 71 TC 268; Nicholson v Morris CA 1977, 51 TC 95* and cf. *Barney v Pybus Ch D 1957, 37 TC 106; R v Special Commrs (ex p. Martin) CA 1971, 48 TC 1* and *Arumugam Pillai v Director General of Inland Revenue PC, [1981] STC 146*). For the standard of proof required, see *Les Croupiers Casino Club v Pattinson CA 1987, 60 TC 196*.

Unexplained capital increases or admitted omissions may be held evidence of fraud or wilful default (*Amis v Colls Ch D 1960, 39 TC 148; Woodrow v Whalley Ch D 1964, 42 TC 249; Hudson v Humbles Ch D 1965, 42 TC 380; Hillenbrand CS 1966, 42 TC 617; Young v Duthie Ch D 1969, 45 TC 624; James v Pope Ch D 1972, 48 TC 142;* and cf. *Brimelow v Price Ch D 1965, 49 TC 41*). Fraud or wilful default may be by an agent (*Clixby v Pountney Ch D 1967, 44 TC 515; Pleasants v Atkinson Ch D 1987, 60 TC 228*).

9.3 NEGLECT

See 9.4 below as regards the replacement of 'fraud, wilful default or neglect' assessments by 'fraudulent or negligent conduct' assessments.

'Neglect' means negligence or a failure to give any notice, make any return, or produce or furnish any document or other information required by or under the *Taxes Acts*. [*TMA 1970, s 118; FA 1989, Sch 17 Pt VIII*]. Neglect may be by an agent (*Mankowitz v Special Commrs Ch D 1971, 46 TC 707*).

9.4 EXTENDED TIME LIMITS

For time limits under SELF-ASSESSMENT effective from 1996/97 onwards see 56.27 .

In other cases the normal time limit for making assessments is six years after the chargeable period concerned. [*TMA 1970, s 34*]. In certain cases, however, extended limits apply to assessments for the purpose of making good a loss of tax, subject to the overriding provision that an assessment may not be made on personal representatives later than three years after that in which the deceased died (see 9.5 below). See 5.5 ASSESSMENTS as regards the date on which an assessment is made.

9.4 Back Duty

Assessments made after 26 July 1989 relating to 1983/84 and subsequent years (or to accounting periods ending after 31 March 1983). Where the loss of tax arises due to the fraudulent or negligent conduct of a person (or of a person acting on his behalf), an assessment may be made at any time not later than 20 years after the end of the chargeable period to which it relates. If the person assessed so requires, the assessment may give effect to reliefs or allowances to which he would have been entitled had he made the necessary claims within the relevant time limits. [*TMA 1970, s 36(1)(3); FA 1989, s 149*].

Assessments made before 27 July 1989 or relating to 1982/83 and earlier years (or to accounting periods ending before 1 April 1983). *Fraud or wilful default.* An assessment to make good tax lost through fraud or wilful default may be made at any time. [*TMA 1970, s 36*]. The leave of a single General or Special Commissioner must be obtained, and the Commissioner must be satisfied that there are reasonable grounds for believing that tax may have been so lost. [*TMA 1970, s 41*]. In applying for leave, the inspector need only provide such information as would allow the Commissioner to so satisfy himself and is not required to embark on a wide-ranging review of all the circumstances of the case (*Re McGuckian CA(NI) 1999, [2000] STC 65*). There is no hearing, and the taxpayer is not entitled to appear or to present his case (*Day v Williams CA 1969, 46 TC 59; Pearlberg v Varty HL 1972, 48 TC 14* and *Nicholson v Morris CA 1977, 51 TC 95*) but contrast *R v Spec Commrs (ex p. Stipplechoice Ltd) (No 1) CA, [1985] STC 248* where a judicial review was granted in the absence of any other adequate remedy. The taxpayer may, of course, appeal against the assessment in the normal way. The Commissioner who gave leave to issue the assessment is not allowed to be present at the hearing of such an appeal. [*TMA 1970, s 41(2)*].

Neglect. Where, for the purpose of recovering tax lost due to fraud, wilful default, or neglect, an assessment has been made not later than six years after the end of the year for which the tax was lost (the '*normal year*'), the Revenue may make assessments for any of the six years prior to that normal year to make good a loss of tax attributable to neglect. Leave of a General or Special Commissioner is required. Such an assessment must be made not later than the end of the year of assessment following that in which the normal year assessment is finally determined. [*TMA 1970, s 37(1)–(3)*]. Thus an assessment made in 1988/89 to recover tax lost for the year 1982/83 may support assessments for 1976/77 onwards. The decision in *O'Mullan v Walmsley QB (NI) 1965, 42 TC 573* that such assessments are invalid unless the assessment for the 'normal year' was expressly stated to be for making good tax lost by fraud, default or neglect was not followed in *Thurgood v Slarke Ch D 1971, 47 TC 130.* 'What matters is not the purpose of the assessor but of the assessment.' See also *R v Spec Commrs (ex p. Rogers) CA 1972, 48 TC 46; Knight v CIR CA 1974, 49 TC 179* and *R v Holborn Commrs (ex p. Frank Rind Settlement Trustees) QB 1974, 49 TC 656.*

The Revenue may go back further if an assessment for any year has been made more than six years after the end of that year. The year for which the assessment has been made is called the '*earlier year*'. One of the following conditions must be satisfied.

(*a*) The assessment has been made under *TMA 1970, s 37(3)* (see above).

(*b*) The assessment is one of a number made under *TMA 1970, s 36* (see above) for years which are not more than six years apart and of which the latest is within six years prior to the normal year.

If (*a*) or (*b*) above applies, the Revenue may make an assessment for any of the six years immediately preceding the earlier year (and so on for other earlier years) with the leave of the General or Special Commissioners. The Commissioners must be satisfied that reasonable grounds exist for believing that tax for that year may have been lost through the taxpayer's neglect. The taxpayer is entitled to appear (or to be represented) and be heard. [*TMA 1970, s 37(4)–(7)*]. The Revenue must apply to the Commissioners not later than the end of the year following that in which liability under the assessment for the earlier year is finally determined.

In determining the tax to be charged for any year, the taxpayer is to be given the reliefs and allowances to which he would have been entitled for that year. [*TMA 1970, s 37(8)*].

The making of an assessment to income tax will not affect the time allowed for the making of a capital gains tax assessment under these provisions, and vice versa. [*TMA 1970, s 37(9)*].

For companies, similar provisions apply, by reference to accounting periods instead of tax years. [*TMA 1970, s 39*].

9.5 **Deceased persons.** Assessments on a deceased's capital gains arising or accruing before death must be made on the deceased's personal representatives on or before the third anniversary of 31 January following the year of assessment in which death occurred (or within three years after the end of that year of assessment where it was 1995/96 or an earlier year), and those made as a result of the deceased's fraudulent or negligent conduct are restricted to years of assessment ending not earlier than six years prior to the death. A fraudulent or negligent act or omission under *TMA 1970, s 98B* (failure etc. to render return relating to European Economic Interest Groupings; see 44.15 OVERSEAS MATTERS, 47.7 PENALTIES and 54.15 RETURNS) on the part of a grouping or a member thereof is deemed to be the act or omission of each member. [*TMA 1970, s 40; FA 1989, s 149(4), Sch 17 Pt VIII; FA 1990, Sch 11 para 4(2), para 5*]. See 5.5 ASSESSMENTS as regards the date on which an assessment is made.

9.6 EVIDENCE

Statements made or documents produced by or on behalf of a taxpayer are admissible as evidence in proceedings against him, notwithstanding that reliance on the Board's practice in cases of full disclosure may have induced him to make or produce them. [*TMA 1970, s 105; FA 1989, s 168(1)(5)*]. See 9.7 and 9.9 and 47.6 PENALTIES below.

9.7 CERTIFICATES OF FULL DISCLOSURE

A certificate of full disclosure may be required by the Revenue from a taxpayer during a back duty enquiry stating that complete disclosure has been made of, inter alia, all banking, savings and loan accounts, deposit receipts, building society and co-operative society accounts; all investments including savings certificates and premium bonds and loans (whether interest-bearing or not); all other assets, including cash and life assurance policies, which the taxpayer and his spouse now possess, or have possessed, or in which they have or have had any interest or power to operate or control during the stated period; all gifts in any form, by the taxpayer or his spouse to their children or to other persons during the stated period; all sources of income and all income derived therefrom; and all facts bearing on liability to income tax, capital gains tax and other duties for the stated period. Great care must be exercised before signing such a certificate, since subsequent discovery of an omission could lead to heavy penalties. See 47 PENALTIES.

9.8 INVESTIGATORY POWERS

Enquiry procedures introduced by SELF-ASSESSMENT from 1996/97 onwards are explained in 56.11.

For these purposes, '*document*' has the same meaning as in *Civil Evidence Act 1968, Pt I* (or Scottish or Northern Ireland equivalent), but does not include personal records or journalistic material (within *Police and Criminal Evidence Act 1984, ss 12, 13*) (and those exclusions apply also to particulars contained in such records or material). The documents concerned are those in the possession or power of the person receiving the notice. Photographic, etc. facsimiles may be supplied provided the originals are produced if called for, and documents relating to any pending tax appeal need not be delivered. There are special provisions relating to computer records (see *FA 1988, s 127*). Documents in a person's 'possession or power' are those actually in existence at the time the notice is given, and not any which would have to be brought into existence in order to satisfy the notice.

(*a*) Where an inspector is of the reasonable opinion that documents contain, or may contain, information relevant to the tax liability of a person, he may (with the Board's authority and the consent of a General or Special Commissioner) by notice in writing require that person to deliver such documents to him (but only after that person has been given reasonable opportunity to produce them).

After 2 May 1994, the inspector must give a written summary of his reasons for applying for consent to the giving of the notice. He is not required to identify any informant in the summary and no summary need be provided if the Special or General Commissioner giving consent so directs, and the Commissioner concerned must not so direct unless he is satisfied that the inspector has reasonable grounds for believing that disclosure of the information in question would prejudice the assessment or collection of tax. The Commissioner concerned must not take part in or be present at any subsequent proceedings concerning an appeal made by the person if the Commissioner concerned has reason to believe that any of the documents which were the subject of the notice is likely to be adduced in evidence in those proceedings.

For an unsuccessful challenge to the validity of a notice, see *Kempton v Special Commrs & CIR Ch D 1992, 66 TC 249.*

(*b*) An inspector may similarly by notice in writing require a person to furnish him with such particulars as he may reasonably require as being relevant to any tax liability of that person.

The notice is subject to the same authority and giving of consent requirements as at (*a*) above, and the requirements there relating to the giving of a written summary and the obligation imposed on the Special or General Commissioner giving consent apply similarly in relation to particulars as they do there to documents.

For an unsuccessful challenge to the validity of a notice, see *Kempton v Special Commrs & CIR Ch D 1992, 66 TC 249.*

(*c*) An inspector may similarly by notice in writing require any other person (including the Director of Savings) to deliver to him (or, if the person so elects, make available for inspection by a named officer of the Board) documents relevant to any tax liability of a 'taxpayer'. A copy of the notice must be given to the taxpayer concerned unless, in a case involving suspected fraud, a General or Special Commissioner so directs. Production of documents originating more than six years before the notice cannot be required (unless the Commissioner who gave consent to the notice specifically allows it on being satisfied that there is reasonable ground for believing loss of tax through fraud).

'*Taxpayer*' includes an individual who has died (but any notice must be given no more than six years after the death) and a company which has ceased to exist.

The notice is subject to the same authority and giving of consent requirements as at (*a*) above, and the requirements there relating to the giving of a written summary and the obligation imposed on the Special or General Commissioner giving consent apply similarly, except that the summary must be given to, and the obligation imposed relates to an appeal brought by, the taxpayer rather than the person to whom the notice is given, and no summary need be given if the taxpayer is not, as above, given a copy of the notice.

A notice cannot require the production by a statutory auditor of his audit papers, nor by a tax adviser of communications with a client (or with any other tax adviser of his client) relating to advice about the client's tax affairs. This exemption does not, however, apply to explanatory documents concerning any other documents prepared with the client for, or for delivery to, the Revenue, unless the Revenue already has access to the information contained therein in some other document. Where the exemption is so disapplied, either the document must be delivered or made available to the Revenue or a copy of the relevant parts must be supplied (which parts must be available if required for inspection).

The Revenue's application of these provisions relating to papers of a statutory auditor or client communications of a tax adviser is set out in Revenue Pamphlet IR 131, SP 5/90. In particular, it is made clear that accountants' working papers will be called for only where voluntary access has not been obtained and it is considered absolutely necessary in order to determine whether a client's accounts or returns are complete and correct. Requests for access may on occasion extend to the whole or a particular part of the working papers, rather than just to information explaining specific entries, and the Revenue will usually be prepared to visit the accountants' or clients' premises to examine the papers and to take copies or extracts.

For guidance on the question of whether documents and records are the property of a statutory auditor or tax adviser, or of the client of such a person, see ICAEW Memorandum TR 781, 23 February 1990.

For an unsuccessful challenge to the validity of a notice, see *R v CIR (ex p. TC Coombs & Co.) HL 1991, 64 TC 124.*

(*d*) An inspector may similarly, on an application authorised by the Board, give a notice in writing as under (*c*) above without naming the taxpayer concerned. Consent to the application must be obtained from a Special Commissioner, who must be satisfied that: it relates to a taxpayer or class of taxpayers whose identity(ies) is (are) not known; there are reasonable grounds to believe the taxpayer(s) to have failed to comply with the *Taxes Acts*, with the likelihood of serious prejudice to the assessment or collection of tax; and the information is not reasonably available from elsewhere. The recipient can object (with a right of appeal to the Special Commissioners), by notice in writing, within 30 days on the ground that it would be onerous for him to comply.

The requirements at (*a*) above relating to the giving of a written summary and the obligation imposed on the Special or General Commissioner giving consent do not apply. The exemption, and disapplication of the exemption, from the requirements of a notice under (*d*) above relating to the production of the papers of a statutory auditor or client communications of a tax adviser apply similarly, except that the exemption does not apply to any document giving the identity or address of any taxpayer to whom the notice relates or of any person who has acted on behalf of any such person, unless the Revenue already has access to the information contained therein in some other document.

The Boards power to authorise an application may be delegated to one of its officers, and the authorisation may be given orally (*R v Special Commr (ex p. CIR); R v CIR (ex p. Ulster Bank Ltd) QB, [2000] STC 537*).

(*e*) An officer may similarly (with the Board's authority and the consent of a Circuit judge in England and Wales, a sheriff in Scotland or a county court judge in

Northern Ireland) by notice in writing require a '*tax accountant*' (i.e. a person who assists another in the preparation of returns, etc. for tax purposes) who has been convicted by or before any UK court of a tax offence or incurred a penalty under *TMA 1970, s 99* (see 47.5 PENALTIES) to deliver documents in his possession or power relevant to any tax liability of any of his clients. The notice must be issued within twelve months of the final determination of the conviction or penalty award.

Neither the requirements at (*a*) above relating to the giving of a written summary nor the exemption from the requirements of a notice under (*d*) above relating to the production of the papers of a statutory auditor or client communications of a tax adviser apply to the giving of a notice as above.

(*f*) The Board may require, by notice in writing, a person to deliver or furnish to a named officer of theirs documents or information as specified in (*a*) and (*b*) above relevant to the tax liability of that person.

The requirements at (*a*) above relating to the giving of consent and a written summary do not apply. However, notices cannot be given on or after 26 July 1990 under this power unless there are reasonable grounds for believing that that person may have failed, or may fail, to comply with any provision of the *Taxes Acts*, and that any such failure is likely to have led, or to lead, to serious prejudice to the proper assessment or collection of tax.

For procedural matters in relation to such a notice, see *R v CIR (ex p. Taylor) (No 1) CA 1988, 62 TC 562; (No 2) CA 1990, 62 TC 578.*

The notice must specify or describe the documents or particulars required, the time limit for production (generally not less than 30 days) and, except as above, the name of the taxpayer or client, as appropriate; and the person to whom they are delivered may take copies.

The penalty for failure to comply with a notice is given by *TMA 1970, s 98* (see 47.7 PENALTIES for this and the penalty for failure to allow access to computers). In addition there are severe penalties (in summary proceedings, a fine of the statutory maximum, and on indictment, imprisonment for two years and/or an unlimited fine) for the falsification, concealment, destruction or disposal of a document which is the subject of a notice, unless strict conditions and time limits are observed.

[*TMA 1970, s 20, s 20A, s 20B(1)(1A)(1B)(2)(4)–(7)(9)–(14), s 20BB, s 20D; FA 1976, Sch 6; FA 1988, s 126(2)(3); FA 1989, ss 142–145, s 148, s 168(1)(2); FA 1990, s 93; FA 1994, s 255; FA 2000, s 149(3)(4)*].

The person to whom notice is to be given is not entitled to attend or be legally represented at the meeting at which the inspector seeks the consent of a Commissioner (*Applicant v Inspector of Taxes (Sp C 189), [1999] SSCD 128*).

Notices other than those under (*d*) and (*e*) above may relate to tax liabilities in EU member States other than the UK [*FA 1990, s 125(1)(2)(6)*] or in any other territory with which the UK has entered into arrangements providing for the obtaining of information [*FA 2000, s 146(3)(4)*].

For an article setting out the Revenue's view on the question of claims to legal or professional privilege in relation to requests for information under these provisions (other than where tax evasion or tax fraud is suspected), see Revenue Tax Bulletin April 2000 pp 743–746.

Order for delivery of documents in serious tax fraud cases. Under *TMA 1970, s 20BA, Sch 1AA*, introduced by *FA 2000, s 149, Sch 39*, the Board may apply to the appropriate judicial authority (a Circuit judge in England and Wales, a sheriff in Scotland or a County Court judge in NI) for an order requiring any person who appears to have in his possession or power documents specified or described in the order to deliver them to an officer of the Board within ten working days after the day of service of the notice, or such longer or shorter period as may be specified in the order. The judicial authority must be satisfied, on information on oath given by an authorised officer of the Board, that there is reasonable ground for suspecting that an offence involving serious tax fraud has been or is about to be committed, and that the documents may be required as evidence in proceedings in respect of the offence. In Scotland, a single sheriff may make orders in respect of persons anywhere in Scotland as long as one of the orders relates to a person residing or having a place of business at an address in the sheriff's own sherriffdom. Orders may not be made in relation to items subject to legal privilege (as defined) unless they are held with the intention of furthering a criminal purpose. Failure to comply with an order is treated as contempt of court, and there are severe penalties for falsification of documents.

Schedule 1AA lays down detailed requirements in relation to such applications, and these may be supplemented by regulations. In particular, a person is entitled to notice of intention to apply for such an order, and to appear and be heard at the application, unless the judicial authority is satisfied that this would seriously prejudice investigation of the offence. Until the application has been dismissed or abandoned, or an order made or complied with, any person given such notice must not conceal, destroy, alter or dispose of any document to which the order sought relates, or disclose information etc. likely to prejudice the investigation, except with the leave of the judicial authority or the written permission of the Board. Professional legal advisers may, however, disclose such information etc. in giving legal advice to a client or in connection with legal proceedings, provided that it is not disclosed with a view to furthering a criminal purpose. Failure to comply with these requirements is treated as failure to comply with an order under these provisions. The procedural rules where documents are delivered in accordance with an order are as for Search and seizure (see below) under *TMA 1970, s 20CC(3)–(9)*.

Search and seizure. Where there is a reasonable suspicion of serious tax fraud, and there are reasonable grounds for believing that use of the procedure under *TMA 1970, s 20BA* (see above under Order for delivery of documents in serious tax fraud cases) might seriously prejudice the investigation, the Board may apply to a Circuit judge (a sheriff in Scotland or a County Court judge in NI) for a warrant to enter premises within 14 days to search and seize any things which may be relevant as evidence. There are detailed procedural rules governing searches and the removal of documents etc. [*TMA 1970, ss 20C, 20CC, 20D; FA 1976, Sch 6; FA 1989, ss 146–148; FA 2000, s 150*].

The taxpayer is not entitled to be told the nature of the offence, the ground of suspicion, or the person suspected (*CIR and Another v Rossminster Ltd and Others HL 1979, 52 TC 160*). For the proper procedure in seeking and obtaining judicial review of a decision to grant a warrant as above, and interim injunctions, see *R v CIR (ex p. Kingston Smith) QB 1996, 70 TC 264*. As regards the validity of warrants, see *R v CIR (ex p. Tamosius & Partners) QB, [1999] STC 1077*.

Barristers, advocates or solicitors. A notice under (*a*), (*b*), (*c*) or (*e*) above to a barrister, advocate or solicitor can be issued only by the Board (who may nevertheless delegate their powers — see *R v CIR (ex p. Davis Frankel & Mead) QB, [2000] STC 595*). The requirements at (*a*) above relating to the giving of consent and a written summary do not apply. The barrister etc. cannot (without his client's consent) be required to deliver under (*c*), (*d*) or (*e*) documents protected by professional privilege but, subject to that, the exemption, and disapplication of the exemption, from the requirements of a notice under, as the case may be, (*c*), (*d*) or (*e*) above relating to the production of the papers of a statutory auditor or client communications of a tax adviser apply similarly. [*TMA 1970, s 20B(3)(8)*]. As regards the Search and seizure powers above, there is similarly an exclusion for documents protected by professional privilege or, from 28 July 2000, 'legal privilege' as more widely defined (but excluding items held with the intention of furthering a criminal purpose) [*TMA 1970, s 20C(4)–(4B); FA 1989, s 146(4); FA 2000, s 150(4)*], and see above as regards similar protection in relation to an order under *TMA 1970, s 20BA* in cases involving serious tax fraud.

See *R v CIR (ex p. Goldberg) QB 1988, 61 TC 403* and cf. *Dubai Bank Ltd v Galadari CA, [1989] 3 WLR 1044* (a non-tax case). In relation to search and seizure, it was held in *R v CIR (ex p. Tamosius & Partners) QB, [1999] STC 1077* that the presence of independent counsel to determine the issue of professional privilege was 'to be encouraged', although it would not prevent action by the courts if counsel was wrong.

For an article setting out the Revenue's view on the question of claims to legal or professional privilege in relation to requests for information under these provisions (other than where tax evasion or tax fraud is suspected), see Revenue Tax Bulletin April 2000 pp 743–746.

9.9 OFFERS BY TAXPAYER

Where back duty arises, the taxpayer may be invited to offer a sum in settlement of liability of tax, interest and penalties (a 'contract settlement') and such offers are often accepted by the Board without assessment of all the tax. A binding agreement so made cannot be repudiated afterwards by the taxpayer or his executors. Where the liability is agreed and the tax etc. paid, this cannot afterwards be set aside, notwithstanding any alleged overcharge and no formal assessment (see cases at 47.10 PENALTIES and *CIR v Nuttall CA 1989, 63 TC 148* and *CIR v Woollen CA 1992, 65 TC 229*). See generally Revenue Pamphlet IR 73 regarding negotiation of settlements.

The practice of the Board in cases of tax fraud is as follows.

(*a*) The Board may accept a money settlement instead of instituting criminal proceedings in respect of fraud alleged to have been committed by a taxpayer.

(*b*) They can give no undertaking that they will accept a money settlement and refrain from instituting criminal proceedings (even if the taxpayer has made a full disclosure and fully facilitated the investigation of the facts) and reserve to themselves full discretion in all cases as to the course they pursue.

(*c*) But in considering whether to accept a money settlement or to institute criminal proceedings, it is their practice to be influenced by the fact that the taxpayer has made a full disclosure and fully facilitated the investigation of his affairs.

(Revenue Press Release of 18 October 1990 reproducing a Parliamentary statement (HC Written answer 18 October 1990 Vol 177 col 882) and replacing the 'Hansard leaflet' statement of 5 October 1944). See also 9.6 above and 47.6 PENALTIES.

A decision by the Revenue to enter into a contract settlement and not to prosecute does not preclude the Crown Prosecution Service (CPS) from instituting criminal proceedings (*R v W and another CA, [1998] STC 550*). However, the Revenue in commenting on this case have stated that the CPS will ordinarily bring proceedings that encompass tax evasion charges only where that evasion is incidental to allegations of non-fiscal criminal conduct (Revenue Tax Bulletin June 1998 pp 544, 545).

A case is more likely to be considered by the Revenue for prosecution if it contains features such as falsification of documents, lying during an investigation, conspiracy, discovery of false statements made during a previous investigation or dishonesty on the part of a professional tax adviser (Revenue Press Release 14 July 1999).

From 1 January 2001, the fraudulent evasion of *income tax* (not capital gains tax) on behalf of oneself or another person is itself a criminal offence. [*FA 2000, s 144*].

10 Charities

Sumption: Capital Gains Tax. See A22.

10.1 DEFINITIONS AND GENERAL PRINCIPLES

For certain income tax purposes, '*charity*' means any body of persons or trust established for charitable purposes only. [*ICTA 1988, s 506(1)*]. The meaning of charity is also governed by general law. These meanings apply for capital gains tax for all practical purposes.

Under *Recreational Charities Act 1958, s 1,* the provision, in the interests of social welfare, of facilities for recreation or other leisure occupation is deemed to be charitable (subject to the principle that, unless the trust is for the relief of poverty (*Dingle v Turner HL, [1972] 1 All E R 878*) a trust or institution to be charitable must be for the public benefit). See in this connection *Guild v CIR HL, [1992] STC 162.*

Charities are regulated under the *Charities Acts 1992* and *1993* in England and Wales by the Charity Commissioners. In Scotland, charities recognised as such by the Inland Revenue are regulated by the Scottish Charities Office, on behalf of the Lord Advocate, under the *Law Reform (Miscellaneous Provisions) (Scotland) Act 1990.* Registers of charities are kept by the Charity Commissioners and the Financial Intermediaries and Claims Office (Scotland), Trinity Park House, South Trinity Road, Edinburgh EH5 3SD (Tel. 031 551 8127), as appropriate. A leaflet CB(1), available from the address quoted, provides further information on how to apply for recognition in Scotland and the tax reliefs available. Under *Charities Act 1993, s 10* and *Law Reform (Miscellaneous Provisions (Scotland) Act 1990, s 1,* the Revenue may disclose information regarding charities to the Charity Commissioners and the Lord Advocate, as appropriate.

Subject to the above, what is a charity rests largely on judicial interpretation. A leading case is *Special Commrs v Pemsel HL 1891, 3 TC 53* in which Lord Macnaghten laid down that 'charity' should be given its technical meaning under English law and comprises 'four principal divisions; trusts for the relief of poverty, trusts for the advancement of education, trusts for the advancement of religion and trusts beneficial to the community and not falling under any of the preceding heads. The trusts last referred to are not the less charitable . . . because incidentally they affect the rich as well as the poor'. In the same case it was held that, in relation to tax, the English definition should be applied to Scottish cases (and cf. *Jackson's Trustees v Lord Advocate CS 1926, 10 TC 460* and *CIR v Glasgow (City) Police Athletic Assn HL 1953, 34 TC 76*). The concept of 'charity' may change with changes in social values (cf. *CIR v Trustees of Football Association Youth Trust HL 1980, 54 TC 413*).

The charity reliefs are not available to charities established overseas (*CIR v Gull KB 1937, 21 TC 374; Dreyfus Foundation Inc v CIR HL 1955, 36 TC 126*). The *Charitable Trusts (Validation) Act 1954* provides for validating as charitable a pre-1953 trust if its property was in fact applied for charitable purposes only, notwithstanding that the trust also authorised its application for non-charitable purposes (cf. *Vernon & Sons Ltd Employees Fund v CIR Ch D 1956, 36 TC 484; Buxton v Public Trustees Ch D 1962, 41 TC 235*).

10.2 CHARITY, CHARITABLE PURPOSES — EXAMPLES

Relevant cases are summarised below under appropriate headings.

(*a*) **Almshouse.** Inmates need not be destitute (*Mary Clark Home Trustees v Anderson KB 1904, 5 TC 48*).

(*b*) **Arts.** A musical festival association and the Royal Choral Society have been held to be charitable (*Glasgow Musical Festival Assn CS 1926, 11 TC 154; Royal Choral Society v CIR CA 1943, 25 TC 263*) but not companies formed to produce plays in association with the Arts Council (*Tennent Plays Ltd v CIR CA 1948, 30 TC 107*) or with the aim of furthering the theatre and dramatic taste (*Associated Artists Ltd v CIR Ch D 1956, 36 TC 499*).

(*c*) **Benevolent funds, etc.** for the relief of widows and orphans of members were held charitable (*Society for the Relief of Widows and Orphans of Medical Men KB 1926, 11 TC 1; Baptist Union, etc. Ltd v CIR KB (NI) 1945, 26 TC 335*) but not a death benefit fund (*Royal Naval etc. Officers' Assn Ch D 1955, 36 TC 187*) nor a fund set up to promote the formation of mutual provident associations (*Nuffield Foundation v CIR; Nuffield Provident Guarantee Fund v CIR KB 1946, 28 TC 479*).

(*d*) **Education.** A trust for the advancement of education does not require an element of poverty to be charitable (*R v Special Commrs (ex p. University College of N. Wales) CA 1909, 5 TC 408*). The technical college of a trade association was held to be charitable (*Scottish Woollen Technical College v CIR CS 1926, 11 TC 139*) as was the Students' Union of a medical college (*London Hospital Medical College Ch D 1976, 51 TC 365*) and a trust to promote sports in schools, etc. (*CIR v Trustees of Football Association Youth Trust HL 1980, 54 TC 413*). See also *Educational Grants Assn Ltd CA 1967, 44 TC 93; Abdul Caffoor Trustees v Ceylon Income Tax Commr PC 1961, 40 ATC 93*. For 'public school' see (*h*) below.

(*e*) **Hospital.** A friendly society's convalescent home was exempted (*Royal Antediluvian Order of Buffaloes v Owens KB 1927, 13 TC 176*).

(*f*) **Political and similar objects** (including the reform of the law) are not charitable purposes. Objects held not to be charitable include the reform of the law on vivisection (*National Anti-Vivisection Society HL 1947, 28 TC 311*) and temperance (*Temperance Council etc. of England KB 1926, 10 TC 748*), the securing of worldwide observance of the Universal Declaration of Human Rights (*McGovern and Others v Attorney-General & CIR Ch D 1981, [1982] 2 WLR 222*), the education of the public in militarism and disarmament (*Southwood & Another v Attorney-General Ch D 9 October 1998, Times 26 October 1998*), simplified spelling (*Hunter 'C' Trustees v CIR KB 1929, 14 TC 427*), fostering Anglo-Swedish relations (*Anglo-Swedish Society v CIR KB 1931, 16 TC 34*), Jewish resettlement (*Keren Kayemeth Le Jisroel Ltd v CIR HL 1932, 17 TC 27*) and a memorial fund for Bonar Law (*Bonar Law Memorial Trust v CIR KB 1933, 17 TC 508*).

(*g*) **Professional associations etc.** Professional associations are generally not admitted to be established for charitable purposes; they benefit their members, any wider public advantage being incidental (*R v Special Commrs (ex p. Headmasters' Conference) KB 1925, 10 TC 73; General Medical Council v CIR CA 1928, 13 TC 819; Geologists' Assn v CIR CA 1928, 14 TC 271; Midland Counties Institution of Engineers v CIR KB 1928, 14 TC 285; General Nursing Council for Scotland v CIR CS 1929, 14 TC 645; Master Mariners (Honourable Company of) v CIR KB 1932, 17 TC 298*). But contrast *Institution of Civil Engineers v CIR CA 1931, 16 TC 158*, where the Institution was held to be charitable, any benefit to members being incidental. Members' clubs and social clubs are not charitable (*Scottish Flying Club v CIR CS 1935, 20 TC 1; Sir H J Williams's Trustees v CIR HL 1947, 27 TC 409*). An agricultural society for the general promotion of agriculture was held charitable (*CIR v Yorkshire Agricultural Society CA 1927, 13 TC 58*) but not a statutory pig marketing board (*Pig Marketing Board (Northern Ireland) v CIR KB (NI) 1945, 26 TC 319*) nor a society to promote foxhound breeding (*Peterborough Royal Foxhound Show Society v CIR KB 1936, 20 TC 249*) (but it was given relief under *ICTA 1988, s 510* on its annual show).

(*h*) **Public school.** A school may be for the public benefit and qualify for the relief notwithstanding that it derives substantial receipts from fees (*Blake v Mayor etc. of London CA 1887, 2 TC 209; Ereaut v Girls' Public Day School Trust Ltd HL 1930, 15 TC 529,* and contrast *Birkenhead School Ltd v Dring KB 1926, 11 TC 273*). A Quaker school exclusively for children of members of the Society of Friends was refused relief (*Ackworth School v Betts KB 1915, 6 TC 642*) but a Roman Catholic school which admitted non-Catholic pupils qualified for relief (*Cardinal Vaughan Memorial School Trustees v Ryall KB 1920, 7 TC 611*).

(*i*) **Religion.** Charitable relief was refused for trusts to advance the 'religious, moral, social and recreative life' of Presbyterians in Londonderry (*Londonderry Presbyterian Church House Trustees v CIR CA (NI) 1946, 27 TC 431*), for the promotion and aiding of 'Roman Catholicism' in a particular district (*Ellis v CIR CA 1949, 31 TC 178*) and for the 'religious, educational and other parochial requirements' of the Roman Catholic inhabitants of a parish (*Cookstown Roman Catholic Church Trustees v CIR QB (NI) 1953, 34 TC 350*). In each case, the objects included non-charitable elements which prevented the whole being charitable. Relief was also refused to the Oxford Group (*Oxford Group v CIR CA 1949, 31 TC 221*).

(*j*) **Miscellaneous.** A nursing home (*Peebleshire Nursing Assn CS 1926, 11 TC 335*) and a holiday home (*Roberts Marine Mansions Trustees CA 1927, 11 TC 425*) providing services for members etc. at reduced fees were held to be charitable, as was a non-profit making company for publishing law reports (*Incorporated Council of Law Reporting v A-G CA 1971, 47 TC 321*). Relief was refused to a trust to maintain an historic building because it also had a non-charitable object (*Trades House of Glasgow v CIR CS 1969, 46 TC 178*) and to a Society established mainly with philanthropic objects which, in the event, were not achieved (*Hugh's Settlement Ltd v CIR KB 1938, 22 TC 281*). A training and enterprise council was denied charitable status, despite having *some* charitable objects, on the grounds that one of its main objects enabled it to 'promote the interests of individuals engaged in trade, commerce or enterprise and provide benefits and services to them' (*CIR v Oldham Training and Enterprise Council Ch D 1996, 69 TC 231*).

10.3 EXEMPTION AVAILABLE

Subject to the restriction in 10.4 below, a gain accruing to a charity is not a chargeable gain provided it is 'applicable and applied for charitable purposes only'. [*TCGA 1992, s 256(1)*]. For the scope of 'applicable and applied for charitable purposes only', see *Lawrence v CIR KB 1940, 23 TC 333, Slater (Helen) Charitable Trust Ltd CA 1981, 55 TC 230* and *Guild and others v CIR CS 1993, 66 TC 1.*

Where a UK charity is a beneficiary of an offshore trust and receives a capital payment, such that a gain would otherwise be treated as accruing to the charity under *TCGA 1992, s 87* (see 43.13 OFFSHORE SETTLEMENTS), the above exemption is available to the extent that the capital payment is applicable and applied for charitable purposes. This represents a change of practice by the Revenue following legal advice and applies to capital payments made on or after 10 August 1998 and also to any earlier payments where the tax liability remained open at that date. The Revenue had previously taken the view that the exemption was unavailable in such circumstances. (Revenue Tax Bulletin August 1998 pp 573, 574).

Where property held on charitable trusts ceases to be subject to those trusts, the trustees are deemed to have disposed of, and immediately reacquired, the property at its market value at that time. Any gain arising is not treated as accruing to a charity. Furthermore, insofar as the property represents, directly or indirectly, the consideration for the disposal of assets by the trustees, any gain accruing on that earlier disposal (and previously exempt) is treated as not having accrued to a charity and capital gains tax is chargeable as if the exemption had never applied. A cumulative liability may therefore arise and an assessment may be made within three years of the end of the year of assessment in which the property ceases to be subject to charitable trusts. [*TCGA 1992, s 256(2)*]. Such an assessment seems to be able to be made even where the gain arising on an earlier disposal is outside the normal time limit for assessment.

By concession, where land given for educational and certain other charitable purposes ceases after 16 August 1987 to be used for such purposes and, under *Reverter of Sites Act 1987*, is held by the trustees on a trust for sale for the benefit of the revertee, then unless the revertee is known to be a charity, there is a deemed disposal and reacquisition for capital gains purposes under *TCGA 1992, s 256(2)* above, which may give rise to a chargeable gain. Any income arising from the property will be liable to income tax, and a chargeable gain may also arise on a subsequent sale of the land. By concession, where the revertee is subsequently identified as a charity or disclaims all entitlement to the property (or where certain orders are made by the Charity Commissioners or the Secretary of State), provided that charitable status is re-established within six years of the date on which the land ceased to be held on the original charitable trust, any capital gains tax paid as above in the interim period will be discharged or repaid (with repayment supplement where appropriate) as will any income tax (provided that the income charged was used for charitable purposes). Partial relief will be given where the above conditions are only satisfied in respect of part of the property concerned. A request by the trustees for postponement of the tax payable will be accepted by the Revenue where the revertee has not been identified and this concession may apply (Revenue Pamphlet IR 1, D47).

10.4 **Restriction of exemption.** A restriction of the exemption in 10.3 above applies in certain circumstances as follows.

If in any chargeable period a charity

(*a*) has 'relevant income and gains' of £10,000 or more (but see below); and

(*b*) has relevant income and gains exceeding the amount of its 'qualifying expenditure'; and

(*c*) incurs, or is treated as incurring 'non-qualifying expenditure',

exemption under *TCGA 1992, s 256* (and *ICTA 1988, s 505(1)* for income tax) is not available for so much of the excess at (*b*) as does not exceed the non-qualifying expenditure incurred in that period. Where the exemption is not so available, the charity may, by notice in writing, specify which items of its relevant income and gains are wholly or partly to be attributed to the amount concerned. Covenanted payments to the charity (within *ICTA 1988, s 347A(7)*) are treated as a single item. If, within thirty days of a request to do so, the charity does not give notice, the Board determines the attribution.

The £10,000 limit in (*a*) above is proportionately reduced where a chargeable period is less than twelve months, and does not apply where two or more charities acting in concert are engaged in transactions aimed at tax avoidance and where the Board, by notice in writing, so direct. An appeal, as against a decision on a claim, may be made against such a notice.

'*Relevant income and gains*'. This means the aggregate of

(i) income which, apart from *ICTA 1988, s 505(1)*, would not be exempt from tax, together with any income which is taxable notwithstanding *ICTA 1988, s 505(1)*; and

(ii) gains which, apart from *TCGA 1992, s 256*, would be chargeable gains, together with any gains which are chargeable gains notwithstanding *TCGA 1992, s 256*.

'*Non-qualifying expenditure*'. This is expenditure other than 'qualifying expenditure'. If the charity invests any funds in an investment which is not a 'qualifying investment' or makes a loan (not as an investment) which is not a 'qualifying loan', the amount invested or lent is treated as non-qualifying expenditure. Where the investment or loan is realised or repaid in whole or in part in the period in which it was made, any further investment or lending of the sum realised or repaid in that period is, to the extent that it does not exceed the sum originally invested or lent, ignored in arriving at non-qualifying expenditure of the period.

Where the aggregate of the qualifying and non-qualifying expenditure incurred in a chargeable period (the '*primary period*') exceeds the relevant income and gains of that period, so much of the excess as does not exceed the non-qualifying expenditure constitutes '*unapplied non-qualifying expenditure*'. Except to the extent (if any) that it represents the expenditure of 'non-taxable sums' received in the primary period, the unapplied non-qualifying expenditure may be treated as non-qualifying expenditure of an '*earlier period*' (a chargeable period ending not more than six years before the end of the primary period). '*Non-taxable sums*' are donations, legacies and other sums of a similar nature which, apart from *ICTA 1988, s 505(1)* and *TCGA 1992, s 256*, are not within the charge to tax.

Where an amount of unapplied non-qualifying expenditure (the '*excess expenditure*') falls to be treated as non-qualifying expenditure of earlier periods, it is attributed only to those periods in which, apart from the attribution in question but taking account of any previous attribution, the relevant income and gains exceed the aggregate of the qualifying and non-qualifying expenditure in that period; and such attribution is not to be greater than the excess. Attributions are made to later periods in priority to earlier periods. Any excess expenditure which cannot be attributed to an earlier period is ignored for attribution purposes altogether. Adjustments by way of further assessment etc. are made in consequence of an attribution to an earlier period.

'*Qualifying expenditure*'. This is expenditure incurred for charitable purposes only. A payment made (or to be made) to a body situated outside the UK is not qualifying expenditure unless the charity concerned has taken such steps as may be reasonable in the circumstances to ensure that the payment will be applied for charitable purposes.

Expenditure incurred in a particular period may be treated as incurred in another period if it is properly chargeable against income of that other period and is referable to commitments (contractual or otherwise) entered into before or during that other period.

'*Qualifying investments*'. These are the following.

(A) Investments within *Trustee Investments Act 1961, Sch 1 Pts I, II* (*para 13* excepted; mortgages etc.) and *III*.

(B) Investments in a common investment fund established under *Charities Act 1993, s 24* (or NI equivalent), a common deposit fund established under *Charities Act 1960, s 25* or similar funds under other enactments.

(C) Any interest in land other than a mortgage, etc.

(D) Shares or securities of a company listed on a recognised stock exchange (within *ICTA 1988, s 841* — see 58.5 SHARES AND SECURITIES) or dealt in on the Unlisted Securities Market (now closed).

(E) Units in unit trusts (as statutorily defined).

(F) Deposits with a recognised bank or licensed institution in respect of which interest is payable at a commercial rate but excluding a deposit made as part of an arrangement whereby the bank, etc. makes a loan to a third party.

(G) Certificates of deposit within *ICTA 1988, s 56(5)*.

(H) Loans or other investments as to which the Board are satisfied, on a claim, that the loans or other investments are made for the benefit of the charity and not for tax avoidance purposes (whether by the charity or by a third party). Loans secured by mortgage etc, over land are eligible.

'*Qualifying loans*'. A loan which is not made by way of investment is a qualifying loan if it is one of the following.

(1) A loan made to another charity for charitable purposes only.

(2) A loan to a beneficiary of the charity which is made in the course of carrying out the purposes of the charity.

(3) Money placed on a current account with a recognised bank or licensed institution otherwise than under arrangements as in (F) above.

(4) A loan, not within (1)–(3) above, as to which the Board are satisfied, on a claim, that the loan is made for the benefit of the charity and not for tax avoidance purposes (whether by the charity or by a third party).

[*ICTA 1988, s 505, s 506, Sch 20; Charities Act 1993, Sch 6 para 25; FA 1995, Sch 17 para 7; FA 1996, s 146, s 198, Sch 37 para 2(3)(4), para 5, para 10, Sch 38 para 6(1)(2)(l)(11)*].

10.5 GIFTS OF ASSETS TO CHARITIES

Where a disposal of an asset is made otherwise than under a bargain at arm's length to a charity, the normal MARKET VALUE (40) provisions (which deem the acquisition and disposal as being made at market value) do not apply.

If the disposal is by way of gift (including a gift into settlement) or for a consideration not exceeding the allowable expenditure which would be available on a disposal of the asset (see 17.3 DISPOSAL) the transaction is treated as made for a consideration producing neither a gain nor a loss. Where the asset is subsequently disposed of by the charity, its acquisition by the person making the original disposal is treated as the acquisition of the asset by the charity. See 8.7 ASSETS HELD ON 31 MARCH 1982 and 26.4 INDEXATION for consequential re-basing and indexation provisions. Where the asset is a qualifying investment for the purposes of *ICTA 1988, s 587B* (gifts of shares and securities to charities) and the disposal qualifies for income tax or corporation tax relief under that *section* (see TOLLEY'S INCOME TAX under Charities), the amount treated as the charity's acquisition cost is reduced by the amount on which income tax or corporation tax is given or, if this would otherwise produce a negative figure, is reduced to nil.

If the disposal to the charity is for a consideration exceeding the allowable expenditure, the market value is not substituted for the actual consideration.

These provisions do not apply to disposals in relation to which venture capital trust relief is available (see 65 VENTURE CAPITAL TRUSTS).

The above provisions do apply to disposals made otherwise than under a bargain at arm's length to any of the bodies mentioned in *IHTA 1984, Sch 3.*

[*TCGA 1992, s 257(1)(2)(4); ICTA 1988, s 587B; FA 1995, s 72(5)(8); FA 2000, s 43*].

The bodies listed in *IHTA 1984, Sch 3* (as amended) comprise

The National Gallery.

The British Museum.

The National Museum of Scotland.

The National Museum of Wales.

The Ulster Museum.

Any other similar national institution which exists wholly or mainly for the purpose of preserving for the public benefit a collection of scientific, historic or artistic interest and which is approved for this purpose by the Treasury.

Any museum or art gallery in the UK which exists wholly or mainly for that purpose and is maintained by a local authority or university in the UK.

Any library the main function of which is to serve the needs of teaching and research at a university in the UK.

The Historic Buildings and Monuments Commission for England.

The National Trust for Places of Historic Interest or Natural Beauty.

The National Trust for Scotland for Places of Historic Interest or Natural Beauty.

The National Art Collections Fund.

The Trustees of the National Heritage Memorial Fund.

The National Endowment for Science, Technology and the Arts.

The Friends of the National Libraries.

The Historic Churches Preservation Trust.

Nature Conservancy Council for England.

Scottish National Heritage.

Countryside Council for Wales.

Any local authority.

Any Government department (including the National Debt Commissioners).

Any university or university college in the UK.

A health service body within *ICTA 1988, s 519A.*

10.6 **Gifts of assets out of settlements.** Where, subject to below, a charity becomes absolutely entitled to any assets (or part thereof) which were previously settled property and those assets are deemed to be disposed of and reacquired by the trustees on that occasion (under *TCGA 1992, s 71*) then, if no consideration is received by any person for or in connection with the transaction, the disposal is deemed to take place on a no gain, no loss basis. This does *not* apply where the charity becomes absolutely entitled to the assets on the termination of a life interest (within the meaning of *TCGA 1992, s 72*, see 57.7 SETTLEMENTS) by the death of the person entitled to it. (On such an event, because of the interaction of *TCGA 1992, s 71* and *s 72*, the assets are revalued to market value at that date but no chargeable gain accrues; see 57.9, 57.11 SETTLEMENTS.)

The above provisions also apply to a gift to any of the bodies mentioned in *IHTA 1984, Sch 3* (gifts for national purposes). See 10.5 above. [*TCGA 1992, s 257(3)*].

In *Prest v Bettinson Ch D 1980, 53 TC 437*, the residue of an estate was held on trust for five institutions, four of which were charities, subject to the payment of annuities to six individuals. No specific fund was set aside, but distributions of capital and income were made annually to the five institutions, the income of the residuary fund being more than sufficient to pay the annuities. The trustee failed in his claim that four-fifths of any capital gain arising was exempt as accruing for charitable purposes. Since no fund had been set aside to pay the annuities, the trustee retained full control of the trust property until the distribution of the proceeds of sale, and any gain from a disposal thereof had accrued to him as trustee and not to the charities.

10.7 GIFT AID DONATIONS BY INDIVIDUALS

Gifts of money made by individuals to charities which are 'qualifying donations' attract relief under the Gift Aid provisions described below. Significant modifications were made to the rules with effect from 6 April 2000, including a change enabling the tax treated as deducted from the gift to be met out of a capital gains tax (CGT) liability. Previously, the requirement was that the donor pay basic rate income tax equal to the tax deducted. The Gift Aid provisions applying before 6 April 2000 had no direct significance for CGT purposes and are not covered here. See TOLLEY'S INCOME TAX under Charities for those provisions. For the Gift Aid provisions applicable to companies, see the corresponding chapter of TOLLEY'S CORPORATION TAX.

The provisions described below apply to gifts made on or after 6 April 2000 which are not covenanted payments, and to covenanted payments due on or after that date. For the purposes of these provisions, '*charity*' has the same meaning as in 10.1 above and also includes the bodies listed in *ICTA 1988, s 507*. [*FA 1990, s 25(12)(a); FA 2000, s 39(10)*].

The donor. Where a qualifying donation is made by an individual ('*the donor*') in a tax year, then, for that year,

(*a*) he is treated for the purposes of income tax and CGT as if:

- the gift had been made after deduction of income tax at the basic rate; and
- the basic rate limit were increased by an amount equal to the 'grossed up amount of the gift' (i.e. the amount which, after deducting income tax at the basic rate for the tax year in which the gift is made, leaves the amount of the gift);

(*b*) references in specified income tax provisions to income tax which an individual is entitled to charge against any person are taken in his case to include a reference to the tax treated as deducted from the gift; and

(*c*) to the extent, if any, necessary to ensure that he is charged to an amount of income tax and CGT equal to the tax treated as deducted from the gift, he is not entitled to income tax personal reliefs.

As the basic rate limit is used in determining the CGT liability of a higher rate taxpayer (see 2.1 ANNUAL RATES AND EXEMPTIONS), the increase mentioned in (*a*) above gives potential CGT relief in a case where *income* is insufficient to fully obtain higher rate relief on the amount of the gift. For this purpose, higher rate relief means relief for the excess of tax at the higher rate over tax at the basic rate for which relief is effectively given at source.

Where the tax treated as deducted from a gift by virtue of (*a*) above exceeds the amount of income tax and CGT with which the donor is charged for the tax year, the donor is liable to income tax at the basic rate on so much of the gift as is necessary to recover an amount of tax equal to the excess. In determining for this purpose the total amount of income tax and CGT with which the donor is charged for the year, the following are disregarded:

- any tax charged at the basic rate by virtue of *ICTA 1988, s 348* or *s 349* (annual payments — see TOLLEY'S INCOME TAX under Deduction of tax at source);
- any notional tax treated as having been paid under *ICTA 1988, s 233(1)(a)* (taxation of certain recipients of distributions), *ICTA 1988, s 249(4)(a)* (stock dividends treated as income), or *ICTA 1988, s 547(5)(a)* (method of charging life policy gain to tax);
- any personal reliefs, or any relief for maintenance payments, falling to be given by way of an income tax reduction;

- any double tax relief (whether given under a double tax agreement or unilaterally);
- any set-off of tax deducted, or treated as deducted, from income *other than*
  - tax treated as deducted from income by virtue of *ICTA 1988, s 421(1)(a)* (taxation of borrower when loan released etc. — see TOLLEY'S INCOME TAX under Excess liability), or
  - tax treated as deducted from a relevant amount within the meaning of *ICTA 1988, s 699A* (untaxed sums comprised in the income of an estate — see TOLLEY'S INCOME TAX under Deceased estates) except to the extent that the relevant amount is or would be paid in respect of a distribution chargeable to income tax under Schedule F; and
- any set-off of tax credits on dividends.

For the purposes of age-related income tax allowances, which are dependent on the level of total income, the donor's total income is treated as reduced by the aggregate grossed up amount of his qualifying donations for the year.

[*FA 1990, s 25(1)(6)–(9A)(12)(d); FA 2000, s 39(1)(6)*].

The charity. The receipt by a charity of a qualifying donation is treated as the receipt, under deduction of income tax at the basic rate for the tax year in which the gift is made, of an annual payment of an amount equal to the 'grossed up amount of the gift' (see (*a*) above). [*FA 1990, s 25(10)*].

Qualifying donations. A '*qualifying donation*' is a gift to a charity by the donor which meets the following conditions:

(i) it takes the form of a payment of a sum of money;

(ii) it is not subject to a condition as to repayment;

(iii) it is not deductible under the payroll deduction scheme — see TOLLEY'S INCOME TAX under Charities);

(iv) neither the donor nor any person connected with him (within *ICTA 1988, s 839*) receives any benefit in consequence of making it which exceeds specified limits (see below);

(v) it is not conditional on or associated with, or part of an arrangement involving, the acquisition of property by the charity, otherwise than by way of gift, from the donor or a person connected with him;

(vi) either

- at the time it is made the donor is UK-resident or performs duties which by virtue of *ICTA 1988, s 132(4)(a)* (Crown employees serving overseas) are treated as being performed in the UK, or
- the grossed up amount of the gift (see (*a*) above) would, if in fact made, be payable out of profits or gains brought into charge to income tax or CGT; and

(vii) the donor gives the charity an 'appropriate declaration' in relation to it.

An '*appropriate declaration*' for the purposes of (vii) above is a declaration which is given in the form and manner prescribed by regulations made by the Board. Draft regulations were published by the Revenue on 21 February 2000 which included provision for declarations to be made orally, in writing or via the internet.

[*FA 1990, s 25(1)–(3A)(11); FA 2000, s 39(1)–(4)*].

10.7 Charities

Limits on donor benefits. Where the donor or a person connected with him receives a benefit or benefits in consequence of making the gift, the gift will not be a qualifying donation if either:

(1) the aggregate value of the benefits received exceeds

- where the gift is £100 or less, 25% of the amount of the gift;
- where the gift is greater than £100 but not more than £1,000, £25;
- where the gift is greater than £1,000, 2.5% of the amount of the gift; or

(2) the aggregate of the value of the benefits received in relation to the gift and the value of any benefits received in relation to any qualifying donations previously made to the charity by the donor in the same tax year exceeds £250.

Where a benefit:

- consists of the right to receive benefits at intervals over a period of less than twelve months;
- relates to a period of less than twelve months; or
- is one of a series of benefits received at intervals in consequence of making a series of gifts at intervals of less than twelve months,

the value of the benefit and the amount of the gift are 'annualised' for the purposes of (1) above. Where a one-off benefit is received in consequence of making a gift which is one of a series of gifts made at intervals of less than twelve months, the amount of the gift (but not the value of the benefit) is likewise annualised. For these purposes a gift or benefit is '*annualised*' by multiplying the amount or value by 365 and dividing the result by the number of days in the period of less than twelve months or the average number of days in the intervals of less than twelve months as appropriate.

In applying the above limits, the benefit of a right of free or reduced-price admission for the donor or a member of his family

- to view property, the preservation of which for the public benefit is the sole or main purpose of the charity; or
- to observe wildlife, the conservation of which for the public benefit is the sole or main purpose of the charity;

is disregarded provided that the opportunity to make gifts which attract such a right is available to members of the public.

[*FA 1990, s 25(2)(e), (4)–(5G)(11); FA 2000, s 39(1)(3)(5)*].

11 Children

Cross-reference. See 52.7 RESIDENCE AND DOMICILE for domicile of children.

11.1 GENERAL

There is no general bar to the chargeable gains made by an infant (i.e. an individual under 18 years of age) being assessed and charged on him personally (see *R v Newmarket Commissioners (ex p. Huxley) CA 1916, 7 TC 49*). The Revenue can, therefore, resort directly to the infant, whether or not there is a guardian etc. to charge. Whether or not, in practice, they will do so will depend on particular circumstances.

A child is entitled to the same capital gains tax reliefs and exemptions as an adult (subject to specific exclusions).

11.2 NOMINEES AND BARE TRUSTEES

Where assets are held by a person as nominee, or as trustee for any person who would be absolutely entitled against him but for being an infant, the provisions of *TCGA 1992* apply as if the acts of the nominee or trustee are the acts of the infant. Acquisitions from or to the trustee or nominee to or from the infant are accordingly disregarded. References in *TCGA 1992* to a person being absolutely entitled against the trustee mean that the person has the exclusive right (subject only to satisfying any outstanding charge, lien or other right of the trustee to resort to the relevant asset(s) for payment of duty, taxes, costs or other outgoings) to direct how the asset(s) shall be dealt with. [*TCGA 1992, s 60*]. For the wider implications of nominees and bare trustees generally, see 57.2 SETTLEMENTS.

11.3 ASSESSMENT OF GUARDIANS ETC.

In practice, the Revenue often makes use of the machinery of *TMA 1970*, which enables it to charge and assess the tax due from an 'incapacitated person' (this term includes an 'infant': see *TMA 1970, s 118*), on the trustee, guardian, tutor, curator or committee, having the direction, control or management of that person's property. Such machinery applies whether or not the incapacitated person resides in the UK. The person chargeable in this way is answerable for all matters required to be done under the capital gains tax provisions, for the purpose of assessment of that tax, but is given a right of retention and indemnity in respect of tax charges or payments made on the incapacitated person's behalf. [*TMA 1970, ss 72, 77*].

11.4 DEFAULT OF INFANT

Where the person chargeable to tax is an infant, then his parent, guardian, or tutor is liable for the tax in the event of the infant's default. On neglect or refusal of payment, the parent etc. may be proceeded against for sums due to the Revenue. [*TMA 1970, ss 73, 77*].

12 Claims

Cross-reference. See 39.3 LOSSES for requirement to notify capital losses.

12.1 For details of the formal procedures applying for 1996/97 and subsequent years of assessment under self-assessment, see 12.2 below.

Previously, claims had to be made to the local Inspector of Taxes (or to the Board of Inland Revenue in certain specified cases) whenever the *Taxes Acts* provided for relief to be given or other thing to be done. Any error or mistake in a claim could be rectified by a supplementary claim made within the time allowed for making the original claim. [*TMA 1970, s 42(1)(2)(8) as originally enacted*].

Companies make certain claims in a corporation tax return (see 54.11 RETURNS).

Claims are personal matters and (except in the case of trustees for persons under disability etc.) can be made only by the person entitled to the relief (cf. *Fulford v Hyslop Ch D 1929, 8 ATC 588*). See 54.4 RETURNS for the signing of claims by an attorney.

From 1998 onwards, the Revenue accept certain income tax claims by telephone (see TOLLEY'S INCOME TAX). At present, this facility does not extend to capital gains tax claims.

12.2 CLAIMS AND ELECTIONS UNDER SELF-ASSESSMENT

A formal procedure applies for 1996/97 and subsequent years of assessment as regards the making of claims, elections and notices. A claim for a relief, allowance or tax repayment (other than one to be given effect by a PAYE coding adjustment) must be for an amount quantified at the time of the claim. Where notice has been given by the Revenue requiring the delivery of a return (see 54.3, 54.14 RETURNS), a claim, etc. (other than one to be given effect by a PAYE coding adjustment) can only be made at any time by inclusion in such a return (or by virtue of an amendment to a return) *unless it could not be so included* either at that time or subsequently (but see below re claims involving two or more years).

In the case of a partnership business, a claim under any of numerous provisions specified in *TMA 1970, s 42(7)* must be made by a partner nominated by the partnership if it cannot be included in a partnership return (or amendment thereto). See 12.3 below for provisions applying where a claim, etc. is made otherwise than by inclusion in a return.

Where a claimant discovers that an error or mistake has been made in a claim (whether or not made in a return), he may make a supplementary claim within the time allowed for making the original claim.

[*TMA 1970, s 42; FA 1994, s 196, s 199(2)(3), Sch 19 para 13; FA 1995, s 103(7), s 107; FA 1996, s 128(1), s 130(1)–(4)(7)–(9)*].

Claims for relief involving two or more years. A claim for a loss incurred or payment made in one year of assessment to be carried back to an earlier year or years need not be made in a return, is treated as a claim for the year of loss or payment (the later year), must be for an amount equal to what would otherwise have been the tax saving for the earlier year, and is given effect *in relation to the later year* by repayment, set-off etc. or by treating the said amount as a tax payment made on account under SELF-ASSESSMENT (56.15). The tax position for the earlier year is not adjusted. [*TMA 1970, Sch 1B para 2; FA 1996, s 128(2)(11), Sch 17*]. See TOLLEY'S INCOME TAX for more details. Whilst the legislation does not specifically cover the situation, the Revenue's view is that, in the event of such a carry-back, interest on overpaid tax accrues only from 31 January following the *later* year (see, for example, Revenue Tax Bulletin December 1996 p 364 and *Taxation 8 January 1998 pp 319–321*). An example of a capital gains provision affected by these rules is the potential three-year carry-back of capital losses incurred by an individual in the tax year in which he dies — see 16.5 DEATH.

12.3 **Claims etc. not included in returns.** Subject to any specific provision requiring a claim, etc. to be made to the Board, an income tax or capital gains tax claim or election made otherwise than in a return (see 12.2 above) must be made to an officer of the Board. The claim, etc. must include a declaration by the claimant that all particulars are correctly stated to the best of his information or belief. No claim requiring a tax repayment can be made unless the claimant has documentary proof that the tax has been paid or deducted. The claim must be made in a form determined by the Board and may require, inter alia, a statement of the amount of tax to be discharged or repaid and supporting information and documentation. In the case of a claim by or on behalf of a person who is not resident (or who claims to be not resident or not ordinarily resident or not domiciled) in the UK, the Revenue may require a statement or declaration in support of the claim to be made by affidavit.

A person who may wish to make a claim must keep all such records as may be requisite for the purpose and must preserve them until such time as the Revenue may no longer enquire into the claim (see below) or such enquiries are treated as completed. There is a maximum penalty of £3,000 for non-compliance in relation to any claim actually made. Similar provisions and exceptions apply as in 56.10 SELF-ASSESSMENT as to the preservation of copies of documents instead of originals.

Provisions similar to those in 54.7 RETURNS above (amendments of self-assessments) apply to enable a claimant (within twelve months of the claim) or officer of the Board (within nine months of the claim) to amend a claim etc. The Revenue has power of enquiry into a claim, etc. (or amendment thereof) similar to that in 56.11 SELF-ASSESSMENT (enquiries into returns). Notice of intention to enquire must be given by the first anniversary of 31 January following the year of assessment (or where the claim relates to a period other than a year of assessment, the first anniversary of the end of that period) or, if later, the quarter day (meaning 31 January, 30 April, etc.) next following the first anniversary of the date of claim, etc. In the event of such an enquiry, the Revenue has power to call for documents similar to that in 56.12 SELF-ASSESSMENT. Where an enquiry is in progress, an officer of the Board may give provisional effect to the claim, etc. (or amendment thereof) to such extent as he thinks fit. Provisions similar to those in 56.13 SELF-ASSESSMENT apply as regards amendments of claims upon completion of an enquiry. The Revenue must give effect to such an amendment, by assessment if necessary, within 30 days after it is made. An appeal may be made against a Revenue amendment to a claim following an enquiry, written notice of appeal to be given normally within 30 days after the amendment is made (extended to three months where certain specified issues concerning residence are involved). If an amendment is varied on appeal, the Revenue has a further 30 days to give effect to the variation.

Where a claim, etc. does not give rise to a discharge or repayment of tax, there are provisions as to disallowance of such claims on enquiry similar to those in 56.11 SELF-ASSESSMENT in respect of claims etc. included in returns, with appeal procedures similar to those above.

Appeals against amendments to claims are normally made to the General Commissioners. Where the claim was made to the Board or under certain specified provisions, appeal is to the Special Commissioners, and in other cases, there are rules, similar to those in 4.5 APPEALS, enabling the taxpayer to elect to bring the appeal before the Special Commissioners. If the taxpayer also has an appeal pending concerning an assessment and the appeals relate to the same income, both appeals must be to the same body of Commissioners.

[*TMA 1970, s 42(11), Sch 1A; FA 1994, s 196, s 199(2)(3), Sch 19 paras 13, 35; FA 1995, s 103(7), s 107(10)(11), Sch 20; FA 1996, s 124(4), s 130(5), Sch 19 paras 8–10, Sch 22 para 9; FA 1998, s 117, Sch 19 paras 20, 42*].

12.4 **Corporation tax self-assessment.** Provisions having broadly similar effect as those in 12.2 above (other than those of *TMA 1970, Sch 1B*) apply to companies under corporation tax self-assessment (for accounting periods ending on or after 1 July 1999 — see 13.2 COMPANIES). Subject to any express provision to the contrary, claims and elections made after notice has been given requiring the delivery of a company tax return must be made in the return, or by amendment of the return, if they can be so made (see 54.11 RETURNS) and must be quantified. A claim etc. made by a company which could have been made by amending the return is treated for this purpose as an amendment of the return. Otherwise, *TMA 1970, Sch 1A* (see 12.3 above) provides the procedure for claims etc. A supplementary claim (where there was an error or mistake in the original claim) may be made within the time limit for the original claim. A group relief or capital allowances claim *must* be made in a return or by amendment of a return. [*FA 1998, Sch 18 paras 9, 10, 54, 56–60*].

12.5 TIME LIMITS FOR CLAIMS

See 61 TIME LIMITS—FIXED DATES and 62 TIME LIMITS—MISCELLANEOUS for check-lists of claims and elections.

The following general time limits apply where no specific time limit is prescribed. For capital gains tax, a claim **for 1995/96 or an earlier year** must be made within **six years** after the end of the year of assessment to which it relates. A claim **for 1996/97 or a subsequent year** must be made within **five years after 31 January** following the year of assessment to which it relates. Under corporation tax self-assessment for accounting periods ending on or after 1 July 1999 (see 13.2 COMPANIES), the general corporation tax time limit remains at **six years** after the end of the accounting period to which the claim relates. [*TMA 1970, s 43(1); FA 1998, s 117, Sch 18 para 55, Sch 19 para 21*].

By concession, where an overpayment of tax arises because of an error by the Inland Revenue or another Government department and where there is no dispute as to the facts, claims to repayment of the tax overpaid made outside of the statutory period will be allowed (Revenue Pamphlet IR 1, B41).

A claim (including a supplementary claim) which could not have been allowed but for the making of an assessment to capital gains tax after the year of assessment to which it relates, may be made at any time before the end of the year of assessment following that in which the assessment was made. [*TMA 1970, s 43(2*].

If an assessment for 1983/84 or later years (or for a company accounting period ending after 31 March 1983) makes good loss of tax arising from fraudulent or negligent conduct (see 9.4 BACK DUTY), the person assessed can require effect to be given to reliefs or allowances to which he would have been entitled had he made the necessary claims within the relevant time limits. [*TMA 1970, s 36(3); FA 1989, s 149; FA 1998, s 117, Sch 18 para 65*].

Discovery etc. In the case of a 'discovery' assessment (see 5.2 ASSESSMENTS), or an assessment to recover excess group relief under *ICTA 1988, s 412(3)* which is made after 26 July 1993, which is *not* for making good loss of tax attributable to fraudulent or negligent conduct (see 9.4 BACK DUTY),

(*a*) any 'relevant' claim, election, application or notice which could have been made or given within the normal time limits of the *Taxes Acts* may be made or given within a year of the end of the chargeable period in which the assessment is made, and

(*b*) any 'relevant' claim, etc. previously made or given, except an irrevocable one, can, with the consent of the person(s) by whom it was made or given (or their personal representatives), be revoked or varied in the manner in which it was made or given.

A claim, etc. is '*relevant*' to an assessment for a chargeable period if

(i) it relates to, or to an event occurring in, the chargeable period, and

(ii) it, or its revocation or variation, reduces, or could reduce,

(A) the increased tax liability resulting from the assessment, or

(B) any other liability of the person for that chargeable period or a later one ending not more than one year after the period in which the assessment is made.

The normal APPEALS (4) provisions apply, with any necessary modifications.

If the making, etc. of a claim, etc. would alter another person's tax liability, the consent of that person (or his personal representatives) is needed. If such alteration is an increase, the other person cannot make, etc. a claim, etc. under the foregoing provisions.

If the reduction in tax liability resulting from one or more claims etc. would exceed the additional tax assessed, relief is not available for the excess. If the reduction involves more than one period, or more than one person, the inspector will specify by notice in writing how it is to be apportioned; but within 30 days of the notice being given, or the last notice being given if there is more than one person, the person (or persons jointly) can specify the apportionment by notice in writing to the inspector. [*TMA 1970, ss 43A, 43B; FA 1989, s 150; FA 1993, Sch 14 para 2; FA 1998, s 117, Sch 19 para 22*]. These provisions broadly continue for companies under corporation tax self-assessment. [*FA 1998, s 117, Sch 18 paras 61–64*].

12.6 APPEALS IN RESPECT OF CLAIMS

1995/96 and earlier years. An unfavourable decision by the inspector, or Board, on a claim, may be appealed against in writing within 30 days of *receipt* of written notice of the decision or within 3 months on matters relating to residence, ordinary residence or domicile. Appeals from decisions of the inspector are to the General Commissioners or (at the taxpayer's option) to the Special Commissioners, and those from decisions of the Board to the Special Commissioners. [*TMA 1970, s 42, Sch 2; FA 1984, s 127, Sch 22 para 3*]. See under 4 APPEALS for this and for appeals to the High Court.

As regards **1996/97 and later years**, see 12.3 above and 56.28, 56.30 SELF-ASSESSMENT.

12.7 ERROR OR MISTAKE RELIEF

Pre-self-assessment. Relief may be claimed in writing, within six years after the end of the chargeable period in which the assessment was made, against any over-assessment due to an error or mistake (including an omission) in any return. The relief is given because the return was wrong and hence does not apply where the assessment is not on the basis of the return. No relief is allowed if the return was made on the basis or in accordance with the practice generally prevailing at the time. Otherwise, the Revenue will give such relief as is reasonable and just, having regard to all the relevant circumstances.

The relief is determined by the Board with appeal from them to the Special Commissioners and from them, but only on a point of law *arising in connection with the computation of profits*, to the High Court. (See *Rose Smith & Co Ltd v CIR KB 1933, 17 TC 586; Carrimore Six Wheelers Ltd v CIR CA 1944, 26 TC 301; R v Special Commrs (ex p. Carrimore Six Wheelers Ltd) CA 1947, 28 TC 422; Arranmore Investment Co Ltd v CIR CA (NI) 1973, 48 TC 623; Eagerpath Ltd v Edwards Ch D, [1999] STC 771.*)

[*TMA 1970, s 33; FA 1971, s 37(2), s 38, Sch 14 Pt II; SI 1994 No 1813, Reg 2(1), Sch 1 paras 1, 2*].

For relief for double assessment, see 5.3 ASSESSMENTS.

Self-assessment. The error or mistake relief provisions of *TMA 1970, s 33* continue to apply for 1996/97 and subsequent years of assessment and company accounting periods ending on or after 1 July 1999. They apply by reference to an overcharge to tax under a self-assessment as well as under any other assessment. The time limit for claiming error or mistake relief, in the case of an income tax or capital gains tax assessment, is five years after 31 January following the year of assessment to which the return in question relates, and, in the case of an assessment to corporation tax, six years after the end of the accounting period to which the return relates. No relief is available in respect of an error or mistake in a claim which is included in a return (but see 12.2 above as regards supplementary claims). [*TMA 1970, s 33; FA 1994, s 196, s 199(2)(3), Sch 19 para 8, Sch 26 Pt V; FA 1998, s 117, Sch 18 para 51, Sch 19 para 15*].

Error or mistake in partnership statement. For 1996/97 and subsequent years of assessment and company accounting periods ending on or after 1 July 1999, error or mistake relief is extended to cover an error or mistake in a partnership statement (see 54.14 RETURNS) by reason of which the partners allege that their self-assessments were excessive. The claim to relief must be made by one of the partners within five years after the filing date for the partnership return (see 54.14 RETURNS). Where the claim results in an amendment to the partnership statement, the Board will, by notice, make any necessary amendments to the self-assessments of all persons who were partners at any time in the period covered by the partnership statement. Otherwise, provisions similar to those above apply, with appropriate modifications. [*TMA 1970, s 33A; FA 1994, s 196, s 199(2)(3), Sch 19 para 9; FA 1996, Sch 22 para 5; FA 1998, s 117, Sch 19 para 16*].

13 Companies

Cross-references. See 7.1, 7.3 ASSETS HELD ON 6 APRIL 1965 and 8.3, 8.6 ASSETS HELD ON 31 MARCH 1982 for irrevocable election by principal company of a group; 38 LOAN RELATIONSHIPS OF COMPANIES; 52.6 RESIDENCE AND DOMICILE for company residence; 58 SHARES AND SECURITIES; 59.11 SHARES AND SECURITIES—IDENTIFICATION RULES for parallel pooling provisions before 1 April 1985; 64 UNIT TRUSTS ETC.; 65 VENTURE CAPITAL TRUSTS.

Sumption: Capital Gains Tax. See A10.

The headings in this chapter are as follows.

13.1 LIABILITY OF COMPANIES TO CORPORATION TAX ON THEIR CHARGEABLE GAINS

Companies resident in the UK (and non-resident companies in respect of UK branch or agency assets, see 44.3 OVERSEAS MATTERS) are liable to corporation tax on their chargeable gains. These gains are included in their profits liable to corporation tax as described in 13.3 below. [*ICTA 1988, s 6, s 11(2); TCGA 1992, s 10(3)*].

Companies accordingly do not pay 'capital gains tax' as such, but their chargeable gains less allowable losses are computed in accordance with provisions relating to capital gains tax, except that

(i) computations are made by reference to accounting periods instead of years of assessment [*TCGA 1992, s 8(3)*],

(ii) provisions in the legislation confined to individuals do not apply to companies [*TCGA 1992, s 8(4)(5)*],

(iii) the indexation allowance and share identification rules apply (subject to transitional provisions) to disposals after 31 March 1982 and again after 31 March 1985 instead of 5 April 1982 and 5 April 1985 respectively,

(iv) an alternative method was available of identifying particular shares and securities which were disposed of after 31 March 1982 and before 1 April 1985 ('parallel pooling'; see 59.11 SHARES AND SECURITIES—IDENTIFICATION RULES),

(v) for disposals by companies after 14 March 1988 and before 30 November 1993, indexation allowance was restricted or excluded in certain cases involving a debt on a security owed by, or shares in, a 'linked company' (see TOLLEY'S CORPORATION TAX under Capital Gains),

(vi) special provisions apply after 31 March 1996 to gilts and loan stock acquired and sold by companies (see 38 LOAN RELATIONSHIPS OF COMPANIES),

(vii) TAPER RELIEF (60) applies to disposals after 5 April 1998 by individuals, trustees etc., but not by companies; but indexation allowance is not frozen at its April 1998 level for companies as it is for individuals etc. (see 26.1 INDEXATION),

(viii) as regards acquisitions after 5 April 1998, the rules for matching shares and securities sold with those acquired are not the same for corporation tax as for capital gains tax (see 59.1 SHARES AND SECURITIES—IDENTIFICATION RULES), and

(ix) certain provisions, as contained in this chapter, apply only to companies.

See TOLLEY'S CORPORATION TAX under Friendly Societies and Life Insurance Companies for provisions of *TCGA 1992* (and related provisions) which are integral with the corporation tax regime applicable to life assurance business carried on by such entities.

See also 5 ASSESSMENTS; 34 INTEREST ON OVERPAID TAX; 35 INTEREST AND SURCHARGES ON UNPAID TAX; 46 PAYMENT OF TAX; 47 PENALTIES; and 54 RETURNS for matters applicable to companies generally.

The definition of 'company' includes any body corporate or unincorporated association but does not include a partnership. [*TCGA 1992, s 288(1)*]. References to 'persons' in the capital gains tax legislation generally include unincorporated associations (*CIR v Worthing Rugby Football Club Trustees CA 1987, 60 TC 482*).

Regulations (*SI 1998 No 3177*) have been made to modify the application of the Taxes Acts on the introduction of the European single currency in certain countries other than the UK on 1 January 1999. The regulations are meant to prevent unintended tax consequences arising as a result of the conversion of the currencies of participating EU Member States into euros. Broadly, they provide for continuity of treatment for assets, contracts, financial instruments etc. redenominated in euros, and grant tax relief, by means of a deduction from profits, for the costs of converting a company's shares or other securities into euros. (Revenue Press Release 17 December 1998). See 6.1 ASSETS, 21.5 EXEMPTIONS AND RELIEFS and 58.11 SHARES AND SECURITIES for specific CGT measures included.

13.2 CORPORATION TAX SELF-ASSESSMENT

There are provisions extending, generally for company accounting periods ending on or after an appointed day, the principles of SELF-ASSESSMENT (56) to the pre-existing Pay and File system for corporation tax payment and returns. The appointed day for corporation tax self-assessment is 1 July 1999. [*SI 1998 No 3173*]. Corporation tax self-assessment is covered in TOLLEY'S CORPORATION TAX. See also Revenue booklet 'A Guide to Corporation Tax Self-Assessment — for Tax Practitioners and Inland Revenue Officers (April 1999)'.

13.3 RATE OF CORPORATION TAX IN RESPECT OF CHARGEABLE GAINS

For accounting periods beginning after 16 March 1987 the whole of the chargeable gains (net of allowable losses under 13.4 below) of a company is included in the profits chargeable to corporation tax. The rate of corporation tax applicable will be dependent upon, inter alia, the residence position of the company, its status, the number of associated companies and the level of the chargeable profits and certain franked investment income but the rate so determined applies to both income and chargeable gains included in the chargeable profits. If the company's accounting period straddles different financial years, chargeable profits are apportioned on a time basis between the years. [*ICTA 1988 s 8(3); TCGA 1992, s 8(1)*]. For the level and applicability of the starting rate and small companies rate of corporation tax, marginal relief and the full corporation tax rate, see TOLLEY'S CORPORATION TAX.

Alternative rules apply as in 64 UNIT TRUSTS ETC. and 65 VENTURE CAPITAL TRUSTS.

13.4 CAPITAL AND INCOME LOSSES

The amount of chargeable gains to be taken into account for an accounting period is the amount of the chargeable gains accruing to the company in that period less the aggregate amount of the allowable losses in that period and allowable losses brought forward from any previous period. Allowable losses include short-term losses accruing under Schedule D, Case VII for years before 1971/72 which remain unrelieved. [*TCGA 1992, s 8(1), Sch 11 para 12*]. It is expressly provided for the purposes of corporation tax on chargeable gains that an allowable loss does not include any loss which, if it had been a gain, would have been exempt from corporation tax in the hands of the company. [*TCGA 1992, s 8(2)*]. Allowable losses for the purposes of corporation tax on chargeable gains cannot normally be offset against trading profits or other income but see 39.15 LOSSES. Since chargeable gains are included in profits chargeable to corporation tax as in 13.1 above, claims under *ICTA 1988, s 393A* to set trading losses against such profits mean that trading losses can be set against chargeable gains arising in the same accounting period and, to the extent permitted by that *section*, preceding accounting periods. See TOLLEY'S CORPORATION TAX under Losses for the detailed provisions.

Management expenses of an investment company may be offset against chargeable gains within the same or succeeding accounting periods. [*ICTA 1988, s 75(3)*].

See 13.24 below for the restriction on set-off of pre-entry losses where a company joins a group, and see 13.35 below for the restriction on set-off of losses against pre-entry gains where a company joins a group.

13.5 LIQUIDATION

The vesting of a company's assets in a liquidator is disregarded. All the acts of the liquidator in relation to such assets are treated as acts of the company. [*TCGA 1992, s 8(6)*].

All expenses properly incurred in a voluntary winding-up, including the remuneration of the liquidator, are payable out of the company's assets in priority to all other claims. [*Insolvency Act 1986, s 115*]. *Insolvency Rules 1986, Rule 4.218(1)* provides that expenses of a liquidation are to be paid out of the assets in the order of priority therein specified, subject to a discretionary power of the court under *Insolvency Act 1986, s 156* to vary the order where assets are insufficient to satisfy liabilities. [*SI 1986 No 1925, Rule 4.218(1), Rule*

4.220]. Included in the normal order of priority is the amount of any corporation tax on chargeable gains accruing on the realisation of any asset of the company (*Rule 4.218(1)(p)*).

Notwithstanding the specific inclusion of corporation tax on chargeable gains, corporation tax chargeable on a company's post-liquidation profits is to be treated as a 'necessary disbursement' of the liquidator (within *Insolvency Rules 1986, Rule 4.218(1)(m)*), and thus as an expense requiring priority as above (*Re Toshoku Finance UK plc; Kahn and another v CIR CA, [2000] STC 301*).

See also 58.14, 58.15 and 58.16 SHARES AND SECURITIES.

13.6 **RECOVERY FROM SHAREHOLDERS**

Where a person connected with a UK resident company (see 14 CONNECTED PERSONS) receives, or becomes entitled to receive, in respect of shares in that company, a capital distribution within *TCGA 1992, s 122* (see 58.14 SHARES AND SECURITIES) which is not a reduction of capital but which constitutes, or is derived from, a disposal of assets from which a chargeable gain accrues to the company, and the company does not pay, within six months after its due date, the corporation tax due for the accounting period in which the gain accrued, the recipient of the distribution may be required (by assessment within two years of the due date) to pay so much of that corporation tax as relates to chargeable gains but not exceeding the lesser of

(i) part of that tax, at the rate in force when the gain accrued, proportionate to his share of the total distribution made by the company, and

(ii) the value of the distribution he received or became entitled to receive.

The person then has a right of recovery against the company. These provisions do not affect any liability of the person in respect of a chargeable gain accruing to him as a result of the capital distribution. For accounting periods ending after 30 September 1993 (Pay and File) the provisions relating to the assessment of the person and the right of recovery are suitably adapted so that, in particular, the right of recovery also extends to any interest on unpaid tax which the person has paid in respect of the outstanding tax. [*TCGA 1992, s 189*].

For coverage of *ICTA 1988, ss 767A–767C*, which broadly allow the Revenue to recover any corporation tax unpaid by a company from persons controlling the company in certain circumstances where there has been a change of ownership of the company, see TOLLEY'S CORPORATION TAX under Payment of Tax.

13.7 **RECONSTRUCTIONS, AMALGAMATIONS ETC.**

See also 58.8 and 58.10 SHARES AND SECURITIES and 13.42 below.

Subject to the following, where a 'scheme of reconstruction or amalgamation' (meaning a scheme for the reconstruction of any company or companies or the amalgamation of any two or more companies) involves the transfer of a company's business to another company for no consideration (other than the assumption of liabilities of the business), capital assets (not used as trading stock by either company) are regarded as being transferred at a 'no gain/no loss' disposal value and the acquiring company takes over the disposing company's acquisition date for the purposes of ASSETS HELD ON 6 APRIL 1965 (7).

For disposals before 1 April 2000, the above is conditional on both companies being UK-resident at the time of transfer. For disposals on or after that date, the conditions are:

- that *either* the transferee company is UK-resident at time of acquisition *or* the assets are 'chargeable assets' in relation to that company immediately after that time; *and*

- that *either* the transferor company is UK-resident at that time *or* the assets are 'chargeable assets' in relation to that company immediately before that time.

For these purposes, an asset is a '*chargeable asset*' in relation to a company at a particular time if, on a disposal by that company at that time, any gain would be a chargeable gain and would be within the charge to corporation tax by virtue of *TCGA 1992, s 10* (non-UK resident company trading in the UK through a branch or agency — see 44.3 OVERSEAS MATTERS).

[*TCGA 1992, s 139(1)(1A)(2)(9); FA 2000, Sch 29 para 5*].

Strictly, the second company should carry on substantially the same business and have substantially the same members as the first, but in practice the identity of shareholdings is not insisted upon where the scheme is for bona fide commercial reasons or where there is segregation of trades or businesses into identifiable parts which are capable of being carried on in their own right (Revenue Pamphlet IR 131, SP 5/85).

Anti-avoidance and disapplication of relief. *TCGA 1992, s 139* will not apply to any transfer unless the scheme is for bona fide commercial reasons and not to avoid corporation tax, capital gains tax or income tax, or the Board, on written application by the acquiring company, has notified its satisfaction with the scheme before the transfer is made. The Board may, within 30 days of receipt, call for further particulars to be supplied within 30 days, or longer if the Board allows; if the information is not supplied, the application lapses. Subject to this, the Board must notify its decision within a further 30 days. If not so notified, or if dissatisfied with the decision, the applicant may within a further 30 days require the Board to refer the application to the Special Commissioners for their decision. All material facts and considerations must be disclosed, otherwise any decision is void. [*TCGA 1992, s 138(2)–(5), s 139(5)*].

Where, if the disposing company had not been wound up, tax could have been assessed on it because of the effect of *TCGA 1992, s 139(5)* above, that tax can be assessed and charged (in the name of the disposing company) on the acquiring company. Subject to this, tax assessed on either company which is unpaid six months after the date when it is payable, may, within two years of that date, be similarly assessed and charged on certain third parties. The third parties are restricted to any person holding all or any part of the assets in respect of which the tax is charged and who either is the acquiring company or subsequently acquired them as a result of one or more disposals within *TCGA 1992, s 139* or *s 171(1)* (companies within same group) without any intervening disposals not within those provisions. Tax assessed on the third party is restricted to the proportion held of the assets in respect of which the tax was originally charged and may be recovered from the company originally assessed. The right of recovery is suitably adapted for accounting periods ending after 30 September 1993 (Pay and File) so that, in particular, the right of recovery also extends to any interest on unpaid tax which the third party has paid in respect of the outstanding tax. [*TCGA 1992, s 139(6)–(8)*].

Written application for clearance should be made (by either company) to Inland Revenue, Capital and Valuation Division (CGT), Sapphire House, 550 Streetsbrook Rd, Solihull, West Midlands, B91 1QU. Tel. 0121–713 4600. It should give full details of the transactions and of all the companies directly involved, their tax districts and references. Copies of accounts for the last two years for which accounts have been prepared should accompany the application, which should be cross-referenced to (though made separately from) any clearance or consent which is being sought under *ICTA 1988, s 215, s 225,* or *s 707* in respect of the same scheme. See also 3.16 ANTI-AVOIDANCE above.

The provisions of *TCGA 1992, s 139* do not apply in the case of a transfer of the whole or part of a company's business to a unit trust scheme, within *TCGA 1992, s 100(2)* or which is an authorised unit trust, to an investment trust or, for transfers after 16 March 1998, to a venture capital trust (see 64 UNIT TRUSTS ETC. and 65 VENTURE CAPITAL TRUSTS). [*TCGA 1992, s 139(4); FA 1998, s 134(1)(4)*].

Where *TCGA 1992, s 139* has applied in relation to a transfer to a company which was not then an investment trust but which subsequently becomes one for an accounting period, then any assets transferred and still owned by the company at the beginning of that accounting period are deemed to have been sold and immediately reacquired by the transferee company, immediately after the transfer, at their market value at that time. For accounting periods ending on or after 1 July 1999 (the appointed day for corporation tax self-assessment — see 13.2 above), the resulting chargeable gain or allowable loss arising is deemed to accrue to the transferee company not at the time of the deemed disposal but at the end of the accounting period preceding the accounting period in which the company becomes an investment trust. Notwithstanding normal time limits, a corporation tax assessment in respect of any resulting liability can be made within six years after the end of the last-mentioned accounting period.

Similar provisions apply where, after a transfer to which *TCGA 1992, s 139* applied and after 16 March 1998, the transferee company becomes a venture capital trust (within *ICTA 1988, s 842AA* — see 65 VENTURE CAPITAL TRUSTS). They apply by reference to the time at which the Board's approval for the purposes of *section 842AA* comes into effect, and the resulting gain or loss is deemed to accrue immediately before that time rather than at the time of the deemed disposal. In a case in which the Board's approval has effect as from the beginning of an accounting period, any consequential corporation tax assessment can be made, notwithstanding normal time limits, within six years after the end of that accounting period. These provisions do not apply if those above relating to investment trusts have already applied (in relation to the same transfer of assets) and *vice versa*.

[*TCGA 1992, ss 101, 101B; FA 1996, s 140; FA 1998, s 134(2)(3)(5)*].

In respect of disposals after 19 March 1990, the provisions of *TCGA 1992, s 139* did not apply in relation to an asset acquired before 30 November 1993 (the latter date being the date of the coming into force of *FA 1994, s 249*; companies otherwise regarded as UK resident but under double tax relief arrangements already regarded as non-UK resident to be treated as non-UK resident for *Taxes Acts* purposes after 29 November 1993; see 52.6 RESIDENCE AND DOMICILE) if the company which acquired it, though resident in the UK, was regarded as resident elsewhere by virtue of DOUBLE TAX RELIEF (18.2) arrangements such that it would not under those arrangements be taxable in the UK on any gain arising on a disposal of the asset immediately after its acquisition. [*TCGA 1992, s 139(3); FA 1994, s 251(1)(5), Sch 26 Pt VIII*].

The following applies where there is a disposal or acquisition of currency; a 'qualifying asset' consisting of the right to settlement under a debt which is not a debt on a security (within *TCGA 1992, s 132*; see 21.5 EXEMPTIONS AND RELIEFS); a 'qualifying asset' consisting of the right to settlement under a debt on a security; or an obligation which by virtue of *TCGA 1992, s 143* (futures contracts; see 17.11 DISPOSAL) is regarded as an asset to the disposal of which *TCGA 1992* applies and which is a duty under a currency contract. Where the disposal or acquisition is by a 'qualifying company' and is made on or after the company's 'commencement day' (the first day of its first accounting period beginning after 22 March 1995, subject to transitional provisions), and immediately before the disposal or after the acquisition, as the case may be, the asset is held wholly for 'qualifying purposes', and *TCGA 1992, s 139* would otherwise apply, the last-mentioned provision does not apply as regards the disposal or acquisition and the corresponding acquisition or disposal. '*Qualifying purposes*' are purposes of long term or mutual insurance business. [*FA 1993, s 169, Sch 17 para 7*]. See 13.44 below for a note of the terms quoted and not otherwise defined.

Life assurance business. The provisions of *TCGA 1992, s 139* are adapted for certain transfers of an insurance company's long term business. See TOLLEY'S CORPORATION TAX under Life Insurance Companies.

Privatisations etc. In connection with privatisations, and reorganisations of public corporations, various specific provisions have been enacted, mainly to cause transfers of assets to be treated on a 'no gain/no loss' basis, and to preclude a liability from arising under *TCGA 1992, s 179* (see 13.19 below) when a company leaves a group. See, for example, *British Telecommunications Act 1981, s 82*; *Telecommunications Act 1984, s 72*; *Trustee Savings Bank Act 1985, Sch 2 paras 2-6*; *Transport Act 1985, s 130(3)(4)*; *Airports Act 1986, s 77*; *Gas Act 1986, s 60*; *ICTA 1988, s 513*; *Water Act 1989, s 95*; *Electricity Act 1989, Sch 11*; *FA 1990, Sch 12* (broadcasting undertakings); *TCGA 1992, s 267* (sharing of transmission facilities); *F(No 2)A 1992, Sch 17* (privatisation of Northern Ireland Electricity); *FA 1994, Sch 24* (provisions relating to *Railways Act 1993*); and *FA 1994, Sch 25* (Northern Ireland Airports Ltd).

Building society's business etc. transferred to a company or other building society. Similar provisions apply as for privatisations etc. above where there is a transfer of the whole of a building society's business to a successor company in accordance with the relevant provisions of *Building Societies Act 1986* [*TCGA 1992, s 216*] and where there is a disposal by one society to another as part of an amalgamation etc. of societies. [*TCGA 1992, s 215*].

Industrial and provident societies etc. Similar provisions apply as for privatisations etc. above where there is a union or amalgamation of two or more registered industrial and provident societies or a transfer of engagements from one society to another. This treatment also applies to certain co-operative associations established and resident in the UK, the primary purposes of which are to assist members in carrying on husbandry in the UK or fishery operations. [*ICTA 1988, s 486(8)(9)*].

13.8 OVERSEAS MATTERS

See 44.3 OVERSEAS MATTERS for the transfer before 1 April 2000 of a UK branch or agency owned by a non-UK resident company to a UK resident company.

Various provisions apply where a UK resident company has an interest in a controlled foreign company. See 44.7 OVERSEAS MATTERS.

Where a UK resident company transfers all or part of a trade carried on by it outside the UK to a company not resident in the UK in exchange, wholly or partly, for shares, see 44.9 OVERSEAS MATTERS. Where the transferee company is resident in an EC member state, see 44.11 OVERSEAS MATTERS. Where the UK company's trade is carried on in the UK and is transferred to a company resident in another EC member state, see 44.10 OVERSEAS MATTERS.

There are 'exit charges' and provisions for the recovery of unpaid tax where a company ceases to be UK resident etc., is a dual resident company or is not resident in the UK. See 44.12 and 44.13 OVERSEAS MATTERS.

13.9 INTEREST CHARGED TO CAPITAL

For interest paid in accounting periods beginning after 31 March 1981, interest on money borrowed by a company for the construction of any building, structure or works, and referable to a time before disposal of it, may be added to the expenditure allowable as a deduction under *TCGA 1992, s 38* in computing the gain on the disposal of the building etc. by the company, provided the expenditure on the construction was itself so allowable. No relief is given for interest which has been allowed as a debit after 31 March 1996 in respect of the loan relationship provisions (see 38 LOAN RELATIONSHIPS OF COMPANIES) or for deductions prior to 1 April 1996 treated as a charge on income under *ICTA 1988, s 338.* This restriction also applies to any amount which is allowable as a deduction in computing income, profits, gains or losses for corporation tax purposes (or would be so but for an insufficiency of profits or gains) or which would be allowable if the building etc. was held as a fixed asset of a trade. For such accounting periods the practical effect of these provisions is that a payment of interest is unlikely to qualify as allowable expenditure in computing a chargeable gain.

For interest paid in accounting periods ending before 1 April 1981, the provisions and comment made in the last two sentences above do not apply. Instead, interest had to be charged to capital in order to qualify as allowable expenditure, which treatment prevented it being treated as a charge on income by virtue of *ICTA 1970, s 248(5)(a) as originally enacted*. [*TCGA 1992, s 40*].

13.10 GILTS AND BONDS

See 24 GOVERNMENT SECURITIES, 38 LOAN RELATIONSHIPS OF COMPANIES and 49 QUALIFYING CORPORATE BONDS for the exemption available for gilt-edged securities and qualifying corporate bonds.

For accounting periods ended on or before 31 March 1996, if gilt-edged securities or qualifying corporate bonds are appropriated by a company *from* trading stock in such circumstances that any gain accruing on their disposal would be exempt from corporation tax on chargeable gains, there is a deemed disposal and re-acquisition at market value immediately before the appropriation. Where the securities are appropriated *to* trading stock, any trading loss arising on a subsequent disposal cannot exceed the loss which would have arisen if the securities had been acquired at their market value at the time of the appropriation. As a consequence of the introduction of the loan relationships provisions (see 38 LOAN RELATIONSHIPS OF COMPANIES), this ceases to be of application for accounting periods ended after 31 March 1996, subject to the transitional provisions outlined in that chapter. [*ICTA 1988, s 126A; TCGA 1992, Sch 10 para 14(6); FA 1996, s 105, Sch 41 Pt V(3)*].

See 6.3 ASSETS for appropriations to and from trading stock generally and see also 13.14 below for intra-group transfers of assets which are trading stock of one of the companies but not of the other.

13.11 GROUPS OF COMPANIES

The following applies for the purposes of this paragraph, and of paragraphs 13.12–13.39 below.

Definition of company. '*Company*' means a company within the meaning of the *Companies Act 1985* or the corresponding enactment in Northern Ireland or which is constituted under any other Act, Royal Charter, or letters patent or under the law of a country outside the UK. It also includes a registered industrial and provident society, a trustee savings bank, a building society and, from 17 March 1998, an incorporated friendly society within the meaning of *Friendly Societies Act 1992*.

Residence requirement. Before, broadly, April 2000, and in all cases, except those referred to in 13.20 below, 13.23 below and 44.3, 44.6 OVERSEAS MATTERS, the company had to be resident in the UK. The law is amended by *FA 2000* to remove this condition and thus enable any company, whatever its country of residence, to be a member of a group for the purposes of UK corporation tax on chargeable gains. The change is generally effective on and after 1 April 2000, though consequential changes to pre-existing anti-avoidance legislation took effect on 21 March 2000. The consequences, and effective dates, of the change in the residence requirement are dealt with in this publication wherever appropriate (see, for example, 13.12 below). Transitional measures ensure continuity of treatment as regards a pre-existing group of companies (see also (3) below).

[*TCGA 1992, s 170(2)(a)(9); FA 1998, s 136(1)(4); FA 2000, s 102, Sch 29 paras 1, 46(1)–(3)*].

Definition of group. A '*group*' comprises

(*a*) a company ('*the principal company of the group*') and

(*b*) that company's '75 per cent subsidiaries' (as in *ICTA 1988, s 838* i.e. where not less than 75 per cent of the 'ordinary share capital' (see below under 'General') is beneficially owned directly or indirectly by the principal company), and those subsidiaries' 75 per cent subsidiaries (and so on), except that any 75 per cent subsidiary which is not 'an effective 51 per cent subsidiary' of the principal company is excluded.

This definition is subject to the following rules.

(1) A company ('the subsidiary') which is a 75 per cent subsidiary of another company cannot be a principal company of a group, unless,

  (i) because of the exclusion in (*b*) above, the two companies are not in the same group,

  (ii) the requirements of the definition of a group in (*a*) and (*b*) are otherwise satisfied, and

  (iii) no further company could, under this provision, be the principal company of a group of which the subsidiary would be a member.

(2) If a company would otherwise belong to more than one group (the principal company of each of which is called the 'head of a group' below), it belongs only to the group which can first be determined under the following tests.

  (i) The group to which it would belong if the exclusion of a company which is not an effective 51 per cent subsidiary in (*b*) above were applied without the inclusion of any amount to which the head of a group is entitled of any profits available for distribution to equity holders of a head of another group or would be entitled of any assets of a head of another group available for distribution to its equity holders on a winding up.

  (ii) The group the head of which is entitled to a greater percentage than any other head of a group of its profits available for distribution to equity holders.

  (iii) The group the head of which would be entitled to a greater percentage than any other head of a group of its assets available for distribution to equity holders on a winding-up.

  (iv) The group the head of which owns (as in *ICTA 1988, s 838(1)(a)*) directly or indirectly more of its ordinary share capital than any other head of a group.

(3) *Transitional.* If a group is regarded as reconstituted purely because of the amendment made by *FA 2000* to the residence requirement (see above), such that the principal company of the 'old' group is not the principal company of the 'new' group, a subsidiary which is not 'an effective 51 per cent subsidiary' of the new principal company remains part of the group for as long as it remains 'an effective 51 per cent subsidiary' of the company which was the principal company of the old group.

A company ('the subsidiary') is '*an effective 51 per cent subsidiary*' of another company ('the parent') at any time if and only if

(A) the parent is entitled to more than 50 per cent of any profits available for distribution to equity holders of the subsidiary, and

(B) the parent would be entitled to more than 50 per cent of any assets available for distribution to the equity holders on a winding up.

ICTA 1988, Sch 18 as amended (group relief: equity holders and profits or assets available for distribution) applies with suitable modifications for the purposes of (2) and (A) and (B) above. One modification for these purposes disapplies the requirement that certain arrangements for changes in profit or asset shares are assumed to take place in applying the 50 per cent tests above.

[*TCGA 1992, s 170(2)(b)(3)–(8); ICTA 1988, s 838; F(No 2)A 1992, s 24, Sch 6 paras 5, 10; FA 2000, Sch 29 para 46(4)–(6), Sch 40 Pt II(11)*].

For consideration of beneficial ownership of a company's shares where they are subject to cross-options by shareholders, see *J Sainsbury plc v O'Connor CA 1991, 64 TC 208.* Although legislation overturning the *Sainsbury* decision in respect of arrangements entered into after 14 November 1991 was introduced by *F(No 2)A 1992* for group relief purposes, it does not apply for the purposes of the taxation of chargeable gains.

A group remains the same group so long as the same company remains the principal company of the group, and if at any time the principal company of a group becomes a member of another group, the first group and the other group are regarded as the same, and the question whether or not a company has ceased to be a member of a group is determined accordingly. [*TCGA 1992, s 170(10)*].

The passing of a resolution, or the making of an order, or any other act for the winding-up of a member of a group is not treated as an occasion on which any company ceases to be a member of the group. [*TCGA 1992, s 170(11)*].

General. '*Ordinary share capital*' means all issued share capital of a company except that carrying a fixed rate of dividend only. Any share capital of a registered industrial and provident society is treated as ordinary share capital.

'*Group*' and '*subsidiary*' are construed with any necessary modifications where applied to a company incorporated under the law of a country outside the UK.

'*Profits*' means income and gains. '*Trade*' includes a vocation, office or employment (including the occupation of UK woodlands before 6 April 1993).

[*TCGA 1992, s 170(1)(2)(c)(d)*].

As regards nationalised industries, etc., see *TCGA 1992, s 170(12)–(14)*.

See also 44.6, 44.9, 44.14 OVERSEAS MATTERS.

13.12 **Disposals of capital assets by one member of a group to another member are treated as if made at a 'no gain/no loss' disposal value except for the following.**

(i) Assumed (as opposed to actual) disposals.

(ii) A disposal of a debt due from a group member effected by satisfying it (or part of it).

(iii) A disposal on redemption of redeemable shares.

(iv) A disposal of an interest in shares in consideration of a capital distribution within *TCGA 1992, s 122* whether or not involving a reduction of capital.

(v) The receipt of compensation for destruction etc. of assets (in that the disposal is treated as being to the insurer or other person who ultimately bears the burden of furnishing the compensation).

(vi) A disposal after 31 March 1980 by or to an investment trust within *ICTA 1988, s 842* (and see also 13.21 below).

(via) A disposal after 16 March 1998 by or to a venture capital trust within *ICTA 1988, s 842AA* (and see 13.22 below).

(vib) A disposal after 16 March 1998 by or to a qualifying friendly society, i.e. an incorporated friendly society within *ICTA 1988, s 461A* which is entitled to income tax and corporation tax exemptions on certain profits.

(vii) A disposal after 31 March 1987 to a 'dual resident investing company' within *ICTA 1988, s 404*.

(viii) An exchange, etc., after 14 March 1988, of shares, etc. in a reorganisation, takeover, etc. which is treated by *TCGA 1992, ss 127, 135* as not involving a disposal by the member of the group first mentioned above (see 58.5 and 58.8 SHARES AND SECURITIES).

The position for exchanges of shares before 14 March 1988 in reorganisations within a group was examined in *Westcott v Woolcombers Ltd CA 1987, 60 TC 575* and *NAP Holdings UK Ltd v Whittles HL 1994, 67 TC 166*. The decision in the former case, which involved consideration of the original *FA 1965* legislation and a reorganisation occurring prior to the introduction by *FA 1968* of certain anti-avoidance provisions was approved in the judgements given in the latter case, which involved a reorganisation which occurred when the provisions of *ICTA 1970* and *CGTA 1979* were extant and subsequent to further anti-avoidance provisions introduced by *FA 1977*.

For the Revenue's views on this topic, see Revenue Capital Gains Manual CG 45550–45573.

(ix) A disposal after 19 March 1990 and before 30 November 1993 (the latter date being the date of the coming into force of *FA 1994, s 249*; companies otherwise regarded as UK resident but under double tax relief arrangements already regarded as non-UK resident to be treated as non-UK resident for *Taxes Acts* purposes after 29 November 1993; see 52.6 RESIDENCE AND DOMICILE) to a company which, though resident in the UK, was regarded as resident elsewhere by virtue of DOUBLE TAX RELIEF (18.2) arrangements such that it would not under those arrangements be taxable in the UK on any gain arising on a disposal of the asset immediately after its acquisition.

The change in the residence requirement in 13.11 above has effect for these purposes in relation to disposals on or after 1 April 2000. The conditions for intra-group transfers of assets on or after that date to be treated as no gain/no loss disposals are:

- that *either* the transferor company is UK-resident at time of disposal *or* the asset is a 'chargeable asset' in relation to that company immediately before that time; *and*
- that *either* the transferee company is UK-resident at time of disposal *or* the asset is a 'chargeable asset' in relation to that company immediately after that time.

For these purposes, an asset is a '*chargeable asset*' in relation to a company at a particular time if, on a disposal by that company at that time, any gain would be a chargeable gain and would be within the charge to corporation tax by virtue of *TCGA 1992, s 10* (non-UK resident company trading in the UK through a branch or agency — see 44.3 OVERSEAS MATTERS).

For disposals before 1 April 2000, the effect of the residence requirement was that both transferor and transferee had to be UK-resident and members of the same group of UK-resident companies.

[*TCGA 1992, s 171; FA 1994, s 251(1)(7), Sch 26 Pt VIII; FA 1998, s 135(1)(4), s 136(2)(3)(5); FA 2000, Sch 29 para 2*].

The following applies where there is a disposal or acquisition of currency; a 'qualifying asset' consisting of the right to settlement under a debt which is not a debt on a security (within *TCGA 1992, s 132*; see 21.5 EXEMPTIONS AND RELIEFS); a 'qualifying asset' consisting of the right to settlement under a debt on a security; or an obligation which by virtue of *TCGA 1992, s 143* (futures contracts; see 17.11 DISPOSAL) is regarded as an asset to the disposal of which *TCGA 1992* applies and which is a duty under a currency contract. Where the disposal or acquisition is by a 'qualifying company' and is made on or after the company's 'commencement day' (the first day of its first accounting period beginning after 22 March 1995, subject to transitional provisions), and immediately before the disposal or after the acquisition, as the case may be, the asset is held wholly for 'qualifying purposes', and *TCGA 1992, s 171* would otherwise apply, the last-mentioned provision does not apply as regards the disposal or acquisition and the corresponding acquisition or disposal. '*Qualifying purposes*' are purposes of long term or mutual insurance business. [*FA 1993, s 169, Sch 17 para 7*]. See 13.44 below for a note of the terms quoted and not otherwise defined.

As regards (iv) above, the assets acquired in the capital distribution are nevertheless transferred at a 'no gain/no loss' price (see *Innocent v Whaddon Estates Ltd Ch D 1981, 55 TC 476*).

For the Revenue's views as to the application of the principles established by *Furniss v Dawson HL 1984, 55 TC 324* with regard to the use of 'capital loss' companies within a group, see ICAEW Guidance Note TR 588, 25 September 1985 (but note the provisions in 13.24 below).

13.13 **Disposal outside a group treated as having been preceded by intra-group transfer.** Where two companies, X and Y, are members of a group, and X disposes of an asset on or after 1 April 2000 to a person outside the group (the actual disposal), X and Y may make a joint election to the effect that for the purposes of corporation tax on chargeable gains:

- the asset (or a specified part of it) be deemed to have been transferred by X to Y immediately before the actual disposal;
- that transfer be deemed to be a no gain/no loss disposal within *TCGA 1992, s 171* (see 13.12 above);
- the actual disposal (or the part of it to which the election relates) be deemed to have been made by Y.

The election must be made in writing to an officer of the Board before the second anniversary of the end of the accounting period of X in which the actual disposal was made. It can be made only if an actual transfer of the asset (or part) from X to Y would have been a no gain/no loss disposal within *TCGA 1992, s 171*. This provision is intended to facilitate the bringing together of chargeable gains and allowable losses within one group company. Any payment made by X to Y, or vice versa, in connection with the election is not to be taken into account in computing profits or losses of either company or treated as a distribution or a charge on income, *provided* it does not exceed the chargeable gain or allowable loss deemed to accrue to Y on the disposal.

[*TCGA 1992, s 171A; FA 2000, s 101*].

13.14 **Intra-group transfers of assets which are trading stock of one of the companies but not of the other.** Where a company (Company A) acquires an asset as trading stock of a trade from another member of the group (Company B), and the asset did not form part of the trading stock of a trade carried on by Company B, Company A is treated for the purposes of *TCGA 1992, s 161* (see 6.3 ASSETS) as acquiring the asset otherwise than as trading stock and immediately appropriating it to trading stock. The effect is that, subject to an election being made for the alternative treatment in 6.3 ASSETS, a chargeable gain or allowable loss accrues to Company A based on the difference between market value and the no gain/no loss (see 13.12 above) transfer value.

Where a company (Company C) disposes of an asset forming part of the trading stock of a trade to another member of the group (Company D), and the asset is acquired by Company D otherwise than as trading stock of a trade carried on by it, Company C is treated for the purposes of *TCGA 1992, s 161* as appropriating the asset immediately before the disposal for a purpose other than use as trading stock. The effect is that Company C is deemed to have acquired the asset at that time at the amount brought into the accounts of the trade for tax purposes (see 6.3 ASSETS).

In relation to acquisitions and disposals on or after 1 April 2000, the change in the residence requirement in 13.11 above applies in determining whether a company is a member of a group for the above purposes, but references above to a trade do not include a trade carried on by a non-UK resident company other than in the UK through a branch or agency.

[*TCGA 1992, s 173; FA 2000, Sch 29 para 11*].

Acquisition 'as trading stock' implies a commercial justification for the acquisition, see *Coates v Arndale Properties Ltd HL 1984, 59 TC 516, Reed v Nova Securities Ltd HL 1985, 59 TC 516* and *N Ltd v Inspector of Taxes (Sp C 90), [1996] SSCD 346.*

13.15 **Intra-group transfers: indexation allowances.** See 8.7 ASSETS HELD ON 31 MARCH 1982 and 26.4 INDEXATION for re-basing and indexation provisions on 'no gain/no loss' disposals.

13.16 **Disposal or acquisition outside a group — miscellaneous.** Where there is a disposal of an asset which was acquired in circumstances in which *TCGA 1992, s 140A* (see 44.10 OVERSEAS MATTERS), *s 171* (see 13.12 above) or (before 1 April 2000) *s 172* (see 44.3 OVERSEAS MATTERS) applied or in which *TCGA 1992, s 171* would have applied but for the exclusions mentioned in 13.12(ii)–(iv)(vi)–(vii)(ix) above, restriction of allowable losses by reference to capital allowances (see 17.5(*j*) DISPOSAL) applies in relation to capital allowances made to the person from whom it was acquired (so far as not taken into account in relation to a disposal by that person) and so on as respects previous such acquisitions. The above does not affect the 'no gain/no loss' consideration for which the asset is deemed under the above-mentioned provisions to have been acquired. [*TCGA 1992, s 41(8), s 174(1)–(3); F(No 2)A 1992, s 46(1)(5); FA 2000, Sch 29 para 12, Sch 40 Pt II(12)*].

Where a company which is or has been a group member disposes of an asset which it acquired from another group member as a result of a no gain/no loss disposal within 13.12 above, the provisions relating to ASSETS HELD ON 6 APRIL 1965 (7) apply as if all group members were one person. As regards acquisitions before 1 April 2000, this provision was dependent on the asset having been acquired at a time when both parties to the transaction were members of the group, regardless of whether or not the transfer was within 13.12 above, except that it did not apply if the transfer was within 13.12(iv) (transfer by or to an investment trust). The change in the residence requirement in 13.11 above applies in determining whether a company is a member of a group for these purposes at any time on or after 1 April 2000. [*TCGA 1992, s 174(4)(5); FA 2000, Sch 29 para 13*].

13.17 **Rollover relief on the replacement of business assets** is granted by *TCGA 1992, ss 152–158.* See 55.5 ROLLOVER RELIEF for provisions relating to groups of companies.

13.18 Collection of unpaid tax from other members of the group and controlling directors

Gains accruing after 31 March 2000. Where a chargeable gain accrues to a company (hereafter referred to as the taxpayer company) after 31 March 2000 and either

- that company is UK-resident at the time the gain accrues, or
- the gain is within the charge to corporation tax by virtue of *TCGA 1992, s 10* (non-UK resident company trading in the UK through a branch or agency — see 44.3 OVERSEAS MATTERS),

the following rules apply where all or part of the corporation tax assessed on the company for the relevant accounting period (i.e. the accounting period in which the gain accrues) remains unpaid six months after it became payable.

The Board may serve on any of the following persons a notice requiring that person to pay, within 30 days, the unpaid tax or, if less, an amount equal to corporation tax on the chargeable gain at the appropriate rate.

(*a*) If the taxpayer company was a member of a 'group' at the time the gain accrued:

- a company which was at that time the 'principal company of the group'; and
- any other company which, in any part of the period of 12 months ending with that time, was a member of the group *and* owned the asset, or any part of the asset, disposed of (or, where that asset is an interest in, or a right over, another asset, owned either asset or any part of either asset).

(*b*) If the gain is within the charge to corporation tax by virtue of *TCGA 1992, s 10*, any person who is, or has been during the 12 months ending with the time the gain accrued, a controlling director of the taxpayer company or of a company which has, or has had within that 12-month period, control over the taxpayer company.

For the purpose of (*a*) above, '*group*' and '*principal company of the group*' are construed as in 13.11 above but as if references there to 75 per cent subsidiaries were references to 51 per cent subsidiaries. The change in the residence requirement in 13.11 above applies in determining whether a company is a member of a group at any time (including a time before 1 April 2000). For the purposes of (*b*) above and in determining whether a director is a controlling director, 'control' is construed in accordance with *ICTA 1988, s 416*, and 'director' has the wide meaning given by *ICTA 1988, s 168(8)(9)* and *ICTA 1988, s 417(5)(6)*.

The notice must state the amount of tax assessed, the original due date and the amount required from the person on whom it is served. It has effect, for the purposes of collection, interest and appeals, as if it were a notice of assessment on that person. The notice must be served within three years beginning with the date on which the liability of the taxpayer company for the relevant accounting period is finally determined. That date varies according to whether the unpaid tax is charged in a self-assessment (and, if so, whether there is an enquiry into the tax return in question), in a discovery assessment (and, if so, whether there is an appeal) or in consequence of a 'determination' (see TOLLEY'S CORPORATION TAX under Self-Assessment). In the simplest case of a self-assessment and no enquiry, the liability is determined on the last date on which notice of enquiry could have been given.

A person paying an amount under these provisions may recover it from the taxpayer company, but such an amount is not deductible for any tax purpose.

[*TCGA 1992, s 190; FA 2000, Sch 29 para 9(1)(3)(4)*].

Gains accruing before 1 April 2000 (and see also 44.13 OVERSEAS MATTERS as regards non-resident companies). If corporation tax on a chargeable gain of a group member is not paid within six months of the time when it becomes payable or it is assessed (whichever is the later), then, within two years after that time, the tax may be assessed on (*a*) the principal company of the group when the gain accrued or (*b*) any other company which at any time in the two years preceding the time the gain accrued was a group member and owned the asset disposed of (or the right, interest, etc. therein). The company paying the tax then has a right of recovery from the company to which the gain accrued, or from the principal company of the group when the gain accrued, if that is a different company. In the latter instance, a right is given to that principal company of recovery from the company to which the gain accrued and, insofar as the tax is not so recovered, of a just proportion from any present member of the group which has previously owned, whilst still a group member, the asset disposed of. These provisions extend to interest on overdue tax. [*TCGA 1992, s 190*].

General. For coverage of

- *ICTA 1988, ss 767A–767C*, which provide for unpaid corporation tax due from a company to be recovered from persons controlling the company, in certain circumstances where there has been a change of ownership; and
- *FA 2000, s 98, Sch 28*, effective for accounting periods ending on or after 1 April 2000, which provide for unpaid corporation tax due from a non-UK resident company to be recovered from other companies within the same group (defined by reference to 51% subsidiaries), from any member of a consortium (defined as for CT group relief purposes) owning the company, or from any member of the same group (defined as for CT group relief purposes) as a member of that consortium,

see TOLLEY'S CORPORATION TAX under Payment of Tax.

13.19 **Company leaving group after acquiring asset intra-group.** Broadly, where a company ceasing to be a member of a group owns a capital asset which has been transferred to it by another group member (such status being determined at the time of transfer) within the preceding six years, that company is treated as if, immediately after its acquisition of the asset, it had sold, and immediately reacquired, the asset at its then market value. There will thus be a gain or loss by reference to the market value of the asset at that time and its 'no gain/no loss' acquisition consideration under 13.12 above (but see below as to the time at which the gain or loss is deemed to accrue). The time limit for electing for 6 April 1965 value (normally two years from the end of the accounting period in which the disposal took place) is concessionally extended (Revenue Pamphlet IR 131, SP D21).

The provision applies to a company ('*the chargeable company*') leaving a group which acquired an asset as described above where it or an 'associated' company also leaving the group at the same time owns (otherwise as trading stock) the asset at that time, property to which a gain on the disposal of the original asset has been carried forward under ROLLOVER RELIEF (55) or an asset the value of which is wholly or partly derived from the original asset.

Companies are '*associated*' if they would form a group by themselves.

These provisions do not apply if, before the chargeable company leaves the group (or leaves a second group — see below), it has already been deemed to have sold and reacquired the asset in question at the time mentioned above by virtue of its having since become an investment trust or a venture capital trust (see, respectively, 13.21 and 13.22 below).

In relation to assets acquired by intra-group transfer on or after 1 April 2000, these provisions apply only if that transfer satisfied the conditions necessary for it to be a no gain/no loss disposal (see 13.12 above).

Any gain or loss on the deemed sale is treated as accruing at whichever is the later of the time immediately after the beginning of the accounting period in which or, as the case may be, at the end of which the company ceases to be a member of the group and the time it is deemed to reacquire the asset concerned above.

Where, for group relief purposes, the accounting period of the claimant or surrendering company ends after 1 July 1997 and the overlapping period for the purposes of *ICTA 1988, s 403A* falls at least partly after that date, *ICTA 1988, ss 403A, 403B* (limits on group relief — see TOLLEY'S CORPORATION TAX) have effect as if the actual circumstances were as they are treated above as having been. For earlier accounting periods, an apportionment under *ICTA 1988, s 409(2)* (profits and losses for group relief etc. when two or more companies join or leave a group) is to take the timing of the gain or loss on the deemed sale into account but not so as to require any reference in that provision to an accounting period to have effect for any of the purposes mentioned in *ICTA 1988, s 409(3)* (surrendering and claimant companies) as a reference to any accounting period other than a true accounting period.

The provision does not apply in relation to transfers of assets between associated companies which cease to be members of the group at the same time.

[*TCGA 1992, s 179(1)(1A)(2)(2C)(2D)(3)(4)(10); FA 1993, s 89; F(No 2)A 1997, Sch 7 para 8; FA 1998, s 133(2)(3), s 135(3)(5); FA 2000, Sch 29 para 4(2)(6)*].

However, where a company in a group transfers an asset intra-group and both transferor and recipient then leave that group to form a second group 'connected' with the first, with the recipient company then departing from the second group after 28 November 1994, the provision will apply (in relation to the departure from the second group) if the intra-group transfer, which is deemed for this purpose to have taken place in the second group, occurred within the preceding six years. The two groups are '*connected*' for this purpose if, broadly, at the time the chargeable company ceases to be a member of the second group, the second group is under the control of the first group or both groups are under the common control of a company which controls or has controlled the first group at any time since the chargeable company left the first group. The general definitions of *ICTA 1988, s 416(2)–(6)* (meaning of 'control') apply for this purpose (except for banking businesses). See TOLLEY'S CORPORATION TAX under Close Companies. Where the recipient company's departure from the second group takes place after 16 March 1998, the definition of '*connected*' groups is widened so that this provision will apply where common control of the two groups is exercised by any person or persons (which thus includes natural persons as well as companies). [*TCGA 1992, s 179(2A)(2B)(9A); FA 1995, s 49; FA 1998, s 139; FA 2000, Sch 29 para 4(3)(4)(6)*].

'*Ceasing to be a member of a group*' does not apply to cases where a company ceases to be a member of a group in consequence of another member of the group ceasing to exist. For a company ceasing to be a member of a group before 15 November 1991, the phrase did not apply to cases where a company ceased to be a member of a group by being wound up or dissolved or in consequence of another member of the group being wound up or dissolved. [*TCGA 1992, s 179(1); F(No 2)A 1992, s 25*]. For events after 14 November 1991, the Revenue takes the view that this 'liquidation let out' only applies to the case of a parent company ceasing to be a member of a group on the occasion of its only subsidiary ceasing to exist on dissolution (or all its subsidiaries ceasing to exist simultaneously on dissolution). (Revenue Capital Gains Manual CG 45441–45445). See also *Burman v Hedges & Butler Ltd Ch D 1978, 52 TC 501*. In relation to events at any time, the Revenue has confirmed it does not apply the deemed sale and reacquisition where the company receiving the asset ceases to be a group member as a result of its only subsidiary leaving the group except where the parent company emigrates, thereby causing the group to break up (Revenue Capital Gains Manual CG 45450 and see *Dunlop International AG v Pardoe CA, [1999] STC 909*).

If

(*a*) a company ceases to be a member of a group only through the principal company becoming a member of another group (e.g. it is not an 'effective 51 per cent subsidiary' of the principal company of the other group as in 13.11 above), and

(*b*) under the provisions described above, it would be treated as selling an asset at any time,

the following provisions apply.

(1) The company in question is not treated as selling the asset at that time.

(2) If

  (i) within six years of that time the company in question ceases at any time ('*the relevant time*') to satisfy the following conditions: namely that it is a '75 per cent subsidiary' (as defined in 13.11 above) of one or more members of the other group mentioned in (*a*) above and an 'effective 51 per cent subsidiary' (as defined in 13.11 above) of one or more of those members; and

  (ii) at the relevant time the company in question or a company in the same group, owns (otherwise than as trading stock) the asset, or property to which a chargeable gain has been rolled over from the asset, or an asset the value of which is wholly or partly derived from the original asset,

  the company in question is treated as if, immediately after acquiring the asset, it had sold and reacquired it at its market value at the time of acquisition.

(3) Any gain or loss on the deemed sale is treated as arising at the relevant time.

[*TCGA 1992, s 179(5)–(8)*].

If under any of the foregoing provisions a deemed sale arises at any time, and if on an actual sale at market value at that time any loss or gain would, under the value shifting provisions (see 3.6–3.12 ANTI-AVOIDANCE), have been calculated as if the consideration were increased by an amount, the market value at the time of the deemed sale is treated as having been greater by that amount. [*TCGA 1992, s 179(9)*].

In relation to gains accruing before 1 April 2000, if any corporation tax assessed on a company in consequence of the above is still unpaid six months after the later of the date when the tax becomes due and payable by the company and the date when the assessment was made on the chargeable company, it may instead be assessed and charged (in the name of the chargeable company), within two years from the date determined above, on the principal company of the group on that date or immediately after the time the chargeable company ceased to be a member of the group, or on a company which owned the asset on that date or immediately after that time. A company paying tax and interest under such an assessment is given a right of recovery against the chargeable company. As regards gains accruing on or after 1 April 2000, see the general recovery provisions at 13.18 above. [*TCGA 1992, s 179(11)(12); FA 2000, Sch 29 para 4(5)(7)*].

Any adjustment of tax or recomputation of liability on a disposal may be made by assessment or otherwise as a result of any deemed disposal and reacquisition mentioned above. [*TCGA 1992, s 179(13)*].

Example

C Ltd had the following transactions.

1.3.86	Purchased a freehold property £20,000.
1.12.95	Sold the freehold to D Ltd (a wholly-owned subsidiary) for £40,000 (market value £100,000).
31.7.2000	Sold its interest in D Ltd (at which time D Ltd continued to own the freehold property).

Both C Ltd and D Ltd prepare accounts to 30 April.

Relevant values of the RPI are: March 1986 96.73, December 1995 150.7.

(i) C Ltd's disposal of the property to D Ltd is to be treated as one on which, after taking account of the indexation allowance, neither gain nor loss arises (see 13.12 above and 26.4 INDEXATION).

Indexation factor

$$\frac{150.7 - 96.73}{96.73} = 0.558$$

	£
Cost to C Ltd	20,000
Indexation allowance £20,000 × 0.558	11,160
Deemed cost to D Ltd	£31,160

(ii) Following the sale of C Ltd's shares in D Ltd on 31.7.2000 (i.e. within six years after the transaction in (i) above), *D Ltd* will have a deemed disposal as follows.

Deemed disposal on 1.12.95

	£
Market value at 1.12.95	100,000
Cost (as above)	31,160
Chargeable gain subject to CT	£68,840
D Ltd's new base cost for future gains	£100,000

Although the deemed disposal occurs on 1 December 1995, i.e. immediately after D Ltd's acquisition, the gain is treated as accruing on 1 May 2000, i.e. the beginning of the accounting period in which D Ltd left the group, being later than the date of the deemed disposal. The gain thus forms part of D Ltd's profits for the year ended 30 April 2001.

13.20 **Exemption from charge on company ceasing to be member of group.** *TCGA 1992, s 179* in 13.19 above does not apply, subject to conditions, where, as part of a 'merger', a company (Company A) ceases to be a member of a group ('the A group'), and it is shown that the merger was carried out for bona fide reasons and that the avoidance of a liability to tax was not the main or one of the main purposes of the merger.

'*Merger*', in broad terms, means an arrangement whereby one or more companies ('the acquiring compan(y)(ies)') not in the A group acquire interests in the business previously carried on by Company A, and one or more members of the A group acquire interests in the business or businesses previously carried on either by the acquiring company or companies or by a company at least 90% of the ordinary share capital of which is owned by two or more of the acquiring companies. For this purpose a group member is treated as carrying on as one business the activities of that group. 25% of the value of the interests acquired must take the form of ordinary share capital, whilst the remainder of the interests acquired by the A group must consist of share capital or debentures or both. The value of the interests acquired must be substantially the same, and the consideration for the interests acquired by the acquiring companies must substantially consist of the interests acquired by the A group.

For these purposes, references to a company include a non-UK resident company, and this applied even before the change in the residence requirement in 13.11 above.

[*TCGA 1992, s 181; FA 2000, Sch 29 para 28*].

See also 13.42 below regarding demergers.

13.21 **Company becoming an investment trust after acquiring asset intra-group.** Similar treatment as in 13.19 above (company leaving group) applies where a company (the '*acquiring company*') becomes an investment trust (within *ICTA 1988, s 842* — see 64.2 UNIT TRUSTS ETC.) for an accounting period beginning after 16 March 1998 and not more than six years after the company acquired an asset from another company in its group, the disposal by which it acquired the asset (the corresponding disposal) having been treated by virtue of *TCGA 1992, s 171* (intra-group transfers — see 13.12 above) as a no gain/no loss disposal. The provisions apply where at the beginning of the said accounting period, the acquiring company owns, otherwise than as trading stock, either the asset itself or replacement property, i.e. property into which a chargeable gain on disposal of the asset has been rolled over as in 55 ROLLOVER RELIEF, whether directly (i.e. as a result of a single rollover relief claim) or indirectly (where two or more such claims have been made). For the purposes of these provisions, an asset acquired is deemed to be the same as an asset owned subsequently if the value of the latter asset is derived, wholly or partly, from the original asset (in particular where the original was a leasehold and the lessee has acquired the freehold reversion). The provisions do not apply if the acquiring company was an investment trust at the time of the corresponding disposal (in which case the no gain/no loss treatment would not have applied — see 13.12(vi) above) nor if it has been an investment trust for any intervening accounting period.

The acquiring company is treated as if, immediately after the corresponding disposal, it had sold and immediately reacquired the asset at its market value at that time. The resulting chargeable gain or allowable loss is treated as accruing immediately before the end of the acquiring company's accounting period which immediately preceded that in which it became an investment trust. Notwithstanding normal time limits, any consequential corporation tax assessment may be made at any time within six years after the end of the accounting period in which the company became an investment trust. These provisions are disapplied if, prior to the company becoming an investment trust, the above treatment has already applied to the asset by virtue either of 13.19 above or 13.22 below (company becoming a venture capital trust).

[*TCGA 1992, s 101A; FA 1998, s 133(1)(3)*].

13.22 **Company becoming a venture capital trust after acquiring asset intra-group.** The same treatment as in 13.21 above (company becoming an investment trust) applies where the acquiring company becomes a venture capital trust (VCT) (within *ICTA 1988, s 842AA* — see 65 VENTURE CAPITAL TRUSTS) after 16 March 1998 and not more than six years after it acquired the asset intra-group by means of a no gain/no loss disposal under *TCGA 1992, s 171* (see 13.12 above). For this purpose, a company becomes a VCT at the time of the coming into effect of the Board's approval for the purposes of *section 842AA* (the time of approval). The provisions apply where at the time of approval, the acquiring company owns, otherwise than as trading stock, either the asset itself (with the same rules as in 13.21 above as to derivation of assets) or replacement property (as in 13.21 above). The provisions do not apply if the acquiring company was a VCT at the time of the intra-group disposal (in which case the no gain/no loss treatment would have applied only if that disposal occurred before 17 March 1998— see 13.12(via) above) nor if it has been a VCT at any time in the intervening period. Nor do they apply if, prior to the company becoming a VCT, the said treatment has already applied to the asset by virtue either of 13.21 above or 13.19 above (company leaving group).

The chargeable gain or allowable loss resulting from the deemed disposal at market value immediately after the intra-group transfer is treated as accruing to the acquiring company immediately before the time of approval. Notwithstanding normal time limits, any consequential corporation tax assessment may, in a case in which the Board's approval has effect as from the beginning of an accounting period, be made at any time within six years after the end of that accounting period.

[*TCGA 1992, s 101C; FA 1998, s 135(2)(5)*].

13.23 **Value shifting to give tax-free benefit, depreciatory transactions and dividend stripping.** See 3.6–3.12 ANTI-AVOIDANCE for value shifting to give a tax-free benefit where groups may be involved. See 3.19 ANTI-AVOIDANCE for depreciatory transactions within a group. See 3.20 ANTI-AVOIDANCE for dividend stripping.

13.24 **Restriction on set-off of pre-entry losses where a company joins a group.** *General outline and commencement.* Under *TCGA 1992, Sch 7A*, a restriction applies to the deduction of allowable losses accruing to a company before the time it becomes a member of a group of companies and losses accruing on assets held by any company at such a time. The restriction is further described in 13.25–13.34 below. For Revenue comment on this legislation, see Revenue Capital Gains Manual CG 47500–47988.

The restriction applies for the calculation of the amount to be included in respect of chargeable gains in a company's total profits for any accounting period ending after 15 March 1993 (including one beginning before 6 April 1992 where the provisions of *TCGA 1992* are applied to the pre-consolidation legislation then in force). However, the restriction applies only in relation to the deduction from chargeable gains accruing after 16 March 1993 of amounts in respect of, or of amounts carried forward in respect of,

(*a*) 'pre-entry losses' accruing before it became a member of a UK CGT group to a company whose membership of that group began or begins after 31 March 1987, and

(*b*) losses accruing on the disposal of any assets so far as it is by reference to such a company that the assets fall to be treated as being or having been 'pre-entry assets' or assets incorporating a part referable to pre-entry assets.

[*TCGA 1992, s 177A; FA 1993, s 88, Sch 8*].

The restriction is widely drawn, and whilst its stated principal intention is to prevent the fiscal effectiveness of an acquisition of a 'capital loss' company (i.e. a company that has a *realised* allowable loss as its only commercial feature), it may also impinge on an acquisition of a company solely for commercial reasons where it becomes a member of a group whilst holding an asset which is later disposed of (whether by the company or another group member to whom the asset has been transferred) outside the group at a loss. Further restrictions were imposed by *FA 1994, s 94* in relation to the deduction of a loss from a chargeable gain where either the gain or the loss accrues after 10 March 1994. After 20 March 2000, the change in the residence requirement (see 13.11 above) as regards groups of companies is applied to these provisions.

For a worked example on pre-entry losses, see TOLLEY'S CORPORATION TAX under Capital Gains.

13.25 *Application and construction of TCGA 1992, Sch 7A. Sch 7A* has effect, in the case of a company which or has been the member of a group of companies ('*the relevant group*'), in relation to any pre-entry losses. A '*pre-entry loss*', in relation to a company, means any allowable loss that accrued to it at a time before it became a member of the relevant group or the 'pre-entry proportion' (see 13.26–13.29 below) of any allowable loss accruing to it on the disposal of any 'pre-entry asset'. [*TCGA 1992, Sch 7A para 1(1)(2)*].

A '*pre-entry asset*', in relation to any disposal, means any asset that was held, at the time immediately before the 'relevant event' occurred in relation to it, by any company (whether or not the one which makes the disposal) which is or has at any time been a member of the relevant group. Originally, the '*relevant event*' occurred in relation to a company when it became a member of the relevant group. This now applies only if the company is UK-resident at that time or the asset is then a 'chargeable asset' (defined as in 13.12 above) in relation to it, but if neither is the case a relevant event subsequently occurs when the company becomes UK-resident or the asset becomes a chargeable asset in relation to it. This amendment is a consequence of the change in the residence requirement for groups of companies (see 13.11 above) and has effect in computing chargeable gains for accounting periods ending after 20 March 2000, but the question of whether a company is a member of a group at any time on or before that date is to be determined by reference to the residence requirement before *FA 2000*. If a company becomes a member of a group on 21 March 2000 purely as a result of the change in the residence requirement, *Sch 7A* is not thereby brought into effect. [*TCGA 1992, Sch 7A para 1(3)(3A); FA 2000, Sch 29 para 7(2)(3)(6)–(9)*].

Subject to 13.27 below, an asset is not, however, a pre-entry asset if the company which held the asset at the time the relevant event occurred in relation to it is not the company which makes the disposal and since that time the asset has been disposed of otherwise than on the no gain/no loss basis of *TCGA 1992, s 171* (general provisions for transfers within a group; see 13.12 above) except where the company making the disposal retains an interest in or over the asset (when the interest is treated as a pre-entry asset). [*TCGA 1992, Sch 7A para 1(4); FA 2000, Sch 29 para 7(4)(6)–(8)*].

Subject to 13.27 below, an asset ('*the second asset*') which derives wholly or partly its value from another asset ('*the first asset*') acquired or held by a company at any time is treated as the same asset if the second asset is held subsequently by the same company, or by any company which is or has been a member of the same group of companies as that company (e.g. a freehold derived from a leasehold where the lessee acquires the reversion). Where this treatment applies, whether under this provision or not (*TCGA 1992, s 43* is similar; see 17.6 DISPOSAL), the second asset is treated as a pre-entry asset in relation to a company if the first asset would have been. [*TCGA 1992, Sch 7A para 1(8)*].

In relation to a pre-entry asset, references to '*the relevant time*' are references to the time when the relevant event occurred in relation to the company by reference to which that asset is a pre-entry asset. Where a relevant event has occurred in relation to a company more than once, an asset is a pre-entry asset in relation to that company if it would be a pre-entry asset in relation to that company in respect of any of those occasions, but in these circumstances any reference to the time when a relevant event occurred in relation to the company is a reference to the last such occasion. [*TCGA 1992, Sch 7A para 1(5); FA 2000, Sch 29 para 7(5)–(8)*].

Subject to so much of *Sch 7A para 9(6)* (see 13.33 below) as requires groups of companies to be treated as separate groups for the purposes of *Sch 7A para 9*, if

(*a*) the principal company of a group of companies ('*the first group*') has at any time become a member of another group ('*the second group*') so that the two groups are treated as the same under *TCGA 1992, s 170(10)* (see 13.11 above), and

(*b*) the second group, together in pursuance of *TCGA 1992, s 170(10)* with the first group, is the relevant group, then, except where the circumstances are as in *Sch 7A para 1(7)* below, the members of the first group are treated for the purposes of *Sch 7A* as having become members of the relevant group at that time, and not by virtue of *TCGA 1992, s 170(10)* at the times when they became members of the first group. [*TCGA 1992, Sch 7A para 1(6)*].

The circumstances mentioned in *Sch 7A para 1(6)* are where

(1) the persons who immediately before the time when the principal company of the first group became a member of the second group owned the shares comprised in the issued share capital of the principal company of the first group are the same as the persons who, immediately after that time, owned the shares comprised in the issued share capital of the principal company of the relevant group; and

(2) the company which is the principal company of the relevant group immediately after that time

 (i) was not the principal company of any group immediately before that time; and

 (ii) immediately after that time had assets consisting entirely, or almost entirely, of shares comprised in the issued share capital of the principal company of the first group.

[*TCGA 1992, Sch 7A para 1(7)*].

Where an allowable loss accrues to a company under *TCGA 1992, s 116(10)(b)* (gain or loss on shares exchanged on reorganisation, conversion or reconstruction for qualifying corporate bonds to crystallise when bonds sold; see 49.3 QUALIFYING CORPORATE BONDS and 13.31 below), that loss is deemed to accrue at the time of the reorganisation etc. for the purposes of deciding whether a loss accrues before a company becomes a member of the relevant group. [*TCGA 1992, Sch 7A para 1(9)*]. Likewise, the annual deemed disposals of unit trust etc. holdings of a life assurance company's long term business fund under *TCGA 1992, s 212* (see TOLLEY'S CORPORATION TAX under Life Insurance Companies) are deemed to occur for this purpose without regard to the 'spreading' provisions of *TCGA 1992, s 213*. [*TCGA 1992, Sch 7A para 1(10)*].

13.26 *Pre-entry proportion of losses on pre-entry assets.* Subject to 13.27–13.29 below, the '*pre-entry proportion*' of an allowable loss accruing on the disposal of a pre-entry asset is the allowable loss that would accrue on that disposal if that loss were the sum of the amounts determined, for every item of relevant allowable expenditure (within *TCGA 1992, s 38(1)(a)* or *(b)*; see 17.3 DISPOSAL), according to the following formula:

$$A \times \frac{B}{C} \times \frac{D}{E} \text{ where}$$

A is the total amount of the allowable loss;

B is the sum of the amount of the item of relevant allowable expenditure concerned and, for disposals before 30 November 1993, the '*indexed rise*' (as in *TCGA 1992, s 54* (see 26.1 INDEXATION) but ignoring the effect of *TCGA 1992, s 110* (see 59.4 SHARES AND SECURITIES—IDENTIFICATION RULES)) where the above formula is applied for the purposes of 13.27 below) in that item;

C is the sum of the total amount of all such expenditure and, for disposals before 30 November 1993, the indexed rises in each of the items comprised in that expenditure;

D is the length of the period beginning with 'the relevant pre-entry date' and ending with the relevant time or, if that date is after that time, nil (i.e. there is no pre-entry proportion if the relevant time precedes the relevant pre-entry date); and

E is the length of the period beginning with the relevant pre-entry date and ending with the day of disposal.

[*TCGA 1992, Sch 7A para 2(1)(9); FA 1994, s 93(8)(a)(d), (11), Sch 26 Pt V*].

'*The relevant pre-entry date*', in relation to any item referred to above, is the later of 1 April 1982 and the date the asset was acquired or provided or, as the case may be, improvement expenditure became due and payable (such date being subject to the assumptions provided for by *Sch 7A para 2(4)(5)(6A)(6B)* below in relation to the deduction of a loss from a chargeable gain where either the gain or the loss accrues after 10 March 1994 and subject to the assumptions provided for by *Sch 7A para 2(4)(5)* in relation to the deduction of a loss from a chargeable gain where both the gain and loss accrue before 11 March 1994). [*TCGA 1992, Sch 7A para 2(3); FA 1994, s 94(1)(2)(4)*].

Where any 'original shares' are treated as the same asset as a 'new holding' (within *TCGA 1992, s 127*; see 58.5 SHARES AND SECURITIES), the above formula and (where applicable) the provisions in 13.27 below are applied (except, for disposals before 30 November 1993, in relation to the calculation of any indexed rise):

(*a*) as if any item referred to above consisting in consideration given for the acquisition of the new holding had been incurred at the time the original shares were acquired; and

(*b*) where there is more than one such time as if that item were incurred at those different times in the same proportions as the consideration for the acquisition of the original shares.

[*TCGA 1992, Sch 7A para 2(4); FA 1994, s 93(8)(b)(d), (11), Sch 26 Pt V*].

Without prejudice to (*a*) and (*b*) above, the formula is applied to any asset which

(A) was held by a company at the time when it became a member of the relevant group, and

(B) is treated as having been acquired by that company on *any* no gain/no loss corresponding disposal,

as if the company and every person who acquired that asset or 'the equivalent asset' (see below) at a 'material time' had been the same person and, accordingly, as if the asset had been acquired by the company when it or the equivalent asset was acquired by the first of those persons to have acquired it at a material time and the time at which any expenditure had been incurred were to be determined accordingly. [*TCGA 1992, Sch 7A para 2(5)*].

A '*material time*' is any time before an acquisition of an asset in circumstances as in (B) above and is, or is after, the last occasion before the occasion on which any person acquired that asset or the equivalent asset otherwise than on an acquisition which is within (B) above or is an acquisition by virtue of which any asset is treated as the equivalent asset; and the formula is applied in relation to any asset within (A) and (B) above without regard to *TCGA 1992, s 56(2)* (consideration on no gain/no loss disposal deemed to include indexation allowance; see 26.4 INDEXATION). [*TCGA 1992, Sch 7A para 2(6)*].

In relation to the deduction of a loss from a chargeable gain where either the gain or the loss accrues after 10 March 1994, and notwithstanding anything in *TCGA 1992, s 56(2)* (see above), where in the case of the disposal of any pre-entry asset any company has, between the relevant time and the time of the disposal, acquired that asset or the equivalent asset, and the acquisition was either an acquisition in pursuance of a no gain/no loss disposal under *TCGA 1992, s 171* (general provisions for no gain/no loss transfers within a group; see 13.12 above) or an acquisition by virtue of which an asset is treated as the equivalent asset, the items of relevant allowable expenditure in the above formula, and the times they are treated as having been incurred, are determined on the assumption that the company by reference to which the asset in question is a pre-entry asset, and the company which acquired the asset or the equivalent asset as above (and every other company which has made such an acquisition), were the same person and, accordingly, that the pre-entry asset had been acquired by the company disposing of it at the time when it or the equivalent asset would have been treated as acquired by the company by reference to which the asset is a pre-entry asset. [*TCGA 1992, Sch 7A para 2(6A)(6B); FA 1994, s 94(1)(2)(4)*].

In relation to the deduction of a loss from a chargeable gain where either the gain or the loss accrues after 10 March 1994, for the purposes of the provisions in *Sch 7A para 2(5)(6)(6A)(6B)* above, '*the equivalent asset*', in relation to another asset acquired or disposed of by any company, is any asset which falls in relation to that company to be treated (whether under *Sch 7A para 1(8)* in 13.25 or otherwise) as the same as the other asset or which would fall to be so treated after applying, as respects other assets, the assumptions for which those provisions provide. In relation to the deduction of a loss from a chargeable gain where both the gain and the loss accrue before 11 March 1994, for the purposes of the provisions in *Sch 7A para 2(5)(6)* above, '*the equivalent asset*', in relation to the acquisition of any asset by any company, is any asset which (whether under *Sch 7A para 1(8)* or otherwise) would be treated in relation to that company as the same as the asset in question. [*TCGA 1992, Sch 7A para 2(7); FA 1994, s 94(1)(2)(4)*].

The above provisions and (where applicable) those in 13.27 below have effect where a loss accrues to a company under *TCGA 1992, s 116(10)(b)* (see *Sch 7A para 1(9)* in 13.25 above), and the shares exchanged for qualifying corporate bonds are treated under 13.27 below as including pre-entry assets, as if the disposal on which the loss accrues were the disposal of the shares assumed to be made by *s 116(10)(a)* at the time of reorganisation etc. [*TCGA 1992, Sch 7A para 2(8)*].

In relation to disposals on or after 30 November 1993, where, under *TCGA 1992, s 55(8)* (rolled-up indexation on no gain/no loss disposals after 31 March 1982 and before 30 November 1993; see 8.7 ASSETS HELD ON 31 MARCH 1982), the allowable loss (or part) accruing on the disposal of a pre-entry asset is attributable to an amount of rolled-up indexation, the total relevant allowable expenditure is treated for the purposes of *Sch 7A para 2* above as increased by that rolled-up amount, each item of expenditure being treated as increased by the attributable proportion of the total. [*TCGA 1992, Sch 7A para 2(8A); FA 1994, s 93(8)(c), (11)*].

Also in relation to disposals on or after 30 November 1993, where *TCGA 1992, s 56(3)* (disapplication of *TCGA 1992, s 56(2)* on any no gain/no loss disposal on or after 30 November 1993; see 26.4 INDEXATION) applies to reduce the total allowable expenditure on the disposal of a pre-entry asset on which an allowable loss accrues, the amount of each item of relevant allowable expenditure is treated for the purposes of *Sch 7A para 2* as reduced by so much of that reduction as is attributable to it. [*TCGA 1992, Sch 7A para 2(8B); FA 1994, s 93(8)(c), (11)*].

13.27 *Disposals of pooled assets.* Subject to 13.28 and 13.29 below, the provisions below apply where any assets acquired by a company fall to be treated with other assets as indistinguishable parts of the same asset ('*a pooled asset*') and the whole or part of that asset is referable to pre-entry assets.

For the purposes of *Sch 7A*, where a pooled asset has at any time contained a pre-entry asset, the pooled asset is treated, until on the assumptions below all the pre-entry assets included in the asset have been disposed of, as incorporating a part which is referable to pre-entry assets, the size of that part being determined as below. [*TCGA 1992, Sch 7A para 3(1)(2)*].

Where there is a disposal of any part of a pooled asset and the proportion of the asset which is disposed of does not exceed the proportion of that asset which is represented by any part of it which is not, at the time of disposal, referable to pre-entry assets, that disposal is treated as confined to assets which are not pre-entry assets. Consequently, no part of any loss accruing on that disposal is treated as a pre-entry loss (except where *Sch 7A para 4(2)* in 13.28 below applies), and the part of the pooled asset which after the disposal is treated as referable to pre-entry assets is correspondingly increased (without prejudice to the effect of any subsequent acquisition of assets to be added to the pool in determining whether, and to what extent, any part of the pooled asset is to be treated as referable to pre-entry assets). [*TCGA 1992, Sch 7A para 3(3)(11)*].

Where there is such an excess as postulated above, the disposal is treated as relating to pre-entry assets only so far as required for the purposes of the excess. Consequently

(*a*) any loss accruing on that disposal is treated for the same purposes as an allowable loss on a pre-entry asset,

(*b*) the pre-entry proportion of that loss is deemed (except where *Sch 7A para 4(3)* in 13.28 below applies) to be the amount (insofar as it does not exceed the amount of the loss actually accruing) which would have been the pre-entry proportion under 13.26 above of any loss accruing on the disposal of the excess if the excess were a separate asset, and

(*c*) the pooled asset is treated after the disposal as referable entirely to pre-entry assets (with the same qualification as appears in parentheses at the end of the previous paragraph regarding any subsequent acquisition).

[*TCGA 1992, Sch 7A para 3(4)(11)*].

Where there is a disposal of the whole or part of a pooled asset at a time when the asset is referable entirely to pre-entry assets, (*a*) and (*b*) above apply to the disposal of the asset or the part as they apply in relation to the assumed disposal of the excess mentioned in the preamble to (*a*) and (*b*) but, where the whole of an asset only part of which is referable to pre-entry assets is disposed of, the reference in (*b*) above to the excess is taken as a reference to that part. [*TCGA 1992, Sch 7A para 3(5)*].

In applying (*b*) above, it is assumed that none of the assets treated as comprised in the separate asset mentioned in (*b*) has ever been comprised in a pooled asset with any assets other than those which are taken to constitute that separate asset for the purposes of determining what would have been the pre-entry proportion of any loss accruing on the disposal of any assets as that separate asset. [*TCGA 1992, Sch 7A para 3(6)*].

Assets comprised in any asset which is treated as separate are identified on the following assumptions:

(A) that assets are disposed of in the order of the relevant pre-entry dates for the acquisition consideration as under 13.26 above;

(B) subject to (A), that assets with earlier relevant times are disposed of before those with later ones;

(C) that disposals made when a company was not a member of the relevant group are made according to the provisions in *Sch 7A para 3(1)–(6)* and (A) and (B) above, as they have effect in relation to the group of companies of which the company was a member at the time of disposal or, as the case may be, of which it had most recently been a member before that time; and

(D) subject to (A)–(C) above, that a company disposes of assets in the order in which it acquires them.

[*TCGA 1992, Sch 7A para 3(7)*].

Where there is more than one pre-entry date in relation to acquisition consideration, the date in (A) above is the earlier or earliest of those dates if any such date relating to an option to acquire the asset is disregarded. [*TCGA 1992, Sch 7A para 3(8)*].

Where a second asset falls to be treated as acquired at the same time as a first asset was earlier acquired (whether under *Sch 7A para 1(8)* in 13.25 above or otherwise), and the second asset is either comprised in a pooled asset partly referable to pre-entry assets or is, or includes, an asset which is to be treated as so comprised, (A)–(D) above apply not only in relation to the second asset as if it were the first asset but also, in the first place, for identifying the asset which is to be treated as the first asset under the above provisions. [*TCGA 1992, Sch 7A para 3(10)*].

Where the formula in 13.26 above is applied to an asset treated as above as a separate asset, the amount or value of the asset's acquisition or disposal consideration and any related incidental costs are determined not under *TCGA 1992, s 129* or *s 130* (see 58.5 SHARES AND SECURITIES) but by apportioning the consideration or costs relating to both that asset and other assets acquired or disposed of at the same time according to the proportion that is borne by that asset to all the assets to which the consideration or costs related. [*TCGA 1992, Sch 7A para 3(9)*].

13.28 *Rules to prevent pre-entry losses on pooled assets being treated as post-entry losses.* The provisions below apply if

(*a*) there is a disposal of any part of a pooled asset which under 13.27 above is treated as including a part referable to pre-entry assets;

(*b*) the assets disposed of are or include assets ('*the post-entry element of the disposal*') which for the purposes of 13.27 are treated as having been included in the part of the pooled asset which is not referable to pre-entry assets;

(*c*) an allowable loss ('*the actual loss*') accrues on the disposal; and

(*d*) the amount which in computing the allowable loss is allowed as a deduction of relevant allowable expenditure ('*the expenditure actually allowed*') exceeds such expenditure attributable to the post-entry element of the disposal.

[*TCGA 1992, Sch 7A para 4(1)*].

Subject to *Sch 7A para 4(6)* below, where the post-entry element of the disposal comprises all of the assets disposed of the actual loss is treated for *Sch 7A* purposes as a loss accruing on the disposal of a pre-entry asset, and the pre-entry proportion of that loss is treated as being the amount (insofar as it does not exceed the amount of the actual loss) of the excess referred to in (*d*) above. [*TCGA 1992, Sch 7A para 4(2)*].

Subject to *Sch 7A para 4(6)* below, where the actual loss is treated under 13.27 above as a loss accruing on a pre-entry asset, and the expenditure actually allowed exceeds the actual cost of the assets to which the disposal is treated as relating, the pre-entry proportion of the loss is treated as being the amount which (insofar as it does not exceed the amount of the actual loss) is equal to the sum of that excess and what would, apart from the provisions in 13.29 and these provisions, be the pre-entry proportion of the loss accruing on the disposal. [*TCGA 1992, Sch 7A para 4(3)*].

For the purposes of *Sch 7A para 4(3)* above, the actual cost of the assets to which the disposal is treated as relating is taken to be the sum of

(A) the relevant allowable expenditure attributable to the post-entry element of the disposal; and

(B) the amount which, in computing the pre-entry proportion of the loss under *Sch 7A para 3(4)(b)* (13.27(*b*) above) and *Sch 7A para 3(6)* (13.27 above), would be treated for the purposes of 'C' in the formula in 13.26 above as the total amount allowable as a deduction of relevant allowable expenditure in respect of such of the assets disposed of as are treated as having been incorporated in the part of the pooled asset referable to pre-entry assets.

[*TCGA 1992, Sch 7A para 4(4)*].

Without prejudice to *Sch 7A para 4(6)* below, where *Sch 7A para 4(2)* or *(3)* above applies for the purpose of determining the pre-entry proportion of any loss, no election can be made under 13.29 below for the purpose of enabling a different amount to be taken as the pre-entry proportion of that loss. [*TCGA 1992, Sch 7A para 4(5)*].

Where

(*aa*) the pre-entry proportion of the loss accruing to any company on the disposal of any part of a pooled asset falls to be determined under *Sch 7A para 4(2)* or *(3)* above,

(*bb*) the amount determined thereunder exceeds the amount determined under *Sch 7A para 4(7)* below ('*the alternative pre-entry loss*'), and

(*cc*) the company makes an election for the purpose,

the pre-entry proportion of the loss determined as specified in (*aa*) above is reduced to the amount of the alternative pre-entry loss. [*TCGA 1992, Sch 7A para 4(6)*]. For this purpose '*the alternative pre-entry loss*' is whatever apart from these provisions would have been the pre-entry proportion of the loss on the disposal in question, if for the purposes of *Sch 7A* the identification of the assets disposed of were to be made disregarding the part of the pooled asset which was not referable to pre-entry assets, except to the extent (if any) by which the part referable to pre-entry assets fell short of what was disposed of. [*TCGA 1992, Sch 7A para 4(7)*].

The election mentioned in (*cc*) above must be made by the company incurring the loss by notice to the inspector given within the period of two years beginning with the end of its accounting period in which the disposal giving rise to the loss is made, or within such longer period as the Board may by notice allow. The provisions in 13.29 below may be taken into account under *Sch 7A para 4(7)* above in determining the amount of the alternative pre-entry loss as if an election had been made under 13.29 below but only if the election under (*cc*) above contains an election corresponding to the election that otherwise might have been made under 13.29 below. [*TCGA 1992, Sch 7A para 4(8)*].

As the rules for pre-entry losses can operate in relation to losses which arise on disposals of assets by companies which became members of the relevant group after 31 March 1987, they may apply in situations where elections would be beneficial but the normal two year time limit has already passed. The Revenue will extend the period for elections for these cases, and others where the time limit would expire less than two years after 27 July 1993. Elections will be accepted as made in time in all cases where made by 27 July 1995. Queries concerning elections can be addressed to Capital & Valuation Division (CGT), Sapphire House, 550 Streetsbrook Road, Solihull B91 1QU (tel. 0121 711-3232 ext 2220) (Revenue Tax Bulletin, May 1994 p 129).

For the purposes of the above the relevant allowable expenditure attributable to the post-entry element of the disposal is the amount which, in computing any allowable loss accruing on a disposal of that element as a separate asset, would have been allowed as a deduction of relevant allowable expenditure if none of the assets comprised in that element had ever been comprised in a pooled asset with any assets other than those which are taken to constitute that separate asset for the purposes of this provision. [*TCGA 1992, Sch 7A para 4(9)*]. To identify the assets which are to be treated for this purpose as comprised in the post-entry element of the disposal, a company is taken to dispose of assets in the order in which it acquired them. [*TCGA 1992, Sch 7A para 4(10)*].

Sch 7A para 3(9) in 13.27 above is applied *mutatis mutandis* for the purposes of *Sch 7A para 4(9)* above, as is *Sch 7A para 3(10)* in 13.27 for the purposes of this provision in relation to *Sch 7A para 4(10)* above. [*TCGA 1992, Sch 7A para 4(11)*].

In the above references to an amount allowed as a deduction of relevant allowable expenditure are references to the amount falling to be so allowed in accordance with *TCGA 1992, s 38(1)(a)* and *(b)* and (so far as applicable) *TCGA 1992, s 42*, together (for disposals before 30 November 1993) with the indexed rises (as in 13.26 above) in the items comprised in that expenditure or, as the case may be, in the appropriate portions of those items. Nothing in the above provisions affects the operation of the rules contained in 13.27 above for determining, for any purposes other than those of *Sch 7A para 4(7)* above, how much of any pooled asset at any time consists of a part which is referable to pre-entry assets. [*TCGA 1992, Sch 7A para 4(12)–(14); FA 1994, s 93(9)(11), Sch 26 Pt V*].

13.29 *Alternative calculation by reference to market value.* Subject to *Sch 7A para 4(5)* in 13.28 above and the following provisions, if an otherwise allowable loss accrues on the disposal by any company of any pre-entry asset, and that company makes an election accordingly, the pre-entry proportion of that loss (instead of being any amount arrived at under the above provisions of *Sch 7A*) is whichever is the smaller of [*TCGA 1992, Sch 7A para 5(1)*]

(*a*) the amount of any loss which would have accrued if that asset had been disposed of at the relevant time at its market value at that time; and

(*b*) the amount of the otherwise allowable loss accruing on the actual disposal of that asset.

[*TCGA 1992, Sch 7A para 5(2)*].

In relation to disposals on or after 30 November 1993, in determining the amount of any notional loss under (*a*) above, it is assumed that the prohibition (and its consequences) of indexation allowance creating or increasing a loss introduced by *FA 1994, s 89(1)–(5)* with effect generally in relation to disposals on or after 30 November 1993 (see 8.7 ASSETS HELD ON 31 MARCH 1982 and 26.1 and 26.4 INDEXATION) has effect for disposals on or after the day on which the relevant time falls. [*TCGA 1992, Sch 7A para 5(2A); FA 1994, s 93(10)(11)*].

Where no loss would have accrued on the deemed disposal in (*a*) above, the loss mentioned in (*b*) above is deemed not to have a pre-entry proportion. [*TCGA 1992, Sch 7A para 5(3)*]. The election mentioned above must be made by the company incurring the loss by notice to the inspector given within the period of two years beginning with the end of its accounting period in which the disposal giving rise to the loss is made, or within such longer period as the Board may by notice allow. [*TCGA 1992, Sch 7A para 5(8)*]. See 13.28 above regarding comments made about adherence to the similar two-year time limit mentioned there which apply equally here.

The provisions in *Sch 7A para 5(5)* below apply where an election as above is made in relation to any loss accruing on the disposal ('*the real disposal*') of the whole or any part of a pooled asset, and the case is one in which (but for the election) the provisions in 13.27 above would apply for determining the pre-entry proportion of a loss accruing on the real disposal. [*TCGA 1992, Sch 7A para 5(4)*]. In these circumstances, these provisions have effect as if the amount specified in (*a*) above were to be calculated

(A) on the basis that the disposal which is assumed to have taken place was a disposal of all the assets falling within (*aa*)–(*cc*) below; and

(B) by apportioning any loss that would have accrued on that disposal between

  (i) such of the assets falling within (*aa*)–(*cc*) below as are assets to which the real disposal is treated as relating, and

(ii) the remainder of the assets so falling,

according to the proportions of any pooled asset whose disposal is assumed which would have been, respectively, represented by assets mentioned in (i) above and by assets mentioned in (ii) above.

Where assets falling within (*aa*)–(*cc*) below have different relevant times there is assumed to have been a different disposal at each of those times. [*TCGA 1992, Sch 7A para 5(5)*].

Assets fall to be included within (A) and (B) above if

(*aa*) immediately before the time which is the relevant time in relation to those assets, they were comprised in a pooled asset which consisted of or included assets which fall to be treated for the purposes of 13.27 above as

(i) comprised in the part of the pooled asset referable to pre-entry assets; and

(ii) disposed of on the real disposal;

(*bb*) they were also comprised in such a pooled asset immediately after that time; and

(*cc*) the pooled asset in which they were so comprised immediately after that time was held by a member of the relevant group.

[*TCGA 1992, Sch 7A para 5(6)*].

Where

(AA) an election is made under *Sch 7A para 4(6)* (see 13.28(*cc*) above) requiring the determination by reference to these provisions of the alternative pre-entry loss accruing on the disposal of any assets comprised in a pooled asset, and

(BB) under that election any amount of the loss that would have accrued on an assumed disposal is apportioned in accordance with (A) and (B) above to assets ('*the relevant assets*') which

(i) are treated for the purposes of that determination as assets to which the disposal related, but

(ii) otherwise continue after the disposal to be treated as incorporated in the part of that pooled asset which is referable to pre-entry assets,

then, on any further application of these provisions for the purpose of determining the pre-entry proportion of the loss accruing on a subsequent disposal of assets comprised in that pooled asset, that amount (without being apportioned elsewhere) is deducted from so much of the loss accruing on the same assumed disposal as, apart from the deduction, would be apportioned to the relevant assets on that further application of these provisions. [*TCGA 1992, Sch 7A para 5(7)*].

13.30 *Restrictions on the deduction of pre-entry losses.* In the calculation of the amount to be included in respect of chargeable gains in any company's total profits for any accounting period

(*a*) if in that period there is any chargeable gain from which the whole or any part of any pre-entry loss accruing in that period is deductible in accordance with the provisions in 13.31 below, the loss or, as the case may be, that part of it is deducted from that gain;

(*b*) if, after all the deductions in (*a*) above have been made, there is in that period any chargeable gain from which the whole or any part of any pre-entry loss carried forward from a previous accounting period is deductible in accordance with the provisions in 13.31, the loss or, as the case may be, that part of it is deducted from that gain;

(*c*) the total of chargeable gains (if any) remaining after all the deductions in (*a*) or (*b*) above is subject to deductions in accordance with *TCGA 1992, s 8(1)* (chargeable gains less allowable losses of company to be included in chargeable profits; see 13.3 above) in respect of any allowable losses that are not pre-entry losses; and

(*d*) any pre-entry loss which has not been the subject of a deduction under (*a*) or (*b*) above (as well as any other losses falling to be carried forward under *section 8(1)*) are carried forward to the following accounting period of that company.

[*TCGA 1992, Sch 7A para 6(1)*].

Subject to (*a*)–(*d*) above, any question as to which or what part of any pre-entry loss has been deducted from any particular chargeable gain is decided

(A) where it falls to be decided in respect of the setting of losses against gains in any accounting period ending before 16 March 1993 as if

(i) pre-entry losses accruing in any such period had been set against chargeable gains before any other allowable losses accruing in that period were set against those gains;

(ii) pre-entry losses carried forward to any such period had been set against chargeable gains before any other allowable losses carried forward to that period were set against those gains; and

(iii) subject to (i) and (ii) above, the pre-entry losses carried forward to any accounting period ending after 15 March 1993 were identified with those losses which are determined in accordance with elections made by the company to which they accrued;

and

(B) in any other case, in accordance with such elections as may be made by the company to which the loss accrued;

and any question as to which or what part of any pre-entry loss has been carried forward from one accounting period to another is decided accordingly. [*TCGA 1992, Sch 7A para 6(2)*].

An election under (A)(iii) above must be made by the company by notice to the inspector given before the end of the period of two years beginning with the end of its accounting period which was current on 16 March 1993. An election under (B) above must similarly be made before the end of the period of two years beginning with the end of the company's accounting period in which the gain in question accrued. [*TCGA 1992, Sch 7A para 6(3)*].

For the purposes of *Sch 7A* where any matter falls to be determined under the above provisions by reference to an election but no election is made, it is assumed, so far as consistent with any elections that have been made that losses are set against gains in the order in which the losses accrued, and that the gains against which they are set are also determined according to the order in which they accrued with losses being set against earlier gains before they are set against later ones. [*TCGA 1992, Sch 7A para 6(4)*].

13.31 *Gains from which pre-entry losses are to be deductible.* A pre-entry loss that accrued to a company before it became a member of the relevant group is deductible from a chargeable gain accruing to that company if the gain is one accruing

(*a*) on a disposal made by that company before the date on which it became a member of the relevant group ('*the entry date*');

(*b*) on the disposal of an asset which was held by that company immediately before the entry date; or

(*c*) on the disposal of any asset which

(i) was acquired by that company on or after the entry date from a person who was not a member of the relevant group at the time of the acquisition; and

(ii) since its acquisition from that person has not been used or held for any purposes other than those of a trade which was being carried on by that company at the time immediately before the entry date and which continued to be carried on by that company until the disposal.

[*TCGA 1992, Sch 7A para 7(1)*].

The pre-entry proportion of an allowable loss accruing to any company on the disposal of a pre-entry asset is deductible from a chargeable gain accruing to that company if

(A) the gain is one accruing on a disposal made, before the date on which it became a member of the relevant group, by that company and that company is the one ('*the initial company*') by reference to which the asset on the disposal of which the loss accrues is a pre-entry asset;

(B) the pre-entry asset and the asset on the disposal of which the gain accrues were each held by the same company at a time immediately before it became a member of the relevant group; or

(C) the gain is one accruing on the disposal of an asset which

(i) was acquired by the initial company (whether before or after it became a member of the relevant group) from a person who, at the time of the acquisition, was not a member of that group; and

(ii) since its acquisition from that person has not been used or held for any purposes other than those of a trade which was being carried on, immediately before it became a member of the relevant group, by the initial company and which continued to be carried on by the initial company until the disposal.

[*TCGA 1992, Sch 7A para 7(2)*].

Where two or more companies become members of the relevant group at the same time and those companies were all members of the same group of companies immediately before they became members of the relevant group, then, without prejudice to the provisions in 13.33 below

(*aa*) an asset is treated for the purposes of (*b*) above as held, immediately before it became a member of the relevant group, by the company to which the pre-entry loss in question accrued if that company is one of those companies and the asset was in fact so held by another of those companies;

(*bb*) two or more assets are treated for the purposes (B) above as assets held by the same company immediately before it became a member of the relevant group wherever they would be so treated if all those companies were treated as a single company; and

(*cc*) the acquisition of an asset is treated for the purposes of (*c*) and (C) above as an acquisition by the company to which the pre-entry loss in question accrued if that company is one of those companies and the asset was in fact acquired (whether before or after they became members of the relevant group) by another of those companies.

[*TCGA 1992, Sch 7A para 7(3)*].

TCGA 1992, Sch 7A para 1(4) in 13.25 above is applied *mutatis mutandis* for determining for the purposes of the above provisions whether an asset on the disposal of which a chargeable gain accrues was held at the time when a company became a member of the relevant group. [*TCGA 1992, Sch 7A para 7(4)*].

Subject to *Sch 7A para 7(6)* below, where a gain accrues on the disposal of the whole or any part of

(1) any asset treated as a single asset but comprising assets only some of which were held at the time mentioned in (*b*) or (B) above, or

(2) an asset which is treated as held at that time by virtue of a provision requiring an asset which was not held at that time to be treated as the same as an asset which was so held (see 13.25 above),

a pre-entry loss is deductible under (*b*) or (B) above from the amount of that gain to the extent only of such proportion of that gain as is attributable to assets held at that time or, as the case may be, represents the gain that would have accrued on the asset so held. [*TCGA 1992, Sch 7A para 7(5)*].

Where

(AA) a chargeable gain accrues under *TCGA 1992, s 116(10)* on the disposal of a qualifying corporate bond which has been exchanged for shares etc. (see 49.3 QUALIFYING CORPORATE BONDS and 13.25 above),

(BB) that bond was not held as required by (*b*) or (B) above at the time mentioned respectively in (*b*) or (B), and

(CC) the whole or any part of the asset which is the 'old asset' for the purposes of *TCGA 1992, s 116* was so held,

the question whether that gain is one accruing on the disposal of an asset the whole or any part of which was held by a particular company at that time is determined for the purposes of *Sch 7A para 7* as if the bond were deemed to have been so held to the same extent as the old asset. [*TCGA 1992, Sch 7A para 7(6)*].

13.32 *Change of a company's nature.* If

(*a*) within any period of three years, a company becomes a member of a group of companies and there is (either earlier or later in that period, or at the same time) 'a major change in the nature or conduct of a trade' carried on by that company, or

(*b*) at any time the scale of the activities in a trade carried on by a company has become small or negligible, and before any considerable revival of the trade, that company becomes a member of a group of companies,

the trade carried on before that change, or which has become small or negligible, is disregarded for the purposes of 13.31(*c*) and (C) above in relation to any time before the company became a member of the group in question.

'*A major change in the conduct of a trade*' includes a reference to a major change in services or facilities provided in the trade or a major change in customers of the trade or a change in the nature of investments held. Regard will also be had to appropriate changes in other factors such as the location of the company's business premises, the identity of the company's suppliers, management or staff, the company's methods of manufacture, or the company's pricing or purchasing policies to the extent that these factors indicate that a major change has occurred. Efficiency changes and technological advancements would not in themselves indicate that a major change in the nature or conduct of a trade has occurred.

The Revenue will compare any two points in three years which include the date of change of ownership of the company. This applies even if the change is the result of a gradual process which began outside the period of three years mentioned in (*a*) above. The Revenue take note of both qualitative and quantitative issues as discussed in the cases *Willis v Peeters Picture Frames Ltd CA (NI) 1982, 56 TC 436* and *Purchase v Tesco Stores Ltd Ch D 1984, 58 TC 46* respectively. (Revenue Pamphlet IR 131, SP 10/91).

Where the operation of the above provisions depends on circumstances or events at a time after the company becomes a member of any group of companies (but not more than three years after), an assessment to give effect to the provisions may be made within six years from that time or the latest such time. [*TCGA 1992, Sch 7A para 8*].

The above provisions are identical *mutatis mutandis* with those in *ICTA 1988, s 768* regarding the disallowance of trading losses on a change in ownership of a company. See TOLLEY'S CORPORATION TAX under Losses for the appropriate case law and Revenue practice applying to that provision which may apply to the above.

13.33 *Identification of the 'relevant group' and application of Sch 7A to every connected group.* The provisions below apply where there is more than one group of companies which would be the relevant group in relation to any company.

Where any loss has accrued on the disposal by any company of any asset, *Sch 7A* does not apply by reference to any group of companies in relation to any loss accruing on that disposal unless

(*a*) that group is a group in relation to which that loss is a pre-entry loss because it is an allowable loss that accrued to that company at a time before it became a member of the group or, if there is more than one such group, the one of which that company most recently became a member;

(*b*) that group, in a case where there is no group falling within (*a*) above, is either

  (i) the group of which that company is a member at the time of the disposal, or

  (ii) if it is not a member of a group of companies at that time, the group of which that company was last a member before that time;

(*c*) that group, in a case where there is a group falling within paragraph (*a*) or, in relation to the deduction of a loss from a chargeable gain where either the gain or the loss accrues after 10 March 1994, paragraph (*b*) above, is a group of which that company was a member at any time in the accounting period of that company in which it became a member of the group falling within that paragraph;

(*d*) that group is a group the principal company (see 13.11 above) of which is or has been, or has been under the control (within *ICTA 1988, s 416*) of

  (i) the company by which the disposal is made, or

  (ii) another company which is or has been a member of a group by reference to which *Sch 7A* applies in relation to the loss in question under (*a*), (*b*) or (*c*) above; or

(*e*) that group is a group of which either

  (i) the principal company of a group by reference to which *Sch 7A* applies, or

  (ii) a company which has had that principal company under its control,

  is or has been a member.

In the case of a loss accruing on the disposal of an asset where, under (*a*)–(*e*) above there are two or more groups ('*connected groups*') by reference to which *Sch 7A* applies, the further provisions in *Sch 7A para 9(3)–(5)* below apply. [*TCGA 1992, Sch 7A para 9(1)(2); FA 1994, s 94(1)(3)(4)*].

Sch 7A is applied separately in relation to each of the connected groups (so far as they are not groups in relation to which the loss is a pre-entry loss because it is a loss that accrued to a company at a time before it became a member of the group) for the purpose of determining whether the loss on the disposal of an asset is a loss on the disposal of a pre-entry asset, and calculating the pre-entry proportion of that loss. [*TCGA 1992, Sch 7A para 9(3)*].

Subject to *Sch 7A para 9(5)* below, the provisions in 13.30 above have effect

(A) as if the pre-entry proportion of any loss accruing on the disposal of an asset which is a pre-entry asset in the case of more than one of the connected groups were the largest pre-entry proportion of that loss as calculated under *Sch 7A para 9(3)* above; and

(B) so that, where the loss accruing on the disposal of an asset is a pre-entry loss because it is an allowable loss that accrued to a company at a time before it became a member of a group in the case of any of the connected groups, that loss is the pre-entry loss for the purposes of 13.30 above, and not any amount which is the pre-entry proportion of that loss in relation to any of the other groups.

[*TCGA 1992, Sch 7A para 9(4)*].

Where, on the separate application of *Sch 7A* in the case of each of the groups by reference to which *Sch 7A* applies, there is, in the case of the disposal of any asset, a pre-entry loss by reference to each of two or more of the connected groups, no amount in respect of the loss accruing on the disposal is to be deductible under the provisions in 13.31 above from any chargeable gain if any of the connected groups is a group in the case of which, on separate applications of those provisions in relation to each group, the amount deductible from that gain in respect of that loss is nil. [*TCGA 1992, Sch 7A para 9(5)*].

Notwithstanding that the principal company of one group ('*the first group*') has become a member of another ('*the second group*'), those two groups are not under *TCGA 1992, s 170(10)* (see 13.11 above) treated for the purposes of the above provisions as the same group if the principal company of the first group was under the control, immediately before it became a member of the second group, of a company which at that time was already a member of the second group. In addition, in relation to accounting periods ending after 16 March 1998, again where the principal company of the first group has become a member of the second group, the two groups are not for those purposes treated, in relation to any company that is (or has become) a member of the second group, as the same group if the time at which that company became a member of the first group falls in the same accounting period as that in which the principal company of the first group became a member of the second group. [*TCGA 1992, Sch 7A para 9(6); FA 1998, s 138*]. For an example, see Revenue Capital Gains Manual CG 47944.

Where, in the case of the disposal of any asset

(*aa*) two or more groups which but for *Sch 7A para 9(6)* above would be treated as the same group are treated as separate groups because of that provision; and

(*bb*) one of those groups is a group of which either

  (i) the principal company of a group by reference to which *Sch 7A* applies by virtue of (*a*), (*b*) or (*c*) above in relation to any loss accruing on the disposal, or

  (ii) a company which has had that principal company under its control,

  is or has been a member,

the above provisions have effect as if that principal company had been a member of each of the groups mentioned in (*aa*) above. [*TCGA 1992, Sch 7A para 9(7)*].

13.34 *Miscellaneous.* Where, but for an election under *TCGA 1992, s 161(3)* (appropriation of asset to trading stock; see 6.3 ASSETS), there would be deemed to have been a disposal at any time by a company of an asset the amount by which the market value of it may be treated as increased under the election does not include the amount of any pre-entry loss that would have accrued on that disposal, and *Sch 7A* has effect as if the pre-entry loss of the last mentioned amount had accrued to the company at that time. [*TCGA 1992, Sch 7A para 10*].

The provisions of *Sch 7A* are prevented from applying where a loss arises, or a company joins a group, as a result of any enactment under which transfers of property etc. are made from a statutory body, a subsidiary of such a body or a company wholly owned by the Crown. [*TCGA 1992, Sch 7A para 11*].

For the purposes of *Sch 7A*, and without prejudice to the provisions in *Sch 7A para 11* above, where

(*a*) a company which is a member of a group of companies becomes at any time a member of another group of companies as the result of a disposal of shares in or other securities of that company or any other company; and

(*b*) that disposal is one of the no gain/no loss disposals mentioned in *TCGA 1992, s 35(3)(d)* (see 8.7 ASSETS HELD ON 31 MARCH 1982),

Sch 7A has effect in relation to the losses that accrued to that company before that time and the assets held by that company at that time as if any time when it was a member of the first group were included in the period during which it is treated as having been a member of the second group. [*TCGA 1992, Sch 7A para 12*].

13.35 Restriction on set-off of losses against pre-entry gains where a company joins a group

General outline and commencement. The provisions of *TCGA 1992, s 177B, Sch 7AA* (added by *FA 1998, s 137, Sch 24*), as described at 13.36–13.39 below, are designed to counter a practice known as 'gain buying'. This involves a group of companies with unrealised capital losses acquiring a company with a realised gain. The assets in question are then transferred to the new group company, and the losses are then realised by that company in the same accounting period as it realised the gain, thus enabling the losses to be utilised against the gain. Under these provisions, the losses that can be set against a gain realised before a company joins a group are restricted to those that arose before it joined the group and those that arise after it joins the group on assets which that company held at the time of its joining the group. This also applies, with the appropriate modifications, where two or more companies leave one group and join another. These restrictions do not extend to the set-off of losses realised in an accounting period later than that in which the company or companies enter the gain-buying group, in view of the fact that losses cannot normally be carried back to preceding accounting periods. There is an exception under *TCGA 1992, s 213* for losses on certain deemed disposals by life assurance companies, for which see TOLLEY'S CORPORATION TAX.

The provisions have effect in relation to accounting periods ending after 16 March 1998 where a company joins a group after that date. [*TCGA 1992, Sch 7AA para 1(3)(b); FA 1998, s 137(1)(2)(5), Sch 24*]. The legislation contains no motive test and thus applies wherever the necessary conditions are satisfied, with the result that innocent transactions are caught.

The change in the residence requirement in 13.11 above is taken into account in determining for the purposes of these provisions whether a company is a member of a group at any time after 20 March 2000. [*FA 2000, Sch 29 para 8*].

Certain provisions, *viz. TCGA 1992, s 213(1)(c)* and *s 214A(2)(b)*, deem gains and losses (on deemed disposals of certain holdings in unit trusts or offshore funds) to have arisen at the end of an accounting period of a life assurance company. For the purposes of the pre-entry gain provisions outlined above, such gains/losses are treated as having accrued *before* any time at which the company concerned joined a group in the accounting period in question (or before the earliest such time). [*TCGA 1992, Sch 7AA para 7*]. See TOLLEY'S CORPORATION TAX for details.

For a worked example on set-off of losses against pre-entry gains, see TOLLEY'S CORPORATION TAX under Capital Gains.

13.36 *The detailed provisions — preamble.* The provisions apply in the case of any company (the '*relevant company*') in relation to any accounting period (the '*gain period*') in which a 'pre-entry gain' has accrued to that company. A '*pre-entry gain*' is a chargeable gain accruing to a company in an accounting period in which it becomes a member of a group of companies after 16 March 1998 and after the gain has accrued to it. When the principal company of a group becomes a member of another group, *TCGA 1992, s 170(10)* (see 13.11 above) does not prevent all the members of the first-mentioned group from being treated for these purposes as having become members of the second-mentioned group. [*TCGA 1992, Sch 7AA para 1*].

The relevant company's total chargeable gains for the gain period are split between pre-entry gains (X) and gains that arose after the company joined the group (Y). To the extent that current year and brought-forward capital losses can be set against X in accordance with the following rules, they cannot additionally be set against Y nor can they be carried forward to a succeeding accounting period. [*TCGA 1992, Sch 7AA para 2*].

Only so much of any allowable capital loss as is a 'qualifying loss' (see 13.37 below) in relation to a pre-entry gain can be set against it (to the extent that it has not been set against another pre-entry gain). If a loss is precluded by the pre-entry losses rules or the connected persons rule at *TCGA 1992, s 18(3)* from being set against a particular gain (see, respectively, 13.31 above and 39.5 LOSSES), those rules override these provisions. [*TCGA 1992, Sch 7AA para 3*]. Losses which are not qualifying losses can be set against post-entry gains of the same accounting period, with any balance being carried forward to subsequent accounting periods, under general principles.

13.37 *Qualifying losses.* The following allowable capital losses are '*qualifying losses*' (for the purposes of 13.36 above) in relation to a pre-entry gain accruing to the relevant company in the gain period (see 13.36 above):

- any loss brought forward from an earlier accounting period.
- any loss accruing in the gain period and accruing before, or at the same time as, the gain accrues.
- any loss accruing in the gain period and accruing after the gain accrues but before the company joined the group;
- any loss accruing in the gain period and accruing after the gain accrues and after the company joined a group of companies but which is a loss on the disposal of an asset which was owned, immediately before the relevant company joined the group, either by the relevant company itself or by another company which joined the group at the same time as the relevant company *and* which immediately before that time had been a member of the same group as the relevant company.

[*TCGA 1992, Sch 7AA para 4*].

As regards the final category above, see 13.38 below for pooled assets and 13.39 below for other cases where an asset is acquired over a period of time or derived from another asset.

13.38 *Pooled assets.* Where a loss-producing disposal is made of (or out of) a pool of shares or securities or similar assets (see 59.3–59.5 SHARES AND SECURITIES—IDENTIFICATION RULES), globally described below as '*securities*', special rules apply to determine to what extent the securities disposed of (or part disposed of) were held at the time the relevant company (or a member of its group) joined the new group (the entry time) (see 13.37 above). The rules apply in respect of any such disposal made in the gain period (see 13.36 above) and at or after the '*relevant entry time*' (being the entry time or, if there is more than one such time in the gain period, the earliest entry time). In practice, the rules need only be applied where the pool has been added to at or after the relevant entry time.

As regards any holding of securities, a 'notional net pre-entry loss' is computed. Actual losses on the disposals referred to above are matched with the notional net pre-entry loss in the order in which the actual losses accrued. The actual aggregate loss is regarded as a loss on disposal of securities held at the entry time to the extent that there is (or, in the case of a second or subsequent entry time, that there remains) an amount with which it can be so matched.

The notional net pre-entry loss is computed as follows. *For these purposes only* (actual losses still being computed under normal pooling rules), securities acquired at or after the relevant entry time ('*post-entry securities*') are not added to the pool existing immediately before the relevant entry time, which thus continues to consist only of securities acquired (and not disposed of) before that time ('*pre-entry securities*'). Disposals within these provisions (see above) are matched with the pool of pre-entry securities in preference to post-entry securities. Gains and losses on those disposals matched with pre-entry securities are computed and aggregated. If the net result of that aggregation is a loss, the amount of that loss is the notional net pre-entry loss. If the net result is a gain, there is no notional net pre-entry loss. See example at Revenue Capital Gains Manual CG 48214.

For the purposes of determining whether securities are pre-entry or post-entry securities, the rules of *TCGA 1992, s 127* applying on a reorganisation of share capital, i.e. the equation of a 'new holding' with the securities originally held (see 58.5 SHARES AND SECURITIES) are to be disregarded in as much as they would treat the 'new holding' as having been acquired at the same time as the original holding. So, for example, securities acquired by means of a bonus or rights issue must be taken as having been acquired at the time they were, in reality, acquired.

There are provisions to ensure that securities held by the relevant company or by any 'associated company' at the relevant entry time are taken to be pre-entry securities if, since the relevant entry time but prior to the disposal in question, they have been disposed of by way of intra-group disposal. For this purpose, an '*associated company*' is one which was a member of the same group as the relevant company immediately before the relevant entry time and which joined the new group, along with the relevant company, at that time.

[*TCGA 1992, Sch 7AA para 5*].

13.39 *Rules for an asset acquired over a period of time or derived from another asset.* An apportionment is necessary if an asset within either of the two categories below (other than a pooled asset as in 13.38 above) is disposed of (or part disposed of) by the relevant company (at a loss) in the gain period (see 13.36 above) and at or after the time that the relevant company (or a member of its group) joined the new group (the entry time) (see 13.37 above). These rules apply (by reference to any entry time) to

- an asset which is treated as a single asset but comprises assets only some of which were held at the entry time by the relevant company or an associated company; or
- an asset which is treated as held at the entry time by the relevant company or an associated company by virtue of any provision which treats an asset not held at that time as one which was so held.

An example of an asset within these rules is a leasehold interest in property held by a company which subsequently acquires the freehold. The proportion of the allowable loss treated as relating to a pre-entry asset and thus a qualifying loss (see 13.37 above) is made up of

(*a*) the proportion of the loss which, on a just and reasonable apportionment, is properly attributable to assets in fact held at the entry time; and

(*b*) such proportion of the loss not within (*a*) above as represents the loss that would have accrued if the asset disposed of had been the asset in fact held at that time.

For the above purposes, an '*associated company*' is one which was a member of the same group as the relevant company immediately before the entry time and which joined the new group, along with the relevant company, at that time.
[*TCGA 1992, Sch 7AA para 6*].

13.40 SHARES—ACQUISITIONS AND DISPOSALS WITHIN SHORT PERIOD

The ordinary rules for matching disposals with 'acquisitions' are modified for disposals by a company of shares (including securities, as defined in 58.11 SHARES AND SECURITIES) if

(*a*) the company acquired shares of the same class within one month before or after the disposal where the disposal was through a stock exchange, or otherwise within six months before or after the disposal, and

(*b*) the number of that class of shares held by the company during the said prescribed period before the disposal was not less than 2% of the number issued.

Shares acquired within (*a*) above are called '*available shares*'.

Where the company making the disposal (Company X) is a member of a group and the prescribed period as above begins on or after 1 April 2000, the following apply.

(A) Where shares of the same class are held by another group member and at any time in the prescribed period before the disposal

   (i) the other group member is UK-resident, or

   (ii) the shares are 'chargeable shares' in relation to that other group member,

   those shares are treated for the purposes of (*b*) above as held by Company X.

(B) Where shares of the same class are acquired by another group member, and either (A)(i) or (A)(ii) applies at the time of acquisition, those shares are treated for the purposes of (*a*) above as acquired by Company X.

(C) Where shares of the same class are acquired by Company X from a company which was a member of the group throughout the prescribed period before and after the disposal, and either (A)(i) or (A)(ii) applies throughout that part of the said period during which the other group member held the shares, those shares are disregarded for the purposes of (*a*) above.

Shares are '*chargeable shares*' in relation to a company at a particular time if, on a disposal by that company at that time, any gain would be a chargeable gain and would be within the charge to corporation tax by virtue of *TCGA 1992, s 10* (non-UK resident company trading in the UK through a branch or agency — see 44.3 OVERSEAS MATTERS). The question whether a company is a member of a group is determined as in 13.11 COMPANIES, taking into account the change in the residence requirement.

Where the company making the disposal is a member of a group and the prescribed period as above begins before 1 April 2000, similar provisions apply but taking into account the fact that under 13.11 above, as it applies before the change in the residence requirement, a group is restricted to UK-resident companies.

Disposals are matched with available shares before other shares and with available shares acquired by the disposing company before those acquired by a fellow group member, and then with acquisitions before the disposal (latest ones first) rather than after (when earlier ones are taken first). Where disposals are identified with acquisitions of another group member, the cost to that member will be allowed to the disposing company plus the usual incidental costs of disposal. Shares identified with one disposal are precluded from further identification with a later disposal.

'*Acquisitions*' do not include shares acquired as trading stock or acquired from another group member.

For disposals after 31 March 1985, the above identification rules have priority over those in 59 SHARES AND SECURITIES—IDENTIFICATION RULES generally, but not where shares acquired and disposed of on the same day are matched under *TCGA 1992, s 105(1)* (see 59.3 SHARES AND SECURITIES—IDENTIFICATION RULES). For disposals after 31 March 1982 and before 1 April 1985 the above rules had priority over the then identification rules pertaining to the indexation provisions. For disposals before 1 April 1982 the above rules were subject to *TCGA 1992, s 105(1)* solely.

[*TCGA 1992, s 106; FA 2000, Sch 29 para 18*].

13.41 CLOSE COMPANY TRANSFERRING ASSET AT UNDERVALUE

See 3.15 ANTI-AVOIDANCE where a close company transfers an asset otherwise than at arm's length for a consideration less than market value.

13.42 DEMERGERS

The provisions of *ICTA 1988, ss 213–218* have effect for facilitating certain transactions whereby trading activities carried on by a single company or 'group' are divided so as to be carried on by two or more companies not belonging to the same group or by two or more independent groups. '*Group*' means a company and all of its 75 per cent subsidiaries (with the effect of direct and indirect ownership of shares held as trading stock being ignored in deciding whether one company is a 75 per cent subsidiary of another).

An exempt distribution (as in *ICTA 1988, s 213(2)*) within *ICTA 1988, s 213(3)(a)* (transfer by company of shares in one or more 75 per cent subsidiaries) is not a capital distribution within *TCGA 1992, s 122* (see 58.14 SHARES AND SECURITIES). *TCGA 1992, ss 126–130* (see generally 58.5 SHARES AND SECURITIES) are applied as if that company and the subsidiary whose shares are transferred were the same company and the distribution were a reorganisation of share capital.

A charge under *TCGA 1992, s 179* (see 13.19 above) on a company ceasing to be a member of a group does not apply where the cessation is by reason only of an exempt distribution. However, this exemption does not apply if there is a chargeable payment (within *ICTA 1988, s 214(2)*: payment not made for *bona fide* reasons or made for tax avoidance purposes) within five years of the exempt distribution, and will result in the *TCGA 1992, s 179* charge being able to be the subject of an assessment made within three years of the chargeable payment.

[*TCGA 1992, s 192; FA 2000, Sch 29 para 29, Sch 40 Pt II(12)*].

For full details of the provisions see TOLLEY'S CORPORATION TAX under Groups of Companies. For the treatment of distributions arising from demergers in the hands of trustees, see Revenue Capital Gains Manual CG 33900–33936.

13.43 **USE OF NON-STERLING CURRENCIES**

Under provisions effective for company accounting periods beginning on or after 23 March 1995, a company which carried on a trade and which prepares its accounts or other financial statements in a currency other than sterling could elect, subject to conditions, for the 'basic profits or losses' (as defined) of the trade to be computed and expressed for corporation tax purposes in that currency. The sterling equivalent of the basic profits or losses, for inclusion in the company's overall corporation tax computation, was calculated by reference to an average arm's length exchange rate for the accounting period concerned, if the company so elected, or otherwise by reference to the London closing exchange rate for the last day of the accounting period. [*FA 1993, ss 92–95, 165(7)(b); SI 1994 Nos 3224, 3230; SI 1998 No 3177, Pt X*]. With effect for accounting periods beginning after 31 December 1999 and ending after 20 March 2000, and subsequent accounting periods, these are replaced by provisions under which all companies automatically follow the currency of the company accounts (or branch accounts/financial statements) in calculating taxable business profits (not just trading profits). Where the company accounts are prepared in a currency other than sterling, it is a condition that this be in accordance with normal accounting practice. There are detailed rules covering translation into sterling for corporation tax purposes. In certain circumstances, companies were allowed a limited period in which they could elect that the new provisions be deferred until their first accounting period beginning after 30 June 2000. [*FA 1993, ss 92–94; FA 2000, s 105*].

Despite the extension of the provisions to non-trading profits generally, **chargeable gains and allowable capital losses are specifically excluded**. [*FA 1993, s 93(5); FA 2000, s 105*]. These should continue to be translated into sterling using the rules at 17.3(*a*) DISPOSAL, subject to the exception there noted.

13.44 **EXCHANGE GAINS AND LOSSES**

The main elements of the provisions in *FA 1993, ss 60, 125–170, Schs 15–18* (as amended), which are described in detail in TOLLEY'S CORPORATION TAX under Exchange Gains and Losses (wherein the terms referred to in the following are defined), are as below.

(*a*) The provisions apply, subject to transitional rules, to 'qualifying companies' (broadly all companies excepting authorised unit trusts, investment trusts and open-ended investment companies) becoming entitled to 'qualifying assets', subject to 'qualifying liabilities', or entitled or subject to 'currency contracts', for accounting periods beginning after 22 March 1995.

(*b*) Exchange gains and losses in respect of qualifying assets and liabilities and currency contracts are recognised as they accrue between set 'translation times'.

(*c*) Trading exchange gains and losses are treated as trading items within Schedule D, Case I, net non-trading exchange gains are assessed under Schedule D, Case VI, and there are special provisions for the relief of net non-trading exchange losses.

(*d*) Certain unrealised exchange gains on long-term capital items may be deferred.

(*e*) Exchange differences are generally calculated in sterling, subject to 13.43 above.

(*f*) A company can elect for 'matching' of exchange differences on borrowings with exchange differences on certain non-qualifying assets (see *SI 1994 No 3227*).

Matched exchange differences are left out of account until the matched asset is disposed of (other than by way of no gain/no loss disposal) and are then treated as chargeable gains or allowable capital losses. See TOLLEY'S CORPORATION TAX for details.

(*g*) The charge to corporation tax in respect of chargeable gains does not apply to qualifying assets (subject to transitional provisions).

(*h*) Anti-avoidance rules operate to prevent abuse of the provisions.

There are a number of exclusions from the operation of the provisions, and special rules in relation to insurance companies and cases where assets or contracts are held, or liabilities owed, in '*exempt circumstances*' (broadly, for the purposes of long term insurance business; for the purposes of mutual insurance business; for the purposes of the occupation for profit of commercial woodlands in the UK; by an approved housing association; or by an approved self-build society).

The principal provisions consequential to (*g*) above are mentioned at 13.7 and 13.12 above; 21.5 and 21.8 EXEMPTIONS AND RELIEFS; 44.3 OVERSEAS MATTERS and 49.2 QUALIFYING CORPORATE BONDS.

See also Tolley's Taxation of Foreign Exchange Gains and Losses.

13.45 FINANCIAL INSTRUMENTS INVOLVING INTEREST RATE AND CURRENCY CONTRACTS

The corporation tax provisions in *FA 1994, Pt IV Ch II* (i.e. *ss 147–177, Sch 18*) relating to the treatment of financial instruments to manage interest rate and currency risk are given in TOLLEY'S CORPORATION TAX under Financial Instruments (wherein the following quoted terms are defined). For the purposes of those provisions, an 'interest rate contract' or 'interest rate option', or a 'currency contract' or 'currency option', is a 'qualifying contract' as regards a 'qualifying company' if the company becomes entitled to rights or subject to duties under the contract or option on or after its 'commencement day', i.e. the first day of its first accounting period beginning after 22 March 1995 (subject to transitional provisions).

Any amount which under or by virtue of the above provisions is chargeable to corporation tax as profits of a qualifying company, or which falls to be taken into account as a receipt in computing for the purposes of those provisions (which are deemed to include certain provisions in 13.44 above dealing with non-trading exchange gains) the profits or losses of such a company, is excluded for the purposes of *TCGA 1992* from the consideration for a disposal of assets taken into account in the computation of the gain. Similarly, any amount (irrespective of whether effect is or would be given to the deduction of it in computing the amount of tax chargeable or by discharge or repayment of tax or in any other way), which is allowable as a deduction in computing for the above purposes (as similarly extended) the profits or losses of a qualifying company, or which under or by virtue of the above provisions is allowable as a deduction in computing any other income or profits or gains or losses of such a company for the purposes of the *Tax Acts*, or which, although not so allowable as a deduction in computing any losses, would be so allowable as a deduction but for an insufficiency of income or profits or gains, is excluded from the sums allowable under *TCGA 1992, s 38* (allowable expenditure on disposal) as a deduction in the computation of the gain. [*FA 1994, s 173*].

Finance Act 1996 extended the *Finance Act 1994* rules [*FA 1994, ss 147–177, Sch 18*], with effect for accounting periods ending after 31 March 1996 but subject to transitional provisions, to debt contracts or options.

A debt contract is a contract which may or may not be subject to conditions whereby a qualifying company has an entitlement or requirement to become a party to a loan relationship, details of which will be contained in the contract.

Payments allowed under the contract apart from those under the loan relationship are:

(*a*) a payment of an amount representing the price for becoming a party to the relationship,

(*b*) a payment of an amount determined by reference to the value at any time of the money debt by which the relationship subsists,

(*c*) a settlement payment of an amount determined by reference at specified times to the difference between—

  (i) the price for becoming a party to the relationship, and

  (ii) the value of the money debt by reference to which the relationship subsists or (if the relationship were in existence) would subsist.

[*FA 1994, s 150A(1)–(6); FA 1996, Sch 12*].

In addition payments under *FA 1994, s 151* are also allowed. These will include payments for entering into a contract or option, arrangement fees, variation or termination fees and compensation fees on non-compliance.

If the contract is a hybrid of debt contract and non-debt contract provisions, the clauses relating to the debt contract shall be treated as a separate contract.

[*FA 1994, s 150A(7)(8); FA 1996, Sch 12*].

A debt contract is not a loan relationship if it is convertible or its value is linked to the value of chargeable assets.

[*FA 1994, s 150A(10); FA 1996, Sch 12*].

See also Tolley's Taxation of Corporate Debt and Financial Instruments.

14 Connected Persons

[*ICTA 1988, s 839; TCGA 1992, s 286; FA 1995, Sch 17 paras 20, 31*]

Cross-references. See 3.13, 3.14 ANTI-AVOIDANCE for certain disposals between connected persons; 39.5 LOSSES for losses on disposals to connected persons; 45.10 PARTNERSHIPS for transactions between partners; and 57.6 SETTLEMENTS for settlors and trustees being connected persons.

14.1 An **individual** is connected with his spouse, any 'relative' (see 14.7 below) of himself or of his spouse, and with the spouse of any such relative. It appears that a widow or widower is no longer a spouse (*Vestey's Exors and Vestey v CIR HL 1949, 31 TC 1*). Spouses divorced by decree nisi remain connected persons until the divorce is made absolute (*Aspden v Hildesley Ch D 1981, 55 TC 609*).

14.2 A **trustee of a 'settlement'**, in his capacity as such, is connected with

(*a*) the 'settlor' (if an individual) (see 14.7 below),

(*b*) any person connected with the settlor, and

(*c*) a 'body corporate connected with the settlement' (see 14.7 below).

The Revenue has confirmed (*a*) above applies as regards the time when a settlement is created and property first transferred to it. On the death of the settlor, neither (*a*) nor (*b*) apply (Revenue Tax Bulletin February 1993 p 56).

14.3 **Partners** are connected with each other and with each other's spouses (see 14.1 above) and relatives (see 14.7 below), except in connection with acquisitions and disposals of partnership assets made pursuant to *bona fide* commercial arrangements. See also 14.5 below.

14.4 **A company is connected with another company** if

(*a*) the same person 'controls' both (see 14.7 below), or

(*b*) one is controlled by a person who has control of the other in conjunction with persons connected with him, or

(*c*) a person controls one company and persons connected with him control the other, or

(*d*) the same group of persons controls both, or

(*e*) the companies are controlled by separate groups which can be regarded as the same by interchanging connected persons.

14.5 **A company is connected with another person who** (either alone or with persons connected with him) **has control of it**. It is understood that the Revenue will accept that a partnership and a company under common control are connected for some purposes (see Tolley's Practical Tax 1981 p 142).

14.6 **Persons acting together to secure or exercise control of a company** are treated in relation to that company as connected with each other and with any other person acting on the direction of any of them to secure or exercise such control (see *Steele v EVC International NV CA 1996, 69 TC 88*). Control may be 'exercised' passively. See *Floor v Davis HL 1979, 52 TC 609*. See 3.20 ANTI-AVOIDANCE for an extension of this provision in connection with dividend stripping.

14.7 '*Company*' includes any body corporate, unincorporated association or unit trust scheme but does not include a partnership.

'*Control*' is as defined in *ICTA 1988, s 416*. [*TCGA 1992, s 288(1)*]. See TOLLEY'S CORPORATION TAX under Close Companies.

'*Relative*' means brother, sister, ancestor or lineal descendant. [*TCGA 1992, s 286(8)*].

'*Settlement*' includes any disposition, trust, covenant, agreement, arrangement or transfer of assets. [*ICTA 1988, s 660G(1); FA 1995, Sch 17 para 1*]. It must contain an element of bounty. It does not include a transfer of assets for full consideration (*CIR v Plummer HL 1979, 54 TC 1*).

'*A body corporate connected with the settlement*' is a close company (or one which would be so if resident in the UK) the participators in which include the trustees of the settlement, or a company controlled by such a close company. Control for these purposes is as under *ICTA 1988, s 840*: namely, the power of a person by shareholding or voting power (whether directly or through another company), or under Articles of Association, to secure that the company's affairs are conducted according to his wishes. Prior to 27 July 1981 it was defined as a close company (or one which would be so if resident in the UK), the participators in which include the trustees of, or a beneficiary under, the settlement. [*ICTA 1988, s 682A; FA 1995, Sch 17 para 11*].

'*Settlor*' is any person by whom the settlement was made or who has directly or indirectly (or by a reciprocal arrangement) provided, or undertaken to provide, funds for the purpose of the settlement. [*ICTA 1988, s 660G(1)(2); FA 1995, Sch 17 para 1*]. See *Countess Fitzwilliam and others v CIR (and related appeals) HL 1993, 67 TC 614*.

15 Corporate Venturing Scheme

15.1 **INTRODUCTION**

For shares issued on or after 1 April 2000 but before 1 April 2010, a scheme is introduced whereby most trading companies are able to obtain corporation tax relief at 20% ('*investment relief*') on corporate venturing investments, i.e. acquisitions (by cash subscription) of minority shareholdings in 'small higher risk' trading companies. In addition, investing companies are able to postpone chargeable gains ('*deferral relief*') on disposals of corporate venturing investments where they reinvest in other shares attracting investment relief. Also, an allowable capital loss on the disposal of a corporate venturing investment, computed net of investment relief, can be relieved against *income* of the accounting period in which the loss arises and accounting periods ending in the previous 12 months (but may alternatively be relieved against chargeable gains in the normal way). [*FA 2000, s 63(1)(4), Sch 15 para 1*].

Investee companies are limited to those with gross assets not exceeding £15 million immediately before the investment and £16 million immediately afterwards. Such companies must exist for the purpose of carrying on trading activities other than the kind of 'lower risk' activity excluded under the ENTERPRISE INVESTMENT SCHEME (20) or the provisions for VENTURE CAPITAL TRUSTS (65). Potential investee companies may request advance clearance from the Revenue. The maximum investment qualifying for relief is 30% of the issued ordinary share capital of the investee company, and no minimum investment is stipulated. It is a further condition that at least 20% of the ordinary share capital of the investee company be held by individuals (other than directors and employees of the investing company). To qualify for the relief, the investing company must retain the shares acquired for at least three years. Investing companies carrying on financial trades (e.g. banking, share dealing etc.) are not eligible.

The remainder of this chapter is set out under the following headings.

15.2 **INVESTMENT RELIEF**

Eligibility. An investing company is eligible for investment relief (see 15.3 below) in respect of an amount subscribed by it for shares in an investee company (the '*issuing company*') if

(*a*) the shares (the '*relevant shares*') are issued to the investing company;

(*b*) the investing company is a 'qualifying investing company' (see 15.5 below);

(*c*) the issuing company is a 'qualifying issuing company' (see 15.6 below) in relation to the relevant shares; and

(*d*) the general requirements at 15.8 below are met.

For advance clearance as regards (*c*) and (*d*) above, see 15.9 below.

Qualification period. In these provisions, the '*qualification period*' is normally the three-year period beginning with the date of issue of the relevant shares. If, however, the money raised by the issue is employed wholly or mainly for the purposes of a qualifying trade (or trades) (see 15.7 below) which, on the date of issue, was not being carried on by the issuing company or a qualifying subsidiary (see 15.6 below), the qualification period begins on the date of issue and ends immediately before the third anniversary of the date of commencement of the trade (or the latest such date where there is more than one such trade). [*FA 2000, Sch 15 paras 2, 3*].

15.3 **Form of relief.** Where an investing company is eligible for investment relief (see 15.2 above) in respect of amounts subscribed by it for shares, its corporation tax liability for the accounting period in which the shares are issued is reduced, on a claim (see 15.4 below), by the lesser of

- **20%** of the amount (or aggregate amount) subscribed, and
- the amount which reduces the liability to nil.

[*FA 2000, Sch 15 para 39*].

Investment relief is said to be 'attributable to shares' if relief as above has been obtained in respect of those shares and has not been withdrawn (as opposed to reduced) — see 15.10 below. Where for any one accounting period relief has been obtained by reason of more than one issue of shares, the relief is attributed to those issues in proportion to the amounts subscribed. Relief attributable to any one issue of shares is attributed *pro rata* to each share in that issue, and any reduction of relief (see 15.10 below) is similarly apportioned between the shares in question. For these purposes, any bonus shares, issued in respect of the original shares and being shares in the same company, of the same class and carrying the same rights, are treated as if comprised in the original issue, and relief is apportioned to them accordingly. This applies only if the original shares have been held continuously since issue (as in 15.20(*a*) below), and, where it does apply, the bonus shares are themselves treated as having been held continuously since the time of the original issue. [*FA 2000, Sch 15 para 45*].

15.4 **Claims for relief.** No deadline is specified for making a claim, so the general six-year time limit applies as in 12.5 CLAIMS. A claim for relief cannot be made in respect of any investment until the 'funded trade' has been carried on by the issuing company or a subsidiary for at least four months (disregarding time spent *preparing* to carry on the trade) and the investing company has received from the issuing company a 'compliance certificate' (see below). No postponement of tax pending appeal (see 46.3 PAYMENT OF TAX) can be made on the grounds of eligibility for investment relief until a claim for that relief can be and has been made. The '*funded trade*' is the trade or trades by reference to which the requirement at 15.8 below as to 'use of money raised' is met (or, where applicable, the notional trade of research and development therein mentioned). A claim *can* be made if the funded trade ceases within less than four months by reason of the winding-up or dissolution of the company or subsidiary concerned or its going into administration or receivership (both as defined), provided that this is for commercial reasons and not part of tax avoidance arrangements.

A '*compliance certificate*' is a certificate issued, with the authority of the Revenue and in such form as they may direct, by the issuing company in respect of the relevant shares and confirming that, from the issuing company's point of view, the requirements for investment relief are for the time being met in relation to the shares. To obtain authority for the issue of a certificate, the issuing company must provide the Revenue with a 'compliance statement' in respect of the issue of shares which includes the relevant shares. Where notice of an event giving rise to withdrawal etc. is given to the Revenue by or in relation to the issuing company (see 15.10 below), any authority already given is invalid unless renewed.

A '*compliance statement*' is a statement, in respect of an issue of shares, to the effect that, from the issuing company's point of view, the requirements for investment relief are for the time being met in relation to the shares and have been met at all times since the shares were issued. The statement must be in required form and must contain any additional information as the Revenue reasonably require, a declaration that it is correct to the best of the company's knowledge and belief, and such other declarations as the Revenue reasonably require. A compliance statement cannot be made until such time as the funded trade has been carried on for at least four months (or such shorter time as is specified above). It *must* be made within two years after the end of the accounting period in which the shares were issued or, if later, two years after the minimum period of trading condition is satisfied.

The issuing company may give notice of appeal, within 30 days, against a Revenue refusal to authorise a compliance certificate (as if that refusal were the disallowance of a claim other than for discharge or repayment of tax — see 12.3 CLAIMS).

The issuing company is liable to a penalty of up to £3,000 for issuing a compliance certificate which is made fraudulently or negligently or without Revenue authority, or for making a compliance statement fraudulently or negligently.

[*FA 2000, Sch 15 paras 40–44, 102(4)*].

15.5 QUALIFYING INVESTING COMPANY

The investing company is a '*qualifying investing company*' (see 15.2(*b*) above) in relation to the relevant shares if it meets all the requirements below as to absence of material interest, reciprocal arrangements, control and tax avoidance, the nature of its activities, and the relevant shares being a chargeable asset. [*FA 2000, Sch 15 para 4*].

'No material interest' requirement. At no time in the qualification period (see 15.2 above) must the investing company have a material interest in the issuing company. For this purpose, a person has a material interest in a company if he (alone or together with any person connected with him — within *ICTA 1988, s 839* — see 14 CONNECTED PERSONS) directly or indirectly possesses, or is entitled (or will in future be entitled) to acquire (at present or at a future date), more than **30%** of

- the 'ordinary share capital' of, or
- the voting power in,

the company or any 51% subsidiary. In applying the test, there must be attributed to a person any rights or powers of any associate of his (as defined by *FA 2000, Sch 15 para 99*). For these purposes, a company's '*ordinary share capital*' comprises

(*a*) all of its issued share capital other than 'relevant preference shares', and

(*b*) all of its loan capital (as widely defined but excluding a bank overdraft or an ordinary business debt) that carries a right to convert into, or to acquire, shares which would fall within (*a*) above.

'*Relevant preference shares*' are, broadly, non-voting, non-convertible shares issued for new consideration and carrying no right to dividends other than dividends which

- are of a fixed amount or at a rate which is fixed or which varies according to a standard published interest rate, a tax rate, a retail price index or an official share price index, and
- which are not dependent on the company's business results or asset values and do not represent more than a reasonable commercial return on the investment.

[*FA 2000, Sch 15 paras 5, 7, 9, 102(3)*].

'No reciprocal arrangements' requirement. The investing company's subscription for the relevant shares must not be part of any arrangements which provide for any other person to subscribe for shares in a 'related company'. A '*related company*' is a company in which the investing company, or any other person who is party to the arrangements, has a material interest (as defined immediately above). Arrangements are disregarded to the extent that they provide for the issuing company to subscribe for shares in any qualifying subsidiary (see 15.6 below). [*FA 2000, Sch 15 para 6*].

'No control' requirement. At no time in the qualification period must the investing company 'control' the issuing company. '*Control*' is determined in accordance with *ICTA 1988, s 416(2)–(6)* as modified for this purpose. [*FA 2000, Sch 15 para 8*].

'No tax avoidance' requirement. The relevant shares must be subscribed for by the investing company for commercial reasons and not as part of a tax avoidance scheme or arrangement. [*FA 2000, Sch 15 para 14*].

Non-financial activities requirement. Throughout the qualification period, the investing company,

- if a single company (i.e. a company which is not a parent company or a 51% subsidiary), must exist wholly for the purpose of carrying on one or more 'non-financial trades'; and,
- if a group company, must be part of a 'non-financial trading group' and must either exist wholly for the purpose of carrying on one or more 'non-financial trades' or businesses other than trades or be the parent company of the group.

In determining the purpose for which a company exists, purposes having no significant effect (other than in relation to incidental matters) on the extent of the company's activities are disregarded. Purposes for which a company exists are also disregarded to the extent that they consist of

- (as regards a single company) the holding and managing of property used by the company for one or more 'non-financial trades' carried on by it;
- (as regards a group company) any activities within (*a*) or (*b*) below; or
- (as regards any company) holding shares to which investment relief is attributable (see 15.3 above) unless the holding of such shares is a substantial part of the company's business.

A trade is a '*non-financial trade*' if

- it is conducted on a commercial basis and with a view to profit, and
- it does not consist, wholly or as to a substantial part, in the carrying on of 'financial activities'.

'*Financial activities*' include for this purpose

- banking, or money-lending, carried on by a bank, building society or other person;
- debt factoring, finance-leasing or hire-purchase financing;
- insurance;
- dealing in shares, securities, currency, debts or other assets of a financial nature; and
- dealing in commodity or financial futures or options.

A group is a '*non-financial trading group*' unless the business of the group (treating the activities of the group companies, taken together, as a single business) consists, wholly or as to a substantial part, in the carrying on of trades other than non-financial trades (as above) and/or businesses other than trades. Activities of a group company are disregarded to the extent that they consist of

(*a*) holding shares in or securities of, or making loans to, another group company;

(*b*) holding and managing property used by a group company for the purposes of one or more non-financial trades carried on by a group company; or

(*c*) holding shares to which investment relief is attributable (see 15.3 above), unless the holding of such shares is a substantial part of the company's business.

Amendments to the non-financial activities requirement may be made in the future by Treasury Order.

[*FA 2000, Sch 15 paras 10–12, 101, 102(1)*].

Requirement as to shares being a chargeable asset. The relevant shares must be a chargeable asset of the investing company immediately after they are issued to it. For this purpose, an asset is a chargeable asset at a particular time if, on a disposal at that time, a gain would be a chargeable gain. [*FA 2000, Sch 15 para 13*].

15.6 QUALIFYING ISSUING COMPANY

The issuing company is a '*qualifying issuing company*' (see 15.2(*c*) above) in relation to the relevant shares if it meets all the requirements below as to unquoted status, independence, individual-owners, partnerships and joint ventures, qualifying subsidiaries, gross assets, and trading activities. [*FA 2000, Sch 15 para 15*].

Unquoted status requirement. At the time of issue of the relevant shares, none of the issuing company's shares, debentures or other securities must be listed on a recognised stock exchange (see 58.5 SHARES AND SECURITIES) or a 'designated' exchange outside the UK or be dealt in outside the UK by 'designated' means, and there must be no arrangements in existence for such a listing or such dealing. This applies whether or not the company is UK-resident. '*Designated*' means designated by order of the Board for the purposes of *ICTA 1988, s 312(1B)* (enterprise investment scheme). The company does not fail to meet the requirement simply because a designation order is made, or a stock exchange obtains recognition, after the time of issue of the shares.

If, at the time of issue of the relevant shares, arrangements are in existence for the issuing company to become a wholly-owned subsidiary of a new holding company by means of a share exchange within 15.24 below, there must be no arrangements made for any of the new company's shares, debentures or other securities to be listed or dealt in as above.

[*FA 2000, Sch 15 para 16*].

Independence requirement. At no time in the qualification period (see 15.2 above) must the issuing company be a 51% subsidiary of another company or otherwise under the control (within *ICTA 1988, s 840*) of another company or of another company and persons connected with it (within *ICTA 1988, s 839* — see 14 CONNECTED PERSONS). No arrangements must exist at any time during that period whereby the company could become such a subsidiary or fall under such control (whether during that period or otherwise). Arrangements with a view to a company reconstruction within 15.24 below are disregarded for this purpose. [*FA 2000, Sch 15 paras 17, 102(3)*].

Individual-owners requirement. Throughout the qualification period, at least **20%** of the issued ordinary share capital of the issuing company must be beneficially owned by one or more 'independent individuals'. An '*independent individual*' is one who is not, at any time during the qualification period when he holds ordinary shares in the issuing company, a director or employee of the investing company or of any company connected with it (within

ICTA 1988, s 839 — see 14 CONNECTED PERSONS), or a relative (i.e. husband, wife, forebear or issue) of such a director or employee. Where an independent individual owned shares immediately prior to his death, they are treated for these purposes as continuing to be owned by an independent individual until they cease to form part of the deceased's estate. [*FA 2000, Sch 15 paras 18, 102(3)*].

Partnerships and joint ventures requirement. At no time in the qualification period must the issuing company or any qualifying subsidiary (see below) be a member of a partnership or a party to a joint venture where

- a trade by reference to which the trading activities requirement (see below) is met by the issuing company is being carried on, or is to be carried on, by the partners in partnership or, as the case may be, by the company or a qualifying subsidiary (see below) as a party to the joint venture;
- the other partners or parties to the joint venture include at least one other company; and
- the same person(s) is/are the beneficial owner(s) of more than 75% of the issued share capital or the ordinary share capital of both the issuing company and at least one of the other partners/parties.

For these purposes, there must be attributed to any person any share capital held by an associate of his (within *FA 2000, Sch 15 para 99*).

[*FA 2000, Sch 15 para 19*].

Qualifying subsidiaries requirement. At no time in the qualification period must the issuing company have a 'subsidiary' other than a 'qualifying subsidiary'. For this purpose, a '*subsidiary*' of a company is any company which it controls (within *ICTA 1988, s 416(2)–(6)*), with or without the aid of CONNECTED PERSONS (14). A subsidiary is a '*qualifying subsidiary*' of another company (the '*relevant company*') if the following conditions are met.

(*a*) The relevant company, or another of its subsidiaries, possesses at least 75% of the issued share capital of, and the voting power in, the subsidiary, and is beneficially entitled to at least 75% of the assets available for distribution to shareholders on a winding-up etc. and of the profits available for distribution to shareholders;

(*b*) No other person has control (within *ICTA 1988, s 840*) of the subsidiary; and

(*c*) No arrangements exist whereby (*a*) or (*b*) could cease to be satisfied (though see also below).

The fact that a subsidiary or another company is wound up or otherwise dissolved or goes into administration or receivership (both as defined) does not mean the subsidiary ceases to be a qualifying subsidiary, provided that the winding-up etc., and anything done as a consequence of administration or receivership, is for genuine commercial reasons and not part of a tax avoidance scheme or arrangements. Similarly, the fact that arrangements may exist to dispose of the entire interest held in the subsidiary does not prevent the subsidiary from being a qualifying subsidiary if the disposal is to be for commercial reasons and not part of a tax avoidance scheme or arrangements.

[*FA 2000, Sch 15 paras 20, 21, 102(3)(4)*].

Gross assets requirement. The value of the company's gross assets must not exceed £15 million immediately before the issue of the relevant shares or £16 million immediately afterwards. If the company is the parent company of a group, those limits apply by reference to the aggregate value of the gross assets of the group (disregarding certain assets held by any member of the group which correspond to liabilities of another member). The limits may be amended in the future by Treasury Order. [*FA 2000, Sch 15 paras 22, 101*].

See Revenue Pamphlet IR 131, SP 5/98 (referred to at 20.5 ENTERPRISE INVESTMENT SCHEME (AND BES)) for the Revenue's approach to the gross assets requirement (in relation, at present, to other legislation but expected to be extended to the corporate venturing scheme).

Trading activities requirement. Throughout the qualification period, the issuing company must meet the trading activities requirement, which is as follows. If the company is a single company (i.e. neither the parent company of a group nor a subsidiary), it must exist wholly for the purpose of carrying on one or more qualifying trades (see 15.7 below) and must actually be carrying on such a trade or preparing to do so. Purposes having no significant effect (other than in relation to incidental matters) on the extent of the company's activities are disregarded.

If the company is a parent company, the business of the group (treating the activities of the group companies, taken together, as a single business) must not consist wholly or as to a substantial part in any 'non-qualifying activities', and at least one company in the group must satisfy the above trading activity requirement for a single company. '*Non-qualifying activities*' means 'excluded activities' (as in 15.7 below, and with similar exceptions in relation to the letting of ships and the receiving of royalties or licence fees) and non-trading activities.

Where the trading activities requirement would otherwise be met by reason of the issuing company or a subsidiary *preparing* to carry on a qualifying trade, the requirement is treated as not having been met at any time if that trade does not commence within two years after the issue of the relevant shares.

Purposes for which a company exists are disregarded to the extent that they consist of

- (as regards a single company) the holding and managing of property used by the company for one or more qualifying trades carried on by it;
- (as regards a group company) any activities within (*a*), (*b*) or (*d*) below; or
- (as regards any company) holding shares to which investment relief is attributable (see 15.3 above), unless the holding of such shares is a substantial part of the company's business.

For the purposes of determining the business of a group, activities of a group company are disregarded to the extent that they consist of

(*a*) holding shares in or securities of, or making loans to, another group company;

(*b*) holding and managing property used by a group company for the purposes of one or more qualifying trades carried on by a group company;

(*c*) holding shares to which investment relief is attributable (see 15.3 above), unless the holding of such shares is a substantial part of the company's business; or

(*d*) incidental activities of a company which meets the above trading activities requirement for a single company.

A company does not cease to meet the trading activities requirement purely by reason of it or a qualifying subsidiary (see above) being wound up or otherwise dissolved, provided that the winding-up or dissolution is for commercial reasons and not part of a tax avoidance scheme or arrangements. A similar let-out applies in relation to a company or its qualifying subsidiary going into administration or receivership (both as defined) and to anything done as a consequence thereof.

Amendments to the trading activities requirement (including the provisions at 15.7 below) may be made in the future by Treasury Order.

[*FA 2000, Sch 15 paras 23, 24, 101, 102(1)(4)*].

15.7 **Qualifying trades.** A trade is a qualifying trade (see the trading activities requirement at 15.6 above) if

(i) it is carried on wholly or mainly in the UK;

(ii) it is conducted on a commercial basis and with a view to profit; and

(iii) it does not consist wholly or as to a 'substantial' part in the carrying on of any 'excluded activities' (see below).

See Revenue Pamphlet IR 131, SP 7/98 (at 20.6 ENTERPRISE INVESTMENT SCHEME (AND BES)) for the Revenue's approach to the requirement at (i) above (in relation, at present, to other legislation but expected to be extended to cover the corporate venturing scheme). '*Substantial*' in (iii) above is not defined, but in its application to similar legislation is taken by the Revenue to mean 20% or more of total activities (see 20.6 ENTERPRISE INVESTMENT SCHEME (AND BES)).

Activities of research and development (within *ICTA 1988, s 837A*) from which it is intended that a 'connected qualifying trade' will be derived or will benefit are treated as a notional qualifying trade, but preparing to carry on such activities is not treated as preparing to carry on a qualifying trade. A '*connected qualifying trade*' is a qualifying trade carried on either by the company carrying out the research and development or, where applicable, by another member of the group.

'*Excluded activities*' are as follows:

(*a*) dealing in land, commodities or futures, or in shares, securities or other financial instruments;

(*b*) dealing in goods otherwise than in an ordinary trade of wholesale or retail distribution (for more detail, see the similar exclusion at 65.3(*b*) VENTURE CAPITAL TRUSTS);

(*c*) banking, insurance, money-lending, debt-factoring, hire purchase financing or other financial activities;

(*d*) leasing or receiving royalties or licence fees (see further below);

(*e*) providing legal or accountancy services;

(*f*) property development (see further below);

(*g*) farming or market gardening;

(*h*) holding, managing or occupying woodlands, any other forestry activities or timber production;

(*j*) operating or managing hotels or comparable establishments (including guest houses, hostels and other establishments whose main purpose is to offer overnight accommodation with or without catering) or property used as such (see further below);

(*k*) operating or managing nursing homes or residential care homes (both as defined) or property used as such (see further below);

(*l*) providing services or facilities for any business consisting to a substantial extent of activities within (*a*)–(*k*) above and carried on by another person, where a person has a controlling interest (see below) in both that business and the business of the provider company.

The term 'leasing' in (*d*) above includes the letting of ships on charter or other assets on hire. A trade will be not be excluded by reason only of its consisting of letting ships, other than oil rigs or pleasure craft (both as defined), on charter, provided certain conditions are satisfied.

As regards the receiving of royalties or licence fees (see (*d*) above), a trade is not excluded from being a qualifying trade solely because at some time in the qualification period (see 15.2 above) it consists to a substantial extent in the receiving of royalties or licence fees substantially attributable (in terms of value) to the exploitation of intangible assets, such as intellectual property, which have been created by the company carrying on the trade or by a fellow group company — for more details, see the similar let-out at 65.3(*b*) VENTURE CAPITAL TRUSTS.

As regards (*f*) above, see the comments at 65.3(*b*) VENTURE CAPITAL TRUSTS, which apply equally here. The exclusions at (*j*) and (*k*) above apply only if the person carrying on the activity has an estate or interest (e.g. a lease) in the property concerned or occupies that property.

As regards (*l*) above, see the comparable exclusion at 65.3(*b*) VENTURE CAPITAL TRUSTS as regards the meaning of 'controlling interest', which applies similarly here, though without the modifications there mentioned to *ICTA 1988, s 416*.

[*FA 2000, Sch 15 paras 25–33, 102(1)*].

15.8 **GENERAL REQUIREMENTS**

For investment relief to be available in respect of the relevant shares (see 15.2 above), the following requirements (see 15.2(*d*) above) must be met as to the shares, the use of money raised by the issue, the absence of pre-arranged exits and the absence of a tax avoidance motive. [*FA 2000, Sch 15 para 34*].

The shares. The relevant shares must be ordinary, fully paid up, shares and must be subscribed for wholly in cash. Shares are not fully paid up for this purpose if there is any undertaking to pay cash to the issuing company at a future date. At no time in the qualification period (see 15.2 above) must the shares carry any present or future preferential right to dividends or to assets on a winding-up, or any present or future right to be redeemed. [*FA 2000, Sch 15 para 35*].

Use of money raised. The money raised by the 'relevant issue of shares' must be employed wholly (disregarding any insignificant amount) for the purposes of a 'relevant trade' not later than

(*a*) the end of the 12 months beginning with the date of issue; or,

(*b*) if later, the end of the 12 months beginning when the issuing company or a subsidiary begins to carry on the relevant trade.

For these purposes, employing money for the purposes of *preparing* to carry on a trade (other than a notional trade of research and development — see 15.7 above) is equivalent to employing it for the purposes of a trade.

The '*relevant issue of shares*' means the issue of shares which includes the relevant shares. A '*relevant trade*' is a trade by reference to which the issuing company meets the trading activities requirement in 15.6 above. Where the trade by reference to which the trading activities requirement is met is a notional trade of research and development (see 15.7 above), the term 'relevant trade' also refers to any qualifying trade which is derived or benefits from that notional trade and is carried on by the issuing company or a qualifying subsidiary (see 15.6 above); in this case, the money raised by the issue must be employed for the purposes of that trade before the third anniversary of the date of issue of the shares, notwithstanding that a later date may be given by (*b*) above.

[*FA 2000, Sch 15 para 36*].

No pre-arranged exits. The arrangements (as very broadly defined) under which the relevant shares are issued to the investing company (including arrangements preceding the issue but relating to it and, in certain cases, arrangements made on or after the issue and within the qualification period) must not

(*a*) provide for the eventual disposal by the investing company of the relevant shares or other shares or securities of the issuing company;

(*b*) provide for the eventual cessation of a trade of the issuing company or a person connected with it;

(*c*) provide for the eventual disposal of all, or a substantial part of, the assets of the issuing company or of a person connected with it; or

(*d*) provide (by means of any insurance, indemnity, guarantee or otherwise) partial or complete protection for investors against the normal risks attaching to the investment (but excluding commercial arrangements which merely protect the issuing company and/or its subsidiaries against normal business risks).

Arrangements with a view to a company reconstruction within 15.24 below are excluded from (*a*) above. Arrangements applicable only on an unanticipated winding-up of the issuing company for commercial reasons are excluded from (*b*) and (*c*) above.

[*FA 2000, Sch 15 paras 37, 102(1)*].

No tax avoidance motive. The relevant shares must be issued for commercial reasons and not as part of a tax avoidance scheme or arrangement. [*FA 2000, Sch 15 para 38*].

15.9 **ADVANCE CLEARANCE**

A *potential* qualifying issuing company (see 15.6 above) may apply to the Board for an advance clearance notice in respect of an issue of shares. An application must contain particulars, declarations and undertakings as required and must disclose all material facts and circumstances. An advance clearance notice states that, on the basis of the particulars etc. provided by the applicant, the Revenue are satisfied that, at the time the shares are issued, the requirements of 15.6–15.8 above will be met (or, in the case of a requirement that can only be met in the future, will for the time being be met).

Within 30 days after receiving an application (or within 30 days after an 'information notice' is complied with), the Board must either issue an information notice (or further information notice), issue an advance clearance notice, or refuse the application. An '*information notice*' is a notice requiring further particulars to be provided within such time, not being less than 30 days, as is stated therein. If the applicant fails to comply timeously with an information notice, the Board need not proceed further with the application. If the shares in question are issued before the advance clearance notice is given or the application refused, then again the Board need not proceed further.

Within 30 days after a refusal of an application, or a failure to give a decision, the applicant can require the Board to transmit the application, together with any information notices given and further particulars provided, to the Special Commissioners, whose approval, if given, has effect as if it were an advance clearance notice given by the Revenue.

An advance clearance notice is rendered void if it transpires that any particulars provided did not fully and accurately disclose all facts and circumstances material for the decision, or if the applicant or any subsidiary (including any new subsidiary) fails to act in accordance with any declaration or undertaking given as part of the application.

[*FA 2000, Sch 15 paras 89–92*].

15.10 **WITHDRAWAL OR REDUCTION OF INVESTMENT RELIEF**

Investment relief falls to be withdrawn or reduced on a disposal of the relevant shares (see 15.11 below), if value is received in respect of the shares (see 15.12–15.15 below), or on the grant of certain options relating to the shares (see 15.16 below).

Where investment relief given falls to be withdrawn or reduced, and also where it is found not to have been due, the withdrawal etc. is achieved by means of an assessment under Schedule D, Case VI for the accounting period of the investing company *in which the relief was given*. For relief to be withdrawn on the grounds that the issuing company is not a qualifying issuing company (see 15.6 above), or that the general requirements at 15.8 above are not met, or by virtue of value received by the investing company (see 15.12 below) or other persons (see 15.15 below), certain statutory notice procedures must be followed. The investing company may give notice of appeal, within 30 days, against a Revenue notice pending withdrawal of relief on such grounds (as if the giving of that notice were the disallowance of a claim other than for discharge or repayment of tax — see 12.3 CLAIMS).

The Revenue cannot make an assessment to withdraw (or reduce) investment relief, or give statutory notice pending withdrawal of relief on the above-mentioned grounds, more than six years after the end of whichever is the later of the following accounting periods:

- the accounting period in which falls the deadline for employing money raised by the issue of the shares (see 15.8 above);
- the accounting period in which occurs the event giving rise to withdrawal (or reduction) of relief.

The above is subject to the extended time limit for assessments in cases of fraud or negligence (see 56.27 SELF-ASSESSMENT).

In most cases, interest on overdue tax runs from the date of the event giving rise to withdrawal (or reduction) of relief, if this is later than the normal due date, or the latest such date, for payment of corporation tax for the accounting period for which the assessment is made (see 46.2 PAYMENT OF TAX).

[*FA 2000, Sch 15 paras 60–63*].

Information. Certain events giving rise to withdrawal or reduction of investment relief must be notified to the Revenue, generally within 60 days, by the investing company or the issuing company (or any person connected with the issuing company and having knowledge of the matter), as the case may be. The Revenue have power to require information from such persons where they have reason to believe that such notice should have been given or from a person whom they believe to have given or received value which would have triggered a requirement to give such notice but for the amount of value being insignificant (see 15.12 below). The penalty provisions of *TMA 1970, s 98* apply in the event of non-compliance with these information provisions. [*FA 2000, Sch 15 paras 64–66, Sch 16 para 1*].

15.11 **Disposal.** Where, during the qualification period (see 15.2 above), the investing company disposes of any shares to which relief is attributable (see 15.3 above) and which it has held continuously since their issue (see 15.20(*a*) below), relief is withdrawn or reduced as set out below. See 15.10 above re consequences of withdrawal etc.

If the disposal is either

- by way of bargain at arm's length for full consideration; or
- by way of a distribution on a dissolution or winding-up of the issuing company; or

- a disposal within *TCGA 1992, s 24(1)* (entire loss, destruction etc. of asset — see 17.7 DISPOSAL); or
- a deemed disposal under *TCGA 1992, s 24(2)* (assets of negligible value — see 39.9 LOSSES),

the relief attributable to the shares disposed of is withdrawn, or is reduced by 20% of the disposal consideration (if such reduction would not amount to full withdrawal). If the relief initially obtained was less than 20% of the amount subscribed for those shares (i.e. because the company's corporation tax liability was insufficient to fully absorb the available relief), the reduction is correspondingly restricted.

In the case of any other disposal, for example a transaction not at arm's length, the relief attributable to the shares disposed of is withdrawn.

[*FA 2000, Sch 15 para 46*].

For the above purposes, shares are regarded as being disposed of if they are so regarded for the purposes of corporation tax on chargeable gains, and see also 15.23 below (certain company reconstructions and amalgamations treated as disposals). [*FA 2000, Sch 15 para 96*]. In the case of a part disposal, see 15.17 below for the rules for identifying shares disposed of.

15.12 **Value received by investing company.** Subject to 15.14 below (replacement value), where during the 'period of restriction' the investing company 'receives value' (see 15.13 below), other than an 'amount of insignificant value', from the issuing company, investment relief attributable to the relevant shares is withdrawn, or is reduced by 20% of the amount of value received (if such reduction would not amount to full withdrawal). If the relief initially obtained was less than 20% of the amount subscribed for those shares (i.e. because the company's corporation tax liability was insufficient to fully absorb the available relief), the reduction is correspondingly restricted. These provisions apply equally to receipts of value by and from persons connected (within *ICTA 1988, s 839* — see 14 CONNECTED PERSONS), at any time in the period of restriction, with the investing company or, as the case may be, the issuing company. See 15.13 below for the meaning of 'value received' and the determination of the amount of value received. See 15.10 above for consequences of withdrawal etc.

The '*period of restriction*' in relation to the relevant shares is the period beginning one year before their issue and ending at the end of the qualification period in 15.2 above.

Where two or more issues of shares have been made by the same issuing company to the same investing company, in relation to each of which investment relief is claimed, and value is received during a period of restriction relating to more than one such issue, the value received is apportioned between them by reference to the amounts subscribed for each of those issues.

An '*amount of insignificant value*' is an amount of value which

- does not exceed £1,000, or
- in any other case is insignificant in relation to the amount subscribed by the investing company for the relevant shares.

If at any time in the period beginning one year before the date of issue of the relevant shares and ending with the date of issue, there are in existence arrangements (as very broadly defined) providing for the investing company to receive, or become entitled to receive, any value from the issuing company at any time in the period of restriction (see above), no amount of value received by the investing company is treated as an amount of insignificant value.

There are provisions to aggregate a receipt of value, whether insignificant or not, with amounts of insignificant value received previously, and treating that aggregate, if it is not itself an amount of insignificant value, as an amount of value received at the time of the latest actual receipt.

Where relief is withdrawn or reduced by reason of a disposal (see 15.11 above), the investing company is not treated as receiving value from the issuing company in respect of the disposal.

[*FA 2000, Sch 15 paras 47, 48, 51–53, 102(1)*].

15.13 *Meaning of, and amount of, value received.* The investing company '*receives value*' from the issuing company if the latter (and see 15.12 above re connected persons)

(*a*) repays, redeems or repurchases any part of the investing company's holding of the issuing company's share capital or securities, or makes any payment to the investing company in respect of the cancellation of any of the issuing company's share capital or any security;

(*b*) repays, in pursuance of any arrangements for or in connection with the acquisition of the relevant shares, any debt owed to the investing company other than one incurred by the issuing company on or after the date of issue of the shares and otherwise than in consideration of the extinguishment of a debt incurred before that date;

(*c*) makes any payment to the investing company in respect of the cancellation of any debt owed to it;

(*d*) releases or waives any liability of the investing company to the issuing company (which it is deemed to have done if discharge of the liability is twelve months or more overdue) or discharges, or undertakes to discharge, any liability of the investing company to a third person;

(*e*) makes a loan or advance to the investing company which has not been repaid in full before the issue of the relevant shares; for this purpose a loan includes any debt incurred, other than an ordinary trade debt (as defined), and any debt due to a third person which is assigned to the issuing company;

(*f*) provides a benefit or facility for the directors or employees of the investing company or any of their associates (as defined), except in circumstances such that, if a *payment* had been made of equal value, it would have been a 'qualifying payment';

(*g*) disposes of an asset to the investing company for no consideration or for consideration less than market value (as defined), or acquires an asset from the investing company for consideration exceeding market value; or

(*h*) makes a payment to the investing company other than a 'qualifying payment'.

References above to a debt or liability do not include one which would be discharged by making a 'qualifying payment'. References to a payment or disposal include one made indirectly to, or to the order of, or for the benefit of, the person in question.

Each of the following is a '*qualifying payment*':

- a reasonable (in relation to their market value) payment for any goods, services or facilities provided by the investing company in the course of trade or otherwise;
- the payment of interest at no more than a reasonable commercial rate on money lent;
- the payment of a dividend or other distribution which represents no more than a normal return on investment;

- a payment to acquire an asset at no more than its market value;
- a payment not exceeding a reasonable and commercial rent for property occupied;
- a payment discharging an ordinary trade debt.

The *amount of value received* is

- in a case within (*a*), (*b*) or (*c*) above, the amount received or, if greater, the market value of the shares, securities or debt in question;
- in a case within (*d*) above, the amount of the liability;
- in a case within (*e*) above, the amount of the loan etc. less any amount repaid before the issue of the relevant shares;
- in a case within (*f*) above, the cost (net of any consideration given for it by the recipient or his associate) of providing the benefit etc.;
- in a case within (*g*) above, the difference between market value and the consideration received (if any); and
- in a case within (*h*) above, the amount of the payment.

[*FA 2000, Sch 15 paras 49, 50, 99, 102(5)*].

15.14 *Replacement value.* The provisions at 15.12 above are disapplied if the person from whom the value was received (the '*original supplier*') receives, by way of a 'qualifying receipt' and whether before or after the original receipt of value, at least equivalent replacement value from the original recipient. A receipt is a '*qualifying receipt*' if it arises by reason of

(*a*) a payment by the original recipient to the original supplier other than a qualifying payment as in 15.13 above or a payment for any shares or securities in any company in circumstances not within (*c*) below;

(*b*) (where the original receipt of value falls within 15.13(*d*) above) an event having the effect of reversing the original event; or

(*c*) (where the original receipt of value falls within 15.13(*g*) above) the acquisition of an asset by the original recipient from the original supplier for consideration exceeding market value (as defined), or the disposal of an asset by the original recipient to the original supplier for no consideration or for consideration less than market value.

The amount of replacement value is

- in a case within (*a*) above, the amount of the payment;
- in a case within (*b*) above, the same as the amount of the original value; and
- in a case within (*c*) above, the difference between market value and the consideration received (if any).

The receipt of replacement value is disregarded if

- it occurs before the start of the period of restriction (see 15.12 above);
- there was an unreasonable delay in its occurrence; or
- it occurs more than 60 days after the relief falling to be withdrawn (or reduced) has been determined on appeal.

Where

- the receipt of replacement value is a qualifying receipt (as above), and
- the event giving rise to the receipt is (or includes) a subscription for shares by the investing company or a person connected (within *ICTA 1988, s 839* — see 14 CONNECTED PERSONS) with it at any time in the period of restriction,

the subscriber is not eligible for investment relief, EIS income tax relief or EIS capital gains deferral relief in relation to those shares or any other shares in the same issue.

[*FA 2000, Sch 15 paras 54, 55, 102(3)(5)*].

15.15 **Value received by other persons.** Investment relief is withdrawn (or reduced) in certain cases of value received by persons other than the investing company (see 15.10 above re consequences of withdrawal etc.). This applies where, during the period of restriction (as in 15.12 above), the issuing company or a 'subsidiary'

- repays, redeems or repurchases any part of its share capital from a member (other than the investing company) who does not thereby suffer a withdrawal or reduction of any investment relief, EIS income tax relief or EIS capital gains deferral relief attributable to his shares; or
- makes any payment to any such member in respect of the cancellation of any of the share capital of the issuing company or subsidiary.

The investment relief attributable to the relevant shares held by the investing company is withdrawn, or is reduced by 20% of the amount received by the member (if such reduction would not amount to full withdrawal). If the relief initially obtained was less than 20% of the amount subscribed for those shares (i.e. because the company's corporation tax liability was insufficient to fully absorb the available relief), the reduction is correspondingly restricted. The amount received is also apportioned between investing companies (by reference to amounts subscribed) where the receipt of value causes a withdrawal or reduction of more than one such company's investment relief. Where the receipt of value falls into overlapping periods of restriction in relation to more than one issue of shares which includes shares to which investment relief is attributable, the value received is similarly apportioned between issues.

If the amount received by the member in question is insignificant in relation to the remaining share capital of the issuing company or, as the case may be, subsidiary, it is disregarded. In applying this test, the market value, immediately before the event concerned, of the shares to which the event relates is substituted for the amount received if this would give a greater amount. The assumption is made that the shares in question are cancelled at the time of the event. This let-out does not apply if at any time in the period beginning one year before the date of issue of the relevant shares and ending with the date of issue, there are in existence arrangements (as very broadly defined) providing for a payment within these provisions to be made, or entitlement to such a payment to come into being, at any time in the period of restriction.

For the above purposes, a '*subsidiary*' is a company which is a 51% subsidiary of the issuing company at any time in the period of restriction, whether or not at the time of receipt of value.

The above provisions do not apply to the redemption, within twelve months of issue, of any share capital of nominal value equal to the authorised minimum issued to comply with *Companies Act 1985, s 117* (or NI equivalent).

[*FA 2000, Sch 15 paras 56–58, 102(1)*].

15.16 **Put options and call options.** Where there is granted during the qualification period (see 15.2 above)

- an option, the exercise of which would bind the grantor to purchase any of the relevant shares from the investing company, or
- an option, the exercise of which would bind the grantor, in this case the investing company, to sell any of the relevant shares,

investment relief attributable (see 15.3 above) to those of the relevant shares which would (on given assumptions) be treated as disposed of on exercise of the option is withdrawn. See 15.10 above re consequences of withdrawal.

[*FA 2000, Sch 15 para 59*].

15.17 **IDENTIFICATION RULES**

The rules below apply, for the purpose of identifying shares disposed of, where a company makes a part disposal of a holding of shares of the same class in the same company, and the holding includes shares to which investment relief is attributable (see 15.3 above) and which have been held continuously (see 15.19(*a*) below) since the time of issue. The rules apply for the purposes of the corporate venturing scheme and for the purposes of corporation tax on chargeable gains generally. As regards the latter, the normal rules at 59.3 SHARES AND SECURITIES — IDENTIFICATION RULES are disapplied.

Where shares comprised in the holding have been acquired on different days, a disposal is identified with acquisitions on a first in/first out basis. In matching the shares disposed of with shares acquired on a particular day, shares to which investment relief is attributable and which have been held continuously since issue are treated as being disposed of *after* any other shares acquired on that day.

If, on a reorganisation of share capital (e.g. a scrip issue), a new holding falls, by virtue of *TCGA 1992, s 127*, to be equated with the original shares (see 58.5 SHARES AND SECURITIES, and see also 15.22 below), shares comprised in the new holding are deemed for the above purposes to have been acquired when the original shares were acquired.

[*FA 2000, Sch 15 para 93*].

15.18 **CHARGEABLE GAINS AND ALLOWABLE LOSSES**

A gain on the disposal at any time by the investing company of shares to which investment relief is attributable (see 15.3 above) is a chargeable gain, though see 15.21 below as regards possibility of deferral relief. A loss on such a disposal is an allowable loss — see 15.19 below as to the computation of the loss and 15.20 below as regards possibility of setting the loss against income rather than gains. For the rules for identifying disposals with acquisitions, see 15.17 above.

15.19 **Computation of allowable loss.** If a loss would otherwise accrue on a disposal by the investing company of shares to which investment relief is attributable, and the investment relief does not fall to be withdrawn (as opposed to reduced) as a result of the disposal (see 15.10 above), the company's acquisition cost for the purposes of corporation tax on chargeable gains is reduced by the amount of investment relief attributable to the shares immediately after the disposal, but not so as to convert the loss into a chargeable gain. This applies only if the condition at 15.20(*a*) below (shares held continuously) is met from issue to disposal. [*FA 2000, Sch 15 para 94*].

15.20 **Set-off of allowable loss against income.** Subject to all the conditions at (*a*)–(*c*) below being satisfied and a claim being made, an allowable loss, on a disposal by the investing company of shares to which investment relief is attributable (see 15.3 above), may be set against *income* (as an alternative to setting it against chargeable gains in the normal way — see 13.4 COMPANIES). The loss is as computed after applying the reduction at 15.19 above. The conditions are as follows.

(*a*) The shares must have been held continuously by the company from time of issue to time of disposal. If, during any period,

- the company was deemed under any provision of *TCGA 1992* to have disposed of and immediately reacquired the shares; or,
- following a scheme of reconstruction or amalgamation within *TCGA 1992, s 136* — see 58.10 SHARES AND SECURITIES (or which would have been within that *section* but for the provisions at 3.16 ANTI-AVOIDANCE) , the company was deemed by virtue of 15.23 below to have made a disposal of shares which it retained under the scheme;

it is not treated for the purposes of the corporate venturing scheme provisions as having held the shares continuously throughout that period.

(*b*) The investment relief must not fall to be withdrawn (as opposed to reduced) as a result of the disposal.

(*c*) The disposal must be either

- by way of bargain at arm's length for full consideration; or
- by way of a distribution on a dissolution or winding-up of the issuing company; or
- a disposal within *TCGA 1992, s 24(1)* (entire loss, destruction etc. of asset — see 17.7 DISPOSAL); or
- a deemed disposal under *TCGA 1992, s 24(2)* (assets of negligible value — see 39.9 LOSSES).

The set-off is against income of the accounting period in which the loss is incurred. As regards any unrelieved balance, the claim may be extended to income of accounting periods ending within the 12 months immediately preceding the accounting period in which the loss is incurred. Income of an accounting period beginning before, and ending within, that 12 months is apportioned on a time basis so as to exclude income thereby deemed to have accrued prior to that 12-month period. The income of each accounting period included in the claim is treated as reduced by the loss, or by so much of it as cannot be relieved in a later accounting period. Losses of earlier accounting periods are relieved in priority to those of later periods. Relief is given before any relief claimed under *ICTA 1988, s 573* (loss incurred by investment company on disposal of unlisted shares — see 39.15 LOSSES) and before any deduction for charges on income or other deductible amounts. Once relief has been obtained under these provisions for an amount of loss, that amount cannot be relieved under *section 573* or against chargeable gains.

Claims must be made within two years after the end of the accounting period in which the loss is incurred.

Where a claim is made under these provisions, *TCGA 1992, s 30* (value shifting to give tax-free benefit) has effect in relation to the disposal if *any* benefit is conferred, whether tax-free or not. No loss relief against income is available if the disposal is the result of a company reconstruction or amalgamation effected for tax avoidance rather than commercial reasons, such that it falls within the ambit of 3.16 ANTI-AVOIDANCE.

[*FA 2000, Sch 15 paras 67–72, 97*].

15.21 **Deferral relief** is available where a chargeable gain would otherwise accrue to the investing company

- on a disposal of shares to which investment relief was attributable (see 15.3 above) immediately before the disposal and which satisfy the condition at 15.20(*a*) above (shares held continuously) from issue to disposal; or
- on the occurrence of a chargeable event under these provisions,

and the company makes a 'qualifying investment'. A '*qualifying investment*' is a subscription for shares ('*qualifying shares*') on which investment relief is obtained under the corporate venturing scheme, other than shares issued by a 'prohibited company'. The qualifying shares must be issued to the investing company within the one year immediately preceding or the three years immediately following the time the chargeable gain in question accrues. If the qualifying shares are issued *before* the gain accrues, they must have been held continuously (see 15.20(*a*) above) by the investing company from issue until the time the gain accrues, and investment relief must still be attributable to them. A '*prohibited company*' means either

(*a*) the company whose shares are disposed of or, or as the case may be, in relation to whose shares the chargeable event occurred; or

(*b*) a company which, when the gain accrues or when the qualifying shares are issued, is a member of the same group as the company in (*a*) above.

Deferral relief is said to be 'attributable to shares' if expenditure on those shares has been used to defer the whole or part of a chargeable gain and no chargeable event has occurred resulting in the deferred gain being brought back into charge.

The following themselves become qualifying shares:

- any bonus shares, issued in respect of the qualifying shares and being shares in the same company, of the same class and carrying the same rights;
- any shares issued on a company reconstruction within 15.24 below in exchange for qualifying shares.

Postponement of the original gain. On a claim by the investing company, the whole or part of the chargeable gain can be deferred. The amount to be deferred is the lower of

- the amount of the gain (or the amount remaining in charge after any previous deferral relief claim);
- the amount subscribed for the qualifying shares (to the extent that it has not been used in previous deferral relief claims); and
- the amount specified by the company in the claim.

No time limit is specified for making a claim, so the general six-year time limit applies as in 12.5 CLAIMS.

Deferred gain becoming chargeable. The deferred gain will become chargeable on the occurrence of, *and at the time of*, one of the following chargeable events:

(i) a disposal of qualifying shares by the investing company; or

(ii) any other event giving rise to a withdrawal of, or reduction in, the investment relief attributable to qualifying shares (see 15.10 above).

If the qualifying investment is made before the gain accrues, there is disregarded for the purposes of (ii) above any reduction made by reason of an event occurring before the gain accrues.

The chargeable gain accruing to the investing company at the time of the chargeable event is equal to so much of the deferred gain as is attributable to the shares in relation to which the chargeable event occurs. For these purposes, a proportionate part of the net deferred gain (i.e. the deferred gain less any amount brought into charge on an earlier chargeable event, e.g. a part disposal) is attributed to each of the qualifying shares held immediately before the chargeable event. Thus, a part disposal of qualifying shares brings into charge a proportionate part of the deferred gain.

Provision is made to ensure that a previously deferred gain accruing as above is brought into charge under *TCGA 1992, s 10* (see 44.3 OVERSEAS MATTERS) in the case of a non-UK resident company carrying on a trade or vocation through a UK branch or agency.

[*FA 2000, Sch 15 paras 73–79*].

15.22 **COMPANY RESTRUCTURING**

Reorganisations of share capital. The following applies where a company holds shares in another company, being shares of the same class, held in the same capacity and forming part of the ordinary share capital of that other company, and there is a reorganisation within the meaning of *TCGA 1992, s 126* (see 58.5 SHARES AND SECURITIES). If the shares fall within two or more of the categories below, *TCGA 1992, s 127* (see 58.5 SHARES AND SECURITIES), or, where appropriate, *TCGA 1992, s 116* (reorganisations involving QUALIFYING CORPORATE BONDS (49.3)), applies separately to each category. (This is subject to the disapplication of those provisions in the circumstances set out below.) The categories are:

- shares to which deferral relief is attributable (see 15.21 above);
- shares to which investment relief, but not deferral relief, is attributable (see 15.3 above) and which have been held continuously (see 15.20(*a*) above) by the company since they were issued; and
- shares in neither of the categories above.

[*FA 2000, Sch 15 para 80*].

Rights issues etc. Where

- a reorganisation (within *TCGA 1992, s 126* — see 58.5 SHARES AND SECURITIES) involves an allotment of shares or debentures in respect of and in proportion to an existing holding,
- investment relief is attributable (see 15.3 above) to the shares in the existing holding or to the allotted shares, and,
- if investment relief is attributable to the shares in the existing holding, those shares have been held continuously (see 15.20(*a*) above) by the company since they were issued,

the share reorganisation rules of *TCGA 1992, ss 127–130* (see 58.5 SHARES AND SECURITIES) are disapplied. The effect is that the allotted shares are treated as a separate holding acquired at the time of the reorganisation. This does not apply in the case of bonus shares where these are issued in respect of shares comprised in the existing holding and are of the same class and carry the same rights as those shares.

If, in a case otherwise within 49.3 QUALIFYING CORPORATE BONDS,

- the old asset consists of shares to which investment relief is attributable and which have been held continuously (see 15.20(*a*) above) by the company since they were issued, and
- the new asset consists of a qualifying corporate bond,

the usual treatment is disapplied. The effect is that the investing company is deemed to have disposed of the shares at the time of the relevant transaction, and the resulting chargeable gain or allowable loss crystallises *at that time.*

[*FA 2000, Sch 15 para 81*].

15.23 **Company reconstructions and amalgamations.** Subject to 15.24 below, *TCGA 1992, s 135* (exchange of securities for those in another company — see 58.8 SHARES AND

SECURITIES)and *s 136* (schemes of reconstruction or amalgamation involving issue of securities — see 58.10 SHARES AND SECURITIES), which equate the new holding with the original shares, are disapplied in the following circumstances:

- a company holds shares in another company (Company A);
- investment relief is attributable (see 15.3 above) to those shares;
- those shares have been held continuously (see 15.20(*a*) above) by the investing company since they were issued, and
- there is a reconstruction or amalgamation whereby a third company issues shares or debentures in exchange for, or in respect of, Company A shares or debentures.

The result is that the transaction is treated, both for the purposes of the corporate venturing scheme provisions and for the purposes of corporation tax on chargeable gains generally, as a disposal of the original shares (and an acquisition of a new holding). [*FA 2000, Sch 15 paras 82, 96*].

15.24 **Issuing company becoming wholly-owned subsidiary of new holding company.** Notwithstanding 15.23 above, *TCGA 1992, s 135* is not disapplied (and there is thus no disposal and acquisition) where, by means entirely of an exchange of shares, all the shares in one company (the '*old shares*') are acquired by another company, and the conditions below are satisfied. Following such a share exchange, the shares thereby issued by the acquiring company (the '*new shares*') stand in place of the old shares, so that

- any investment relief or deferral relief attributable to the old shares (see, respectively, 15.3, 15.21 above) is attributed to the new shares for which they were exchanged;
- the new shares are treated as having been issued at the time the old shares were issued and as having been held continuously (see 15.20(*a*) above) by the investing company since that time (provided the old shares had been so held);
- generally speaking, anything done, or required to be done, by or in relation to the acquired company is treated as having been done etc. by or in relation to the acquiring company; and
- certain of the requirements of 15.5, 15.6 above which were met to any extent in relation to the old shares are deemed to be met to the same extent in relation to the new shares.

The conditions to be satisfied are as follows.

(*a*) The consideration for the old shares consists entirely of the issue of the new shares.

(*b*) New shares are issued only at a time when the issued shares in the acquiring company consist entirely of subscriber shares (and any new shares already issued in consideration of old shares).

(*c*) The consideration for new shares of each description consists entirely of old shares of the 'corresponding description'.

(*d*) New shares of each description are issued to holders of old shares of the 'corresponding description' in respect of, and in proportion to, their holdings.

(*e*) Before any exchange of shares takes place, the Revenue have given an 'approval notification'.

For the purposes of (*c*) and (*d*) above, old and new shares are of a '*corresponding description*' if, assuming they were shares in the same company, they would be of the same class and carry the same rights. All references above to 'shares' (other than to 'subscriber shares') include references to 'securities'. An '*approval notification*' (see (*e*) above) is given by the Revenue, on an application by either company involved, if they are satisfied that the share exchange will be effected for commercial reasons and does not form part of a scheme or arrangements to avoid liability to corporation tax or capital gains tax.

The provisions of *FA 2000, Sch 15 para 80* (see 15.23 above) are applied to a reconstruction within the above provisions where a company's holding of 'old shares' falls within more than one of the categories there mentioned.

[*FA 2000, Sch 15 paras 83–87*].

16 Death

Cross-references. See 33.2 INTERACTION WITH OTHER TAXES for inheritance tax (or capital transfer tax); 35.9 INTEREST AND SURCHARGES ON UNPAID TAX for relief given if probate is delayed; 40 MARKET VALUE; 57.2 SETTLEMENTS for death of a bankrupt etc. and 57.9–57.11 for termination of a life interest by the death of the person entitled thereto; 58.19 SHARES AND SECURITIES.

Sumption: Capital Gains Tax. See A7.

16.1 GENERAL PROVISIONS

All 'assets of which a deceased person was competent to dispose' are deemed to have been acquired on his death by his personal representatives (or other person on whom they devolve) for a consideration equal to their market value at the date of death. However, they are not deemed to be disposed of by the deceased on his death (whether or not they were the subject of a testamentary disposition), i.e. no chargeable gain or allowable loss arises on death and any gain or loss arising on the disposal of the asset by the personal representatives, etc. after the death is calculated by reference to the market value of the asset at the date of death (subject to the further provisions in this chapter).

'*Assets of which the deceased was competent to dispose*' are those assets which (otherwise than in right of a power of appointment or of the testamentary power conferred by statute to dispose of entailed interests) he could, if of full age and capacity, have disposed of by his will, assuming that all the assets were situated in England and, if he was not domiciled in the United Kingdom, that he was domiciled in England, and include references to his severable share in any assets to which, immediately before his death, he was beneficially entitled as joint tenant. [*TCGA 1992, s 62(1)(10)*].

16.2 **Scotland.** So far as the provisions in *TCGA 1992* relate to the consequences of the death of

(*a*) an heir of entail in possession of any property in Scotland subject to an entail (whether *sui juris* or not), or

(*b*) a proper liferenter of any property,

then, on the death of any such heir or liferenter, the heir next entitled or, as the case may be, the person (if any) who, on the death of the liferenter, becomes entitled to possession of the property as fiar, is deemed to have acquired all the assets forming part of the property at the date of the deceased's death for a consideration equal to their market value at that date. [*TCGA 1992, s 63*].

16.3 **Valuation.** Where on the death of any person, inheritance tax is chargeable on the value of his estate immediately before his death and the value of an asset forming part of his estate has been ascertained for those purposes, that value is taken to be the market value at the date of death for capital gains tax purposes. [*TCGA 1992, s 274*]. See also Revenue Tax Bulletin April 1995 p 209. In practice (see Revenue Pamphlet IHT 15 page 15), unless there are special circumstances, quoted shares and securities are valued in the same way as for capital gains tax (see 40.2 MARKET VALUE). In the case of land and quoted shares and securities, proceeds of certain post-death sales within a specified period may be substituted for values at date of death for inheritance tax purposes. The value of related property (as defined for inheritance tax purposes) may also be revised in the event of a post-death sale. If such substitutions/revisions are made for inheritance tax purposes, they must be made for CGT purposes also. See TOLLEY'S INHERITANCE TAX for details and also Revenue Capital Gains Manual CG 32290–32310.

Where, in consequence of a death before 31 March 1971 (when death *was* an occasion of charge for CGT), capital gains tax was chargeable or an allowable loss accrued, then if the market value of any property on the date of death which was subject to charge has been depreciated *by reason of the death*, then any later estimate of the market value is to take that depreciation into account. [*TCGA 1992, Sch 11 para 8*]. This provision may still, therefore, be relevant in computing allowable expenditure on a first disposal subsequent to the date of death. The legislation now refers to deaths before 31 March 1973 but the reasoning for this is not clear; see *FA 1965, s 44(2) proviso* as repealed by *FA 1971, Sch 14 Pt V* for deaths occurring after 30 March 1971 and cf. *CGTA 1979, Sch 6 para 2(2)*).

Following the decision in *Gray v CIR CA, [1994] STC 360*, the Revenue's view is that two or more different assets comprised in an estate can be treated as a single unit of property if disposal as one unit was the course that a prudent hypothetical vendor would have adopted in order to obtain the most favourable price without undue expenditure of time and effort.

This principle will apply for capital gains tax purposes in the following cases:

(*a*) An acquisition by personal representatives or legatees under *TCGA 1992, s 62* of assets which a deceased person was competent to dispose.

(*b*) An acquisition of settled property under *TCGA 1992, s 71(1)* on the occasion of a person becoming absolutely entitled to that settled property.

There are certain situations when a single valuation will still apply, such as in the cases of:

(i) the disposal of an asset for consideration deemed to be equal to its market value under *TCGA 1992, s 17*;

(ii) when a valuation of an asset is required for the purpose of re-basing to 31 March 1992 under *TCGA 1992, s 35*.

The single asset valuation for *TCGA 1992, s 17* is modified by *TCGA 1992, s 19* where there is a series of linked transactions between connected persons. Each disposal in the series may be treated as being made for consideration equal to a proportion of the aggregate value of all the assets in the series.

16.4 **Donatio mortis causa.** No chargeable gain arises on the making of a disposal by way of '*donatio mortis causa*' i.e. a gift of personal property made in 'contemplation of the conceived approach of death' (see *Duffield v Elwes Ch D 1827, 1 Bligh's Reports (New Series) 497*), and the recipient is treated as a legatee acquiring it at the date of death. [*TCGA 1992, s 62(5), s 64(2)*].

16.5 CARRY-BACK OF LOSSES

Allowable losses in excess of chargeable gains incurred by the deceased in the year of assessment in which death occurs can be carried back and set off against chargeable gains in the preceding three years of assessment. See 2.5 ANNUAL RATES AND EXEMPTIONS for the interaction between losses carried back and the annual exempt amount. Subject to this, chargeable gains accruing in a later year must be relieved before those of an earlier year. Losses carried back to 1998/99 or a subsequent year cannot be set against any of the following that might be attributed to the individual:

- gains treated under *TCGA 1992, s 77* as accruing to him as settlor from a UK resident settlement in which he has an interest (see 57.3 SETTLEMENTS);

- gains treated under *TCGA 1992, s 86* as accruing to him as settlor from a non-UK resident settlement in which he has an interest (see 43.4 OFFSHORE SETTLEMENTS);
- gains treated under *TCGA 1992, s 87* or *s 89(2)* as accruing to him as a beneficiary of a non-UK resident settlement (an offshore trust) (see 43.13 OFFSHORE SETTLEMENTS).

Losses carried back are treated in the same way as current year and brought-forward losses for the purposes of the application of TAPER RELIEF (60) and are thus set against chargeable gains *before* applying that relief (see 60.2).

[*TCGA 1992, s 62(2)–(2B); FA 1998, s 121(3)(4), Sch 21 para 5*].

Any remaining unused losses *cannot* be carried forward and set off against gains made by the personal representatives or legatees.

Where the year of death is **1996/97 or a later year** (i.e. where self-assessment applies), a carry-back of a loss under *TCGA 1992, s 62(2)* is brought within the scope of *TMA 1970, Sch 1B* (claims for relief involving two or more years). This provision is fully covered in TOLLEY'S INCOME TAX (and see also 12.2 CLAIMS) and its effect is that whilst the resulting tax saving/repayment is computed by reference to the facts for the tax year(s) to which the loss is carried back (the earlier year), it is then treated as a reduction or repayment of tax for the tax year in which the loss is incurred (the later year). The tax position for the earlier year is not adjusted. The general requirement that claims be made in a self-assessment tax return (see 12.2 CLAIMS) does not apply to a carry-back under *section 62(2)*. [*TMA 1970, Sch 1B para 2; FA 1996, s 128(2)(11), Sch 17*]. Whilst *TCGA 1992, s 283* (repayment supplement — see 34 INTEREST ON OVERPAID TAX) does not specifically cover the situation, the Revenue's view is that, in the event of a loss carry-back, supplement accrues only from 31 January following the *later* year (see, for example, Revenue Tax Bulletin December 1996 p 364 and *Taxation 8 January 1998 pp 319–321*).

16.6 DEEDS OF FAMILY ARRANGEMENT ETC.

Variations or disclaimers of the dispositions (whether effected by will, under the intestacy rules or otherwise) of the 'property of which the deceased was competent to dispose' (see 16.1 above) which are made by deed of family arrangement (or similar instrument in writing) within two years of death do not constitute disposals but are related back to the date of death. However, in the case of a variation, an appropriate election (under *TCGA 1992, s 62(7)*) is required for this treatment to apply. Such treatment does not apply in respect of variations or disclaimers made for any consideration in money or money's worth other than consideration consisting of the making of a variation or disclaimer in respect of another of the dispositions. The election in respect of a variation must be made to the Board in writing by the parties to the instrument within six months after the date of the instrument or such longer time as the Board may allow. The provisions apply whether or not the administration of the estate is complete or the property has been distributed in accordance with the original dispositions. [*TCGA 1992, s 62(6)–(9)*]. In the Revenue's view, these provisions apply to a variation of the deceased's interest in jointly held assets, which pass on death to the surviving joint owner(s) (Revenue Tax Bulletin October 1995 p 254).

In a case based upon the original *FA 1965* legislation, it was held that the equivalent provisions to *TCGA 1992, s 62(6)* above and *s 62(4)* (see 16.9 below), although deeming provisions, were to be given their normal and natural meaning. But, where such construction would lead to an injustice or absurdity, the application of the statutory fiction should be limited to the extent needed to avoid such injustice or absurdity. Thus, nothing in *TCGA 1992, s 62(6)* requires one to assume something which is inconsistent with the legatee under an original will, who then varies dispositions under *TCGA 1992, s 62(6)* to a third party, as having been the actual settlor of the arrangement. The deeming provisions apply only to assets of which the testator was competent to dispose at his death. However, the property settled by the legatee comprised, not the assets in the deceased's estate which eventually came to be vested in the third party, but a separate chose in action, i.e. the right to due administration of the estate, and this could only have been settled by the legatee and not by the deceased (*Marshall v Kerr HL 1994, 67 TC 56*). Where, in the rare event, the administration of an estate has been completed before a deed of variation is made, a different analysis may follow.

For the Revenue's comments on the provisions affecting the variation of the devolution of a deceased estate, see Revenue Capital Gains Manual CG 31400–32100.

For cases bearing on the effectiveness of similar deeds used for inheritance tax purposes, see TOLLEY'S INHERITANCE TAX under Deeds Varying Dispositions on Death.

16.7 PERSONAL REPRESENTATIVES

Personal representatives are treated as a single and continuing body (distinct from persons who may from time to time be the personal representatives) which has the deceased's residence, ordinary residence and domicile at the date of death. [*TCGA 1992, s 62(3)*].

They are liable to capital gains tax on disposals of assets made by them by reference to the disposal proceeds and the market value at the date of death (but see 16.8 below). They may be assessed in respect of disposals made by the deceased prior to death as well as in respect of their own disposals. See 5.6, 5.7 ASSESSMENTS.

For the year of assessment in which death occurs and the following two years of assessment, the personal representatives are entitled to the same annual exempt amount as individuals, with the same general provisions applying. [*TCGA 1992, s 3(7)*]. See 2.5 ANNUAL RATES AND EXEMPTIONS.

See 2.3 ANNUAL RATES AND EXEMPTIONS for the rate of capital gains tax applicable to personal representatives.

Losses made by personal representatives during the administration period cannot be passed on to the legatees. The position should be compared with that for losses made by trustees as in 57.9 SETTLEMENTS.

For 1996/97 and subsequent years, CGT due from personal representatives may be assessed and charged on and in the name of any one or more of the 'relevant personal representatives'. In relation to chargeable gains, the '*relevant personal representatives*' means the personal representatives in the tax year in which the gains accrue and any subsequent personal representatives of the deceased. Previously, CGT could be assessed on any personal representative, except that where an assessment was raised otherwise than on all the personal representatives the persons assessed could not include a person who was not resident or ordinarily resident in the UK. [*TCGA 1992, s 65(1)((4); FA 1995, s 103(7), s 114*].

16.8 **Allowable expenditure.** The decision in *Richards' Executors HL 1971, 46 TC 626* enables personal representatives, in computing chargeable gains on the disposal of assets, to add to the cost of acquiring the assets from the testator (i.e. the market value at the date of death) those legal and accountancy costs that are involved in preparing the inheritance tax or capital transfer tax account and obtaining the grant of probate etc. See also 17.3 DISPOSAL.

16.8 Death

Because of the practical difficulty of identifying the costs applicable to individual assets comprised in the estate, the Board of Inland Revenue has agreed expenditure based on the following scales (Revenue Pamphlet IR 131, SPs 7/81 and 8/94).

Personal representatives

Deaths after 5 April 1993

	Gross value of estate	*Allowable expenditure*
A	Up to £40,000	1.75% of the probate value of the assets sold by the personal representatives.
B	Between £40,001 and £70,000	A fixed amount of £700, to be divided between all the assets in the estate in proportion to the probate values, and allowed in those proportions on assets sold by the personal representatives.
C	Between £70,001 and £300,000	1% of the probate value of the assets sold.
D	Between £300,001 and £400,000	A fixed amount of £3,000, to be divided as at B above.
E	Between £400,001 and £750,000	0.75% of the probate value of the assets sold.

Deaths after 5 April 1981 and before 6 April 1993

	Gross value of estate	*Allowable expenditure*
(*a*)	Up to £20,000	1.5% of the probate value of the assets sold by the personal representatives.
(*b*)	Between £20,001 and £30,000	A fixed amount of £300 to be divided among all the assets in the estate in proportion to their probate values, and allowed in those proportions on assets sold by the personal representatives.
(*c*)	Between £30,001 and £150,000	1% of the probate value of the assets sold.
(*d*)	Between £150,001 and £200,000	A fixed amount of £1,500, to be divided as in (b) above.
(*e*)	Between £200,001 and £400,000	0.75% of the probate value of the assets sold.

The scales do not extend to gross estates that exceed £750,000 for deaths after 5 April 1993 (or £400,000 for deaths before 6 April 1993). In those cases, the allowable expenditure has to be negotiated by the inspector and the personal representatives, according to the facts of the particular case.

In practice, the Board will accept computations based either on these scales or on the actual expenditure incurred.

Corporate trustees

The Board of Inland Revenue have also agreed the following scale of allowable expenditure for expenses incurred by corporate trustees in the administration of estates and trusts. The Board will accept computations based either on this scale or on the actual allowable expenditure incurred.

Acquisitions and disposals, or deemed disposals, after 5 April 1993

(a) *Transfers of assets to beneficiaries etc.*

(1)	Quoted stocks and shares	
	(A) One beneficiary	£20 per holding.
	(B) More than one beneficiary between whom a holding must be divided	As (A), to be divided in equal shares between the beneficiaries.
(2)	Unquoted shares	As (1) above, with the addition of any exceptional expenditure.
(3)	Other assets	As (1) above, with the addition of any exceptional expenditure.

(b) *Actual disposals and acquisitions*

(1)	Quoted stocks and shares	The investment fee as charged by the trustee.
(2)	Unquoted shares	As (1) above, plus actual valuation costs.
(3)	Other assets	The investment fee as charged by the trustee, subject to a maximum of £60, plus actual valuation costs.

Where a comprehensive annual management fee is charged, covering both the cost of administering the trust and the expenses of actual disposals and acquisitions, the investment fee for (1)–(3) above will be taken to be £0.25 per £100 on the sale or purchase moneys.

(c) *Deemed disposals by trustees*

(1)	Quoted stocks and shares	£6 per holding.
(2)	Unquoted shares	Actual valuation costs.
(3)	Other assets	Actual valuation costs.

16.9 LEGATEES

A '*legatee*' includes any person taking under a testamentary disposition or an intestacy or partial intestacy, whether he takes beneficially or as trustee. [*TCGA 1992, s 64(2)*].

On a 'person acquiring any asset as legatee', no chargeable gain accrues to the personal representatives, and the legatee is treated as if the personal representatives' acquisition of the asset had been his acquisition of it. [*TCGA 1992, s 62(4)*]. The consequences of this are that the asset is taken as acquired at either the market value at the date of death or, if the asset was acquired subsequent to death, the allowable expenditure incurred by the personal representatives in providing etc. the asset. See also 16.6 above.

For the purposes of '*legatee*' and '*person acquiring an asset as legatee*', property taken under a testamentary disposition or on an intestacy or partial intestacy includes any asset appropriated by the personal representative in or towards satisfaction of a pecuniary legacy or any other interest or share in the property devolving. [*TCGA 1992, s 64(3)*].

Where a person disposes of an asset to which he became absolutely entitled as legatee, any incidental expenditure incurred by that person or the personal representatives in relation to the transfer of the asset to him is allowable as a deduction in the computation of the gain arising on the disposal. [*TCGA 1992, s 64(1)*]. The expenditure incurred by the person concerned, but not that incurred by the personal representatives, qualifies for indexation allowance (Revenue Capital Gains Manual CG 31192).

17 Disposal

Cross-references. See 2.5 ANNUAL RATES AND EXEMPTIONS; 3.4 ANTI-AVOIDANCE for transactions treated as disposals; 7 ASSETS HELD ON 6 APRIL 1965; 8 ASSETS HELD ON 31 MARCH 1982; 26 INDEXATION; 33 INTERACTION WITH OTHER TAXES; 36 LAND for disposals of land and leases; 37.2 LIFE ASSURANCE POLICIES AND DEFERRED ANNUITIES; 39 LOSSES; 40 MARKET VALUE; 58 SHARES AND SECURITIES; 66 WASTING ASSETS.

17.1 GENERAL

Gains and losses accruing on disposals of assets are computed by deducting allowable expenditure (see 17.3–17.5 below) from the amount realised or deemed to be realised on the disposal (i.e. the actual or deemed consideration). [*TCGA 1992, ss 15, 38*]. The consideration for the sale of an asset is the agreed purchase price regardless of how it is to be applied (*Spectros International plc v Madden Ch D 1996, 70 TC 349*). No deduction is allowable more than once from any sum or from more than one sum. [*TCGA 1992, s 52(1)*]. See 17.2 below for date of disposal. See 17.6 below for part disposals.

There is a disposal of assets where a capital sum is derived from them. See 17.7–17.9 below. Options are dealt with at 17.10, commodity and financial futures at 17.11 and forfeited deposits of purchase money at 17.12.

'*Disposal*' is not defined in the legislation. It does not, however, include a conveyance or transfer of an asset or of a right therein *by way of security* (e.g. a mortgage), but if the creditor or any person appointed as receiver, manager, etc. deals with the asset in order to enforce the security, his activities are imputed to the giver of the security. The existence of a security is ignored for both acquisition and disposal of an asset save that the amount of liability assumed forms part of the acquisition and disposal consideration in addition to any other consideration. [*TCGA 1992, s 26*]. Relief is available if there has been a sale of an asset at arm's length in circumstances such that the vendor granted the purchaser a mortgage (in full or in part) in order for the purchaser to buy and where there has later been a default on the mortgage loan. If, as a result, the vendor regains beneficial ownership of the asset he has contracted to sell he may elect that the gain realised by him on that sale be taken as limited to the net proceeds (after incidental costs of disposal) retained by him and the loan be treated as never coming into existence (although interest on the loan would be subject to income tax in the usual way). On any subsequent disposal of the asset concerned, the computation will be by reference to the original date and costs of acquisition etc. (Revenue Pamphlet IR 1, D18).

For disposals after 5 April 1998, a taper relief applies to gains realised by individuals, trustees and personal representatives, whereby the otherwise chargeable gain (after deducting any indexation allowance available — see below) is reduced according to the length of time the asset has been held after 5 April 1998 and whether it is a business or non-business asset. See 60 TAPER RELIEF.

For disposals after 29 November 1993, the gain (if any) arrived at as above is termed the '*unindexed gain*'. Any indexation allowance due is deducted from the unindexed gain to give the gain for the purposes of *TCGA 1992* unless otherwise provided. If the allowance equals or exceeds the unindexed gain, no gain or loss arises. If a loss arises as above, no indexation allowance is available. For disposals after 5 April 1998 for capital gains tax purposes (though not those of corporation tax on chargeable gains), indexation allowance is frozen at its April 1998 level and is not available at all in respect of expenditure incurred after 31 March 1998. See 26.1 INDEXATION and note the transitional relief for 'indexation losses' which may be due for 1993/94 and 1994/95 as in 26.2 INDEXATION in the case of disposals by individuals and trustees of settlements made before 30 November 1993.

For disposals after 5 April 1985 (31 March 1985 for companies) and before 30 November 1993, the gain or loss (if any) arrived at by deducting allowable expenditure from disposal consideration received was termed the '*unindexed gain or loss*'. Any indexation allowance due was deducted from the unindexed gain (and so as to create a loss if greater than the unindexed gain) or was added to the unindexed loss. If the unindexed gain or loss was nil, the indexation allowance itself was the loss arising. The resulting net figure was the gain or loss for the purposes of *TCGA 1992* unless otherwise provided. See 26.1 INDEXATION.

For disposals after 5 April 1982 and before 6 April 1985 (after 31 March 1982 and before 1 April 1985 for companies), the gain (if any) arrived at by deducting allowable expenditure from disposal consideration received was termed the 'gross gain'. Any indexation allowance due was deducted from the gross gain to arrive at the gain for the purposes of *CGTA 1979* unless otherwise provided. If the allowance exceeded or was equal to the gross gain, no gain or loss arose. If a loss was produced by deducting allowable expenditure from disposal consideration received, no indexation allowance was available. See 26.1 INDEXATION.

For disposals before 6 April 1982 (1 April 1982 for companies), indexation allowance did not apply. The gain, if any, arrived at above, was, unless the legislation provided otherwise, the chargeable gain.

17.2 DATE OF DISPOSAL

Contracts. Where an asset is disposed of and acquired under a contract, the disposal and acquisition are made at the time the contract is made (and not, if different, the time at which the asset is conveyed or transferred, e.g. on a contract for the sale of land). This rule applies even if the contract is unenforceable, provided that the disposal is actually completed (*Thompson v Salah Ch D 1971, 47 TC 559*). (However, the Revenue points out that the authority of this case is no longer valid where the general law provides that contracts entered into in respect of land must be made in writing (as is required under *Law of Property (Miscellaneous Provisions) Act 1989* and which applies in England and Wales although a similar requirement applies in Scotland (Revenue Capital Gains Manual CG 18162, 25860 and 70280)). If the contract is conditional (and, in particular, if it is conditional on the exercise of an option), the disposal and acquisition are made at the time the condition is satisfied. [*TCGA 1992, s 28*]. See *Eastham v Leigh London & Provincial Properties Ltd CA 1971, 46 TC 687* and *Johnson v Edwards Ch D 1981, 54 TC 488*. See also under hire purchase below.

Gifts. A gift is treated as having been made when the donor has done everything within his power to transfer the property to the donee (*Re Rose, Rose and Others v CIR CA, [1952] 1 All ER 1217*).

Hire purchase. A transaction under which the assets may pass to the hirer at the end of the hire is treated as a disposal of the whole asset at the beginning of that period, with subsequent adjustments if the agreement terminates without the hirer acquiring the asset. [*TCGA 1992, s 27*]. For consideration of hire-purchase and conditional contracts (see above), see *Lyon v Pettigrew Ch D 1985, 58 TC 452*.

Capital sums. Deemed disposals covered by 17.7 below take place on the receipt of the capital sum. [*TCGA 1992, s 22(2)*]. See *Chaloner v Pellipar Investments Ltd Ch D 1996, 68 TC 238* in which it was held, by reference to the particular facts of the case, that a capital sum received by the taxpayer in 'money's worth' fell outside *section 22* and that the date of disposal had thus to be determined by reference to the contract date as above.

Options. See 17.10 below.

Assets lost or destroyed are deemed to be disposed of at the time of loss etc. [*TCGA 1992, s 24(1)*]. It seems that this provision does not override *TCGA 1992, s 22(2)* above where an actual capital sum is received subsequent to the loss etc. (see comments by Hoffman J in the Ch D in *Powlson v Welbeck Securities Ltd CA 1987, 60 TC 269*).

Assets becoming of negligible value. See 39.9 LOSSES.

Land compulsorily acquired. See 36.9 LAND for acquisition of land by an authority possessing any power of compulsory purchase.

Rollover relief. See 55.1 ROLLOVER RELIEF.

17.3 **ALLOWABLE EXPENDITURE—GENERAL PROVISIONS**

Except as otherwise expressly provided, the sums allowable as a deduction from the consideration in the computation of any gain accruing to a person on the disposal of an asset are restricted to the following.

(*a*) **The amount or value of the consideration, in money or money's worth, given wholly and exclusively for the acquisition of the asset** (plus 'incidental costs') or expenditure incurred wholly and exclusively in providing the asset [*TCGA 1992, s 38(1)(a)*]. See *Cleveleys Investment Trust Co v CIR (No 2) CS 1975, 51 TC 26; Allison v Murray Ch D 1975, 51 TC 57; Garner v Pounds Shipowners & Shipbreakers Ltd (and related appeal) HL, [2000] STC 420.*

'*Incidental costs*' of acquisition are (strictly) limited to expenditure wholly and exclusively incurred for the purposes of the acquisition, being

(i) fees, commission or remuneration for the professional services of a surveyor, valuer, auctioneer, accountant, agent or legal adviser;

(ii) transfer/conveyancing charges (including stamp duty); and

(iii) advertising to find a seller.

[*TCGA 1992, s 38(2)*].

Where the purchaser is a company, and the purchase price is satisfied by the issue of fully paid-up shares in the company, the consideration is the shares and their value is normally that placed on them by the parties, i.e. the purchase price satisfied by the issue. 'Value' in *TCGA 1992, s 38(1)(a)* (see above) does not mean 'market value' (*Stanton v Drayton Commercial Investment Co Ltd HL 1982, 55 TC 286*). Disposals which are deemed to take place at market value will, generally speaking, give rise to an equivalent base cost in the acquirer's hands (but see 40.1 MARKET VALUE). No allowance is given for notional costs of disposal or reacquisition, where there is a deemed disposal and reacquisition. [*TCGA 1992, s 17, s 38(4)*].

Where the cost (or deemed cost) of an asset is in foreign currency, it is converted into sterling at the exchange rate ruling at the time of acquisition. Similarly, consideration is converted at the date of disposal. (*Bentley v Pike Ch D 1981, 53 TC 590; Capcount Trading v Evans CA 1992, 65 TC 545*). However, the principle laid down by these cases is superseded, in the case of a 'qualifying company', where the taxation regime for exchange gains and losses noted at 13.44 COMPANIES and covered in TOLLEY'S CORPORATION TAX has effect. By contrast (and where that regime had not come into force), where a company borrowed foreign currency and entered into a forward contract to purchase sufficient foreign currency to repay the loan some ten months later, which in effect commercially was a single composite transaction, these were treated as separate transactions for capital gains purposes. As a result, the forward currency contract produced a chargeable gain and the repayment of the currency loan produced a loss on exchange that was not an allowable loss for capital gains tax. (*Whittles v Uniholdings Ltd (No 3) CA, [1996] STC 914*).

See (*b*) below for capital contributions by shareholders.

A company with an annual turnover of not less than £5 million may round incidental costs of acquisition to the nearest £1,000 subject to certain conditions and exceptions (Revenue Pamphlet IR 131, SP 15/93).

(*b*) **Expenditure wholly and exclusively incurred for the purpose of enhancing the value of the asset being expenditure reflected in the state or nature of the asset at the time of disposal.** [*TCGA 1992, s 38(1)(b)*]. Expenditure on initial repairs (including decoration) to a property, undertaken to put it into a fit state for letting, and not allowable for Schedule A purposes, is regarded as allowable expenditure under this heading (Revenue Pamphlet IR 131, SP D24). The Revenue consider that capital contributions made to a company by shareholders are not allowable expenditure under this heading, but that if made at the time of issue of the shares they might be treated as in the nature of a share premium (ICAEW Guidance Note TR 713, 23 August 1988 and Revenue Capital Gains Manual CG 43500). See also 17.5(A) below.

'*Expenditure*' does not include the value of personal labour and skill (*Oram v Johnson Ch D 1980, 53 TC 319*). However, it may be in the form of providing money's worth and may be first reflected in the state or nature of the asset before completion even if this is after the time of disposal (*Chaney v Watkis Ch D 1985, 58 TC 707*).

(*c*) **Expenditure wholly and exclusively incurred in establishing, preserving or defending title to, or to a right over, the asset.** [*TCGA 1992, s 38(1)(b)*]. This includes resealing Scottish confirmation and other probate etc. expenses incurred to establish the title of the personal representatives (*Richards' Executors HL 1971, 46 TC 626* and see 16.8 DEATH) and see 57.9 SETTLEMENTS.

(*d*) **Incidental costs of disposal.** [*TCGA 1992, s 38(1)(c)*]. Strictly, such costs are limited to expenditure wholly and exclusively incurred for the purposes of the disposal, being

(i) fees, commission or remuneration for the professional services of a surveyor, valuer, auctioneer, accountant, agent or legal adviser;

(ii) transfer/conveyancing charges (including stamp duty);

(iii) advertising to find a buyer; and

(iv) any other costs reasonably incurred in making any valuation or apportionment for capital gains tax purposes, including, in particular, expenses reasonably incurred in ascertaining market value where this is required under *TCGA 1992*.

[*TCGA 1992, s 38(2)*].

Stamp duty and other expenses of terminating a settlement incurred to bring about a chargeable occasion within *TCGA 1992, s 71* are allowable (*Chubb's Trustee CS 1971, 47 TC 353*).

Costs within (iv) above extend only to costs reasonably incurred in making the valuation or apportionment, and not to any subsequent costs incurred in negotiating a value with the Revenue or in litigation with it concerning the value (Revenue Tax Bulletin February 1994 p 116) and see *Caton's Administrators v Couch CA 1997, 70 TC 10*. The costs of obtaining post-transaction valuation checks (see 54.5 RETURNS) are not deductible (Revenue Capital Gains Manual CG 15261, 16615).

A company with an annual turnover of not less than £5 million may round incidental costs of disposal to the nearest £1,000 subject to certain conditions and exceptions (Revenue Pamphlet IR 131, SP 15/93).

17.4 **ALLOWABLE EXPENDITURE—SPECIAL CASES**

In addition to the general provisions relating to allowable expenditure in 17.3 above, specific items of expenditure are allowed as follows.

(*a*) **Interest in certain (now very rare) circumstances** on money borrowed by a *company* for financing allowable expenditure on the construction of a building, structure, or work. There is no such provision for individuals, trustees, etc. See 13.9 COMPANIES.

(*b*) **Income tax paid by a close company participator** on income which has been apportioned to him (broadly in relation only to accounting periods ending before 1 April 1989) but which remains undistributed is an allowable deduction. [*TCGA 1992, s 124*]. Alternatively, the Revenue will restrict a participator's 'excess liability' on an apportionment for a period after commencement of winding-up to the excess, if any, over capital gains tax paid on distributions made in respect of the participator's share by the liquidator during that period. Where post liquidation income is apportioned to trust beneficiaries or residuary legatees, account will be taken of any relevant capital gains tax paid by the trustees or personal representatives (see Revenue Pamphlet IR 1, A36). Where tax on the apportioned income is borne by a beneficiary under a trust or by a residuary legatee, the relief is extended to a disposal of the relevant shares by the trustees or by the personal representatives (see Revenue Pamphlet IR 1, D12). The reliefs in IR 1, A36 and D12 are in the alternative. See also 3.15 ANTI-AVOIDANCE regarding *TCGA 1992, s 125* (close company transferring assets at undervalue).

(*c*) **Foreign tax** borne by the disposer on the disposal is deductible. See 18.5 DOUBLE TAX RELIEF.

(*d*) **Inheritance tax** is a deduction in some circumstances. See 33.2 INTERACTION WITH OTHER TAXES.

(*e*) **Acquisitions from persons neither resident nor ordinarily resident in the UK.** Where, *after 9 March 1981 and before 6 April 1983*,

(i) a person acquired an asset for no valuable consideration, or for a consideration lower than the asset's market value, and no other amount or value was imputed to the consideration by operation of *CGTA 1979* (e.g. under the MARKET VALUE (40) rules); and

(ii) there was a corresponding disposal of the asset by a person neither resident nor ordinarily resident in the UK; and

(iii) a charge to income tax, corporation tax or capital gains tax arose in respect of the acquisition in (i) above;

a deduction is given on the subsequent disposal of the asset by the acquirer, equal to the amount in respect of which the charge in (iii) above arises. The condition in (iii) above was taken to be satisfied where, under *FA 1981, s 80(3)* (now *TCGA 1992, s 87(4)*; see 43.13 OFFSHORE SETTLEMENTS), in any year of assessment, gains were attributed to a beneficiary of a non-resident settlement, by reason of that beneficiary's acquisition of an asset in that or an earlier fiscal year. In such circumstances, the deduction is the amount of the gains attributed to the beneficiary because of the acquisition of the said asset.

After 5 April 1983, the market value rules were amended so that, subject to the election below, an acquisition under the circumstances in (i) to (iii) is treated as being made at market value and the above provisions do not apply. Where, however, the corresponding disposal under (ii) is made *after 5 April 1983 and before 6 April 1985* the persons acquiring and disposing of the asset may jointly elect that both the acquisition and disposal are excepted from the amended market value rules in which case the above provisions still apply. [*CGTA 1979, s 32(5)(6); FA 1981, s 90(2); FA 1984, s 66(3)*]. See 40.1 MARKET VALUE for further details.

(*f*) **Stock dividends.** The 'appropriate amount in cash' relating to a stock dividend is deductible. See 58.13 SHARES AND SECURITIES.

(*g*) **Offshore funds and deep discount securities.** Certain sums charged to income tax on the disposal of interests in offshore funds and on the disposal of deep discount securities. See 44.8 OVERSEAS MATTERS and 58.20 SHARES AND SECURITIES.

(*h*) **Shares acquired by employees.** See 19 EMPLOYEE SHARE SCHEMES.

(*j*) **Legatees and beneficiaries.** Where a person disposes of an asset to which he became absolutely entitled as legatee or as against the trustees of settled property, any incidental expenditure incurred by that person, the personal representatives or the trustees in relation to the transfer of the asset to him, is allowable. [*TCGA 1992, s 64(1)*]. See 16.9 DEATH and 57.9 SETTLEMENTS.

(*k*) **Devaluation of sterling in November 1967.** In computing gains on the disposal of foreign securities purchased out of foreign currency borrowed before 19 November 1967 for that purpose (by permission given, subject to specified conditions, under *Exchange Control Act 1947*) the deduction under 17.3(A) above is increased by one-sixth. A similar increase applies to disposals after 18 November 1967 of foreign securities which at that date formed part of a trust fund established abroad by a Lloyd's underwriter, etc., or a company engaged in marine protection or indemnity assurance on a mutual basis, which consists of premiums received and used mainly for meeting business liabilities arising in the country in which the fund is set up. [*TCGA 1992, Sch 11 paras 13, 14*].

17.5 NON-ALLOWABLE EXPENDITURE

In no case is allowance given for the following.

(*a*) Expenditure which is deductible in computing profits or losses for income tax purposes [*TCGA 1992, s 39(1)*] or would be so deductible if the asset were held as a fixed asset of a trade [*TCGA 1992, s 39(2)*]. See *Emmerson v Computer Time International Ltd CA 1977, 50 TC 628.*

(*b*) Premiums paid to cover the risk of damage to, or loss or depreciation of, the asset. [*TCGA 1992, s 205*].

(*c*) Any expenditure recoverable from any government or public or local authority in the UK or elsewhere. Where such a grant is subsequently repaid, the consideration on disposal of the asset may be treated, by concession, as reduced by the amount repaid. (Revenue Pamphlet IR 1, D53). [*TCGA 1992, s 50*]. (See Revenue Tax Bulletin April 1999 pp 642–645 (in particular, Example 2) re the application of this provision to land introduced by a public sector body into a Private Finance Initiative contract as a contribution to the private sector operator's construction costs.)

(*d*) Interest, except as under 17.4(*a*) above. [*TCGA 1992, s 38(3)*].

(*e*) Income tax chargeable on shares acquired under certain employee schemes. See 19 EMPLOYEE SHARE SCHEMES.

(*f*) Liabilities remaining with, or assumed by, the disposer contingent upon the default of the assignee of a lease, or upon the breach of covenants in a conveyance or lease of land, or of warranties, or representations made on the sale or lease of other property. If the contingent liability subsequently becomes enforceable and is enforced, relief is given by way of discharge or repayment. [*TCGA 1992, s 49; FA*

1996, Sch 20 para 49]. An amount received under a warranty or indemnity is normally deductible from acquisition cost (Revenue Pamphlet IR 1, D33 and Revenue Capital Gains Manual CG 13043, 13044). See further 36.23 LAND.

(*g*) Any discount for postponement of receipt of the consideration and, in the first instance, for any risk of non-recovery, or for any contingency in the right to receive any part of the consideration. If, however, any part of the consideration subsequently proves to be irrecoverable, on a claim to that effect the tax liability will be adjusted accordingly which may result in a discharge or repayment of tax. [*TCGA 1992, s 48; FA 1996, Sch 20 para 48*]. (See *Marson v Marriage Ch D 1979, 54 TC 59.*) See also 17.7 below and 46.6 PAYMENT OF TAX for the possibility of payment by instalments.

Where consideration for a disposal is fixed in a foreign currency, any subsequent loss on exchange is not irrecoverable consideration for the purposes of a claim under *TCGA 1992, s 48*. See *Goodbrand v Loffland Bros North Sea Inc CA 1998, 71 TC 57*.

A subsequent payment, by the vendor of an option to a third party, to release restrictive covenants did not alter the consideration received for the option and was not allowable expenditure in computing the gain (*Garner v Pounds Shipowners & Shipbreakers Ltd (and related appeal) HL, [2000] STC 420*).

(*h*) Notional expenses on deemed disposals and acquisitions. [*TCGA 1992, s 38(4)*].

(*j*) Where a 'loss' would otherwise be shown, expenditure otherwise allowable as a deduction is reduced to the extent that capital allowances have been made in respect of it. The capital allowances taken into account are those granted (less any balancing charge) to the disposer. Where the asset was treated for capital allowance purposes as acquired at written-down value, allowances granted to any former owner which were not taken into account in restricting his loss are also deducted from allowable expenditure. '*Loss*' seemed to refer to the unindexed loss for disposals before 30 November 1993 and after 5 April 1985 (after 31 March 1985 for companies), when the restriction of allowable expenditure above also applied in the calculation of the indexation allowance so that, broadly, the allowable loss was the indexation allowance arising. The Revenue maintain that '*loss*' is the indexed loss, i.e. the loss after indexation (Revenue Capital Gains Manual CG 17450), though this is arguable. Where the loss-making disposal is of machinery or plant in relation to expenditure on which allowances or charges have been made for capital allowance purposes and which has been used solely for trade purposes and has not attracted wear and tear subsidies which would deny capital allowances, the capital allowances (if any) are deemed to be the difference between the expenditure incurred (or treated as incurred) by the disposer, and the disposal value. [*TCGA 1992, s 41(1)–(7), s 53(3)*]. See also 7.13 ASSETS HELD ON 6 APRIL 1965, 8.8 ASSETS HELD ON 31 MARCH 1982 and 13.16 COMPANIES for further applications of these rules.

17.6 PART DISPOSALS

References to a disposal for the purposes of the capital gains tax legislation include, unless otherwise required, references to a part disposal. There is a part disposal of an asset where an interest or right in or over the asset is created by the disposal, as well as where it subsists before the disposal, and generally, there is a part disposal of an asset where, on a person making a disposal, any description of property derived from the asset remains undisposed of. [*TCGA 1992, s 21(2)*].

Where a disposal is partial, those deductions which are not wholly attributable either to the part retained or to the part disposed of are apportioned over the total value of the asset, including the part retained, and only the portion relative to the part disposed of is deductible from the consideration received for it. This apportionment also applies for indexation allowance purposes. The apportioned allowable expenditure is calculated by reference to the formula

$$\frac{A}{A + B}$$

where

A is the consideration received or deemed to have been received; and

B is the market value of the part retained.

Any such apportionment is to be made before applying the following provisions.

(*a*) *TCGA 1992, s 41* (restriction of losses by reference to capital allowances, see 17.5(*j*) above). (If after the part disposal there is a subsequent disposal of the asset, the capital allowances to be taken into account on that subsequent disposal are those referable to the expenditure incurred under 17.3(*a*)–(*c*) above whether before or after the part disposal, but those allowances are reduced by the amount, if any, by which the loss on the earlier disposal was restricted under *TCGA 1992, s 41*.)

(*b*) *TCGA 1992, s 58(1)* (transfers between husband and wife, see 41.3 MARRIED PERSONS).

(*c*) *TCGA 1992, ss 152-158* (replacement of business assets, see 55 ROLLOVER RELIEF).

(*d*) *TCGA 1992, s 171(1)* (transfers within a group of companies, see 13.12 COMPANIES).

(*e*) Any other provision making an adjustment to secure that neither a gain nor a loss occurs on disposal.

(*f*) The computation of any indexation allowance. [*TCGA 1992, s 56(1); FA 1994, Sch 26 Pt V*].

[*TCGA 1992, s 42*].

Similar apportionments of allowable deductions are made where assets have been merged or divided, have changed their nature, or have had interests created out of them, etc. [*TCGA 1992, s 43*].

See 8 ASSETS HELD ON 31 MARCH 1982 for further applications of *TCGA 1992, s 42* and *s 43*.

Any other necessary apportionment is to be made as may be 'just and reasonable'. [*TCGA 1992, s 52(4), Sch 11 para 11; FA 1996, Sch 20 para 50*]. The Revenue cites the case of *EV Booth (Holdings) Ltd v Buckwell Ch D 1980, 53 TC 425* as authority for its view that if the inspector is satisfied with the allocation contained in a contract made between parties bargaining at arm's length, it is not open to either the vendor or the purchaser to seek to alter that apportionment for capital gains tax purposes. In contrast, where the terms of the contract are artificial it takes the view that *TCGA 1992, s 52(4)* may be applied irrespective of the way in which the vendor and purchaser have agreed to allocate the overall price (Revenue Capital Gains Manual CG 14772).

Example

X buys a piece of land in 1986 for £182,000. He subsequently sells half of it to Y in May 2000 for £150,000. The remainder of the land, because of its better position, is estimated to be then worth £200,000.

X's unindexed gain is computed as follows

A = £150,000

B = £200,000

Allowable expenditure attributable to the part disposed of

$$\frac{150{,}000}{(150{,}000\ +\ 200{,}000)} \times £182{,}000 = \underline{£78{,}000}$$

Unindexed gain (subject to indexation to April 1998 and TAPER RELIEF (60)): £150,000 – £78,000 = $\underline{£72{,}000}$

The allowable expenditure on a disposal of the remaining land will be £104,000, i.e. £182,000 less £78,000.

In *Anders Utkilens Rederi A/S v O/Y Lovisa Stevedoring Co A/B and Another Ch D 1984, [1985] STC 301*, a plaintiff had initially obtained judgement for a liquidated sum against a defendant, but the action was then compromised by an agreement for the defendant's property to be sold and the proceeds divided between the parties. It was held that there had been a part disposal of an interest in the property by the defendant to the plaintiff followed by a disposal by each party of his interest then held to the final purchaser.

See 36.7 LAND for relief for certain part disposals of land and 36.16 where part of the premium received for a lease is liable to income tax.

17.7 CAPITAL SUMS DERIVED FROM ASSETS

Subject to 17.8 and 17.9 below, there is a disposal of assets by their owner where any 'capital sum' is *derived from* them, 'notwithstanding that no asset is acquired by the person paying the capital sum' (which means 'whether or not an asset is acquired', see *Marren v Ingles HL 1980, 54 TC 76*, and thus not following *CIR v Montgomery Ch D 1974, 49 TC 679*). See also *Zim Properties Ltd v Proctor Ch D 1984, 58 TC 371* (which has been superseded by extra-statutory concession; see 6.1 ASSETS) and *Kirby v Thorn EMI plc CA 1987, 60 TC 519*.

For general consideration of what constitutes an 'asset' for tax purposes, see 6.1 ASSETS.

'*Capital sum*' means any money or money's worth which is not otherwise excluded from the computation of chargeable gains.

The provisions apply in particular to capital sums received as follows (other than those brought into charge to income tax — see Revenue Tax Bulletin December 1997 pp 490, 491 for the treatment of compensation received by a business).

(*a*) By way of compensation for any kind of damage or injury to assets or for the loss, destruction or dissipation of assets or for any depreciation or risk of depreciation of an asset.

Where compensation is paid for the acquisition of business property by an authority possessing powers of compulsory acquisition, any amount included for temporary loss of profits was formerly treated as part of the consideration for the premises for capital gains tax purposes (Revenue Press Release 13 December 1972). However, following *Stoke-on-Trent City Council v Wood Mitchell & Co Ltd CA 1978, [1979]*

STC 197, any element of such compensation representing temporary loss of profits is treated as a trading receipt after 27 July 1978. Compensation for losses on trading stock and to reimburse revenue expenditure, such as removal expenses and interest, are similarly treated (Revenue Pamphlet IR 131, SP 8/79). See also *Lang v Rice CA (NI) 1983, 57 TC 80* and 33.1 INTERACTION WITH OTHER TAXES.

In *Pennine Raceway Ltd v Kirklees Metropolitan Borough Council CA, 1988, [1989] STC 122*, to which the Revenue was not a party, the company held a licence to conduct motor racing in accordance with existing planning permission. Compensation under *Town and Country Planning Act 1971* paid by the local authority for revoking the planning permission was held to be derived from the licence, the value of which had been depreciated.

See 6.6 ASSETS re compensation receivable in respect of milk quota.

(*b*) Under a policy of insurance of the risk of any kind of damage or injury to, or the loss or depreciation of, assets.

(*c*) In return for the forfeiture or surrender of rights or for refraining from exercising rights.

Statutory compensation payable to agricultural tenants under *Agricultural Holdings Act 1986, ss 60, 64* or under *Agricultural Tenancies Act 1995, s 16* and to business tenants under *Landlord and Tenant Act 1954, s 37* is not chargeable to capital gains tax. This follows the decision in *(Davis v Powell Ch D 1976, 51 TC 492)* where a tenant quit the holding in consequence of a notice to quit.

Following the decisions in *Davis v Henderson (Sp C 46), [1995] SSCD 308* and *Pritchard v Purves (Sp C 47), [1995] SSCD 316*, where a tenant is issued with a notice to quit and quits before the expiry of the notice period in return for payments made by his landlord under a surrender agreement, the Revenue does not consider that the part of the landlord's payment that represents statutory compensation is chargeable to capital gains tax. (Revenue Tax Bulletin April 1996 pp 303, 304). (Grants for giving up agricultural land may be specifically exempt. See 21.17 EXEMPTIONS AND RELIEFS.) Compensation under *Landlord and Tenant Act 1954, Pt II* to a tenant giving up possession is similarly excluded (*Drummond v Austin Brown CA 1984, 58 TC 67*).

(*d*) As consideration for use or exploitation of assets.

Time of disposal under (*a*) to (*d*) above is when the capital sum is received.

[*TCGA 1992, s 22*].

A right to unquantified and contingent future consideration on the disposal of an asset is itself an asset and the future consideration, if received, is a capital sum derived from that asset (*Marren v Ingles* above and *Marson v Marriage Ch D 1979, 54 TC 59*) but see 58.9 SHARES AND SECURITIES for mitigation of this principle in the case of 'earn-outs'.

A grant received under *Farm Amalgamations Scheme 1973* is regarded as a capital sum derived from an asset (an interest in land) within *TCGA 1992, s 22* (Revenue Capital Gains Manual CG 15290).

The *entire* loss, destruction, dissipation or extinction of an asset (whether or not any capital sum is received as above) constitutes a disposal of that asset (with certain exceptions for options as in 17.10 below). (The fact that the asset may be a capital asset employed in a business makes no difference to this tax treatment — see Revenue Tax Bulletin December 1997 pp 490, 491.) For this purpose, land and buildings may be regarded as separate assets so that where there is a deemed disposal of a building, the land comprising the site of the building (including any land occupied for purposes ancillary to the use of that building) is treated as if it were sold and immediately reacquired at its then market value. [*TCGA 1992, s 24(1)(3)*]. Cf. the treatment under *TCGA 1992, s 23(4)(5)* in 17.9 below. For relief where the value of an asset becomes *negligible*, see 39.9 LOSSES.

Subject to certain conditions (see below), a gain will be treated as exempt where it arises on compensation received after 18 December 1994 (or where appeals are not determined by 19 December 1994) deriving from an overseas government for property lost or confiscated which is paid under the *Foreign Compensation Act 1950*, or under circumstances directly analogous thereto (including certain arrangements with Germany, Uganda and Iraq) other than where the compensation arises from a right to payment under the law of the country concerned at the time the property is confiscated or destroyed or under contractual or similar arrangements. This concession applies to a person entitled to compensation:

(1) who was the owner of the property at the time it was confiscated, expropriated or destroyed, or

(2) who has since acquired their title, directly or otherwise from the owner of the property at that time.

This concession will not apply to a person who is not the owner of the relevant property and who has acquired directly or otherwise the right to receive compensation in money or money's worth. Transfers within the no gain/no loss provisions of *TCGA 1992, s 58* (inter-spouse transfers) and *TCGA 1992, s 171* (inter-group transfers) are to be ignored in deciding whether the concession applies. Claims for the concessionary treatment should be made to the Capital and Valuation Division, CGT (Foreign Compensation), Duchy Rooms, Somerset House, WC2R 2LL (Revenue Pamphlet IR 1, D50).

The Revenue considers that *TCGA 1992, s 22* does not change the normal meaning of the word 'owner' so all that the provision needs for it to apply is that the person receiving the capital sum has, or had, beneficial ownership of the asset, and the receipt of a capital sum derived from that ownership. It cites the case of an asset being damaged prior to its sale where a claim for compensation results in compensation being received after the time of sale. Unless the owner has assigned his rights to compensation, the receipt of compensation will be chargeable within the provision. In certain cases, the sale itself will require to be treated as a part disposal depending on the 'hope value' of the compensation (Revenue Capital Gains Manual CG 12975, 12976).

Sumption: Capital Gains Tax. See A18.01.

17.8 **Capital sums applied in restoring assets and small capital sums.** Where a capital sum within 17.7(*a*)–(*d*) above is derived from an asset which is not lost or destroyed, the recipient may claim under *TCGA 1992, s 23(1)* that the asset is not treated as disposed of provided the capital sum is

(*a*) wholly applied in restoring the asset (not being a wasting asset in relation to a capital sum received before 6 April 1996); or

(*b*) (subject to the following) applied in restoring the asset (not being a wasting asset) except for a part which is not reasonably required for the purpose and which is 'small' compared with the whole capital sum; or (*c*) (subject to the following) 'small' as compared with the value of the asset (not being a wasting asset).

'*Small*' for the purposes of (*b*) and (*c*) above has normally been taken by the Revenue to mean not exceeding 5%. With effect from **24 February 1997**, the Revenue also regard any amount of £3,000 or less as being 'small', whether or not it would pass the 5% test (Revenue Tax Bulletin February 1997 p 397). Additionally, for small part disposals of land, see 36.8 and 36.10 LAND.

If the receipt is not treated as a disposal, the capital sum is deducted from the allowable expenditure on a subsequent disposal. [*TCGA 1992, s 23(1)(6)(8)(a); FA 1996, Sch 39 para 3*].

Where the allowable expenditure relating to the asset (not being a wasting asset) immediately prior to the receipt of the capital sum (including the cost of any restoration work before receipt) is less than the capital sum (or is nil), (*b*) and (*c*) above do not apply but the recipient may elect under *TCGA 1992, s 23(2)* to reduce the capital sum by the amount of any allowable expenditure. The balance of the capital sum is treated as a part disposal. The capital sum so utilised cannot be deducted again either on the part disposal or any subsequent disposal of the asset by the recipient. [*TCGA 1992, s 23(2)(6)(8)(a); FA 1996, Sch 39 para 3*]. Where the capital sum received is subsequently wholly applied in restoring the asset, the recipient may alternatively make a claim as under (*a*) above for the asset not to be disposed of.

If part only of the capital sum within 17.7(*a*) or (*b*) derived from an asset (not being a wasting asset in relation to capital sums received before 6 April 1996) is applied in restoring the asset (but not sufficient so as to fall within (*b*) above) the recipient may claim under *TCGA 1992, s 23(3)* to have the part so applied deducted from any allowable expenditure on a subsequent disposal. The balance of the capital sum is treated as a part disposal of the asset. [*TCGA 1992, s 23(3)(6)(8); FA 1996, Sch 39 para 3*]. In the part disposal computation, the Revenue take the market value after any restoration work.

Where *TCGA 1992, s 23(1)* or *(3)* above applies in the case of a wasting asset in relation to capital sums received after 5 April 1996, the amount of the allowable expenditure from which the appropriate deduction is made is the amount that would have been allowable if the asset had been disposed of immediately after the application of the capital sum. [*TCGA 1992, s 23(8)(b); FA 1996, Sch 39 para 3*].

The above provisions supersede ESC D1 (see 36.21 LAND) in respect of capital sums received after 5 April 1996.

Examples

An Old Master painting belonging to X and worth £100,000 (in its undamaged state) is damaged in June 2000. Subsequently X successfully claims £20,000 from his insurance company. The picture cost X £40,000 in 1993 and in its damaged state in 2000 is valued at £60,000. The following possibilities arise, the capital gains tax calculations being as shown.

(i) X retains the insurance moneys and does nothing to restore the picture. He is treated as having made a part disposal, and the unindexed gain is computed according to the formula described in 17.6 above. The allowable expenditure apportioned to the disposal is thus £10,000.

(ii) X subsequently expends the whole of the sum on restoration of the picture, but *does not* make a claim under (*a*) above. He will be treated as having made a part disposal as in (i) above, and his allowable expenditure on a future disposal is computed as follows.

	£
Original allowable expenditure	40,000
Deduct: apportioned allowable expenditure	10,000
	30,000
Add: Expenditure on restoration	20,000
Revised allowable expenditure	£50,000

(iii) X expends the whole of the sum on restoration of the asset *and* makes a claim under (*a*) above. The position is as follows

	£
Original allowable expenditure	40,000
Deduct: compensation moneys received	20,000
	20,000
Add: Expenditure incurred on the asset after compensation received	20,000
Revised allowable expenditure	£40,000

(iv) X expends £19,000 on restoration of the asset and makes a claim under (*b*) above. The shortfall of £1,000 is small in relation to the compensation moneys received, and will effectively be treated as a deferred capital gain.

	£
Original allowable expenditure	40,000
Deduct: compensation	20,000
	20,000
Add: Expenditure out of compensation	19,000
Revised allowable expenditure	£39,000

(v) X manages to have the asset restored for £15,000. The shortfall is not small in relation to the compensation moneys received. X makes a claim under *TCGA 1992, s 23(3)*. The market value of the restored asset is £95,000.

	£
Consideration deemed to have been received for the part disposal (£20,000 – £15,000)	5,000
Deduct: Allowable expenditure on that disposal	
$\frac{5,000}{(5,000 + 95,000)} \times$ £(40,000 + 15,000)	2,750
Unindexed gain	£2,250

The allowable expenditure on a future disposal is as follows

	£
Allowable expenditure after part disposal £(40,000 + 15,000 – 2,750)	52,250
Deduct: Compensation expended on asset	15,000
Revised allowable expenditure	£37,250

Indexation allowance will be computed at (i), (ii) and (v) above in respect of the expenditure attributable to the part disposed of as in 26.3 INDEXATION, but not beyond April 1998. All gains are subject to TAPER RELIEF (60).

17.9 **Assets lost and replaced out of compensation.** Where an asset (other than a wasting asset in relation to capital sums received before 6 April 1996) is lost or destroyed and a capital sum is received in compensation, there is a disposal of the asset under *TCGA 1992, s 22(1)* as in 17.7 above. Where, however, within one year of receipt (or such longer period as the inspector allows; inspectors are instructed to allow two years from receipt where the delay can reasonably be regarded as unavoidable (Revenue Capital Gains Manual CG 15744)) the whole capital sum is applied in acquiring a replacement asset (other than a wasting asset in relation to capital sums received before 6 April 1996), the owner may claim under *TCGA 1992, s 23(4)* to have the disposal of the old asset (if otherwise greater) treated as made at a consideration giving rise to neither a gain nor a loss. The consideration for the acquisition of the new asset is then reduced by the amount of the excess of the capital sum received plus any residual or scrap value of the old asset over the amount of the deemed consideration. [*TCGA 1992, s 23(4)(6)(8); FA 1996, Sch 39 para 3*].

Where all of the gain on the disposal of the old asset is not chargeable as it was acquired before 6 April 1965, the amount of the reduction in the acquisition cost of the new asset is the amount of the chargeable gain and not the whole amount of the gain. [*TCGA 1992, Sch 2 para 23*].

If part only of the capital sum received in respect of the old asset (other than a wasting asset in relation to capital sums received before 6 April 1996) is applied in acquiring the new asset (other than a wasting asset in relation to capital sums received before 6 April 1996), the relief above cannot be claimed. However, provided that the amount not applied is less than the gain (whether chargeable or not) accruing on the disposal of the old asset, the owner can claim under *TCGA 1992, s 23(5)* to reduce the gain arising to the amount not applied (and if not all chargeable, with a proportionate reduction in the amount of the chargeable gain). The amount of the consideration for the acquisition of the new asset is reduced by the same amount as the original gain. [*TCGA 1992, s 23(5)(6)(8); FA 1996, Sch 39 para 3*].

Where all of the gain on the disposal of the old asset is not chargeable as it was acquired before 6 April 1965, the amount of the reduction in acquisition cost is the amount by which the chargeable gain is reduced and not the amount by which the original gain is reduced. [*TCGA 1992, Sch 2 para 23*].

If a building (including a structure in the nature of a building) is destroyed or irreparably damaged, and all or part of any capital sum received after 5 April 1996 is applied by the recipient in constructing or otherwise acquiring a replacement building (but excluding the land on which the building stands) situated elsewhere, then for the purposes of a claim under *TCGA 1992, s 23(4)* or *(5)* above each of the old building and the new building are regarded as an asset separate from the land on which it is or was situated and the old building treated as lost or destroyed. Just and reasonable apportionments of expenditure, compensation or consideration are made for this purpose. [*TCGA 1992, s 23(6)(7); FA 1996, Sch 39 para 3*]. Cf. the treatment under *TCGA 1992, s 24(1)(3)* in 17.7 above.

In respect of capital sums received after 5 April 1996 the provisions of *TCGA 1992, s 23(6)(7)* replace ESC D19 which was similar in its effect but did not apply where the interest in the land on which the old building stood was a wasting asset.

Examples

(*a*) A bought an asset for £50,000 in February 1991. It is subsequently destroyed by fire in October 2000 and A receives £90,000 compensation later in that month. A buys a new asset six months later for £100,000 and makes a claim under *TCGA 1992, s 23(4)*. The indexation factor for the period February 1991 to April 1998 is 0.242.

		£
Cost of destroyed asset		50,000
Indexation allowance £50,000 × 0.242		12,100
Deemed consideration		£62,100
Compensation received		90,000
Deemed consideration		62,100
Excess (i.e. the gain otherwise accruing)		£27,900
Consideration for acquisition of new asset		100,000
Excess as above		27,900
Reduced allowable expenditure on new asset		£72,100

(*b*) Facts as in *Example* (*a*) above except that A buys another asset to replace the old at a cost of £80,000 and makes a claim under *TCGA 1992, s 23(5)*.

	£	
Gain on disposal (see above)		£27,900
Compensation moneys received	90,000	
Compensation moneys expended	80,000	
Excess (being less than the gain of £27,900)	£10,000	
The chargeable gain is treated as reduced to the balance arrived at as above and, subject to TAPER RELIEF (60), is		£10,000
Amount by which the gain otherwise chargeable is reduced (£27,900 – £10,000)		£17,900

The allowable expenditure on the new asset is reduced as follows

	£
Actual expenditure	80,000
Amount by which chargeable gain is reduced	17,900
Total allowable expenditure	£62,100

17.10 OPTIONS

Cross-reference. See also 19 EMPLOYEE SHARE SCHEMES.

The grant of an option is the disposal of an asset (i.e. the option). This applies in particular to the grant of an option under which the grantor binds himself to sell what he does not own, and because the option is abandoned, never has occasion to own, and the grant of an option under which the grantor binds himself to buy what, because the option is abandoned, he does not acquire. This treatment is without prejudice to *TCGA 1992, s 21* (see 6.1 ASSETS and 17.6 above) and is subject to the provisions below as to treating the grant of an option as part of a larger transaction. [*TCGA 1992, s 144(1)*]. A grant of an option is not a part disposal of an asset which was the subject of the option even though the grantor possessed that asset at the time of the grant (*Strange v Openshaw Ch D 1983, 57 TC 544*).

Subject to the treatment of cash-settled options below, if an option is exercised, the grant of the option and the transaction entered into by the grantor in fulfilment of his obligations under the option are treated as a single transaction, so if a sale by the grantor can be called for under the option, the option consideration is part of the consideration for the sale, and if the grantor can be called on to buy, the option consideration is deducted from the acquisition cost incurred by him in buying in accordance with his option obligations. The exercise of an option by the grantee is not a disposal, but on that event the acquisition of the option (whether directly from the grantor or not) and the transaction entered into by the grantee (or his assignee etc.) on the exercise are treated as a single transaction, so if a sale by the grantor can be called for under the option, the option cost is part of the cost of acquiring what is sold, and if the grantor can be called on to buy, the option cost is treated as an incidental cost of disposal of what is bought by the grantor. [*TCGA 1992, s 144(2)(3)*]. The time of the 'single transaction' is taken to be the time the option is exercised (and see below re taper relief). [*TCGA 1992, s 28(2)*].

As a consequence of the option being exercised, any tax paid on the gain arising on the grant of the option should be set off or repaid (and, for years before self-assessment, any assessment should be discharged) (Revenue Capital Gains Manual CG 12317).

If an option binds the grantor both to sell and to buy, it is treated as two separate options with half the consideration attributable to each. [*TCGA 1992, s 144(5)*]. Any reference to an 'option' includes a reference to an option binding the grantor to grant a lease for a premium, or enter into any other transaction which is not a sale, so that references to 'buying' and 'selling' under an option are construed accordingly. [*TCGA 1992, s 144(6)*].

For the purposes of TAPER RELIEF (60), the time of disposal of any asset disposed of in pursuance of the 'single transaction' referred to above, is as follows:

- where the option binds the grantor to sell, the time of the disposal made in fulfilment of the grantor's obligations under the option; and
- where the option binds the grantor to buy, the time of the disposal made to the grantor in consequence of the exercise of the option.

Any question as to whether the asset disposed of or acquired was a business asset (see 60.4 TAPER RELIEF) at any time is determined by reference to the asset to which the option related and not the option. The time of acquisition for taper relief purposes of any asset acquired in pursuance of an option, or in consequence of its exercise, is the time of the exercise of the option.

[*TCGA 1992, Sch A1 para 13; FA 1998, s 121(2)(4), Sch 20*].

Cash-settled options. In relation to an option granted after 29 November 1993, alternative provisions to those in *TCGA 1992, s 144(2)(3)* above apply to a 'cash-settled' option, i.e. an option which is exercised where the nature of the option (or its exercise) is such that the grantor is liable to make, and the grantee is entitled to receive, a payment in full settlement (for partial settlement, see below) of all obligations under the option. [*TCGA 1992, s 144A(1); FA 1994, s 96*].

Under the alternative provisions, the grantor of a cash-settled option is treated as having disposed of an asset consisting of the liability to make the payment, the payment being treated as an incidental cost of making the disposal, and the grant of the option and the disposal are treated as a single transaction, the consideration for the option being treated as the consideration for the disposal. The grantee of the cash-settled option is treated as having disposed of an asset consisting of the entitlement to receive the payment, the payment received being treated as the consideration for the disposal, and the acquisition of the option and the disposal are treated as a single transaction, the cost of acquiring the option and related expenses being treated as allowable expenditure deductible under *TCGA*

1992, s 38(1)(a) (acquisition and incidental costs; see 17.3 above). [*TCGA 1992, s 144A(2)(3)(a)(b); FA 1994, s 96*].

Where a payment is only in partial settlement of all obligations under a cash-settled option, *TCGA 1992, s 144(2)(3)* and *s 144A(2)(3)* above both apply subject to the modification that, in those provisions, any reference to the grant or acquisition of an option is replaced by a reference to the grant or acquisition of so much of the option as relates to the making and receipt of the payment or, as the case may be, the sale or purchase by the grantor, and any reference to the consideration for, or the cost of or of acquiring, the option is replaced by a reference to a just and reasonable proportion of that consideration or cost. [*TCGA 1992, s 144A(4)(5); FA 1994, s 96*].

Other matters. The above applies generally but the further treatment of options depends on the circumstances as under.

(*a*) **Options to acquire assets for trading use.** An option to acquire an asset exercisable by a person intending to use it, if acquired, for the purpose of a trade carried on by him, is not a wasting asset, and abandonment of such an option constitutes a disposal of it (such that an allowable loss may accrue). [*TCGA 1992, s 144(4)(c), s 146(1)(c)*].

(*b*) **Traded options.** A 'traded option', i.e. an option listed on a 'recognised stock exchange' or on a 'recognised futures exchange', is not a wasting asset, and an abandonment of such an option constitutes a disposal of it (such that an allowable loss may accrue). [*TCGA 1992, s 144(4)(b), (8)(b), s 146(1)(b), (4)(a); FA 1996, Sch 38 para 10(1)–(3)*].

'*Recognised stock exchange*' means the London Stock Exchange and any overseas stock exchange designated as such by Order of the Board. [*ICTA 1988, s 841; TCGA 1992, s 288(1)*]. A list of designated overseas stock exchanges is given in Revenue Tax Bulletin April 1999 p 657. A list of recognised stock exchanges also appears in Simon's Direct Tax Service, Binder 1, p 7521 *et seq.*

'*Recognised futures exchange*' means the London International Financial Futures and Options Exchange and any other UK or non-UK futures exchange designated by an order made by the Board. [*TCGA 1992, s 288(6)(7)*]. A list of recognised futures exchanges appears in Simon's Direct Tax Service, Binder 1, p 7521 *et seq.*

After 5 April 1985, gains arising in the course of dealing in traded options, which would previously have been chargeable to income tax under Schedule D otherwise than as profits of a trade were instead brought within the scope of capital gains tax. Losses are treated similarly. [*TCGA 1992, s 143(1)(2)(b)*]. See also 17.11 below.

Where a person ('the grantor') who has granted a traded option ('the original option') closes it out by acquiring a traded option of the same description ('the second option'), any disposal by the grantor involved in closing out the original option is disregarded for the purposes of capital gains tax. The allowable expenditure attributable to the incidental costs to the grantor of making the disposal constituted by the original option is treated as increased by the aggregate of the amount or value of the consideration, in money or money's worth, given by him or on his behalf wholly and exclusively for the acquisition of the second option and the incidental costs of that acquisition. [*TCGA 1992, s 148*].

(*c*) **Quoted options to subscribe for shares.** An option to *subscribe* for shares in a company, which option is itself quoted on a recognised stock exchange (see (*b*) above), is not a wasting asset and an abandonment of such an option constitutes a disposal of it (such that an allowable loss may accrue). [*TCGA 1992, s 144(4)(a), (8)(a), s 146(1)(a), (4)(a)*]. (The term 'quoted option' is understood to have become virtually otiose following the introduction of the term 'traded option'; the technical differences between the definitions, which have changed from time to time, are believed to have few, if any, practical consequences.)

(*d*) **Financial options.** 'Financial options' are treated in the same way as traded options in (*b*) above except that *TCGA 1992, s 148* does not apply to financial options. A '*financial option*' is an option, other than a traded option, which

(i) relates to currency, shares, securities or an interest rate and is granted (otherwise than as agent) by a member of a recognised stock exchange, an 'authorised person' (as in *Financial Services Act 1986*) or a 'listed institution' (as in *Financial Services Act 1986, s 43*); or

(ii) relates to shares or securities which are quoted on a recognised stock exchange (see (*b*) above) and is granted by a member of such an exchange, acting as agent; or

(iii) relates to currency, shares, securities or an interest rate and is granted to an authorised person or listed institution and concurrently and in association with an option falling within (i) above which is granted by the authorised person or listed institution concerned to the grantor of the first-mentioned option; or

(iv) relates to shares or securities which are quoted on a recognised stock exchange and is granted to a member of such an exchange, including such a member acting as agent; or

(v) is of a description specified in a Treasury order.

[*TCGA 1992, s 144(4)(b), (8)(c), (9), s 146(1)(b), (4)(a)*].

Two options, purchased by the taxpayer company from the same fellow group company, intended to have effect together, and undoubtedly financial options within *(i)* above when considered separately, could not be re-characterised as a loan (*Citibank Investments Ltd v Griffin (Sp C 228), [2000] SSCD 92*).

(*e*) **Options to acquire or dispose of gilt-edged securities and qualifying corporate bonds.** Disposals of any such options are exempt. [*TCGA 1992, s 115(1)(b)*].

(*f*) **Options not within (a)–(e) above.** Such options are WASTING ASSETS (66) and the abandonment of such an option is not a disposal. Options (other than those in (*b*), (*c*) or (*d*) above) to buy or sell quoted shares and securities (being shares or securities which are listed on a recognised stock exchange in the UK or elsewhere) are regarded as wasting assets, the life of which ends when the right to exercise the option ends, or when the option becomes valueless, whichever is the earlier. [*TCGA 1992, s 144(4), s 146(2)(3)(4)(b); FA 1996, Sch 38 para 11*].

Example

On 1 February 1997 F granted an option to G for £10,000 to acquire freehold land bought by F for £50,000 in September 1993. The option is for a period of 5 years, and the option price is £100,000 plus 1% thereof for each month since the option was granted. On 1 February 1999, G sold the option to H for £20,000. On 30 June 2000, H exercises the option and pays F £141,000 for the land. Neither G nor H intended to use the land for the purposes of a trade.

Indexation factors	September 1993 to April 1998	0.146
	February 1997 to April 1998	0.049

1997 Grant of option by F

	£
Disposal proceeds	10,000
Allowable cost	—
Chargeable gain	£10,000

1999 Disposal of option by G

	£	£
Disposal proceeds		20,000
Allowable cost	10,000	
Less: Wasted — $\frac{2}{5}$ × £10,000	4,000	
		6,000
Unindexed gain		14,000
Indexation allowance £6,000 × 0.049		294
Chargeable gain		£13,706

2000 Exercise of option

	£
(i) Earlier assessment on F vacated	
(ii) Aggregate disposal proceeds (£10,000 + £141,000)	151,000
Allowable cost of land	50,000
Unindexed gain	101,000
Indexation allowance £50,000 × 0.146	7,300
Chargeable gain (on F) (subject to TAPER RELIEF (60))	£93,700

H's allowable expenditure is

	£
Cost of option (month of acquisition Feb. 1999, so no indexation due)	20,000
Cost of land (month of acquisition June 2000, so no indexation due)	141,000
	£161,000

A sum paid to a person to relinquish his rights to call on another person to buy property from him (a put option) is a capital sum derived from an asset (the option) and can bring about a chargeable event as regards gains although such a transaction is not able to give rise to an allowable loss. Properly construed, the provision above that an abandonment of an option is not to be treated as a disposal is a specific exception to the general rule that the extinction of an asset constitutes a disposal of it (see 17.7 above) for the purpose of allowable losses but it does not exempt a gain made from such a transaction (*Golding v Kaufman Ch D 1984, 58 TC 296; Powlson v Welbeck Securities Ltd CA, 1987, 60 TC 269*). The consideration to be taken into account in respect of the receipt of a contingently repayable sum in return for the grant of an option to purchase land is valued subject to the contingency provided the contingency is not within 17.5(*f*) and (*g*) above (*Randall v Plumb Ch D 1974, 50 TC 392*). If, however, a contingency is related to matters which do not directly bear upon the value of the consideration, it does not necessarily have to be taken into account (*Garner v Pounds Shipowners & Shipbreakers Ltd (and related appeal) HL, [2000] STC 420*).

If, under *Building Societies Act 1986*, the whole of a building society's business is transferred to a successor company, and in connection therewith rights are conferred on members to acquire shares in priority to other persons, at a discount or for no payment, the rights are treated as options within *TCGA 1992, s 144* having no value and granted for no consideration. [*TCGA 1992, s 216(1), s 217(1)(6)*]. See also 58.26 SHARES AND SECURITIES. Similar provisions apply where a building society confers on its members or former members (or any class of them) similar acquisition rights after 24 July 1991 over 'qualifying shares' in the society (meaning, generally, permanent interest bearing shares (PIBs) — see 49.2 QUALIFYING CORPORATE BONDS for full definition). [*TCGA 1992, s 149*].

The Revenue have expressed their views on whether transactions in financial futures and options amount to trading where carried out by: investment trusts; unauthorised unit trusts; charities; companies; non-resident collective investment vehicles and non-resident pension funds, which either do not trade or whose principal trade is outside the financial area.

In general, while an individual is unlikely to be regarded as trading as a result of speculative transactions in futures or options, case law suggests that a corporate body cannot speculate and that transactions by it must be either trading or capital in nature. Transactions in futures or options by a company may be treated as giving rise to trading profits if they are ancillary to a trading transaction on current account or, if they are not clearly ancillary to another transaction, they may be treated as trading transactions in their own right. A transaction may be regarded as capital when it is clearly ancillary to a transaction which is not a trading transaction on current account.

A number of factors must be considered in determining whether an ancillary relationship exists between a futures or options transaction and another transaction.

(1) There must actually be another transaction which has been undertaken, or there must be a firm intention to undertake it in the future.

(2) The futures or options transaction must be

    (i) undertaken to reduce or eliminate risk, or to reduce costs, in respect of the other transaction, and

    (ii) 'economically appropriate' to the reduction of those risks or costs.

    An 'economically appropriate' futures or options transaction is one which, by virtue of the fluctuations in its price and the value of the other transaction, may reasonably be regarded as appropriate to the reduction of risk. Futures or options transactions which are based on an index of some kind are not necessarily considered inappropriate in this connection. However, in general, the amount of principal on which the futures or options transaction is based should not materially exceed the principal of the other transaction.

(3) One futures and options transaction may be ancillary to a number of other transactions and, similarly, a number of futures and options transactions may be ancillary to one other transaction.

(4) Where the value of the assets or liabilities resulting from the other transaction varies, it may be necessary to terminate existing futures or options transactions or to enter into new ones.

(5) Where a financial futures transaction to buy or sell currency forward is entered into, the taxpayer's 'base currency' may be relevant in determining whether or not that futures transaction is ancillary to a capital transaction. The 'base currency' is the

currency in which value is measured and, for UK resident taxpayers, that will normally be sterling. Where the Revenue is called on to determine whether there is a non-sterling currency base, they will have regard to the following factors:

(i) the currency in which accounts are prepared;

(ii) the currency in which share capital is denominated; and

(iii) evidence of the taxpayer's intentions (in a published prospectus, for example).

(Revenue Pamphlet IR 131, SP 14/91). See also 21.50 EXEMPTIONS AND RELIEFS (in the case of pension funds) and 64.1 UNIT TRUSTS ETC. (in the case of unit trusts).

For the Revenue's views on whether transactions in financial futures and options constitute investment transactions for the purposes of *TMA 1970, s 78(3)* (relief for agents carrying out investment transactions) see Revenue Pamphlet IR 131, SP 15/91.

See also 58.12 and 19 EMPLOYEE SHARE SCHEMES for quoted options granted following a reorganisation and options granted to employees respectively.

See 55.3 ROLLOVER RELIEF for options over land as regards that relief.

See 26.8 INDEXATION for indexation allowance provisions relating to options generally.

See 13.44 and 13.45 COMPANIES for, respectively, exchange gains and losses, and financial instruments involving interest rate and currency contracts, for certain provisions which may supersede those above in the case of certain companies.

Transactions with guaranteed returns. For chargeable periods ending **after 4 March 1997** in relation to profits realised, and losses sustained, after that date, special provisions apply to a disposal of futures or options if it is one of two or more related transactions and it is reasonable to assume that a main purpose of the transactions, taken together, is or was to produce a guaranteed return, either from the disposal itself or together with another such disposal or disposals. Broadly, any profits arising are treated as income chargeable under Schedule D, Case VI rather than, where such would otherwise be the case, as capital gains (and any losses are treated accordingly). For these purposes, the existence or timing of a disposal is determined in accordance with *TCGA 1992, s 143(5)(6)* (see 17.11 below) and *ss 144, 144A* (see above), modified as necessary. [*ICTA 1988, s 127A, Sch 5AA; FA 1997, s 80, Sch 11*]. With effect from 6 February 1998, these provisions are extended to cover the exercise, as well as the disposal, of an option. [*FA 1998, s 99*]. See TOLLEY'S INCOME TAX under Anti-Avoidance for detailed coverage.

Derivatives over assets which are the subject of euroconversion. The following applies where (A) a 'derivative' represents rights or obligations in respect of an asset, liability or other amount, (B) there is a 'euroconversion' of the underlying asset, (C) a transaction is entered into that would otherwise result in a disposal of the original derivative and the acquisition of a new derivative, (D) the terms of the new derivative differ from those of the original only to the extent necessary to reflect the euroconversion, *and* (E) no party to the transaction receives any consideration other than the new derivative. The transaction is not treated as involving a disposal or acquisition for CGT purposes. Instead, the original derivative and the new derivative are treated as the same asset, acquired as the original derivative was acquired. '*Derivative*' means any commodity or financial futures or an option. A '*euroconversion*', in relation to an asset, liability, contract or instrument, is the redenomination into euros of that asset etc. where it was previously expressed in the currency of an EU Member State participating in the European single currency. [*SI 1998 No 3177, Regs 2, 3, 38*].

17.11 **FUTURES CONTRACTS**

Commodity and financial futures. *After 5 April 1985*, gains arising in the course of dealing in '*commodity or financial futures*' (which here means commodity futures or financial futures which are for the time being dealt in on a 'recognised futures exchange' (as in 17.10(*b*) above)) which would otherwise (apart from *ICTA 1988, s 128*; corresponding treatment for Schedule D) have been chargeable to income tax under Schedule D otherwise than as profits of a trade are instead brought within the scope of capital gains tax. Losses are treated similarly. In addition, *after 28 April 1988*, the following transactions, not being entered into in the course of dealing on a recognised futures exchange and except in so far as any gain or loss arising to any person from any such transaction arises in the course of a trade, are regarded as being so dealt in.

(*a*) A transaction under which an 'authorised person' (as in *Financial Services Act 1986*) or 'listed institution' (as in *Financial Services Act 1986, s 43*) enters into a commodity or financial futures contract with another person.

(*b*) A transaction under which the outstanding obligations under a commodity or financial futures contract to which an authorised person or listed institution is a party are brought to an end by a further contract between the parties to the futures contract.

[*TCGA 1992, s 143(1)(2)(a), (3)(4)(8); FA 1994, s 95, Sch 26 Pt V*].

For the purposes of *TCGA 1992*, where, *after 5 April 1985*, in the course of dealing in commodity or financial futures (whether or not, it seems, ones dealt in on a recognised futures exchange) a person who has entered into a futures contract closes out that contract by entering into another futures contract with reciprocal obligations to those of the first contract, the transaction is regarded as the disposal of an asset consisting of the outstanding obligations under the first contract, and any money's worth received or paid by him on the transaction is treated, respectively, as consideration for the disposal or as incidental costs of the disposal. [*TCGA 1992, s 143(5)*].

In any case where, in the course of dealing in commodity or financial futures (whether or not, it seems, ones dealt in on a recognised futures exchange) a person has entered into, *after 29 November 1993*, a futures contract and has not closed out that contract as above, and he becomes entitled to receive or liable to make a payment, whether under the contract or otherwise, in full or partial settlement of any obligations under the contract, he is treated for the purposes of *TCGA 1992* as having disposed of an asset consisting of that entitlement or liability, and the payment received or made is treated, respectively, as consideration for, or as incidental costs of, the disposal. Previously, in any case where a person who, in the course of dealing in financial futures (whether or not, it seems, ones dealt in on a recognised futures exchange) had entered into, *after 5 April 1985 and before 30 November 1993*, a futures contract did not close out that contract as above, and the nature of the futures contract was such that, at its expiry date, he was entitled to receive or liable to make a payment in full settlement of all obligations under the contract, was treated for the purposes of *TCGA 1992* as having disposed of an asset consisting of the outstanding obligations under the futures contract, and the payment received or made was treated, respectively, as consideration for, or as incidental costs of, the disposal. [*TCGA 1992, s 143(6); FA 1994, s 95*].

In relation to contracts entered into *after 29 November 1993*, *TCGA 1992, s 46* (WASTING ASSETS (66)) does not apply to obligations under a commodity or financial futures contract which is entered into by a person in the course of dealing in such futures on a recognised futures exchange, or a commodity or financial futures contract to which an authorised person or listed institution is a party. [*TCGA 1992, s 143(7)(8); FA 1994, s 95*].

See 17.10 above for the further tax treatment of transactions in commodity and financial futures in certain cases.

Case VI losses arising from transactions in futures before 6 April 1985 cannot be set against chargeable gains arising from similar transactions carried out after 5 April 1985. Instead another Case VI source of income may be used to offset the losses (Tolley's Practical Tax 1986 pp 96, 112).

See 21.50 EXEMPTIONS AND RELIEFS and 64.1 UNIT TRUSTS ETC. for futures contracts entered into by pension schemes etc. and unit trusts respectively.

See 13.44 and 13.45 COMPANIES for, respectively, exchange gains and losses, and financial instruments involving interest rate and currency contracts, for certain provisions which may supersede those above in the case of certain companies.

Gilt-edged securities and qualifying corporate bonds. *After 1 July 1986*, the disposal of the outstanding obligation under any contract to acquire or dispose of such securities and bonds is exempt. Without prejudice to the provisions within *TCGA 1992, s 143(5)* above regarding the closing out of futures contracts generally, where a person closes out a contract for gilts or bonds as above by entering into another, reciprocal, contract, that transaction is treated as a disposal of the outstanding obligation under the first-mentioned contract. [*TCGA 1992, s 115(1)(b), (2)(3)*].

Transactions with guaranteed returns. For chargeable periods ending **after 4 March 1997** in relation to profits realised, and losses sustained, after that date, special provisions apply to a disposal of futures or options if it is one of two or more related transactions and it is reasonable to assume that a main purpose of the transactions, taken together, is or was to produce a guaranteed return, either from the disposal itself or together with another such disposal or disposals. Broadly, any profits arising are treated as income chargeable under Schedule D, Case VI rather than, where such would otherwise be the case, as capital gains (and any losses are treated accordingly). For these purposes, the existence or timing of a disposal is determined in accordance with *TCGA 1992, s 143(5)(6)* (see above) and *ss 144, 144A* (see 17.10 above), modified as necessary. [*ICTA 1988, s 127A, Sch 5AA; FA 1997, s 80, Sch 11*]. With effect from 6 February 1998, these provisions are extended so as to apply in the case of the exercise of an option or the running to delivery of a futures contract. [*FA 1998, s 99*]. See TOLLEY'S INCOME TAX under Anti-Avoidance for detailed coverage.

Derivatives over assets which are the subject of euroconversion. See 17.10 above.

17.12 FORFEITED DEPOSIT OF PURCHASE MONEY

A forfeited deposit of purchase money or other consideration money for a prospective purchase or other transaction which is abandoned is treated in the same way as consideration given for an option to purchase which is not exercised. [*TCGA 1992, s 144(7)*]. There is no disposal for capital gains tax purposes by the person who abandons his deposit and no loss relief is available (except, in consequence of 17.10(*a*) above, in the case of a forfeited deposit on an asset intended to be used, if acquired, for the purposes of a trade carried on by the forfeiter). There is, however, a disposal of an asset to which no allowable expenditure attaches by the person receiving the forfeited deposit the amount of which is treated as the consideration received. See 17.10 above.

18 Double Tax Relief

(See also Revenue Pamphlets IR 6 and IR 20 and Capital Gains Manual CG 14380–14427.)

Cross-references. See 43 OFFSHORE SETTLEMENTS; 44 OVERSEAS MATTERS; 45.4 PARTNERSHIPS; 51 REMITTANCE BASIS; and 52 RESIDENCE AND DOMICILE.

Sumption: Capital Gains Tax. See A3.40.

18.1 Where the same gains are liable to be taxed in both the UK and another country, relief may be available as follows.

(*a*) Under the specific terms of a double tax agreement between the UK and that other country — see 18.2 below.

(*b*) Under special arrangements with Ireland — see 18.3 below.

(*c*) Under the unilateral double tax relief provisions contained in UK tax legislation — see 18.4 below.

(*d*) By deduction — see 18.5 below.

18.2 **DOUBLE TAX AGREEMENTS** [*TCGA 1992, s 277; ICTA 1988, ss 788, 789, 791–816, 828 as amended*]

A list is given below of the bilateral agreements made by the UK which are currently operative. Under these agreements, exemption from taxes in the country where they arise may be granted for gains realised by UK residents, whether individuals or companies. Reciprocal relief is given to overseas residents from UK capital gains tax and corporation tax. See 18.6(*b*) below as regards claims.

The specific provisions of the particular agreement concerned must be examined carefully. For relevant court decisions, see TOLLEY'S TAX CASES. Where tax on overseas gains is not relieved, or is only partly relieved, under an agreement, unilateral relief (see 18.4 below) will normally apply.

Where double tax relief by agreement applies, no deduction for foreign tax is allowed in computing the foreign gains (see 18.6(*a*)(ii) below). If a taxpayer chooses not to take relief by way of credit, any foreign tax paid is treated as allowable expenditure for the purposes of the UK assessment. See 18.5 below.

Reciprocal agreements with the following countries supersede the provisions of *ICTA 1988, s 790* (unilateral relief) to the extent, and as from the operative dates, specified therein (SI numbers in round brackets).

Antigua and Barbuda (1947/2865; 1968/1096), **Argentina** (1997/1777), **Australia** (1968/305; 1980/707), **Austria** (1970/1947; 1979/117; 1994/768), **Azerbaijan** (1995/762),

Bangladesh (1980/708), **Barbados** (1970/952; 1973/2096), **Belarus** (1995/2706 — see note below), **Belgium** (1970/636; 1987/2053), **Belize** (1947/2866; 1968/573; 1973/2097), **Bolivia** (1995/2707), **Botswana** (1978/183), **Brunei** (1950/1977; 1968/306; 1973/2098), **Bulgaria** (1987/2054), **Burma** (see Myanmar below),

Canada (1980/709; 1980/780; 1980/1528; 1985/1996; 1987/2071; 1996/1782), **China** (1981/1119; 1984/1826; 1996/3164), **Croatia** (see note below), **Cyprus** (1975/425; 1980/1529), **Czech Republic** (see note below),

Denmark (1980/1960; 1991/2877; 1996/3165),

Egypt (1980/1091), **Estonia** (1994/3207),

Falkland Islands (1984/363; 1992/3206; 1997/2985), **Faroe Islands** (1961/579; 1971/717; 1975/2190 until 6 April 1997), **Fiji** (1976/1342), **Finland** (1970/153; 1980/710; 1985/1997; 1991/2878; 1996/3166), **France** (1968/1869; 1973/1328; 1987/466; 1987/2055),

Gambia (1980/1963), **Germany** (1967/25; 1971/874), **Ghana** (1993/1800), **Greece** (1954/142), **Grenada** (1949/361; 1968/1867), **Guernsey** (1952/1215; 1994/3209), **Guyana** (1992/3207),

Hungary (1978/1056),

Iceland (1991/2879), **India** (1981/1120; 1993/1801), **Indonesia** (1994/769), **Ireland** (see 18.3 below), **Isle of Man** (1955/1205; 1991/2880; 1994/3208), **Israel** (1963/616; 1971/391), **Italy** (1990/2590), **Ivory Coast** (1987/169),

Jamaica (1973/1329), **Japan** (1970/1948; 1980/1530), **Jersey** (1952/1216; 1994/3210),

Kazakhstan (1994/3211; 1998/2567), **Kenya** (1977/1299), **Kiribati** (as Tuvalu), **Korea, Republic of (South)** (1996/3168), **Kuwait** (1999/2036 — see note below),

Latvia (1996/3167), **Lesotho** (1949/2197; 1968/1868; 1997/2986), **Luxembourg** (1968/1100; 1980/567; 1984/364),

Macedonia (see note below), **Malawi** (1956/619; 1964/1401; 1968/1101; 1979/302), **Malaysia** (1973/1330; 1987/2056; 1997/2987), **Malta** (1995/763), **Mauritius** (1981/1121; 1987/467), **Mexico** (1994/3212), **Mongolia** (1996/2598), **Montserrat** (1947/2869; 1968/576), **Morocco** (1991/2881), **Myanmar** (1952/751),

Namibia (1962/2788; 1967/1490), **Netherlands** (1967/1063; 1980/1961; 1983/1902; 1990/2152), **New Zealand** (1984/365), **Nigeria** (1987/2057), **Norway** (1985/1998),

Oman (1998/2568),

Pakistan (1987/2058), **Papua New Guinea** (1991/2882), **Philippines** (1978/184), **Poland** (1978/282), **Portugal** (1969/599),

Romania (1977/57), **Russia** (1994/3213 and see note below),

St. Christopher (St. Kitts) and Nevis (1947/2872), **Sierra Leone** (1947/2873; 1968/1104), **Singapore** (1967/483; 1978/787; 1997/2988), **Slovak Republic** (see note below), **Slovenia** (see note below), **Solomon Islands** (1950/748; 1968/574; 1974/1270), **South Africa** (1969/864), **Spain** (1976/1919; 1995/765), **Sri Lanka** (1980/713), **Sudan** (1977/1719), **Swaziland** (1969/380), **Sweden** (1961/619; 1984/366), **Switzerland** (1978/1408; 1982/714; 1994/3215),

Thailand (1981/1546), **Trinidad and Tobago** (1983/1903), **Tunisia** (1984/133), **Turkey** (1988/932), **Tuvalu** (1950/750; 1968/309; 1974/1271),

Uganda (1952/1213; 1993/1802), **Ukraine** (1993/1803), **U.S.A.** (1946/1331; 1955/499; 1961/985; 1980/568; 1980/779; 1994/418; 1996/1781), **U.S.S.R.** (see note below), **Uzbekistan** (1994/770),

Venezuela (1996/2599), **Vietnam** (1994/3216),

Yugoslavia (1981/1815 and see note below),

Zambia (1972/1721; 1981/1816), **Zimbabwe** (1982/1842).

Shipping & Air Transport only—Algeria (Air Transport only) (1984/362), Brazil (1968/572), Cameroon (Air Transport only) (1982/1841), Ethiopia (Air Transport only) (1977/1297), Hong Kong (Air Transport only) (1998/2566), Iran (Air Transport only) (1960/2419), Jordan (1979/300), Kuwait (Air Transport only) (1984/1825), Lebanon (1964/278), Saudi Arabia (Air Transport only) (1994/767), Zaire (1977/1298).

Notes.

Agreements not yet in force. The above-mentioned Agreements with Belarus and Kuwait had not yet entered into force at 1 April 2000. (Revenue Tax Bulletin June 2000 p 765).

China. The Agreement published as *SI 1984 No 1826* does not apply to the Hong Kong Special Administrative Region which came into existence on 1 July 1997. (Revenue Tax Bulletin October 1996 p 357).

Czechoslovakia. The Agreement published as *SI 1991 No 2876* between the UK and Czechoslovakia is treated as remaining in force between the UK and, respectively, the Czech Republic and the Slovak Republic. (Revenue Pamphlet IR 131, SP 5/93).

U.S.S.R. The Agreement published as *SI 1986 No 224* (which also continued in force the Air Transport agreement published as *SI 1974 No 1269*) between the UK and the former Soviet Union is to be regarded as still in force between the UK and the former Soviet Republics until such time as new agreements take effect with particular countries. In such cases, the stance of the foreign authorities should be clarified with them. (Revenue Pamphlet IR 131, SP 5/93 and Revenue Tax Bulletin June 2000 p 765).

Yugoslavia. The Agreement published as *SI 1981 No 1815* between the UK and Yugoslavia is regarded as remaining in force between the UK and, respectively, Croatia, Slovenia, Macedonia and the Federal Republic of Yugoslavia. The position as at 1 April 2000 with regard to the remainder of former Yugoslavia was undetermined. (Revenue Tax Bulletin June 2000 p 765).

Representations about new double tax treaties, or suggestions about desirable changes to existing ones, should be made to Inland Revenue, International Division, 2nd Floor, Victory House, 30–34 Kingsway, London, WC2B 6ES (Tel. 020–7438 6745). Questions about a particular double tax treaty and its effects on an individual's own tax affairs should be addressed to his local tax office.

Representations for new or revised double tax treaties in connection with estates, inheritances and gifts should be made to Inland Revenue, Capital and Savings Division, Room 121, 3rd Floor, New Wing, Somerset House, Strand, London WC2R 1LB (Tel. 020–7438 7741). Questions regarding a particular treaty on estates, inheritances and gifts should be addressed to Inland Revenue, Capital Taxes Office, Ferrers House, PO Box 38, Castle Meadow Road, Nottingham NG2 1BB (Tel. 0115 974 2416).

18.3 IRELAND [*TCGA 1992, s 277; ICTA 1988, ss 788, 789, 791–816, 828 as amended; SI 1976 Nos 2151, 2152; SI 1995 No 764; SI 1998 No 3151*]

Broadly, capital gains on immovable property (and on business assets of a permanent establishment) are taxed in the country where it is situate. The same applies to gains on certain assets deriving their value from immovable property. Gains on other property are normally taxed in the taxpayer's country of residence. See also 52.10 RESIDENCE AND DOMICILE.

18.4 UNILATERAL RELIEF BY UK [*TCGA 1992, s 277; ICTA 1988, ss 790, 794 as amended*]

Tax on chargeable gains, *other than that for which credit is available under the bilateral double tax agreements in* 18.2 *above*, payable under the law of any territory outside the UK (and see 18.3 above for Ireland) and computed by reference to gains *arising in that territory* is allowed (to the extent defined below) as a credit against UK tax paid on those gains by *UK residents.* The machinery and limits (with modifications as below) are substantially the same as those under which the bilateral agreements operate and the credit given is, basically, such as would be allowable were a double taxation agreement in force with the territory concerned.

The modifications are as follows.

(*a*) The foreign taxes must be charged on gains and correspond to capital gains tax in the UK but may include similar taxes payable under the law of a province, state or part of a country, or a municipality or other local body. See *Yates v GCA International Ltd (and cross-appeal) Ch D 1991, 64 TC 37*. Following that decision, the Revenue amended its practice from 13 February 1991. For claims made on or after that date, and earlier claims unsettled at that date, foreign taxes will be examined to determine whether, in their own legislative context, they serve the same function as UK taxes, and are thus eligible for unilateral relief. (Revenue Pamphlet IR 131, SP 7/91). The overseas taxes which the Revenue consider admissible or inadmissible for relief are listed country by country in the Revenue Double Taxation relief Manual at D2100 *et seq.*. See also Revenue Inspector's Manual IM 1121 and Revenue Tax Bulletins August 1995 p 244 and October 1996 p 358 as regards recent reclassification of certain South African, Algerian, Argentine, Brazilian and Peruvian taxes.

(*b*) The restriction to tax on '*income arising in the territory*' does not apply in the case of the Channel Islands or the Isle of Man, and credit is given for CI or IOM tax if the claimant is resident for the particular year of assessment or accounting period *either in the UK or the Channel Islands or IOM*, as the case may be.

For accounting periods ending after 20 March 2000, unilateral relief is extended to foreign tax paid in respect of the chargeable gains of a UK branch or agency of a non-UK resident person. The relief does not extend to taxes of the non-resident's home state, and it is limited to that which would have been available if the branch or agency had been a UK-resident person to whom such gains had accrued.

In relation to double tax agreements made after 20 March 2000, unilateral relief will not be given in particular circumstances if the agreement expressly precludes relief by credit under the agreement in those circumstances. As regards claims made after 20 March 2000, it is made expressly clear that where relief or credit for foreign tax is available under a double tax agreement, unilateral relief cannot be claimed. [*ICTA 1988, s 793A; FA 2000, Sch 30 para 5*].

18.5 RELIEF BY DEDUCTION

Subject to 18.2–18.4 above and 18.6 below, foreign tax on the disposal of an asset which is borne by the disposer is an *allowable deduction* in computing UK chargeable gains. This is on the assumption that no relief is claimed by way of credit. See Revenue Capital Gains Manual CG 14410, 14425–14427. Where the amount of any deduction allowed is rendered excessive or insufficient by reason of any adjustment made after 20 March 2000 of any tax payable either in the UK or under the law of any other territory, the time limit for revising the UK liability accordingly is extended to six years after the time when all material assessments etc. have been made to give effect to the adjustment. In a case where a deduction is rendered excessive by reason of adjustment after 20 March 2000 of a foreign tax charge, the taxpayer must give the Revenue written notification of the adjustment within one year of its being made. The maximum penalty for non-compliance is equal to the additional tax payable for the tax year or company accounting period in question. [*TCGA 1992, s 278; FA 2000, Sch 30 para 30*].

18.6 SPECIFIC MATTERS

(*a*) (i) **Amounts assessable in UK on the remittance basis.** Where double tax credit for foreign tax is allowable in respect of it, any gain which is assessable on the basis of remittance is treated, for UK assessment purposes, as increased by the foreign tax on that gain. [*ICTA 1988, s 795(1)(3)*].

(ii) **Amounts assessable in UK on the arising basis.** Where gains are assessable to capital gains tax on the basis of the full amount arising (not on remittances as in (i) above) and double tax credit is allowable in respect of foreign tax suffered on a gain, no deduction may be made in the computation of the gain for foreign tax on that, or any other gain. [*ICTA 1988, s 795(2)*].

(*b*) **Claims** for credit under double tax arrangements must normally be made on or before the fifth anniversary of 31 January following the year of assessment for which the gain is chargeable to CGT; or within six years after the end of the company accounting period for which the gain is chargeable to corporation tax. For years before 1996/97, a six-year time limit applied for CGT. In relation to claims made after 20 March 2000, the deadline is extended to 31 January following the year of assessment in which the foreign tax is paid or one year after the end of the company accounting period in which the foreign tax is paid, where this is later than the deadline given above. [*ICTA 1988, s 806(1); TCGA 1992, s 277; FA 1996, Sch 21 para 23; FA 2000, Sch 30 para 20*]. Claims for credit are made to the inspector responsible for the relevant assessment but other claims for relief are to the Board. [*ICTA 1988, s 788(6)*]. Pending final agreement, a provisional allowance can usually be obtained on application to the inspector.

Written notice must be given to the Revenue where any credit allowed for foreign tax has become excessive by reason of an adjustment of the amount of any foreign tax payable (except in the case of UNDERWRITERS AT LLOYD'S (63) where the consequences of such an adjustment are dealt with under regulations). This applies to adjustments made on or after 17 March 1998, and the notice must be given within one year after the making of the adjustment. The maximum penalty for failure to comply is the amount by which the credit was rendered excessive by the adjustment. [*ICTA 1988, s 806(3)–(6); FA 1998, s 107*]. For what constitutes an adjustment and when an adjustment should be considered to have been made for these purposes, see Revenue Tax Bulletin June 1999 p 673.

(*c*) **Limit of relief.** Where gains are chargeable to UK capital gains tax, credit for foreign tax suffered on a gain is set against the capital gains tax chargeable in respect of the double-taxed gain. [*ICTA 1988, s 790(4), s 793*]. See *George Wimpey International Ltd v Rolfe Ch D 1989, 62 TC 597* and *Yates v GCA International Ltd (and cross-appeal) Ch D 1991, 64 TC 37.* But the relief is limited to the difference between the capital gains tax (before double tax relief) which would be payable by the claimant

(i) if he were charged on his total capital gains (as computed under (*a*) above), and

(ii) if he were charged on those gains excluding the gains in respect of which the credit is to be allowed.

Where double tax relief is due from more than one source, the above limitation is applied successively to each source, but so that on each successive application, (i) above applies to the total capital gains exclusive of the capital gains to which the limitation has already been applied. [*ICTA 1988, s 796(1)(2)*].

In no case may total double tax credits exceed the total capital gains tax payable by the claimant for the year of assessment. [*ICTA 1988, s 796(3)*].

The Revenue take the view that if the UK chargeable gain (before deducting any losses and taper relief) is less than the sterling equivalent of the gain chargeable in the overseas territory, the foreign tax eligible for relief must be proportionately restricted. They are also of the view that where the gain chargeable abroad has accrued over a longer period than the UK chargeable gain, the foreign tax must again be proportionately restricted. See, in both cases, Revenue Helpsheet IR 261 (as in 29.3 INLAND REVENUE EXPLANATORY PUBLICATIONS). Neither of these views appears to have any basis in either statute or case law, and they are thus open to challenge.

(*d*) **Minimisation of foreign tax.** In relation to claims made after 20 March 2000, relief by credit under double tax arrangements is restricted to the foreign tax that would have been payable had all reasonable steps been taken, under the law of the territory concerned and under the agreement itself, and on the assumption that no double tax relief were available, to minimise the liability. Such steps include the claiming of available reliefs and allowances and the making of available elections. [*ICTA 1988, s 795A; FA 2000, Sch 30 para 6*].

18.7 **Revenue practice.** The standard credit article in double tax agreements provides for overseas tax to be allowed as a credit against UK tax on the gain in respect of which the overseas tax was computed. Unilateral relief operates similarly. There is no requirement for the two liabilities to arise at the same time or on the same persons; and therefore the Revenue consider that relief is available in the following situations.

(*a*) A capital gain is taxed overseas as income.

(*b*) Tax is charged overseas on a no gain, no loss transfer within a group of companies, and a UK liability arises on a subsequent disposal (see 13.12, 13.19 COMPANIES).

(*c*) An overseas trade carried on through a branch or agency is transferred to a local subsidiary, with an immediate overseas tax charge; and a UK tax charge arises on a subsequent disposal of the securities or on a disposal of the assets by the subsidiary within six years (see 44.9 OVERSEAS MATTERS).

(*d*) UK liability arises on a disposal of assets after overseas tax has become payable by reference to an increase in value without a disposal.

This relief is not available where a gain is rolled over in the UK (see 55 ROLLOVER RELIEF); but the overseas tax can be deducted from the gain (see 18.5 above) (Revenue Pamphlet IR 131, SP 6/88).

19 Employee Share Schemes

Cross-reference. See also 21.79 EXEMPTIONS AND RELIEFS re employee trusts.

19.1 INTRODUCTION

Income tax and capital gains tax (CGT) legislation applies where there are arrangements to allow employees (which term includes for these purposes directors) to acquire shares in their employing companies. Tax reliefs and exemptions apply where such arrangements take the form of one or more of the various statutory schemes and have been granted Revenue approval. This chapter is concerned with the CGT consequences of both approved schemes and unapproved schemes (and for these purposes the term 'scheme' encompasses any such arrangements as mentioned above). For context, the coverage includes in most cases a brief note of the income tax position, but for the full provisions (and, as regards approved schemes, the conditions for approval) see TOLLEY'S INCOME TAX under Share Incentives and Options. For the general income tax liability in respect of shares given to employees as part of their emoluments see TOLLEY'S INCOME TAX under Schedule E. See Revenue Capital Gains Manual CG 56300–56554 for the Revenue's own notes on the CGT provisions, and see generally Simon's Direct Tax Service at E4.5

The remainder of this chapter is set out under the following headings.

See 59.2, 59.4 SHARES AND SECURITIES—IDENTIFICATION RULES for special rule where shares are acquired as an employee and are subject to restricted disposal rights.

See also 17.10 DISPOSAL and 66 WASTING ASSETS for CGT treatment of options generally.

19.2 CONSIDERATION FOR GRANT OF SHARE OPTION

Where an option to acquire shares in a company is granted after 27 November 1995 to an individual by reason of his office or employment as a director or other employee of that or any other company, *TCGA 1992, s 17(1)* (see 40.1 MARKET VALUE) is disapplied (where it would otherwise apply), so that, for CGT purposes, the amount or value of the consideration for the grant, as regards both the company and employee, is the actual value or consideration passing (if any). However, in computing actual value for this purpose, any value put on the employee's services, past or present, is ignored. [*TCGA 1992, s 149A; FA 1993, s 104; FA 1996, s 111*]. Before 28 November 1995, the above applied only to options granted under approved schemes (see 19.18 below) and then only as regards the company and not the employee.

19.3 RELEASE AND REPLACEMENT OF OPTIONS

The following applies where an option to acquire shares in a company ('*the old option*') which was obtained by an individual by reason of his office or employment as director or other employee of that or any other company is released after 27 November 1995 in whole or in part for a consideration which consists of or includes the grant to him of another option ('*the new option*') to acquire shares in that or any other company. The new option is not regarded for CGT purposes as consideration received by him for the release of the old option. Any consideration given by him for the old option is taken to be the consideration given for the new option and any additional expenditure paid by him for the acquisition of the new option is treated as allowable expenditure. The release of the old option is disregarded in determining the consideration received for the new option by the grantor company. [*TCGA 1992, s 237A; FA 1996, s 112*].

19.4 UNAPPROVED EMPLOYEE SHARE SCHEMES

Where an employee (including a director) receives shares by reason of his employment and otherwise than under an approved scheme (see 19.12–19.23 below), he is generally treated by virtue of *TCGA 1992, s 17* (see 40.1 MARKET VALUE) as acquiring them at their market value at the time of acquisition. Likewise, any disposal by the employer is treated as made at market value (but see Revenue Tax Bulletin December 1994 p 181 for concessional treatment applied in certain cases to pre-6 April 1995 transactions). As regards certain shares subject to risk of forfeiture, *section 17* is disapplied as regards the employee only (see 19.10 below).

See also, at 40.1 MARKET VALUE, the **exception to the market value rule** where an asset is acquired for nil consideration or at less than its market value *and* there is no corresponding disposal. This would apply, for example, where *new* shares are *issued* by a company to an employee (as opposed to existing shares being transferred), as an issue of shares is not a disposal by a company for the purposes of corporation tax on chargeable gains; in such a case, the employee's CGT acquisition cost of the shares is restricted to the actual consideration given (if any). (This exception to the rule did not apply to pre-10 March 1981 transactions.)

A transfer of shares to a director or other employee for nil consideration or at less than market value normally gives rise to a charge to income tax under Schedule E by virtue of *ICTA 1988, s 19(1)* if regarded as part of his emoluments. The amount so charged does not form part of the acquisition cost of the shares for CGT purposes (cf. 19.5 below re shares acquired on the exercise of an option).

See 19.33 below for disapplication of market value rules where employees receive priority allocations in public share offers.

Before 28 November 1995, the market value rule of *TCGA 1992, s 17* could also be applied in determining the cost of acquisition of an *option* to acquire shares, but see now 19.2 above. The market value rule does not normally apply to shares acquired as a result of the *exercise* of an option (Revenue Capital Gains Manual CG 56379, 56380 and see 19.5 below).

19.5 **Exercise of unapproved employee share option.** The acquisition of an option and the transaction entered into by the grantee on the exercise of the option, being in this case an acquisition of shares, are treated for CGT purposes as a single transaction taking place at the time the option is exercised (see also 17.10 DISPOSAL).

Where a person realises a gain by the exercise of an OPTION to acquire shares in a company which he obtained as a director or employee (within Schedule E, Case I) of that, or any other, company, he is chargeable to income tax under Schedule E by virtue of *ICTA 1988, s 135* on the difference between the open market value of the acquired shares at the time of exercise and the aggregate of the consideration given for the shares and any given for the option. Consideration given for an option does not include any value placed on the performance of duties in connection with the employment. (In specified circumstances, a person is chargeable under these provisions even though the gain in question is realised by another person.) The amount so chargeable to income tax forms part of the cost of acquisition of the shares for CGT purposes (within *TCGA 1992, s 38(1)(a)* — see 17.3(*a*) DISPOSAL). Such cost therefore consists of the aggregate of

- the amount chargeable to income tax,
- the consideration given for the shares acquired on the exercise of the option, and
- any consideration given for the option (for options granted before 28 November 1995, the market value of the option at the time it was granted — see 19.2 above).

[*TCGA 1992, s 120(2)(4), s 144(3)*].

For the above purposes, the amount chargeable to income tax is the amount that would be so chargeable if there were disregarded any deduction available in respect of any employer's national insurance contributions borne by the employee who realised the share option gain (see TOLLEY'S INCOME TAX under Share Incentives and Options). [*ICTA 1988, s 187A(5)(a); FA 2000, s 56(1)*].

19.6 **Assignment, release or abandonment of unapproved share option.** *ICTA 1988, s 135* also imposes an income tax charge on a gain realised on the assignment or release (including the cancellation or surrender) of an unapproved employee share option. Whilst this is also a CGT disposal, the amount charged to income tax is excluded by *TCGA 1992, s 37* (see 33.1 INTERACTION WITH OTHER TAXES) from the proceeds to be taken into account for CGT purposes (Revenue Capital Gains Manual CG 56387). See 19.3 above re the release of an option in return for a replacement option. By virtue of *TCGA 1992, s 144(4)* (see 17.10(*f*) DISPOSAL), the abandonment (i.e. the lapse) of an employee share option is not a disposal for CGT purposes, so no capital loss may be claimed in respect of any consideration given for the option.

19.7 EMPLOYEE SHARE INCENTIVES — FURTHER PROVISIONS

Shares acquired at under-value. Where, after 6 April 1976, a current or prospective employee earning £8,500 a year or director acquires shares (or an interest in shares) in a company (whether or not the employing company) at an under-value (as defined by *ICTA*

1988, s 162(2)) in pursuance of a right or opportunity available by reason of the employment, and an income tax charge does not arise under any other provision (see 19.4, 19.5 above), he is regarded as having the benefit of an interest-free loan (which attracts a charge under the Schedule E benefits rules). The notional loan terminates on the happening of specified events, viz. (i) the making good of the loan by payments or further payments for the shares, (ii) the release or transfer of any obligation to make further payment, (iii) the disposal of the shares, or (iv) the death of the employee. Where the notional loan terminates as a result of either (ii) or (iii), then, under *ICTA 1988, s 162(5)*, a charge to income tax under Schedule E arises at that time on the amount of the loan thus deemed to be written off. See TOLLEY'S INCOME TAX under Schedule E for further detail. Where the chargeable event is also a disposal of the shares for CGT purposes, and in any other case on the first disposal after the chargeable event, the amount charged to income tax forms part of the CGT acquisition cost (within *TCGA 1992, s 38(1)(a)* — see 17.3(*a*) DISPOSAL). [*TCGA 1992, s 120(2)(3)*]. These provisions are most likely to be applied where shares are issued partly-paid, where payment is due in instalments or on the exercise of an option where the employment is within Schedule E, Case II or III and thus outside the scope of *ICTA 1988, s 135* in 19.5 above.

19.8 **Employee protected from subsequent fall in value of shares.** Where, after 6 April 1976, a current or prospective employee earning £8,500 a year or director acquires shares (or an interest in shares) in a company (whether or not the employing company), *whether or not at an under-value*, in pursuance of a right or opportunity available by reason of the employment, and the shares are subsequently disposed of (such that neither the employee nor any person connected with him (within *ICTA 1988, s 839*) any longer has a beneficial interest) at more than their market value at the time of disposal, the excess over market value is chargeable to income tax under Schedule E. [*ICTA 1988, s 162(6)*]. The amount charged to income tax is excluded by *TCGA 1992, s 37* (see 33.1 INTERACTION WITH OTHER TAXES) from the proceeds to be taken into account for CGT purposes (Revenue Schedule E Manual SE 3646).

19.9 **Chargeable events occurring subsequent to an acquisition of shares.** As regards shares (or an interest in shares) in a company acquired (other than in pursuance of a public offer) by a person after 25 October 1987 (and subject to *ICTA 1988, s 140A* in 19.10 below for interests acquired after 16 March 1998) by reason of his being a director or other employee, past, present or future, within Schedule E, Case I, of that or any other company, a subsequent income tax charge may arise in either of the following circumstances (in addition to any charge arising on acquisition).

- The imposition, removal or variation of a restriction, or the creation, removal or variation of a right, relating to the acquired shares or to other shares in the company, such that the acquired shares increase in value (or would do so but for another event). [*FA 1988, s 78*].
- The receipt by the employee of a 'special benefit' by virtue of his ownership of the shares. [*FA 1988, s 80; F(No 2)A 1992, s 37*].

In addition, where the company concerned is a 'dependent subsidiary' (as defined by *FA 1988, s 86*), an income tax charge arises on any increase in value of the acquired shares from time of acquisition to the earlier of

- the employee's ceasing to have a beneficial interest in the shares (such an interest normally being treated as retained for this purpose where a disposal is made to a connected person and/or other than at arm's length — see *FA 1988, s 83(2)(3)*), and
- seven years after acquisition.

Slightly different rules apply where the company becomes a dependent subsidiary after the acquisition in question. [*FA 1988, s 79; FA 1998, s 50(3), s 51(2)*].

Where a person acquires shares (or an interest in shares) by reason of his being connected (within *ICTA 1988, s 839*) with a director or employee, the shares are deemed for the purposes of these provisions to have been acquired by the director or employee. [*FA 1988, s 83(1)*].

Where an amount is chargeable under these provisions on a person who acquires (or is treated as acquiring) shares (or an interest in shares), then on the first disposal of the shares following that acquisition (whether that disposal is made by that or any other person, for example a connected person), the amount so chargeable forms part of the CGT acquisition cost of the shares to the person making the disposal. [*TCGA 1992, s 120(1)*].

The above provisions replaced the broadly comparable provisions of *ICTA 1988, s 138*, which continue to apply, subject to transitional provisions in *FA 1988, s 88*, in respect of shares acquired before 26 October 1987. The earlier provisions and the transition continue to be covered in TOLLEY'S INCOME TAX under Share Incentives and Options. Where an amount is chargeable under *section 138* on a person who acquired shares (or an interest in shares), then on the first disposal of the shares following that acquisition (whether that disposal is made by that or any other person), the amount so chargeable forms part of the CGT acquisition cost of the shares to the person making the disposal. [*TCGA 1992, s 120(2)(5)*].

19.10 **CONDITIONAL ACQUISITION OF SHARES**

An income tax charge under Schedule E may apply where, after 16 March 1998, a beneficial interest in shares in or securities of a company is acquired by an employee or director (of that or another company) on terms such that, subject to certain exclusions, his interest is only conditional, i.e. subject to the risk of forfeiture. The charge arises on the interest ceasing to be conditional or on an earlier disposal. As regards shares acquired after 16 March 1998 and before 27 July 1999, there was also a specific income tax charge under these provisions on the employee's acquisition of the shares if the terms were such that his interest might have remained conditional for more than five years. For shares acquired on or after 27 July 1999 on such terms, no charge arises under *ICTA 1988, s 140A*, but a charge may still arise under the general Schedule E charging provision, *ICTA 1988, s 19*, referred to at 19.4 above. There is no charge on acquisition, whether before, on or after 27 July 1999, if the terms are such that the interest will cease to be conditional within five years or less, except for any charge that may arise under *ICTA 1988, s 135* (see 19.5 above) or *s 162* (see 19.7, 19.8 above). [*ICTA 1988, ss 140A, 140C; FA 1998, s 50; FA 1999, ss 42, 43*]. For CGT purposes, the consideration given for the interest (see below) is increased by any amount chargeable to income tax under *ICTA 1988, s 140A*. [*TCGA 1992, s 120(2)(5A)(8); FA 1998, s 54(2)(4)(6)*].

TCGA 1992, s 17 (see 40.1 MARKET VALUE) is disapplied (where it would otherwise apply) so that, instead of his being deemed to have acquired the interest at market value, the consideration given by the individual for the interest is the actual amount or value of the consideration given as computed under *ICTA 1988, s 140B* (which does not include the value of duties performed in the office or employment concerned). However, this does not apply in calculating the consideration received for the interest by the person from whom the individual acquired it. [*TCGA 1992, s 149B; FA 1998, s 54(5)(6)*].

As regards shares acquired before 17 March 1998 and subject to risk of forfeiture, it was originally the Revenue's view that an income tax charge arose when that risk was lifted and by reference to the value of the shares at that time. Following legal advice received on 26 May 1995, they now take the view that a charge arises at the time of acquisition and by reference to the then value of the shares taking into account the risk of forfeiture, with no charge arising on the risk being lifted. The CGT acquisition cost of the shares is whatever value has been taken into account for income tax purposes. See Revenue Tax Bulletin June 1998 pp 545–548.

19.11 **CONVERTIBLE SHARES**

Where convertible shares in a company are acquired after 16 March 1998 by a director or employee of that or another company, an income tax charge under Schedule E arises on the conversion of the shares to shares of a different class whilst the employee etc. still has a beneficial interest. [*ICTA 1988, s 140D; FA 1998, s 51*]. For CGT purposes, the cost of acquiring the shares is increased by the amount so chargeable to income tax. [*TCGA 1992, s 120(2)(5B); FA 1998, s 54(2)(6)*].

19.12 **EMPLOYEE SHARE OWNERSHIP PLANS**

Subject to Revenue approval **on or after 28 July 2000**, a company may set up an employee share ownership plan (ESOP), which is a tax-advantaged all-employee share plan of which the main features are as follows.

- A plan is operated by trustees, who buy or subscribe for shares with funds provided by the company (or, in the case of partnership shares, the employees) and appropriate them to the participating employees.
- With limited exceptions, the plan must be open to all employees (other than those with a material interest where the company is a close company), but may incorporate performance-related awards within certain parameters.
- An employer can appropriate to an employee free shares in the company valued at up to £3,000 per tax year without any charge to income tax at that time (‘*free share plans*’).
- An employee can buy shares in the company out of amounts deducted from his salary up to a limit of £125 per month or, if less, 10% of salary (or such lower limits as the employer's particular plan may specify), these being allowable deductions for income tax (‘*partnership share plans*’).
- In respect of each partnership share an employee buys, the employer may appropriate to him up to two free ‘*matching shares*’, again without any charge to income tax at that time.
- Free and matching shares must normally be kept in the plan for a specified period which must be not less than three years nor more than five (the ‘*holding period*’) — no such restriction applies to partnership shares. The employer's plan may provide that free and/or matching shares be forfeited in certain circumstances (see further below under Capital gains tax)
- An employee who keeps shares in the plan for at least five years after they are awarded to him receives them free of income tax. With some exceptions (e.g. on death, disability, normal retirement or redundancy), an employee who withdraws shares from the plan within three to five years pays income tax on the lower of their value at the time of award (or, for partnership shares, their cost) and their value at withdrawal. With similar exceptions, an employee who withdraws shares from the plan within three years of appropriation pays income tax on their value at withdrawal.
- An employer's plan may provide for reinvestment of up to £1,500 worth of dividends on plan shares, in which case such dividends are tax-free. Shares acquired by such reinvestment are known as ‘*dividend shares*’.

- The employer's costs of setting up and running the scheme are tax deductible as is the market value at acquisition of free and matching shares appropriated to employees under the plan.

[*FA 2000, s 47, Sch 8*].

For detailed coverage of the above, see TOLLEY'S INCOME TAX under Share Incentives and Options.

Capital gains tax. Notwithstanding anything in the plan or the trust instrument, an employee (a '*participant*') is treated for CGT purposes as absolutely entitled as against the plan trustees to any shares awarded to him under an approved ESOP. [*FA 2000, Sch 8 para 99*]. Shares are awarded to a participant when free or matching shares are appropriated to him or when partnership shares are acquired on his behalf. [*FA 2000, Sch 8 para 3(1)*]. For the purpose of applying 59.2 SHARES AND SECURITIES — IDENTIFICATION RULES, plan shares (including free, matching, partnership and dividend shares) are treated as of a different class from any shares (otherwise of the same class) held by the participant outside the plan. [*FA 2000, Sch 8 para 100(1)*].

Shares cease to be subject to a plan when either the shares are withdrawn from the plan, or the participant ceases to be in relevant employment, or in certain circumstances the trustees dispose of shares in order to meet PAYE obligations. See TOLLEY'S INCOME TAX for full details. Shares are withdrawn from the plan when the participant directs (or, after his death, his personal representatives direct) the plan trustees to transfer them (to the participant etc. or to another person) or to dispose of them and similarly account for the proceeds, or when the participant etc. assigns, charges or otherwise disposes of his beneficial interest in them. [*FA 2000, Sch 8 para 122*]. Shares which cease to be subject to a plan at any time are deemed to have been disposed of and immediately reacquired by the participant at their then market value, but no chargeable gain (or allowable loss) arises on the deemed disposal. [*FA 2000, Sch 8 para 101*].

Plan trustees. A gain (or loss) accruing in respect of shares to the trustees of an approved ESOP is not a chargeable gain (or an allowable loss) if the shares

- satisfy the requirements of *FA 2000, Sch 8 paras 59–67* as to the type of share that may be used in a plan (see TOLLEY'S INCOME TAX); and
- are awarded to employees (see above), or acquired on their behalf as dividend shares, in accordance with the plan within the 'relevant period'; for these purposes, shares of a particular class acquired by the trustees are deemed to be awarded on a first in/first out basis (subject to special rules for shares acquired by qualifying transfer from an employee share ownership trust).

The '*relevant period*' depends on whether or not the shares are 'readily convertible assets' within *ICTA 1988, s 203F* — broadly, whether or not they are capable of being readily converted into cash (see TOLLEY'S INCOME TAX under Pay As You Earn). In determining whether shares are readily convertible assets, one may disregard any market for the shares which is created by virtue of the trustees acquiring shares for the plan and exists solely for the purposes of the plan. If the shares are readily convertible assets at the time of acquisition by the trustees, the relevant period is the two years beginning with that time. If they are not, the relevant period is extended to five years, but if within that period the shares become readily convertible assets the relevant period ends no later than two years beginning with the date on which they did so.

[*FA 2000, Sch 8 paras 98, 128*].

If the plan trustees acquire shares from the trustees of an approved profit sharing scheme (see 19.22 below), the disposal by the scheme trustees and acquisition by the plan trustees are deemed to be made for such consideration as to secure that neither a gain nor a loss accrues on the disposal. For the purpose *only* of determining the relevant period as above (and *not* for taper relief purposes), the shares are deemed to have been acquired by the plan trustees at the time they were acquired by the trustees of the profit sharing scheme. [*FA 2000, Sch 8 para 103*].

An approved ESOP *may* provide for free or matching shares to be forfeited in certain circumstances, i.e. if, other than for a permitted reason, the participant leaves the relevant employment within a specified forfeiture period of up to three years or withdraws the shares, or any related partnership shares, from the plan within that period. [*FA 2000, Sch 8 para 65*]. Forfeited shares are deemed to have been disposed of by the participant and acquired by the plan trustees at their market value at the date of forfeiture, but no chargeable gain (or allowable loss) arises on the deemed disposal. [*FA 2000, Sch 8 para 102*].

Subject to their duty to act in accordance with the participant's directions, the plan trustees may dispose of some of the rights under a rights issue in respect of a participant's plan shares in order to raise funds to take up other rights under the issue. [*FA 2000, Sch 8 para 72*]. Provided similar rights are conferred in respect of all ordinary shares in the company, the gain (or loss) arising on such a disposal is not a chargeable gain (or an allowable loss). [*FA 2000, Sch 8 para 104*].

For the purpose of applying 59.2 SHARES AND SECURITIES — IDENTIFICATION RULES, any shares transferred to the plan trustees by way of qualifying transfer from an employee share ownership trust (see TOLLEY'S INCOME TAX) are treated as of a different class from any other shares (otherwise of the same class) held by the trustees. [*FA 2000, Sch 8 para 100(2)(3)*].

19.13 **Rollover relief on disposals of shares to an ESOP.** A form of capital gains rollover relief is available, as described below, on a disposal of shares, or an interest in shares, to the trustees of an approved employee share ownership plan and the reinvestment of the proceeds into a chargeable asset. The relief is not available where the person making the disposal is a company. [*TCGA 1992, s 236A, Sch 7C; FA 2000, s 48, Sch 9*].

Requirements for relief. The relief (see 19.14 below) applies only where all the following requirements are met.

(*a*) The person making the disposal (the claimant) obtains consideration for the disposal and, at any time in the '*acquisition period*' (the period of 6 months beginning with the date of disposal or, if later, the date on which the requirement at (*d*) below is first met) or under an unconditional contract made within that period, he either

(i) applies the whole of the consideration in acquiring 'replacement assets', or

(ii) applies part of the consideration as in (i) above, and the part *not* so applied is less than the gain on the disposal (whether all chargeable gain or not).

A '*replacement asset*' is one which, immediately after the acquisition, is a 'chargeable asset' in relation to the claimant. The term includes an interest in an asset but does not include shares in, or debentures of, the company whose shares are the subject of the disposal or a company which, at the time of the acquisition, is in the same CGT group (see 13.11 COMPANIES, as amended by *FA 2000*) as that company. A '*chargeable asset*' is broadly an asset the immediate disposal of which would give rise to a chargeable gain which would not be outside the charge to CGT as a result of the claimant's residence status or the terms of a double tax agreement.

(*b*) The employee share ownership plan is Revenue-approved at the time of the disposal.

(*c*) The shares disposed of

- are not of a class listed on a recognised stock exchange (within *ICTA 1988, s 841* — see 58.5 SHARES AND SECURITIES),
- are not shares in a company which is under the control (within *ICTA 1988, s 840*) of a company (other than a close company or non-resident equivalent) whose shares are so listed,

but otherwise meet the requirements of *FA 2000, Sch 8 paras 59–67* (see TOLLEY'S INCOME TAX) as to the types of share that may be used in an approved plan. (This appears to be what the draftsman intended, though his wording is ambiguous.)

(*d*) At some time in the '*entitlement period*' (the period of 12 months beginning with the date of disposal), the plan trustees hold (for the beneficiaries) shares in the company concerned that constitute at least 10% of ordinary share capital and carry rights to at least 10% of distributable profits and of distributable assets on a winding-up. Shares appropriated under the plan, or acquired on a beneficiary's behalf, but still subject to the plan count towards this requirement.

(*e*) At no time in the '*proscribed period*' (the period beginning with the date of disposal and ending with the date of acquisition of the replacement asset or, if later, the date on which the requirement at (*d*) above is first met) are there any unauthorised arrangements under which the claimant (or a person connected with him — see 14 CONNECTED PERSONS) may be entitled to acquire (directly or indirectly) from the plan trustees any shares (or an interest in or right deriving from any shares). For this purpose, all arrangements are unauthorised unless they only allow shares to be appropriated to or acquired on behalf of an individual under the plan.

[*TCGA 1992, Sch 7C paras 1–4, 8; FA 2000, Sch 29 para 40*].

19.14 *Form of relief.* Where the requirements at 19.13 are met, the person making the disposal may make a claim for rollover relief under these provisions, such claim to be made within the two years beginning with the acquisition.

Where the whole of the consideration was reinvested (as in 19.13(*a*)(i) above), the effect of the claim is that for CGT purposes the disposal is deemed to have been made for such consideration (if it would otherwise be greater) as would result in no gain and no loss. The acquisition cost of the replacement asset is reduced by the excess of the actual consideration over the deemed consideration.

Where part only of the consideration was reinvested (as in 19.13(*a*)(ii) above), the effect of the claim is that for CGT purposes the gain on the disposal is reduced to the amount of consideration not reinvested. The acquisition cost of the replacement asset is reduced by the amount by which the gain is reduced.

The other parties to the disposal and acquisition are not affected by a claim for relief. Any provision of *TCGA 1992* fixing deemed consideration for a disposal or acquisition is applied before the above adjustments are made.

[*TCGA 1992, Sch 7C para 5*].

19.15 *Special rules where replacement asset is a dwelling-house.* Special rules may apply where

- a rollover relief claim is made under 19.14 above,
- any replacement asset (as in 19.13(*a*) above) is a dwelling-house, part of a dwelling-house or land, and,
- as is required, that asset was a chargeable asset in relation to the claimant immediately after the acquisition.

The said rules apply where the property later comes within the private residence exemption (see 48 PRIVATE RESIDENCES) (or would do if it were disposed of) by reference to the claimant or the claimant's spouse (whether as an individual taxpayer or as a person entitled to occupy the property under the terms of a settlement).

If there is a time after the acquisition and *before* the making of the rollover relief claim when the dwelling-house etc. would fall within the private residence exemption, it is treated as if it had not been a chargeable asset in relation to the claimant immediately after the acquisition, with the result that the rollover relief claim fails. If, instead, there is a time *after* the making of the rollover relief claim when the dwelling-house etc. would fall within the private residence exemption, it is similarly treated, but in this case the gain rolled over is treated as not having accrued until that time (or until the earliest of such times if there is more than one).

Similar rules apply where the replacement asset is an option to acquire (or to acquire an interest in) a dwelling-house etc., and the option is exercised.

[*TCGA 1992, Sch 7C para 6*].

19.16 *Special rules where replacement asset is EIS shares.* Special rules apply where

- a rollover relief claim is made under 19.14 above,
- any replacement asset (as in 19.13(*a*) above) is shares,
- that asset was a chargeable asset in relation to the claimant immediately after the acquisition, and
- the claimant makes a claim for Enterprise Investment Scheme (EIS) income tax relief in respect of the shares (see 20.2 ENTERPRISE INVESTMENT SCHEME (AND BES)).

Regardless of whether the EIS relief claim is made before or after the rollover relief claim, the shares are treated if they had not been a chargeable asset in relation to the claimant immediately after the acquisition, with the result that the rollover relief claim fails (and any relief already given is treated as if never due).

[*TCGA 1992, Sch 7C para 7*].

19.17 **ENTERPRISE MANAGEMENT INCENTIVES**

With effect **on and after 28 July 2000**, 'small higher risk' trading companies are able to grant options over shares worth up to £100,000 (at time of grant) to each of up to 15 eligible employees without income tax consequences (except to the extent that the option is to acquire shares at less than their market value at time of grant). The company may be quoted or unquoted but must be an independent company trading or preparing to trade wholly or mainly in the UK and whose gross assets do not exceed £15 million. A company carrying on certain specified activities deemed to be lower risk activities does not qualify, such exclusions being similar to those at 65.3(*b*) VENTURE CAPITAL TRUSTS. Broadly, an employee is eligible if he is employed by the company for at least 25 hours per week or, if less, at least 75% of his total working time, and he controls no more than 30% of the company's ordinary share capital. Companies are not required to obtain Revenue approval to schemes but must give notification to the Revenue within 30 days after an option is granted. [*FA 2000, s 62, Sch 14*]. For full details, see TOLLEY'S INCOME TAX under Share Incentives and Options.

Capital gains tax. On a disposal of shares acquired under an option satisfying the requirements of the enterprise management incentives scheme (hereafter referred to as a '*qualifying option*'), the cost of acquisition of the shares for CGT purposes (within *TCGA 1992, s 38(1)(a)* — see 17.3(*a*) DISPOSAL) consists of the aggregate of

- the consideration given for the shares acquired on the exercise of the option,
- any consideration given for the option, and
- (by virtue of *TCGA 1992, s 120(2)(4)*) any amount charged to income tax under *ICTA 1988, s 135*, which might be the case if the option was to acquire shares at less than their market value at the time of grant or if a disqualifying event (see below) occurred while the option remained unexercised.

The provisions at 19.6 above (as regards release of options), 19.8 above, 19.9 above (as regards the charge on removal of restrictions and on special benefits), and 19.10 above (charge on shares ceasing to be conditional) apply to options under an EMI scheme and to shares acquired under such options. Those at 19.7 above are disapplied (see TOLLEY'S INCOME TAX).

Modification of taper relief provisions. On a disposal of 'qualifying shares', the shares are treated for the purposes of taper relief as if they had been acquired when the option was granted. Thus, the qualifying holding period (see 60.2 TAPER RELIEF) begins with the date of grant and not with the date of exercise (which is contrary to the normal rule in 17.10 DISPOSAL).

'*Qualifying shares*' are shares acquired by the exercise of a qualifying option, but also include 'replacement shares'. '*Replacement shares*' are shares treated under *TCGA 1992, s 127* (reorganisation of share capital — see 58.5 SHARES AND SECURITIES) as the same asset as shares acquired under a qualifying option and which meet the statutory requirements as to the type of share that may be acquired under such an option (broadly, fully paid up, non-redeemable ordinary shares). A 'disqualifying event' occurs in relation to a qualifying option if any of a number of specified conditions ceases to be satisfied whilst the option remains unexercised (for details, see TOLLEY'S INCOME TAX under Share Incentives and Options). Where such an event occurs (whether in relation to the original option or a replacement option — see below), shares acquired by the exercise of the option are qualifying shares only if the option is exercised within 40 days after that event.

Where a qualifying option is exchanged on one or more occasions for a 'replacement option', the above modification to the taper relief rules applies by reference to the time the original option was granted. A '*replacement option*' is an option issued by a company which in specified circumstances takes over the company that granted the original qualifying option and which is issued, on equivalent terms, in place of the original option (see TOLLEY'S INCOME TAX for details).

Rights issues. If there is a rights issue affecting qualifying shares, the share reorganisation rules of *TCGA 1992, ss 127–130* (see 58.5 SHARES AND SECURITIES) are disapplied, with the result that the rights shares are treated as a separate acquisition and are not qualifying shares.

[*FA 2000, Sch 14 paras 56–58*].

19.18 OTHER APPROVED SHARE OPTION SCHEMES

Assignment, release or abandonment of approved employee share option. The same comments apply as for unapproved options at 19.6 above.

Earlier CGT provisions applicable to approved schemes generally. The following applied as regards all Revenue-approved share option schemes.

Consideration for grant of share option. Where an option to acquire shares in a company was granted after 15 March 1993 and before 28 November 1995 under an approved share option scheme, the grantor company was treated for CGT purposes as if *TCGA 1992, s 17(1)* (see 40.1 MARKET VALUE) did not apply so that the company was treated as if the amount or value of the consideration for the grant was the actual value or consideration passing (if any). In computing actual value for this purpose, any value put on the employee's services, past or present, was ignored. These provisions did not affect the CGT position of the person to whom the option was granted. [*TCGA 1992, s 149A; FA 1993, s 104*]. This treatment applies to *all* employee share options granted after 27 November 1995 and does so with regard to both grantor and grantee (see 19.2 above).

Release and replacement of options. Where, under *ICTA 1988, Sch 9 para 15*, approved share option schemes are permitted to make provision for the release of options over one company's shares in consideration of the grant of options over another company's shares (for example on a company takeover), any such transaction before 28 November 1995 was not treated as a disposal or acquisition, the new options and old options being treated as the same asset. [*TCGA 1992, s 238(4); FA 1996, s 112(2)(3)*]. For transactions after 27 November 1995, the position as regards *all* employee share options is governed by *TCGA 1992, s 237A* — see 19.3 above.

19.19 **Savings-related share option schemes.** Under a savings-related share option scheme approved by the Revenue, a company grants to an employee of itself or its group an option to acquire ordinary shares in the company at a specified price (the option price) at a specified future date. No income tax charge arises on either the grant of the option or, on exercise of the option, on any excess of the then value of the shares over the option price. The option price must not be manifestly less than 80% of the market value of shares of the same class at the time the option is granted. The scheme is linked to an approved Save As You Earn (SAYE) scheme with a bank, building society or other authorised provider, to which the employee makes regular contributions by deduction from salary and to which a tax-free bonus is added at maturity (the bonus date), the funds then being used to purchase the agreed number of shares at the option price (though the funds may alternatively be repaid to the employee if he so chooses, the option being allowed to lapse). Savings contracts of between three years and five years are available (the former from April 1996), and five-year contracts may offer the choice of an extension to seven years. Aggregate monthly contributions to all such schemes to which an employee contributes at any one time cannot exceed £250, and the minimum monthly contribution set for any scheme must not exceed £10 (although monthly contributions as low as £5 are permitted).

Other than in specified circumstances, the option cannot be exercised before the bonus date, nor can it be exercised, except in the case of death (for which special rules apply), more than six months after that date. The circumstances under which early exercise may be permitted include *inter alia* (i) the takeover of the company whose shares are scheme shares, (ii) where the eligible employment is in a subsidiary company, the company which established the scheme ceasing to have control of that subsidiary, and (iii) the transfer (to a person other than a subsidiary or associated company) of the business (or part thereof) to which the employment relates. In each case, the option can be exercised within six months of the change but if, in any of these three instances, the option is thus exercised within three years of its being granted, the income tax exemption on exercise is lost and a charge may arise under *ICTA 1988, s 135* (see 19.5 above); the income tax exemption on the *grant* of the option does, however, continue to apply.

The scheme *must* be available on similar terms (subject to any variations by reference to salary level, period of service etc.) to all employees and full-time directors within Schedule E, Case I and with a stipulated minimum period of service, which cannot be more than five years. It *may* be made available to other employees and directors. Where the company is a close company, those with material interests are excluded.

[*ICTA 1988, s 185(1)–(4)(10), s 187, Sch 9*].

See TOLLEY'S INCOME TAX for the full provisions and conditions for approval. See also Revenue Pamphlets IR 97 (outline for employees) and IR 98 (explanatory notes).

Capital gains tax. Other than where early exercise of the option results in the loss of the income tax exemption as mentioned above (in which case see 19.5 above), the provisions of *TCGA 1992, s 17* (see 40.1 MARKET VALUE) are specifically disapplied both in calculating the CGT acquisition cost of the shares to the employee and for the purposes of any corresponding disposal to him. [*ICTA 1988, s 185(3)(b), (4); FA 1991, s 39(2)(4)(8)*]. On a disposal of the shares by the employee, his allowable expenditure consists of the actual consideration given on the exercise of the option, i.e. the amount saved plus the tax-free bonus (plus, if applicable, any consideration given for the option itself, or, for options granted before 28 November 1995, the market value, if any, of the option at the time it was granted — see 19.2 above). The date of acquisition of the shares for CGT purposes is the date the option is exercised.

Shares acquired through an approved savings-related share option scheme may be transferred without CGT consequences to an Individual Savings Account (see 21.27 EXEMPTIONS AND RELIEFS), or, before 6 April 1999, to a single company PEP (see 58.22 SHARES AND SECURITIES), subject to the annual subscription limits for those investment vehicles (applied by reference to market value transferred) and provided the transfer is made within 90 days after the option is exercised.

19.20 **Company share option plans** were introduced by *FA 1996* to replace executive share option schemes (see 19.21 below). Unlike savings-related share option schemes and profit sharing schemes, company share option plans and their predecessors are not required to be open to all employees, and are more likely to be used to reward directors and key employees. Company share option plans are more restrictive than their predecessors in that they place a lower ceiling on the value of options an individual may hold at any one time and do not permit the option price to be discounted by reference to the current share price. New company share option plans could be established from 29 April 1996, but under transitional provisions the new rules also apply to pre-existing approved executive schemes with effect for options granted on or after 17 July 1995 (other than within 30 days of a written offer or invitation to apply for them made before that date). An executive share option scheme had until 1 January 1997 to opt out of the new rules if it wished and thus cease to be an approved scheme.

Under a company share option plan approved by the Revenue, a company grants to an employee of itself or its group an option to acquire ordinary shares in the company at a specified price (the option price) at a specified future date. The option price should not be manifestly less than the market value of the shares at the time of the grant. Normally, no income tax charge arises on either the grant of the option or, on exercise of the option, on any excess of the then value of the shares over the option price. In the exceptional case where the aggregate of the option price and any amount paid for the option itself is less than the market value of the shares at the time of the grant, an income tax charge under Schedule E arises in the tax year of grant on the amount of the difference. The normal tax exemption on *exercise* of the option does not apply if the scheme is no longer approved at the time of exercise or if the option is exercised less than three years or more than ten years after it was granted. The exemption is also forgone if at the time of exercise the individual concerned had within the last three years (other than earlier that same day) exercised an option under the scheme or under another approved share option scheme (other than a savings-related scheme) and obtained the tax exemption. Special rules apply in cases of death.

Only full-time directors (generally taken to mean those working at least 25 hours per week) are eligible. For schemes approved after 30 April 1995, or altered accordingly after that date, part-time employees (other than directors) may be included. Where the company is a close company, employees and directors with material interests are excluded.

It is a condition of approval that the aggregate market value (at the time of grant) of shares over which an individual may hold unexercised rights under the scheme (and any other approved share option scheme, other than a savings-related scheme, established by the company or an associated company) must at no time exceed £30,000.

[*ICTA 1988, ss 185, 187, Sch 9; FA 1996, s 114, Sch 16*].

See TOLLEY'S INCOME TAX for the full provisions and conditions for approval. See also Revenue Pamphlets IR 101 (outline for employees) and IR 102 (explanatory notes).

Capital gains tax. Where the income tax exemption on exercise of the option applies (see above), the provisions of *TCGA 1992, s 17* (see 40.1 MARKET VALUE) are specifically disapplied both in calculating the CGT acquisition cost of the shares to the employee and for the purposes of any corresponding disposal to him. [*ICTA 1988, s 185(3)(b)*]. Where, exceptionally, an income tax liability arises on the grant of the option (due to the option price being discounted — see above), the amount chargeable to income tax is included in the cost of acquisition of the shares for CGT purposes. This applies whether or not the exercise is in accordance with the provisions of the scheme and whether or not the scheme is still approved at the time of the exercise. [*TCGA 1992, s 120(2)(6)(c); ICTA 1988, s 185(7); FA 1996, s 114(7)(8)*]. Thus, on a disposal of the shares by the employee, his allowable expenditure within *TCGA 1992, s 38(1)(a)* (see 17.3(*a*) DISPOSAL) consists of

- the actual consideration given on the exercise of the option,
- any consideration given for the option itself (or, for options granted before 28 November 1995, the market value, if any, of the option at the time it was granted — see 19.2 above), and
- the amount, if any, on which income tax is chargeable.

The date of acquisition of the shares for CGT purposes is the date the option is exercised. Any deemed expenditure corresponding to an amount chargeable to income tax is also deemed to have been incurred on that date.

19.21 **Executive share option schemes** were superseded by company share option plans in relation to (broadly) options granted on or after 17 July 1995. See 19.20 above for the new plans and for transitional provisions.

The executive share option scheme rules differed from the current rules for company share option plans in the following respects.

(*a*) The aggregate market value (at the time of grant) of shares over which an individual could hold unexercised rights under the scheme (and any other approved share option scheme, other than a savings-related scheme, established by the company or an associated company) could at no time exceed the greater of £100,000 and four times his emoluments (as defined).

(*b*) Subject to certain conditions being fulfilled, and with effect after 31 December 1991, the scheme could contain provision for the option price (i.e. the price at which shares may be acquired) to be set at 85% (at least) of the market value of the shares at the time of grant.

Where the conditions referred to in (*b*) above were fulfilled and the scheme contained the appropriate provision, an income tax charge on grant of the option arose only if the aggregate of the option price and any consideration for the option itself was less than 85% of the then market value of the shares.

[*ICTA 1988, ss 185, 187, Sch 9; FA 1991, s 39*].

See TOLLEY'S INCOME TAX for the full provisions and conditions for approval.

Capital gains tax. The same comments apply as for company share option plans in 19.20 above. [*TCGA 1992, s 120(2)(6)(a)(b); ICTA 1988, s 185(7); FA 1991, s 39*].

19.22 APPROVED PROFIT SHARING SCHEMES

Approved profit sharing schemes are being **phased out** following the introduction of employee share ownership plans (see 19.12 above). A scheme will not be approved by the Revenue unless the application for approval, accompanied by necessary particulars, is received by them before 6 April 2001. No appropriations of shares to employees may be made after 31 December 2002 under approved schemes. [*ICTA 1988, s 186(1); FA 2000, s 49*]. In the meantime, approval will be withdrawn if shares are appropriated to a participant who has already had *free shares* appropriated to him in the same tax year under an approved employee share ownership plan established by the same company (or by a 'connected company', as defined) (or to a participant who would have had such shares appropriated to him but for his failure to meet set performance targets). [*ICTA 1988, Sch 9 para 3(2)(4)–(6); FA 2000, s 51*].

Otherwise, under a profit sharing scheme approved by the Revenue, a company provides funds to trustees who use them to acquire ordinary shares in the company for appropriation free-of-charge to employees of the company or group. The scheme *must* be available on similar terms (subject to any variations by reference to salary level, period of service etc.) to all employees and full-time directors within Schedule E, Case I and with a stipulated minimum period of service, which cannot be more than five years. It *may* be made available to other employees and directors with at least 18 months' service. Where the company is a close company, those with material interests are excluded. The limit on the market value of shares which may be appropriated to any one individual in any tax year is the greater of £3,000 and 10% of salary (excluding benefits and net of pension contributions) for that year or, if greater, the preceding year, subject to a ceiling of £8,000.

There is no income tax charge on the appropriation of shares to an eligible employee (the participant) nor on the transfer of shares to him after three years. On a disposal before the third anniversary of the date of appropriation (the release date), the participant incurs an income tax charge under Schedule E for the tax year of disposal on 100% of the 'locked-in value'. The '*locked-in value*' is normally the market value of the shares at date of appropriation (less any capital receipts previously giving rise to an income tax charge — see below) or, if less, the disposal proceeds. The charge is reduced to 50% of the locked-in value if the disposal follows the cessation of employment due to injury, disability, redundancy or on reaching a specified retirement age of between 60 and 75. Before 29 April 1996, the release date was the fifth anniversary of the date of appropriation but the normal charge was reduced to 75% of the locked-in value if the disposal occurred between the fourth and fifth anniversaries. Where an appropriation of shares is made to a non-eligible employee or in excess of the permitted limit (see above), a Schedule E charge arises at the earlier of the date of disposal, the release date or the employee's death and is on the market value at that time.

[*ICTA 1988, ss 186, 187, Schs 9, 10*].

There is also an income tax charge on any capital receipts (e.g. proceeds of a sale of rights) between date of appropriation and release date. The charge varies according to the length of time that has elapsed since appropriation. [*ICTA 1988, s 186(3)(12), Sch 10 para 4; FA 1996, s 118*].

See TOLLEY'S INCOME TAX for the full provisions and conditions for approval. See also Revenue Pamphlets IR 95 (outline for employees) and IR 96 (explanatory notes).

19.23 **Capital gains tax.** Notwithstanding any period of retention or other restriction imposed by an approved profit sharing scheme, the participant who has shares appropriated to him in pursuance of such a scheme is treated as absolutely entitled as against the trustees for CGT purposes. [*TCGA 1992, s 238(1)(3)*]. The date of the participant's acquisition of the shares for CGT purposes is the date of appropriation. By virtue of *TCGA 1992, s 17* (see 40.1 MARKET VALUE), the participant's acquisition cost is the market value of the shares at the date of appropriation (Revenue Capital Gains Manual CG 56479). On a disposal of the shares, neither this acquisition cost nor the proceeds are adjusted to take account of any income tax payable as in 19.22 above in relation to the shares at that or any earlier time. [*TCGA 1992, s 238(2)(a)*].

The fact that a capital receipt may have been charged to income tax under the provisions in 19.22 above does not prevent its being a capital distribution within *TCGA 1992, s 122* (see 58.14 SHARES AND SECURITIES). [*TCGA 1992, s 238(2)(b)*].

Part disposals of scheme shares acquired at different times are subject to the normal IDENTIFICATION RULES (59) notwithstanding anything to the contrary in the income tax provisions. [*TCGA 1992, s 238(2)(c)*]. For as long as the shares remain subject to restrictions on their disposal, i.e. until the release date (see 19.22 above), they are regarded as a separate holding as compared to other shares of the same class in the same company held by the participant. [*TCGA 1992, s 104(4); FA 1998, s 123(4)*]. Thus, scheme shares cannot be pooled with non-scheme shares before 6 April 1998 and disposals of scheme shares cannot be identified with acquisitions of non-scheme shares (and *vice versa*) on or after that date. See 59.2, 59.4 SHARES AND SECURITIES — IDENTIFICATION RULES. See also Revenue Capital Gains Manual CG 56480.

Shares acquired through an approved profit sharing scheme may be transferred without CGT consequences to an Individual Savings Account (see 21.27 EXEMPTIONS AND RELIEFS), or, before 6 April 1999, to a single company PEP (see 58.22 SHARES AND SECURITIES), subject to the annual subscription limits for those investment vehicles (applied by reference to market value transferred) and provided the transfer is made within 90 days after the shares leave the scheme.

Trustees. The appropriation of shares to participants is a disposal by the trustees. However, no chargeable gain (or allowable loss) arises to the extent that shares are appropriated within a period of 18 months beginning with the date of their acquisition by the trustees. For the purpose of deciding whether or not this condition has been met, shares are deemed to be appropriated on a first in/first out basis. [*TCGA 1992, s 238(2)(d); ICTA 1988, s 186(11)*]. Following appropriation, the trustees act as bare trustees (see 57.2 SETTLEMENTS) for the participant, so the eventual transfer of the shares to the participant does not constitute a disposal (Revenue Capital Gains Manual CG 56482).

19.24 EMPLOYEE SHARE OWNERSHIP TRUSTS

Under provisions contained in *FA 1989, ss 67–74, Sch 5*, payments made by a UK resident company to a 'qualifying employee share ownership trust' (broadly, a trust set up to acquire shares in a company and distribute them to employees of that company) are, subject to conditions, deductible for corporation tax purposes. On the happening of a 'chargeable event', any tax relief given to the company is clawed back by means of a charge under Schedule D, Case VI on the trustees of the trust, and if they fail to pay the tax it can be recovered from the company. An employee share ownership trust and its beneficiaries do not qualify for any special income tax or CGT reliefs, but may be used in conjunction with an approved savings-related share option scheme (see 19.19 above) or an approved profit sharing scheme (see 19.22 above). See TOLLEY'S INCOME TAX under Schedule D, Cases I and II and Share Incentives and Options for the detailed provisions.

19.25 **Rollover relief on disposals of shares to a trust.** On a disposal of shares, or an interest in shares, **before 6 April 2001** to a qualifying employee share ownership trust, a relief in the form of a rollover of a chargeable gain applies subject to the detailed conditions below. The relief is abolished for disposals on or after that date by *FA 2000, s 54*.

The relief given under *TCGA 1992, s 229(1)* below is available where the following conditions are met.

(*a*) The claimant makes a disposal of, or of his interest in, shares to the trustees of a trust which is a 'qualifying employee share ownership trust' at the time of the disposal and which was established by a company (the 'founding company') which, immediately after the disposal, was a 'trading company' or the 'holding company' of a 'trading group'.

(*b*) The shares are fully paid up, not redeemable, form part of the 'ordinary share capital' of the founding company, and are not subject to any restrictions other than those which attach to all shares of the same class or are authorised by *FA 1989, Sch 5 para 7(2)*.

(*c*) At any time in the 'entitlement period', the trustees are beneficially entitled to at least 10% of the 'ordinary share capital' of the founding company and of any 'profits available for distribution to equity holders' therein, and would be beneficially entitled to at least 10% of any of the founding company's 'assets available for distribution to equity holders' on a winding-up.

(*d*) The claimant obtains consideration for the disposal and, at any time in the 'acquisition period', applies all (but see below under *TCGA 1992, s 229(2)(3)*) the consideration in acquiring assets ('replacement assets') (or an interest therein) which are, immediately thereafter, 'chargeable assets' in relation to the claimant and which are not shares in, or debentures issued by, the founding company or a company which, at the time of the acquisition, is in the same 'group' as the founding company. The requirement that the consideration be applied in the 'acquisition period' is satisfied if the acquisition is made pursuant to an unconditional contract entered into in that period.

(*e*) At all times in the 'proscribed period', there are no 'unauthorised arrangements' under which the claimant or a person connected with him may be entitled to acquire any of the shares, or an interest in or right deriving from any of the shares, which are the subject of the disposal by the claimant.

(*f*) No 'chargeable event' occurs in relation to the trustees in the chargeable period(s) in which the claimant makes the disposal and acquisition or in any other chargeable period between those of the disposal and the acquisition, 'chargeable period' meaning year of assessment or (if the claimant is a company) claimant company accounting period.

[*TCGA 1992, s 227*].

Where relief is available as above, the claimant may, within two years of the acquisition, claim that, for the purposes of *TCGA 1992*, the disposal be treated as made at a no gain/no loss consideration (if it otherwise would be greater), the consideration for the acquisition being treated as reduced by the excess of the actual consideration for the disposal over that no gain/no loss consideration. [*TCGA 1992, s 229(1)*].

Partial relief is available on a claim made within the same time limit where part only of the consideration for the disposal is applied as under (*d*) above and the amount of the consideration not so applied is less than the gain (whether all chargeable gain or not) accruing on the disposal. In such a case, the amount of the gain on the disposal is treated as reduced to the amount of the consideration not so applied, and the consideration for the acquisition is treated as reduced by the reduction so made to the amount of the gain. [*TCGA 1992, s 229(2)(3)*].

The other parties to the disposal and acquisition are not affected by such claims for relief. Any provision of *TCGA 1992* fixing deemed consideration for a disposal or acquisition is applied before the above adjustments are made. [*TCGA 1992, s 229(4)(5)*].

For the purposes of *TCGA 1992, s 227* above, the following applies.

(A) The '*entitlement period*' is the period beginning with the disposal and ending twelve months after the date of the disposal.

(B) The '*acquisition period*' is the period beginning with the disposal and ending six months after the date of the disposal or, if later, the date on which the condition at (*c*) above first becomes fulfilled.

(C) The '*proscribed period*' is the period beginning with the disposal and ending on the date of the acquisition or, if later, the date on which the condition at (*c*) above first becomes fulfilled.

(D) Arrangements are '*unauthorised arrangements*' unless either they arise wholly from a restriction authorised by *FA 1989, Sch 5 para 7(2)*, or they only allow, as regards shares, interests or rights, acquisition by a beneficiary under the trust and/or appropriation under an approved profit sharing scheme (within *ICTA 1988, Sch 9*).

(E) An asset is a '*chargeable asset*' at a particular time in relation to the claimant if

(i) he is at that time resident or ordinarily resident in the UK and, were the asset to be disposed of at that time, a gain accruing to him would be a chargeable gain; or

(ii) were it to be disposed of at that time, any gain accruing to him would be a chargeable gain under *TCGA 1992, s 10(1)* or form part of his corporation tax profits under *ICTA 1988, s 11(2)(b)* (see 44.3 OVERSEAS MATTERS),

but not if, were he to dispose of it at that time, double tax relief arrangements under *ICTA 1988, s 788* (as extended to CGT by *TCGA 1992, s 277*) would render him not liable to UK tax on any gain accruing to him on the disposal.

(F) '*Qualifying employee share ownership trust*' has the same meaning as under *FA 1989, Sch 5*, and '*chargeable event*' in relation to the trustees has the same meaning as under *FA 1989, s 69*.

(G) '*Holding company*', '*trading company*' and '*trading group*' have the same meanings as under *TCGA 1992, Sch 6 para 1* (see 53.4 RETIREMENT RELIEF); and '*group*' (except in the expression 'trading group') is construed in accordance with 13.11 COMPANIES, with the change in the residence requirement there mentioned having effect in relation to disposals on or after 1 April 2000.

(H) '*Ordinary share capital*' means all issued share capital other than that carrying a right to a dividend at a fixed rate but with no other right to share in profits.

(J) As regards the condition at (*c*) above, the provisions of *ICTA 1988, Sch 18* (suitably adapted) apply as appropriate.

[*TCGA 1992, s 228, s 288(1); FA 2000, Sch 29 para 33, Sch 40 Pt II(11)*].

19.26 *Chargeable event when replacement assets owned.* Where

(*a*) relief under *TCGA 1992, s 229(1)* or *(3)* is given as in 19.25 above,

(*b*) a 'chargeable event' in relation to the trustees (within *FA 1989, s 69* as amended) occurs on or after the date on which the disposal is made, (*c*) the claimant was neither an individual who died before the occurrence of the chargeable event nor trustees of a settlement which ceased to exist before that occurrence, and

(*d*) at the time of the occurrence of the chargeable event, the claimant or a person connected with him (within *TCGA 1992, s 286*) is beneficially entitled to all the replacement assets acquired as under 19.25(*d*) above,

the claimant or the connected person (as the case may be) is deemed, immediately before the occurrence of the chargeable event, to have disposed of, and immediately reacquired, all the replacement assets at the 'relevant value'.

The '*relevant value*' is such value as secures on the deemed disposal a chargeable gain equal to the amount of the gain carried forward by virtue of *TCGA 1992, s 229(1)* or *(3)*, i.e. the amount by which the consideration for the acquisition was treated as reduced as a result of a claim for that relief to apply.

Where only a part of the replacement assets falls within 19.25(*d*) above, there is a deemed disposal and reacquisition of that part, the relevant value being reduced as is just and reasonable.

An adjustment may be made where there is a deemed disposal and reacquisition under these provisions, and before the occurrence of the chargeable event it can be said that, because of something which has happened as regards any of the replacement assets, a charge has accrued in respect of any gain carried forward as a result of relief having been given under *TCGA 1992, s 229(1)* or *(3)*. In these circumstances, the deemed disposal and reacquisition rules apply, if it is just and reasonable, as if the relevant value either were such value as secures that the deemed disposal produces neither gain nor loss (if that is just and reasonable), or, unless it produces a lower value, were reduced to whatever value is just and reasonable.

[*TCGA 1992, s 232*].

Where a charge can be said, on a just and reasonable basis, to accrue by virtue of a deemed disposal as above in respect of any of the gain carried forward by virtue of *TCGA 1992, s 229(1)* or *(3)*, so much of the gain charged is not to be capable of being carried forward for the purposes of ROLLOVER RELIEF (55) under *TCGA 1992, ss 152–158*. For the purposes of ROLLOVER RELIEF (55.5) under *TCGA 1992, s 154* (new assets which are depreciating assets), a charge will arise under that provision by reference to the earlier of the disposal of the replacement asset, the deemed disposal of it under the above and the expiration of ten years beginning with the acquisition of the replacement asset. [*TCGA 1992, s 154(3), s 236(1)(2)*].

19.27 *Chargeable event when replacement property owned.* Where

(*a*) the conditions described in 19.26(*a*)–(*c*) above are fulfilled,

(*b*) before the time when the chargeable event occurs all the gain carried forward by virtue of *TCGA 1992, s 229(1)* or *(3)* (see 19.25 above) was in turn carried forward from all the replacement assets to other property by virtue of a claim for ROLLOVER RELIEF (55) to apply under *TCGA 1992, ss 152–158*, and

(*c*) at the time of the occurrence of the chargeable event, the claimant or a person then connected with him (as above) is beneficially entitled to all the property,

the claimant or the connected person (as the case may be) is deemed, immediately before the occurrence of the chargeable event, to have disposed of, and immediately reacquired, all the property at the 'relevant value'.

The '*relevant value*' is as defined for *TCGA 1992, s 232* in 19.26 above.

Where the conditions at (*b*) and (*c*) above were satisfied as regards only part of the gain carried forward, the replacement assets from which it was in turn carried forward or the beneficial entitlement to the property into which it was further carried forward, there is a deemed disposal and reacquisition of the property concerned, the relevant value being reduced as is just and reasonable.

An adjustment may be made where there is a deemed disposal and reacquisition under these provisions, and before the occurrence of the chargeable event it can be said that, because of something which has happened as regards any of the replacement assets or any other property, a charge has accrued in respect of any gain carried forward by virtue of *TCGA 1992, s 229(1)* or *(3)*. In these circumstances, the deemed disposal and reacquisition rules apply, if it is just and reasonable, as if the relevant value either were such value as secures that the deemed disposal produces neither gain nor loss (if that is just and reasonable), or, unless it produces a lower value, were reduced to whatever value is just and reasonable.

[*TCGA 1992, s 233*].

Where a charge can be said to accrue, on a just and reasonable basis, by virtue of a deemed disposal as above in respect of any of the gain carried forward by virtue of *TCGA 1992, s 229(1)* or *(3)*, so much of the gain charged is not to be capable of being carried forward for the purposes of ROLLOVER RELIEF (55) under *TCGA 1992, ss 152–158*. [*TCGA 1992, s 236(1)(2)*].

19.28 *Chargeable event when qualifying corporate bonds owned.* Where

(*a*) the conditions described in 19.26(*a*)–(*c*) above are fulfilled,

(*b*) all the replacement assets were shares in a company or companies (referred to below as 'new shares'),

(*c*) there has been a transaction within *TCGA 1992, s 116(10)* (see 49.3 QUALIFYING CORPORATE BONDS) as regards which all the new shares constitute the 'old asset' and qualifying corporate bonds constitute the 'new asset', and

(*d*) at the time of the occurrence of the chargeable event, the claimant or a person then connected with him (as above) is beneficially entitled to all the bonds,

a chargeable gain of the 'relevant amount' is deemed to have accrued to the claimant or the connected person (as the case may be) immediately before the time when the chargeable event occurs.

The '*relevant amount*' is the lesser of the 'first amount' and the 'second amount'.

The '*first amount*' is the amount of the chargeable gain that would be deemed to accrue under *TCGA 1992, s 116(10)(b)* if there were a disposal of all the bonds at the time the chargeable event occurs (or nil if an allowable loss would arise). The '*second amount*' is the relevant value as for *TCGA 1992, s 232* in 19.26 above.

Where the conditions at (*b*), (*c*) and (*d*) above were satisfied as regards only part of the replacement assets, the new shares constituting the old asset or the bonds to which there is beneficial entitlement, a chargeable gain is nevertheless deemed to arise as above, but the first amount is determined only by reference to the bonds concerned, the second amount is reduced as is just and reasonable, and the relevant amount is reduced accordingly.

An adjustment may be made where a chargeable gain arises as above, and before the occurrence of the chargeable event it can be said that, because of something which has happened as regards any of the new shares or any of the bonds, a charge has accrued in respect of any gain carried forward by virtue of *TCGA 1992, s 229(1)* or *(3)* (see 19.25 above). In these circumstances, the chargeable gain is, if it is just and reasonable, calculated as if the second amount were reduced as is just and reasonable (but not so as to reduce it below nil) and the relevant amount reduced (if appropriate) accordingly.

[*TCGA 1992, s 234*].

Where a charge arises as above in the case of qualifying corporate bonds and subsequently a chargeable gain accrues under *TCGA 1992, s 116(10)(b)* on a disposal of them (see above), the chargeable gain is reduced by the relevant amount or (if the amount exceeds the gain) reduced to nil. The relevant amount is apportioned for this purpose where the subsequent disposal is of only some of the bonds. [*TCGA 1992, s 236(3)(4)*].

19.29 *Dwelling-houses: special provisions.* As regards 19.25(*d*) above, a replacement asset which is a dwelling-house (or part thereof) or land is not treated (where it would otherwise be so treated) as being a chargeable asset in relation to the claimant immediately after the asset's acquisition if on a disposal of it (or an interest in it) at some time in the period from its acquisition to the time a claim is made under *TCGA 1992, s 229(1)* or *(3)* (see 19.25 above), the PRIVATE RESIDENCES (48.1) exemption of *TCGA 1992, s 222(1)* would apply to the asset (or interest in it) and the 'individual' (which includes references to a person entitled to occupy the dwelling-house etc. under the terms of a settlement; see 48.6 PRIVATE RESIDENCES) mentioned in *TCGA 1992, s 222(1)* would be the claimant or his spouse.

A similar treatment applies retrospectively where the replacement asset is a dwelling-house etc. which would otherwise be a chargeable asset in relation to the claimant immediately after its acquisition and which becomes eligible for the private residences exemption at some time after a claim under *TCGA 1992, s 229(1)* or *(3)* is made. In such a case, any gain thereby treated as having accrued is deemed not to have accrued until the time (or the earliest time) on which a disposal of the dwelling-house would be within the private residences exemption.

Similar provisions apply in relation to a replacement asset which is an option to acquire (or to acquire an interest in) a dwelling-house and the application of the private residences exemption in the period from the exercise of the option and the time of claim, and subsequent to the time of claim, respectively.

[*TCGA 1992, s 230*].

19.30 *Shares qualifying for EIS relief: special provisions.* As regards 19.25(*d*) above, a replacement asset which consists of shares is not treated (where it would otherwise be so treated) as being a chargeable asset in relation to the claimant immediately after the asset's acquisition if at some time in the period from its acquisition to the time a claim is made under *TCGA 1992, s 229(1)* or *(3)* (see 19.25 above) Enterprise Investment Scheme (EIS) income tax relief (see 20.2 ENTERPRISE INVESTMENT SCHEME (AND BES)) is claimed in respect of it.

A similar treatment applies retrospectively where the replacement asset consists of shares which would otherwise be a chargeable asset in relation to the claimant immediately after their acquisition and EIS relief is claimed at some time after a claim under *TCGA 1992, s 229(1)* or *(3)* is made.

Similar provisions applied as regards relief under the Business Expansion Scheme for shares issued before 1 January 1994 (see 20.15, 20.16 ENTERPRISE INVESTMENT SCHEME (AND BES)).

[*TCGA 1992, s 231; FA 1994, s 137, Sch 15 para 34*].

19.31 *Information powers.* The Inspector may, by notice in writing, require a return containing specified information by the trustees of an employee share ownership trust (within *FA 1989, Sch 5*) where a disposal of shares (or an interest therein) has been made to them and a claim is made under *TCGA 1992, s 229(1)* or *(3)* (see 19.25 above). The information specified must be needed for the purposes of *TCGA 1992, ss 232–234* (see 19.26–19.28 above), and may include information about: expenditure incurred by the trustees (including the purpose of the expenditure and the recipients); assets acquired by them (including the persons from whom the assets were acquired and the consideration); and transfers of assets made by them (including the persons to whom they were transferred and the consideration). Penalties under *TMA 1970, s 98* apply for failure to comply with a notice. Where relief has been given by virtue of *TCGA 1992, s 229(1)* or *(3)*, the Inspector must send to the trustees a certificate that it has been given, stating the effect on the consideration for the disposal or on the gain accruing on the disposal. [*TCGA 1992, s 235*].

19.32 *Clearance procedure.* Trustees are able to seek and obtain confirmation that a particular trust is a qualifying employee share ownership trust and so facilitate a sale by a potential vendor who would be able to claim the relief in 19.25 above. A written request should be sent to Inland Revenue, Business Profits Division (Employee Share Schemes), Room 111A, New Wing, Somerset House, Strand, London WC2R 1LB (Tel. 020–7438 7801 or 020–7438 7803). The request should be accompanied by copies of the executed trust deed and any other relevant information that may be required by the Revenue (Revenue Press Release 9 May 1990). The Revenue will also examine and comment on draft trust deeds submitted to them (Revenue Press Release 14 December 1990).

19.33 PRIORITY ALLOCATIONS IN PUBLIC SHARE OFFERS

If a benefit derived by an employee from a priority allocation of shares in a public offer made after 22 September 1987 is exempted from income tax by *FA 1988, s 68* (see TOLLEY'S INCOME TAX under Schedule E), the usual MARKET VALUE (40) rules do not apply and the allowable expenditure for CGT on a disposal of the shares is the consideration given. [*FA 1988, s 68(4)*].

20 Enterprise Investment Scheme (and BES)

Cross-references. See 19.16, 19.30 EMPLOYEE SHARE SCHEMES for restriction on rollover relief arising from disposal of shares to, respectively, an approved employee share ownership plan and, before 6 April 2001, an employee share ownership trust, where replacement asset is shares and a claim for EIS income tax relief is made; 50 REINVESTMENT RELIEF; 58 SHARES AND SECURITIES; 65 VENTURE CAPITAL TRUSTS.

Sumption: Capital Gains Tax. See A15A.

The headings in this chapter are as follows.

20.1 INTRODUCTION

The Enterprise Investment Scheme (EIS) offers income tax relief to a qualifying individual to whom eligible shares (see 20.4 below) in a qualifying company (see 20.5 below) have been issued after 31 December 1993 by subscription. The company concerned must use the money raised within the specified time limit for a qualifying business activity (see 20.6 below). See 20.2(*a*) below.

These rules have some similarities with the BES rules in 20.15 *et seq.* below which they replaced. [*ICTA 1988, s 289(11); FA 1994, s 137(1)(2), Sch 15 para 12*].

For more detailed coverage of the income tax provisions, see TOLLEY'S INCOME TAX under Enterprise Investment Scheme (and BES). As regards both income tax and CGT, see also Revenue Pamphlet IR 137.

See 20.9 below re capital gains deferral relief.

20.2 INCOME TAX RELIEF

(*a*) **Conditions for relief.** A qualifying individual (see 20.3 below) is eligible for income tax relief under the Enterprise Investment Scheme (EIS) if

- eligible shares (see 20.4 below) in a qualifying company (see 20.5 below) for which he has subscribed are issued to him (for shares issued after 5 April 1998, and see below, the subscription must be wholly in cash and the shares fully paid up at time of issue),
- those shares (and, for shares issued after 5 April 1998, all other shares comprised in the same issue) are issued to raise money for the purpose of a qualifying business activity (see 20.6 below), and
- the money so raised (or all but an insignificant amount of it) is employed wholly for that purpose by the end of the twelve months following the issue

or, if the only qualifying business activity falls within 20.6(*a*) below, and if later, by the end of the twelve months starting when the company (or subsidiary) began to carry on the qualifying trade (see 20.6 below).

[*ICTA 1988, s 289(1)(3); FA 1994, Sch 15 para 2; FA 1998, Sch 13 para 1(1)*].

The Revenue would consider it implicit in the legislation that shares issued before 6 April 1998 also had to be issued for a money consideration and not for money's worth, and that view was supported by the Court in the BES case of *Thompson v Hart Ch D, [2000] STC 381*.

With effect from 27 November 1996, there is an additional condition that the 'active company' must, throughout the relevant period (as defined in 20.6 below), either:

(i) be within 20.5(*a*) below; or

(ii) fall within (i) above if the company's purposes were disregarded to the extent that they consist

- in holding shares in or securities of, or making loans to, any of the company's subsidiaries, or
- in holding and managing property used by the company or any of its subsidiaries either for research and development (as defined) from which a qualifying trade (see 20.6 below) to be carried on by any of them is intended to be derived, or for the purposes of a 'qualifying trade' or trades carried on by any of them, or
- in making loans to the parent company; or

(iii) be a '90% subsidiary' of the qualifying company which either

- apart from purposes capable of having no significant effect (other than on incidental matters) on the extent of its activities, exists wholly for the purpose of carrying on activities consisting in holding and managing property used by the company or any of its subsidiaries either for research and development (as defined) from which a qualifying trade to be carried on by any of them is intended to be derived, or for the purposes of a qualifying trade or trades carried on by any of them, or
- has no corporation tax profits and no part of its business consists in the making of investments.

The '*active company*' is the qualifying company unless the qualifying business activity consists in a subsidiary of the qualifying company carrying on or preparing to carry on a qualifying trade, research and development or oil exploration, in which case it is that subsidiary. Due to a defect in *Finance Act 1998*, it was sufficient as regards shares issued after 5 April 1998 and before 6 April 1999 for the active subsidiary to be a 75% subsidiary of the qualifying company (except for the purpose of satisfying condition (iii) above). As regards shares issued after 5 April 1999, reverting to the rules for those issued before 6 April 1998, it must be a '90% subsidiary'.

For these purposes, a '*90% subsidiary*' is a subsidiary that would satisfy the conditions given at 20.5(A) below if references to 90% were substituted for references to 75% and the let-out for *bona fide* commercial disposals of interests in the subsidiary were disregarded.

Although a winding-up or dissolution in the 'relevant period' (as in 20.6 below) generally prevents a company meeting the above conditions, they are deemed met if the winding-up or dissolution is for *bona fide* commercial reasons and not part of a scheme a main purpose of which is tax avoidance, with the additional proviso before 21 March 2000 that any net assets are distributed to members (or dealt with as *bona vacantia*) before the end of the relevant period or (if later) the end of three years from the commencement of winding-up. After 20 March 2000 (both in relation to shares issued after that date and to pre-existing shares to which EIS income tax relief or capital gains tax deferral relief remains attributable), a company does not cease to meet the above conditions by reason of anything done as a consequence of its being in administration or receivership (both as defined by *ICTA 1988, s 312(2A)*), provided everything so done and the making of the relevant order are for *bona fide* commercial (and not tax avoidance) reasons.

[*ICTA 1988, s 289(1A)–(1D)(9), s 312(1)(2A); FA 1997, Sch 8 paras 1, 2; FA 1998, s 74, Sch 13 para 1(2)(5); FA 1999, s 71; FA 2000, Sch 17 para 9(2)(4), paras 12, 15*].

(*b*) **Method of relief**. On the making of a claim (see 20.7 below), EIS income tax relief is given in the year of assessment in which the subscription is made. The relief is given as a reduction from the individual's income tax liability, the reduction being equal to the smaller of tax at the lower rate (currently 20%) of the amount subscribed for the shares (subject to (*c*) below) and the amount which reduces the tax liability to nil. For the purposes of calculating an individual's total tax liability, EIS income tax relief is given before any other reliefs or allowances granted in terms of tax except for top-slicing relief on chargeable event gains and Venture Capital Trust relief (see Revenue Independent Taxation Manual, para 336). [*ICTA 1988, s 289A(1)(2)(5); FA 1994, s 137(1)(2), Sch 15 para 2*].

Income tax relief is said to be attributable to EIS shares if a reduction has been made in the individual's income tax liability in respect of them, and that relief has not been fully withdrawn. [*ICTA 1988, s 289B(1); FA 1994, s 137(1)(2), Sch 15 para 2*].

Example

W is a married man who on 2 January 2001 subscribes £20,000 for 20,000 EIS shares in E Co Ltd. His Schedule E income for the year ended 5 April 2001 amounts to £60,000. PAYE deducted amounts to £16,751.60. He has no other sources of income. W and his wife were born on 27 April 1941 and 25 September 1934 respectively.

W's 2000/01 income tax liability is calculated as follows:

	£
Schedule E	60,000
Less Personal Allowance	4,385
Taxable Income	£55,615
Tax Liability	
£1,520 @ 10%	152.00
£26,880 @ 22%	5,913.60
£27,215 @ 40%	10,886.00
£55,615	16,951.60
Less EIS relief £20,000 @ 20%	4,000.00
Carried forward	£12,951.60

Brought forward	£12,951.60
Less Married Couple's Allowance (minimum) £2,000 @ 10%	200.00
Income tax liability	12,751.60
Less PAYE deducted	16,751.60
Income tax repayment due	£4,000.00

(*c*) **Maximum and minimum amounts.** The respective total maximum and minimum amounts per tax year on which income tax relief is granted to an individual are £150,000 (£100,000 as regards shares issued before 6 April 1998) and £500 respectively. The relief is granted for the year of assessment in which the shares were issued. [*ICTA 1988, s 290(1)(2); FA 1994, Sch 15 paras 1, 3; FA 1998, s 74, Sch 13 para 4*]. The individual will obtain Form EIS 3 from the EIS company for the purposes of making the claim. Where the shares in the company are issued between 6 April and 5 October inclusive in any year the investor can request that up to one half of those shares be treated as being issued in the previous tax year, subject to an overall limit of £25,000 (£15,000 as regards shares issued before 6 April 1998) on the amount of subscriptions which may be so treated. [*ICTA 1988, s 289A(3)(4); FA 1994, s 137(1)(2), Sch 15 paras 1, 2; FA 1998, s 74, Sch 13 para 2*].

(*d*) **Approved Investment Funds.** Income tax relief for investments made through approved investment funds is due in the year of assessment in which the fund closes and should be claimed on Form EIS 5 obtainable from the fund manager. For any fund closing before 6 October the investor may treat part of the investment as relating to the previous year as described in (*c*) above. [*ICTA 1988, s 311(2B); FA 1994, s 137(1)(2), Sch 15 para 26*].

(*e*) **Issue of shares.** Shares or debentures shall be treated as issued if they are included in a letter of allotment or similar instrument except in circumstances where the allotment is dependent upon acceptance and such acceptance is not obtained. [*TCGA 1992, s 288(5)*].

(*f*) **Withdrawal of relief on disposal.** Where the investor disposes of EIS shares before the end of the 'relevant period' (as in 20.3(*a*) below), EIS income tax relief given falls to be withdrawn. This does not apply on an inter-spouse transfer made at a time they are living together; the transferee stands in the shoes of the transferor as regards any subsequent disposal. If a disposal is not made by way of bargain at arm's length, the relief is fully withdrawn in all cases. Otherwise, the relief given is fully withdrawn unless it is greater than tax at the lower rate (for the tax year for which the relief was given) on the amount or value of the consideration received on disposal, in which case only the lower amount is withdrawn. [*ICTA 1988, s 299(1)–(3), s 304; FA 1994, Sch 15 paras 12, 18; FA 1998, s 74, Sch 13 para 12(1)(2)(8), para 16*]. Withdrawal is given effect by Schedule D, Case VI assessment for the tax year for which the relief was given. [*ICTA 1988, s 307(1)*]. Disposals are identified with acquisitions on a first in/first out (FIFO) basis, and for disposals after 5 April 1998 further rules apply as to the order in which shares acquired on the same day are deemed to be disposed of where only some of those shares have attracted income tax relief and/or CGT deferral relief (see 20.9 below). These rules are the same as those described at 20.8 below (under 'Identification rules') for CGT purposes. [*ICTA 1988, s 299(6)–(6D); FA 1998, Sch 13 para 12(5)(6)(8)*]. A share exchange is treated as a disposal for these purposes (Revenue Assessment Procedures Manual, AP 4977), unless it occurs after 5 April 1998 and is within *ICTA 1988, s 304A* — see 20.5 below. For further details and for other circumstances in which EIS income tax relief falls to be withdrawn, see TOLLEY'S INCOME TAX.

(*g*) **Loan-linked investments.** An individual is not eligible for income tax relief in respect of EIS shares if there is a loan made by any person at any time in the 'relevant period' (as in 20.3(*a*) below) to that individual or to an associate of his, and the loan would not have been made (or would not have been made on the same terms) if the individual had not subscribed for the shares or had not been proposing to do so. The giving of credit, and the assignment of a debt due from the individual or an associate, are also caught by these provisions. [*ICTA 1988, s 299A; FA 1993, s 111(1)(4); FA 1994, Sch 15 para 13*]. For the Revenue's views on loan-linked investments, see Revenue Pamphlet IR 131, SP 6/98.

(*h*) **Pre-arranged exits.** In relation to shares issued after 1 July 1997, an individual is not eligible for income tax relief in respect of EIS shares if arrangements (as very broadly defined) under which the shares are issued to him (or arrangements preceding the issue but relating to it)

- provide for the eventual disposal by the investor of the shares in question or other shares or securities of the company; or
- provide for the eventual cessation of a trade of the company or of a person connected with it; or
- provide for the eventual disposal of all, or a substantial part of, the assets of the company or of a person connected with it; or
- provide (by means of any insurance, indemnity, guarantee or otherwise) complete or partial protection for investors against the normal risks attaching to EIS investment (but excluding arrangements which merely protect the company and/or its subsidiaries against normal trading risks).

Certain types of arrangements, i.e. those applicable only on an unanticipated winding-up of the company for commercial reasons and those for certain share exchanges not counted as a disposal by the investor, are excluded from the above.

[*ICTA 1988, ss 299B, 312(1); FA 1998, s 71(1)(5); FA 2000, Sch 17 para 14, Sch 40 Pt II(5)*].

20.3 QUALIFYING INDIVIDUAL

(*a*) **Unconnected with the company.** The individual must be unconnected with the company throughout the designated period (as regards shares issued before 6 April 1998 at any time in the 'relevant period') and must subscribe for the shares on his own behalf. Relief is not available to individuals acting in the capacity of trustees.

The designated period for these purposes is

- (for shares issued after 5 April 2000) the period beginning two years before the issue of the shares and ending immediately before the third anniversary of the issue date or, if later and where relevant, the third anniversary of the date of commencement of the intended trade referred to in 20.6(*a*) below; or
- (for shares issued before 6 April 2000) the seven-year period beginning two years before the issue of the shares.

The '*relevant period*' for the purposes of this and certain other specified EIS provisions is the period beginning with the incorporation of the company or, if later, two years before the date of issue of the shares and ending

- (for shares issued after 5 April 2000, where relevant) immediately before the third anniversary of the issue date or, if later and where relevant, the third anniversary of the date of commencement of the intended trade referred to in 20.6(*a*) below; or

- (for shares issued before 6 April 2000) five years after the issue date.

[*ICTA 1988, s 291(1)(5)(6), s 312(1)(1A)(a); FA 1994, s 137(1)(2), Sch 15 paras 1, 5; FA 1998, s 74, Sch 13 para 6(1)(4); FA 2000, Sch 17 paras 2, 6(2)–(4), para 8*].

(*b*) **Residence.** There is no requirement for the individual to be UK resident and ordinarily resident at the time the shares are issued but EIS relief is only available against income chargeable to UK income tax.

(*c*) **Circumstances in which an individual/director may be connected with the company.** An individual is connected with the issuing company if he or an 'associate' of his is

- employed by the company (or a subsidiary) or by a partner of the company (or of a subsidiary);
- a partner of the company (or a subsidiary); or
- (subject to what is said below) a director of the company (or a subsidiary) or of a company which is a partner of the company (or of a subsidiary);

and see also the provisions of *ICTA 1988, s 291B* outlined below.

References above to a subsidiary are to any company which is a 51% subsidiary of the issuing company at any time in the 'relevant period' (see (*a*) above) regardless of whether or not the individual etc. was an employee etc. at that particular time.

[*ICTA 1988, s 291(2)–(5), s 312(1)(1A)(a); FA 1994, s 137(1)(2), Sch 15 paras 1, 5; FA 1998, s 74, Sch 13 para 6(2)(3), Sch 27 Pt III(14)); FA 2000, Sch 17 para 6(3)(4), para 8*].

If the individual or his associate is a director he will *not* be regarded as connected with the company unless the company or a related person (as defined) makes or accrues a payment to him (or to his associate or his or his associate's partnership) during the designated period — see (*a*) above (as regards shares issued before 6 April 1998, the 'relevant period' — see (*a*) above). The following normal business expenditure is disregarded for this purpose:

- reimbursement of travelling or other expenses wholly, exclusively and necessarily incurred by the individual or his associate in the performance of the individual's duties as a director;
- interest at a commercial rate for money lent to the company;
- distributions at a reasonable return for the investment;
- payment for use of goods at a commercial rate;
- rent for any property occupied by the issuing company and related person that does not exceed a reasonable and commercial rent;
- remuneration at a reasonable rate for services supplied by the director, excluding secretarial or managerial services, which are deductible by the company in its Schedule D, Case I corporation tax computation.

A director who receives reasonable remuneration *can* receive EIS relief if, when the shares are issued,

- he has never been connected with the issuing company, and
- he has never been involved (as sole trader, employee, partner or director) in carrying on its (or its subsidiary's) trade (or any part thereof) (in relation to shares issued before 6 April 1998, he has never been an employee of a person who had previously carried on the issuing company's trade).

If additional EIS shares are issued within three years (five years for shares issued before 6 April 2000) after the previous EIS issue these new shares will also qualify for relief. Where relevant, and in relation only to shares issued after 5 April 2000, the said three-year period is replaced by a longer period beginning with the date of the last such issue and ending with the third anniversary of the date of commencement of the intended trade referred to in 20.6(*a*) below.

[*ICTA 1988, ss 291A, 312(1)(1A)(a); FA 1994, s 137(1)(2), Sch 15 paras 1, 5; FA 1998, s 74, Sch 13 para 7, Sch 27 Pt III(14); FA 2000, Sch 17 paras 3, 6(2)–(4), para 8*].

Individuals who own or are entitled to acquire more than 30% of the issued ordinary share capital, loan capital, voting power or the assets available to equity holders on a winding-up are deemed to be connected with the company. [*ICTA 1988, s 291B(1)–(3); FA 1994, s 137(1)(2), Sch 15 paras 1, 5*]. For this purpose, the interests of an individual and his associates are *not* aggregated (*Cook v Billings & Others Ch D, [1999] STC 661*, a BES case which is nevertheless considered relevant to the EIS as the wording of the disputed provisions is identical). An individual is also connected if he controls the voting power by holding a majority of shares or has the power granted to him in the Articles of Association or other document [*ICTA 1988, s 291B(4); FA 1994, s 137(1)(2), Sch 15 paras 1, 5*]. Bank overdrafts arising in the normal course of banking business are not treated as loan capital for this purpose. [*ICTA 1988, s 291B(9)*]. An individual is not connected with the company by virtue only of the fact that he or an associate is a shareholder if at that time the company has issued no shares other than subscriber shares and has neither commenced business nor made preparations for doing so. [*ICTA 1988, s 291B(5A); FA 1998, s 74, Sch 13 para 8*]. This applies by statute in relation to shares issued after 5 April 1998, but a similar exclusion previously applied by concession (ESC A76 now withdrawn).

'*Associate*' for the above purposes has the same meaning as *ICTA 1988, s 417(3)(4)* except that a 'relative' does not include a brother or sister. See TOLLEY'S CORPORATION TAX under Close Companies.

20.4 ELIGIBLE SHARES

Types of share. The shares must be new ordinary shares issued for *bona fide* commercial purposes and not as part of a scheme or arrangement the main purpose of which is the avoidance of tax. Throughout the three years beginning with the date of issue (five years for shares issued before 6 April 2000) the shares must carry no present or future preferential right to dividends or to a company's assets on its winding up and no present or future right (for shares issued before 6 April 1998, present or future preferential right) to redemption. If, for shares issued after 5 April 2000, the company satisfied the qualifying business activity requirement by virtue of 20.6(*a*) below and the trade had not yet commenced on the issue date, this condition must be satisfied throughout the period from date of issue to immediately before the third anniversary of commencement. [*ICTA 1988, s 289(6)(7), s 312(1); FA 1994, s 137(1)(2), Sch 15 paras 1, 2; FA 1998, s 74, Sch 13 para 1(3)(4), Sch 27 Pt III(14); FA 2000, Sch 17 paras 1, 6(3), para 8*]. Shares are not issued until the company's register of members has been completed. (*National Westminster Bank plc v CIR; Barclays Bank plc v CIR HL 1994, 67 TC 1* and see Revenue Tax Bulletin June 1995 p 217).

Permitted maximum. As regards shares issued before 6 April 1998, there was a restriction on the total amount of eligible shares which could be issued by a company within a specified period (see below) and attract relief. Where the money raised in such a period exceeded

£1m (£5m in the case of certain shipping concerns) the excess did not qualify for relief. The period specified was the longer of

(*a*) six months ending with the date of issue of the shares, and

(*b*) the period from the preceding 6 April to the date of issue.

Amounts raised which did not attract relief because the subscriber was not a qualifying individual (see 20.3 above), or had exceeded his personal limit or invested under the permitted minimum (see 20.2(*c*) above), or because of an earlier application of these provisions, were not taken into account for the purposes of this restriction.

There were provisions which reduced the limit where the issuing company or a subsidiary carried on a trade in partnership, or as a joint venture, with other companies.

Where the application of the permitted maximum restricted the amount of relief available to two or more individuals, the total relief available was apportioned amongst them according to the respective amounts subscribed for shares giving rise to the restriction and which would otherwise be eligible for the relief.

The permitted maximum is abolished as regards shares issued after 5 April 1998.

[*ICTA 1988, s 290A; FA 1988, s 51(1); FA 1994, Sch 15 para 4; FA 1997, Sch 8 paras 1, 3; FA 1998, s 74, Sch 13 para 5, Sch 27 Pt III(14)*].

20.5 **QUALIFYING COMPANY**

A '*qualifying company*' may be resident in the UK or elsewhere. It must, throughout the 'relevant period' (defined as in 20.6 below), be 'unquoted' and either

(*a*) exist wholly for the purpose of carrying on one or more 'qualifying trades' (see 20.6 below) (disregarding purposes incapable of having any significant effect on the company's activities), or

(*b*) be 'the parent company of a trading group'.

Before 27 November 1996, condition (*b*) above required the business of the company to consist of holding shares in or securities of, or making loans to, 'qualifying subsidiaries', with or without the carrying on of one or more qualifying trades.

The above conditions are not considered to be breached by reason only of the winding-up or dissolution of a company, or anything done after 20 March 2000 as a consequence of its being in administration or receivership, provided certain conditions are met.

A company is '*unquoted*' if none of its shares etc. are listed on a recognised stock exchange or designated foreign exchange, or dealt in outside the UK by such means as may be designated. Securities on the Alternative Investment Market ('AIM') are treated as unquoted for these purposes. (Revenue Press Release 20 February 1995).

The '*parent company of a trading group*' is a company all of whose subsidiaries are 'qualifying subsidiaries' provided that, in relation to the business consisting of the activities, taken together, of the company and its subsidiaries, neither the business nor a 'substantial part' of it consists in either or both of

(I) excluded activities within 20.6(A)–(M) below, and

(II) non-trading activities (not including, as regards shares issued after 5 April 1998, research and development (as defined) and oil exploration).

Activities are for this purpose disregarded to the extent that they consist (*a*) in holding shares in or securities of, or making loans to, any of the company's subsidiaries, or (*b*) in holding and managing property used by the company or any of its subsidiaries either for research and development (as defined) from which a 'qualifying trade' (see 20.6 below) to be carried on by any of them is intended to be derived, or for the purposes of a 'qualifying trade' or trades carried on by any of them. They are similarly disregarded to the extent that they consist in making loans to the company or, in the case of a 'mainly trading subsidiary' (as defined), in activities not in pursuance of its main purpose.

During the debates on the 1997 Finance Bill, the Government stated that a '*substantial part*' means 80% of the business activity (HC Official Report, Standing Committee B (Twelfth sitting), cols 418, 419).

The company must not at any time in the 'relevant period' (defined as in 20.6 below) either

(i) (in relation to shares issued before 6 April 1998) have share capital which includes any issued shares not fully paid up (or which would not be fully paid up if any undertaking to pay cash to the company at a future date were disregarded), or

(ii) control another company other than a 'qualifying subsidiary' (see below), 'control' being construed in accordance with *ICTA 1988, s 416(2)–(6)* and being considered with or without connected persons within *ICTA 1988, s 839*, or

(iii) be a 51% subsidiary of another company or otherwise under the control of another company, 'control' being construed in accordance with *ICTA 1988, s 840* (after 20 March 2000, previously in accordance with *ICTA 1988, s 416(2)–(6)*) and again being considered with or without connected persons, or

(iv) be capable of falling within (ii) or (iii) by virtue of any arrangements (as very broadly defined).

The above is subject to provisions in *ICTA 1988, s 304A* (inserted by *FA 1998, Sch 13 para 17*) which enable an EIS company to become, after 5 April 1998, a wholly-owned subsidiary of a new holding company in certain circumstances. The investors receive shares in the new company in exchange for their original shares, and the new shares then stand in the shoes of the old for the purposes of EIS income tax relief. See TOLLEY'S INCOME TAX for details.

Gross assets test. In relation to shares issued after 5 April 1998, the value of the company's gross assets must not exceed £15 million immediately before the issue of EIS shares and must not exceed £16 million immediately afterwards. If the company has 'qualifying subsidiaries', the test applies by reference to the aggregate gross assets of the company and all such subsidiaries (disregarding certain assets held by any such company which correspond to liabilities of another). The value of a company's gross assets at any time is the aggregate of the values of its assets (without any deduction for liabilities) as would be shown in a balance sheet drawn up as at that time. Any advance payment received for the share issue itself is ignored immediately before the issue but the right to the unpaid portion of shares issued partly paid is taken as included in gross assets immediately after the issue. See Revenue Pamphlet IR 131, SP 5/98.

As regards shares issued after 16 March 1998, any of the above provisions may be amended by Treasury Order.

[*ICTA 1988, s 293, s 298(4), s 312(1)–(1E); FA 1994, Sch 15 para 7; FA 1997, Sch 8 paras 1, 4; FA 1998, s 70(2)(4), s 74, Sch 13 paras 9, 23, Sch 27 Pt III(14); FA 2000, Sch 17 para 9(1)(4), paras 10–12, 14, 15*].

Land and buildings. Subject to an exemption for small issues, there was an additional exclusion if at any time during the relevant period (defined as in 20.6 below) and before 29 November 1994, the value of the company's 'interests in land' exceeded half the value of all its assets. See TOLLEY'S INCOME TAX for full details.

Advance provisional approval. A company may submit its proposals for using the EIS to the inspector who normally deals with its tax affairs. If satisfied as to the purposes for which the money raised will be used, the company's status as a qualifying company and the eligibility of the shares to be issued under the proposals, the inspector may grant advance provisional approval, of which investors may be informed, although in the end the question of whether the company qualifies for the scheme is one of fact which cannot be determined in advance. (Revenue Pamphlet IR 137, page 30).

Subsidiaries. The existence of certain subsidiaries in the 'relevant period' (defined as in 20.6 below) does not prevent the parent being a qualifying company. The conditions imposed on any such subsidiary (a '*qualifying subsidiary*') are that:

(A) (i) the qualifying company, or another of its subsidiaries, must possess at least 75% (90% in relation to EIS shares issued before 6 April 1998) of both the issued share capital and the voting power, and be beneficially entitled to at least 75% (90% in relation to EIS shares issued before 6 April 1998) of the assets available for distribution to equity holders on a winding-up etc. (see *ICTA 1988, Sch 18 paras 1, 3*) and of the profits available for distribution to equity holders,

(ii) no other person may have control (within *ICTA 1988, s 840*) of the subsidiary, and

(iii) no arrangements (as very broadly defined) may exist whereby (i) or (ii) could cease to be satisfied; and

(B) (before 27 November 1997), it must either exist wholly, or substantially wholly, for the purpose of carrying on one or more qualifying trades (see 20.6 below), or be a 'property managing' or 'dormant' subsidiary.

The condition at (A) above must continue to be satisfied until the end of the relevant period, except that the winding-up or dissolution, during that period, of the subsidiary or of the qualifying company does not prevent those conditions being satisfied, provided that the winding-up meets certain conditions. The above conditions are also not regarded as ceasing to be satisfied by reason only of the disposal of the interest in the subsidiary within the relevant period if it can be shown to be for *bona fide* commercial reasons and not part of a tax-avoidance scheme.

A '*property managing subsidiary*' is one which exists wholly (or substantially wholly) for the purpose of holding and managing property used by the qualifying company, or a subsidiary, for the purposes of a qualifying trade or trades carried on by the qualifying company or a subsidiary, or for the purposes of research and development (as defined) from which such a qualifying trade is intended to be derived. A '*dormant*' subsidiary is one with no corporation tax profits, and no part of whose business consists in the making of investments.

[*ICTA 1988, s 293(3), ss 308, 312(1); FA 1994, Sch 15 paras 23, 24; FA 1997, Sch 8 paras 1, 6; FA 1998, s 74, Sch 13 para 21; FA 2000, Sch 17 paras 14, 15*].

20.6 QUALIFYING BUSINESS ACTIVITY

Any of the following is a '*qualifying business activity*' (see 20.1 above) in relation to the issuing company, provided that, at any time in the 'relevant period' (see below) when it is carried on, it is carried on wholly or mainly in the UK.

(*a*) The issuing company or any 'qualifying subsidiary' (see 20.5 above) carrying on a 'qualifying trade' (see below) which it is carrying on on the date of issue of the shares, or preparing to carry on such a trade which, on the date of issue of the shares, it intends to carry on wholly or mainly in the UK and which it begins to carry on within two years after that date.

(*b*) The issuing company or any subsidiary carrying on either research and development (as defined) or oil exploration which it is carrying on on the date of issue of the shares, or which it begins to carry on immediately afterwards, and from which it is intended will be derived a 'qualifying trade' which the company or a subsidiary will carry on wholly or mainly in the UK.

As regards (*a*) above, 'preparing' to carrying on a trade refers to the setting up of the trade, and not, for example, to market research aimed at discovering whether it would be worthwhile starting a trade, or to preparatory research and development or exploration. (Revenue Inspector's Manual, IM 6974). As regards (*b*) above, in relation to oil exploration, there are further conditions relating to exploration and appraisal or development licenses.

In considering whether a trade is carried on '*wholly or mainly in the UK*', the totality of the trade activities is taken into account. (Revenue Pamphlet IR 131, SP 7/98). As to how the schemes operates where a company raises money by a single share issue for more than one qualifying business activity, see Revenue Tax Bulletin April 1996 pp 305, 306.

Relevant period. The '*relevant period*' for these purposes is the period beginning with the date of issue of the shares and ending three years after that date or, where (*a*) above applies and the company (or subsidiary) was not carrying on the 'qualifying trade' on that date, three years after the date on which it begins to carry on the trade.

[*ICTA 1988, s 289(2)(4)(5)(8), s 312(1)(1A)(b); FA 1994, Sch 15 para 2; FA 2000, Sch 17 para 6(4), paras 8, 15*].

Qualifying trades. To be a '*qualifying trade*' a trade may *not*, at any time in the relevant period (as defined above) consist to a substantial extent of, or of a combination of:

(A) dealing in land, commodities or futures, or in shares, securities or other financial instruments; or

(B) dealing in goods otherwise than in an ordinary trade of wholesale or retail distribution (see the similar exclusion at 65.3(*b*) VENTURE CAPITAL TRUSTS for further details); or

(C) banking, insurance or any other financial activities; or

(D) oil extraction activities (but without prejudice to relief in respect of oil exploration (see (*b*) above) for which the activities would otherwise qualify), or

(E) leasing or letting or receiving royalties or licence fees (see below re letting of ships, and see the similar exclusion at 65.3(*b*) VENTURE CAPITAL TRUSTS for further details as regards these items generally); or

(F) providing legal or accountancy services;

(G) 'property development' (see below);

(H) farming or market gardening;

(J) holding, managing or occupying woodlands, any other forestry activities or timber production;

(K) operating or managing hotels or comparable establishments (including guest houses, hostels and other establishments whose main purpose is to offer overnight accommodation with or without catering) or property used as such;

(L) operating or managing nursing homes or residential care homes (both as defined in *ICTA 1988, s 298(5)*) or property used as such;

(M) providing services or facilities for any trade, profession or vocation consisting to a substantial extent of activities within (A)–(L) above and carried on by another person (other than a parent company), where one person has a controlling interest (as defined) in both trades.

Exclusions (G)–(L) (and the reference to those in exclusion (M)) apply in relation to shares issued **after 16 March 1998**. Exclusions (K) and (L) apply only if the person carrying on the activity in question has an estate or interest (e.g. a lease) in the property concerned or occupies that property.

Adventures and concerns in the nature of trade, and trades not carried on commercially and with a view to the realisation of profits, are also generally excluded.

The Revenue regard as 'substantial' for the above purposes a part of a trade which consists of 20% or more of total activities, judged by any reasonable measure (normally turnover or capital employed). (Revenue Inspector's Manual, IM 6997).

'Property development' in (G) above means the development of land by a company, which has (or has had at any time) an 'interest in the land' (as defined by *ICTA 1988, s 298(5B)(5C)*), with the sole or main object of realising a gain from the disposal of an interest in the developed land.

As regards (E) above, a trade will not be excluded by reason only of its consisting of letting ships, other than oil rigs or pleasure craft (as defined), on charter, provided certain conditions are satisfied.

[*ICTA 1988, ss 297, 298; FA 1994, Sch 15 paras 10, 11; FA 1997, Sch 8 para 5; FA 1998, s 70(1), Sch 12 paras 1, 2, 5(1); FA 2000, Sch 17 para 13*].

20.7 CLAIMS FOR RELIEF

A claim by the individual for EIS income tax relief cannot be made until the company has carried on the trade or other qualifying business activity for at least four months. It cannot be made later than the fifth anniversary of 31 January following the tax year in which the shares were issued (or treated as issued, in a case where relief is carried back one year as in 20.2(*c*) above). A claim cannot be made until, with the authority of the Revenue, the company has furnished the individual with a certificate (on form EIS 3) to the effect that, from its point of view, the conditions for the relief are satisfied. [*ICTA 1988, s 289A(6)–(8A), s 306; FA 1994, Sch 15 para 21; FA 1996, Sch 20 para 22, Sch 21 para 7; FA 1998, s 74, Sch 13 para 19, Sch 27 Pt III(14); FA 2000, Sch 17 para 9(3), para 12*]. For more details, see TOLLEY'S INCOME TAX.

20.8 CAPITAL GAINS TAX

See also 20.9 below re EIS deferral relief.

Gains arising on the disposal by the investor, after the end of the 'relevant period' (see below), of shares on which EIS income tax relief has been given are not chargeable gains. (There is no such exemption for shares disposed of before the end of the relevant period, and any EIS income tax relief given will be withdrawn — see 20.2(*f*) above.) Where EIS income tax relief was not given on the full amount subscribed for the shares (other than by reason of the income tax liability being insufficient to support the relief), the capital gains tax exemption is restricted to a proportion of the gain. Where this arises, it will usually be because the investor's EIS subscriptions exceeded the annual maximum on which relief is available (see 20.2(*c*) above). The exempt gain is the proportion of the gain (after any indexation allowance available) found by applying the multiple A/B where

A = the actual income tax relief given (expressed in terms of the reduction in the tax liability); and

B = tax at the lower rate (for the tax year for which EIS relief was given) on the amount subscribed for the issue.

The '*relevant period*' for these purposes is the period beginning with the incorporation of the company or, if later, two years before the date of issue of the shares and ending

- (for shares issued after 5 April 2000) immediately before the third anniversary of the issue date or, if later and where relevant, the third anniversary of the date of commencement of the intended trade referred to in 20.6(*a*) above; or
- (for shares issued before 6 April 2000) five years after the issue date.

[*TCGA 1992, s 150A(2)(3); ICTA 1988, s 312(1A)(a); FA 1994, Sch 15 paras 28–30; FA 1995, Sch 13 para 2(3); FA 1998, Sch 13 para 24(1)(8); FA 2000, Sch 17 para 6(4), para 8*].

See *Example 1* below. See also 20.13 below for special taper relief rules where a gain on EIS shares is chargeable but is deferred by reinvestment in further EIS shares.

Losses. If a disposal of shares on which EIS income tax relief has been given results in a capital loss, the loss is allowable *regardless* of whether the disposal occurs within or without the 'relevant period' (see above). However, in calculating the loss, or in ascertaining whether a loss has indeed arisen, the cost of the shares for CGT purposes is reduced by the amount of EIS income tax relief attributable to the shares disposed of (expressed in terms of the reduction in the tax liability) to the extent that this has not been, or does not fall to be, withdrawn. See *Examples 2 & 3* below. The loss qualifies for relief against income, if claimed, under the provisions of *ICTA 1988, ss 574–576* (losses on shares in unlisted trading companies), which are specifically applied for these purposes — see 39.13 LOSSES.

[*TCGA 1992, s 150A(1)(2A); ICTA 1988, s 305A; FA 1994, Sch 15 paras 20, 28–30; FA 1995, Sch 13 para 2(2); FA 1998, Sch 13 paras 18, 24(1)(8)*].

Example 1

On 8 November 2000 P subscribes £675,000 for 450,000 shares in the EIS company, S Ltd, and obtains the maximum EIS income tax relief of £30,000 (£150,000 × 20%) for 2000/01. On 3 April 2006 he sells the entire holding for £1,395,000.

The chargeable gain arising is calculated as follows:

	£
Disposal proceeds	1,395,000
Cost	675,000
Gain	720,000
Less TCGA 1992, s 150A(3) exemption	
$£720,000 \times \dfrac{30,000(A)}{135,000(B)}$	160,000
Chargeable gain (subject to TAPER RELIEF (60))	£560,000

Note:

A = relief given (£150,000 × 20%)	£30,000
B = £675,000 × 20%	£135,000

Example 2

Assuming the facts are as in *Example 1* above except that the shares are sold for £450,000 on 3 April 2006.

The allowable loss arising is calculated as follows:

	£	£
Disposal proceeds		450,000
Less Cost	675,000	
Less income tax relief given (and not withdrawn)	30,000	645,000
Allowable loss		£195,000

Example 3

Assuming the facts are as in *Example 1* above except that the shares are sold on 3 April 2002 for £450,000, income tax relief of £450,000 × 20% × $\frac{30,000}{135,000}$ = £20,000 would be withdrawn (see below). The balance of £10,000 is not withdrawn and is attributable to the shares sold.

	£	£
Disposal proceeds		450,000
Less Cost	675,000	
Less income tax relief given (and not withdrawn)	10,000	665,000
Allowable loss		£215,000

In calculating the EIS withdrawal, as not all the subscriber shares qualified for EIS income tax relief, the consideration must be reduced by applying the formula A/B, to the amount of the consideration received. [*ICTA 1988, s 299(4); FA 1994, Sch 15 para 12; FA 1998, s 74, Sch 13 para 12(3)(8)*]. For this purpose, A is the actual income tax reduction and B is the tax at the lower rate for that year on the amount subscribed for the issue, i.e. £450,000 × $\frac{30,000}{135,000}$ = £100,000. The EIS relief withdrawn is then calculated on this result, i.e. £100,000 × 20% = £20,000.

See Revenue Capital Gains Manual CG 62819 for an example involving a part disposal.

Identification rules. The normal pooling arrangements for shares acquired before 6 April 1998 (see 59.3, 59.4 SHARES AND SECURITIES—IDENTIFICATION RULES) and the normal identification rules for disposals on or after that date (see 59.2 SHARES AND SECURITIES—IDENTIFICATION RULES) are each disapplied as regards EIS shares. Instead, the rules described below apply to match disposals with acquisitions of shares of the same class in the same company, and they apply where at least some of those shares have attracted EIS income tax relief. Shares are not treated as being of the same class unless they would be so treated if dealt with on the Stock Exchange.

Disposals **after 5 April 1998** are identified with acquisitions on different days on a first in/first out (FIFO) basis. Shares transferred between spouses living together are treated as if they were acquired by the transferee spouse on the day they were issued. Shares comprised in a 'new holding' following a reorganisation to which *TCGA 1992, s 127* applies (see 58.5, 58.8 SHARES AND SECURITIES) are treated as having been acquired when the original shares were acquired. Where shares within two or more of the categories listed below were acquired on the same day, any of those shares disposed of (applying the FIFO basis) are treated as disposed of in the order in which they are listed, as follows:

- shares to which neither EIS income tax relief nor EIS deferral relief (see 20.9 below) is attributable;
- shares to which EIS deferral relief, but not EIS income tax relief, is attributable;
- shares to which EIS income tax relief, but not EIS deferral relief, is attributable;
- shares to which both of those reliefs are attributable.

Any shares within either of the last two categories which are treated as issued on an earlier day by virtue of the carry-back provisions at 20.2(*c*) above are to be treated as disposed of before any other shares within the same category.

Disposals before 6 April 1998 are identified with acquisitions on a FIFO basis.

[*TCGA 1992, s 150A(4)(5); ICTA 1988, s 299(6)–(6D)(8)(a), s 312(4B); FA 1994, Sch 15 paras 12, 28, 30; FA 1998, Sch 13 para 12(5)(7)(8), para 23(5), para 24(2)(3)(8), Sch 27 Pt III(14)*].

Reorganisations of share capital. Where EIS income tax relief has been given on some shares in a particular company but not others and there is a reorganisation (including a bonus issue) within the meaning of *TCGA 1992, s 126*, then *TCGA 1992, s 127* (see 58.5 SHARES AND SECURITIES) applies separately as regards the shares attracting and not attracting relief so that, in each case, the new shares will stand in the place of the old shares. For reorganisations taking effect after 5 April 1998, a distinction is also made, as regards shares attracting income tax relief, between those (if any) to which EIS deferral relief (see 20.9 below) is attributable and those to which it is not, and the separate treatment described above also applies to each of those two categories.

Rights issues. If, immediately following a rights issue, EIS relief is attributable either to the original holding or the rights shares, the share reorganisation rules of *TCGA 1992, ss 127–130* (see 58.5 SHARES AND SECURITIES) are disapplied, with the result that the rights shares are treated as a separate acquisition.

[*TCGA 1992, s 150A(6)(6A)(7); FA 1994, Sch 15 paras 28, 30; FA 1998, Sch 13 para 24(4)(8)*].

Special rules applied to reduce the EIS relief given where a rights issue occurred before 29 November 1994 and the market value of the shares immediately afterwards was less than both the market value immediately before the rights issue and the amount subscribed for the shares. The rules applied *mutatis mutandis* where the individual sold his rights instead of taking up his allotment. [*ICTA 1988, s 305; FA 1995, s 66(4)*]. In any case where these rules have applied, an amount equal to the reduction made is added to the cost for CGT purposes of the allotted shares and deducted from the cost for CGT purposes of the original shares, in each case being apportioned between shares in a just and reasonable manner. [*TCGA 1992, s 150A(9); FA 1994, Sch 15 paras 28, 30; FA 1996, Sch 20 para 54*].

Company reconstructions and amalgamations. If as part of a reconstruction, shares or debentures in another company are issued to an EIS shareholder in exchange for EIS shares to which income tax relief remains attributable, then the shares in the new company are not generally deemed to stand in the place of shares in the old company under *TCGA 1992, s 135* or *s 136* (see 58.8, 58.10 SHARES AND SECURITIES) and there is thus a disposal of the shares in the old company. However, *section 135* or *136* does apply in the normal way if

- the new holding consists of new ordinary shares issued after 28 November 1994 and after the end of the 'relevant period' (as defined above under Gains and applied by reference to the original shares and the company which issued them) and carrying no present or future preferential rights to dividends or assets or right to redemption (no preferential right to redemption where the new shares were issued before 6 April 1998); and
- the company issuing the new shares has previously issued shares under the EIS and has issued the appropriate certificate (see 20.7 above) enabling investors to obtain relief on that earlier issue.

In addition, *TCGA 1992, s 135* is not disapplied in a case to which *ICTA 1988, s 304A* (inserted by *FA 1998, Sch 13 para 17*) applies. That provision enables an EIS company to become, after 5 April 1998, a wholly-owned subsidiary of a new holding company in certain circumstances. The investors receive shares in the new company in exchange for their original shares, and the new shares then stand in the shoes of the old for the purposes of EIS income tax relief. This treatment is generally applied for CGT purposes also. See TOLLEY'S INCOME TAX for details.

[*TCGA 1992, s 150A(8)(8A)–(8D); FA 1994, Sch 15 paras 28, 30; FA 1995, Sch 13 para 2(4); FA 1998, Sch 13 para 24(5)(6)(8), Sch 27 Pt III(14)*].

Reduction of relief where value received etc. Where a gain on disposal of EIS shares would otherwise be exempt due to their having been held until after the end of the 'relevant period' (see above), a special rule applies if EIS income tax relief has been, or falls to be, reduced (though not fully withdrawn) as a result of either or both of the following events occurring before the disposal and after 28 November 1994:

- the investor receives value from the company within the meaning of *ICTA 1988, s 300* (see TOLLEY'S INCOME TAX);
- there is a repayment, redemption, repurchase or payment in circumstances within *ICTA 1988, s 303* (see TOLLEY'S INCOME TAX).

The CGT exemption applies only to so much of the gain as remains after deducting so much of it as is represented by the fraction $\frac{X}{Y}$ where

X = the reduction(s) made, as mentioned above, to the income tax relief given, and

Y = the income tax relief given before applying such reductions.

Where the CGT exemption has already been restricted because EIS income tax relief was not given on the full amount subscribed for the shares (see above), the fraction is applied to the part of the gain otherwise exempt and the deduction made from that part.

[*TCGA 1992, s 150B; FA 1995, Sch 13 para 3; FA 1998, Sch 13 para 25, Sch 27 Pt III(14)*].

Example 4

On 9 November 2000, Q subscribed for 20,000 EIS £1 shares at par in H Ltd. The EIS relief given was £4,000. On 2 January 2002 he received £2,000 from the company, as a result of which EIS relief of £2,000 @ 20% = £400 is withdrawn under *ICTA 1988, s 300(1B)*. In June 2006, the shares were sold for £60,000.

The CGT computation is as follows:

	£
Disposal consideration	60,000
Less Cost	20,000
Gain	£40,000
Chargeable gain (subject to TAPER RELIEF (60))	
$£40{,}000 \times \frac{400}{4{,}000}$ (*TCGA 1992, s 150B*)	£4,000
Exempt gain (balance)	£36,000

If only £3,000 EIS relief were given (say because the investor was also given £27,000 EIS relief on another investment in 2000/01, the maximum relief for that year being £30,000)

the relief withdrawn would be $\frac{3,000}{4,000}$ × £2,000 × 20% = £300 (see *ICTA 1988, s 300(1B)* applying *ICTA 1988, s 299(4)*).

The chargeable gain restriction would be calculated in two stages:

Gain as above	£40,000
Stage 1 (*TCGA 1992, s 150A(3)* restriction)	
Gain exempt:	
£40,000 × $\frac{3,000}{4,000}$	£30,000
Gain chargeable (balance)	£10,000

Stage 2 (*TCGA 1992, s 150B* restriction)

	Exempt £	Chargeable £
Gain chargeable as above		10,000
Gain otherwise exempt	30,000	
Reduced by value received		
£30,000 × $\frac{300}{3,000}$	(3,000)	3,000
Total chargeable gain (subject to TAPER RELIEF (60))		£13,000
Exempt gain	£27,000	

20.9 **EIS: CAPITAL GAINS DEFERRAL RELIEF**

Introduction. General reinvestment relief was available for reinvestment into qualifying shares acquired before 6 April 1998 (see 50.1 REINVESTMENT RELIEF) but relief under those rules for reinvestment into shares on which EIS income tax relief is claimed was prohibited by *TCGA 1992, s 164MA* (see 50.16). However, a specific relief was introduced by *FA 1995, s 67, Sch 13 para 4(3)* whereby any chargeable gain accruing after 28 November 1994 could be deferred to the extent that it could be matched with an investment in EIS shares to which income tax relief (see 20.2 above) was attributable.

In relation to EIS shares issued after 5 April 1998, significant changes were made to the deferral relief provisions. In particular, it is no longer a requirement that the shares qualify for income tax relief nor that the individual be unconnected with the company. The provisions are also extended to trustees. These changes are intended to compensate for the abolition of general reinvestment relief. There is no limit on the amount of the gain that can be deferred under the new provisions (previously the income tax relief annual maximum at 20.2(*c*) above would have applied), but the gross assets test at 20.5 above does limit the amount that may be invested in any one EIS company (or group).

The main provisions of the revamped EIS deferral relief are described at 20.10 below, with further provisions at 20.12 below. Their application to trustees is covered at 20.11 below. Special rules on the application of taper relief in certain cases are dealt with at 20.13 below. The provisions as they related to shares issued before 6 April 1998 are described at 20.14 below.

Deferral relief is attributable to any EIS shares if expenditure on them has been used to defer the whole or part of any gain and there has been no chargeable event (see 20.10 and 20.14 below) in relation to those shares resulting in the deferred gain being brought back into charge. [*TCGA 1992, Sch 5B para 19(2)*].

20.10 **Reinvestment into EIS shares issued after 5 April 1998.** Deferral relief applies where

- a chargeable gain would otherwise accrue to an individual
  - on the disposal by him of any asset; or
  - on the occurrence of a chargeable event under these provisions or the provisions governing reinvestment into VCT shares (see 65.10 VENTURE CAPITAL TRUSTS); or
  - to give effect to a withdrawal under *TCGA 1992, s 164F* or *s 164FA* of general reinvestment relief (see 50.11, 50.12 REINVESTMENT RELIEF);
- the individual makes a 'qualifying investment'; and
- the individual is UK resident or ordinarily resident both when the chargeable gain accrues to him and when he makes the qualifying investment, and is not, at the time he makes the investment, regarded as resident outside the UK for the purposes of any double taxation arrangements the effect of which would be that he would not be liable to tax on a gain arising on a disposal, immediately after their acquisition, of the shares comprising the qualifying investment, disregarding any exemption available under *TCGA 1992, s 150A* (see 20.8 above).

See 20.11 below re the application of these provisions to trustees.

Subject to the further conditions below, a '*qualifying investment*' is a subscription *wholly in cash* for eligible shares (broadly, *new* ordinary, non-preferential, shares — see 20.4 above) in a company which are issued within the one year immediately preceding or the three years immediately following the time the chargeable gain in question accrues. These time limits may be extended by the Board in individual cases. If the shares are issued *before* the gain accrues, they must still be held at the time it accrues. For these purposes, shares are not treated as issued merely by being comprised in a letter of allotment or similar instrument. The further conditions are as follows:

(*a*) the company must be a qualifying company (within 20.5 above) in relation to the shares;

(*b*) the shares must be fully paid up at time of issue (disregarding any undertaking to pay cash to the company at a future date);

(*c*) the shares must be subscribed for and issued for *bona fide* commercial purposes and not as part of tax avoidance arrangements;

(*d*) the requirements of *ICTA 1988, s 289(1A)* (see 20.2(*a*)(i)–(iii) above) must be satisfied in relation to the company; in practice, this condition need be considered only if the company is part of a group (Revenue Capital Gains Manual CG 62902);

(*e*) all the shares comprised in the issue are issued to raise money for the purpose of a qualifying business activity (see 20.6 above); and

(*f*) the money so raised (or all but an insignificant amount of it) is employed wholly for that purpose by the end of the twelve months following the issue or, if the only qualifying business activity falls within 20.6(*a*) above, and if later, by the end of the twelve months starting when the company (or subsidiary) began to carry on the qualifying trade (see 20.6 above).

These conditions draw on those applicable to income tax relief (see 20.2(*a*) above). However, there is no requirement that any income tax relief be attributable to the shares, and, in contrast to the position for income tax relief, the individual does not have to be unconnected with the company.

Postponement of the original gain. Where a chargeable gain would otherwise accrue to an individual ('the investor'), and he acquires a qualifying investment, a claim can be made by him to defer the whole or part of that gain against his investment up to an amount specified in the claim (limited to the amount of the gain or, where applicable, the amount of the gain not already relieved under either these provisions or those at 65.10 VENTURE CAPITAL TRUSTS). The amount of investment available to be matched with gains in this way is limited to the amount of the qualifying investment (to the extent that it has not already been so matched). The gain eligible for deferral is the gain after all available reliefs (including retirement relief and indexation allowance) other than taper relief (see *Example* below and also 20.13 below) (Revenue Capital Gains Manual CG 62901).

Claims. Subject to what is said at 56.29 SELF-ASSESSMENT re claims being included in a self-assessment tax return if possible, there is no statutory form in which a claim *must* be made (though the claim form attached to form EIS 3 — see below — *may* be used, with or without a tax return). The provisions for income tax relief claims (see 20.7 above) are applied, with modifications, to deferral relief claims. Thus, a deferral relief claim cannot be made until the company has carried on the trade or other qualifying business activity for at least four months and cannot be made later than the fifth anniversary of 31 January following the tax year in which the shares were issued. A claim cannot be made until, with the authority of the Revenue, the company has furnished the individual with a certificate (on form EIS 3) to the effect that, from its point of view, the conditions for deferral relief are satisfied. For more details relating to the issue of the certificate, see TOLLEY'S INCOME TAX.

Deferred gain becoming chargeable. The deferred gain will become chargeable upon the occurrence of, *and at the time of*, any of the chargeable events listed below. The amount of the gain accruing at the time of the chargeable event is equal to so much of the deferred gain as is attributable to the EIS shares in relation to which the chargeable event occurs. For these purposes, a proportionate part of the net deferred gain (i.e. the deferred gain less any amount brought into charge on an earlier part disposal) is attributed to each of the 'relevant shares' held, immediately before the chargeable event, by the investor or by a person who acquired them from the investor on an inter-spouse transfer within *TCGA 1992, s 58*. The '*relevant shares*' are the shares acquired in making the qualifying investment and, in a case where the original gain accrued at a later time than the making of the qualifying investment, still held at that time. They also include any bonus shares issued in respect of the relevant shares and of the same class and carrying the same rights. These rules were modified by *FA 1999, Sch 8* and are described here in their modified form. The modifications affect part disposals (see the *Example* below) and give statutory effect in relation to shares issued after 5 April 1999 to the Revenue's interpretation of the previous rules (Treasury Explanatory Notes to Finance Bill 1999). The said chargeable events are as follows.

(i) The investor disposes of the EIS shares otherwise than by way of an inter-spouse transfer to which *TCGA 1992, s 58* applies.

(ii) Subsequent to an inter-spouse transfer within *TCGA 1992, s 58*, the shares are disposed of by the investor's spouse (otherwise than by way of transfer back to the investor).

(iii) Within the designated period (see below), the investor becomes neither resident nor ordinarily resident in the UK.

(iv) Within the designated period (see below), the investor's spouse, having acquired the shares by way of inter-spouse transfer within *TCGA 1992, s 58*, becomes neither resident nor ordinarily resident in the UK.

(v) The shares cease to be eligible shares or are treated as so ceasing (see below).

For these purposes, the designated period is

- (for shares issued after 5 April 2000) the period beginning two years before the issue of the shares and ending immediately before the third anniversary of the issue date or, if later and where relevant, the third anniversary of the date of commencement of the intended trade referred to in 20.6(*a*) above; or
- (for shares issued before 6 April 2000) the five years beginning with the issue of the shares.

In the case of (iii) or (iv) above (non-residence), the deferred gain does not become chargeable where the investor (or, where applicable, spouse) becomes neither resident nor ordinarily resident through temporary working outside the UK and again becomes resident or ordinarily resident within three years of that event, without having disposed of any of the relevant shares in the meantime in circumstances such that a chargeable event would have occurred had he been UK resident. No assessment is to be made until it is clear that the person concerned will not regain UK resident status within the three-year period.

EIS shares are *treated* as ceasing to be eligible shares (in which case a chargeable event occurs under (v) above) in any of the following circumstances (and see also the further provisions in 20.12 below).

(1) The condition at (*a*) above (qualifying company) ceases to be satisfied in consequence of an event occurring after the issue of the shares: the shares cease to be eligible shares at the time of that event. The Revenue have confirmed that the company is required to retain its qualifying status only for the duration of the 'relevant period' (as defined in 20.6 above), so no chargeable event can occur under this heading by reason of anything happening beyond the end of that period (*Taxation 18 February 1999 p 486*).

(2) The condition at (*d*) above (compliance with *ICTA 1988, s 289(1A)*) ceases to be satisfied in consequence of an event occurring after the issue of the shares: the shares cease to be eligible shares at the time of that event.

(3) The condition at (*f*) above (money raised to be used for purpose of qualifying business activity within a specified time period) is not satisfied and the deferral claim was made before the end of the time period allowed: the shares cease to be eligible shares at the end of that time period. (If the deferral claim has not been made by then, or if the condition at (*e*) above is not satisfied at all, the shares are treated as never having been eligible shares.)

Death. The deferred gain does not become chargeable on the death of the investor (or, where applicable, spouse) or on the occurrence after death of any event which would otherwise have been a chargeable event.

Identification rules. In determining whether any shares disposed of after 5 April 1998 are shares to which deferral relief is attributable (see 20.9 above), the normal identification rules (see 59.2 SHARES AND SECURITIES—IDENTIFICATION RULES) are disapplied and, instead, the same rules as in 20.8 above apply (broadly, first in/first out but with special rules where shares acquired on the same day fall into different specified categories — see examples at Revenue Capital Gains Manual CG 62919–62921).

Where at the time of the chargeable event, any of the relevant shares are regarded under capital gains tax legislation as represented by assets which consist of or include assets other than such shares, the deferred gain attributable to those shares is to be apportioned between those assets on a just and reasonable basis. As between different assets regarded as representing the same shares, the identification of those assets follows the same identification rules as for shares.

Persons chargeable. The chargeable gain is treated as accruing, depending on which type of chargeable event occurs, to

- the individual who makes the disposal;
- the individual who becomes non-resident;
- the individual who holds the shares in question when they cease (or are treated as ceasing) to be eligible shares.

Where the last category applies and some of the shares are held by the investor and some by a person who acquired them from the investor by way of inter-spouse transfer within *TCGA 1992, s 58*, the gain is computed separately as regards each individual without reference to the shares held by the other.

[*TCGA 1992, s 150C, Sch 5B paras 1–6, 19; FA 1995, s 67, Sch 13 para 4(3)(4); FA 1998, s 74, Sch 13 paras 26–33, 36, Sch 27 Pt III(14); FA 1999, s 73, Sch 8; FA 2000, Sch 17 para 7(2)(3), para 8*].

See the further provisions at 20.12 below.

Example

Frank realises a gain of £270,000 (before taper relief) in May 2000 on the disposal of a business asset he had owned since 1992. He makes no other disposals in 2000/01. On 1 March 2002, he subscribes £234,000 for 60% of the issued ordinary share capital in a new company, ABC Ltd. The investment is a qualifying investment for the purposes of EIS deferral relief, and the shares represent a business asset for the purposes of taper relief. Frank makes a claim to defer the maximum £234,000 of the May 2000 gain against the qualifying investment.

The CGT position for 2000/01 is as follows.

	£
Gain	270,000
Less deferred under EIS provisions	234,000
	36,000
Less taper relief £36,000 @ 25%	9,000
	27,000
Less annual exemption	7,200
Taxable gain 2000/01	£19,800

On 1 August 2007, he sells 40% of his holding of ABC Ltd shares for £213,600. He makes no other disposals in 2007/08. His CGT position for that year is as follows.

	£
Gain on ABC Ltd shares	
Disposal proceeds	213,600
Less cost (£234,000 × 40%)	93,600
	120,000
Less taper relief £120,000 @ 75%	90,000
Gain	£30,000
Deferred gain brought into charge	
Total gain deferred	£234,000
	£
Clawback restricted to expenditure to which disposal relates	93,600
Less taper relief £93,600 @ 25%	23,400
Gain	£70,200

Taxable gains 2007/08 (subject to annual exemption) (£30,000 + £70,200)	£100,200
Gain remaining deferred until any future chargeable event (£234,000 – £93,600)	£140,400

Notes to the example

(*a*) Frank's subscription for ABC Ltd shares cannot qualify for EIS income tax relief. He is connected with the company by virtue of his shareholding being greater than 30%. (In practice, the holdings of his associates, e.g. wife and children, need to be taken into account as well.) See 20.3(*c*) above.

(*b*) As the ABC Ltd shares do not qualify for income tax relief, there is no exemption as in 20.8 above for the gain arising on part disposal, despite the shares having been held for over three years.

(*c*) Taper relief on the deferred gain becoming chargeable is given by reference to the time and circumstances of the original disposal, not the disposal of the EIS shares which gives rise to the chargeable event (see 60.12 TAPER RELIEF), but see 20.13 below re cases of serial reinvestment. See 60.2 for the calculation of taper relief and 60.4 for the definition of a business asset.

20.11 **Reinvestment into EIS shares issued after 5 April 1998 — application to trustees.** The deferral provisions for individuals at 20.10 above (and the further provisions at 20.12 below) also apply to trustees of a settlement where, in a case where the gain to be deferred accrues to them on the disposal of an asset, that asset (the '*trust asset*') is comprised in settled property of the kind mentioned in either (*a*) or (*b*) below.

(*a*) Settled property on discretionary trusts (i.e. settlements where the beneficiaries' interests are not interests in possession, an interest in possession for this purpose excluding an interest for a fixed term; and see generally 57.7 SETTLEMENTS) where all of the beneficiaries are either individuals or charities.

(*b*) Settled property on non-discretionary trusts (i.e. settlements where the beneficiaries' interests are interests in possession as in (*a*) above) where any of the beneficiaries is an individual or a charity.

Where there is at least one beneficiary holding a non-discretionary interest and at least one beneficiary holding a discretionary interest (i.e. a mixed settlement), all of the discretionary interests are treated for these purposes as if they were a single interest in possession, and as if that interest were held, where all the discretionary beneficiaries are individuals or charities, by an individual or charity, and, in any other case, by a person who is not an individual or charity.

If, at the time of the disposal of the trust asset, the settled property comprising that asset is within (*b*) above but not all of the beneficiaries are individuals or charities, then only the 'relevant proportion' of the gain on the disposal is taken into account for the purposes of deferral relief. The '*relevant proportion*' at any time is the proportion which the aggregate amount of the income of the settled property interests in which are held by individuals or charities bears to the total amount of all of the income of the settled property.

If the settled property qualifies under (*a*) above at the time of the disposal of the trust asset, deferral relief is available only if, immediately after the acquisition of the EIS shares, the settled property comprising the EIS shares also qualifies under (*a*) above. This also applies *mutatis mutandis* to settled property qualifying under (*b*) above but, if not all the beneficiaries are individuals or charities, with the additional condition that the relevant proportion immediately after the acquisition of the EIS shares must be not less than the relevant proportion at the time of the disposal of the trust asset.

[*TCGA 1992, Sch 5B para 17; FA 1998, s 74, Sch 13 para 36*].

The above provisions mirror those applicable for the purposes of general reinvestment relief for qualifying shares acquired before 6 April 1998 (see 50.4 REINVESTMENT RELIEF). Revenue Capital Gains Manual CG 63056 summarises the provisions in the form of a flow chart.

20.12 **Reinvestment into EIS shares issued after 5 April 1998 — further provisions**

(1) *Reorganisations.* Provisions identical to those of *TCGA 1992, s 150A(6)(6A)(7)* (see 20.8 above under 'Reorganisations of share capital'), as they apply for reorganisations taking effect after 5 April 1998, apply in relation to shares to which deferral relief is attributable (see 20.9 above).

Acquisition of share capital by new company. Provisions similar to those of *ICTA 1988, s 304A* (which enables an EIS company to become a wholly-owned subsidiary of a new holding company in certain circumstances — see 20.8 above under 'Company reconstructions and amalgamations' and also TOLLEY'S INCOME TAX) apply for the purposes of deferral relief. Provided all the conditions are satisfied, deferral relief attributable to shares in the original EIS company is regarded as being attributable to the shares in the new company for which the original shares are exchanged.

Other reconstructions and amalgamations. Provisions similar to those of *TCGA 1992, s 150A(8)(8A)–(8D)* (see 20.8 above under 'Company reconstructions and amalgamations') apply in relation to shares to which deferral relief is attributable. These provisions treat an exchange of shares as a disposal, except in specified circumstances.

[*TCGA 1992, Sch 5B paras 7–9, 19; FA 1998, s 74, Sch 13 paras 34, 36; FA 1999, Sch 8 para 3*].

(2) *Anti-avoidance provisions.*

Reinvestment in same company etc. If an individual realises a gain on disposal of shares in or securities of a company (Company A), he cannot defer that gain by virtue of a subscription for shares in an EIS company which is either Company A itself or is, either at the time of the disposal or the time of the issue of the EIS shares, a member of the same group as Company A. Further provisions apply where an individual defers a gain by subscribing for EIS shares, disposes of any of those shares and makes a further subscription for shares in the same company (or member of the same group); no deferral relief is allowed in respect of the second subscription. This also applies where there has been no disposal of the original EIS shares but the further subscription is for shares in a company a disposal of shares in which resulted in the initial deferral (or a member of the same group as that company).

Investment-linked loans. Provisions analogous to those at 20.2(*g*) above apply where an investment-linked loan etc. is made to the investor or his associate in the 'relevant period' (as in 20.3(*a*) above). For deferral relief purposes, the EIS shares are treated as never having been eligible shares (with the result that no such relief is available) if the loan is made on or before the date of their issue and as otherwise ceasing to be eligible shares (with the result that a chargeable event occurs in respect of deferral relief claimed — see 20.10(v) above) on the date the loan is made.

Where the shares are subscribed for by trustees, and relief claimed by virtue of 20.11 above, the above applies to loans made not only to the trustees but to any individual (or associate) or charity (or connected person) by virtue of whose interest (at the time the shares are issued and/or at the time the loan is made) deferral relief is available in respect of the settled property.

Pre-arranged exits. Provisions identical to those at 20.2(*h*) above apply to prevent EIS shares from being eligible shares for deferral relief purposes where certain exit arrangements are made in relation to their issue.

Put and call options. The granting of a put option or call option prevents the EIS shares to which it relates from being eligible shares for deferral relief purposes if the option is granted on or before the date of issue of the shares, or otherwise causes them to be treated as ceasing to be eligible shares (with the result that a chargeable event occurs in respect of deferral relief claimed — see 20.10(v) above) at the time the option is granted. The provisions apply where an individual subscribes for EIS shares (or acquires them on a no gain/no loss transfer from a subscriber spouse) and, during the 'relevant period' (defined as in 20.3(*a*) above), either

- an option for the grantor to purchase such shares (a '*put option*') is granted to the individual, or
- an option for the individual to sell such shares (a '*call option*') is granted by the individual.

Comparable provisions apply for the purposes of EIS income tax relief.

Value received by the investor from the EIS company. Where the EIS investor (or his associate — within 20.3(*c*) above) receives any value from the company during the designated period (see below), the shares are treated as never having been eligible shares for deferral relief purposes if the value is received on or before the date of the share issue or as otherwise ceasing to be eligible shares (with the result that a chargeable event occurs in respect of deferral relief claimed — see 20.10(v) above) at the time value is received. Note that the full amount of the deferred gain falls to be clawed back even if the investor receives back only a proportion of the value of his investment. The provisions of *TCGA 1992, Sch 5B para 13* which determine whether value is received from a company are based on the EIS income tax relief withdrawal provisions of *ICTA 1988, s 300* (for which see TOLLEY'S INCOME TAX). They are fairly widely drawn but *not* so as to catch, for example, reasonable remuneration (or reimbursement of expenses) to the individual as an officer or employee of the company, interest at a commercial rate on a loan made to the company or dividends which represent no more than a normal return on investment in that company. The provisions *do* include, for example, any repayment, redemption or repurchase by the company of any of its share capital or securities which belong to the individual, any loan or advance by the company to the individual which is not repaid before the EIS shares are issued, and the provision of a benefit or facility for the individual. Value received from a connected person of the company (within *TCGA 1992, s 286* — see 14 CONNECTED PERSONS) falls within the provisions if it would do so had it been received from the EIS company itself.

Where the shares are subscribed for by trustees, and relief claimed by virtue of 20.11 above, the above applies to value received not only by the trustees but by any individual (or associate) or charity (or connected person) by virtue of whose interest (at the time the shares are issued and/or at the time the value is received) deferral relief is available in respect of the settled property.

For these purposes, the designated period is

- (for shares issued after 5 April 2000) the period beginning two years before the issue of the shares and ending immediately before the third anniversary of the issue date or, if later and where relevant, the third anniversary of the date of commencement of the intended trade referred to in 20.6(*a*) above; or
- (for shares issued before 6 April 2000) the seven-year period beginning two years before, and ending five years after, the issue of the shares.

Value received by other persons from the EIS company. Provisions based on the EIS income tax relief withdrawal provisions of *ICTA 1988, ss 303, 303A* (for which see TOLLEY'S INCOME TAX) apply where, at any time in the designated period defined immediately above, the EIS company (or one which is a 51% subsidiary at some time in the 'relevant period' — defined as in 20.3(*a*) above) repays, redeems or repurchases any of its share capital from a member (other than the EIS investor in question) who does not thereby lose EIS income tax relief or deferral relief or CORPORATE VENTURING SCHEME (15) investment relief. They apply equally where the company or such subsidiary makes any payment to any such member for the giving up of rights to share capital on its cancellation or extinguishment. The shares are treated as never having been eligible shares for deferral relief purposes if such an event occurs on or before the date of the share issue or as otherwise ceasing to be eligible shares (with the result that a chargeable event occurs in respect of deferral relief claimed — see 20.10(v) above) at the time such event occurs.

[*TCGA 1992, Sch 5B paras 10–15, 18, 19; FA 1998, s 74, Sch 13 para 35); FA 2000, Sch 16 para 4, Sch 17 para 7(4), para 8*].

(3) *Information.* Certain chargeable events and failures of conditions must be notified to the inspector, generally within 60 days, by either the investor, the EIS company or any person connected with the EIS company having knowledge of the matter. The inspector may require such notice where he has reason to believe it should have been made, and is given broad powers to require information generally.

[*TCGA 1992, Sch 5B para 16; FA 1998, s 74, Sch 13 para 36; FA 1999, Sch 8 para 4(i); FA 2000, Sch 17 para 7(3), para 8*].

20.13 **Taper relief.** Except where the special rule below has effect, taper relief is applied to a gain deferred under 20.10 above at the time it becomes chargeable but by reference to the period for which the original asset was held — see 60.12 TAPER RELIEF.

A special rule applies in consequence of the disposal after 5 April 1999 of a holding of EIS shares (the initial investment) which were issued after 5 April 1998 and to which either (or both) CGT deferral relief or income tax relief is attributable (see, respectively, 20.9 and 20.2(*b*) above). The rule has effect only where the whole or part of the gain otherwise accruing is deferred under 20.10 (or 20.11) above by reinvestment in further EIS shares (the second investment). Upon a disposal of the second investment (the '*relevant disposal*'), with the result that all or part of the deferred gain on the initial investment is revived (i.e. becomes chargeable), taper relief is calculated in respect of the revived gain as if the qualifying holding period (see 60.2 TAPER RELIEF) for the initial investment began with the date of acquisition of that investment and ended with the date of the relevant disposal. In other words, the holding periods of the two investments are combined. Where all or part of the revived gain is itself deferred by means of a third EIS investment, such that taper relief does not fall to be calculated until the third investment is disposed of, the holding periods of all three investments are combined to form the qualifying holding period, and so on as regards fourth and subsequent investments.

The above applies only to the revived gain and not to any other gain accruing on the relevant disposal or to any part of the original gain which was not deferred. The extension of the qualifying holding period as above is subject to the anti-avoidance provisions at 60.16, 60.17 TAPER RELIEF, which provide *inter alia* for certain periods to be left out of account for taper relief purposes. In addition, any gap in time between disposal of the initial investment and acquisition of the second investment (or between disposal and acquisition of subsequent investments in the chain) does not count towards the qualifying holding period or the relevant period of ownership (see 60.8 TAPER RELIEF).

In determining the extent (if any) to which the revived gain is a gain on a business asset and thus the rate of taper relief to be applied (see 60.2, 60.4 TAPER RELIEF), the combined period of ownership is calculated as above. The initial investment and each subsequent investment in the chain is treated as having been held for the actual time it was held and its character (as a business or non-business asset) resolved accordingly. For the duration of any overlap period during which more than one such investment was held, it is assumed for these purposes that only the first-acquired of those investments was held. If these rules result in the revived gain being of mixed character, the rules at 60.9 TAPER RELIEF apply to determine the relief available.

[*TCGA 1992, s 150D, Sch 5BA; FA 1999, s 72, Sch 7*].

Example

Annabelle realises a gain of £270,000 (before taper relief) on 1 May 2000 on the disposal of a complete holding of shares in ABC Ltd (an EIS company) for which she had subscribed on 1 May 1999 and in respect of which she had deferred a gain of £50,000 which would otherwise have accrued in 1998/99 on a disposal of quoted shares. The ABC Ltd shares were a business asset throughout for taper relief purposes. She makes no other disposals in 2000/01. On 1 November 2001, she subscribes £210,000 for new ordinary shares in a new company, EIS Ltd. The investment is a qualifying investment for the purposes of EIS deferral relief (but not income tax relief) and a business asset for the purposes of taper relief. Annabelle makes a claim to defer the maximum £210,000 of the May 2000 gain against her investment in EIS Ltd.

The CGT position for 2000/01 is as follows.

	£
Gain on ABC Ltd shares	270,000
Less deferred under EIS provisions	210,000
	60,000
Less taper relief £60,000 @ 12.5%	
(Qualifying holding period 1.5.99–1.5.2000 = 1 year)	7,500
	52,500
Previously deferred gain now chargeable*	50,000
	102,500
Less annual exemption	7,200
Taxable gain 2000/01	£95,300

* The taper relief period for the first asset (a non-EIS investment) ends on the date of disposal of that asset (see 60.12 TAPER RELIEF) and does not fall to be extended under these provisions. No taper relief is due in this case as the asset is a non-business asset held for less than three years.

On 1 May 2005, Annabelle sells her holding of EIS Ltd shares for £500,000. She makes no other disposals in 2005/06. Her CGT position for that year is as follows.

	£
Gain on EIS Ltd shares	
Disposal proceeds	500,000
Less cost	210,000
	290,000
Less taper relief £290,000 @ 50%	
(Qualifying holding period 1.11.01 –1.5.05 = 3 years)	145,000
Gain	£145,000

Deferred gain brought into charge	£
Gain deferred	210,000
Less taper relief £210,000 @ 75%*	157,500
Gain	£52,500

* Qualifying holding period:
1.5.99–1.5.2000 — 1 year
1.11.01–1.5.05 — 3.5 years
Total — 4.5 years

Number of whole years in qualifying holding period = 4

Taxable gains 2005/06 (subject to annual exemption) (£145,000 + £52,500)	£197,500

20.14 **Reinvestment into EIS shares issued before 6 April 1998.** The deferral rules described below apply where the EIS shares are issued before 6 April 1998 (see 20.10 above re later issues and 20.9 above generally).

The relief applies where

(*a*) a chargeable gain would otherwise accrue to an individual after 28 November 1994 on the disposal by him of any asset (or on the occurrence of a chargeable event either under these provisions or the similar provisions governing reinvestment into VCT shares (SEE 65.10 VENTURE CAPITAL TRUSTS));

(*b*) the individual makes a 'qualifying investment'; and

(*c*) the individual is UK resident or ordinarily resident both when the chargeable gain accrues to him and when he makes the 'qualifying investment', and is not, at the time he makes the investment, regarded as resident outside the UK for the purposes of any double taxation arrangements the effect of which would be that he would not be liable to tax on a gain arising on a disposal, immediately after their acquisition, of the shares comprising the 'qualifying investment', disregarding the exemption under *TCGA 1992, s 150A* (see 20.8 above).

A '*qualifying investment*' is a subscription for shares to which any income tax relief given under the EIS to the individual is attributable and which are issued within the one year immediately preceding or the three years immediately following the time the chargeable gain in question accrues. These time limits may be extended by the Board in individual cases. If the shares are issued *before* the gain accrues, they must still be held at the latter time. For these purposes, shares are not treated as issued merely by being comprised in a letter of allotment or similar instrument.

Postponement of the original gain. Where a chargeable gain would otherwise accrue to an individual ('the investor'), and he acquires a qualifying investment, a claim can be made by him to defer the whole or part of that gain against his investment up to an amount specified in the claim (limited to the amount of the gain or, where applicable, the amount of the gain not already relieved under either these provisions or those at 65.10 VENTURE CAPITAL TRUSTS). The amount of investment available to be matched with gains in this way is limited to the amount in respect of which income tax relief is given under the EIS and which has not already been so matched.

Subject to what is said at 56.29 SELF-ASSESSMENT re claims being included in a self-assessment tax return if possible, there is no statutory form in which a claim must be made. The deferral claim must be made by the fifth anniversary of 31 January following the 'relevant tax year' (for 1995/96 and earlier years, within six years after the end of the relevant tax year). The '*relevant tax year*' is the tax year in which the *later* of the following events occurred:

- the gain to be deferred arose;
- the EIS shares were issued.

(Revenue Capital Gains Manual CG 62860).

Deferred gain becoming chargeable. The deferred gain will become chargeable upon the occurrence of, *and at the time of*, any of the chargeable events listed below. The amount of the gain accruing at the time of the chargeable event is equal to so much of the original gain as was matched under these provisions with expenditure on the EIS shares in question.

(i) The investor disposes of the EIS shares otherwise than by way of an inter-spouse transfer to which *TCGA 1992, s 58* applies. As regards part disposals, the Revenue interpret the law as requiring a proportionate part of the deferred gain to be brought into account.

(ii) Subsequent to an inter-spouse transfer within *TCGA 1992, s 58*, the shares are disposed of by the investor's spouse (otherwise than by way of transfer back to the investor).

(iii) Within five years after the issue of the shares, the investor becomes neither resident nor ordinarily resident in the UK.

(iv) Within five years after the issue of the shares, the investor's spouse, having acquired the shares by way of inter-spouse transfer within *TCGA 1992, s 58*, becomes neither resident nor ordinarily resident in the UK.

(v) The company which issued the shares ceases to be a qualifying company under the EIS (see 20.5 above) within the 'relevant period' (defined as in 20.6 above).

(vi) The EIS income tax relief is withdrawn or reduced (see TOLLEY'S INCOME TAX) in circumstances not falling within (i)–(v) above.

In the case of (iii) or (iv) above (non-residence), the deferred gain does not become chargeable where the investor (or, where applicable, spouse) becomes neither resident nor ordinarily resident through temporary working outside the UK and again becomes resident or ordinarily resident within three years of that event, without having disposed of any of the relevant EIS shares in the meantime in circumstances such that a chargeable event would have occurred had he been UK resident. No assessment is to be made until it is clear that the person concerned will not regain UK resident status within the three-year period.

Death. The deferred gain does not become chargeable on the death of the investor (or, where applicable, spouse) or on the occurrence after death of any event which would otherwise have been a chargeable event.

Identification rules. In determining whether any EIS shares to which a chargeable event relates are shares the expenditure on which has been matched with any gain, disposals of shares are first identified with those acquired earlier rather than later (i.e. first in, first out). On a part disposal of shares in a company acquired by the same person on the same day, shares the expenditure on which has been matched under these provisions are regarded as disposed of subsequent to any others (see Revenue Capital Gains Manual CG 62851–62854).

Where at the time of the chargeable event, the relevant EIS shares are regarded under capital gains tax legislation as represented by assets which consist of or include assets other than such shares, the expenditure on those shares is to be apportioned between those assets on a just and reasonable basis. As between different assets regarded as representing the same shares, the identification of those assets follows the share identification rules above.

Persons chargeable. The chargeable gain is treated as accruing, depending on which type of chargeable event occurs, to

(A) the individual who makes the disposal;

(B) the individual who becomes non-resident;

(C) the individual who holds the shares in question at the time that the company ceases to be a qualifying company; or

(D) the individual who holds the shares in question at the time that the EIS income tax relief is withdrawn or reduced.

Where (C) or (D) apply and some of the shares are held by the investor and some by a person who acquired them from the investor by way of inter-spouse transfer within *TCGA 1992, s 58*, the gain is computed separately as regards each individual without reference to the shares held by the other.

[*TCGA 1992, s 150C, Sch 5B; FA 1995, s 67, Sch 13 para 4(3)(4)*].

20.15 BUSINESS EXPANSION SCHEME

(*a*) **Introduction.** The Business Expansion Scheme (BES) was replaced by the Enterprise Investment Scheme and was available in respect of shares issued after 5 April 1983 and before 1 January 1994.

(*b*) **Tax relief** was available to a qualifying individual who subscribed for eligible shares between 6 April 1983 and 31 December 1993 (both inclusive) in a qualifying company which uses the funds raised for a qualifying purpose. [*ICTA 1988, s 289(1)*].

(*c*) **Amount of investment.** The minimum investment was £500 and the maximum was £40,000 per individual. The minimum investment criteria did not apply if the investment was made through an approved investment fund. £5,000 of investments made within the first 6 months of the tax year during the period 6 April 1987 to 1 January 1994 could be deemed to be made in the previous year.

(*d*) **Residence.** The individual concerned must have been resident and ordinarily resident at the time the shares were issued and have subscribed for the shares on his own behalf. Nor could he be connected with the company at any time during the relevant period being the shorter of two years before the share issue or the date of incorporation until five years after share issue. [*ICTA 1988, s 312(1A)(a)*].

The company must be incorporated in the UK and throughout the period from the date of issue of the shares until three years following it must be resident in the UK, unquoted and exist wholly for the purposes of carrying on one or more qualifying trades.

20.16 **BES income tax relief.** Relief for income tax purposes was given by allowing a deduction against total income of the individual who subscribes for the shares for the year in which the shares are issued. The allowance is excluded from total income for the purposes of calculating age allowance, life assurance relief or dependent relative relief and top-slicing relief. Relief in respect of shares issued before 6 October in the tax year could be carried back to the previous tax year up to a maximum of £5,000.

Withdrawn relief. Relief is withdrawn if the shares are disposed of within five years from date of issue. A share exchange is treated as a disposal for this purpose (although provisions effective after 5 April 1998 enable a BES company to become a wholly-owned subsidiary of a new holding company in certain circumstances without loss of relief). The relief allowed is reduced by the sale proceeds. Relief is also withdrawn if value is received from the company, e.g. redemption of share capital, company repays a debt, company waivers any liability of an individual etc.

See TOLLEY'S INCOME TAX for the full provisions.

20.17 **BES capital gains.** Any gain accruing to an individual, to whom BES relief has been given, on the disposal of eligible shares **issued after 18 March 1986** is exempt from capital gains tax provided relief has not been withdrawn. Similarly, any loss is not allowable. [*TCGA 1992, s 150(2)*]. If the BES shares have been disposed of to a spouse and the inter-spouse exemption applies under *TCGA 1992, s 58*, the BES exemption for capital gains will still apply to disposals by the recipient spouse to third parties (see 41.3 MARRIED PERSONS).

Only a complete withdrawal of relief, and not a partial one, will affect the capital gains tax position, i.e. exemption for a gain, no allowance for a loss (Tolley's Practical Tax 1987, p 115). If relief is withdrawn completely, any allowable loss which results on a disposal of the shares may be eligible for relief under *ICTA 1988, s 574* — capital gains tax loss accruing to individual in respect of unquoted shares in a trading company converted to an income tax loss; see 39.13 LOSSES.

Further rules dealing with identification and other matters apply as follows.

(*a*) The normal share identification rules (and, for shares acquired before 6 April 1998, share pooling arrangements) (see 59 SHARES AND SECURITIES—IDENTIFICATION RULES) do not apply to BES shares. Each acquisition is treated as a separate acquisition and shares are matched on a first in/first out (FIFO) basis. Where a disposal after 5 April 1998 is so matched with shares acquired on the same day as one another, only some of which still have BES income tax relief attributable to them, it is first matched with shares in respect of which no such relief is still attributable. For these purposes and that in (*d*) below shares are only treated as being of the same class if they would be so treated if dealt with on the Stock Exchange and the grant after 18 March 1986 of an option the exercise of which would bind the grantor to sell shares is treated as a disposal of those shares.

(*b*) If there is a reorganisation within the meaning of *TCGA 1992, s 126* then the new ordinary shares will stand in the place of the old ordinary shares and each is treated as a new holding.

(*c*) If, as part of a reconstruction, shares or debentures in another company are issued to a BES shareholder in exchange for the BES shares, then, unless the income tax relief is withdrawn, the shares in the new company are not generally deemed to stand in the place of shares in the old company under *TCGA 1992, s 135* or *s 136* (see 58.8, 58.10 SHARES AND SECURITIES) and there is thus a disposal of the shares in the old company. However, *section 135* or *136* does apply in the normal way if

- the new holding consists of new ordinary shares issued after 28 November 1994 and more than five years after the issue of the original shares and carrying no present or future preferential rights to dividends or assets or right to redemption (no preferential right to redemption where the new shares were issued before 6 April 1998); and
- the company issuing the new shares has previously issued shares under the BES and has issued the appropriate certificate enabling investors to obtain relief on that earlier issue.

In addition, *TCGA 1992, s 135* is not disapplied in a case to which *ICTA 1988, s 304A* (inserted by *FA 1998, Sch 13 para 41*) applies. That provision enables a BES company to become, after 5 April 1998, a wholly-owned subsidiary of a new holding company in certain circumstances. The investors receive shares in the new company in exchange for their original shares, and the new shares then stand in the shoes of the old for the purposes of BES income tax relief. This treatment is generally applied for CGT purposes also.

(*d*) Where an original holding has been subject to the relief, a disposal of the whole or part of a new holding, allotted other than for payment as a result of a reorganisation within *TCGA 1992, s 126(2)(a)* after 18 March 1986 (allotments in respect of, and in proportion to, existing holdings or of any class of shares, e.g. a bonus issue within 58.5 SHARES AND SECURITIES above), will be treated, for the purposes of deciding whether relief given is to be withdrawn, as a disposal of the whole or a corresponding part of the original holding with which, by reason of *TCGA 1992, s 127*, the new holding is identified. Any reallocated shares under *section 127* will be deemed to stand in the place of the original shares.

(*e*) The general share reorganisation provisions of *TCGA 1992, ss 127–130* (see 58.5–58.7 SHARES AND SECURITIES above) do not apply after 18 March 1986 to ordinary shares in respect of which relief has been given if

(i) there is, by virtue of an allotment for payment within *TCGA 1992, s 126(2)(a)* (see also (*d*) above), a reorganisation affecting those shares; and

(ii) immediately following the reorganisation, the relief has not been withdrawn in respect of those shares or relief has been given in respect of the allotted shares and not withdrawn.

On such reorganisations occurring before 29 November 1994 where immediately before it the relief has not been withdrawn, and where both the amount of relief (or the amount remaining where it has been reduced) and the market value of the shares immediately before the reorganisation exceed their market value immediately after the reorganisation, the relief is reduced by an amount equal to whichever is the smaller of those excesses. This reduction also applies *mutatis mutandis* where the individual sells his rights instead of taking up his allotment. Where the relief is so reduced an amount equal to the reduction is treated as additional expenditure for capital gains tax purposes on a disposal of the allotted shares or debentures and such expenditure is apportioned between the allotted shares etc. in a just and reasonable manner. Where a disposal of the original holding of ordinary shares is not ultimately exempt (e.g. because all relief has been withdrawn), the allowable expenditure relating to such shares is reduced by an amount equal to the above reduction and is again apportioned in a just and reasonable manner.

In computing gains or losses arising on an individual's disposal of shares **issued before 19 March 1986** in respect of which BES relief has been given and not withdrawn, that relief is disregarded *except* to the extent that an unindexed loss would otherwise accrue in which case the deductible expenditure is reduced by the smaller of the BES relief given (and not withdrawn) and the amount of the loss. [*TCGA 1992, s 150(3)*]. It was held in *Quinn v Cooper Ch D 1998, 71 TC 44* that indexation allowance should be based on the reduced cost. *Section 150(3)* does not apply to disposals within *TCGA 1992, s 58(1)* (inter-spouse transfers) but will apply on a subsequent disposal to a third party by the transferee spouse. In determining whether any sums are excluded under *TCGA 1992, s 39(1)(2)* (exclusion of expenditure allowable against income; see 17.5 DISPOSAL), the existence of any relief given and not withdrawn is ignored.

The provisions in (*a*) (except in relation to a grant of an option etc.), and (*b*) above also apply to shares issued before 19 March 1986 as do those in (*d*) in respect of reorganisations before that date. The provisions in (*c*) do not apply to shares issued before 19 March 1986 and those in (*e*) do not apply to reorganisations before that date. (*Note.* A Revenue Press

Release of 19 December 1989 announced that an unintended change in the law had been made by *ICTA 1988* so as to apply the provisions in (*c*) above to shares issued before 19 March 1986 where a reconstruction or amalgamation involving an exchange or cancellation of shares occurs after 5 April 1988 with the result that the exchange or cancellation would give rise to a disposal. *FA 1990, Sch 14 paras 17, 19* restored the position for exchanges etc. occurring after 5 April 1988 save that in respect of an exchange before 1 January 1990 the shareholder could irrevocably elect to have the exchange treated as a disposal by giving written notice at any time before 6 April 1991.)

Where an allowable loss still arose after the above reduction in consideration, the loss may have been eligible for relief under *ICTA 1988, s 574* (capital gains tax loss accruing to individual in respect of unquoted shares in a trading company converted to an income tax loss; see 39.13 LOSSES).

General. Where relief has been granted or withdrawn, consequential adjustments may be made to the individual's capital gains tax position.

[*TCGA 1992, s 39(3), s 150; FA 1985, Sch 19 para 16(3); ICTA 1988, ss 289, 299, 305; FA 1991, s 99(2)(4); F(No 2)A 1992, s 38; FA 1994, s 137, Sch 15 para 29; FA 1995, ss 68, 69; FA 1998, s 74, Sch 13 paras 37, 39, 42*].

It should be noted that 'relief' refers to the deduction falling to be made from a person's income and not to any amount of income tax which is not chargeable due to such a deduction.

For consideration of the determination of the time shares are issued under the scheme, see *National Westminster Bank plc v CIR; Barclays Bank plc v CIR HL 1994, 67 TC 1.*

21 Exemptions and Reliefs

Cross-references. See 7 ASSETS HELD ON 6 APRIL 1965; 8 ASSETS HELD ON 31 MARCH 1982; 10 CHARITIES; 16 DEATH; 18 DOUBLE TAX RELIEF; 24 GOVERNMENT SECURITIES; 25 HOLD-OVER RELIEFS; 26 INDEXATION; 39 LOSSES; 44 OVERSEAS MATTERS; 48 PRIVATE RESIDENCES; 49 QUALIFYING CORPORATE BONDS; 50 REINVESTMENT RELIEF; 52 RESIDENCE AND DOMICILE; 53 RETIREMENT RELIEF; 55 ROLLOVER RELIEF; 58 SHARES AND SECURITIES; 64 UNIT TRUSTS ETC.; 65 VENTURE CAPITAL TRUSTS.

21.1 INTRODUCTION

A person is chargeable to capital gains tax on chargeable gains accruing to him on the disposal of assets in any year of assessment during any part of which he is resident in the UK, or during which he is ordinarily resident in the UK. [*TCGA 1992, s 1(1), s 2(1)*]. All forms of property except sterling are regarded as assets for these purposes [*TCGA 1992, s 21(1)*] and every gain, except as otherwise expressly provided, is a chargeable gain. [*TCGA 1992, s 28(2)*]. There are, however, a number of exemptions and reliefs. These may broadly be classified as follows.

(*a*) Exempt assets (see 21.2–21.15 below).

(*b*) Exempt gains and transactions (see 21.16–21.33 below).

(*c*) Exempt organisations and individuals (see 21.34–21.56 below).

In addition, a number of reliefs are available to reduce or defer the amount of capital gains tax payable. See 21.57–21.82 and certain provisions in 21.44 and 21.52 below.

21.2 EXEMPT ASSETS

Gains accruing on the disposal of certain assets are exempt from capital gains tax. The exemption (total or partial) of the various types of asset is examined in 21.3–21.15 below. Losses arising from such disposals are similarly not allowable unless expressly provided otherwise. [*TCGA 1992, s 16(2)*].

21.3 **Annuities and annual payments.** A gain accruing on the disposal of a right to or to any part of an allowance, annuity, or capital sum from a *superannuation fund* or any other annuity (not under a deferred annuity policy, but see 21.10 below), or annual payments receivable under a 'covenant' not secured on property, is exempt. [*TCGA 1992, s 237*].

'*Covenant*' means a gratuitous promise enforceable solely due to the form in which it is evidenced (i.e., in England, in a document under seal). It does not include contracts enforceable as such (*Rank Xerox Ltd v Lane HL 1979, 53 TC 185*).

21.4 **Chattels.** A tangible movable asset (other than a commodity disposed of by or through a dealer on a terminal market) is entirely exempt, provided that the asset is not 'currency of any description' and that the disposal is for a consideration of £6,000 or less. If the consideration exceeds £6,000, the chargeable gain is limited to five-thirds of the excess. [*TCGA 1992, s 262(1)(2)(6)*]. Sovereigns minted before 1837 are not legal tender and are thus within the exemption (Revenue Capital Gains Manual CG 78309).

Examples

(i) A chattel which cost £5,000 in 1996 is disposed of in May 2000 for £8,000. Assume an indexation allowance (to April 1998) of £400 and expenses of disposal of £300. The chargeable gain is ascertained as follows.

Excess of consideration over £6,000	£2,000
£2,000 × $\frac{5}{3}$	£3,333
Actual gain (after indexation) is £2,300 which is less than £3,333	
Chargeable gain (subject to TAPER RELIEF (60))	£2,300

(ii) A chattel which cost £2,000 in 1996 is disposed of in May 2000 for £8,000. Assume an indexation allowance of £160 and expenses of disposal of £180.

Excess of consideration over £6,000	£2,000
£2,000 × $\frac{5}{3}$	£3,333
Actual gain (after indexation) is £5,660 which is more than £3,333	
Chargeable gain (subject to TAPER RELIEF (60))	£3,333

Part disposal. Where the disposal is of a right or interest in or over a tangible movable asset, and the sum of the consideration received plus the value of what remains exceeds £6,000, a similar limitation of the chargeable gain applies but the excess for this purpose is computed as follows.

$$(\text{consideration received} + \text{value of remainder} - £6{,}000) \times \frac{\text{consideration received}}{\text{total value}}$$

[*TCGA 1992, s 262(5)*].

Losses. For the purposes of loss relief, a disposal of a tangible movable asset for a consideration of less than £6,000 is deemed to be made for a consideration of £6,000. In the case of a partial disposal of an asset the total value of which is less than £6,000, the deemed consideration for loss relief purposes is computed as follows.

$$(£6{,}000 - \text{total value}) \times \left(\frac{\text{consideration received}}{\text{total value}}\right) + \text{consideration received}$$

Simplified, this becomes (£6,000 × consideration/total value).

[*TCGA 1992, s 262(3)*].

Assets forming a set. Where these are owned by the same disposer they are to be treated as a single asset where they are disposed of, whether on the same or on different occasions, to the same person or to persons acting in concert, or to CONNECTED PERSONS (14). [*TCGA 1992, s 262(4)*]. For the Revenue's views on the circumstances in which a number of bottles of wine may constitute a set, see Revenue Tax Bulletin August 1999 p 686. For an article on pairs of shotguns, see Revenue Tax Bulletin February 2000 pp 726, 727.

Wasting assets. Tangible movable assets which are WASTING ASSETS (66) are exempt whatever the consideration received, but this exemption is restricted or eliminated to the extent that the asset, by reason of its having been used in trade or otherwise, has been or could have been the subject of a capital allowance. This exemption is not applicable to a disposal of commodities on a terminal market. [*TCGA 1992, s 45*]. Where capital allowances were initially granted in respect of qualifying expenditure on movable machinery but were later withdrawn because the machinery was sold without it having been brought into use by the taxpayer, it was held that the taxpayer should be treated as if the allowance had never been made, with the result that the disposal on sale was exempt (*Burman v Westminster Press Ltd Ch D 1987, 60 TC 418*). If a restriction by reference to capital allowances would otherwise arise, relief as under *TCGA 1992, s 262* above may be available.

The Revenue accept that any of the following is machinery and is thus a tangible movable wasting asset (see 66.1 WASTING ASSETS) which will be exempt where owned privately and not used in a business: antique clocks and watches; motor vehicles which are not normal private passenger vehicles and are thus outside the exemption at 21.11 below, e.g. taxi cabs, vans, motor cycles etc.; trawlers, fishing vessels, tankers and other vessels propelled by engines (and see below re boats generally). (Revenue Tax Bulletin October 1994 pp 166, 167). They 'generally accept' that all types of gun are within the general description of machinery (Revenue Tax Bulletin February 2000 p 727).

Boats 'will generally be tangible movable wasting assets' and thus exempt (except where qualifying for capital allowances). (Revenue Capital Gains Manual CG 64328 and see also above). This will not always apply to yachts, barges or boats used as a residence, as these may have a longer useful life. A houseboat which is permanently located on a site and connected to all mains services may in some circumstances be regarded as a dwelling house. (Revenue Capital Gains Manual CG 64329, 64330).

For the Revenue's views on the circumstances in which *bottled wine* may qualify as a wasting asset and thus an exempt chattel, see Revenue Tax Bulletin August 1999 p 686.

21.5 **Debts.** A debt, other than a 'debt on a security' (see below), disposed of by the original creditor or his personal representative or legatee is exempt. Where the original creditor is a trustee and the debt, when created, is settled property, a person becoming absolutely entitled to the debt is treated as a personal representative or legatee as is his own personal representative or legatee. [*TCGA 1992, s 251(1)(5)*].

The foregoing does not apply to the disposal of a bank balance in foreign currency, except to the extent that it represents currency acquired by an individual for purposes similar to those in *TCGA 1992, s 269* or, in the case of a company, the disposal is exempted under *FA 1993, Sch 17 paras 1–3* (see, in both cases, 21.8 below). [*TCGA 1992, s 252*]. A taxpayer may treat all bank accounts in his name containing a particular foreign currency as one account and so disregard direct transfers among such accounts which would otherwise constitute disposals and acquisitions under this last provision. The practice, once adopted, must be applied to all future direct transfers among bank accounts in the taxpayer's name designated in that currency until such time as all debt represented in the accounts has been repaid to the taxpayer. The practice may be applied to all cases where computations have not been settled as at 19 December 1984. Accounts held as in 6.2(*l*) ASSETS (non-domiciled individuals) do not qualify for this treatment (Revenue Pamphlet IR 131, SP 10/84).

The redenomination into euros of a debt, other than a debt on a security, from the currency of a State participating in the European single currency on or after 1 January 1999 is not treated as involving the disposal of that debt or the acquisition of a new debt. The original debt and the new debt are treated as the same asset, acquired as the original debt was acquired. [*SI 1998 No 3177, Reg 37*]. Accordingly the disposal of the new debt by the original creditor retains its exemption.

No chargeable gain or allowable loss accrues on the disposal before 1 April 1996 by a 'qualifying company', on or after its 'commencement day', of a debt the right to settlement under which is a 'qualifying asset' (see 13.44 COMPANIES for a note of these terms), and the settlement currency of which is a currency other than sterling, provided that immediately before the disposal the company did not hold the debt in 'exempt circumstances', and that the debt is not a debt on a security (security for this purpose including a debenture deemed to be a security under *TCGA 1992, s 251(6)* below). (For later disposals, these provisions are superseded by the rules referred to at 38.1 LOAN RELATIONSHIPS OF COMPANIES.) '*Exempt circumstances*' are when the debt is held

(*a*) for the purposes of long term insurance business;

(*b*) for the purposes of mutual insurance business;

(*c*) for the purposes of the occupation for profit of commercial woodlands in the UK;

(*d*) by an approved housing association; or

(*e*) by an approved self-build society.

No chargeable gain or allowable loss accrues on the disposal of a foreign currency debenture issued on a reorganisation or other transaction which meets the above conditions. [*FA 1993, s 169, Sch 17 para 4; FA 1995, Sch 24 para 5; FA 1996, Sch 41 Pt V(3)*]. See also 21.8 below.

Loss relief is available to the maker of a 'qualifying loan' or a guarantor of a qualifying loan. See 39.10 LOSSES. See 39.11 LOSSES for a corresponding relief where the borrower's debt is a debt on a security which is a qualifying corporate bond.

A right possibly to receive an unidentifiable sum at an unascertainable date is not a 'debt' (*Marren v Ingles HL 1980, 54 TC 76; Marson v Marriage Ch D 1979, 54 TC 59*).

Subject to the foregoing, the satisfaction of a debt (including a debt on a security) or part of it is treated as a disposal of the debt by the creditor made at the time when the debt is satisfied. Where a debt on a security is involved this rule is subject to the provisions in *TCGA 1992, ss 132, 135* covering the reorganisation of share capital (see 58.8 and 58.11 SHARES AND SECURITIES). [*TCGA 1992, s 251(2)*].

Where property is acquired by a creditor in satisfaction of a debt then, subject to any reorganisation of share capital as above, the property is not treated as disposed of by the debtor or acquired by the creditor for a consideration greater than its market value at the time of the creditor's acquisition of it. But if no chargeable gain accrues as regards the debt either because the creditor is the original creditor or under the share capital reorganisation rules *and* a chargeable gain accrues to the creditor on a disposal by him of the property, then any resulting chargeable gain is reduced so as not to exceed the chargeable gain that would have accrued if he had acquired the property for a consideration equal to the amount of the debt. [*TCGA 1992, s 251(3)*].

Where the original creditor and a subsequent creditor are CONNECTED PERSONS (14), a loss incurred by the subsequent creditor on the disposal of a debt is not an allowable loss. See 39.5 LOSSES.

A '*debt on a security*' is defined by reference to *TCGA 1992, s 132(3)(b)*, '*security*' thereby including any loan stock or similar security of any government or public or local authority in the UK or elsewhere, or of any company, and whether secured or unsecured. The existence of a document may be indicative of a 'debt on a security', but it cannot be concluded from the absence of a document that the debt is not 'on a security' (*Aberdeen Construction Group Ltd v CIR HL 1978, 52 TC 281; W T Ramsay Ltd v CIR HL 1981, 54 TC 101; Cleveleys Investment Trust Co v CIR (No 1) CS 1971, 47 TC 300*). An intra-group loan secured on a promissory note was held not to be a marketable security in any realistic sense and was not a 'debt on a security' (*Taylor Clark International Ltd v Lewis CA 1998, 71 TC 226*). For further discussion of the meaning of debt on security see *Tarmac Roadstone Holdings Ltd v Williams (Sp C 95), [1996] SSCD 409*.

In the opinion of the Revenue the following characteristics must be satisfied before a debt can qualify as a debt on security.

(A) The debtor should be a government, a public or a local authority, or a company.

(B) The debt should be capable of being marketed, sold or assigned.

(C) Interest should be payable to the lender (or at least the terms of the debt must be such that it is capable of being held as an investment, e.g. it would be so capable if it were issued at a discount or repayable at a premium).

(D) There should be stated terms for the repayment of the debt.

(E) The debt should be for a specified amount and for a definite term (normally for a period of years rather than months or days).

(F) The debt should be capable of being issued or subscribed for (even if the procedure involved is simple, and if only one lender is involved).

(Tolley's Practical Tax 1983 p 119).

In relation to any chargeable period ending after 15 March 1993, a debenture issued by any company after 15 March 1993 is deemed to be a security within *TCGA 1992, s 132(3)(b)* above if

(1) it is issued on a reorganisation or reduction of a company's share capital or in pursuance of its allotment on any such reorganisation or reduction;

(2) it is issued in exchange for shares in or debentures of another company and in a case unaffected by *TCGA 1992, s 137* (restriction on application of share reorganisation rules in *TCGA 1992, ss 135, 136*; see 3.16 ANTI-AVOIDANCE and 58.8 and 58.10 SHARES AND SECURITIES) where one or more of the conditions mentioned in *s 135(1)(a)–(c)* (25% of ordinary share capital, view to control or greater part of the voting power) is satisfied in relation to the exchange;

(3) it is issued under any such arrangements as are mentioned in *TCGA 1992, s 136(1)(a)* (arrangement between company and share or debenture holders in connection with a scheme of reconstruction or amalgamation) and in a case unaffected by *TCGA 1992, s 137* where *s 136* requires shares or debentures in another company to be treated as exchanged for, or for anything that includes, that debenture; or

(4) it is issued in pursuance of rights attached to any debenture issued after 15 March 1993 and falling within (1), (2) or (3) above.

In relation to any disposal after 25 November 1996, any debenture resulting from a conversion of securities (within *TCGA 1992, s 132*—see 58.11 SHARES AND SECURITIES —and whether occurring before or after that date), or which is issued in pursuance of rights attaching to such a debenture, is similarly deemed to be a security.

[*TCGA 1992, s 251(6); FA 1993, s 84(2)(3); FA 1997, s 88(5)(6)*].

For the purposes of *section 251*, the following instruments are deemed to be 'securities' where this would not otherwise be the case, but this fiction does not apply for the purposes of determining what is or is not an allowable loss in any case.

(i) Any instrument falling to be treated as an asset representing a company loan relationship if it were not for the exclusions at 38.8 LOAN RELATIONSHIPS OF COMPANIES.

(ii) Any instrument which, even apart from the exclusions mentioned in (i) above, is not a loan relationship of a company but which would be a relevant discounted security if it were not an 'excluded indexed security' (see 58.20 SHARES AND SECURITIES).

[*TCGA 1992, s 251(7)(8); FA 1996, s 104, s 105(1), Sch 14 para 64*].

The definition of a relevant discounted security was widened to take further account of potential redemptions before maturity (see 58.20 SHARES AND SECURITIES). For the immediately-above purposes, the widened definition has effect in relation to any disposal or part disposal of an asset after 14 February 1999. [*FA 1999, s 65(11)*].

See also 49.2 QUALIFYING CORPORATE BONDS for a provision corresponding to *TCGA 1992, s 251(6)* and regarding the definition of 'corporate bond', so that combined the two provisions prevent, in the circumstances stated, the issue of a debenture which neither represents a debt on a security nor is a qualifying corporate bond.

21.6 **Decorations.** A decoration for valour or gallantry (unless acquired by the vendor for money or money's worth) is exempt. [*TCGA 1992, s 268*].

21.7 **Dwelling-houses.** A gain accruing to an individual on the disposal of (or of an interest in) a dwelling-house which has been his only or main residence during his period of ownership is exempt (or partly exempt). See 48 PRIVATE RESIDENCES for this exemption which is also extended, in certain circumstances, to trustees and personal representatives.

21.8 **Foreign currency** acquired for an individual's (or his dependant's) personal expenditure outside the UK (including the provision or maintenance of his residence outside the UK) is exempt. [*TCGA 1992, s 269*].

No chargeable gain or allowable loss accrues on the disposal by a 'qualifying company' (see 13.44 COMPANIES), on or after its 'commencement day' (the first day of its first accounting period beginning after 22 March 1995), of currency other than sterling, provided that immediately before the disposal the company did not hold the currency in 'exempt circumstances'. '*Exempt circumstances*' are when the currency is held

(*a*) for the purposes of long term insurance business;

(*b*) for the purposes of mutual insurance business;

(*c*) for the purposes of the occupation for profit of commercial woodlands in the UK;

(*d*) by an approved housing association; or

(*e*) by an approved self-build society.

[*FA 1993, s 169, Sch 17 paras 1–3*].

See also 21.5 above.

21.9 **Government securities.** Disposals of specified government and public corporation securities are exempt from capital gains tax whatever the period of ownership. This also applies to options or contracts to acquire or dispose of such securities. See 24 GOVERNMENT SECURITIES, 38 LOAN RELATIONSHIPS OF COMPANIES, and also 17.10, 17.11 DISPOSAL as regards options and contracts.

21.10 **Insurance policies.** The disposal of rights under any insurance policy (other than a life policy) *by the insurer* is exempt, but the disposal of rights *of the insured* under any policy for damage to, or loss or depreciation of, assets is chargeable so far as the rights relate to assets which on a disposal could give rise to a chargeable gain. (Sums received under such policies for loss, damage, etc. to assets are chargeable; see 17.7–17.9 DISPOSAL.) [*TCGA 1992, s 204(1)(2)(4)*].

See also 37 LIFE ASSURANCE POLICIES AND DEFERRED ANNUITIES.

21.11 **Motor cars etc.** A mechanically propelled road vehicle constructed or adapted for the carriage of passengers, except for a vehicle of a type not commonly used as a private vehicle and unsuitable to be so used, is not a chargeable asset, and thus no chargeable gain or allowable loss accrues on its disposal. [*TCGA 1992, s 263*]. This exemption applies regardless of whether or not the vehicle was eligible for capital allowances (cf. 21.4 above). For the interpretation of 'commonly used as a private vehicle' in relation to capital allowances, see cases mentioned in Tolley's Capital Allowances. Vehicles outside this exemption include taxi cabs, racing cars, single seat sports cars, vans, lorries, other commercial vehicles, motor cycles, scooters and motor cycle/sidecar combinations (Revenue Capital Gains Manual CG 76907).

Motor vehicles which are outside the above exemption, and which are privately owned and not used in a business, are exempt as tangible movable wasting assets (see 21.4 above and Revenue Tax Bulletin October 1994 p 166).

Personalised car number plates are not covered by either exemption. The value of the number plate itself is usually negligible, and the plate is regarded as part of the car when sold attached thereto. However, the disposal of the inherent intangible right to use a specific combination of letters or numbers when registering a vehicle is neither a disposal of a motor car as above nor of a chattel as in 21.4 above, and any gain arising will be a chargeable gain. (Revenue Capital Gains Manual CG 76920–76928).

21.12 **Qualifying corporate bonds.** Qualifying corporate bonds are exempt whatever the period of ownership. This also applies to options or contracts to acquire or dispose of such bonds. See 49 QUALIFYING CORPORATE BONDS, and see 17.10 and 17.11 DISPOSAL as regards options and contracts. For loans to traders evidenced by qualifying corporate bonds, see 39.11 LOSSES.

21.13 **Savings certificates, savings schemes and savings accounts etc.** Savings certificates, and non-marketable securities issued under the *National Loans Acts 1939* and *1968* and corresponding NI enactments are not 'chargeable assets' and accordingly no chargeable gain accrues on their disposal. Bonuses resulting from certified contractual savings schemes and tax-exempt special savings accounts are ignored for capital gains tax purposes. [*TCGA 1992, s 121, s 271(4)*]. No provision of *TCGA 1992* defines 'chargeable asset' but the subsequent words of the provision seem to put the position beyond doubt.

21.14 **Settlements.** With certain exceptions, no chargeable gain accrues on the disposal of an interest created by or arising under a settlement by the original beneficiary or any other person (other than one who acquired, or derives his title from one who acquired, his interest for money or money's worth). See 57.8 SETTLEMENTS.

21.15 **Ships and other assets within the tonnage tax regime.** Under this ring-fenced regime introduced for accounting periods beginning on or after 1 January 2000, a shipping company or group may elect to have its taxable profits computed by reference to the net tonnage of each of the qualifying ships it operates. The initial period for making an election is the 12 months beginning with 28 July 2000 (the date of Royal Assent to *FA 2000*). An election is normally expected to remain in force for at least 10 years. Qualifying ships must be seagoing, of at least 100 tons gross tonnage and be engaged in qualifying activities, e.g. the transportation of goods or passengers by sea. Certain vessels are excluded, e.g. fishing and factory support vessels, harbour and river ferries, oil rigs, pleasure craft, floating restaurants etc. The strategic and commercial management of ships within the regime must be undertaken from the UK. *Capital gains* accruing during the currency of the election are not chargeable gains (and losses are not allowable losses) to the extent that the assets disposed of were used exclusively for the qualifying shipping activity. In the event of a company leaving the regime for certain specified reasons, anti-avoidance provisions apply to bring into charge a previously exempt gain arising in the last six years. [*FA 2000, s 82, Sch 22*].

21.16 EXEMPT GAINS AND TRANSACTIONS

The gains or transactions detailed in 21.17–21.33 below do not give rise to a liability to capital gains tax.

21.17 **Agricultural grants.** Grants made to an individual under *Agriculture Act 1967, s 27* (grants for relinquishing occupation of uncommercial agricultural units) are not treated as part of the consideration obtained, or otherwise accruing, on the disposal of any asset. [*TCGA 1992, s 249*]. See also 17.7(*c*) DISPOSAL.

21.18 **Betting, lottery etc.** Winnings from betting, including pool betting, or lotteries or games with prizes are not chargeable gains, and no chargeable gain or allowable loss accrues on the disposal of rights to such winnings obtained by participating. [*TCGA 1992, s 51(1)*]. Included is the betting on future price movements of precious and base metals, soft commodities and currencies etc. (see Tolley's Practical Tax 1982 p 59).

Where prize winnings take the form of an asset, the recipient is regarded as having acquired the asset at its market value at the time of acquisition (Revenue Capital Gains Manual CG 12604).

21.19 **Business expansion scheme.** In respect of shares issued after 18 March 1986 and before 1 January 1994, any gain or loss arising on a disposal of shares in respect of which such relief has been given and not totally withdrawn is exempt. In respect of such shares issued before 19 March 1986 there was no such exemption but a reduction was made in the amount of allowable expenditure where that amount exceeded the disposal consideration. See 20.17 ENTERPRISE INVESTMENT SCHEME (AND BES).

21.20 **Cashbacks.** A cashback is a lump sum received by a customer as an inducement for entering into a transaction for the purchase of goods, investments or services and received as a direct consequence of having entered into that transaction. An example of such a transaction is the taking out of a mortgage. The payer may be either the provider of the goods etc. or an interested third party. The term 'cashback' does not include a cash payment by a building society to its members on a takeover or conversion (for which see 58.26 SHARES AND SECURITIES), or by other mutual organisations such as insurance companies or friendly societies to their policy holders on demutualisation.

A cashback does not derive from a chargeable asset for CGT purposes. No chargeable gain therefore arises on its receipt. (An ordinary retail customer purchasing goods etc. at arm's length will not be liable to income tax on a cashback either.)

(Revenue Pamphlet IR 131, SP 4/97).

21.21 **Damages and compensation.** Sums received by way of compensation or damages for any wrong or injury suffered by an individual 'in his person' or in his profession or vocation are not chargeable gains. [*TCGA 1992, s 51(2)*]. The words 'in his person' contrast with 'in his finances', but are construed widely. The exemption given in relation to vocation is extended by concession to an individual's trade or employment. See Revenue Pamphlet IR 1, D33. If the compensation relates to an asset (e.g. insurance recoveries), payment does constitute a disposal; see 17.7–17.9 DISPOSAL.

21.22 **Enterprise investment scheme (EIS).** In respect of shares issued after 31 December 1993, any gain arising on a disposal more than, broadly, three years after the issue of them (five years for shares issued before 6 April 2000), where an amount of EIS income tax relief is attributable to them, is wholly or partly exempt. If a loss would otherwise arise on a disposal of shares where an amount of such relief is attributable to them, a reduction is made in the amount of allowable expenditure equal to the amount of relief. See 20 ENTERPRISE INVESTMENT SCHEME (AND BES).

Venture capital trusts. In respect of shares issued after 5 April 1995, any gain arising on a disposal of them where an amount of such relief is attributable to them is wholly or partly exempt. A loss arising on a disposal of shares is not an allowable loss, except to the extent that a gain on the disposal would have been a chargeable gain. See 65.9 VENTURE CAPITAL TRUSTS.

21.23 **Compensation from foreign governments.** Gains on sums received by individuals from foreign governments by way of compensation for assets confiscated, destroyed or expropriated are exempt provided certain conditions are met. See 17.7 DISPOSAL.

21.24 **Exempt amount for the year.** A specified amount of the taxable amount of gains for a year of assessment is exempt. See 2.5 ANNUAL RATES AND EXEMPTIONS.

21.25 **Gains arising partly before 6.4.1965 or 31.3.1982.** Assets held on, and gains arising partly before, these dates are subject to special provisions. See 7 ASSETS HELD ON 6 APRIL 1965 and 8 ASSETS HELD ON 31 MARCH 1982.

21.26 **Gifts for public benefit.** Gifts **before 17 March 1998** of 'eligible property' to bodies not established or conducted for profit will, if the Board so direct (whether before or after the transfer), be exempt from capital gains tax.

'*Eligible property*' is

(*a*) land which in the opinion of the Board is of outstanding scenic, historic or scientific interest;

(*b*) a building for the preservation of which special steps should in the opinion of the Board be taken by reason of its outstanding historic, architectural or aesthetic interest and the cost of preserving it;

(*c*) land used as the grounds of a building within (*b*) above;

(*d*) an object which at the time of the transfer is ordinarily kept in, and is given with, a building within (*b*) above;

(*e*) property given as a source of income for the upkeep of property within these sub-paragraphs;

(*f*) a picture, print, book, manuscript, work of art or scientific collection which in the opinion of the Board is of national, scientific, historic or artistic interest. ('*National interest*' includes interest within any part of the UK.)

The Board must not give a direction (i) unless in their opinion, the body who receives the property is an appropriate one to be responsible for its preservation; or (ii) in relation to property within (*e*) above, if or to the extent that the property will, in their opinion, produce more income than is needed (with a reasonable margin) for the upkeep of the other property in question.

Before giving a direction, the Board may require undertakings (which may be varied by agreement) concerning the use, disposal, and preservation of the property and reasonable access to it for the public.

The above exemption is abolished for disposals after 16 March 1998.

[*TCGA 1992, s 258(1); IHTA 1984, s 26; FA 1998, s 143(1), Sch 27 Pt IV*].

See also 25.7 HOLD-OVER RELIEFS for relief for gifts for public benefit.

21.27 **Individual Savings Accounts (ISAs).** ISAs are available **after 5 April 1999** to individuals over 18 who are both resident and ordinarily resident in the UK and will continue to be available for a minimum of ten years. The accounts can be made up of cash, life assurance and stocks and shares and are intended as a replacement for PEPs and TESSAs, although see 21.29 below as regards PEPS already in existence at the end of 1998/99 and note that neither the value of PEP holdings nor any capital transferred to an ISA from a TESSA (tax-exempt special savings account) will affect the amount which can be subscribed to an ISA. Investors can subscribe up to £5,000 to an ISA in each tax year, of which a maximum of £1,000 can go into cash and £1,000 into life assurance. See further details below. **For 1999/2000 and 2000/01 only**, the overall subscription limit is £7,000 and the cash limit is £3,000. There is no statutory lock-in, minimum subscription, minimum holding period or lifetime subscription limit. Withdrawals may be made at any time without loss of tax relief but not so as to allow further subscriptions in breach of the annual maximum.

Interest and dividends are free of income tax (and a 10% tax credit is payable on dividends received from UK equities before 6 April 2004). Gains arising from assets held within an ISA are not chargeable gains for CGT purposes (and losses are not allowable).

[*TCGA 1992, s 151; ICTA 1988, ss 333, 333A; FA 1998, ss 75, 76, Sch 27 Pt III(15)*].

The Individual Savings Account Regulations 1998 (*SI 1998 No 1870* as amended) provide for the setting up by Revenue-approved accounts managers of plans in the form of an account (an ISA) under which individuals may make certain investments, for the conditions under which they may invest and under which the accounts are to operate, for relief from tax in respect of account investments, and for general administration. The regulations generally took effect on 6 April 1999, although earlier applications could be made to subscribe to an account for 1999/2000 or to obtain approval as an account manager, and are summarised below.

General. An application to subscribe to an ISA may be made by an individual who is 18 or over and who is resident and ordinarily resident in the UK (or is a non-UK resident Crown employee performing duties treated under *ICTA 1988, s 132(4)(a)* (see TOLLEY'S INCOME TAX) as performed in the UK). Joint accounts are not permitted. An investor who subsequently fails to meet the residence requirement may retain the account and the right to tax exemptions thereunder but can make no further subscriptions to the account until he again comes to meet that requirement. In Scotland, a *curator bonis* appointed in respect of an individual qualifying as above but incapable of managing his affairs may subscribe to an ISA in his capacity as such without affecting his right to subscribe in any other capacity.

An ISA is made up of *one or more* of the following: a stocks and shares component, a cash component and an insurance component (see below re qualifying investments for each of these components). It must be designated from the outset as a maxi-account, mini-account or TESSA only account, such designation continuing to have effect for any year in which the investor makes a subscription to the account.

A *maxi-account* must comprise a stocks and shares component (*with or without* other components). The maximum subscription per tax year is £5,000 (£7,000 for 1999/2000 and 2000/01 only) of which a maximum of £1,000 (£3,000 for 1999/2000 and 2000/01) may be allocated to a cash component and £1,000 to an insurance component. In any tax year in which an investor subscribes to a maxi-account he cannot subscribe to any other ISA apart from a TESSA only account.

A *mini-account* must consist of a single specified component. The maximum subscription (per tax year) is £3,000 if that component is stocks and shares, £1,000 if it is insurance and £1,000 (£3,000 for 1999/2000 and 2000/01 only) if it is cash. In any tax year in which an investor subscribes to a mini-account, he cannot subscribe to another mini-account consisting of the same component or to a maxi-account.

A *TESSA only account* is an account consisting of a cash component only and limited to capital (*not* accumulated interest) transferred from a TESSA (see TOLLEY'S INCOME TAX) within six months following its maturity after 5 April 1999 (or after 5 January 1999 where no follow-up TESSA is opened). Such transfers are not subject to any annual subscription limit, and may also be made to a maxi-account or to a cash component mini-account without counting towards the annual subscription limits for such accounts. Continuing subscriptions after 5 April 1999 to a TESSA or follow-up TESSA do not affect an individual's ISA annual subscription limits.

Subscriptions to an ISA must be made in cash (and must be allocated irrevocably to the agreed component or single component) except that shares acquired by the investor under a savings-related (SAYE) share option scheme (see 19.19 EMPLOYEE SHARE SCHEMES) or appropriated to him under an approved profit sharing scheme (see 19.22 EMPLOYEE SHARE SCHEMES) may be transferred to a stocks and shares component. Such transfers count towards the annual subscription limits, by reference to the market value of the shares at the date of transfer. No chargeable gain or allowable loss arises on the transfer. A transfer of SAYE scheme shares must be made within 90 days after the exercise of the option. A transfer of shares appropriated under a profit sharing scheme must be made within 90 days after the earlier of the release date (see TOLLEY'S INCOME TAX) and the date on which the investor instructed the scheme trustees to transfer ownership of the shares to him.

ISA investments cannot be purchased otherwise than out of cash held by the account manager and allocated to the particular component concerned, and cannot be purchased from the investor or his spouse.

The title to ISA investments (other than cash deposits, national savings products and certain insurance policies) is vested in the account manager (or his nominee) either alone or jointly with the investor, though all ISA investments are in the beneficial ownership of the investor. The investor may elect to receive annual reports and accounts etc. in respect of ISA investments and/or to attend and vote at shareholders' etc. meetings.

The statements and declarations to be made when applying to subscribe to an ISA are specified. The maximum penalty for an incorrect statement or declaration is the amount (if any) of income tax and/or capital gains tax underpaid as a result. Assessments to withdraw tax relief or otherwise recover tax underpaid may be made (under Schedule D, Case VI in the case of income tax) on the account manager or investor. The Revenue have power to require information from, and to inspect records of, account managers and investors.

Tax exemptions. Except as stated below, no income tax or capital gains tax is chargeable on the account manager or the investor in respect of interest, dividends, distributions or gains on ISA investments. Capital losses are not allowable. As stated in the introduction above, tax credits on UK dividends paid before 6 April 2004 are repayable (via the account manager). An investor who ceases to be UK-resident is treated as continuing to be so resident as regards his entitlement to repayment of tax credits.

Interest on a cash deposit held within a stocks and shares component or insurance component is, however, taxable at the lower rate of income tax, such tax to be accounted for by the account manager (by set-off against tax repayments or otherwise). There is no further liability; the interest does not form part of the investor's total income and the tax paid cannot be repaid to the investor.

Life assurance gains on policies held within an insurance component are not subject to income tax (and a deficiency on termination is not deductible from the investor's total income). If it comes to the account manager's notice that such a policy is invalid, i.e. its terms and conditions do not provide (or no longer provide) that it be held only as a qualifying insurance component investment, a chargeable event then occurs, with any gain taxable under Schedule D, Case VI. If the policy has already terminated, the chargeable event is deemed to have occurred at the end of the final policy year (see TOLLEY'S INCOME TAX). Any previous chargeable event which actually occurred in relation to the policy is similarly taxed, by reference to the time it occurred. Basic rate income tax is payable by the account manager (with the Revenue also having power to assess the investor). Any higher rate tax due is payable by the investor by assessment within five years after 31 January following the year of assessment in which the chargeable event occurred or was deemed to occur. Top-slicing relief (see TOLLEY'S INCOME TAX) is available in the same way as for non-ISA-related chargeable events.

Exempt income and gains do not have to be reported in the investor's personal tax return.

Further capital gains matters. A transfer of ISA investments by an account manager to an investor is deemed to be made at market value, with no capital gain or allowable loss arising. An investor is treated as holding shares or securities in an ISA in a capacity other than that in which he holds any other shares etc. of the same class in the same company, so that share identification rules (see 59.1 SHARES AND SECURITIES—IDENTIFICATION RULES) are applied separately to ISA investments (and separately as between different ISAs held by the same investor). The normal share reorganisation rules are disapplied in respect of ISA investments in the event of a reorganisation of share capital involving an allotment for payment, e.g. a rights issue. Shares transferred to an ISA in the limited circumstances described above are deemed for these purposes to have been ISA investments from, in the case of SAYE option scheme shares, their acquisition by the investor and, in the case of profit sharing scheme shares, the earlier of the release date and the date on which the investor instructed the scheme trustees to transfer ownership of the shares to him. Where the investor held shares eligible for transfer to an ISA and other shares of the same class but not so eligible, disposals are generally identified primarily with the latter, thus preserving to the greatest possible extent the eligibility of the remaining shares.

Qualifying investments

Stocks and shares component. Qualifying investments for a stocks and shares component are as follows.

(*a*) Shares issued by a company (other than an investment trust, but see (*e*) below) wherever incorporated, and officially listed on a recognised stock exchange. There are rules to allow the official listing condition to be treated as satisfied in the case of shares issued under a public offer and due to be listed.

(*b*) Securities (i.e. secured or unsecured loan stock and similar) issued by a company wherever incorporated, and with a minimum residual term of five years from the date when first held under the ISA. Either the securities must be officially listed on a recognised stock exchange or the shares in the issuing company or its 75% holding company must be so listed. In the case of securities of an investment trust, the trust must satisfy the two qualifying conditions at (*e*) below.

(*c*) Gilt-edged securities and gilt strips with at least five years to run to maturity from the date when first held under the ISA.

(*d*) Securities issued by or on behalf of a government of a European Economic Area State (comprising the EU plus Norway, Iceland and Liechtenstein and excluding for this purpose the UK), and strips of such securities, with at least five years to run to maturity from the date when first held under the ISA.

(*e*) Shares in a qualifying investment trust listed in the Official List of the Stock Exchange. Broadly, in order to qualify, an investment trust must have no 'eligible rental income' (within *ICTA 1988, s 508A* — see TOLLEY'S CORPORATION TAX) *and* not more than 50% in value of its investments can be securities otherwise within any of (*b*)–(*d*) above but having less than five years to run to maturity from the date when first acquired by the trust.

(*f*) Units in

- a securities fund (broadly an authorised unit trust or part of an umbrella scheme — see 64.1 UNIT TRUSTS ETC.); or
- a warrant fund (broadly a type of authorised unit trust investing in warrants or part of an umbrella scheme of that category);

or shares in

- a securities company (broadly an open-ended investment company (OEIC) or part of an umbrella company — see 64.4 UNIT TRUSTS ETC.); or
- a warrant company (broadly a type of OEIC investing in warrants or part of an umbrella company of that category);

or units in, or shares of,

- a relevant UCITS (an Undertaking for Collective Investment in Transferable Securities situated in and authorised by an EU Member State other than the UK, or part of such an undertaking equivalent to part of an umbrella scheme or umbrella company);

where the fund, company or UCITS satisfies the equivalent of the 50% condition in (*e*) above.

(*g*) Units in a fund of funds (as defined), subject to the condition that not more than 50% in value of its investments can be investments which would otherwise be within (*f*) above but do not themselves satisfy the 50% condition therein mentioned.

(*h*) Shares acquired by the investor under a SAYE share option scheme (see 19.19 EMPLOYEE SHARE SCHEMES) or appropriated to him under an approved profit sharing scheme (see 19.22 EMPLOYEE SHARE SCHEMES) which are transferred into the ISA as mentioned under 'General' above.

(*j*) Cash held on deposit pending investment in any of the above.

The term '*company*' does not for the above purposes include an OEIC, a UCITS or an industrial and provident society (or 51% subsidiary thereof).

Cash component. Qualifying investments for a cash component are as follows.

(i) Cash deposited in a deposit account with a building society, an institution authorised under *Banking Act 1987* or certain European institutions entitled to accept deposits in the UK.

(ii) Cash deposited in a building society share account.

(iii) Units in a money market fund (as defined).

(iv) Units in a fund of funds (as defined) which permits investment only in units in money market funds.

(v) Designated national savings products.

A deposit or share account within (i) or (ii) above is not a qualifying investment if is 'connected' with any other account held within those categories (whether or not by the investor). For this purpose, accounts are '*connected*' if either was opened with reference to the other or with a view to enabling the other to be opened, or facilitating the opening of the other, on particular terms *and* the terms on which the cash component account was opened would have been significantly less favourable to the investor if the other had not been opened. The Revenue will accept that an account is not a connected account if it is a 'feeder' account opened to enable investors to fund future deposits into an ISA, provided that the interest on the feeder account is in line with the interest paid on the account manager's other savings accounts (Revenue Guidance Notes for ISA Managers).

Insurance component. Qualifying investments for an insurance component are policies of life insurance satisfying specified conditions and cash held on deposit pending investment in such policies. The insurance must be on the life of the ISA investor only and its terms and conditions must provide

(A) that the policy may only be owned or held as a qualifying investment for an ISA insurance component;

(B) that, if found to be in breach of (A) above, it shall automatically terminate (and see also above under 'Tax exemptions');

(C) for an express prohibition of any transfer to the investor of the policy or the rights conferred thereby or any share or interest therein (other than cash proceeds on termination or partial surrender); and

(D) that the policy etc. cannot be assigned other than by transfer of title between approved ISA managers or by its vesting in the investor's personal representatives.

The policy must constitute long-term insurance business (as defined) and must not be a contract to pay a life annuity, a personal portfolio bond (see TOLLEY'S INCOME TAX) or a contract constituting pension business (as defined). There must be no contractual obligation to pay any premium other than the first (so regular premium policies are excluded). 'Connected' policies are excluded in much the same way as connected accounts are excluded from a cash component (see above). The making of loans by, or by arrangement with, the insurer to, or at the direction of, the ISA investor is prohibited.

Account managers. The regulations cover qualification as an account manager, Revenue approval and withdrawal thereof, appointment of UK tax representatives of non-UK account managers, account managers ceasing to act or to qualify, claims for tax relief and agreement of liabilities, annual returns of income and of information, annual and interim tax repayment claims, record-keeping, and information to be provided to investors. Subject to conditions, an ISA (or part thereof) may at the investor's request be transferred from one Revenue-approved account manager to another.

[*SI 1998 Nos 1870, 3174; SI 2000 No 809*].

Separate regulations modify existing tax legislation so far as it concerns individual savings account business of insurance companies. [*SI 1998 Nos 1871, 3174*].

Closure and death. Subject to the ISA terms and conditions, an investor may close an ISA at any time without affecting tax exemptions up to the date of closure. Where an investor dies, income and gains in respect of ISA investments which arise after the date of death but before the date of closure are not exempt.

See generally Revenue Pamphlet ISA 1.

21.28 **Legatees.** No chargeable gain accrues to the personal representatives where a person acquires an asset from them as legatee, and the legatee is treated as if the personal representatives' acquisition of the asset had been his acquisition of it. See 16.9 DEATH.

21.29 **Personal Equity Plans (PEPs). Before 6 April 1999**, an individual could make, subject to conditions, investments under a plan and obtain exemption from capital gains tax (as well as income tax) in respect of transactions covered by the plan. No further subscriptions to PEPs can be made after 5 April 1999, but existing PEPs continue under the same rules as before and independently of individual savings accounts (see 21.27 above). See 58.22 SHARES AND SECURITIES.

21.30 **Settled property.** No charge to capital gains tax arises

(*a*) where a person disposes of an interest in settled property provided the interest either was created for his benefit or was not acquired for money or money's worth (see 57.8 SETTLEMENTS); or

(*b*) when a person becomes absolutely entitled to settled property on the termination of a life interest by the death of the person entitled to it (see 57.9 and 57.11 SETTLEMENTS); or

(*c*) on the termination, on the death of the person entitled to it, of a life interest in possession in settled property where the property does not cease at that time to be settled property (see 57.10 SETTLEMENTS).

21.31 **Special reserve funds of individual Lloyd's underwriters.** Disposals of assets held in an individual underwriter's special reserve fund set up in respect of the 1992 or a subsequent underwriting year of account are exempt. See 63.1 UNDERWRITERS AT LLOYD'S.

21.32 **Woodlands.** Where woodlands are managed by the occupier on a commercial basis and with a view to the realisation of profits (before 6 April 1988, where land is assessed to either income tax or corporation tax under Schedule B)

(*a*) any consideration for the disposal of trees (whether standing, felled or cut thereon) and saleable underwood; and

(*b*) any capital sum received under an insurance policy in respect of the destruction of, or damage or injury to, trees or saleable underwood by fire or other hazard thereon

is excluded from any capital gains tax computation on the disposal if the person making the disposal is the occupier (before 6 April 1988, the person assessed under Schedule B).

In *any* capital gains tax computation on the sale of woodlands in the UK, there is excluded so much of the cost of the woodlands and/or consideration for the disposal as is attributable to trees, including saleable underwood, growing on the land. [*TCGA 1992, s 250*].

From 29 November 1994, the cultivation of 'short rotation coppice' is regarded as farming for capital gains purposes and not as forestry, and any land on which such activity takes place is regarded as farm land or agricultural land, as the case may be, and not as woodlands. '*Short rotation coppice*' means a perennial crop of tree species at high density, the stems of which are harvested above ground level at intervals of less than ten years. [*FA 1995, s 154*].

The Revenue regard the initial cultivation of the land including any spraying, ploughing, fencing and planting of the cuttings as capital costs against which any Woodland Grants received should be matched. The stools from planting form part of the land and as such will be allowable for capital gains purposes. The cost of the stools will not be allowable for capital gains if they are grubbed up before the land is sold. Revenue Tax Bulletin October 1995 p 253.

21.33 **Works of art etc.** A gain is not a chargeable gain if it accrues on the disposal of an asset with respect to which an undertaking has been given and where the disposal is

(*a*) by way of sale by private treaty to a body mentioned in *IHTA 1984, Sch 3* (see 10.5 CHARITIES); or

(*b*) to such a body as in (*a*) above otherwise than by sale; or (*c*) to the Board in satisfaction of the payment of inheritance tax or capital transfer tax.

[*TCGA 1992, s 258(2)*].

See 21.74(*a*)–(*e*) below for types of national heritage property which may be sold by private treaty within (*a*) above and also the undertakings required generally. See also 25.7 HOLD-OVER RELIEFS for relief for gifts of works of art etc.

The standard of objects which can be accepted under (*c*) above is very much higher. They have to satisfy a test of 'pre-eminence' either in the context of a national, local authority, or university collection, or through association with a particular building.

21.34 **EXEMPT ORGANISATIONS AND INDIVIDUALS**

The organisations and individuals detailed in 21.35–21.56 below are completely exempt from capital gains tax except where otherwise indicated.

21.35 **Atomic Energy Authority.** The authority is exempt from corporation tax in respect of chargeable gains. In addition, gains arising from investments or deposits held by a pension scheme provided and maintained by the Authority are exempt. [*TCGA 1992, s 271(7)*].

21.36 **Bare trustees and nominees.** Where assets are held by bare trustees or nominees for another person, capital gains tax is chargeable as if the assets were held by that other person. Consequently, there is no liability where the assets are transferred from the bare trustees etc. to that other person. [*TCGA 1992, s 60*]. See further 57.2 SETTLEMENTS.

21.37 **British Museum** and the **Natural History Museum** are entitled, on a claim to the Board, to exemption from tax on chargeable gains. [*TCGA 1992, s 271(6)(a); Museums and Galleries Act 1992, Sch 8 para 1(8)(9)*].

21.38 **Central banks.** Non-resident central banks as specified by Order in Council and the issue departments of the Reserve Bank of India and the State Bank of Pakistan are exempt from tax on chargeable gains. [*ICTA 1988, s 516(3)–(5); TCGA 1992, s 271(8)*].

21.39 **Charities.** Subject to restrictions after 11 June 1986, a gain is not a chargeable gain if it accrues to a charity and is applicable and applied for charitable purposes. See 10.3 and 10.4 CHARITIES.

21.40 **The Crown** is not liable to tax unless statute otherwise provides; see *Bank voor Handel v Administrator of Hungarian Property HL 1954, 35 TC 311* and *Boarland v Madras Electric Supply Corporation HL 1955, 35 TC 612*. In addition, gains arising on the disposal of stock belonging to the Crown, or in the name of the Treasury or National Debt Commissioners under statutory schemes under which transfers are made in accounts at the Bank of England, are not chargeable gains. [*TCGA 1992, s 271(1)(a)*]. Property held under trusts contained in *Chevening Estate Act 1959* is exempt from capital gains tax. [*TCGA 1992, s 270*].

21.41 **Diplomatic agents** (i.e. heads of mission or members of the diplomatic staff) of foreign states are exempt from capital gains tax except on gains arising from private investments or immovable property in the UK. [*Diplomatic Privileges Act 1964*]. Similar exemption is given to agents-general and to their personal staffs. Consular officers and their personal staffs are exempt from gains arising out of disposals of assets which are situated outside the UK at the time of disposal. [*TCGA 1992, s 11(2)–(4), s 271(1)(f); ICTA 1988, ss 320, 322*].

An order made *Arms Control and Disarmament (Privileges and Immunities) Act 1988, s 1(2)* can extend a similar exemption to the above to persons designated by states other than the UK.

21.42 **Friendly societies.** A friendly society registered under *Friendly Societies Act 1974* (a registered friendly society) is an unincorporated society of individuals. Under *Friendly Societies Act 1992*, societies are able to incorporate, take on new powers and form subsidiary companies. *TCGA 1992, ss 217A–217C* provide continuity of tax treatment between registered societies and incorporated societies and removes adverse tax consequences which would otherwise arise as a result of incorporation.

Friendly societies which are neither registered nor incorporated, the incomes of which do not exceed £160 per annum, are wholly exempt from corporation tax on chargeable gains, but a claim must be made. Exemption for other friendly societies is broadly restricted in respect of life or endowment business to the assurance of gross sums under contracts under which the total premiums payable in any period of twelve months do not exceed £270 or the granting of annuities not exceeding £156. The figure of £270 is reduced to £200 for contracts made after 24 July 1992 and before 1 May 1995, and to £150 for contracts made after 31 August 1990 and before 25 July 1991, previously £100. Where the premium under a contract made after 31 August 1987 and before 1 May 1995 is increased by a variation after 24 July 1991 and before 1 August 1992, or after 1 May 1995 and before 1 April 1996, the contract is treated for these purposes as having been made at the time of the variation. For contracts before 1 September 1987 the restriction was by reference to the assurance of gross sums not exceeding £750 and of annuities not exceeding £156. The limits were £500 for gross sums and £104 for annuities for contracts before 14 March 1984. Exemption also applied before that date provided that the society's rules did not enable it to write business above £2,000 and £416 respectively for years of account ending after 31 May 1980. Some policies made before 20 March 1991 were written on the mistaken assumption that they fell outside the required conditions for the tax-exempt policies above. A society may treat the policies as not being tax-exempt by election made before 1 August 1992, but a member surrendering or allowing a policy to mature will not be affected (see Revenue Press Release 12 June 1991). [*ICTA 1970, ss 331–337; FA 1976, s 48; FA 1980, s 57; FA 1984, s 73; Friendly Societies Act 1984, s 2(4); FA 1985, s 41, Sch 8; FA 1987, s 30; F(No 2)A 1987, Sch 2 para 2; ICTA 1988, ss 459–466; FA 1990, ss 49, 50; FA 1991, s 50, Sch 9; TCGA 1992, ss 217A–217C; F(No 2)A 1992, s 56, Sch 9; SI 1993 No 236; FA 1995, Sch 10 para 1; FA 2000, Sch 29 para 32*]. See also TOLLEY'S INCOME TAX and TOLLEY'S CORPORATION TAX under Friendly Societies.

21.43 **The Historic Buildings and Monuments Commission for England** is exempt from tax in respect of chargeable gains. [*TCGA 1992, s 271(7)*].

21.44 **Housing associations** approved under *ICTA 1988, s 488* (see TOLLEY'S CORPORATION TAX under Housing Associations Etc.) may make a claim to the inspector (within two years of the end of the relevant accounting period) for exemption from corporation tax on chargeable gains arising from the sale of property which is, or has been, occupied by a tenant of the association. [*ICTA 1988, s 488(5)*].

Relief from corporation tax generally by specific grant made by the Secretary of State for the Environment may also be obtainable under *Housing Act 1988, s 54* for registered non-profit making housing associations which are approved as above. See TOLLEY'S CORPORATION TAX under Housing Associations Etc.

Disposals of land and other assets by a housing association (as defined) to the Housing Corporation (or the Secretary of State (formerly Housing for Wales) or Scottish Homes) under certain statutory schemes, and subsequent disposals of those assets by the Corporation etc. to a single housing association, are treated as taking place on a no gain/no loss basis. The same applies to

(*a*) transfers of land between the Housing Corporation etc. and registered housing associations (as defined and see 21.52 below regarding self-build societies);

(*b*) transfers of land between such associations; and

(*c*) transfers under a direction from the Corporation etc. of property other than land between such associations.

Similar relief applies to NI housing associations.

[*TCGA 1992, ss 218–220; Government of Wales Act 1998, Sch 16 paras 77–80; SI 1996 No 2325; SI 1998 No 2244*].

The disposal and corresponding acquisition of an estate or interest in land in the UK made after 13 March 1989 otherwise than under a bargain at arm's length to a registered housing association (as defined) is treated as being made for a no gain/no loss consideration (or for the actual consideration if the latter exceeds the disposer's allowable expenditure; see 17.3 DISPOSAL) if a joint claim for such relief is made. On a subsequent disposal of the land by the association after a no gain/no loss acquisition its acquisition by the original donor is treated as the acquisition of the association. [*TCGA 1992, s 259*]. See 8.7 ASSETS HELD ON 33 MARCH 1982 and 26.4 INDEXATION for the consequential re-basing and indexation provisions which apply.

21.45 **International organisations** (e.g. the United Nations) may be specified by Order in Council as exempt from certain taxes [*International Organisations Act 1968*], as may certain financial bodies under the *Bretton Woods Agreement Act 1945* (e.g. the International Monetary Fund). Also exempt are the International Development Association [*International Development Association Act 1960, s 3* and *SI 1960 No 1383*]; the International Finance Corporation [*International Finance Corporation Act 1955, s 3* and *SI 1955 No 1954*]; and signatories to the Convention on the International Maritime Satellite Organisation in respect of capital gains tax on any payment received by the signatory from the Organisation in accordance with the Convention. [*TCGA 1992, s 271(5)*]. Bodies may be specified by Order as exempt under *European Communities Act 1972, s 2(2)*.

Securities issued by designated international organisations are treated as situated outside the UK. See 6.2 ASSETS.

21.46 **Local authorities, local authority associations and health service bodies** (as defined) are exempt from capital gains tax. [*TCGA 1992, s 271(3)*].

21.47 **National Debt.** Gains accruing to trustees of a settlement the property of which is for the reduction of the National Debt and which qualifies under statute are not chargeable. [*TCGA 1992, s 271(1)(e)*].

21.48 **The National Heritage Memorial Fund** is exempt from tax on chargeable gains. [*TCGA 1992, s 271(7)*].

21.49 **The National Radiological Protection Board** is exempt from tax on chargeable gains. [*TCGA 1992, s 271(7)*].

21.50 **Pension schemes, i.e. exempt approved schemes, retirement annuity schemes, approved personal pension schemes and pension business funds of life assurance companies and registered friendly societies.** Subject to the following, such schemes or the person deriving the benefit from them together with parliamentary pension schemes, National Insurance supplementary benefit schemes and certain overseas pension funds are exempt on gains arising from investments forming part of the fund or from the disposal of units in an authorised unit trust which is also an approved personal pension scheme. For disposals after 26 July 1990, futures contracts and options contracts are included as investments (notwithstanding that one party to the contract will not be involved with a transfer of assets other than money) as regards exempt approved schemes and approved personal pension schemes. (Income arising after 26 July 1990 from transactions relating to such contracts is regarded as income derived from, or income from, such contracts (and therefore exempt from income tax).) For disposals after 25 July 1984 and before 27 July 1990 a contract entered into by exempt approved schemes or approved personal pension schemes in the course of dealing in financial futures or 'traded options' is regarded as an investment. A '*traded option*' means an option which is for the time being quoted on a recognised stock exchange (within *ICTA 1988, s 841* — see 58.5 SHARES AND SECURITIES) or on the London International Financial Futures Exchange. For the Revenue's treatment of options and futures in other cases, see 17.10 DISPOSAL. [*TCGA 1992, s 271(1)(b)(c)(d)(g)(h)(j), (10)(11); FA 1984, s 45; F(No 2)A 1987, s 39(2), s 40(2), Sch 2 paras 1, 2, 5, Sch 3 para 5; ICTA 1988, s 438(1), s 460(1)(2), s 461(1), s 463, s 466, s 659; FA 1990, s 81(3)(4)(6)(8)*]. Before 26 July 1984, in the case of a covered option, the sale of the shares was normally treated as a disposal of an investment, and any gain was exempt under this provision. In the case of an uncovered option, whether the shares used to fulfil the obligation were regarded as an investment depended on the circumstances and, in particular, on whether they were acquired solely for resale.

Pension scheme surpluses. From 6 April 1987, the exemption provided by *TCGA 1992, s 271(1)(g)* will apply only to a prescribed percentage of any gain accruing on a disposal where an exempt approved scheme of a prescribed kind fails to carry out a reduction of its actuarial surplus. [*ICTA 1988, s 603, Sch 22; SI 1987 No 412*]. For full coverage, see TOLLEY'S INCOME TAX under Retirement Schemes for Employees.

Non-approved pension schemes. The rules for non-approved or 'top-up' pension schemes introduced by *FA 1989* are explained in an Inland Revenue explanatory booklet, 'The Tax Treatment of Non-approved Pension Schemes'. Copies are available, price £1.50, from the Inland Revenue Reference Room, Room 8, New Wing, Somerset House, London WC2R 1LB.

Where a retirement benefits scheme ceases to be tax approved under *ICTA 1988, s 591C* after 1 November 1994 (other than one which had its approval removed before that date), assets of the scheme are treated as having been acquired at their market value immediately before the date of cessation of approval, ensuring that on a future disposal of assets, only the gain accruing on these assets since approval was withdrawn will be brought into account. [*TCGA 1992, s 239A; FA 1995, s 61(2)(3)*].

Mis-sold pensions. Capital sums received by way of compensation for 'bad investment advice' received during the period beginning on 29 April 1988 and ending on 30 June 1994 in connection with a person's membership of certain occupational pension schemes and his entry into a personal pension scheme or retirement annuity contract is not regarded as the disposal of an asset for capital gains tax purposes. [*FA 1996, s 148(2)*]. The same applies, by concession, to capital sums received by way of compensation for mis-sold free standing additional voluntary contribution schemes (FSAVCS), where such compensation is paid as a result of the Financial Services Authority (FSA)/Personal Investment Authority Policy Statement issued on 28 February 2000 and is determined under the related FSA Guidance. The Policy Statement required a review of specified categories of FSAVCS sold during the period 28 April 1988 to 15 August 1999 inclusive. (Revenue ESC A99, 28 February 2000).

Withdrawal of tax approval of personal pensions. Where an approved personal pension scheme has its tax approval withdrawn by the Board on or after 17 March 1998 (otherwise than where the Revenue notice withdrawing approval was given before that date), an income tax charge under Schedule D, Case VI arises on the scheme administrator at the rate of 40% on the value, immediately before the date of withdrawal of approval, of the assets properly attributable to the scheme. [*ICTA 1988, s 650A; FA 1998, s 95(1)(4)*]. See TOLLEY'S INCOME TAX for details. For capital gains tax purposes, the assets in question are deemed to have been acquired immediately before the date of withdrawal of approval (without any corresponding disposal) by the person who would be chargeable if there had been a disposal at that time giving rise to a gain, and the acquisition cost of the assets is deemed to be equal to the amount on which income tax is charged as above. [*TCGA 1992, s 239B; FA 1998, s 95(3)(4)*]. The effect is similar to that under *TCGA 1992, s 239A* which applies where an occupational pension scheme has its approval withdrawn (see above).

21.51 **Scientific research associations**, provided that in each case its object is research in the fields of natural or applied science which may lead to an extension of trade and which is approved by the Department of Trade and Industry (DTI), and that it is prohibited by its Memorandum or similar instrument from distributing its income or property to its members in any form other than that of reasonable payments for supplies, labour, power, services, interest and rent. [*TCGA 1992, s 271(6)(b); ICTA 1988, s 508*]. On 4 September 1998, the DTI issued new guidance on the criteria for approval. By concession, the tax exemption continued for accounting periods beginning before 1 September 1999 as regards scientific research associations established before 4 September 1998 which either were approved or would have obtained approval under DTI practice before 1 January 1997. Capital gains on disposals of assets on or after 4 September 1998 qualify for exemption under this concession provided the proceeds are applied for qualifying scientific research by a body approved by the DTI for accounting periods beginning on or after 1 September 1999. (Revenue Pamphlet IR 1, C31).

21.52 **Self-build society.** An approved self-build society (as defined) may claim relief from corporation tax on chargeable gains arising on the disposal of any land to a member, provided that none of its land is occupied by a non-member. Claims must be made to the inspector within two years of the end of the accounting period. [*ICTA 1988, s 489*]. Disposals of land by unregistered self-build societies (as defined) to the Housing Corporation (or the Secretary of State (formerly Housing for Wales) or Scottish Homes) are treated as made at a no gain/no loss price. [*TCGA 1992, s 219; Government of Wales Act 1998, Sch 16 para 79; SI 1996 No 2325; SI 1998 No 2244*]. See TOLLEY'S CORPORATION TAX under Housing Associations Etc. and 21.44 above.

21.53 **Superannuation funds.** Approved superannuation funds which, immediately before 6 April 1980, enjoyed exemption under *ICTA 1970, s 208* (repealed after 5 April 1980 by *FA 1971, Sch 3 para 1*) may claim exemption for chargeable gains arising from the disposal of investments (for which see 21.50 above) held for the purposes of the fund. The following conditions must be satisfied.

(*a*) The fund has not been approved under *FA 1970, Pt II Ch II* or *ICTA 1988, Pt XIV Ch I*.

(*b*) No contribution has been made to it since 5 April 1980.

(*c*) The terms on which benefits are payable from the fund have remained unaltered since 5 April 1980.

[*TCGA 1992, s 271(2)(10)(11); FA 1980, s 36; FA 1984, s 45; FA 1987, Sch 16 Pt VI; ICTA 1988, s 431(5), s 608, s 659, Sch 29 para 26; FA 1990, s 81(3)(4)(6)(8); FA 1994, s 146, Sch 17 para 4; FA 1996, Sch 20 para 63*].

21.54 **Trade unions.** Registered trade unions, provided that they are precluded from assuring more than £4,000 by way of gross sum or £825 by way of annuity (excluding approved annuities under *ICTA 1988, s 620(9)*) in respect of any one person. (Prior to 1 April 1991 the appropriate sums were £3,000 and £625 respectively, and before 17 March 1987 they were £2,400 and £500 respectively. Following the enactment of *FA 1991, s 74*, the Treasury has power to increase the limits by order.) Exemption is granted in respect of chargeable gains which are applicable and are applied to 'provident benefits' i.e. sickness, injury and superannuation payments, payment for loss of tools, etc. [*ICTA 1988, s 467; FA 1991, s 74*]. Provident benefits also include legal expenses incurred in representing members at Industrial Tribunal hearings of cases alleging unfair dismissal, or incurred in connection with a member's claim in respect of accident or injury suffered, and general administrative expenses of providing provident benefits (Revenue Pamphlet IR 131, SP 1/84).

The above exemption also applies to employers' associations registered as trade unions [*ICTA 1988, s 467(4)(b)*], and to the Police Federations for England and Wales, Scotland, and Northern Ireland and other police organisations with similar functions. [*ICTA 1988, s 467(4)(c)*].

21.55 **Unit and investment trusts, open-ended investment companies and venture capital trusts.** Authorised unit trusts, investment trusts, open-ended investment companies and venture capital trusts are exempt from corporation tax on their chargeable gains. See 64 UNIT TRUSTS ETC. and 65.8 VENTURE CAPITAL TRUSTS.

21.56 **Visiting forces etc.** A period during which a member of a visiting force to whom *ICTA 1988, s 323(1)* applies is in the UK solely because of such membership is not treated either as a period of residence here or as creating a change in his residence or domicile. [*TCGA 1992, s 11(1); ICTA 1988, s 323*].

21.57 **RELIEFS AND DEFERRALS**

In addition to the exemption from capital gains tax detailed in 21.2–21.56 above, a number of reliefs are available to reduce or defer the amount of tax payable. The more common of these are outlined in 21.58–21.82 below as well as in certain provisions in 21.44 and 21.52 above.

21.58 **Amalgamations and reconstructions.** These do not normally constitute disposals, the original holding and the new holding being treated as the same asset acquired at the same date as the original shares. See 58.8 and 58.10 SHARES AND SECURITIES and 13.7 COMPANIES.

21.59 **Capital distributions and sale of rights.** If small as compared with the value of the shares in respect of which it is made, a capital distribution may be treated not as a disposal but the proceeds deducted from the acquisition cost of the shares on a subsequent disposal. See 58.14 SHARES AND SECURITIES. This treatment also applies to any consideration received for the disposal of rights. See 58.7 SHARES AND SECURITIES.

21.60 **Companies.**

(*a*) *Intra-group transfers of capital assets* are treated as if made at a no gain, no loss consideration (with certain exceptions). See 13.12 COMPANIES.

(*b*) *Transfers of assets to non-UK resident company.* Where a UK resident company carrying on a trade outside the UK through a branch or agency transfers that trade and its assets to a non-UK resident company partly or wholly for shares in that company, a proportion of the net chargeable gains relating to those shares may be claimed by the transferor company as being deferred. See 44.9 OVERSEAS MATTERS.

(*c*) *Transfers of UK trades between companies resident in different EC member States* are treated as if made at a no gain, no loss consideration. See 44.10 OVERSEAS MATTERS.

21.61 **Constituency associations.** Where, as a result of the redistribution of parliamentary constituencies, an existing constituency association in a former parliamentary constituency disposes, after 5 April 1983, of any land

(*a*) to a new association which is its successor, or

(*b*) to a body which is an organ of the political party (within *IHTA 1984, s 24*) and which, as soon as practicable thereafter, disposes of the land to a new association which is a successor to the existing association,

the disposal is treated as being made for such consideration as would secure that neither a gain nor loss accrues on disposal.

If the asset was originally held on 6 April 1965, time apportionment will be available (see 7.9 ASSETS HELD ON 6 APRIL 1965) to the new association as if it had held the land from the original date of acquisition.

Where, as a result of the redistribution of parliamentary constituencies, an existing constituency association in a former parliamentary constituency disposes, after 5 April 1983, of any land used and occupied by it for the purposes of its functions and transfers the whole or part of the proceeds to a new association which is its successor, ROLLOVER RELIEF (55) may be claimed as if the land disposed of had been the property of the new association since its acquisition. Where only part of the proceeds is transferred, rollover relief may be claimed on a corresponding share. [*TCGA 1992, s 264*].

21.62 **Corporate venturing scheme.** Companies may defer all or part of a chargeable gain on a corporate venturing scheme investment against a further subscription for shares (other than those of the same company or a company in its group) on which investment relief is obtained under the corporate venturing scheme. The deferred gain becomes chargeable on a disposal of the shares and in certain other circumstances. See 15.21 CORPORATE VENTURING SCHEME.

21.63 **Disposals: capital sums received as compensation etc.** Where such a sum is received in respect of an asset which is damaged or, alternatively, lost or destroyed, a number of reliefs are available provided the capital sum is expended on restoration of, or a replacement for, the asset. See 17.8 and 17.9 DISPOSAL.

21.64 **Enterprise investment scheme (EIS).** Individuals and most trustees may defer all or part of a chargeable gain against a subscription for eligible shares under the EIS. The deferred gain becomes chargeable on a disposal of the EIS shares and in certain other circumstances. See 20.9 ENTERPRISE INVESTMENT SCHEME (AND BES).

21.65 **Gifts of business assets and assets on which inheritance tax is chargeable etc.** A form of holdover relief applies to (*a*) gifts of business assets before 14 March 1989 (see 25.6 HOLD-OVER RELIEFS);

(*b*) gifts of business assets after 13 March 1989 (see 25.1 HOLD-OVER RELIEFS); and

(*c*) gifts after 13 March 1989 of assets on which inheritance tax is chargeable etc. (see 25.7 HOLD-OVER RELIEFS).

21.66 **Gifts to charities etc.** Disposals (otherwise than under a bargain at arm's length), by way of gift or at a consideration not exceeding the allowable expenditure, to charities or any of the bodies mentioned in *IHTA 1984, Sch 3* are deemed to have been made for a consideration giving neither a gain nor a loss. See 10.5 CHARITIES.

21.67 **Harbour reorganisation schemes.** Where the trade of any body corporate, other than a limited company, is transferred to a harbour authority by or under a certified harbour reorganisation scheme which provides for the dissolution of the transferor, any assets transferred on the transfer of trade are treated as giving rise to neither gain nor loss and, for the purposes of any assets acquired before 6 April 1965, the transferor's acquisition of the asset is treated as the transferee's acquisition of it. The transferee is also entitled to relief for any amount for which the transferor would have been entitled to claim relief in respect of allowable losses if it had continued to trade. [*TCGA 1992, s 221; ICTA 1988, s 518*].

21.68 **Hold-over: general relief for gifts.** After 5 April 1980 and before 14 March 1989, a general relief for gifts applied to the disposal of an asset otherwise than at arm's length. Any gain otherwise chargeable could be deferred by deduction from the transferee's acquisition cost. For full details of the relief and claims required, together with the possible clawback of relief, see 25.9 HOLD-OVER RELIEFS.

21.69 **Hops Marketing Board.** Certain transfers of assets by the Hops Marketing Board were deemed to be for a consideration which gives rise to neither a gain nor a loss and the Board's period of ownership is imputed to the transferee for the purposes of applying (where relevant) the provisions relating to ASSETS HELD ON 6 APRIL 1965 (7). [*FA 1982, s 148; TCGA 1992, Sch 12*].

21.70 **Land — compulsory acquisition.** Where *part* of a holding of land is transferred under a compulsory acquisition order, in certain circumstances the transferor may claim not to treat the transfer as a disposal and the consideration is then deducted from the allowable expenditure on a subsequent disposal. See 36.10 LAND for this and 36.11 for deferral of any gain arising on the compulsory purchase of land by means of a claim for rollover relief where the proceeds are re-invested in new land.

21.71 **Land — part disposals.** Where the value of the consideration for a part disposal of a larger holding of land does not exceed £20,000, in certain circumstances the transferor may claim that the transfer is not treated as a disposal and the consideration is then deducted from the allowable expenditure on a subsequent disposal. See 36.7 LAND.

21.72 **Maintenance funds for historic buildings.** After 5 April 1982 and before 6 April 1984, assets disposed of by a person to trustees for the purposes of maintenance, repair, preservation or reasonable improvement of, or for making provision for public access to, property of historic, scientific, etc. interest (see 21.74 below) where the transfer was exempt from capital transfer tax were deemed to be made for a consideration which gave neither a gain nor a loss for capital gains tax purposes. These provisions also applied in certain other circumstances. [*CGTA 1979, s 148; FA 1980, s 82; FA 1982, s 85; FA 1984, s 68*]. Broadly similar capital gains tax provisions existed for disposals after 30 July 1980 and before 6 April 1982, except that there was no provision for *improvement* of the buildings concerned.

In view of the general relief for gifts (see 25.9 HOLD-OVER RELIEFS but note that relief in turn was abolished for gifts after 13 March 1989) the above relief was abolished for disposals after 5 April 1984. For gifts after 13 March 1989, a specific deferral relief is again introduced in the form of the hold-over relief for gifts on which inheritance tax is chargeable etc. See 25.7 HOLD-OVER RELIEFS.

21.73 **Married persons.** Transfers between married persons are regarded as made on a no gain, no loss basis where the spouses are living together. See 41.3 MARRIED PERSONS.

21.74 **National heritage property.** The following types of property are within the term 'national heritage property' provided they are so designated by the Board.

(*a*) Any picture, print, book, manuscript, work of art or scientific object, any collection or group of such items taken as a whole, and any other item not yielding income, which appears to the Board to be pre-eminent for its national, scientific, historic or artistic interest (with regard being taken of any significant association of the item, collection or group with a particular place). Slightly less stringent criteria applied before 31 July 1998. '*National interest*' includes interest within any part of the UK;

(*b*) Land which in the opinion of the Board is of outstanding scenic or historic or scientific interest;

(*c*) A building for the preservation of which special steps should in the opinion of the Board be taken by reason of its outstanding historic or architectural interest;

(*d*) Any area of land which in the opinion of the Board is essential for the protection of the character and amenities of such a building as is mentioned in (*c*) above. For events before 19 March 1985 the land had to *adjoin* the building;

(*e*) An object which in the opinion of the Board is historically associated with such a building as is mentioned in (*c*) above.

[*IHTA 1984, s 31(1)(5); FA 1985, s 94, Sch 26 para 2(1)(2); FA 1998, Sch 25 para 4*].

Where any of the above assets, which have been (or could be) designated by the Board under *IHTA 1984, s 31*, are disposed of by gift (including a gift into settlement) or deemed to be disposed of by trustees on a person becoming absolutely entitled to settled property (other than on the death of the life tenant), then the person making the disposal and the person acquiring the asset are treated for capital gains tax purposes as making the transaction for a consideration giving neither gain nor loss. [*TCGA 1992, s 258(3)(4)*].

Certain undertakings must be given by such persons as the Board think appropriate in the circumstances of the case that, until the person beneficially entitled to the property dies or the property is disposed of, certain conditions regarding the property are kept, e.g. reasonable access to the public. [*TCGA 1992, s 258(9); IHTA 1984, s 30(1), s 31(2)(4); FA 1985, s 94, Sch 26 para 2(2)–(4)*]. An undertaking given on or after 31 July 1998 may be varied by agreement between the Revenue and the person bound by the undertaking or, in the absence of such agreement, by a Special Commissioner at the Revenue's behest. Earlier undertakings, where access to the asset is by public appointment only (disregarding special exhibitions), may be similarly varied so as to include an extended access requirement and/or a requirement that certain information be published. This does not apply to earlier undertakings in relation to which a chargeable event for inheritance tax purposes (see TOLLEY'S INHERITANCE TAX) occurs before 31 July 1998. [*TCGA 1992, s 258(8A); IHTA 1984, s 35A; FA 1998, Sch 25 para 8(1)(4), para 9, para 10*].

If the asset is sold and inheritance tax is chargeable under *IHTA 1984, s 32* (or would be chargeable if an undertaking under that provision had been given), the person selling the asset is treated as having sold the asset for its market value. Similarly, if the Board are satisfied that at any time during the period for which any undertaking was given that it has not been observed in a material respect, the owner is treated as having sold and immediately reacquired the asset for its market value. An undertaking for the purposes of these provisions is given for the period until the person beneficially entitled to the asset dies or disposes of the asset (whether by sale, gift or otherwise). [*TCGA 1992, s 258(5)(6)*].

If the asset subject to the undertaking is disposed of otherwise than on sale and without a further undertaking being given, the asset is treated as having been sold to an individual for its market value. [*TCGA 1992, s 258(6)*].

Where a person is treated as having sold for market value any asset within (*c*), (*d*) or (*e*) above, he is also treated as having sold and immediately reacquired at market value any asset 'associated' with it (unless the Board directs otherwise). '*Associated*' assets are a building within (*c*) above and land or objects which, in relation to that building, fall within (*d*) or (*e*) above. [*TCGA 1992, s 258(7)*].

Where a person is treated as having sold an asset under these provisions and inheritance tax becomes chargeable on the same occasion, any capital gains tax payable is deductible in determining the value of the asset for inheritance tax purposes. [*TCGA 1992, s 258(8)*].

See also 25.7 HOLD-OVER RELIEFS for relief for gifts of works of art etc.

Exceptions. The above provisions do not apply where the disposal is by way of gift or sale by private treaty to a body within *IHTA 1984, Sch 3* or if the disposal is to the Board in satisfaction of inheritance tax (or capital transfer tax). Such disposals are exempt. See 21.33 above.

21.75 **Reinvestment relief.** An individual or trustees could claim, subject to conditions, to defer a chargeable gain by deducting an amount equal to the gain (or such smaller amount as they choose) from the consideration given for the acquisition before 6 April 1998 of qualifying shares. See 50 REINVESTMENT RELIEF. Separate deferral provisions continue to apply for investment in enterprise investment scheme companies (see 21.64 above) and in venture capital trusts (see 21.82 below).

21.76 **Reorganisation of share capital.** Reorganisations do not normally constitute disposals, the original holding and the new holding being treated as the same asset acquired at the same date as the original shares. See 58.5 SHARES AND SECURITIES. See also 58.11 for conversion of securities into shares where the same principles apply.

21.77 **Retirement relief.** Subject to certain conditions, where an individual who has attained the age of 50 (or at a lesser age through ill-health) makes, at a gain, a 'material disposal of business assets', the gains qualifying for relief are reduced in accordance with the provisions in 53 RETIREMENT RELIEF.

21.78 **Rollover relief: replacement of business assets.** A person disposing of certain qualifying assets used exclusively for the purposes of a trade who used the proceeds to purchase other qualifying assets so used may claim to defer the capital gains tax payable by deducting the otherwise chargeable gain on the old asset from the cost of the newly acquired one. See 55 ROLLOVER RELIEF.

21.79 **Settlements for the benefit of employees.** Where the circumstances surrounding a disposal are as in one of (*a*)–(*c*) below, the MARKET VALUE (40.1) rules do not apply to it; and if made gratuitously or for a consideration of an amount not exceeding the allowable expenditure attributable to the asset, the disposal, and the corresponding acquisition by the trustees, is treated as taking place on a no gain/no loss basis and the transferor's acquisition of the asset is imputed to the trustees.

The circumstances mentioned above are as follows.

(*a*) A close company (as in *ICTA 1988, ss 414, 415* but additionally including a non-UK resident company which would be close as defined by those provisions) disposes of an asset to trustees in circumstances such that the disposition is not a transfer of value for IHT purposes by virtue of *IHTA 1984, s 13* (employee trusts).

(*b*) An individual disposes of an asset to trustees in circumstances such that the disposal is an exempt transfer for IHT purposes by virtue of *IHTA 1984, s 28* (employee trusts).

(*c*) A company other than a close company (as in (*a*) above) disposes of property to trustees otherwise than under a bargain at arm's length in circumstances such that, broadly, had the disposition been made by a close company it would not be a transfer of value by virtue of *IHTA 1984, s 13*.

[*TCGA 1992, s 239(1)(2)(4)–(8)*].

For coverage of *IHTA 1984, s 13* and *s 28* (each of which refers to the provisions of *IHTA 1984, s 86*), see TOLLEY'S INHERITANCE TAX under Trusts for Employees.

If the trustees of an 'employee trust' transfer an asset to a beneficiary for no payment, no charge under *TCGA 1992, s 71* will, by concession, be levied on the trustees provided there is a Schedule E income tax charge of the full market value of the asset on the employee. For this purpose, '*employee trust*' means a trust within *IHTA 1984, s 86* but ignoring the restriction in *s 86(3)* (class defined by employment with a particular body to include all or most employees), and the employee must not be a person of the kind described in *IHTA 1984, s 28(4)* (participators, connected persons etc.) and not excluded by *s 28(5)* (participators with 5% or more of a class of shares etc.). The concession does not apply where special statutory rules restrict either the liability to capital gains tax or the Schedule E liability (Revenue Pamphlet IR 1, D35). For notes on the application of ESC D35 in given situations, see Revenue Tax Bulletin April 2000 p 738.

For the position of the shareholders in a close company transferor which makes a transfer within (*a*)–(*c*) above at less than market value, see 3.15 ANTI-AVOIDANCE.

See also 25 HOLD-OVER RELIEFS and 19.13, 19.25 EMPLOYEE SHARE SCHEMES for alternative reliefs which may be available in respect of transfers to settlements for the benefit of employees.

21.80 **Transfer of a business to a company.** Where a person transfers a business and its assets to a company in return for shares in that company, any chargeable gain on disposal of the assets is deferred by reducing the amount otherwise chargeable in the proportion of the value of the shares received to the value of the overall consideration received by the transferor in exchange for the business. See 25.10 HOLD-OVER RELIEFS.

21.81 **Unremittable overseas gains.** On a claim, such gains may be treated as gains of the year in which conditions preventing remittance cease to apply. See 44.5 OVERSEAS MATTERS. See also 35.7 INTEREST AND SURCHARGES ON UNPAID TAX.

21.82 **Venture capital trusts (VCTs).** Individuals may defer all or part of a chargeable gain against subscriptions of up to £100,000 per tax year for shares in VCT companies by reference to which income tax investment relief is obtained. The deferred gain becomes chargeable on a disposal of the VCT shares and in certain other circumstances. See 65.10 VENTURE CAPITAL TRUSTS.

22 Furnished Holiday Accommodation

22.1 DEFINITIONS

Special provisions apply to the treatment for the purposes of tax on chargeable gains of the commercial letting of furnished holiday accommodation in the UK.

'*Commercial letting*' is letting (whether or not under a lease) on a commercial basis and with a view to the realisation of profits (see *Brown v Richardson (Sp C 129), [1997] SSCD 233* and Revenue Tax Bulletin October 1997 p 472), and accommodation is let '*furnished*' if the tenant is entitled to the use of furniture.

'*Holiday accommodation*' is accommodation which

(*a*) must be available for commercial letting to the public generally as holiday accommodation for at least 140 days in a twelve month period (see below), and

(*b*) is so let for at least 70 such days.

It must, however, not normally be in the same occupation for more than 31 consecutive days at any time during a period (although not necessarily a continuous period) of seven months in that twelve month period which includes any months in which it is let as in (*b*) above. In the case of an individual or partnership, these conditions must be satisfied in the year of assessment in which the profits or gains arise, unless

(i) the accommodation was not let furnished in the preceding year of assessment but is so let in the following year of assessment, in which case they must be satisfied in the twelve months from the date such letting commenced in the year of assessment, or

(ii) the accommodation was let furnished in the preceding year of assessment but is not so let in the following year of assessment, in which case they must be satisfied in the twelve months ending with the date such letting ceased in the year of assessment.

In the case of a company, the conditions must be satisfied in the twelve months ending on the last day of the accounting period in which the profits or gains arise, with similar variations as in (i) and (ii) above where the accommodation was not let furnished in the twelve months preceding or following the period in question.

In satisfying the 70 day test ((*b*) above) averaging may be applied to letting periods of holiday accommodation already treated as such ('*qualifying accommodation*') and letting periods of any or all of other accommodation let by the same person which would be holiday accommodation if it satisfied the 70 day test. Any such other accommodation is then treated as holiday accommodation if the average of the days let in the twelve month period is at least 70. For 1996/97 onwards, for persons other than companies, a claim under *ICTA 1988, s 504(6)* for averaging must be made on or before the first anniversary of 31 January following the year of assessment for which it is to apply. Previously, the time limit was two years after the end of that year of assessment. For companies, the time limit is two years after the end of the accounting period for which the averaging claim is to apply. Only one such claim may be made in respect of qualifying accommodation in any year of assessment or accounting period.

Where there is a letting of accommodation only part of which is holiday accommodation, apportionments are made as are just and reasonable.

[*ICTA 1988, s 504; TCGA 1992, s 241(1)(2)(7); FA 1996, Sch 20 para 62, Sch 21 para 14*].

Furnished holiday accommodation may include caravans (Revenue Press Release 17 May 1984).

See TOLLEY'S INCOME TAX regarding income tax provisions in respect of furnished holiday accommodation.

22.2 CAPITAL GAINS TAX TREATMENT

For the purposes of the following provisions, the commercial letting of furnished holiday accommodation in the UK in respect of which the profits are chargeable under Schedule A (previously Schedule D, Case VI) is treated as a trade, and all such lettings made by a particular person, partnership or body of persons are treated as one trade.

(*a*) RETIREMENT RELIEF (53).

(*b*) ROLLOVER RELIEF (55).

(*c*) Relief for gifts of business assets (see 25.1–25.6 HOLD-OVER RELIEFS).

(*d*) Relief for loans to traders (see 39.10 LOSSES).

(*e*) TAPER RELIEF (60).

A notable omission from (*a*)–(*e*) above, which may be of advantage to the taxpayer, are the provisions applying in respect of a non-UK resident trading in the UK through a branch or agency (see 44.3 OVERSEAS MATTERS).

Where, in any chargeable period, a person makes a commercial letting within these provisions, the let property is to be taken for the purposes of (*a*)–(*e*) above as being used throughout that period only for the purposes of the deemed trade of making such lettings except for any period when it is neither commercially let nor available to be so let (unless it is only works of construction or repair that make this the case).

For the purposes of (*b*) above, the replacement asset must be acquired after 5 April 1982. However, where the only or main residence exemption in *TCGA 1992, s 222* (see 48 PRIVATE RESIDENCES) is also available to any extent, the gain to which *TCGA 1992, s 222* applies is reduced by the amount of the rolled-over gain.

[*TCGA 1992, s 241(3)–(6)(8); FA 1995, Sch 6 para 36; FA 1998, s 121(3)(4), Sch 5 para 62, Sch 21 para 8*].

The Revenue consider that the relief at (*a*) or (*b*) is available if the holiday accommodation is sold within three years of its ceasing to be let so long as the owner does not occupy it or use it for some other non-qualifying purpose (CCAB Statement TR 551, June 1984). Where periods before 6 April 1982 need to be considered, then, for the purposes of (*a*)–(*d*) above, those periods would be judged by the Revenue on the basis of the actual activity carried on and whether that activity would have qualified in relation to the period after 5 April 1982 (Tolley's Practical Tax 1985 p 96).

Sumption: Capital Gains Tax. See A16.08.

23 Gifts

Cross-references. See 33.2 INTERACTION WITH OTHER TAXES for inheritance tax interaction on lifetime gifts; and 46.6 PAYMENT OF TAX for payment by instalments on certain gifts etc.

23.1 GENERAL

The fact that no proceeds are received on a disposal of an asset does not mean that capital gains tax will not apply. With certain exceptions, where a person acquires or disposes of an asset, otherwise than by way of a bargain made at arm's length *and in particular where he acquires or disposes of it by way of gift*, his acquisition or disposal of the asset is deemed to be for a consideration equal to the market value of the asset. [*TCGA 1992, s 17(1)(a)*]. See 40 MARKET VALUE for the full market value rules and the exceptions where the provisions do not apply.

Thus, the donor of an asset is normally treated as incurring a chargeable gain computed by reference to market value at the date of disposal. For the purposes of gifts, the date of disposal is the time when the donor has done everything within his power to transfer the property to the donee (see *Re Rose, Rose and Others v CIR CA, [1952] 1 All E R 1217*).

23.2 GENERAL RELIEF FOR GIFTS FROM 1980 TO 1989

After 5 April 1980 and before 14 March 1989, a general relief for gifts applied to the disposal of an asset otherwise than at arm's length. Any gain otherwise chargeable could be deferred by deduction from the transferee's acquisition cost. For full details of the relief and claims required, together with the possibility of clawback of relief, see 25.9 HOLD-OVER RELIEFS.

23.3 SPECIAL EXEMPTIONS RELATING TO GIFTS

Once the market value of a gift has been established, the ordinary capital gains tax provisions relating to exemptions apply to that gift. See 21 EXEMPTIONS AND RELIEFS. For example, the gift of a chattel with a market value of £6,000 (£3,000 for gifts before 6 April 1989) or less is exempt. The following gifts are expressly exempt.

(*a*) Gifts for public benefit (see 21.26 EXEMPTIONS AND RELIEFS).

(*b*) Gifts of property to bodies mentioned in *IHTA 1984, Sch 3* for national purposes (see 21.33 EXEMPTIONS AND RELIEFS).

(*c*) Donatio mortis causa (see 16.3 DEATH).

23.4 SPECIAL RELIEFS RELATING TO GIFTS

Apart from the general relief for gifts from 1980 to 1989 outlined in 23.2 above, reliefs are also available for

(*a*) gifts of business assets before 14 March 1989 (see 25.6 HOLD-OVER RELIEFS);

(*b*) gifts of business assets after 13 March 1989 (see 25.1 HOLD-OVER RELIEFS);

(*c*) gifts to charities (see 10.5 CHARITIES);

(*d*) gifts after 13 March 1989 of assets on which inheritance tax etc. is chargeable (see 25.7 HOLD-OVER RELIEFS);

(*e*) gifts to housing associations after 13 March 1989 (see 21.44 EXEMPTIONS AND RELIEFS);

(*f*) gifts to maintenance trusts for historic buildings before 6 April 1984 (see 21.72 EXEMPTIONS AND RELIEFS);

(*g*) gifts of national heritage property subject to certain undertakings (see 21.74 EXEMPTIONS AND RELIEFS); and

(*h*) gifts to settlements for the benefit of employees (see 21.79 EXEMPTIONS AND RELIEFS).

23.5 RECOVERY OF TAX FROM DONEE

Where capital gains tax arising on a disposal made by way of gift (including any transaction otherwise than at arm's length) is not paid by the donor (or, if he being an individual has died, his personal representatives) within twelve months from the date it became payable, it may be recovered, subject to the coverage below, from the donee within two years after the date on which it became payable. The donee then has a right of recovery from the donor or his personal representatives. The recovery is done by assessment and the donee is assessed and charged (in the name of the donor) to capital gains tax on an amount not exceeding the amount of the chargeable gain arising on the disposal, and not exceeding the grossed-up amount of the capital gains tax unpaid at the time such assessment is made, grossing up at the marginal rate of tax (i.e. by taking capital gains tax on a chargeable gain at the amount which would not have been chargeable but for that chargeable gain). [*TCGA 1992, s 282*].

24 Government Securities

Cross-reference. See also 38 LOAN RELATIONSHIPS OF COMPANIES.

24.1 EXEMPTION RULES

Gains on disposals of any of the UK government and public corporation stocks ('gilts') specified in 24.2 below are not chargeable gains, and losses are not allowable. [*TCGA 1992, s 115(1)(a)*].

The same applies to disposals of options or contracts to acquire or dispose of such gilts. See 17.10 and 17.11 DISPOSAL.

The above applies to companies as well as persons chargeable to capital gains tax. However, from 1 April 1996, gains and losses on disposals by companies of such assets are within the company loan relationship provisions described in 38 LOAN RELATIONSHIPS OF COMPANIES. They are thus treated for corporation tax purposes as *income* (and not capital) gains and losses, and are chargeable/allowable accordingly. Note the specific exceptions for low coupon gilts at 38.19 LOAN RELATIONSHIPS OF COMPANIES.

See 13.10 COMPANIES for appropriations of gilts to and from trading stock by companies.

See 58.11 SHARES AND SECURITIES regarding government stock issued as compensation for shares compulsorily acquired.

24.2 EXEMPT SECURITIES

Government (and certain public corporation securities guaranteed by the Treasury) are specified as exempt, as described in 24.1 above, by the Treasury in the form of a statutory instrument. In practice, all UK government securities charged on the National Loans Fund are so specified.

Any security which is a strip (within *FA 1942, s 47*) of a security which is a gilt specified as exempt is also itself a gilt specified for the purposes of the exemption. The Treasury are given powers to amend the legislation by regulations in connection with the introduction of gilt strips. [*TCGA 1992, s 288(8), Sch 9 Pt I; FA 1996, s 202, Sch 40 para 8*].

Those securities specified as exempt of which the latest redemption date falls after 31 December 1991 are now listed in *TCGA 1992, Sch 9 Pt II* as supplemented by *SI 1993 No 950*, *SI 1994 No 2656* and *SI 1996 No 1031*. The position of securities with an earlier redemption date is protected by *TCGA 1992, Sch 11 para 15*.

25 Hold-Over Reliefs

Cross-references. See 8.12 ASSETS HELD ON 31 MARCH 1982 for 50% relief etc. on held-over gains relating to an asset acquired before 31 March 1982; 13.7 COMPANIES for the relief available on a scheme of reconstruction or amalgamation and 13.12 for relief on disposals within a group; 17.8, 17.9 DISPOSAL for reliefs available where capital sums received as compensation are expended on restoration or replacement; 21 EXEMPTIONS AND RELIEFS generally; 23.4 GIFTS for summary of special reliefs relating to gifts; 36.8, 36.10, 36.11 LAND for reliefs available on small part disposals and compulsory purchase of land; 44.3 OVERSEAS MATTERS for transfer of UK branch or agency to UK resident company, 44.9 for transfers of assets to a non-UK resident company, 44.10 for transfer of trade between companies in different EC member States and 44.11 for transfer of non-UK trade between companies in different EC member States; 50 REINVESTMENT RELIEF for a relief which may be able to be used as an alternative to the reliefs in this chapter in relation to disposals after 29 November 1993 where a qualifying investment is made before 6 April 1998; 55 ROLLOVER RELIEF; 60.13 TAPER RELIEF.

See also Tolley's Roll-Over, Hold-Over and Retirement Reliefs.

25.1 RELIEF FOR GIFTS OF BUSINESS ASSETS AFTER 13 MARCH 1989

Where, after 13 March 1989,

(*a*) an individual ('*the transferor*') makes a disposal not at arm's length (e.g. a gift) of an asset specified below, and

(*b*) a joint claim for relief is made by him and the transferee, or, where the transferee is a trustee of a settlement, by him alone,

then, subject to *TCGA 1992, s 165(3)* below and the provisions in 25.5 below, the hold-over relief described below is to apply. [*TCGA 1992, s 165(1); FA 2000, s 90(1)*]. Note that the transferee need not be an individual and may, for example, be a company. See also 25.2 below re agricultural property and 25.3 below re settled property.

An asset is within (*a*) above if

(i) it is, or is an interest in, an asset used for the purposes of a trade, profession or vocation carried on by the transferor, his 'personal company' ('family company' for disposals before 16 March 1993) or a member of a 'trading group' of which the 'holding company' is his personal company (family company for disposals before 16 March 1993), or

(ii) it consists of shares or securities of a 'trading company', or of the holding company of a trading group, where *either* the shares etc. are neither listed on a recognised stock exchange (within *ICTA 1988, s 841* — see 58.5 SHARES AND SECURITIES) nor dealt in on the Unlisted Securities Market (now closed) *or* the trading company or holding company is the transferor's personal company (family company for disposals before 16 March 1993).

[*TCGA 1992, s 165(2); FA 1993, s 87, Sch 7 para 1, Sch 23 Pt III; FA 1996, Sch 38 para 10(1)–(3); FA 2000, s 90(3)*].

Nature of relief. Where there is no actual consideration for the disposal (as opposed to a deemed MARKET VALUE (40.1) consideration under *TCGA 1992, s 17(1)*), or where an actual consideration does not exceed the allowable expenditure within *TCGA 1992, s 38* (see 17.3 DISPOSAL) relating to the asset, the effect of a claim is that the gain otherwise chargeable on the transferor apart from this relief and the transferee's acquisition cost are each reduced by the '*held-over gain*', i.e. the gain otherwise chargeable apart from this relief and, where relevant, retirement relief (termed the '*unrelieved gain*') but subject to the reductions described below. Where actual consideration exceeds the allowable expenditure, the held-over gain is the unrelieved gain less that excess but again subject to the reductions below. (*Note.* Indexation allowance is deductible in arriving at the gain otherwise chargeable but it is not allowable expenditure within *TCGA 1992, s 38*.) [*TCGA 1992, s 165(4)(6)(7)*]. See also 60.13 TAPER RELIEF.

Hold-over relief does not apply on a disposal if

- the disposal is a transfer of shares or securities after 8 November 1999, and the transferee is a company; or
- the gain arising is wholly relieved by RETIREMENT RELIEF (53); or
- the disposal is of shares or securities, and the 'appropriate proportion' of the gain is wholly relieved by retirement relief (see 53.9 RETIREMENT RELIEF); or
- the gain arises by virtue of *TCGA 1992, s 116(10)(b)* (disposal of qualifying corporate bonds derived from shares giving rise to deferred gain, see 49.3 QUALIFYING CORPORATE BONDS); or
- hold-over relief is available (or would be if a claim were made) under *TCGA 1992, s 260* in 25.7 below for gifts after 13 March 1989 on which inheritance tax is chargeable etc.

[*TCGA 1992, s 165(3); FA 2000, s 90(4)(5)*].

Under self-assessment from 1996/97 onwards, hold-over relief claims must be made on a standard claim form (which can be found attached to Revenue Helpsheet IR 295). As they are usually bilateral claims, they cannot be made in the self-assessment tax return itself and will fall within the provisions of *TMA 1970, Sch 1A* (claims not included in returns — see 12.3 CLAIMS). A unilateral claim by a settlor will usually form part of his tax return. (Revenue Tax Bulletin April 1997 pp 417, 418).

In most circumstances, the Revenue will admit a hold-over relief claim without requiring a computation of the gain, which would involve ascertaining the market value of the asset at the date of the transfer. Transferor and transferee must jointly request this in writing (for 1996/97 onwards, in the standard claim form — see above) and must provide, in particular, a calculation incorporating informally estimated valuations and a statement that the claimants are satisfied that the value of the asset exceeds the allowable expenditure plus any indexation allowance due. Once accepted by the Revenue, a claim made on this basis cannot be withdrawn. In many cases, a formal valuation will never become necessary; in others, for example where the gain partially attracts retirement relief, valuation may still be deferred until a subsequent disposal of the asset by the transferee (or, in a retirement relief case, if and when the transferor makes a further gain attracting retirement relief). This practice applies equally to valuations on dates other than the date of transfer, where these are relevant to the computation of the gain. Where the asset was held by the transferor on 31 March 1982, then unless the transferee has paid *some* consideration, it will normally be necessary to agree a 31 March 1982 valuation only when the transferee disposes of the asset. (Revenue Pamphlet IR 131, November 1998 Supplement, SP 8/92). The informal valuations referred to above need not be made by an expert and are non-binding. (Revenue Tax Bulletin April 1997 pp 417, 418).

The definitions of '*family company*' (for disposals before 16 March 1993), '*holding company*', '*personal company*' (for disposals after 15 March 1993), '*trading company*' and '*trading group*' have the meanings given by *TCGA 1992, Sch 6 para 1* (see 53.4 RETIREMENT RELIEF). '*Trade*', '*profession*' and '*vocation*' generally have the same meanings as in the *Income Tax Acts* but the commercial letting of FURNISHED HOLIDAY ACCOMMODATION (22) in the UK in respect of which the profits, etc. are chargeable under Schedule A or Schedule D, Case VI is treated as a trade for relief purposes; and for the same purposes in determining whether a company is a trading company, '*trade*' includes the occupation of woodlands managed on a commercial basis by the occupier with a view to profit. [*TCGA 1992, s 165(8)(9), s 241(3); FA 1993, s 87, Sch 7 para 1, Sch 23 Pt III*].

There is nothing in the legislation to deny relief if consideration for the use of the asset passes between an individual and a company, e.g. under a lease or tenancy agreement, and similarly there is no requirement that the individual need be a 'full-time working officer or employee' ('full-time working director' for disposals before 16 March 1993) (see 53.4 RETIREMENT RELIEF). It is understood that the Revenue will apply SP D11 (see 55 ROLLOVER RELIEF) *mutatis mutandis* for this hold-over relief as it applies to rollover relief (Tolley's Practical Tax 1990 p 143). As a claim applies separately to each asset, the comments made about the general relief for gifts from 1980 to 1989 in 25.9 below regarding the treatment of property as separate assets would seem also to apply to the above relief.

Where a hold-over relief claim is made, the transferee may deduct for capital gains tax purposes on a subsequent disposal made by him any inheritance tax attributable to the value of the asset on the transfer to him which qualified for relief and which is either a chargeable transfer or a potentially exempt transfer which proves to be a chargeable transfer. The tax deductible may be varied on the subsequent death of the transferor within seven years or otherwise but it cannot in any circumstances give rise to an allowable loss on the subsequent disposal. [*TCGA 1992, s 165(10)(11)*]. See also 33.2 INTERACTION WITH OTHER TAXES.

Reductions in the held-over gain. If the qualifying asset disposed of was not used for the purposes of the trade, profession or vocation concerned throughout the period of its ownership by the transferor, the held-over gain is reduced by multiplying it by the fraction of which the denominator is the total period of ownership and the numerator the number of days in the period during which the asset was so used. (*Note.* In the determination of the period of ownership there is no exclusion of any period before 31 March 1982, cf. 55.6 ROLLOVER RELIEF.) Where the qualifying asset disposed of is a building or structure part only of which has been used for the trade etc. concerned over all or a 'substantial' part of the period of its ownership, the held-over gain is reduced as is 'just and reasonable'. [*TCGA 1992, Sch 7 para 4, para 5(1), para 6(1)*].

If the disposal of shares or securities of a company qualifies for relief and the company or group (as appropriate) then has 'chargeable assets' which are not 'business assets' and *either* at any time in the twelve months before the disposal the transferor could exercise 25% or more of the company's voting rights (as exercisable in general meeting) *or* the company is the personal company (family company for disposals before 16 March 1993) (see above) of an individual transferor at any time within that period of twelve months, the held-over gain is reduced by multiplying it by the fraction of which the denominator is the then market value of all of the company's or group's chargeable assets and the numerator is the then market value of the company's or group's business assets. In considering a group, a holding in the ordinary share capital of one group member by another is ignored, and if a 51% subsidiary is not wholly owned directly or indirectly by the holding company the values of its chargeable and business assets are reduced in proportion to the share capital owned; and for both purposes the expressions used are as in *ICTA 1988, s 838*. An asset is a '*business asset*' if it is or is an interest in an asset used for the purposes of a trade etc. carried on by the company or another group member, and an asset is a '*chargeable asset*' if a gain accruing on its disposal by the company or another group member would be a chargeable gain. [*TCGA 1992, Sch 7 paras 4, 7; FA 1993, s 87, Sch 7 para 1, Sch 23 Pt III*].

If the asset disposed of is a 'chargeable business asset' for the purposes of retirement relief (see 53.9 RETIREMENT RELIEF) and the held-over gain (as reduced under the above) would exceed the gain otherwise chargeable (ignoring hold-over relief itself but allowing for any deduction of retirement relief), the held-over gain is reduced by the amount of the excess. In the case of a disposal of shares or securities qualifying for retirement relief where the held-over gain (as reduced under the above) would exceed an amount equal to the 'appropriate proportion' of the gain otherwise chargeable (ignoring hold-over relief itself but allowing for any deduction of retirement relief), the held-over gain is reduced by the amount of the excess. [*TCGA 1992, Sch 7 paras 4, 8*].

25.2 **Agricultural property.** If an asset, or an interest in an asset,

(*a*) is 'agricultural property' within the inheritance tax provisions of *IHTA 1984, Pt V Ch II* and *either* qualifies for an inheritance tax reduction in value in relation to a chargeable transfer made simultaneously with the disposal *or* would so qualify if there were a chargeable transfer on the disposal *or* would so qualify but for *IHTA 1984, s 124A* (additional conditions for transfers within seven years before death of transferor) (assuming, where there is no chargeable transfer, that there were); but

(*b*) it fails to qualify for hold-over relief solely because the agricultural property is not used for the purposes of a trade etc. carried on as in 25.1(i) above,

then, notwithstanding (*b*) above, hold-over relief is granted to the individual transferor. Hold-over relief is also granted *mutatis mutandis* to trustees (see under settled property below) where the agricultural property would not otherwise qualify for relief solely because it is not used for the purposes of a trade etc. carried on as in 25.3(i) below. In these circumstances *TCGA 1992, Sch 7 para 4, para 5(1), para 6(1)* in 25.1 above do not apply. [*TCGA 1992, s 165(5), Sch 7 para 1, para 3, para 5(2), para 6(2)*]. Where development value over and above the agricultural value of the land is inherent in the property transferred, hold-over relief is available in respect of the whole of the gain, i.e. not just that part which reflects the land's agricultural value (Revenue Tax Bulletin November 1991 p 5).

25.3 **Settled property.** If

(*a*) trustees of a settlement make a non-arm's length disposal of an asset specified below, and

(*b*) a claim for relief under *TCGA 1992, s 165* is made by the trustees and the transferee or, if trustees are also the transferee, by the trustees making the disposal alone,

then, subject to *TCGA 1992, s 165(3)* (see 25.1 above) and the provisions in 25.5 below, hold-over relief given by *TCGA 1992, s 165(4)* (see 25.1 above) applies to the disposal.

An asset is within (*a*) above if

(i) it is, or is an interest in, an asset used for the purposes of a trade, profession or vocation carried on by the trustees making the disposal or a beneficiary who had an interest in possession in the settled property immediately before the disposal, or

(ii) it consists of shares or securities of a trading company, or of the holding company of a trading group, where *either* the shares etc. are neither listed on a recognised stock exchange nor dealt in on the Unlisted Securities Market (now closed) *or* not less than 25% of the voting rights as exercisable in general meeting are held by the trustees at the time of disposal.

Where hold-over relief is granted to trustees in this way, references to the trustees are substituted for references to the transferor in *TCGA 1992, s 165(4)(a)* above and *CGTA 1979, s 126C* in 25.5 below; and where hold-over relief is granted on a disposal deemed to occur by virtue of *TCGA 1992, s 71(1)* or *s 72(1)* (see 57.9–57.11 SETTLEMENTS and 25.5 below), no reduction in the held-over gain is made under *TCGA 1992, s 165(7)* in 25.1

above (reduction by excess of actual consideration over allowable expenditure). [*TCGA 1992, s 165(5), Sch 7 para 2; CGTA 1979, Sch 4 para 2; FA 1989, Sch 14 para 3(3); FA 1996, Sch 38 para 10(1)–(3); FA 2000, s 90(3)*]. See also 25.2 above re agricultural property.

25.4 *Example*

S has carried on his antique dealing business for 10 years. The assets of the business are valued as follows

	£
Freehold shop and office	245,000
Goodwill	75,000
Stocks	50,000
Debtors	9,500
Cash	4,500

Before the business began, S let the shop premises for one year. In October 2000, S transfers the business as a going concern to a company which he has formed with share capital of £1,000, held wholly by him. The transfer consideration is £1. At the time of the transfer S is 51. The gain arising in respect of the freehold is £165,000 and on goodwill it is £45,000 (both after deducting indexation allowance to April 1998).

	£	£
Gains eligible for retirement relief		
(£165,000 + £45,000)		210,000
Relief £150,000 × 100%	150,000	
£60,000 × 50%	30,000	180,000
Chargeable gain		£30,000

If S and the company jointly claim relief under *TCGA 1992, s 165*, part of the chargeable gain may be rolled over, as follows

	Freehold	Goodwill	
	£	£	£
Total gain	165,000	45,000	
Reduction for non-trade use [*TCGA 1992, Sch 7 para 5*] ($\frac{1}{11}$)	15,000		
	£150,000	£45,000	
Held–over gain before adjustment			195,000
Chargeable gain after retirement relief [*TCGA 1992, Sch 7 para 8*]			30,000
Excess			£165,000
Held–over gain (£195,000 – £165,000)			£30,000
Chargeable gain			Nil

Notes to the example

(*a*) There is no statutory formula for apportioning the held-over gain after retirement relief between different assets. The following is one possible method of computing the revised base costs in the hands of the company.

Freehold

Gain held over $\frac{165{,}000}{210{,}000} \times £30{,}000$ £23,571

Revised base cost (£245,000 – £23,571) £221,429

Goodwill

Gain held over $\frac{45{,}000}{210{,}000} \times £30{,}000$ £6,429

Revised base cost (£75,000 – £6,429) £68,571

(*b*) If S had transferred the business to the company in consideration for the issue of shares, *TCGA 1992, s 162* would have applied, but business assets relief under *TCGA 1992, s 165* would not. Retirement relief would still have applied in priority, so that the chargeable gain would have been £30,000. This gain would then have been rolled over against the base cost of the shares acquired by S.

(*c*) If the chargeable gain, after retirement relief, of £30,000 were not held over, business asset taper relief of 25% would have reduced it to £22,500. As a result of the hold-over claim, taper relief is forgone. The availability and quantum of taper relief needs to be taken into account in the decision-making.

25.5 Restrictions on, and clawback of, hold-over relief under TCGA 1992, s 165, Sch 7 as applicable to disposals after 13 March 1989

Gifts to non-residents. The hold-over relief of *TCGA 1992, s 165(4)* in 25.1–25.3 above is not to apply where the transferee is neither resident nor ordinarily resident in the UK. It also does not apply where the transferee is an individual or, for disposals before 30 November 1993 (this date being the date of the coming into force of *FA 1994, s 249*; companies otherwise regarded as UK resident but under double tax relief arrangements already regarded as non-UK resident to be treated as non-UK resident for *Taxes Acts* purposes after 29 November 1993; see 52.6 RESIDENCE AND DOMICILE), a company if that individual or, for disposals before 30 November 1993, company, though resident or ordinarily resident in the UK, is regarded as resident elsewhere by virtue of DOUBLE TAX RELIEF (18.2) arrangements such that it would not under those arrangements be taxable in the UK on a gain arising on a disposal of the asset immediately after its acquisition. [*TCGA 1992, s 166; FA 1994, s 251(1)(7), Sch 26 Pt VIII*].

Gifts to foreign-controlled companies. Relief under *TCGA 1992, s 165(4)* is also denied where the transferee is a company which is controlled by a person who, or by persons each of whom, is neither UK-resident nor ordinarily resident and is connected (see 14 CONNECTED PERSONS) with the person making the disposal; and in determining a person's residence status, a person who either alone or with others controls a company by virtue of holding assets relating to that or any other company and who is UK-resident or ordinarily resident is regarded as neither UK-resident nor ordinarily resident if he is regarded under a double tax agreement as resident overseas in circumstances in which he would not be liable to a UK tax charge on a gain arising on a disposal of the assets. [*TCGA 1992, s 167*].

Emigration of controlling trustees before 19 March 1991. If relief under *TCGA 1992, s 165* (formerly *CGTA 1979, s 126*) was given on a disposal of an asset to a company which was controlled by trustees of a settlement ('the relevant disposal') at a time when the person making the disposal was connected with the trustees, and at a time when the company had not disposed of the asset and the trustees still controlled the company the trustees became before 19 March 1991 neither UK-resident nor ordinarily resident (determined as above for *TCGA 1992, s 167*), then a gain equal to the held-over gain was deemed to accrue to the trustees immediately before the change in residence status. Provision was made for a corresponding reduction in the gain deemed to accrue to the trustees where before the change in residence status some of the held-over gain had been brought into charge on a disposal within the UK tax charge, e.g. on a part disposal, but this did not include a disposal under *TCGA 1992, s 171* (transfers within a group, see 13.12 COMPANIES) or *TCGA 1992, s 172* (transfer of UK branch or agency, see 44.3 OVERSEAS MATTERS) although the first subsequent disposal of the asset to which neither of these provisions applied was taken into account as if it had been made by the company. If tax assessed on the trustees as a result of the above was not paid within twelve months of the date when it became payable, the transferor could be assessed, within six years after the end of the year of assessment in which the relevant disposal was made, and he was then given a right of recovery against the trustees. Where an amount was assessed in this way, the consideration deemed to have been given for the asset in question was no longer deemed to have been reduced by the amount of the held-over gain. [*CGTA 1979, s 126C: FA 1989, Sch 14 para 2; FA 1990, s 70(5)(9); FA 1991, s 92(1)(5)*]. For changes in residence status after 18 April 1991, see 43.2 OFFSHORE SETTLEMENTS.

Gifts into dual resident trusts. Hold-over relief under *TCGA 1992, s 165* is not available where the transferees are trustees who fall to be treated as UK-resident although the general administration of the trust is carried on overseas, and where, on a notional disposal of the asset by the trustees immediately after the disposal of it to them, the trustees would be regarded for double tax relief arrangements as resident overseas and as not liable to UK tax arising on the notional disposal. Where relief has been allowed under *TCGA 1992, s 165* in respect of a disposal made after 13 March 1989 and subsequently the trustees' circumstances become before 19 March 1991 such that a disposal to them would not then qualify for relief in view of the above, a clawback of relief under *TCGA 1992, s 168* (formerly *FA 1981, s 79*) (see under emigration of transferee below) is to have effect (subject to any previous clawback under that provision) as if the trustees had become neither resident nor ordinarily resident in the UK. [*FA 1986, s 58; FA 1989, Sch 14 para 6(4); FA 1991, s 92(4)(7)*]. For trustees becoming dual resident after 18 March 1991, see 43.2 OFFSHORE SETTLEMENTS.

Emigration of transferee. Subject to the exception mentioned below, a gain held over under *TCGA 1992, s 165* will be clawed back if the individual transferee concerned becomes neither resident nor ordinarily resident in the UK or if the transferee trustees concerned become neither resident nor ordinarily resident in the UK before 19 March 1991. If the transferee is an individual the clawback may be made within six years after the end of the year of assessment in which the disposal for which hold-over relief was claimed was made; otherwise (e.g. where trustees are the transferee) no time limit is specified. The charge, which is on a gain deemed to have accrued just prior to the cessation of UK residence and ordinary residence, is reduced to the extent that the held-over gain has already been taken into account in a disposal by the transferee (e.g. on a part disposal). For the latter purpose, a disposal does not include a no gain/no loss disposal between MARRIED PERSONS (41.3) under *TCGA 1992, s 58*. If such an inter-spouse transfer occurs, a disposal by the acquiring spouse is treated as made by the spouse who originally acquired the asset to which the held-over gain related. If not paid within twelve months from the due date of payment, tax on the deemed gain assessed on the transferee can be assessed on the transferor within six years after the end of the year of assessment in which the disposal for which hold-over relief was claimed was made, although the transferor then has the right to recover any tax so paid from the transferee.

Where a deemed gain relating to a previously held-over gain has been assessed under the above, then on a subsequent disposal of the asset in question the allowable expenditure relating to it is not reduced by the held-over gain.

An exception to the above applies where the disposal for which relief was claimed was made to an individual, and

(*a*) the reason for his becoming neither resident nor ordinarily resident in the UK is that he works in an employment or office, all of the duties of which are performed abroad, and

(*b*) he again becomes UK-resident or ordinarily resident within three years of ceasing to be so, and

(*c*) in the meantime, the asset which is the subject of the hold-over relief has not been subject to a disposal by him in connection with which the allowable expenditure attaching to the asset, if the individual had been UK-resident, would have been reduced by the held-over gain; for this purpose the same provisions as above for inter-spouse transfers apply.

Where (*a*) applies, and (*b*) and (*c*) *may* apply, no assessment under the main provisions outlined above will be made before the end of the three-year period. [*TCGA 1992, s 168; FA 1991, s 92(2)(6)*]. For changes of residence of trustees after 18 March 1991, see 43.2 OFFSHORE SETTLEMENTS.

Clawback of relief on life tenant's death. The exemption otherwise available for gains arising on deemed disposals under *TCGA 1992, s 71(1)* or *s 72(1)(a)* (formerly *CGTA 1979, s 54(1)* or *s 55(1)(a)*) on the death of a life tenant etc. (see 57.9–57.11 SETTLEMENTS) does not apply to an asset (or part asset) where a claim for hold-over relief was made under *TCGA 1992, s 165* in relation to an original disposal of that asset after 13 March 1989 to the trustees. Any chargeable gain accruing to the trustees will, however, be restricted to the held-over gain (or corresponding part) on the original disposal of the asset. Where the life tenant's interest was in part only of the settled property, and that property is subject to a deemed disposal under *TCGA 1992, s 71(1)*, the clawback is proportional to the life tenant's interest. [*TCGA 1992, s 74*]. By analogy with the position when *FA 1980, s 79* (general relief for gifts) was extant before 14 March 1989, it seems to be possible for the trustees to claim hold-over relief under *TCGA 1992, s 165* (provided all the conditions are met) in respect of any gain arising from this clawback provision (Tolley's Practical Tax 1983 p 142).

25.6 RELIEF FOR GIFTS OF BUSINESS ASSETS BEFORE 14 MARCH 1989

As a result of the availability of the general relief for gifts in 25.9 below, the rules relating specifically to gifts of business assets were of restricted application for gifts after 5 April 1980 and before 14 March 1989. The scope of the provisions is given at the end of the coverage below. None of the provisions in 25.5 above applied to the hold-over relief described below.

If an individual ('*the transferor*') made a disposal not at arm's length (e.g. a gift) to a person resident or ordinarily resident in the UK ('*the transferee*') of

(*a*) an asset which was, or was an interest in, an asset which was used for the purposes of a trade, profession or vocation carried on by the transferor or by a company which was his 'family company', or

(*b*) shares or securities of a 'trading company' which was the transferor's family company,

then, subject to *CGTA 1979, s 126(2)* below, the hold-over relief described below applied on a joint claim made by the transferor and transferee. [*CGTA 1979, s 126(1)*].

Hold-over relief did not apply on a disposal if

(A) the gain arising was wholly relieved by RETIREMENT RELIEF (53), or

(B) it related to shares or securities where the 'appropriate proportion' of the gain arising was wholly relieved by RETIREMENT RELIEF (53).

Where there was no actual consideration for the disposal (as opposed to a deemed MARKET VALUE (40.1) consideration under *TCGA 1992, s 17(1)*), or where an actual consideration does not exceed the allowable expenditure within *TCGA 1992, s 38* (see 17.3 DISPOSAL) relating to the asset, the effect of a claim was that the gain otherwise chargeable on the transferor apart from this relief and the transferee's acquisition cost were each reduced by the '*held-over gain*', i.e. the gain otherwise chargeable apart from this relief and, where relevant, retirement relief (termed the '*unrelieved gain*' for the provision mentioned in the next sentence) but subject to the reductions described below. Where actual consideration exceeded the allowable expenditure, the held-over gain was the unrelieved gain less that excess but again subject to the reductions below. (*Note.* Indexation allowance was deductible in arriving at the gain otherwise chargeable but it was not allowable expenditure within *TCGA 1992, s 38.*) [*CGTA 1979, s 126(3)(5)(6)*].

The definition of '*family company*' had the meaning given by *TCGA 1992, Sch 6 para 1* (see 53.4 RETIREMENT RELIEF). '*Trade*', '*profession*' and '*vocation*' generally have the same meanings as in the *Income Tax Acts* but the commercial letting of FURNISHED HOLIDAY ACCOMMODATION (22) in the UK in respect of which the profits, etc. were chargeable under Schedule D, Case VI was treated as a trade for relief purposes in relation to disposals after 5 April 1982. A '*trading company*' was any company which exists wholly or mainly for the purpose of carrying on a trade, and any other company whose income does not consist wholly or mainly of investment income, i.e. income which, if the company were an individual, would not be earned income; and for the purpose of determining whether a company is a trading company, '*trade*' includes the occupation of woodlands managed on a commercial basis by the occupier with a view to profit. [*CGTA 1979, s 126(7)(8); FA 1984, Sch 11 para 1; ICTA 1988, Sch 19 para 7*].

Reductions in the held-over gain. If the qualifying asset disposed of was not used for the purposes of the trade, profession or vocation concerned throughout the period of its ownership by the transferor, the held-over gain was reduced by multiplying it by the fraction of which the denominator was the total period of ownership and the numerator the number of days in the period during which the asset was so used. (*Note.* In the determination of the period of ownership there was no exclusion of any period before 31 March 1982 in relation to disposals after 5 April 1988, cf. 55.6 ROLLOVER RELIEF.) Where the qualifying asset disposed of was a building or structure part only of which has been used for the trade etc. concerned over all or a 'substantial' part of the period of its ownership, the held-over gain was reduced as was 'just and reasonable'. [*CGTA 1979, Sch 4 paras 5, 6*].

If the disposal of shares or securities of a company qualified for relief and the company then had 'chargeable assets' which were not 'business assets' the held-over gain was reduced by multiplying it by the fraction of which the denominator was the then market value of the whole of the company's chargeable assets and the numerator was the then market value of the company's business assets. An asset was a '*business asset*' if it was or was an interest in an asset used for the purposes of a trade etc. carried on by the company; and an asset was a '*chargeable asset*' if on its disposal a chargeable gain would accrue. [*CGTA 1979, Sch 4 para 7*].

If the asset disposed of was a 'chargeable business asset' for the purposes of retirement relief (see 53.9 RETIREMENT RELIEF) and the held-over gain (as reduced under the above) would exceed the gain otherwise chargeable (ignoring hold-over relief itself but allowing for any deduction of retirement relief), the held-over gain was reduced by the amount of the excess. In the case of a disposal of shares or securities qualifying for retirement relief where the held-over gain (as reduced under the above) would exceed an amount equal to the 'appropriate proportion' of the gain otherwise chargeable (ignoring hold-over relief itself but allowing for any deduction of retirement relief), the held-over gain was reduced by the amount of the excess. [*CGTA 1979, Sch 4 para 8*].

Agricultural property. If an asset, or an interest in an asset,

(I) was 'agricultural property' within the inheritance tax (previously capital transfer tax) provisions of *IHTA 1984, Pt V Ch II* and either qualified for 50% inheritance tax relief in relation to a chargeable transfer made simultaneously with the disposal or would have qualified if there were a chargeable transfer on the disposal; but

(II) it failed to qualify for hold-over relief solely because the agricultural property was not used for the purposes of a trade etc. carried on as in (*a*) above,

then, notwithstanding (II) above, hold-over relief was granted to the individual transferor. Hold-over relief was also granted *mutatis mutandis* to trustees (see under settled property below) on deemed disposals under *TCGA 1992, s 71(1)* after 5 April 1982 where the agricultural property would not otherwise qualify for relief solely because it was not used for the purposes of a trade etc. carried on as in (*aa*) below. Before 10 March 1981, hold-over relief was not restricted to cases where 50% capital transfer tax relief was given. [*CGTA 1979, Sch 4 paras 1, 3; FA 1981, s 96(3)(e), (4), Sch 19 Pt VIII; FA 1989, Sch 17 Pt VII*].

Settled property. If a trustee was deemed under *TCGA 1992, s 71(1)* (see 57.9 and 57.11 SETTLEMENTS) after 5 April 1982 to have disposed of, and immediately reacquired

(*aa*) an asset which was, or was an interest in, an asset used for the purposes of a trade carried on by the trustee or by a 'relevant beneficiary', or

(*bb*) shares or securities of a trading company which conferred on the trustee not less than 25 per cent of the total voting rights then exercisable,

then hold-over relief given by *CGTA 1979, s 126(3)* (see above) applied to the disposal on a claim made by the trustee.

Where hold-over relief was granted to trustees in this way, references to the trustees were substituted for references to the transferor and transferee in *CGTA 1979, s 126(3)* above and no reduction in the held-over gain was made under *CGTA 1979, s 126(6)* above (reduction of excess of actual consideration over allowable expenditure). A '*relevant beneficiary*' was a beneficiary having an interest in possession in the settled property immediately before the deemed disposal. [*CGTA 1979, Sch 4 para 2; FA 1982, Sch 22 Pt VI*]. See also under agricultural property above.

Disposals after 5 April 1982 and before 14 March 1989. Hold-over relief as described above under *CGTA 1979, s 126, Sch 4* did not apply to any disposals or deemed disposals from individuals or trustees to individuals or trustees resident or ordinarily resident in the UK. [*FA 1982, s 82*]. The relief could therefore in practice only cover gifts by individuals to companies.

Disposals after 5 April 1981 and before 6 April 1982. Hold-over relief as described above under *CGTA 1979, s 126, Sch 4* did not apply to any disposals by individuals to individuals or trustees resident or ordinarily resident in the UK. *CGTA 1979, Sch 4 para 2* (see agricultural property and settled property above) additionally applied to deemed disposals under *CGTA 1979, s 55(1)* (as originally enacted) in relation to terminations of life interests in settled property. [*FA 1981, s 78*].

Disposals after 5 April 1980 and before 6 April 1981. Hold-over relief as described above under *CGTA 1979, s 126, Sch 4* did not apply to any disposals by individuals to individuals resident or ordinarily resident in the UK. *CGTA 1979, Sch 4 para 2* additionally applied to deemed disposals under *CGTA 1979, s 55(1)* (as originally enacted). [*FA 1980, s 79*].

25.7 GIFTS ON WHICH INHERITANCE TAX IS CHARGEABLE ETC. AFTER 13 MARCH 1989

After 13 March 1989, if

(*a*) an individual or trustees ('the transferor') make a disposal within (i)–(vi) below of an asset,

(*b*) the asset is acquired by an individual or trustees ('the transferee'), and

(*c*) a claim for relief is made by the transferor and transferee or, where trustees are the transferee, by the transferor alone,

then, subject to the conditions below and in 25.8 below, hold-over relief is available as under *TCGA 1992, s 260(3)* below. [*TCGA 1992, s 260(1); FA 2000, s 90(2)*].

A disposal is within (*a*) above if it is made otherwise than under a bargain at arm's length (e.g. a gift) and it

(i) is a chargeable transfer within *IHTA 1984* (or would be but for annual exemptions under *IHTA 1984, s 19*) and is not a potentially exempt transfer within the meaning of *IHTA 1984*, or

(ii) is an exempt transfer by virtue of *IHTA 1984, s 24, s 27* or *s 30* (political parties, maintenance funds for historic buildings (see also 21.72 EXEMPTIONS AND RELIEFS) and designated property), or, for gifts before 16 March 1998, *IHTA 1984, s 26* (gifts for public benefit — see also 21.26 EXEMPTIONS AND RELIEFS), or

(iii) is a disposition to which *IHTA 1984, s 57A* applies and by which the property disposed of becomes held on trusts referred to in *IHTA 1984, s 57A(1)(b)* (maintenance funds for historic buildings), or

(iv) by virtue of *IHTA 1984, s 71(4)* (accumulation and maintenance trusts) does not constitute an occasion on which tax is chargeable under that provision, or

(v) by virtue of *IHTA 1984, s 78(1)* (works of art etc., see also 21.33 and 21.74 EXEMPTIONS AND RELIEFS) does not constitute an occasion on which tax is chargeable under *IHTA 1984, Pt III Ch III*, or

(vi) is a disposal of an asset comprised in a settlement where, as a result of the asset or part of it becoming comprised in another settlement, there is no charge, or a reduced charge, to inheritance tax by virtue of *IHTA 1984, Sch 4 para 9, para 16* or *para 17* (maintenance funds for historic buildings).

[*TCGA 1992, s 260(2); FA 1998, Sch 27 Pt IV*].

The '*held-over gain*' on a disposal is the chargeable gain otherwise accruing and relief is given by deducting this amount from the gain otherwise accruing to the transferor and from the consideration otherwise regarded as being given by the transferee. [*TCGA 1992, s 260(3)(4)*].

Hold-over relief is reduced or eliminated to nil on a disposal where there is actual consideration (as opposed to any deemed MARKET VALUE (40) consideration) which exceeds the allowable expenditure under *TCGA 1992, s 38* (see 17.3 DISPOSAL), any such excess being deducted from the held-over gain; but no deduction is made of any such excess where *TCGA 1992, s 260(3)* above applies to a deemed disposal under *TCGA 1992, s 71(1)* or *s 72(1)* (see 57.9–57.11 SETTLEMENTS). (*Note.* Indexation allowance is deductible in arriving at the gain otherwise chargeable but it is not allowable expenditure within *TCGA 1992, s 38.*) Where part of a gain is relieved by RETIREMENT RELIEF (53), the held-over gain is reduced by so much, if any, of the excess of actual consideration over allowable expenditure as exceeds the part so relieved. [*TCGA 1992, s 260(5)(9)*].

Hold-over relief does not apply to a disposal if it arises by virtue of *TCGA 1992, s 116(10)(b)* (disposal of qualifying corporate bonds derived from shares giving rise to deferred gain, see 49.3 QUALIFYING CORPORATE BONDS). [*TCGA 1992, s 260(6)*].

Hold-over relief does not apply, so far as any gain accruing in accordance with *TCGA 1992, Sch 5B paras 4, 5* (crystallisation of a deferred gain on the happening of a chargeable event in relation to enterprise investment scheme shares, see 20 ENTERPRISE INVESTMENT SCHEME (AND BES)) is concerned. [*TCGA 1992, s 260(6A); FA 1995, Sch 13 para 4(2)*].

Hold-over relief does not apply, so far as any gain accruing in accordance with *TCGA 1992, Sch 5C paras 4, 5* (crystallisation of a deferred gain on the happening of a chargeable event in relation to venture capital trust shares, see 65.10 VENTURE CAPITAL TRUSTS) is concerned. [*TCGA 1992, s 260(6B); FA 1995, s 72(6)(8)*].

Where hold-over relief is claimed on a transfer within (i) above, the transferee may deduct for capital gains tax purposes on a subsequent disposal made by him any inheritance tax attributable to the value of the asset on the transfer to him which qualified for hold-over relief. The tax deductible may be varied if the inheritance tax itself is varied but it cannot in any circumstances give rise to an allowable loss. [*TCGA 1992, s 260(7)(8)*]. The same treatment applies if a hold-over relief claim *could have been made* (Revenue Capital Gains Manual CG 67050). See also 33.2 INTERACTION WITH OTHER TAXES.

Where a disposal is only partly within (i)–(v) above, or is a disposal within (vi) above on which there is a reduced charge as mentioned therein, the foregoing provisions apply to an appropriate part of the disposal. [*TCGA 1992, s 260(10)*].

As a claim applies separately to each asset, the comments made about the general relief for gifts from 1980 to 1989 in 25.9 below regarding the treatment of property as separate assets would seem also to apply to the above relief.

25.8 **Restrictions on, and clawback of, hold-over relief under TCGA 1992, s 260**

Gifts to non-residents. Relief is denied under *TCGA 1992, s 260* where the transferee is neither UK-resident nor ordinarily resident. Relief is also denied where the transferee is an individual who though UK-resident or ordinarily resident is regarded under a double tax agreement as resident overseas in circumstances where he would not be liable to a UK tax charge on a gain arising on a disposal of an asset immediately after its acquisition. [*TCGA 1992, s 261*].

Gifts into dual resident trusts. TCGA 1992, s 169 (formerly *FA 1986, s 58*) (see 25.5 above) operates *mutatis mutandis* for hold-over relief claimed under *TCGA 1992, s 260* in respect of gifts after 13 March 1989 as it does for hold-over relief under *TCGA 1992, s 165* in respect of gifts made after that date. [*TCGA 1992, s 169*].

Emigration of transferee. TCGA 1992, s 168 (formerly *FA 1981, s 79*) (see 25.5 above) operates *mutatis mutandis* for hold-over relief claimed under *TCGA 1992, s 260* in respect of gifts after 13 March 1989 as it does for hold-over relief under *TCGA 1992, s 165* in respect of gifts made after that date. [*TCGA 1992, s 168*].

Clawback of relief on life tenant's death. TCGA 1992, s 74 (see 25.5 above) operates *mutatis mutandis* for hold-over relief claimed under *TCGA 1992, s 260* in respect of gifts after 13 March 1989 as it does for hold-over relief under *TCGA 1992, s 165* in respect of gifts made after that date. [*TCGA 1992, s 74*].

25.9 GENERAL RELIEF FOR GIFTS FROM 1980 TO 1989

A general relief for gifts applied after 5 April 1980 and before 14 March 1989.

After 5 April 1982 and before 14 March 1989, relief could be claimed where the transferor, who could be either (*a*) an individual; or

(*b*) the trustees of a settlement

disposed of an asset otherwise than at arm's length to

(i) an individual resident or ordinarily resident in the UK; or

(ii) trustees resident or ordinarily resident in the UK (but see under gifts into dual resident trusts).

The effect of a claim was that the gain otherwise chargeable (less any RETIREMENT RELIEF (53)), and the transferee's acquisition cost, were each reduced by the '*held-over gain*', i.e. the gain otherwise chargeable (less any retirement relief) less any excess of actual consideration over the aggregate of allowable expenditure within *TCGA 1992, s 38* and any retirement relief.

Whilst indexation allowance was deductible in arriving at the gain otherwise chargeable, it was not allowable expenditure within *TCGA 1992, s 38* (see 17.3 DISPOSAL). Ignoring cases involving retirement relief this meant that where there was no consideration or where the consideration was not greater than the allowable expenditure, the whole of the gain otherwise chargeable could be held over. In other cases not involving retirement relief a gain was left in charge equal to the lower of the excess of consideration over the allowable expenditure and the gain otherwise chargeable.

A claim had to be made jointly by the transferor and transferee unless the transfer was to trustees when only the transferor needed to claim.

In computing any chargeable gain accruing on the subsequent disposal of the asset, the transferee may deduct any inheritance tax (or capital transfer tax) attributable to the value of the asset on the original transfer, being either a chargeable transfer or a potentially exempt transfer which proves to be a chargeable transfer. The tax deductible may be varied on the subsequent death of the original transferor or otherwise but cannot create an allowable loss on the subsequent disposal. See also 33.2 INTERACTION WITH OTHER TAXES.

Gifts into dual resident trusts. TCGA 1992, s 169 (formerly *FA 1986, s 58*; see 25.5 above and note certain changes for trustees becoming dual resident after 18 March 1991) operated (and continues to operate after 13 March 1989) *mutatis mutandis* for hold-over relief claimed under the above provisions in respect of gifts made after 17 March 1986 and before 14 March 1989 as it does to hold-over relief under *TCGA 1992, s 165* in respect of gifts made after 13 March 1989. However, the clawback of relief when trustees became dual resident after 17 March 1986 and before 18 March 1991 operated in respect of gifts made before, on or after 18 March 1986.

Emigration of transferee. TCGA 1992, s 168 (see 25.5 above and note certain changes for trustees emigrating after 18 March 1991) operated (and continues to operate after 13 March 1989) *mutatis mutandis* for hold-over relief claimed under the above provisions in respect of gifts made after 5 April 1981 and before 14 March 1989 as it does to hold-over relief under *TCGA 1992, s 165* in respect of gifts made after 13 March 1989.

Clawback of relief on life tenant's death. TCGA 1992, s 74 (see 25.5 above) operated (and continues to operate after 13 March 1989) *mutatis mutandis* for hold-over relief claimed under the above provisions in respect of interests terminating after 5 April 1982 and where the original gift to the trustees was after 5 April 1981 and before 14 March 1989 as it does to hold-over relief under *TCGA 1992, s 165* in respect of gifts made after 13 March 1989. See 8.12 ASSETS HELD ON 31 MARCH 1982 for the treatment by the Revenue of the clawback in relevant cases occurring after 5 April 1988.

After 5 April 1981 and before 6 April 1982, (*b*) above did not apply.

Before 6 April 1981, neither (*b*) nor (ii) above applied.

[*TCGA 1992, ss 67, 74, 168, 169; CGTA 1979, s 56A; FA 1980, s 79; FA 1981, ss 78, 79; FA 1982, s 82, s 84(3); FA 1986, s 58, s 101(2); FA 1989, s 124(1)(3), Sch 17 Pt VII; FA 1991, s 92(2)(4)(6)(7)*].

Where the property transferred consisted in law of two or more separate assets, the claim applied separately to each asset, and so some gains could be left in charge to be covered by annual exemptions or losses etc. Similarly, where freehold land was transferred to two or more joint tenants or tenants in common, a claim could be made individually in relation to the interest transferred to each recipient (Tolley's Practical Tax 1983 p 178, 1984 p 2 and 1985 p 195).

25.10 TRANSFER OF BUSINESS TO A COMPANY

Where a person who is not a company transfers to a company a business as a going concern, together with the whole assets of the business (or together with the whole of such assets other than cash) ('the old assets') and the transfer is made wholly or partly in exchange for shares issued by the company to the transferor ('the new assets'), the chargeable gain on the disposal of the old assets (or part thereof) is deferred by reducing the amount otherwise chargeable, by the fraction A/B, where 'A' is the 'cost of the new assets' and 'B' the value of the overall consideration received by the transferor in exchange for the business.

'*The cost of the new assets*' means the total allowable expenditure under *TCGA 1992, s 38(1)(a)* if the new assets were disposed of as a whole in circumstances giving rise to a chargeable gain. (See 17.3 DISPOSAL.) The total expenditure otherwise allowable on the new assets is reduced by the amount of the chargeable gain deferred, and if the new assets comprise different classes of share, the reduction is apportioned by reference to the market value of each class of share at the time of their acquisition by the transferor. Deferment on part of the gain on the old assets therefore remains until the new assets are disposed of. [*TCGA 1992, s 162*].

The only point of time at which the test should be made as to whether a business is being transferred 'as a going concern' is at the time of transfer, so that if the business continues without interruption past that time relief will be available notwithstanding the existence of a planned move of the entire assets of the business from one place to another (*Gordon v CIR (and cross-appeal) CS 1991, 64 TC 173*).

The Revenue are prepared not to treat the assumption of liabilities by the transferee company as consideration for the transfer, and the relief is not precluded if some or all of the liabilities of the business are not taken over by the company (Revenue Pamphlet IR 1, D32). However, it seems that the Revenue treat the assumption of provisions for partnership income tax liabilities as denying relief (Tolley's Practical Tax 1984 p 26 and Revenue Capital Gains Manual CG 65748). If some of the assets are retained by the original owner, relief under *TCGA 1992, s 162* above is not available and liability to capital gains tax arises by reference to the market value of any chargeable assets transferred, e.g. goodwill. If the market value of such an asset exceeds the consideration given by the company, the Revenue will accept that the excess represents a gift and that the capital gain may be deferred by means of a joint election under *TCGA 1992, s 165* (see 25.1–25.6 above) (Tolley's Practical Tax 1983 pp 24, 188). Where a partner is a company, *TCGA 1992, s 162* strictly cannot apply because individual partners are not transferring the whole business but only their collective shares. However, the Revenue will view each partner separately thus enabling individual, but not company, partners to obtain relief. In addition, relief will be granted to individual partners taking shares even though others take purely cash. In all cases the whole of the business must be exchanged wholly or partly for shares (Tolley's Practical Tax 1986 p 23 and Revenue Capital Gains Manual CG 65757).

Although the above relief is mandatory, the Revenue is prepared to allow rollover relief as an alternative if appropriate. See 55.1 ROLLOVER RELIEF. However, it is not clear whether the Revenue will allow the above relief *not* to apply in the absence of a rollover relief claim (e.g. so as to utilise allowable losses, annual exempt amount etc.).

Example

W carries on an antiquarian bookselling business. He decides to form an unquoted company, P Ltd, to carry on the business. He transfers, in August 2000, the whole of the business undertaking, assets and liabilities to P Ltd, in consideration for the issue of shares, plus an amount left outstanding on interest-free loan. The business assets and liabilities transferred are valued as follows

		Value	Chargeable gain (after indexation to April 1998)
	£	£	£
Freehold shop premises		80,000	52,000
Goodwill		36,000	26,000
Fixtures and fittings		4,000	—
Trading stock		52,000	—
Debtors		28,000	—
		200,000	
Mortgage on shop	50,000		
Trade creditors	20,000	70,000	—
		£130,000	£78,000

The company issues 100,000 £1 ordinary shares, valued at par, to W in August 2000, and the amount left outstanding is £30,000. In March 2001, W sells 20,000 of his shares for £45,000 to X. W's remaining shareholding is then worth, say, £155,000.

(i) Amount of chargeable gain rolled over on transfer of the business

$$\frac{100,000}{130,000} \times £78,000 \qquad £60,000$$

Of the chargeable gain, £18,000 (£78,000 – £60,000) remains taxable but is subject to TAPER RELIEF (60).

The allowable cost of W's shares is £40,000 (£100,000 – £60,000).

(ii) On the sale of shares to X, W realises a chargeable gain

	£
Disposal consideration	45,000
Allowable cost $£40,000 \times \dfrac{45,000}{45,000 + 155,000}$	9,000
Chargeable gain*	£36,000

* No indexation due as shares acquired after March 1998 and no taper relief due as shares held for less than 12 months

Sumption: Capital Gains Tax. See A14.08.

26 Indexation

Cross-references. See 7 ASSETS HELD ON 6 APRIL 1965; 8 ASSETS HELD ON 31 MARCH 1982; 17 DISPOSAL; 36.13 LAND for concessionary treatment of indexation allowance on the merger of leases; 59 SHARES AND SECURITIES—IDENTIFICATION RULES; 64.1, 64.2, 64.4 UNIT TRUSTS ETC. for Revenue practice in the case of unit trust units, investment trust shares and open-ended investment company shares acquired under monthly savings schemes.

Sumption: Capital Gains Tax. See A4B.

26.1 INDEXATION ALLOWANCE

General. In respect of disposals after 5 April 1982 (31 March 1982 for companies) an indexation allowance is deductible under certain circumstances from the 'unindexed' or 'gross' gain, or is added, for disposals on or after the '1985 date' and before 30 November 1993, to the 'unindexed' loss. For the purposes of capital gains tax, though not those of corporation tax on chargeable gains, no indexation allowance is available in respect of expenditure incurred after 31 March 1998, and for expenditure incurred on or before that date and falling to be deducted on a disposal after 5 April 1998 indexation allowance is computed up to and including April 1998 only.

For disposals after 5 April 1998 by individuals, trustees and personal representatives, indexation allowance, where available, is deducted before applying TAPER RELIEF (60) to the gain.

Special provisions apply to the calculation of the allowance in relation to disposals involving ASSETS HELD ON 31 MARCH 1982 (8) where made on or after the '1985 date' or, again, on or after 6 April 1988. See that chapter for details.

Disposal on or after 30 November 1993. For disposals on or after 30 November 1993 the gain (if any) arrived at by deducting an amount of allowable expenditure from the amount of consideration realised (see 17 DISPOSAL), or deemed to be realised, on the disposal is termed an '*unindexed gain*'. There is to be allowed against the unindexed gain an 'indexation allowance', which is the aggregate of the 'indexed rise' in each item of 'relevant allowable expenditure', so as to give the gain for the purposes of *TCGA 1992*.

An indexation allowance is only allowed against an unindexed gain. If the disposal gives rise to a loss, no indexation allowance is allowed notwithstanding anything in *TCGA 1992, s 16* (computation of losses; see 39.2 LOSSES), and if the indexation allowance equals or exceeds the unindexed gain on a disposal so as to extinguish it, the disposal is one on which, after taking account of the indexation allowance, neither a gain nor a loss accrues.

The rules outlined above are subject to the special provisions in 26.3–26.8 below. In addition, a transitional relief applies as in 26.2 below for 1993/94 and 1994/95 in respect of 'indexation losses' in the case of individuals and trustees of settlements made before 30 November 1993.

'*Relevant allowable expenditure*' is allowable expenditure within *TCGA 1992, s 38(1)(a)* and *s 38(1)(b)*, i.e. basically acquisition cost or value, taken for these purposes as incurred when the asset is acquired or provided, and expenditure on enhancement and on establishing, preserving and defending title and rights to the asset, such expenditure being taken for these purposes as incurred when it becomes due and payable (see 17.3(*a*)–(*c*) DISPOSAL). Disposal costs are excluded. In determining relevant allowable expenditure, account is taken of any provision of any enactment which, for the purpose of computing gains, increases, excludes or reduces any item of expenditure, or provides for it to be written down. For the purposes of capital gains tax, though not those of corporation tax on chargeable gains, 'relevant allowable expenditure' *excludes* any item of expenditure incurred **after 31 March 1998**.

The '*indexed rise*' in each item of relevant allowable expenditure is computed by multiplying that item by a figure (rounded to the nearest third decimal place) calculated by the formula

$$\frac{RD - RI}{RI}, \text{ where}$$

RD = retail prices index for the month in which the disposal occurs or, if earlier and for capital gains tax (not corporation tax) purposes, April 1998; and

RI = retail prices index for March 1982 or the month in which the expenditure was incurred, whichever is the later.

If, in relation to any item of expenditure, RD in the formula is equal to, or less than, RI, there is no indexed rise for that item.

The freezing of indexation allowance at its April 1998 level for capital gains tax (not corporation tax) disposals after 5 April 1998 does not affect the computation of a gain which arose on an actual or deemed disposal on or before that date but by virtue of any CGT enactment does not come into charge until after that date. Examples might be the coming into charge of a gain previously deferred by reinvestment in an EIS company (see 20.9 ENTERPRISE INVESTMENT SCHEME (AND BES)) or a VCT (see 65.10 VENTURE CAPITAL TRUSTS).

[*TCGA 1992, s 53, s 54, s 288(1); ICTA 1988, s 833(2); FA 1994, s 93(1)–(3)(11); FA 1998, s 122(1)–(3)(6)(7), s 123(3)–(5)*].

The above rules do not apply to 'section 104 holdings' (i.e. single asset pools) of shares or securities, for which see 59.4 SHARES AND SECURITIES—IDENTIFICATION RULES.

The figure given by the formula is commonly called the '*indexation factor*'. The consistent calculation of the indexation factor to more than three decimal places is generally accepted.

The Revenue publishes the retail prices index and the associated indexation factors in a monthly press release. Yearly tables of indexation factors are contained in Tolley's Tax Data. Both the retail prices index and the April 1998 indexation factors are reproduced below.

Values of the retail prices index (RPI) for March 1982 and subsequent months are as follows.

	1982	**1983**	**1984**	**1985**	**1986**	**1987**	**1988**	**1989**	**1990**	**1991**
January	—	82.61	86.84	91.20	96.25	100.0	103.3	111.0	119.5	130.2
February	—	82.97	87.20	91.94	96.60	100.4	103.7	111.8	120.2	130.9
March	79.44	83.12	87.48	92.80	96.73	100.6	104.1	112.3	121.4	131.4
April	81.04	84.28	88.64	94.78	97.67	101.8	105.8	114.3	125.1	133.1
May	81.62	84.64	88.97	95.21	97.85	101.9	106.2	115.0	126.2	133.5
June	81.85	84.84	89.20	95.41	97.79	101.9	106.6	115.4	126.7	134.1
July	81.88	85.30	89.10	95.23	97.52	101.8	106.7	115.5	126.8	133.8
August	81.90	85.68	89.94	95.49	97.82	102.1	107.9	115.8	128.1	134.1
September	81.85	86.06	90.11	95.44	98.30	102.4	108.4	116.6	129.3	134.6
October	82.26	86.36	90.67	95.59	98.45	102.9	109.5	117.5	130.3	135.1
November	82.66	86.67	90.95	95.92	99.29	103.4	110.0	118.5	130.0	135.6
December	82.51	86.89	90.87	96.05	99.62	103.3	110.3	118.8	129.9	135.7

26.1 Indexation

	1992	1993	1994	1995	1996	1997	1998	1999	2000
January	135.6	137.9	141.3	146.0	150.2	154.4	159.5	163.4	166.6
February	136.3	138.8	142.1	146.9	150.9	155.0	160.3	163.7	167.5
March	136.7	139.3	142.5	147.5	151.5	155.4	160.8	164.1	168.4
April	138.8	140.6	144.2	149.0	152.6	156.3	162.6	165.2	170.1
May	139.3	141.1	144.7	149.6	152.9	156.9	163.5	165.6	170.7
June	139.3	141.0	144.7	149.8	153.0	157.5	163.4	165.6	171.1
July	138.8	140.7	144.0	149.1	152.4	157.5	163.0	165.1	
August	138.9	141.3	144.7	149.9	153.1	158.5	163.7	165.5	
September	139.4	141.9	145.0	150.6	153.8	159.3	164.4	166.2	
October	139.9	141.8	145.2	149.8	153.8	159.5	164.5	166.5	
November	139.7	141.6	145.3	149.8	153.9	159.6	164.4	166.7	
December	139.2	141.9	146.0	150.7	154.4	160.0	164.4	167.3	

Re-referencing of retail prices index. The index is calculated by the Office for National Statistics and was re-referenced so as to make January 1987 = 100.0 and equivalent to 394.5 on the former index where January 1974 = 100.0. In the above table, all the index figures for months before January 1987 have been re-indexed to the January 1987 base. This has been done by dividing the index on the January 1974 base for such a month by 3.945 (i.e. 394.5 divided by 100.0) and rounding to two places of decimals (e.g. the index for December 1985 is 393.0 on the January 1974 base, which would have been the figure announced at the time, and is 96.05 on the January 1987 base). By so rounding the re-indexed figures, the same level of accuracy (to 1 in 10,000) is maintained compared with the figures quoted for months after December 1986.

The Revenue originally announced an incorrect RPI figure of 144.7 for September 1994 (the correct figure being 145.0 as shown above) and the error was repeated in notes to the 1996/97 self-assessment tax return. Errors consequently made in tax returns already submitted for 1994/95 and 1995/96 and resulting in tax underpayments will not be corrected by the Revenue. Any taxpayer who made a disposal in September 1994 and has consequently overpaid tax should write to his tax office. (Revenue Press Release 13 August 1997).

The indexation factors for disposals in April 1998 are also relevant (other than for corporation tax purposes) for disposals after April 1998 of assets acquired before April 1998 (see above). In view of their added importance, those indexation factors are set out in full below.

Indexation factors for CGT disposals in or after April 1998 (per Revenue Press Release 20 May 1998)

	1982	*1983*	*1984*	*1985*	*1986*	*1987*	*1988*	*1989*	*1990*
January	—	0.968	0.872	0.783	0.689	0.626	0.574	0.465	0.361
February	—	0.960	0.865	0.769	0.683	0.620	0.568	0.454	0.353
March	1.047	0.956	0.859	0.752	0.681	0.616	0.562	0.448	0.339
April	1.006	0.929	0.834	0.716	0.665	0.597	0.537	0.423	0.300
May	0.992	0.921	0.828	0.708	0.662	0.596	0.531	0.414	0.288
June	0.987	0.917	0.823	0.704	0.663	0.596	0.525	0.409	0.283
July	0.986	0.906	0.825	0.707	0.667	0.597	0.524	0.408	0.282
August	0.985	0.898	0.808	0.703	0.662	0.593	0.507	0.404	0.269
September	0.987	0.889	0.804	0.704	0.654	0.588	0.500	0.395	0.258
October	0.977	0.883	0.793	0.701	0.652	0.580	0.485	0.384	0.248
November	0.967	0.876	0.788	0.695	0.638	0.573	0.478	0.372	0.251
December	0.971	0.871	0.789	0.693	0.632	0.574	0.474	0.369	0.252

	1991	1992	1993	1994	1995	1996	1997	1998
January	0.249	0.199	0.179	0.151	0.114	0.083	0.053	0.019
February	0.242	0.193	0.171	0.144	0.107	0.078	0.049	0.014
March	0.237	0.189	0.167	0.141	0.102	0.073	0.046	0.011
April	0.222	0.171	0.156	0.128	0.091	0.066	0.040	—
May	0.218	0.167	0.152	0.124	0.087	0.063	0.036	—
June	0.213	0.167	0.153	0.124	0.085	0.063	0.032	—
July	0.215	0.171	0.156	0.129	0.091	0.067	0.032	—
August	0.213	0.171	0.151	0.124	0.085	0.062	0.026	—
September	0.208	0.166	0.146	0.121	0.080	0.057	0.021	—
October	0.204	0.162	0.147	0.120	0.085	0.057	0.019	—
November	0.199	0.164	0.148	0.119	0.085	0.057	0.019	—
December	0.198	0.168	0.146	0.114	0.079	0.053	0.016	—

Examples

(1) X acquired an asset in November 1984 for £28,000. He disposes of the asset on 11 May 2000 for £99,000. The retail prices index for November 1984 is 90.95 and for April 1998 it is 162.6.

	£
Sale consideration	99,000
Cost of asset	28,000
Unindexed gain	71,000
Indexation allowance	

$$\frac{162.6 - 90.95}{90.95} = 0.788$$

0.788 × £28,000	22,064
Chargeable gain (subject to TAPER RELIEF (60))	£48,936

(2) Facts as in (1) above except that X receives consideration of £18,000.

	£
Sale consideration	18,000
Cost of asset	28,000
Allowable loss (no indexation allowance available)	£10,000

(3) Facts as in (1) above except that X received consideration of £40,000.

	£
Sale consideration	40,000
Cost of asset	28,000
Unindexed gain	£12,000

Indexation allowance is as in (1) above (£22,064) but as this exceeds the amount of the unindexed gain, the disposal gives rise neither to a gain nor to a loss.

(4) Facts as in (1) above except that the acquisition and disposal are by a company, X Ltd. The retail prices index for May 2000 is 170.7.

	£
Sale consideration	99,000
Cost of asset	28,000
Unindexed gain carried forward	£71,000

Unindexed gain brought forward	£71,000
Indexation allowance	
$\frac{170.7 - 90.95}{90.95} = 0.877$	
0.877 × £28,000	24,556
Chargeable gain	£46,444

Disposal on or after the '1985' date and before 30 November 1993. Subject to below, for disposals on or after 6 April 1985 or, for companies, 1 April 1985 (the '1985 date') and before 30 November 1993, the gain or loss arrived at by deducting allowable expenditure from the amount realised, or deemed to be realised, on the disposal was termed the '*unindexed gain or loss*'. There was to be deducted from the unindexed gain or, as the case may have been, added to the unindexed loss, an 'indexation allowance' which was the aggregate of the indexed rise in each item of 'relevant allowable expenditure'.

The indexation allowance was set against the unindexed gain or, as the case may have been, added to the unindexed loss. If the allowance exceeded any unindexed gain, the excess constituted an allowable loss. Where there was no unindexed gain or loss, there was an allowable loss equal to the indexation allowance.

[*TCGA 1992, ss 53, 54, s 288(1); ICTA 1988, s 833(2)*].

See above for 'relevant allowable expenditure', 'indexed rise', 'indexation factor' and values of the retail prices index for March 1982 and subsequent months.

The rules outlined above are subject to the special provisions in 26.3–26.8 below. In addition, a transitional relief applies as in 26.2 below for 1993/94 and 1994/95 in respect of 'indexation losses' in the case of individuals and trustees of settlements made before 30 November 1993.

For disposals after 3 July 1987 and before 30 November 1993, the allowance was not available in respect of disposals of shares in a building society (within *Building Societies Act 1986*) or shares in a registered industrial and provident society (as defined by *ICTA 1988, s 486*). [*TCGA 1992, s 111, s 288(1); FA 1994, s 93(7)(11), Sch 26 Pt V*].

For disposals by companies after 14 March 1988 and before 30 November 1993, the allowance was restricted or excluded in certain cases involving a debt on a security owed by, or shares in, a 'linked company'. [*TCGA 1992, ss 182–184; F(No 2)A 1992, s 46(1)(7); FA 1994, s 93(7)(11), Sch 26 Pt V*]. Full details are given in TOLLEY'S CORPORATION TAX under Capital Gains.

For disposals after 19 March 1990 and before 30 November 1993, the allowance was not available in respect of disposals of rights in property to which '*collective investment arrangements*' (i.e. arrangements constituting a 'collective investment scheme' within *Financial Services Act 1986*) related where at some time in the 'relevant ownership period' at least 90 per cent of the then market value of all of the property (except cash awaiting investment) then within the arrangements was represented by assets (including currency and debts other than securities disposed of as in *FA 1993, Sch 17 para 2* and *para 4*) gains on the disposal of which at the time the rights were disposed of by a UK resident person would not be chargeable gains, shares in a building society (within *Building Societies Act 1986*), or both such assets and such shares. If under the arrangements the participants' contributions, and the profits etc. out of which payments were to be made to the participants, were pooled in relation to separate parts of the property, and the disposal was of rights in property falling within a separate part, this 90 per cent test applied only to that part. The '*relevant ownership period*' was the period beginning on 1 April 1982 or, if later, the earliest date on which any 'relevant consideration' was given for the rights, and ending on the date of the disposal. '*Relevant consideration*' was consideration which would be taken into account as allowable expenditure on the disposal, including consideration given by or on behalf of a predecessor in title whose acquisition cost represented (directly or indirectly) the whole or any part of the acquisition cost of the disposer. [*TCGA 1992, s 103; FA 1993, s 169, Sch 17 para 8; FA 1994, s 93(7)(11), Sch 26 Pt V*].

In respect of disposals on or after the '1985 date' (see above) and before 2 July 1986, there was no indexation allowance in respect of a disposal of 24 GOVERNMENT SECURITIES or 49 QUALIFYING CORPORATE BONDS. Disposals after 27 February 1986 and before 30 November 1993 of securities within the accrued income scheme (see 59.6 SHARES AND SECURITIES—IDENTIFICATION RULES) had indexation allowance calculated and allowed as above for assets generally but, for disposals on or after the '1985 date' and before 27 February 1986, the indexation provisions which applied generally for disposal on or after the '1982 date' and before the '1985 date' (see below) applied. [*FA 1985, s 68(2)*].

Disposals on or after the '1982 date' and before the '1985 date'. For disposals on or after 6 April 1982 or, for companies, 1 April 1982 (the '1982 date') and before the '1985 date' (see above), the gain (if any) arrived at by deducting allowable expenditure from the amount realised, or deemed to be realised, on the disposal was termed a '*gross gain*'. There was to be deducted from it an 'indexation allowance' which was the aggregate of the 'indexed rise' in each item of 'relevant expenditure', provided the asset had been held for the 'qualifying period'.

The '*qualifying period*' was twelve months, beginning on the date on which the asset in question was acquired or provided.

See above for '*relevant allowable expenditure*'.

The '*indexed rise*' in each item of relevant allowable expenditure was computed by multiplying that item by a figure (rounded to the nearest third decimal place) calculated by the formula

$$\frac{RD - RI}{RI}, \text{ where}$$

RD = retail prices index for the month in which the disposal occurred; and

RI = retail prices index for the later of March 1982 or for the twelfth month after the expenditure was incurred.

If, in relation to any particular expenditure item, the month in which that item was incurred was less than thirteen months before the month of disposal, or RD in the above formula was equal to, or less than, RI, there was no indexed rise for that item.

An indexation allowance was only given where there was a gross gain (see above). Where there was a loss, there was no indexation allowance and no allowable loss could be created by such an allowance. Where the allowance exceeded the gross gain, there was to be neither a chargeable gain nor an allowable loss. [*FA 1982, ss 86, 87*].

See above for 'indexation factor' and values of the retail prices index for March 1982 and subsequent months.

The rules outlined above are subject to the special provisions in 26.3–26.8 below.

26.2 **Indexation losses: transitional relief in respect of 1993/94 and 1994/95 for individuals and trustees of settlements made before 30 November 1993**

(1) *Introduction.* Consequent to, inter alia, the provisions in 26.1 above which, broadly, for disposals after 29 November 1993 deny the giving of indexation allowance where it would otherwise create or increase a loss, a transitional form of relief applies to mitigate this denial

for 1993/94 and 1994/95 in relation to chargeable gains and allowable losses accruing to an individual or trustees of a settlement made before 30 November 1993 ('*the taxpayer*'). Companies and personal representatives are excluded from the relief. [*FA 1994, s 93(11), Sch 12 para 1*].

(2) *Determinations of indexation losses under old indexation rules.* If

(*a*) an allowable loss accrues on a disposal made after 29 November 1993 and, under 'the old indexation rules', a greater allowable loss would have accrued, there is an '*indexation loss*' in respect of the disposal equal to the amount by which the allowable loss which would have accrued under the old indexation rules exceeds the allowable loss accruing on the disposal; or

(*b*) a disposal made after 29 November 1993 is one on which neither a gain nor a loss accrues and, under the old indexation rules, an allowable loss would have accrued, there is an indexation loss in respect of the disposal equal to the amount of the allowable loss that would have accrued under the old indexation rules.

If the total amount of chargeable gains accruing to the taxpayer in either 1993/94 or 1994/95 exceeds the allowable losses accruing in that year, there is a '*relevant gain*' for that year equal to the excess.

The foregoing determinations of any amount of indexation loss and relevant gain are made without regard to *FA 1994, Sch 12 paras 4–7* below. [*FA 1994, Sch 12 para 2*].

'*The old indexation rules*' means *TCGA 1992* as it would have effect if *FA 1994, s 93(1)–(5)* (see 26.1 above for *subsections (1)–(3)*, 8.7 ASSETS HELD ON 31 MARCH 1982 for *subsection (4)* and 26.4 below for *subsection (5)*) and the repeal of *TCGA 1992, s 103* and *s 111* by *FA 1994, s 93(7)* (see 26.1 above; collective investment schemes and building society shares) had not come into force. [*FA 1994, Sch 12 para 8(1)(2)*]. In broad terms, the old indexation rules therefore means the provisions of *TCGA 1992* pertaining for disposals immediately before 30 November 1993 (when indexation allowance could increase or create a loss).

(3) *Appropriation of capital asset to trading stock and capital loss on disposal of shares treated as deduction from income.* The cases in which the appropriation of an asset by the taxpayer is treated under *TCGA 1992, s 161(1)* (appropriation of capital asset to trading stock; see 6.3 ASSETS) as a disposal of the asset include cases in which, if he sold the asset for its market value, an allowable loss would have accrued to him under the old indexation rules. Where, but for an election under *TCGA 1992, s 161(3)* (gain or loss treated as arising under *TCGA 1992, s 161(1)* taken into account for Schedule D, Case I rather than capital gains tax; see 6.3 ASSETS), an asset appropriated (an event called a '*relevant appropriation*') by the taxpayer would have been treated as disposed of under *TCGA 1992, s 161(1)* and (2)(*a*) or (*b*) above would have applied on the disposal, *FA 1994, Sch 12 para 1* and *para 2* (above) and *FA 1994, Sch 12 para 6* and *para 7* (see below) apply as if the asset had been so treated, to determine for the purposes of *TCGA 1992, s 161(3)* any increase (references to an increase in any loss, where (2)(*b*) above applies, include a reference to the creation of the loss for the purposes of this provision (*FA 1994, Sch 12 para 3*) and *FA 1994, Sch 12 para 6* and *para 7* below) to be made in the amount of any allowable loss.

ICTA 1988, ss 574–576 (loss incurred by individual on shares subscribed for in unquoted trading companies treated as income deduction; see 39.13 LOSSES) apply if an individual who has subscribed for shares as mentioned in *ICTA 1988, s 574(1)* disposes of them in circumstances where (2)(*b*) above applies as they apply in other cases. Where an individual makes a claim for relief under *ICTA 1988, s 574(1)* in the case of a disposal in respect of which there is an indexation loss, *FA 1994, Sch 12 para 6* and *para 7* below apply to determine any increase to be made, for the purposes of that provision, in the amount of the allowable loss, and *FA 1994, Sch 12 para 4* and *para 5* below apply to so much only of the indexation loss as is not relieved under *ICTA 1988, s 574*. [*FA 1994, Sch 12 para 3*].

(4) *Relief against chargeable gains for 1993/94.* Where in the case of any taxpayer,

(*a*) there is a relevant gain (see (2) above) for 1993/94,

(*b*) the relevant gain exceeds the exempt amount for that year (i.e. £5,800 for individuals and settlements for the disabled and £2,900 for other settlements, subject to reduction for 'grouping' of both kinds of settlement as in 57.4 and 57.5 SETTLEMENTS), and

(*c*) there are indexation losses (see (2) above) in respect of any disposals made in that year (which, by definition, would have to be disposals made after 29 November 1993),

then, for the purposes of *TCGA 1992*, the amount by which the total amount of chargeable gains accruing to the taxpayer in that year exceeds the allowable losses accruing in that year (i.e. such excess being the amount of the relevant gain although not so stated in the legislation) is reduced (including reducing an amount to nil) by the amount mentioned below, and is so reduced before the deduction of any allowable losses carried forward from any previous year or carried back under *TCGA 1992, s 62* (losses of year of death carried back against gains of previous three years; see 16.5 DEATH) from any subsequent year. [*FA 1994, Sch 12 para 4(1), para 8(3)*].

The amount of the reduction referred to above is so much of the total of indexation losses in respect of disposals made in 1993/94 as does not exceed £10,000 or the amount by which the relevant gain exceeds the exempt amount, whichever is the smaller. [*FA 1994, Sch 12 para 4(2)*].

(5) *Relief against chargeable gains for 1994/95.* Where in the case of any taxpayer,

(*a*) there is a relevant gain for 1994/95,

(*b*) the relevant gain exceeds the exempt amount for that year (i.e. the same amounts mentioned in (4)(*b*) above for 1993/94 but subject to the same conditions as regards 'grouping' of settlements), and

(*c*) there are indexation losses in respect of any disposals made in 1994/95 or 'unused indexation losses' for 1993/94,

then, for the purposes of *TCGA 1992*, the amount by which the total amount of chargeable gains accruing to the taxpayer in 1994/95 exceeds the allowable losses accruing in that year is reduced by the amount mentioned below, and is so reduced before the deduction of any allowable losses carried forward from any previous year or carried back under *TCGA 1992, s 62* from any subsequent year. [*FA 1994, Sch 12 para 5(1)*].

The amount of the reduction referred to above is so much of the total of indexation losses in respect of disposals made in 1994/95, plus any unused indexation losses for 1993/94, as does not exceed

(A) £10,000 less the aggregate of

(i) the amount of any reduction made under *FA 1994, Sch 12 para 4(1)* above for 1993/94, and

(ii) any increase made under *FA 1994, Sch 12 para 6(2)* below for 1993/94,

or

(B) the amount by which the relevant gain exceeds the exempt amount for 1994/95,

whichever is the smaller. [*FA 1994, Sch 12 para 5(2)*].

For the purposes of *FA 1994, Sch 12 para 5(1)* and *(2)* above, if the total amount of indexation losses in respect of disposals made by the taxpayer in 1993/94 exceeds the aggregate of the amount of any reduction made under *FA 1994, Sch 12 para 4(1)* for that year and any increase made under *FA 1994, Sch 12 para 6(2)* for that year, there are '*unused indexation losses*' for that year of an amount equal to the excess. [*FA 1994, Sch 12 para 5(3)*].

(6) *Relief against chargeable gains and income for 1993/94 where there is an appropriation of a capital asset to trading stock or a capital loss on a disposal of shares is treated as a deduction from income.* The following provisions apply where, at any time in the period beginning with 30 November 1993 and ending with 5 April 1994, the taxpayer makes any relevant appropriation or any *ICTA 1988, s 574* disposal, and for the purposes of those provisions the following amounts must be determined:

(*a*) the amount of any reduction for the year 1993/94 which (disregarding relevant appropriations and *ICTA 1988, s 574* disposals) would be made under *FA 1994, Sch 12 para 4(1)* above, and

(*b*) the amounts of any indexation losses in respect of relevant appropriations or *ICTA 1988, s 574* disposals made in that period.

[*FA 1994, Sch 12 para 6(1)*].

If the aggregate of the amounts in (*a*) and (*b*) above does not exceed £10,000, the amount of any allowable loss referable to such an appropriation or disposal is increased by any indexation loss in respect of it. [*FA 1994, Sch 12 para 6(2)*].

In any other case, notwithstanding anything in *FA 1994, Sch 12 para 4* and *para 5* above,

(A) the aggregate of

(i) the amount of any reduction for the year 1993/94 to be made under *FA 1994, Sch 12 para 4(1)* above, and

(ii) the amount of any indexation losses in respect of relevant appropriations or *ICTA 1988, s 574* disposals made in the period beginning with 30 November 1993 and ending with 5 April 1994,

is deemed to be equal to £10,000 and is allocated as the taxpayer determines between that reduction and increases in allowable losses referable to such appropriations or disposals, and

(B) no reduction is made for the year 1994/95 under *FA 1994, Sch 12 para 5* (above) or *para 7* (below).

[*FA 1994, Sch 12 para 6(3)*].

(7) *Relief against income and chargeable gains for 1994/95 where there is an appropriation of a capital asset to trading stock or a capital loss on a disposal of shares is treated as a deduction from income.* The following provisions apply where, at any time in 1994/95, the taxpayer makes any relevant appropriation or any *ICTA 1988, s 574* disposal, and for the purposes of those provisions the following amounts must be determined:

(*a*) the amount of any reduction for the year 1994/95 which (disregarding relevant appropriations and *ICTA 1988, s 574* disposals) would be made under *FA 1994, Sch 12 para 5(1)* above, and

(*b*) the amounts of any indexation losses in respect of relevant appropriations or *ICTA 1988, s 574* disposals made in that year.

[*FA 1994, Sch 12 para 7(1)*].

If the aggregate of the amounts in (*a*) and (*b*) above does not exceed the limit for 1994/95 (that limit being £10,000 less the aggregate of the amount of any reduction made under *FA 1994, Sch 12 para 4(1)* above for the year 1993/94 and of any increases made under *FA 1994, Sch 12 para 6(2)* above for that year), the amount of any allowable loss referable to such an appropriation or disposal is increased by any indexation loss in respect of it. [*FA 1994, Sch 12 para 7(2)*].

In any other case, notwithstanding anything in *FA 1994, Sch 12 para 5* above, the aggregate of any reduction for the year 1994/95 to be made under *FA 1994, Sch 12 para 5(1)* above and of the amount of any indexation losses in respect of relevant appropriations or *ICTA 1988, s 574* disposals made in that year is deemed to be equal to the limit for 1994/95 and is allocated as the taxpayer determines between that reduction and increases in allowable losses referable to such appropriations or disposals. [*FA 1994, Sch 12 para 7(3)*].

Example

At the beginning of 1993/94 individual G had allowable losses of £1,000 available to carry forward against general chargeable gains. In May 1993, he disposes of Asset 1 which gives rise to a chargeable gain of £9,000. In January 1994 he disposes of Asset 2 for a consideration of £26,000 which he had originally acquired in September 1985 for a consideration of £20,932. The retail prices index is 95.44 for September 1985 and 141.3 for January 1994. The computation of the gain or loss arising on the disposal of Asset 2 proceeds as follows.

	£
Disposal proceeds of Asset 2	26,000
Acquisition consideration of Asset 2	20,932
Unindexed gain arising on disposal	£5,068
Indexation allowance otherwise available:	

$$\frac{141.3 - 95.44}{95.44} = 0.481$$

0.481 × £20,932	£10,068

An indexation allowance of £10,068 would extinguish the unindexed gain of £5,068, so the disposal is treated as giving rise to neither a gain nor a loss. However, the indexation loss is £5,000 in respect of the January 1994 disposal because, under the old indexation rules, G would have had an allowable loss of that amount (i.e. £10,068 – £5,068).

If the May 1993 and January 1994 disposals are the only ones occurring in 1993/94, the relevant gain (because there are no allowable losses arising in that year) is £9,000. This is greater than the annual exempt amount of £5,800 by £3,200. The amount of £3,200 is less than £10,000 so, as the indexation losses for 1993/94 amount to £5,000, £3,200 is deducted from the net chargeable gains (ignoring, at this stage, the brought forward allowable losses of £1,000) of 1993/94 (£9,000) to give net chargeable gains for that year of £5,800, such net gains being exempt by virtue of the exempt amount of the year. There are unused indexation losses of £1,800 (£5,000 – £3,200) available for utilisation in 1994/95 only and unused allowable losses of £1,000 available for utilisation generally.

Suppose, for 1994/95, G has chargeable gains less allowable losses (ignoring, at this stage, the brought forward allowable losses of £1,000) of £20,000 (i.e. the relevant gain) and indexation losses of £7,600. As the relevant gain exceeds the exempt amount for the year of £5,800, the excess being £14,200, relief is available as follows.

	£
Indexation losses of 1994/95	7,600
Unused indexation losses of 1993/94	1,800
Aggregate of available indexation losses	£9,400

However, this aggregate is limited to the lower of:

£10,000 – £3,200 = £6,800

£20,000 – £5,800 = £14,200

	£
Net chargeable gains of 1994/95 before reduction	20,000
Restricted reduction for indexation losses	6,800
	13,200
Allowable losses brought forward	1,000
	12,200
Exempt amount for the year	5,800
Net chargeable gains for 1994/95	£6,400

Notes to the example

(*a*) Indexation losses of £2,600 (£9,400 – £6,800) remaining unutilised in 1994/95 cannot be carried forward.

(*b*) The example illustrates that all three conditions mentioned above, at (4)(*a*)–(*c*) for 1993/94 and (5)(*a*)–(*c*) for 1994/95, have to be fulfilled before relief is available for the year concerned.

26.3 **Part disposals.** Apportionment of relevant allowable expenditure is to take place before computing the indexation allowance. The allowance is then only calculated for relevant allowable expenditure attributable to the part disposed of. [*TCGA 1992, s 56(1); FA 1994, Sch 26 Pt V*].

Example

X sells part of a plot of land on 18 January 2001 for £100,000. The then market value of the remaining part of the plot is £30,000. The cost, in September 1983, of the whole plot was £25,000. The retail prices index at September 1983 is 86.06 and for April 1998 it is 162.6.

	£
Allowable expenditure attributable to the part disposed of	
$\frac{100,000}{100,000 + 30,000} \times £25,000$	£19,231
Unindexed gain: £100,000 – £19,231	80,769
Indexation allowance	
$\frac{162.6 - 86.06}{86.06} = 0.889$	
0.889 × £19,231	17,096
Chargeable gain (subject to TAPER RELIEF (60))	£63,673

Notes to the example

(*a*) Indexation allowance cannot be computed to a month later than April 1998 (other than for the purposes of corporation tax on chargeable gains). See 26.1 above.

(*b*) No indexation allowance is computed at this stage on the balance of expenditure to be carried forward of £5,769 (£25,000 – £19,231).

26.4 **Disposals on a no gain/no loss basis.** *Disposals on or after 30 November 1993.* On a 'no gain/no loss disposal' on or after 30 November 1993, both the disposal consideration of the transferor and the corresponding acquisition consideration of the transferee are calculated for the purposes of *TCGA 1992* on the assumption that, on the disposal, an unindexed gain accrues to the transferor which is equal to the indexation allowance on that disposal, and so that after taking account of the indexation allowance the disposal is one on which neither a gain nor a loss accrues.

For the purposes of calculating indexation allowance under *TCGA 1992, ss 53, 54* (see 26.1 above), any enactment is disregarded to the extent to which it provides that, on a subsequent disposal of an asset by the transferee which was acquired by him on a no gain/no loss disposal as above, the transferor's acquisition of the asset is to be treated as the transferee's acquisition of it. [*TCGA 1992, s 56(2); FA 1994, s 93(5)(11)*]. For further applications of this provision, see 8.7 ASSETS HELD ON 31 MARCH 1982 and 59.4 SHARES AND SECURITIES—IDENTIFICATION RULES.

Where otherwise a loss would accrue on the disposal of an asset, and the sums allowable as a deduction in computing the loss would include an amount attributable to the application of the assumption contained in *TCGA 1992, s 56(2)* above on any no gain/no loss disposal on or after 30 November 1993, those sums are determined as if *TCGA 1992, s 56(2)* had not applied on any such disposal made on or after that date and the loss is reduced accordingly or, if those sums are then equal to or less than the consideration for the disposal, the disposal is to be one on which neither a gain nor a loss accrues. [*TCGA 1992, s 56(3); FA 1994, s 93(5)(11)*].

For the purposes of *TCGA 1992, s 56(1)* (part disposals; see 26.3 above) and *TCGA 1992, s 56(2)(3)* above, a '*no gain/no loss disposal*' is one which, by virtue of any enactment other than *TCGA 1992, s 35(4)* (no gain/no loss disposal where the general re-basing rule of *TCGA 1992, s 35(1)(2)* would otherwise convert a gain into a loss and vice versa; see 8.2 ASSETS HELD ON 31 MARCH 1982), *s 53(1)* (no gain/no loss disposal where indexation allowance equals or exceeds indexation allowance; see 26.1 above) or *s 56* itself, is treated as a disposal on which neither a gain nor a loss accrues. [*TCGA 1992, s 56(4); FA 1994, s 93(5)(11)*]. For these purposes the definition is not therefore confined to those no gain/no loss disposals mentioned in *TCGA 1992, s 35(3)(d)* (see 8.7 ASSETS HELD ON 31 MARCH 1982), being disposals to which the general re-basing rule of *TCGA 1992, s 35(1)(2)* does not apply.

Disposals on or after the '1985 date' and before 30 November 1993. On a 'no gain/no loss disposal' on or after the '1985 date' and before 30 November 1993, the provisions of *TCGA 1992, s 56(2)* applied similarly as above but *TCGA 1992, s 56(3)(4)* did not apply. A '*no gain/no loss disposal*' was, in effect, a disposal which, by virtue of any enactment (other than, in practice, *TCGA 1992, s 35(4)* (as above), *s 53(1) (as originally enacted)* (indexation allowance equal to unindexed gain so as to produce neither gain nor loss) or *s 56* itself) was treated as one on which neither a gain nor a loss accrued. [*TCGA 1992, s 56(2)*].

Examples

(1) In January 1993, Y gives his wife X an asset which is worth £170,000. The asset was purchased from a third party in May 1983 for £80,000. The retail prices index for May 1983 is 84.64 and for January 1993 it is 137.9.

	£
Cost of asset	80,000
Indexation allowance	
$\frac{137.9 - 84.64}{84.64} = 0.629$	
0.629 × £80,000	50,320
Deemed consideration	£130,320

X is deemed to acquire the asset for a consideration of £130,320.

(2) Facts in (1) above but Y and X subsequently divorce, with X retaining the asset. X later marries Z to whom the asset is transferred in February 1998 when it is worth £120,000. In May 2001 the asset is sold by Z to a third party for £130,000. The retail prices index for February 1998 is 160.3.

	£
Cost of asset	130,320
Indexation allowance	
$\frac{160.3 - 137.9}{137.9} = 0.162$	
0.162 × £130,320	21,112
Deemed consideration (X to Z)	£151,432

	£
Sale consideration	130,000
Cost of asset	151,432
Loss (indexation allowance unavailable)	21,432
Less: Reduction under *TCGA 1992, s 56(3)* of £21,112 which was the indexation uplift on the no gain/no loss disposal of February 1998	21,112
Allowable loss accruing to Z	£320

Disposals on or after the '1982 date' and before the '1985 date'. On any no gain/no loss disposal (other than one occurring only by reason of the indexation provisions on the disposal of an asset outside the twelve month qualifying period) the consideration (and corresponding base cost) was adjusted so that after such adjustment, the transaction still gave rise to neither a gain nor a loss. In effect the disposal consideration (and corresponding base cost) was uplifted by the indexation allowance.

Except as provided below, for indexation purposes, any enactment was disregarded which provided that, on the subsequent disposal by the transferee of an asset acquired by him on a no gain/no loss disposal, the transferor's acquisition of the asset was imputed to the transferee.

If a *loss* accrued on a subsequent disposal of the same asset (a 'subsequent disposal'), the loss was to be reduced by the lesser of (*a*) the indexation allowance on the initial disposal; and

(*b*) the amount required to secure that, on the subsequent disposal, neither a gain nor a loss accrued.

If a *gain* accrued on a subsequent disposal, the indexation allowance (if any) was calculated in the normal way, unless the no gain/no loss position on the initial disposal arose only by reason of any of the following enactments, viz. *TCGA 1992, s 139* (transfer of assets on amalgamation, see 13.7 COMPANIES); *TCGA 1992, s 171* (intra-group asset transfers, see 13.12 COMPANIES); *TCGA 1992, s 58* (inter-spouse transfers, see 41.3 MARRIED PERSONS); *FA 1982, s 148* (certain transfers of assets of the Hops Marketing Board, see 21.69 EXEMPTIONS AND RELIEFS); or *TCGA 1992, s 264* (certain transactions by local constituency associations, see 21.61 EXEMPTIONS AND RELIEFS). In those circumstances, if the transferor on the initial disposal had held the asset for at least the usual twelve month qualifying period, the requirement that the transferee must have held the asset for twelve months was removed, and the indexed rise in the deemed acquisition cost was taken from the month in which the expenditure was incurred (or March 1982 if later), and not the twelfth month thereafter. This provision applied both where the initial disposal took place on or after the '1982 date' and, in the Revenue's view, where it took place before that date (Revenue Pamphlet IR 131, SP 3/82). If the initial no gain/no loss disposal was within the above enactments, and was within the usual twelve-month qualifying period and thus ineligible for indexation allowance, the original transferor's acquisition was imputed to the second or subsequent transferee on further no gain/no loss disposals occurring within the twelve months of the initial no gain/no loss disposal. [*FA 1982, Sch 13 paras 2, 3*].

26.5 **Receipts affecting allowable expenditure.** Where account is to be taken, in determining relevant allowable expenditure (see 26.1 above) of any provision which, for the purposes of computing gains, reduces such expenditure by reference to a '*relevant event*' (i.e. any event which is not treated as a capital gains tax disposal), the computation of the indexation allowance proceeds in three stages.

(i) The 'indexed rise' (see 26.1 above) is calculated for each item of expenditure ignoring the reduction.

(ii) The 'indexed rise' is calculated of a notional item of expenditure equal to the amount of the reduction, as if that notional amount had actually been incurred on the date of the 'relevant event'.

(iii) The figure calculated in (ii) above is deducted from that in (i) above.

[*TCGA 1992, s 57*]. Examples of such 'relevant events' are small part disposals of land as in 36.8 LAND and the sale of rights nil paid where the consideration received is small as in 58.5 SHARES AND SECURITIES.

For disposals on or after the '1982 date' and before the '1985 date', the above provisions also applied, subject to the twelve month qualifying period, i.e. no adjustment under (ii) above was required if the asset was sold within twelve months of the 'relevant event'. [*FA 1982, Sch 13 para 4*].

Example

Z purchases a large area of land in April 1990 for £800,000. In June 1993, he sells a small part of that land at arm's length for £2,000. In May 2000, he sells all the remaining land for £4,500,000. The retail prices index for April 1990 is 125.1, for June 1993 it is 141.0 and for April 1998 it is 162.6.

		£
Sale consideration		4,500,000
Cost	800,000	
Small sale not treated as a disposal	2,000	798,000
Unindexed gain		£3,702,000
Indexation allowance on cost		
$\frac{162.6 - 125.1}{125.1} = 0.300$		
0.300 × £800,000		240,000
Indexation allowance on notional expenditure equal to small sale consideration		
$\frac{162.6 - 141.0}{141.0} = 0.153$		
0.153 × £2,000		306
Reduced indexation allowance		£239,694
Chargeable gain = £(3,702,000 – 239,694)		£3,462,306

Notes to the example

(*a*) Indexation allowance cannot be computed to a month later than April 1998 (other than for the purposes of corporation tax on chargeable gains). See 26.1 above.

(*b*) The chargeable gain is subject to TAPER RELIEF (60).

26.6 **Reorganisation, reconstructions etc.** In computing indexation allowance, any consideration given for 'the new holding' (treated under *TCGA 1992, s 127* as the same asset as 'the original shares' on a reorganisation or reduction of a company's share capital) is to be treated as an item of relevant allowable expenditure incurred when the consideration was, or was liable to be, given, i.e. not related back to the acquisition date of 'the original shares', as would normally be the case under *TCGA 1992, s 128(1)*.

'*Reorganisation*', the '*original shares*' and '*the new holding*' are as defined in *TCGA 1992, s 126(1)*. In addition the above provisions also apply where the treatment under *TCGA 1992, s 127* is adapted for a conversion of securities and company reconstructions and amalgamations. See 58.5–58.11 SHARES AND SECURITIES. [*TCGA 1992, s 131, s 132(1), s 135(3)*].

Example

In November 1987, Y purchases 5,000 shares in A plc for £3,500. In June 1989, he acquires, for £960, 1,000 further shares by way of a 1 for 5 rights issue. In January 2001, he sells all his holding for £8,000. The retail prices index for November 1987 is 103.4, for June 1989 it is 115.4 and for April 1998 it is 162.6.

		£
Sale consideration		8,000
Original cost	3,500	
Cost of rights	960	
		4,460
Unindexed gain		£3,540

Indexation allowance on original cost

$$\frac{162.6 - 103.4}{103.4} = 0.573$$

0.573 × £3,500	2,006

Indexation allowance on cost of taking up rights

$$\frac{162.6 - 115.4}{115.4} = 0.409$$

0.409 × £960	393
Total indexation allowance	£2,399
Chargeable gain = £(3,540 – 2,399)	£1,141

Notes to the example

(*a*) Technically, the pooling provisions in 59.4 SHARES AND SECURITIES—IDENTIFICATION RULES apply, as the acquisition in November 1987 is a 'section 104 holding'. For practical purposes, where, as in this example, there is a single acquisition and disposal, the above computation gives essentially the same result.

(*b*) Indexation allowance cannot be computed to a month later than April 1998 (other than for the purposes of corporation tax on chargeable gains). See 26.1 above.

(*c*) The chargeable gain is subject to TAPER RELIEF (60).

26.7 **Calls on shares.** Where the whole or part of the consideration for the issue of shares, securities or debentures is given after the period of twelve months beginning on the date of the issue of the shares etc., that consideration (or part) is treated as a separate item of expenditure for indexation purposes, incurred at the time it is given and not at the time at which the shares etc. were acquired or provided. [*TCGA 1992, s 113*]. Any calls paid within the twelve-month period are thus treated as incurred at the time the shares etc. were acquired or provided.

The above does not apply to privatisation issues, for which see 58.17 SHARES AND SECURITIES.

26.8 **Options.** Where, on a disposal, relevant allowable expenditure includes both

(*a*) the cost of acquiring an option binding the grantor to sell ('*the option consideration*'); and

(*b*) the cost of acquiring what was sold as a result of the exercise of the option ('*the sale consideration*') the option consideration and sale consideration are regarded as separate items of expenditure incurred when the option was acquired and when the sale took place respectively. An option binding the grantor both to sell and to buy is treated for these purposes as two separate options with one half of the consideration attributable to each. These provisions do not apply where those at 59.4 SHARES AND SECURITIES—IDENTIFICATION RULES (under 'Consideration for options') apply. Where the whole of the option consideration is incurred after 31 March 1998, the above provisions apply only for corporation tax purposes, this being in consequence of the freezing of indexation allowance for CGT purposes at its April 1998 level (see 26.1 above). [*TCGA 1992, s 145; FA 1998, s 122(5)*].

As in 17.10 DISPOSAL, the reference above to an 'option' includes a reference to an option binding the grantor to grant a lease for a premium, or enter into any other transaction which is not a sale. [*TCGA 1992, s 144(6), s 145(3)*].

In the case of the grantee of a 'cash-settled' option granted *after 29 November 1993* (see 17.10 DISPOSAL), the cost of the option is treated as incurred when the option was acquired for the purposes of calculating any indexation allowance. [*TCGA 1992, s 144A(3)(c); FA 1994, s 96*].

Disposals on or after the '1982 date' and before the '1985 date'. The above provisions of what is now *TCGA 1992, s 145* applied to such disposals but the qualifying period did not begin until the date of the sale resulting from the exercise of the option, i.e. it began with the date of acquisition of the asset and not, for example, the date of the grant of the option. [*FA 1982, Sch 13 para 7*].

27 Inland Revenue: Administration

27.1 The levying and collection of capital gains tax is administered by the **Commissioners of Inland Revenue** (normally referred to as **'the Board'**), Somerset House, London WC2R 1LB. [*TMA 1970, s 1(1)*].

Under them are local **inspectors of taxes** who are permanent civil servants responsible for making most assessments and dealing with claims and allowances and to whom all enquiries should be addressed.

27.2 **Collectors of Taxes** are also permanent civil servants and their duties for the most part relate only to the collection of tax. [*TMA 1970, ss 60–70*].

27.3 **Commissioners.** Except as otherwise provided, assessments are made by officers of the Board [*TMA 1970, s 30A; FA 1994, Sch 19 para 5*] and appeals against such assessments are heard by

(*a*) the *General Commissioners* (local people appointed on a voluntary basis by the Lord Chancellor for divisions in England and Wales and, from 3 April 1989, Northern Ireland or, for divisions in Scotland, by the Secretary of State) [*TMA 1970, s 2; FA 1975, s 57; FA 1988, s 125*], or

(*b*) the *Special Commissioners* (full-time civil servants, being barristers, advocates or solicitors of at least ten years' standing) [*TMA 1970, s 4; FA 1984, s 127, Sch 22 para 1*].

The Lord Chancellor has powers, by regulation, to change the appellations 'General Commissioners' and 'Special Commissioners' to something different. [*F(No 2)A 1992, s 75*].

See 4.5 and 4.8 APPEALS as regards jurisdiction of appeal Commissioners and the conduct of appeals before them.

27.4 **'Care and management' powers.** For the validity of amnesties by the Board, see *R v CIR (ex p. National Federation of Self-Employed and Small Businesses Ltd) HL 1981, 55 TC 133*. INLAND REVENUE EXTRA-STATUTORY CONCESSIONS (30) have been the subject of frequent judicial criticism but their validity has never been directly challenged in the Courts. In *R v CIR (ex p. Fulford-Dobson) QB 1987, 60 TC 168*, it was held that there had been no unfair treatment by the Revenue when it failed to apply a published extra-statutory concession because it was clear from the facts of the case that it was one of tax avoidance and this was a clearly stated general circumstance in which concessions would not be applied (cf. *R v Inspector of Taxes, Hull, ex p. Brumfield and others QB 1988, 61 TC 589* at 4.10 APPEALS). For a general discussion of the Board's care and management powers and an example of a ruling by the Court that the Board had acted reasonably, see *R v CIR (ex p. Preston) HL 1985, 59 TC 1*. See also *R v Attorney-General (ex p. ICI plc) CA 1986, 60 TC 1*, *R v CIR (ex p. MFK Underwriting Agencies Ltd and others) QB 1989, 62 TC 607* and *R v CIR (ex p. Matrix-Securities Ltd) HL 1994, 66 TC 587*. See also 4.10 APPEALS regarding judicial review of Revenue powers.

The Revenue policy of selective prosecution for criminal offences (see 47.6 PENALTIES) in connection with tax evasion does not render a decision in a particular case unlawful or *ultra vires*, provided that the case is considered on its merits fairly and dispassionately to see whether the criteria for prosecution were satisfied, and that the decision to prosecute is then taken in good faith for the purpose of collecting taxes and not for some ulterior, extraneous or improper purpose (*R v CIR (ex p. Mead and Cook) QB 1992, 65 TC 1*).

See 46.13 PAYMENT OF TAX for the Revenue's practice as regards reduced payments under 'equitable liability'.

27.5 **Mistakes by the Revenue.** If the Revenue makes a 'serious' mistake in dealing with a taxpayer's affairs, it will pay any costs he incurs as a direct result of the mistake. This practice is now embodied in the Revenue's Code of Practice 1 'Mistakes by the Inland Revenue' issued in February 1993 but this replaced SP A31 which dated from 1975 and was similar. Under the Code, the same practice also applies in relation to 'persistent' Revenue errors. The Code of Practice provides examples of what the Revenue envisage by the terms 'serious' and 'persistent'.

Further practices relating to Revenue mistakes are mentioned at 34.5 INTEREST ON OVERPAID TAX, 35.9 INTEREST AND SURCHARGES ON UNPAID TAX and 46.8 PAYMENT OF TAX.

27.6 **Taxpayer's Charter.** The Board of Inland Revenue and HM Customs and Excise have jointly produced a Taxpayer's Charter setting out the principles they try to meet in their dealings with taxpayers, the standards they believe the taxpayer has a right to expect, and what people can do if they wish to appeal or complain. Copies are available from local tax or collection offices and from local VAT offices. The Revenue version is contained in Pamphlet IR 167.

A series of codes of practice, available from local tax offices, setting out the standards of service people can expect in relation to specific aspects of the Revenue's work, was announced in a Revenue Press Release of 17 February 1993 to support the Taxpayer's Charter. The codes are not meant to represent any change of practice although some practices mentioned in them were not previously publicly available.

27.7 **Revenue Adjudicator.** A taxpayer who is not satisfied with the Revenue response to a complaint has the option of putting the case to a Revenue Adjudicator. The Adjudicator's office considers complaints about the Revenue's handling of a taxpayer's affairs, e.g. excessive delays, errors, discourtesy or the exercise of Revenue discretion. Matters subject to existing rights of appeal are excluded.

Complaints will normally go to the Adjudicator only after they have been considered by the Controller of the relevant Revenue office, and where the taxpayer is still not satisfied with the response received. The alternatives of pursuing the complaint to the Revenue's Head Office, to an MP, or (through an MP) to the Parliamentary Ombudsman continue to be available. The Adjudicator will review all the facts, consider whether the complaint is justified, and, if so, make recommendations as to what should be done. The Revenue will normally accept the recommendations 'unless there are very exceptional circumstances'.

The Adjudicator publishes an annual report to the Board. (Revenue Press Release 17 February 1993 and Tax Bulletin May 1993 p 75), the first of which was published on 13 September 1994. Contact should be made with Revenue Adjudicator, 3rd Floor, Haymarket House, 28 Haymarket, London SW1Y 4SP. Tel: 020–7930 2292. Fax: 020–7930 2298. An explanatory leaflet is available from the Adjudicator which describes the actions a taxpayer should take and how the Adjudicator will respond to complaints.

27.8 **Open Government.** Under the Government's 'Code of Practice on Access to Government Information', the Revenue (in common with other Government departments) is to make information about its policies and decisions more widely available. Revenue Pamphlet IR 141 ('Open Government') sets out the information to be made available, and how it may be obtained, and the basis on which a fee may be charged in certain circumstances to offset the cost of providing the information. Copies of the Code of Practice may be obtained by writing to Open Government, Room 417b, Office of Public Service and Science, 70 Whitehall, London SW1A 2AS (tel. 0345 223242).

27.9 **Use of electronic communications.** The Commissioners of Inland Revenue (and Customs & Excise) are given broad powers to make regulations, by statutory instrument (see now *SI 2000 No 945*), to facilitate two-way electronic communication in the delivery of information, e.g. tax returns and the making of tax payments. The regulations may allow or require the use of intermediaries such as Internet service providers. They will have effect notwithstanding any existing legislation requiring delivery or payment in a manner which would otherwise preclude the use of electronic communications or intermediaries. [*FA 1999, ss 132, 133*].

The two departments are given further regulatory powers to provide tax-free incentives to use electronic communications as above or otherwise in connection with tax matters. These may, in particular, take the form of discounts, the allowing of additional time for compliance or for payment of tax, or the facility to deliver information or make payments at more convenient intervals. [*FA 2000, s 143, Sch 38*]. In this connection, for one year from April 2000, individual taxpayers who personally file their self-assessment tax return via the internet and pay any tax due electronically will receive a discount of £10 (Revenue Press Release 16 February 2000). For notes on electronic filing and payment, see Revenue Tax Bulletin June 2000 pp 757, 758 and see the Revenue's e-business website at www.inlandrevenue.gov.uk/ebu/info.htm For the pre-existing system of electronic lodgement of returns, normally by agents, see 54.16 RETURNS.

28 Inland Revenue: Confidentiality of Information

28.1 The Revenue consider that the confidentiality of information maintained by their Department 'is essential to their traditional approach to their task and is deeply embedded in their practice' (*Royal Commission on Standards of Conduct in Public Life 1976, para 111*). All officers of the Inland Revenue, together with General and Special Commissioners, are required to make declarations that information received in the course of their duty will not be disclosed except for the purposes of such duty or for the purposes of the prosecution of revenue offences or as may be required by law. [*TMA 1970, s 6, Sch 1*]. As to production in Court proceedings of documents in the possession of the Revenue or copies of documents previously submitted to the Revenue which are held by a party to the proceedings, see *Brown's Trustees v Hay SCS 1897, 3 TC 598; In re Joseph Hargreaves Ltd CA 1900, 4 TC 173; Shaw v Kay SCS 1904, 5 TC 74; Soul v Irving CA 1963, 41 TC 517; H v H Fam D 1980, 52 TC 454; R v CIR (ex p. J Rothschild Holdings plc) CA 1987, 61 TC 178; Lonrho plc v Fayed and Others (No 4) CA 1993, 66 TC 220.*

28.2 The Inland Revenue are authorised to disclose information to the following (and see also written reply in HC Official Report, 20 February 1990, col 685).

(*a*) **Charity Commissioners for England and Wales**. The Revenue is authorised to disclose certain information to the Charity Commissioners regarding bodies which are or have been charities. Similar provisions apply in Scotland as regards disclosure to the Lord Advocate. [*Charities Act 1993, s 10; Law Reform (Miscellaneous Provisions) (Scotland) Act 1990, s 1*].

(*b*) **Department of Trade and Industry, Department of Employment or Office for National Statistics.** The Revenue are authorised to disclose, for the purposes of statistical surveys, the names and addresses of employers and information concerning the number of persons employed by individual concerns. [*FA 1969, s 58; F(No 2)A 1987, s 69*].

(*c*) **Tax authorities of other countries**. The Revenue are authorised to disclose information concerning individual taxpayers where it is necessary to do so for the operation of double taxation agreements. After 14 May 1987, provision is made for double taxation agreements to include arrangements for the exchange of information relating to the taxes covered by an agreement including, in particular, those concerned with the prevention of fiscal evasion. The Board may also be required to disclose information to an advisory commission set up under the Arbitration Convention (*90/436/EEC*). [*TCGA 1992, s 277(4); FA 1975, Sch 7 para 7(5); IHTA 1984, s 158; ICTA 1988, s 788(2), s 816; F(No 2)A 1992, s 51(2)*]. Disclosure may also be made to the tax authorities of other member states of the EEC which observe similar confidentiality and use the information only for taxation purposes. [*FA 1978, s 77; EEC Directive 19 December 1977 No 77/799 EEC*]. See also the working arrangement between USA and UK in Revenue Press Release 2 March 1978.

With effect from 28 July 2000, the UK may also enter into Tax Information Exchange Agreements with other countries, under which information relating to income tax, capital gains tax and corporation tax, and foreign equivalents, may be exchanged. The Revenue may disclose information under such agreements only if satisfied that the confidentiality rules applied by the foreign government concerned with respect to the information are no less strict than the equivalent UK rules. [*ICTA 1988, ss 815C, 816(2ZA); FA 2000, s 146(1)(2)*].

(*d*) **Customs and Excise.** The Revenue and the Customs and Excise are authorised to disclose information to each other for the purpose of their respective duties. [*FA 1972, s 127*].

(*e*) **Occupational Pensions Board.** The Revenue are authorised to disclose information about pension schemes. [*Social Security Act 1973, s 89(2)*].

(*f*) **Social Security Departments.** The Revenue may disclose information obtained in connection with the assessment or collection of income tax but for self-employed persons they may only disclose the fact that a person has commenced or ceased self-employment together with the identity of that person and information relating to earners employed by that person. [*Social Security Administration Act 1992, s 122*]. Information under this authority will be disclosed in connection with the tracing of absent parents liable to maintain lone-parent families receiving income support (Revenue Press Release 9 May 1990).

From 5 October 1999, the Board may, and *must* if an authorised social security officer so requires, supply to the social security authorities information held for the purposes of functions relating to working families' tax credit and disabled person's tax credit (for which see TOLLEY'S INCOME TAX under Social Security) for use by those authorities for the purposes of functions relating to social security benefits, child support or war pensions. [*Tax Credits Act 1999, Sch 5 para 2*].

From 2 July 1997, social security authorities are permitted to supply information to the Revenue for investigative purposes. [*FA 1997, s 110; Tax Credits Act 1999, Sch 5 para 7; SI 1997 No 1603*].

(*g*) **Police.** To assist investigation into suspected murder or treason. (*Royal Commission on Standards of Conduct in Public Life 1976, para 93*).

(*h*) **Non-UK resident entertainers and sportsmen.** In connection with the deduction of sums representing income tax from certain payments to such persons after 5 April 1987, the Board may disclose relevant matters to any person who appears to the Board to have an interest. [*ICTA 1988, s 558(4)*].

(*j*) From 5 October 1999 and only as regards information held for the purposes of functions relating to working families' tax credit and disabled person's tax credit (for which see TOLLEY'S INCOME TAX under Social Security), a **local authority** (or authorised delegate) for use in the administration of housing benefit or council tax benefit. Information must also be provided in the opposite direction if the Board so require but only for use for purposes relating to the aforementioned tax credits. [*Tax Credits Act 1999, Sch 5 paras 4, 5*].

28.3 From 5 October 1999, consequent upon the introduction of working families' tax credit and disabled person's tax credit (for which see TOLLEY'S INCOME TAX under Social Security), the Board may pool the information they hold for the purposes of their functions relating to those tax credits and to tax, national insurance contributions, statutory sick pay, statutory maternity pay and certain functions under *Pension Schemes Act 1993* (and corresponding NI legislation). There is also provision for the exchange of information held for the purposes of functions relating to the aforementioned tax credits between the Board and persons providing services to the Board, for use in the exercise of those functions. [*Tax Credits Act 1999, Sch 5 para 1*].

From 28 July 2000, information obtained by officers of the Board for the purposes of enforcing the *National Minimum Wage Act 1998* may be used for the purpose of any of the Board's other functions. Information obtained by other officers for similar purposes may likewise be supplied to the Board. [*FA 2000, s 148*].

28.4 Inland Revenue: Confidentiality of Information

28.4 It is a criminal offence for a person to disclose tax information of an identifiable person held by him in the exercise of 'tax functions' or as a member of an advisory commission set up under the Arbitration Convention (*90/436/EEC*). '*Tax functions*' include functions relating to the General and Special Commissioners, the Board and their officers and any other persons providing, or employed in the provision of, services to the aforementioned persons. This does not apply if the person has (or believes he has) lawful authority or the information has lawfully been made available to the public, or if the person involved has consented. The maximum penalty for an offence is imprisonment for up to two years, a fine, or both. The above applies equally as regards national insurance contributions, statutory sick pay, statutory maternity pay, working families' tax credit and disabled person's tax credit. [*FA 1989, ss 182, 182A; F(No 2)A 1992, s 51(3); FA 1995, Sch 29 Pt VIII(16); Government of Wales Act 1998, Sch 12 para 31; Social Security Contributions (Transfer of Functions, etc) Act 1999, Sch 6 para 9; Tax Credits Act 1999, s 12; SI 1999 No 527*].

29 Inland Revenue Explanatory Publications

29.1 INLAND REVENUE EXPLANATORY PAMPHLETS

The Board publish explanatory pamphlets (with supplements from time to time) on Inland Revenue taxes. Those having a bearing on capital gains tax and corporation tax on chargeable gains are listed below, with the date of the latest edition in brackets, and are obtainable free of charge (except where otherwise stated) from local tax offices or, where unobtainable locally, the Inland Revenue Information Centre, Ground Floor, South West Wing, Bush House, Strand, London WC2B 4RD (Tel. 020–7438 7772), unless otherwise stated. Pamphlets are also available on the Revenue web site at www.inlandrevenue.gov.uk/home.htm

CGT 1 Capital Gains Tax — An Introduction (December 1998).
IR 1 Extra-Statutory Concessions as at 31 August 1999 (January 2000).
IR 6 Double taxation relief for companies (March 1994).
IR 16 Share acquisitions by directors and employees: Explanatory notes (March 1997).
IR 20 Residents and Non-residents: Liability to Tax in the United Kingdom (December 1999).
IR 37 Appeals against Tax (April 1999).
IR 45 Income Tax; Capital Gains Tax; Inheritance Tax: What to do about tax when someone dies (September 1997).
IR 46 Clubs, Societies and Voluntary Associations (January 2000).
IR 64 Giving to Charity: How businesses can get tax relief (November 1993).
IR 65 Giving to Charity: How individuals can get tax relief (November 1993).
IR 73 Inland Revenue Investigations: How Settlements are Negotiated (January 1994).
IR 75 Tax Reliefs for Charities (June 1987).
IR 83 Independent Taxation: A guide for Tax Practitioners (January 1990).
IR 87 Letting and your home (December 1999).
IR 89 Personal Equity Plans (PEPs) (October 1998).
IR 95 Approved profit sharing schemes: An outline for employees (June 1996).
IR 96 Approved profit sharing schemes: Explanatory notes (June 1996).
IR 97 Approved SAYE share option schemes: An outline for employees (June 1996).
IR 98 Approved SAYE share option schemes: Explanatory notes (June 1996).
IR 101 Approved company share option plans—An outline for employees (June 1996).
IR 102 Company share options: Explanatory notes (June 1996).
IR 120 You and the Inland Revenue: Tax, Collection and Accounts Offices (April 1999).
IR 126 Corporation Tax Pay and File: A General Guide (July 1995).
IR 128 Corporation Tax Pay and File: Company Leaflet (July 1993).
IR 131 Statements of Practice as at 31 August 1999 (January 2000).
IR 137 The Enterprise Investment Scheme (July 1999).
IR 152 Trusts – An Introduction (September 1996).
IR 160 Inland Revenue enquiries under self-assessment (December 1999).
IR 162 A better approach to local office enquiry work under self-assessment (March 1998).
IR 166 The Euro — Tax and National Insurance options for UK businesses from 1 January 1999 (December 1998).
IR 167 Charter for Inland Revenue taxpayers (April 1999).
IR 169 Venture Capital Trusts (February 2000).
— Capital Gains Tax Reform: The 1998 Finance Act — A Guide for Inland Revenue Officers and Tax Practitioners, providing a detailed explanation of the capital gains tax legislation in Finance Act 1998 including, *inter alia*, taper relief. (Obtainable by post from Inland Revenue Library, Room 28, New Wing, Somerset House, Strand, London WC2R 1LB or in person from the Inland Revenue Information Centre as above — price £5.00 post-free.) (November 1998).

29.2 Inland Revenue Explanatory Publications

—	A Guide to Corporation Tax Self-Assessment — for Tax Practitioners and Inland Revenue Officers, explaining the rules of CTSA. (Obtainable by post from Inland Revenue Library, Room 28, New Wing, Somerset House, Strand, London WC2R 1LB or in person from the Inland Revenue Information Centre as above — price £15.00 post-free.) (April 1999).
SAT 2	Self-Assessment — The Legal Framework, explaining the rules on the assessment and collection of income tax and capital gains tax. Also available on disk. (Obtainable from Inland Revenue Library, Room 28, New Wing, Somerset House, Strand, London WC2R 1LB — price £5.00.) (July 1995).
SA/BK4	Self-Assessment — A General Guide to Keeping Records (December 1997).
SA/BK6	Self-Assessment — Penalties for Late Tax Returns (October 1997)
SA/BK7	Self-Assessment — Surcharges for Late Payment of Tax (October 1997).
SA/BK8	Self-Assessment — Your Guide (October 1997).
ISA 1	The answers on ISAs — Your Guide (March 1999).
COP 1	Mistakes by the Inland Revenue (April 1999).
COP 10	Information and advice (April 1999).
COP 11	Enquiries into tax returns (July 1996).
COP 14	Enquiries into company tax returns (July 1999).
AO1	How to complain about the Inland Revenue and the Valuation Office Agency (February 2000).
CB(1)	Setting up a charity in Scotland (see 10.1 CHARITIES for address).

IR 83, IR 96, IR 98 and IR 102 are available from the Inland Revenue Information Centre (see above).

29.2 INLAND REVENUE GUIDANCE MANUALS

The Inland Revenue Guidance Manuals provide guidance to Revenue staff on the operation and application of tax law and the tax system and are also available to the public, either by inspection free of charge at any Inland Revenue Enquiry Centre or by purchase (with updating service). The Capital Gains Manual comprises Volumes I–VIII to which references are made throughout this book.

29.3 INLAND REVENUE TAX BULLETIN

The Revenue publish a bi-monthly Tax Bulletin aimed at tax practitioners and giving the views of Revenue technical specialists on various issues. The annual subscription is £22, and applications should be made to Inland Revenue, Finance Division, Barrington Road, Worthing, West Sussex, BN12 4XH. Telephone enquiries can be made on 020–7438 7700 (subscription or distribution) and 020–7438 7842 (more general information).

29.4 INLAND REVENUE HELPSHEETS

The Revenue produce a number of free helpsheets designed to explain different aspects of the tax system and to assist in the completion of self-assessment tax returns. These can be ordered via the Revenue Orderline (Tel. 0645 000404, fax 0645 000604, between 8 a.m. and 10 p.m. seven days a week). Those concerned with capital gains tax are listed below.

IR 261*	Tax credit relief: capital gains (i.e. double tax relief).
IR 278	Temporary non-residents and capital gains tax.
IR 279	Taper relief.
IR 280	Re-basing — assets held at 31 March 1982.
IR 281	Husband and wife, divorce and separation.

IR 282	Death, personal representatives and legatees.
IR 283	Private residence relief.
IR 284	Shares and capital gains tax.
IR 285	Share reorganisations, company takeovers and capital gains tax.
IR 286	Income tax losses for shares you have subscribed for in unlisted trading companies.
IR 287	Employee share schemes and capital gains tax.
IR 288	Partnerships and capital gains tax.
IR 289	Retirement relief and capital gains tax.
IR 290	Business asset rollover relief.
IR 292	Land and leases, the valuation of land and capital gains tax.
IR 293	Chattels and capital gains tax.
IR 294	Trusts and capital gains tax.
IR 295	Relief for gifts and similar transactions.
IR 296	Debts and capital gains tax.
IR 297	Enterprise Investment Scheme and capital gains tax.
IR 298	Venture Capital Trusts and capital gains tax.
IR 299	Non-resident trusts and capital gains tax.
IR 301	Capital gains on benefits from non-resident and dual resident trusts.

* Supports foreign supplementary pages of self-assessment tax return; the remaining helpsheets support the capital gains supplementary pages.

29.5 INLAND REVENUE WEB SITE

The Revenue web site is at www.inlandrevenue.gov.uk/home.htm It has copies of, *inter alia*, recent press releases, extra-statutory concessions, statements of practice, consultative documents, Tax Bulletins, explanatory pamphlets and helpsheets.

29.6 TAX LAW REWRITE PLANS

The Inland Revenue plans over a number of years to rewrite the tax law in 'clearer and simpler language'. (Revenue Press Releases 11 December 1996, 31 July 1997, 19 May 1998, 29 October 1998 and Revenue Tax Bulletins June 1998 pp 549–551, October 1998 pp 592, 593).

30 Inland Revenue Extra-Statutory Concessions

Below are summarised the concessions relating to tax on capital gains published (or to be published) in Revenue Pamphlet IR 1 (January 2000). Any concessions announced in Press Releases but not yet designated by a formal prefix (see below) are summarised in date order at the end of the chapter. Copies of recently announced concessions are also available (with the relevant press release) on the Revenue web site at www.inlandrevenue.gov.uk/home.htm In the pamphlet it is stated: 'The concessions described within are of general application, but it must be borne in mind that in a particular case there may be special circumstances which will require to be taken into account in considering the application of the concession. A concession will not be given in any case where an attempt is made to use it for tax avoidance'. See also 27.4 INLAND REVENUE: ADMINISTRATION. Fuller coverage in context is normally given in the appropriate chapter referred to below. Except where the context otherwise requires, each concession relates to both individuals and companies. The full text of all current Extra-Statutory Concessions is reproduced in Tolley's Tax Link.

See 3.23 ANTI-AVOIDANCE for the charge arising where concessions involving deferral of gains are abused.

D 2 **Residence in the UK: year of commencement or cessation of residence.** Where a person's UK residence status is determined by reference to the period of actual residence in the UK, tax will only be charged on disposals made during the period of residence. (See also A11 below). This concession does not apply in certain cases. It was amended for individuals arriving in the UK on or after 6 April 1998 or leaving the UK after 16 March 1998, and ceased to apply to companies for disposals after 5 April 1998. See 52.3 RESIDENCE AND DOMICILE.

D 3 **Private residence exemption: periods of absence (a).** Periods of absence are ignored where husband and wife are living together and the conditions are satisfied by the spouse who is not the owner. See 48.2 PRIVATE RESIDENCES.

D 4 **Private residence exemption: periods of absence (b).** Resumption of occupation after certain periods of absence will not be necessary if the terms of his employment require the taxpayer to work elsewhere. See 48.2 PRIVATE RESIDENCES.

D 5 **Private residence exemption** is extended to cover a residence disposed of by personal representatives and occupied before and after the death of the deceased as an only or main residence by an individual entitled to the whole or a substantial part of the proceeds of sale either absolutely or for life. See 48.6 PRIVATE RESIDENCES.

D 6 **Private residence exemption: separated couples.** If, as the result of a breakdown of the marriage, one spouse ceases to occupy the matrimonial home and later transfers it (or part of it) as part of a financial settlement to the other spouse who has continued in occupation, no gain will be chargeable unless election has been made for some other house to be the main residence of the transferring spouse. See 48.2 PRIVATE RESIDENCES.

D10 **Unquoted shares acquired before 6 April 1965: disposals following reorganisation of share capital.** Tax is not charged on a disposal of the entire new shareholding on more than the actual gains realised. See 7.12 ASSETS HELD ON 6 APRIL 1965.

D15 **Rollover relief: unincorporated associations.** Where property is held via the medium of a company in which at least 90% of the shares are held by the association or its members, the relief is available provided the other conditions are satisfied. See 55.5 ROLLOVER RELIEF.

D16 **Rollover relief: repurchase of the same asset.** An asset which is repurchased for purely commercial reasons after having been sold as part of a business may be treated as the 'new asset' for the purposes of the relief. See 55.3 ROLLOVER RELIEF.

D17 **Unit trusts for exempt unit holders.** The exemption available to the unit trust is not withdrawn because of the intermittent holding of units by the trust managers under statutory arrangements. See 64.3 UNIT TRUSTS ETC..

D18 **Mortgage granted by vendor: subsequent default by purchaser as mortgagor.** In such circumstances and where the vendor regains beneficial ownership of the asset and so elects, the original sale is ignored and the chargeable gain arising is limited to the net proceeds obtained from the transactions. See 17.1 DISPOSAL.

D21 **Private residence exemption: late elections in dual residence cases.** The two-year time limit will be extended in cases where the capital value of each of the residences, or each of them except one, is negligible. See 48.5 PRIVATE RESIDENCES.

D22 **Rollover relief: expenditure on improvements to existing assets.** Such expenditure is treated as incurred in acquiring other assets provided certain conditions are met. See 55.3 ROLLOVER RELIEF.

D23 **Rollover relief: partition of land and other assets on the dissolution of a partnership.** Partitioned assets are treated as 'new assets' for the purposes of the relief provided that the partnership is dissolved immediately thereafter. See 55.1 ROLLOVER RELIEF.

D24 **Rollover relief: assets not brought immediately into trading use.** The 'new asset' will qualify for relief even if not immediately taken into use for the purposes of the trade provided certain conditions are met. Land to be used for the site of a qualifying building will also qualify as the 'new asset' for the purposes of this concession subject to conditions. See 55.3 ROLLOVER RELIEF.

D25 **Rollover relief: acquisition of a further interest in an existing asset.** The further interest is treated as a 'new asset' for the purposes of the relief. See 55.3 ROLLOVER RELIEF.

D26 **Exchange of joint interests in land: form of rollover relief.** A form of rollover relief as on the compulsory purchase of land (see 36.11 LAND) is allowed on a disposal caused by the exchange of interests in land which is in the joint beneficial ownership of two or more persons. This relief is not confined to traders. The relief applies also to certain exchanges of milk or potato quota associated with such land. See 36.12 LAND.

D27 **Earn-outs.** *TCGA 1992, s 135* may be applied to a takeover which includes an 'earn-out' element. Superseded by *FA 1997, s 89*. See 58.9 SHARES AND SECURITIES.

D31 **Retirement relief: date of disposal.** If business activities continue beyond the date an unconditional contract is made, the date of completion will be accepted as the date of disposal. See 53.3 RETIREMENT RELIEF.

D32 **Transfer of a business to a company.** For the purposes of *TCGA 1992, s 162*, liabilities taken over by a company on the transfer are not treated as consideration so that no gain arises. See 25.10 HOLD-OVER RELIEFS.

D33 **Compensation and damages.** These are treated as derived from any underlying asset, and exempt or taxable accordingly, and as exempt if there is no underlying asset. See 6.1 ASSETS and 21.21 EXEMPTIONS AND RELIEFS.

D34 **Rebasing and indexation: shares held on 31 March 1982.** A single holding treatment will apply even if the shares were acquired on or before 6 April 1965. See 8.2 ASSETS HELD ON 31 MARCH 1982.

D35 **Employee trusts.** Concessional treatment will apply where an asset is transferred to a beneficiary who as a result suffers a Schedule E income tax charge. See 21.79 EXEMPTIONS AND RELIEFS.

D37 **Relocation of employees.** The exemption for a gain arising on the disposal of an employee's private residence is extended similarly to his right to share in any profits made by a relocation business or his employer to whom he sells property and which later sells it to a third party. See 48.2 PRIVATE RESIDENCES.

D38 **Loans to traders evidenced by qualifying corporate bonds.** A further concessional relief will apply in certain circumstances where the bonds concerned only became qualifying corporate bonds because of a change in definition, even though they are not evidenced by a qualifying loan. Obsolete as regards loans made on or after 17 March 1998. See 39.12 LOSSES.

D39 **Extension of leases.** No capital gains tax is payable where a lessee surrenders an existing lease and is granted, in an arm's length transaction (or equivalent), a new, longer lease on the same property at a different rent, but otherwise on the same terms. See 36.14 LAND.

D40 **Non-resident trusts.** The definition of 'participator' in *ICTA 1988, s 417(1)* is concessionally restricted for the purposes of *TCGA 1992, s 96* and specified provisions of *TCGA 1992, Sch 5.* See 43.8, 43.13 OFFSHORE SETTLEMENTS.

D42 **Mergers of leases.** Where a superior interest in leasehold land is acquired (being either a superior lease or the reversion of freehold), and the land is disposed of after 28 June 1992, indexation allowance on the expenditure incurred on the inferior lease will be calculated by reference to the date of its acquisition. See 36.13 LAND.

D44 **Re-basing and indexation: shares derived from larger holdings held at 31 March 1982.** In certain circumstances a valuation of a shareholding held or treated as having been held at 31 March 1982 can be calculated by reference to the size of the shareholding held by a spouse or group member at that date. See 8.7 ASSETS HELD ON 31 MARCH 1982.

D45 **Rollover into depreciating assets.** Where an asset employed in a trade carried on by a claimant to rollover relief ceases to be used due to the claimant's death, no charge to tax will arise under *TCGA 1992, s 154(2)(b)*. See 55.7 ROLLOVER RELIEF.

D46 **Relief against income for capital losses on the disposal of unquoted shares in a trading company.** Where an unquoted trading company devoid of assets is wound up, a holder of shares in that company who has not made a negligible value claim under *TCGA 1992, s 24(2)* and did not receive a distribution during the course of winding up will, by concession, be able to claim relief under either *ICTA 1988, s 573* or *s 574* despite the requirements of *ICTA 1988, s 575(1)* not being met, provided all other conditions for relief are met. Superseded by statutory provision for events treated as disposals after 5 April 2000 (on or after 1 April 2000 as regards companies). See 39.13 and 39.15 LOSSES.

D47 **Temporary loss of charitable status due to reverter of school and other sites.** A temporary loss of charitable status will in general be ignored for tax purposes. See 10.3 CHARITIES.

D49 **Private residence exemption: short delay by owner occupier in taking up residence.** Restriction of relief is removed in certain circumstances where an individual acquires a property but does not immediately use it as his only or main residence. See 48.2 PRIVATE RESIDENCES. This replaces SP D4.

D50 **Compensation from foreign governments.** Exemption from tax is granted for gains arising on compensation from foreign governments in certain circumstances. See 17.7 DISPOSAL.

D51 **Close company transferring asset at undervalue.** An anti-avoidance provision is not applied in two sets of circumstances. See 3.15 ANTI-AVOIDANCE.

D52 **Share exchanges and company reconstructions and amalgamations: incidental costs of acquisition and disposal and warranty payments in respect of contingent liabilities.** Any such costs or payments are treated as allowable expenditure referable to the new holding of shares. See 58.8 and 58.10 SHARES AND SECURITIES.

D53 **TCGA 1992, s 50; Grants repaid.** Where a grant is repaid, and acquisition cost has been restricted by the amount of the grant, the consideration on disposal may be reduced by the amount repaid. See 17.5(*c*) DISPOSAL.

The following income tax and corporation tax concessions are also relevant for the purposes of capital gains tax.

A11 **Residence in the UK: year of commencement or cessation of residence.** Although there is no provision for splitting a tax year in relation to residence, liability to UK tax which is affected by residence is computed by reference to the period of actual residence in the UK during the year. This concession was revised by Revenue Press Releases of 14 September 1993 and 29 January 1996. See also D2 above. See TOLLEY'S INCOME TAX.

A17 **Death of taxpayer before due date for payment of tax.** For notices of assessment issued after 31 July 1975, personal representatives unable to pay tax before obtaining probate may have concessional treatment so that interest on tax falling due after the date of death runs from the later of the expiration of thirty days after the grant of probate and the statutory date for interest to run. See 35.9 INTEREST AND SURCHARGES ON UNPAID TAX.

A19 **Arrears of tax arising through official error.** Arrears of tax arising due to the Revenue's failure to make proper and timely use of information supplied by an *individual* taxpayer will be waived in certain cases. See 46.8 PAYMENT OF TAX.

A78 **Residence in the UK—accompanying spouse.** Where an employee leaving the UK to work abroad satisfies the conditions of A11 above, the residence treatment of the employee may be extended to an accompanying spouse in certain circumstances. This concession was revised by Revenue Press Release of 14 September 1993. See 52.3–52.5 RESIDENCE AND DOMICILE.

A82 **Repayment supplement paid to individuals etc. resident in EC member states.** Residents of EC member states other than the UK will be treated on the same basis as UK residents in relation to a repayment supplement on a repayment of income tax. It is understood that this concession will also apply to repayments of capital gains tax. See 34.2 INTEREST ON OVERPAID TAX.

A99 **Tax treatment of compensation for mis-sold free standing additional voluntary contribution schemes.** Certain capital sums received by way of compensation are not regarded for capital gains tax purposes as the disposal of an asset (Revenue Press Release 28 February 2000). See 21.50 EXEMPTIONS AND RELIEFS.

B41 **Claims to repayment of tax.** Where an overpayment of tax arises because of an error by the Inland Revenue or another Government department and where there is no dispute as to the facts, claims to repayment of the tax overpaid made outside of the statutory period will be allowed. See 46.8 PAYMENT OF TAX.

C31 **Scientific research associations (SRAs).** Following changes announced on 4 September 1998 to the criteria for granting Government approval to SRAs, and to allow existing SRAs time to restructure accordingly, tax exemption is temporarily extended to SRAs which were approved or would have obtained approval under earlier criteria. See 21.51 EXEMPTIONS AND RELIEFS.

31 Inland Revenue Press Releases

The following is a summary, in date order, of Press Releases referred to in this Annual other than those designated as containing Extra-Statutory Concessions or Statements of Practice.

Copies of any individual Press Release may be obtained from: Inland Revenue Information Centre, South West Wing, Bush House, Strand, London WC2B 4RD (Tel. 020–7438 6420/6425/7772). A charge (currently £100) is made for Press Releases (including Extra-Statutory Concessions and Statements of Practice) mailed weekly throughout a calendar year. To receive Press Releases, application can be made to Tolley, 2 Addiscombe Road, Croydon, Surrey CR9 5AF (Tel. 020–8686 9141). A separate application is needed to subscribe to the Revenue's Tax Bulletin for an annual charge of £22, which should be made to Inland Revenue, Finance Division, Barrington Road, Worthing, West Sussex, BN12 4XH. Copies of recent press releases (and Tax Bulletin) are also available on the Revenue web site at www.inlandrevenue.gov.uk/home.htm

13.12.72 **Compensation for acquisition of property under compulsory powers.** Compensation for temporary loss of profits was formerly included in overall compensation on compulsory purchase is treated as part of the consideration on disposal for capital gains tax purposes. This practice ceased with effect from 28 July 1978 and the present provisions are to be found in Revenue Pamphlet IR 131, SP 8/79. See 17.7 DISPOSAL.

1.8.77 **Investigation of incorrect business accounts and tax returns.** The Board may mitigate penalties where the taxpayer shows a willingness to co-operate. See 47.10 PENALTIES.

2.3.78 **Double taxation: exchange of information with the USA.** Terms of a working arrangement between the USA and UK for the examination of the affairs of taxpayers with substantial operations in both countries. See 28.2 INLAND REVENUE: CONFIDENTIALITY OF INFORMATION.

25.6.82 **Deep discounted stock.** The Revenue indicate their view of the tax treatment of deep discounted stock, including zero-coupon bonds. The treatment of certain indexed stocks is also clarified. Subsequent legislation has modified this statement. See 58.20 SHARES AND SECURITIES.

23.2.84 **Building societies and the taxation of gains on the disposal of gilt-edged securities.** The Revenue indicate their view of the tax treatment of such disposals. See 33.1 INTERACTION WITH OTHER TAXES.

17.5.84 **Furnished holiday lettings and caravans.** The Revenue indicate their practice as to the tax treatment of such accommodation. See 22.1 FURNISHED HOLIDAY ACCOMMODATION.

27.12.84 **Assets disposed of in a series of transactions.** The Revenue give their views on anti-avoidance legislation applying before 20 March 1985.
See 3.14 ANTI-AVOIDANCE.

16.4.85 **Retirement relief and ill-health.** The Revenue explain the procedures they will adopt in obtaining evidence of ill-health. See 53.4 RETIREMENT RELIEF.

8.7.88 **Capital gains deferred between 1982 and 1988.** Guidance is given as to the availability of the 50% relief where rollover relief was claimed in respect of the disposal of the old asset before 31 March 1982, and the replacement asset was acquired afterwards. See 8.12 ASSETS HELD ON 31 MARCH 1982.

3.5.89 **Personal equity plans.** The requirements that unit trusts and authorised unit trusts have to meet will be relaxed. See 58.22 SHARES AND SECURITIES.

6.10.89 **Personal equity plans.** New issue shares generally on offer to the public will not be disqualified from being transferred to a plan even though concurrent separate offers are made on slightly different terms to, for example, employees of the company concerned. See 58.22 SHARES AND SECURITIES.

19.12.89 **Business expansion scheme: shares issued before 19 March 1986.** An unintended change in the law made by *ICTA 1988* is to be corrected.
See 20.17 ENTERPRISE INVESTMENT SCHEME (AND BES).

26.2.90 **Elections for an appeal to be heard by the Special Commissioners.** The procedure to be adopted by inspectors of taxes is explained. See 4.5 APPEALS.

20.3.90 **Value added tax capital goods scheme: implication for capital gains tax.** See 33.3 INTERACTION WITH OTHER TAXES.

9.5.90 **Confidentiality of information.** The Revenue will disclose details of absent parents liable to support lone-parent families. See 28.2 INLAND REVENUE: CONFIDENTIALITY OF INFORMATION.

9.5.90 **Clearance procedure for employee share ownership trusts.** The Revenue are prepared to give an opinion whether a trust qualifies for relief. See 19.32 EMPLOYEE SHARE SCHEMES.

17.10.90 **Personal equity plans.** Pending the issue of revised regulations, certain changes to the rules for qualifying investments are applied by concession. See 58.22 SHARES AND SECURITIES.

18.10.90 **Tax fraud: 'Hansard' extract.** The Board's policy as to whether they will accept a money settlement instead of instituting fraud proceedings is explained. See 9.9 BACK DUTY.

21.11.90 **Married persons owning jointly held property.** The Revenue explain how gains should be allocated between spouses under independent taxation. See 41.1 MARRIED PERSONS.

14.12.90 **Clearance procedure for employee share ownership trusts.** The Revenue are prepared to give an opinion whether a draft trust deed (as well as any substantive one) qualifies for relief. See 19.32 EMPLOYEE SHARE SCHEMES.

19.12.90 **Revenue practice regarding validity of trust deeds for general and tax law purposes.** From 6 April 1991 new trust deeds will not normally be examined by the Revenue to check their validity. See 57.6 SETTLEMENTS.

31.1.91 **Double taxation: Ghana.** Details of claims able to be made by taxpayers are given following the discovery that an earlier agreement was still in force because a later agreement, which had been operated in practice for many years, had never been formally ratified. See 18.2 DOUBLE TAX RELIEF.

12.6.91 **Friendly societies: tax-exempt policies.** Deals with certain pre-20 March 1991 policies written on the mistaken assumption that they were not tax-exempt. See 21.42 EXEMPTIONS AND RELIEFS.

18.11.91 **Valuation of unquoted shares at 31 March 1982.** Shares Valuation Division may initiate valuation procedures, in certain circumstances, before receiving a formal request to do so from the inspector. See 8.2 ASSETS HELD ON 31 MARCH 1982.

15.9.92 **Rollover relief and groups of companies.** Depending on the outcome of a court case, steps may be taken to ensure that the established practice in relation to roll-over relief and groups of companies will continue to apply. See 55.5 ROLLOVER RELIEF.

31 Inland Revenue Press Releases

17.2.93 **Revenue Adjudicator and Codes of Practice.** The appointment of the Adjudicator and publication of a series of Codes of Practice are announced. See 27.6 and 27.7 INLAND REVENUE: ADMINISTRATION.

16.3.93 **Temporary residents in the UK: available accommodation.** Available accommodation in the UK, though ignored for certain temporary visitors to the UK after 1992/93, will still be taken into determining an individual's residence or ordinary residence status in other circumstances. See 52.3–52.5 RESIDENCE AND DOMICILE.

1.4.93 **Payment of tax by electronic funds transfer.** An effective date of payment of tax is provided. See 46.5 PAYMENT OF TAX.

23.7.93 **Tax repayments to EC resident companies.** Such companies can qualify for repayment supplement in respect of accounting periods ending before 1 October 1993 in certain circumstances. See 34.3 INTEREST ON OVERPAID TAX.

9.2.94 **European Economic Area Agreement.** The coming into force of the European Economic Area Agreement from 1 January 1994 affects European Economic Interest Groupings. See 44.15 OVERSEAS MATTERS.

7.4.94 **Repayments of overpaid tax made automatically.** From 5 April 1994, the Revenue will use computer systems that identify and repay overpayments automatically in most cases. See 46.10 PAYMENT OF TAX.

29.11.94 **Claims for rollover relief.** After 28 November 1994 claims for rollover relief must be made in writing specifying certain details. See 55.2 ROLLOVER RELIEF.

14.9.95 **Venture capital trusts: proportion of investments to be held in 'qualifying holdings'.** An inadvertent breach of the minimum proportion requirement will not lead to withdrawal of approval as a venture capital trust. See 65.2 VENTURE CAPITAL TRUSTS.

8.2.96 **Profits and Losses of Theatre Backers (Angels).** Revenue treatment.
See 39.17 LOSSES.

11.3.96 **Remission and Repayment of tax in cases of Official Error.** New procedures introduced from 11 March 1996. See 46.8 PAYMENT OF TAX.

21.3.96 **CGT treatment of certain payments by banks and building societies.** The Revenue give their views on the treatment of cashbacks and other lump sum payments (on mergers, takeovers and conversions) by banks and building societies. Partly superseded by Revenue Press Release of 27 March 1997 (see below) and, as regards cashbacks, by SP 4/97. See 58.26 SHARES AND SECURITIES.

31.5.96 **Disclosure and discovery under self-assessment.** A Revenue paper discusses disclosure requirements, with particular reference to the possibility of a discovery assessment. See 5.2 ASSESSMENTS, 56.5 SELF-ASSESSMENT.

20.1.97 **Self-assessment — the tax obligations of trustees and beneficiaries of certain bare trusts.** Trustees are not required to make self-assessment returns or payments on account. See 56.33 SELF-ASSESSMENT.

27.1.97 **Self-assessment— payments on account — calculation of interest following late issue of statements of account.** See 56.19 SELF-ASSESSMENT.

4.2.97 **Self-assessment — valuations for capital gains tax.** The Revenue will, on request, check post-transaction asset valuations for capital gains tax computation purposes. See 54.5 RETURNS.

27.3.97 **Cash payments to investors in Cheltenham and Gloucester Building Society on takeover by Lloyds Bank.** The Revenue explain their revised treatment of cash received by investors as a result of building society conversions and takeovers. See 58.26 SHARES AND SECURITIES.

13.8.97 **Indexation allowance — correction to RPI figure for September 1994.** The Revenue announce that an incorrect retail price index figure was published for September 1994 and explain the ramifications. See 26.1 INDEXATION.

12.12.97 **Self-assessment — provision of information from taxpayer statements of account to authorised agents.** The Revenue will continue to provide such information to agents. See 56.15 SELF-ASSESSMENT.

31.3.98 **'Faster Working' scheme for self-assessment enquiries.** Self-employed people whose tax returns are selected for enquiry will be invited to participate in 'Faster Working', which involves setting an agreed timetable for the enquiry. See 56.11 SELF-ASSESSMENT.

31.7.98 **Payment of tax in euros.** After 1 January 1999, British businesses may, if they wish, pay tax in euros (the European single currency). See 46.14 PAYMENT OF TAX.

17.12.98 **The European Single Currency (Taxes) Regulations** are introduced. Their purpose is to prevent unintended UK tax consequences arising from the introduction of the euro in certain other EU Member States from 1 January 1999. See 13.1 COMPANIES, 44.1 OVERSEAS MATTERS.

2.3.99 **Fish quota** are added to the classes of assets qualifying for rollover relief. See 55.3 ROLLOVER RELIEF—REPLACEMENT OF BUSINESS ASSETS.

11.3.99 **Interest factor tables** for pre-self-assessment repayment supplement and interest on overdue tax are published by the Revenue. See 34.2 INTEREST ON OVERPAID TAX and 35.2 INTEREST AND SURCHARGES ON UNPAID TAX.

8.6.99 **Corporation tax payable in instalments by large companies.** The Revenue outline the way in which they will use the information and penalty powers contained in the instalment payments regulations. See 46.2 PAYMENT OF TAX.

18.6.99 **Controlled Foreign Companies.** The Revenue publish guidance notes on the CFC legislation. See 44.7 OVERSEAS MATTERS.

13.8.99 **Payment of tax.** As an experiment, the Revenue offer a limited facility to pay tax by debit card over the telephone. See 56.15 SELF-ASSESSMENT.

10.1.2000 The Revenue's service of offering **post-transaction (pre-return) valuation checks** is extended to companies (in relation to their chargeable gains). See 54.11 RETURNS.

16.2.2000 **Discounts to boost use of internet.** For one year from April 2000, individual taxpayers who file their self-assessment tax return via the internet and pay any tax due electronically will receive a discount of £10. See 27.9 INLAND REVENUE: ADMINISTRATION, 54.4 RETURNS.

21.3.2000 **Rollover relief for gains on company shareholdings.** The Government is to consult on the possibility of introducing a rollover relief for gains on substantial shareholdings held by companies, with a view to including legislation in Finance Act 2001 (Revenue News Release BN2C). See 55.1 ROLLOVER RELIEF.

21.3.2000 **31 March 1982 valuations.** Companies and groups may ask the Revenue to agree the value at 31 March 1982 of large portfolios of land and buildings held since then. (Revenue News Release BN2G). See 8.2 ASSETS HELD ON 31 MARCH 1982.

23.6.2000 **Rollover relief for gains on company shareholdings.** The Revenue issue a technical note exploring the above-mentioned proposals of 21 March 2000. See 55.1 ROLLOVER RELIEF.

32 Inland Revenue Statements of Practice

The following is a summary of those current Statements of Practice published in Revenue Pamphlet IR 131 (January 2000) or subsequently announced for inclusion therein, which are referred to in this book.

Statements are divided into those originally published before 18 July 1978 (which are given a reference letter (according to the subject matter) and consecutive number, e.g. E11) and later Statements (which are numbered consecutively in each year, e.g. SP 10/86).

Copies of individual SP-denominated Statements are available free of charge from Inland Revenue Information Centre, Ground Floor, South West Wing, Bush House, Strand, London, WC2B 4RD (large SAE to accompany postal applications).

Copies of recently published Statements are also available (with the relevant press release) on the Revenue web site at www.inlandrevenue.gov.uk/home.htm

A8 **Stock dividends.** The interpretation of *ICTA 1988, s 251(2)* is clarified. See 58.13 SHARES AND SECURITIES.

A13 **Completion of return forms by attorneys.** In cases of age and infirmity of the taxpayer the Revenue will accept the signature of an attorney who has full knowledge of the taxpayer's affairs. See 54.9 RETURNS.

B1 **Treatment of VAT.** The position of partly exempt persons is considered. See 33.3 INTERACTION WITH OTHER TAXES.

D1 **Part disposals of land.** Where part of an estate is disposed of, the Revenue will accept that that part can be treated as a separate asset and the total cost apportioned accordingly (i.e. on an alternative basis to the usual part disposal formula). See 36.7 LAND.

D3 **Company liquidations: shareholders' capital gains tax.** Special rules can be applied where a shareholder receives more than one distribution in the liquidation. See 7.12 ASSETS HELD ON 6 APRIL 1965 and 58.15 SHARES AND SECURITIES.

D4 **Short delay by owner-occupier in taking up residence.** The period of occupation of a house will, in certain circumstances, include one year prior to taking up residence. This statement was replaced by ESC D49 on 18 October 1994. See 48.2 PRIVATE RESIDENCES.

D6 **Replacement of business assets: time limit.** Where land is acquired under a compulsory purchase order and leased back to the vendor, the Revenue will, under certain conditions, extend the time limit for replacement.
See 36.11 LAND.

D7 **Treatment of VAT.** See 33.3 INTERACTION WITH OTHER TAXES.

D10 **Termination of interest in possession in part of settled property.** The Revenue will agree with the trustees what assets are to be identified with the termination. See 57.9 SETTLEMENTS.

D11 **Partnership: assets owned by a partner.** Rollover relief may be available. See 45.12 PARTNERSHIPS and 55.1 ROLLOVER RELIEF.

D12 **Partnerships.** This statement sets out a number of points of general practice agreed in discussions with the Law Society and the Allied Accountancy Bodies on the capital gains tax treatment of partnerships. See 45 PARTNERSHIPS.

D18 **Value-shifting: TCGA 1992, s 30, Sch 11 para 10(1).** These provisions do not apply when a farmer retires, leases the farm to his son, and sells the freehold, subject to the lease, to an outside investor. See 3.6 ANTI-AVOIDANCE.

D19 **Replacement of business assets in groups of companies.** To obtain rollover relief, the Revenue do not insist that a company be a member of the group at the time of the transaction carried out by the other company. See 55.5 ROLLOVER RELIEF.

D21 **Time limit for an election for valuation on 6 April 1965 under TCGA 1992, Sch 2 para 17: company leaving a group: TCGA 1992, s 179.** See 13.19 COMPANIES.

D23 **Overseas resident company.** The appropriate proportion of any overseas tax payable by a non-resident company is deductible in computing the gain chargeable on a UK participator under *TCGA 1992, s 13.* See 44.6 OVERSEAS MATTERS.

D24 **Initial repairs to property.** Such expense, including the cost of decorating, not allowable for Schedule A purposes, is regarded as allowable for capital gains tax purposes. See 17.3(*b*) DISPOSAL.

SP 1/79 **Partnerships: extension of SP D12 above.** The practice whereby the capitalised value of an annuity paid to a retired partner is not treated as consideration for the disposal of his share in the partnership assets in certain circumstances is extended to cases where a lump sum is paid in addition. See 45.8 PARTNERSHIPS.

SP 8/79 **Compensation for acquisition of property under compulsory powers.** As from 28 July 1978, any compensation for temporary loss of profits is taxable under Schedule D, Case I or II. See 17.7 DISPOSAL.

SP 10/79 **Power for trustees to allow a beneficiary to occupy a dwelling-house.** Depending upon the circumstances, this may be treated as giving rise to an interest in possession. See 57.7 SETTLEMENTS.

SP 14/79 **Unquoted shares or securities held on 6 April 1965: computation of chargeable gains where there has been a reorganisation of share capital.** See 7.12 ASSETS HELD ON 6 APRIL 1965.

SP 14/80 **Relief for owner-occupiers.** This statement explains the relief for owner-occupiers who let living accommodation in their homes. See 48.3, 48.8 PRIVATE RESIDENCES.

SP 18/80 **Securities dealt in on The Stock Exchange Unlisted Securities Market: status and valuation for tax purposes** (now obsolete). Such securities are not regarded as 'quoted' or 'listed' but are 'authorised to be dealt in'. See 40.4 MARKET VALUE.

SP 3/81 **Individuals coming to the UK: ordinary residence.** The ordinary residence position is further explained, regarding individuals coming to, or leaving, the UK who have, or acquire, accommodation for their use in the UK. See 52.4 RESIDENCE AND DOMICILE.

SP 8/81 **Rollover relief for replacement of business assets: trades carried on successively.** The Board's practice in deciding whether trades are carried on successively, how acquisitions in the interval between trades are to be regarded, and how this treatment is to be applied to groups of companies, is explained. See 55.4 ROLLOVER RELIEF.

SP 3/82 **Capital gains tax indexation before the 1985 date.** The Revenue gives guidance on the practice that will be adopted in relation to (*a*) the identification of securities disposed of during the twelve months before indexation came into effect (see 59.10 SHARES AND SECURITIES—IDENTIFICATION RULES); (*b*) the time apportionment rules for assets acquired before 6 April 1965 (see 7.9 ASSETS HELD ON 6 APRIL 1965); and (*c*) disposals of assets on a no gain/no loss basis (see 26.4 INDEXATION). This practice is of limited application for disposals after 5 April 1985 (31 March 1985 for companies).

32 Inland Revenue Statements of Practice

SP 5/83 **Use of schedules in making personal tax returns.** Schedules supporting a return are acceptable provided the taxpayer signs the official declaration and all material in the schedules is clearly linked to the official return form. See 54.9 RETURNS.

SP 1/84 **Trade unions: provident benefits** include legal expenses in connection with a member's accident or injury claim or unfair dismissal. See 21.54 EXEMPTIONS AND RELIEFS.

SP 6/84 **Leasing of mobile drilling rigs etc. by overseas residents.** The Revenue indicate their practice. See 44.14 OVERSEAS MATTERS.

SP 7/84 **Exercise of a power of appointment or advancement over settled property.** The Revenue indicate how they will decide whether a new settlement has been created. See 57.6 SETTLEMENTS.

SP 10/84 **Foreign bank accounts.** The Revenue give their practice regarding direct transfers from one foreign bank account to another. See 21.5 EXEMPTIONS AND RELIEFS.

SP 5/85 **Division of a company on a share for share basis.** The special treatment accorded to a company reconstruction under *TCGA 1992, s 136(1)(2)* and *s 139* is extended to cover a division, for *bona fide* commercial reasons, of a company's undertakings into two or more companies owned by different sets of shareholders. See 3.16 ANTI-AVOIDANCE; 13.7 COMPANIES and 58.10 SHARES AND SECURITIES.

SP 5/86 **Rollover relief for employees and office-holders.** In certain circumstances relief is available to such persons where the land or building owned is in general use in the trade carried on by the employer. See 55.4 ROLLOVER RELIEF.

SP 5/87 **Tax returns: use of substitute forms.** The Revenue states its requirements. See 54.9 RETURNS.

SP 2/88 **Civil tax penalties and criminal prosecution cases.** The Revenue explain a change of practice on seeking civil money penalties from certain taxpayers whom they have prosecuted. See 47.6 PENALTIES.

SP 6/88 **Double taxation relief.** The Revenue describe some situations where double taxation relief is available. See 18.7 DOUBLE TAX RELIEF.

SP 1/89 **Partnerships.** The practice concerning changes in partnership sharing ratios (see D12 above) is extended to cover the 1988 re-basing provisions. See 45.5 PARTNERSHIPS.

SP 4/89 **Company purchasing own shares.** The Revenue's practice where a purchase gives rise to a distribution is explained. See 58.18 SHARES AND SECURITIES.

SP 5/89 **Capital gains re-basing and indexation: shares held at 31 March 1982.** A single holding treatment will apply if some shares were held on 31 March 1982 and the remainder are treated as held on that date. See 8.7 ASSETS HELD ON 31 MARCH 1982.

SP 6/89 **Delay in rendering tax returns: interest on unpaid tax.** The Revenue's practice is explained. See 54.4 RETURNS.

SP 1/90 **Company residence.** The Revenue's approach to the determination of a company's residence is explained. See 52.6 RESIDENCE AND DOMICILE.

SP 2/90 **Company migration: notice and arrangements under FA 1988, s 130.** Guidance is given on the procedure, information and arrangements the Revenue will require under the provision. See 44.13 OVERSEAS MATTERS.

SP 5/90 **Accountants' working papers.** The Revenue's investigatory powers as regards the disclosure of accountants' working papers are explained. See 9.8 BACK DUTY.

SP 8/90 **Loans to traders evidenced by qualifying corporate bonds.** Loss relief will still be available where the security concerned ceases to have any value because it is redeemed early. See 39.11 LOSSES.

SP 2/91 **Residence in the UK: visits extended because of exceptional circumstances.** In deciding a person's residence status, days spent in the UK because of exceptional circumstances beyond the person's control will be ignored in certain cases. See 52.3 RESIDENCE AND DOMICILE.

SP 4/91 **Tax returns.** The principles adopted by the Revenue are explained. See 54.9 RETURNS.

SP 7/91 **Double taxation: business profits: unilateral relief.** The practice as regards admission of foreign taxes for unilateral relief is revised. See 18.4 DOUBLE TAX RELIEF.

SP 8/91 **Discovery assessments.** The Revenue practice as regards the making of further assessments following 'discovery' is explained. See 5.2 ASSESSMENTS.

SP 10/91 **Corporation tax: a major change in the nature or conduct of a trade or business.** The Revenue set out some of the circumstances which may amount to a major change in the nature or conduct of a trade for the purposes of, *inter alia*, *TCGA 1992, Sch 7A* (restriction of set-off of pre-entry losses where a company joins a group). See 13.24 , 13.32 COMPANIES.

SP 14/91 **Tax treatment of transactions in financial futures and options.** The Revenue give their views. See 17.10 DISPOSAL and 64.2 UNIT TRUSTS ETC.

SP 15/91 **Treatment of investment managers and their overseas clients.** The Revenue give their views. See 17.10 DISPOSAL.

SP 17/91 **Ordinary residence in the UK.** The practice regarding the commencement of ordinary residence where the period to be spent in the UK is less than three years is explained. See 52.4 RESIDENCE AND DOMICILE.

SP 3/92 **Double taxation agreement with the USSR.** The Revenue clarify the position following the disintegration of the old Soviet Union. See 18.2 DOUBLE TAX RELIEF.

SP 4/92 **Capital gains tax re-basing elections.** The Revenue describe the three kinds of disposal which will not be treated as the first relevant disposal for a re-basing election. See 8.3 ASSETS HELD ON 31 MARCH 1982.

SP 5/92 **Non-resident trusts.** The Revenue give their views on a number of detailed matters in connection with: the residence of trustees; past trustees' liabilities; the settlor's right to repayment from the trustees; trusts created before 19 March 1991; transactions entered into at arm's length; close companies; transactions with wholly-owned companies; loans made to settlements; loans made by trustees; failure to exercise rights to reimbursement; administrative expenses; life tenants; indemnities and guarantees; variations; *ultra vires* payments; and intra-group transfers. See 43 OFFSHORE SETTLEMENTS.

SP 8/92 **Hold-over relief: valuation of assets.** The circumstances in which the Inland Revenue will require a valuation of assets in respect of which a claim to hold-over relief is made are described. See 25.1 HOLD-OVER RELIEFS and 53.3 RETIREMENT RELIEF.

SP 5/93 **Double taxation agreement with Czechoslovakia.** The Revenue clarify the position following the split of Czechoslovakia into separate Czech and Slovak republics. See 18.2 DOUBLE TAX RELIEF.

SP 6/93 **Double taxation agreement with Yugoslavia.** The Revenue clarify the position following the disintegration of the former Yugoslavia into separate republics. See 18.2 DOUBLE TAX RELIEF.

32 Inland Revenue Statements of Practice

SP 9/93 **Corporation tax Pay and File: corporation tax returns.** The Revenue explain how its statutory powers will be exercised in relation to corporation tax returns under Pay and File. See 54.11 RETURNS.

SP 10/93 **Corporation tax Pay and File: special arrangement for groups of companies.** For companies dealt with mainly in one tax district simplified procedures can operate regarding claims to group relief and giving consents to surrender such relief. Superseded by *Regulations* for accounting periods ending on or after 1 July 1999. See 54.11 RETURNS.

SP 11/93 **Corporation tax Pay and File: claims to capital allowances and group relief made outside the normal time limit.** The Revenue's power to exercise a discretion with regard to such late claims is explained. See 54.11 RETURNS.

SP 13/93 **Compulsory acquisition of freehold by tenant.** The Revenue will accept a rollover relief claim from a landlord whose tenant has exercised certain statutory rights to acquire the freehold reversion or extension of the lease. See 36.11 LAND.

SP 15/93 **Incidental costs of acquisition and disposal.** In certain cases, large companies may round these costs to the nearest £1,000. See 17.3 DISPOSAL.

SP 4/94 **Enhanced stock dividends received by trustees of interest in possession trusts.** Revenue set out their view on tax treatment. See 58.13 SHARES AND SECURITIES.

SP 8/94 **Allowable expenditure: expenses incurred by personal representatives and corporate trustees under TCGA 1992, s 38(1)(b).** For deaths after 5 April 1993, a revised scale of expenditure is allowable for costs of establishing title in computing gains or losses of personal representatives on the sale of assets in a deceased person's estate. See 16.8 DEATH.

SP 8/95 **Venture capital trusts: default terms in loan agreements.** Certain standard terms will be ignored in deciding whether a loan qualifies as a security. See 65.2 VENTURE CAPITAL TRUSTS.

SP 1/97 **The electronic lodgement service.** The Revenue provide details and procedures for filing self-assessment returns electronically. See 54.16 RETURNS.

SP 3/97 **Investment trusts investing in authorised unit trusts or open-ended investment companies.** The Revenue express their views of the tax implications of such investment. Replaces SP 7/94 with effect from 18 July 1997. See 64.2 UNIT TRUSTS ETC.

SP 4/97 **Taxation of commissions, cashbacks and discounts.** No chargeable gain arises on receipt of a cashback. See 21.20 EXEMPTIONS AND RELIEFS. See TOLLEY'S INCOME TAX for income tax consequences of the receipt of commissions, cashbacks and discounts.

SP 4/98 **Partnerships including companies.** The Revenue issue guidance on the application of, *inter alia*, the loan relationships legislation to partnerships which include one or more company partners. See 38.4 LOAN RELATIONSHIPS OF COMPANIES.

SP 5/98 **EIS and venture capital trusts: value of gross assets.** The Revenue set out their approach in applying the 'gross assets test'. Replaces SP 7/95 which applied only to venture capital trusts. See 20.5 ENTERPRISE INVESTMENT SCHEME (AND BES) and 65.3(*e*) VENTURE CAPITAL TRUSTS.

SP 6/98 **EIS, BES, reinvestment relief and venture capital trusts: loans to investors.** The Revenue explain how they apply the rules which deny or withdraw the above reliefs where investors receive loans linked to their investments. Replaces SP 3/94. See 20.2(*g*) ENTERPRISE INVESTMENT SCHEME (AND BES), 50.16 REINVESTMENT RELIEF and 65.5(*d*) VENTURE CAPITAL TRUSTS.

SP 7/98 **EIS, reinvestment relief and venture capital trusts: location of activity.** The Revenue give their interpretation of the requirement that qualifying trades or activities for the purposes of the above reliefs should be carried on wholly or mainly in the UK. Replaces SP 2/94. See 20.6 ENTERPRISE INVESTMENT SCHEME (AND BES), 50.15 REINVESTMENT RELIEF and 65.3(*b*) VENTURE CAPITAL TRUSTS.

SP 1/99 **Self-assessment enquiries.** Where an enquiry into a personal, partnership or trust return remains open pending agreement of a CGT valuation, the Revenue will not use the open enquiry to raise new issues which they would not otherwise have been able to raise. See 56.11 SELF-ASSESSMENT.

SP 2/99 **Authorised unit trusts, approved investment trusts and open-ended investment companies — monthly savings schemes.** A simplified method of calculating the chargeable gain arising on a disposal can be used as regards acquisitions in accounting years of funds ending before 6 April 1999 where savings commenced before 6 April 1998. Replaces SP 2/97 which itself replaced SP 3/89. See 64.1, 64.2, 64.4 UNIT TRUSTS ETC.

33 Interaction with Other Taxes

Cross-references. See 2 ANNUAL RATES AND EXEMPTIONS for rates applicable to gains by reference to lower, basic and higher rates of income tax; 13.44 COMPANIES as regards the taxation regime for exchange gains and losses of a 'qualifying company' whereby such transactions are only taken into account for the charge of corporation tax on income; 13.45 COMPANIES as regards the taxation regime for financial instruments involving interest rate and currency contracts of a 'qualifying company' whereby such transactions are only taken into account for the charge of corporation tax on income; 17 DISPOSAL for acquisition and disposal consideration taken into account for capital gains tax purposes generally; 25.7 HOLD-OVER RELIEFS for relief given to gifts after 13 March 1989 on which inheritance tax is chargeable etc; 36.15–36.18 LAND for premiums on leases of land charged to income tax; 58 SHARES AND SECURITIES for interaction with income tax provisions; 63.1 UNDERWRITERS AT LLOYD'S for treatment of assets in premiums trust funds.

33.1 GENERAL AND INCOME TAX

Any money or money's worth charged to income tax as income of, or taken into account as a receipt in computing income or profits or gains or losses of (except in relation to the computation under *ICTA 1988, s 76(2)* of management expenses of life assurance companies), the person making the disposal is excluded from the consideration for the disposal of the asset for capital gains tax purposes. However,

(*a*) this is not to be taken as excluding any money or money's worth taken into account in making a balancing charge for capital allowance purposes or brought into account as the disposal value of machinery or plant for such purposes (see *Hirsch v Crowthers Cloth Ltd Ch D 1989, 62 TC 759*);

(*b*) the capitalised value of a rentcharge (as in the case where a rentcharge is exchanged for another asset), ground annual or feu duty, or of a right of any other description to income or to payments in the nature of income over a period, or to a series of payments in the nature of income may be taken into account for capital gains tax purposes; and

(*c*) amounts chargeable to tax under *ICTA 1988, s 348* or *s 349* (deduction of basic rate income tax from annual payments) are not excluded from the disposal consideration for capital gains tax purposes.

[*TCGA 1992, s 37, s 52(2)(3)(5), Sch 8 para 5(6)*].

For income tax matters relating to know-how and patents (and which have a capital gains tax effect), see 6.4, 6.5 ASSETS). See also 44.8 OVERSEAS MATTERS for offshore funds.

Expenditure which is deductible in computing profits or losses for income tax purposes (or would be so deductible if the asset were held as a fixed asset of a trade) is excluded from being allowable expenditure for capital gains tax purposes. [*TCGA 1992, s 39(1)(2)*]. See 17.5 DISPOSAL.

Any assessment to income tax or decision on a claim under the *Income Tax Acts*, and any decision on an appeal in connection therewith, is conclusive for capital gains tax purposes where liability to tax depends on the provisions of the *Income Tax Acts*. [*TCGA 1992, s 284*]. Where *alternative* income tax and capital gains tax assessments are made in respect of the same transactions, the fact that the capital gains tax assessment becomes final does not preclude the income tax assessment taking effect instead (*Bye v Coren CA 1986, 60 TC 116*). See also *Lord Advocate v McKenna CS 1989, 61 TC 688* and *CIR v Wilkinson CA 1992, 65 TC 28*.

Income or capital? Whether the gain arising on the disposal of an asset is of income or capital nature has been tested in the courts on numerous occasions and the outcome is likely to be one of fact and degree. In particular, see 36.3 LAND for isolated and speculative transactions in land. 'No part of our law of taxation presents such almost insoluble conundrums as the decision whether a receipt or outgoing is capital or income for tax purposes' (Lord Upjohn in *Strick v Regent Oil Co Ltd HL 1965, 43 TC 1* which see for a comprehensive review of the law). A widely used test is the 'enduring benefit' one given by Viscount Cave in *Atherton v British Insulated & Helsby Cables Ltd HL 1925, 10 TC 155.*

Building societies and gilts. In the light of legal advice received, the Inland Revenue decided to treat gains of building societies arising from the realisation of gilt-edged securities and similar stock after 23 February 1984 as part of trading profits and not as chargeable gains subject to the rules of capital gains tax (Revenue Press Release 23 February 1984).

Investment trusts and the tax treatment of forward currency transactions. See 64.2 UNIT TRUSTS ETC.

Transactions in certain options and futures by certain taxpayers. See 17.10 and 17.11 DISPOSAL.

33.2 INHERITANCE TAX

A lifetime disposal which contains an element of gift may incur liability to inheritance tax (IHT) as well as capital gains tax. For the purposes of IHT, no account is taken of any capital gains tax borne by the transferor in determining the reduction in value in his estate. [*IHTA 1984, s 164*].

Example

A makes a gift of land, to a non-UK resident discretionary trustee, B, which is valued at £20,000 and on which there is a capital gains tax liability of £3,000. The value for IHT purposes (subject to grossing-up for the IHT payable) is £20,000 (i.e. the same as if A had sold the land and given the £20,000 proceeds to B).

Relief for CGT against IHT

Capital gains tax paid will be taken into account for IHT purposes in the following instances.

(*a*) If the transferor fails to pay all or part of the capital gains tax within twelve months of the due date, an assessment may be made on the donee (see 23.5 GIFTS) and the amount of such tax borne by the donee is treated as reducing the value transferred. There is a similar effect when the transfer is from a settlement but, after 8 March 1982, this only applies if the capital gains tax is borne by a person who becomes absolutely entitled to the settled property concerned. [*IHTA 1984, s 165(1)(2)*]

Example

In the *Example* above, if A fails to pay the £3,000 capital gains tax and it is borne by B, the value transferred by A is £17,000 for the purposes of IHT (again subject to grossing-up for the IHT payable).

(*b*) Where a person sells, or is treated as having sold, national heritage property on the breach or termination of an undertaking (see 21.74 EXEMPTIONS AND RELIEFS) any capital gains tax payable is deductible in determining the value of the asset for IHT purposes. [*TCGA 1992, s 258(8)*].

Relief for IHT against CGT

Where hold-over relief is granted under

(i) *TCGA 1992, s 165* in relation to gifts made after 13 March 1989 (see 25.1 HOLD-OVER RELIEFS),

(ii) *TCGA 1992, s 260* in relation to gifts after 13 March 1989 (see 25.7 HOLD-OVER RELIEFS), or

(iii) *FA 1980, s 79* in relation to gifts after 5 April 1980 and before 14 March 1989 (see 25.9 HOLD-OVER RELIEFS),

the transferee may deduct on a subsequent disposal any IHT attributable to the value of the asset on the original transfer (being either a chargeable transfer or a potentially exempt transfer which proves to be a chargeable transfer). The tax deductible may be varied on the subsequent death of the transferor or otherwise but it cannot in any circumstances create an allowable loss on the subsequent disposal. [*TCGA 1992, s 67(1)–(3), s 165(10)(11), s 260(7)(8)*]. In the case of (ii) above, the same treatment applies if a hold-over relief claim *could have been made* (Revenue Capital Gains Manual CG 67050).

There is no relief for IHT under (i) and (iii) above if hold-over relief is *not* claimed, so that even where the gain otherwise arising is negligible or covered by reliefs a hold-over relief claim may still be beneficial overall (Tolley's Practical Tax 1984 p 198). A hold-over relief claim can be made even if an allowable loss arises on the original gift and so give rise to an IHT deduction on a subsequent disposal by the donee whilst not affecting the loss relief position of the donor. Where only part of the asset gifted is subsequently disposed of, the Revenue accept that any IHT paid on the original gift can still be deducted in full on the part disposal (subject to the size of the gain arising) and there is no need to apportion IHT paid between the part disposed of and the part retained (Taxation 5 October 1989 pp 12, 14). There is no provision for indexation allowance to be calculated by reference to the IHT that can be deducted.

Valuation of assets. Valuations of assets made *at death* for the purpose of an inheritance tax charge on the value of a person's estate immediately before death are binding for capital gains tax purposes. [*TCGA 1992, s 274; IHTA 1984, s 168*]. See also Revenue Tax Bulletin April 1995 p 209. In practice (see Revenue Pamphlet IHT 15 p 15), unless there are special circumstances, quoted shares and securities are valued in the same way as for capital gains tax (see 40.2 MARKET VALUE). In the case of land and quoted shares and securities, proceeds of certain post-death sales within a specified period may be substituted for values at date of death for inheritance tax purposes. The value of related property (as defined for inheritance tax purposes) may also be revised in the event of a post-death sale. If such substitutions/revisions are made for inheritance tax purposes, they must be made for CGT purposes also. See TOLLEY'S INHERITANCE TAX for details and also Revenue Capital Gains Manual CG 32290–32310.

33.3 VALUE ADDED TAX

If VAT is suffered on the purchase of an asset, but is available for set-off in full in the purchaser's VAT account (e.g. a capital asset purchased by a trader who is registered for VAT), then the cost of the asset for capital gains tax purposes is the cost exclusive of VAT. Where no VAT set-off is available, the cost is inclusive of VAT borne. On the disposal of an asset, VAT chargeable is disregarded in computing the disposal consideration for capital gains tax purposes (Revenue Pamphlet IR 131, SP D7).

A person whose output is partly exempt and partly taxable may set off only part of his VAT on inputs against his VAT on outputs. In such a case, although the computation of disposal proceeds is as above, it will be necessary to allocate the VAT ultimately suffered to the various expense payments made. Inspectors will be prepared to consider any reasonable arrangements made to carry out this apportionment. A taxable person making both taxable and exempt supplies may therefore treat as part of the capital gains tax cost of an asset the input tax that was not available for credit in respect of the acquisition (Revenue Pamphlet IR 131, SP B1).

The above practices should be read in the light of a Revenue Press Release of 20 March 1990 which mentioned that VAT on certain inputs (broadly land, buildings and computers with values above certain levels) after 31 March 1990 may require annual adjustment for a period of up to ten years after the input concerned. In certain circumstances a VAT adjustment may reduce the amount of expenditure on an asset qualifying for ROLLOVER RELIEF (55). Where a VAT adjustment is made after a claim to rollover relief has been determined, the Revenue will not normally seek to reopen the claim.

34 Interest on Overpaid Tax

Cross-reference. See 46 PAYMENT OF TAX.

34.1 PERSONS OTHER THAN COMPANIES — 1996/97 ONWARDS (SELF-ASSESSMENT)

Under self-assessment **for 1996/97 and subsequent years**, a repayment by the Revenue of capital gains tax paid by or on behalf of an individual (or trust or personal representatives of a deceased person) carries interest at the rate(s) listed below. The amount by which the repayment is so increased is known as a **repayment supplement**. The interest runs from the date the tax is paid until the date on which the order for the repayment is issued by the Revenue. [*TCGA 1992, s 283(1)(2)(4); FA 1994, s 196, s 199(2), Sch 19 para 46, Sch 26 Pt V(23); FA 1997, s 92(5)(6)*]. A repayment supplement is not taxable in the hands of the recipient. [*ICTA 1988, s 824(8)*].

Rates of interest are:

4.00% p.a. from 6 February 2000

3.00% p.a. from 6 March 1999 to 5 February 2000

4.00% p.a. from 6 January 1999 to 5 March 1999

4.75% p.a. from 6 August 1997 to 5 January 1999

4.00% p.a. from 31 January 1997 to 5 August 1997

It will be noted that the rates are considerably lower than those by reference to which interest is charged on late paid tax (see 35.1 INTEREST AND SURCHARGES ON UNPAID TAX). The rates are adjusted automatically by reference to changes in the average of base lending rates of certain clearing banks, and are announced by Revenue Press Release. For the relationship to base rates, see *SI 1989 No 1297, Reg 3AB* as inserted from 31 January 1997 by *SI 1996 No 3187*.

In contrast to the position prior to 1996/97 (see 34.2 below), there is no requirement that the taxpayer be resident in the UK or European Community.

Although repayment supplement runs from the date the tax was paid, even if this falls before the due date, the Revenue state that they will not pay repayment supplement on any amount deliberately overpaid (Revenue Press Release 12 November 1996). This is intended to deter taxpayers from using the Revenue as a source of tax-free interest. Where a payment of tax is not set against any liability and repayment is not claimed, the payment remains on record until the next liability arises, but no repayment supplement will be given. (Revenue Tax Bulletin June 1999 p 674). As regards the date on which payment is treated as made, see 46.5 PAYMENT OF TAX and 56.21 SELF-ASSESSMENT. Interest is not payable on repayments made by order or judgement of a court having power to allow interest (for which see 46.4 PAYMENT OF TAX). [*TCGA 1992, s 283(3)*].

Repayment supplement is added in similar fashion to any repayment of a penalty imposed under any provision of *TMA 1970* (see 47 PENALTIES and 56.22–56.26 SELF-ASSESSMENT) or of a surcharge imposed under *TMA 1970, s 59C* (see 35.5 INTEREST AND SURCHARGES ON UNPAID TAX). [*ICTA 1988, s 824*]. For full details of repayment supplement under *section 824*, see 56.20 SELF-ASSESSMENT and also TOLLEY'S INCOME TAX.

34.2 PERSONS OTHER THAN COMPANIES — 1995/96 AND EARLIER YEARS

The provisions described below apply where the tax repayable relates to 1995/96 and/or earlier years.

A repayment (or set-off) to an individual by the Revenue of capital gains tax, repaid more than twelve months after the end of the year of assessment to which it relates, carries interest ('*a repayment supplement*'), provided that the individual was resident in the UK for that year. However, repayment supplement will also be paid by concession where the individual was resident elsewhere in the European Community for that year provided all the other conditions are met. The Revenue will also accept claims on a similar basis from persons who were resident elsewhere in the EC for a year of assessment for which a repayment without supplement has been made since 12 July 1987 (Revenue Pamphlet IR 1, A82). (*Note.* Although stated by the Revenue to be a concession, there may be a legal requirement not to discriminate against individuals resident elsewhere in the EC; see 34.3 below regarding company accounting periods ending before 1 October 1993. Although phrased in terms of income tax and repayment supplement under *ICTA 1988, s 824*, it is understood that the concession applies equally to capital gains tax and repayment supplement under *TCGA 1992, s 283*.)

The repayment supplement will not constitute income of the recipient for any tax purpose. The interest will run to the end of the tax month (i.e. 6th day of one calendar month to 5th day of following month) in which the repayment order is issued, and will commence as follows.

Tax originally paid	*Interest commences*
More than twelve months after year of assessment	From end of year of assessment in which tax was paid
In any other case	From end of twelve months following year of assessment

Rates of interest are:

4.00% p.a. from 6 February 2000

3.00% p.a. from 6 March 1999 to 5 February 2000

4.00% p.a. from 6 January 1999 to 5 March 1999

4.75% p.a. from 6 August 1997 to 5 January 1999

4.00% p.a. from 31 January 1997 to 5 August 1997

6.25% p.a. from 6 February 1996 to 30 January 1997

7.00% p.a. from 6 March 1995 to 5 February 1996

6.25% p.a. from 6 October 1994 to 5 March 1995

5.50% p.a. from 6 January 1994 to 5 October 1994

6.25% p.a. from 6 March 1993 to 5 January 1994

7.00% p.a. from 6 December 1992 to 5 March 1993

7.75% p.a. from 6 November 1992 to 5 December 1992

9.25% p.a. from 6 October 1991 to 5 November 1992

10.00% p.a. from 6 July 1991 to 5 October 1991

10.75% p.a. from 6 May 1991 to 5 July 1991

11.50% p.a. from 6 March 1991 to 5 May 1991

12.25% p.a. from 6 November 1990 to 5 March 1991

13.00% p.a. from 6 November 1989 to 5 November 1990

12.25% p.a. from 6 July 1989 to 5 November 1989

34.2 Interest on Overpaid Tax

11.50% p.a. from 6 January 1989 to 5 July 1989

10.50% p.a. from 6 October 1988 to 5 January 1989

9.75% p.a. from 6 August 1988 to 5 October 1988

7.75% p.a. from 6 May 1988 to 5 August 1988

8.25% p.a. from 6 December 1987 to 5 May 1988

9.00% p.a. from 6 September 1987 to 5 December 1987

8.25% p.a. from 6 June 1987 to 5 September 1987

9.00% p.a. from 6 April 1987 to 5 June 1987

9.50% p.a. from 6 November 1986 to 5 April 1987

8.50% p.a. from 6 August 1986 to 5 November 1986

11.00% p.a. from 6 May 1985 to 5 August 1986

8.00% p.a. from 6 December 1982 to 5 May 1985

12.00% p.a. from 6 January 1980 to 5 December 1982

9.00% p.a. from 6 April 1974 to 5 January 1980

6.00% p.a. previously

The rates of interest are adjusted automatically by reference to changes in the average of base lending rates of certain clearing banks, and are announced in Revenue Press Releases. (Revenue Press Release 1 August 1989). Before 1990, they were prescribed by statutory instrument. The relationship to base rates was revised from 31 January 1997 (see *SI 1996 No 3187*).

Where a repayment relates to tax paid in two or more years of assessment, it is treated, as far as possible, as representing payments made in later rather than earlier years.

Trustees of a 'United Kingdom trust' (within *ICTA 1988, s 231(5)*), 'personal representatives' (within *ICTA 1988, s 701(4)*) of a deceased person whose estate is a 'United Kingdom estate' (within *ICTA 1988, s 701(9)*) and partnerships are treated similarly to individuals (including the concessional practice mentioned above (Revenue Pamphlet IR 1, A82)).

The above provisions do not apply to companies (see 34.3 below) or to payments or repayments made by order or judgement of a court having power to allow interest (for which see 46.4 PAYMENT OF TAX).

[*TCGA 1992, s 283; ICTA 1988, s 824(8); SI 1974 No 966; SI 1979 No 1687; SI 1982 No 1587; SI 1985 No 563; SI 1986 Nos 1181, 1832; SI 1987 Nos 513, 898, 1492, 1988; SI 1988 Nos 756, 1278, 1621, 2185; SI 1989 No 1000; FA 1989, s 158(2)(5)(6), s 178, s 179(1)(4), Sch 17 Pt IV; SI 1989 Nos 1297, 1298; SI 1996 No 3187*].

For the above purposes and for those in 34.3 below for accounting periods ended before 1 October 1993, the Board publish ready-reckoner tables of interest factors which may be used in calculating repayment supplement. These are updated as rates change (but not beyond 5 April 1999). They cannot be used where the supplement is payable under 34.1 above for 1996/97 onwards or under 34.3 below for company accounting periods ending after 30 September 1993. (Revenue Press Release 11 March 1999).

Example

L realised net chargeable gains (after the annual exemption) of £20,000 in 1995/96. An assessment was raised on 15 January 1997, charging tax of £8,000. L paid the tax on 30 January 1997. In December 1998, L made a claim under *TCGA 1992, s 152* (rollover relief) and the 1995/96 assessment was reduced to £8,000, with tax payable of £3,200. A repayment of £4,800 was made by payable order issued on 15 January 1999.

Repayment supplement is	£
6.4.97 – 5.8.97 £4,800 × 4% × $\frac{4}{12}$	64.00
6.8.97 – 5.1.99 £4,800 × 4.75% × $\frac{17}{12}$	323.00
6.1.99 – 5.2.99 £4,800 × 4% × $\frac{1}{12}$	16.00
	£403.00

34.3 COMPANIES

Accounting periods ending after 30 September 1993

Where a repayment of corporation tax falls to be made to a company for an accounting period ending after 30 September 1993 (Pay and File), the repayment carries interest (under *ICTA 1988, s 826*) from the 'material date' until the order for repayment is issued.

The *'material date'* is the later of the date the corporation tax was paid and the date on which it became (or would have become) due and payable, i.e. subject to the payment of tax in quarterly instalments where applicable, the day following the expiry of nine months from the end of the accounting period (see 46.2 PAYMENT OF TAX).

The interest rate is determined by criteria contained in Treasury regulations made by statutory instrument so that when such criteria change so as to alter the rate, the Board must specify in an order the new rate and the day from which it has effect. For the criteria, see *SI 1989 No 1297, Reg 3B* and, as regards accounting periods ending on or after 1 July 1999, *Regs 3BA, 3BB* as inserted by *SI 1998 No 3176* and amended by *SI 1999 No 1928.*

Rates of interest for accounting periods ending before 1 July 1999 are:

3.50% p.a. from 6 February 2000

2.75% p.a. from 6 March 1999 to 5 February 2000

3.25% p.a. from 6 January 1999 to 5 March 1999

4.00% p.a. from 6 August 1997 to 5 January 1999

3.25% p.a. from 6 February 1996 to 5 August 1997

4.00% p.a. from 6 March 1995 to 5 February 1996

3.25% p.a. from 6 October 1994 to 5 March 1995

2.50% p.a. from 6 January 1994 to 5 October 1994

3.25% p.a. from 1 October 1993 to 5 January 1994

The rate of interest for accounting periods ending on or after 1 July 1999 (such interest being chargeable to tax — see below) has been set at **5.00% p.a.** for amounts overpaid on or after the normal due date for payment of corporation tax (see above) (Revenue Press Release 2 February 2000). The rates for amounts overpaid before that date, **for example under the quarterly accounting rules for large companies** (see 46.2 PAYMENT OF TAX), are

5.75% p.a. from 21 February 2000

5.50% p.a. from 24 January 2000 to 20 February 2000

5.25% p.a. from 15 November 1999 to 23 January 2000

5.00% p.a. from 20 September 1999 to 14 November 1999

4.75% p.a. from 21 June 1999 to 19 September 1999

5.00% p.a. from 19 April 1999 to 20 June 1999

5.25% p.a. from 15 February 1999 to 18 April 1999

5.75% p.a. from 18 January 1999 to 14 February 1999

6.00% p.a. from 7 January 1999 to 17 January 1999

The latter set of rates applies up to the earlier of the date of repayment and the normal due date (whereafter the normal rates apply).

There are restrictions on the amount of the interest where surplus advance corporation tax of a later accounting period displaces mainstream corporation tax paid in respect of an earlier accounting period, or trading losses or non-trading deficits of a later accounting period are offset against profits of an earlier period or there is a combination of such events.

Interest is paid without deduction of income tax and, for accounting periods ending before 1 July 1999, is not brought into account in computing profits or income. Interest on repayments of tax paid for later accounting periods is chargeable to corporation tax as a non-trading credit under the loan relationship rules (see 38 LOAN RELATIONSHIPS OF COMPANIES and TOLLEY'S CORPORATION TAX). Corporation tax repayments are as far as possible treated as repayments of tax paid on a later date rather than an earlier date.

For accounting periods ending on or after 1 July 1999 (i.e. under corporation tax self-assessment), interest on overpaid tax paid to a company which becomes recoverable because of a change in the company's assessed corporation tax liability and not because of Revenue error can be recovered without an assessment.

[*ICTA 1988, ss 826, 826A; FA 1989, s 178, s 179(1)(c)(ii), s 180(6); FA 1991, Sch 15 para 23; FA 1993, ss 120, 170, Sch 14 para 10, Sch 18 para 5; SI 1989 No 1297; SI 1993 No 2212; FA 1996, s 100(4A), Sch 18 para 13; FA 1998, ss 34, 35, Sch 4 paras 1–3, 5, 7; SI 1998 No 3175, Reg 8*].

Accounting periods ending before 1 October 1993

A repayment after 31 July 1975 to a company by the Revenue of corporation tax on chargeable gains (amounting to £100 or more for repayments prior to 6 April 1993) and repaid more than twelve months after the 'material date' carries interest ('*a repayment supplement*'), which is disregarded for all tax purposes. Prior to 31 January 1997, rates of interest were the same as those on overpaid capital gains tax (see 34.1 above), but have since diversified as follows:

6.50% p.a. from 6 February 2000

5.75% p.a. from 6 March 1999 to 5 February 2000

6.50% p.a. from 6 January 1999 to 5 March 1999

7.25% p.a. from 6 August 1997 to 5 January 1999

6.25% p.a. from 6 February 1996 to 5 August 1997

The interest will run to the end of the tax month (i.e. 6th day of one calendar month to 5th day of the following month) in which the order for repayment is issued and will commence as follows. (Where a repayment relates to corporation tax paid on different dates, it is treated, as far as possible, as being for a later rather than an earlier date.)

Tax originally paid	**Interest commences**
On or after the first anniversary of the 'material date'	At the beginning of the tax month following the next anniversary of the 'material date' after the tax was paid.
In any other case	At the beginning of the tax month following the first anniversary of the 'material date'.

'*Material date*' means the earliest due date for payment of corporation tax for the accounting period in question (for which see 46.2 PAYMENT OF TAX).

In order to qualify for the repayment supplement, the company must have been resident in the UK for the accounting period in connection with which the repayment is made. However, the Revenue, following the case of *R v CIR (ex p. Commerzbank AG) CJEC, [1993] STC 605* decided on 13 July 1993 in which it was held that refusal to pay repayment supplement on a tax repayment to a company resident elsewhere in the European Community was discriminatory and breached the Treaty of Rome, has invited claims for repayment supplement from companies resident elsewhere in the EC in an accounting period for which a repayment without supplement has been made more than twelve months after the end of the accounting period and within the six years before 13 July 1993 (Revenue Press Release 23 July 1993). This practice presumably applies to subsequent accounting periods ending before 1 October 1993.

The provisions do not apply to amounts paid by order of a court having power to allow interest (for which see 46.4 PAYMENT OF TAX). There are restrictions on the amount of the supplement where surplus advance corporation tax of a later accounting period displaces mainstream corporation tax of an earlier period, or trading losses of a later accounting period are offset against profits of an earlier period, or there is a combination of such events. [*ICTA 1988, s 825; FA 1989, s 158(2)(5)(6), s 178, s 179(1)(4); FA 1991, Sch 15 para 22; FA 1993, s 120, Sch 14 para 10; FA 1996, Sch 18 para 13*].

34.4 OVER-PAYMENTS

See 46.10 PAYMENT OF TAX as regards assessment of repayment supplement or interest overpaid.

34.5 MISCELLANEOUS

Unauthorised demands for tax. There is a general right to interest under *Supreme Court Act 1981, s 35A* in a case where the taxpayer submits to an unauthorised demand for tax, provided that the payment is not made voluntarily to close a transaction (*Woolwich Equitable Building Society v CIR HL 1992, 65 TC 265*).

Mistakes by the Revenue. Where there is no good reason for a delay in excess of six months, over and above their own 28-day target, before the Revenue replies to a letter or enquiry,

- they will not charge interest on tax unpaid during the period of the delay,
- they will pay repayment supplement or interest (as appropriate) on tax overpaid during that period, and
- they will pay any reasonable costs the taxpayer has incurred as a direct result of the delay.

(Revenue Code of Practice 1).

35 Interest and Surcharges on Unpaid Tax

Cross-references. See 5 ASSESSMENTS; 9 BACK DUTY; 46 PAYMENT OF TAX; 47 PENALTIES.

35.1 PERSONS OTHER THAN COMPANIES — 1996/97 ONWARDS (SELF-ASSESSMENT) AND ASSESSMENTS RAISED AFTER 5 APRIL 1998

The provisions of *TMA 1970, s 86* as amended for self-assessment and described below apply in respect of capital gains tax **for 1996/97 and subsequent years,** i.e. under self-assessment, **and also** in respect of capital gains tax for an earlier year which is charged by an assessment first raised after 5 April 1998. [*FA 1995, s 110(2)*]. Where these provisions have effect, *TMA 1970, s 88* (interest on tax recovered to make good loss of tax due to taxpayer's fault — see 35.8 below) does not have effect. Capital gains tax paid more than 28 days after the due date is also subject to a surcharge, with an additional surcharge where payment is more than six months late (see 35.5 below).

Interest is charged by the Revenue on late payments of capital gains tax, whether payable under a self-assessment or an assessment made by the Revenue or as a result of a Revenue amendment to a self-assessment following an enquiry. (For details of interest charged on late payment of income tax, including interim payments, see 56.19 SELF-ASSESSMENT and also TOLLEY'S INCOME TAX.) Interest at the rates listed below accrues from the 'relevant date' (even if a non-business day) to the date of payment. The '*relevant date*' is, with one statutory exception, 31 January following the year of assessment. This applies equally to liabilities under pre-1996/97 assessments raised after 5 April 1998. The exception is that where the due date for payment of tax is deferred until three months after notice is given to deliver a self-assessment tax return (see 46.1 PAYMENT OF TAX), the relevant date is identically deferred. Where the due date of payment is later than the relevant date, either under the circumstances in 46.1 PAYMENT OF TAX or because a successful application is made to postpone tax on a pre-1996/97 assessment (see 46.3 PAYMENT OF TAX), this does *not* alter the relevant date for interest purposes.

[*TMA 1970, s 86(1)–(3); FA 1995, s 110; FA 1996, s 131(2)*].

In practice, where a self-assessment return is submitted by 30 September for calculation by the Revenue of the tax due (see 54.6 RETURNS), the relevant date is deferred until 30 days after notification of the liability to the taxpayer if this occurs later than 31 December following the tax year (Revenue Self-Assessment Manual — Interest, penalties and surcharge section — para 1.2.1), and see 35.9 below re personal representatives.

As regards the date on which payment of tax is treated as made, see 46.5 PAYMENT OF TAX and 56.21 SELF-ASSESSMENT.

Rates of interest are:

8.50% p.a. from 6 February 2000

7.50% p.a. from 6 March 1999 to 5 February 2000

8.50% p.a. from 6 January 1999 to 5 March 1999

9.50% p.a. from 6 August 1997 to 5 January 1999

8.50% p.a. from 31 January 1997 to 5 August 1997

See 35.2 below for earlier rates, which will still apply under these provisions where an assessment for 1994/95 or an earlier year is raised after 5 April 1998.

Interest charges are calculated automatically and, however small, will appear on taxpayer statements of account under self-assessment. There is no de minimis limit for charging interest. It will be noted that the above rates are greater than those by reference to which interest is paid by the Revenue (see 34.1 INTEREST ON OVERPAID TAX). The rates are adjusted automatically by reference to changes in the average of base lending rates of certain clearing banks, and are announced by Revenue Press Release. For the relationship to base rates, see *SI 1989 No 1297, Reg 3* as substituted from 31 January 1997 by *SI 1996 No 3187*.

Interest is also chargeable at the above rates from 9 March 1998 on late payment of surcharges (see 35.5 below) and penalties (see 56.22 SELF-ASSESSMENT). [*TMA 1970, s 59C(6), s 103A; SI 1989 No 1297, Reg 3; SI 1998 Nos 310, 311*].

Interest is payable gross and recoverable (as if it were tax charged and due and payable under the assessment to which it relates) as a Crown debt; it is *not deductible from profits or income* [*TMA 1970, ss 69, 90*] and is refundable to the extent that the tax concerned is subsequently cancelled. [*TMA 1970, s 91*].

35.2 PERSONS OTHER THAN COMPANIES — ASSESSMENTS FOR 1995/96 AND EARLIER YEARS RAISED BEFORE 6 APRIL 1998

The provisions of *TMA 1970, s 86* described below, and in 35.3, 35.4, apply where the capital gains tax payable relates to **1995/96 and earlier years**. However, **they do not apply** where an assessment for 1995/96 or earlier is first raised on or after 6 April 1998.

If tax is not paid on the date it becomes due and payable (see 46 PAYMENT OF TAX), interest is chargeable from that date (even if it is a non-business day) on each assessment. This applies to all assessments but additional rules apply where an appeal is entered against the assessment (see 35.3 below). The Board could remit interest of £30 or less arising on any assessment notice of which was issued before 19 April 1993 (and it is understood an administrative de minimis limit applied subsequently). [*TMA 1970, s 86(1)(2)(5)(6); F(No 2)A 1975, s 46(1); FA 1980, s 62; FA 1989, s 158(1)(3)(6); FA 1996, Sch 6 para 1*].

Rates of interest are:

8.50% p.a. from 6 February 2000

7.50% p.a. from 6 March 1999 to 5 February 2000

8.50% p.a. from 6 January 1999 to 5 March 1999

9.50% p.a. from 6 August 1997 to 5 January 1999

8.50% p.a. from 31 January 1997 to 5 August 1997

6.25% p.a. from 6 February 1996 to 30 January 1997

7.00% p.a. from 6 March 1995 to 5 February 1996

6.25% p.a. from 6 October 1994 to 5 March 1995

5.50% p.a. from 6 January 1994 to 5 October 1994

6.25% p.a. from 6 March 1993 to 5 January 1994

7.00% p.a. from 6 December 1992 to 5 March 1993

7.75% p.a. from 6 November 1992 to 5 December 1992

9.25% p.a. from 6 October 1991 to 5 November 1992

10.00% p.a. from 6 July 1991 to 5 October 1991

10.75% p.a. from 6 May 1991 to 5 July 1991

11.50% p.a. from 6 March 1991 to 5 May 1991

12.25% p.a. from 6 November 1990 to 5 March 1991

13.00% p.a. from 6 November 1989 to 5 November 1990

12.25% p.a. from 6 July 1989 to 5 November 1989

11.50% p.a. from 6 January 1989 to 5 July 1989

10.50% p.a. from 6 October 1988 to 5 January 1989

9.75% p.a. from 6 August 1988 to 5 October 1988

7.75% p.a. from 6 May 1988 to 5 August 1988

8.25% p.a. from 6 December 1987 to 5 May 1988

9.00% p.a. from 6 September 1987 to 5 December 1987

8.25% p.a. from 6 June 1987 to 5 September 1987

9.00% p.a. from 6 April 1987 to 5 June 1987

9.50% p.a. from 6 November 1986 to 5 April 1987

8.50% p.a. from 6 August 1986 to 5 November 1986

11.00% p.a. from 1 May 1985 to 5 August 1986

8.00% p.a. from 1 December 1982 to 30 April 1985

12.00% p.a. from 1 January 1980 to 30 November 1982

9.00% p.a. from 1 July 1974 to 31 December 1979

Rates of interest are, from 18 August 1989, adjusted automatically by reference to changes in the average of base lending rates of certain clearing banks, and are announced in Revenue Press Releases. (Revenue Press Release 1 August 1989). Before that date, they were prescribed by statutory instrument. The relationship to base rates was revised from 31 January 1997 (see *SI 1996 No 3187*).

[*TMA 1970, s 89; F(No 2)A 1987, s 89; SI 1974 No 966; SI 1979 No 1687; SI 1982 No 1587; SI 1985 No 563; SI 1986 Nos 1181, 1832; SI 1987 Nos 513, 898, 1492, 1988; SI 1988 Nos 756, 1278, 1621, 2185; SI 1989 No 1000; FA 1989, s 178, s 179(1)(4); SI 1989 Nos 1297, 1298; SI 1996 No 3187*].

Interest factor tables for use as ready reckoners in calculating interest on overdue tax are published by the Revenue and updated as rates change (but not beyond 5 April 1999). They cannot be used where the interest is chargeable under 35.1 above. (Revenue Press Release 11 March 1999).

See 46 PAYMENT OF TAX for collection.

The provisions of *TMA 1970, ss 69, 90, 91* apply as they do under 35.1 above.

35.3 **Tax becoming due after appeal against assessment.** On application by the taxpayer, the inspector may agree (or the Commissioners may determine) that part of the tax charged by an assessment may be postponed (see 46 PAYMENT OF TAX). Any tax which is *not postponed* then becomes due and payable as if it were tax charged by an assessment notice of which was issued on the date of the determination or agreement and in respect of which there had been no appeal, or, if later, on the due date had there been no appeal. On the determination of the substantive appeal, any *postponed tax* and/or *extra tax* (the latter being the tax additional to that charged by the original assessment) which then becomes payable is due and payable as if it were tax charged by an assessment notice of which was issued on the date on which the inspector issues to the appellant a notice of the total amount payable in accordance with the determination, or, if later, on the due date for the original assessment had there been no appeal. [*TMA 1970, s 55(3)(6)(9); F(No 2)A 1975, s 45(1); FA 1989, s 156(2)(4)*]. For assessments raised before 6 April 1998 for 1995/96 and/or earlier years, interest on non-postponed and any postponed or extra tax will then run from a '*reckonable date*', which is the *later* of

(*a*) the due date if there had been no appeal (i.e. under the original assessment, see 46.1 PAYMENT OF TAX), and

(*b*) the *earlier* of

  (i) the date on which the tax actually becomes due and payable (see 46 PAYMENT OF TAX), and

  (ii) 1 June in the year next following that for which the assessment is made—e.g. 1 June 1992 for a 1990/91 assessment. [*TMA 1970, s 86(3)(3A)(4); FA 1989, s 156(1)*].

General. Adequate payments made on account of assessments under dispute or the use of certificates of tax deposit (see 46.11 PAYMENT OF TAX) may help prevent or reduce a charge to interest.

35.4 **Interest on tax becoming due after determination of an appeal by the courts.** Any outstanding tax charged in accordance with a Commissioners' decision must be paid before an appeal can be heard by the High Court, and if, on the determination of the appeal, further tax is found to be chargeable, it becomes due and payable thirty days from the date on which the inspector issues to the taxpayer a notice of the total amount payable. As regards assessments raised before 6 April 1998 for 1995/96 and/or earlier years, interest under *TMA 1970, s 86* runs from the later of 1 June in the year next following that for which the assessment was made and the date on which the tax would have become due and payable if charged by the original assessment (without an appeal being made). [*TMA 1970, s 56(9), s 86(3A); F(No 2)A 1975, s 45(3); FA 1989, s 156(1)(3)(4)*]. See 46.4 PAYMENT OF TAX.

35.5 SURCHARGES ON UNPAID TAX

The provisions described below apply in respect of capital gains tax (and income tax) **for 1996/97 and subsequent years** and **also apply** in respect of assessments for 1995/96 and/or earlier years which are raised after 5 April 1998. [*FA 1995, s 109(2)*].

An initial surcharge is payable where an amount of CGT (and/or income tax), whether payable under a self-assessment or an assessment made by the Revenue or as a result of a Revenue amendment to a self-assessment following an enquiry, remains unpaid more than 28 days after the due date for payment. The due date for payment of CGT is normally 31 January following the year of assessment, but see 46.1 PAYMENT OF TAX for exceptions. As regards a pre-1996/97 assessment first raised after 5 April 1998, the due date is 30 days after the issue of the notice of assessment, though this is deferred to the extent that any tax is postponed on appeal (see 46.1, 46.3 , 46.4 PAYMENT OF TAX). The surcharge is equal to **5%** of the amount of tax unpaid. **A further 5%** surcharge is payable on any of that tax which remains unpaid more than six months after the due date. Interest accrues on an unpaid surcharge with effect from the expiry of 30 days beginning with the date of the notice imposing the surcharge. An appeal may be made, within the same 30-day period, against the imposition of a surcharge as if it were an assessment to tax, and the surcharge may be set aside if it appears that, *throughout* the period from the due date until payment of the tax, the taxpayer had a 'reasonable excuse' for non-payment. Inability to pay the tax, i.e. due to insufficient funds, is not to be regarded as a reasonable excuse. Revenue booklet SA/BK7 'Self-assessment: surcharges for late payment of tax' includes, *inter alia*, examples of what the Revenue may regard and will not regard as a reasonable excuse, although the decision rests ultimately with the Appeal Commissioners. See also Revenue Tax Bulletin April 1998 pp 527–529. In practice, the Revenue allow a further 14 days for payment to be made after a reasonable excuse has ceased to exist (SA/BK7).

There are provisions to prevent a double charge where tax has been taken into account in determining the tax-geared penalties of *TMA 1970, s 7* (see 54.2 RETURNS), *s 93(5)* (tax-geared penalty for failure to make return for income tax and capital gains tax; see 56.23 SELF-ASSESSMENT), *s 95* (incorrect return etc. for income tax or capital gains tax; see 47.4 PENALTIES, 56.25 SELF-ASSESSMENT) and *s 95A* (incorrect return etc. for partnerships; see 56.25 SELF-ASSESSMENT). Any such tax will not be subject to a surcharge. The Board have discretion to mitigate, or to stay or compound proceedings for recovery of, a surcharge and may also, after judgement, entirely remit the surcharge.

[*TMA 1970, s 59C; FA 1994, s 194, s 199(2); FA 1995, s 109*].

In practice, where a self-assessment return is submitted by 30 September for calculation by the Revenue of the tax due (see 54.6 RETURNS), the due date by reference to which any surcharge is triggered is delayed until 30 days after notification by the Revenue of the amount due, where this occurs after 31 December following the tax year (ICAEW Technical Release TAX 9/94, June 1994).

No surcharge will be imposed where a taxpayer has entered into a 'Time to Pay' arrangement (see 46.6 PAYMENT OF TAX), provided that the payment proposals are received by the Revenue before the relevant surcharge date, they lead to an acceptable agreement to settle the full liability for the self-assessment year, and the terms of the arrangement are adhered to, such that it is not cancelled. (Revenue Self-Assessment Manual — Payments section — para 7.2.48).

35.6 COMPANIES

Accounting periods ending after 30 September 1993. In relation to accounting periods ending after 30 September 1993 (Pay and File), corporation tax carries interest (under *TMA 1970, s 87A*) from the due and payable date (see 46.2 PAYMENT OF TAX), even if it is a non-business day, until payment. Where corporation tax assessed on a company may be assessed on other persons in certain circumstances, the due and payable date is that which refers to the company's liability.

The interest rate is determined by criteria contained in Treasury regulations made by statutory instrument so that when such criteria change so as to alter the rate, the Board must specify in an order the new rate and the day from which it has effect. For the criteria, see *SI 1989 No 1297, Reg 3A* and, as regards accounting periods ending on or after 1 July 1999, *Regs 3ZA, 3ZB* as inserted by *SI 1998 No 3176* and amended by *SI 2000 No 893*.

Rates of interest for accounting periods ending before 1 July 1999 are:

6.75% p.a. from 6 February 2000

5.75% p.a. from 6 March 1999 to 5 February 2000

6.50% p.a. from 6 January 1999 to 5 March 1999

7.50% p.a. from 6 August 1997 to 5 January 1999

6.25% p.a. from 6 February 1996 to 5 August 1997

7.00% p.a. from 6 March 1995 to 5 February 1996

6.25% p.a. from 6 October 1994 to 5 March 1995

5.50% p.a. from 6 January 1994 to 5 October 1994

6.25% p.a. from 1 October 1993 to 5 January 1994

The rate of interest for accounting periods ending on or after 1 July 1999 (such interest being deductible for tax purposes — see below) has been set at **8.50% p.a.** as regards corporation tax becoming due on or after the normal due date (nine months and one day after the end of the accounting period) (Revenue Press Release 2 February 2000). The rates for corporation tax payable by earlier **instalments**, under the quarterly accounting rules for large companies (see 46.2 PAYMENT OF TAX), are

7.00% p.a. from 20 April 2000

8.00% p.a. from 21 February 2000 to 19 April 2000

7.75% p.a. from 24 January 2000 to 20 February 2000

7.50% p.a. from 15 November 1999 to 23 January 2000

7.25% p.a. from 20 September 1999 to 14 November 1999

7.00% p.a. from 21 June 1999 to 19 September 1999

7.25% p.a. from 19 April 1999 to 20 June 1999

7.50% p.a. from 15 February 1999 to 18 April 1999

8.00% p.a. from 18 January 1999 to 14 February 1999

8.25% p.a. from 7 January 1999 to 17 January 1999

The latter set of rates applies up to the earlier of the date of payment and the normal due date (whereafter the normal rates apply).

Interest on tax subsequently discharged is adjusted or repaid so as to secure that the total is as it would have been had the tax discharged never been charged. However, where surplus advance corporation tax of a later accounting period displaces mainstream corporation tax paid in respect of an earlier accounting period, or trading losses or non-trading deficits of a later accounting period are offset against profits of an earlier period, or there is a combination of such events, any such adjustment or repayment of interest is restricted. In considering an adjustment or repayment of interest, then, where relief for tax paid for an accounting period is given by way of repayment of tax, the amount repaid is, as far as possible, treated as if it were a discharge of the corporation tax charged for that period.

Interest is paid without deduction of income tax and, for accounting periods ending before 1 July 1999, is not brought into account in computing profits or income. It is recoverable (as if it were tax charged and due and payable under an assessment) as a Crown debt. Interest paid for later accounting periods is deductible in computing profits (as a non-trading debit under the loan relationship rules — see 38 LOAN RELATIONSHIPS OF COMPANIES and TOLLEY'S CORPORATION TAX).

[*TMA 1970, ss 69, 87A, 90, s 91(1A)(2A); F(No 2)A 1987, s 85, s 86(5)(6); FA 1989, s 178; FA 1991, Sch 15 para 2; FA 1993, ss 120, 170, Sch 14 para 4, 5, Sch 18 para 1; SI 1989 No 1297; SI 1993 No 2212; FA 1996, s 100(4A), Sch 18 para 13; FA 1998, ss 33, 35, Sch 4 para 4, 7; SI 1998 No 3175, Reg 7; FA 2000, Sch 29 para 9(2)(3), Sch 40 Pt II(12)*].

Accounting periods ending before 1 October 1993. The provisions in 35.2–35.4 above generally apply to corporation tax (including that in respect of chargeable gains) except that the '*reckonable date*' in 35.3 above is the *later* of

(*a*) the due date if there had been no appeal (see 46.2 PAYMENT OF TAX), and

(*b*) the *earlier* of

(i) the date on which the tax becomes due and payable, and

(ii) the last day of the six months following the payment interval given in 46.2 PAYMENT OF TAX.

Prior to 31 January 1997, **rates of interest** were the same as those on unpaid capital gains tax (see 35.1 above), but have since diversified as follows:

6.50% p.a. from 6 February 2000

5.75% p.a. from 6 March 1999 to 5 February 2000

6.50% p.a. from 6 January 1999 to 5 March 1999

7.25% p.a. from 6 August 1997 to 5 January 1999

6.25% p.a. from 6 February 1996 to 5 August 1997

As a transitional measure, where

(1) a notice is served under *TMA 1970, s 11* (return of profits; see 54.11 RETURNS) after 31 December 1993 (post-Pay and File),

(2) the notice relates to an accounting period ending before 1 October 1993 (pre-Pay and File), and

(3) the tax charged by any corporation tax assessment for that accounting period does not become due and payable until after the date nine months after the end of that accounting period,

the reckonable date is the date mentioned in (3) above rather than the date determined under (*a*) and (*b*) above. The Board are given power to mitigate any interest falling due as a result of this provision and to stay or compound any proceedings for its recovery (see Revenue Tax Bulletin August 1993 pp 83–85 for guidance on the approach to be taken as regards mitigation etc.). [*TMA 1970, s 86; F(No 2)A 1975, s 46(1); FA 1980, s 61(3)(5), s 62; FA 1982, s 69; FA 1987, Sch 6 paras 6, 12; ICTA 1988, s 478(6), Sch 30 para 1(7); FA 1989, s 156(1)(4); FA 1993, s 170, Sch 18 para 3*].

Where surplus advance corporation tax of a later accounting period displaces mainstream corporation tax paid in respect of an earlier accounting period, or trading losses of a later accounting period are offset against profits of an earlier period, any adjustment or repayment of interest under *TMA 1970, s 91* is restricted. [*FA 1989, s 157; FA 1991, Sch 15 para 1*].

35.7 EXCHANGE RESTRICTIONS AND DELAYED REMITTANCES

Where gains arising overseas cannot be remitted to the UK due to government action in the country of origin etc., and the Revenue agree to defer collection of the tax, interest ceases to run from the date on which the Board were first in possession of information necessary to enable them to agree to deferment. If that date is three months or less from the due and payable date, no interest is payable. But where a demand is later made for payment of the deferred tax, interest (from the date of demand) is only assessable if the tax is not paid within three months of that demand. [*TMA 1970, s 92; F(No 2)A 1987, s 86(2)(a)*]. The Board may defer collection indefinitely. See 44.5 OVERSEAS MATTERS for an alternative relief under *TCGA 1992, s 279*.

35.8 FAILURE OR ERROR, AND FRAUD, WILFUL DEFAULT OR NEGLECT

The charge to interest under *TMA 1970, s 88*, as described below, no longer applies where the new self-assessment interest provisions of *TMA 1970, s 86* have effect (see 35.1 above).

Where an assessment is made for making good 'tax' lost, after 26 July 1989, through (*a*) a 'failure' to give a notice, make a return, or provide a document or other information, or

(*b*) an error in any information, return, etc. supplied,

the tax attributable to that failure or error is chargeable with interest if an inspector or the Board so determines.

'*Tax*' includes capital gains tax and, with respect to accounting periods ending before 1 October 1993 (pre-Pay and File), corporation tax (including that in respect of chargeable gains). (For accounting periods ending after 30 September 1993 (Pay and File), corporation tax instead carries a *TMA 1970, s 87A* interest charge if paid late; see 35.6 above).

'*Failure*' includes failure to do something at a particular time or within a particular period; and the exclusion in *TMA 1970, s 118(2)* (see 54.8 RETURNS) does not apply to it. [*TMA 1970, s 88(1)(7); F(No 2)A 1987, s 86(4); FA 1989, s 159, s 160(1)*].

Determination. A determination under these provisions can be made at any time within six years of the end of the chargeable period for which the tax is charged or within three years of the final determination of the amount of that tax. It must specify

(i) the date of issue,

(ii) the amount of tax carrying interest, and the assessment by which it was charged,

(iii) the date when, for *TMA 1970, s 88*, it ought to have been paid, and

(iv) the time within which an appeal against the determination may be made.

The general APPEALS (4) provisions apply, except *TMA 1970, s 50(6)–(8)* (see 4.8 APPEALS). On appeal, the Commissioners can set aside or confirm the determination, or alter it in respect of the amount of tax or the date. [*TMA 1970, s 70, s 88A(1)–(5); FA 1989, s 160(2)(3)*].

Where an assessment is made for making good tax lost by fraud, wilful default or neglect (see 9.4 BACK DUTY) which occurred before 27 July 1989, the tax attributable to that fraud, etc. is chargeable with interest. [*TMA 1970, s 88(1)*]. The amount of interest is certified by the General or Special Commissioners under *TMA 1970, s 70(3)*, following an application by the Revenue at which the taxpayer is entitled to appear and be heard (*Nicholson v Morris CA 1977, 51 TC 95*). There is no appeal by way of case stated (*R v Holborn Commissioners (ex p. Frank Rind Settlement Trustees) QB 1974, 49 TC 656*).

Tax carrying interest under these provisions does not also carry interest under *TMA 1970, s 86* (see 35.2, 35.3 and 35.6 above). It is payable gross (and not deductible for tax purposes) from the date when the tax ought originally to have been paid (but without the alternative of thirty days from the date of the issue of the notice of assessment, see 46.1 PAYMENT OF TAX) to the date of actual payment. The Board have power to mitigate interest payable and stay or compound any proceedings for recovery. Interest is refundable to the extent that the tax concerned is subsequently cancelled. [*TMA 1970, ss 88–91; F(No 2)A 1975, s 46(4); FA 1980, s 61(4)(5); FA 1987, Sch 6 para 7; ICTA 1988, Sch 30 para 1(8); FA 1989, s 161*]. See also 9.9 BACK DUTY, 47 PENALTIES and 54.4 RETURNS.

Rates of interest are the same as in 35.2 above except that a rate of 4% p.a. applied from 19 April 1967 to 30 June 1974 and a rate of 3% p.a. applied for periods up to and including 18 April 1967. [*TMA 1970, s 89; F(No 2)A 1987, s 89; FA 1989, s 178, s 179(1)(4)*].

The Board publish ready-reckoner tables of interest factors which may be used in calculating interest in BACK DUTY (9) investigation settlements.

Where a *TMA 1970, s 88* interest charge arises as regards one assessment and there is an amount of overpaid tax on a different assessment, a set-off will be given where requested (HC Official Report Standing Committee H col 746, 2 July 1975). It seems the set-off will only apply from the date of the request but in relation to non-corporate taxpayers, and corporate taxpayers before the introduction of Pay and File, it would usually be advantageous because of the disparity in the pre-self-assessment rules for INTEREST ON OVERPAID TAX (34) and *TMA 1970, s 88* interest.

The Revenue has pointed out that there is no element of culpability regarding the charging of interest under *TMA 1970, s 88* as it has effect **after 26 July 1989**. *Any* error in a return etc. which delays the payment of tax is sufficient for the provision to be operated. This may cover the case where a chargeable gain is returned based upon a valuation which is subsequently agreed or determined in such an amount as to increase the gain returned. Interest can be mitigated in such circumstances by making appropriate payments on account (specifying to the Collector precisely what liability it is intended to cover) or by purchasing a certificate of tax deposit in an appropriate amount before the normal due date of the tax. An assessment issued before the normal due date of the tax payment will not carry *TMA 1970, s 88* interest (though it may carry *TMA 1970, s 86* interest). Where such an assessment has been made which has not been appealed, a further assessment carrying *section 88* interest will normally be made on the basis that the return contained an error (subject to the restrictions on discovery assessments contained in Revenue Statement of Practice SP 8/91; see 5.2 ASSESSMENTS). Where an appeal is lodged against such an assessment, any interest charge will normally be under *section 86*, although exceptionally the power to make a further assessment carrying *section 88* interest whilst an original assessment is under appeal (see 5.2 ASSESSMENTS) will be used. The decision to make such a further assessment will be operated centrally, the main factor being the possible loss of interest to the public revenue. Where no assessment has been made before the earliest due date, any subsequent assessment based on an incomplete, misleading or erroneous return, even one submitted within the time limits specified by Revenue Statement of Practice 6/89 (late returns and charging of interest and penalties; see 54.4 RETURNS), will carry *section 88* interest as regards the tax lost due to the error etc. but will not carry such interest where, following the submission of a fully completed return within the time limits mentioned, the delay in issuing the assessment is due to the operation of the Revenue's procedures (Revenue Tax Bulletin May 1993 p 61).

For the limited extent to which regard should be had to events after the making of an assessment in determining whether *TMA 1970, s 88* applies, see *Billingham v Myers CA, [1996] STC 593.*

35.9 MISCELLANEOUS

Mistakes by the Revenue. Where there is no good reason for a delay in excess of six months, over and above their own 28-day target, before the Revenue replies to a letter or enquiry,

- they will not charge interest on tax unpaid during the period of the delay,
- they will pay repayment supplement or interest (as appropriate) on tax overpaid during that period, and
- they will pay any reasonable costs the taxpayer has incurred as a direct result of the delay.

(Revenue Code of Practice 1).

Personal representatives. For notices of assessment issued after 31 July 1975, personal representatives unable to pay tax before obtaining probate may have concessional treatment so that interest on tax falling due after the date of death runs from the expiration of thirty days after the date of grant of probate or letters of administration (if this is later than the date arrived at under 35.2 or 35.3 above). (Revenue Pamphlet IR 1, A17). This concession continues to apply under self-assessment (Revenue Self-Assessment Manual — Interest, penalties and surcharges section — para 1.2.1).

36 Land

Cross-references. See 6.6 ASSETS re milk quota; 7.8 ASSETS HELD ON 6 APRIL 1965 for land reflecting development value and 7.9–7.14 for other land held at that date; 17.7 DISPOSAL for treatment of statutory compensation received by tenants of land, 17.9 for buildings destroyed and replaced out of compensation and 17.10 for granting of options; 21.17 EXEMPTIONS AND RELIEFS for certain agricultural grants; 21.32 for woodlands, 21.44 for housing associations, 21.52 for self-build societies and 21.74 for disposal by gift of national heritage property; 39.9 LOSSES for buildings becoming of negligible value; 40.6 MARKET VALUE; 42 MINERAL ROYALTIES; 46.6 PAYMENT OF TAX for payment by instalments on gifts of land; 48 PRIVATE RESIDENCES with land attached; 55 ROLLOVER RELIEF for a claim on disposal of land occupied for trade purposes.

Sumption: Capital Gains Tax. See A16.

The headings in this chapter are as follows.

36.1 INTRODUCTION

There are a number of special provisions in the capital gains tax legislation relating to land. For disposals of land generally, see 36.2–36.12 below. For provisions relating to leases of land, see 36.13–34.22. For contingent liabilities on the disposal of land, see 36.23 below.

36.2 GENERAL

The general principles of capital gains tax apply to disposals of land. There are, however, particular problems concerning land transactions.

(*a*) An isolated or speculative transaction may be liable to income tax rather than to capital gains tax as amounting to an adventure or concern in the nature of trade (see 36.3 below).

(*b*) Even where (*a*) above does not apply, capital gains from certain transactions in land may be treated as income (see 36.4 and 36.5 below).

(*c*) The definition of 'land' for the purposes of *TCGA 1992* is not exclusive and may lead to difficulties of interpretation, especially where property derives its existence from the existence of the physical land. '*Land*' includes for such purposes, except where the context otherwise requires, messuages, tenements and hereditaments, houses and buildings of any tenure. [*TCGA 1992, s 288(1)*]. This is the original 1851 definition and should be compared with the current *Interpretation Act 1978* definition which is that '*land*' includes buildings and other structures, land covered with water, and any estate, interest, easement, servitude or right in or over land. (Apart from the specific definition for certain transactions in land under *ICTA 1988, ss 776–778* in 36.4 below, it is not entirely clear which of the above definitions applies for purposes of *ICTA 1988*.) That said, many provisions in *TCGA 1992* refer to 'land' as including any interest in or right over land or to an interest in an asset which can include land or buildings etc. (e.g. *TCGA 1992, s 152* (ROLLOVER RELIEF (55), although *TCGA 1992, s 155* treats buildings and the underlying land as separate) and *TCGA 1992, s 247* (36.11 below)). Deciding whether property is an interest or right over land can thus depend on general legal principles and the surrounding facts. Milk quota does not constitute such an interest or right (see 6.6 ASSETS).

36.3 ISOLATED OR SPECULATIVE TRANSACTIONS

A line is drawn between realisations of property held as investment or as a residence and transactions amounting to an adventure or concern in the nature of a trade. Whether the surplus on the purchase and resale of land, otherwise than in the course of an established commercial enterprise, is derived from an adventure or concern in the nature of trade depends upon the facts.

Para. 116 of the Final Report of the Royal Commission on the Taxation of Profits and Income (1955 HMSO Cmd. 9474) lists six 'badges of trade'.

(*a*) The subject matter of the realisation.

(*b*) The length of period of ownership.

(*c*) The frequency or number of similar transactions.

(*d*) Supplementary work on assets sold.

(*e*) Reason for the sale.

(*f*) Motive.

Other relevant factors may be the degree of organisation, whether the taxpayer is or has been associated with a recognised business dealing in similar assets and how the purchases were financed.

In *Leeming v Jones HL 1930, 15 TC 333* an income tax assessment on the acquisitions and disposal of options over rubber estates was confirmed by Commissioners. The Crown had defended the assessment under both Schedule D, Case I and Case VI. In a Supplementary Case the Commissioners found there had been no concern in the nature of trade. The Court held there was no liability. Per Lawrence LJ 'in the case of an isolated transaction . . . there is really no middle course open. It is either an adventure in the nature of trade, or else it is simply a case of sale and resale of property.' See also *Pearn v Miller KB 1927, 11 TC 610* and *Williams v Davies* below.

Property transactions by companies were held to be trading in *Californian Copper Syndicate v Harris CES 1904, 5 TC 159* (purchase of copper bearing land shortly afterwards resold); *Thew v South West Africa Co CA 1924, 9 TC 141* (numerous sales of land acquired by concession for exploitation); *Cayzer, Irvine & Co v CIR CS 1942, 24 TC 491* (exploitation of landed estate acquired by shipping company); *Emro Investments v Aller and Webb (Lance) Estates v Aller Ch D 1954, 35 TC 305* (profits carried to capital reserve on numerous purchases and sales); *Orchard Parks v Pogson Ch D 1964, 42 TC 442* (land compulsorily purchased after development plan dropped); *Parkstone Estates v Blair Ch D 1966, 43 TC 246* (industrial estate developed—land disposed of by sub-leases for premiums); *Eames v Stepnell Properties Ltd CA 1966, 43 TC 678* (sale of land acquired from associated company while resale being negotiated). See also *Bath & West Counties Property Trust Ltd v Thomas Ch D 1977, 52 TC 20.* Realisations were held to be capital in *Hudson's Bay Co v Stevens CA 1909, 5 TC 424* (numerous sales of land acquired under Royal Charter—contrast *South West Africa Co* above); *Tebrau (Johore) Rubber Syndicate v Farmer CES 1910, 5 TC 658* (purchase and resale of rubber estates—contrast *Californian Copper* above); *Mamor Sendirian Berhad v Director-General of Inland Revenue PC, [1985] STC 801* (sales of timber in the course of developing forest land into an oil palm plantation). See also *Lim Foo Yong Sendirian Berhad v Comptroller-General of Inland Revenue PC, [1986] STC 255* where it was held that a company may hold property on both trading and capital account and the fact that acquisitions and disposals have taken place on the former does not automatically determine for all time the company's intention in acquiring, holding and developing other property; and contrast *Richfield International Land and Investment Co Ltd v Inland Revenue Commissioner PC, [1989] STC 820* where an initial finding that a property sale had been on trading account was upheld, such finding only being inferred from previous property sales which had either been taxed or accounted for as trading transactions.

In *Rand v Alberni Land Co Ltd KB 1920, 7 TC 629* sales of land held in trust were held not to be trading but contrast *Alabama Coal etc. Co Ltd v Mylam KB 1926, 11 TC 232; Balgownie Land Trust v CIR CS 1929, 14 TC 684; St Aubyn Estates v Strick KB 1932, 17 TC 412; Tempest Estates Ltd v Walmsley Ch D 1975, 51 TC 305.* Sales of property after a period of letting were held to be realisations of investments or not trading in *CIR v Hyndland Investment Co Ltd CS 1929, 14 TC 694; Glasgow Heritable Trust v CIR CS 1954, 35 TC 196; Lucy & Sunderland Ltd v Hunt Ch D 1961, 40 TC 132* but were held to be trading in *Rellim Ltd v Vise CA 1951, 32 TC 254* (notwithstanding that the company was previously admitted as an investment company); *CIR v Toll Property Co CS 1952, 34 TC 13; Forest Side Properties (Chingford) v Pearce CA 1961, 39 TC 665.* But sales by the liquidator of property owned by companies following the abandonment of a plan for their public flotation were held to be not trading in *Simmons v CIR HL 1980, 53 TC 461* (reversing Commissioners' decision).

Property transactions by individuals and partnerships. Profits were held assessable as income in *Reynold's Exors v Bennett KB 1943, 25 TC 401; Broadbridge v Beattie KB 1944, 26 TC 63; Gray & Gillitt v Tiley KB 1944, 26 TC 80; Laver v Wilkinson KB 1944, 26 TC 105; Foulds v Clayton Ch D 1953, 34 TC 382; Kirkby v Hughes Ch D 1992, 65 TC 532; Lynch v Edmondson (Sp C 164), [1998] SSCD 185* in all of which the taxpayers were or had been associated with building or estate development, and contrast *Williams v Davies KB 1945, 26 TC 371* in which the taxpayers were closely associated with land development but a profit on transactions in undeveloped land belonging to their wives was held not assessable as income. The acquisition and resale of land for which planning permission had been or was obtained was held as trading in *Cooke v Haddock Ch D 1960, 39 TC 64; Turner v Last Ch D 1965, 42 TC 517* and *Pilkington v Randall CA 1966, 42 TC 662* (and cf. *Iswera v Ceylon Commr PC 1965, 44 ATC 157*), but contrast *Taylor v Good CA 1974, 49 TC 277* (in which a house bought as a residence was found unsuitable and resold to a developer after obtaining planning permission) and *Kirkham v Williams CA 1991, 64 TC 253* (in which a site was acquired principally as a capital asset to be used in the taxpayer's trade but which was later developed and sold), in both of which cases it was held that there had not been an adventure. In *Burrell v Davis Ch D 1948, 38 TC 307; Johnston v Heath Ch D 1970, 46 TC 463; Reeves v Evans, Boyce & Northcott Ch D 1971, 48 TC 495* and *Clark v Follett Ch D 1973, 48 TC 677* the short period of ownership or other evidence showed an intention to purchase for resale at a profit and not for investment, and contrast *CIR v Reinhold CS 1953, 34 TC 389, Taylor v Good* above and *Marson v Morton Ch D 1986, 59 TC 381.* For other cases in which profits were held assessable as income see *Hudson v Wrightson KB 1934,*

26 TC 55, MacMahon v CIR CS 1951, 32 TC 311 and *Eckel v Board of Inland Revenue PC 1989, 62 TC 331.*

36.4 TRANSACTIONS IN LAND [*ICTA 1988, ss 776–778*]

The following provisions apply to all persons, whether UK residents or not, if all or any part of the 'land' in question is in the UK.

Where

(*a*) land (or any 'property deriving its value from land') is acquired with the sole or main object of realising a gain from disposing of it, or

(*b*) land is held as trading stock, or

(*c*) land is developed with the sole or main object of realising a gain from disposing of it when developed,

any capital gain from 'disposal' of the land or any part of it (i.e. any amount not otherwise able to be included in any computation of income for tax purposes) which is realised (for himself or for any other person) by the person acquiring, holding or developing it (or by CONNECTED PERSONS (14), or a person party to, or concerned in, any arrangement or scheme to realise the gain indirectly or by a series of transactions) is, subject as below, treated for all tax purposes as income of the person realising the gain (or the person who transmitted to him, directly or indirectly, the opportunity of making that gain) assessable, under Schedule D, Case VI, for the chargeable period in which the gain is realised. See *Yuill v Wilson HL 1980, 52 TC 674* and its sequel *Yuill v Fletcher CA 1984, 58 TC 145, Winterton v Edwards Ch D 1979, 52 TC 655* and *Sugarwhite v Budd CA 1988, 60 TC 679. Bona fide* transactions, not entered into with tax avoidance in view, may be caught by the legislation. See *Page v Lowther and Another CA 1983, 57 TC 199.*

'*Land*' includes buildings, and any estate or interest in land or buildings.

'*Property deriving its value from land*' includes any shareholding in a company, partnership interest, or interest in settled property, deriving its value, directly or indirectly, from land, and any option, consent or embargo affecting the disposition of land. But see 'Exemptions' below.

'*Disposal*' of land occurs for the above purposes if, by any one or more transactions or by any arrangement or scheme (whether concerning the land or any property deriving its value therefrom), the property in, or control over, the land is effectively disposed of. Any number of transactions may be treated as a single arrangement or scheme if they have, or there is evidence of, a common purpose. For the date of disposal where instalments are involved see *Yuill v Fletcher* above. See also under 'General' below.

Exemptions

(i) An individual's gain made from the sale, etc., of his residence exempted from capital gains tax under *TCGA 1992, ss 222–226* or which would be so exempt but for *TCGA 1992, s 224(3)* (acquired for purpose of making a gain, see 48.4 PRIVATE RESIDENCES).

(ii) A gain on the sale of shares in a company holding land as trading stock (or a company owning, directly or indirectly, 90% of the ordinary share capital of such a company) *provided that* the company disposes of the land by normal trade and makes all possible profit from it, and the share sale is not part of an arrangement or scheme to realise a land gain indirectly. See *Chilcott v CIR Ch D 1981, 55 TC 446.*

(iii) If the liability arises solely under (*c*) above, any part of the gain fairly attributable to a period before the intention was formed to develop the land.

36.5 Land

Gains are to be computed 'as is just and reasonable in the circumstances', allowance being given only for expenses attributable to the land disposed of, and the following may be taken into account.

(A) If a leasehold interest is disposed of out of a freehold, the Schedule D, Case I treatment in such a case of a person dealing in land.

(B) Any adjustment under *ICTA 1988, s 99(2)(3)* for the amount of any lease premium charged to income tax under Schedule A by *ICTA 1988, s 34* (see TOLLEY'S INCOME TAX).

Where the computation of a gain in respect of the development of land (as under (*c*) above) is made on the footing that the land or property was appropriated as trading stock, that land, etc., is also to be treated for purposes of capital gains tax (under *TCGA 1992, s 161*; see 6.3 ASSETS) as having been transferred to stock.

Where, under *ICTA 1988, s 776,* tax is assessed on, and paid by, a person other than the one who actually realised the gain, the person paying the tax may recover it from the other party (for which purpose the Revenue will, on request, supply a certificate of income in respect of which tax has been paid).

Clearance. The person who made or would make the gain may (if he considers that (*a*) or (*c*) above may apply), submit to his inspector particulars of any completed or proposed transactions. If he does so, the inspector must, within 30 days of receiving those particulars, notify the taxpayer whether or not he is satisfied that liability under above does not arise. If the inspector is so satisfied no assessment can thereafter be made on that gain under the provisions above, provided that all material facts and considerations have been fully and accurately disclosed.

General. There are also provisions to prevent avoidance by the use of indirect means to transfer any property or right, or enhance or diminish its value, e.g., by sales at less, or more, than full consideration, assigning share capital or rights in a company or partnership or an interest in settled property, disposal on the winding-up of any company, partnership or trust etc. For ascertaining whether, and to what extent, the value of any property or right is derived from any other property or right, value may be traced through any number of companies, partnerships and trusts, at each stage attributing property held by the company etc. to its shareholders etc., 'in such manner as is appropriate to the circumstances'.

For the above purposes the Revenue may require, under penalty, any person to supply them with any particulars thought necessary, including particulars of

(I) transactions, etc., in which he acts, or acted, on behalf of others, and

(II) transactions, etc., which in the opinion of the Revenue should be investigated, and

(III) what part, if any, he has taken, or is taking, in specified transactions, etc. (Under this heading a *solicitor* who has merely acted as professional adviser is not compelled to do more than state that he acted and give his client's name and address.)

The transactions of which particulars are required need not be identified transactions (*Essex v CIR CA 1980, 53 TC 720*).

The Valuation Office Agency has published its internal guidance manuals on the valuation of property (Revenue Press Release 19 February 1996).

36.5 **LAND SOLD WITH RIGHT OF RECONVEYANCE**

Where an interest in land is sold on terms requiring it to be subsequently *reconveyed* two years or more after the sale (or leased back one month or more after the sale) *to the vendor,* or a person connected with him, and the price at which the interest is sold exceeds that at which it is to be reconveyed (or, in the case of a lease-back, the value of the reversionary interest plus any premium for the lease), the excess less $\frac{1}{50}$th for each full year (minus one) between the sale and the date of the earliest possible reconveyance (or lease-back) is assessed on the vendor as income under Schedule A (previously Schedule D, Case VI). [*ICTA 1988, s 36; FA 1998, Sch 5 para 17*].

Any amount (as adjusted under *ICTA 1988, s 36(2)(b)*; price on reconveyance varying with time) brought into account as a receipt of a Schedule A business under these provisions is excluded from the consideration brought into account in the computation for capital gains tax purposes *except* in the denominator of the part disposal fraction (A/(A+B); see 17.6 DISPOSAL). This does not apply where what is disposed of is the remainder of a lease or a sub-lease out of a lease the duration of which does not exceed 50 years. See 36.17 below for the alternative provisions which apply. [*TCGA 1992, Sch 8 para 5(3)(4), para 6(3); FA 1998, Sch 5 para 63(2)*].

36.6 BETTERMENT LEVY

Betterment levy paid in respect of certain development land is deductible as expenditure wholly and exclusively incurred in enhancing the value of the asset in the CGT computation arising on the disposal or part disposal of that land. [*TCGA 1992, Sch 11 para 17*].

36.7 PART DISPOSALS

The general provisions for part disposals in *TCGA 1992, s 42* apply to disposals of land. See 17.6 DISPOSAL. These require the use of the market value of the part retained. The Revenue will, however, accept an alternative basis of calculation in the case of land. Under this, the part disposed of will be treated as a separate asset and any fair and reasonable method of apportioning part of the total cost to it will be accepted — e.g. a reasonable valuation of that part at the acquisition date. Where the market value at 6 April 1965 is to be taken as the cost, a reasonable valuation of the part at that date will similarly be accepted.

The cost of the part disposed of will be deducted from the total cost of the estate (or the balance of total cost) to determine the cost of the remainder of the estate; thus the total of the separate amounts adopted for the parts will not exceed the total cost. The cost attributed to each part must also be realistic in itself and the Board reserves the right to apply the general rule if not satisfied that apportionments are fair and reasonable. The taxpayer can always require that the general rule should be applied (except in cases already settled on the alternative basis). If he chooses the general rule it will normally be necessary to apply this rule to all subsequent disposals out of the estate; but where the general rule has been applied for a part disposal before the introduction of the alternative basis and it produced a result broadly the same as under the alternative basis, the alternative basis may be used for subsequent part disposals out of the estate.

So long as disposals out of an estate acquired before 6 April 1965 are dealt with on the alternative basis, each part disposal will carry a separate right to elect for acquisition at market value on 6 April 1965. Similarly, where part is sold with development value, the mandatory valuation at 6 April 1965 will apply only to that part. Even where the part is to be treated as acquired at market value on 6 April 1965, however, it will still be necessary to agree how much of the actual cost should be attributed to the part disposed of: first, to ensure that any allowable loss does not exceed the actual loss, and second, to produce a balance of total cost for subsequent disposals.

Adoption of the alternative basis is without prejudice to the treatment of small disposals set out in 36.8 below (Revenue Pamphlet IR 131, SP D1).

For provisions which apply to land held on 6 April 1965 generally, see 7.8–7.14 ASSETS HELD ON 6 APRIL 1965. Although the Revenue have yet to confirm it, it seems the above practice could be applied to land held on 31 March 1982 with suitable modifications. See generally, 8 ASSETS HELD ON 31 MARCH 1982.

36.8 **Small part disposals.** Where there is a transfer of land forming part only of a holding of land (or an estate or interest therein) and the amount or value of the consideration does not exceed one-fifth of the market value of the holding as it existed immediately before the disposal, the transferor may claim under *TCGA 1992, s 242(2)* that the transfer is not treated as a disposal. The consideration which would have been brought into account in the capital gains tax computation is then treated as a reduction of allowable expenditure in relation to any subsequent disposal of the remaining holding.

The consideration for the transfer or, if the transfer is not for full consideration, the market value of the land transferred, must not exceed a limit of £20,000. Where the transferor has made other disposals of land in the year of assessment, the total amount or value of the consideration for all such disposals of land (other than those within 36.10 below) must not exceed the limit.

The provisions do not apply to

(*a*) transfers treated as giving rise to neither a gain nor a loss between husband and wife (see 41.3 MARRIED PERSONS) or between companies in the same group (see 13.11 COMPANIES); or

(*b*) an estate or interest in land which is a wasting asset (e.g. a short lease under 36.14 below).

A claim for small part disposals must be made for the purposes of capital gains tax on or before the first anniversary of the 31 January next following the year of assessment in which the transfer is made; and in the case of corporation tax within two years after the end of the accounting period in which the transfer is made.

Where the allowable expenditure is less than the consideration for the part disposal (or is nil) the claim referred to above cannot be made but, if the recipient elects under *TCGA 1992, s 244(2)* and there is allowable expenditure, the consideration for the part disposal is reduced by the amount of the allowable expenditure. None of that expenditure is then allowable as a deduction in computing the gain accruing on the part disposal or any subsequent disposal. [*TCGA 1992, ss 242, 244; FA 1996, Sch 21 para 37*].

Example

C owns farmland which cost £134,000 in May 1987. In February 1995, a small plot of land is exchanged with an adjoining landowner for another piece of land. The value placed on the transaction is £18,000. The value of the remaining estate excluding the new piece of land is estimated at £250,000. In March 2001, C sells the whole estate for £300,000.

Indexation factors	May 1987 to February 1995	0.442
	February 1995 to April 1998	0.107
	May 1987 to April 1998	0.596

(i) No claim made under *TCGA 1992, s 242(2)*

		£	£
(*a*)	*Disposal in February 1995*		
	Disposal proceeds		18,000
	Allowable cost $\frac{18,000}{18,000 + 250,000} \times £134,000$		9,000
	Unindexed gain		9,000
	Indexation allowance £9,000 × 0.442		3,978
	Chargeable gain 1994/95		£5,022
(*b*)	*Disposal in March 2001*		
	Disposal proceeds		300,000
	Allowable cost		
	Original land £(134,000 – 9,000)	125,000	
	Exchanged land	18,000	143,000
	Unindexed gain		157,000
	Indexation allowance		
	Original land £125,000 × 0.596	74,500	
	Exchanged land £18,000 × 0.107	1,926	76,426
	Chargeable gain 2000/01 (subject to TAPER RELIEF (60))		£80,574

(ii) Claim made under *TCGA 1992, s 242(2)*

		£	£
(*a*)	*No disposal in February 1995*		
	Allowable cost of original land		134,000
	Deduct disposal proceeds		18,000
	Adjusted allowable cost		£116,000
	Allowable cost of additional land		£18,000
(*b*)	*Disposal in March 2001*		
	Disposal proceeds		300,000
	Allowable cost		
	Original land	116,000	
	Additional land	18,000	134,000
	Unindexed gain		166,000
	Indexation allowance		
	Original land £134,000 × 0.596	79,864	
	Additional land £18,000 × 0.107	1,926	
		81,790	
	Receipt set-off £18,000 × 0.107	1,926	79,864
	Chargeable gain 2000/01 (subject to TAPER RELIEF (60))		£86,136

36.9 COMPULSORY PURCHASE

The transfer of an interest in land to an 'authority exercising or having compulsory powers' (see 36.10 below) is a disposal for capital gains tax purposes. If the land is acquired under a contract, the date of disposal is the time the contract is made (and not, if different, the time at which the asset is conveyed or transferred). If the contract is conditional, the date of disposal is the time when the condition is satisfied. See also 17.2 DISPOSAL. Otherwise, the disposal and acquisition are made at the time at which compensation for the acquisition is agreed or otherwise determined (any variation on appeal against the original determination being disregarded). For 1995/96 and earlier years, the time when the local authority entered on the land in pursuance of its powers, if earlier than the time given by the aforementioned rule, was taken instead. This continues to be the case as regards interests owned by companies as respects accounting periods ending before 1 July 1999, i.e. the appointed day for corporation tax self-assessment (see 13.2 COMPANIES).

[*TCGA 1992, ss 28, 246; FA 1996, s 121(8), s 141(4), Sch 41 Pt V(6)*].

Relief is available for small part disposals (see 36.10 below). Rollover relief may be claimed in certain circumstances (see 36.11 below). In addition, where land or an interest in or right over land is acquired and the acquisition is (or could have been) made under compulsory powers, then the existence of the compulsory powers and any statutory provision treating the purchase price, compensation or other consideration as exclusively paid in respect of the land itself is disregarded in considering whether, under *TCGA 1992, s 52(4)* (just and reasonable apportionments), the purchase price etc. should be apportioned on a just and reasonable basis and treated in part as a capital sum within *TCGA 1992, s 22(1)(a)* (whether as compensation for loss of goodwill, for disturbance or otherwise) or should be apportioned in any other way. [*TCGA 1992, s 245(1)*]. The effect of this is that, where it is just and reasonable, part of the proceeds may be treated as a capital sum derived from an asset. See 17.7(A) DISPOSAL.

The receipt of severance compensation or compensation for injurious affection where part of a holding of land is or could have been compulsorily purchased is treated as a part disposal of the remaining land. [*TCGA 1992, s 245(2)*]. Where the conditions are satisfied, a claim for rollover relief may be made (see 36.11 below) in which case the consideration rolled over will include such compensation and there will be no deemed disposal of the remaining land. [*TCGA 1992, s 247(6)*].

Example

(i) Rollover not claimed

D owns freehold land purchased for £77,000 in 1978. Part of the land is made the subject of a compulsory purchase order. The compensation of £70,000 is agreed on 10 August 2000. The market value of the remaining land is £175,000. The value of the total freehold land at 31 March 1982 was £98,000. The indexation factor for the period March 1982 to April 1998 is 1.047.

	£	£
Disposal consideration	70,000	70,000
Cost £77,000 × $\frac{70,000}{70,000 + 175,000}$	22,000	
Market value 31.3.82		
£98,000 × $\frac{70,000}{70,000 + 175,000}$		28,000
Unindexed gain	48,000	42,000
Indexation allowance £28,000 × 1.047	29,316	29,316
Gain after indexation	£18,684	£12,684
Chargeable gain (subject to TAPER RELIEF (60))		£12,684

(ii) Rollover claimed under *TCGA 1992, s 247*

If, in (i), D acquires new land costing, say, £80,000 in, say, December 2000, relief may be claimed as follows.

	£
Allowable cost of land compulsorily purchased	28,000
Indexation allowance	29,316
Deemed consideration for disposal	57,316
Actual consideration	70,000
Chargeable gain rolled over	£12,684
Allowable cost of new land (£80,000 – £12,684)	£67,316

36.10 **Small part disposals.** Where a part of a holding of land (or an interest therein) is transferred to an 'authority exercising or having compulsory powers', the transferor may claim under *TCGA 1992, s 243(2)* that the transfer is not treated as a disposal, in which case the consideration which would have been brought into account is treated as a reduction of allowable expenditure in relation to any subsequent disposal of the remaining holding. A claim shall be made for the purposes of capital gains tax on or before the first anniversary of the 31 January next following the year of assessment in which the transfer is made; and in the case of corporation tax within two years after the end of the accounting period in which the transfer is made. [*TCGA 1992, s 243(2A); FA 1996, Sch 21 para 38*]. A holding of land for these purposes comprises only the land in respect of which allowable expenditure would be apportioned under *TCGA 1992, s 42* if the transfer had been treated as a part disposal. The consideration for the transfer (or, if the transfer is not for full consideration, the market value of the land transferred) must be 'small' as compared with the market value of the holding immediately before the transfer. For this purpose, the Revenue have regarded 'small' as meaning 5% or less (see Revenue Capital Gains Manual CG 57836, 72201). With effect from **24 February 1997**, they additionally regard an amount of £3,000 or less as 'small', regardless of whether or not it would pass the 5% test (Revenue Tax Bulletin February 1997 p 397).

The transferor must not have taken any steps, by advertising or otherwise, to dispose of any part of the holding or to make his willingness to dispose of it known to anyone. The provisions do not apply to wasting interests in land (e.g. a short lease under 36.14 below) but subject to this any estate or interest in land is included as a holding.

Where the allowable expenditure is less than the consideration for the part disposal (or is nil) the claim referred to above cannot be made but, if the recipient elects under *TCGA 1992, s 244(2)* and there is allowable expenditure, the consideration for the part disposal is reduced by the amount of the allowable expenditure. An election shall be made for the purposes of capital gains tax on or before the first anniversary of the 31st January next following the year of assessment in which part disposal is made; and in the case of corporation tax within two years after the end of the accounting period in which the part disposal is made. None of that expenditure is then allowable as a deduction in computing the gain accruing on the part disposal or any subsequent disposal.

'*Authority exercising or having compulsory powers*' means, in relation to the land transferred, a person or body of persons acquiring it compulsorily or who has or have been, or could be, authorised to acquire it compulsorily for the purposes for which it is acquired, or for whom another person or body of persons has or have been, or could be, authorised so to acquire it. [*TCGA 1992, ss 243, 244; FA 1996, Sch 21 para 39*].

36.11 Land

Example

(i) No rollover relief claimed

T inherited land in June 1987 at a probate value of £290,000. Under a compulsory purchase order, a part of the land is acquired for highway improvements. Compensation of £32,000 and a further £10,000 for severance, neither sum including any amount in respect of loss of profits, is agreed on 15 May 2000. The value of the remaining land is £900,000. Prior to the compulsory purchase, the value of all the land had been £950,000. The indexation factor for the period June 1987 to April 1998 is 0.596.

	£
Total consideration for disposal (£32,000 + £10,000)	42,000
Deduct allowable cost $\frac{42,000}{42,000 + 9000,000} \times$ £290,000	12,930
Unindexed gain	29,070
Indexation allowance £12,930 × 0.596	7,706
Chargeable gain (subject to TAPER RELIEF (60))	£21,364

(ii) Rollover relief claimed under ***TCGA 1992, s 243***

Total consideration for disposal is £42,000, less than 5% of the value of the estate before the disposal (£950,000). T may therefore claim that the consideration be deducted from the allowable cost of the estate.

Revised allowable cost (£290,000 – £42,000)	£248,000

An indexation adjustment in respect of the amount deducted will be required on a subsequent disposal of the estate. [*TCGA 1992, s 53(3), s 57*].

36.11 **Rollover relief.** ROLLOVER RELIEF (55) is extended to *any landowner* (i.e. not confined to land (or any interest in or right over land) which is used and occupied for the purposes of a trade) who disposes of land to an 'authority exercising or having compulsory powers' (see 36.10 above) where the landowner reinvests part or the whole of the proceeds in acquiring new land. Any land which is a dwelling-house or part of one and on which the whole or part of the gain on a subsequent disposal within six years would be covered by the exemptions for PRIVATE RESIDENCES (48) is excluded. Where any land is not so excluded at the time of its acquisition, but becomes so within six years, relief is withdrawn notwithstanding time limits for the making of assessments.

The effect of a claim (under *TCGA 1992, s 247(2)*) is to defer capital gains tax by deducting the otherwise chargeable gain on the original land from the acquisition cost of the newly acquired land. Relief is restricted where part only of the proceeds is reinvested in qualifying land. See 55.6 ROLLOVER RELIEF.

The following further matters should be noted.

(*a*) The landowner must not have taken any steps, by advertising or otherwise, to dispose of the old land or to make his willingness to dispose of it known. In practice, any event which occurred more than three years before the date of disposal is ignored. (CCAB Statements TR 476 and 477, May and June 1982 and Revenue Capital Gains Manual CG 61902, 72202).

(*b*) The new land must be acquired in the period beginning twelve months before and ending three years after the disposal or such longer period as the Board may allow e.g. where it has not been practical to acquire new land within the time limit.

New town corporations and similar authorities may purchase land for development and then grant the previous owner a lease or tenancy of the land until they are ready to commence building. Where land is so acquired under a compulsory purchase order or under the threat of such an order and is immediately leased back to the previous owner the Board is prepared, so long as there is a clear continuing intention that the sale proceeds will be used to acquire assets qualifying for rollover relief, to extend the time limit to a date three years after the land ceases to be used by him for his trade. An assurance to this effect will be given in appropriate cases subject to the reservation that it would be necessary to raise a protective assessment on the gain arising if exceptionally the lease or tenancy continued so long as to extend beyond the statutory time limit for making assessments (Revenue Pamphlet IR 131, SP D6). See Revenue Capital Gains Manual CG 60660–60665.

(*c*) Where the new land is a depreciating asset, similar provisions apply as in 55.7 ROLLOVER RELIEF except that the gain is held over for ten years or until the new asset is disposed of, whichever is the sooner. A gain previously held over is never deemed to accrue in consequence of an event occurring after 5 April 1988 if the application of this provision would be directly attributable to the disposal of an asset before 1 April 1982.

(*d*) The normal treatment of severance compensation as a part disposal (see 36.9 above) is expressly excluded. Such compensation is treated as additional consideration for the old land.

(*e*) Claims under these provisions and under *TCGA 1992, s 243* (see 36.10 above) are mutually exclusive.

(*f*) Subject to all other conditions for the granting of relief being met, the Revenue will accept a claim from a landlord whose leasehold tenant has exercised the following statutory rights:

- his right under the *Leasehold Reform Act 1967* or the *Leasehold Reform, Housing and Urban Development Act 1993* to acquire the freehold reversion of a property or an extension of the lease, or
- his right to buy or to acquire the freehold or an extension of the lease under the *Housing Acts 1985* to *1996* (which covers the situation where a tenant's right to buy is preserved following a transfer of housing stock into the private sector).

(Revenue Pamphlet IR 131, SP 13/93).

(*g*) In relation to a group of companies, where there is a compulsory purchase from one group member and acquisition of land by another, ROLLOVER RELIEF (55) is available where the compulsory purchase or the acquisition is after 28 November 1994. The previous ability to 'frank' a compulsory purchase from one group member to another by an intra-group acquisition was ended with effect to acquisitions after 28 November 1994.

[*TCGA 1992, ss 247, 248, Sch 4 para 4(5); FA 1995, s 48(2)(6); FA 1996, s 121(8), s 141(5)*].

For a concessionary application of this relief to the exchange of joint interests in land, see 36.12 below.

Provisional claims are permitted under self-assessment, in much the same way as for ROLLOVER RELIEF (55.2), for disposals after 5 April 1996 for capital gains tax purposes and in company accounting periods ending on or after 1 July 1999 (the commencement date for corporation tax self-assessment — see 13.2 COMPANIES).

The claimant may make a declaration in his tax return for a tax year or company accounting period in which he has made a qualifying disposal of land that the whole or a specified part of the consideration will be invested, within the requisite time limits (see (*b*) above), in new land (or an interest in or right over land) and that the new land is not excluded by virtue of the availability of the private residence exemption (see above). As long as the declaration continues to have effect, the same consequences ensue as if both an acquisition and a valid rollover relief claim had been made. The declaration ceases to have effect on the day, and to the extent that, it is withdrawn or is superseded by a valid claim, if either occurs before the 'relevant day'. It otherwise ceases to have effect on the relevant day itself. On its ceasing to have effect, all necessary adjustments will be made to the claimant's tax position, even if they would otherwise be out of time.

The '*relevant day*' means

- in relation to capital gains tax, the third anniversary of 31 January following the tax year of disposal, e.g. 31 January 2003 for disposals in 1998/99; and
- in relation to corporation tax, the fourth anniversary of the last day of the accounting period of disposal.

[*TCGA 1992, s 247A; FA 1996, s 121(8), s 141(6)*].

To the extent that a provisional claim is withdrawn or lapses, interest on unpaid tax is chargeable as if no such claim had been made.

36.12 **CONCESSIONARY ROLLOVER RELIEF FOR EXCHANGE OF JOINT INTERESTS IN LAND**

A form of rollover relief is available by concession for exchanges made after 19 December 1984 on the lines provided in 36.11 above (i.e. not confined to land which is used and occupied for the purposes of a trade) where

(*a*) a 'holding of land' is held jointly and as a result of the exchange each joint owner becomes sole owner of part of the 'land' formerly owned jointly; or

(*b*) a number of separate holdings of land are held jointly and as a result of the exchange each joint owner becomes sole owner of one or more holdings.

The interest relinquished will be treated as the 'old land' and the interest acquired as the 'new land'. '*Land*' includes any interest or right over land and '*holding of land*' includes an estate or interest in a holding of land and is to be construed in accordance with *TCGA 1992, s 243(3)* (see 36.10 above).

Relief will be denied under the concession to the extent that the new land is, or becomes, a dwelling-house (or part) within the meaning of *TCGA 1992, ss 222–226* (see 48 PRIVATE RESIDENCES) but subject to this, relief will be restricted as in 36.11 above where there is only part re-investment or only part of the gain is chargeable because of time apportionment.

However, where individuals who are joint beneficial owners of dwelling-houses which are their respective residences become sole owners of those houses in consequence of an exchange of interests, an alternative concessionary relief may be claimed if the gain accruing on the disposal of each dwelling-house immediately after the exchange would be exempt under the provisions contained in 48.1–48.5 PRIVATE RESIDENCES. Each individual must undertake to accept that he is deemed to have acquired the other's interest in the dwelling-house at the original base cost and at the time at which that joint interest was acquired.

For the purposes of this concession, a married couple is treated as an individual, so that an exchange of interests which results in a married couple alone becoming joint owners of land or of a dwelling house will meet the terms of the concession.

Where

(i) the concession applies to an exchange of interests in land after 29 October 1987,

(ii) there is a parallel exchange of interests in milk or potato quota associated with the land, and

(iii) each joint owner becomes sole owner of the part of the quota relating to the land he now owns,

the concession applies also to the exchange of interests in quota. (Revenue Pamphlet IR 1, D26).

The operation of the concession should be read in the light of the decision of *Warrington v Brown and related appeals Ch D 1989, 62 TC 226.*

36.13 LEASES

For capital gains tax purposes, a '*lease*' in relation to land includes an underlease, sub-lease or any tenancy or licence, and any agreement for a lease, underlease, sub-lease or tenancy or licence. In the case of land outside the UK, any interest corresponding to a lease as so defined is included. '*Lessor*', '*lessee*' and '*rent*' are construed accordingly. [*TCGA 1992, s 240, Sch 8 para 10(1)*].

Where a leaseholder of land acquires a superior interest in that land (whether a superior lease or the freehold reversion) so that the first lease is extinguished, the two interests are merged within the meaning of *TCGA 1992, s 43* (assets derived from other assets). On a subsequent disposal the allowable expenditure relating to the merged interest will include the cost of the first lease, after exclusion, in the case of a lease with less than 50 years to run, of the part which was wasted under *TCGA 1992, Sch 8* to the date of the acquisition of the superior interest (see 36.14 below) and the cost of the superior interest. Where the superior interest is itself a lease with less than 50 years to run, the total of these two amounts will also be wasted under *TCGA 1992, Sch 8* down to the date of disposal. Strictly, indexation allowance should be calculated on the total of these two amounts by reference to the date of acquisition of the superior interest, but, by concession, for disposals after 28 June 1992, indexation on the expenditure on the earlier, inferior lease, will be calculated by reference to the date of its acquisition.

For disposals before 29 June 1992, indexation allowance for the total of the two amounts is, by concession, calculated by reference to the date of acquisition of the inferior interest (Revenue Pamphlet IR 1, D42).

36.14 LEASES AS WASTING ASSETS

A lease of land is not a wasting asset until the time when its duration does not exceed fifty years. [*TCGA 1992, Sch 8 para 1(1)*]. The **duration** of a lease is to be decided by reference to the facts known or ascertainable at the time when the lease was acquired or created. In determining the duration, the following provisions apply.

(*a*) Where the terms of the lease include provision for the determination of the lease by notice given by the landlord, the lease is not to be treated as granted for a term longer than one ending at the earliest date on which it could be determined by notice given by the landlord.

(*b*) Where any of the terms of the lease or any other circumstances render it unlikely that the lease will continue beyond a date earlier than the expiration of the terms of the lease, the lease is not to be treated as having been granted for a longer term than one ending on that date. This applies in particular where the lease provides for rent to go up after a given date, or for the tenant's obligation to become more onerous after a given date, but includes provision for the determination of the lease on that date, by notice given by the tenant, and those provisions render it unlikely that the lease will continue beyond that date.

(*c*) Where the terms of the lease include provision for the extension of the lease beyond a given date by notice given by the tenant, the duration of the lease applies as if the term of the lease extended for as long as it could be extended by the tenant, but subject to any right of the landlord to determine the lease by notice.

[*TCGA 1992, Sch 8 para 8*].

A lease granted under *Landlord and Tenant Act 1954* to follow on from another is not a continuation of the old lease and is to be treated as having been acquired on the date it was granted (*Bayley v Rogers Ch D 1980, 53 TC 420*).

A similar view was taken in *Lewis v Walters Ch D 1992, 64 TC 489* regarding the right of a tenant to be granted a lease under *Leasehold Reform Act 1967* to follow on from another and where it was also held that (*c*) above did not apply since such a right was not included in the terms of the original lease.

Where a lease is 'extended' by the surrender of an old lease and the grant of a new one for a longer term, a disposal of the old lease will in strictness occur, the consideration for it normally being the value, if any, of the new lease. By concession, a disposal is not treated as arising in these circumstances provided that

- the parties are not connected and the transaction is at arm's length (or the parties *are* connected but the terms of the transaction are equivalent to those to be expected in an arm's length transaction between unconnected parties);
- the transaction is not part of or connected with a larger scheme or series of transactions;
- no capital sum is received by the lessee;
- the extent of the property in which the lessee has an interest is unchanged; and
- the terms of the leases remain the same except as regards the duration and amount of rent payable. For this purpose, trivial differences will be ignored.

(Revenue Pamphlet IR 1, D39). (See 3.23 ANTI-AVOIDANCE for the charge arising where concessions involving deferral of gains are abused.)

Computation. If a lease of land is a wasting asset, its original cost and any enhancement expenditure are not written off on a straight line basis (as would otherwise be required under *TCGA 1992, s 46*) but on a reducing basis as set out in the table below.

Table for depreciation of leases

Years	Percentage	Years	Percentage	Years	Percentage
50 (or more)	100	33	90.280	16	64.116
49	99.657	32	89.354	15	61.617
48	99.289	31	88.371	14	58.971
47	98.902	30	87.330	13	56.167
46	98.490	29	86.226	12	53.191
45	98.059	28	85.053	11	50.038
44	97.595	27	83.816	10	46.695
43	97.107	26	82.496	9	43.154
42	96.593	25	81.100	8	39.399
41	96.041	24	79.622	7	35.414
40	95.457	23	78.055	6	31.195
39	94.842	22	76.399	5	26.722
38	94.189	21	74.635	4	21.983
37	93.497	20	72.770	3	16.959
36	92.761	19	70.791	2	11.629
35	91.981	18	68.697	1	5.983
34	91.156	17	66.470	0	0

The fraction of the *original cost* which is not allowed is given by the fraction

$$\frac{P(1) - P(3)}{P(1)}$$

where

P(1) = the percentage derived from the table for the duration of the lease at acquisition

P(3) = the percentage derived from the table for the duration of the lease at the time of disposal

The fraction of any *enhancement expenditure* which is not allowed is given by the fraction

$$\frac{P(2) - P(3)}{P(2)}$$

where

P(2) = the percentage derived from the table for the duration of the lease at the time when the item of expenditure is first reflected in the nature of the lease

P(3) = as above

If the duration of the lease is not an exact number of years, the percentage is that for the whole number of years plus one twelfth of the difference between that and the percentage of the next higher number of years for each odd month, counting an odd 14 days or more as one month.

The provisions above apply even if the period of ownership of the lease exceeds 50 years. Accordingly, in such a case, any cost or enhancement expenditure incurred before the lease becomes a wasting asset is not reduced until the lease does become a wasting asset. [*TCGA 1992, Sch 8 para 1(3)–(5)*]. In these circumstances P(1) and P(2) will each be 100 in the fractions given above.

Example

X purchases a 30-year lease of business premises in 1994 for £250,000. In 1997, when 27 years of the lease remain, he spends £25,000 on improvements which are at once reflected in the value of the lease and continue to be so until he disposes of it with 24 years remaining in 2000. His allowable expenditure is reduced as follows

$$\text{Original cost } (£250{,}000) \times \frac{(87.330 - 79.622)}{87.330} = £22{,}066$$

$$\text{Additional cost } (£25{,}000) \times \frac{(83.816 - 79.622)}{83.816} = £1{,}251$$

£23,317

The total allowable expenditure is then (£275,000 – £23,317) = £251,683

Exceptions. The above provisions do not apply in the following circumstances.

(i) If at the beginning of the period of ownership of a lease, it is subject to a *sub-lease not at a rackrent* and the value of the lease at the end of the sub-lease (estimated at the beginning of the period of ownership) exceeds the expenditure allowable in computing the gain accruing on the disposal of the lease (see 17.3(*a*) DISPOSAL), the lease is *not* a wasting asset until the end of the duration of the sub-lease. [*TCGA 1992, Sch 8 para 1(2)*].

(ii) Where the land, throughout the ownership of the person making the disposal, is used solely for the purposes of a trade, profession or vocation, and capital allowances have, or could have, been claimed in respect of its cost, or in respect of any enhancement expenditure. This also applies where the cost of land has otherwise qualified in full for any capital allowances. Where, however, the land disposed of has been used partly for non-business purposes, or has only partly qualified for capital allowances, the expenditure and consideration are apportioned and the restriction of allowable expenditure as above applies only to that portion of expenditure which has not qualified for capital allowances, or which relates to the period of non-business use. [*TCGA 1992, s 47, Sch 8 para 1(6)*].

36.15 PREMIUMS FOR LEASES

Where the payment of a 'premium' is required under a lease (or otherwise under the terms subject to which the lease is granted) there is a part disposal of the freehold or other interest out of which that lease is granted. [*TCGA 1992, Sch 8 para 2(1)*].

In the part disposal computation (which follows the normal rules in *TCGA 1992, s 42,* see 17.6 DISPOSAL) the property which remains undisposed of includes a right to any rent or other payments (other than a premium) payable under the lease, and that right is valued at the time of the part disposal. [*TCGA 1992, Sch 8 para 2(2)*].

'*Premium*' includes any like sum, whether payable to the intermediate or superior landlord and includes any sum (other than rent) paid on or in connection with the granting of a tenancy except when the other sufficient consideration for the payment can be shown to have been given. In Scotland, '*premium*' includes in particular a *grassum* payable to any landlord or intermediate landlord on the creation of a sub-lease. [*TCGA 1992, Sch 8 para 10(2)(3); FA 1996, Sch 20 para 67*].

Capital sums treated as premiums. The legislation provides for other capital amounts payable under leases to be treated as if they were premiums. Where the landlord is a freeholder, or is a leaseholder and that lease has more than 50 years to run, and (*a*) *under the terms of a lease*, a sum becomes payable by the tenant in lieu of the whole or part of the rent for any period ('commutation of rent'), or as consideration for the surrender of the lease, or

(*b*) a sum becomes payable by the tenant (otherwise than by way of rent) as consideration for the variation or waiver of any of the terms of the lease,

the lease is deemed to have required payment of a premium to the landlord (in addition to any actual premium) of the amount of that sum. This premium is treated as being due when the sum is payable by the tenant and as being in respect of, where (*a*) applies, the period in relation to which it is payable or, where (*b*) applies, the period from the time the variation or waiver takes effect to the time it ceases to have effect. The deemed receipt of the premium does not require a chargeable gain arising from the receipt of any other premium to be recomputed. Instead, it is regarded as a separate transaction effected at the time the premium is deemed to be due and as a part disposal (or further part disposal) of the freehold (or other asset out of which the lease is granted) or, in the case of a payment for surrender, as a disposal by the landlord of his interest in the lease.

Where a sum falls within (*b*) above and the transaction is not at arm's length and/or is entered into gratuitously, the amount actually payable is replaced in the tax computation by such sum as might have been required of the tenant in an arm's length transaction.

The above provisions apply as regards sums payable after 5 April 1996, having been changed to facilitate self-assessment. The previous rules were broadly similar but with the fundamental difference that, except in the case of consideration for the surrender of a lease, the premium was deemed to have been received by the landlord at the time the lease was originally granted. Any capital gains computation relating to a premium actually received on the grant of the lease had to be reworked to take the additional premium into account, and the requisite assessment could if necessary be made outside the normal six-year time limit then applicable.

The rules are modified (both before and after 5 April 1996 but not where the payment is consideration for the surrender of a lease) if the landlord is himself a tenant under a lease with 50 years or less to run at the time the capital sum is paid. The premium is deemed to have been given by way of consideration for the grant of the part of the sub-lease covered by the period in respect of which the premium is treated as having been paid. It is *not* thereby treated as having been received at the time the sub-lease was granted; the date of disposal is determined under general principles — see 17.2 DISPOSAL. See the worked example at Revenue Capital Gains Manual CG 71371. As far as the sub-lessee is concerned, the payment is treated as allowable enhancement expenditure (see 17.3(*b*) DISPOSAL) incurred by him and attributable to the aforementioned part of the sub-lease.

[*TCGA 1992, Sch 8 para 3; FA 1996, s 142*].

See Revenue Capital Gains Manual CG 71350–71371 for further commentary on the above and worked examples.

If a capital sum is paid by a tenant for commutation of rent and the terms of the lease do *not* provide for such a payment, the above rules do not apply. The transaction is treated as a part disposal within *TCGA 1992, s 22* (capital sums derived from assets — see 17.7 DISPOSAL). (Revenue Capital Gains Manual CG 71351, 71372).

Reverse premiums. In a New Zealand case, a substantial lump sum received by an accountancy firm as an inducement to enter into a lease of premises at a rent above the market rent, i.e. a payment *by* a lessor *to* a lessee (known as a reverse premium), was held to be a capital receipt (*New Zealand Commissioner of Inland Revenue v Wattie and another PC, [1998] STC 1160*). As a result of this case, legislation was introduced in the UK to ensure that a reverse premium (as defined therein) is chargeable to income tax or corporation tax as a *revenue* receipt. This applies to a premium received on or after 9 March

1999 unless, disregarding any arrangements made on or after that date, the recipient was entitled to it immediately before that date. As regards earlier premiums, the Revenue will be guided by the decision in *Wattie*, although a reverse premium could still be a revenue receipt if, on the evidence, it is a contribution to revenue expenditure, e.g. relocation costs, although the linkage of the premium to an increased rental does not of itself give it the character of a revenue receipt. Where a reverse premium is a capital receipt, it gives rise to a chargeable gain *only* if derived from an asset held by the tenant. If the premium was paid before the tenant entered into the lease, this could be the case only if it were derived from some other asset, for example if it is a payment to induce the tenant to surrender an existing lease. See *FA 1999, s 54, Sch 6* and Revenue Tax Bulletin April 1999 p 641, and see TOLLEY'S INCOME TAX for full coverage.

General. In *Clarke v United Real (Moorgate) Ltd Ch D 1987, 61 TC 353*, the taxpayer company contracted for a freehold site which it owned to be developed by a third party. Subsequently it entered into an 'agreement for a lease' with another third party ('A') under which A agreed to reimburse the company's development costs and the company was to grant him a long lease of the developed site at a rent below market value, which was to be ascertained by reference to his reimbursement payments to the company. The granting of the lease was agreed to be a part disposal. The reimbursement payments were held to be a premium within *TCGA 1992, Sch 8 para 2(1), para 10(2)*, because they were made to the company in its capacity as landlord, and not to meet an obligation incurred by the company on behalf of A.

36.16 **Premiums taxed under Schedule A.** Where a premium is received for a lease not exceeding 50 years and part of it is liable to tax under *ICTA 1988, s 34* as a receipt of a Schedule A business, that part is excluded from the computation for capital gains tax purposes *except* in the denominator of the part disposal fraction of A/(A+B) given by *TCGA 1992, s 42*. '*Premium*' includes a deemed premium under *ICTA 1988, s 34(4)* or *(5)* (which correspond to a premium deemed to arise under (*a*) or (*b*) in 36.15 above). [*TCGA 1992, Sch 8 para 5(1)(5); FA 1998, Sch 5 para 63(2)*].

Where the terms of a lease impose an obligation on the tenant to carry out work on the premises concerned, an amount equal to the increase in value of the landlord's interest occasioned by the work is treated as a premium under *ICTA 1988, s 34* above except insofar as the obligation relates to work which, had it been carried out by the landlord, would have been deductible as an expense of any Schedule A business carried on by the landlord. [*ICTA 1988, s 34(2)(3); FA 1998, Sch 5 para 15(3)*]. For capital gains tax purposes the consequential effect is that the landlord is treated as incurring enhancement expenditure of that amount on the premises at the time of the grant of the lease. [*TCGA 1992, Sch 8 paras 7, 7A; FA 1995, s 41(4); FA 1998, Sch 5 para 63(4)(5)*].

Example

X grants a 14-year lease of premises for a premium of £5,000 in 2000/01 and retains the freehold interest. The amount chargeable to income tax for that year is

	£
Premium	5,000
Deduct $\frac{14 - 1}{50} \times$ £5,000	1,300
Chargeable to income tax	£3,700

If the allowable expenditure on the original unencumbered freehold (acquired in 1995) is £30,000 and the value of the reversion £47,000, the unindexed gain is computed as follows

	£
Consideration received (i.e. the premium)	5,000
Deduct amount chargeable to income tax	3,700
	£1,300

Allowable expenditure attributable to the part disposal

$$\frac{1,300}{(5,000 + 47,000)} \times £30,000 = \qquad £750$$

Unindexed gain: £1,300 – £750 = £550

36.17 **Sub-leases granted out of short leases.** Where a sub-lease is granted out of a head-lease with less than 50 years to run, the normal part disposal rules do not apply. Instead, subject to below, a proportion of the cost and enhancement expenditure attributable to the lease is apportioned to the part disposed of as follows

$$\frac{P(1) - P(3)}{P(2)}$$

where

P(1) = the percentage derived from the table in 36.14 above for the duration of the lease at the date of granting the sub-lease

P(3) = the percentage for the duration of the lease at the date of termination of the sub-lease

P(2) = the percentage for the duration of the lease at the date of acquisition (for apportionment of cost) *or* the date when expenditure is first reflected in the nature of the lease (for apportionment of enhancement expenditure)

If the amount of the premium is less than what would be obtainable by way of premium for the sub-lease if the rent payable under the sub-lease were the same as the rent payable under the lease, the percentage attributable to the sub-lease as calculated above must be multiplied by the premium received over the premium so obtainable before being applied to cost or enhancement expenditure. [*TCGA 1992, Sch 8 para 4(1)(2)*].

Example

X purchases a 40-year lease of a flat in 1995 for £15,000. In 2000, he sub-lets the flat to Y for 20 years for a premium of £8,000. The premium obtainable on the basis of the rent paid under the head-lease is £10,000. X's original expenditure of £15,000 is apportioned as follows

$$\frac{91.981 - 61.617}{95.457} = 0.3180908 \times \frac{8,000}{10,000} = 0.2544726$$

0.2544726 × £15,000 = £3,817

The expenditure attributable to the part disposal is therefore £3,817 as against £4,771 (£15,000 × 0.3180908) if the premium had been the maximum obtainable, £10,000.

Where the sub-lease is a sub-lease of part only of the land comprised in the lease, the cost and enhancement expenditure of the head-lease must be apportioned between the sub-lease and the remainder in proportion to their respective values. [*TCGA 1992, Sch 8 para 4(3)*].

Where a premium (including a deemed premium as in 36.16 above) is paid for the sub-lease, an amount of which is liable to tax under *ICTA 1988, s 34* as a receipt of a Schedule A business, that amount is deducted from any *gain* accruing on the disposal for which the premium is consideration but not so as to convert the gain into a loss or to increase any loss. [*TCGA 1992, Sch 8 para 5(2)(5); FA 1998, Sch 5 para 63(2)*]. Similar provisions apply where, under *ICTA 1988, s 36* (see 36.5 above) what is disposed of is the remainder of a lease or a sub-lease out of a lease the duration of which does not exceed 50 years. [*TCGA 1992, Sch 8 para 5(4)*].

36.18 **Allowances to payer for premiums paid.** Where a lease, granted for a premium which gave rise to a liability under *ICTA 1988, s 34* (see 36.16 above) or *35* (see 36.19 below) on the landlord, is sub-leased or sold for a premium, any potential liability on that latter event is compared with the 'appropriate fraction' of the liability on the first transaction (proportionate to the period covered by the sub-lease as compared with that covered by the first lease) and only the excess is chargeable. [*ICTA 1988, s 37(1)(2)(3)(7); FA 1998, Sch 5 para 18*].

Where the 'appropriate fraction' of the amount chargeable on the superior landlord exceeds the amount of the premium chargeable on the intermediate landlord, the surplus is treated under *ICTA 1988, s 37(4)* as 'additional rent' allowable against property income. In this event, if a *loss* accrues for capital gains tax purposes to the intermediate landlord on the disposal by way of the grant of the sub-lease, the loss is reduced by the total amount of the additional rent but not so as to convert the loss into a gain. Any adjustment under *ICTA 1988, s 36(2)(b)* (see 36.5 above) is taken into account. [*TCGA 1992, Sch 8 para 6(1)(3)*].

Example

On 21 January 1994 C is granted a lease of a shop for 21 years for a rent and a premium of £12,800. On 21 January 2001 he grants a sub-lease for a period of 7 years for a premium of £1,000 and a rent equal to that payable under the terms of the head-lease.

	£	£
Schedule A		
Premium	1,000	
Deduct $\dfrac{7-1}{50} \times £1{,}000$	120	880
Allowances for premium paid		
$\dfrac{\text{Duration of sub-lease}}{\text{Duration of head-lease}} = \dfrac{7}{21}$		
Amount chargeable on superior landlord		
$£12{,}800 - \left(\dfrac{21-1}{50} \times £12{,}800\right) - £7{,}680$		
Allowance = $£7{,}680 \times \frac{7}{21}$		2,560
Amount allowable under Schedule A against rent received		£1,680

		£
Capital gains tax		
Premium received		1,000
Consideration given for lease	£12,800	
Percentage applicable to lease of 21 years	74.635	
Percentage applicable to lease of 14 years	58.971	
Percentage applicable to lease of 7 years	35.414	
Amount allowable $\frac{58.971 - 35.414}{74.635} \times$ £12,800		4,040
Loss		3,040
Deduct amount allowable under Schedule A		1,680
Allowable loss		£1,360

36.19 **Anti-avoidance provisions.** Where a lease not exceeding 50 years granted at *less than market value* is assigned for a consideration exceeding any premium for which it was granted (or the consideration on any previous assignment) the excess, up to the limit of the amount of any premium, or additional premium, which the grantor forwent when granting the lease, is assessed on him, but under Schedule A (previously Schedule D, Case VI), to the same extent that an additional premium would have been assessed under *ICTA 1988, s 34(1)* (see 36.16 above). [*ICTA 1988, s 35; FA 1998, Sch 5 para 16*].

Any assessment to income or corporation tax under these provisions is not taken into account in any capital gains computation. [*TCGA 1992, Sch 8 para 6(2); FA 1998, Sch 5 para 63(3)*]. There may, therefore, be a double charge to tax.

36.20 LAND SOLD AND LEASED BACK — PROPORTION OF CAPITAL SUM RECEIVED TO BE TAXED AS INCOME IN CERTAIN CIRCUMSTANCES

As regards arrangements within *ICTA 1988, s 779* (land sold and leased back), where the lease when sold has no more than 50 years still to run and the period for which the premises are leased back is *15 years or less*, any increased rent payable, so far as it does not exceed a commercial rent, is allowable as a deduction from profits, but of the consideration received by the lessee for giving up the original lease (or undertaking to pay an increased rent) a proportion equivalent to one-fifteenth of that consideration multiplied by the number of years by which the term of the lease-back falls short of 16 years will be treated as an income receipt instead of a capital one. Appropriate adjustment is made where the lease-back is of part only of the property previously leased. For the above purposes the term of the new lease is deemed to end on any date whereafter the rent payable is reduced, or, if the lessor or lessee has power to determine the lease or the lessee has power to vary its terms, on the earliest date on which the lease can be so determined or varied. [*ICTA 1988, s 780*].

36.21 INSURANCE RECOVERIES: SHORT LEASES

Where property is held on a lease which has 50 years or less to run, insurance payments received by the lessee before 6 April 1996 in respect of the property will not be treated as a capital sum derived from the lease within the meaning of *TCGA 1992, s 22(1)* to the extent that they are applied by the lessee in discharging an obligation to restore any damage to the property. (Revenue Pamphlet IR 1, D1). See generally 17.7(*a*) DISPOSAL. Subsequent legislation at 17.8 DISPOSAL has superseded this concessionary treatment.

36.22 **VALUE SHIFTING — ADJUSTMENT OF LEASEHOLD RIGHTS**

Where an owner of land (or of any other description of property) enters into a transaction whereby he becomes the lessee of that property (e.g. a sale and lease-back) and there is a subsequent adjustment of rights and liabilities under the lease (whether or not involving the grant of a new lease) which is on the whole favourable to the lessor, such an adjustment is a disposal by the lessee of an interest in the property. [*TCGA 1992, s 29(4)*]. See 3.4 ANTI-AVOIDANCE for full coverage.

36.23 **CONTINGENT LIABILITIES**

In the first instance, no allowance is made in a capital gains tax computation for

(*a*) in the case of a disposal by way of assigning a lease of land or other property, any liability remaining with, or assumed by, the person making the disposal which is contingent on a default in respect of liabilities thereby or subsequently assumed by the assignee under the terms and conditions of the lease; and

(*b*) any contingent liability of the person making the disposal in respect of any covenant for quiet enjoyment or other obligation assumed as vendor of land, or of any estate or interest in land, or as a lessor.

If it is subsequently shown to the satisfaction of the inspector that any such contingent liability has become enforceable, and is being or has been enforced, such adjustment is made as is required in consequence. [*TCGA 1992, s 49(1)(a)(b), (2)(3)*].

The receipt of a contingently repayable deposit in return for the grant of an option to purchase land was valued subject to the contingency because on the facts the contingency was not within (*b*) above (*Randall v Plumb Ch D 1974, 50 TC 392*).

37 Life Assurance Policies and Deferred Annuities

37.1 The disposal of rights under, or of an interest in, a life assurance policy or deferred annuity does not give rise to a chargeable gain unless it is made by a person other than the original beneficial owner who has acquired the rights or interest for money or money's worth.

Subject to this, the payment of the sum assured by the policy or of the first instalment of the deferred annuity, the transfer of investments or other assets to the owner in accordance with the policy and the surrender of the policy or of rights thereunder, are each treated as a disposal of rights under the policy. The amount of the consideration for the disposal of a deferred annuity is deemed to be the then market value of the outstanding annuity payments. [*TCGA 1992, s 210*]. Any transfer of investments or other assets is deemed to be made at market value. [*TCGA 1992, s 204(3)*].

In computing any chargeable gain, allowable expenditure will be

(*a*) the base cost of the policy to the person to whom the gain accrues (normally, this will be what the purchaser paid for the policy), and

(*b*) any premiums paid by the purchaser.

37.2 *ICTA 1988, ss 539–554* provide for income tax to be charged on the profits arising on certain life policies and life annuity contracts. Before 26 June 1982, where such policies or contracts were assigned for money or money's worth, any profit subsequently arising was taken out of charge to income tax and was subject instead to capital gains tax. To counter the tax advantages previously gained by the use of such policies and contracts, any profit on policies etc. taken out after 25 June 1982 cease to escape the charge to income tax. The former provisions also cease to apply to policies etc. issued and assigned for money or money's worth before 26 June 1982 if, after 23 August 1982,

(i) the rights under the policy etc. are again assigned for money or money's worth; or

(ii) further capital is injected; or

(iii) subject to certain conditions, loans are taken against the security of the policy etc.

[*ICTA 1988, s 540(3), s 542(3), s 544*].

For full details, see TOLLEY'S INCOME TAX.

37.3 For gains made in connection with life assurance policies which are assessable to income tax or corporation tax, not capital gains tax, see TOLLEY'S INCOME TAX or TOLLEY'S CORPORATION TAX respectively.

37.4 For the treatment of other kinds of policy, see 21.10 EXEMPTIONS AND RELIEFS.

38 Loan Relationships of Companies

Cross-references. See also 24 GOVERNMENT SECURITIES; 49 QUALIFYING CORPORATE BONDS.

The headings in this chapter are as follows.

38.1 **INTRODUCTION**

New rules regarding the taxation of corporate and government debt together with some consequential changes to income tax and capital gains provisions were introduced by *Finance Act 1996, ss 80–110, Schs 8–15*. Subject to transitional provisions, the rules apply for company accounting periods ending after 31 March 1996. [*FA 1996, s 105*].

38.2 **TAXATION OF CORPORATE AND GOVERNMENT DEBT — SUMMARY**

Full coverage of the *Finance Act 1996* rules affecting companies is given in TOLLEY'S CORPORATION TAX under Loan Relationships. The rules for individual investors in this respect remain unchanged.

The intention is for the corporate taxation of income and expenditure from corporate and government debt to equate with its accepted accounting treatment. This is brought about by first establishing the existence of a 'loan relationship' and secondly, by treating all company profits and losses from such relationships as income and not capital, regardless of whether the company is borrower or lender.

38.3 A **loan relationship** exists whenever a company is in the position of debtor or creditor to a money debt which arises from the lending of money. [*FA 1996, s 81(1)*].

A *money debt* is defined as a debt which falls to be settled

(*a*) by the payment of money; or

(*b*) by the transfer of a right to settlement under a debt which is itself a money debt.

[*FA 1996, s 81(2)*].

The legislation does not define a *debtor* or *creditor* and therefore the accepted meaning is understood to apply.

Examples of loan relationships are: bank overdrafts, bank borrowings and third party borrowings plus corporate bonds and gilt-edged securities (except $3\frac{1}{2}$% Funding Stock 1999–2004 and $5\frac{1}{2}$% Treasury Stock 2008–2012) held by non-financial traders.

However, normal debtor/creditor relationships are not included as these do not arise from the lending of money and a debt arising from shareholders' rights is specifically excluded. Thus, ordinary shares and preference shares are not loan relationships. The same applies as regards permanent interest bearing shares (PIBs) issued by building societies, although only in respect of gains (and losses), which are, therefore, brought within the charge to corporation tax on chargeable gains. Interest on PIBs is within the loan relationship rules by virtue of *ICTA 1988, s 477A(3)*. (See Revenue Company Taxation Manual para 12119 and Life Assurance Manual para 3B.44.)

The legislation does not provide a definition of *money* but it is not restricted to sterling. [*FA 1996, s 81(5)(6)*].

38.4 **Charge to and relief from tax.** Profits, gains and deficits arising from loan relationships to which a company is party are computed according to the purposes for which those loan relationships are arranged and currently exist.

In the case of existing loan relationships arranged for trading purposes any receipts and expenses are attributable to the trade and any profit or gain is taxable under Schedule D, Case I with relief provided for any deficit. It is understood that if only part of the loan relates to trading purposes the receipts and expenses should be apportioned accordingly. [*FA 1996, s 82(1)*].

Profits, gains and deficits in respect of loans arranged for non-trading purposes are taxable under Schedule D, Case III with relief for deficits.

The Revenue have issued guidance on the application of the loan relationships provisions to a partnership which includes one or more companies. Broadly, the partnership itself is treated as the party to the relationship, and the debits and credits computed as if the partnership were a company. They are then apportioned to the corporate partners in accordance with the partnership agreement. See Revenue Pamphlet IR 131, SP 4/98.

38.5 COMPUTATION

As the underlying criteria is for the tax treatment of each loan relationship to follow normal accountancy practice the terms *debit* and *credit* have been introduced to statute to describe the method of accounting for individual items of income and expenditure. All debits and credits, both of a revenue and of a capital nature must be accounted for using an authorised accounting method prescribed by *Finance Act 1996* of which there are two:

(*a*) the authorised accruals basis; and

(*b*) the authorised mark to market basis.

The debits and credits will include all profits, gains, losses, interest payments, charges and expenses appertaining to the company's loan relationship or its attributed rights and liabilities. Charges and expenses appertaining to a loan relationship will only include those incurred directly. [*FA 1996, s 84*].

The loan relationship provisions relate not only to profits and gain reported in the profit and loss account but also to any item which following normal accountancy practice is transferred to or included in reserves but not any amount which is required to be transferred to the share premium account. [*FA 1996, s 84(2)*].

Charges and expenses include only those incurred directly

(*a*) in bringing any of the loan relationships into existence, (*b*) in entering into or giving effect to any of the related transactions,

(*c*) in making payments under any of the relationships or in pursuance of any of the related transactions, or

(*d*) in taking steps for ensuring the receipt of payments under any of the relationships or in pursuance of any of the related transactions.

Foreign exchange gains and losses remain subject to the *Finance Act 1993* provisions.

38.6 **AUTHORISED ACCOUNTING METHODS**

(*a*) *The authorised accruals basis* must allocate receipts and expenses to the period to which they relate rather than to the period in which they are made or received or in which they become due and payable.

(*b*) *The mark to market basis* allocates receipts and expenses to the period in which they become due and payable and brings the value of every existing loan relationship into account at fair value at the end of each period.

[*FA 1996, s 85*].

Different authorised methods of accounting may be used as respects different loan relationships and for different accounting periods (or parts) as respects the same loan relationship. If a company uses an authorised method of accounting for its statutory accounts that method must be used for the whole period covered by those accounts. If the company does not use an authorised accruals basis of accounting the Revenue will substitute the authorised accruals basis. [*FA 1996, s 86*].

38.7 **CAPITAL GAINS**

The **general rule** is that no chargeable gain will arise on the disposal of any loan relationship because, for disposals after 31 March 1996, every asset representing a loan relationship of a company is a QUALIFYING CORPORATE BOND (see 49.2). [*TCGA 1992, s 117(A1); FA 1996, Sch 14 para 61, Sch 15 para 7(c)*].

Exceptions to the general rule and the transitional provisions are described below.

38.8 **ASSETS REMAINING WITHIN THE SCOPE OF CAPITAL GAINS**

(i) Convertible securities etc. held by companies as *non-trading assets* are outside the scope of the *Finance Act 1996* provisions as regards capital but not as regards interest. Interest receipts and payments must be brought to account using the *Finance Act 1996* prescribed authorised accruals basis of accounting. (See TOLLEY'S CORPORATION TAX under Loan Relationships). Securities are '*convertible securities*' if

(i) they carry a right to acquire shares in a company, which need not necessarily be in the company which issued the securities;

(ii) the shares that are to be acquired are not determined by a cash value specified in the loan terms;

(iii) at the outset it was judged there was more than a negligible likelihood that the rights will in due course be exercised to a significant extent;

(iv) the security is not a 'relevant discounted security' (see 58.20 SHARES AND SECURITIES and see also below);

(v) the security is a non-trading asset and as such a disposal would not form an *integral* part of the company's trade.

The value on disposal of any convertible security is adjusted for interest accrued but not received. Disposal for this purpose means any disposal within the meaning of *TCGA 1992* (see 17 DISPOSAL) and any reorganisation, conversion or reconstruction within the meaning of *TCGA 1992, s 127* and *s 116* (see 49.3 and 58.5).

[*FA 1996, s 92(1)–(6)*].

As regards (iv) above, the definition of 'relevant discounted security' has been widened to take further account of potential redemptions before maturity (see 58.20 SHARES AND SECURITIES). For the purposes of the above provisions, this has effect in relation to company accounting periods ending after 14 February 1999 but not so as to affect disposals or part disposals completed on or before that date. [*FA 1999, s 65(9)*]. If an asset continuing to represent a creditor relationship of the company ceases after that date to be a convertible security within these provisions (which would be the case if it becomes a relevant discounted security), there is deemed to be a disposal and reacquisition by the company at its current value (adjusted for accrued interest) under the company's chosen accounting method, with the resulting gain or loss deferred under the provisions at 49.3 QUALIFYING CORPORATE BONDS covering share reorganisations etc. involving the issue of a qualifying corporate bond. [*FA 1996, s 92(7)–(11); FA 1999, s 65(7)(9)*].

(ii) Relationships linked to the value of chargeable assets.

Where a debt i.e. a loan relationship is linked to the value of a non-trading chargeable asset for capital gains purposes or linked to an index of the value of non-trading chargeable assets it will be outside the scope of the *Finance Act 1996* provisions for both issuer and holder except for interest purposes.

A trading asset is one the disposal of which would fall to be treated as a disposal in the course of activities forming an integral part of a trade carried on by the company.

The interest is to be accounted for using the authorised accruals basis. The value on disposal of any loan relationship linked to the value of chargeable assets is adjusted by a 'just and reasonable' apportionment of any interest accrual that is made by the company which because of the terms of the acquisition or disposal of the asset is not paid or payable to the company. Disposal for this purpose means any disposal within the meaning of *TCGA 1992* (see 17 DISPOSAL) and any reorganisation, conversion or reconstruction within the meaning of *TCGA 1992, s 127* and *s 116* (see 49.3 and 58.5).

A linkage to the value of a non-trading chargeable asset is determined where the following formula applies:

Amount to discharge the money debt	=	Value of non–trading chargeable assets × relevant % change in value of such chargeable assets over the relevant period.

Notes

1. The amount to discharge the money debt may be by redemption of that security or other arrangement.
2. The value of the chargeable assets is deemed to be the amount of the original loan from which the money debt arises.
3. The relevant change in the value of such chargeable assets is the percentage change applicable to that type of asset. The retail price index is not to be used nor any similar general index of prices published by the government of any territory or by the agent of any such government because these are not specific to the type of assets.
4. The relevant period is the period between the date of the original loan and the date of its discharge. If it is impractical to use this period for valuation reasons, a different

period is allowed, provided the loan relationship existed for practically the whole of that period.

If the amount payable to discharge the debt is determined by another provision of the taxes legislation and the amount so calculated is less than 10% of the original loan as in (2) above that provision shall be ignored for these purposes in determining whether the relationship is linked to the value of chargeable assets.

[*FA 1996, s 93*].

38.9 **TRANSITIONAL RULES**

The following definitions apply for the purposes of this chapter:

A *relevant event* occurs on the first occasion after 31 March 1996 when any company falls to be treated as making a disposal (other than a no gain, no loss disposal) of the asset or of any asset falling to be treated the same as that asset. Where the disposal is by a company other than the one holding the asset on 31 March 1996 the chargeable gain or allowable loss is brought into account on that company.

'*Market value*' in relation to any assets means the price which those assets might reasonably be expected to fetch on a sale in the open market.

'*Relevant qualifying asset*' in relation to a company means any qualifying asset for the purposes of *Chapter II* of *Part II* of the *Finance Act 1993* the value of which has been determined as at the company's commencement day for the purpose of calculating any attributed amount.

'*First relevant accounting period*' the first accounting period of the company to end after 31 March 1996.

'*Transitional accounting period*' any accounting period of the company beginning before and ending on or after 1 April 1996.

'*Relevant asset*' means a chargeable asset or a relevant qualifying asset.

'*Chargeable asset*' any asset which if disposed of at 31 March 1996 would have given rise to a chargeable gain or any asset on which a chargeable gain or allowable loss would be deemed to have accrued to the company on any disposal of that asset on that date.

38.10 **Chargeable assets continuing to be held after commencement.** This provision applies where on 31 March 1996 a company held any asset representing (in whole or in part) a loan relationship to which it was a party and the company did not dispose of that asset on that date and is not otherwise deemed to have done so. It does not apply where the asset is

(*a*) an asset to which *FA 1996, s 92* (convertible securities etc., see 38.8 (I) above) or *FA 1996, Sch 15 para 15* (certain unit trust holdings of insurance companies) applies, or

(*b*) an asset representing a loan relationship to which *FA 1996, s 93* (relationships linked to the value of chargeable assets see 38.8 (II) above) applies, or

(*c*) a relevant qualifying asset.

The asset is deemed to be disposed of at 31 March 1996 and the gain or loss on disposal is calculated using market value as the disposal consideration. No amount brought into account for the authorised accrual or mark to market basis shall also be brought into account for the purposes of calculating the chargeable gain.

The gain or loss adjustment is brought into account in the accounting period in which the relevant event (see 38.9 above and see also below) occurs.

Where the company was non-UK resident at any time before 1 April 1996 when it held the asset other than through a UK branch or agency, the company is treated for these purposes as having acquired the asset at market value on the first day on which a gain on the asset could have been included in the company's profits chargeable to corporation tax. This applies through any chain of no gain, no loss disposals.

For these purposes a company ceasing to be within the charge to corporation tax at any time is treated as disposing of all its assets at market value immediately before that time.

A relevant event for these purposes does not include a no gain, no loss disposal under *TCGA 1992, s 139* (reconstruction or amalgamation involving transfer of business), *TCGA 1992, s 140A* (transfer of a UK trade), *TCGA 1992, s 171(1)* (transfers within a group) or *TCGA 1992, s 172* (now repealed — see 44.3 OVERSEAS MATTERS).

[*FA 1996, Sch 15 para 8; FA 1997, Sch 13 paras 1, 5, 7(1); FA 2000, Sch 29, para 45*].

Where a company uses a mark to market basis of accounting for a loan relationship that is represented by a chargeable asset (that is not a qualifying corporate bond) held at 31 March 1996, the value of that chargeable asset is taken to be its market value at 31 March 1996 for opening valuation at 1 April 1996.

[*FA 1996, Sch 15 para 10*].

38.11 **Election for alternative treatment.** Where the provision at 38.10 above results in an amount being brought into account for an accounting period as an allowable loss the company may instead elect for that amount to be treated as a debit under the current provisions for that period. The debit is a trading or non-trading debit according to the treatment which would apply to any other debits as respects the same loan relationship for that period. The election must be made within two years after the relevant event. No election can be made in respect of a loss on an asset which as at 1 April 1996 fell under *TCGA 1992, s 127* or *s 214(9)* to be treated as the same as an asset not representing a loan relationship or would have done so but for *TCGA 1992, s 116(5)*.

[*FA 1996, Sch 15 para 9*].

38.12 **Other adjustments in the case of chargeable assets etc.** Where a company holds chargeable assets and assets which would have been chargeable but for the *Finance Act 1993* foreign exchange provisions, it is the intention that the overall profits and losses reflect the pre-1 April 1996 capital gains and foreign exchange positions. This only applies to companies who adopt the authorised accruals basis of accounting.

The provisions only apply to assets not dealt with under existing legislation in computing trading profits which are either chargeable assets at 31 March 1996 or would be chargeable assets apart from the Foreign Exchange provisions of *Finance Act 1993*.

An adjustment is to be made when the difference between the amount deemed to accrue in the profit and loss account for the company's accounting period using the authorised accruals basis that will be applied to the whole accounting period and the amount deemed to accrue from 1 April 1996 to the end of the accounting period assuming a notional closing value of the assets. This will be either the market value at 31 March 1996 or the closing value for the purposes of the *Finance Act 1993* foreign exchange provisions. The amount will be taken into account as a non-trading debit on the earlier of the company ceasing to be a party to the loan relationship or the company ceasing to be within the charge to corporation tax.

The company may elect in writing to an officer of the Board by 1 October 1996 for the 31 March 1996 valuation to be applied to all its assets within this provision.

[*FA 1996, Sch 15 paras 11, 12*].

38.13 **Accrued income scheme.** Where a company would otherwise have been treated under *ICTA 1988, s 714(2)* or *(4)* (accrued income scheme — see 58.19 SHARES AND SECURITIES and see further TOLLEY'S INCOME TAX under Schedule D, Case VI) as receiving any amount at the end of a period straddling 1 April 1996, or as entitled to an allowance of any amount for such a period, that amount is instead brought into account under the current provisions as a non-trading credit or debit respectively for the first accounting period ending after 31 March 1996. A debit in respect of an allowance relating to a security will not, however, be brought into account where the security was transferred to the company with accrued interest in an accounting period straddling 1 April 1996, and an authorised accruals basis of accounting is used for that period as respects the creditor relationship represented by the security. Credit for foreign tax under *ICTA 1988, s 807* may continue to be given in relation to such amounts, and *FA 1993, s 63* (which deals with debts between associated companies etc.) continues to apply up to 31 March 1996, which is for this purpose treated as the last day of an accounting period.

A special relief applies to certain excess reliefs brought forward by overseas life insurance companies.

[*FA 1996, s 105, Sch 15 para 18*].

38.14 **Deep discount securities — disposals after 31 March 1996** (see also 58.20 SHARES AND SECURITIES). Accounting periods straddling 31 March 1996 will be deemed to end on that date and for taxation purposes the deep discount security will be deemed to be disposed of at 31 March 1996 under the previous provisions of *ICTA 1988, Sch 4 para 4*. The amount that would have been charged to tax is carried forward as a non-trading credit that will crystallise during the accounting period in which the earlier of three possible events occurs:

- the earliest day after 31 March 1996 when the security may be redeemed under its issue terms,
- the actual date of redemption,
- the date the company disposes of the security.

Where a company issued a deep discount security before 1 April 1996 which was not redeemed before that date and there is a difference between the *adjusted issue price* of the security at 31 March 1996 and the *adjusted closing value* at that date the difference is brought to account accordingly as a non-trading debit or credit in the accounting period in which the security is deemed to be redeemed, which occurs on the earliest of the three dates described above. The adjusted closing value is defined as the opening value at 1 April 1996 of the company's rights and liabilities under the loan relationship as represented by that security. The adjusted issue price at 31 March 1996 is defined as whatever for the purposes of *ICTA 1988, Sch 4 para 4* would have been the adjusted issue price of that security for an income period beginning on 1 April 1996.

[*FA 1996, s 105, Sch 15 para 19*].

38.15 **Deep gain securities — disposals after 31 March 1996** (see also 58.20 SHARES AND SECURITIES). Similar rules apply to the issuers of deep gain securities as to deep discount securities. Accounting periods straddling 31 March 1996 will for these purposes be deemed to end on 31 March 1996.

For taxation purposes the security is deemed to be disposed of at 31 March 1996 at its adjusted closing value and the amount that would have been charged to tax under the previous *FA 1989, Sch 11 para 5* provisions is carried forward as a non-trading credit that will crystallise during the accounting period in which the earlier of three possible events occurs:

- the earliest day after 31 March 1996 when the security may be redeemed under its issue terms,
- the actual date of redemption,
- the date the company disposes of the security.

The adjusted closing value is defined as the opening value at 1 April 1996 of the company's rights and liabilities under the loan relationship as represented by that security.

[*FA 1996, s 105, Sch 15 para 20*].

38.16 **Convertible securities** (see also 58.20 SHARES AND SECURITIES). Similar rules apply to the issuers of qualifying convertible securities as to deep discount and deep gain securities. Accounting periods straddling 31 March 1996 will be deemed to end on 31 March 1996.

For taxation purposes the security is deemed to be disposed of at 31 March 1996 under the previous *FA 1990, Sch 10 para 12* provisions and the amount that would have been charged to tax is carried forward as a non-trading credit that will crystallise during the accounting period in which the earlier of three possible events occurs:

- the earliest day after 31 March 1996 when the security may be redeemed under its issue terms,
- the actual date of redemption,
- the date the company disposes of the security.

[*FA 1996, s 105, Sch 15 para 21*].

38.17 **Transition for debt contracts and options to which Chapter II of Part IV of the Finance Act 1994 is applied.** As regards debt contracts and options in existence at 1 April 1996, provisions ensure that the Finance Act 1994 provisions apply to the whole of the company's accounting period ending on or after 31 March 1996 instead of as from 1 April 1996.

[*FA 1996, Sch 15 para 25*].

38.18 **Transitional rules affecting individuals.**

(a) Qualifying Indexed Securities

No chargeable gain will arise where a 'relevant person' holds a qualifying indexed security at 5 April 1996 for which there is no disposal neither actual nor deemed. However if at any time after 5 April 1996 a relevant event occurs the chargeable gain will be calculated as if the disposal had occurred at 5 April 1996 and the consideration was equal to the market value at 5 April 1996. This does not apply to inter-spouse disposals under *TCGA 1992, s 58* (see 41.3 MARRIED PERSONS) but will apply to a subsequent disposal by the other spouse.

[*FA 1996, s 105, Sch 15 para 27*].

(b) Qualifying Corporate Bonds

If as a result of a share reorganisation on or after 5 April 1996 within *TCGA 1992, s 127* (see 58.5 SHARES AND SECURITIES), a person holds a relevant discounted security (see 58.20 SHARES AND SECURITIES) that is not a qualifying indexed security and would not have been a qualifying corporate bond at that date, *TCGA 1992, s 116* (reorganisations etc. involving qualifying corporate bonds — see 49.3 QUALIFYING CORPORATE BONDS) is deemed to take effect and the asset is treated as having been disposed of and immediately re-acquired as a qualifying corporate bond. The capital gain or loss to 5 April 1996 is thereby preserved.

[*FA 1996, s 105, Sch 15 para 30*].

38.19 **Low coupon gilts.** If a company holds the following low-coupon gilts for non-trading purposes, they will be exempt from a charge on profits under the loan relationship provisions introduced from 1 April 1996. The low coupon gilts are:

$3\frac{1}{2}$% Funding Stock (1999–2004)

$5\frac{1}{2}$% Treasury Stock (2008–2012)

[*FA 1996, s 96*].

38.20 **Chargeable gains: general savings.** As regards changes to the capital gains tax legislation these do not apply to any disposal made or deemed to be made before 1 April 1996 or where a loan has become irrecoverable or its value negligible before that date. [*FA 1996, Sch 15 para 7*].

39 Losses

Cross-references. See also 15.19, 15.20 CORPORATE VENTURING SCHEME; 20.8 ENTERPRISE INVESTMENT SCHEME (AND BES); 57.9, 57.14 SETTLEMENTS.

The headings in this chapter are as follows.

39.1 GENERAL

Subject to the annual exempt amount (see 2.5 ANNUAL RATES AND EXEMPTIONS) and TAPER RELIEF (60), the charge to capital gains tax is on all chargeable gains accruing to the taxpayer in the year of assessment, less any allowable losses accruing to him in that year and, so far as not allowed as a deduction from chargeable gains accruing in any previous year of assessment, any allowable losses accruing to him in any previous year (but not earlier than 1965/66), subject to 39.8 below (interaction with annual exempt amount). [*TCGA 1992, s 2(2)*].

For 1998/99 onwards, an individual's allowable capital losses, whether of the current year of assessment or brought forward from previous years (or brought back from the year of death — see 16.5 DEATH), cannot be set off against any of the following that might be attributed to him:

- gains treated under *TCGA 1992, s 77* as accruing to him as settlor from a UK resident settlement in which he has an interest (see 57.3 SETTLEMENTS);
- gains treated under *TCGA 1992, s 86* as accruing to him as settlor from a non-UK resident settlement in which he has an interest (see 43.4 OFFSHORE SETTLEMENTS);
- gains treated under *TCGA 1992, s 87* or *s 89(2)* as accruing to him as a beneficiary of a non-UK resident settlement (see 43.13 OFFSHORE SETTLEMENTS).

[*TCGA 1992, s 2(4)(5); FA 1998, s 121(3)(4), Sch 21 para 2*].

See 26.2 INDEXATION for transitional relief for 'indexation losses' in 1993/94 and 1994/95 only in the case of disposals by individuals and trustees of settlements made before 30 November 1993.

Short-term losses which accrued before 1971/72 but which were not relieved under Schedule D, Case VII may be brought forward against gains chargeable to capital gains tax. [*TCGA 1992, Sch 11 para 12*]. This is the only instance where losses incurred before 6 April 1965 can be carried forward.

A person may be able to enjoy the benefit of unutilised losses of trustees which have accrued to them in respect of property to which the person has become absolutely entitled. However, where a person becomes so entitled after 15 June 1999, the previously unfettered right to utilise such losses is significantly restricted. See 57.9 SETTLEMENTS. This facility to transfer losses does not apply as regards personal representatives and legatees (see 16.7 DEATH).

Where a loss accrues on the disposal of an asset held on 6 April 1965 there are provisions (e.g. time apportionment), which may restrict the loss allowable. See 7 ASSETS HELD ON 6 APRIL 1965. Similar observations may apply to disposals after 5 April 1988 of assets held on 31 March 1982. See 8 ASSETS HELD ON 31 MARCH 1982. See also 17.5(*j*) DISPOSAL where an asset has qualified for capital allowances.

A loss accruing to a person in a year of assessment during no part of which he is resident or ordinarily resident in the UK is not allowable unless

(*a*) if there had been a gain instead of a loss, he would have been chargeable under *TCGA 1992, s 10* (see 44.3 OVERSEAS MATTERS), in respect of that gain; or

(*b*) it is a loss accruing to trustees in a year of assessment for which *CGTA 1979, s 17* or *TCGA 1992, s 87* (see 43 OFFSHORE SETTLEMENTS) applies to the settlement.

[*TCGA 1992, s 16(3), s 97(6)*].

A loss arising to an individual not domiciled in the UK but resident or ordinarily resident here in respect of the disposal of an asset overseas is not allowable. See 44.2 OVERSEAS MATTERS. [*TCGA 1992, s 16(4)*].

An agreement under *TMA 1970, s 54* (see 4.6 APPEALS) allied to the existence of a loss for a chargeable period does not preclude the Revenue from challenging its size or existence in a later chargeable period (*Tod v South Essex Motors (Basildon) Ltd Ch D 1987, 60 TC 598*).

39.2 **Computation.** Losses are computed as for gains except as in *FA 1991, s 72* (see 39.7 below) and where expressly provided otherwise (e.g. as in 26.1 INDEXATION). Wherever an exemption is given under *TCGA 1992* (or under any provision which is to be construed as one with it) so as to make a gain not a chargeable gain, that exemption applies similarly to losses so that they are not to be allowable losses. [*TCGA 1992, s 16(1)(2); ICTA 1988, s 834(1)*].

Losses are not deductible if, and so far as, other tax relief can be claimed in respect of them and may only be deducted once for capital gains tax purposes. They may not be deducted at all if already given relief for income tax (see 39.13 and 39.15 below regarding an election for capital losses arising on the disposal of certain shares in unquoted trading companies to be set off against general income). [*TCGA 1992, s 2(3)*].

Example

On 30 April 2000 Q sells for £40,000 a part of the land which he owns. The market value of the remaining estate is £160,000. Q bought the land for £250,000 in March 1991.

	£
Disposal consideration	40,000
Allowable cost $\dfrac{40{,}000}{40{,}000 + 160{,}000} \times £250{,}000$	50,000
Allowable loss	£10,000

39.3 **Notification of capital losses.** Under self-assessment, for 1996/97 and subsequent years for capital gains tax and for accounting periods ending on or after 1 July 1999 (see 13.2 COMPANIES) for corporation tax, a capital loss is not an allowable loss unless its amount is quantified and notified to the Revenue, such notice being subject to the provisions of *TMA 1970, s 42*, and to the enquiry regime (see 56.11 SELF-ASSESSMENT, 12.3 CLAIMS), as if it were a claim for relief (see 12.2 CLAIMS). For capital gains tax purposes, losses must, if possible, be notified on the self-assessment tax return or in an amendment thereto, or failing that may be notified on or before the fifth anniversary of 31 January following the year of assessment in which they arose (regardless of whether they are utilised within that period — there is no time limit on the utilisation of losses brought forward). The equivalent time limit for corporation tax purposes is six years after the end of the accounting period in which the loss arose. [*TCGA 1992, s 16(2A); FA 1995, s 103(7), s 113(1)*]. Notice may be given outside the tax return either by making an entry for allowable losses brought forward in a subsequent year's return (within the time limit) and/or by giving the Inspector a separate notice (see Self-Assessment Tax Return Notes on Capital Gains Tax).

No notification time limit applies to capital losses arising in 1995/96 and earlier years or in company accounting periods ending before 1 July 1999.

Order of set-off. Losses arising to individuals and trustees in the year 1996/97 and subsequent years are to be treated as utilised before losses arising in earlier years. Similarly, losses accruing to companies for accounting periods ending on or after 1 July 1999 (see 13.2 COMPANIES) will have preference to losses arising in accounting periods ending before that date. [*FA 1995, s 113(2)*].

39.4 **Carry-back prohibited.** Losses may not be carried back against the gains of an earlier year (except from the year of death, see 16.5 DEATH). [*TCGA 1992, s 2(3)*].

39.5 **Connected persons.** A loss on a disposal to a CONNECTED PERSON (14) is deductible only from chargeable gains arising on other disposals to that same person while he is still connected. A disposal, whereby capital and income are settled wholly or primarily for educational, cultural or recreational purposes, the beneficiaries being 'an association of persons' most of whom are *not* connected persons, is not subject to this restriction on losses. [*TCGA 1992, s 18(3)(4)*]. The restriction does not apply where a person becomes absolutely entitled as against the trustee to property in a settlement (see 57.9 SETTLEMENTS).

Where the disposal is of an option to enter into a transaction with the disposer, no loss accruing to a connected person who acquires the option is allowable unless it accrues on the disposal of the option at arm's length to a person unconnected with the acquirer. [*TCGA 1992, s 18(5)*].

See 3.13 ANTI-AVOIDANCE for special market value provisions for disposals between connected persons.

Debts. A loss accruing on the disposal of a debt by a person making the disposal (the 'subsequent creditor') who acquired it from the 'original creditor' at a time when the original creditor or his personal representative or legatee was connected with the subsequent creditor, is not an allowable loss. Purchases through persons all of whom are connected with the subsequent creditor are also included as are acquisitions from the original creditor's personal representative or legatee. Where the original creditor is a trustee and the debt, when created, is settled property, any loss accruing to the subsequent creditor is not allowable if he is connected with any person (or his personal representative or legatee) who becomes absolutely entitled to the debt on its ceasing to be settled property. [*TCGA 1992, s 251(4)(5)*]. The Revenue takes the view that these provisions do not apply to debts on a security (Revenue Capital Gains Manual CG 53451). For debts generally, see 21.5 EXEMPTIONS AND RELIEFS.

39.6 **Anti-avoidance.** Where a deemed disposal arises under *TCGA 1992, s 29(2)* on the transfer of value between different shares or rights in a company by the person controlling it, no loss is allowable on such a disposal. See 3.4 ANTI-AVOIDANCE. Value-shifting to give a tax free benefit may result in losses being allowable only to such extent as is just and reasonable. See 3.6–3.12 ANTI-AVOIDANCE.

Where there are depreciatory transactions within a group of companies or where there is 'dividend stripping' by one company holding 10% or more of a class of shares in another company, any related loss is only allowable to the extent that it is just and reasonable. See 3.19, 3.20 ANTI-AVOIDANCE.

A restriction of a loss accruing to a company which is a member of a group of companies may occur where the loss is wholly or partly referable to a time before it joined the group or the disposal of an asset which was held by another group member when that member company joined the group. See 13.24 COMPANIES.

Trading losses effectively converted into allowable capital losses under *FA 1991, s 72* in 39.7 below cannot be carried forward as a deduction against chargeable gains after the time the trade concerned ceases.

39.7 SET-OFF OF TRADING LOSSES ETC. AGAINST CHARGEABLE GAINS

General. A person other than a company cannot normally set off his allowable losses for capital gains tax purposes against his income. A company, also, cannot normally set off its allowable losses for the purposes of corporation tax on chargeable gains against income but trading losses or management expenses of a company can, in certain cases, be set off against profits chargeable to corporation tax, such profits including chargeable gains. See 13.3, 13.4 COMPANIES. See, however, 39.13 and 39.15 below for the allowance of capital losses arising on the disposal of certain shares in unquoted trading companies against general income of *individuals* and *investment companies* respectively.

There are specific provisions enabling trading losses and certain other expenditure for income tax purposes to be set off against chargeable gains to the extent that they cannot be relieved against income (due to an insufficiency of income) for the year of assessment in question. These are described below.

Set-off of trading losses against chargeable gains of a person other than a company. Where trading losses arise in 1991/92 and subsequent years of assessment and a person makes a claim for relief under *ICTA 1988, s 380* (set-off for income tax purposes of trading losses against general income; see TOLLEY'S INCOME TAX under Losses) for a year of assessment in respect of an amount ('the trading loss') which is available for relief under that provision, he may, in the notice by which the claim is made, make a further claim (under *FA 1991, s 72(1)*) for 'the relevant amount for the year' to be determined. Where such a claim is finally determined (see below), the relevant amount for the year (or the 'maximum amount' if lower) is treated as an allowable loss for capital gains tax purposes accruing to the claimant in the year. (This means that in effect capital losses flowing from a claim are treated as current year losses rather than losses brought forward from prior years; see 39.1 above and 39.8 below.) However, an amount treated as an allowable loss under the foregoing is not allowed as a deduction from chargeable gains accruing to a person in any year of assessment beginning after he has ceased to carry on the trade, profession etc. in which the relevant trading loss was sustained. (The Revenue have indicated that a continuing partner in a partnership which has a technical discontinuance for income tax purposes under *ICTA 1988, s 113* will not be prejudiced by this restriction. However, this ceases to be of relevance after 1993/94 in respect of trades set up after 5 April 1994 or after 1995/96 for other trades since, in such circumstances, the effect of the changes made by *FA 1994, s 216(1)(2), Sch 26 Pt V* to that provision is that only a total change in the persons carrying on the trade will bring about such a discontinuance.)

'*The relevant amount for the year*' is so much of the trading loss as

(*a*) cannot be set off against the claimant's income for the year, and

(*b*) has not already been taken into account for the purposes of giving relief (under *ICTA 1988, s 380*, this relief provision or otherwise) for any year.

'*The maximum amount*' is the amount on which the claimant would be chargeable to capital gains tax for the year, disregarding the annual exemption available under *TCGA 1992, s 3(1)* and the effect of this relief provision. In ascertaining the maximum amount, no account is taken of any event occurring after the date on which the claim for relief is finally determined, and in consequence of which the maximum amount is reduced by virtue of any capital gains tax provision (e.g. a claim for rollover relief in a later year having the effect of reducing the amount chargeable for the year for which this relief provision is claimed; in such a case the allowable capital losses flowing from a claim under this provision would be displaced by the effect of the rollover claim but would be available for carry forward to subsequent years). A claim for relief is not deemed finally to be determined until the relevant amount for the year can no longer be varied, whether by the Commissioners on appeal or on the order of any court.

Trading losses relieved under the above are treated similarly to losses relieved under *ICTA 1988, s 380* as regards *ICTA 1988, s 382(3)* (prevention of double allowances), *s 383(6)–(8)* (extension of right of set-off to capital allowances before 1994/95 in respect of trades set up after 5 April 1994 or before 1997/98 for other trades) and *s 385(1)* (carry-forward of trading losses against subsequent profits reduced by other set-offs claimed).

[*FA 1991, s 72; FA 1994, s 209(1), s 211(2), s 215(4)(5), s 218(1)(5), Sch 20 para 8, Sch 26 Pt V*].

The years of assessment for which relief may be claimed under *ICTA 1988, s 380* against income, and consequently under *FA 1991, s 72* against gains, are as follows:

- from the outset for businesses commenced after 5 April 1994 and for 1996/97 onwards for other businesses, the year in which the trading loss is incurred or the preceding year;
- for 1995/96 and earlier years as regards businesses commenced before 6 April 1994, the year in which the trading loss is incurred or the following year.

Time limits for claims are as follows:

- for losses incurred in 1996/97 and subsequent years, the first anniversary of 31 January following the tax year in which the loss is incurred;
- for losses incurred in 1994/95 and 1995/96 by businesses commenced after 5 April 1994, two years after the end of the tax year in which the loss is incurred;
- for losses incurred before 1996/97 by businesses commenced before 6 April 1994, two years after the end of the tax year for which relief is claimed.

A claim under *FA 1991, s 72* may be made even though there is no income for the year in question to justify making a claim under *ICTA 1988, s 380* alone (Revenue Inspector's Manual IM 3517).

Although in strictness the two claims should be made in the same notice, the Revenue are prepared to accept a separate claim under *FA 1991, s 72* where: the trader has previously made a claim under *ICTA 1988, s 380* to which a *section 72* claim could have been added; a separate *section 72* claim is made within the time limits for the original *section 380* claim;

after giving relief under *section 380* there is a balance of trading losses which have not otherwise been relieved; and all the other conditions for the relief are satisfied (Revenue Tax Bulletin August 1993 p 87).

See TOLLEY'S INCOME TAX under Losses for the possible augmentation under *ICTA 1988, s 383* of a loss determined under *ICTA 1988, s 380* by an amount of capital allowances for years before 1994/95 in respect of trades set up after 5 April 1994 or for years before 1997/98 for other trades. In other circumstances, capital allowances will be treated as a trading expense. See TOLLEY'S INCOME TAX under Capital Allowances.

Example

M has carried on a trade for some years, preparing accounts to 30 June each year. For the year ended 30 June 2000 he makes a trading loss of £17,000. His taxable profit for 1999/2000 is £5,000, and his other income for both 1999/2000 and 2000/01 amounts to £2,000. He makes a capital gain of £12,200 and a capital loss of £1,000 for 2000/01 and has capital losses brought forward of £5,800. The gain is after indexation allowance to April 1998 and qualifies for a 25% deduction for TAPER RELIEF (60). M makes claims for loss relief, against income of 1999/2000 and income and gains of 2000/01, under *ICTA 1988, s 380(1)(b)*, *ICTA 1988, s 380(1)(a)* and *FA 1991, s 72* respectively.

Calculation of 'relevant amount'

	£
Trading loss—year ended 30.6.2000	17,000
Relieved against other income for 2000/01 (*ICTA 1988, s 380(1)(a)*)	(2,000)
Relieved against income for 1999/2000 (*ICTA 1988, s 380(1)(b)*)	(7,000)
Relevant amount	£8,000

Calculation of 'maximum amount'

	£
Gains for 2000/01	12,200
Deduct Losses for 2000/01	(1,000)
Unrelieved losses brought forward	(5,800)
	5,400
Deduct Taper relief — £5,400 @ 25%	1,350
Maximum amount	£4,050

Relief under *FA 1991, s 72*

	£	£
Gains for the year		12,200
Losses for the year	1,000	
Relief under *FA 1991, s 72*	4,050	
		5,050
Gain (covered by annual exemption)		£7,150
Capital losses brought forward and carried forward		£5,800

Loss memorandum

	£
Trading loss	17,000
Claimed under *ICTA 1988, s 380(1)(a)*	(2,000)
Claimed under *ICTA 1988*, s *380(1)(b)*	(7,000)
Claimed under *FA 1991, s 72*	(4,050)
Unutilised loss	£3,950

Note to the example

(*a*) In this example, £50 of the capital gains tax annual exemption of £7,200 is wasted, but the brought forward capital losses are preserved for carry-forward against gains of future years. If M had *not* made the claim under *FA 1991, s 72*, his net gains for the year of £11,200 would have been reduced to the annual exempt amount by deducting £4,000 of the losses brought forward. (Taper relief would be irrelevant as the untapered net gains would be exempt in any case.) A further £1,800 of capital losses would remain available for carry-forward against future gains and a further £4,050 of trading losses would have been available for carry-forward against future trading profits. So the effect of the claim is to preserve capital losses at the expense of trading losses.

Set-off of post-cessation expenditure of a trade against capital gains. Relief is available against both income and capital gains for individuals who incur qualifying business expenditure after 28 November 1994 in connection with a trade or profession which has ceased within seven years of its ceasing. Broadly, qualifying expenditure includes costs of remedying defective work or services rendered and damages in respect thereof, insurance premiums paid to insure against such costs and legal and other professional expenses incurred in connection therewith. Relief is also given for bad debts which prove to be bad or which are released in whole or in part after 28 November 1994, and for the costs of collecting debts which have been taken into account in the final accounts. The relief is reduced by accruals for costs in the final accounting period which remain unpaid. On a claim, the relief may be set against income and then against capital gains of the year of assessment in which the qualifying expenditure is incurred, otherwise it will have to be carried forward to be set only against any post-cessation receipts under *ICTA 1988, s 105*. Claims for relief in respect of 1994/95 and 1995/96 must be made within two years after the end of the year of assessment in which the expenditure is incurred. For 1996/97 onwards claims must be made within twelve months after 31 January following the year of assessment in which the expenditure was incurred. A claim for relief cannot exceed the capital gains available, disregarding losses brought forward, the annual exemption and trading losses set against gains under *FA 1991, s 72*. For full details of the provisions see TOLLEY'S INCOME TAX under Post-Cessation Etc. Receipts and Expenditure. [*ICTA 1988, s 109A; FA 1995, s 90; FA 1996, Sch 20 para 5*].

Set-off of post-employment deductions against capital gains. For 1995/96 onwards relief against income or capital gains will be given to former employees who bear the costs of indemnity insurance or certain work-related uninsured liabilities relating to their former employment where such costs are incurred by them up to six years after the year in which the employment ended. On a claim, the relief may be set against income and then against capital gains of the year of assessment in which the qualifying expenditure is incurred, otherwise it will be lost. Claims for relief in respect of 1995/96 must be made before 6 April 2002. For 1996/97 onwards claims must be made within five years after 31 January following the year of assessment to which the claim relates. A claim for relief cannot exceed the capital gains available, disregarding losses brought forward, the annual exemption and trading losses set against gains under *FA 1991, s 72*. For full details of the provisions see TOLLEY'S INCOME TAX under Schedule E — Emoluments. [*ICTA 1988, s 201AA; FA 1995, ss 91, 92*].

39.8 INTERACTION WITH ANNUAL EXEMPTION

In giving relief for capital losses brought forward from earlier years (or carried back from a subsequent year in which the taxpayer dies — see 16.5 DEATH), such losses are deducted from the net chargeable gains (i.e. chargeable gains less allowable losses) for the year only to the extent necessary to reduce those net gains to the amount of the annual exemption for the year, thus avoiding any wastage of losses brought forward (or back). Any balance of losses remains available to carry forward (or back). For 1998/99 and subsequent years, the deduction is made from, and by reference to, the 'adjusted net gains' rather than the net chargeable gains, the '*adjusted net gains*' being the net chargeable gains before applying TAPER RELIEF (60). [*TCGA 1992, s 3(5)–(5C); FA 1998, s 121(3)(4), Sch 21 para 3*]. See also 2.5 ANNUAL RATES AND EXEMPTIONS (including worked examples) and 60.3 TAPER RELIEF.

39.9 **ASSETS OF NEGLIGIBLE VALUE**

Where the owner of an asset which has become of negligible value makes a claim under *TCGA 1992, s 24(2)* after 5 April 1996 to that effect he is treated as if he had sold, and immediately reacquired, the asset at the time of the claim or (subject to the following) at any earlier time specified in the claim for a consideration of an amount equal to the value specified in the claim. An earlier time can be specified in the claim if the claimant owned the asset at that time, the asset had become of negligible value at that time and that time is not more than two years before the beginning of the year of assessment in which the claim is made or, for corporation tax, is on or after the first day of the earliest accounting period ending not more than two years before the time of the claim. *FA 1994, s 93, Sch 12* (indexation losses and transitional relief; see 26.1 and 26.2 INDEXATION) apply to an asset for which relief is claimed as if the sale and reacquisition occurred at the time of the claim and not at any earlier time. [*TCGA 1992, s 24(2); FA 1996, Sch 39 para 4*].

A claim under *TCGA 1992, s 24(2)* made before 6 April 1996 could only be made by reference to a deemed sale and reacquisition on the date of claim and not at any earlier date. [*TCGA 1992, s 24(2)*]. However, ESC D28 operated to give broadly similar provisions to those applying in relation to claims made after 5 April 1996 so that an earlier date as specified above could be included in a claim. The concession was explicit in that the asset had to be of negligible value at both the time of claim and the earlier specified date but this is not so in the legislation relating to claims made after 5 April 1996. The concession also applied to claims within 39.13 and 39.15 below (losses on shares in unquoted trading companies).

For the purposes of a claim under *TCGA 1992, s 24(2)*, a building may be regarded as a separate asset from the land on which it stands so that where there is a deemed sale of a building, the land comprising the site of the building (including any land occupied for purposes ancillary to the use of the building) is treated as if it was sold, and immediately reacquired, at its then market value. [*TCGA 1992, s 24(3)*].

'*Negligible*', in relation to the value of shares, is regarded as 'considerably less' than 5% of the nominal value, 5% of nominal value being regarded as 'small'. See CCAB Statement June 1971 and 58.14 SHARES AND SECURITIES.

In *Director v Inspector of Taxes (Sp C 161), [1998] SSCD 172*, a negligible value claim was refused on the grounds that the shares in question had a nil acquisition cost by virtue of *TCGA 1992, s 17* (see 40.1 MARKET VALUE) and thus could not *become* of negligible value.

For certain qualifying corporate bonds becoming of negligible value where evidencing a 'qualifying loan', see 39.11 below.

Quoted securities. The Inland Revenue have accepted that certain quoted securities have become of negligible value within the meaning of *TCGA 1992, s 24(2)*. For securities so accepted in recent years, see Tolley's Tax Data. For additional securities so accepted, see the quarterly list in Tolley's Practical Tax or Simon's Weekly Tax Intelligence.

39.10 LOANS TO TRADERS

Relief for lender on loan becoming irrecoverable. Provided that, at the time of the claim, the claimant and borrower were neither spouses living together nor companies in the same 'group' when the loan was made or at any subsequent time, and that the claimant has not assigned his right of recovery, loss relief is available to the extent that any outstanding amount of the principal of a 'qualifying loan' made by the claimant after 11 April 1978 has become irrecoverable otherwise than under the express terms of the loan or related arrangements, or by reason of any act or omission by the lender (or, as appropriate, the guarantor of a loan claiming the relief below). The loss is treated as accruing either when the claim under *TCGA 1992, s 253(3)* is made or, within limits (see below), at an earlier specified time. As regards loans the principal on which became irrecoverable on or after 1 April 1996 the amount of the loss cannot include any amount falling to be relieved by way of a debit under the loan relationship provisions in 38 LOAN RELATIONSHIPS OF COMPANIES. [*TCGA 1992, s 253(3)(12)(14)(a), (15); FA 1996, Sch 14 para 65, Sch 15 para 7(a), Sch 39 para 8*]. For a case in which the Revenue failed in contending that the loans became irrecoverable by reason of acts of the lender, see *Cann v Woods (Sp C 183), [1999] SSCD 77*.

A '*qualifying loan*' is a loan to a UK resident borrower in the case of which the money lent is used by him wholly for the purposes of a trade, profession or vocation (not being a trade which consists of or includes the lending of money) carried on by him (and for this purpose money used by a borrower for setting up a trade which is subsequently carried on by him is treated as used for the purposes of that trade), and which is not a 'debt on a security'. However, for guarantees see below, and for loans evidenced by securities which are qualifying corporate bonds, see 39.11 below.

The 'commercial letting' of 'furnished holiday accommodation' in the UK is treated as a trade for losses arising after 5 April 1982. See 22 FURNISHED HOLIDAY ACCOMMODATION.

A '*debt on security*' is defined by reference to *TCGA 1992, s 132*, security thereby embracing any loan stock or similar security of any government or public or local authority in the UK or elsewhere, or of any company, and whether secured or unsecured. See further 21.5 EXEMPTIONS AND RELIEFS. [*TCGA 1992, s 253(1)(2)*].

Where a company re-lends money to a 'trading company' in the same group, the original loan is treated as having been used by the first company as it is used by the second while the second remains a member of the group. '*Trading company*' has the meaning given by *TCGA 1992, Sch 6 para 1* as in 53.4 RETIREMENT RELIEF. For the purposes of these provisions, a group of companies is construed in accordance with 13.11 COMPANIES, with the change in the residence requirement there mentioned having effect in relation to loans made (and guarantees given — see below) on or after 1 April 2000. [*TCGA 1992, s 253(2)(14)(b)(c); FA 1989, Sch 12 para 6; FA 2000, Sch 29 para 34*].

Relief is not available and nor is a clawback of relief made (see below) if the amount in question is taken into account for computing income for the purposes of income tax or corporation tax. [*TCGA 1992, s 253(10)*].

The allowable loss accrues at the time of the claim or at whatever earlier time is specified in the claim, so long as the amount claimed was also irrecoverable at that earlier time. For capital gains tax purposes, the time specified cannot be earlier than two years before the beginning of the tax year in which the claim is made. For corporation tax purposes, the time specified must fall on or after the first day of the earliest accounting period ending within the two years ending with the date of claim. This facility to backdate claims applies to claims made after 5 April 1996, but a similar facility previously operated by concession (ESC D36, now withdrawn). [*TCGA 1992, s 253(3)(3A); FA 1996, Sch 39 para 8*].

Relief for payment made under guarantee. The relief given above to a lender also applies (with the exception of ESC D36 above; see Revenue Capital Gains Manual CG 65943) to a guarantor of a qualifying loan who makes a claim under *TCGA 1992, s 253(4)* and who must additionally have made a payment under the guarantee to the lender or a co-guarantor. The claimant is treated as if an allowable loss of the amount of the payment had accrued to him when the payment was made. Where loss relief is given, no allowable loss and no chargeable gain (otherwise than on a clawback of relief as below) will accrue on the disposal of rights consequent on his having made a payment (which may include a payment in respect of interest as well as principal) under the guarantee. The guarantee must have been given after 11 April 1978. Relief is available to a guarantor even though the original loan is a 'debt on a security' (see above and 39.11 below). Relief is reduced to the extent that any contribution is 'payable' to the claimant by any co-guarantor. [*TCGA 1992, s 253(4)(11)(15); FA 1996, Sch 39 para 8*].

A claim shall be made for the purposes of capital gains tax on or before the fifth anniversary of the 31st January next following the year of assessment in which the payment was made; and in the case of corporation tax within six years after the end of the accounting period in which the payment was made. [*TCGA 1992, s 253(4A); FA 1996, Sch 21 para 40*].

'*Payable*' has its ordinary meaning, so that if under general legal principles the claimant could have made a recovery against one or more co-guarantors of part of a sum paid by him under a guarantee but chose not to do so, the relief given to him is reduced proportionately (*Leisureking Ltd v Cushing Ch D 1992, 65 TC 400*).

'*Guarantee*' covers the case where a person's property is charged as security for a qualifying loan. It does not include an indemnity, which creates a primary liability. A guarantee can apply to the repayment of an overdraft but not a hire purchase agreement. (CCAB Memorandum TR 308, 4 October 1978). Presumably, therefore, an indemnity could itself be treated as a qualifying loan.

The Revenue have stated that they interpret the provision in *TCGA 1992, s 253(4)* concerning reduction of relief where any contribution is 'payable' by a co-guarantor as limiting the relief available to the level it would be if all *possible* recoveries had been made. (Tolley's Practical Tax 1986 p 40 and cf. the *Leisureking* case above which was heard subsequently). The Revenue ignore voluntary payments, only those being made as a consequence of the formal calling in of a guarantee being covered by the relief. (Tolley's Practical Tax 1987 p 147). The Revenue have confirmed that a trading debt arising from the supply of stock to a trading company is considered capable of being treated as a qualifying loan as regards a guarantee made in respect of the debt. (Tolley's Practical Tax 1988 p 40).

Clawback of relief. Where loss relief has been obtained by the person who made the loan or a guarantor of it, and all or part of the outstanding amount of, or of interest in respect of (in the case of a guarantor), the principal of the loan is recovered, a chargeable gain is deemed to accrue to him at the time of recovery equal to so much of the allowable loss (for which relief was claimed) as corresponds to the amount recovered. Where a claimant has obtained loss relief in respect of a payment under a guarantee and recovers, at any time after 19 March 1990, the whole or any part of that payment, he will be treated as if there had accrued to him at that time a chargeable gain equal to so much of the allowable loss as corresponds to the amount recovered. A similar treatment will apply to a company ('the second company') which, at any time after 19 March 1990, recovers the whole or any part of the outstanding amount of the principal of a loan which has become irrecoverable in circumstances where a company ('the first company'), which made the loan originally and is in the same group as the second company when the loan was made or at any subsequent time, has obtained loss relief in respect of that loan becoming irrecoverable. Where the first company has obtained loss relief in relation to a payment made under a guarantee in respect of a loan which has become irrecoverable, a similar treatment of the second company applies if it recovers, at any time after 19 March 1990, the whole or any part of the outstanding amount of, or of interest in respect of, the principal of the loan, or the whole or any part of the guarantee payment made by the first company. An amount is treated as recovered if money or money's worth is received in satisfaction of the right of recovery. If this right is assigned otherwise than at arm's length, its full market value at that time is deemed to have been received. [*TCGA 1992, s 253(5)–(9)(13)*].

39.11 LOANS TO TRADERS EVIDENCED BY QUALIFYING CORPORATE BONDS

Relief to lender on loan becoming irrecoverable etc. A loss incurred on a qualifying corporate bond is not an allowable loss (see 49.1 QUALIFYING CORPORATE BONDS). However, special provisions apply whereby if, at the time of a claim under *TCGA 1992, s 254* by a person who has made a 'qualifying loan' **before 17 March 1998**, one of the three conditions given below is fulfilled, the claimant is treated as if an allowable loss equal to the 'allowable amount' had accrued to him either at the time of the claim or, within limits (see below), at an earlier specified time. For accounting periods ending after 31 March 1996, to which the regime in 38 LOAN RELATIONSHIPS OF COMPANIES applies, these provisions do not apply for the purposes of corporation tax, but, by virtue of *FA 1996, Sch 15 para 7(b)*, this does not prevent a company making a claim in respect of any security whose value became negligible before 1 April 1996. The provisions are **repealed** for capital gains tax purposes in relation to loans made after 16 March 1998.

A '*qualifying loan*' means a loan in the case of which

(*a*) the borrower's debt is a debt on a security within *TCGA 1992, s 132* (see 39.10 above) which was issued after 14 March 1989, or issued before 15 March 1989 but held on 15 March 1989 by the person who made the loan,

(*b*) but for the borrower's debt being a debt on a security, the loan would be a qualifying loan within *TCGA 1992, s 253* (see 39.10 above), and

(*c*) the security is a QUALIFYING CORPORATE BOND (49), other than a relevant discounted security (see 58.20 SHARES AND SECURITIES) and with certain other modifications (see *TCGA 1992, s 117(13)*), in particular so as to exclude building society permanent interest bearing shares). (The definition of 'relevant discounted security' was widened to take further account of potential redemptions before maturity: the widened definition has effect in relation to any claim made under these provisions after 14 February 1999. [*FA 1999, s 65(12)*].)

The first condition is that

(i) the value of the security has become negligible (but relief will still be available where the security ceases to have any value because it is redeemed early; Revenue Pamphlet IR 131, SP 8/90 and see (1) below for 'redemption date'),

(ii) the claimant has not assigned his right to recover any outstanding amount of the principal of the loan, and

(iii) the claimant and the borrower are not companies which have been in the same group (within *TCGA 1992, s 170*, see 13.11 COMPANIES) at any time after the loan was made.

The second condition is that

(1) the security's 'redemption date' (i.e. the latest date on which, under the terms under which the security was issued, the company or body which issued it can be required to redeem it) has passed,

(2) all the outstanding amount of the principal of the loan was irrecoverable (taking the facts existing on that date) or proved to be irrecoverable (taking the facts existing on a later date), and

(3) the requirements in (ii) and (iii) above are fulfilled.

The third condition is that

(A) the security's redemption date (as at (1) above) has passed,

(B) sub-condition (2) of the second condition above was fulfilled on a similar basis as regards part (rather than the whole) of the outstanding principal of the loan, and

(C) the requirements in (ii) and (iii) above are fulfilled.

Where the first or second condition is fulfilled, '*the allowable amount*' is the lesser of the outstanding amount of the principal of the loan and the amount of the security's acquisition cost (i.e. the amount or value of the consideration in money or money's worth given, by or on behalf of the person who made the loan, wholly and exclusively for the acquisition of the security, together with the incidental costs to him of the acquisition). However, if any amount of the principal of the loan has been recovered the amount of the security's acquisition cost is for this purpose reduced (but not beyond nil) by the amount recovered. An amount is treated as recovered if money or money's worth is received in satisfaction of the right of recovery. If this right is assigned otherwise than at arm's length, its full market value at that time is deemed to have been received.

Where the third condition is fulfilled, then '*the allowable amount*' is an amount equal to the excess (if any) of the security's acquisition cost over the 'relevant amount' or nil (if there is no such excess). The '*relevant amount*' is the aggregate of the amount (if any) of the principal of the loan which has been recovered (as above) and the amount (if any) of the principal of the loan which has not been recovered but which is recoverable.

The allowable loss accrues at the time of the claim or at whatever earlier time is specified in the claim, so long as the relevant condition was also fulfilled at that earlier time. The time specified cannot be earlier than two years before the beginning of the tax year in which the claim is made. For corporation tax purposes, the time specified cannot be 1 April 1996 or later (see above) and, subject to that, must fall on or after the first day of the earliest accounting period ending within the two years ending with the date of claim. This facility to backdate claims applies to claims made after 5 April 1996, but a similar facility previously operated by concession (ESC D36, now withdrawn).

Relief is not available and nor is a clawback of relief made (see below) if the amount in question is taken into account for computing income for the purposes of income tax or corporation tax. An amount is not treated as irrecoverable for the purposes of the relief if it becomes irrecoverable under the express terms of the loan or related arrangements, or by reason of any act or omission by the lender.

[*TCGA 1992, s 254(1)–(8)(12), s 255(1)(2)(4)(5); FA 1996, Sch 14 para 66, Sch 39 para 9; FA 1998, s 141(1)(b), (2)(b), Sch 27 Pt III(32)*].

Clawback of relief. Where an allowable loss has been treated under the above as accruing to any person and the whole or any part of the 'relevant outstanding amount' is at any time recovered (as above) by him, he is treated as if there had accrued to him at that time a chargeable gain equal to so much of the allowable loss as corresponds to the amount recovered. A similar treatment applies to a company ('the second company') where an allowable loss has been treated under the above as accruing to a company ('the first company'), and the whole or any part of the relevant outstanding amount is at any time recovered by the second company which is in the same group (as above) as the first company at any time after the loan was made. The '*relevant outstanding amount*' means, in a case where the first or second condition was fulfilled, the amount of the principal of the loan outstanding when the claim was allowed or, in a case where the third condition was fulfilled, the amount of the part (or the greater or greatest part) arrived at by the inspector under sub-condition (B) of the third condition above.

[*TCGA 1992, s 254(9)–(11), s 255(3)–(5); FA 1996, Sch 39 para 9; FA 1998, s 141(1)(b), (2)(b), Sch 27 Pt III(32)*].

39.12 **Qualifying corporate bonds: reorganisations etc. thereof and relief under** 39.11 **above.** *TCGA 1992, s 116(10)(11)* deals with the situation where, on a reorganisation etc. of shares (which are not qualifying corporate bonds), such shares ('the old asset') are replaced by securities ('the new asset') which are qualifying corporate bonds (and thus exempt from capital gains tax). The broad effect is to defer the chargeable gain or allowable loss that would have accrued on a disposal of the old asset at its market value immediately before the reorganisation until such time as a part or the whole of the new asset is disposed of, at which time the corresponding part or the whole of the deferred gain or loss is deemed to accrue. See 49.3 QUALIFYING CORPORATE BONDS for full details. In such a case and where the new asset is a qualifying corporate bond in respect of which an allowable loss is treated as accruing under *TCGA 1992, s 254(2)* in 39.11 above, and the loss is treated as so accruing at a time falling after the reorganisation but before any actual disposal of the new asset subsequent to the reorganisation, then, for the purposes of *TCGA 1992, s 116(10)(11)*, a disposal of the new asset is deemed to have occurred at (and only at) the time the loss is deemed to have accrued. This applies whatever the time the reorganisation occurs. [*TCGA 1992, s 116(15)*]. The effect is that the deferred gain or loss relating to the old asset will be deemed to accrue at the same time as the loss arising on a claim under *TCGA 1992, s 254(2)* above in respect of the new asset is deemed to accrue, and any later disposal of the new asset is ignored for the purposes of ascertaining when and in what amount the deferred gain or loss is treated as arising.

A concessional practice, contained in Revenue Pamphlet IR 1, D38, applies as follows. Where a person acquired corporate bonds in respect of shares and securities and those bonds became, or would fall to be treated as, qualifying corporate bonds by virtue only of *FA 1989, s 139* (extension of definition to include a wider range of sterling bonds; see 49.2 and 49.3 QUALIFYING CORPORATE BONDS), an allowable loss, computed in accordance with the rules in *TCGA 1992, s 116* (see 39.11 above), will accrue if

(*a*) the qualifying corporate bonds were issued in respect of shares or other securities before 14 March 1989 and were still retained at that date by the person to whom they were issued;

(*b*) the bonds were acquired in a transaction within *TCGA 1992, s 116(10)(11)* (see above) and on disposal after 13 March 1989 fall to be treated as qualifying corporate bonds as a result of *FA 1989, s 139*;

(*c*) relief under *TCGA 1992, s 254* would have been available had the loan been a qualifying loan within *TCGA 1992, s 254(1)*;

(*d*) the taxpayer claiming the concessional relief agrees that if all or part of the amount relieved is subsequently recovered the relief will be clawed back in the same way as if *TCGA 1992, s 254* had applied, save that in all cases the chargeable gain will be treated as accruing to the claimant; and

(*e*) when this concession applies, any gain or loss on the original shares or securities will be treated as accruing at the same time as the loss on the bonds in accordance with *TCGA 1992, s 116(15)* (see above and also 49.3 QUALIFYING CORPORATE BONDS for an additional relief which may apply in such circumstances where the bonds are gifted to a charity).

Under the concession the allowable loss will be treated as arising when a claim is made but it will be treated as arising in an earlier year of assessment or accounting period provided the claim is made not later than two years after the end of that year of assessment or accounting period, all the conditions for relief are satisfied at the date of claim, and the relief would have been available at the end of the year of assessment or accounting period for which relief is claimed.

39.13 LOSSES ON SHARES IN UNLISTED TRADING COMPANIES: INDIVIDUALS

Where an individual who has 'subscribed' for 'shares' in a 'qualifying trading company' incurs an allowable loss (for capital gains tax purposes) on the disposal of the shares in any year of assessment, he may, by written notice given within twelve months from 31 January next following that year, make a claim for relief from income tax on

(1) so much of his income for that year as is equal to the amount of the loss or, where it is less than that amount, the whole of that income; or

(2) so much of his income for the last preceding year as is equal to the amount of the loss as remains after deducting any part of the loss utilised under (1) above or, where it is less than that remaining amount, the whole of that income.

Where such relief is given in respect of the loss or any part of it, no deduction from chargeable gains is available in respect of the loss or (as the case may be) that part. Relief claimed under (1) above in respect of any income is given in priority to any relief claimed under (2) in respect of that income; and relief claimed under either (1) or (2) in respect of any income is given in priority to relief claimed under *ICTA 1988, s 380* (trading losses set against general income) or *ICTA 1988, s 381* (further relief for trading losses to be set against general income in early years of a trade) in respect of that income.

The relief described above applies for 1994/95 onwards (except that for 1994/95 and 1995/96 the time limit for claims was two years after the end of the tax year in which the loss was incurred). The relief applied similarly for years before 1994/95, except that it applied to reduce income for the tax year in which the loss was incurred and the *next following* year rather than that year and the *last preceding* year. There is no statutory order of priority between the relief due under the old rules and that due under the new rules. In practice, a claimant can choose the order in which these reliefs are given (Revenue Tax Bulletin December 1994, p 184).

Relief is available only if

(*a*) the disposal is at arm's length for full consideration, or

(*b*) it is by way of a distribution on a winding-up or dissolution, or

(*c*) the value of the shares has become negligible and a claim to that effect made under *TCGA 1992, s 24(2)* (see 39.9 above and note there the application of ESC D28 as regards claims before 6 April 1996, which also applies to this relief), or

(*d*) a deemed disposal occurs after 5 April 2000 under *TCGA 1992, s 24(1)* (which deems the entire loss, destruction, dissipation or extinction of an asset to be a disposal — see 17.7 DISPOSAL).

By concession, relating to events before 6 April 2000, relief is not denied, provided that all the other conditions are fulfilled, where an unquoted trading company devoid of assets is wound up and a shareholder has not made a negligible value claim and did not receive a distribution during the course of winding-up. (Revenue Pamphlet IR 1, D46). This concession is effectively replaced by (*d*) above.

An individual '*subscribes*' for shares if they are issued to him by the company for money or money's worth, or if they were so issued to his 'spouse', who transferred them to him by a transaction inter vivos. '*Spouse*' refers to one of two spouses who are living together (see 41.2 MARRIED PERSONS).

As regards shares issued **after 5 April 1998**, a '*qualifying trading company*' is a company which at all times in the 'relevant period' has been an unquoted company (as defined for EIS purposes — see 20.5 ENTERPRISE INVESTMENT SCHEME (AND BES)) and which

- either
  - (i) is an 'eligible trading company' at the date of disposal, or
  - (ii) has ceased to be an eligible trading company within three years before that date and has not since that cessation been an 'excluded company', an 'investment company' or a non-eligible trading company, *and*
- either
  - (i) has been an eligible trading company for a continuous period of at least six years prior to the disposal (or prior to the cessation, as the case may be), or
  - (ii) has been an eligible trading company for a shorter continuous period ending with the disposal or cessation and has not previously been an excluded company, an investment company or a non-eligible trading company, *and*
- has carried on its business wholly or mainly in the UK throughout the 'relevant period'.

As regards shares issued **before 6 April 1998**, a '*qualifying trading company*' is a company none of the shares in which have at any time in the 'relevant period' been listed on a recognised stock exchange (within *ICTA 1988, s 841* — see 58.5 SHARES AND SECURITIES) and which

- either
  - (i) is a 'trading company' at the date of disposal, or
  - (ii) has ceased to be a trading company within three years before that date and has not since that cessation been an 'excluded company' or an 'investment company', *and*
- either
  - (i) has been a trading company for a continuous period of at least six years prior to the disposal (or prior to the cessation, as the case may be), or
  - (ii) has been a trading company for a shorter continuous period ending with the disposal or cessation and has not previously been an excluded company or an investment company, *and*
- has been resident in the UK throughout the period from incorporation to the date of disposal.

The '*relevant period*' is the period ending with the disposal of the shares and beginning with the incorporation of the company or, if later, one year before the date on which the shares were issued (one year before they were subscribed for as regards shares issued before 6 April 1998).

An '*eligible trading company*' is a company which is, or would be, a qualifying company for the purposes of the EIS (see 20.5, 20.6 ENTERPRISE INVESTMENT SCHEME (AND BES)). For this purpose, the EIS legislation is applied (by *ICTA 1988, s 576(4A)(4B)*) with appropriate minor modifications; for example, certain references to the relevant period for EIS purposes are replaced with references to the date of disposal or ceasing to be an eligible trading company (whichever is relevant) or whichever is the relevant continuous period (see definition of 'qualifying trading company' above). This represents a narrowing of the loss relief against income rules as regards shares issued after 5 April 1998 in that the company which issued the shares must satisfy the EIS requirements as to, inter alia, qualifying activities, qualifying trades, gross assets and, where applicable, group structure. However, it is not a condition that the company issued the shares under the EIS, that the shares be held for a minimum period, or that any EIS income tax relief has been, or could have been, claimed in respect of them.

'*Trading company*' is any company (other than an excluded company—see below) whose business consists wholly or mainly of the carrying on of a trade or trades (for disposals before 1 April 1989, any company which exists wholly or mainly for the purpose of carrying on a trade, or the income of which does not consist wholly or mainly of investment income). The 'holding company' of a 'trading group' is also included.

'*Excluded company*' means a company the trade of which consists wholly or mainly of dealing in land, in commodities or futures or in shares, securities or other financial instruments (as regards shares issued before 6 April 1998, dealing in shares, securities, land, trades or commodity futures). A company which does not carry on its trade on a commercial basis and with a reasonable expectation of profit is within this definition, as are the holding company of a non-trading group, a building society or a registered industrial and provident society.

'*Trading group*' means a 'group' the business of the members of which, taken together, consists wholly or mainly in the carrying on of a trade or trades. Any trade carried on by a subsidiary which is an excluded company (or, as regards shares issued before 6 April 1998, which is non-UK resident) is disregarded.

'*Group*' means a company and its 51% subsidiary or subsidiaries, and a 'holding company' is one the business of which consists wholly or mainly in the holding of shares or securities in its 51% subsidiary or subsidiaries. 51% subsidiaries are as defined by *ICTA 1988, s 838*.

'*Investment company*' has the meaning given by *ICTA 1988, s 130* (i.e. any company the business of which consists wholly or mainly in the making of investments and the principal part of the income of which is derived therefrom but including banks and other banks for savings (except trustee savings banks)) except that it does not include the holding company of a trading group. In *Tintern Close Residents Society Ltd v Winter (Sp C 7), [1995] SSCD 57*, it was decided that property management companies which collect income from residents for the upkeep of relevant properties are not investment companies within the meaning of *ICTA 1988, s 130*.

'*Shares*' (except in the definition of 'excluded company', when all shares and stock are covered) means 'ordinary share capital' as defined in *ICTA 1988, s 832(1)* (see 58.8 SHARES AND SECURITIES).

Identification rules. Where an individual who has subscribed for shares in a company has also acquired shares of the same class in the same company by other means, and both the subscription shares and the other shares form part of the same holding (i.e. a number of shares of the same class held by one person in one capacity, whether or not pooled for CGT purposes), then in determining the extent (if any) to which a disposal relates to shares subscribed for (qualifying shares), disposals are to be identified with acquisitions on a last in/first out (LIFO) basis.

For disposals after 5 April 1998, there is an exception to the above rule where the holding includes any of the following:

- Shares in respect of which Business Expansion Scheme (BES) relief has been given and not withdrawn (see 20.15 ENTERPRISE INVESTMENT SCHEME (AND BES));
- Shares to which Enterprise Investment Scheme (EIS) income tax relief is attributable (see 20.2 ENTERPRISE INVESTMENT SCHEME (AND BES));

- Shares to which EIS capital gains deferral relief is attributable (see 20.9 ENTERPRISE INVESTMENT SCHEME (AND BES)).

In such a case, disposals are identified in accordance with the identification rules generally applicable to BES and EIS shares (first in/first out (FIFO), subject to certain special rules — see 20.8, 20.17 ENTERPRISE INVESTMENT SCHEME (AND BES)). (See below as regards the application of these loss relief provisions to EIS and BES shares.)

Loss relief under these provisions on the disposal of qualifying shares forming part of a larger holding is restricted to the sums that would have been allowable as deductions in computing the loss if the qualifying shares had been acquired and disposed of as a separate holding (see Step 4 in the example at 39.14 below). (Note that even for disposals before 30 November 1993 when indexation allowance could create or increase a loss, the term 'deductions' here did not include indexation allowance — see Revenue Capital Gains Manual CG 58378.)

Revenue Capital Gains Manual CG 58377 identifies four steps in the computation of loss relief under these provisions where a share pool does not entirely consist of qualifying shares. Step 1 is to compute the allowable loss for CGT purposes under normal CGT principles and identification rules (see 59 SHARES AND SECURITIES—IDENTIFICATION RULES). Step 2 is to identify the qualifying and non-qualifying shares included in the disposal (using the special identification rules described above). If it is found that the disposal comprises both, Step 3 is to apportion the loss, on a just and reasonable basis, between qualifying and non-qualifying shares. Step 4 is to compare the loss so attributed to the qualifying shares with the actual allowable expenditure incurred on those shares and to apply, if necessary, the restriction mentioned above. See the example at 39.14 below.

Note that, for capital gains tax (but not corporation tax) purposes, share pooling is abolished for acquisitions after 5 April 1998 (see 59.1 SHARES AND SECURITIES—IDENTIFICATION RULES).

Miscellaneous. Relief is not available in respect of a 'new holding' (within *TCGA 1992, s 127*) unless relief could have been given (assuming the legislation to have been in force) on the disposal which would have occurred on the reorganisation but for *TCGA 1992, s 127* *or* unless the claimant gave 'new consideration' for the new holding, in which latter case the relief is restricted to such amount or value of the new consideration as represents allowable expenditure. See, generally, 58.5 SHARES AND SECURITIES and see Revenue Capital Gains Manual CG 58400 *et seq.*

'*New consideration*' means consideration in money or money's worth (other than the surrender of rights etc. and that met out of the company's assets).

An amalgamation or scheme of reconstruction which is undertaken for tax avoidance purposes or other than for *bona fide* commercial reasons, and therefore gives rise to a chargeable disposal under *TCGA 1992, s 137*, cannot support a claim under these provisions. See 3.16 ANTI-AVOIDANCE.

Where a claim is made under these provisions, *TCGA 1992, s 30* (value shifting to give tax-free benefit, see 3.6 ANTI-AVOIDANCE) has effect in relation to the disposal if *any* benefit is conferred, whether tax-free or not.

[*ICTA 1988, ss 574–576; FA 1988, Sch 14 Pt VIII; FA 1989, Sch 12 para 14; FA 1994, s 146, s 210, s 218(5), Sch 17 para 6, Sch 20 para 8; FA 1995, s 119; FA 1996, Sch 38 para 6(1)(2)(h), (9); FA 1998, s 80, Sch 27 Pt III(16); FA 2000, s 63(2)(3), Sch 16 para 3(3)*].

See 26.2 INDEXATION for transitional relief for 1993/94 and 1994/95 in respect of 'indexation losses' referable to disposals of shares within the above provisions.

For the Revenue's views on the above provisions (and those in 39.15 below), see Revenue Capital Gains Manual CG 58300–58445.

Application to EIS shares. It is formally provided that the provisions described above apply to a loss on the disposal by an individual of shares to which EIS income tax relief is attributable (see 20 ENTERPRISE INVESTMENT SCHEME (AND BES)), except that the above-mentioned LIFO identification rules do not apply to such disposals (whether made before or on or after 6 April 1998). [*ICTA 1988, s 305A; FA 1994, s 137, Sch 15 para 20; FA 1998, Sch 13 para 18*].

Application to BES shares. There is no equivalent to *ICTA 1988, s 305A* in respect of a loss arising on shares issued after 18 March 1986 and before 1 January 1994 in respect of which BES relief (see 20.15 ENTERPRISE INVESTMENT SCHEME (AND BES)) has been given and not withdrawn, because any loss so arising was not allowable for capital gains tax purposes. A complete withdrawal of relief would mean that any loss was allowable for such purposes and, all conditions being met, there seems nothing to prevent the above relief from applying. The position would appear to be the same in respect of a loss arising on shares issued before 19 March 1986 in respect of which BES relief has been given but completely withdrawn. A loss arising on shares issued before 19 March 1986 in respect of which BES relief has been given and not withdrawn, could give rise to an allowable (albeit reduced) loss so that, again, there seems nothing to prevent the reduced loss from being similarly set against income if all conditions are met.

39.14 *Example*

P subscribed for 3,000 £1 ordinary shares at par in W Ltd, a qualifying trading company, in June 1988. In September 1995, P acquired a further 2,200 shares at £3 per share from another shareholder. In December 2000, P sold 3,900 shares at 40p per share.

Indexation factors	June 1988 to September 1995	0.413
	September 1995 to April 1998	0.080

Establish 'section 104 holding' pool.

	Shares	Qualifying expenditure	Indexed pool
		£	£
June 1988 subscription	3,000	3,000	3,000
Indexation to September 1995			
£3,000 × 0.413			1,239
September 1995 acquisition	2,200	6,600	6,600
	5,200	9,600	10,839
Indexed rise: September 1995 to April 1998			
£10,839 × 0.080			867
	5,200	9,600	11,706
December 2000 disposal	(3,900)	(7,200)	(8,780)
Pool carried forward	1,300	£2,400	£2,926

Step 1. Calculate the CGT loss in the normal way, as follows

	£
Disposal consideration 3,900 × £0.40	1,560
Allowable cost $\frac{3,900}{5,200}$ × £9,600	7,200
Allowable loss	£5,640

Step 2. Applying a LIFO basis, identify the qualifying shares (1,700) and the non-qualifying shares (2,200) comprised in the disposal.

Step 3. Calculate the proportion of the loss attributable to the qualifying shares.

Loss referable to 1,700 qualifying shares $\frac{1,700}{3,900} \times$ £5,640 £2,458

Step 4. Compare the loss in *Step 3* with the actual cost of the qualifying shares, *viz.*

Cost of 1,700 qualifying shares $\frac{1,700}{3,000} \times$ £3,000 £1,700

The loss available against income is restricted to £1,700 (being lower than £2,458).

The loss not relieved against income remains an allowable loss for CGT purposes.

£5,640 – £1,700 = £3,940

39.15 LOSSES ON SHARES IN UNLISTED TRADING COMPANIES: INVESTMENT COMPANIES

Where an 'investment company' disposes of shares in a 'qualifying trading company' for which it has subscribed (i.e. not purchased in the open market), and thereby incurs an allowable capital loss in an accounting period, it may claim relief for the loss against income of that accounting period, instead of against gains chargeable to corporation tax. Additionally, if it was an investment company at that earlier time, it may claim to set off any balance of the loss remaining, after relief above, against income of the twelve months immediately preceding the accounting period in which the loss was incurred (income of the relevant accounting periods being time apportioned for this purpose).

The investment company must have been such on the date of the relevant disposal and must either

(*a*) have been an investment company for a continuous period of six years ending on that date; or

(*b*) have been an investment company for a shorter continuous period ending on that date, and must not have been, before the beginning of that period, a 'trading company' or an 'excluded company'.

It must also not have been 'associated' with, or have been a member of the same 'group' as, the qualifying trading company, at any time in the period beginning with the date of its (the investment company's) subscription for the shares, and ending with the date of disposal.

Companies are '*associated*' with each other, for this purpose, if one controls the other, or both are under the control of the same person or persons. The general definitions of *ICTA 1988, s 416(2)(6)* (meaning of 'control') apply for this purpose. See TOLLEY'S CORPORATION TAX under Close Companies.

Subject to the above, the definitions of '*excluded company*', '*group*', '*investment company*', '*qualifying trading company*', '*eligible trading company*', '*trading company*', and the other general definitions and provisions (including identification rules and concessionary treatment under ESCs D28 and D46) relating to the similar relief for individuals outlined in 39.13 above, apply, *mutatis mutandis*, to this relief. Note that 39.13(*d*) above applies in this case to deemed disposals on or after 1 April 2000. Just as the normal identification rule for this relief is disapplied in the case of EIS and BES shares held by individuals, so is it disapplied where the investment company's holding includes shares issued on or after 1 April 2000 to which investment relief under the Corporate Venturing Scheme is attributable and which have been held continuously (see 15.20 CORPORATE VENTURING SCHEME) by the company; the identification rules at 15.17 CORPORATE VENTURING SCHEME (generally first in/first out) apply instead.

Relief must be claimed within two years of the end of the accounting period in which the loss arises and before any deduction for charges on income, expenses of management or other deductions, except that a claim for a loss on a Corporate Venturing Scheme investment to be relieved against income does take priority (see 15.20 CORPORATE VENTURING SCHEME).

[*ICTA 1988, ss 573, 575, 576; FA 1989, Sch 12 para 14; FA 1994, s 146, Sch 17 para 6; FA 1998, s 80, Sch 27 Pt III(16); FA 2000, s 63(2)(3), Sch 16 para 3(2)–(4)*].

For accounting periods beginning before 2 July 1997, and subject to the general provisions of the foregoing, a capital loss could be relieved against surplus franked investment income, by means of a claim, under *ICTA 1988, s 242*, made within two years of the end of the accounting period in which the loss was incurred. *Section 242* was repealed by *F(No 2)A 1997, s 20, Sch 8 Pt II(4)* (which also restrict relief for accounting periods straddling 2 July 1997). See, generally, TOLLEY'S CORPORATION TAX under Franked Investment Income.

39.16 WRITE-OFF OF GOVERNMENT INVESTMENT

Where any amount of an investment, by the Government, in a *corporate body*, is written off, an equal amount is to be set off against the body's tax 'losses', starting with losses available at the end of the accounting period ended before the write-off, and continuing for subsequent periods, until the investment is covered. The definition of '*losses*', for this purpose, includes, inter alia, unrelieved allowable losses under *TCGA 1992, s 8* (capital losses of companies). It should be noted, however, that the investment is only written off against capital losses as a last resort, i.e. after the extinction of other losses, unrelieved capital allowances, management expenses and charges. The investment can also be written off against the losses of any member of the same 51% group within *ICTA 1988, s 838*. An investment is written off if the liability to repay any money lent is extinguished; if any shares subscribed for out of public funds are cancelled; or if 'commencing capital debts' (as defined) or 'public dividend capital' (as defined) is reduced otherwise than by being paid off or repaid. These provisions do not apply where the investment written off is replaced in some other form. [*ICTA 1988, s 400*]. See TOLLEY'S CORPORATION TAX under Losses for further details.

39.17 PROFIT AND LOSSES OF THEATRE BACKERS (ANGELS)

Angels are theatrical backers who invest in productions. An investment which occurs in the normal course of a backer's trade falls within the Schedule D, Case I rules (see TOLLEY'S INCOME TAX). Special tax treatment applies to non-trading backers.

The Revenue's view is that the profits of non-trading theatre angels are assessable under Schedule D, Case III whilst a loss forms an allowable loss for capital gains tax.

A '*profit*' for these purposes is the return the angel receives over and above the original investment. A '*loss*' arises where there is no further prospect of a return from the investment. The contract is viewed in normal circumstances as an asset for capital gains purposes (although most certainly this would have to be established on the facts of each case).

However, by concession the Revenue will allow the profits and losses of non-trading theatre angels resident in the UK to be assessed and relieved accordingly under Schedule D, Case VI. (Press Release 8 February 1996).

40 Market Value

Cross-references. See 3.13 and 3.14 ANTI-AVOIDANCE for anti-avoidance provisions which may override or amend the general rules given below; 4.2 and 4.5 APPEALS for appeals relating to market values; 7.2 ASSETS HELD ON 6 APRIL 1965 for valuation of quoted shares and securities held on 6 April 1965; 16.3 DEATH for valuation at death; 17.3 DISPOSAL for allowable expenditure relating to acquisition of assets at market value; 39.9 LOSSES for loss relief where the market value of an asset has become negligible; 45 PARTNERSHIPS for further valuation rules which apply to partnership assets.

40.1 Market value is the price which assets might reasonably fetch in the open market, sold individually, with no allowance being made for any reduction in market value arising out of the whole of the assets being placed on the market at one and the same time. [*TCGA 1992, s 272(1)(2)*].

After 9 March 1981, acquisition and disposal are treated as being made at market value (subject to any other provision and the exception below) if the transaction is

(*a*) not at arm's length (which includes, in particular, a transaction between CONNECTED PERSONS (14), or

(*b*) by way of gift, or

(*c*) on a transfer into settlement by a settlor, or

(*d*) a distribution from a company in respect of shares in that company, or

(*e*) wholly or partly for a consideration that cannot be valued (see *Fielder v Vedlynn Ltd Ch D 1992, 65 TC 145*), or

(*f*) in connection with his own or another's loss of office or employment, diminution of emoluments (see *Whitehouse v Ellam Ch D, [1995] STC 503*), or in consideration for or recognition of his or another's services (in any office, employment or otherwise), past or future.

Exception. The market value provisions in (*a*)–(*f*) above do not apply to the *acquisition* of an asset if there is no corresponding disposal of it *and* there is no consideration in money or money's worth (or the consideration is of an amount or value lower than the market value of the asset).

[*TCGA 1992, s 17*].

An attempt by a taxpayer to substitute market value for actual price paid in a transaction between unconnected persons failed in *Bullivant Holdings Ltd v CIR Ch D 1998, 71 TC 22*.

Special rules applied to disposals by 'excluded persons' after 9 March 1981 and before 6 April 1985. '*Excluded persons*' meant

(i) a person neither resident nor ordinarily resident in the UK;

(ii) a person wholly exempt from tax in respect of chargeable gains (or who would have been so exempt on making a claim for exemption);

(iii) a charity;

(iv) a registered friendly society; or

(v) a person making the disposal for the purposes of a pension fund (as defined) which was exempt from tax.

Where the corresponding disposal (see the exception above) was made by an excluded person, the following provisions applied.

(A) *For disposals after 9 March 1981 and before 6 April 1983,* the market value rules in (*a*)–(*f*) above did not apply (with one exception) to the *acquisition* or *disposal* of the asset. The exception was the *acquisition*, by an individual, of currency or tangible movable property (excluding commodities of a kind dealt with on a terminal market or a mere right in, or over, any property) in circumstances where there was a corresponding disposal by an individual who was neither resident nor ordinarily resident in the UK. In this case the acquisition was treated as being made at market value.

(B) *For disposals after 5 April 1983 and before 6 April 1985* by an excluded person who would be chargeable in respect of any chargeable gain thereon, then provided there was no consideration in money or money's worth (or the consideration was of an amount or value lower than the market value of the asset), the person acquiring the asset and the excluded person could jointly elect that the deemed market value rules in (*a*)–(*f*) above did not apply to the acquisition and corresponding disposal. The election had to be made in writing within two years of the end of the chargeable period in which the corresponding disposal occurred. Any adjustments of capital gains tax (or corporation tax in respect of chargeable gains) in consequence of the election were to be made by way of assessment, discharge or repayment of tax.

[*CGTA 1979, s 29A(3)–(5); FA 1981, s 90(1); FA 1984, s 66(2)*].

See also 43.13 OFFSHORE SETTLEMENTS and 17.4 DISPOSAL.

Before 10 March 1981, (*c*) above was not expressly stated to apply and the exception to (*a*)–(*f*) above also did not apply (but see *CGTA 1979, s 76* regarding share option schemes). See *Harrison v Nairn Williamson Ltd CA 1977, 51 TC 135*, where the earlier provisions, found in *CGTA 1979, s 19(3) (as originally enacted)*, were held to operate where there was an acquisition but no corresponding disposal.

40.2 QUOTED SHARES AND SECURITIES

The market value of shares and securities quoted in The Stock Exchange Daily Official List is the lesser of

(*a*) the lower of the two prices quoted in The Stock Exchange Daily Official List for the relevant date, plus a quarter of the difference between those prices (*'the quarter-up rule'*), and

(*b*) the average of the highest and lowest prices for normal bargains recorded on that date, if any.

If the London trading floor is closed on the relevant date, the prices are to be taken by reference to the latest previous date or to the earliest subsequent date, whichever produces the lower figure.

The above method of valuation does not apply for computing the value of shares as at 6 April 1965 (see 7.2 ASSETS HELD ON 6 APRIL 1965), nor where special circumstances may affect the value. [*TCGA 1992, s 272(3)(4)(6), Sch 11 para 6(1)(2)(4), para 7(1); FA 1996, Sch 38 para 12*]. See *Hinchcliffe v Crabtree HL 1971, 47 TC 419.*

The Board may make regulations extending, inter alia, provisions relating to tax on chargeable gains and referring to The Stock Exchange to any or all other investment exchanges within the meaning of *Financial Services Act 1986*. [*TCGA 1992, ss 285, 287*].

Units in unit trusts, subject to similar valuation rules at 6 April 1965 (as above), are valued at the lower of the two prices published by the managers on the relevant date or if no price is published at that time, on the latest date before the relevant date. [*TCGA 1992, s 272(5)(6), Sch 11 para 6(1)(3)*].

Sumption: Capital Gains Tax. See A23.02.

40.3 UNQUOTED SHARES

Market value of unquoted shares is determined on the assumption that all information is available which a prudent prospective purchaser might reasonably require before purchase by private treaty at arm's length from a willing vendor. [*TCGA 1992, s 273*]. This counteracts *In re Lynall HL 1971, 47 TC 375.*

This provision applies to disposals after 5 July 1973 and valuations are made on the present basis in connection both with acquisition (even if before 6 July 1973, or 6 April 1965) and disposal. Otherwise, the chargeable gain on a part disposal before 6 July 1973 is not itself affected but it is re-computed on the present basis for the purpose of calculating the gain on a subsequent disposal after 5 July 1973. As regards deemed acquisitions on death after 30 March 1971 and before 6 July 1973, the present basis does not apply if the shares constituted a controlling holding and were valued on the assets basis for estate duty purposes. [*TCGA 1992, Sch 11 paras 3–5*].

In arriving at a valuation, unpublished information concerning the company's profits may be taken into account (*Caton's Administrators v Couch (Sp C 6), [1995] SSCD 34; Clark (Clark's Executor) v Green & CIR (Sp C 5), [1995] SSCD 99*).

Other cases concerning disputes as to the value of unquoted shares include *Hawkings-Byass v Sassen (and related appeals) (Sp C 88), [1996] SSCD 319* and *Denekamp v Pearce Ch D 1998, 71 TC 213.*

Sumption: Capital Gains Tax. See A23.04.

40.4 UNLISTED SECURITIES MARKET (USM) (NOW CLOSED)

Securities dealt in on the USM were not treated as 'listed' or 'quoted' for those provisions of the *Taxes Acts* which use such terms in relation to securities. Evidence of the open-market value of such securities would have been suggested, initially, by details of the bargains done at, or near, the relevant date. Where other factors needed to be weighed, the Shares Valuation Division of the Capital Taxes Office would consider whether a value offered on the basis of those bargains could be accepted as an adequate reflection of the open-market value. The Revenue stated that securities dealt in on the USM would satisfy the tests of being 'authorised to be dealt in' and 'dealt in (regularly or from time to time)' on a recognised stock exchange (SP 18/80 — now obsolete). It appears that the Revenue applied similar criteria to securities covered by Rule 4.2 of The Stock Exchange. This may also have been the position as regards the Third Market of The Stock Exchange which closed on 31 December 1990.

The USM is now closed.

40.5 ALTERNATIVE INVESTMENT MARKET (AIM)

Companies not wishing to apply for a full listing have access to the Alternative Investment Market (AIM) launched on 19 June 1995. AIM replaced the existing Rule 4.2 (of the Stock Exchange) dealing facility, and transitional provisions were available to assist companies already under Rule 4.2 to migrate to the AIM at minimum cost. AIM companies are not treated as 'quoted' or 'listed' for those provisions of the Taxes Acts which use such terms in relation to securities. (Revenue Press Release 20 February 1995).

40.6 LAND

Where, at a certain date, freehold land was subject to a tenancy by a company controlled by the freeholder, the valuation had to be of the reversion in the land expectant on the determination of the tenancy and not of the unencumbered freehold (*Henderson v Karmel's Exors Ch D 1984, 58 TC 201*).

40.7 **EXCHANGE CONTROL**

In relation to assets of a kind the sale of which was subject to restrictions imposed under the *Exchange Control Act 1947*, a determination of market value at any time before 13 December 1979 is subject to adjustment for the premium which would have been payable by a purchaser but not receivable by a seller. [*TCGA 1992, Sch 11 para 7(2)*].

41 Married Persons

Cross-references. See 2 ANNUAL RATES AND EXEMPTIONS; 7.1 and 7.3 ASSETS HELD ON 6 APRIL 1965; 8.5 ASSETS HELD ON 31 MARCH 1982; 25 HOLD-OVER RELIEFS; 26.4 INDEXATION for certain transfers between spouses before 6 April 1985 and after 5 April 1982; 39.10 LOSSES for loss relief restrictions on qualifying loans between spouses; 48.1 and 48.2 PRIVATE RESIDENCES; 52 RESIDENCE AND DOMICILE for treatment of spouses; 53.10 RETIREMENT RELIEF for reliefs applicable to spouses; 54.9 RETURNS for returns required by spouses; 60.11 TAPER RELIEF.

41.1 INTRODUCTION

For 1990/91 and subsequent years of assessment, the spouses, whether or not 'living together' (see 41.2 below), are each treated as separate individuals so that

(*a*) each spouse is assessed and charged by reference only to their own gains and circumstances (e.g. the rate of tax applicable);

(*b*) losses of one spouse are not deductible from the gains of the other; and

(*c*) each spouse has a separate right to the whole of the annual exempt amount available to individuals generally.

Where a husband and wife have made a declaration under *ICTA 1988, s 282B* in respect of their individual beneficial interests in, and in the income from, jointly held property (see TOLLEY'S INCOME TAX under Married Persons) and the declaration is still effective at the time of disposal of the property, there is a presumption that the declared split of interests is effective for capital gains tax purposes. Where there is no declaration which has effect at the time of disposal but it is clear that there is a particular split of ownership (e.g. a separate agreement may provide for the spouses' respective rights or that one spouse is merely a nominee and has no beneficial interest in the property) any gain on a disposal should be reported to the Revenue on that basis. In other cases where the split of ownership is not clear the Revenue will normally accept that the spouses hold the property in equal shares (Revenue Press Release 21 November 1990).

Transfers of assets between spouses living together are treated as made on a 'no gain, no loss basis' as in 41.3 below.

Where

(i) the husband makes a claim under *TCGA 1992, s 279* (previously *CGTA 1979, s 13*; enforced delay in remitting gains from disposals of overseas assets, see 44.5 OVERSEAS MATTERS) in respect of gains accruing to the wife before 6 April 1990 (when gains of the wife were, with certain exceptions, assessed on the husband), and

(ii) under that provision the amount of the gains falls to be assessed as if it were an amount of gains accruing after 5 April 1990,

the assessment is to be made on the wife (or her personal representatives). [*TCGA 1992, s 279(7)*].

Gains accruing to one spouse as trustee or personal representative cannot affect the position of the other spouse. [*TCGA 1992, s 65(2)*].

Spouses living together may claim exemption in respect of only one main residence. See 48.1 PRIVATE RESIDENCES.

See 59.2 SHARES AND SECURITIES—IDENTIFICATION RULES as regards joint husband and wife shareholdings.

41.2 **'LIVING TOGETHER'**

For 1990/91 and subsequent years of assessment, a husband and wife are treated as living together unless they are

(*a*) separated under a court order or separation deed, or

(*b*) in fact separated in circumstances which render permanent separation likely.

[*ICTA 1988, s 282; TCGA 1992, s 288(3)*].

41.3 **TRANSFERS BETWEEN SPOUSES**

Transfers of assets, in a year of assessment, between spouses who are living together (see 41.2 above) in any part of that year are regarded as made on a 'no gain, no loss' basis, both parties being treated as identical. This treatment also seems to apply for transfers between spouses in the part of a year following marriage and in the whole of the year in which separation takes place even though the spouses may not be 'living together' at the time of transfer. The no gain, no loss treatment does not apply to transfers (i) by way of *donatio mortis causa* (see 16.4 DEATH); (ii) to or from trading stock of either spouse; or (iii) after decree absolute. [*TCGA 1992, s 58*].

See 17.6 DISPOSAL for part disposals between spouses and 36.8 LAND for small part disposals of land. See 60.11 TAPER RELIEF for the application of that relief on a disposal by the transferee of an asset acquired inter-spouse.

Example

(A) No inter-spouse transfer

Paul and Heidi are a married couple with total income of £30,500 and £35,500 respectively for 2000/01. On 4 April 2001, Heidi sells a painting which she had acquired in June 1994 at a cost of £5,000. Net sale proceeds amount to £18,000 and the indexation factor for the period June 1994 to April 1998 is 0.124. Neither spouse disposed of any other chargeable assets during 2000/01.

Chargeable gain — Heidi

	£
Net proceeds	18,000
Cost	5,000
Unindexed gain	13,000
Indexation allowance £5,000 × 0.124	620
Chargeable gain	12,380
Taper relief @ 5%	619
	11,761
Annual exemption	7,200
Taxable gain	£4,561
Total income	35,500
Personal allowance	4,385
Taxable income	£31,115

Basic rate limit = £28,400, so gain of £4,561 is all taxed at 40%.

Tax payable £4,561 × 40%	£1,824.40

(B) Inter-spouse transfer

The facts are as in (A) above except that in January 2001, Heidi gives the painting to Paul who then makes the sale on 4 April 2001.

Chargeable gain — Heidi

	£
Deemed consideration (January 2001) note (*a*)	5,620
Cost	5,000
Unindexed gain	620
Indexation allowance (to April 1998) £5,000 × 0.124	620
Chargeable gain	Nil

Chargeable gain — Paul

	£
Net proceeds (4.4.2001)	18,000
Cost (January 2001)	5,620
Chargeable gain	12,380
Taper relief @ 5% (note (*b*))	619
	11,761
Annual exemption	7,200
Taxable gain	£4,561
Total income	30,500
Personal allowance	4,385
Taxable income	£26,115

Taxable income falls short of the basic rate limit (£28,400) by £2,285, so gain of £4,561 is taxed as follows.

£2,285 at 20%	457.00
£2,276 at 40%	910.40
Tax payable	£1,367.40
Tax saving compared with (A) above	£457.00

Notes to the example

(*a*) The inter-spouse transfer is deemed to be for such consideration as to ensure that no gain or loss accrues. Effectively, the consideration is equal to cost plus indexation to April 1998 (see 26.1 INDEXATION).

(*b*) Taper relief is computed by reference to the combined period of ownership after 5 April 1998 (see 60.11 TAPER RELIEF). In this instance, relief is at the non-business asset rate of 5% by reference to a qualifying holding period of three complete years (including the bonus year for assets acquired before 17 March 1998).

(*c*) The fact that transfers of assets between husband and wife are no gain/no loss transfers enables savings to be made by ensuring that disposals are made by a spouse with an unused annual exemption and/or basic rate band.

(*d*) An inter-spouse transfer followed by a sale could be attacked by the Revenue as an anti-avoidance device. To minimise the risk, there should be a clear time interval between the two transactions and no arrangements made to effect the ultimate sale until after the transfer. The gift should be outright with no strings attached and with no 'arrangement' for eventual proceeds to be passed to the transferor.

Transfers whilst spouses separated or treated as separated. In a case in which spouses, after several years of separation, were divorced and the court order (by consent) on the decree nisi provided for the transfer of certain property (which was not otherwise exempt) it was held that the property had been disposed of at the time of the decree nisi. As the divorce was not then absolute, the spouses were still connected persons and the consideration was to be taken as the market value. See 14.1 CONNECTED PERSONS and 40.1 MARKET VALUE and Revenue Capital Gains Manual CG 22400/510. The normal 'no gain, no loss' basis (see above) did not apply as the spouses were not living together (*Aspden v Hildesley Ch D 1981, 55 TC 609*). Such transfers after 5 April 1980 and before 14 March 1989 prima facie qualified for the general hold-over relief for gifts but the Revenue normally rejected a claim in the usual case where the transfer of an asset had been made in consideration of the giving up of rights to take action under the various provisions concerning matrimonial proceedings. See 25.9 HOLD-OVER RELIEFS and Tolley's Practical Tax 1984 p 145 and 1986 p 96.

42 Mineral Royalties

Cross-reference. See 36 LAND.

42.1 Where a person resident or ordinarily resident in the UK is entitled to receive mineral royalties (i.e. so much of any rents, tolls, royalties or periodical payments as relates to the winning and working of minerals other than water, peat, topsoil, etc.) under a lease, licence or agreement conferring a right to win and work minerals in the UK or under a sale or conveyance of such minerals, only one-half of any such royalties receivable, after 5 April 1970, in any year of assessment or accounting period is treated as income for the purposes of income tax or for corporation tax on profits other than chargeable gains (except for the deduction of income tax under *ICTA 1988, s 348* or *s 349* for payments before 1 May 1995). The other half of the royalties is treated as a chargeable gain to which no allowable expenditure attaches.

A 'terminal loss' which accrues on a 'relevant event' may (if the taxpayer so claims within six years of the event) be carried back and set against chargeable gains accruing in the years of assessment or accounting periods falling wholly or partly within a period of 15 years before the relevant event, taking later years first.

A '*relevant event*' occurs on the expiry or termination of the mineral lease or the disposal (or deemed disposal under any provision) of the interest held in the land to which the lease relates ('*the relevant interest*'). The taxpayer must have been entitled to receive mineral royalties under the mineral lease and held the interest immediately before the relevant event.

A '*terminal loss*' is an allowable loss for capital gains tax purposes which arises

(*a*) on the expiry or termination of the mineral lease, and on an additional claim within the same time limit as above, by which the taxpayer is treated as if he had disposed of and immediately re-acquired the relevant interest at its market value; or

(*b*) on the actual disposal (or any other deemed disposal under any provision) of the relevant interest.

Relief in any one year or accounting period is restricted to the chargeable gains previously assessed by reason of the treatment above in respect of the mineral lease in question, except that any unrelieved balance is treated as accruing at the date of the relevant event and as allowable against general gains. If no claim is made for the terminal loss to be treated as above, the whole of such loss is treated as accruing at the date of the relevant event and as an allowable loss against general gains. Repayments of tax are made as may be necessary.

Regulations may be made by the Board to facilitate the above provisions. [*SI 1971, No 1035*]. These deal with apportionments of payments where they relate to other matters as well as mineral royalties.

Where, on the last disposal (before 23 July 1970) affecting a mineral lease, betterment levy was chargeable under Case B (as defined by *Land Commission Act 1967, Pt III*) the chargeable gain was limited to a fraction (base value of that disposition/consideration received) of one half of the royalties received. After 5 April 1988, this limitation applies only if it applied in a chargeable period ending before 6 April 1988. But if such a lease has been renewed, extended or varied after 22 July 1970, one half of any subsequent royalty receipt is treated as a chargeable gain. [*TCGA 1992, ss 201–203; ICTA 1988, s 122(1)(5)–(7); FA 1995, Sch 29 Pt VIII(22)*].

Example

L Ltd, an investment company preparing accounts to 31 December, is the holder of a lease of land acquired in 1987 for £66,000, when the lease had an unexpired term of 65 years. In January 1995, L Ltd grants a 10-year licence to a mining company to search for and exploit minerals beneath the land. The licence is granted for £60,000 plus a mineral royalty calculated on the basis of the value of any minerals won by the licensee. The market value of the retained land (exclusive of the mineral rights) is then £10,000. L Ltd receives mineral royalties as follows

		£
Year ended	31 December 1995	12,000
	31 December 1996	19,000
	31 December 1997	29,000
	31 December 1998	38,000
	31 December 1999	17,000
	31 December 2000	10,000

On 2 January 2001, L Ltd relinquishes its rights under the lease and receives no consideration from the lessor.

(i) Chargeable gains 1995

		£
(*a*)	Disposal proceeds	60,000
	Allowable cost $\dfrac{60,000}{60,000 + 10,000} \times £66,000$	56,571
	Chargeable gain subject to indexation	£3,429
(*b*)	$\frac{1}{2} \times £12,000$	£6,000

(ii) Chargeable gains 1996 to 2000

	£
1996 $\frac{1}{2} \times £19,000$	9,500
1997 $\frac{1}{2} \times £29,000$	14,500
1998 $\frac{1}{2} \times £38,000$	19,000
1999 $\frac{1}{2} \times £17,000$	8,500
2000 $\frac{1}{2} \times £10,000$	5,000

(iii) Loss 2001

Proceeds of disposal of lease	Nil
Allowable cost £66,000 – £56,571	9,429
Allowable loss	£9,429

(iv) The loss may be set off against the chargeable gains arising on the mineral royalties as follows

	£
2000 (whole)	5,000
1999 (part)	4,429
	£9,429

43 Offshore Settlements

Cross-references. See 44.3 OVERSEAS MATTERS for non-UK residents trading in the UK through branch or agency; 52 RESIDENCE AND DOMICILE for the determination of a person's residence, ordinary residence and domicile status; and 57 SETTLEMENTS for settlements generally and provisions relating to UK resident settlements.

Sumption: Capital Gains Tax. See A3.08–18

43.1 INTRODUCTION

The provisions set out in this chapter apply generally in relation to settlements whose trustees are, or become, not resident and not ordinarily resident in the United Kingdom or where the trustees are regarded for the purposes of DOUBLE TAX RELIEF (18) arrangements as resident outside the UK. Such trustees are not, in general, chargeable to capital gains tax (see 44.1 and 44.3 OVERSEAS MATTERS) but trustees becoming non-resident are subject to an 'exit charge', and charges arise in certain circumstances on settlors and beneficiaries of such offshore settlements. For these purposes, trustees are treated as a single and continuing body (distinct from the persons who may from time to time be trustees) which is resident and ordinarily resident in the UK unless the administration of the settlement is ordinarily carried on outside the UK and the trustees or a majority of them for the time being are not resident or not ordinarily resident in the UK. A person carrying on the business of managing settlements (and acting as trustee in the course of that business) is treated as not resident in relation to a settlement if the entire settled property consists of, or is derived from, property provided by a person not at the time (or, in the case of a will trust, at death) domiciled, resident or ordinarily resident in the UK. If, in such a case, the trustees or a majority of them are, or are treated as, not resident in the UK, the administration of the settlement is treated as ordinarily carried on outside the UK. [*TCGA 1992, s 69(1)(2)*]. See also 52.3 and 52.4 RESIDENCE AND DOMICILE for the meaning of resident and ordinarily resident.

The remainder of this chapter is set out under the following headings.

43.2 CHARGE ON TRUSTEES CEASING TO BE RESIDENT IN THE UK

Where, at any time ('*the relevant time*') after 18 March 1991, trustees of a settlement become neither resident nor ordinarily resident in the UK (see 43.1 above), they are deemed for capital gains tax purposes to have disposed of 'the defined assets' immediately before the relevant time, and immediately to have reacquired them, at their market value at that time.

'*The defined assets*' are all assets constituting settled property of the settlement immediately before the relevant time. However, if immediately after the relevant time the trustees carry on a trade in the UK through a branch or agency, and any assets are situated in the UK and either used in or for the purposes of the trade or used or held for the purposes of the branch or agency, those assets are not defined assets (see also 44.3 OVERSEAS MATTERS). In addition, assets are not defined assets if they are of a description specified in any DOUBLE TAX RELIEF (18.2) arrangements, and were the trustees to dispose of them immediately before the relevant time, the trustees would fall to be regarded for the purposes of those arrangements as not liable in the UK to tax on gains accruing to them on the disposal (but see below under Dual resident trustees).

TCGA 1992, s 152 (55 ROLLOVER RELIEF) is not to apply where the trustees have disposed of, or their interest in, 'the old assets' before the relevant time, and acquire 'the new assets', or their interest in them, after that time. However, this denial of relief does not apply to new assets if, at the time they are acquired, the trustees carry on a trade in the UK through a branch or agency, and any new assets are situated in the UK and either used in or for the purposes of the trade or used or held for the purposes of the branch or agency. '*The old assets*' and '*the new assets*' have the same meanings as in *TCGA 1992, s 152.*

[*TCGA 1992, s 80*].

For the Revenue's practice in this area, see Revenue Pamphlet IR 131, SP 5/92, paras 2 and 3.

For 1996/97 onwards, the normal rules for assessment of trustees (see 5.6 ASSESSMENTS) are disapplied so that no assessment to CGT payable under *TCGA 1992, s 80* by the migrating trustees can be made on a person who ceased to be a trustee of the settlement before the relevant time and who shows that, when he did so cease, there was no proposal that the trustees might migrate. [*TCGA 1992, s 65(3)(4); FA 1995, s 103(7), s 114*].

Death of trustee: special rules. Special rules apply where *TCGA 1992, s 80* above applies as a result of the death of a trustee of the settlement, and within the period of six months beginning with the death, the trustees of the settlement become resident and ordinarily resident in the UK. In such circumstances, *TCGA 1992, s 80* is to apply as if the defined assets were restricted to such assets (if any) as would, apart from this special rule, be defined assets and which either:

- are disposed of by the trustees in the period which begins with the death and ends when the trustees become resident and ordinarily resident in the UK, or
- are of a description specified in any double tax relief arrangements; constitute settled property of the settlement immediately after the trustees become resident and ordinarily resident in the UK; and, were the trustees to dispose of them at that time, the trustees would fall to be regarded for the purposes of the arrangements as not liable in the UK to tax on gains accruing to them on the disposal.

Further special rules apply where at any time (whether before, on or after 19 March 1991) the trustees of a settlement become resident and ordinarily resident in the UK as a result of the death of a trustee of the settlement, and *TCGA 1992, s 80* above applies as regards the trustees of the settlement in circumstances where the relevant time (within the meaning of that provision) falls within the period of six months beginning with the death. In such circumstances, *TCGA 1992, s 80* is to apply as if the defined assets were restricted to such assets (if any) as would, apart from this special rule, be defined assets and which the trustees acquired in the period beginning with the death and ending with the relevant time as a result of a disposal in respect of which relief is given under *TCGA 1992, s 165* (hold-over relief for gifts of business assets; see 25.1 HOLD-OVER RELIEFS) or in relation to which *TCGA 1992, s 260(3)* (hold-over relief for gifts on which inheritance tax is chargeable etc; see 25.7 HOLD-OVER RELIEFS) applies. [*TCGA 1992, s 81*].

Past trustees: liability for tax. Where *TCGA 1992, s 80* above applies as regards the trustees of a settlement ('*the migrating trustees*'), and any resulting capital gains tax which is payable by the migrating trustees is not paid within six months from the time when it became payable, the Board may act as below.

The Board may, at any time before the end of the period of three years beginning with the time when the amount of tax is finally determined, serve on any person who, at any time within the 'relevant period', was a trustee of the settlement (but not so as to include a person ceasing to be a trustee before the end of the relevant period who can show that at the time he ceased to be a trustee there was no proposal that the trustees might become neither resident nor ordinarily resident in the UK), a notice requiring the payment of outstanding tax and interest within 30 days from the service of the notice. The notified amount can be recovered from the person concerned as if it were tax due and payable; and he may recover from the migrating trustees any amount paid by him. No tax relief is given on any such payment in computing taxable profits etc.

The '*relevant period*' is the period of twelve months ending with the relevant time. (Where the relevant time for the purposes of *TCGA 1992, s 80* above was within the period of twelve months beginning with 19 March 1991, the relevant period was restricted to the period beginning with that date and ending with that time.) [*TCGA 1992, s 82*].

For the Revenue's practice in this area, see Revenue Pamphlet IR 131, SP 5/92, paras 4–6.

Dual resident trustees. *Charge on becoming dual resident.* Where, at any time ('*the time concerned*') after 18 March 1991, the trustees of a settlement, while continuing to be resident and ordinarily resident in the UK, become trustees who fall to be regarded for the purposes of any DOUBLE TAX RELIEF (18.2) arrangements as resident overseas and as not liable in the UK to tax on gains accruing on disposals of assets ('*relevant assets*') which constitute settled property of the settlement and fall within descriptions specified in the arrangements, they are deemed for capital gains tax purposes to have disposed of the relevant assets immediately before the time concerned, and immediately to have reacquired them, at their market value at that time. [*TCGA 1992, s 83*].

Disapplication of rollover relief provision. TCGA 1992, s 152 (55.1 ROLLOVER RELIEF) is not to apply where

- the new assets (as in 55.1 ROLLOVER RELIEF) are, or the interest in them is, acquired after 18 March 1991 by the trustees of a settlement;
- at the time of acquisition the trustees are resident and ordinarily resident in the UK and fall to be regarded for the purposes of any double tax relief arrangements as resident overseas;
- the assets are of a description specified in the arrangements; and
- were the trustees to dispose of the assets immediately after the acquisition, the trustees would fall to be regarded for the purposes of the arrangements as not liable in the UK to tax on gains accruing to them on the disposal.

[*TCGA 1992, s 84*].

43.3 **DISPOSAL OF SETTLED INTEREST**

The exemption in *TCGA 1992, s 76(1)* (see 57.8 SETTLEMENTS) by virtue of which no chargeable gain accrues in certain circumstances on the disposal of an interest created by or arising under a settlement does not apply to such disposals in either of the following circumstances.

(*a*) At the time of disposal, the trustees are neither resident nor ordinarily resident in the UK (see 43.1 above) and the disposal is not one which arises on a person becoming absolutely entitled to settled property as against the trustees and accordingly treated under *TCGA 1992, s 76(2)* (see 57.8 SETTLEMENTS) as made in consideration of his obtaining the settled property. [*TCGA 1992, s 85(1)*].

(*b*) Subject to the same exclusion as in (*a*) above, the disposal is made **after 5 March 1998** and there has ever been a time (whether before, on or after that date) when the trustees of the settlement were not resident or ordinarily resident in the UK or fell to be treated under a double tax agreement as resident in a territory outside the UK. Nor does the exemption apply if any property comprised in the settlement in question derives directly or indirectly from a settlement which is caught by this provision. [*TCGA 1992, s 76(1A)(1B)(3); FA 1998, s 128*].

Calculation of gain on disposal of interest after trustees becoming non-resident. Subject to the exceptions below, for the purpose only of calculating any chargeable gain accruing to a person on the disposal of an interest created by or arising under a settlement, where

(i) *TCGA 1992, s 80* at 43.2 above (charge on trustees becoming non-resident) applies as regards the trustees of the settlement;

(ii) the disposal is made after the 'relevant time' (see 43.2 above) and the circumstances are such that the exemption for disposal of an interest in a settlement is prevented from applying by (*a*) above; and

(iii) the interest was created for his benefit, or he otherwise acquired it, before the relevant time,

he is treated as if he had disposed of the interest immediately before the relevant time, and immediately reacquired it, at its market value at that time.

This treatment does not apply where

- *TCGA 1992, s 83* at 43.2 above (charge on trustees ceasing to be liable to UK tax under double tax relief arrangements) applied as regards the trustees in circumstances where 'the time concerned' (see 43.2 above) fell before the time when the interest was created for the benefit of the person disposing of it or when he otherwise acquired it; or

- the relevant time fell after 20 March 2000 and the settlement had 'relevant offshore gains' at that time.

A settlement has '*relevant offshore gains*' at any time if, were the tax year to end at that time, there would be an amount of trust gains which by virtue of *TCGA 1992, s 89(2)* (see 43.13 below) or *TCGA 1992, Sch 4C para 8(3)* (see 43.18 below) would be available to be treated as chargeable gains accruing to any beneficiaries of the settlement receiving capital payments in the following tax year.

The above treatment is also disapplied where conditions (i)–(iii) above apply but, in addition, *TCGA 1992, s 83* at 43.2 above applied as regards the trustees in circumstances where 'the time concerned' (see 43.2 above) fell in the 'relevant period' (see below). In these circumstances, for the purposes only of calculating any chargeable gain accruing on the disposal of the interest, the person disposing of it is instead treated as if he had disposed of it immediately before the time concerned (where there is only one such time) or the earliest time concerned (where there is more than one because *TCGA 1992, s 83* applied more than once), and had immediately reacquired it, at its market value at that time. This treatment does not apply where the time concerned or, as the case may be, the earliest time concerned, fell after 20 March 2000 and the settlement had relevant offshore gains (as defined above) at that time.

For this purpose, the '*relevant period*' is the period which begins when the interest was created for the benefit of the person disposing of it or when he otherwise acquired it, and ends with the relevant time (within the meaning of *TCGA 1992, s 80* at 43.2 above).

[*TCGA 1992, s 85(2)–(11); FA 2000, s 95*].

43.4 CHARGE ON SETTLOR WITH INTEREST IN SETTLEMENT

Where all the conditions listed below are fulfilled, chargeable gains of an amount equal to that referred to in (*e*) below are treated as accruing in a particular year of assessment to 'the settlor' (see 43.8 below) of a settlement such that they are treated as forming the highest part of the amount on which he is chargeable to capital gains tax for the year. See also 43.12 below.

The conditions are

(*a*) the settlement is a 'qualifying settlement' (see 43.9 below) in a particular year of assessment;

(*b*) *either*

  (i) the trustees are not resident or ordinarily resident in the UK during any part of the year (see 43.1 above); or

  (ii) the trustees are resident in the UK during any part of the year or ordinarily resident in the UK during the year, but at any time of such residence or ordinary residence they fall to be regarded for the purposes of any DOUBLE TAX RELIEF (18.2) arrangements as resident overseas;

(*c*) the person who is the settlor in relation to the settlement is domiciled in the UK at some time in the year and is either resident in the UK during any part of the year or ordinarily resident in the UK during the year (and see 44.4 OVERSEAS MATTERS re 'temporary' non-residence);

(*d*) at any time during the year the settlor has an 'interest' (see 43.5 below) in the settlement;

(*e*) by virtue of disposals of any of the settled property 'originating' from the settlor (see 43.8 below), there is an amount on which the trustees would be chargeable to tax for the year under *TCGA 1992, s 2(2)* (i.e. an amount of chargeable gains less current and brought forward allowable losses — see 39.1 LOSSES) if the assumption as to residence below were made; and

(*f*) the provisions in 43.7 below do not preclude a charge.

Where the residence condition specified in (*b*)(i) above applies, the assumption as to residence in (*e*) above is that the trustees are resident or ordinarily resident in the UK throughout the year; and where the residence condition specified in (*b*)(ii) above applies, the assumption as to residence in (*e*) above is that the double tax relief arrangements do not apply.

In arriving at the amount to be charged on the settlor for a particular year of assessment, the effects of *TCGA 1992, s 3* (annual exempt amount — see 57.4 and 57.5 SETTLEMENTS) and *TCGA 1992, ss 77–79* (settlor having interest in UK resident settlement chargeable instead of trustees in certain circumstances — see 57.3 SETTLEMENTS) are ignored. In addition, any deductions provided for by *TCGA 1992, s 2(2)* (current and brought forward allowable losses) are to be made in respect of disposals of any of the settled property originating from the settlor, and *TCGA 1992, s 16(3)* (losses of non-resident not to be allowable — see 44.3 OVERSEAS MATTERS) is to be assumed not to prevent losses accruing to trustees in one year of assessment from being allowed as a deduction from chargeable gains in a later year (so far as not previously set against gains).

Where trustees are participators in a company in respect of property which originates (for gains accruing before 28 November 1995, hold shares in a company which originate) from the settlor, and under *TCGA 1992, s 13* (gains of non-resident close company assessable on shareholder — see 44.6 OVERSEAS MATTERS) gains or losses would be treated as accruing to the trustees in a particular year of assessment by virtue of so much of their interest as participators as arises from that property (for gains accruing before 28 November 1995, the shares) if the assumption as to residence in (*e*) above were made, the gains or losses are taken into account in arriving at the amount charged on the settlor as regards that year as if they had accrued by virtue of disposals of settled property originating from the settlor.

Where the trustees fall within the residence condition specified in (*b*)(i) above, further rules apply to arrive at the amount to be charged on the settlor as regards a particular year of assessment ('*the year concerned*'). If the conditions for the charge to apply are not fulfilled as regards the settlement in any year of assessment falling before the year concerned, no deductions are made for losses accruing before the year concerned. If those conditions are fulfilled as regards the settlement in any year or years of assessment falling before the year concerned, no deductions are made for losses accruing before that year (or the first of the years) so falling. However, these two prohibitions on deductions being made for losses are not to prevent deductions being made in respect of losses accruing in a year of assessment in which the conditions in (*a*) to (*d*) and (*f*) above are fulfilled as regards the settlement. As regards a particular year of assessment and in relation to a settlement created before 19 March 1991, no account is taken of disposals made before 19 March 1991 (whether for the purpose of arriving at gains or losses).

Where, as regards a particular year of assessment, there would otherwise be an amount to be charged on the settlor and the trustees fall within the residence condition specified in (*b*)(ii) above, the following assumptions and adjustments to the amount are made. It is to be assumed that references in the foregoing to settled property originating from the settlor were to such of it as constitutes 'protected assets' and that references in the foregoing to shares originating from the settlor were to such of them as constitute protected assets. The amount (if any) to be charged on the settlor is found on those assumptions, and if there is no amount found there is deemed to be no amount to be charged on the settlor, and if an amount is found on these assumptions it is compared with the amount which would otherwise be charged on the settlor, and the smaller of the two is taken to be the amount to be charged on the settlor.

Assets are '*protected assets*' if they are of a description specified in the double tax relief arrangements mentioned in connection with the residence condition specified in (*b*)(ii) above, and were the trustees to dispose of them at any 'relevant time', the trustees would fall to be regarded for the purposes of the arrangements as not liable in the UK to tax on gains accruing to them on the disposal. For this purpose, the alternative assumptions as to residence in (*e*) above are ignored, the '*relevant time*' is any time, in the year of assessment concerned, when the trustees fall to be regarded for the purposes of the arrangements as resident overseas, and if different assets are identified by reference to different relevant times, all of them are protected assets.

[*TCGA 1992, s 86(1)–(4)(5), Sch 5 para 1; FA 1996, s 174(10)(11)*].

43.5 **Test whether settlor has an interest.** A settlor has an interest in a settlement if

(*a*) any property originating from the settlor ('*relevant property*') which is or may at any time be comprised in the settlement is, or will or may become, applicable for the benefit of or payable to a 'defined person' in any circumstances whatever;

(*b*) any income originating from the settlor ('*relevant income*') which arises or may arise under the settlement is, or will or may become, applicable for the benefit of or payable to a defined person in any circumstances whatever; or

(*c*) any defined person enjoys a benefit directly or indirectly from any relevant property which is comprised in the settlement or any relevant income arising under the settlement.

Each of the following is a '*defined person*':

- the settlor;
- the settlor's spouse;
- any child (which term includes stepchild) of the settlor or of the settlor's spouse;
- the spouse of any such child;
- any grandchild of the settlor or of the settlor's spouse (see 43.6 below as regards the addition of grandchildren to the list of defined persons); ('*grandchild*' includes a child of a stepchild or a stepchild of a child or stepchild);
- the spouse of any such grandchild (see 43.6 below as regards the addition of grandchildren and their spouses to the list of defined persons);
- a company controlled by a person or persons mentioned in the foregoing (see 43.6 below as regards the addition of grandchildren and their spouses to the fore-mentioned categories); ('*control*' is construed as in *ICTA 1988, s 416* but for these purposes no rights or powers of (or attributed to) an associate or associates of a person are attributed to him under *ICTA 1988, s 416(6)* if he is not a participator (within *ICTA 1988, s 417(1)*, but subject to ESC D40 (see 43.8 below)) in the company);
- a company associated with any such company; ('*associated*' is construed as in *ICTA 1988, s 416* but for these purposes where it falls to be decided whether a company is controlled by a person or persons, a similar relaxation to that for 'control' applies as above).

A settlor does not have an interest in a settlement at any time when none of the property or income concerned can become applicable or payable as mentioned above except in the event of:

- the bankruptcy of some person who is or may become beneficially entitled to that property or income;
- any assignment of or charge on the property or income being made or given by some such person;
- in the case of a marriage settlement, the death of both parties to the marriage and of all or any of the children of the marriage; or
- the death under the age of 25 or some lower age of some person who would be beneficially entitled to the property or income on attaining that age.

He also does not have an interest in a settlement under (*a*) above at any time when some person is alive and under the age of 25 if during that person's life none of the property or income concerned can become applicable or payable as mentioned in (*a*) above except in the event of that person becoming bankrupt or assigning or charging his interest in the property or income concerned.

[*TCGA 1992, Sch 5 para 2; FA 1998, s 131, Sch 22 para 2*].

43.6 **Addition of grandchildren to list of defined persons**. Grandchildren and their spouses (and companies which they control or which are associated with such companies) are included in the list of defined persons in 43.5 above **in relation to disposals made on or after 17 March 1998**. Their inclusion applies as regards all disposals by settlements created on or after that date. As regards **settlements created before that date**, post-16 March 1998 disposals (whether giving rise to gains or losses) to which the 'charge on settlor' provisions would not apply if the addition of the said categories to the above-mentioned list were disregarded are left out of account (i.e. are regarded as not falling within 43.4(*e*) above) unless they are made in a tax year in which one of the following events occurs or in a subsequent tax year. (Where the tax year in question is 1997/98, only post-16 March 1998 events are taken into account.)

(*a*) Property or income is provided directly or indirectly for the purposes of the settlement (i.e. is added to the settlement) otherwise than under an arm's length transaction and otherwise than in pursuance of a liability incurred by any person before 17 March 1998. Property or income provided towards (and not beyond) an excess for a tax year of trust expenses (relating to administration and taxation) over trust income is ignored.

(*b*) The trustees become neither resident nor ordinarily resident in the UK or begin to fall to be regarded under a double tax agreement as resident in a territory outside the UK.

(*c*) The terms of the settlement are varied so as to enable for the first time any one or more of the persons mentioned below to benefit from the settlement.

(*d*) Any one or more of the persons mentioned below does enjoy a benefit for the first time but would not have been capable of doing so by reference to the terms of the settlement as they stood immediately before 17 March 1998.

The persons mentioned in (*c*) and (*d*) above are: any grandchild (as in 43.5 above) of the settlor or of the settlor's spouse, the spouse of any such grandchild, a company controlled by any such grandchildren and/or their spouses (with or without other defined persons — see 43.5 above) and a company associated with any such company. (For these purposes, '*control*' and '*associated*' are to be construed as in 43.5 above.)

[*TCGA 1992, Sch 5 para 2A; FA 1998, Sch 22 para 2*].

43.7 **Exceptions to charge.** There is no charge on the settlor if he dies in the year.

There is also no charge on the settlor where **both** (*a*) and (*b*) below apply.

(*a*) The settlor has no interest in the settlement at any time in the year except for one (or, where they are satisfied by reference to the same person, for two or all) of the following reasons:

- property is, or will or may become, applicable for the benefit of or payable to a person, being the settlor's spouse, any child (which term includes stepchild) or grandchild (defined as in 43.5 above, and see below for the addition of grandchildren to this list) of the settlor or of the settlor's spouse, or the spouse of any such child or grandchild;
- income is, or will or may become applicable for the benefit of or payable to such a person; or
- such a person enjoys a benefit from property or income.

(*b*) Either

- the person referred to in (*a*) above dies in the year; or
- where the person referred to in (*a*) above is the settlor's spouse or the spouse of any child or grandchild of the settlor or of the settlor's spouse, that person ceases to be married to the settlor, the child or the grandchild concerned (as the case may be) during the year.

Again no charge arises on the settlor in the following circumstances:

(i) the settlor has no interest in the settlement at any time in the year except for the reason that there are two or more persons, each of whom is one of the following: the settlor's spouse, any child (which term includes stepchild) or grandchild (defined as in 43.5 above, and see below for the addition of grandchildren to this list) of the settlor or of the settlor's spouse, or the spouse of any such child or grandchild and stands to gain for one or more of the following reasons:

- property is, or will or may become, applicable for his benefit or payable to him;
- the income is, or will or may become, applicable for his benefit or payable to him; or
- he enjoys a benefit from property or income, *and*

(ii) each of the persons referred to in (i) dies in the year.

References above to grandchildren apply only in relation to disposals made **on or after 17 March 1998** to which the 'charge on settlor' provisions would otherwise apply by reference to grandchildren (see 43.5 and 43.6 above).

[*TCGA 1992, Sch 5 paras 3–5; FA 1998, Sch 22 para 3*].

43.8 **Meaning of 'settlor'.** For the purposes of these provisions, a person is a '*settlor*' in relation to a settlement if the settled property consists of or includes property originating from him. [*TCGA 1992, Sch 5 para 7*].

Meaning of 'originating'. References to property originating from a person are taken as references to property provided by that person, property representing property provided by that person, and so much of any property provided by that person and other property as, on a just apportionment, can be taken to represent property provided by that person. References to income originating from a person are taken as references to income from property originating from that person and income provided by that person.

Where a person who is a settlor in relation to a settlement makes reciprocal arrangements with another person for the provision of property or income, then the property or income provided by the other person under the arrangements is treated as provided by the settlor, but property or income provided by the settlor under the arrangements is treated as provided by the other person (and not by the settlor).

Where property is provided by a '*qualifying company*' (i.e. a company which is a close company within *ICTA 1988, ss 414, 415* or which would be a close company if it were resident in the UK) controlled (construed as in *ICTA 1988, s 416* but with the same relaxation as in 43.5 above) by one person alone at the time it is provided, that person is taken to provide it. Where property is provided by a qualifying company controlled by two or more persons (taking each one separately) at the time it is provided, those persons are taken to provide the property in equal shares. Where property is provided by a qualifying company controlled by two or more persons (taking them together) at the time it is provided, the persons who are participators (construed as in *ICTA 1988, s 417(1)*) in the company at the time it is provided are taken to provide it in just proportions (save that where a person would otherwise be treated under this last provision as providing less than 5% of any property, he is not taken as providing any property). By concession, a beneficiary in the settlement is not to be regarded as a participator in the company solely by virtue of his status as beneficiary (Revenue Pamphlet IR 1, D40).

References to property representing other property include references to property representing accumulated income from that other property. A person is treated as providing property or income if he provides it directly or indirectly. For gains accruing before 28 November 1995, the above provisions for determining whether property of any kind originates from a person apply equally to determine whether shares held by the trustees of a company whose gains and losses are taken into account in arriving at the amount to be charged on the settlor (see 43.4 above) originate from the settlor.
[*TCGA 1992, Sch 5 para 8; FA 1996, Sch 41 Pt V(30)*].

43.9 **Qualifying settlements, and commencement.** A settlement **created on or after 19 March 1991** is a '*qualifying settlement*' for the purposes of 43.4(*a*) above in the year of assessment in which it is created and subsequent years of assessment.

A settlement **created before 19 March 1991** which was not previously a qualifying settlement (see also below) becomes a qualifying settlement with effect **in and after the tax year 1999/2000**. (Disposals made before 6 April 1999, whether giving rise to gains or losses, are left out of account in arriving at any figure within 43.4(*e*) above.) The above does **not** apply if the settlement is a 'protected settlement' immediately after the beginning of 6 April 1999 in which case it becomes a qualifying settlement with effect in and after any tax year in which *either* the settlement ceases to be a protected settlement *or* any of the four conditions set out below becomes fulfilled. See 43.10 below for provisions bringing into charge certain **gains realised in the transitional period** between the announcement of these rules on 17 March 1998 and their first coming into effect in 1999/2000.

A settlement is a '*protected settlement*' at any time if at that time the 'beneficiaries' are confined to persons falling within some or all of the following categories:

- children of a settlor or of a spouse of a settlor who are under 18 either at that time or at the end of the immediately preceding tax year;
- unborn children of a settlor, of a spouse of a settlor, or of a future spouse of a settlor;
- future spouses of any children or future children of a settlor, a spouse of a settlor or any future spouse of a settlor;
- a future spouse of a settlor;

- persons who are not at that time defined persons (see 43.5 above) in relation to the settlement and by reference to any current settlor.

  Despite the addition of grandchildren to the list of defined persons (see 43.6 above), the Revenue do *not* regard the existence as beneficiaries of the settlor's (or his spouse's) grandchildren (of whatever age) as denying protected settlement status (Revenue Tax Bulletin December 1998 p 620).

The term 'children' includes stepchildren. For these purposes, a person is a '*beneficiary*' of a settlement if

- there are any circumstances whatever in which

  (*a*) 'relevant property' which is, or may become, comprised in the settlement, or

  (*b*) 'relevant income' which arises, or may arise, under the settlement,

  is, or will or may become, applicable for his benefit or payable to him; or
- he enjoys a benefit directly or indirectly from any 'relevant property' comprised in, or 'relevant income' arising under, the settlement.

'*Relevant property*' and '*relevant income*' mean, respectively, property and income originating (see 43.8 above) from a settlor.

A settlement created **before 19 March 1991** is also a qualifying settlement **in any year of assessment before 1999/2000** in which any of the four conditions set out below becomes fulfilled and in subsequent years of assessment.

The **four conditions** twice referred to above are as follows.

- The first condition is that after 18 March 1991 property or income is provided directly or indirectly for the purposes of the settlement otherwise than under a transaction entered into at arm's length and otherwise than in pursuance of a liability incurred by any person before 19 March 1991. However, if the settlement's expenses relating to administration and taxation for a year of assessment exceed its income for the year, property or income provided towards meeting those expenses is ignored for the purposes of this condition if the value of the property or income so provided does not exceed the difference between the amount of those expenses and the amount of the settlement's income for the year. By concession, a repayable on demand loan which was made to a relevant trust on non-commercial terms before 19 March 1991 was not caught by this condition provided that, before 31 July 1992, it was either repaid in full with any outstanding interest or made subject to fully commercial terms (Revenue Pamphlet IR 1, D41 — this concession contained further detailed notes on the treatment of amounts paid where the loan was put on a commercial basis. See also Revenue Tax Bulletin August 1993 p 83).
- The second condition is that the trustees become after 18 March 1991 neither resident nor ordinarily resident in the UK, or the trustees, while continuing to be resident and ordinarily resident in the UK, become after 18 March 1991 trustees who fall to be regarded for the purposes of any double tax relief arrangements as resident overseas.
- The third condition is that after 18 March 1991 the terms of the settlement are varied so that a defined person (see 43.5 above) becomes for the first time a person who will or might benefit from the settlement.
- The fourth condition is that after 18 March 1991 a defined person enjoys a benefit from the settlement for the first time and the person concerned is not one who (looking only at the terms of the settlement immediately before 19 March 1991) would be capable of enjoying a benefit from the settlement on or after that date.

For the purposes of the third and fourth conditions above, grandchildren (as in 43.5 above) and their spouses (and companies which they control or which are associated with such companies) are not defined persons in relation to events before 17 March 1998 (see also 43.6 above).

[*TCGA 1992, Sch 5 para 9; FA 1998, s 132, Sch 22 para 4, Sch 27 Pt III(30)*].

For the Revenue's practice in this area, see Revenue Pamphlet IR 131, SP 5/92, paras 11–37, Revenue Tax Bulletin August 1993 p 82 and April 1995 pp 204, 205, and ICAEW guidance note TAX 20/92, 14 December 1992, paras 7–23.

43.10 **Pre-19 March 1991 settlements in the transitional period 17 March 1998 to 5 April 1999.** The decision to bring remaining non-qualifying pre-19 March 1991 settlements (except for protected settlements) within the 'charge on settlor' provisions (see 43.9 above) was announced on 17 March 1998 but its coming into effect was delayed until 1999/2000 in order to allow time for those affected to reorganise their affairs if they so wished. However, the rules in (*a*)–(*c*) below were introduced to prevent certain gains in the **transitional period (17 March 1998 to 5 April 1999 inclusive)** from escaping tax.

(*a*) *Settlements that become qualified in 1999/2000.* Where a pre-19 March 1991 settlement was not a qualifying settlement (see 43.9 above) in 1998/99 but becomes one in 1999/2000 (without having been a 'protected settlement' immediately after the beginning of 6 April 1999), then, in the case of any settlor of the settlement, gains and losses actually accruing to the trustees in the transitional period are deemed to have accrued on 6 April 1999, with the result that the 'charge on settlor' provisions apply in relation to such gains etc. in the year 1999/2000. Any gains/losses realised in a tax year in which the residence condition in 43.4(*b*) above is not fulfilled (broadly, a year in which the trustees are UK-resident) are left out of account. If the trustees do not fulfil the residence condition in 1999/2000, they are treated (only for the purpose of applying this transitional provision) as having done so. For these purposes, a '*protected settlement*' is defined as in 43.9 above but also includes a settlement which would be within that definition if the settlor under consideration were the only settlor of the settlement.

(*b*) *Transfers to another settlement.* The treatment described below applies where

- a gain or loss accrues on the disposal of an asset in the transitional period by the trustees of a pre-19 March 1991 settlement (the '*transferor settlement*');
- the disposal is made in a tax year in which the trustees fulfil the residence condition in 43.4(*b*) above (broadly a year in which they are non-UK resident) but the settlement is not a qualifying settlement;
- a person who is a settlor in relation to the transferor settlement (the '*chargeable settlor*') is UK-domiciled at some time in both 1999/2000 and the tax year of disposal, is either UK-resident during any part of each of those years or ordinarily resident during each of those years *and* is alive at the end of the tax year 1999/2000;
- the asset disposed of is property originating (see 43.8 above) from the chargeable settlor;
- there is property comprised in another settlement (the '*transferee settlement*') at some time after the said disposal and *before 6 April 1999* which is or includes (whether or not in consequence of the disposal) the asset disposed of or any 'relevant property';
- the transferor settlement has a 'relevant connection' with the transferee settlement;

- the said gain/loss is not one treated under (*a*) above as accruing on 6 April 1999 to the trustees of the transferor settlement.

The 'charge on settlor' provisions are applied for the tax year 1999/2000 in relation to the *transferee* settlement as if the above-mentioned gain/loss had accrued on 6 April 1999 to the trustees of that settlement on a disposal by them of property originating from the chargeable settlor. Where those provisions would not otherwise have applied in relation to that settlement in the case of the chargeable settlor, they are treated as if they did apply, but only for the purpose of so taking into account the said gain/loss. Where the same gain/loss would be treated as accruing to trustees of more than one settlement, it is to be apportioned between them in a just and reasonable manner. These provisions are disapplied if, for the tax year of disposal, the exceptions in 43.7 above would have prevented the 'charge on settlor' provisions from applying (on the assumption that they would otherwise have applied) in the case of the chargeable settlor in relation to the transferor settlement or from so applying in relation to the transferee settlement.

'*Relevant property*', in relation to a disposal by the trustees of the transferor settlement, means any property (other than the asset disposed of) which is (or represents) property or income originating from the chargeable settlor, has been comprised in (or has arisen to) the transferor settlement at any time after the disposal *and* is property or income of the trustees of the transferee settlement acquired or otherwise deriving (directly or indirectly) from the trustees of the transferor settlement.

A transferor settlement has, in relation to a disposal by its trustees, a '*relevant connection*' with a transferee settlement if

- immediately before the disposal, the 'beneficiaries' (as very broadly defined by *FA 1998, Sch 23 para 6(5)*) of the transferor settlement are, or include, defined persons (as in 43.5 above and by reference to the chargeable settlor) in relation to that settlement at that time;
- the transferor settlement is not a 'protected settlement' at that time in relation to the chargeable settlor; ('*protected settlement*' is defined as in 43.9 above but on the assumption that the chargeable settlor is the only settlor and with the omission of the reference to children under 18 at the end of the immediately preceding tax year);
- at the beginning of 6 April 1999 the beneficiaries of the transferee settlement are, or include, persons aged 18 or over who have been defined persons in relation to the transferor settlement; and
- the property comprised in the transferee settlement in respect of which some or all of the persons mentioned immediately above are beneficiaries at the beginning of 6 April 1999 is, or includes, anything which, in relation to either the transferee settlement or the transferor settlement, is property or income originating from the chargeable settlor.

(*c*) *Transfers to a foreign institution.* Provisions broadly similar to those in (*b*) above apply, with appropriate modifications, where the effective transfer of property by the pre-19 March 1991 settlement is not to another settlement but to a '*foreign institution*', meaning a company or other institution resident outside the UK, with which the transferor settlement has a 'relevant connection'. In this case, the gain/loss is treated as accruing on 6 April 1999 to the trustees of the *transferor* settlement, and for this purpose the transferor settlement is deemed to exist in 1999/2000 even if it does not actually do so. The gain/loss is not brought into account under this provision if it falls to be brought into account under (*a*) or (*b*) above. The transferor settlement has, in relation to a disposal by its trustees, a '*relevant connection*' with the transferee institution if

- immediately before the disposal, the beneficiaries of the transferor settlement are, or include, defined persons (as in 43.5 above and by reference to the chargeable settlor) in relation to that settlement at that time;
- the transferor settlement is not a 'protected settlement' (defined as in (*b*) above) at that time in relation to the chargeable settlor; and
- the transferee institution is one
  - (i) in which a 'relevant defined person' is a participator (within *ICTA 1988, s 417(1)*) at the beginning of 6 April 1999; or
  - (ii) which is under the control of a company in which (or two or more companies in any of which) a relevant defined person is a participator at that time; or
  - (iii) whose 'relevant property' or 'relevant income' includes property or income in which a relevant defined person has an interest (as very broadly defined by *FA 1998, Sch 23 para 3(10)*) at that time.

A person is a '*relevant defined person*' at any time if he is 18 or over and has been, by reference to the chargeable settlor, a defined person in relation to the transferor settlement. '*Relevant property*' and '*relevant income*', in relation to a foreign institution, mean, respectively, property or income of that institution which, if the institution were a settlement, would be treated for the purposes of the 'charge on settlor' provisions as originating from the chargeable settlor.

Prevention of double charge. There are provisions (*FA 1998, Sch 23 paras 4, 5*) to ensure that gains realised in the transitional period, and falling to be brought into account under (*a*), (*b*) or (*c*) above, are not charged twice, i.e. on the settlor and also on beneficiaries under the provisions of *TCGA 1992, s 87* or *s 89(2)* (the 'charge on beneficiaries' provisions — see 43.13 below). The provisions are applied separately as regards each settlor of the settlement. Broadly, any excess of capital payments to beneficiaries over trust gains unattributed at 17 March 1998 is regarded as referable to trust gains on disposals in the transitional period and is deducted from the amount that would otherwise fall to be treated as gains of the settlor for 1999/2000 under (*a*)–(*c*) above. Only so much of any capital payment or trust gains as is properly referable to property originating from the settlor in question is to be taken into account for this purpose, any necessary apportionments being made on a just and reasonable basis. These provisions interact with those of *TCGA 1992, s 87(3)* (see 43.13 below) under which trust gains potentially chargeable on beneficiaries are reduced by amounts chargeable on settlors of the settlement.

[*FA 1998, s 132(6), Sch 23*].

43.11 **Right of recovery.** Where a charge is made on a settlor, any tax he pays as a result may be recovered by him from any person who is a trustee of the settlement. For this purpose, the settlor may require certificated proof from the Revenue of the amount of the gains concerned and the amount of tax paid. [*TCGA 1992, Sch 5 para 6*].

For the Revenue's practice in this area, see Revenue Pamphlet IR 131, SP 5/92, paras 7–10 and ICAEW guidance note TAX 20/92, 14 December 1992, paras 5, 6 and 24–26.

Revenue information powers. The Revenue can by notice require a trustee, beneficiary or settlor to provide, within a specified time limit of at least 28 days beginning with the day the notice is given, particulars they think necessary for the purposes of these provisions. PENALTIES (47.7) under *TMA 1970, s 98* apply for failure. [*TCGA 1992, Sch 5 para 10*].

43.12 **Interaction with other provisions.** 'The trust gains for the year' of *TCGA 1992, s 87(2)* (gains of overseas resident settlements chargeable on beneficiaries — see 43.13 below) and the 'Schedule 4B trust gains' of *TCGA 1992, Sch 4C* (gains chargeable on beneficiaries accruing on transfer of value linked with borrowing by trustees of overseas resident settlement — see 43.18 below) are reduced by the amount or the aggregate of the amounts chargeable on the settlor under the provisions in 43.4 above. [*TCGA 1992, s 87(3), Sch 4C paras 3, 6; FA 2000, s 92(4)(5), Sch 26 para 1*]. Where amounts chargeable on the settlor are so chargeable by virtue of *TCGA 1992, s 10A* (charge on temporary non-residents — see 44.4 OVERSEAS MATTERS), there are provisions (see below) to prevent a double tax charge where gains have been charged on beneficiaries.

Both the 'charge on settlor' provisions at 43.4 above and the provisions of *TCGA 1992, ss 77–79* (charge on settlor with interest in UK resident settlement) contain a direction that the charge on the settlor is to be treated as the highest part of the amount on which he is chargeable to capital gains tax for a year of assessment. Where charges under both provisions apply to the same person in the same year, then the direction under *TCGA 1992, ss 77–79* takes effect subject to the similar direction under the provisions at 43.4 above. [*TCGA 1992, s 78(3)*].

Offset of losses and application of taper relief. The amount treated as accruing to the settlor under the provisions in 43.4 above will be net of TAPER RELIEF (60) where this is available. No further taper relief is available to the settlor. In addition, for 1998/99 and subsequent years of assessment, the settlor's own, untapered, losses, whether of the current year of assessment or brought forward from previous years, cannot be set off against gains treated as accruing to him as above. [*TCGA 1992, s 2(4)(5), s 86(4A); FA 1998, s 121(3)(4), Sch 21 paras 2, 6(2)*].

Settlor temporarily non-resident. Where a charge on a settlor arises under the provisions in 43.4 above by virtue of the charge under *TCGA 1992, s 10A* (the charge on individuals temporarily non-resident in the UK — see 44.4 OVERSEAS MATTERS) in the year of his return to the UK, there is a limitation on the amount to be so charged. The limitation applies if for any intervening year (i.e. any complete tax year between the 'year of departure' and the 'year of return' — see 44.4 OVERSEAS MATTERS), beneficiaries of the settlement were charged to tax in respect of any capital payments received by them from the settlement under *TCGA 1992, s 87* or *s 89(2)* (see 43.13 below) or *TCGA 1992, Sch 4C* (see 43.18 below).

Where the beneficiaries were charged to tax under *TCGA 1992, s 87* or *s 89(2)*, the limitation applies by reducing the amount falling within the charge on the settlor under these provisions for the intervening year (or years), and to be attributed to the settlor for the year of return, by the excess (if any) of the 'relevant chargeable amounts for the non-residence period' over the amount of the 'section 87 pool' at the end of the 'year of departure' (as defined in 44.4 OVERSEAS MATTERS and which must be 1997/98 or a subsequent year of assessment).

The '*relevant chargeable amounts for the non-residence period*' is the aggregate of the amounts on which beneficiaries of the settlement are charged to capital gains tax in respect of any capital payments received by them from the settlement under *TCGA 1992, s 87* or *s 89(2)* for the intervening year or years. The '*section 87 pool*' at the end of a year of assessment is the amount (if any), under that section, of 'the trust gains for the year' (see 43.13 below) which are to be carried forward from that year to be included in the amount of the trust gains for the immediately following year of assessment. In calculating the above amounts, where the settlement property has at any time included property not originating from the settlor, only so much (if any) of any capital payment or amount of trust gains for the year carried forward as, on a just and reasonable apportionment, is properly referable to property originating from the settlor (see 43.8 above) is taken into account.

These provisions interact with those of *TCGA 1992, s 87(3)* (see 43.13 below) under which trust gains potentially chargeable on beneficiaries are reduced by amounts chargeable on settlors of the settlement.

[*TCGA 1992, s 86A; FA 1998, s 129(1)(3)*].

Where the beneficiaries were charged to tax under *TCGA 1992, Sch 4C*, the provisions of *TCGA 1992, s 86A* above do not apply. Instead, the limitation applies by taking the amount of the gains accruing under *TCGA 1992, Sch 4B* (see 57.13 SETTLEMENTS) which fall within the charge on the settlor under these provisions for the intervening years, and which are to be attributed to the settlor for the year of return, and reducing it by the total of the amounts on which beneficiaries of the transferor or transferee settlements (see 43.18 below) were charged to tax under *TCGA 1992, Sch 4C* in respect of those gains for all the intervening years. In calculating the amount on which the beneficiaries have been so charged to tax, where the property comprised in the transferor settlement has at any time included property not originating from the settlor, only so much (if any) of any capital payment taken into account for the purposes of *TCGA 1992, Sch 4C* as, on a just and reasonable apportionment, is properly referable to property originating from the settlor (see 43.8 above) is taken into account.

[*TCGA 1992, Sch 4C paras 1, 12; FA 2000, Sch 26 para 1*].

43.13 **CHARGE ON BENEFICIARY IN RESPECT OF CAPITAL PAYMENTS RECEIVED FROM SETTLEMENT**

A 'beneficiary' of an overseas resident settlement is liable to capital gains tax on the gains of the settlement in the following circumstances.

- The trustees must be neither resident nor ordinarily resident in the UK (see 43.1 above) during any part of the year of assessment.
- The beneficiary must be domiciled in the UK at some time during the year of assessment.
- There must be 'trust gains for the year'.
- The beneficiary must have received 'capital payments' from the trustees.

For 1996/97 and earlier years, and also for any subsequent year as regards gains and losses accruing to the trustees **before 17 March 1998** and capital payments received by beneficiaries before that date, these provisions applied **only** if (in addition to the above conditions being satisfied) the 'settlor', or one of the settlors, either at some time during the tax year in question or when the settlement was made, was domiciled and either resident or ordinarily resident in the UK. (A settlement arising under a will or intestacy is treated as made by the testator or intestate at the time of his death.)

[*TCGA 1992, s 87(1)(2)(4)(7)(9)(10); FA 1998, s 130(1)(3)(4), Sch 27 Pt III(30)*].

Note that the provisions of *TCGA 1992, Sch 4C* (see 43.18 below) apply in place of these provisions where capital payments are received by beneficiaries and are attributed to 'Schedule 4B trust gains' (as defined) accruing by virtue of a transfer of value by trustees linked to trustee borrowing (see 43.17 below). [*TCGA 1992, Sch 4C para 1(2); FA 2000, s 92(4)(5), Sch 26 para 1*].

'*Settlement*' and '*settlor*' are defined by the references in *ICTA 1988, s 660G(1)(2)* (see 14.7 CONNECTED PERSONS) and 'settled property' is construed accordingly and as regards 'settlor' includes, in the case of a settlement arising under a will or intestacy, the testator or intestate. [*TCGA 1992, s 97(7); FA 1995, Sch 17 para 30*]. In a case where a residuary legatee (who was domiciled, resident and ordinarily resident in the UK) settled the unadministered residue of the estate of a testator (who was domiciled, resident and ordinarily resident outside the UK) under a deed of family arrangement within *TCGA 1992, s 62(6)* (see 16.6 DEATH), it was held that the legatee was the settlor for the purposes of *TCGA 1992, s 87* (*Marshall v Kerr HL 1994, 67 TC 56*).

'*Beneficiary*' is not otherwise defined, but in any case where:

(1) at any time after 18 March 1991 a capital payment is received from the trustees of a settlement or is treated as so received by virtue of *TCGA 1992, s 96(1)* (see below under Payments by and to companies);

(2) it is received by a person, or treated as received by a person by virtue of *TCGA 1992, s 96(2)–(5)* (see below under Payments by and to companies);

(3) at the time it is received or treated as received, the person is not otherwise a beneficiary of the settlement; and

(4) certain exceptions do not apply;

then for the purposes of *TCGA 1992, ss 87–90* (for which see further below) and *TCGA 1992, Sch 4C* (see 43.18 below) the person is treated as a beneficiary of the settlement as regards events occurring on or after that time. The first exception is where a payment within (1) above is made in circumstances where it is treated (otherwise than under the provision in the last sentence) as received by a beneficiary. The second exception is where the trustees of the settlement concerned or trustees of any other settlement are beneficiaries of the settlement concerned. [*TCGA 1992, s 97(8)–(10); FA 2000, s 92(4)(5), Sch 26 para 4*].

The trust gains for a year of assessment are treated as chargeable gains accruing in that year to beneficiaries of the settlement who receive capital payments from the trustees in that year or have received such payments in any earlier year, such attribution being made in proportion to, but not exceeding, the amounts of capital payments received by them. A capital payment is left out of account for these purposes to the extent that chargeable gains have by reason of the payment been treated as accruing to the recipient in an earlier year. A capital payment is also left out of account to the extent that chargeable gains have, by reason of it, been treated as accruing to the recipient under *TCGA 1992, Sch 4C* (see 43.18 below). [*TCGA 1992, s 87(4)–(6), Sch 4C para 9(1); FA 2000, s 92(4)(5), Sch 26 para 1*].

Note that the trust gains for a year are attributed to capital payments in priority to any 'Schedule 4B trust gains' (as defined for the purpose of the charge on beneficiaries receiving capital payments where trustees have made a transfer of value linked with trustee borrowing — see 43.18 below). [*TCGA 1992, Sch 4C para 8(2); FA 2000, s 92(4)(5), Sch 26 para 1*].

'*Trust gains for the year*'. This is an amount which is the aggregate of

(i) an amount computed for the current year, being the amount which would have been chargeable on the trustees under *TCGA 1992, s 2(2)* (i.e. chargeable gains less current year and brought forward losses), had they been resident or ordinarily resident in the UK in that year; and

(ii) the corresponding amount for any earlier year(s) (1981/82 onwards) which has not yet been attributed under *TCGA 1992, s 87(4)* (see above) or *TCGA 1992, s 89(2)* (see below under Migrant settlements) to beneficiaries.

[*TCGA 1992, s 87(2)*].

Example

T and M are the only beneficiaries under a Jersey settlement set up by their grandfather.

T is resident in the UK but M is neither resident nor ordinarily resident in the UK. Both beneficiaries have a UK domicile. In 1999/2000, the trustees sell shares realising a chargeable gain of £102,000. No disposals are made in 2000/01.

The trustees make capital payments of £60,000 to M in 1999/2000. In 2000/01 they make capital payments of £60,000 to T and £10,000 to M.

1999/2000	£
Trust gains	102,000
Capital payment	60,000
Trust gains carried forward	£42,000

M has chargeable gains of £60,000 but is not subject to CGT.

2000/01	£
Trust gains (brought forward)	42,000
Capital payments (£60,000 + £10,000)	70,000
Balance of capital payments carried forward	£28,000

The chargeable gains are apportioned as follows

	£
T $\dfrac{60,000}{70,000} \times$ £42,000	36,000
M $\dfrac{10,000}{70,000} \times$ £42,000 (not assessable)	6,000
	£42,000

The capital payments carried forward are apportioned as follows

	£
T £60,000 – £36,000	24,000
M £10,000 – £6,000	4,000
	£28,000

Where as regards the same settlement and for the same year of assessment chargeable gains, whether of one amount or of two or more amounts, are treated as accruing by virtue of *TCGA 1992, s 86(4)* (offshore settlement where settlor has interest — see 43.4 above), and an amount falls to be computed under *TCGA 1992, s 87(2)* above, the amount so computed is treated as reduced by the amount, or aggregate of the amounts, mentioned in 43.4 above. [*TCGA 1992, s 87(3)*]. In addition, in computing an amount under *TCGA 1992, s 87(2)* for years of assessment after 1990/91, the effect of *TCGA 1992, ss 77–79* (charge on settlor with interest in UK resident settlement — see 57.3 SETTLEMENTS) is ignored. (The interaction between these two charging provisions is not explicitly stated for 1988/89, 1989/90 and 1990/91 but in *De Rothschild v Lawrenson CA 1995, 67 TC 300*, it was held that a practically similar position applied for those years.) [*TCGA 1992, s 87(8)*].

Where a loss accrues to the trustees in a year of assessment for which these provisions apply, or *CGTA 1979, s 17* applied (see 43.20 below), the loss is allowable against gains accruing to the trustees in any later year (1981/82 onwards) insofar as it has not previously been set against gains for the purpose of a computation under these provisions, those of *CGTA 1979, s 17* or otherwise. [*TCGA 1992, s 97(6)*].

'*Capital payments*'. These are any 'payments' received after 9 March 1981 which either are not chargeable to income tax on the 'recipient' (formerly 'beneficiary' for payments etc. before 19 March 1991), or, in the case of a recipient neither resident nor ordinarily resident in the UK, are payments received otherwise than as income. However, payments received *after 9 March 1981 and before 6 April 1984* and which represent chargeable gains accruing to the trustees *before 6 April 1981* are dealt with under the previous legislation (see 43.20 below), subject to provisions which avoid double taxation. For payments received after 18 March 1991, a capital payment does not include a payment under a transaction entered into at arm's length. [*TCGA 1992, s 87(10), s 97(1); FA 1995, Sch 17 para 30*].

A beneficiary is regarded as having received a capital payment from the trustees where

- the beneficiary receives the payment from them, whether directly or indirectly;
- the trustees, directly or indirectly, apply the payment in settlement of any of the beneficiary's debts, or it is otherwise paid or applied for his benefit; or
- a third party receives it at the beneficiary's direction.

[*TCGA 1992, s 97(5)*].

'*Payment*' includes the transfer of an asset and the conferring of any other benefit. It also includes any occasion where settled property becomes property to which *TCGA 1992, s 60* applies (e.g. property held by nominees or on bare trusts for persons absolutely entitled). [*TCGA 1992, s 97(2)*]. A benefit treated (in whole or in part), under *ICTA 1988, s 740(2)(b)* (transfer of assets abroad: liability of non-transferors on benefits received — see TOLLEY'S INCOME TAX under Anti-Avoidance), as the recipient's income for a year of assessment *later* than the year of receipt, is not precluded from being treated as a capital payment in relation to any year *prior* to the year of assessment for which it is treated as income. It cannot, however, be treated as a capital payment in relation to the year for which it is treated as income, or in relation to any *subsequent* year. [*TCGA 1992, s 97(3)*].

The amount of capital payment made by way of loan, and of any other capital payment which is not an outright payment of money, is to be taken as the value of the benefit conferred by it. [*TCGA 1992, s 97(4)*]. Where trustees made loans which were repayable on demand they conferred a continuing benefit on the borrower by leaving the loans outstanding for any period, and were thus making annual capital payments, which were taken in this case to be equal to the interest that would have been payable had the loans (interest-free in this case) been taken from a commercial lender (*Billingham v Cooper; Edwards v Fisher Ch D, [2000] STC 122*).

A beneficiary would not be chargeable if he was neither resident nor ordinarily resident (despite being domiciled) in the UK for the year of assessment in question under the general rules of *TCGA 1992, s 2(1)* (see 44.1 OVERSEAS MATTERS). Thus, in respect of capital payments received by a beneficiary in these circumstances, whilst trust gains are attributed to those capital payments, no charge to tax can be made in respect of them.

As regards capital payments received by UK charities as beneficiaries, see 10.3 CHARITIES.

For allowable expenditure on a subsequent disposal of an asset transferred to a beneficiary, see 40.1 MARKET VALUE. Where beneficiaries resident or ordinarily resident in the UK became absolutely entitled to settled property (see 57.9 SETTLEMENTS) after 5 April 1982 and before 14 March 1989 hold-over relief was available as in 25.9 HOLD-OVER RELIEFS (Tolley's Practical Tax 1984 p 25). By analogy, the other current HOLD-OVER RELIEFS (25) would be available in such circumstances (provided all the conditions for the relief in question are met).

Offset of losses and application of taper relief. The amount treated as accruing to the beneficiary under the above provisions will be net of TAPER RELIEF (60) where this is available. No further taper relief is available to the beneficiary. In addition, for 1998/99 and subsequent years of assessment, the beneficiary's own, untapered, losses, whether of the current year of assessment or brought forward from previous years, cannot be set off against gains treated as accruing to him as above. [*TCGA 1992, s 2(4)(5), s 87(6A); FA 1998, s 121(3)(4), Sch 21 paras 2, 6(3)*].

Dual resident settlements. *TCGA 1992, s 87* above also applies to a settlement for years of assessment beginning after 1990/91 if the trustees are resident in the UK during any part of the year or ordinarily resident in the UK during the year *and* at any time of such residence or ordinary residence they fall to be regarded for the purposes of a double tax agreement as resident overseas. For 1996/97 and earlier years, and also for any subsequent year as regards gains and losses accruing to the trustees **before 17 March 1998** and capital payments received by beneficiaries before that date, these provisions applied **only** if (in addition to the above conditions being satisfied) the settlor, or one of the settlors, either at some time during the tax year in question or when the settlement was made, was domiciled and either resident or ordinarily resident in the UK.

In the above circumstances, *TCGA 1992, s 87* is to have effect for every year of assessment as if the amount to be computed under *TCGA 1992, s 87(2)* (see (i) above) were 'the assumed chargeable amount'; and the reference in *TCGA 1992, s 87(2)* to 'the corresponding amount' in respect of any earlier year(s) (see (ii) above) is to be construed as a reference to the amount computed under *TCGA 1992, s 87(2)* apart from this provision (*TCGA 1992, s 88*) or (as the case may be) the amount computed under *TCGA 1992, s 87(2)* by virtue of this provision.

'*The assumed chargeable amount*' in respect of a year of assessment is the lesser of: the amount on which the trustees would be chargeable to tax for the year under *TCGA 1992, s 2(2)* on the assumption that the double tax relief arrangements did not apply; and the amount on which, by virtue of disposals of protected assets, the trustees would be chargeable to tax for the year under *TCGA 1992, s 2(2)* on the assumption that those arrangements did not apply. Assets are '*protected assets*' if they are of a description specified in the double tax relief arrangements, and were the trustees to dispose of them at any 'relevant time', the trustees would fall to be regarded for the purposes of the arrangements as not liable in the UK to tax on gains accruing to them on the disposal. For the purposes of this definition of protected assets: the second assumption in the first sentence of this paragraph is ignored; '*the relevant time*' is any time, in the year of assessment concerned, when the trustees fall to be regarded for the purposes of the arrangements as resident overseas; and if different assets are identified by reference to different relevant times, all of them are protected assets. In computing the assumed chargeable amount in respect of a particular year of assessment, the effect of *TCGA 1992, ss 77–79* (charge on settlor with interest in UK resident settlement — see 57.3 SETTLEMENTS) is ignored. For the purposes of *TCGA 1992, s 87* as it applies by virtue of this provision, capital payments received before 6 April 1991 are disregarded.

[*TCGA 1992, s 88; FA 1998, s 130(2)–(4), Sch 27 Pt III(30)*].

Migrant settlements. A capital payment (see above) made to a beneficiary in a period of one or more years of assessment 'for each of which *TCGA 1992, s 87* above does not apply to the settlement' (formerly 'in each of which the trustees were at some time resident or ordinarily resident in the UK' before 25 July 1991) (a '*resident period*') is disregarded provided that the payment is not anticipatory of a disposal by the trustees in a succeeding period of one or more years of assessment for which *TCGA 1992, s 87* applies to the settlement (a '*non-resident period*'). Where a resident period follows a non-resident period and part or whole of the trust gains for the last year of the non-resident period have not yet been apportioned and charged to beneficiaries, the outstanding trust gains are, to the extent, each year, that the beneficiaries receive capital payments, apportioned and charged to them for the first year of the resident period and so on for successive years, until the outstanding gains are exhausted. [*TCGA 1992, s 89(2)*]. *TCGA 1992, s 87(5)(7)* is applied to *TCGA 1992, s 89(2)* as it applies to *TCGA 1992, s 87(4)*. [*TCGA 1992, s 89(3)*].

Offset of losses and application of taper relief. The amount treated as accruing to the beneficiary under the above provisions will be net of TAPER RELIEF (60) where this is available. No further taper relief is available to the beneficiary. In addition, for 1998/99 and subsequent years of assessment, the beneficiary's own, untapered, losses, whether of the current year of assessment or brought forward from previous years, cannot be set off against gains treated as accruing to him as above. [*TCGA 1992, s 2(4)(5), s 87(6A), s 89(3); FA 1998, s 121(3)(4), Sch 21 paras 2, 6(4)*].

Transfers between settlements. There are provisions for the carry-over of unattributed trust gains under *TCGA 1992, s 87* or *s 89(2)* (apportioned where necessary), in cases where transfers of settled property are made from one settlement to another other than for consideration in money or money's worth. If neither of the last mentioned provisions would otherwise apply to the transferee settlement for the year of transfer, *TCGA 1992, s 89(2)* is deemed to apply to it as if the year were the first year of a resident period following a non-resident period, and the trust gains equal to the trust gains for the last year of the non-resident period. These provisions do not apply to a transfer treated as linked with trustee borrowing, or to any chargeable gain arising, under *TCGA 1992, Sch 4B* (transfers of value by trustees linked with trustee borrowing — see 57.13 SETTLEMENTS). [*TCGA 1992, s 90; FA 2000, s 92(4)(5), Sch 26 para 2*].

Payments by and to companies. By virtue of *TCGA 1992, s 96(1)*, where a capital payment is received after 18 March 1991 from a 'qualifying company' which is 'controlled' by the trustees of a settlement at the time it is received, it is treated for the purposes of *TCGA 1992, ss 87–90* above and (for capital payments received after 20 March 2000) *TCGA 1992, Sch 4C* (see 43.18 below) as received from the trustees. A '*qualifying company*' is a close company within *ICTA 1988, ss 414, 415* or a company which would be a close company if it were UK resident. For this purpose, a company is 'controlled' by the trustees of a settlement if it is 'controlled' by the trustees alone or by the trustees together with a person who (or persons each of whom) is a settlor in relation to the settlement or is connected (see 14 CONNECTED PERSONS) with such a settlor. '*Control*' is to be construed in accordance with *ICTA 1988, s 416* except that for this purpose no rights or powers of (or attributed to) an associate or associates of a person are attributed to him under *ICTA 1988, s 416(6)* if he is not a participator (within *ICTA 1988, s 417(1)*) in the company. By concession, a beneficiary in the settlement is not to be regarded as a participator in the company solely by virtue of his status as beneficiary (Revenue Pamphlet IR 1, D40).

By virtue of *TCGA 1992, s 96(2)–(5), w*here a capital payment is received after 18 March 1991 from trustees of a settlement (or treated as so received under the foregoing) and it is received by a '*non-resident qualifying company*' (i.e. a company which is not resident in the UK and would be a close company if it were so resident), the following provisions apply for the purposes of *TCGA 1992, ss 87–90* above and (for capital payments received after 20 March 2000) *TCGA 1992, Sch 4C* (see 43.18 below).

If the company is 'controlled' (construed as above) by one person alone at the time the payment is received, and that person is (or is deemed to be) then resident or ordinarily resident in the UK, it is treated as a capital payment received by that person.

If the company is controlled by two or more persons (taking each one separately) at the time the payment is received, then: if one of them is (or is deemed to be) then resident or ordinarily resident in the UK, it is treated as a capital payment received by that person; and if two or more persons are (or are deemed to be) then resident or ordinarily resident in the UK ('*the residents*') it is treated as being as many equal capital payments as there are residents and each of them is treated as receiving one of the payments.

If the company is controlled by two or more persons (taking them together) at the time the payment is received and, where the payment is received before 21 March 2000, each of them is (or is deemed to be) then resident or ordinarily resident in the UK: it is treated as being as many capital payments as there are participators in the company at the time it is received; and each such participator (whatever his residence or ordinary residence) is treated as receiving one of the payments, quantified on the basis of just and reasonable apportionment. But where a participator would otherwise be treated as receiving less than 5% of the payment actually received by the company, he is not treated as receiving anything by virtue of the foregoing.

For the Revenue's practice in this area, see SP 5/92, paras 38–40.

For the above purposes, an *individual* is deemed to be resident in the UK at any time in any year of assessment which is an intervening year for the purposes of the charge to capital gains tax on temporary non-residents (see 44.4 OVERSEAS MATTERS). Where it appears after the end of a year of assessment that this does apply to an individual and consequential adjustments are required to the amounts of tax chargeable on any person under the above provisions, no time limits for making any assessment or claim prevent the making of those adjustments (whether by assessment, amended assessment, tax repayment or otherwise). [*TCGA 1992, s 96; FA 1998, s 127(3); FA 2000, s 92(4)(5), s 95, Sch 26 para 3*].

Revenue information powers. The Board may, by notice in writing, require any person, within such time as it directs (not less than 28 days), to furnish it with such particulars as it thinks necessary for the purposes of *TCGA 1992, ss 87–90* above and *TCGA 1992, Sch 4C* (see 43.18 below). The very wide information powers of *ICTA 1988, s 745(2)–(5)*, suitably adapted, are also expressly stated to apply. [*TCGA 1992, s 98; FA 2000, s 92(4)(5), s 95, Sch 26 para 5*].

43.14 FURTHER CHARGE ON BENEFICIARY IN RESPECT OF CAPITAL PAYMENTS RECEIVED FROM SETTLEMENT

Further provisions apply as regards the regime of provisions in 43.13 above for taxing beneficiaries of overseas resident settlements. They provide for an increased tax charge on the beneficiary in certain cases.

The provisions apply where

(*a*) a 'capital payment' (see 43.13 above) is made by the trustees of a settlement after 5 April 1992;

(*b*) the payment is made in a year of assessment for which *TCGA 1992, s 87* applies to the settlement or in circumstances where *TCGA 1992, s 89(2)* treats chargeable gains as accruing in respect of the payment;

(*c*) the whole payment is matched with a 'qualifying amount' of the settlement for a year of assessment falling at some time before that immediately preceding the one in which the payment is made (but see 43.15 below for the application of the provisions where a capital payment is matched with more than one qualifying amount, only part of a capital payment is matched with a qualifying amount, or a payment or part of a payment is matched with part of a qualifying amount); and

(*d*) a beneficiary is charged to tax in respect of the payment by virtue of *TCGA 1992, s 87* or *s 89(2)*.

In the above circumstances the tax payable by the beneficiary in respect of the payment is increased by the amount found below, except that it cannot be increased beyond the amount of the payment.

The amount is equal to the interest that would be yielded if an amount equal to the tax which would be otherwise payable by him in respect of the payment carried interest for 'the chargeable period' at the rate of 10% per annum. The percentage may be amended by Treasury Order.

'*The chargeable period*' is the period which begins with the later of 1 December in the year of assessment following that for which the qualifying amount mentioned in (*c*) above is the qualifying amount and 1 December falling six years before 1 December in the year of assessment following that in which the capital payment is made, and ends with 30 November in the year of assessment following that in which the capital payment is made.

In arriving, for the above purposes, at the amount of CGT payable by the beneficiary in respect of the capital payment, that payment is deemed to form the lowest slice of the beneficiary's total gains (Revenue Helpsheet IR 301 p 1). Therefore, it may, for example, be reduced by the annual exemption.

Qualifying amounts. If *TCGA 1992, s 87* applies to a settlement for the year 1991/92 or a subsequent year of assessment, the settlement has a qualifying amount for the year, and that amount is the amount computed for the settlement in respect of the year concerned under *TCGA 1992, s 87(2)* (i.e. the amount in 43.13(i) above).

If *TCGA 1992, s 87* applied to a settlement for the year 1990/91, the settlement had a '*qualifying amount*' for the year, and that amount was the amount constituting the 'trust gains for the year' (see 43.13 above) less so much of them as were by virtue of *TCGA 1992, s 87* treated as chargeable gains accruing in that year to the beneficiaries.

A qualifying amount for 1990/91 is also determined where

(i) there was a period ('*a non-resident period*') of one or more years of assessment for each of which *TCGA 1992, s 87* applied to a settlement and each of which fell before the year 1990/91;

(ii) *TCGA 1992, s 87* did not apply to the settlement for the year 1990/91; and

(iii) there were trust gains for the last year of the non-resident period which were not (or were not wholly) treated by virtue of *TCGA 1992, s 87* or *s 89(2)* as chargeable gains accruing to beneficiaries before the year 1990/91.

In such a case the settlement had a qualifying amount for the year 1990/91 of the amount constituting the trust gains mentioned in (iii) above (or the outstanding part of them) less so much of them as were by virtue of *TCGA 1992, s 87(2)* treated as chargeable gains accruing in that year to beneficiaries.

Matching capital payments. Where capital payments are made by the trustees of a settlement after 5 April 1991 and the payments are made in a year or years of assessment for which *TCGA 1992, s 87* applies to the settlement or in circumstances where *TCGA 1992, s 89(2)* treats chargeable gains as accruing in respect of the payments, the payments are matched with qualifying amounts of the settlement for the year 1990/91 and subsequent years of assessment (so far as the amounts are not already matched with payments by virtue of this provision). Payments are matched with qualifying amounts so that: earlier payments are matched with earlier amounts; payments are carried forward to be matched with future amounts (so far as not matched with past amounts); a payment which is less than an unmatched amount (or part) is matched to the extent of the payment; and a payment which is more than an unmatched amount (or part) is matched, as to the excess, with other unmatched amounts.

Where part only of a capital payment is taxable, the part which is not taxable does not fall to be matched until taxable parts of other capital payments (if any) made in the same year of assessment have been matched, and the provisions in the paragraph above have effect accordingly. For this purpose a part of a capital payment is taxable if the part results in chargeable gains accruing under *TCGA 1992, s 87* or *s 89(2)*.

See 43.15 and 43.16 below for matching in certain special cases. For an example of matching, see Tolley's Tax Computations or Tolley's Capital Gains Tax Workbook.

[*TCGA 1992, ss 91, 92*].

43.15 **Matching: special cases.** Where, applying the matching rules in 43.14 above, a capital payment is matched with more than one qualifying amount, only part of the capital payment is matched with a qualifying amount, or a payment or part of a payment is matched with part of a qualifying amount (so that condition (*c*) at 43.14 above is not strictly met), the further charge in 43.14 above applies as follows.

More than one qualifying amount. Where the whole capital payment is matched with qualifying amounts of the settlement for different years of assessment, each falling at some time before that immediately preceding the one in which the payment is made, the capital payment ('*the main payment*') is treated as being as many payments ('*subsidiary payments*') as there are qualifying amounts. A qualifying amount is attributed to each subsidiary payment and each payment is quantified accordingly, and the tax in respect of the main payment is divided up and attributed to the subsidiary payment on the basis of a just and reasonable apportionment. The provisions in 43.14 above then apply in the case of each subsidiary payment, the qualifying amount attributed to it and the tax attributed to it.

Payment partly ignored. Where part of the capital payment is matched with a qualifying amount of the settlement for a year of assessment falling at some time before that immediately preceding the one in which the payment is made, or with qualifying amounts of the settlement for different years of assessment each so falling, only the tax in respect of so much of the payment as is so matched is taken into account, and references below to the tax are to be construed accordingly. The capital payment is divided into two, the first part representing so much as is matched as mentioned above and the second so much as is not. The second part is ignored, and the first part is treated as a capital payment, the whole of which is matched with the qualifying amount or amounts mentioned above, and the whole of which is charged to tax. The provisions in 43.14 above and the above provisions relating to the matching of a payment with more than one qualifying amount (as the case may be) are then applied in the case of the capital payment divided as above, the qualifying amount or amounts, and the tax.

Parts of amounts matched. The above provisions and the provisions in 43.14 above apply (with suitable modifications) where a payment or part of a payment is to any extent matched with part of an amount.

[*TCGA 1992, s 93*].

43.16 **Transfers between settlements.** For the purposes of the provisions at 43.14 and 43.15 above, the following applies if: in the year 1990/91 or a subsequent year of assessment the trustees of a settlement ('*the transferor settlement*') transfer all or part of the settled property to the trustees of another settlement ('*the transferee settlement*'), and looking at the state of affairs at the end of the year of assessment in which the transfer is made, there is a qualifying amount of the transferor settlement for a particular year of assessment ('*the year concerned*') and the amount is not (or not wholly) matched with capital payments.

In the above circumstances, if the whole of the settled property is transferred, the transferor settlement's qualifying amount for the year concerned is treated as reduced by so much of it as is not matched, and so much of that amount as is not matched is treated as (or as an addition to) the transferee settlement's qualifying amount for the year concerned.

If, in the above circumstances, only part of the settled property is transferred, so much of the transferor settlement's qualifying amount for the year concerned as is not matched is apportioned on a just and reasonable basis, part being attributed to the transferred property and part to the property not transferred. The transferor settlement's qualifying amount for the year concerned is treated as reduced by the part attributed to the transferred property; and that part is treated as (or as an addition to) the transferee settlement's qualifying amount for the year concerned.

If the transferee settlement did not in fact exist in the year concerned, then it is treated as having been made at the beginning of that year. If the transferee settlement did in fact exist in the year concerned, the foregoing provisions are to apply whether or not *TCGA 1992, s 87* applies to the settlement for that year or for any year of assessment falling before that year.

Matching after transfer. In the case of a transferee settlement, matching is to be made in accordance with the provisions in 43.14 and 43.15 above by reference to the state of affairs existing immediately before the beginning of the year of assessment in which the transfer is made, and the transfer is not to affect matching so made. Subject to this, payments are matched with amounts in accordance with the provisions in 43.14 and 43.15 above and by reference to amounts arrived at under the 'transfer between settlements' provisions above.

[*TCGA 1992, ss 94, 95*].

43.17 ANTI-AVOIDANCE: TRANSFERS OF VALUE BY TRUSTEES LINKED WITH TRUSTEE BORROWING

See 57.13 SETTLEMENTS for provisions deeming chargeable gains to arise to trustees of a settlement where they make a 'transfer of value' (as defined). Where the trustees are at no time in the tax year in which the transfer of value is made resident or ordinarily resident in the UK or they are treated as non-resident under double tax relief arrangements, the resulting gains are, in certain circumstances, chargeable either on the settlor (see 43.4 above) or on beneficiaries who receive capital payments under *TCGA 1992, Sch 4C* (see 43.18 below). Note that the latter provisions apply in place of, but with broadly similar effect to, the provisions of 43.13 and 43.14 above (and for the interaction of *TCGA 1992, Sch 4C* with those provisions see 43.18 below).

43.18 TRANSFERS OF VALUE: ATTRIBUTION OF GAINS TO BENEFICIARIES

The provisions described below apply where in any tax year a chargeable gain or allowable loss accrues under *TCGA 1992, Sch 4B* (see 57.13 SETTLEMENTS) to trustees of a 'settlement' 'within *TCGA 1992, s 87*' in respect of a 'transfer of value' (within 57.13 SETTLEMENTS) made after 20 March 2000. They apply in place of the provisions of *TCGA 1992, ss 87-95* (the normal provisions attributing gains to beneficiaries receiving capital payments from offshore settlements — see 43.13 above), so that

- in computing the trust gains for a tax year in accordance with *TCGA 1992, ss 87-89* no account is taken of any such chargeable gain or allowable loss; and
- in computing the 'Schedule 4B trust gains' (see below) in accordance with these provisions, no account is taken of any chargeable gain or allowable loss to which *TCGA 1992, ss 87-89* apply.

For this purpose a '*settlement*' (defined by the references in *ICTA 1988, s 660G(1)(2)* — see 14.7 CONNECTED PERSONS) is '*within TCGA 1992, s 87*' for a tax year if in that year the trustees are at no time resident or ordinarily resident in the UK or they fall to be regarded for the purpose of any DOUBLE TAX RELIEF (18) arrangements as resident outside the UK.

Schedule 4B trust gains computed as below and relating to a transfer of value by trustees of such a settlement are treated as chargeable gains accruing to 'beneficiaries' of the 'transferor settlement' (being the settlement the trustees of which made the transfer of value) or of any 'transferee settlement' (i.e. any settlement of which the settled property includes property representing, directly or indirectly, the proceeds of the transfer of value), who

- receive 'capital payments' (as defined by *TCGA 1992, s 97(1)* — see 43.13 above) from the trustees in the tax year in which the transfer of value is made, or
- have received such payments in any earlier year,

to the extent that such payments exceed the amount of any gains attributed to the beneficiaries under *TCGA 1992, s 87(4)* or *s 89(2)* (see 43.13 above). Any Schedule 4B trust gains remaining are carried forward to the following tax year and treated as if they were gains from a transfer of value made in that year.

A capital payment is left out of account to the extent that chargeable gains have, by reason of it, been treated as accruing to the recipient in an earlier year of assessment. Capital payments received before 21 March 2000 or before the tax year preceding that in which the transfer of value is made are also disregarded.

The attribution of chargeable gains to beneficiaries is made in proportion to, but not exceeding, the amounts of the capital payments received by them. A beneficiary is not charged to tax on chargeable gains so treated as accruing to him in any year unless he is domiciled in the UK at some time in that year.

To the extent that chargeable gains have, by reason of a capital payment, been treated as accruing to the recipient under these provisions, the payment is left out of account for the purposes of *TCGA 1992, s 87(4)(5)* and *s 89(2)* (see 43.13 above).

For the above purposes, '*beneficiaries*' include

- persons who have ceased to be beneficiaries by the time the chargeable gains accrue, and
- persons who were beneficiaries of the settlement before it ceased to exist (where this is the case),

but who were beneficiaries of the settlement at a time in a previous tax year when a capital payment was made to them. See 43.13 above for a further circumstance in which, by virtue of *TCGA 1992, s 97(8)–(10)*, a person is treated as a beneficiary.

Payments by and to companies. See 43.13 above for the application of these provisions where capital payments are made by or to certain companies.

Residence of trustees from whom capital payment received. Subject to the following exception, it is immaterial for the purposes of the above provisions that the trustees of the transferor settlement, or any transferee settlement, are or have at any time been resident or ordinarily resident in the UK. A capital payment received by a beneficiary of a settlement from the trustees in a tax year during the whole of which the trustees are resident in the UK, or in which the trustees are ordinarily resident in the UK, is disregarded for the purposes of the above provisions if it was made before, but was not made in anticipation of, chargeable gains accruing under the provisions of *TCGA 1992, Sch 4B* or of a transfer of value being made to which those provisions apply. For these purposes, trustees are not regarded as resident or ordinarily resident in the UK at any time when they fall to be treated as resident outside the UK for the purposes of any double tax relief arrangements.

Application of taper relief. The amount treated as accruing to the beneficiary under the above provisions will be net of TAPER RELIEF (60) where this is available. No further taper relief is available to the beneficiary.

Revenue information powers. See 43.13 above for details of the Revenue's information powers in relation to the above provisions.

[*TCGA 1992, ss 85A, 97(7), Sch 4C paras 1, 2, 8–11, 14; FA 2000, s 92(3)–(5), Sch 26 paras 1, 4*].

Computation of Schedule 4B trust gains. The amount of the '*Schedule 4B trust gains*', which is to be computed for the above purposes in relation to each transfer of value, is given by

CA – SG – AL, where

CA = the 'chargeable amount' (see below),

SG = the amount of any gains attributed to the settlor (within the meaning below), and

AL = the amount of any allowable losses that may be deducted as described below.

Chargeable amount. If the transfer of value is made in a tax year during which the trustees of the transferor settlement are at no time resident or ordinarily resident in the UK, the '*chargeable amount*' is the amount on which the trustees would have been chargeable to CGT by virtue of *TCGA 1992, Sch 4B* (i.e. the chargeable gains, net of allowable losses, on the disposals deemed to occur at the time of the transfer of value — see 57.13 SETTLEMENTS) if they had been resident or ordinarily resident in the UK in the year.

If the transfer of value is made in a tax year where the trustees of the transferor settlement are treated as resident outside the UK for the purposes of any double tax relief arrangements at a time when they are, in fact, UK-resident or ordinarily resident, the chargeable amount is the lesser of

- the amount on which the trustees would be chargeable to CGT by virtue of *TCGA 1992, Sch 4B* on the assumption that the double tax relief arrangements did not apply, and
- the amount on which the trustees would be so chargeable to CGT by virtue of disposals of 'protected assets' (as defined by *TCGA 1992, s 88(4)* — see 43.13 above under Dual resident settlements).

In computing the chargeable amount the effect of *TCGA 1992, ss 77-79* (under which a settlor having an interest in a UK-resident settlement is chargeable on gains of the trustees in certain circumstances — see 57.3 SETTLEMENTS) is ignored.

Gains attributed to the settlor means any chargeable gains arising by virtue of the transfer of value that

(*a*) are treated as accruing to the settlor under *TCGA 1992, s 86(4)* (see 43.4 above), disregarding any losses arising otherwise than under *TCGA 1992, Sch 4B*, or

(*b*) where *TCGA 1992, s 10A* applies (charge on individuals temporarily non-resident in the UK — see 44.4 OVERSEAS MATTERS and also 43.12 above), are treated as accruing to the settlor in the year of his return to the UK.

Allowable losses. The allowable losses that may be deducted in arriving at the Schedule 4B trust gains in relation to a transfer of value by the trustees of a settlement are losses arising under *TCGA 1992, Sch 4B* in relation to other transfers of value by those trustees, and any such loss is deductible *only* in accordance with the following rules.

- The loss is deducted first from chargeable amounts arising from other transfers of value made in the same tax year.
- If there is more than one chargeable amount and the aggregate allowable losses is less than the aggregate chargeable amounts, each of the chargeable amounts is reduced proportionately.
- If in any tax year the aggregate allowable losses exceeds the aggregate chargeable amounts, the excess is carried forward to the following tax year and treated as if it were an allowable loss arising in relation to a transfer of value made in that following year.

Losses are deducted from chargeable amounts after any deduction for gains attributed to the settlor as above.

[*TCGA 1992, Sch 4C paras 3–7*].

43.19 **Increase in tax payable by beneficiary receiving capital payments.** Where

- a capital payment is made by the trustees of a settlement;
- chargeable gains are treated as accruing in respect of the payment under 43.18 above; and
- a beneficiary is accordingly charged to tax in respect of the payment,

the tax payable is increased by an amount equal to the interest that would be yielded if an amount equal to that tax carried interest for the 'chargeable period' at the rate specified in *TCGA 1992, s 91(3)* (i.e. 10% per annum — see 43.14 above), except that it cannot be increased beyond the amount of the payment.

The '*chargeable period*' is the period which

(*a*) begins with the later of

(i) 1 December in the tax year following that in which the transfer of value was made, and

(ii) 1 December falling 6 years before 1 December in the tax year following that in which the capital payment is made; and

(*b*) ends with 30 November in the tax year following that in which the capital payment is made.

[*TCGA 1992, Sch 4C para 13*].

43.20 **CHARGE ON BENEFICIARY IN RESPECT OF SETTLEMENT GAINS BEFORE 1981/82**

The provisions applied to chargeable gains accruing to the trustees of a settlement if the trustees were not resident and not ordinarily resident in the UK, and if the settlor (or any one of them) was domiciled and either resident or ordinarily resident in the UK when the gains accrued (or was domiciled and either resident or ordinarily resident in the UK when he made the settlement). Any beneficiary under the settlement who was domiciled and either resident or ordinarily resident in the UK during any year of assessment was treated as if an apportioned part of the amount, if any, on which the trustees would have been chargeable to capital gains tax (i.e. if domiciled and either resident or ordinarily resident in the UK in that year of assessment) had been chargeable gains accruing to the beneficiary in that year of assessment. The amount of such gains was apportionable in such manner as was 'just and reasonable' between persons having interests in the settled property, whether that interest was a life interest or an interest in reversion and so that, as near as maybe, the gains were apportioned according to the respective values of those interests, disregarding in the case of a defeasible interest the possibility of defeasance. [*CGTA 1979, s 17(1)(2)*].

Following *Ritchie v McKay Ch D 1984, 57 TC 719* it appears that losses accruing to trustees are treated similarly to the provisions outlined in 43.13 above.

Where in the three years ending with the year of the gain, a person had received a discretionary payment of income from the settlement, he was regarded as having an interest in the settled property of a value equal to that of an annuity of a yearly amount equal to one-third of the payments so received by him in that time. [*CGTA 1979, s 17(3)(a)*].

Where a person received at any time after the chargeable gain accrued (but before 6 April 1984) a capital payment out of the settled property in exercise of the trustee's discretion, insofar as it represented a chargeable gain which had accrued to the trustees before 6 April 1981 but which had not already been attributed to any other person domiciled and resident or ordinarily resident in the UK, that person (if domiciled and resident or ordinarily resident in the UK) was treated as if the chargeable gain (or part) represented by the capital payment had accrued to him at the time he received the capital payment. [*CGTA 1979, s 17(3)(b); FA 1984, s 70(2)*]. See *Ewart v Taylor Ch D 1983, 57 TC 401* and *Jones v Lincoln-Lewis and Others Ch D 1991, 64 TC 112.* Tax paid by the trustees was not regarded as a payment to the beneficiary. [*CGTA 1979, s 17(5)*]. Similar payments made after 5 April 1984 are dealt with under the present legislation (see 43.13 above) even where the payments represent chargeable gains which accrued to the trustees before 6 April 1981.

Where the settlement was made before 6 April 1965

(i) payment of the capital gains tax apportioned to a beneficiary in respect of an interest in reversion in any part of the trust capital could be postponed until that beneficiary became absolutely entitled or disposed of all or part of his interest unless he could, with or without the consent of another person, obtain any of the capital at an earlier date. [*CGTA 1979, s 17(4)(b); TCGA 1992, Sch 11 para 18(a)*].

(ii) a beneficiary who had an interest in income only and who could not, whether with or without the consent of another person, obtain any part of the capital of the settlement, was not within these provisions. [*CGTA 1979, s 17(4)(a)*].

'*Settlor*' and '*settlement*' were as defined in *ICTA 1970, s 454(3)* and settled property was construed accordingly. [*CGTA 1979, s 17(7)*].

In *Leedale v Lewis HL 1982, 56 TC 501* it was held that a discretionary interest was an interest in settled property and the direction that the gain should be apportioned 'as near as may be, according to the respective values of the interests' envisaged not a strict apportionment by reference to actuarial valuations but a much looser apportionment by reference to what was just and reasonable in view of the real probabilities under the particular settlement.

To mitigate the effect of this decision, legislation as summarised in 43.21 below allows postponement of tax due in certain circumstances.

43.21 POSTPONEMENT OF TAX DUE FROM BENEFICIARY IN RESPECT OF SETTLEMENT GAINS BEFORE 1981/82

Under certain circumstances, the UK beneficiary of an overseas resident settlement who has been assessed under *CGTA 1979, s 17* to capital gains tax on trust gains arising before 6 April 1981 (see 43.20 above) may postpone payment of that tax, without incurring further interest on unpaid tax, until he or a '*close relative*' (i.e. spouse, child or remoter descendant) of his obtains some benefit from the trust.

For the rules to apply, the following conditions must be satisfied.

(*a*) A chargeable gain accruing to an overseas resident settlement before 6 April 1981 falls within *CGTA 1979, s 17.*

(*b*) Under *CGTA 1979, s 17,* a beneficiary is assessed to capital gains tax on all or part of that gain for any year of assessment before 1984/85.

(*c*) Any of the capital gains tax thereby due had not been paid at 29 March 1983.

A claim to postpone payment had to be made before 1 July 1985 or, if later, within 30 days of the date of issue of a notice of assessment requiring payment.

For full details of the relief see the 1984/85 edition of Tolley's Capital Gains Tax where full coverage is given of the relevant provisions *viz. FA 1984, s 70, Sch 14* (which are preserved by *TCGA 1992, Sch 11 para 18(b)*).

43.22 INFORMATION REQUIRED TO BE RETURNED IN RESPECT OF SETTLEMENTS WITH A FOREIGN ELEMENT

With effect after 2 May 1994, there are extensive requirements for information relating to 'settlements with a foreign element' to be returned to the Revenue within certain time limits *without a notice to make a return having to be given by the Revenue.* PENALTIES (47.7) under *TMA 1970, s 98* apply for failure to comply although no failure will arise where information already has been returned or will be returned later under any other provision. In particular, the following requirements should be observed.

(*a*) Where property is transferred after 16 March 1998, otherwise than by way of an arm's length transaction or in pursuance of a liability incurred on or before that date, to a settlement created before 17 March 1998 which is non-UK resident at the time of transfer, a return of certain particulars must be made by the transferor within twelve months of the day ('the relevant day') of the transfer if he knows, or has reason to believe, the residence status of the settlement. (Before 17 March 1998, this requirement operated only in relation to transfers to settlements created before 19 March 1991.)

(*b*) Where a settlement is created at a time after 18 March 1991 which, at that time, is either non-UK resident or both UK resident and, under double tax relief arrangements, resident elsewhere, a return of certain particulars must be made by the settlor within twelve months of the day ('*the relevant day*') he first fulfils after 2 May 1994 the condition that he is UK domiciled and UK resident or ordinarily resident, not having met that condition at the time of the settlement's creation. Similarly, where such a settlement is created after 2 May 1994, a return of certain particulars must be made by the settlor who meets the above condition at the time of the settlement's creation within *three months* of the day ('*the relevant day*') on which the settlement was created.

(*c*) Where a settlement becomes at any time ('*the relevant time*') after 2 May 1994 non-UK resident or, whilst continuing to be UK resident becomes at any time ('*the relevant time*') after 2 May 1994, under double tax relief arrangements, resident elsewhere, a return of certain particulars must be made by a person who was a trustee immediately before the relevant time within *twelve months* of the day ('*the relevant day*') when the relevant time falls.

[*TCGA 1992, s 98A, Sch 5A; FA 1994, s 97(1)–(3)(6); FA 1998, Sch 22 para 5*].

Returns of information should be made to Financial Intermediaries and Claims Office (FICO) (Foreign Trusts Section), St John's House, Merton Road, Stanley Precinct, Bootle, Merseyside L69 9BB. Tel. 0151–472 6000.

44 Overseas Matters

Cross-references. See 6.2 ASSETS for location of assets; 17.4 DISPOSAL for acquisitions from persons neither resident nor ordinarily resident in the UK after 9 March 1981 and before 6 April 1985; 18 DOUBLE TAX RELIEF for relief which may be claimable and for double tax agreements which may override or amend statutory provisions; 25 HOLD-OVER RELIEFS for clawback of relief where transferee becomes before 19 March 1991 neither resident nor ordinarily resident in the UK; 40.1 MARKET VALUE for special market value rules which apply to disposals by persons neither resident nor ordinarily resident in the UK after 9 March 1981 and before 6 April 1985; 43 OFFSHORE SETTLEMENTS for provisions dealing with settlements whose trustees are, or become, neither resident nor ordinarily resident in the UK; 45.4 PARTNERSHIPS for partnerships controlled and managed abroad; 52 RESIDENCE AND DOMICILE for the determination of a person's residence, ordinary residence and domicile status; 57.3 SETTLEMENTS for the residence status of settlements; and 63.7 UNDERWRITERS AT LLOYD'S for overseas resident underwriters.

Sumption: Capital Gains Tax. See A3.

The headings in this chapter are as follows.

44.1 INTRODUCTION

As a general rule a person is chargeable to capital gains tax in respect of chargeable gains accruing to him in a year of assessment during any part of which he is resident in the UK, or during which he is ordinarily resident in the UK. [*TCGA 1992, s 2(1)*]. However, where an individual is not domiciled in the UK but resident or ordinarily resident here, and where a person neither resident nor ordinarily resident in the UK trades etc. in the UK through a branch or agency, alternative rules apply. See 44.2 and 44.3 below. See 44.3 also for the relief applying when a non-UK resident company transfers the trade of a UK branch or agency to a UK resident company. Gains on assets acquired by an individual whilst UK resident and disposed of during a period of temporary non-residence (less than five full tax years) beginning after 16 March 1998 are charged in the tax year of his resuming UK residence — see 44.4 below.

Where a person is within the ambit of *TCGA 1992, s 2(1)* he may be unable to remit overseas gains to the UK. See 44.5 below for the special relief available in such circumstances.

Persons within *TCGA 1992, s 2(1)* may also be assessed by reference to chargeable gains accruing to non-UK resident persons with whom they have certain specified relationships. See 44.6 below for circumstances where a UK resident is a shareholder in a closely-held overseas resident company; and see 43 OFFSHORE SETTLEMENTS where a UK domiciled individual is a beneficiary of an overseas resident settlement and where a UK domiciled settlor has an interest in an overseas resident settlement.

Where a UK resident company has an interest in a 'controlled foreign company' and where a UK resident has 'offshore income gains' arising out of certain interests in 'offshore funds', there may be a capital gains tax effect. See 44.7 and 44.8 below.

A special relief is available where a UK resident company transfers the assets of an overseas trading branch or agency to an overseas resident company in exchange for shares in that company. See 44.9 below.

See 44.10 below for the special relief claimable where a UK trade is transferred between companies in different EC member States and 44.11 for the claim and double taxation relief available where a non-UK trade is transferred between companies in different EC member States.

There are 'exit charges' and provisions for the recovery of unpaid tax where a company ceases to be UK resident etc., is a dual resident company (before 30 November 1993) or is not resident in the UK. See 44.12 and 44.13 below. See also 43.2 OFFSHORE SETTLEMENTS for the 'exit charge' where trustees of a settlement cease to be UK-resident etc.

For exploration and exploitation rights to the UK territorial sea-bed, see 44.14 below.

For European Economic Interest Groupings, see 44.15 below.

For the collection of tax where an overseas element is involved, see 44.16 below.

Regulations (*SI 1998 No 3177*) have been made to modify the application of the Taxes Acts on the introduction of the European single currency in certain countries other than the UK on 1 January 1999. The regulations are meant to prevent unintended tax consequences arising as a result of the conversion of the currencies of participating EU Member States into euros. Broadly, they provide for continuity of treatment for assets, contracts, financial instruments etc. redenominated in euros, and grant tax relief, by means of a deduction from profits, for the costs of converting a company's shares or other securities into euros. (Revenue Press Release 17 December 1998). See 6.1 ASSETS, 21.5 EXEMPTIONS AND RELIEFS and 58.11 SHARES AND SECURITIES for specific CGT measures included.

44.2 INDIVIDUALS NOT DOMICILED IN THE UK DISPOSING OF OVERSEAS ASSETS

Individuals not domiciled in the UK, but resident or ordinarily resident here, are liable on gains arising in the UK, but gains accruing after 5 April 1965 from disposals of assets abroad are chargeable if, and only so far as, remitted here (with no allowance for losses arising abroad). [*TCGA 1992, s 12(1), s 16(4)*]. For this purpose, gains effectively transferred to the UK through loan, etc. transactions as under the REMITTANCE BASIS (51) are treated as if remitted here. [*TCGA 1992, s 12(2)*].

44.3 NON-UK RESIDENT TRADING ETC. IN THE UK THROUGH BRANCH OR AGENCY

Disposals and other events after 13 March 1989. Subject to transitional provisions and any other exceptions in the legislation, for disposals after 13 March 1989 a person is chargeable to capital gains tax in respect of chargeable gains accruing to him in a year of assessment in which he is not resident and not ordinarily resident in the UK and which are made at a time when he is carrying on a trade, profession or vocation in the UK through a 'branch or agency', and is so chargeable on chargeable gains accruing on the disposal

(*a*) of assets situated in the UK and used in or for the purposes of the trade, profession or vocation at or before the time when the gain accrued, or

(*b*) of assets situated in the UK and used or held for the purposes of the branch or agency at or before that time, or assets acquired for use by or for the purposes of the branch or agency.

These provisions are applied to companies not resident in the UK carrying on a trade or vocation through a UK branch or agency as for individuals not resident and not ordinarily resident in the UK in arriving at their chargeable profits for an accounting period. [*TCGA 1992, s 10(1)–(3)(5)*].

The commercial letting of FURNISHED HOLIDAY ACCOMMODATION (22.2) in the UK, although treated as a trade for certain capital gains tax provisions, is not so treated for the purposes of *TCGA 1992, s 10.*

Transitional provisions. Under transitional provisions, a person was chargeable under *TCGA 1992, s 10(1)* (formerly *CGTA 1979, s 12(1)*) above for 1988/89 in respect of a disposal made after 13 March 1989 if he ceased to carry on a *trade* (but not a *profession or vocation*) in the UK through a branch or agency before 14 March 1989 but a person is not to be chargeable under *TCGA 1992, s 10(1)* for 1988/89 and later years of assessment where he carries on a profession or vocation in the UK through a branch or agency in respect of chargeable gains accruing on the disposal of assets only used in or for the purposes of the profession or vocation before 14 March 1989 or only used or held for the purposes of the branch or agency before that date. [*TCGA 1992, s 10(5)*].

As a further transitional measure, where immediately before 14 March 1989 a person was not resident and not ordinarily resident in the UK but was carrying on a *profession* or *vocation* (but not a *trade*) in the UK through a branch or agency, he was deemed to have disposed immediately before 14 March 1989 of every specified asset and to have immediately reacquired every such asset, all such deemed transactions being treated as made at market value at that time. An asset was specified for this purpose if it was held by the person concerned immediately before 14 March 1989 and if at the beginning of 14 March 1989 it was a 'chargeable asset' in relation to him by virtue of his carrying on the profession or vocation. For this purpose an asset was at the beginning of 14 March 1989 a '*chargeable asset*' in relation to the person if, had it been disposed of at that time, any chargeable gains accruing would have been chargeable under *TCGA 1992, s 10(1)* above. [*FA 1989, s 126(3)–(5)*]. (No chargeable gain actually arose on the deemed disposal immediately before 14 March 1989 as professions and vocations were not then within the charge of *TCGA 1992, s 10(1)* (see below) and the broad effect was that the assets of a person carrying on a profession or vocation which became within the charge of *TCGA 1992, s 10(1)* were re-based to their market value on that date.)

Deemed disposals. Where an asset ceases after 13 March 1989 by virtue of becoming situated outside the UK to be a 'chargeable asset' (as below) in relation to a person, he is deemed to have disposed of the asset immediately before the time when the asset becomes situated outside the UK and immediately to have reacquired it, both such transactions being treated as made at market value. This does not apply where the asset becomes situated outside the UK contemporaneously with the person involved ceasing to carry on a trade, profession or vocation in the UK through a branch or agency (see below) or where the asset is an '*exploration or exploitation asset*' (i.e. an asset used in connection with 'exploration or exploitation activities' carried on in the UK or a 'designated area' as defined by *TCGA 1992, s 276* in 44.14 below; in this case comparable provisions apply). [*TCGA 1992, s 25(1)(2)(8)*].

Where an asset ceases to be a chargeable asset in relation to a person by virtue of his ceasing after 13 March 1989 to carry on a trade, profession or vocation in the UK through a branch or agency, he is deemed to have disposed of the asset immediately before the time when he ceased to carry on the trade, profession or vocation in the UK through the branch or agency and immediately to have reacquired it, both such transactions being treated as made at market value. The deemed disposal and reacquisition does not apply to an asset which is a chargeable asset in relation to the person concerned at any time after he ceases to carry on the trade, profession or vocation in the UK through a branch or agency and before the end of the chargeable period in which he does so. There is no deemed disposal and reacquisition of an asset to which a claim for relief under *TCGA 1992, s 172* applies (see below under transfer of UK branch or agency before 1 April 2000). The Revenue take a similar view as regards a claim for relief under *TCGA 1992, s 162* (see 25.10 HOLD-OVER RELIEFS) (Taxation Practitioner May 1990 p 232). Similarly, there is no deemed disposal and reacquisition on a transfer within *TCGA 1992, s 140A* of a UK trade between companies in different EC member States (see 44.10 below).

There is no deemed disposal and reacquisition of an asset by reason of the transfer of the trade by a company to another company in circumstances such that the assets transferred are transferred on or after 1 April 2000 at no gain/no loss by virtue of *TCGA 1992, s 139* or *s 171* (see, respectively, 13.7 and 13.12 COMPANIES). Previously, there was no deemed disposal and reacquisition of an asset by reason of a transfer of the whole or part of the long term business of an insurance company to another company if *TCGA 1992, s 139* had effect in relation to the asset by virtue of *TCGA 1992, s 211* (see TOLLEY'S CORPORATION TAX under Life Insurance Companies).

[*TCGA 1992, s 25(3)–(6)(8), s 140A(4)(b), s 172(2)(b); F(No 2)A 1992, s 44; FA 2000, Sch 29 para 6*].

For the purposes of *TCGA 1992, s 25* above, an asset is at any time a '*chargeable asset*' in relation to a person if, were it to be disposed of at that time, any chargeable gains accruing to him on the disposal either would be chargeable under *TCGA 1992, s 10(1)* or would form part of his chargeable profits for corporation tax purposes by virtue of *TCGA 1992, s 10(3)*. [*TCGA 1992, s 25(7)*].

Rollover relief. Where the disposal of the 'old assets' or the acquisition of the 'new assets' (or both) (within the meaning of *TCGA 1992, s 152*, see 55 ROLLOVER RELIEF) takes place after 13 March 1989, rollover relief under that provision is not to apply if the old assets are 'chargeable assets' (having the same meaning as in *TCGA 1992, s 25* above) in relation to the person concerned at the time of disposal unless the new assets are chargeable assets in relation to him immediately after the time they are acquired.

References to acquisition of the new assets include references to acquisition of an interest in them or to entering into an unconditional contract for the acquisition of them. However, rollover relief may apply where the acquisition of the new assets occurs before 14 March 1989 and the disposal of the old assets is after 13 March 1989 but within twelve months (or such longer period as is allowed by written notice given by the Board) of the acquisition of the new assets.

Rollover relief will, however, apply, where the acquisition of the new assets takes place after the disposal of the old assets and immediately after the time of acquisition the person concerned is resident or ordinarily resident in the UK, unless he is also then a 'dual resident' and the new assets are 'prescribed assets'. A '*dual resident*' is a person who is resident or ordinarily resident in the UK and falls to be regarded under any DOUBLE TAX RELIEF (18.2) arrangements as resident overseas. A '*prescribed asset*', in relation to a dual resident, is one which under any double tax relief arrangements would not give rise to a UK tax charge on him in respect of a gain accruing to him on a disposal of it.

[*TCGA 1992, s 159*].

Non-payment of tax attributable to TCGA 1992, s 10(3) by non-resident company. See 44.13 below.

Disposals and other events before 14 March 1989. Subject to the commencement and transitional provisions for disposals and other events after 13 March 1989 above and any other exceptions in the legislation, for disposals before 14 March 1989 a person was chargeable to capital gains tax in respect of chargeable gains accruing to him in a year of assessment in which he was not resident and not ordinarily resident in the UK but was carrying on a trade in the UK through a 'branch or agency', and was so chargeable on chargeable gains accruing on the disposal

(A) of assets situated in the UK and used in or for the purposes of the trade at or before the time when the gain accrued, or

(B) of assets situated in the UK and used or held for the purposes of the branch or agency at or before that time, or assets acquired for use by or for the purposes of the branch or agency.

These provisions were applied to companies not resident in the UK carrying on a trade or vocation through a UK branch or agency as for individuals not resident and not ordinarily resident in the UK in arriving at its chargeable profits for an accounting period. [*CGTA 1979, s 12(1); ICTA 1988, s 11(2)(b)*].

In effect, the charge to tax applied only to trades and not to professions or vocations, and could where relevant be avoided by removing an asset from the UK before disposal even though the UK trade continued or disposing of an asset situated in the UK in a chargeable period subsequent to that in which the UK trade ceased.

General provisions for disposals. No charge to tax under *TCGA 1992, s 10* applies to a person who, by virtue of any relevant double tax agreement, is exempt from income tax for the particular year in respect of profits or gains from the branch or agency. [*TCGA 1992, s 10(4)*].

'*Branch or agency*' means, for *TCGA 1992, s 10* and capital gains tax provisions generally, any factorship, agency, receivership, branch or management but excludes any general agents or brokers carrying on *bona fide* business as such who act for non-residents and are exempt under *TMA 1970, s 82*. [*TCGA 1992, s 10(6)*]. For consideration of this definition in relation to a partnership where two of the partners were resident outside the UK at the time of disposal of a partnership asset but the third partner was UK resident at that time, see *White v Carline (Sp C 33), [1995] SSCD 186*. See also *Puddu v Doleman (Sp C 38), [1995] SSCD 236* (where a non-UK resident sole trader employed a supervisor to manage the UK trading activity) and *Willson v Hooker Ch D 1995, 67 TC 585* (where a UK resident individual was held to be an agent, not exempted by *TMA 1970, s 82*, of a non-UK resident company in relation to the company's purchase and subsequent sale of UK land, being transactions in which the individual was closely involved).

Losses accruing to a person in a year of assessment during no part of which he is resident or ordinarily resident in the UK are not allowable unless, under *TCGA 1992, s 10* above, he would be chargeable in respect of a chargeable gain if there had been a gain instead of a loss on that occasion. [*TCGA 1992, s 16(3)*].

Where a non-resident etc. person is chargeable under *TCGA 1992, s 10* he is assessable and chargeable in the name of the branch or agent. Any person so chargeable in the name of a non-resident is responsible for all matters required to be done by a taxpayer under the capital gains tax provisions. The person so chargeable may retain, out of money coming into his hands on behalf of the non-resident, any tax or interest on unpaid tax under *TMA 1970, s 87A* required to be paid and is indemnified for all such payments made. [*TMA 1970, ss 84, 85; F(No 2)A 1987, Sch 6 para 7*].

See 52.3 RESIDENCE AND DOMICILE for the exclusion, after 5 April 1989, of extra-statutory concession D2 in respect of the period from the cessation of UK residence to the end of the year of assessment.

Transfer of UK branch or agency before 1 April 2000. For disposals after 19 March 1990 and before 1 April 2000 a relief for the purposes of corporation tax on chargeable gains applies where

(*a*) there is a scheme for the transfer by a non-UK resident 'company' ('company A') which carries on a trade in the UK through a branch or agency of the whole or part of the trade to a UK resident company ('company B'),

(*b*) company A disposes of an asset to company B in accordance with the scheme at a time when both companies are members of the same 'group', and

(*c*) a claim under *TCGA 1992, s 172(1)* relating to the asset is made by both companies within two years after the end of the accounting period of company B during which the disposal is made.

'Company' and 'group' have the same meanings as in *TCGA 1992, s 170* but ignoring *subsections (2)(a)* and *(9)* thereof (references to company only to include UK resident companies etc. incorporated under UK and overseas legislation etc.). For disposals on or after 1 April 2000, the relief is made redundant by the change in the residence requirement as regards groups of companies. See 13.11 COMPANIES.

The relief given is that, firstly, the asset is treated as disposed of by company A and acquired by company B for a no gain, no loss consideration and, secondly, *TCGA 1992, s 25(3)* (deemed disposal by non-resident on ceasing to trade in the UK through a branch or agency; see above under disposals and other events after 13 March 1989) is not to apply to the asset by reason of the transfer.

The relief did not apply on a disposal before 30 November 1993 where company B was UK resident but under any double tax relief arrangements was regarded as resident elsewhere and would not have been liable to UK tax on a gain arising on the disposal of the asset occurring immediately after its acquisition. Relief is also denied if company B is a 'dual resident investing company' within *ICTA 1988, s 404* or an 'investment trust' within *ICTA 1988, s 842*. No relief is given unless any gain accruing to company A on the disposal of the asset in accordance with the scheme, or, where that disposal occurs after the transfer has taken place, on a disposal of the asset immediately before the transfer, would be a chargeable gain and would, under *TCGA 1992, s 10(3)* above, form part of its profits for corporation tax purposes.

[*TCGA 1992, s 172; FA 1994, s 251(1)(7), Sch 26 Pt VIII; FA 2000, Sch 29 para 3*].

The following applies where there is a disposal or acquisition of currency; a 'qualifying asset' consisting of the right to settlement under a debt which is not a debt on a security (within *TCGA 1992, s 132*; see 21.5 EXEMPTIONS AND RELIEFS); a 'qualifying asset' consisting of the right to settlement under a debt on a security; or an obligation which by virtue of *TCGA 1992, s 143* (futures contracts; see 17.11 DISPOSAL) is regarded as an asset to the disposal of which *TCGA 1992* applies and which is a duty under a currency contract. Where the disposal or acquisition is by a 'qualifying company' and is made on or after the company's 'commencement day', and immediately before the disposal or after the acquisition, as the case may be, the asset is held wholly for 'qualifying purposes', and *TCGA 1992, s 172* would otherwise apply, the last-mentioned provision does not apply as regards the disposal or acquisition and the corresponding acquisition or disposal. '*Qualifying purposes*' are purposes of long term or mutual insurance business. [*FA 1993, s 169, Sch 17 para 7; FA 2000, Sch 29 para 43*]. See 13.44 COMPANIES for a note of the terms quoted and not otherwise defined.

44.4 INDIVIDUALS TEMPORARILY NON-RESIDENT IN THE UK

Conditions. The following provisions apply where an individual leaves the UK **after 16 March 1998** for a period of temporary residence outside the UK, and

- four out of the seven years of assessment immediately preceding the 'year of departure' were years for which the individual satisfied 'the residence requirements', and
- there are fewer than five years of assessment (the '*intervening years*') falling between (and not including) the 'year of departure' and the 'year of return'.

For the purposes of these provisions, the '*year of departure*' means the last year of assessment before the year of return for which the taxpayer satisfied the 'residence requirements'. The '*year of return*' is any year of assessment for which the individual satisfies the 'residence requirements' and which immediately follows one or more years of assessment for which he did not satisfy those requirements.

An individual satisfies the '*residence requirements*' for a year of assessment if that year is one during any part of which he is resident in the UK or during which he is ordinarily resident in the UK. (For the meaning of 'resident' and 'ordinarily resident' see 52 RESIDENCE AND DOMICILE.)

The charge. Where the above conditions apply, and subject to the exclusions below, the individual is chargeable to capital gains tax as if all the chargeable gains and losses which accrued to him in the intervening years were gains or losses accruing to him in the year of return. Any gains or losses accruing in the year of departure (whether accruing before or after the date of departure), and any gains or losses accruing in the year of return (whether accruing before or after the date of return) are chargeable to capital gains tax in the year of departure or return under general principles (*TCGA 1992, s 2(1)* — see 44.1 above). The treatment otherwise available under ESC D2 (whereby, subject to certain conditions, an individual is charged to capital gains tax in respect of gains accruing in a year in which his residence status changes only to the extent that the gains accrued from disposals made before his departure or, as the case may be, after his return) does not apply where the above conditions are satisfied. See 52.3 RESIDENCE AND DOMICILE.

The chargeable gains to be treated as accruing in the year of return include any chargeable gains which would have been treated as having accrued to him in any intervening year, if he had been resident in the UK throughout that year, under

(i) *TCGA 1992, s 13* (gains of non-resident companies attributed to members — see 44.6 below); or

(ii) *TCGA 1992, s 86* (attribution of gains to settlers with an interest in non-resident or dual-resident settlements — see 43.4 OFFSHORE SETTLEMENTS).

Where (i) above applies, any losses accruing to the non-resident company in an intervening year which, under 44.6 below, would have been allowable to the individual if he had been UK-resident throughout that year are treated as accruing in the year of return but only to the extent that such losses do not exceed the amount of the gains of the company (or another non-resident company) attributed to the individual for that same year and similarly treated.

Where (ii) above applies, see 43.12 OFFSHORE SETTLEMENTS for details of the limitation on the amount to be brought into charge where beneficiaries of the settlement have been charged in respect of capital payments from the settlement.

Where these provisions apply, any assessment to capital gains tax may be made for the year of departure at any time before the second anniversary of 31st January following the year of return.

The provisions do not prejudice any right to claim DOUBLE TAX RELIEF (18) under a bilateral agreement.

Exclusions from the charge. The gains or losses treated as accruing in the year of return do not include a gain or loss on the disposal of an asset in the intervening years if it was acquired by the taxpayer at a time either in the year of departure or in an intervening year when he was neither resident nor ordinarily resident in the UK, provided that

(a) the asset was not acquired by means of a 'relevant disposal' (see below) which is treated as having been a disposal on which neither a gain nor a loss accrued, by virtue of *TCGA 1992, s 58* (transfer between husband and wife — see 41.3 MARRIED PERSONS), *TCGA 1992, s 73* (reversion of settled property to settlor on death of person entitled to interest in possession — see 57.11 SETTLEMENTS) or *TCGA 1992, s 258(4)* (gifts of national heritage property — see 21.74 EXEMPTIONS AND RELIEFS);

(*b*) that asset is not an interest created by or arising under a settlement; and

(*c*) the acquisition cost of the asset to the taxpayer does not fall, by reference to any 'relevant disposal' (see below), to be treated as reduced under any of the following provisions:

- *TCGA 1992, s 23(4)(b)* or *(5)(b)* (rollover where the replacement asset is acquired after receipt of compensation or insurance money — see 17.9 DISPOSAL);
- *TCGA 1992, s 152(1)(b)* (ROLLOVER RELIEF (55) on business assets);
- *TCGA 1992, s 162(3)(b)* (hold-over relief where shares are acquired on the disposal of a business to a company — see 25.10 HOLD-OVER RELIEFS);
- *TCGA 1992, s 247(2)(b)* or *(3)(b)* (rollover relief where replacement land is acquired on the compulsory acquisition of other land — see 36.11 LAND).

For the purposes of (*a*) and (*c*) above, a '*relevant disposal*' is a disposal of an asset acquired by the person making the disposal at a time when that person was resident or ordinarily resident in the UK.

Note that this exclusion does not apply to assets acquired within a non-resident trust to which the provisions of *TCGA 1992, ss 86, 87* (see 43.4, 43.13 OFFSHORE SETTLEMENTS) apply or a non-resident company to which *TCGA 1992, s 13* (see 44.6 below) applies.

Where a chargeable gain has accrued on the disposal of an asset which is not within (*a*)–(*c*) above, but the gain falls to be postponed by virtue of one of the following CGT deferral provisions and treated as accruing on the disposal of the whole or part of another asset which *is* within (*a*)–(*c*) above, the above exclusion from the charge does not apply. The said provisions are:

- *TCGA 1992, s 116(10)* or *(11)* (deferral of gain arising on a company reconstruction where the new asset is a QUALIFYING CORPORATE BOND (see 49.3));
- *TCGA 1992, s 134* (deferral of gain arising where gilts are acquired as compensation for compulsory acquisition of SHARES AND SECURITIES (see 58.11);
- *TCGA 1992, s 154(2)* or *(4)* (deferral of gain on a business asset where a depreciating asset is acquired as replacement — see 55.7 ROLLOVER RELIEF).

Also excluded from the charge is any chargeable gain or allowable loss accruing to the taxpayer in an intervening year which is brought into account for that year under *TCGA 1992, s 10, s 16(3)* (non-residents carrying on a trade etc. in the UK through a branch or agency — see 44.3 above).

[*TCGA 1992, s 10A; FA 1998, s 127(1)(4)*].

44.5 RELIEF FOR UNREMITTABLE OVERSEAS GAINS

Where chargeable gains accrue from assets situated abroad and the taxpayer is unable with reasonable endeavour to transfer those gains to the UK due to the laws of the territory where the assets were situated at the time of disposal, or to the executive action of its government, or to the impossibility of obtaining foreign currency in that territory, he may claim under *TCGA 1992, s 279(1)* that they be left out of account. No claim shall be made for the purposes of capital gains tax later than the fifth anniversary of 31 January following the year of assessment in which the gains arose; or in the case of corporation tax more than six years after the end of the accounting period in which the gains arose. Prior to the introduction of self-assessment from 1996/97, the claim for CGT purposes had to be made within six years after the year of assessment in which the gains arose. The gains are then treated as gains of the year, if any, in which the conditions cease to apply. The claim is open to personal representatives.

For capital gains tax purposes, the gain to be left out of account in the first instance is the untapered gain. The availability of taper relief when the gain is brought into charge is determined by reference to the original disposal date (see 60.12 TAPER RELIEF).

[*TCGA 1992, s 279(1)–(3)(5)(6)(8); FA 1996, Sch 20 para 64, Sch 21 para 41; FA 1998, s 121(3)(4), Sch 21 para 9*].

These provisions cannot be relied upon as a defence against an assessment under *TCGA 1992, s 13* (see 44.6 below) if the taxpayer's inability to transfer the gain to the UK is owing to the company's failure to distribute the gain. Relief can only be given if the gain is represented by money, or money's worth, in the hands of the taxpayer (*Van Arkadie v Plunket, Ch D 1982, 56 TC 310*).

See 35.7 INTEREST AND SURCHARGES ON UNPAID TAX for an alternative relief given to interest on tax overdue, where collection of tax is deferred in similar circumstances. See also 41.1 MARRIED PERSONS where a claim for the relief above has effect before 1990/91 in respect of a wife's gains which would otherwise have been assessed on the husband.

Gains which are subject to payments made by the Export Credits Guarantee Department under statutory arrangements for export guarantees do not qualify for the relief above to the extent of such payments. [*TCGA 1992, s 279(4)*].

44.6 UK RESIDENT SHAREHOLDER IN OVERSEAS RESIDENT COMPANY

Gains accruing after 27 November 1995. The following provisions apply where chargeable gains accrue after 27 November 1995 to a company which is not resident in the UK but which would be a close company (within *ICTA 1988, ss 414, 415*; see TOLLEY'S CORPORATION TAX under Close Companies) if it were resident in the UK. Subject to the following, every person who at the time when the gain accrues to the company is resident or ordinarily resident in the UK, who, if an individual, is domiciled in the UK, and who is a participator (within *ICTA 1988, s 417(1)*) in the company, is treated for capital gains tax purposes as if part of the chargeable gain had accrued to him. The amount of the gain accruing to the company is computed (where it is not the case) as if the company were within the charge to UK corporation tax on chargeable gains. The gain is not eligible for taper relief.

The part that is taken as accruing to the participator is equal to the proportion of the gain that corresponds to the extent of the participator's interest as a participator in the company. However, there is no charge on him where the aggregate amount otherwise falling to be apportioned to him and to persons connected (see 14 CONNECTED PERSONS) with him does not exceed one-twentieth of the gain.

References to a person's interest as a participator in a company are references to the interest in the company which is represented by all the factors by reference to which he falls to be treated as such a participator. References to the extent of such an interest are references to the proportion of the interests as participators of all the participators in the company (including any who are not resident or ordinarily resident in the UK) which on a just and reasonable apportionment is represented by that interest. Any appeal involving any question as to the extent of a person's interest as a participator is made to the Special Commissioners.

These provisions do not apply in relation to a gain accruing on the disposal of tangible property (or a lease thereof) used solely for a trade carried on by the company wholly outside the UK, a gain chargeable to UK tax under *TCGA 1992, s 10(3)* (UK branch or agency, see 44.3 above) or a gain from the disposal of foreign currency or of a debt within *TCGA 1992, s 252(1)* (see 21.5 EXEMPTIONS AND RELIEFS) where the currency or debt is or represents money used for the purposes of a trade carried on by the company wholly outside the UK.

Where any amount of capital gains tax is paid by a participator as a result of the charge above and an amount in respect of the gain charged is distributed (either by way of dividend or distribution of capital or on the dissolution of the company) within two years from the time when the chargeable gain accrued to the company, that amount of tax (so far as neither reimbursed by the company nor applied as a deduction under the further provisions below) is applied for reducing or extinguishing any liability of his to income tax in respect of the distribution or (in the case of a distribution falling to be treated as a disposal on which a chargeable gain accrues to that person) to any capital gains tax in respect of the distribution.

Any capital gains tax paid by the participator resulting from the above treatment (so far as neither reimbursed by the company nor applied as above for reducing any liability to tax) is treated as allowable expenditure in the computation of the gain arising on his disposal of any asset representing his interest as a participator in the company (e.g. shares in the company by reference to which he is a participator).

In ascertaining for the purposes above the amount of capital gains tax or income tax chargeable on a participator for any year on or in respect of any chargeable gain or distribution

(*a*) any distribution as is mentioned above which falls to be treated as his income for that year is regarded as forming the highest part of the income on which he is chargeable to tax for the year;

(*b*) any gain accruing in that year on the disposal of any asset representing his interest as a participator in the company is regarded as forming the highest part of the gains on which he is chargeable to tax for that year;

(*c*) where any distribution as is mentioned above falls to be treated as a disposal on which a gain accrues on which he is so chargeable, that gain is regarded as forming the next highest part of the gains on which he is so chargeable, after any gains falling within (*b*) above; and

(*d*) any gain treated as accruing as above to him in that year by virtue of a chargeable gain accruing to a company is regarded as the next highest part of the gains on which he is so chargeable, after any gains falling within (*c*) above.

Any loss arising on the disposal of assets by the company can be similarly treated as accruing to the participator concerned, but only insofar as it reduces or extinguishes gains accruing in the same year of assessment which are charged on him by reference to that company.

If a person who is a participator in the company at the time when the chargeable gain accrues to the company is itself a company which is not resident in the UK but which would be a close company if it were resident in the UK, an amount equal to the amount which would otherwise have been apportioned as above out of the chargeable gain to the participating company's interest as a participator in the company to which the gain accrues is further apportioned among the participators in the participating company according to the extent of their respective interests as participators, and an amount is apportioned to them as above accordingly in relation to the amounts further apportioned, and so on through any number of companies.

Beneficial interests are regarded as interests of the trustees of the settlement.

The person treated by these provisions as if a part of a chargeable gain accruing to a company had accrued to them expressly include trustees who are participators in the company, or in any company amongst the participators in which the gain is apportioned as above, if when the gain accrues to the company the trustees are neither resident nor ordinarily resident in the UK. See further in 43 OFFSHORE SETTLEMENTS. For anti-avoidance provisions concerning the attribution of gains under these provisions to trustees of a UK-resident trust, see 57.15 SETTLEMENTS.

If any tax payable by a participator as a result of a gain accruing to a company is paid by that company, or in a case where there are other intervening non-UK resident companies as above is paid by any such other company, the amount so paid is left out of account in relation to that person for income tax, capital gains tax and corporation tax purposes.

[*TCGA 1992, s 13; FA 1996, s 174(1)–(9); FA 1998, s 121(3)(4), s 120(4), Sch 21 para 4*].

The appropriate proportion of any overseas tax in respect of its gain which the company pays in its country of residence is deductible in computing the gain chargeable on the UK participator; alternatively, tax credit relief may be allowable for the overseas tax (Revenue Pamphlet IR 131, SP D23).

An individual who is 'temporarily' non-UK resident, such as to be within the charge to tax under *TCGA 1992, s 10A* on his return to the UK, is chargeable for the tax year of return on gains that would have been attributed to him under the above provisions had he remained UK-resident. See 44.4 above.

Gains accruing before 28 November 1995. The following provisions apply where chargeable gains accrue before 28 November 1995 to a company which is not resident in the UK but which would be a close company (within *ICTA 1988, ss 414, 415*; see TOLLEY'S CORPORATION TAX under Close Companies) if it were resident in the UK. Subject to the following, every person who at the time when the gain accrues to the company is resident or ordinarily resident in the UK, who, if an individual, is domiciled in the UK, and who holds shares in the company, is treated for capital gains tax purposes as if part of the chargeable gain had accrued to him.

The part that is taken is equal to the proportion of the assets of the company to which the person concerned would be entitled on a liquidation of the company at the time when the gain accrues to the company. However, there is no charge on him where the part is less than one-twentieth.

These provisions do not apply in relation to any amount in respect of the gain which is distributed, whether by way of dividend or distribution of capital or on dissolution of the company, to persons holding shares in the company, or creditors of the company, within two years from the time when the gain accrued to the company. Notwithstanding any intention to distribute any part of the gain within this two-year period, an assessment may be made on the person concerned, although it may be adjusted as necessary if the distribution is subsequently made within that period.

These provisions do not apply in relation to a gain accruing on the disposal of tangible property (or a lease thereof) used solely for a trade carried on by the company wholly outside the UK, a gain chargeable to UK tax under *TCGA 1992, s 10(3)* (UK branch or agency; see 44.3 above) or a gain from the disposal of foreign currency or of a debt within *TCGA 1992, s 252(1)* (see 21.5 EXEMPTIONS AND RELIEFS) where the currency or debt is or represents money used for the purposes of a trade carried on by the company wholly outside the UK.

Any capital gains tax paid by the shareholder resulting from the above treatment (so far as not reimbursed by the company) is treated as allowable expenditure in the computation of the gain arising on his disposal of the shares by reason of which the tax was paid.

Any loss arising on the disposal of assets by the company can be similarly treated as accruing to the shareholder concerned, but only insofar as it reduces or extinguishes gains accruing in the same year of assessment which are charged on him by reference to that company.

If the shareholder at the time when the chargeable gain accrues to the company is itself a company which is not resident in the UK but which would be a close company if it were resident in the UK, an amount equal to the amount which would otherwise have been apportioned as above out of the chargeable gain to the shares so owned is further apportioned among the issued shares of the second-mentioned company, and the holders of those shares are treated as if part of the gain had accrued to them, and so on through any number of companies.

The persons treated by these provisions as if a part of a chargeable gain accruing to a company had accrued to them expressly include, in respect of gains accruing after 9 March 1981, trustees owning shares in the company if when the gain accrues to the company the trustees are neither resident nor ordinarily resident in the UK. See further in 43 OFFSHORE SETTLEMENTS.

If any tax payable by any shareholder as a result of a gain accruing to a company is paid by that company, or in a case where there are other intervening non-UK resident companies as above is paid by any such other company, the amount so paid is left out of account in relation to that person for income tax, capital gains tax and corporation tax purposes.

[*TCGA 1992, s 13*].

General. For the purposes of the above, the provisions at 13.12, 13.14, 13.16, 13.19 COMPANIES, *TCGA 1992, s 172* (now repealed) at 44.3 above, and *TCGA 1992, s 175(1)* at 55.5 ROLLOVER RELIEF apply, with appropriate modifications, in relation to non-UK resident companies which are members of a non-UK resident group of companies as they apply in relation to members of a CGT group as in 13.11 COMPANIES. [*TCGA 1992, s 14; FA 2000, Sch 29 para 16*]. The provisions mentioned in *section 14* are so applied not only where the UK-resident participator or shareholder on whom gains fall to be assessed is subject to corporation tax on chargeable gains but also where he is within the charge to capital gains tax (Revenue Tax Bulletin May 1993 p 74).

A person who holds shares in an overseas resident company can be required by notice from the Board to provide sufficient information to give effect to the above provisions. [*TMA 1970, s 28; TCGA 1992, Sch 10 para 2(5)*].

The appropriate proportion of any overseas tax in respect of its gain which the company pays in its country of residence is deductible in computing the gain chargeable on the shareholder; alternatively, tax credit relief may be allowable for the overseas tax (Revenue Pamphlet IR 131, SP D23). The Revenue has confirmed that where the overseas resident company is a subsidiary of a UK resident parent company and the relevant double taxation agreement has an article exempting residents of the overseas territory from a charge to UK capital gains tax, then such an article may prevent the imposition of a charge under the above provisions (CCAB Statement TR 500 March 1983).

The relief for unremittable overseas gains (see 44.5 above) is not a defence to an assessment under the above provisions. See also 44.7 below for a UK resident company having an interest in a 'controlled foreign company'.

44.7 UK RESIDENT COMPANY HAVING AN INTEREST IN A CONTROLLED FOREIGN COMPANY

Legislation relating to controlled foreign companies ('CFC's') is contained in *ICTA 1988, ss 747–756, Schs 24–26* (as amended). For full coverage of these provisions see TOLLEY'S CORPORATION TAX under Controlled Foreign Companies. Broadly, the Board of Inland Revenue used to be able to direct that the provisions should apply in relation to an accounting period of a 'CFC'. For accounting periods ending on or after the appointed day for corporation tax self-assessment (1 July 1999), the provisions (as significantly amended by *FA 1998, Sch 17* and *FA 2000, Sch 31*) apply automatically whenever the conditions are met, and the Board are no longer required to make a direction. The Revenue have published guidance notes on the CFC legislation, which include the position under self-assessment and details of a comprehensive CFC clearance procedure introduced on 1 January 1999 (Revenue Press Release 18 June 1999).

A '*CFC*' is a company which is

(i) resident outside the UK for the purposes of the provisions;

(ii) 'controlled' by persons resident in the UK; and

(iii) subject to a 'lower level of taxation' in the territory in which it is 'resident'.

Where the provisions apply, a UK resident company which has an 'interest' in the CFC at any time in the accounting period is then liable to a sum as if it were corporation tax. Such sum is computed by multiplying the part of the 'chargeable profits' arising in an accounting period of the CFC that is proportionate to the interest held by the UK resident company and the 'appropriate rate' of UK corporation tax. The foregoing is subject to further detailed rules. See TOLLEY'S CORPORATION TAX for these and the definitions assigned to the terms given above. Rules specifically relating to corporation tax on chargeable gains are given below.

(*a*) **Gains on disposal of shares.** Relief may be claimed where

  (i) an apportionment falls to be made (before self-assessment, a direction is given) in respect of a CFC's accounting period;

  (ii) a UK resident company (the '*claimant company*') disposes of shares, acquired before the end of that accounting period, in either the CFC or another company whose shares give rise to the claimant company's interest in the CFC; and

  (iii) chargeable profits of the CFC are apportioned to the claimant company, and a sum is accordingly chargeable on it as if it were corporation tax.

  Where a claim is made, in the computation of the chargeable gain accruing on the disposal in (ii) above, a deduction is allowed of the sum assessed as in (iii) above, reduced to the proportion thereof that the average market value, in the period for which the apportionment falls to be made, of the interest in the CFC in respect of which the charge as in (iii) above arose bears to the average market value in that period of the shares disposed of. A sum assessed as at (iii) above may only be relieved once in this way.

  Relief may, however, be restricted where, before the disposal, a dividend is paid by the CFC out of profits from which the chargeable profits in (iii) above derived. If either

(1) the effect of the payment of the dividend is to reduce the value of the shares disposed of as in (ii) above; or

(2) the claimant company obtains relief (see (*b*) below) in respect of a dividend paid on the shares disposed of as in (ii) above, by reference to sums including that referred to in (iii) above,

then relief is denied in respect of so much of the sum chargeable as corresponds to the part of the chargeable profits in (iii) above corresponding to the profits which the dividend represents.

Claims for relief must be made within three months of the later of the end of the accounting period in which the disposal occurs and the date the assessment in (iii) above becomes final and conclusive. Such claims are outside the main provisions governing claims under corporation tax self-assessment (included in returns or otherwise).

Identification of shares disposed of for this purpose is with those acquired earlier before those acquired later.

[*ICTA 1988, Sch 26 para 3; FA 1998, Sch 17 paras 35, 37*].

(*b*) **Dividends from the CFC.** The total of assessments on UK resident companies under the provisions in respect of a CFC's chargeable profits (the '*gross attributed tax*') is treated as underlying tax for double taxation relief purposes (see TOLLEY'S CORPORATION TAX under Double Taxation Relief) where a dividend is paid by the CFC wholly or partly out of profits from which those chargeable profits derive. The gross attributed tax is *not*, however, treated as increasing the amount of the dividend income in determining liability on that income.

If *ICTA 1988, s 796* or *s 797(1)* act to limit the foreign tax credit by reference to the UK tax on the dividends concerned, the amount so debarred from relief, insofar as it does not exceed the foreign tax *other than* underlying tax attributable to the dividend, is set against the gross attributed tax chargeable on UK resident companies. On a claim by any of those companies, the tax so chargeable on it is reduced and, if appropriate, repaid.

Any condition for double tax relief under *ICTA 1988, s 788* or *s 789* (by agreement with other countries) or *s 790* (unilateral relief) (see 18 DOUBLE TAX RELIEF) requiring a particular degree of control of the company paying the dividend is treated as satisfied for these purposes.

Where the CFC dividend is paid out of unspecified profits, and any part of its chargeable profits is apportioned other than to UK resident companies, the gross attributed tax is attributed to the proportion of the chargeable profits apportioned to UK resident companies (the '*taxed profits*'). So much of the dividend as is received by, or by a 'successor in title' of, any such company is regarded as paid primarily out of the taxed profits. '*Successor in title*' for this purpose refers to a successor in respect of the whole or part of the interest in the CFC giving rise to a charge under these provisions.

If

(i) relief has been allowed for the purposes of corporation tax on chargeable gains, on a disposal of shares, in respect of a sum chargeable under these provisions (see (*a*) above); and

(ii) that sum forms part of the gross attributed tax in relation to a dividend, as above; and

(iii) a person receiving the dividend in respect of the shares referred to in (i) above (the '*primary dividend*'), or any other dividend in respect of shares in a company resident outside the UK representing profits consisting directly or indirectly of or including the primary dividend, is entitled to relief by way of underlying tax (as above) by reference to the whole or part of the gross attributed tax,

then the relief available as in (iii) above is reduced or extinguished by deducting therefrom the amount allowed by way of relief as in (i) above.

[*ICTA 1988, Sch 26 paras 4–6; FA 1998, Sch 17 paras 36, 37*].

44.8 OFFSHORE FUNDS

For disposals after 31 December 1983 'offshore income gains' arising out of certain interests in 'offshore funds' which are considered not to distribute sufficient income are charged to income tax or corporation tax under Schedule D, Case VI rather than to capital gains tax or corporation tax in respect of chargeable gains. Broadly, a capital gains tax treatment applies to any part of such a gain accruing before 1 January 1984 but the whole of the gain arising thereafter (without indexation allowance) is taxed as income. [*ICTA 1988, s 437(2)(a), s 441, s 660B(4), ss 757–764, Schs 27, 28; FA 1990, Sch 7 para 3; FA 1995, Sch 17 para 1*]. Interests held were identified under the rules applicable to securities generally before 6 April 1985 (1 April 1985 for companies). After 5 April 1985 (31 March 1985 for companies) interests are designated 'relevant securities' and amended identification rules apply. See 59.6 SHARES AND SECURITIES—IDENTIFICATION RULES. See TOLLEY'S INCOME TAX under Overseas Matters for general coverage and definitions assigned to terms used in the provisions. Rules relating to capital gains tax are given below.

Deduction of offshore income gain in determining capital gain. There are provisions in substitution of *TCGA 1992, s 37(1)* (deduction of consideration chargeable to tax on income) to prevent a double charge to tax when a disposal gives rise to both an offshore income gain and a chargeable gain for capital gains tax purposes.

(i) Where an offshore income gain arises on a 'material disposal' that gain is deducted from the sum which would otherwise constitute the amount or value of the consideration in the calculation of the capital gain arising under *TCGA 1992* although the offshore gain is not to be deducted in calculating the figure 'A' in the A/(A + B) fraction under the rules relating to part disposal. See 17.6 DISPOSAL.

(ii) Where a capital gains tax disposal forms part of a transfer within *TCGA 1992, s 162* (see 25.10 HOLD-OVER RELIEFS) the offshore income gain is taken into account to reduce 'B' in the A/B fraction determined under those provisions.

(iii) Where a reorganisation of shares or securities (see 58.5 SHARES AND SECURITIES) constitutes a disposal of an interest in an offshore fund the amount of any offshore income gain to which the disposal gives rise is treated as consideration for the new holding.

[*ICTA 1988, s 763(1)–(6)*].

44.9 UK RESIDENT COMPANY TRANSFERRING ASSETS TO OVERSEAS RESIDENT COMPANY

Where a UK resident company carrying on a trade (which includes vocations, offices and employments) outside the UK through a branch or agency transfers the whole or part of that trade together with its assets, or its assets other than cash, to a company not resident in the UK in exchange, wholly or partly, for shares (or shares and loan stock) in that company, so that thereafter it holds one quarter or more of the transferee company's ordinary share capital, and the chargeable gains on the transfer exceed the allowable losses, a proportion of the resulting net chargeable gains relating to the shares (in the proportion that the market value of the shares at the time of the transfer bears to the market value of the whole consideration received) may be claimed by the transferor company as being deferred and not treated as arising until the happening of one of the following events.

(i) The transferor company disposes of all or any of the shares received. The 'appropriate proportion' of the deferred gain (insofar as not already charged under this specific provision or under (ii) below) is then added to the consideration received on the disposal. The '*appropriate proportion*' is the proportion which the market value of the shares disposed of bears to the market value of the shares held immediately before the disposal. However, where the disposal of the shares received occurs after 5 April 1988 no addition to the consideration is made under this provision if its application would be directly attributable to the disposal of an asset before 1 April 1982.

(ii) The transferee company disposes, within six years of the transfer, of the whole or part of the assets on which chargeable gains were deferred. The gain chargeable (insofar as it has not already been charged under this provision, or under (i) above) is the proportion which the deferred gain on the assets disposed of bears to the total deferred gain on assets held immediately before the disposal.

The following disposals are disregarded: for the purposes of (i) above, intra-group transfers within *TCGA 1992, s 171* (see 13.12 COMPANIES); for the purposes of (ii) above, intra-group transfers which would be within *TCGA 1992, s 171* if for those purposes a group included (without qualification) non-UK resident companies. A charge will arise when a subsequent group company makes a disposal outside the group. A claim under *TCGA 1992, s 140C* (transfer of non-UK trade between different EC member States; see 44.11 below) as regards a transfer precludes a claim under the above.

[*TCGA 1992, s 140, Sch 4 para 4(5); F(No 2)A 1992, s 46(4); FA 2000, Sch 29 para 23*].

Insurance companies. Where a UK resident insurance company (i.e. not confined to life assurance companies) transfers its foreign branch or agency business and assets to an overseas company in exchange wholly or partly for shares in that company in circumstances corresponding to those set out above any profit or loss on the assets transferred which would otherwise be included in the computation of profits or losses under Schedule D, Case I will be disregarded for that purpose (otherwise than in restricting management expenses under *ICTA 1988, s 76(2)*) and treated as chargeable gains or allowable losses. Any net chargeable gain may then be deferred as given above. [*ICTA 1988, s 442(1)–(3)*]. *ICTA 1988, s 442(3)* is ignored in calculating any relief given under *TCGA 1992, s 140C* (transfer of non-UK trade between different EC member States; see 44.11 below). [*TCGA 1992, s 140C(8); F(No 2)A 1992, s 45*].

44.10 TRANSFER OF UK TRADE BETWEEN COMPANIES IN DIFFERENT EC MEMBER STATES

A special relief may be claimed where, **after 31 December 1991**, a 'qualifying company' resident in one EC member State transfers the whole or part of a trade carried on by it in the UK to a qualifying company resident in another member State wholly in exchange for securities (including shares) in the latter company, provided that certain conditions (see below) are met. On such a claim made by both companies (under *TCGA 1992, s 140A*), any assets included in the transfer are treated for the purposes of corporation tax on chargeable gains as transferred for a no gain/no loss consideration, and *TCGA 1992, s 25(3)* (deemed disposal by non-resident on ceasing to trade in the UK through a branch or agency, see 44.3 above) does not apply to the assets by reason of the transfer.

A '*qualifying company*' is a body incorporated under the law of a member State.

A company is regarded for the above purposes as resident in a member State under the laws of which it is chargeable to tax because it is regarded as so resident (unless it is regarded under DOUBLE TAX RELIEF (18.2) arrangements entered into by the member State as resident in a territory not within any of the member States).

The conditions referred to above are:

(*a*) (i) if the transferee company is non-UK resident immediately after the transfer, any chargeable gain accruing to it on a disposal of the assets included in the transfer would form part of its corporation tax profits under *TCGA 1992, s 10(3)*, or

(ii) if it is UK resident at that time, none of the assets included in the transfer is exempt from UK tax on disposal under double tax relief arrangements; and

(*b*) the transfer is effected for *bona fide* commercial reasons and not as part of a scheme or arrangement a main purpose of which is avoidance of income, corporation or capital gains taxes.

Advance clearance in relation to (*b*) above may be obtained from the Board on the application of the companies, subject to the same conditions and appeal procedures as apply to clearances under *TCGA 1992, s 138* (see 3.16 ANTI-AVOIDANCE). [*TCGA 1992, ss 140A, 140B; F(No 2)A 1992, s 44*].

The above provisions were introduced to comply with EEC Directive No 90/434/EEC.

44.11 TRANSFER OF NON-UK TRADE BETWEEN COMPANIES IN DIFFERENT EC MEMBER STATES

Where, **after 31 December 1991,**

(*a*) a 'qualifying company' resident in the UK transfers to a qualifying company resident in another member State the whole or part of a trade carried on by the UK company immediately before the transfer through a branch or agency in a member State other than the UK,

(*b*) the transfer includes all the UK company's assets used in that trade or part (with the possible exception of cash),

(*c*) the transfer is wholly or partly in exchange for securities (including shares) in the non-UK company,

(*d*) the aggregate of the chargeable gains accruing to the UK company on the transfer exceeds the aggregate of the allowable losses so accruing, and

(*e*) the transfer is effected for *bona fide* commercial reasons and not as part of a scheme or arrangement a main purpose of which is avoidance of income, corporation or capital gains taxes,

the UK company may claim that the transfer be treated as giving rise to a single chargeable gain of the excess at (*d*) above. No claim may, however, be made where a claim is made under *TCGA 1992, s 140* at 44.9 above in relation to the same transfer. As regards insurance companies, *ICTA 1988, s 442(3)* (also see 44.9 above) is ignored in arriving at the chargeable gains and allowable losses accruing on the transfer.

A '*qualifying company*' is a body incorporated under the law of a member State.

For the purposes of (*a*) above, a company is not regarded as resident in the UK if it is regarded under any DOUBLE TAX RELIEF (18.2) arrangements to which the UK is a party as resident in a territory not within any of the member States. A company is regarded as resident in another member State under the laws of which it is chargeable to tax because it is regarded as so resident (unless it is regarded under a double tax relief arrangement entered into by the member State as resident in a territory not within any of the member States).

Advance clearance in relation to (*e*) above may be obtained from the Board on the application of the UK company, subject to the same conditions and appeal procedures as apply to clearances under *TCGA 1992, s 138* (see 3.16 ANTI-AVOIDANCE). [*TCGA 1992, ss 140C, 140D; F(No 2)A 1992, s 45*].

The above provisions were introduced to comply with EEC Directive No 90/434/EEC.

Double tax relief. Where the above provisions apply, and the UK company produces to the inspector an 'appropriate certificate' from the tax authorities of the Member State in which the company carried on the trade immediately before the transfer, the amount stated in the certificate is treated for double tax relief purposes as tax paid in that other member State.

An '*appropriate certificate*' is one which states that gains accruing to the UK company on the transfer would, but for the Mergers Directive (*90/434/EEC*), have been chargeable to tax in the other member State, and which states the amount of tax which would, but for that Directive, have been payable in respect of the gains. The tax must be calculated after any permissible set-off of losses arising on the transfer and on the assumption that any available reliefs are claimed.

Where the UK company is unable to obtain an appropriate certificate and the Board is satisfied that this is the case, the company may make a claim to the Board to have the amount of tax computed which, in the opinion of the Board, would have been payable under the law of the relevant member State in respect of the gains accruing to it on the transfer but for the Mergers Directive. The company is required to provide such information and documents in connection with the claim as the Board may require. [*ICTA 1988, s 815A(3); F(No 2)A 1992, s 50; FA 1996, Sch 20 para 39*].

44.12 COMPANY CEASING TO BE UK RESIDENT ETC., DUAL RESIDENT COMPANIES (BEFORE 30 NOVEMBER 1993) AND NON-RESIDENT COMPANIES

Company ceasing to be UK resident etc. If, at any time ('*the relevant time*') after 14 March 1988, a company ceases to be resident in the UK, except with Treasury consent under *ICTA 1988, s 765(1)(a)* on an application made before 15 March 1988, and does not cease to exist,

(*a*) it is deemed to dispose of immediately before the relevant time, and immediately reacquire, all its 'assets' at market value at that time, and

(*b*) ROLLOVER RELIEF (55) under *TCGA 1992, s 152* is not subsequently available by reference to disposals of old assets made before that time and acquisitions of new assets after that time.

If at any later time the company carries on a trade in the UK through a branch or agency (as defined in 44.3 above), the foregoing does not apply

(i) for (*a*) above, to any assets which, immediately after the relevant time, or

(ii) for (*b*) above, to any new assets which, after the relevant time,

are situated in the UK and are used in or for a trade, or are used or held for the branch or agency. '*Assets*' include various assets and rights relating to exploration or exploitation activities in the UK or a designated area of the sea, within *TCGA 1992, s 276* in 44.14 below. [*TCGA 1992, s 185*].

The Revenue takes the view that any gain resulting from a deemed disposal within paragraph (*a*) above cannot be the subject of a rollover relief claim by reference to a deemed acquisition within that paragraph because only the same and not a different asset is being acquired (Revenue International Tax Handbook ITH 408).

Where the company concerned ceases to be resident in the UK on 30 November 1993 solely by virtue of the coming into force of *FA 1994, s 249* (companies otherwise regarded as UK resident but under double tax relief arrangements already regarded as non-UK resident to be treated as non-UK resident for *Taxes Acts* purposes after 29 November 1993; see 52.6 RESIDENCE AND DOMICILE) and a deemed disposal under (*a*) above occurs, further provisions apply. Where an actual disposal of the assets is made on or before the day when corporation tax would otherwise be due and payable in respect of the deemed disposal, the tax is due and payable on that day; otherwise the tax is due and payable on the earlier of the day the assets are actually disposed of and 30 November 1999. Interest on unpaid tax in respect of the deemed disposal will only run from the due and payable date as determined above. If an actual part disposal of the assets is made, these further provisions are applied separately to the different parts, and the tax apportioned (and carrying interest) accordingly. [*FA 1994, s 250(3)–(6)*].

Where, at any time after 14 March 1988 and before 30 November 1993 (the latter date being the date of the coming into force of *FA 1994, s 249* above), a company, while continuing to be UK resident, commenced to be regarded, for the purposes of any DOUBLE TAX RELIEF (18.2) arrangements, as resident in a territory outside the UK, and as not liable to UK tax on gains on disposals of assets specified in those arrangements, (*a*) and (*b*) above applied to those assets. [*TCGA 1992, s 186; FA 1994, s 251(1)(9), Sch 26 Pt VIII*].

If the deemed disposal described in paragraph (*a*) above includes any '*foreign assets*' (i.e. assets which are situated, and are used in or for a trade carried on, outside the UK), any charge to tax will be postponed, as described below, if

(A) immediately after the relevant time the company was a '75% subsidiary' (see below) of a company ('*the principal company*') which was resident in the UK, and

(B) both companies elect in writing within two years after that time.

The excess of gains over losses arising on the foreign assets included in the deemed disposal is treated as a single chargeable gain not accruing to the company on the disposal. An equal amount ('*the postponed gain*') is instead treated as follows.

If within six years after the relevant time the company disposes of any assets (the '*relevant assets*') capital gains on which were taken into account in arriving at the postponed gain, a chargeable gain equal to the whole, or 'the appropriate proportion', of the postponed gain, so far as this has not already been treated as a chargeable gain under these provisions, is deemed to accrue to the principal company. '*The appropriate proportion*' is the proportion which the chargeable gain taken into account in arriving at the postponed gain in respect of the part of the relevant assets disposed of bears to the aggregate of the chargeable gains so taken into account in respect of the relevant assets held immediately before the time of the disposal.

If at any time

(I) the company ceases to be a 75% subsidiary of the principal company on a disposal by the principal company of ordinary shares in it, or

(II) after the company otherwise ceases to be a 75% subsidiary, the principal company disposes of ordinary shares in it, or

(III) the principal company ceases to be resident in the UK,

a chargeable gain, equal to so much of the postponed gain as has not previously been charged under these provisions, is deemed to arise.

If any part of the postponed gain becomes chargeable, and the subsidiary has unrelieved capital losses, the companies can elect within two years for part or all of the losses to be set against the amount chargeable.

For the purposes of the above provisions a company is a '*75% subsidiary*' of another company if and so long as not less than 75% of its ordinary share capital is owned *directly* by that other company. [*TCGA 1992, s 187; FA 1994, s 251(1)(9), Sch 26 Pt VIII*].

Dual resident companies. Where, at any time after 14 March 1988 and before 30 November 1993 (the latter date being the date of the coming into force of *FA 1994, s 249* above), an asset of a 'dual resident company' became a 'prescribed asset', the company was deemed immediately before that time to have disposed of and immediately reacquired it, both transactions being treated as carried out at the then market value. No deemed disposal and acquisition was to take place under this provision, however, where the asset became a prescribed asset on the company becoming to be regarded as a dual resident company as this already took place on such an event under *TCGA 1992, s 186* above. A company was a '*dual resident company*' if it was UK resident and fell to be regarded under any double tax relief arrangements as resident in another territory elsewhere. A '*prescribed asset*', in relation to a dual resident company, was an asset treated under any double tax relief arrangements as not giving rise to a UK tax charge on the company in respect of a gain arising on its disposal. [*TCGA 1992, s 188; FA 1994, s 251(1)(10), Sch 26 Pt VIII*].

Where either the disposal of the 'old assets' (or of the interest in them) or the acquisition of the 'new assets' is made (or the acquisition of the interest in them is made or the unconditional contract for their acquisition is entered into) (or both such events) occurred after 13 March 1989, then, if either such event occurred before 30 November 1993 (the latter date being the date of the coming into force of *FA 1994, s 249* above), ROLLOVER RELIEF (55) under *TCGA 1992, s 152* (the above quoted terms having the same meaning as in that provision) did not apply where a company was a 'dual resident company' (having the same meaning as in *TCGA 1992, s 188* above) at the time of disposal and at the time of acquisition, and the old assets were not 'prescribed assets' (defined as for in *TCGA 1992, s 188* above) at the time of disposal, unless the new assets were not prescribed assets immediately after the time of acquisition. However, rollover relief could apply where the acquisition of the new assets occurred before 14 March 1989 and the disposal of the old assets was after 13 March 1989 but within twelve months (or such longer period as is allowed by written notice given by the Board) of the acquisition of the new assets. [*TCGA 1992, s 160; FA 1994, s 251(1)(6), Sch 26 Pt VIII*].

44.13 **Company ceasing to be UK resident etc: compliance.** Before a company, after 14 March 1988, ceases to be resident in the UK, otherwise than with Treasury consent under *ICTA 1988, s 765(1)(a)*, it must give the Board

(*a*) notice of its intention to cease to be resident, specifying the time when it intends to do so,

(*b*) a statement of the amount of tax which it considers payable for periods beginning before that time, and

(*c*) particulars of the arrangements which it proposes to make to secure the payment of that tax.

It must also make arrangements to secure the payment of that tax; and the arrangements must be approved by the Board.

References to tax payable are not defined but include specified liabilities such as certain income tax payments, sub-contractors' deductions and amounts payable under *FA 1973, Sch 15 para 4* (territorial extension of charge of tax as in 44.14 below). Interest on unpaid tax is included in certain circumstances.

Any question as to the amount of tax payable is to be determined by the Special Commissioners. If any information provided by the company does not fully and accurately disclose all the material facts and considerations, any resulting approval is void. [*FA 1988, s 130*].

A person who is, or is deemed to be, involved in a failure to comply with the foregoing provisions is liable to a penalty not exceeding the amount of unpaid tax for periods beginning before the failure occurred. [*FA 1988, s 131*].

The requirements of *FA 1988, s 130* and the penalty that can be exacted under *FA 1988, s 131* above do not apply where the company concerned ceases to be resident in the UK on 30 November 1993 solely by virtue of the coming into force of *FA 1994, s 249* (companies otherwise regarded as UK resident but under double tax relief arrangements already regarded as non-UK resident to be treated as non-UK resident for *Taxes Acts* purposes after 29 November 1993; see 52.6 RESIDENCE AND DOMICILE). [*FA 1994, s 250(1)*].

Any tax in respect of accounting periods beginning before the cessation of UK residence which is still unpaid six months after the time when it became payable can (see also 44.12 above), within three years of final determination of the tax due, be recovered from a person who is, or in the twelve months before the cessation of UK residence (or, if less, the period after 14 March 1988) was, a member of the same group of companies (as in *TCGA 1992, s 170* (see 13.11 COMPANIES) but disregarding the pre-FA 2000 UK residence requirement and substituting 51 per cent subsidiary for '75 per cent subsidiary') or a controlling director (as defined). [*FA 1988, s 132; FA 2000, Sch 29 para 15*].

Guidance on the procedure to be followed under these provisions is given in Revenue Pamphlet IR 131, SP 2/90. In particular, notice under (*a*) above should be sent to Inland Revenue, International Division (Company Migrations) (at Room 312, Melbourne House, Aldwych, London WC2B 4LL) to whom an initial enquiry may be made via the Inland Revenue Information Centre (Tel. 020–7438 6945).

Non-resident companies. Where a non-UK resident company makes a gain on the disposal after 13 March 1989 and before 1 April 2000 of an asset, the gain forms part of its chargeable profits for corporation tax purposes under *TCGA 1992, s 10(3)* (non-UK resident trading etc. in the UK, see 44.3 above), and any of the corporation tax assessed relating to the accounting period in which the gain accrued remains unpaid after six months from it becoming payable, then the unpaid tax (or an amount equal to corporation tax on the amount of the gain at the rate in force at the time when the gain accrued if lower) can be recovered by the Board within three years from the amount being determined from a person who is, or in the twelve months before the disposal occurred (or, if less, the period after 13 March 1989) was, a member of the same group of companies (as in *TCGA 1992, s 170* but excluding any references to UK residence and substituting '51 per cent subsidiary' for '75 per cent subsidiary') or a controlling director (as defined). For gains accruing after 31 March 2000, these provisions are superseded by those at 13.18 COMPANIES. [*TCGA 1992, s 191; FA 2000, Sch 29 para 9(1)(3)(4)*].

44.14 EXPLORATION AND EXPLOITATION RIGHTS TO TERRITORIAL SEA-BED AND CONTINENTAL SHELF

Any gains accruing on the disposal of 'exploration or exploitation rights' are treated for the purposes of *TCGA 1992* as gains accruing on the disposal of assets situated in the UK. For this and all other purposes of the taxation of chargeable gains, the territorial sea of the UK is deemed to be part of the UK. (Under the *Territorial Sea Act 1987, s 1*, the breadth of the territorial sea adjacent to the UK is 12 nautical miles, a nautical mile being approximately 1,852 metres.)

Gains accruing on the disposal of 'exploration or exploitation assets' which are situated in a 'designated area', or 'unquoted shares' (i.e. not listed on a recognised stock exchange) deriving their value or the greater part of their value directly or indirectly from exploration or exploitation assets situated in the UK or a designated area or from such assets and exploration or exploitation rights taken together, are treated for the purposes of *TCGA 1992* as gains accruing on the disposal of assets situated in the UK. Gains accruing to a person not resident in the UK on the disposal of such rights or of such assets (the latter including for this purpose unquoted shares of the description above) are treated for the same purposes as gains accruing on the disposal of assets used for the purposes of a trade carried on by that person in the UK through a branch or agency (for which see 44.3 above).

If exploration or exploitation rights or exploration or exploitation assets (the latter including for this purpose unquoted shares of the description above) are disposed of by a company resident in an overseas territory to either a company resident in the same territory or a UK-resident company, or by one UK-resident company to another, the provisions at 13.12, 13.14, 13.16, 13.19, 13.20 COMPANIES, and *TCGA 1992, s 172* (now repealed) at 44.3 above apply, with appropriate modifications.

'*Exploration or exploitation rights*' means rights to assets to be produced by 'exploration or exploitation activities' or to interests in or to the benefit of such assets. '*Exploration or exploitation activities*' means activities carried on in connection with the exploration or exploitation of so much of the seabed and subsoil and their natural resources as is situated in the UK or a designated area.

References in the above to the disposal of exploration or exploitation rights include references to the disposal of shares deriving their value or the greater part of their value directly or indirectly from such rights, other than shares listed on a recognised stock exchange. '*Shares*' includes stock and any security as defined in *ICTA 1988, s 254(1)*. '*Designated area*' means an area designated by Order in Council under the *Continental Shelf Act 1964, s 1(7)*.

For the above purposes, an asset disposed of is an '*exploration or exploitation asset*' if either

(*a*) it is not a mobile asset and it is being or has at some time (for disposals before 14 March 1989, being a time within the period of two years ending at the date of disposal) been used in connection with exploration or exploitation activities carried on in the UK or a designated area; or

(*b*) it is a mobile asset which has at some time (for disposals before 14 March 1989, being a time within the period of two years ending at the date of disposal) been used in connection with exploration or exploitation activities so carried on and is dedicated to an oil field in which the person making the disposal, or a person connected with him, is or has been a participator;

and expressions used in (*a*) and (*b*) above have the same meanings there as if those paragraphs were included in *Oil Taxation Act 1975, Pt I*.

[*TCGA 1992, s 276; FA 1989, s 130, Sch 17 Pt VII; FA 1996, Sch 38 para 10(2)(d); FA 2000, Sch 29 para 35*].

There are comprehensive information and enforcement powers in relation to tax assessed by virtue of *TCGA 1992, s 276* above. In particular, unpaid tax so assessed on an overseas resident person may be recovered together with interest thereon from the holder of a licence granted under *Petroleum (Production) Act 1934* in respect of chargeable gains accruing on the disposal of exploration or exploitation rights connected with activities authorised, or carried on in connection with activities authorised, by the licence. An overseas resident liable to charge and who the Board are satisfied will meet his obligations under the *Taxes Acts* may apply for a certificate to be issued to the licence holder exempting him (subject to detailed conditions) from a charge on the default of the applicant. [*FA 1973, s 38(2)(8), Sch 15*].

Where an 'exploration or exploitation asset' (for this purpose, an asset used in connection with 'exploration or exploitation activities' carried on in the UK or a 'designated area', both expressions having the same meanings as in *TCGA 1992, s 276* above) ceases to be 'chargeable' in relation to a person by virtue of ceasing after 13 March 1989 to be 'dedicated to an oil field' in which he, or a person connected with him, is or has been a 'participator' (these last two expressions having the same meanings as in *Oil Taxation Act 1975, Pt I*), he is deemed for all purposes of *TCGA 1992* to have disposed of the asset immediately before the time when it ceased to be so dedicated, and immediately to have reacquired it, at its market value at that time.

An asset is a '*chargeable*' asset at any time in relation to a person if, were it to be disposed of at that time, any chargeable gains accruing to him on the disposal would be brought into charge for capital gains tax or corporation tax by virtue of *TCGA 1992, s 10(1)* or *(3)* respectively.

A similar deemed disposal and acquisition takes place where a person who is not resident or ordinarily resident ceases after 13 March 1989 to carry on a trade through a branch or agency in respect of any exploration or exploitation asset, other than a mobile asset, used in or for the purposes of the trade at or before the time of the deemed disposal. No such deemed disposal and reacquisition takes place if, immediately after the cessation of the trade carried on through the UK branch or agency, the asset is used in or for the purposes of exploration or exploitation activities carried on by him in the UK or a designated area. However, on a person ceasing after 13 March 1989 so to use the asset, there will be a deemed disposal and reacquisition. [*TCGA 1992, s 199*].

As regards leasing of mobile drilling rigs and other assets by overseas resident companies, see Revenue Pamphlet IR 131, SP 6/84.

See also 52.9 RESIDENCE AND DOMICILE for the territorial extent of the UK.

44.15 EUROPEAN ECONOMIC INTEREST GROUPINGS

With retrospective effect after 30 June 1989, new provisions are introduced governing the tax treatment of European Economic Interest Groupings ('groupings'), wherever registered, within *EEC Council Regulation No 2137/85* dated 25 July 1985. For the purposes of charging tax in respect of gains and subject to exceptions as below, a grouping is regarded as acting as the agent of its members. Its activities are regarded for such purposes as those of its members acting jointly, each member being regarded as having a share of its property, rights and liabilities, and a person is regarded as acquiring or disposing of a share of its assets not only where there is an acquisition or disposal by it while he is a member but also where he becomes or ceases to be a member or there is a change in his share of its property. A member's share in a grouping's property, rights or liabilities is that determined under the contract establishing the grouping or, if there is no provision determining such shares, it will correspond to the profit share to which he is entitled under the provisions of the contract (or if the contract makes no such provision, members are regarded as having equal shares). Where the grouping carries on a trade or profession, the members are regarded for the purposes of tax on gains as carrying on that trade or profession in partnership.

[*ICTA 1988, s 510A; FA 1990, s 69, Sch 11; FA 1995, Sch 29 Pt VIII(16)*].

The EEC provision of 25 July 1985 mentioned above covers all groupings established within the European Economic Area on the coming into force of the European Economic Area Agreement on 1 January 1994 (Revenue Press Release 9 February 1994).

See also 54.15 RETURNS, and 47.7 PENALTIES, 56.24 SELF-ASSESSMENT regarding non-compliance.

44.16 **COLLECTION OF TAX**

Although tax is legally assessable by notice served abroad, there are difficulties in collection. The UK courts will not enforce the revenue laws of other countries, see *Government of India v Taylor (re Delhi Electric Supply & Traction Co. Ltd) HL, [1955] AC 491* and *Brokaw v Seatrain UK Ltd, CA, [1971] 2 All ER 98.* See also 44.3 above for the assessment of UK resident agents of overseas resident traders and 44.13 above for arrangements required to secure payment of tax by a company ceasing to be UK resident or by a non-UK resident company. See also 43.2 OFFSHORE SETTLEMENTS for the arrangements where trustees become non-resident.

45 Partnerships

Cross-references. See 44.15 OVERSEAS MATTERS for European Economic Interest Groupings deemed to carry on a trade in partnership; 53 RETIREMENT RELIEF; 54.14 RETURNS; 55 ROLLOVER RELIEF and 56 SELF-ASSESSMENT.

Sumption: Capital Gains Tax. See A9.

45.1 A partnership is defined in *Partnership Act 1890, s 1* as 'the relation which subsists between persons carrying on a business in common with a view of profit'. This does not include purely capital transactions, e.g. the sale of a house by joint tenants.

45.2 An English partnership or firm is not a legal entity distinct from the partners themselves, but a collection of separate persons (which may be companies or individuals). In Scotland a firm is a legal person, but in general this does not affect the application of the *Taxes Acts*. A partnership cannot be a company for the purposes of *TCGA 1992*. [*TCGA 1992, s 288(1)*].

45.3 The taxation of partnership gains is based on a body of Revenue practice superimposed on the general capital gains rules. There are few specific references to partnerships in the capital gains legislation. For a useful codification of Revenue practice, reference should be made to Revenue Pamphlet IR 131, SPs D12, 1/79 and 1/89 on which much of this chapter is based. See also SP D11 regarding rollover relief.

Unless otherwise stated paragraph references in the remainder of this chapter are to SP D12.

For details of **returns under self-assessment** for 1996/97 and subsequent years, see 54.14 RETURNS.

45.4 **TREATMENT AND ASSESSMENT GENERALLY**

Where two or more persons carry on a trade or business in partnership, tax is assessed and charged on them separately in respect of chargeable gains accruing to them on the disposal of any partnership assets. (The treatment of partnerships in Scotland as a legal person is ignored for this purpose.) Any partnership dealings are treated as dealings by the partners and not by the firm as such. [*TCGA 1992, s 59(a)(b)*].

In general terms, because of the separate assessment and charging procedure of capital gains tax (and the charge to corporation tax in respect of chargeable gains), it will be the residence and domicile circumstances of each partner (whether an individual or company) that will dictate the basis of charge on him (although prior to the introduction of self-assessment this was not made explicitly clear; see *TCGA 1992, s 59(c)* applying *ICTA 1988, s 112(1)(2) (as originally enacted)* (partnerships controlled abroad). For example, an individual partner who is resident or ordinarily resident in the UK and domiciled there will be assessable wherever partnership gains arise and whether remitted to the UK or not. An individual partner neither resident nor ordinarily resident in the UK would only be liable in respect of partnership assets under *TCGA 1992, s 10* (UK branch or agency; see 44.3 OVERSEAS MATTERS). However, it is specifically provided that, if, under a double tax agreement, any income or capital gains of a partnership 'which resides outside the UK or which carries on any trade, profession or business the control or management of which is situated outside the UK' (prior to self-assessment, 'which resides or is deemed to reside outside the UK') is relieved from tax in the UK, such relief is not to affect the liability of any UK resident partner's share of the income or capital gains. Such treatment is always deemed to have applied (thus overruling *Padmore v CIR CA 1989, 62 TC 352*) except as regards cases where proceedings had before 17 March 1987 been determined by Commissioners or had a judgement given in court in respect of them before that date. [*ICTA 1988, s 112(4), s 115(5); TCGA 1992, s 59(c); FA 1995, s 125(1)(3)(5), Sch 29 Pt VIII(16)*].

Each partner is regarded as owning a fractional share of each asset which is calculated by reference to his asset-surplus-sharing ratio. Where no such ratio is specified, the share will follow the treatment in the accounts, subject to any external agreement. Failing that, regard will be had to the normal profit-sharing ratios. For appeals regarding apportionments of amounts etc., see 4 APPEALS and *White v Carline (Sp C 33), [1995] SSCD 186*.

The fraction is applied to the value of the total partnership interest in the asset disposed of, and no discount is allowed against market value for the size of an individual partner's share.

Expenditure on the acquisition of partnership assets will be allocated for capital gains tax purposes, in similar fashion to gains/losses, at the time of acquisition, subject to adjustment on any subsequent change in partnership sharing ratios (*paragraphs 1 and 2*).

Examples

Each of the following partnerships disposes of its offices to outside parties at arm's length at a chargeable gain of £30,000. No reliefs (e.g. rollover) are otherwise claimed. The gain is apportioned among the partners in the manner shown.

(*a*) *A & Co.* The partnership agreement states that each of the three partners shall be entitled to share equally in any surplus arising from assets disposed of by the partnership. Each partner is therefore treated as if he had made a gain of £10,000.

(*b*) *B & Co.* The three partners in B & Co have no formal agreement, but interest on capital contributed to the partnership is shown in the accounts at the same sum for each. The inference is that the capital has been equally contributed and can be equally withdrawn, so that the apportioned gain is £10,000 to each partner.

(*c*) *C & Co.* The three partners in C & Co, X, Y, and Z, have no formal agreement and the capital is shown in the accounts as a global sum. The profit-sharing ratio is 3:2:1, so that the apportioned gain is X–£15,000, Y–£10,000, and Z–£5,000.

45.5 CHANGES IN SHARING RATIOS

Where changes occur in partnership sharing ratios (including partners joining or leaving the firm), each partner is treated as acquiring or disposing of part or the whole of a share in each of the partnership assets, insofar as his share increases or decreases. Subject to certain qualifications (see below) the disposal consideration of each chargeable asset is regarded as being equal to the relevant fraction of the *current balance sheet value*. The balance sheet value could therefore be less than, equal to (i.e. on a no loss/no gain basis subject to any indexation allowance as below), or more than the cost for capital gains tax purposes, depending on what adjustments, if any, have been made in the accounts since acquisition of the assets. The cost of any part disposal under these provisions is calculated as a corresponding fraction of the total acquisition cost, and not by way of apportionment under *TCGA 1992, s 42* as in 17.6 DISPOSAL (*paragraph 4*).

A figure other than balance sheet value may have to be used in the following cases.

(*a*) Where a direct payment is made in connection with the change in sharing ratios (see 45.7 below).

(*b*) Where the change in sharing ratios results from a transaction made otherwise than at arm's length or made between CONNECTED PERSONS (14). The meaning of connected persons for these purposes is narrowed. See 45.10 below.

Re-basing to 1982, deferred charges and indexation allowance. The Revenue have agreed that a disposal of a share of partnership assets which is treated under *paragraph 4* above as on a no gain/no loss basis (before indexation, for disposals before 6 April 1988) may be treated as if it were a no gain/no loss disposal within *TCGA 1992, s 35(3)(d)* (see 8.7 ASSETS HELD ON 31 MARCH 1982). Such a disposal may also be treated as if it were a no gain/no loss disposal within that provision for the purposes of *TCGA 1992, s 36, Sch 4* (deferred charges; see 8.12 ASSETS HELD ON 31 MARCH 1982). Where such a disposal occurs after 5 April 1988, the amount of the consideration will be calculated on the assumption that an unindexed gain will accrue to the transferor equal to the indexation allowance, so that after taking into account the indexation allowance due, neither a gain nor a loss accrues. Where under the above a partner is treated as having owned the asset on 31 March 1982 in relation to a disposal after 5 April 1988 of all or part of his share of partnership assets, the indexation allowance on the disposal may be calculated as if he had acquired the share on 31 March 1982. A disposal of a share in a partnership asset on or after 31 March 1982 which is treated under *paragraph 4* above as on a no gain/no loss basis may be treated for the purposes of *TCGA 1992, s 55(5)(6)* as if it were a no gain/no loss disposal within those provisions (see 8.7 ASSETS HELD ON 31 MARCH 1982). A special rule will however apply where the share changed hands after 5 April 1985 (31 March 1985 in the case of an acquisition from a company) and before 6 April 1988: in these circumstances the indexation allowance will be calculated by reference to the 31 March 1982 value *but* from the date of the last disposal of the share before 6 April 1988 (Revenue Pamphlet IR 131, SP 1/89). This practice should be read in the light of the changes made regarding indexation allowance for disposals on or after 30 November 1993.

Example

J and K have traded in partnership for several years, sharing capital and income equally. The acquisition costs and 31 March 1982 values of the chargeable assets of the firm are as follows

	Cost	31.3.82 value
	£	£
Premises	60,000	150,000
Goodwill	10,000	50,000

The assets have not been revalued in the firm's balance sheet. On 1 June 2000, J and K admit L to the partnership, and the sharing ratio is J 35%, K 45% and L 20%. The indexation factor for March 1982 to April 1998 is 1.047.

J and K are regarded as disposing of part of their interest in the firm's assets to L as follows

	£	£
J		
Premises		
Deemed consideration		
£60,000 × (50% – 35%)	9,000	
Add indexation allowance (see below)	23,558	
Total deemed consideration	32,558	
Allowable cost	9,000	
Unindexed gain	23,558	
Indexation allowance (50% – 35%) × £150,000 × 1.047	23,558	—
Goodwill		
Deemed consideration		
£10,000 × (50% – 35%)	1,500	
Add indexation allowance (see below)	7,853	
Total deemed consideration	9,353	
Allowable cost	1,500	
Unindexed gain	7,853	
Indexation allowance (50% – 35%) × £50,000 × 1.047	7,853	—
Chargeable gain/allowable loss		Nil
K		
Premises		
Deemed consideration		
£60,000 × (50% – 45%)	3,000	
Add indexation allowance (see below)	7,853	
Total deemed consideration	10,853	
Allowable cost	3,000	
Unindexed gain	7,853	
Indexation allowance (50% – 45%) × £150,000 × 1.047	7,853	—
Goodwill		
Deemed consideration		
£10,000 × (50% – 45%)	500	
Add indexation allowance (see below)	2,618	
Total deemed consideration	3,118	
Allowable cost	500	
Unindexed gain	2,618	
Indexation allowance (50% – 45%) × £50,000 × 1.047	2,618	—
Chargeable gain/allowable loss		Nil

The allowable costs (inclusive, in L's case, of indexation allowance to April 1998) of the three partners are now

	Freehold land	Goodwill
	£	£
J	21,000	3,500
K	27,000	4,500
L (note (*b*))	43,411	12,471

Notes to the example

(*a*) The treatment illustrated above is taken from Revenue Pamphlet IR 131, SP D12 (17.1.75), para. 4 as extended by SP 1/89. Each partner's disposal consideration is equal to his share of current balance sheet value of the asset concerned plus, for disposals after 5 April 1988, indexation allowance, and each disposal treated as producing no gain and no loss.

(*b*) L's allowable costs comprise 20% of original cost, plus indexation allowance to April 1998 (see 26.1 INDEXATION) based on 20% of 31 March 1982 value.

General rules. Where a partner is treated as making a disposal it may also qualify for HOLD-OVER RELIEFS (25), RETIREMENT RELIEF (53) or ROLLOVER RELIEF (55). As regards an acquisition, this may be used to cover a chargeable gain as in ROLLOVER RELIEF (55). A partner treated as disposing of a partnership asset (or share) seems to be able to roll over any chargeable gain arising against an acquisition in another trade carried on, whether as sole trader or in another partnership trade, and vice versa.

45.6 ACCOUNTING ADJUSTMENTS

An upward revaluation of a partnership asset with the consequent credit to a partner's current or capital account does not give rise to a chargeable gain, but if after such a revaluation, a change occurs in a partner's sharing ratio (see 45.5 above), the disposal which he is thereby treated as making takes place at the increased value and may therefore give rise to a chargeable gain. Any acquisition is similarly treated.

Examples (ignoring indexation)

(*a*) X, Y and Z are partners in D & Co and share both capital and income profits and losses in the ratio 3:2:1. X wishes to take a less active part in the business, and Z to devote more time to it. The asset-surplus-sharing ratio is amended to 2:2:2. X is treated as having disposed of a one-sixth interest in each chargeable asset belonging to the partnership for a consideration equal to one-sixth of their respective book values, and Z as having acquired that interest for the same consideration.

(*b*) The facts are as (*a*) above, save that before the ratio is altered, the partnership premises are written up in the books from £120,000 to £180,000. No charge arises on this occasion. On the change in sharing ratio, however, X is treated as having made a gain of £10,000 (one-sixth of the book gain), subject to indexation and taper relief, and this forms part of Z's acquisition cost on a future disposal.

A downward revaluation, even if following an upward revaluation, is similarly not treated as giving rise to an allowable loss, but a change in partnership shares following such a revaluation may do so (*paragraph 5*).

45.7 CONSIDERATION OUTSIDE THE ACCOUNTS

Where actual consideration is given in connection with an alteration in partnership sharing ratios (see 45.5 above), it is added to the consideration deemed to have been received under the rules in 45.5 and 45.6 above, and may therefore give rise to a chargeable gain or increased gain, the payer's acquisition cost being adjusted accordingly. Where such an extraneous payment is expressed to be in respect of goodwill not included in the balance sheet, it is only deductible by the payer from a subsequent disposal (including a reduction in his share) of the goodwill, or on the payer's leaving the partnership (*paragraph 6*). It is understood that the Revenue do not accept that the writing down to nil of the value of goodwill by a professional partnership is able to form the basis of a 'negligible value' loss claim (see 39.9 LOSSES) by a partner who has previously given consideration for goodwill (see further Revenue Capital Gains Manual CG 27700–27733).

Example

D, E and F are partners in a firm of accountants who share all profits in the ratio 7:7:6. G is admitted as a partner in May 2000 and pays the other partners £10,000 for goodwill. The new partnership shares are D $\frac{3}{10}$, E $\frac{3}{10}$, F $\frac{1}{4}$ and G $\frac{3}{20}$. The book value of goodwill is £18,000, its cost on acquisition of the practice from the predecessor in 1988.

The partners are treated as having disposed of shares in goodwill as follows

	£	£
D		
$\frac{7}{20} - \frac{3}{10} = \frac{1}{20}$		
Disposal consideration		
Notional $\frac{1}{20} \times$ £18,000	900	
Actual $\frac{7}{20} \times$ £10,000	3,500	
		4,400
Allowable cost $\frac{1}{20} \times$ £18,000		900
Unindexed gain		£3,500
E		
$\frac{7}{20} - \frac{3}{10} = \frac{1}{20}$		
Disposal consideration (as for D)		4,400
Allowable cost (as for D)		900
Unindexed gain		£3,500
F		
$\frac{6}{20} - \frac{1}{4} = \frac{1}{20}$		
Disposal consideration		
Notional $\frac{1}{20} \times$ £18,000	900	
Actual $\frac{6}{20} \times$ £10,000	3,000	
		3,900
Allowable cost		900
Unindexed gain		£3,000
G's allowable cost of his share of goodwill is therefore		
Actual consideration paid		10,000
Notional consideration paid $\frac{3}{20} \times$ £18,000		2,700
		£12,700

Note to the example

(*a*) In practice, the above calculations must be adjusted for indexation allowance to April 1998 (see 26.1 INDEXATION) which is added to the notional consideration and deducted from the unindexed gain (see *Example* at 45.5 above). Any chargeable gains remaining after indexation are reduced by TAPER RELIEF (60).

45.8 Insofar as **annual payments** (whether under covenant or not) **to a retired partner** exceed an amount regarded as reasonable in view of the partner's past work for the firm, the capitalised value of the annuity is treated as consideration for the disposal of his partnership share (and as allowable expenditure by the remaining partners). If he had been a partner for at least ten years, the maximum 'reasonable' annuity is two-thirds of his average share of the partnership profits (before capital allowances or charges on income) in the best three of the last seven years in which he was required to devote substantially the whole of his time to the partnership. The ten-year period includes any period during which the partner was a member of another firm which has been merged with the existing firm. For periods less than ten years, the relevant fractions are as follows (instead of two-thirds).

Complete years	*Fraction*
1–5	$\frac{1}{60}$ for each year
6	$\frac{8}{60}$
7	$\frac{16}{60}$
8	$\frac{24}{60}$
9	$\frac{32}{60}$

This treatment applies to certain cases in which a lump sum is paid as well as the annuity (*paragraph 8*). Where the aggregate of the annuity and one-ninth of the lump sum does not exceed the appropriate fraction of the retired partner's average share of the profits (as above), the capitalised value is not treated as consideration in his hands. The lump sum continues to be treated as consideration (Revenue Pamphlet IR 131, SP 1/79).

45.9 SHARES ACQUIRED IN STAGES

Where a share in a partnership asset was acquired in stages wholly after 5 April 1965 then, on a part disposal (e.g. on a decrease in a partner's asset-surplus-sharing ratio) the acquisitions are pooled. Where a share built up in stages was acquired wholly or partly before 6 April 1965 the rules given in 7 ASSETS HELD ON 6 APRIL 1965 normally apply on a disposal or part disposal to identify the acquisition cost of the share in each asset i.e. the disposal is normally identified firstly with shares held on 6 April 1965 on a 'first in, first out basis' and then on a 'pool' basis with shares acquired after 6 April 1965. The Revenue give special consideration to situations where this rule appears to produce an unreasonable result when applied to temporary changes in the shares of a partnership, e.g. those occurring when a partner's departure and a new partner's arrival do not exactly coincide (*paragraph 10*). Presumably each partner has a separate right of election for 6 April 1965 value in addition to the election in 45.13 below as regards quoted shares and securities.

Example

Q is a partner in a medical practice. The partnership's only chargeable asset is a freehold house used as a surgery. The cost of the house to the partnership was £3,600 in 1962 and it was revalued in the partnership accounts to £50,000 in 1989. Q was admitted to the partnership in June 1964 with a share of $\frac{1}{6}$ of all profits. As a result of partnership changes, Q's profit share altered as follows

1970 $\frac{1}{5}$

1981 $\frac{1}{4}$

2000 $\frac{3}{10}$

For capital gains tax, Q's allowable cost of his share of the freehold house is calculated as follows

	£	
1964 $\frac{1}{6} \times$ £3,600		£600
1970 $(\frac{1}{5} - \frac{1}{6}) \times$ £3,600	120	
1981 $(\frac{1}{4} - \frac{1}{5}) \times$ £3,600	180	
2000 $(\frac{3}{10} - \frac{1}{4}) \times$ £50,000	2,500	£2,800

Notes to the example

(*a*) The pre-6.4.65 costs are not pooled.

(*b*) On Q's acquisition of an increased share of the property in 2000 (subsequent to the revaluation in 1989), any partner with a reduced share will be treated as having made a disposal and thus a chargeable gain. The re-basing rules will apply to the disposal (subject to the usual comparison with the gain or loss without re-basing).

45.10 TRANSACTIONS BETWEEN PERSONS NOT AT ARM'S LENGTH

Transactions within the partnership are not treated as made between CONNECTED PERSONS (14), provided they are pursuant to bona fide commercial arrangements, unless the partners are otherwise connected. Market value will be substituted for actual consideration only if the consideration would have been different had the parties been at arm's length. Where market value is applied, the deemed disposal proceeds are treated as in 45.7 above (*paragraph 7*).

45.11 PARTNERSHIP ASSETS DISTRIBUTED IN KIND

The disposal of a partnership asset to one or more of the partners is treated as being made at market value which is apportioned among all the partners as in 45.5 above. Chargeable gains thus attributable to partners receiving no asset are taxed at the time of the disposal. Any gain notionally accruing to a receiving partner is treated as reducing his allowable expenditure on a subsequent disposal of the asset. The same principle applies where a loss arises (*paragraph 3*).

Example

R, S and T are partners sharing all profits in the ratio 4:3:3. Farmland owned by the firm is transferred in November 2000 to T for future use by him as a market gardening enterprise separate from the partnership business. No payment is made by T to the other partners but a reduction is made in T's future share of income profits. The book value of the farmland is £5,000, its cost in 1989, but the present market value is £15,000.

		£
R		
Deemed disposal consideration	$\frac{4}{10} \times$ £15,000	6,000
Allowable cost	$\frac{4}{10} \times$ £5,000	2,000
Gain (subject to indexation allowance to April 1998 and TAPER RELIEF (60))		£4,000
S		
Deemed disposal consideration	$\frac{3}{10} \times$ £15,000	4,500
Allowable cost	$\frac{3}{10} \times$ £5,000	1,500
Gain (subject to indexation allowance to April 1998 and TAPER RELIEF (60))		£3,000

		£
T		
Partnership share	$\frac{3}{10} \times$ £5,000	1,500
Market value of R's share		6,000
Market value of S's share		4,500
Allowable cost of land for future disposal		£12,000

45.12 MERGERS

Mergers of existing partnerships are treated as in 45.5–45.7 above. If gains arise for reasons similar to 45.6 and 45.7 above, a continuing partner may claim ROLLOVER RELIEF (55) insofar as he disposes of his share of assets of the old firm and acquires a share in other assets of the new firm (*paragraph 9*).

45.13 6 APRIL 1965 AND 31 MARCH 1982 ELECTIONS

The election under *TCGA 1992, Sch 2 para 4* for quoted securities, whereby 6 April 1965 market value is substituted for acquisition cost and the securities form part of the '1982 holding' for identification purposes (see 7.3, 7.4 ASSETS HELD ON 6 APRIL 1965) is available separately to each partner as regards his share of partnership assets. Each partner's right to elect is distinct from his right to elect in respect of securities held by him in his personal capacity. The time limit for making the election in respect of a particular partner's share of partnership securities operates by reference to the earlier of the first relevant disposal by the partnership and the first post-19 March 1968 reduction of his share of partnership assets (*paragraph 11*).

A universal re-basing election made under *TCGA 1992, s 35(5)* (see 8.3 ASSETS HELD ON 31 MARCH 1982) by a person in one capacity does not cover disposals made by him in a different capacity. [*TCGA 1992, s 35(7)*]. The Revenue have confirmed that an election for assets held privately will not apply to assets held in the capacity of partner, and *vice versa*. As regards partnership assets, the election is available separately to each partner in respect of his share. (Revenue Tax Bulletin November 1991 p 5).

45.14 COMPANIES

The above rules apply, *mutatis mutandis*, to company partners.

46 Payment of Tax

Cross-references. See 4 APPEALS; 5 ASSESSMENTS; 9 BACK DUTY; 35 INTEREST AND SURCHARGES ON UNPAID TAX; 43.2 OFFSHORE SETTLEMENTS as regards the liability of migrating trustees of a settlement; 44.5 OVERSEAS MATTERS for relief for unremittable overseas gains and 44.13 for companies ceasing to be UK resident and non-resident companies; 56 SELF-ASSESSMENT.

46.1 CAPITAL GAINS TAX

For 1996/97 and subsequent years, capital gains tax becomes due and payable as part of a taxpayer's self-assessment. The due date for payment (or repayment) is 31 January following the year of assessment. The one exception is where the taxpayer gave notice of chargeability under *TMA 1970, s 7* (see 54.2 RETURNS) within six months after the end of the year of assessment, but was not given notice under *TMA 1970, s 8* or *s 8A* (personal and trustee's return; see 54.3 RETURNS) until after 31 October following the year of assessment; in such case, the due date is the last day of the three months beginning with the date of the said notice. The tax payable is reduced by any income tax overpayment for the year. [*TMA 1970, s 59B(1)–(4)(7)(8); FA 1994, s 193, s 196, s 199(2), Sch 19 para 45; FA 1996, s 122(2), s 126(2)*].

Where a person's self-assessment is amended under the relevant provisions in 54.7 RETURNS, 56.13 SELF-ASSESSMENT or under the partnership 'discovery' provisions (see 5.2 ASSESSMENTS), the due date for the final payment (or repayment) is normally as above but is deferred, as regards any tax payable (or repayable) by virtue of the amendment and subject to the appeal and postponement provisions in 56.28 SELF-ASSESSMENT, until, if later, 30 days after the date of notice of the amendment (but note that this does not defer the date from which interest accrues on unpaid tax; see 35.1 INTEREST AND SURCHARGES ON UNPAID TAX).

Where an officer of the Board enquires into the return (see 56.11 SELF-ASSESSMENT) and a repayment is otherwise due, the repayment is not required to be made until the enquiry is completed (see 56.13 SELF-ASSESSMENT) although the officer may make a provisional repayment at his discretion. This does not affect the due date of repayment for interest purposes (see 34.1 INTEREST ON OVERPAID TAX).

Subject to the appeal and postponement provisions in 56.28 SELF-ASSESSMENT, the due date for payment of tax charged by assessment otherwise than by self-assessment, e.g. a discovery assessment under *TMA 1970, s 29* (see 5.2 ASSESSMENTS), is 30 days after the date of the assessment (but see also 35.1 INTEREST AND SURCHARGES ON UNPAID TAX).

[*TMA 1970, s 59B(4A)(5)(6); FA 1994, s 193, s 199(2)(3); FA 1995, s 103(7), s 115(6); FA 1996, s 127*].

For 1995/96 and earlier years, capital gains tax became due and payable on 1 December following the end of the year of assessment to which it related, or 30 days after the issue of the notice of assessment, whichever was the later. [*TCGA 1992, s 7*].

46.2 CORPORATION TAX (ON CHARGEABLE GAINS)

The following applies *for accounting periods ending after 30 September 1993* (Pay and File). Corporation tax (including that in respect of chargeable gains) is due and payable without assessment on the day following the expiry of nine months from the end of the period. The amount shown in the return for the period under *TMA 1970, s 11* (see 54.11 RETURNS) as the corporation tax due for the period is treated for collection purposes as tax charged and due and payable under an assessment on the company.

If the company subsequently has grounds for believing that a change in circumstances has rendered payment for a period excessive, it may, by notice to the inspector stating the grounds and the amount it considers should be repaid, claim repayment of the excess. Such notice may not be given before the date on which the tax became (or would have become) due and payable as above, or after an assessment for the period has become final. If the company wishes to claim repayment at a time when an assessment for the period is under appeal, the company must apply to the Appeal Commissioners concerned for a determination of the amount to be repaid pending determination of the appeal. Such an application may be combined with an application for postponement of tax pending an appeal (see 46.3 below). [*ICTA 1988, s 10; FA 1990, s 106; FA 1998, s 117, Sch 19 para 1, Sch 27 Pt III(28); SI 1992 No 3066*].

Under corporation tax self-assessment for accounting periods ending on or after 1 July 1999 (see 56.2 SELF-ASSESSMENT), comparable provisions generally apply (except that assessments are replaced by self-assessments). [*TMA 1970, ss 59D, 59DA; FA 1998, s 117, Sch 19 para 29*]. For 'large' companies, however, this is subject to the rules outlined below for payment of corporation tax by quarterly instalments.

A system of *quarterly accounting* for corporation tax (i.e. payment by instalments) by 'large' companies is introduced for accounting periods ending on or after 1 July 1999 (to coincide with the introduction of corporation tax self-assessment). [*TMA 1970, s 59E; FA 1998, s 30*]. Under the *Corporation Tax (Instalment Payments) Regulations 1998*, '*large*' companies are those liable to the full rate of corporation tax, i.e. those with profits (including UK dividend income, other than intra-group dividends, plus tax credits) exceeding £1,500,000 in a year, divided by one plus the number of active associated companies if any. However, such a company is not treated as 'large' in respect of an accounting period if its total corporation tax liability for that period does not exceed £10,000 (£5,000 for accounting periods ending before 1 July 2000), which might be the case if it would otherwise be large only by reference to the number of its associates or the level of its dividend income. A company is also exempt from payment by instalments for an accounting period if it was not 'large' in the 12 months preceding the accounting period and its profits for the accounting period do not exceed £10 million, divided by one plus the number of active associated companies as at the end of the preceding accounting period. Each of these monetary limits is proportionately reduced for accounting periods of less than 12 months.

The switch to full payment by instalments is being achieved over a transitional period ending on 30 June 2002. For accounting periods ending before 1 July 2000, 60% of the total liability is payable by a maximum of four instalments, increasing to 72% for those ending in the year to 30 June 2001, 88% for those ending in the year to 30 June 2002 and finally to 100% for all subsequent accounting periods. During the transitional period, the balance not payable by instalments is payable by the normal due date (see above). The first instalment is due 6 months and 14 days into the accounting period and the last is due 3 months and 14 days after the end of the accounting period. Interim instalments are due at quarterly intervals. Except for accounting periods of less than 12 months, the amount of each instalment should be one quarter of the total payable by instalments. Interest on tax underpaid by any instalment will run from the due date of that instalment. In cases of deliberate or reckless non-payment or underpayment, a penalty of up to twice the amount of interest may be charged. Subject to similar penalty for fraud or negligence, a company may claim repayment of tax paid by instalments if its circumstances change such that the total liability is likely to be less than previously calculated. See Revenue Tax Bulletin February 2000 pp 723–726 for a practical article on the operation of the system. The Revenue are given extensive powers to require information and records to ascertain reasons for non-payment of an instalment, the validity of a repayment claim or whether the amount of an instalment is consistent with the quality and quantity of information available as to the company's likely corporation tax liability. See below re Revenue guidance on use of their information and penalty powers.

In the absence of counteraction, companies could delay the commencement of instalments or obtain excessive benefit from the transition (by, for example, arranging that more than one year's corporation tax liability fell in the first year of the transition); they could do so by changing their accounting date and/or transferring profitable activities to companies in the same group but with different accounting dates. There are anti-forestalling provisions to counteract this. Changes of accounting date decided upon, or based on facts in existence, before 25 November 1997 or occasioned by the company being taken over and aligning its accounting date with that of its new ultimate parent company are exempted, as are transfers of profits not exceeding £5 million, reduced proportionately for accounting periods of less than 12 months.

[*SI 1998 No 3175; SI 1999 No 1929; SI 2000 No 892*].

The Revenue have published guidance outlining the way in which they will use their information and penalty powers under the above regulations; the information powers are not intended for routine use, and the majority of cases of late or inadequate payment will attract only an interest charge, not a penalty. A penalty will be sought in only the most serious cases involving flagrant abuse of the regulations. (Revenue Press Release 8 June 1999).

Penalties are also chargeable for non-compliance with a notice to produce information, records etc. [*TMA 1970, s 98; FA 1999, s 89(1)(3)*].

Under corporation tax self-assessment, the Revenue are given power to enter into arrangements ('Group Payment Arrangements') with some or all of the members of a group of companies (defined to include all 51% subsidiaries) for one of them to discharge any liability of each of them for the accounting period to which the arrangements relate. [*FA 1998, s 36*]. This facility will be in place for accounting periods ending on or after 31 December 1999 (Revenue Press Release 26 February 1999). See Revenue Tax Bulletin April 1999 pp 647–650.

There are already provisions to allow two companies within a group (as defined for group relief purposes under *ICTA 1988, Pt X Ch IV*) to jointly give notice to the inspector that a 'tax refund relating to an accounting period' which falls to be made to one of them should be surrendered in whole or part to the other. The surrendering company is then treated as having received on the 'relevant date' a payment equal to the refund (or part), and the recipient company as having paid on that date corporation tax equal to the amount of the refund (or part). [*FA 1989, s 102; FA 1993, Sch 14 para 11; FA 1999, s 89(2)(3), s 93, Sch 11 para 3; SI 1998 No 3175, Reg 9; SI 1999 No 1929, Reg 3*]. These provisions are designed to enable group members to rearrange their tax liabilities without suffering a disadvantage because of the higher rates for interest on unpaid tax as compared with those for interest on overpaid tax. See TOLLEY'S CORPORATION TAX under Groups of Companies for full coverage of the provisions.

For accounting periods ending before 1 October 1993, corporation tax (including that in respect of chargeable gains) assessed for an accounting period is due and payable within nine months from the end of the period or, if later, within 30 days from the date of issue of the notice of assessment. [*ICTA 1988, s 10(1)(b)*].

46.3 POSTPONEMENT OF TAX PENDING APPEAL

If a taxpayer has grounds for believing that he is overcharged to tax by an assessment, he (or his agent) may, by notice in writing stating those grounds and given to the inspector within thirty days after the issue of the notice of assessment, apply for postponement of a specified amount of tax. Application may be made outside the normal thirty-day time limit if there is a change in circumstances giving grounds for belief that the appellant is overcharged by the assessment. The Revenue have said that a 'change in circumstances' is not just a 'change of mind' but a change in the circumstances in which the decision not to apply for postponement was made. Two examples cited by the Revenue are (*a*) where further work on the preparation of accounts indicates that the estimated assessment is 'wide of the mark' and (*b*) where it has become apparent that further relief (e.g. loss or group relief) is due (CCAB Statement TR 477, 28 June 1982). The taxpayer and the inspector may then come to an agreement in writing as to the amount of tax to be postponed (if any), and the giving by either party to the other of written notice confirming the existence of an agreement and the terms thereof is treated as a written agreement for this purpose. Where the parties cannot (or do not attempt to) come to an agreement, the matter is referred to the Commissioners, who, if they consider that there are reasonable grounds for believing that an amount of tax has been overcharged, must postpone that amount pending determination of the substantive appeal (which consideration of the issue of postponement does not preclude them from hearing). [*TMA 1970, s 55(1)(d), (3)(3A)(4)(8)(10); F(No 2)A 1975, s 45(1); FA 1982, s 68; FA 1990, s 104(2)(4)*].

On the determination of (or agreement on) the amount of tax to be postponed, the balance which is *not postponed* becomes due and payable as if it had been charged by an assessment, notice of which was issued on the date of that determination or agreement (or on the date of notice of confirmation of the latter) and in respect of which there had been no appeal (see example at 46.4 below). [*TMA 1970, s 55(6)(a); F(No 2)A 1975, s 45(1); FA 1989, s 156(2)(4)*].

If, after the determination of an amount of tax to be postponed, the inspector or the taxpayer has grounds, as a result of a change in the circumstances of the case, for believing that that amount is excessive or insufficient, as the case may be, he may, by notice in writing given to the other party at any time before the determination of the substantive appeal, apply to the Commissioners for a further determination of that amount. The notice must state the amount in which the postponement is believed to be discrepant and the grounds for that belief. Any tax which then ceases to be postponed is treated as charged by an assessment, notice of which was issued on the date of the further determination and in respect of which no appeal is pending. Any tax overpaid is repaid. [*TMA 1970, s 55(4)(6)(b); F(No 2)A 1975, s 45(1); FA 1989, s 156(2)(4)*].

46.4 PAYMENT OF TAX ON DETERMINATION OF APPEAL

Any tax payable in accordance with the determination of the substantive appeal, the payment of which had been postponed (see 46.3 above), or which would not have been charged by the assessment if there had been no appeal (i.e. further tax found to be due on the appeal), becomes due and payable as if it were charged by an assessment, notice of which was issued on the date on which the inspector issued to the taxpayer a notice of the total amount payable in accordance with the determination and in respect of which there had been no appeal, and any tax overpaid is repaid. [*TMA 1970, s 55(9); F(No 2)A 1975, s 45(1); FA 1989, s 156(2)(4)*].

Any outstanding tax charged in accordance with the Commissioners' decision must be paid as above before an appeal can be heard by the High Court (or Court of Appeal in NI). If, on the determination of the appeal by the High Court, further tax is found to be chargeable, it becomes due and payable thirty days from the date on which the inspector issues to the taxpayer a notice of the total amount payable. [*TMA 1970, s 56(9); F(No 2)A 1975, s 45(3); FA 1989, s 156(3)(4)*]. Tax overpaid consequent on the decision of the High Court (or Court of Appeal in NI) is repaid (with, at the Court's discretion, interest) even though further appeal is possible (*T & E Homes Ltd v Robinson CA 1979, 52 TC 567*). [*TMA 1970, s 55(9); FA 1989, s 156(2)(4)*]. See also 34 INTEREST ON OVERPAID TAX.

46.5 DATE OF PAYMENT

With effect from 6 April 1996, the Revenue consider that in respect of each method of payment the following dates of payment apply:

- Cheques, cash, postal orders handed in at Revenue offices or received by post (except in the case of (ii) below): the day of receipt by the Revenue.
- Cheques, cash, postal orders received by post following a day when the Office has been closed for whatever reason (including a weekend): the day the office was first closed (for payments received on Monday the effective date will be the previous Saturday).
- Electronic Funds transfer (EFT) — payment by BACS or CHAPS (Clearing House Automated Payment System: one working day immediately before the date that the value is received (Working day for this purpose is a Bank of England working day). This practice was announced in a Revenue press release dated 1 April 1993. Prior to this the practice was to treat the date value was received as the effective date of payment.
- Bank Giro or Girobank: three working days prior to the date of processing by the Revenue.

(Revenue Press Release 1 April 1996).

Prior to this, the Revenue considered that the effective dates of payment for the various methods by which tax may be paid were as follows.

- In-date cheques tendered by post: the third working day before the day on which the Collector receives the cheque.
- Cash and in-date cheques (other than those returned to the drawer) tendered personally: the date of tender.
- Post-dated cheques: the date of the cheque.
- Bank giro credit: the date stamped on the payslip by the bank's cashier.
- National Giro bank in-payment: the date stamped on the payslip by the Post Office counter clerk.
- National Giro bank transfer: the date of the Revenue's National Giro bank statement on which the item appears.

(Tolley's Practical Tax 1981, p 42).

46.6 PAYMENT BY INSTALMENTS ETC.

Where the whole or part of the consideration for a disposal is receivable by instalments over a period exceeding 18 months, beginning not earlier than the date of disposal, the tax arising may at the option of the person making the disposal be paid by such instalments as the Revenue allows, over a period not exceeding eight years (and ending not later than the time at which the last of the instalments of the consideration is payable). Prior to 6 April 1996 it was necessary to satisfy the Revenue that payment in one sum would cause the taxpayer undue hardship. Under self-assessment, the Revenue has general powers within *TMA 1970* to enquire into any return, claim or election. [*TCGA 1992, s 280; FA 1996, Sch 20 para 65*]. For guidance given to inspectors on the practical operation of this relief, see Revenue Capital Gains Manual CG 14910–14922.

Interest on unpaid tax will be charged only if an instalment is paid late. It will be charged on that instalment, and will run from the date when the instalment was due (Tolley's Practical Tax 1988, p 176 and 1989, p 5).

For postponed or contingent future consideration, see 17.5 and 17.7 DISPOSAL.

Gifts etc. Subject to the conditions below, capital gains tax chargeable on a gift made after 13 March 1989 may, on election in writing, be paid by ten equal yearly instalments. The first instalment is due on the ordinary due date and the unpaid tax will attract interest on unpaid tax in the usual way and which will be payable with each instalment. The outstanding balance together with accrued interest may be paid at any time. The deferral of payment is available where the whole or any part of specified assets is disposed of by way of gift or is deemed to be disposed of by trustees under *TCGA 1992, s 71(1)* or *s 72(1)* (see 57.9–57.11 SETTLEMENTS) and the disposal is *either* one to which neither *TCGA 1992, s 165(4)* nor *s 260(3)* (see 25.1 and 25.7 HOLD-OVER RELIEFS) applies (or would apply if a claim was made) *or* one to which either of those *sections* does apply but on which the held-over gain only partly reduces the gain otherwise arising or is nil. The assets specified for this purpose are: land or any interest or estate in land; any shares or securities of a company which, immediately before the disposal, gave control to the person making or deemed to be making the disposal; and any shares or securities of a company not falling within the foregoing and not listed on a recognised stock exchange nor dealt in on the Unlisted Securities Market. Tax and any accrued interest is payable immediately if the disposal was by way of a gift to a person connected (see 14 CONNECTED PERSONS) with the donor or was deemed to be made under *TCGA 1992, s 71(1)* or *s 72(1)* and the assets are disposed of for a valuable consideration under a subsequent disposal (whether or not made by the original donee). Interest on unpaid tax is chargeable on each instalment as if no election to pay by instalments had been made. Instalments and interest may be paid at any time with the interest calculation adjusted accordingly.

[*TCGA 1992, s 281; FA 1996, Sch 18 para 15, para 17(3), Sch 38 para 10(1)–(3)*].

For a summary of other reliefs available to disposals by way of gift etc., see 23.4 GIFTS.

'Time to Pay' arrangements. By concession, under a 'time to pay' arrangement, a taxpayer enters into a negotiated agreement with the Revenue, which takes full account of his circumstances (e.g. illness, unemployment, unforeseen short-term business difficulties), and thereby commits to settle his tax liabilities by regular instalments. Clear reasons for allowing settlement over an extended period that runs beyond the due date must be established during negotiations and any such arrangement is normally subject to adequate provision being made to settle future liabilities on time. Interest on unpaid tax is chargeable in the normal way on the full amount unpaid at the due date and not just on overdue instalments. However, a surcharge may be avoided where a 'Time to Pay' arrangement is in force (see 35.5 INTEREST AND SURCHARGES ON UNPAID TAX). (Revenue Self-Assessment Manual — Payments section — para 7.2.1, Personal Contact Manual para 4.8).

46.7 COLLECTION AND GENERALLY

The Collector of Taxes may distrain (poind in Scotland). [*TMA 1970, ss 61–64; FA 1989, ss 152–155; SI 1994, Nos 87, 236; SI 1995 No 2151*]. See also *Herbert Berry Associates Ltd v CIR HL 1977, 52 TC 113*. Where an amount due (or any instalment) is less than £1,000, the Collector may within six months of the due date take summary magistrates' court proceedings. The limit is raised to £2,000 for 1996/97 onwards under SELF-ASSESSMENT (56.32). The Collector may also recover the tax by proceedings in the county court. [*TMA 1970, ss 65, 66; FA 1984, s 57; SI 1989 No 1300; SI 1991 Nos 724, 1625, 1877*]. But for limitations in Scotland and NI see *TMA 1970, s 65(4), s 66(3)(4), s 67; FA 1976, s 58; FA 1995, s 156*, and see *Mann v Cleaver KB 1930, 15 TC 367*. Unpaid tax (and arrears) may also be recovered (with full costs) as a *Crown debt in the High Court*. [*TMA 1970, s 68*]. The amount of an assessment which has become final cannot be re-opened in proceedings to collect the tax (*CIR v Pearlberg CA 1953, 34 TC 57; CIR v Soul CA 1976, 51 TC 86*), and it is not open to the taxpayer to raise the defence that the Revenue acted *ultra vires* in raising the assessment (*CIR v Aken CA 1990, 63 TC 395*).

For whether unpaid tax is a business liability for commercial etc. purposes, see *Conway v Wingate CA, [1952] 1 All ER 782; Stevens v Britten CA, [1954] 3 All ER 385; R v Vaccari CCA, [1958] 1 All ER 468; In re Hollebone's Agreement CA, [1959] 2 All ER 152.*

For the limited priority given to payment of corporation tax in a winding-up of a company, see 13.5 COMPANIES.

46.8 **REMISSION AND REPAYMENT OF TAX IN CASES OF OFFICIAL ERROR**

Arrears of income tax or capital gains tax may be given up if they result from the Inland Revenue's failure to make proper and timely use of information supplied by:

(*a*) a taxpayer about his or her own income, gains or personal circumstances;

(*b*) an employer where the information affects a taxpayer's coding; or

(*c*) the Department of Social Security about a taxpayer's State retirement disability or widow's pension.

From 11 March 1996, tax will normally be given up only where the taxpayer could reasonably have believed that his or her tax affairs were in order and was notified of an over-repayment after the end of the tax year following the year in which the repayment was made.

In exceptional circumstances arrears of tax notified twelve months or less after the end of the relevant tax year may be given up if the revenue either failed more than once to make proper use of the facts they had been given about one source of income or allowed the arrears of tax to build up over two years in succession by failing to make proper and timely use of information they had been given. (Revenue Press Release 11 March 1996).

Prior to 11 March 1996 the amount of tax remitted was directly related to the taxpayer's gross income according to the following table:

Taxpayer's Gross Annual Income	*Remission*
Up to £15,500	All
£15,501–£18,000	75%
£18,001–£22,000	50%
£22,001–£26,000	25%
£26,001–£40,000	10%
Over £40,000	Nil

The income to be considered is that for the year in which the arrears were met, although in practice the preceding year's income was considered. If this produced an anomaly, income of the current year could be estimated (ICAEW Technical Memorandum TR 627, August 1986).

All these limits apply to arrears where the actual or likely amount of which is notified after 16 February 1993 and before 11 March 1996.

Inspectors could give discretionary relief if the taxpayer's gross income (before personal allowances, deductions etc.) marginally exceeded the above limits and he had large or exceptional family responsibilities. Arrears notified by the end of the tax year following that in which they arose are not remitted except where the Revenue has made repeated errors within that period or the arrears have built up over two whole years in succession as a direct result of the Revenue's failure to make proper and timely use of information. The relief applies for income and capital gains tax purposes, and, for arrears notified after 5 April 1990, the income limits will apply only to the income of the spouse assessed rather than, as previously, to the joint incomes of a husband and wife (Revenue Press Releases 17 February 1993 and 26 April 1994 and Revenue Pamphlet IR 1, A19).

Under *TMA 1970*, unless a longer or shorter period is prescribed, no statutory claim for relief is allowed unless it is made within six years from the end of the tax year to which it relates.

However, repayments of tax will be made in respect of claims made outside the statutory time limit where an overpayment of tax has arisen because of an error by the Inland Revenue or another Government department, and where there is no dispute or doubt as to the facts (Revenue Pamphlet IR 1, B41).

46.9 RECOVERY OF TAX FROM OFFICERS

Tax which has fallen due may be recovered from the treasurer or acting treasurer (the 'proper officer') of a company which is not a body corporate or not incorporated under a UK enactment or by charter. That officer then has a right of reimbursement out of moneys coming into his hands on behalf of that company, and to be indemnified by the company for any balance. [*TMA 1970, s 108(2)(3)*].

46.10 REPAYMENTS AND OVER-REPAYMENTS

Repayments. From 5 April 1994, whilst the onus still seems to be on the taxpayer to claim any repayment that is due, either by reason of mistake, over-estimate or the settling of an appeal, the Revenue has brought into force computer systems that will identify and repay automatically, unless there is an outstanding liability in respect of the same taxpayer when in most cases there will be a set-off made, overpaid income tax under Schedules A and D, capital gains tax, higher rate tax, Class 4 national insurance contributions and associated interest. A letter will accompany the payable order setting out details of the overpayment and the way it has been dealt with. Although computations of revised and repaid interest and repayment supplement will not be produced with the letter they can be requested if desired. Taxpayers can still authorise the Revenue to make the repayment to an agent by sending the authority to the tax office dealing with their affairs (Revenue Press Release 7 April 1994).

For an article on Revenue practice re allocations of overpayments under SELF-ASSESSMENT (56), see Revenue Tax Bulletin June 1999 pp 673, 674.

Over-repayments. If not otherwise assessable under *TMA 1970, s 29* (see 5 ASSESSMENTS), tax over-repaid may be assessed under Schedule D, Case VI as if it were unpaid tax. Any associated excess repayment supplement (see 34 INTEREST ON OVERPAID TAX) may be included in the assessment. The time limit for such assessments is extended to the end of the year of assessment (chargeable period for a company) following that in which the repayment was made if it would otherwise have passed and is subject to the usual fraudulent or negligent conduct extensions. See 56.31 as regards SELF-ASSESSMENT.

Similar provisions to the above apply to companies to enable excess set-offs of advance corporation tax and excess set-offs or payments of tax credit to be recovered, including any INTEREST ON OVERPAID TAX (34).

Where an assessment on a company is to recover repayment of tax paid for an accounting period ending after 30 September 1993, or a repayment of tax received in such a period, the assessment is treated as being for that accounting period, and the sum assessed carries interest under *TMA 1970, s 87A* (see 35.6 INTEREST AND SURCHARGES ON UNPAID TAX) from the date the payment being recovered was made until payment. For this purpose, and where appropriate, sums recovered in respect of repayments are as far as possible identified with later repayments in respect of the accounting period rather than earlier ones.

[*TMA 1970, s 30; FA 1982, s 149; F(No 2)A 1987, s 88; ICTA 1988, s 252; FA 1989, s 149(3); FA 1990, s 105*].

46.11 CERTIFICATES OF TAX DEPOSIT

Such certificates, which enable money to be set aside for payment of future tax liability, may be used in payment of capital gains tax. Interest is received on these certificates from the date of purchase until the date on which the tax in respect of which they are surrendered falls due. Certificates may also be encashed (with interest to the date of encashment) but a lower rate of interest is then paid. Certificates for use against corporation tax liabilities ceased to be available for purchase after 30 September 1993 as a result of the introduction of Pay and File procedures. For further details, see TOLLEY'S INCOME TAX.

46.12 RECOVERY OF TAX IN RESPECT OF DISPOSALS BY OTHERS

There are instances in the legislation whereby the Revenue can assess, and/or recover tax from, persons other than the person actually making the disposal which gives rise to the chargeable event. This right usually follows from the non-payment of tax by the person originally assessed in respect of the chargeable disposal by him but may also arise because of specific legislation (e.g. UK residents charged in respect of disposals made by certain overseas resident companies, see 44.6 OVERSEAS MATTERS). The person from whom tax is recovered is normally given a right of recovery from any person originally assessed.

Specific occurrences of the foregoing are to be found at: 3.16 ANTI-AVOIDANCE; 11.3 and 11.4 CHILDREN; 13.6, 13.7, 13.18, 13.19 and 13.20 COMPANIES; 23.5 GIFTS; 25.5, 25.8 and 25.9 HOLD-OVER RELIEFS; 36.4 LAND; 43.2 and 43.11 OFFSHORE SETTLEMENTS; 44.13 and 44.14 OVERSEAS MATTERS; and 57.3 and 57.8 SETTLEMENTS.

46.13 REDUCED PAYMENTS UNDER 'EQUITABLE LIABILITY'

TMA 1970, s 29(6) (as it applies for 1995/96 and earlier years and for company accounting periods ending before 1 July 1999, i.e. before self-assessment) provides that after a notice of assessment has been served on the person assessed, the assessment is not to be altered except in accordance with the express provisions of the *Taxes Acts*. Thus an assessment not appealed against or for which a late appeal application is refused becomes final and conclusive and the Revenue is able to take recovery proceedings accordingly for the full amount charged even though this may be in excess of the actual liability. Whilst there is no legal right to adjustment of the liability, where the taxpayer has exhausted all other possible remedies, the Revenue may, depending on the circumstances, be prepared not to pursue its legal right to recover the full amount due where it would be unscrupulous to do so.

The Revenue may be prepared to operate this practice of 'equitable liability' where, depending on the circumstances and in the light of all the evidence, it is clearly demonstrated that the liability assessed is greater than the amount which would have been charged had the returns etc. required been submitted at the proper time, and acceptable evidence (not an estimate) is provided of what the correct liability should have been. This treatment is conditional on the taxpayer's affairs being brought fully up to date and full payment of the reduced tax being made, and only most unusually will it be applied more than once in favour of the same taxpayer.

Under self-assessment procedures, there would normally be no need for the Revenue to operate the above practice because of the ability of the taxpayer to displace the Revenue's determination of tax liability by a self-assessment made within the later of the first anniversary of the date of determination and the fifth anniversary of the statutory filing date for the year of assessment concerned. Where exceptionally a determination can no longer be displaced and the conditions of the practice described above are fulfilled, the Revenue will be prepared to consider extending its practice to meet this situation.

Cases are dealt with in the Revenue's Enforcement Offices in Worthing and Belfast and Enforcement Section in Edinburgh but local inspectors will be involved in considering the quantum of any claims for reduction in liability and the acceptability of the supporting evidence (Revenue Tax Bulletin August 1995 p 245).

46.14 PAYMENT OF TAX IN EUROS

From 1 January 1999, British businesses may, if they wish, pay tax in euros (the European single currency). The taxpayer will be credited with the sterling value actually received by the Revenue after conversion at the prevailing rate. There is no facility for making tax repayments in euros. (Revenue Press Release 31 July 1998). See also Revenue Pamphlet IR 166.

47 Penalties

Cross-references. See 9 BACK DUTY; 35 INTEREST AND SURCHARGES ON UNPAID TAX; 44.13 OVERSEAS MATTERS for companies ceasing to be UK resident; 46 PAYMENT OF TAX; 54 RETURNS; 56 SELF-ASSESSMENT for changes from 1996/97.

47.1 NOTIFICATION OF CHARGEABILITY

See 54.2 RETURNS for details of the self-assessment provisions for capital gains tax effective for 1995/96 and subsequent years of assessment.

For failure to notify chargeability to capital gains tax or corporation tax as described in 54.8, 54.11 RETURNS for a year of assessment after 1987/88 and before 1995/96, or an accounting period ending after 31 March 1989, the following maximum penalties apply.

(i) For a person chargeable to capital gains tax: the tax liability on chargeable gains for the year under assessments made more than twelve months after the end of the year.

(ii) For a company where the accounting period ends after 30 September 1993 (Pay and File): the amount by which so much of the corporation tax chargeable on its profits for the period as remains unpaid twelve months after the end of the period exceeds any income tax which, under *ICTA 1988, s 7(2)* or *s 11(3)*, is to be set off against the corporation tax so chargeable. In relation to earlier accounting periods, the maximum penalty is the corporation tax liability for the period under assessments made more than twelve months after the end of the period. In both cases, the amount of the corporation tax outstanding is determined disregarding the discharge of any liability for that tax attributable to surplus advance corporation tax carried back under *ICTA 1988, s 239(3)*.

[*TMA 1970, s 10, s 11A(2); FA 1988, ss 121, 122; FA 1993, s 120, Sch 14 para 1*].

For failure to notify chargeability for an earlier year of assessment or accounting period, there was a maximum penalty of £100. [*TMA 1970, ss 7, 10, 12*].

47.2 FAILURE TO RENDER CAPITAL GAINS TAX RETURN

See 56.22–56.23 for details of the SELF-ASSESSMENT provisions.

Notices served after 5 April 1989. If a person other than a company fails to make a return when required to do so under *TMA 1970, s 8, s 8A*, or s *9* (as applied for capital gains tax purposes by *TMA 1970, s 12*), he incurs a maximum penalty of £300. If his failure continues beyond the end of the tax year following that in which notice was served under one of those provisions, he is liable to a further penalty not exceeding the amount of tax (no amount being taken into account more than once) charged under assessments made on him or his personal representatives after that year on gains which should have been included in the return. A further penalty of up to £60 per day, not continuing after the failure has been remedied, is incurred if the failure continues after the non-tax-based penalty has been imposed (but not for any day for which such a daily penalty has already been imposed). Except in cases where a tax-based penalty is incurred, the rendering of the return prevents the imposition of a penalty. In addition, if the person proves that there was no income or chargeable gain to be included in the return, the overall penalty under the foregoing cannot exceed £100. [*TMA 1970, s 93(1)(2)(5)–(8); FA 1988, Sch 3 para 28; FA 1989, s 162; FA 1990, s 90(3)*].

47.3 FAILURE TO RENDER CORPORATION TAX RETURN

Notices served after 31 December 1993. A company which fails to make a return for any period ('*the return period*') (normally limited in practice to a period ending after 30 September 1993; see Revenue Press Release 7 December 1992), when required to do so by a notice served under *TMA 1970, s 11* (see 54.11 RETURNS) after 31 December 1993 (Pay and File), is liable to penalty of £200 (£100 if the return is delivered within three months of the final day for delivery). (The Revenue will apply administrative transitional measures where a notice is served after 31 December 1993 requiring a return to be made for an accounting period ending before 1 October 1993 (Revenue Tax Bulletin August 1993 pp 83–85). By concession, the £100 penalty will not be charged provided the return is received by the Revenue on or before the last business day within seven days following the final day for delivery; for returns required to be lodged before October 1995, fourteen days of grace were allowed (Revenue Pamphlet IR 1, B45 and Press Release 14 September 1995).) If the return period is one for which accounts are required under *Companies Act 1985*, these penalties do not apply provided that the return is delivered by the last day for delivery of those accounts. These penalties are increased to £1,000 and £500 respectively for failure in relation to a return for an accounting period where such a penalty or a tax-based penalty (see below) was incurred under these provisions for each of the two immediately preceding accounting periods, and the company was within the charge to corporation tax for the whole of the three accounting periods (each accounting period being a return period). A further penalty is imposed (without prejudice to the fixed penalties mentioned above) where the return has not been delivered before the later of the end of the final day for the delivery of the return and the end of the day falling 18 months after the end of the return period. This further penalty is 10% of 'the tax unpaid' at the end of the 18-month period referred to, increased to 20% of the tax unpaid at the end of that 18-month period if the return still has not been delivered before the end of the day falling two years after the end of the return period. '*The tax unpaid*' at any time is the unpaid corporation tax chargeable on the profits for the return period less any income tax which, under *ICTA 1988, s 7(2)* or *s 11(3)*, is to be set off against the corporation tax so chargeable, disregarding any discharge of liability by set-off of surplus advance corporation tax under *ICTA 1988, s 239(3)* arising in an accounting period ending more than two years after the end of the return period. [*TMA 1970, s 94; F(No 2)A 1987, s 83; FA 1993, s 120, Sch 14 para 6*].

Notices served before 1 January 1994. In relation to notices served before 1 January 1994 (and, normally, accounting periods ending before 1 October 1993; see Revenue Press Release 7 December 1992), a company which fails to make a return when required to do so under *TMA 1970, s 11* incurs a maximum penalty of £50. If the failure continues beyond two years from the date of service of notice to make the return, there is an additional penalty of the total amount of tax charged under assessments made after the end of the two-year period on profits that should have been included in the return. In either case, a further penalty of £10 per day is incurred if the failure continues after having been declared by the Court or Appeal Commissioners before whom penalty proceedings have been commenced. If the company can show that there was no profit to be included in the return, the total penalty under these provisions cannot exceed £5. Except in cases where a tax-based penalty is incurred, the rendering of a return before proceedings for recovery are commenced will avoid a penalty. [*TMA 1970, s 94*].

47.4 NEGLIGENCE OR FRAUD

The maximum penalty for negligently or fraudulently delivering, making or submitting an incorrect return or claim for allowance or relief etc., or incorrect accounts, is the amount of tax underpaid by reason of the incorrectness, for the tax year in which the return, etc. was delivered, the year after, and any preceding year, or, in the case of a company, for the chargeable period(s) covered. For returns, etc. before 27 July 1989, the maximum penalty is £50 plus, in the case of negligence, the amount of tax so underpaid, and, in the case of fraud, twice the latter amount.

In each case the amount is additional to any tax or interest actually chargeable. See also 56.25.

'*Negligence*' for this purpose includes any innocent error not rectified without unreasonable delay after its discovery by the taxpayer. Accounts are deemed to have been submitted by the taxpayer unless he proves they were submitted without his consent or connivance. [*TMA 1970, ss 95, 96, 97; FA 1988, Sch 3 para 28; FA 1989, s 163; FA 1990, s 90(4)*].

47.5 For the position if an agent is negligent or fraudulent, see *Mankowitz v Special Commrs Ch D 1971, 46 TC 707* and cf. *Clixby v Pountney Ch D 1967, 44 TC 515* and *Pleasants v Atkinson Ch D, [1987] STC 728.* **After 26 July 1989**, assisting in or inducing the preparation or delivery of any information, return, accounts or other document known to be incorrect and to be, or to be likely to be, used for any tax purpose carries a maximum penalty of £3,000. **Before 27 July 1989**, assisting in, or inducing, the making or delivery of a return or accounts known to be incorrect carried a maximum penalty of £500. [*TMA 1970, s 99; FA 1989, s 166*].

47.6 LIABILITY UNDER CRIMINAL LAW

'False statements to the prejudice of the Crown and public revenue' are criminal offences (*R v Hudson CCA 1956, 36 TC 561*). False statements in income tax returns, or for obtaining any allowance, reduction or repayment may involve liability to imprisonment for up to two years, under *Perjury Act 1911, s 5,* for 'knowingly and wilfully' making materially false statements or returns for tax purposes. Also, in Scotland, summary proceedings may be taken under *TMA 1970, s 107.*

For the Revenue's practice in considering whether to accept a money settlement or institute criminal proceedings for fraud, see 9.9 BACK DUTY.

In relation to any criminal prosecution case which comes to court after 10 May 1988, the Revenue will

(*a*) refrain (as previously) from taking steps to recover civil money penalties on the basis of fraud in respect of an offence which has been before the criminal courts;

(*b*) seek appropriate civil money penalties in respect of any offence which has not been brought before the courts; and

(*c*) reserve the right to seek, where there are grounds to do so, a civil penalty in respect of negligence by a taxpayer who has been acquitted of criminal intent in respect of a prosecution for fraud.

Previously, when the Revenue prosecuted, the practice had been not to seek a civil money penalty, whether for fraud or negligence, in respect of any offence brought before the criminal courts and any other tax offence committed by the person concerned which was brought to light in the course of the same investigation but which, for some reason, it was not appropriate to bring before the criminal courts (Revenue Pamphlet IR 131, SP 2/88). See also 27.4 INLAND REVENUE: ADMINISTRATION.

Falsification etc. of documents after 26 July 1989 which are required to be produced as in 9.8 BACK DUTY is a criminal offence punishable, on summary conviction, by a fine of the statutory maximum or, on indictment, by a fine or imprisonment for up to two years or both. [*TMA 1970, s 20BB; FA 1989, s 145*].

47.7 **OTHER RETURNS ETC.**

Failure to render any information or particulars or any return, certificate, statement or other document which is required, whether by notice or otherwise, under the provisions listed in *TMA 1970, s 98* is the subject of a maximum penalty of £300, plus £60 for each day the failure continues after that penalty is imposed (but not for any day for which such a daily penalty has already been imposed). These penalties are increased by a factor of ten in the case of a failure under *ICTA 1988, s 765A* (movements of capital after 30 June 1990 between residents of EEC member States). (Before 27 July 1989 the penalties were £50 and £10 respectively, and the latter applied for each day the failure continued after having been declared by a court or Commissioners before whom penalty proceedings have been commenced.) The maximum penalty for an incorrect return, etc. given fraudulently or negligently is £3,000. (Before 27 July 1989 it was £250 for negligence and £500 for fraud). Penalties for failure to render information etc. required by notice cannot be imposed after the failure is rectified, and daily penalties can similarly not be imposed where the information etc. was required other than by notice. (Before 27 July 1989 penalties could not be imposed if the failure had been rectified before proceedings for the recovery of penalties had been commenced.) [*TMA 1970, s 98; FA 1980, s 121; FA 1989, s 164(1)–(4)(7); FA 1990, s 68(3)(4)*].

Failure to allow access to computers renders a person liable to a £500 penalty. [*FA 1988, s 127*].

Failure to render a return under *TMA 1970, s 12A* (European Economic Interest Groupings as in 44.15 OVERSEAS MATTERS) renders the grouping or a member of it liable to penalties similar to those imposed by *TMA 1970, s 98* above except that a limit of £100 applies if there is no income or gain to be included in a return and the maximum penalty for an incorrect return given fraudulently or negligently is £3,000 multiplied by the number of members of the grouping at the time of delivery. [*TMA 1970, s 98B; FA 1990, Sch 11 para 3(1), para 5*].

47.8 **COMMISSIONERS' PRECEPTS**

Summary penalties (to be treated as tax assessed and due and payable) may be determined by Commissioners against any party to proceedings before them who fails to comply with a precept, order for inspection etc. (see 4.8 APPEALS). The maximum penalty is £300 in the case of the General Commissioners, £10,000 in the case of the Special Commissioners (and in the case of the General Commissioners, a daily penalty up to £60 may also be imposed for continuing failure). A penalty up to £10,000 may similarly be imposed for failure to comply with any other direction of the Special Commissioners (including in relation to a preliminary hearing). [*SI 1994 No 1811, Reg 24(1)(3); SI 1994 No 1812, Reg 10(1)(3)(4)*]. If a person on whom a witness summons is served (see 4.8 APPEALS) fails to attend in obedience thereto, or attends but refuses to be sworn or to affirm, or refuses to answer any lawful question, or refuses to produce any document required by the summons, the Commissioners may summarily determine a penalty against that person, to be treated as tax assessed and due and payable. The maximum penalty is £1,000 in the case of the General Commissioners, £10,000 in the case of the Special Commissioners. [*SI 1994 No 1811, Reg 24(2)(3); SI 1994 No 1812, Reg 4(12)(13)*]. Before 1 September 1994, similar provisions applied under *TMA 1970, ss 51–53*, except that the maximum penalty for failure to comply with precepts etc. was in all cases £300 plus £60 per day (£3,000 in cases of fraudulently or negligently incorrect returns) under *TMA 1970, s 98* (see 47.7 above), and the maximum penalty in relation to a witness summons was £50 in all cases.

Appeal against such summary penalties lies to the High Court (or Court of Session). [*TMA 1970, s 53 (as inserted by SI 1994 No 1813)*]. For the procedure on such appeals, see *QT Discount Foodstores Ltd v Warley Commrs Ch D 1981, 57 TC 268* and, for a case in which penalties were quashed because the taxpayer's evidence that he was unable to supply the information in question was not properly tested, *Boulton v Poole Commrs Ch D 1988, 60 TC 718.*

For appeals against penalties for non-compliance with precepts etc. see *Shah v Hampstead Commrs Ch D 1974, 49 TC 651; Chapman v Sheaf Commrs Ch D 1975, 49 TC 689; Toogood v Bristol Commrs Ch D 1976, 51 TC 634 and [1977] STC 116; Campbell v Rochdale Commrs Ch D 1975, 50 TC 411; B & S Displays Ltd v Special Commrs Ch D 1978, 52 TC 318; Galleri v Wirral Commrs Ch D 1978, [1979] STC 216; Beach v Willesden Commrs Ch D 1981, 55 TC 663; Stoll v High Wycombe Commrs and CIR Ch D 1992, 64 TC 587; Wilson v Leek Commrs and CIR Ch D 1993, 66 TC 537.*

47.9 PROCEDURE FOR OCCURRENCES AFTER 26 JULY 1989

Except in the case of

(*a*) penalties instituted for suspected fraud (see 47.10 below),

(*b*) penalties imposed for failure to comply with Commissioners' precepts (see 47.8 above), and

(*c*) penalties (see 47.10 below) under

- (i) *TMA 1970, s 93(1)* before amendment by *FA 1989, s 162*, or *TMA 1970, s 93(1)(a)* after such amendment (see 47.2 above),
- (ii) *TMA 1970, s 94(1)* before the substitution made by *F(No 2)A 1987, s 83* (see 47.3 above), and
- (iii) *TMA 1970, s 98(1)* before amendment by *FA 1989, s 164*, or *TMA 1970, s 98(1)(i)* after such amendment (see 47.7 above),
- (iv) *TMA 1970, s 98B(2)(a)* (European Economic Interest Groupings as in 47.7 above),

an authorised officer of the Board may make a determination imposing a penalty of an amount which he considers correct or appropriate. The amendments referred to in (*c*) (i) and (*c*) (iii) above refer to notices served after 5 April 1989 and to failures etc. occurring after 26 July 1989 respectively, and in relation to such notices or failures etc. only the fixed penalty, and not the daily penalty, is excluded from imposition by determination by the Board's officer. The substitution referred to in (*c*)(ii) above refers to notices served after 31 December 1993.

The notice of determination must state the date of issue and the time within which an appeal can be made. It cannot be altered unless

(A) there is an appeal (see 47.10 below), or

(B) an authorised officer discovers that the penalty is or has become insufficient (in which case he may make a further determination), or

(C) the penalty arises under *TMA 1970, s 94(6)*, and an authorised officer subsequently discovers that the amount of tax is or has become excessive (in which case it is to be revised accordingly).

A penalty under these provisions is due 30 days after the issue of the notice of determination, and is treated as tax charged in an assessment which is due and payable. A determination which could have been made on a person who has died can be made on his personal representatives, and is then payable out of his estate. [*TMA 1970, ss 100, 100A; FA 1989, s 167; FA 1990, Sch 11 para 3(2); SI 1994 No 1813*].

47.10 **Appeals.** Subject to the following points, the general APPEALS (4) provisions apply to an appeal against a determination.

TMA 1970, s 50(6)–(8) (see 4.8 APPEALS) does not apply. Instead on appeal the Commissioners can

(*a*) in the case of a penalty which is required to be of a particular amount, set the determination aside, confirm it, or alter it to the correct amount, and

(*b*) in any other case, set the determination aside, confirm it if it seems appropriate, or reduce it (including to nil) or increase it as seems appropriate (but not beyond the permitted maximum, as above).

Without prejudice to *TMA 1970, s 56* (see 4.9 APPEALS), an appeal lies to the High Court (in Scotland, the Court of Session). [*TMA 1970, s 100B; FA 1989, s 167*].

Proceedings before Commissioners. For a penalty within 47.9(C) above, an authorised officer can commence proceedings before the General or Special Commissioners. The proceedings are by information in writing, upon summons to the defendant (or defender); and they are heard in a summary way. An appeal lies to the High Court (or Court of Session) on a question of law, or by the defendant (defender) against the amount. The court can set the determination aside, confirm it if it seems appropriate, or reduce it (including to nil) or increase it as seems appropriate. The penalty is treated as tax charged in an assessment and due and payable. [*TMA 1970, s 100C; FA 1989, s 167*].

Proceedings before court. If the Board considers that liability of any person for a penalty arises from fraud of any person, proceedings can be brought in the High Court (or Court of Session). If the court does not find fraud proved, it can nevertheless impose a penalty to which it considers the person liable. [*TMA 1970, s 100D; FA 1989, s 167*].

Interpretation. See 47.11 below for cases on the interpretation of earlier legislation.

Mitigation etc. The Board may mitigate penalties before or after judgement. [*TMA 1970, s 102; FA 1989, s 168(1)(4)*]. In doing so they will give credit for co-operation by the taxpayer (Revenue Press Release 1 August 1977). A binding agreement by a taxpayer to pay an amount in composition cannot be repudiated afterwards by him or his personal representatives (*A-G v Johnstone KB 1926, 10 TC 758; A-G v Midland Bank Executor and Trustee Co Ltd KB 1934, 19 TC 136; CIR v Richards KB 1950, 33 TC 1*). Statements made or documents produced by or on behalf of a taxpayer are admissible evidence in proceedings against him, notwithstanding that reliance on the Board's practice in cases of full disclosure may have induced him to make or produce them. [*TMA 1970, s 105; FA 1989, s 168(1)(4)*].

If two or more penalties determined by reference to tax chargeable are incurred

(*a*) by a person in respect of capital gains tax for 1988/89 or later, or

(*b*) by a company in respect of corporation tax for an accounting period ending after 31 March 1989,

each one after the first is reduced so that the aggregate referable to any particular part of the tax does not exceed whichever penalty so far determined would otherwise have been the greatest. [*TMA 1970, s 97A; FA 1988, s 129*].

In mitigating penalties, the Revenue regard the weight to be attached to specified circumstances (the amount of tax lost being 100%) as follows.

(i) Disclosure (if any) and its completeness or otherwise, 20–30%.

(ii) Co-operation by the taxpayer and production of information, up to 40%.

(iii) Size and gravity of the offence(s), up to 40%.

(Revenue Pamphlet IR 73). See also *Caesar v Inspector of Taxes 1997 (Sp C 142), [1998] SSCD 1.*

See also 54.8 RETURNS as regards *TMA 1970, s 118(2)* (reasonable excuse for failure, etc.).

For the validity of tax amnesties see *R v CIR (ex p. National Federation of Self-Employed and Small Businesses Ltd) HL 1981, 55 TC 133.*

47.11 PROCEDURE FOR OCCURRENCES BEFORE 27 JULY 1989

In the case of a person's failure to make a capital gains tax return (and that of any person to make a special return or provide the documents or information required by the provisions listed in *TMA 1970, s 98* (see 47.7 above), the inspector may himself commence penalty proceedings before the General Commissioners (or, before 3 April 1989, the Special Commissioners in Northern Ireland), but the Commissioners then have no power to award a penalty based on tax due (see 47.2 above). Penalties for failure to comply with precepts etc. are awarded by Commissioners summarily. Penalties awarded are treated as tax charged by an assessment which is due and payable. Subject to this, penalty proceedings require an order of the Board and may be commenced before the General or the Special Commissioners, the High Court or the Court of Session in Scotland. From the Commissioners, an appeal lies to the High Court or the Court of Session on a point of law or (in the taxpayer's case only) against the amount of the penalty awarded. [*TMA 1970, s 100; FA 1988, Sch 14 Pt IX*].

Interpretation. Non-receipt of notice of the hearing at which the Commissioners awarded penalties is not a ground of appeal to the courts (*Kenny v Wirral Commrs Ch D 1974, 50 TC 405; Campbell v Rochdale Commrs Ch D 1975, 50 TC 411*). A mere denial of liability to penalties implies an intention by the taxpayer to set up a case in refutation, and details must be supplied (*CIR v Jackson CA 1960, 39 TC 357*).

For the validity of penalty proceedings while assessments remain open, see *A-G for Irish Free State v White SC (RI) 1931, 38 TC 666* and *R v Havering Commrs (ex p. Knight) CA 1973, 49 TC 161.* For other procedural matters, see *Collins v Croydon Commrs Ch D 1969, 45 TC 566; Bales v Rochford Commrs Ch D 1964, 42 TC 17; Sparks v West Brixton Commrs Ch D, [1977] STC 212; Moschi v Kensington Commrs Ch D 1979, 54 TC 403;* and for other appeals against penalties for failure to make returns, see *Dunk v Havant Commrs Ch D 1976, 51 TC 519; Napier v Farnham Commrs CA, [1978] TR 403; Garnham v Haywards Heath Commrs Ch D 1977, [1978] TR 303; Cox v Poole Commrs and CIR (No 1) Ch D 1987, 60 TC 445; Montague v Hampstead Commrs & Others Ch D 1989, 63 TC 145; Cox v Poole Commrs (No 2) Ch D 1989, 63 TC 277.*

Variation, mitigation or limitation of penalties. On appeal by the taxpayer, the court may confirm, reduce or increase any penalty imposed by Commissioners. [*TMA 1970, s 100(6)(7)*]. See *Dawes v Wallington Commrs Ch D 1964, 42 TC 200; Salmon v Havering Commrs CA 1968, 45 TC 77; Williams v Special Commrs Ch D 1974, 49 TC 670; Wells v Croydon Commrs Ch D 1968, 47 ATC 356; Taylor v Bethnal Green Commrs Ch D 1976, [1977] STC 44; Stableford v Liverpool Commrs Ch D 1982, [1983] STC 162; Sen v St. Anne, Westminster Commrs Ch D, [1983] STC 415; Jolley v Bolton Commrs Ch D 1986, 65 TC 242; Lear v Leek Commrs Ch D 1986, 59 TC 247; Brodt v Wells Commrs Ch D 1987, 60 TC 436; Walsh v Croydon Commrs Ch D 1987, 60 TC 442.*

See also 47.10 above: mitigation, etc.

47.12 BANKRUPTS

Penalties awarded after a bankruptcy are provable debts, but in practice the Revenue does not proceed for penalties during a bankruptcy where there are other creditors. The trustee may agree to compromise any penalties awarded but the compromise must also be agreed by the bankrupt (*Re Hurren Ch D 1982, 56 TC 494*).

47.13 TIME LIMITS

Occurrences after 26 July 1989. The time within which a penalty can be determined, or proceedings can be commenced, depends on the penalty, as follows.

(*a*) If the penalty is ascertainable by reference to tax payable, the time is

- (i) six years after the penalty was incurred, or
- (ii) a later time within three years after the final determination of the amount of tax (except that this alternative does not apply if the tax was payable by a person who has died, it is charged in an assessment made more than six years after the chargeable period for which it is charged, and the determination would be made in relation to the personal representatives).

(*b*) If the penalty arises under *TMA 1970, s 99* (in relation to provision of inaccurate information etc., see 47.5 above) the time is twenty years after the date when it was incurred.

(*c*) In other cases the time is six years from the time when the penalty was, or began to be, incurred.

[*TMA 1970, s 103; FA 1989, s 169*].

Occurrences before 27 July 1989. Normally, penalty proceedings must be commenced within six years after the date the penalty was incurred [*TMA 1970, s 103(1)*], but, in cases of fraud or wilful default, this limit is extended to three years after final determination of tax liability. [*TMA 1970, s 103(2)*].

This time limit is also extended in cases where a penalty is calculated (e.g. under *TMA 1970, s 93(2)*) by reference to tax charged under an assessment for any chargeable period which is made within six years after the end of that chargeable period. Proceedings may be commenced within three years of the final determination of that tax. [*TMA 1970, s 103(3)*]. But where proceedings could not have been commenced but for this extension, tax on assessments under *TMA 1970, s 37, s 39* or *s 40(2)* (see 9 BACK DUTY) is left out of account in penalty calculations. [*TMA 1970, s 103(4)*].

The effect of the above provisions is to limit the recovery of a penalty attributable to neglect to years for which assessments can be made within normal time limits. For this reason (among others) the Revenue will usually make an assessment within the normal time limits for every year which goes out of date in the course of a back duty enquiry.

Deceased persons. Any proceedings under *TMA 1970, s 103* which were, or could have been, commenced against the deceased may be commenced or continued against his personal representatives, any fine or penalty thereunder being a debt of his estate. [*TMA 1970, s 100(5)*]. The extension of time referred to above for fraud and wilful default does not, however, apply. [*TMA 1970, s 103(2)*].

Provisional agreement of the amount due subject to the inspector being satisfied later with statements of assets, etc. is not final determination (*Carco Accessories Ltd v CIR CS 1985, 59 TC 45*).

48 Private Residences

Cross-references. See 36 LAND generally; 19.15, 19.29 EMPLOYEE SHARE SCHEMES for restriction on rollover relief arising from disposal of shares to, respectively, an approved employee share ownership plan and, before 6 April 2001, an employee share ownership trust, where replacement asset is or becomes exempt as a private residence.

Sumption: Capital Gains Tax. See A16.51–59A.

48.1 EXEMPTION GENERALLY

Where a gain accrues to an individual so far as attributable to the disposal of, or of an interest in,

(*a*) a dwelling-house or part of a dwelling-house which is, or has at any time in his period of ownership been, his only or main residence, or

(*b*) land which he has for his own occupation and enjoyment with that residence as its garden or grounds up to the 'permitted area',

then either the whole or a fraction of the gain is exempt as below. [*TCGA 1992, s 222(1)*].

Any loss accruing is similarly treated as being wholly or partly a non-allowable loss. [*TCGA 1992, s 16(2)*].

The '*permitted area*' means an area of 0.5 hectares (i.e. 5,980 sq. yards or 5,000 sq. metres) or larger area if required for the reasonable enjoyment of the whole or part of the dwelling-house as a residence having regards to its size and character. For disposals before 19 March 1991, the permitted area was an area of one acre (i.e. 4,840 sq. yards; 4,047 sq. metres; or 0.4047 hectares). Prior to the introduction of self-assessment on 6 April 1996 an appeal to the Commissioners determined whether a larger area was reasonable for the enjoyment of the whole or part of the residence. Under self-assessment the Revenue has general powers within *TMA 1970* to enquire into any return, claim or election (see 56 SELF-ASSESSMENT).

Where part of the land occupied with a residence is and part is not within (*b*) above, then (up to the permitted area) the part that is to be taken within (*b*) is that part which would be most suitable for occupation and enjoyment with the residence if the remainder were separately occupied.

[*TCGA 1992, s 222(2)–(4); FA 1991, s 93*].

See below for case law on the 'permitted area' and the extent to which subsidiary buildings may form part of the residence.

There can only be one main residence in the case of a man and his wife living with him, so long as they are 'living together' (see 41.2 MARRIED PERSONS). [*TCGA 1992, s 222(6)*]. As regards separation or divorce, see 48.2(*c*) below.

Total exemption (under *TCGA 1992, s 223(1)*) applies to a gain within *TCGA 1992, s 222(1)* above if the dwelling-house or part of a dwelling-house has been the individual's only or main residence throughout the period of ownership, or throughout the period of ownership except for all or any part of the last 36 months (24 months for disposals before 19 March 1991; however, the Treasury has the power under the 'negative' statutory instrument procedure to reduce the period to twenty-four months again, and then increase it again to thirty-six months, and so on down or up to these levels) of that period. The power cannot be used retrospectively and in practice reasonable notice of any variation will be given (HC Official Report Standing Committee B 7th sitting col 312, 13 June 1991).

Fractional exemption (under *TCGA 1992, s 223(2)*) applies where total exemption does not apply to a gain within *TCGA 1992, s 222(1)*. The fraction of the gain that is exempt is given by

(i) the length of the part or parts of the period of ownership during which the dwelling-house (or part) was the individual's only or main residence, but inclusive of the last thirty-six months (twenty-four months for disposals before 19 March 1991; however, the above Treasury power applies) of the period of ownership in any event, divided by

(ii) the length of the period of ownership.

In considering 'period of ownership' for the purposes of the total or fractional exemption (but *not* for determining for the purposes of *TCGA 1992, s 222(1)* above whether the dwelling-house (or part) has at any time in the period of ownership been the only or main residence), any period before 31 March 1982 (6 April 1965 for disposals before 6 April 1988) is ignored, and if time apportionment applies (see 7.9 ASSETS HELD ON 6 APRIL 1965 but subject to the rules in 8 ASSETS HELD ON 31 MARCH 1982), the resulting fraction is applied only to that part of the gain that would otherwise be chargeable after the time apportionment. [*TCGA 1992, s 223(1)(2)(5)–(7), Sch 2 para 16(10); FA 1988, Sch 8 para 8; FA 1991, s 94*].

See 48.2 below for certain periods of ownership that additionally qualify for the purposes of total and fractional exemption.

Where the individual has had different interests at different times, the period of ownership is taken for the purposes of *TCGA 1992, ss 222–226* generally (i.e. all the provisions contained in this chapter) to begin from the first acquisition taken into account in arriving at the amount of the allowable expenditure deductible in the computation of the gain to which *TCGA 1992, s 222(1)* above applies. In the case of a man and his wife living with him

(A) if one disposes of, or of his interest in, the dwelling-house (or part) which is their only or main residence to the other, and in particular if it passes on death to the other as legatee, the other's period of ownership is treated as beginning with the beginning of the period of ownership of the one making the disposal, and

(B) if (A) above applies, but the dwelling-house (or part) was not the only or main residence of both throughout the period of ownership of the one making the disposal, account is taken of any part of that period during which it was his only or main residence as if it was also that of the other.

[*TCGA 1992, s 222(7)*].

For the purposes of *TCGA 1992, ss 222–226*, apportionments of consideration are to be made wherever required, and, in particular, where a person disposes of a dwelling-house only part of which is his only or main residence. [*TCGA 1992, s 222(10)*].

TCGA 1992, s 222(10) seems to override *TCGA 1992, s 52(4)* (apportionments to be on just and reasonable basis; see 17.6 DISPOSAL) so that, because of the absence of the 'just and reasonable' criterion, there may be an argument that a different basis of apportionment may apply, e.g. where the residence and the permitted area of land block access to other land outside the permitted area but sold together with the residence etc. it may fall that the value of the other land should reflect the situation as if the two areas were in separate ownership (Taxation 7 December 1995 p 256 and Revenue Capital Gains Manual CG 64900, 64901 and 74162).

An immobilised caravan with main services installed has been held to be a dwelling-house (*Makins v Elson Ch D 1976, 51 TC 437*) but one still on wheels and with no services installed was not so held (*Moore v Thompson Ch D 1986, 61 TC 15*). A houseboat will often be an exempt asset in its own right (see 21.4 EXEMPTIONS AND RELIEFS regarding tangible movable wasting assets). If this is not the case, it may qualify as a dwelling-house if it is permanently located on a site and connected to all mains services. Such a houseboat *will* be regarded as a dwelling-house if it has been used as an immobile residence for a period of six months or more and has had its engines removed. Other cases will be considered on their merits. (Revenue Capital Gains Manual CG 64329).

A lodge built for occupation rent-free by a caretaker/gardener and his wife, the housekeeper, and separated from the main house by the width of a tennis court (around nine yards) with the total area of land involved being around 1.1 acres, was held to be within the exemption (*Batey v Wakefield CA 1981, 55 TC 550*). A residence for exemption purposes was declared to be a dwelling-house and all of those buildings which are part and parcel of the whole, where each part is appurtenant to and occupied for the purposes of the building occupied by the taxpayer. However, this is a question of fact and degree.

Whereas *Batey v Wakefield* was concerned with buildings physically separate from the main dwelling-house, *Green v CIR CS 1982, 56 TC 10*, in contrast, involved the disposal of a mansion (occupied by the taxpayer) and its two wings. The Commissioners' finding that the wings were not part of his dwelling-house was upheld.

In *Markey v Sanders Ch D 1987, 60 TC 245*, a finding by Commissioners that a staff bungalow situated 130 metres away from the main dwelling-house and screened from it by a belt of trees, formed part of the taxpayer's residence was not accepted. It was held that *Batey v Wakefield* laid down two tests:

(1) the occupation of the building must increase the taxpayer's enjoyment of the main dwelling-house, and

(2) the building must be 'very closely adjacent to' the main dwelling-house.

Each of these was held to be a necessary, but not by itself sufficient, test and in the present case the first test was satisfied but not the second. The total area of land involved was around twelve acres.

However, *Markey v Sanders* was expressly not followed in *Williams v Merrylees Ch D 1987, 60 TC 297*, so that a finding by Commissioners that a lodge situated 200 metres from the main dwelling-house formed part of the taxpayer's residence during his occupation of the latter was upheld. The total area of the property was around four acres. In the latter case doubt was expressed whether the *Batey v Wakefield* decision did require the satisfaction of two distinct conditions and it was concluded that all the circumstances should be looked at to see whether there is 'an entity which could sensibly be described as being a dwelling-house though split up into different buildings performing different functions'.

The *Williams v Merrylees* decision was itself disapproved by the Court of Appeal in *Lewis v Rook CA 1992, 64 TC 567*. A finding by Commissioners that a gardener's cottage some 170 metres from the main dwelling-house formed part of the taxpayer's residence was initially upheld in the High Court, but was rejected in the Court of Appeal. The true test was declared to be whether the cottage was 'within the curtilage of, and appurtenant to [the main house], so as to be part of the entity which, together with [the main house], constituted the dwelling-house occupied by the taxpayer as her residence'. The curtilage concept was derived from a non-tax case, *Methuen-Campbell v Walters CA, [1979] QB 525* (and see also *Dyer v Dorset County Council CA, [1989] QB 346*), in which Buckley LJ stated that 'for one corporeal hereditament to fall within the curtilage of another, the former must be so intimately associated with the latter as to lead to the conclusion that the former in truth forms part and parcel of the latter'. The cottage in *Lewis v Rook* was not 'intimately associated' with the main house as it was some way off and separated from it by a large garden. The total area of land involved was around 10.5 acres and Balcombe LJ remarked that as 'the 'permitted area' of garden and grounds which is exempt from capital gains tax is limited to one acre [now 0.5 hectares] or such larger area as the [Appeal] Commissioners may determine as required for the reasonable enjoyment of the dwelling-house as a residence, it does seem to me to be remarkable that a separate lodge or cottage which by any reasonable measurement must be outside the permitted area can nevertheless be part of the entity of the dwelling-house'. It should also be noted that Counsel for the Inland Revenue reserved the right to argue in the House of Lords, had the case proceeded that far, that the reference in *TCGA 1992, s 222(1)(a)* to a 'dwelling-house' in the singular meant that buildings which are separate from the main house cannot be included within the exemption if they form separate, self-contained dwelling-houses in their own right. See Revenue Tax Bulletin, August 1994, p 148 for further discussion of this matter.

In *Honour v Norris Ch D 1992, 64 TC 599*, the taxpayer owned four separate, self-contained flats in a London square. Two of these were adjacent and were converted to form a single property, the other two being some way off and not adjacent to each other. Although the taxpayer and his wife had occasionally used the non-adjacent flats themselves, their main function was to provide sleeping accommodation for guests and a nanny. The Commissioners upheld the taxpayer's contention that one of the distant flats, which had been sold, was part of his main residence. However, the Revenue's appeal was upheld in the High Court, Vinelott J remarking that the proposition that the flat which had been sold formed part of the taxpayer's main residence was 'an affront to common sense'.

In *Varty v Lynes Ch D 1976, 51 TC 419,* the taxpayer owned and occupied a house and garden (together comprising an area less than one acre, the latter being the then 'maximum' permitted area subject to an appeal Commissioners' determination). He sold the house and part of the garden in June 1971. In May 1972, he sold at a substantial profit the rest of the garden for which he had meanwhile obtained planning permission. An assessment on the gain accruing on the disposal of the remainder of the garden was upheld. The exemption provided by (*b*) above related only to the actual moment of disposal of the land, and in relation to land formerly used as garden and grounds did not apply to a disposal subsequent to the disposal of the residence. The judgement of Brightman J pointed to anomalies in the legislation. In particular, he stated 'The anomaly which I find most striking [is] the disregard for the purposes of [the provisions providing for total exemption] of the last twelve months [this period being the then period disregarded above] of the period of ownership in respect of the dwelling-house. On the construction advanced by the Crown it must follow, I am disposed to think, that if the taxpayer goes out of occupation of the dwelling-house a month before he sells it, the exemption will be lost in respect of the garden. That, however, is merely my impression, and I do not intend so to decide because it is not a matter for decision before me'. The Revenue did say that they would not take this point unless the garden had development value (CCAB Statements TR 211 December 1976 and TR 233 June 1977). However, the Revenue no longer seek to apply arguments based on the dicta in this case, but will apply the decision itself, so that no relief is due on any sale of a garden taking place after a prior sale of the dwelling house (Revenue Tax Bulletin, August 1994, pp 148, 149 and see Revenue Capital Gains Manual CG 64377–64387).

For a useful summary of the considerations made by the Revenue in arriving at the 'permitted area' and whether a subsidiary building forms part of the residence as a whole, see Revenue Tax Bulletin, February 1992, p 10. The Revenue makes the point that land, other than that taken by the site of the dwelling-house, must be 'garden or grounds' at the time of sale if it is to be within the permitted area. In deciding whether an area of garden or grounds larger than 0.5 hectares is 'required for the reasonable enjoyment' of the dwelling-house as a residence, it considers the following words of Du Parcq J in the compulsory purchase case of *In Re Newhill Compulsory Purchase Order 1937, Payne's Application KB 1937, [1938] 2 All ER 163* to be useful guidance: ' "Required", I think, in this Section does not mean merely that the occupiers of the house would like to have it, or that they would miss it if they lost it, or that anyone proposing to buy the house would think less of the house without it than he would if it was preserved to it. "Required" means, I suppose that without it there will be such a substantial deprivation of amenities or convenience that a real injury would be done to the property owner.' However, it can be argued that the Revenue has taken the words spoken out of context since the case mentioned concerned legislation which prohibited compulsory purchase of 'any land . . . which . . . forms part of any park, garden or leisure ground, or is otherwise required for the amenity or convenience of any house'. The construction of this legislation suggests that, in interpreting it, a garden, park or leisure ground should automatically be considered as required for the amenity or convenience of a dwelling-house. The application of Du Parcq J's words may therefore be invalid in the context of capital gains tax and the private residence exemption.

In *Longson v Baker (Sp C 238), [2000] SSCD 244*, the Commissioner concluded that while it may have been desirable or convenient for the taxpayer to have a total area of 7.56 hectares to enjoy with the dwelling-house (which for this purpose included a farmhouse, stables and outhouse), such an area was not *required* for the reasonable enjoyment of the dwelling-house.

It should be noted that the Revenue considers that a separate disposal of part of the garden or grounds of a residence may be prima facie evidence that the part disposed of was not required for the reasonable enjoyment of the dwelling-house as a residence although this only becomes of relevance where the area of the garden or grounds exceeds 0.5 hectares. It states that in practice any land disposed of separately is likely to be from that part of the garden or grounds which can be disposed of while detracting least from the enjoyment of the residence. In such circumstances it believes the disposal itself presents strong evidence that the land could not have been required for the reasonable enjoyment of the residence so that the permitted area should exclude the area disposed of. However, it accepts that there are two common circumstances where this inference may be incorrect. The first is where the owner of the land makes a disposal to a member of his family where he may be prepared to tolerate some curtailment of the reasonable enjoyment of the residence. The second is where financial necessity may force the owner to sell land which would be regarded as part of the most suitable area of garden or grounds to be included in the permitted area (Revenue Capital Gains Manual CG 64832–64834).

As regards the exemption granted by (*b*) above, there is no requirement that the land occupied and used with the residence as garden or grounds at the time of disposal has to adjoin the land on which the dwelling-house stands. See *Wakeling v Pearce (Sp C 32), [1995] SSCD 96* where the distance between the garden (which was disposed of) and the land including the dwelling-house (which was retained) was less than 10 metres. However, the Revenue considers the facts of the case and the decision do not affect its interpretation of the underlying provisions and that it will be rare for exemption to be given to land (even if used as a garden) separated from the residence by other land which is not in the same ownership as the residence (see Revenue Tax Bulletin August 1995 p 239).

See *Taxation* 5 January 1989, p 311 for a case where the Ombudsman considered the District Valuer to have been wrong in taking the view that the presence of a tennis court and swimming pool must be regarded as irrelevant in deciding what was the permitted area.

For the question of whether or not a dwelling-house is a 'main residence', see *Frost v Feltham Ch D 1980, 55 TC 10* which concerned mortgage interest relief for income tax purposes but note that that question may be determined, for capital gains tax purposes only, by election as in 48.5 below.

See 48.3 to 48.8 below for provisions supplementary to the above.

48.2 PERIODS OF OWNERSHIP QUALIFYING FOR EXEMPTION

For the purposes of the total or fractional exemption of a gain to which *TCGA 1992, s 222(1)* in 48.1 above applies the following provisions apply.

(*a*) **Periods of absence.** A '*period of absence*' means a period during which the dwelling-house (or part) was not the individual's only or main residence and throughout which he had no residence or main residence eligible for relief under the provisions of *TCGA 1992, s 223* in 48.1 above. In applying the total or fractional exemption provided by *TCGA 1992, s 223(1)* and *(2)* respectively in 48.1 above (i.e. ignoring periods of ownership before 31 March 1982 (6 April 1965 for disposals before 6 April 1988))

(i) a period of absence not exceeding three years (or periods of absence which together did not exceed three years), and in addition

(ii) any period of absence throughout which the individual worked in an employment or office all the duties of which were performed outside the UK (holidays spent in the UK are ignored but any duties, even incidental ones, carried out in the UK will not be; Revenue Capital Gains Manual CG 65042), and in addition

(iii) any period of absence not exceeding four years (or periods of absence which together did not exceed four years) throughout which the individual was prevented from residing in the dwelling-house (or part) in consequence of the situation of his place of work or in consequence of any condition imposed by his employer requiring him to reside elsewhere, being a condition reasonably imposed to secure the effective performance by the employee of his duties (the individual may be self-employed or the holder of an office or employment for these purposes; see Revenue Capital Gains Manual CG 65043, 65044),

is treated as if in that period of absence the dwelling-house (or part) was the individual's only or main residence *provided* both before and after the period there was a time when the dwelling-house (or part) was the individual's only or main residence. [*TCGA 1992, s 223(3)(7)*].

The Revenue will view residence as a question of fact. A minimum period is not specified and the Revenue do not attempt to impose one. They take the view that it is quality of occupation rather than length of occupation which determines whether a dwelling house is its owner's residence. Miller J in *Moore v Thompson Ch D 1986, 61 TC 15* commented that 'the Commissioners were alive to the fact that even occasional and short residence in a place can make that a residence; but the question was one of fact and degree' (Revenue Tax Bulletin, August 1994, p 149). In *Goodwin v Curtis CA 1998, 70 TC 478*, it was held that the nature, quality, length and circumstances of the taxpayer's 32-day occupation of a farmhouse was such that he had moved into it on a temporary basis and his occupation did not qualify as residence. *Dicta* of Viscount Cave in *Levene v CIR* (see 52.4 RESIDENCE AND DOMICILE) applied.

Where the periods of absence exceed the three or four years mentioned in (i) and (iii) above, it is only the excess which does not qualify for the exemption treatment (CCAB Statement TR 500, 10 March 1983). Where in the case of a husband and wife who are living together the conditions in (i) to (iii) above are satisfied as regards the spouse who is not the owner of the dwelling-house, they are deemed satisfied as regards the spouse who is the owner. Also, the condition requiring the dwelling-house to be the only or main residence after absence under (ii) and (iii) above will be treated as satisfied if the individual is unable to resume residence because the terms of his employment require him to work elsewhere (Revenue Pamphlet IR 1, D3, D4).

The requirement that the period of absence is a period throughout which the individual has no residence or main residence eligible for relief under *TCGA 1992, s 223* may be difficult to meet in practice given the view (see commentary in 48.5 below) of the Revenue that any residence in which the individual has a legal or equitable interest or, broadly before 17 October 1994, which the individual occupies under licence can constitute an individual's residence eligible for relief, albeit that it may only have a negligible capital value. However, the Revenue will accept a main residence election as in 48.5 below nominating the residence from which the taxpayer is absent even though he is not using it as a residence. No other residence is then eligible for relief, so the requirement is satisfied. See Revenue Capital Gains Manual CG 65048.

Example

T purchased a house on 1 August 1981 from which date it was used as her only residence until 10 February 1982 when she moved to France to live in rent-free accommodation provided by her employer whilst she carried out all the duties of the employment there. She returned from France on 4 August 1990 when she again occupied the house as her only residence. On 30 November 1993 she left the house empty and moved to live with her elderly father in a residence owned by him, intending to sell her own house. In the event, the house was not sold until 1 November 2000 when an otherwise chargeable gain (before taper relief) of £52,186 was realised.

	£
Gain on sale	52,186
Deduct $\dfrac{\text{8y 4m + 3y 4m + 3y}}{\text{18y 7m}} \times$ £52,186	41,186
Chargeable gain (subject to TAPER RELIEF (60))	£11,000

Notes to the example

(1) The period of ownership for the exemption calculation does not include any period before 31 March 1982. This applies regardless of whether the gain has been calculated by reference to cost or 31 March 1982 value under the re-basing rules.

(2) All of the period spent in France (ignoring the period before 31 March 1982) counts as a period of residence under (ii) above. It is assumed that the supply of accommodation to T in France was such that it was not eligible for relief under *TCGA 1992, s 223* (e.g. a licence; see 48.5 below for Revenue comment). None of the period from 30 November 1993 to 1 November 2000 can count as a period of residence under (i) above as there was not a time afterwards that the house was T's only or main residence. However, under *TCGA 1992, s 223(1)* the last 36 months of ownership are exempt provided the house has at some time during the period of ownership (not restricted to periods after 31 March 1982) been the only or main residence.

(3) For the purposes of taper relief, the gain to be tapered is the gain *after* applying the private residence exemption, i.e. the gain of £11,000.

(*b*) **Delay in taking up residence.** The treatment as the individual's only or main residence applies during the twelve months (or longer period up to a maximum of two years if a good reason can be shown) prior to taking up residence during which the dwelling-house was built, alterations etc. were made to it or the necessary steps were being taken to dispose of the individual's previous residence. (Revenue Pamphlet IR 1, D49 replacing SP D4). The period will not be extended beyond twenty-four months. If the twelve-month or longer period allowed is exceeded, none of the period of ownership prior to taking up residence is treated as a period of residence. No main residence election (see 48.5 below) is required if the effect of this concession is to treat an individual as having two residences for a period since relief will be available for both residences for that period (Revenue Capital Gains Manual CG 65009–65014).

(*c*) **Separation or divorce of married persons.** Where a married couple separate or are divorced and one partner ceases to occupy the matrimonial home and subsequently, as part of a financial settlement, disposes of the home, or an interest in it, to the other partner, the home may be regarded for the purposes of the exemption as continuing to be a residence of the transferring partner from the date his or her occupation ceases until the date of transfer, provided that it has throughout this period been the other partner's only or main residence. Thus where a husband leaves the matrimonial home while still owning it, the exemption for the only or main residence would be given on the subsequent transfer to the wife, provided she has continued to live in the house and the husband has not elected that some other house should be treated as his main residence for this period (Revenue Pamphlet IR 1, D6). See also 41.3 MARRIED PERSONS.

(*d*) **'Job-related' accommodation.** If at any time during an individual's period of ownership (as for *TCGA 1992, s 222(1)* in 48.1 above so that a period before 31 March 1982 is *not* ignored) of part or the whole of a dwelling-house he resides in 'job-related' living accommodation and he intends in due course to occupy the dwelling-house (or part) as his only or main residence, he is deemed at that time to occupy the dwelling-house (or part) as a residence for the purposes of *TCGA 1992, ss 222–226* (i.e. all the provisions contained in this chapter). Living accommodation is 'job-related' for these purposes if it is provided for a taxpayer by reason of his (or for his spouse by reason of her) employment, in any of the following cases.

(i) Where it is necessary for the proper performance of the duties of the employment that the employee should reside in that accommodation.

(ii) Where the provision of such accommodation is customary and it is provided for the better performance of the duties of employment.

(iii) Where there is a special threat to the employee's security, special security arrangements are in force, and the employee resides in the accommodation as part of those arrangements.

With certain exceptions, (i) and (ii) above do not apply to accommodation provided to its directors by a company (or associated company).

In respect of residence after 5 April 1983, living accommodation is also job-related if either the person claiming the relief or his or her spouse is carrying on a trade, profession or vocation on premises or other land provided by another person, under tenancy or otherwise, and is bound under an arm's length contract to live in those premises or on other premises provided. Relief is not given if the accommodation is provided, in whole or in part, by a company in which the borrower, or his or her spouse, has a material interest (as defined) or by any person or persons with whom he or she carries on a business in partnership. [*TCGA 1992, s 222(8)(8A)–(8D)(9); ICTA 1988, s 356; FA 1999, Sch 4 para 17, para 18(4)*].

The above treatment still applies if the dwelling-house is disposed of without having been occupied by the individual (but subject to the test of intention to occupy being satisfied previously) or if the property has been let (see 48.8 below). It appears that the above provisions do not obviate the need to consider, subject to the Revenue's views there mentioned, a main residence election as in 48.5 below.

(*e*) **Relocation of employees.** Where liabilities are agreed after 13 January 1991, the Revenue are prepared concessionally to extend the exemption for a private residence where an employee sells his home to a relocation business or his employer and is given the right to share in any profits made when that business or his employer later sells the home, so that the right will generally be exempt to the same extent as the home itself. Relocation arrangements must be set up under arm's length agreements whereby the employee moves home because of the requirements of his place of work or employer and the right to a profit share by the employee must not exceed three years. The concession applies equally to office holders and any other joint owners of the home provided the employee qualifies for his interest in it (Revenue Pamphlet IR 1, D37).

48.3 EXCLUSIVE PART-BUSINESS USE, CHANGES OF USE ETC.

If a gain accrues from the disposal of a dwelling-house or part of a dwelling-house part of which is used *exclusively* for the purposes of a trade or business, or of a profession or vocation, the gain is apportioned and *TCGA 1992, s 223* applied in relation to the part of the gain apportioned to the part which is not exclusively used for those purposes. [*TCGA 1992, s 224(1)*]. If at any time in the period of ownership there is a change in what is occupied as the individual's residence, whether on account of a reconstruction or conversion of a building or for any other reason, or there have been changes as regards the use of part of the dwelling-house for the purpose of a trade etc. or for any other purpose, the relief given under *TCGA 1992, s 223* may be adjusted in such manner as is 'just and reasonable'. [*TCGA 1992, s 224(2); FA 1996, Sch 20 para 60*].

Prior to the introduction of self-assessment on 6 April 1996 the Commissioners on appeal would determine what was considered to be 'just and reasonable'. Under the self-assessment rules the Revenue has general powers within *TMA 1970* to enquire into any return, claim or election. (See 56 SELF-ASSESSMENT).

The Revenue's approach in cases falling within *TCGA 1992, s 224(2)* is to deal with each case on its merits, and to require an adjustment which as far as possible reflects the extent to which, and the length of time over which, each part of the dwelling house has been used as part of residence. It is not normally considered appropriate to take into account intervening market values when apportioning gains to different periods in such cases since *TCGA 1992, s 223* clearly provides for time apportionment as the appropriate method (Revenue Tax Bulletin August 1994 p 149).

ROLLOVER RELIEF (55) may be available in respect of any chargeable gain arising because of the foregoing provisions if a new dwelling-house is acquired, part of which will also be used *exclusively* for the purposes of a trade etc. so that relief will apply to the acquisition costs of that part. Although the treatment by the Revenue is not always consistent, it seems that where an individual, assessable to income tax under Schedule E, uses part of his home exclusively for the purposes of his employment, no restriction of the exemption can be made under the foregoing provisions (Tolley's Practical Tax 1981, p 178).

Letting the dwelling-house may restrict the exemption given by 48.1 and 48.2 above (but see 48.8 below) but there is no restriction where a lodger (but a restriction is applied if there are two or more lodgers; see Revenue Capital Gains Manual CG 64702) lives as part of a family, sharing their living accommodation and taking meals with them (Revenue Pamphlet IR 131, SP 14/80). In addition, participation in the 'rent a room' income tax relief scheme of *F(No 2)A 1992, s 59, Sch 10* will not normally lead to any capital gains tax liability (HL Written Answers, 27 January 1993, Vol 514 col 94).

48.4 EXCLUSION OF EXEMPTION WHERE DWELLING-HOUSE ACQUIRED FOR PROFIT

The exemption given by *TCGA 1992, s 223* does not apply in relation to a gain if the acquisition of, or of the interest in, the dwelling-house (or part) was made wholly or partly for the purpose of realising a gain from the disposal of it, and does not apply in relation to a gain *so far as attributable to* any expenditure which was incurred after the beginning of the period of ownership and was incurred wholly or partly for the purpose of realising a gain from the disposal. [*TCGA 1992, s 224(3)*]. The Revenue's practice is not to take into account expenditure incurred in obtaining planning permission or in removing restrictive covenants when considering whether to apply the second leg of *TCGA 1992, s 224(3)* (Revenue Tax Bulletin, August 1994, p 150). The three most common applications of the second leg are

- acquisition by a leaseholder of a superior interest in the property,
- conversion of an undivided house into self-contained flats, and
- redevelopment of part of the garden or grounds, e.g. barn conversions.

(Revenue Capital Gains Manual CG 65245, 65274).

In *Jones v Wilcock (Sp C 92), [1996] SSCD 389*, a married couple incurred a loss on the sale of their house. They contended that the house had been purchased 'wholly or partly for the purpose of realising a gain'. However, from the facts of the case it was decided that the house was purchased to use as the couple's home.

48.5 ELECTION FOR MAIN RESIDENCE

So far as it is necessary for the purposes of *TCGA 1992, s 222* to determine which of two or more residences is an individual's main residence for any period, the individual may conclude that question by written notice to the inspector given within two years from the beginning of that period but subject to a right to vary that notice by a further written notice to the inspector as respects any period beginning not earlier than two years before the giving of the further notice. [*TCGA 1992, s 222(5); FA 1996, Sch 20 para 59(3)*].

Prior to the introduction of self-assessment on 6 April 1996, in the absence of conclusive notice by the individual, the Revenue were able to determine the main residence, subject to right of appeal to the Commissioners. Under self-assessment the Revenue has general powers within *TMA 1970* to enquire into any return, claim or election. (See 56 SELF-ASSESSMENT).

In the case of a man and his wife living with him, there can only be one residence or main residence for both, so long as 'living together' (see 41.2 MARRIED PERSONS) and, where a notice specifying the main residence under (*a*) above affects both husband and wife, it must be given by both. [*TCGA 1992, s 222(6); FA 1996, Sch 20 para 59(4)*]. See Revenue Tax Bulletin, August 1994, pp 149, 150 for further discussion on elections by married couples.

The case of *Griffin v Craig-Harvey Ch D 1993, 66 TC 396* upheld the Revenue's long-standing view (see Revenue Capital Gains Manual CG 64495) that, broadly and subject to the following, initial notice nominating the main residence must be given within two years of the time the individual first begins to have two or more residences if it is to be effective from that time. Further notice(s) of variation can then only be made subsequent to such an effective initial notice but not so as to vary the nomination of the main residence more than two years before the giving of the further notice. The *ratio decidendi* (supported by certain words in the original *FA 1965* legislation and the *CGTA 1979* consolidation and, under principles established in *Pepper v Hart HL 1992, 65 TC 421*, by a Minister's statement in the HC Official Report relevant to the enactment of the *FA 1965* legislation) of the judgement of Vinelott J appears to be that 'the reference to "any period" in the opening part of [*TCGA 1992, s 222(5)* as above] and to "that period" [as above] are most naturally read as referring to "the whole or any part of the period of ownership in question" that being the period in relation to which in default of agreement or of any notice under [*section 222(5)*] the inspector's determination is to be made'. However, in the judgement the following hypothetical situations were put forward.

(1) The taxpayer owns two houses, each of which he occupies as a residence. More than two years have elapsed since he began to have two residences. He then begins to use a third house as a residence. A new two-year period begins to run at that time so that he can make an election as between all three residences during that two-year period.

(2) If on the same facts the taxpayer ceased, after acquiring a third residence, to use one of them as a residence a new period will begin at the time of cesser so that, again, he will have a period of two years during which he can elect between the remaining residences.

(3) The taxpayer owns two houses which he occupies as residences. The taxpayer conveys one of the houses to the trustees of the settlement under which he has a beneficial interest and the trustees have power which they exercise to permit him to continue to reside in the residence. A new two-year period begins at the time when he creates the settlement and again an election can be made (jointly by the taxpayer and the trustees; see 48.6 below) within the subsequent two years.

(4) The taxpayer has two residences, one owned by him and the other by the trustees of a settlement under which the trustees have power to permit the taxpayer to occupy it as a residence. No election is made during the two years following the inception of this state of affairs. If the trustees have and exercise a power to transfer the residence which they own to the taxpayer he can elect that that residence is to be his main residence at any time during the subsequent two years.

In *obiter dicta* comment on these examples, Vinelott J said (1) and (2) 'do no more than illustrate the inevitable consequence of [*TCGA 1992, s 222(5)*], namely that it becomes necessary to determine which of two or more residences is an individual's main residence whenever there is a change in the number of properties which he occupies as a residence; apart from an election . . . that question has to be determined afresh by the inspector (unless, of course, the disposal of one property occupied as a residence leaves him with only one residence)'. However, although not stated but crucial in the instant case, it appears implicit in the overall judgement that, in relation to examples similar to (1) and (2) above, an initial notice and a further notice . . . can only affect the position since the last change of circumstances in which the individual has two or more residences; they cannot change the main residence nomination for a previous combination of two or more residences which existed before that change even though such notices are made within the time limits. Vinelott J found it unnecessary to comment on a submission given in evidence that the taxpayer can give a initial notice of election and so preserve a right to vary an election even if at the time he has only one residence.

As regards the examples at (3) and (4) above, Vinelott J said they 'seem to be altogether unsurprising consequences of the legislation. If [there is a transfer as in (3) and (4) above], the transfer of the house to the trustees or from the trustees to the taxpayer is a disposal giving rise to a charge to capital gains tax on any gain so far as not exempt under [*TCGA 1992, s 222*]. The position is the same as if he had bought the house from or sold it to a stranger'.

The decision in *Griffin v Craig-Harvey* also led to doubt as to when an election under *TCGA 1992, s 222(5)* was necessary where, for example, the individual used one or more residences with a minimal capital value. With effect after 16 October 1994, the Revenue takes the view that any election or inspector's determination made or given under *TCGA 1992, s 222(5)* cannot be valid if it relies on the existence of a residence which is occupied under a licence so that after that date such an election or determination can only be valid where there is a legal or equitable interest (which includes all forms of ownership, from that of the sole owner of the fee simple absolute in possession to that of the co-owner of a minimal tenancy) in the residence. Job-related accommodation (see 48.2 above) may be occupied under either a service occupancy (i.e. under a licence) or a tenancy.

An election made before 17 October 1994 in favour of a residence in which there is a legal or equitable interest will continue to be regarded as valid even if it relied on the existence of a residence occupied under licence for its effect. An election made before 17 October 1994 in favour of a residence occupied under licence will be regarded as ceasing to have effect after 16 October 1994. Where there is only one other residence in which a legal or equitable interest is held that residence will after 16 October 1994 become the only or main residence subject to the rules for total or fractional exemption in 48.1 above. Where an election was made before 17 October 1994 in favour of a residence occupied under licence and there are two (or, presumably, more) residences in which a legal or equitable interest is held, a new two-year period for making an election between them will be regarded as beginning when the existing election ceases to take effect after 16 October 1994. Only this cessation will be regarded as giving rise to a change in the combination of residences held so that any new election made within two years after 16 October 1994 cannot be backdated to before 17 October 1994. However, this does not mean that an election made after 16 October 1994 cannot be backdated to before 17 October 1994 if there was an earlier change of residences giving rise to a two-year period which has not expired. Finally, the Revenue state that where an assessment is still open an individual may choose to disregard an election made before 17 October 1994 which relied for its effect on the existence of a residence occupied under licence, in which case the strict statutory rules will be applied in accordance with its new view to the whole of the period affected although this might mean, for example, that an election was out of time as regards two residences in which a legal or equitable interest is held (Revenue Tax Bulletin October 1994 p 167).

Prior to the above change of view regarding the validity of an election where a licence to occupy a residence is held, the Revenue had announced on 17 May 1985 a concessional practice which is presumably only applicable after 16 October 1994 to interests in residences which are not licences. Under the concession, where for any period an individual has, or is treated by the *Taxes Acts* as having, more than one residence but his interest in each of them, or in each of them except one, is such as to have no more than a negligible capital value on the open market (e.g. a weekly rented flat or accommodation provided by an employer), the two-year time limit laid down by *TCGA 1992, s 222(5)* for nominating one of those residences as the individual's main residence will be extended where the individual was unaware that such a nomination could be made. In such cases the nomination may be made within a reasonable time of the individual becoming aware of the possibility of so doing, and it will be regarded as effective from the date on which the individual first had more than one residence (Revenue Pamphlet IR 1, D21).

Example

S purchased the long lease of a London flat on 1 June 1992. He occupied the flat as his sole residence until 31 July 1994 when he acquired a property in Shropshire. Both properties were thereafter occupied as residences by S until the lease of the London flat was sold on 28 February 2001, realising an otherwise chargeable gain of £75,000.

The possibilities open to S are

(i) Election for London flat to be treated as main residence throughout

Exempt gain	£75,000

(ii) Election for Shropshire property to be treated as main residence from 31.7.94 onwards

Exempt gain £75,000 × $\frac{2y\ 2m + 3y}{8y\ 9m}$ £44,286

(iii) Election for London flat to be treated as main residence up to 28 February 1998, with election for the Shropshire property to be so treated thereafter

Exempt gain £75,000 × $\frac{5y\ 9m + 3y}{8y\ 9m}$ £75,000

Note to the example

(*a*) The elections in (iii) are the most favourable, provided they could have been made by 31 July 1996 in respect of the London flat, and by 28 February 2000 in respect of the Shropshire property. Note that the last three years' ownership of the London flat is an exempt period in any case. The advantage of (iii) over (i) is that the period of ownership 1 March 1998 to 28 February 2001 of the Shropshire property will be treated as a period of residence as regards any future disposal of that property.

48.6 OCCUPATION UNDER TERMS OF SETTLEMENT OR BY WILL OR INTESTACY

The provisions of *TCGA 1992, ss 222–224* (see 48.1–48.5 above) also apply in relation to a gain accruing to a trustee on a disposal of settled property being an asset within *TCGA 1992, s 222(1)* (see 48.1 above) where, during the period of ownership of the trustee, the dwelling-house (or part) has been the only or main residence of a person entitled to occupy it under the terms of the settlement. In the application of those provisions, references to the individual are taken as references to the trustee except in relation to the occupation of the dwelling-house. Any election for main residence treatment under 48.5 above is to be a joint notice by the trustee and the person entitled to occupy. [*TCGA 1992, s 225*].

A person is 'entitled' to occupy if he does so by permission of the trustees of a discretionary trust of which he is a beneficiary (*Sansom v Peay Ch D 1976, 52 TC 1*). See 57.7 SETTLEMENTS as to the Revenue's views on whether an 'interest in possession' is created in such circumstances.

Relief is given similarly to the above where personal representatives dispose of a dwelling-house which *before and after* the deceased's death has been used as their only or main residence by individuals who, under the will or intestacy, are entitled to the whole (or substantially the whole, interpreted by the Revenue as 75% or more) of the proceeds of the dwelling-house either absolutely or for life (Revenue Pamphlet IR 1, D5). See Revenue Tax Bulletin, August 1994, pp 150, 151 for further discussion on this point.

48.7 OCCUPATION BY DEPENDENT RELATIVE

If an individual so claims, relief as in 48.1–48.5 above is given to a gain accruing to him so far as attributable to the disposal of, or of an interest in, a dwelling-house (or part) which, on 5 April 1988 or at any earlier time in his period of ownership, was the *sole* residence of a 'dependent relative' of the individual, provided 'rent-free and without any other consideration'. Such relief is given in respect of the dwelling-house and its garden and grounds as would be given under *TCGA 1992, ss 222–224* if the dwelling-house had been the individual's only or main residence in the period of residence by the dependent relative; and any such relief is to be in addition to any relief already available under those provisions. Not more than one dwelling-house (or part) may qualify for relief as the residence of a dependent relative at any one time. In the case of a man and his wife living with him, no more than one dwelling-house may qualify as the residence of a dependent relative of the claimant or of the claimant's husband or wife at any one time. The inspector, before allowing a claim, may require the claimant to show that the giving of the relief claimed will not preclude the giving of relief to the claimant's spouse or that a claim for any such relief has been relinquished. [*TCGA 1992, s 226(1)(2)(4)(5)*].

If in a case within *TCGA 1992, s 226(1)* above the dwelling-house (or part) ceases, whether before 6 April 1988 or later, to be the sole residence (provided as mentioned above) of the dependent relative, any subsequent period of residence beginning after 5 April 1988 by that or any other dependent relative is disregarded for the purposes of the above relief. [*TCGA 1992, s 226(3)*]. If a dependent relative is obliged temporarily to live elsewhere (e.g. in a nursing home), the absence will not normally be treated as bringing this provision into play (ICAEW Statement TR 739, 13 February 1989).

For disposals before 6 April 1988, the dwelling-house (or part) merely had to be, or had to have been at some time in the period of ownership, the sole residence; and *TCGA 1992, s 226(3)* did not apply. [*FA 1988, s 111*].

The condition that the dwelling-house must have been provided 'rent-free and without any other consideration' will be regarded as satisfied where the dependent relative paid all or part of the occupier's rates or council tax and the cost of repairs to the dwelling-house attributable to normal wear and tear. In addition, the exemption will not be lost where the dependent relative made other payments in respect of the property either to the individual claiming the exemption or to a third party, provided that no net income was receivable by the individual, taking one year with another. For this purpose, the income receivable and allowable deductions will be computed in accordance with normal Schedule A income tax rules, except that account will be taken of mortgage payments (including both income and capital elements) and of other payments made by the dependent relative as consideration for the provision of the property, whether such payments were made directly to the mortgagee or other recipient or indirectly via the individual (Revenue Pamphlet IR 1, D20).

'*Dependent relative*' means, in relation to an individual

(*a*) any 'relative' of the individual or of his spouse who is incapacitated by old age or infirmity from maintaining himself, or

(*b*) the mother of the individual or of his spouse who, whether or not incapacitated, is widowed, separated, or a single woman in consequence of dissolution or annulment of marriage.

[*TCGA 1992, s 226(5)(6); FA 1996, Sch 20 para 61*].

This definition seems to exclude the mother of a child born out of wedlock (unless the mother either is incapacitated or has married subsequent to the child's birth and then become widowed etc.) but the Revenue have confirmed that such persons will in practice be included (Tolley's Practical Tax 1986 p 143). Also included, it seems in (*a*), is the incapacitated widowed stepmother of an individual, or of an individual's spouse, where the father has remarried and subsequently died. (Tolley's Practical Tax 1981 p 171 and 1984 p 198). '*Relative*' is undefined but may be compared with a specific meaning for other provisions as in 14.7 CONNECTED PERSONS i.e. brother, sister, ancestor or lineal descendant.

Old age, according to the Revenue, is reached at an age of 65 years in any case, and can be reached at an age greater than 54 years if the individual becomes, only because of age, not capable of working again 'in his own industry' (i.e. a man aged 57 years is not considered to have reached old age if he chooses not to work again or is unemployed because of a general lack of jobs). An individual is regarded as infirm if he is prevented by physical or mental illness from supporting himself by working. (Revenue Capital Gains Manual CG 65575–65577).

Where a property qualifies for the main private residence exemption only by virtue of these provisions, it is the Revenue's view that the residential lettings exemption at 48.8 below is *not* available. (Revenue Capital Gains Manual CG 65562, 64718).

48.8 EXEMPTION FOR LETTING AS RESIDENTIAL ACCOMMODATION

Where a gain to which *TCGA 1992, s 222* (see 48.1 above) applies accrues to an individual and the dwelling-house in question, or any part of it, is or has at any time in his 'period of ownership' been wholly or partly let (thus including any tenancy or licence or agreement for a lease, tenancy or licence; see *TCGA 1992, Sch 8 para 10*) by him as residential accommodation, the part of the gain, if any, which otherwise would be a chargeable gain by reason of the letting is exempt to the extent of the lower of

(*a*) £40,000 (£20,000 for disposals before 19 March 1991); and

(*b*) the amount of the gain otherwise exempt under *TCGA 1992, s 222(1)–(3)* (see 48.1 and 48.2 above) or those provisions as applied by *TCGA 1992, s 225* (see 48.6 above).

[*TCGA 1992, s 223(4)*].

'*Period of ownership*' does not include any period before 31 March 1982. [*TCGA 1992, s 223(7)*].

Note that the exemption applies to gains arising both from a residential letting of the entire residence whilst the owner is not occupying the property and to a partial residential letting whilst the owner is in residence.

The length of a letting is not determinative and the words 'residential accommodation' do not limit the above relief to accommodation which is used by a tenant etc. as his home (*Owen v Elliott CA 1990, 63 TC 319*). (In this case the taxpayer let short- and long-term accommodation in private hotel premises which he also occupied different parts of at different times of the year as his main residence in such a way that every part of the premises had at some time in his period of ownership been his main residence and it was agreed that on a disposal of the premises one-third of the gain arising was exempt under *TCGA 1992, ss 222–224*. The CA held that the above relief was also available in respect of the remaining non-exempt gain but Leggatt LJ indicated that it would not be available 'to a taxpayer the whole or part of whose dwelling-house is exclusively used as an hotel or boarding house. It will apply only where a dwelling-house has at any time been used wholly or partly for that or a like purpose by a person whose only or main residence it is'. Cf. the Revenue's practice below as to whether let accommodation forms part of the dwelling-house.)

Whether the let accommodation is part of the owner's dwelling-house, or is itself a separate dwelling-house, will depend on the facts of particular cases. In the Revenue's view, the relief will apply to the common case where the owner of a house, which was previously occupied as his or the family home, lets part as a flat or set of rooms without structural alteration, or with only minor adaptations. Whether or not the tenants have separate washing or cooking facilities will not affect the relief. Where a property, although part of the same building, forms a dwelling-house separate from that which is, or has been, the owner's dwelling-house, e.g. a fully self-contained flat with its own access from the road, relief will not be granted. (Revenue Pamphlet IR 131, SP 14/80).

The maximum gain that can be relieved under these provisions is the gain arising by reason of the letting. In a simple case in which a dwelling-house has at all times either been used as the owner's only or main residence or been let as residential accommodation, the gain remaining after the main private residence relief can be taken to be the gain arising by reason of the letting. See also *Example 2* below.

Where husband and wife are joint owners, they are treated like any other joint owners for the purposes of this exemption, with the result that relief of up to £80,000 is potentially available to the couple. However, Revenue officers have instructions to investigate the fact of a property being in joint ownership of husband and wife where the tax is significant. (Revenue Capital Gains Manual CG 64716, 64738).

The availability of the residential lettings exemption extends to gains accruing to trustees and qualifying for the main private residence exemption under *TCGA 1992, s 225* (see 48.6 above). (Revenue Capital Gains Manual CG 64717).

Where a dwelling-house qualifies for the main private residence exemption due only to its having been occupied by a dependent relative on or before 5 April 1988 (see 48.7 above), it is the Revenue's view that the residential lettings exemption is *not* available. (Revenue Capital Gains Manual CG 64718).

These provisions do not apply to restrict an allowable loss.

For the capital gains tax consequences of eligibility for 'rent a room' income tax relief, see 48.3 above.

For reliefs applicable to the commercial letting of furnished holiday accommodation in the UK, see 22 FURNISHED HOLIDAY ACCOMMODATION.

Example 1

P sold a house on 1 July 2000 realising an otherwise chargeable gain (before taper relief) of £48,667. The house was purchased on 1 February 1980 and was occupied as a residence until 30 June 1987 when P moved to another residence, letting the house as residential accommodation. He did not re-occupy the house prior to its sale.

	£
Gain on sale	48,667
Deduct Exempt amount under main residence rules	
$\dfrac{5y\ 3m + 3y}{18y\ 3m} \times £48,667$	22,000
	26,667
Deduct Let property exemption (see note (2))	22,000
Net chargeable gain (subject to TAPER RELIEF (60))	£4,667

Notes to the example

(1) The period of ownership for the exemption calculation does not include any period before 31 March 1982. This applies regardless of whether the gain has been calculated by reference to cost or to 31 March 1982 value under the re-basing rules.

(2) The gain attributable to the letting (£26,667) is exempt to the extent that it does not exceed the lesser of £40,000 and the gain otherwise exempt (£22,000 in this example).

Example 2

Q purchased a house on 1 February 1989, moved in immediately and occupied it as his main residence until 31 January 1990. It was let as residential accommodation from 1 February 1990 to 31 January 1991, was then empty until 31 January 1994, was again let as residential accommodation until 31 January 1996 and was subsequently let as office accommodation until being sold on 31 January 2001 at an otherwise chargeable gain (before taper relief) of £72,000.

		£
Gain on sale		72,000
Deduct Exempt amount under main residence rules		
$\frac{1y + \text{last } 3y}{12y} \times £72,000$		24,000
		48,000
Deduct Let property exemption:		
Lowest of: main residence relief	£24,000	
statutory limit	£40,000	
gain attributable to residential letting*	£18,000	18,000
Chargeable gain (subject to TAPER RELIEF (60))		£30,000

$$\frac{*\ 1\ y + 2\ y}{12y} \times £72,000 = £18,000$$

49 Qualifying Corporate Bonds

Sumption: Capital Gains Tax. See A12.17.

49.1 EXEMPTION RULES

A gain on the disposal of a qualifying corporate bond (as defined in 49.2 below) is not a chargeable gain, and a loss is not an allowable loss. [*TCGA 1992, s 115(1)(a)*].

The same applies to disposals of options or contracts to acquire or dispose of qualifying corporate bonds (see 17.10, 17.11 DISPOSAL).

See 49.3 below re share capital reorganisations involving qualifying corporate bonds.

See 39.11 LOSSES for allowable loss relief in respect of certain qualifying corporate bonds evidencing loans made before 17 March 1998 which become irrecoverable etc.

See 13.10 COMPANIES for appropriations of qualifying corporate bonds to and from trading stock by companies.

49.2 DEFINITIONS

Position for companies after 31 March 1996. For corporation tax purposes as regards disposals after 31 March 1996, with certain exceptions (see below) and subject to transitional provisions (see 38.9–38.20 LOAN RELATIONSHIPS OF COMPANIES), the definition of 'qualifying corporate bond' is extended so as to include *any* asset representing a loan relationship of a company (see 38.3 LOAN RELATIONSHIPS OF COMPANIES). Exceptions are as follows:

- convertible securities held as non-trading assets (as in 38.8(i) LOAN RELATIONSHIPS OF COMPANIES);
- certain debts linked to the value of non-trading chargeable assets (as in 38.8(ii) LOAN RELATIONSHIPS OF COMPANIES);
- an asset held in 'exempt circumstances' (defined by reference to *FA 1993, Sch 17 para 3* — see 21.8 EXEMPTIONS AND RELIEFS) where the debt to which it relates is not a debt on a security (see 21.5 EXEMPTIONS AND RELIEFS) and its settlement currency is not sterling or is a debt on a security and is 'a debt in a foreign currency' (as defined) (see *TCGA 1992, s 117A*);
- certain rights under a unit trust scheme or interests in an offshore fund which fall to be treated under *FA 1996, Sch 10 para 4* as rights under a creditor relationship of a company and which are denominated in a currency other than sterling and held in 'exempt circumstances' (as defined by reference to *FA 1993, Sch 17 para 3* — see 21.8 EXEMPTIONS AND RELIEFS) (see *TCGA 1992, s 117B*).

[*TCGA 1992, s 117(A1), s 117A, s 117B; FA 1996, s 92(4), s 93(4), s 104, s 105, Sch 14 paras 61, 62, Sch 15 para 7(c); FA 2000, Sch 29 paras 20, 21*].

Definition of corporate bond. The following is subject to the overriding rule for company disposals after 31 March 1996 (as above). Before defining a 'qualifying corporate bond', it is first necessary to define a 'corporate bond'. Subject to the specific inclusion of certain securities within this definition (see below) and the exclusion of some (again, see below), a '*corporate bond*' is a 'security' which fulfils both the following conditions.

(*a*) The debt on the security represents, and has at all times represented, a 'normal commercial loan'.

'*Normal commercial loan*' is as would be defined by *ICTA 1988, Sch 18 para 1(5)* if, for *para (a)(i)–(iii)* of *sub-para (5)*, there were substituted the words 'corporate bonds (within the meaning of *TCGA 1992, s 117*)'. The broad effect of the modification is that securities can be treated as corporate bonds if they carry conversion rights into other corporate bonds but not if the conversion rights relate to securities other than corporate bonds.

(*b*) The security is expressed in sterling and no provision is made for its conversion into, or redemption in, a currency other than sterling.

A security is *not* treated as expressed in sterling if the amount of sterling falls to be determined by reference to the value at any time of any other currency or asset. A provision for redemption in a currency other than sterling is disregarded provided the rate of exchange to be used is that prevailing at redemption.

[*TCGA 1992, s 117(1)(2)*].

'*Security*' includes any loan stock or similar security of any government or public or local authority in the UK or elsewhere, or of any company, and whether secured or unsecured. [*TCGA 1992, s 117(1), s 132(3)(b)*].

Inclusion of other securities within the definition of corporate bond. For 1996/97 onwards, a **relevant discounted security** (within 58.20 SHARES AND SECURITIES) is a corporate bond (and is also a qualifying corporate bond — see below). [*TCGA 1992, s 117(2AA); FA 1996, Sch 14 para 61*]. For this purpose, the widened definition of 'relevant discounted security' (i.e. taking further account of potential redemptions before maturity) applies as regards any disposal or part disposal of an asset after 14 February 1999. [*FA 1999, s 65(11)*].

Save in relation to the application of this definition for the purposes of *TCGA 1992, s 254* (loss relief for irrecoverable loans made before 17 March 1998 to traders and evidenced by qualifying corporate bonds — see 39.11 LOSSES), 'corporate bond' also includes a **share in a building society** (within *Building Societies Act 1986*) which meets the condition in (*b*) above and which is a 'qualifying share' (i.e. a share which is either a 'permanent interest bearing share' — as defined in *SI 1991 No 702* as modified — or is of a description specified in Treasury regulations for this purpose). [*TCGA 1992, s 117(4)–(6)(11)(b), (12)(13); SI 1999 No 1953*].

In relation to chargeable periods ended after 15 March 1993, 'corporate bond' also includes any debenture issued after that date which is not a 'security' as defined above but would fall to be treated as such under *TCGA 1992, s 251(6)* (see 21.5 EXEMPTIONS AND RELIEFS). This does not apply to debentures acquired by a person following a prior disposal of a qualifying corporate bond derived from shares giving rise to a deferred gain (where the general exemption in *TCGA 1992, s 115* has had effect in accordance with *TCGA 1992, s 116(10)(c)* — see 49.3 below). (This provision and *TCGA 1992, s 251(6)* prevent, in certain circumstances, the issue of a debenture which neither represents a debt on a security nor is a qualifying corporate bond.) [*TCGA 1992, s 117(6A); FA 1993, s 84(1)(3)*].

For disposals **before 6 April 1996**, a 'corporate bond' included a security not qualifying under (*a*) and (*b*) above and which was a **deep gain security** for the purposes of *FA 1989, Sch 11* or fell to be treated as a deep gain security under *FA 1989, Sch 11 para 21(2)* (non-gilts: special rules) or *para 22(2)* (indexed securities: special rules). A 'corporate bond' also included a security not qualifying under (*a*) and (*b*) above and which fell to be treated as a deep gain security under *FA 1989, Sch 11 para 22A(2)* (convertible securities: special rules (1)) or *para 22B(3)* (convertible securities: special rules (2)). [*TCGA 1992, s 117(3); FA 1996, Sch 41 Pt V(3)*].The provisions of *FA 1989, Sch 11* were repealed for 1996/97 onwards (see 58.20 SHARES AND SECURITIES).

Securities excluded from being corporate bonds. An **excluded indexed security** (as defined by *FA 1996, Sch 13 para 13* and meaning broadly a security the amount payable on redemption of which is linked to the value of chargeable assets) issued **after 5 April 1996** is *not* a corporate bond. An excluded indexed security issued before that date is a corporate bond only if it satisfies the general conditions above and if the question of whether or not it is a corporate bond arises only for the purposes of *TCGA 1992, s 116(10)* (reorganisation of share capital involving the issue of a qualifying corporate bond — see 49.3 below). [*TCGA 1992, s 117(6B)(6C); FA 1996, Sch 14 para 61*].

After 28 November 1994 and before 6 April 1996, a security (whenever issued) was *not* a corporate bond where it fell to be treated as a **quoted indexed security** for the purposes of the now repealed *FA 1989, Sch 11 para 2(2)(c)*. [*TCGA 1992, s 117(2A); FA 1995, s 50; FA 1996, Sch 41 Pt V(3)*].

Definition of qualifying corporate bond. The following is subject to the overriding rule for company disposals after 31 March 1996 (as above). A corporate bond

(A) is a '*qualifying corporate bond*' if it is issued after 13 March 1984; and

(B) becomes a '*qualifying corporate bond*' if, having been issued before 14 March 1984, it is acquired by any person after 13 March 1984 unless

   (i) the acquisition is as the result of *any* disposal treated as a no gain/no loss transaction or a disposal where the consideration is reduced by an amount of held-over gain under *TCGA 1992, s 165* or *s 260* (see 25.1–25.9 HOLD-OVER RELIEFS); and

   (ii) the bond was not a qualifying corporate bond before the disposal.

[*TCGA 1992, s 117(7)(8)*].

See the example below.

Where a right to a security is comprised in a provisional letter of allotment or similar instrument, the security is not deemed to be issued until acceptance has been made. [*TCGA 1992, s 117(11)(a)*].

A security which is a corporate bond due to its being a **relevant discounted security** (see above) is a qualifying corporate bond whatever its date of issue. [*TCGA 1992, s 117(8A); FA 1996, Sch 14 para 61*].

Example

B has the following transactions in 5% unsecured loan stock issued in 1983 by F Ltd.

	£
11.11.83 Purchase £2,000	1,800
10.7.89 Gift from wife £1,000 (original cost £800)	—
30.9.97 Purchase £2,000	2,100
5.6.2000 Sale £4,000	(3,300)

Apart from the gift on 10.7.89, all acquisitions were arm's length purchases. B's wife acquired her £1,000 holding on 11.11.83. Indexation allowance of £266 arose on the transfer from wife to husband.

For the purposes of the accrued income scheme, the sale is without accrued interest and the rebate amount is £20. The stock is a corporate bond as defined by *TCGA 1992, s 117(1)* and a 'relevant security' as defined by *TCGA 1992, s 108(1)*.

Under the rules for matching relevant securities in *TCGA 1992, s 106A* (see 59.2 SHARES AND SECURITIES—IDENTIFICATION RULES), the stock disposed of is identified with acquisitions as follows.

(i) Identify £2,000 with purchase on 30.9.97 (LIFO)

	£
Disposal consideration £3,300 × $\frac{2,000}{4,000}$	1,650
Add rebate amount £20 × $\frac{2,000}{4,000}$	10
	1,660
Allowable cost	2,100
Loss	£440

The loss is *not* allowable as the £2,000 stock purchased on 30.9.97 is a qualifying corporate bond (note (*a*)). [*TCGA 1992, s 115*].

(ii) Identify £1,000 with acquisition on 10.7.89

	£
Disposal consideration £3,300 × $\frac{1,000}{4,000}$	825
Add rebate amount £20 × $\frac{1,000}{4,000}$	5
	830
Allowable cost (including indexation to 10.7.89)	1,066
Allowable loss	£236

The loss is allowable as the stock acquired on 10.7.89 is not a qualifying corporate bond (note (*b*)).

(iii) Identify £1,000 with part of purchase on 11.11.83

	£
Disposal consideration £3,300 × $\frac{1,000}{4,000}$	825
Add rebate amount £20 × $\frac{1,000}{4,000}$	5
	830
Allowable cost £1,800 × $\frac{1,000}{2,000}$	900
Allowable loss	£70

The loss is allowable as the stock acquired on 11.11.83 is not a qualifying corporate bond (note (*c*)).

Notes to the example

(*a*) The acquisition on 30.9.97 is a qualifying corporate bond as it was acquired after 13 March 1984 otherwise than as a result of an excluded disposal.

(*b*) The acquisition on 10.7.89 was the result of an excluded disposal, being a no gain/no loss transfer between spouses where the first spouse had acquired the stock before 14 March 1984. It is therefore not a qualifying corporate bond.

(*c*) Securities acquired before 14 March 1984 cannot be qualifying corporate bonds in the hands of the person who so acquired them.

Miscellaneous provisions no longer applicable. TCGA 1992, s 117(7)(8) (see above) did not apply to a security which fell to be treated as a corporate bond by virtue of being a **deep gain security** under *FA 1989, Sch 11*. Such a corporate bond was a qualifying corporate bond whatever its date of issue. Neither did they apply to a security which fell to be treated as a corporate bond by virtue of its being treated as a deep gain security under (i) *FA 1989, Sch 11 para 21(2)*, (ii) *Sch 11 para 22(2)*, (iii) *Sch 11 para 22A(2)* or (iv) *Sch 11 para 22B(3)* (see above). Such a corporate bond was a qualifying corporate bond as regards a disposal made after the time mentioned in, respectively, (i) *Sch 11 para 21(1)(c)*, (iii) *Sch 11 para 22A(1)(c)* or (iv) *Sch 11 para 22B(2)(b)*, or, as regards (ii), after the time the agreement mentioned in *Sch 11 para 22(1)(b)* was made. [*TCGA 1992, s 117(9); FA 1996, Sch 41 Pt V(3)*]. The provisions of *FA 1989, Sch 11* were repealed for 1996/97 onwards.

A security issued by a member of a group (within *TCGA 1992, s 170*; see 13.11 COMPANIES) to another member of the same group was excluded from being a qualifying corporate bond except in relation to a disposal by a person who (at the time of the disposal) was not a member of the same group as the company which issued the security. [*TCGA 1992, s 117(10); FA 1996, Sch 41 Pt V(3)*].

The capital element of a deep discount security within *ICTA 1988, Sch 4* (see 58.20 SHARES AND SECURITIES) could be a qualifying corporate bond (CCAB Statement TR 551, July 1984). The deep discount security provisions are repealed for 1996/97 onwards.

Company exchange gains and losses. The provisions below are repealed for disposals after 31 March 1996 as a consequence of the changed position for companies as regards such disposals (see the beginning of this paragraph).

The following applied where a 'qualifying asset' consisted of a right to settlement under a debt on a security, and on or after the first day of its first accounting period beginning after 22 March 1995, a 'qualifying company' (see 13.44 COMPANIES) disposed of the security (or engaged in an event which would be a disposal of the security in the absence of *TCGA 1992, s 127* (reorganisations)) and immediately before the disposal or other event the company did not hold the security in 'exempt circumstances'. '*Exempt circumstances*' are when the security is held for the purposes of long term insurance business; for the purposes of mutual insurance business; for the purposes of the occupation for profit of commercial woodlands in the UK; by an approved housing association; or by an approved self-build society. Where these conditions were fulfilled, then in applying *TCGA 1992, s 117* above in relation to the disposal or other event or a transaction as specified below:

(1) the requirement that the security be expressed in sterling as in (*b*) above was omitted, and

(2) where the settlement currency of the debt was a currency other than sterling, the definition of 'normal commercial loan' in (*a*) above had effect, and was treated as always having had effect, as if *ICTA 1988, Sch 18 para 1(5)(b)(c)* (which broadly requires the return on the security not to depend on results or exceed a commercial return and the repayment of the security not to exceed the new consideration lent or what is generally available on similar securities) had always been omitted, and *TCGA 1992, s 117(10)* above (relating to securities issued within a group) was treated as omitted.

A transaction is taken into account as above if it is a transaction in relation to which *TCGA 1992, ss 127–130* (reorganisations) apply by virtue of any provision within *TCGA 1992, Pt IV Ch II* (reorganisation of share capital, conversion of securities etc.), or would apply apart from *TCGA 1992, s 116* (see 49.3 below); it is a transaction under which the company becomes entitled to the right; it occurs on or after the company's commencement day but before the disposal or other event; and the company holds the right at all times following the time when it becomes entitled to it and preceding the disposal or other event. [*FA 1993, s 169, Sch 17 paras 3, 5; FA 1995, Sch 24 para 6; FA 1996, Sch 15 para 22(6), Sch 41 Pt V(3)*].

The following applied where a 'qualifying company' (see 13.44 COMPANIES) had made a loan under which the debt is a debt on a security, and the right to settlement under the debt was a 'qualifying asset'. In these circumstances the following applied in relation to relief claims made on or after the first day of the company's first accounting period beginning after 22 March 1995.

(*aa*) In applying *TCGA 1992, s 117* above for the purposes of *TCGA 1992, s 254* (see above), the requirement that the security be expressed in sterling as in (*b*) above was ignored.

(*bb*) Where the settlement currency of the debt was a currency other than sterling, then in applying *TCGA 1992, s 117* for the purposes of *TCGA 1992, s 254*:

- (i) the definition of 'normal commercial loan' in (*a*) above had effect as if *ICTA 1988, Sch 18 para 1(5)(b)(c)* (see (2) above) were omitted; and
- (ii) *TCGA 1992, s 117(10)* above (relating to securities issued within a group) was ignored.

(*cc*) In applying *TCGA 1992, s 254(6)* (allowable amount if first or second condition fulfilled) in a case where a security would not be a qualifying corporate bond but for (*aa*) or (*bb*) above, the 'allowable amount' under that provision was found by deducting, from what the amount would otherwise be, the amount of any exchange loss or losses (whether trading or non-trading) accruing to the company as regards the asset for a period or periods ending on or before the 'relevant date'. The '*relevant date*' was the date when the security's value became negligible or the outstanding amount of the principal of the loan was or proved to be irrecoverable. The amount of an exchange loss expressed in a currency other than the basic currency (i.e. the currency in which the allowable amount is expressed) was for these purposes treated as the basic currency equivalent on the day the related claim is made, calculated by reference to the London closing exchange rate for that day.

[*FA 1993, s 169, Sch 17 para 6; FA 1996, Sch 15 para 22(6), Sch 41 Pt V(3)*].

49.3 REORGANISATION OF SHARE CAPITAL

Special provisions apply to a transaction ('*relevant transaction*') where otherwise *TCGA 1992, ss 127–130* (share reorganisation rules for 'original shares' and 'new holding'; see 58.5 SHARES AND SECURITIES) would otherwise apply under any provision contained in *TCGA 1992, Pt IV Ch II* (reorganisation of share capital, conversion of securities etc.), and either the original shares would consist of or include a qualifying corporate bond and the new holding would not, or the original shares would not and the new holding would consist of or include such a bond. In relation to any disposal after 25 November 1996, the provisions apply equally to a conversion of securities occurring before or after that date and effected other than by means of a transaction, for example in consequence of the terms of the security. Where the qualifying corporate bond would constitute the original shares it is referred to as '*the old asset*', the shares and securities constituting the new holding being referred to as '*the new asset*'. Where the qualifying corporate bond would constitute the new holding it is referred to as '*the new asset*', the shares and securities constituting the original shares being referred to as '*the old asset*'.

TCGA 1992, ss 127–130 do not apply to the relevant transaction so far as the latter relates to the old asset and the new asset. (The Revenue has stated that where shares (or other chargeable securities) are exchanged, converted etc. for a new holding consisting partly of qualifying corporate bonds and partly of shares etc., then *TCGA 1992, ss 127–130* are only disapplied to the extent that the consideration takes the form of qualifying corporate bonds, any apportionment of the base cost of the original shares being on a just and reasonable basis under *TCGA 1992, s 52(4)* by reference to the respective market values at the time of exchange etc. of the shares etc. and qualifying corporate bonds received in exchange etc. (Revenue Tax Bulletin February 1993 p 57).)

Where the qualifying corporate bond would constitute the old asset, the shares or securities which constitute the new asset are to be treated as being acquired on the date of the relevant transaction and for a consideration of the market value of the old asset immediately before the relevant transaction. Similar provisions apply where the qualifying corporate bond constitutes the new asset. Where a sum of money by way of consideration for the old asset is received, in addition to the new asset, that sum is to be deducted from the deemed market value consideration and where a sum of money is paid by way of consideration, in addition to the old asset, that sum is to be added to the deemed market value consideration. See also (ii) below.

Where the old asset consists of a qualifying corporate bond, then so far as it relates to the old and the new asset, the relevant transaction is to be treated as a disposal of the old asset and an acquisition of the new asset.

In all other cases (e.g. **where the new asset consists of a qualifying corporate bond**) then so far as it relates to the old asset and to the new asset the relevant transaction is *not* to be treated as a disposal of the old asset but

(*a*) the chargeable gain or allowable loss is calculated that would have accrued had the old asset been disposed of at the time of the relevant transaction at its market value immediately before that time, and

(*b*) subject to the exclusions below, the whole or a corresponding part of the calculated chargeable gain or allowable loss at (*a*) above is to be deemed to accrue on a subsequent disposal of the whole or part of the new asset. The exemption provided by 49.1 above applies only to the gain or loss that actually accrues on that disposal and not to the gain or loss that is deemed to accrue.

The following exclusions are made to the above provisions.

(i) The provisions in (*b*) above do not apply to disposals falling within: *TCGA 1992, s 58(1)* (see 41.3 MARRIED PERSONS); *s 62(4)* (see 16.9 DEATH); *s 139* in respect of disposals after 13 March 1989 (see 13.7 COMPANIES); *s 140A* (see 44.10 OVERSEAS MATTERS); *s 171(1)* (see 13.12 COMPANIES); or *s 172* (now repealed — see 44.3 OVERSEAS MATTERS). Where there is such a disposal (and without there having been a previous disposal other than such a disposal or a devolution on death) the person who has acquired the new asset is treated for the purposes of (*b*) above as if the new asset had been acquired by him at the same time and for the same consideration as it was acquired by the person making the disposal.

(ii) Where a chargeable gain arises under (*a*) above *and* part of the consideration for the old asset is received as money, a proportion of the chargeable gain is deemed to accrue at that time. The proportion is the ratio which the sum of money bears to the market value of the old asset immediately before the relevant transaction. On a later disposal of a part or the whole of the new asset, the proportion already deemed to have accrued is to be deducted from the gain accruing under (*b*) above. However, if the sum of money is 'small' in comparison with the market value of the old asset immediately before the relevant transaction, the Revenue may direct that no chargeable gain accrues at that time. The money consideration is then deducted from allowable expenditure on any subsequent disposal (see 17.8 DISPOSAL).

For the purpose of the above, the Revenue have regarded 'small' as meaning 5% or less (see Revenue Capital Gains Manual CG 53857, 57836). With effect from **24 February 1997**, they additionally regard an amount of £3,000 or less as 'small', regardless of whether or not it would pass the 5% test (Revenue Tax Bulletin February 1997 p 397).

[*TCGA 1992, s 116(1)–(14); FA 1985, s 67(2)(c), Sch 27 Part VII; FA 1989, s 139(6); FA 1990, s 70(6)(9); F(No 2)A 1992, s 46(1)(3); FA 1997, s 88(4)(6); FA 2000, Sch 29 para 19*].

In relation to disposals after 13 March 1989, the changes made by *FA 1989, s 139* are to be regarded as always having had effect. [*TCGA 1992, Sch 11 para 16*].

Where the new asset is a qualifying corporate bond which is subsequently gifted to a charity, the Revenue take the view that no deferred gain or loss will arise to the donor under (*b*) above (Revenue Tax Bulletin May 1992 p 21). This will be advantageous if the loss relief for loans becoming irrecoverable etc. and evidenced by qualifying corporate bonds is unavailable (see below).

A special rule has effect where, before 15 February 1999, there occurred a transaction (the original transaction) to which *TCGA 1992, ss 127–130* applied and the new holding consisted of or included something (the new asset) which becomes a 'relevant discounted security' (and thus a qualifying corporate bond — see 49.2 above) by virtue of the widening of the definition of that term to take further account of potential redemptions before maturity (see 58.20 SHARES AND SECURITIES). In relation to any disposal or part disposal of the new asset after 14 February 1999, there is deemed to have been a transaction subsequent to the original transaction whereby the holder of the new asset disposed of it and immediately re-acquired it. The re-acquired asset is deemed to consist of a qualifying corporate bond and the subsequent transaction is deemed to be one to which *TCGA 1992, s 116* applies, with the same consequences as in (*a*) and (*b*) above. The subsequent transaction is deemed to have occurred immediately after the original transaction, except that where the original transaction occurred before 5 April 1996 the subsequent transaction is deemed to have occurred on that date. [*FA 1999, s 66*].

See 19.28 EMPLOYEE SHARE SCHEMES for the interaction of the provisions above with those relating to certain disposals to employee share ownership trusts.

See 60.12 TAPER RELIEF for the application of that relief to the postponed gain where the new asset is a qualifying corporate bond.

See 39.11 LOSSES for the interaction of the provisions above with the now repealed provisions relating to loss relief by reference to certain qualifying corporate bonds evidencing loans which become irrecoverable etc.

Example

D holds 5,000 £1 ordinary shares in H Ltd. He acquired the shares in April 1991 by subscription at par. On 1 August 1994, he accepted an offer for the shares from J plc. The terms of the offer were one 25p ordinary share of J plc and £10 J plc 10% unsecured loan stock (a qualifying corporate bond) for each H Ltd ordinary share. Both the shares and the loan stock are listed on the Stock Exchange. In December 2000, D sells £20,000 loan stock at its quoted price of £105 per cent.

The value of J plc ordinary shares at 1 August 1994 was £3.52 per share and the loan stock was £99.20 per cent. The indexation factor for April 1991 to August 1994 is 0.087.

The cost of the H Ltd shares must be apportioned between the J plc ordinary shares and loan stock.

	£
Value of J plc shares 5,000 × £3.52	17,600
Value of J plc loan stock £50,000 × 99.2%	49,600
	£67,200

Allowable cost of J plc shares

$\frac{17,600}{67,200} \times £5,000$ — £1,310

Allowable cost of J plc loan stock

$\frac{49,600}{67,200} \times £5,000$ — £3,690

Chargeable gain on H Ltd shares attributable to J plc loan stock to date of exchange

	£
Deemed disposal consideration	49,600
Allowable cost	3,690
Unindexed gain	45,910
Indexation allowance £3,690 × 0.087	321
Deferred chargeable gain	£45,589

Deferred chargeable gain accruing on disposal of loan stock in December 2000

Loan stock sold (nominal)	£20,000
Total holding of loan stock before disposal (nominal)	£50,000

Deferred chargeable gain accruing in 2000/01

$\frac{20,000}{50,000} \times £45,589$ — £18,236

Notes to the example

(*a*) The gain on the sale of J plc loan stock is exempt (as the stock is a qualifying corporate bond) except for that part which relates to the gain on the previous holding of H Ltd shares. [*TCGA 1992, s 115, s 116(10)*]. There will also be income tax consequences under the accrued income scheme.

(*b*) For taper relief purposes, the deferred gain is deemed to arise in August 1994 (and not in December 2000) — see 60.12 TAPER RELIEF. Thus, there can be no taper relief due in this example.

(*c*) The qualifying corporate bond is treated as acquired at the date of the reorganisation, so even if the original shares had been held at 31 March 1982, re-basing could *not* apply on the subsequent disposal, after 5 April 1988, of the loan stock. However, where the original shares were acquired before 31 March 1982, the reorganisation took place before 6 April 1988, and the qualifying corporate bonds are disposed of after 5 April 1988, the deferred chargeable gain is halved (under the provisions at 8.12 ASSETS HELD ON 31 MARCH 1982).

(*d*) The exchange of J plc ordinary shares for H Ltd shares is dealt with under *TCGA 1992, ss 127–130* (see 58.5 SHARES AND SECURITIES), and no gain or loss will arise until the J plc shares are disposed of.

50 Reinvestment Relief

Cross-references. See 20.9 ENTERPRISE INVESTMENT SCHEME (AND BES); 49 QUALIFYING CORPORATE BONDS; 53 RETIREMENT RELIEF; 55 ROLLOVER RELIEF; 58 SHARES AND SECURITIES; 65.10 VENTURE CAPITAL TRUSTS.

Sumption: Capital Gains Tax. See A15A.

See also Tolley's Roll-over, Hold-over and Retirement Reliefs.

The headings in this chapter are as follows.

50.1 BACKGROUND AND ENDING OF RELIEF

In respect of disposals after 15 March 1993, *Chapter IA* of *Part V* of *TCGA 1992* (referred to below as '*Chapter IA*'), as inserted by *FA 1993, s 87, Sch 7 para 3*, provides, subject to conditions, for relief as described in this chapter where reinvestment is made in shares in a company. *Chapter IA* has been **repealed** so as to have no effect where the shares in which the reinvestment is made are **acquired after 5 April 1998**. Separate deferral reliefs apply for reinvestment in EIS and VCT shares — see respectively 20.9 ENTERPRISE INVESTMENT SCHEME (AND BES) and 65.10 VENTURE CAPITAL TRUSTS — and these continue, the former in revised form, as regards acquisitions after 5 April 1998. [*FA 1998, s 141(1)(a), (2)(a), Sch 27 Pt III(32)*].

Chapter IA is entitled 'rollover relief on reinvestment', but in order to avoid confusion with the rollover relief for replacement of business assets (see 55 ROLLOVER RELIEF), the appellation 'reinvestment relief' is generally used and is adopted in this publication.

In its original form, which existed for disposals occurring after 15 March 1993 but before 30 November 1993, the relief required the gain which could be rolled over to arise, broadly, in respect of an individual's disposal of unquoted shares in or other securities of a trading company in circumstances where the individual had throughout a minimum period of one year before the disposal both exercised at least 5% of the voting rights and worked full-time for the company as an officer or employee. However, for disposals after 29 November 1993, the main change to the relief made by *FA 1994, s 91(1)(2), Sch 11* was to allow a gain on any asset arising to an individual to qualify for relief. Similarly, the original requirement to acquire, broadly, at least a 5% holding of the ordinary shares in the company in order for the acquisition cost of that shareholding to be reduced was removed.

Trustees of certain settlements are treated similarly to individuals in the claiming of relief.

The broad approach taken in the coverage below is to describe the relief as it relates to disposals after 29 November 1993, the relief for disposals after 15 March 1993 and before 30 November 1993 being explained by way of contrast in view of its restricted application and relatively short currency before amendment.

A clearance scheme enables companies to obtain an advance ruling from the Revenue on whether their shares are eligible for relief. See 50.17 below.

50.2 **RELIEF FOR INDIVIDUALS—DISPOSALS AFTER 29 NOVEMBER 1993**

Individuals may claim to roll-over chargeable gains accruing on any assets if the disposal proceeds are reinvested in a 'qualifying investment' within the specified time period and before 6 April 1998. The relief is effected by reducing the sale proceeds of the disposed assets and the acquisition cost of the newly acquired investment by the lower of the following amounts:

(*a*) the otherwise chargeable gain (net of any amount deferred by virtue of a previous claim for reinvestment relief),

(*b*) the acquisition cost of the new asset,

(*c*) if the new asset is not acquired at arm's length, the market value at the time of its acquisition,

(*d*) the amount specified by the individual in the claim.

[*TCGA 1992, s 164A(1)(2)(a); FA 1993, Sch 7 para 3; FA 1994, Sch 11 para 2(a)*].

These adjustments only affect the reinvestor claiming the relief and there is no consequential effect for either the complementary purchaser or vendor.

[*TCGA 1992, s 164A(2)(b); FA 1993, Sch 7 para 3; FA 1994, Sch 11 para 2(a)*].

The relief is not available in respect of disposals and re-acquisition of shares in the same company or of shares in a company in the same group.

The specified time limit for reinvestment is the period beginning 12 months before and ending 3 years after the date of the disposal. The Board of Inland Revenue may at their discretion allow an extension. No reinvestment relief is available under these provisions where the reinvestment takes place after 5 April 1998 (see 50.1 above).

If both a qualifying and a non-qualifying asset is purchased the disposal proceeds should be distributed in a just and reasonable manner.

In the case of the crystallisation of a deferred gain under *TCGA 1992, s 116(10)(a)* (gains deferred where shares exchanged for qualifying corporate bonds; see 49.3 QUALIFYING CORPORATE BONDS), the reduction provided under (*a*) above is made from the deemed consideration (i.e. the market value of the shares) when the shares were exchanged for the bonds. When there is a disposal of only some of the bonds, the bonds disposed of are treated as a separate asset, and the chargeable gain and consideration to be reduced under the claim are treated as relating to a corresponding part of what were the shares. In the case of a gain crystallising under *TCGA 1992, s 116(12)* (part of gain referable to cash element to crystallise on exchange where shares exchanged partly for cash and partly for qualifying corporate bonds), the reduction provided under (*a*) is made from the cash element which, with the qualifying bonds, is exchanged for the shares. [*TCGA 1992, s 164A(2A)(2B); FA 1996, s 177*].

In the normal case of the reinvestor acquiring the qualifying investment at arm's length and in the absence of other reliefs and time apportionment, the effect of (*a*)(i) and (ii) above is to provide full deferral of the gain otherwise accruing on the disposal of the asset disposed of where the acquisition consideration given for the qualifying investment is equal to or exceeds the amount of that gain (and *not* where it is equal to or exceeds the amount of the disposal consideration given for the asset disposed of, cf. ROLLOVER RELIEF (55)). It was difficult to ascertain whether the legislation allowed relief under (*a*)(ii) above where the qualifying investment was acquired by way of gift (when other provisions in *TCGA 1992* would substitute a deemed consideration e.g. market value or at a no gain/no loss consideration). *FA 1995* removed any doubt by preventing excess relief being claimed in respect of shares acquired by way of gift if the qualifying investment was acquired after 19 June 1994, or a claim under *TCGA 1992, s 164A(2)* above relating to a disposal is made after that date. Thus, where a claim for the above relief is made after 19 June 1994 and the qualifying investment in respect of which the claim is made was acquired by the reinvestor through an inter-spouse (no gain/no loss) transfer under *TCGA 1992, s 58*, the relief claimed cannot exceed the transferor spouse's allowable base cost of the qualifying investment, after any reduction in that cost due to gains already rolled over into that investment, irrespective of the re-basing rules in *TCGA 1992, s 35, Sch 3 para 1* or *TCGA 1992, s 55* in situations where the qualifying investment was held by the transferor spouse since 31 March 1982. Similarly, the re-basing provisions are disapplied where the claimant returns the qualifying investment to his spouse on a no gain/no loss basis. The reduction provided by (*a*)(iii) would only seem to be in point, having regard to *TCGA 1992, s 164A(10)* below, where the amount of the consideration deemed to be given for the qualifying investment (e.g. at a no gain/no loss transfer consideration) is greater than its market value at the time of its acquisition. The reduction at (*a*)(iv) above is most likely to be useful in cases where the annual exempt amount, allowable losses or other reliefs (e.g. retirement relief; see 50.6 below) are available. In all cases, the reduction provided by (*a*) above is from the disposal consideration, again subject to *TCGA 1992, s 164A(10)* below, of the asset disposed of (and *not* from the gain otherwise arising on that disposal; see further in 50.6 below).

For the purposes of the relief, a person who acquires any 'eligible shares' (see below) in a 'qualifying company' (see 50.14 below) is regarded as acquiring a '*qualifying investment*' unless, where the asset disposed of consisted of shares in or securities of any company ('*the initial holding*'), the qualifying company

(1) is the company in which the holding subsisted, or

(2) is a company that was, at the time of the disposal of the initial holding, or is, at the time of the acquisition of the qualifying investment, a member of the same '*group of companies*' (as in *TCGA 1992, Sch 6 para 1*; see 53.4 RETIREMENT RELIEF) as the company in which the initial holding subsisted.

[*TCGA 1992, s 164A(8)(14), s 164FF; FA 1993, Sch 7 para 3; FA 1994, Sch 11 para 7; FA 1995, s 47(1)(2)(4)(6)(8); FA 1997, Sch 17 para 2(1)*].

After 26 November 1996, where 'eligible shares' are acquired by a person in a 'qualifying company' by their being issued to him, that acquisition is not a qualifying investment unless the company or a 'qualifying subsidiary' (see 50.14 below) intends to employ the money raised by the issue wholly for the purposes of a qualifying trade carried on by it (or for the purposes of preparing to carry on a qualifying trade). This applies equally to shares acquired on or before 26 November 1996, held until that time and continuing throughout to be eligible shares in a qualifying company, but not so as to prevent such shares from being shares in a qualifying company at any time after 26 November 1996 and within three years after their acquisition. For reinvestment relief purposes, an allotment of shares before their issue is disregarded in determining whether and when a person acquires shares by their issue to him. [*TCGA 1992, s 164A(8A)(8B), s 164N(5); FA 1997, Sch 17 para 2(2), para 6(2), para 7*].

It is the Revenue's view that the provisions described immediately above have introduced a requirement that qualifying investments acquired by subscription *must* be acquired wholly for cash (Revenue Capital Gains Manual CG 62490). Their argument is that the condition requiring an intention for the 'money' raised by the issue to be employed as stated above cannot possibly be satisfied if no money is raised. Some commentators argue that this view is unsustainable in law, others that, even if it can be so sustained, it is indefensible to insist on interpreting the legislation in such a way as to introduce a fundamental change which restricts the availability of reinvestment relief but which was not formally announced by either the Government or the Revenue. See, for example, an article in *Taxation 22 January 1998 p 387*. That article suggested various means of avoiding the consequences of the Revenue view. As long as *some* cash was raised by an issue of eligible shares, it is apparent (though not to the Revenue) that the said condition *can* then be satisfied in relation to the entire issue, even if the company also raised other assets thereby.

'*Eligible shares*' means (subject to *TCGA 1992, ss 164L, 164M* in 50.16 below) any 'ordinary shares' in a company which do not carry any present or future preferential rights to dividends or the company's assets on a winding up or right to be redeemed. '*Ordinary shares*' means shares forming part of a company's '*ordinary share capital*' (i.e. all the issued share capital of the company, other than capital the holders of which only have a right to a fixed rate of dividend). [*TCGA 1992, s 164N(1); FA 1993, Sch 7 para 3*].

For the purposes of the relief the acquisition of a qualifying investment is taken to be in the '*qualifying period*' if, and only if, it takes place at any time in the period beginning twelve months before and ending three years after the disposal of the asset disposed of, or at such time before the beginning of that period or after it ends as the Board may by notice allow. [*TCGA 1992, s 164A(9); FA 1993, Sch 7 para 3; FA 1994, Sch 11 para 2(d)*]. No reinvestment relief is available under these provisions where the reinvestment takes place after 5 April 1998 (see 50.1 above).

The provisions of *TCGA 1992* fixing the amount of consideration deemed to be given for the acquisition or disposal of assets are applied before the relief given by the above provisions is applied; and without prejudice to the generality of this, *TCGA 1992, s 42(5)* (apportionment on part disposal to be operated before certain provisions including those deeming a no gain/no loss disposal consideration; see 17.6 DISPOSAL) is applied in relation to an adjustment by way of the above relief of the consideration for the acquisition of any shares as it applies to an adjustment in relation to a deemed no gain/no loss disposal consideration. [*TCGA 1992, s 164A(10); FA 1993, Sch 7 para 3*].

Without prejudice to *TCGA 1992, s 52(4)* (apportionment of consideration or expenditure to be just and reasonable; see 17.6 DISPOSAL), where consideration is given for the acquisition of any assets some of which are shares to the acquisition of which a claim for relief relates and some of which are not, the consideration is to be apportioned in a just and reasonable manner. [*TCGA 1992, s 164A(12); FA 1993, Sch 7 para 3; FA 1994, Sch 11 para 2(e)*].

Where an acquisition is made after 28 November 1994, *TCGA 1992, s 164H* (interests in land rule, see 50.14 below) no longer applies in deciding whether it is an acquisition of a qualifying investment for the purposes of the above relief. [*TCGA 1992, s 164A(13); FA 1995, s 46(1)(2)*].

FA 1995 introduced rules with regard to the making of multiple claims for relief against the same qualifying investment to ensure that aggregate gains rolled over do not exceed the cost thereof. These rules have effect where a qualifying investment is acquired after 19 June 1994, or claims under *TCGA 1992, s 164A(2)* are made in respect of the same qualifying investment for disposals after that date. Where multiple reductions are claimed under the above relief in respect of the same qualifying investment, the reductions shall be treated as claimed separately in such order as the claimant elects or, in default, the Board determines.

On the second and subsequent claims the amount of gain able to be rolled over will be limited to the remaining acquisition cost ((*a*)(ii) above) or market value ((*a*)(iii) above) of the qualifying investment left after any previous claims have been made. A claim that has become final (i.e. it may not be amended or is finally determined, whichever occurs first) will be treated as made earlier than any claim which is not final. [*TCGA 1992, s 164A(14), s 164FG; FA 1995, s 47(1)(2)(5)(7)(8)*].

Claims for relief. As no time limit is specified, the general time limits in *TMA 1970, s 43* apply (see 12.5 CLAIMS). For reinvestment relief purposes, the period of time allowed for the making of a claim begins with the *later* of

- the end of the year of assessment in which the disposal takes place, and
- the end of the year of assessment in which the qualifying investment is acquired,

and ends on the fifth anniversary of 31 January following the year of assessment in question (six years after the end of that year where it is 1995/96 or an earlier year).

A claim to relief is not prevented by the finality of an assessment on chargeable gains.

(Revenue Capital Gains Manual CG 62215, 62216).

For years before 1996/97, if the claimant provides satisfactory evidence of a definite intention to acquire a qualifying investment shortly after the normal payable date for the tax and within the time limit for reinvestment, a postponement application should be accepted. Under self-assessment, for disposals in 1996/97 onwards, there is no provision for postponement of tax in these circumstances. A claim can only be made after a qualifying investment has been acquired. (Revenue Capital Gains Manual CG 62217, 62218). There is no reinvestment relief equivalent of the provisional claim procedure available from 1996/97 for business asset rollover relief (see 55.2 ROLLOVER RELIEF).

As regards 1996/97 onwards, Revenue Helpsheet IR 291 (Reinvestment Relief) contains a form on which an individual may make a claim. The completed form can be attached to the Capital Gains supplementary pages of the self-assessment tax return.

Example

In May 1998 R sells a painting for £200,000 which he purchased in June 1987 for £61,500. In October 1997, R acquired 30,000 ordinary shares in A Ltd for £150,000. A Ltd is an unquoted company which exists wholly for the purpose of carrying on a manufacturing trade. R has no other chargeable gains in 1998/99. He wishes to make a claim under *TCGA 1992, s 164A* for reinvestment relief but so as to leave sufficient gains in charge to utilise £2,000 worth of capital losses brought forward and his annual exemption of £6,800. All transactions are at arm's length. The indexation factor for the period June 1987 to April 1998 is 0.596.

The chargeable gain on the disposal of the painting is calculated as follows

	£
Disposal consideration	200,000
Cost	61,500
Unindexed gain	138,500
Indexation allowance £61,500 × 0.596	36,654
Gain after indexation (no taper relief due)	£101,846

The disposal consideration received is treated as reduced by the smallest of

(i)	the chargeable gain	£101,846
(ii)	the amount reinvested	£150,000
(iii)	the amount specified in the claim for relief (£101,846 – £(2,000 + 6,800))	£93,046

The chargeable gain is recalculated as follows

	£
Disposal consideration	200,000
Less reduction (see (iii) above)	93,046
	106,954
Cost	61,500
Unindexed gain	45,454
Indexation allowance as above	36,654
Gain after indexation	8,800
Less losses brought forward	2,000
Net gain (covered by annual exemption)	£6,800

The base cost of R's acquired shares in A Ltd is reduced by the same amount as above and thus becomes £56,954 (£150,000 – £93,046).

The cost of the painting in the hands of the purchaser is not affected by R's claim for reinvestment relief and is thus £200,000.

50.3 **Relief for disposals after 15 March 1993 and before 30 November 1993.** Subject to the following provisions of *TCGA 1992, Pt V Ch IA*, relief was available where a chargeable gain would otherwise accrue to any individual ('*the reinvestor*') on any 'material disposal' by him of shares in or other securities of any company ('*the initial holding*'), and that individual acquires a 'qualifying investment' at any time in the 'qualifying period' (these three terms being defined below). [*TCGA 1992, s 164A(1); FA 1993, Sch 7 para 3*].

The relief under *TCGA 1992, s 164A(2)* before amendment by *FA 1994, Sch 11 para 2(b)* (see 50.2 above) operated similarly but by reference to the 'initial holding' instead of the 'asset disposed of' and was subject to *TCGA 1992, s 164C* in 50.8 below. *TCGA 1992, s 164A(2A)(2B)* in 50.2 above operated similarly. [*TCGA 1992, s 164A(2), s 164N(4); FA 1993, Sch 7 para 3*].

Subject to the following, the disposal of shares in or other securities of a company was a '*material disposal*' for these purposes if the conditions specified in (*a*)–(*d*) below were satisfied in relation to a period of one year ending with the date of disposal or, if the company ceased at any time in the '*permitted period*' (broadly, one year or such longer period as is allowed by the Board) before the disposal to be a '*trading company*' or the '*holding company*' of a '*trading group*' (these last four terms having the same meaning as in *TCGA 1992, Sch 6 para 1*; see 53.4 RETIREMENT RELIEF), that time. [*TCGA 1992, s 164A(3), s 164N(3)(4); FA 1993, Sch 7 para 3; FA 1994, Sch 11 para 2(c), Sch 26 Pt V*].

The conditions mentioned above were satisfied in relation to any period if throughout that period

(*a*) the company was a trading company or the holding company of a trading group;

(*b*) the company was an '*unquoted company*' (being a company none of the shares in or other securities of which were listed on any recognised stock exchange or were dealt in on the Unlisted Securities Market) (but see below for the relaxation of this condition in certain circumstances);

(*c*) the company was the reinvestor's '*personal company*' (within *TCGA 1992, Sch 6 para 1*; see 53.4 RETIREMENT RELIEF; broadly, he must have had a minimum of 5% of the voting rights in the company); and

(*d*) the reinvestor was a '*full-time working officer or employee*' of the company or, if that company was a member of a '*group of companies*' or '*commercial association of companies*' (these three terms having the same meaning as in *TCGA 1992, Sch 6 para 1*; see 53.4 RETIREMENT RELIEF), of one or more companies which were members of the group or association.

[*TCGA 1992, s 164A(4), s 164N(1)(3); FA 1993, Sch 7 para 3; FA 1994, Sch 11 para 2(c), Sch 26 Pt V; FA 1996, Sch 38 para 10(1)(2)(4)*].

Where, throughout a period ending at the same time as the one-year period referred to in relation to the definition of 'material disposal' in *TCGA 1992, s 164A(3)* above and beginning at a time ('*the time of partial retirement*') when the reinvestor ceased to be such a full-time working officer or employee as is mentioned in (*d*) above

(1) the conditions specified in (*a*)–(*c*) above were satisfied in relation to any company,

(2) the reinvestor was an officer or employee of that company or, as the case may have been, of one or more companies of the group or association in question, and

(3) in that capacity, the reinvestor devoted at least ten hours per week (averaged over the period) to the service of the company or companies in a technical or managerial capacity,

the disposal of shares in or other securities of that company was a material disposal for the purposes of the relief if the conditions specified in (*a*)–(*d*) above were satisfied in relation to the period of one year ending with the time of partial retirement. [*TCGA 1992, s 164A(5); FA 1993, Sch 7 para 3; FA 1994, Sch 11 para 2(c), Sch 26 Pt V*].

Where any company ceased to be an unquoted company and all of the conditions specified in (*a*)–(*d*) above were satisfied in relation to the period of one year ending with the time when the company ceased to be unquoted, *TCGA 1992, s 164A* had effect in relation to an initial holding acquired by the reinvestor at the time when the company in question was an unquoted company as if the company continued to be an unquoted company after that time until the disposal of that holding and as if the one-year period referred to in relation to the definition of 'material disposal' in *TCGA 1992, s 164A(3)* above included all such time (if any) as fell after the company's ceasing to be an unquoted company and before what would otherwise have been the beginning of that period. For the purposes of this treatment, to determine when the shares or other securities comprised in a pool which formed the initial holding were acquired, it had to be assumed that later acquisitions were disposed of before earlier acquisitions. [*TCGA 1992, s 164A(6)(7); FA 1993, Sch 7 para 3; FA 1994, Sch 11 para 2(c), Sch 26 Pt V*].

For the purposes of the relief a person was regarded as acquiring a '*qualifying investment*' where he acquired any 'eligible shares' (defined as in 50.2 above) in a 'qualifying company' (see 50.14 below) if

(A) he held 5% or more of the eligible shares in that company

  (i) at any time after making the acquisition and in the period of three years after the disposal of the initial holding, or

  (ii) at such time after the end of that period as the Board by notice allowed;

(B) that company did not cease to be a qualifying company between the acquisition of those shares and that time; and

(C) that company was neither the company in which the initial holding subsisted nor a company that was a member of the same group of companies (as in (*d*) above) as that company at the time of disposal of the initial holding or of the acquisition of the qualifying investment.

[*TCGA 1992, s 164A(8), s 164N(1)(3); FA 1993, Sch 7 para 3*].

The acquisition of a qualifying investment was taken to be in the '*qualifying period*' if, and only if, it took place at any time in the period beginning twelve months before and ending three years after the disposal of the asset disposed of, or at such time before the beginning of that period or after it ended as the Board by notice allowed. [*TCGA 1992, s 164A(9); FA 1993, Sch 7 para 3*].

TCGA 1992, s 164A(9) before amendment by *FA 1994, Sch 11 para 2(d)* (see 50.2 above) operated similarly by reference to the 'initial holding' instead of the 'asset disposed of'. *TCGA 1992, s 164A(10)* (see 50.2) above also operated similarly. *TCGA 1992, s 164A(12)* although substituted by *FA 1994, Sch 11 para 2(e)* (see 50.2 above) operated similarly *mutatis mutandis* but applied additionally in relation to consideration given for the disposal of any assets. [*TCGA 1992, s 164A(10)(12); FA 1993, Sch 7 para 3*].

For interaction of the above relief with retirement relief, see 50.7 below.

50.4 **RELIEF FOR TRUSTEES**

Subject to the following, *TCGA 1992, s 164A* in 50.2 above (after amendment by *FA 1994, Sch 11*) applies, as it applies in the circumstances mentioned in *TCGA 1992, s 164A(1)* mentioned there, where there is

(*a*) a disposal made **after 29 November 1993** by the trustees of a settlement of any asset comprised in any settled property of the kinds mentioned in (1) and (2) below, and

(*b*) such an acquisition by those trustees of 'eligible shares' (as in 50.2 above) in a 'qualifying company' (see 50.14 below) as would under *TCGA 1992, s 164A* be an acquisition of a 'qualifying investment' at a time in the 'qualifying period' (these two last terms being defined as in 47.2 above).

[*TCGA 1992, s 164B(1); FA 1993, Sch 7 para 3; FA 1994, Sch 11 para 3*].

No reinvestment relief is available under these provisions where the reinvestment takes place after 5 April 1998 (see 50.1 above).

The kinds of settled property referred to in (*a*) above are

(1) settled property on discretionary trusts (i.e. settlements where the beneficiaries' interests are not interests in possession, an interest in possession for this purpose not including an interest for a fixed term; and see generally 57.7 SETTLEMENTS) where all of the beneficiaries are either individuals or charities, and

(2) settled property on non-discretionary trusts (i.e. settlements where the beneficiaries' interests are interests in possession as in (1) above) where any of the beneficiaries is an individual or a charity.

[*TCGA 1992, s 164B(2); FA 1993, Sch 7 para 3; FA 1994, Sch 11 para 3*].

For the purposes of (1) and (2) above and *TCGA 1992, s 164B* generally, where there is at least one beneficiary holding a non-discretionary interest and at least one beneficiary holding a discretionary interest, all of the discretionary interests are treated as if they were a single interest in possession, and that interest held, where all the discretionary beneficiaries are individuals or charities, by an individual or charity, and in any other case, by a person who is not an individual or charity. [*TCGA 1992, s 164B(7); FA 1993, Sch 7 para 3; FA 1994, Sch 11 para 3*]. The broad effect for such 'mixed' settlements, is that the settled property will fall within (2) above if either any non-discretionary interest is held by an individual or charity or all discretionary interests are held by individuals or charities, or both such situations arise. This is subject to the provisions below (in particular, regarding the calculation of the 'relevant proportion').

If, at the time of the disposal of the asset in relation to which relief is to be claimed, the settled property comprising that asset is within (2) above but not all of the beneficiaries are individuals or charities, then

(A) only the 'relevant proportion' of the gain which would accrue to the trustees on the disposal is taken into account for the purposes of 50.2(*a*)(i) above (reduction in disposal consideration of gain otherwise accruing), and

(B) no reduction from disposal or acquisition consideration is made under 50.2(*b*) above for the whole or any part of the balance of the gain.

[*TCGA 1992, s 164B(3); FA 1993, Sch 7 para 3; FA 1994, Sch 11 para 3*].

At any time, the '*relevant proportion*' at that time is the proportion the aggregate amount of the income of the settled property interests in which are held by individuals or charities bears to the total amount of all of the income of the settled property. [*TCGA 1992, s 164B(6); FA 1993, Sch 7 para 3; FA 1994, Sch 11 para 3*].

If the settled property qualifies under (1) above at the time of the disposal of the asset comprised in it for which relief is to be claimed, relief under *TCGA 1992, s 164A* is not applied as above unless, immediately after the acquisition of the eligible shares, the settled property comprising the shares also qualifies under (1) above. This also applies *mutatis mutandis* to settled property qualifying under (2) above but, if not all the beneficiaries are individuals or charities, with the additional condition that the relevant proportion immediately after the acquisition of the shares must be not less than that proportion at the time of the disposal of the asset concerned. [*TCGA 1992, s 164B(4)(5); FA 1993, Sch 7 para 3; FA 1994, Sch 11 para 3*].

For interaction of the above relief with retirement relief, see 50.6 below. For a point concerning withdrawal of relief given to trustees, see 50.11 below.

50.5 **Relief for disposals after 15 March 1993 and before 30 November 1993.** Subject to the following, the provisions of *TCGA 1992, s 164A* in 50.3 above applied, as they applied to an individual, where there was

(*a*) a disposal by trustees of a settlement of any shares in or other securities of a company which were part of the settled property; and

(*b*) such an acquisition by those trustees of 'eligible shares' (see 50.3 above) in a 'qualifying company' (see 50.14 below) as would for the purposes of *TCGA 1992, s 164A* have been an acquisition of a 'qualifying investment' at a time in the 'qualifying period' (these two last terms being defined as in 50.3 above),

but as if the disposal were a 'material disposal' if, and only if, the conditions specified below were satisfied in relation to the one-year period ending with the date of the disposal or, if the case was as contemplated by *TCGA 1992, s 164A(3)* in 50.3 above, the date in the 'permitted period' before the disposal the company ceased to be a 'trading company' or the 'holding company' of a 'trading group'. [*TCGA 1992, s 164B(1); FA 1993, Sch 7 para 3*].

The conditions mentioned above were satisfied *mutatis mutandis* in relation to any period and a 'relevant beneficiary' as they were in *TCGA 1992, s 164A(4)* in 50.3(*a*)–(*d*) above in relation to any period and a reinvestor. [*TCGA 1992, s 164B(2); FA 1993, Sch 7 para 3*].

A '*relevant beneficiary*' was any beneficiary who, under the settlement concerned, had an interest in possession (other than, for this purpose, an interest for a fixed term; and see generally 57.7 SETTLEMENTS) in the whole of the settled property or, as the case may have been, in a part of it which consisted of or included the shares or securities that were disposed of by the trustees of the settlement. [*TCGA 1992, s 164B(3); FA 1993, Sch 7 para 3*].

Where, in addition to the interest in possession held by a relevant beneficiary who satisfied the conditions *mutatis mutandis* in 50.3(*d*) above in relation to a reinvestor ('*the qualifying beneficiary*'), one or more other beneficiaries had such an interest at the 'relevant time' in the shares or securities being disposed of by the trustees, virtually identical provisions to *TCGA 1992, s 164B(3)* as substituted by *FA 1994, Sch 11 para 3* (see 50.4(A) and (B) above) applied regarding the treatment of the 'relevant proportion' of the gain eligible for relief. [*TCGA 1992, s 164B(4); FA 1993, Sch 7 para 3*].

The '*relevant proportion*' was the proportion of the qualifying beneficiary's interest at the relevant time in the income of the part of the settled property comprising the shares and securities bore to the interests at that time in that income of all the beneficiaries (including the qualifying beneficiary) who at that time had interests in possession in that part. For this purpose, the qualifying beneficiary's interest was only to take into account the interest by virtue of which he was a qualifying beneficiary and not any other interest he may have held. [*TCGA 1992, s 164B(5)(6); FA 1993, Sch 7 para 3*].

Relief was unavailable to trustees unless, immediately after the acquisition by them of eligible shares in a qualifying company, the qualifying beneficiary had an interest in possession in the whole of the settled property, or in the part of it in which the acquired shares were comprised, which was the same as or, as the case may have been, was equivalent to the interest at the relevant time by virtue of which he was a qualifying beneficiary. [*TCGA 1992, s 164B(7); FA 1993, Sch 7 para 3*].

The '*relevant time*', in relation to a disposal of shares or other securities, meant the time of disposal or, if the case was as contemplated by *TCGA 1992, s 164A(3)* in 50.3 above, the date in the 'permitted period' before the disposal the company ceased to be a 'trading company' or the 'holding company' of a 'trading group'. [*TCGA 1992, s 164B(8); FA 1993, Sch 7 para 3*].

50.6 INTERACTION WITH RETIREMENT AND OTHER RELIEFS

Reinvestment relief is given in preference to retirement relief. Where reinvestment relief is claimed in part but not in whole the order of set off is first against the portion of gain not qualifying for retirement relief leaving a balance against which reinvestment relief may be claimed. [*TCGA 1992, s 164BA; FA 1994, Sch 11 para 8*].

In order to calculate the amount of available retirement relief, the provisions of *TCGA 1992, s 164A* in 50.2 above for making a reduction from disposal and acquisition consideration in respect of disposals made **after 29 November 1993** must be applied before any provisions for calculating the amount of, or giving effect to, any RETIREMENT RELIEF (53) under *TCGA 1992, s 163* or *s 164*. Accordingly, references in *TCGA 1992, s 164A* to a 'chargeable gain' must be construed ignoring retirement relief. However, if a claim is made under *TCGA 1992, s 164A* in respect of a chargeable gain (ignoring retirement relief), and apart from *TCGA 1992, Pt V Ch IA* (reinvestment relief), the whole or any part of the gain would be relieved by retirement relief, then further provisions apply. For the purpose of giving retirement relief, reinvestment relief under *TCGA 1992, s 164A* is treated as having been made first against 'the unrelieved part of the chargeable gain'; and only the amount (if any) which is equal to the unrelieved part of the chargeable gain (ignoring retirement relief) after that reduction is treated as exceeding 'the amount available for relief'.

'*The unrelieved part of a chargeable gain*' is so much of a chargeable gain, ignoring retirement relief and apart from *TCGA 1992, Pt V Ch IA*, as would constitute a chargeable gain after the application of the retirement relief provisions in, as the case may be, *TCGA 1992, Sch 6 para 6, para 7(1)(b)* or *para 8* (see 53.9 RETIREMENT RELIEF). '*The amount available for relief*' is in practical terms the amount of retirement relief given by way of deduction from chargeable gains. [*TCGA 1992, s 164BA; FA 1994, Sch 11 para 8*].

The above provisions are intended to obviate some of the practical difficulties caused by the previous legislation relevant to the interaction of reinvestment relief with retirement relief applying in respect of disposals after 15 March 1993 and before 30 November 1993 and which are mentioned in 50.7 below. The problem mentioned there caused by time apportionment of gains is not dealt with by the above provisions but re-basing to 1982 will in most cases mean that time apportionment is now rarely met.

In correspondence, the Revenue has indicated, that where reinvestment relief is contemplated in circumstances where retirement relief is to be given (whether or not on a claim because of ill-health), the steps to be taken are illustrated by the Example below.

Example

F, on 10 October 1997 when aged 56, sells all of the 100% shareholding in a trading company (which has no subsidiaries) of which F has been a full-time working officer or employee since 1986. At the date of disposal, the proportion by value of chargeable business assets to chargeable assets held by the company was 80%. Subject to this, all of the other conditions for retirement relief are satisfied. The consideration received for the shares is £1,000,000 and their indexed cost to the date of disposal is £125,000. On 17 October 1997 F acquires for £1,200,000 shares in a company, the acquisition qualifying for reinvestment relief in relation to the 10 October 1997 disposal. F has the 1997/98 annual exempt amount of £6,500 available as well as allowable losses of £93,500. F does not anticipate any further disposals in 1997/98.

In the absence of a claim under *TCGA 1992, s 164A* and before giving effect to retirement relief under *TCGA 1992, s 163* or *s 164*, the chargeable gain arising on the 10 October disposal is £875,000 (£1,000,000–£125,000). Under *TCGA 1992, Sch 6 para 7(1)(b)*, only 80% of this gain can be eligible for retirement relief, the balance of £175,000 remaining chargeable and unaffected by retirement relief. Thus £700,000 of the gain is eligible for retirement relief. In the absence of a claim under *TCGA 1992, s 164A*, the amount of retirement relief to be given by way of deduction is as follows.

Chargeable gains eligible for retirement relief		£700,000
Amount available for relief		£
100% relief: 100% × £250,000		250,000
50% relief:	£	
Excess of eligible gains before retirement relief over £250,000	450,000	
100% × £750,000	750,000	
Half of lower of £450,000 and £750,000		225,000
Retirement relief given by way of deduction		£475,000
Thus chargeable gains remaining after deduction of retirement relief are:		
£175,000 + (£700,000 – £475,000)		*£400,000
Allowable losses and 1996/97 annual exempt amount (£93,500 + £6,500)		100,000
Chargeable gains assessable 1997/98		£300,000

* The amount of £400,000 is the amount referred to as '*the unrelieved amount of the chargeable gain*' above. If a claim is made under *TCGA 1992, s 164A* for a reduction of £300,000 (see 50.2(*a*)(iv) above), the position is as follows.

	£
Consideration received	1,000,000
Reinvestment relief	300,000
	700,000
Indexed cost	125,000
Chargeable gains before retirement relief	575,000
Retirement relief given by deduction	**475,000
Chargeable gains after retirement relief	**100,000
Allowable losses and 1997/98 annual exempt amount	100,000
Chargeable gains assessable 1997/98	£ Nil

** For the purposes of retirement relief only, the reinvestment relief deduction of £300,000 is 'first' set against the £400,000 of unrelieved gains, so that there are only £100,000 of gains left in charge. This means that the retirement relief *actually given by deduction* is still £475,000, £250,000 having been given at the 100% relief level and £225,000 at the 50% relief level. This will be relevant if F makes a disposal in the future (before 6 April 2003) qualifying for retirement relief. The acquisition cost of the shares acquired is reduced by £300,000 from £1,200,000 to £900,000.

With regard to the classes of assets qualifying for ROLLOVER RELIEF (see 55.3), on a disposal after 29 November 1993 it is possible to dispose of an asset in such a class and, rather than claim rollover relief by reference to that disposal and an acquisition of an asset in such a class, claim reinvestment relief in relation to that disposal and an acquisition of eligible shares. Shares are not within the classes of assets qualifying for rollover relief, so it is not possible to claim that relief where either the asset being disposed of or the one acquired consists of shares.

50.7 **Disposals after 15 March 1993 and before 30 November 1993.** The provisions of *TCGA 1992, s 164A* in 50.3 above for making a reduction from disposal and acquisition consideration had to be applied before any provisions for calculating the amount of, or giving effect to, any RETIREMENT RELIEF (53) under *TCGA 1992, s 163* or *s 164*. Accordingly, references in *TCGA 1992, s 164A* to a 'chargeable gain' had to be construed ignoring retirement relief. [*TCGA 1992, s 164A(11); FA 1993, Sch 7 para 3; FA 1994, Sch 11 para 8, Sch 26 Pt V*].

It was intended that those who were eligible both for retirement relief and reinvestment relief should have been able to claim either relief or any combination of the two reliefs (HC Official Report, Standing Committee A, Sixth Sitting, 15 June 1993, Part III, col 423). This statement not only ignored the fact that retirement relief is not the subject of a claim unless ill-health grounds are involved but also the seemingly anomalous result the legislation produced. The operation of time apportionment or retirement relief at the 50% level (i.e. permanent but partial reliefs rather than reliefs by way of deferral) subsequent to a reduction of the disposal consideration by way of an amount of reinvestment relief (i.e. a relief by way of deferral) meant that gains had to be left in charge, despite that latter relief, even though a greater amount of reinvestment relief could have been claimed such as to reduce the gains left in charge to nil, so that no time apportionment or retirement relief could have been given (*Taxation*, 12 August 1993 p 469 and 11 November 1993 p 126). In correspondence, the Revenue indicated that it did not find this situation anomalous but merely a consequence of the way the legislation was drafted.

50.8 RESTRICTION OF RELIEF: DISPOSALS AFTER 15 MARCH 1993 AND BEFORE 30 NOVEMBER 1993

The following provisions applied to disposals made **after 15 March 1993 and before 30 November 1993.**

Subject to the following, where a claim was made under 50.3 above in respect of a disposal of shares in or other securities of a company

(*a*) the gains which (apart from RETIREMENT RELIEF (53) under *TCGA 1992, ss 163, 164* and relief under 50.3 and 50.5 above) would have accrued on the disposal to the individual or trustees concerned were aggregated,

(*b*) the amount available in respect of the disposal for retirement relief and for the making of deductions from disposal and acquisition consideration under 50.3 above was deemed to be confined to 'the appropriate proportion' of the aggregated gains, and

(*c*) the amount by which the aggregated gains exceeded the amount so available was disregarded for the reliefs mentioned in (*a*), so that that amount constituted chargeable gains.

In relation to a company which was not a holding company of a trading group (see 50.3 above), '*the appropriate proportion*' was the proportion that the value of the company's 'chargeable business assets' bore at the relevant time (as in 50.5 above) to the value at that time of the company's 'chargeable assets', and in any other case, it was the proportion that the value of the trading group's 'chargeable business assets' bore at the relevant time to the value at that time of the trading group's 'chargeable assets'. Where the company or trading group had no chargeable assets, the appropriate proportion was deemed to be the whole.

Every asset was a '*chargeable asset*' except one, on the disposal of which by the company at the relevant time, no gain accruing to the company would have been a chargeable gain. A '*chargeable business asset*' of a company meant a chargeable asset (including goodwill but not including any shares or other securities or any assets held as investments) of it which was, or was an interest in, an asset used for the purposes of a trade, profession, vocation, office or employment (these terms having the same meaning as in *ICTA 1988*) carried on by the individual concerned, the personal company (as in 50.3 above) of that individual, a member of a trading group of which the holding company was a personal company of that individual, or a partnership of which that individual was a member. References in the foregoing to the individual were taken as references to the qualifying beneficiary where trustees disposed of any shares or other securities.

A trading group's chargeable business assets and chargeable assets comprised those assets respectively of every member of a trading group, but for this purpose a holding by one member of the group of the ordinary share capital (see 50.2 above) of another member was not a chargeable asset. Where the whole of the ordinary share capital of a 51% subsidiary (within *ICTA 1988, s 838*) of a holding company was not owned directly or indirectly by that company, the value of the subsidiary's chargeable business assets and chargeable assets were reduced respectively according to the formula

$A \times \frac{B}{C}$ where

'A' was the value falling to be reduced of the subsidiary's chargeable business assets or chargeable assets;

'B' was the amount of the subsidiary's ordinary share capital owned, directly or indirectly (as in *ICTA 1988, s 838*), by the holding company; and

'C' was the whole of the subsidiary's ordinary share capital.

The above provisions were without prejudice to *TCGA 1992, Sch 6 paras 7–11* (which apply a similar restriction to the above in the case of retirement relief; see 53.9 RETIREMENT RELIEF). [*TCGA 1992, s 164C, s 164N(1)(3); FA 1993, Sch 7 para 3; FA 1994, Sch 11 para 4, Sch 26 Pt V*].

50.9 **RELIEF CARRIED FORWARD INTO REPLACEMENT SHARES: DISPOSALS AFTER 15 MARCH 1993 AND BEFORE 30 NOVEMBER 1993**

The following provisions applied to disposals made **after 15 March 1993 and before 30 November 1993**.

Further provisions applied as below where a person acquired any eligible shares (see 50.3 above) in a qualifying company (see 50.14 below) ('*the acquired holding*') for a consideration which was treated as reduced, under 50.3 above or by the provisions below, by any amount ('*the held-over gain*').

If

(*a*) the person who acquired the acquired holding disposed of eligible shares in the company in question ('*the acquired shares*'),

(*b*) that person at any time in 'the relevant period' (see below) acquired other eligible shares ('*the replacement shares*') in a qualifying company which was not a 'relevant company' (see below),

(*c*) the acquisition of the replacement shares would have, in relation to the disposal of the acquired shares, been treated (had the disposal been a material disposal) as an acquisition of a qualifying investment for the purposes of the provisions in 50.3 above, and

(*d*) relief was not available under 50.3 above in relation to the acquisition of the replacement shares,

that person, on making a claim in respect of the acquisition of the replacement shares, was treated as below.

In relation to the acquisition, the person was treated

(1) as if the disposal consideration of the acquired shares were reduced by the smallest of the following amounts:

  (i) the amount of the held-over gain on the acquisition of the acquired holding, so far as that amount had not already been carried forward under this provision from any disposal of eligible shares in the company in question or been charged (see below) on a disposal or under *TCGA 1992, s 164F* in 50.13 below,

  (ii) the actual amount or value of the consideration for the acquisition of the replacement shares,

  (iii) in the case of replacement shares acquired otherwise than by a transaction at arm's length, the market value of the replacement shares at the time of their acquisition, and

  (iv) the amount specified for the purposes of this provision in the claim;

  and

(2) as if the amount or value of the consideration for the acquisition of the replacement shares were reduced by the amount of the reduction made under (1) above.

Neither (1) nor (2) affected the treatment under *TCGA 1992* of the other party to the transaction involving the acquired shares or of the other party to the transaction involving the replacement shares.

In (1)(i) above, the reference to an amount which was carried forward from a disposal of eligible shares was a reference to the reduction by that amount under (1) above of the amount of the consideration for the disposal of those shares. Similarly, in (1)(i), the whole or any part of any held-over gain on the acquisition of the acquired holding was treated

(A) under (*aa*) and (*bb*) below as charged on any disposal in relation to which the whole or any part of the held-over gain was taken into account in determining the chargeable gain or allowable loss on the disposal; and

(B) as charged under *TCGA 1992, s 164F* in 50.13 below so far as it fell to be disregarded in accordance with *TCGA 1992, s 164F(11)* which provided that an amount of the held-over gain was disregarded in certain circumstances.

In the case of a disposal within (A) above, the amount of the held-over gain charged on that disposal

(*aa*) was, except for a part disposal, so much of the amount taken into account within (A) above as was not carried forward under this provision from the disposal in question; and

(*bb*) for a part disposal, was calculated by multiplying so much of the amount of the held-over gain as was not carried forward under this provision from the disposal in question and had not already been either charged on a previous disposal or carried forward under this provision from a previous disposal by the A/(A + B) fraction of *TCGA 1992, s 42(2)* (see 17.6 DISPOSAL) used, subject to any deductions under the reinvestment relief provisions, in computing the apportioned allowable expenditure on the disposal in question.

Where *TCGA 1992, s 58* (transfers between spouses at no gain/no loss; see 41.3 MARRIED PERSONS) applied to any disposal of the whole or any part of the acquired holding to any individual, that individual was not regarded under the foregoing as acquiring eligible shares for a consideration which was treated as reduced, and the amount of the held-over gain that was to be treated under the above as charged on the disposal was the amount that would have been charged on the disposal if it had been a disposal at market value.

TCGA 1992, s 164A(10)(12) in 50.3 above, which concern deemed amounts of consideration and apportionment of expenditure, and *TCGA 1992, s 164A(11)* in 50.7 above, which concerns interaction with retirement relief, all apply similarly for these provisions as they do there.

A company was a '*relevant company*' for these purposes if it was

(AA) the company in which the acquired holding subsisted or a company which was a member of the same group of companies (see 50.3 above) as that company at the time of the disposal of the acquired holding or of the acquisition of the replacement shares;

(BB) a company in relation to the disposal of any shares in which there had been a claim under the reinvestment relief provisions such that without that or an equivalent claim there would have been no held-over gain in relation to the acquired holding; or

(CC) a company which, at the time of the disposal or acquisition to which the claim related, was a member of the same group of companies as a company falling within (BB) above.

For the above, '*relevant period*' meant the period (not including any period before the acquisition of the acquired holding) which began twelve months before and ended three years after the disposal of the acquired shares, together with any such further period after the disposal as the Board by notice allowed. [*TCGA 1992, s 164D, s 164N(1)(3); FA 1993, Sch 7 para 3; FA 1994, Sch 11 para 4, Sch 26 Pt V*].

50.10 RELIEF WHERE SHARES ARE EXCHANGED: DISPOSALS AFTER 15 MARCH 1993 AND BEFORE 30 NOVEMBER 1993

The following provisions applied to disposals made **after 15 March 1993 and before 30 November 1993**.

Where

(*a*) there was a transaction involving the issue of any shares in or debentures of any company in exchange for any shares in or debentures of another company ('*the exchanged securities*'),

(*b*) but for this provision, *TCGA 1992, s 127* would have had effect in pursuance of *TCGA 1992, s 135* for requiring the transaction to have been treated for the purposes of *TCGA 1992* as one that did not involve a disposal of the exchanged securities (see 58.5 and 58.8 SHARES AND SECURITIES),

(*c*) any person would have been entitled, if the transaction had been treated as involving such a disposal, to make a claim for relief under the reinvestment relief provisions by reference to that disposal and an acquisition of eligible shares in a qualifying company, and

(*d*) that person made an election under this provision (*TCGA 1992, s 164E*) for the transaction to be treated as involving the disposal of the exchanged securities and claimed that relief,

TCGA 1992, Pt V Ch IA and the other provisions of *TCGA 1992* had effect as if *TCGA 1992, s 127* did not apply in the case of that transaction and, accordingly, as if that transaction did involve such a disposal, together with an acquisition of the shares or debentures that were issued in exchange.

The election mentioned in (*d*) above had to be made by notice given to the Board not more than two years after the end of, as the case may have been, the qualifying period mentioned in 50.3 above or the relevant period mentioned in 50.9 above. Such an election made in connection with a claim for relief under 50.5 above had to be made jointly by the trustees of the settlement and the qualifying beneficiary.

Any adjustment by way of an assessment on any person to give effect to an election was not out of time if the assessment was made within one year of the final determination of the claim for relief in connection with which the election was made. For this purpose a claim for relief was not deemed to be finally determined until the amount of the relief allowed under the claim could no longer be varied, whether on appeal or by the order of any court or otherwise. [*TCGA 1992, s 164E, s 164N(1)(3); FA 1993, Sch 7 para 3; FA 1994, Sch 11 para 4, Sch 26 Pt V*].

50.11 WITHDRAWAL OF RELIEF

In certain circumstances and in relation to disposals **after 29 November 1993**, an effective withdrawal of relief applies as below where a person has acquired any eligible shares (see 50.2 above) in a qualifying company (see 50.14 below) ('*the acquired holding*') for a consideration which is treated as reduced, under *TCGA 1992, s 164A* in 50.2 above (consideration treated as reduced under *TCGA 1992, s 164D* in 50.9 above as extant for disposals after 15 March 1993 and before 30 November 1993 being treated as such a reduction) or the provisions below or in 50.12 below, by any amount ('*the held-over gain*'). [*TCGA 1992, s 164F(1), s 164N(1); FA 1993, Sch 7 para 3; FA 1994, Sch 11 para 9(1)(a), (2)(a); FA 1997, Sch 17 para 3(1)*].

Subject to the following, if at any time in the 'relevant period' (see below),

(*a*) the shares forming the acquired holding cease to be eligible shares, (*b*) the company whose shares form the acquired holding ceases to be a qualifying company,

(*c*) the person who acquired the acquired holding becomes neither resident nor ordinarily resident in the UK, or

(*d*) any of the shares forming the acquired holding are, on a reorganisation, conversion or reconstruction, exchanged for qualifying corporate bonds so that the transaction is within *TCGA 1992, s 116* (gain on original shares not deemed to crystallise until bonds disposed of; see 49.3 QUALIFYING CORPORATE BONDS),

a chargeable gain equal to 'the appropriate proportion' of the held-over gain is treated as accruing to that person immediately before that time or, in a case within (*d*) above, immediately before the disposal that is hypothecated under *TCGA 1992, s 116(10)(a)* immediately before the transaction concerned. [*TCGA 1992, s 164F(2), s 164N(1); FA 1993, Sch 7 para 3*].

In deciding for the purposes of (*b*) above whether a company is a qualifying company at a time falling after 28 November 1994, *TCGA 1992, s 164H* (interests in land rule, see 50.14 below) no longer applies. [*TCGA 1992, s 164F(2A); FA 1995, s 40(1)(3)*].

'*The appropriate proportion*' of the held-over gain is so much, if any, of that gain as has not already been charged on any disposal (such reference to a gain having been charged on a disposal includes the amount of reduction made under *TCGA 1992, s 164D(3)(a)* in 50.9(1) above as extant for disposals after 15 March 1993 and before 30 November 1993 from the disposal consideration received for acquired shares) or under the provisions below. However, where (*d*) above applies, or where (*a*) or (*b*) above applies in accordance with (A)–(D) below, the proportion is a just and reasonable one having regard to the extent to which the acquired holding forms the original shares. [*TCGA 1992, s 164F(3); FA 1993, Sch 7 para 3; FA 1994, Sch 11 para 9(1)(b), (2)(b), (3)*].

The whole or a part of any held-over gain on the acquisition of the acquired holding is treated as below as charged on any disposal in relation to which the whole or any part of the held-over gain falls to be taken into account in determining the chargeable gain or allowable loss on the disposal, and as charged under these provisions so far as it falls to be disregarded under *TCGA 1992, s 164F(11)* below. For a disposal other than a part disposal, the amount of the held-over gain charged on that disposal is the amount taken into account in determining the amount of the chargeable gain etc. as above (but any such amount is reduced by the amount of any reduction made under *TCGA 1992, s 164D(3)(a)* in 50.9(1) above as extant for disposals after 15 March 1993 and before 30 November 1993 from the disposal consideration received for acquired shares). In the case of a part disposal, the corresponding amount charged on that disposal is calculated by multiplying so much of the amount of the held-over gain as has not already been charged on a previous disposal (as similarly reduced by any reduction made under *TCGA 1992, s 164D(3)(a)*) by the A/(A + B) fraction of *TCGA 1992, s 42(2)* (see 17.6 DISPOSAL) used, subject to any deductions under the reinvestment relief provisions, in computing the apportioned allowable expenditure on the disposal in question. [*TCGA 1992, s 164F(4)(4A); FA 1993, Sch 7 para 3; FA 1994, Sch 11 para 9(1)(c), (2)(c), (3)*].

Where the acquired holding or any asset treated as comprised in a single asset (e.g. a share pool) with the whole or any part of that holding has been disposed of under *TCGA 1992, s 58* (transfers between spouses at no gain/no loss; see 41.3 MARRIED PERSONS) by the individual who acquired that holding to another person ('*the spouse*')

(I) the spouse is not (subject to below) treated for the purposes of these provisions as a person who has acquired eligible shares for a consideration which is treated as reduced under *TCGA 1992, s 164A* in 50.2 above;

(II) the disposal is not included in the disposals on which the whole or any part of the held-over gain may be treated as charged for the purposes of these provisions;

(III) disposals by the spouse, as well as disposals by that individual, are taken into account under *TCGA 1992, s 164F(4)(4A)* above;

(IV) any charge under (*a*), (*b*) or (*d*) above is apportioned between that individual and the spouse according to the extent to which the appropriate proportion of the held-over gain would be charged on the disposal by each of them of their respective holdings (if any);

(V) (*c*) above has effect as if the reference there to that individual included a reference to the spouse;

(VI) a charge under (*c*) above is imposed only on a person who becomes neither resident nor ordinarily resident in the UK; and

(VII) the amount of the charge imposed on any person under (*c*) above is that part of the charge on the appropriate proportion of the held-over gain which would be apportioned to that person under (IV) above.

[*TCGA 1992, s 164F(5); FA 1993, Sch 7 para 3; FA 1994, Sch 11 para 9(1)(d)*].

Subject to (A)–(D) below, where the qualifying company in which the acquired holding subsists ceases to be an unquoted company (see 50.2 above) these provisions have effect as if the relevant period ended immediately before it so ceased. (Because, under 50.14 below, a company to be a qualifying company has to be unquoted, this provision seems to prevent a charge arising under (*b*) above because the cessation of qualifying status will not arise in the relevant period.) Subject to this, '*the relevant period*' means the period of three years after the acquisition of the acquired holding. [*TCGA 1992, s 164F(6)(12), s 164N(1); FA 1993, Sch 7 para 3*].

Where there is a transaction involving shares in a company which applies *TCGA 1992, s 127* (see 58.5 SHARES AND SECURITIES) so that those shares are regarded as the same asset as the acquired holding or the whole or any part of an asset comprising that holding, no charge arises as a result of the event in (*a*) or (*b*) above except where

(A) those shares are not, or cease to be, eligible shares in that company;

(B) neither that company nor (if different) the company in which the acquired holding subsisted is or continues to be a qualifying company, or would be or continue to be a qualifying company if it were an unquoted company;

(C) the transaction is one resulting in the shares comprised in the acquired holding ceasing to be eligible shares under *TCGA 1992, s 164L* (anti-avoidance; see 50.16 below); or

(D) there is a transaction under which any shares at any time comprised in the acquired holding would have ceased to be eligible shares under *TCGA 1992, s 164L.*

[*TCGA 1992, s 164F(7), s 164N(1); FA 1993, Sch 7 para 3*].

A charge (*a*) or (*b*) above does not apply where the company in which the acquired holding subsists is wound up or dissolved without winding up and

(*aa*) the winding-up or dissolution is for bona fide commercial reasons and not part of a scheme or arrangement the main purpose of which, or one of the main purposes of which, is the avoidance of tax; and

(*bb*) the company's net assets (if any) are distributed to its members or dealt with as bona vacantia before the end of the period of three years from the commencement of the winding up or dissolution.

[*TCGA 1992, s 164F(8); FA 1993, Sch 7 para 3; FA 1996, Sch 20 para 55*].

A charge will not apply under (*c*) above in relation to any person if

(AA) the reason for his becoming neither resident nor ordinarily resident in the UK is that he works in an employment or office all the duties of which are performed outside the UK, and

(BB) he again becomes resident or ordinarily resident in the UK within the period of three years from the time he ceases to be so, without having meanwhile disposed of any eligible shares in the company in question.

The Revenue are precluded from making an assessment under (*c*) above before the end of the three year period mentioned in (BB) above where the person has satisfied the condition in (AA) above and may satisfy that in (BB). A person is taken to have disposed of an asset under (BB) if there has been such a disposal as would, if the person making the disposal had been resident in the UK, have been a disposal on which the whole or any part of the held-over gain would have been charged. [*TCGA 1992, s 164F(9)(10), s 164N(1); FA 1993, Sch 7 para 3*].

Where otherwise a chargeable gain would arise under (*a*)–(*d*) above but the person who acquired the acquired holding also acquires, within a specified period, a qualifying investment (as in 50.2 above), he is treated as respects the qualifying investment on making a claim

(1) as if the amount of the gain were reduced by whichever is the smallest of the following amounts:

  (i) the actual amount or value of the consideration for the acquisition of the qualifying investment,

  (ii) in the case of a qualifying investment acquired otherwise than by a transaction at arm's length, the market value of that investment at the time of its acquisition,

  (iii) the amount specified for these purposes in the claim;

  and

(2) as if the amount or value of the consideration for the acquisition of the qualifying investment were reduced by the amount of the reduction made under (1) above (but without affecting the treatment for the purposes of *TCGA 1992* of the other party to the transaction involving the qualifying investment).

FA 1995 introduced measures to prevent excess relief being claimed in respect of shares acquired by way of gift if the qualifying investment was acquired after 19 June 1994, or a claim under the preceding paragraph is made in relation to a gain which would otherwise accrue after that date. Thus, where a claim for the above relief is made after 19 June 1994 and the qualifying investment in respect of which the claim is made was acquired by the reinvestor through an inter-spouse (no gain/no loss) transfer under *TCGA 1992, s 58*, the relief claimed cannot exceed the transferor spouse's allowable base cost of the qualifying investment, after any reduction in that cost due to gains already rolled over into that investment, irrespective of the re-basing rules in *TCGA 1992, s 35, Sch 3 para 1* or *TCGA 1992, s 55* in situations where the qualifying investment was held by the transferor spouse since 31 March 1982. Similarly, the re-basing provisions are disapplied where the claimant returns the qualifying investment to his spouse on a no gain/no loss basis.

In addition, rules were introduced with regard to the making of multiple claims for relief against the same qualifying investment to ensure that aggregate gains rolled over do not exceed the cost thereof. These rules have effect where claims under the penultimate paragraph above are made in respect of gains which would otherwise accrue after 19 June

1994. Where multiple reductions are claimed under the above relief in respect of the same qualifying investment, the reductions shall be treated as claimed separately in such order as the claimant elects. On the second and subsequent claims the amount of gain able to be rolled over will be limited to the remaining acquisition cost ((1)(i) above) or market value ((1)(ii) above) of the qualifying investment left after any previous claims have been made. A claim that has become final (i.e. it may not be amended or is finally determined, whichever occurs first) will be treated as made earlier than any claim which is not final.

The specified period mentioned above is the period (not including any period before the acquisition of the acquired holding) beginning twelve months before and ending three years after the time the chargeable gain accrues or would otherwise accrue, together with any such further time after the disposal as the Board may by notice allow. [*TCGA 1992, s 164F(10A)–(10C), s 164FF, s 164FG; FA 1993, Sch 7 para 3; FA 1994, Sch 11 para 9(1)(f); FA 1995, s 47(1)(3)–(8); FA 1996, Sch 20 para 56*].

Gains on disposals made after a chargeable gain has been deemed to accrue under (*a*)–(*d*) above to any person in respect of the acquired holding are computed as if so much of the held-over gain as is equal to the amount of the chargeable gain were to be disregarded. [*TCGA 1992, s 164F(11); FA 1993, Sch 7 para 3*].

Where a withdrawal is of reinvestment relief given to trustees (see 50.4 above), the resulting chargeable gain is taxable at whichever is the relevant of the rates given at 57.1 SETTLEMENTS. This applies even if the settlor has an interest in the settlement, as the 'charge on settlor' provisions in *TCGA 1992, s 77* (see 57.3 SETTLEMENTS) apply only in the event of a disposal whilst the withdrawal of relief provisions above treat a gain as accruing without any disposal being deemed to have occurred. (See *Taxation 15 May 1997 p 194*).

A clawback of relief under the above provisions or those of 50.12 below can be sheltered by a qualifying investment in EIS shares issued after 5 April 1998 (see 20.10 ENTERPRISE INVESTMENT SCHEME (AND BES)).

50.12 **Additional withdrawal provisions** detailed below apply after 26 November 1996 where a person acquired the shares by their being issued to him. They apply equally to shares acquired on or before 26 November 1996, held until that time and continuing until that time to be eligible shares in a qualifying company; however, in their application to such shares the provisions cannot give rise to a withdrawal of relief at any time within three years after the acquisition of the shares. For reinvestment relief purposes, an allotment of shares before their issue is disregarded in determining whether and when a person acquires shares by their issue to him.

Where a person acquired eligible shares in a qualifying company by their being issued to him and the consideration given has been treated as reduced by a held-over gain under the reinvestment relief provisions, a loss of relief applies in *any* of the following circumstances.

(*a*) The money raised by the issue was, at the time of acquisition, intended to be employed for the purposes of a 'qualifying trade' (see 50.15 below) then being carried on, but that money has not been wholly employed for 'permissible purposes' (see below) by the end of the 'initial utilisation period' (see below).

(*b*) The money raised by the issue was, at the time of acquisition, intended to be employed for the purposes of a 'qualifying trade' *not* then being carried on, the trade begins to be carried on within two years after that time, but that money has not been wholly employed for the purposes of the trade by the end of one year from commencement of trading. (Any part of the money wholly employed for 'permissible purposes' within the 'initial utilisation period' is disregarded for this purpose.)

(*c*) The money raised by the issue was, at the time of acquisition, intended to be employed for the purposes of a 'qualifying trade' *not* then being carried on, the trade *does not begin* to be carried on within two years after that time and that money has not been wholly employed for 'permissible purposes' by the end of the 'initial utilisation period'.

'*Permissible purposes*' means the purposes of any qualifying trade carried on by the company concerned or by any of its 'qualifying subsidiaries' (see 50.14 below). The '*initial utilisation period*' is the period of one year after the acquisition of the shares in question. Money is treated as employed wholly for particular purposes even if an amount thereof is employed for other purposes, provided such amount is not significant. Money employed for the purpose of preparing to carry on a qualifying trade is taken to be employed for the purposes of that trade.

Where any of the above circumstances applies, the held-over gain (or such part of it as has not been charged on any disposal, or under 50.11 above or under these provisions) is treated as accruing to the person in question immediately before the end of,

(i) where (*a*) above applies, the initial utilisation period;

(ii) where (*b*) above applies, the first year of trading; or

(iii) where (*c*) above applies, the period of two years therein mentioned.

Where only part of the money raised by the issue of shares has been permissibly employed within the time allowed in (*a*), (*b*) or (*c*) above (and the other part is a significant amount), there are provisions whereby a person's shareholding is treated for reinvestment relief purposes as two separate holdings, one from which that part of the money was raised and one from which the remainder was raised, the value of the holding being apportioned accordingly between the two notional holdings.

TCGA 1992, s 164F(4)(4A)(5)(11) (see 50.11 above) apply for the purposes of these provisions, except that 50.11(V)–(VII) do not so apply. *TCGA 1992, s 164F(10A)–(10C)* also apply, so that, as in 50.11 above, the gain treated as accruing under these provisions may itself be deferred upon the acquisition of a further qualifying investment.

[*TCGA 1992, s 164FA, s 164N(5); FA 1997, Sch 17 para 3(2), para 6(2), para 7*].

50.13 **Disposals after 15 March 1993 and before 30 November 1993.** In certain circumstances, an effective withdrawal of relief applied as below where a person had acquired any eligible shares (see 50.3 above) in a qualifying company (see 50.14 above) ('*the acquired holding*') for a consideration which was treated as reduced, under *TCGA 1992, s 164A* in 50.3 or *TCGA 1992, s 164D* in 50.9 above by any amount ('*the held-over gain*'). [*TCGA 1992, s 164F(1), s 164N(1); FA 1993, Sch 7 para 3*].

The provisions of *TCGA 1992, s 164F(2)* (see 50.11(*a*)–(*d*) above) applied similarly regarding 'the appropriate proportion' of the held-over gain. [*TCGA 1992, s 164F(2), s 164N(1); FA 1993, Sch 7 para 3*].

'*The appropriate proportion*' of the held-over gain was so much, if any, of that gain as had not already been *either* charged on any disposal or under these provisions *or* carried forward under *TCGA 1992, s 164D* in 50.9 above. However, where 50.11(*d*) above applied, or where 50.11(*a*) and (*b*) applied in accordance with 50.11(A)–(D), the proportion was a just and reasonable one having regard to the extent to which the acquired holding represented the original shares. [*TCGA 1992, s 164F(3); FA 1993, Sch 7 para 3*].

Subject to *TCGA 1992, s 164F(5)* below, references in the above to an amount carried forward from a disposal were as in 50.9 above, and the provisions contained there in (A) and (B) and (*aa*) and (*bb*) were applied to these provisions as they applied there. [*TCGA 1992, s 164F(4); FA 1993, Sch 7 para 3*].

The provisions of *TCGA 1992, s 164F(5)* in 50.11 applied similarly, except that 50.11(I) above referred to a reduction under *TCGA 1992, s 164A* or *s 164D*, and 50.11(III) referred to disposals taken into account under 50.9(A) and (B) and (*aa*) and (*bb*) as applied above instead of disposals taken into account under *TCGA 1992, s 164F(4)(4A)*. [*TCGA 1992, s 164F(5); FA 1993, Sch 7 para 3*].

TCGA 1992, s 164F(6)(12) in 50.11 above regarding the definition of 'relevant period' applied similarly. [*TCGA 1992, s 164F(6)(12), s 164N(1); FA 1993, Sch 7 para 3*].

TCGA 1992, s 164F(7) in 50.11(A)–(D) above regarding the effect of *TCGA 1992, s 127* applied similarly. [*TCGA 1992, s 164F(7), s 164N(1); FA 1993, Sch 7 para 3*].

TCGA 1992, s 164F(8) in 50.11(*aa*)–(*bb*) above regarding winding up and dissolution applied similarly. [*TCGA 1992, s 164F(8); FA 1993, Sch 7 para 3*].

TCGA 1992, s 164F(9)(10) in 50.11(AA)–(BB) above regarding non-UK residents etc. applied similarly but by reference to a disposal on which (within the meaning of *TCGA 1992, s 164D*) the whole or any part of the held-over gain would have been charged. [*TCGA 1992, s 164F(9)(10), s 164N(1); FA 1993, Sch 7 para 3*].

TCGA 1992, s 164F(11) in 50.11 above concerning the disregarding of an amount of the held-over gain applied similarly. [*TCGA 1992, s 164F(11); FA 1993, Sch 7 para 3*].

50.14 DEFINITION OF QUALIFYING COMPANY

Except where otherwise stated, the provisions below apply to disposals made after **15 March 1993.**

A company is a '*qualifying company*' for the purposes of *TCGA 1992, Pt V Ch IA* (reinvestment relief) if it complies with the following conditions.

Subject to the further provisions below a company is a qualifying company if it is

(*a*) an unquoted company (being a company none of the shares in or other securities of which were quoted on any recognised stock exchange or were dealt in on the Unlisted Securities Market) which exists wholly for the purpose of carrying on one or more 'qualifying trades' (see 50.15 below) (but purposes capable of having no significant effect, other than in relation to incidental matters, on the extent of the company's activities are ignored). (The case of *Lord v Tustain*; *Lord v Chapple Ch D 1993, 65 TC 761* concerning interest relief had as its main issue the meaning of the phrase 'any company which exists wholly or mainly for the purpose of carrying on a trade' in a similar context.); or

(*b*) an unquoted company which is the 'parent company of a trading group'.

A company is not a qualifying company if

(1) it controls (within *ICTA 1988, s 416*; see TOLLEY'S CORPORATION TAX under Close Companies) (whether on its own or together with any persons connected (within *TCGA 1992, s 286*) with it) any company which is not a 'qualifying subsidiary' or, without controlling it, has a 51% subsidiary (within *ICTA 1988, s 838*) which is not a qualifying subsidiary;

(2) it is under the control of another company (or of another company and a person connected with the other company) or, without being controlled by it, is a 51% subsidiary of another company; or

(3) arrangements are in existence under which the company could fall within (1) or (2) above.

A '*qualifying subsidiary*', in relation to a company (the holding company), is any company which is a member of a 'group of companies' of which the holding company is the principal company. *TCGA 1992, s 170* (see 13.11 COMPANIES) applies to define a '*group of companies*' except that it is not necessary for all members of the group to be resident in the UK (although a 'qualifying trade' must be carried on wholly or mainly in the UK — see also 50.15 below).

A company is the '*parent company of a trading group*' if it is the principal company of a group of companies (defined as above) and, treating all the activities of the company and its qualifying subsidiaries as one business, its business is carried on wholly or mainly in the UK and neither the business nor a substantial part of it consists in excluded activities or activities carried on otherwise than in the course of a trade. In practice, investment in a group will qualify where approximately 80% of the group's activities qualify (Revenue Press Release 26 November 1996). Excluded activities are those in 50.15(*a*)–(*h*) below with similar let-outs as in 50.15 below as regards the receiving of royalties or licence fees and the letting of ships on charter.

For the above purpose, activities of a company or of any of its qualifying subsidiaries are disregarded to the extent that they consist in

(i) the holding of shares in or securities of, or the making of loans to, one or more of the company's qualifying subsidiaries; or

(ii) the holding and managing of property used by the company or any qualifying subsidiary for one or more qualifying trades (see 50.15 below) or for research and development intended to result in a qualifying trade.

In addition, activities of a qualifying subsidiary are disregarded to the extent that they consist in making loans to the company or, in the case of a mainly trading subsidiary (as defined), in activities carried on in pursuance of a purpose capable of having no significant effect (other than in relation to incidental matters) on the extent of its activities.

Without prejudice to the generality of (*a*) and (*b*) above or *TCGA 1992, s 164F(8)* in 50.11 and 50.13 above, a company ceases to be a qualifying company if a resolution is passed or an order is made for its winding up, or any other act is done for a like purpose under foreign law or the company is dissolved without winding up.

[*TCGA 1992, s 164G, s 164N(1)(2); FA 1993, Sch 7 para 3; FA 1997, Sch 17 para 4, para 6(1)*].

The above provisions apply in relation to shares acquired **after 26 November 1996**. They also apply in relation to shares acquired by a person **on or before that date**, held by him until that date and continuing throughout to be eligible shares in a qualifying company, but do not prevent those shares from being shares in a qualifying company at any time after 26 November 1996 and within three years after their acquisition if they would have been so under the provisions described below. [*FA 1997, Sch 17 para 7*].

Previously, instead of the condition at (*b*) above the company had to be

(A) an unquoted company whose business consisted entirely in the holding of shares in or other securities of, or the making of loans to, one or more 'qualifying subsidiaries' (defined as below) of the company; or

(B) an unquoted company whose business consisted entirely in the holding of such shares or securities, or the making of such loans and the carrying on of one or more 'qualifying trades' (see 50.15 below).

For the purposes of the previous rules, in relation to a company ('*the holding company*'), a '*qualifying subsidiary*' means a company which is a member of a 'group of companies' (within *TCGA 1992, s 170*; see 13.11 COMPANIES) of which the holding company is the 'principal company' (within *TCGA 1992, s 170*), and of which each of the members, or each of the members other than the holding company, is a company satisfying one of the following conditions, namely (*aa*) it is such a company as is mentioned in (*a*) above;

(*bb*) it exists wholly for the purposes of holding and managing property used by the holding company or any of the holding company's other subsidiaries for the purposes of

(i) research and development (as defined) from which it is intended that a qualifying trade to be carried on by the holding company or any of those other subsidiaries will be derived, or

(ii) one or more qualifying trades so carried on;

(*cc*) it would exist wholly for such a purpose apart from purposes capable of having no significant effect (other than in relation to incidental matters) on the extent of the company's activities; or

(*dd*) it has no profits for the purposes of corporation tax and no part of its business consists in the making of investments.

Under the pre-26 November 1996 rules, a company which was a member of a group that included one or more non-resident companies could not be a qualifying company, because of the application, without modification, of *TCGA 1992, s 170*. It is, however, the Revenue view that a company with no subsidiaries does not have to be UK resident to be a qualifying company. See Revenue Tax Bulletin May 1994 p 128.

The following rules with regard to determining whether a company is a qualifying company do *not* apply where an acquisition is made after **28 November 1994** of shares in a company.

In determining whether a company is a qualifying company for the purposes of *TCGA 1992, Pt V Ch IA* after **29 November 1993 and before 29 November 1994**, a company is not a qualifying company at any time when the value of the 'interests in land' held by the company exceeds the greater of half the value of the company's 'chargeable assets' and half the value of the company's assets as a whole (this latter value being determined *mutatis mutandis* as in *ICTA 1988, s 294(3)(4)* for the purposes of enterprise investment scheme relief or, before 1 January 1994, business expansion scheme relief). Under *ICTA 1988, s 294(3)(4)*, the value of a company's assets as a whole is arrived at by first aggregating the market value of each of those assets and then deducting the amount of the debts and liabilities of the company, for which purpose a debt includes the amount paid up in respect of any of the shares of the company which carry a present or future preferential right to the company's assets in a winding up and the company's other share capital, share premium account and reserves are not treated as debts or liabilities. In determining whether a company was a qualifying company for the purposes of *TCGA 1992, Pt V Ch IA* before **30 November 1993**, a company was not a qualifying company at any time when the value of the interests in land held by the company was greater than half the value of the company's chargeable assets.

For disposals **after 29 November 1993**, a '*chargeable asset*' of a company at any time is every asset of that company, except one on the disposal of which by the company at that time no gain accruing to the company would be a chargeable gain. For disposals **after 15 March 1993 and before 30 November 1993**, the definition of the term was as in 50.8 above, although both definitions are virtually identical.

'*Interest in land*' is widely defined to include rights related to land, and rights to obtain an interest etc. from another which depend on that other's ability to grant the interest etc., but excludes the interest of a creditor secured by any mortgage or charge over land.

Valuation of an interest in land excludes any plant or machinery which is, in law, part of the land etc. An interest is valued on the assumption that there is no source of mineral deposits on the land exploitable other than by opencast mining or quarrying and that the existence of any oil exploration (as defined) borehole is disregarded.

Where a company is a member of a partnership, the value of any interest in land held by the partnership is apportioned as on a dissolution of the partnership. Where a company is a member of a group (within *TCGA 1992, s 170*) all the group members are treated as one company for the above purposes, but ignoring any debts and liabilities as between the members. [*TCGA 1992, s 164A(13), s 164H, s 164N(1)(1A)(2); FA 1993, Sch 7 para 3; FA 1994, s 91(3)(4), Sch 11 para 5, Sch 26 Pt V; FA 1995, s 46(1)(2)*].

50.15 DEFINITION OF QUALIFYING TRADE

The provisions below apply to disposals made after **15 March 1993**.

A trade is a '*qualifying trade*' for the purposes of *TCGA 1992, Pt V Ch IA* (reinvestment relief) if it complies with the requirements below, and for this purpose the carrying on of any activities of research and development (as defined) from which it is intended that a trade meeting those requirements will be derived is treated as the carrying on of a qualifying trade. A trade cannot be a qualifying trade unless it is conducted on a commercial basis and with a view to profit realisation. In relation to shares acquired **after 26 November 1996**, there is the additional requirement that the trade be carried on wholly or mainly in the UK. This also applies in relation to shares acquired by a person **on or before that date**, held by him until that date and continuing throughout to be eligible shares in a qualifying company, but does not prevent those shares from being shares in a qualifying company at any time after 26 November 1996 and within three years after their acquisition if they would have been so if this requirement had not been introduced. In considering whether a trade is carried on 'wholly or mainly in the UK', the totality of the trade activities is taken into account. (Revenue Pamphlet IR 131, SP 7/98).

Subject to the following, a trade is a qualifying trade if neither that trade nor a substantial part (the Revenue suggests 20% or more in Revenue Capital Gains Manual CG 62571) of it consists in one or more of the following activities:

(*a*) dealing in land, in commodities or futures or in shares, securities or other financial instruments;

(*b*) dealing in goods, otherwise than in the course of an ordinary trade of wholesale or retail distribution;

(*c*) banking, insurance, money-lending, debt-factoring, hire-purchase financing or other financial activities;

(*d*) leasing (including letting ships on charter or other assets on hire) or receiving royalties or licence fees;

(*e*) providing legal or accountancy services;

(*f*) providing services or facilities for any trade which consists, to a substantial extent, in activities within (*a*)–(*e*) above and is carried on by another person (except the principal company of a group of companies, these terms being as defined in *TCGA 1992, s 170*; see 13.11 COMPANIES) who has a 'controlling interest' (see below) in both trades;

(*g*) property development (broadly land development for disposal when developed at a profit); this is treated as a qualifying trade for determinations after 28 November 1994;

(*h*) farming (broadly husbandry in the UK other than market gardening); this is treated as a qualifying trade for determinations after 28 November 1994.

With effect from, broadly, **26 November 1996**, the application of *TCGA 1992, s 170* in defining 'group of companies' in (*f*) above is modified so as no longer to exclude from the definition groups that include non-resident companies.

In relation to (*b*) above

(1) a trade of wholesale distribution is one in which the goods are offered for sale and sold to persons for resale (with or without processing) by them to the general public;

(2) a trade of retail distribution is one in which the goods are offered for sale and sold to the general public; and

(3) a trade is not an ordinary trade within (1) or (2) above if it consists, to a substantial extent, in dealing in goods which are collected or held as an investment (or of that and any other activity in (*a*)–(*h*) above), and a substantial proportion of those goods is held for a significantly longer period than might reasonably be expected of a vendor trying to dispose of them at market value.

In determining whether a trade is an ordinary one within (1) and (2) above, regard is had to the extent the following features are present, with (A)–(C) below being regarded as indicative features whilst (D)–(H) are regarded as contra-indicative ones.

(A) The breaking of bulk between purchase and resale.

(B) The purchase and sale of goods in different markets.

(C) The employment of staff and incurring of expenses in the course of a trade other than the cost of goods or, in the case of a company carrying on a trade, of remuneration of persons connected with it.

(D) The purchase and sale of goods from persons connected with the trader.

(E) The matching of purchases with sales.

(F) The holding of goods for longer than normal for goods of the kind in question.

(G) The carrying on of the trade at a place not commonly used for wholesale or retail trading.

(H) No physical possession of the goods being taken by the trader.

As regards (*d*) above, a trade carried on by a company engaged in the production of films (as defined, and with or without the distribution of films within three years of their production) is not disqualified from being a qualifying trade by reason only of all royalties and licence fees received relating to films (or sound or other by-products arising therefrom) produced within the preceding three years. Similar comments apply to a trade carried on by a company engaged in research and development where all royalties and licence fees received are attributable to such activities it has carried out. Likewise, a trade is not disqualified by reason only of its consisting in the letting of ships, other than oil rigs or pleasure craft (as both defined), on charter if

(*aa*) the company beneficially owns all the ships it so lets;

(*bb*) every ship beneficially owned by the company is UK registered;

(*cc*) the company is solely responsible for arranging the marketing of the services of its ships; and

(*dd*) the further conditions below are satisfied in relation to every letting on charter.

If any of the conditions in (*aa*)–(*dd*) above are not satisfied for any lettings, only those lettings are taken into account, when taken together with any other activity within (*a*)–(*h*) above, in deciding whether a substantial part of the trade consists of activities within (*a*)–(*h*).

The conditions mentioned in (*dd*) above require, broadly, that each letting is for no more than twelve months and is by way of an arm's length bargain, and that chartering is conducted by the company as principal bearing the responsibility or making management decisions and paying expenses between voyages.

Under (*f*) above, a person has a '*controlling interest*' in a trade carried on by a company, or carried on by a person other than a company (when trade also includes any business, profession or vocation), if (AA) or (BB), or (CC), below applies respectively. For this purpose there is attributed to any person any rights or powers of any other person who is an '*associate*' (as in *ICTA 1988, s 417(3)(4)* except that, for these purposes, a brother or sister is not treated as a relative) of his.

(AA) The person controls (within *ICTA 1988, s 416*) the company.

(BB) The company is a close company (within *ICTA 1988, ss 414, 415*) and he or an associate of his is a director (within *ICTA 1988, s 417(5)*) of the company and either the beneficial owner of, or able to control directly or in any indirect manner, more than 30 per cent. of the company, or not less than half the trade could be regarded under *ICTA 1988, s 344(2)* as belonging to him.

(CC) The person is entitled to not less than half the assets used for, or the income arising, from the trade.

As regards (*g*) and (*h*) above, these conditions no longer apply in deciding whether a company is conducting a qualifying trade after 28 November 1994.

[*TCGA 1992, s 164I, s 164J, s 164N(1)(2); FA 1993, Sch 7 para 3; FA 1995, s 46(1)(4); FA 1997, Sch 17 para 5, para 6(1), para 7*].

See TOLLEY'S CORPORATION TAX under Losses for *ICTA 1988, s 344(2)*, and under Close Companies for *ICTA 1988, s 414, s 415, s 416, s 417(3)(4)(5)*.

50.16 DENIAL OF RELIEF

General. The following provisions apply to disposals **after 15 March 1993 unless otherwise stated**.

Overseas residents. Relief under *TCGA 1992, Pt V Ch IA* (reinvestment relief) does not apply in relation to any person in respect of his acquisition of any eligible shares (see 50.2 and 50.3 above) in a qualifying company (see 50.14 above) if at the time when he acquires them he is neither resident nor ordinarily resident in the UK. The same restriction applies to a person who, though resident or ordinarily resident in the UK at the time of acquisition, is regarded under double taxation relief arrangements as resident outside the UK, and under the arrangements would not be liable in the UK to tax on a gain arising on a disposal of the shares immediately after their acquisition. [*TCGA 1992, s 164K; FA 1993, Sch 7 para 3*].

Anti-avoidance. For the purposes of *TCGA 1992, Pt V Ch IA* (reinvestment relief), an acquisition of shares in a qualifying company (see 50.14 above) is not treated as an acquisition of eligible shares (see 50.2 and 50.3 above) if the arrangements (including any scheme, agreement or understanding, whether or not legally enforceable) for the acquisition of those shares, or any prior preliminary arrangements, include: arrangements with a view to the subsequent reacquisition, exchange or other disposal of the shares; arrangements for or with a view to the cessation of the company's trade or the disposal of all or a substantial part of its 'chargeable business assets'; or arrangements for the return of the whole or part of the value of an individual's investment.

For disposals **after 29 November 1993**, a '*chargeable business asset*' of a company means a 'chargeable asset' (including goodwill but not including any shares or other securities or any assets held as investments) which is, or is an interest in, an asset used for the purposes of a trade, profession, vocation, office or employment (these terms having the same meaning as in *ICTA 1988*) carried on by the individual acquiring the shares, any 'personal company' of that individual, a member of a 'trading group' of which the 'holding company' (these last three terms being defined as in *TCGA 1992, Sch 6 para 1*; see 53.4 RETIREMENT RELIEF) is a personal company of that individual or a partnership of which that individual is a member. For disposals **after 15 March 1993 and before 30 November 1993**, the definition of the term was as in 50.8 above, although both definitions are virtually identical. Similarly, for disposals **after 29 November 1993**, a '*chargeable asset*' of a company at any time is every asset of that company, except one on the disposal of which by the company at that time no gain accruing to the company would be a chargeable gain. For disposals **after 15 March 1993 and before 30 November 1993**, the definition of the term was as in 50.8 above, although again both definitions are virtually identical.

If an individual, having acquired eligible shares in a qualifying company, has returned to him afterwards the whole or any part of the value of his investment, the shares are treated as ceasing to be eligible shares under *TCGA 1992, Pt V Ch IA* (reinvestment relief) (for the consequences of which event when it occurs in the relevant period, see 50.11 above). A return of the whole or part of the value of the investment of an individual who is to acquire or has acquired shares in a company is treated as being made if the company

(*a*) repays, redeems or repurchases any of its shares or other securities belonging to that individual or makes any payment to him for giving up rights on the cancellation or extinguishment of any of the company's shares or securities;

(*b*) repays any debt owed to that individual, other than a debt that was incurred by the company on or after the acquisition of the shares and otherwise than in consideration of the extinguishment of a debt incurred before the acquisition;

(*c*) makes any payment to that individual for giving up his rights to any debt on its extinguishment;

(*d*) releases or waives any liability of that individual to the company (which is deemed to occur if the liability remains undischarged twelve months after the time it should have been discharged) or discharges, or undertakes to discharge, any liability of his to a third party;

(*e*) provides a benefit or facility for that individual;

(*f*) disposes of an asset to that individual for no or an insufficient consideration;

(*g*) acquires an asset from that individual for more than a sufficient consideration; or

(*h*) makes any payment to that individual other than a 'qualifying payment'.

Similarly, a whole or partial return of the value of an individual's investment is treated as being made where there is a loan made (including the giving of credit and the assignment of debt) by any person to that individual such that either no loan would have been made or the terms of it would have been different had the individual not have acquired, or been proposing to acquire, the shares. For the Revenue's views on 'loan-linked' investments, see Revenue Pamphlet IR 131, SP 6/98.

Debts and liabilities that could be discharged by the company making a qualifying payment are ignored for the purposes of the above, as are benefits or facilities provided in circumstances such that a payment made to the value of them would be a 'qualifying payment'. A '*qualifying payment*' means

(1) reasonable payment by a company of remuneration to an officer or employee;

(2) reimbursement by a company of an officer's or employee's travel or other expenses incurred wholly, exclusively and necessarily in the performance of his duties;

(3) interest paid by a company on money lent to it on reasonable commercial terms;

(4) payment by a company of a dividend etc. not exceeding a normal return on the investment in shares etc. of the company;

(5) a payment not exceeding market value for the supply of goods;

(6) a payment by a company, as rent for any property occupied by the company, of an amount not exceeding a reasonable and commercial rent for the property;

(7) any reasonable and necessary remuneration paid by a company for services rendered to it in the course of a trade assessed under Schedule D, Case I or II;

(8) a payment in discharge of an '*ordinary trade debt*' (meaning any debt for goods or services supplied in the ordinary course of trade or business where any credit given does not exceed six months and is not longer than that normally given to customers generally).

In relation to disposals **after 29 November 1993**, for the purposes of *TCGA 1992, Pt V Ch IA* (reinvestment relief), where a person has acquired any eligible shares in a qualifying company ('*the acquired holding*') for a consideration which is treated as reduced under *Pt V Ch IA* by any amount ('*the held-over gain*') and after that acquisition, he acquires eligible shares in a 'relevant company', his acquisition of the eligible shares in the relevant company is not regarded as the acquisition of a qualifying investment for the purposes of *TCGA 1992, s 164A* in 50.2 above. A company is a '*relevant company*' if

(A) where that person has disposed of any of the acquired holding, it is the company in which the acquired holding has subsisted or a company which was a member of the same '*group of companies*' (as in *TCGA 1992, Sch 6 para 1*; see 53.4 RETIREMENT RELIEF) as that company at any time since the acquisition of the acquired holding,

(B) it is a company in relation to the disposal of any shares in which there has been a claim under *Pt V Ch IA* such that, without that or an equivalent claim, there would have been no held-over gain in relation to the acquired holding, or

(C) it is a company which, at the time of the disposal or acquisition to which the claim relates, was a member of the same group of companies as a company falling within (B) above.

In the above provisions, a payment or disposal made indirectly to an individual, or to his order or benefit, is treated as made to him, and any reference to an individual includes a reference to any associate (as in 50.15 above) of his, and any reference to a company includes a reference to any person connected (within *TCGA 1992, s 286*) with the company.

For disposals after **29 November 1993**, the above provisions have effect in relation to the acquisition of shares by the trustees of a settlement as if references to an individual acquiring the shares were references to those trustees or any individual or charity by virtue of whose interest, at the time of acquisition, the relief given under *TCGA 1992, s 164B* in 50.4 above applies to the settled property. For disposals **after 15 March 1993 and before 30 November 1993**, the above provisions had effect in relation to the acquisition of shares by the trustees of a settlement as if references to an individual acquiring the shares were references to those trustees or the individual who was the qualifying beneficiary (see 50.5 above) by reference to whom *Pt V Ch IA* had or, as the case may have been, would have had effect in relation to the acquisition. [*TCGA 1992, s 164L, s 164N(1)(1A)(3); FA 1993, Sch 7 para 3; FA 1994, Sch 11 paras 6, 10, 11*].

Relief excluded where enterprise investment scheme relief claimed. In relation to shares issued **after 31 December 1993**, if a person makes a claim for relief under *ICTA 1988, Pt VII Ch III* in respect of any shares, those shares cannot be, or be treated as ever having been, eligible shares within 50.2 and 50.3 above. [*TCGA 1992, s 164MA, s 164N(1);*

FA 1994, s 137, Sch 15 paras 32, 33]. This provision would seem to override *TCGA 1992, s 164F* in 50.11 and 50.13 above regarding the withdrawal of reinvestment relief and so provide for denial or withdrawal of relief in all circumstances (and see Revenue Capital Gains Manual CG 62635). Contrast with *TCGA 1992, s 164M* regarding business expansion scheme relief below.

Relief excluded where business expansion scheme relief claimed. In relation to shares issued **before 1 January 1994**, where a person acquires any shares in a company those shares cannot be eligible shares within 50.2 and 50.3 above or, as the case may be, cease to be eligible shares if that person or any person connected (within *TCGA 1992, s 286*) with him has made or makes a claim for relief in relation to those shares under *ICTA 1988, Pt VII Ch III*. [*TCGA 1992, s 164M, s 164N(1); FA 1993, Sch 7 para 3; FA 1994, s 137, Sch 15 paras 31, 33*]. This provision seems to allow for the application of *TCGA 1992, s 164F* in 50.11 and 50.13 above regarding the withdrawal of reinvestment relief (and see Revenue Capital Gains Manual CG 62635). If so, it is arguable that in certain unusual circumstances (e.g. company not beginning to trade until up to two years after issue of shares) a valid claim to business expansion scheme relief would not lead to the withdrawal of reinvestment relief. If the former relief is not itself withdrawn, any gain arising on the shares is exempt (see 20.17 ENTERPRISE INVESTMENT SCHEME (AND BES)). However, the shares to be eligible shares must be in a qualifying company as in 50.14 above and it is not clear whether any delay between the issue of shares and the commencement of trading would prejudice such status.

See 20.9 ENTERPRISE INVESTMENT SCHEME (AND BES) for provisions on deferral of gains on re-investment in enterprise investment schemes, and 65.10 VENTURE CAPITAL TRUSTS for similar provisions.

50.17 CLEARANCE SCHEME

A reinvestment relief clearance scheme is effective from 26 November 1996 onwards whereby the Revenue is able to give *provisional* clearance to companies who consider they may be qualifying companies (see 50.14 above). Whether investment in a company will qualify cannot be ultimately determined until the investment has been made and the Revenue have been able to confirm that the information supplied by the company still applied at the time of the investment.

If companies wish to make use of the scheme they are first asked to complete a questionnaire (obtainable from any tax office) which contains a check list of reinvestment relief key requirements. If the company then considers it *can* qualify for reinvestment relief it should contact the Revenue to obtain a ruling about whether it is eligible and as a consequence will be able to advise potential investors accordingly. In order to give an informed ruling the Revenue will require a company to supply, where it is not already held, all information which may be relevant including:

(*a*) copy of the latest accounts if applicable;

(*b*) an up-to-date copy of the memorandum and articles of association with details of any changes proposed;

(*c*) a copy of the draft of any prospectus or similar document to be issued to potential investors;

(*d*) details of the trade or activities carried on or proposed to be carried on;

(*e*) any further information which the company believes is necessary for an informed decision or which the inspector may ask for.

Where the company is the parent company of a group, details of the group's structure including any anticipated changes should also be supplied together with details of the trade or activities carried on, or proposed to be carried on, by each subsidiary.

Any ruling can be based only on the information supplied. If the company's circumstances change materially it will need to draw the Inland Revenue's attention to any changes which might influence the availability of relief.

Potential investors may still approach their own tax inspector for advice on reinvestment relief, but guidance given in such circumstances will inevitably be less reliable than a ruling obtained by a company under the clearance scheme.

(Revenue Press Release 2 December 1996).

51 Remittance Basis

Cross-references. See 6.2 ASSETS for the location of assets; 18.6 DOUBLE TAX RELIEF for relief available where remittance basis applies; 44.5 OVERSEAS MATTERS for relief available where overseas gains are unremittable to the UK; 52 RESIDENCE AND DOMICILE.

Sumption: Capital Gains Tax. See A3.05.

51.1 The remittance basis implies that assessments to UK capital gains tax on gains arising abroad are restricted to sums actually remitted (or deemed to have been remitted) into the UK out of those gains, such remittances being treated as gains accruing when received in the UK. Subject to any relevant double taxation agreement, it applies to disposals by individuals *resident or ordinarily resident but not domiciled* in the UK of assets situated abroad (with no allowance for losses arising abroad). [*TCGA 1992, s 12(1), s 16(4)*].

Revenue practice appears to be to leave out of account remittances made out of the proceeds of disposals made whilst a non-UK domiciled individual was neither resident nor ordinarily resident in the UK and, subject to this, to treat a remittance as taxable to the extent given by the proportion which represents chargeable gain on normal disposal principles (see 17.3 DISPOSAL for allowable expenditure and proceeds in foreign currency). This practice even seems to extend to the case where the taxpayer divides the proceeds of disposal but only makes remittances from that part which represents the original allowable expenditure and indexation allowance.

In an appeal to General Commissioners, the Revenue were successful in applying the provisions where the individual was at all material times resident and ordinarily resident in the UK but acquired a UK domicile between the realisation of the gains in question and the time, in a later year of assessment, when the proceeds of the gains were remitted to the UK (Taxation, 6 June 1991, p 257).

Taper relief is computed by reference to actual time of disposal and not time of remittance (see 60.12 TAPER RELIEF).

For the situation where an individual becomes, or ceases to be, resident or ordinarily resident in the UK, see 52.3 RESIDENCE AND DOMICILE.

The Revenue's views on the practical operation of the remittance basis are contained in Revenue Capital Gains Manual CG 25300/440.

51.2 REMITTANCES GENERALLY

By analogy with cases relating to income tax, a taxable remittance may include the repatriation of reinvested gains, provided those gains were made whilst the disposer was resident or ordinarily resident in the UK (*Scottish Provident Institution v Farmer CS 1912, 6 TC 34* and *Kneen v Martin CA 1934, 19 TC 33*). Similarly, a remittance from a foreign bank account into which overseas gains have been paid may be assessable, depending on the circumstances, see *Walsh v Randall KB 1940, 23 TC 55* (sterling draft on foreign bank received by UK resident drawer before handing to UK payee) and *Thomson v Moyse HL 1960, 39 TC 291* (dollar cheques on US bank sold to the Bank of England held to be remitted) but cf. *Carter v Sharon KB 1936, 20 TC 229* (drafts on foreign bank posted abroad by UK drawer for daughter's maintenance; held no remittance as, under relevant foreign law, gift to daughter complete on posting of draft). In *Harmel v Wright Ch D 1973, 49 TC 149* an amount received via two South African companies, ending as a loan from one of them, was held to be a remittance. An erroneous remittance by a bank, contrary to the customer's instructions, was held not liable in *Duke of Roxburghe's Exors v CIR CS 1936, 20 TC 711*.

51.3 **CONSTRUCTIVE REMITTANCES**

Gains arising abroad to a person ordinarily resident in the UK and which he applies abroad towards the satisfaction of

(*a*) a debt (or interest thereon) for money lent to him in the UK, or

(*b*) a debt for money lent to him abroad and brought here, or

(*c*) a loan incurred to satisfy such debts,

are treated as received by him in the UK.

Where an ordinarily resident person imports money lent to him abroad, the debt for which has at that time already been wholly or partly satisfied, the imported money (up to the amount of the original loan) is treated as a remittance at the date of importation, and the provisions at (*a*)–(*c*) above apply accordingly.

Gains available in any form to the 'lender' so that the amount of a loan debt, or the time of its repayment, depends directly or indirectly on the amount of property so available to the lender, are treated as having been applied towards satisfaction of the loan.

'*Lender*' includes any person for the time being entitled to repayment. [*TCGA 1992, s 12(2); ICTA 1988, s 65(6)–(9)*].

Example

X, ordinarily resident but not domiciled in the UK, borrows £28,000 in the UK in order to buy a residence here. Out of a later loan of US $50,000 raised abroad, he uses $40,000 to repay the loan incurred in the UK. He repays the $50,000 loan out of the disposal proceeds of assets situated abroad but he uses the balance ($10,000) of the actual dollars borrowed in improving his UK residence. The disposal proceeds of the overseas assets were $140,000 and the disposal would have given rise to a chargeable gain of £60,000 on normal disposal principles. Subject to double taxation arrangements the gain arising abroad will be liable to UK capital gains tax as follows.

(i) $40,000 under (*c*) above, treated as remitted on the repayment of the dollar loan.

(ii) $10,000 treated as remitted at the date of importation, representing money lent abroad.

Thus, for example, in (i) above the chargeable gain arising is

$$£60,000 \times \frac{40,000}{140,000} = £17,143$$

The balance of the disposal proceeds $(140,000 – 50,000) will remain exempt unless and until it is remitted (or deemed remitted) to the UK.

(*Note.* Foreign currency and bank balances denominated therein are themselves chargeable assets in certain cases. See 6.2 ASSETS and 21.5 and 21.8 EXEMPTIONS AND RELIEFS.)

52 Residence and Domicile

Cross-references. See 16.7 DEATH for residence etc. status of personal representatives; 18 DOUBLE TAX RELIEF for double tax agreements which may override or amend statutory provisions or Revenue practice for the purposes of such agreements; 43 OFFSHORE SETTLEMENTS; 44 OVERSEAS MATTERS; 45.4 PARTNERSHIPS for overseas resident partners and partnerships; and 57.3 SETTLEMENTS for residence etc. status of trustees.

52.1 The legislation contains few specific directions as to the ascertainment of a person's 'residence' and 'ordinary residence' status in a particular year of assessment for general tax purposes and this is especially so of capital gains tax. Consequently, it is a body of case law that has brought about the view that these terms are to be interpreted according to their normal meanings and that each case must rest on its own facts and particular circumstances. The Revenue have taken case decisions, *inter alia*, in formulating their own practice as to the determination of residence and ordinary residence (see 52.3–52.5 below for individuals and 52.6 for companies). The term 'domicile' is governed by the general legal meaning rather than any specific definitions for tax purposes but again, each case rests on its own facts. See 52.7 below. For appeals relating to residence and domicile generally, see 52.8 below.

The extent of the UK for tax purposes is given in 52.9 below and special rules relating to residence status in connection with the double taxation agreement between the UK and Ireland are in 52.10 below.

52.2 **Revenue administrative procedures.** Individuals who come to the UK to take up employment are asked to complete Form P86 to enable their residence status to be considered. This form also now includes a section on domicile so that, in straightforward cases (where, e.g., a person never domiciled in the UK comes here only to work and with the intention of leaving the UK when the employment ceases) the two matters may be dealt with together. In less straightforward cases, Form DOM1 was introduced to obtain the information necessary to the determination of domicile. On leaving the UK, a shortened form P85 (Form P85(S)) was introduced to enable any repayment to be claimed in straightforward cases. Otherwise, Form P85 continues to be used.

Under self-assessment from 1996/97 onwards, Forms P85, P85(S), P86 and DOM 1 continue in operation, but individuals who regard themselves as not resident, not ordinarily resident or not domiciled in the UK are required to self-certify their status in the self-assessment tax return and to complete the 'NON-RESIDENCE ETC.' supplementary pages to the return. The Revenue no longer provide residence 'rulings' but will give specific advice in limited circumstances. Revenue queries on residence status and domicile aspects may be made as part of an enquiry into the self-assessment return or into an initial claim made outside the return (see 56.11 SELF-ASSESSMENT, 12.3 CLAIMS). See Revenue Tax Bulletin June 1997 pp 425–427.

52.3 **RESIDENCE**

An individual can be resident for a particular year of assessment in one or more countries for tax purposes so that a claim not to be UK resident merely because of resident status in another country will usually fail. Unusually, an individual may be regarded as not resident in any country.

Subject to the foregoing an individual is resident in the UK for a year of assessment if any one of the following applies.

(*a*) He is in the UK for some temporary purpose only and not with any view or intent to establish his residence in the UK and if, and only if, the period (or the sum of the periods) for which he is resident (i.e. physically present) in the UK in the year of assessment exceeds six months. [*TCGA 1992, s 9(3); FA 1998, s 127(2)*]. After 1992/93, the question whether for the purposes of this provision an individual is in the UK for some temporary purpose only and not with any view or intent to establish his residence in the UK is decided without regard to any living accommodation available in the UK for his use. [*TCGA 1992, s 9(4); FA 1993, s 208(2)(4)*].

The six months' rule is rigidly applied, even in cases of force majeure, and in borderline cases hours may be significant. See *Wilkie v CIR Ch D 1951, 32 TC 495* where 'six months' was held to mean six calendar months. Otherwise, to be regarded by the Revenue as UK resident for a year of assessment an individual would normally have to be physically present in the UK at some time in the tax year and would also depend on the circumstances. The Revenue treat, *with no exceptions* (including years after 1992/93), an individual as resident if he is in the UK for six months or more during the year. Six months are regarded as 183 days and days of arrival and departure are normally ignored (Revenue Pamphlet IR 20, December 1999 edition, para 1.2).

(*b*) He *visits the UK year after year* (so that his visits become in effect 'part of his habit of life') and the annual visits are for a substantial period or periods of time. The Revenue would normally regard an average annual period or periods which amount to 91 days or more as substantial. Where, after four years, the individual's visits average 91 days or more per year, he is treated as resident from the beginning of the fifth year. However, he will be treated as resident from the beginning of the first year if it is clear at the time of his first visit that he intends to make such visits. Also, if the individual decides that he will make such visits before the beginning of the fifth year, he will be treated as resident from the beginning of the year in which that decision is made (Revenue Pamphlet IR 20, para 3.3). For an example of the averaging calculation, see Revenue Pamphlet IR 20, para 2.10.

Where the Revenue apply the above averaging treatment it will exclude any days spent in the UK because of exceptional circumstances beyond the individual's control (e.g. illness of the individual or a member of his immediate family) although each case will be examined on its facts and the exclusion will not apply for the purposes of the six months' rule in (*a*) above (Revenue Pamphlet IR 131, SP 2/91 and Revenue Pamphlet IR 20, para 3.3).

For further discussion on the position of visitors to the UK see Revenue Tax Bulletin, May 1994, p 130.

(*c*) For years prior to 1993/94, he has *accommodation* (e.g. a house or flat) available for his use in the UK and makes one visit to the UK, however short, in the tax year.

After 1992/93, the enactment of *TCGA 1992, s 9(4)* in (*a*) above (no regard to be had for the purposes of *TCGA 1992, s 9(3)* to any living accommodation available in the UK for an individual's use) means that this Revenue practice (which is based on case law prior to 1993/94) ceases. However, the Revenue have said that there will be no change in the practice of treating as resident and ordinarily resident an individual who comes to and remains in the UK where he owns or acquires on a lease of three years or more accommodation in the UK. Similarly, where an individual leaves the UK, the retention of a home here will continue to be a factor in considering whether he has left the UK permanently (Revenue Pamphlet IR 20, paras 2.8, 3.11 and Revenue Press Release 16 March 1993).

Subject to the above, if an individual works full-time in a trade, profession or vocation which does not have a branch or place of business in the UK, or in an office or employment the whole of the duties under which (apart from mere 'incidental' duties) are performed outside the UK, or in a combination of such activities, any accommodation maintained in the UK for his use is disregarded in determining whether or not he is resident in the UK (although the legislation is unclear whether this provision applies equally to capital gains tax as well as income tax). [*TCGA 1992, s 9(1); ICTA 1988, s 335*]. As to whether duties are 'incidental', see *Robson v Dixon Ch D 1972, 48 TC 527* where an airline pilot was employed abroad but occasionally landed in the UK where the family home was maintained. Held, the UK duties were more than incidental. See also Revenue Pamphlet IR 20, paras 5.7 and 5.8. In deciding whether an individual works full-time in the activities mentioned, the Revenue will consider the particular facts of the case, such as whether there is a standard or irregular number of hours to be worked, a formal job structure, concurrent part-time appointments or a mix of employments and self-employments (Revenue Tax Bulletin February 1993 p 57).

Where available accommodation in the UK is to be taken into account for the determination of an individual's residence or ordinary residence status, it does not depend on ownership, but on whether any accommodation is in fact available for use. Accommodation may be treated as not available for an individual's use if it is:

(i) let on a lease which denies his right to stay in the property;

(ii) left unfurnished so that it is not possible to live in it;

(iii) only available for the individual's use when he is not in the UK;

(iv) too far away from the place visited to be reasonably used when the individual makes one brief business visit to the UK during the tax year;

(v) owned purely for investment purposes and is neither used nor usable by the individual when he is in the UK;

(vi) rented furnished for the individual's use for a period of less than two years;

(vii) rented unfurnished for the individual's use for a period of less than one year.

A house owned or rented by one spouse would (subject to the above) normally be considered available for the use of the other.

(*d*) He is a *Commonwealth* or *Eire* citizen, having been ordinarily resident (see 52.4 below) in the UK, who has left the UK for the purpose only of 'occasional residence' abroad (although the legislation is unclear whether the provisions apply equally to capital gains tax as well as income tax). [*TCGA 1992, s 9(1); ICTA 1988, s 334*].

For a discussion of the meaning of 'occasional residence', see *Reed v Clark Ch D 1985, 58 TC 528.*

Change in residence status. In general, residence status in the UK for part of a year is taken to apply for a whole year (see *Neubergh v CIR Ch D 1977, 52 TC 79* and *Gubay v Kington HL 1984, 57 TC 601*) and, for capital gains tax in particular, disposals are chargeable where they accrue to a person in a year of assessment *during any part of which* he is resident in the UK. [*TCGA 1992, s 2(1)*]. Concessional treatment for a year in which an individual's residence status changes is, however, available in the following circumstances.

- Where an individual comes to live in the UK and is treated as resident in the UK for any year of assessment from the date of arrival, he or she is charged to capital gains tax only in respect of chargeable gains from disposals made after arrival, provided that,

- where the individual arrives on or after 6 April 1998, he or she has not been resident or ordinarily resident in the UK at any time during the five years of assessment immediately preceding the year of assessment in which he or she arrived in the UK; or
- where the individual arrived before 6 April 1998, he or she had not been regarded at any time within the period of 36 months immediately preceding the date of arrival as resident or ordinarily resident in the UK.

- Where an individual leaves the UK and is treated on departure as not resident and not ordinarily resident in the UK, he or she is not charged to capital gains tax on gains from disposals made after the date of departure, provided that, where the date of departure is after 16 March 1998, the individual was not resident and not ordinarily resident in the UK for the whole of at least four out of the seven years of assessment immediately preceding the tax year of departure.

(Revenue Pamphlet IR 1, D2).

The more stringent conditions which apply for arrivals on or after 6 April 1998 and departures after 16 March 1998 result from the introduction of the charge on individuals who become temporarily non-resident in the UK — see 44.4 OVERSEAS MATTERS. In its original form, the concession applied also to companies but ceased to so apply as regards disposals after 5 April 1998 (Revenue Capital Gains Manual CG 42370).

The circumstances in which an individual will be treated by the Revenue on departure as not resident and not ordinarily resident in the UK or on arrival as resident and ordinarily resident are those set out in Revenue Concession A11 (see Revenue Pamphlet IR 20, paras 1.5–1.7, and TOLLEY'S INCOME TAX).

The D2 concession does not apply to

- any person in relation to gains accruing to him on the disposal of assets in the UK which, at any time between his departure and the end of the year, are used for a trade, profession or vocation carried on by him in the UK through a branch or agency, or are used for or acquired for use by or for such a branch or agency (see also 44.3 OVERSEAS MATTERS);
- trustees who commence or cease residence in the UK (see 43.2, 43.3 OFFSHORE SETTLEMENTS);
- a settlor who commences or ceases UK residence during a year in relation to gains of a settlement which are assessed on him as in 57.3 SETTLEMENTS; or
- a settlor on whom gains are taxed under *TCGA 1992, s 86, Sch 5* (see 43.4 OFFSHORE SETTLEMENTS).

As with all published extra-statutory concessions, the D2 concession will not be applied in cases where it would have been part of a tax avoidance arrangement (see Revenue Pamphlet IR 1 and *R v CIR (ex p. Fulford-Dobson) QB 1987, 60 TC 168*). In straightforward cases where the terms of a disposal are negotiated before emigration but the contract is not signed until after the date of departure from the UK, the Board will not withhold the concession merely on the grounds that the disposal was arranged to take place after departure. On its own, a genuine postponement of the disposal is not regarded as an attempt to use the concession for tax avoidance, but where coupled with other arrangements it might be so regarded. (Revenue Capital Gains Manual CG 25982).

Where this split year basis is applied, the day of departure from, or arrival in, the UK is treated as falling into the period of UK residence or ordinary residence (Revenue Pamphlet IR 20, para 1.6).

For visits to the UK for educational purposes, see 52.4 below. For visits abroad generally, see 52.5 below.

Temporary employment in the UK. An individual coming to the UK to work for a period of *at least two years* is treated as resident for the whole period from the day of arrival to the day of departure. Otherwise the normal rules are applied e.g. the six months' or, before 1993/94, the accommodation available rule. (Revenue Pamphlet IR 20, para 3.7).

Examples

(*Note.* After 1992/93, the case law decisions below, which all predate 1993/94, should be read in the light of the enactment of *TCGA 1992, s 9(4)* mentioned in (*a*) and (*c*) above (no regard to be had for the purposes of *TCGA 1992, s 9(3)* to any living accommodation available in the UK for an individual's use) and the comments mentioned there made by the Revenue.)

A resident of Eire making monthly visits here as director of a British company, having no place of abode here, but a permanent one in Eire, was held to be resident and ordinarily resident (*Lysaght v CIR HL 1928, 13 TC 511*). However, compare *CIR v Combe CS 1932, 17 TC 405*. An officer succeeding to an Eire estate, intending to return there permanently but prevented by military duties in the UK, was held, on the facts, to be resident in both countries (*Inchiquin v CIR CA 1948, 31 TC 125*).

In *CIR v Brown KB 1926, 11 TC 292*, and *CIR v Zorab KB 1926, 11 TC 289*, it was held that retired Indian civil servants making periodical visits to, but having no business interests in, the UK, were not resident.

An American holding a lease of a shooting box in Scotland and spending two months there every year (*Cooper v Cadwalader CES 1904, 5 TC 101*), and a merchant physically present and carrying on business in Italy, but owning a house in the UK where he resided for less than six months (*Lloyd v Sulley CES 1884, 2 TC 37*) have both been held to be resident.

A Belgian who had at his disposal for the visits he paid here a house owned not by him but by a company which he controlled, so that it was in fact available whenever he chose to come, was held to be taxable as a resident (*Loewenstein v De Salis KB 1926, 10 TC 424*). But in *Withers v Wynyard KB 1938, 21 TC 724*, an actress (after 18 months abroad) performing in the UK and occupying for $3\frac{1}{2}$ months in 1933/34 a leasehold flat (unable to be disposed of and sub-let when possible), was held not to be UK resident for that year.

A husband and wife who were not actually physically present during the year, although their children were in the UK, were held not to be UK resident (*Turnbull v Foster CES 1904, 6 TC 206*). In *Reed v Clark Ch D 1985, 58 TC 528* the taxpayer had left the UK with the intention to remain abroad throughout a year of assessment and, in the event, did so remain abroad. He was held not to be resident in the UK for the year of absence since his purpose was not only of 'occasional residence' abroad (see (*d*) above).

The taxpayer's presence in the UK need not be voluntary, see *In re Mackenzie decd Ch D 1940, 19 ATC 399* (taxpayer confined in a lunatic asylum).

52.4 ORDINARY RESIDENCE

The term 'ordinary residence' is not defined in the *Taxes Acts*. Broadly, it denotes greater permanence than the term 'residence' (see 52.3 above), and is equivalent to habitual residence; if an individual is resident year after year, he is ordinarily resident. An individual, whose home has been abroad, coming to the UK to live here permanently or intending to stay here for three years or more is treated as resident and ordinarily resident here from the date of his arrival (Revenue Pamphlet IR 20, para 3.1). An individual may be resident in the

UK under the six months' rule of *TCGA 1992, s 9(3)* (see 52.3(*a*) above) without becoming ordinarily resident. Equally, he may be ordinarily resident without being resident in a particular year, e.g. because he usually lives in the UK but is absent on an extended holiday throughout a tax year. (Revenue Pamphlet IR 20, para 1.3).

Accommodation. The availability of accommodation (see 52.3(*c*) above) in the UK for the use of an individual has an important bearing on the determination of ordinary residence status. An individual who has accommodation available and who visits the UK regularly for only limited periods in one or more tax years is regarded as ordinarily resident for each of those years. If such accommodation is not available, he will only be so regarded after such visits have averaged 91 days or more per tax year for four consecutive years (although if he intends such visits from the start of the period, ordinary residence may commence earlier on the same basis as in 52.3(*b*) above). (Revenue Pamphlet IR 131, SP 3/81 and Revenue Pamphlet IR 20, paras 3.4, 3.5, 3.11).

If an individual regarded as ordinarily resident solely because of the availability of accommodation disposes of it and leaves the UK within three years of arrival, he is normally treated as not ordinarily resident for the duration of his stay (assuming this is to his advantage). (Revenue Pamphlet IR 131, SP 3/81 and Revenue Pamphlet IR 20, para 3.12).

Longer term visitors—commencement of ordinary residence. The Revenue practice is to treat an individual coming to the UK but not intending to stay more than three years (and not buying or leasing for three years or more accommodation for use in the UK), as ordinarily resident from the beginning of the tax year following the third anniversary of arrival. If, before the beginning of that tax year, either there is a change in the individual's intention (i.e. to an intention to stay in the UK for three years or more in all) or accommodation for use in the UK is bought (or leased for three years or more), ordinary residence is treated as commencing at the beginning of the tax year in which either of those events happens (or from the date of arrival in the UK if later). (Revenue Pamphlet IR 131, SP 17/91 and Revenue Pamphlet IR 20, paras 3.1 and 3.8–3.11).

Education. An individual who comes to the UK for a period of study or education which is not expected to exceed four years will be treated as not ordinarily resident provided that

(i) he does not own or buy accommodation here, or acquire it on a lease of three years or more; or

(ii) on leaving the UK he will not be returning regularly for visits which average 91 days or more in each tax year.

(Revenue Pamphlet IR 20, para 3.13).

Spouse accompanying employee working overseas. See 52.5(*b*) below.

Averaging of visits to UK over a period. Where this applies in the foregoing, see 52.3(*b*) above for the Revenue's practice in applying averaging treatment.

Examples

(*Note.* After 1992/93, the case law decisions below, all of which predate 1993/94, should be read in the light of the enactment of *TCGA 1992, s 9(4)* mentioned in 52.3(*a*) and (*c*) above (no regard to be had for the purposes of *TCGA 1992, s 9(3)* to any living accommodation available in the UK for an individual's use) and the comments mentioned there made by the Revenue.)

In *Reid v CIR CS 1926, 10 TC 673*, a British subject was held ordinarily resident in the UK although she had no fixed residence either here or abroad and was regularly absent abroad for $8\frac{1}{2}$ months every year. She had here an address, family ties, bank account and furniture in store. *Levene v CIR HL 1928, 13 TC 486*, was decided similarly (British subject abroad for health reasons since 1918, no fixed residence here since (or abroad until 1925), but having ties with this country and in the usual ordering of his life making habitual visits to the UK for 20 weeks yearly for definite purposes). The judgements in this case interpreted the meaning of 'ordinarily resident' by the following phrases: 'habitually resident', 'residence in a place with some degree of continuity' and 'according to the way a man's life is usually ordered'. In *Peel v CIR CS 1927, 13 TC 443*, although the taxpayer had his business and house in Egypt, he was held ordinarily resident in the UK because he also had a house here, and spent an average of 139 days of each year in the UK.

In *Kinloch v CIR KB 1929, 14 TC 736*, a widow living mainly abroad with a son at school in the UK, who had won an appeal in previous years but continued regular annual visits, was held to be resident and ordinarily resident. In *Elmhirst v CIR KB 1937, 21 TC 381* the taxpayer was held to have been ordinarily resident although denying any intention at the time of becoming so. See *Miesegaes v CIR CA 1957, 37 TC 493* (minor at school here for five years, spending the occasional vacation with his father in Switzerland, held ordinarily resident).

In *R v Barnet London Borough Council, ex p. Nilish Shah HL 1982, [1983] 1 All E R 226*, a non-tax case, the words 'ordinarily resident' were held to refer to a man's abode in a particular place or country which he has adopted voluntarily and for settled purposes (i.e. with a sufficient degree of continuity) as part of the regular order of his life for the time being, whether of short or long duration. In *Reed v Clark Ch D 1985, 58 TC 528*, ordinary residence was held to be the converse of 'occasional residence' (see 52.3(*d*) above).

See also the cases under 52.3 above.

52.5 VISITS ABROAD AND CLAIMS TO NON-UK RESIDENCE AND TO NON-UK ORDINARY RESIDENCE

Visits abroad are broadly differentiated by the Inland Revenue as follows.

(*a*) **Visits abroad for short periods.** An individual who has been ordinarily resident in the UK is regarded as remaining resident and ordinarily resident in the UK if he only makes short visits abroad, i.e. for less than a complete tax year. (Revenue Pamphlet IR 20, para 2.1). See also 52.3(*d*) above.

(*b*) **Going abroad for full-time service under a contract of employment.** In such circumstances, where specified conditions are satisfied, the employee is normally regarded as not resident and not ordinarily resident in the UK from the day following the date of his departure until the day preceding the day of return. On his return (if at all), the individual is treated as a new permanent resident. On both occasions (going abroad and eventual return) the year of assessment will be 'split' because of the change in ordinary residence as in 52.3 above (Revenue Pamphlet IR 1, A11; see also Revenue Pamphlet IR 20, paras 2.2, 2.3).

Although the residence status of each spouse is determined independently, the following concessional treatment applies where an individual going abroad for full-time employment meets the specified conditions and is accompanied, or later joined, by his or her spouse who is not in full-time employment. Where the accompanying spouse is abroad for a complete tax year and interim visits to the UK do not amount to 183 days or more in any tax year, or an average of 91 days or more in a tax year over the period of absence (up to a maximum of four years), then the accompanying spouse's liability to UK tax which is affected by residence, for the years of departure and return at the beginning and end of the period spent abroad, is determined by reference to the period of his or her residence in the UK during the year. However, for this treatment to apply for years before 1993/94 in circumstances where accommodation in the UK was available for use by the accompanying spouse, the latter had to ensure that there were no visits to the UK between the date of departure and the following 5 April or, for the year of return, between 6 April and the date of return. In addition, for years before 1993/94, an accompanying spouse who had available accommodation in the UK was regarded as not ordinarily resident in the UK from the day after leaving the UK to the day before the date of return, provided that the absence was for three years or more and visits to the UK averaged less than 91 days in a tax year over the period of absence. If the absence abroad was expected to be for three years or more but was cut short because the period of the spouse's employment was terminated unexpectedly, the shorter absence 'might' (the Revenue do not specify further conditions so presumably 'would normally' is intended) qualify for this treatment provided that it included a complete tax year and any visits to the UK averaged less than 91 days in a tax year over the period of absence (Revenue Pamphlet IR 1, A78; see also Revenue Pamphlet IR 20, para 2.6). For the Revenue's practice in applying averaging treatment, see 52.3(*b*) above.

(*c*) **Permanent emigration for reasons other than a full-time service contract abroad.** Despite *actual* permanent residence abroad, the taxpayer may still fall into one of the *tax* residence traps in 52.3(*a*)–(*c*) above. If, e.g. on retirement abroad, he claims that he has ceased residence and ordinary residence, and requires an immediate provisional Revenue ruling to that effect, he must show, in general terms, that he has completely cut his ties with the UK (e.g. that he has taken steps to acquire accommodation abroad to live in as a permanent home, and if he continues to own property in the UK, the reason is consistent with his stated aim of permanent residence abroad; see the comments made about available accommodation in the UK at 52.3(*c*) above). If he can do this, the claim is usually provisionally admitted with effect from the day after departure and the ruling is confirmed after absence for a period including a complete fiscal year during which any visits to this country have been for an annual average of less than 91 days (for the Revenue's practice in applying this averaging treatment, see 52.3(*b*) above). If the individual cannot produce sufficient evidence to the Revenue to obtain a ruling at the start of his absence, the Revenue adopt a 'wait and see' approach for a period of three years, during which the individual's tax liabilities are computed provisionally on the basis that the individual is UK resident. That liability is adjusted, if necessary, when a final Revenue decision is made at the end of the three-year period. Again a tax year may be split as in 52.3 above if a claim for a change of status is sustained (Revenue Pamphlet IR 20, paras 2.7–2.9).

52.6 COMPANIES

Subject to *FA 1994, s 249* below, after 14 March 1988, a company incorporated in the UK is regarded for the purposes of the *Taxes Acts* as resident there, irrespective of any rule of law giving a different place of residence. [*FA 1988, s 66(1)*].

This 'incorporation' test does not, however, apply in the following circumstances.

(*a*) Where, immediately before 15 March 1988, a company was carrying on business and was not UK resident, having ceased to be so resident in pursuance of a Treasury consent given under *ICTA 1988, s 765* (or any predecessor legislation), and, where the consent was a general consent, the company was liable, by reason of domicile, residence or place of management, to tax on income in a territory outside the UK. If, after 14 March 1988, the company ceases to carry on business or, where the consent was a general consent, ceases to be taxable in a territory outside the UK, the incorporation test applies after that time (or after 14 March 1993 if later).

(*b*) Where a company which carried on business at any time before 15 March 1988 ceases to be UK resident after 14 March 1988 in pursuance of a Treasury consent, and immediately thereafter carries on business. If, after ceasing to be UK resident, the company at any time ceases to carry on business, the incorporation test applies after that time (or after 14 March 1993 if later).

(*c*) Where a company not within (*a*) above carried on business at any time before 15 March 1988, and was not UK resident immediately before that date, the incorporation test applies only after 14 March 1993.

(*d*) Where a company not within (*b*) above carried on business at any time before 15 March 1988, and ceases to be UK resident on or after that date in pursuance of a Treasury consent, the incorporation test applies only after 14 March 1993.

If a company within (*a*)–(*d*) above becomes UK resident at a time after 14 March 1988, the incorporation test applies to it after that time.

Residence for the purposes of (*a*)–(*d*) above is determined without reference to the incorporation test. [*FA 1988, Sch 7*].

A company which is no longer carrying on any business, or is being wound up outside the UK, is treated as continuing to be resident in the UK if it was regarded as resident immediately before it ceased business or any of its activities came under the control of a person exercising the functions which in the UK a liquidator would exercise. [*FA 1988, s 66(2)*].

Revenue Pamphlet IR 131, SP 1/90 clarifies the Revenue's interpretation of three points in relation to *FA 1988, s 66, Sch 7*.

(i) As regards whether a company is 'carrying on business' at a particular time, 'business' has a wider meaning than 'trade', and can include, for instance, the purchase of stock prior to trading, or the holding of investments (which could include the holding of shares in a subsidiary company, or a holding consisting of a single non-income producing investment). A company (e.g. a 'shelf' company) whose transactions have been limited to those formalities necessary to maintain its registration is not regarded as carrying on business. Where, in terms of the application of general case law to the question of residence (see below), a company can demonstrate that it is or was resident outside the UK by reference to the place 'where its real business is carried on', it will have carried on business for the above purposes.

(ii) As regards the requirement under (*a*) that a company be taxable in a territory outside the UK, the liability must be to tax on income, so that liability to a flat rate fee or lump sum duty does not fulfil the test. It is, however, satisfied where the company is within the charge to tax, even though it may pay no tax because, for example, it makes losses or claims double taxation relief.

(iii) The exceptions granted to companies who have ceased to be resident in pursuance of a Treasury consent do not apply to companies who ceased to be resident without Treasury consent but who were subsequently informed by letter that no action would be taken against them.

The Revenue set up a telephone helpline to assist companies becoming resident in the UK after 14 March 1993 under *FA 1988, s 66, Sch 7* above. The telephone number is 020–7438 7551. Alternatively, contact should be made with Inland Revenue International Division, Melbourne House, Aldwych, London WC2B 4LL.

After 29 November 1993, a company which would otherwise be regarded as resident in the UK for the purposes of the *Taxes Acts*, and is regarded for the purposes of any double tax relief arrangements within *ICTA 1988, s 788* as resident in a territory outside the UK and not resident in the UK (on the assumption that a claim for relief under those arrangements has been made and under the claim it falls to be decided whether the company is to be so regarded for the purposes of those arrangements), is treated for the purposes of the *Taxes Acts* as resident outside the UK and not resident in the UK. This treatment applies whether the company would otherwise be regarded as resident in the UK for the purposes of the *Taxes Acts* under the 'incorporation test' of *FA 1988, s 66(1)* above or by virtue of some other rule of law. [*FA 1994, s 249*].

There is no statutory definition of residence; and before the enactment of the deeming provisions described above the courts had determined that a company resides where its real business is carried on, i.e. '*where its central management and control actually abide*'. This criterion continues to apply for companies incorporated outside the UK and for companies covered by the transitional provisions of *FA 1988, Sch 7* above.

Although no general rules for determining company residence are laid down by statute, it is clear, as stated above, from case law that a company resides '*where its central management and control actually abide*' and therefore a company doing business abroad but controlled from the UK is resident in the UK subject to any overriding provisions contained in relevant double taxation agreements. In the following cases, the company was held to be managed and controlled from, and hence resident in, the UK; *Calcutta Jute Mills Co Ltd v Nicholson Ex D 1876, 1 TC 83* (UK company operating abroad but directors and shareholders meeting in UK); *De Beers Consolidated Mines Ltd v Howe HL 1906, 5 TC 198* (South African company operating there but important affairs controlled from UK where majority of directors resided); *New Zealand Shipping Co Ltd v Thew HL 1922, 8 TC 208* (New Zealand company with New Zealand directors, but overall control lay with separate London board); *American Thread Co v Joyce HL 1913, 6 TC 163* (UK company operating in USA with US directors in charge of current business, but overall control in London); *John Hood & Co Ltd v Magee KB (I) 1918, 7 TC 327* (company registered in both UK and USA, with the only director resident in USA, but general meetings and material trading activities in UK). But in *A-G v Alexander Ex D, [1874] 10 Ex 20*, a foreign state bank with a UK branch was held resident abroad, notwithstanding that shareholders' meetings were held in London.

The Revenue's approach to applying the basic test of the place of central management and control is first to ascertain whether the directors in fact themselves exercise central management and control; if so, to determine where that central management and control is exercised (not necessarily where they meet); if not, to establish where and by whom it is exercised. The concept of the place of central management and control is directed at the highest level of control of the company's business, rather than the place where the main business operations are to be found. This must always be a question of fact in any particular case, but the place of directors' meetings will usually be of significance if they are the medium through which central management and control is exercised. If, however, central management and control is in reality exercised by, for example, a single individual, the company's residence will be where that individual exercises his powers. With regard to the particular problem of residence of a subsidiary, the Revenue would not normally seek to impute to the subsidiary the residence of its parent unless the parent in effect usurps the functions of the Board of the subsidiary. Matters taken into account would include the extent to which the directors of the subsidiary take decisions on their own authority as to investment, production, marketing and procurement without reference to the parent (and see below).

In all cases, the Revenue will seek to determine whether a major objective of the existence of any particular factors bearing on residence is the obtaining of tax benefits from residence or non-residence, and to establish the reality of the central management and control (Revenue Pamphlet IR 131, SP 1/90).

Incorporation in the UK and compliance with the requirements of the *Companies Act 1985* did not in themselves render a company resident there before 15 March 1988. See *Todd v Egyptian Delta Land and Investment Co Ltd HL 1928, 14 TC 119* and cf. *Eccott v Aramayo*

Francke Mines Ltd HL 1925, 9 TC 445. A company may be resident in more than one country. See *Swedish Central Railway Co Ltd v Thompson HL 1925, 9 TC 342*, and for an authoritative discussion of dual residence, *Union Corporation Ltd v CIR HL 1953, 34 TC 207*.

A company may have a domicile (see *Gasque v CIR KB 1940, 23 TC 210*), but it would seem from the *Union Corporation* case above that, for a company, ordinary residence and residence are synonymous. In the light of *ICTA 1988, s 11* and *TCGA 1992, s 10* it would seem, anyway, that ordinary residence is not relevant to the chargeable gains of companies.

52.7 DOMICILE

An individual may have only one domicile at any given time, denoting the country or state considered his natural home. Domicile does not necessarily correspond with either residence or nationality and is essentially a question of fact (*Earl of Iveagh v Revenue Commissioners SC (RI), [1930] IR 431*). A *domicile of origin* is acquired at birth (normally that of the taxpayer's father, see below), but may be replaced by a *domicile of choice* (to be proved by subsequent conduct). A domicile of choice may be replaced by another domicile of choice (if the necessary proof is forthcoming), but if a domicile of choice is lost without another being acquired, the domicile of origin immediately revives (*Fielden v CIR Ch D 1965, 42 TC 501*).

It is normally more difficult to show the displacement of a domicile of origin than that of a domicile of choice. See *CIR v Bullock CA 1976, 51 TC 522* where a taxpayer with a domicile of origin in Canada lived in England and intended to remain here during his wife's lifetime. He was held not to have acquired an English domicile of choice (the judgements in this case give a useful review of the law relating to domicile). In *Buswell v CIR CA 1974, 49 TC 334*, the taxpayer had a domicile of origin in South Africa. He came to England to school in 1928, and was called up into the British Army during the Second World War, serving in India. On his return, he signed a written declaration that he intended to remain permanently in the UK. In 1955, he took out a South African passport. In 1961, he married an English lady and their children were brought up in the UK, though registered as South African nationals. In 1968, he and his wife visited South Africa for the first time for 40 years and, with the intention of eventually settling there permanently, bought property there in which they spent three months in each year. He was held never to have abandoned his domicile of origin. In *Re Clore (decd.) (No 2), Official Solicitor v Clore and Others Ch D, [1984] STC 609*, it was held that an English domicile of origin was never lost as, on the evidence, the taxpayer never formed a settled intention to reside permanently elsewhere. Contrast *Qureshi v Qureshi Fam D, [1972] Fam D 173*, and *In re Lawton Ch D 1958, 37 ATC 216*. Actual settlement abroad is necessary as well as intention; see *Plummer v CIR Ch D 1987, 60 TC 452*.

In *Steiner v CIR CA 1973, 49 TC 13*, a Jew who had acquired a German domicile of choice, but who fled to England in 1939 and obtained British naturalisation was held to have acquired an English domicile of choice. In *F and Another (Personal Representatives of F deceased) v CIR 1999 (Sp C 219), [2000] SSCD 1*, an Iranian who had obtained British naturalisation following the 1979 Islamic Revolution was held on the facts to have had a settled intention to return to Iran permanently and thus not to have abandoned his domicile of origin.

In determining domicile for capital gains tax on or after 6 April 1996, relevant action taken by a person in connection with electoral rights is disregarded unless otherwise requested by the person whose liability is in question. Relevant action refers to prospective or actual registration as an overseas elector or use of such vote. [*FA 1996, s 200*].

Married women. Up to 31 December 1973, a woman automatically acquired the domicile of her husband on marriage. From 1 January 1974 onwards, the domicile of a married woman is ascertained in the same way as any other individual capable of having an independent domicile, except that a woman already married on that date will retain her husband's domicile until it is changed by acquisition or revival of another domicile. [*Domicile and Matrimonial Proceedings Act 1973, ss 1, 17(5)*]. See *CIR v Duchess of Portland Ch D 1981, 54 TC 648*. But a woman who is a national of the USA and who married a man with UK domicile before 1974 will be treated (after 5 April 1976) in determining her domicile, as if the marriage had taken place in 1974. See Article 4(4) of the US/UK Double Tax Agreement and any similar provisions in double tax agreements with other countries. A widow retains her late husband's domicile unless she later acquires a domicile of choice (or reverts to a domicile of origin) (*In re Wallach PDA 1949, [1950] 1 All E R 199*).

Minors. The domicile of a minor follows that of a person on whom he is legally dependent (usually his father). Under *Domicile and Matrimonial Proceedings Act 1973, s 3* (which does not extend to Scotland), a person first becomes capable of having an independent domicile when he attains 16 (in Scotland, 14 for boys and 12 for girls) or marries under that age. Under *section 4* thereof, where a child's father and mother are living apart, his domicile is that of his mother if he has his home with her and has no home with his father.

52.8 APPEALS

Ordinary residence and domicile in relation to capital gains tax are determined by the Board. Any appeal from a Board decision is to the Special Commissioners and the normal time limit of thirty days from the receipt of written notice of the decision is extended to three months if the appeal concerns residence, ordinary residence or domicile. [*ICTA 1988, s 207; TCGA 1992, s 9(2)*]. Other disputes regarding residence are settled by appeal against the relevant assessment in the ordinary way. See generally, 4 APPEALS.

52.9 UNITED KINGDOM

The United Kingdom for tax purposes comprises England, Scotland, Wales and Northern Ireland. The Channel Islands (Jersey, Guernsey, Alderney, Sark, Herm and Jethou) and the Isle of Man are excluded. Great Britain comprises England, Scotland and Wales only.

See 44.14 OVERSEAS MATTERS for the territorial extension of the UK in certain circumstances.

52.10 IRELAND

For double taxation relief purposes a person cannot be resident in both the UK and Ireland. The residence of an *individual* is first determined under normal tax rules relating to abode, domicile etc. If this results in him being technically resident in both States the question is decided by reference successively to permanent home, personal and economic ties, habitual abode, and nationality, and if necessary is decided by agreement between the States. A *company or body of persons* is deemed to be resident where its place of effective management is situated. [*SI 1976 Nos 2151, 2152; ICTA 1988, s 68(1)–(4), s 192(1), Sch 3 para 15*]. See also 18.3 DOUBLE TAXATION RELIEF.

53 Retirement Relief

Cross-references. See 22.2 FURNISHED HOLIDAY ACCOMMODATION for application of retirement relief to such accommodation in the UK; 25 HOLD-OVER RELIEFS for interaction of retirement relief and those reliefs; 50.6, 50.7 and 50.8 REINVESTMENT RELIEF for interaction of retirement relief and the now repealed reinvestment relief.

Sumption: Capital Gains Tax. See A15.

See also Tolley's Roll-Over, Hold-Over and Retirement Reliefs.

53.1 BACKGROUND

In respect of disposals made after 5 April 1985, the retirement relief provisions in *CGTA 1979, ss 124, 125* ceased to apply and were replaced by the provisions of what are now *TCGA 1992, ss 163, 164, Sch 6*.

Under transitional provisions, where a disposal took place after 5 April 1985 but the 'qualifying period' (as defined in the current provisions) relating to the disposal ended before 6 April 1985, the provisions of *CGTA 1979, ss 124, 125* applied to the disposal. [*TCGA 1992, Sch 6 para 5(1); FA 1985, s 69(1), Sch 27 Pt VII*].

53.2 PHASED ABOLITION OF RETIREMENT RELIEF

Retirement relief is to be **abolished for 2003/04 and subsequent years**. *TCGA 1992, ss 163, 164, Sch 6* are repealed accordingly. Prior to abolition, the maximum relief available is being reduced annually in equal stages for disposals in the years 1999/2000 to 2002/03 inclusive (see 53.10 below for the figures). [*FA 1998, s 140(2), Sch 27 Pt III(31)*]. See Revenue Tax Bulletin April 1999 pp 653, 654 for examples of situations in which disposals will not qualify for retirement relief, because the requisite associated event occurs after 5 April 2003.

53.3 RELIEF FOR DISPOSALS AFTER 5 APRIL 1985

Relief is given for material disposals of business assets by individuals on retirement from their own, partnership or corporate personal (corporate family, for disposals before 16 March 1993) business provided the necessary conditions are met (see 53.5 below). In addition, relief may also be given for disposals, associated with retirement, of

(*a*) assets used in an office or employment (see 53.6 below);

(*b*) assets owned by a partner, or by an officer or employee (director only, for disposals before 16 March 1993) of a company, and used in the business of the partnership or, as the case may be, the company (see 53.7 below); and

(*c*) settled property consisting of shares or assets used for business purposes if a beneficiary has an interest in possession in the settled property (see 53.8 below).

Except in the case of a disposal made by an individual who has attained the age of 50 (55 for disposals before 28 November 1995 and 60 for disposals before 19 March 1991), relief is subject to a claim being made (under *TCGA 1992, Sch 6 para 5(2)*) on or before the first anniversary of the 31st January next following the end of the year of assessment in which the disposal occurred. Prior to 6 April 1996 the claim had to be made not later than two years after the end of the year of assessment in which the disposal occurred. In the case of a trustees' disposal, the claim (under *TCGA 1992, Sch 6 para 5(3)*) must be made jointly by the trustees and the beneficiary concerned. Where a claim is dependent upon an individual having retired on ill-health grounds below the age of 50 (55 for disposals before 28 November 1995 and 60 for disposals before 19 March 1991), the claim must be made to the Board. [*TCGA 1992, Sch 6 para 5(2)–(4); FA 1996, s 176, Sch 21 para 44(3)*].

Husband and wife. A husband and wife are each eligible for the relief if they individually meet the qualifying conditions. See also 53.10 below.

Date of disposal. For an unconditional contract this is strictly the date the contract is made but if business activities continue beyond that date pending completion of the contract, the date of completion will be accepted as the date of disposal, but *solely* for the purposes of calculating the relief (Revenue Pamphlet IR 1, D31). This treatment applies even to the extent of allowing relief where the individual's 50th birthday falls in the intervening period. It cannot, however, shift the disposal into a later tax year. (Revenue Capital Gains Manual, CG 63290, 63291). Where the concession is claimed, the completion date applies to all aspects of retirement relief including the limit of relief available (see 53.10(*a*) & (*b*) below) in the tax year of completion (Revenue Tax Bulletin April 1999 p 653).

Valuation where hold-over relief also claimed. Where the gain arising on the disposal of an asset is partly relieved by retirement relief and partly by hold-over relief, the Inland Revenue will require a valuation of the asset. However, unless the claimants request otherwise, the valuation may be deferred until either:

(*a*) it is necessary to determine the amount of retirement relief due, for example where the transferor makes another disposal which attracts retirement relief; or

(*b*) it is necessary to determine the transferee's cost of the asset.

(Revenue Pamphlet IR 131, November 1998 Supplement, SP 8/92). For further details, see 25.1 HOLD-OVER RELIEFS.

53.4 **Definitions.** The following definitions apply for the purposes of 53.5–53.10 below.

'*Business*' is not defined but is effectively limited to trades (which includes for retirement relief purposes commercial letting of FURNISHED HOLIDAY ACCOMMODATION (22) in the UK and the activities of both parties to a share farming agreement, provided the landowner takes an active part in the venture (see Country Landowners Association statement of 19 December 1991 reproduced at 1992 STI 189)), professions, vocations, offices or employments as in 53.9 below. Except as regards holiday lettings as mentioned above, retirement relief does not extend to furnished lettings (*Hatt v Newman Ch D, [2000] STC 113*).

'*Commercial association of companies*' means a company together with such associated companies (within *ICTA 1988, s 416*, see TOLLEY'S CORPORATION TAX under Close Companies) as carry on businesses of such a nature that the businesses of all the companies together may be reasonably considered to make up a single composite undertaking.

'*Family company*', in relation to disposals before 16 March 1993 and an individual, is a company where either (i) not less than 25% of the voting rights are 'exercisable' by the individual; or (ii) more than 50% of the voting rights are exercisable by the individual and his family (spouse and brother, sister, ancestor or lineal descendant of the individual or spouse) with not less than 5% being exercisable by the individual himself. '*Exercisable*' means capable of being exercised, whether in fact exercised (*Hepworth v Smith Ch D 1981, 54 TC 396*). Voting rights of trustees are included as those of a member of the family where the individual or a member of his family is a beneficiary of the settlement and no other person is for the time being entitled to receive any income or capital from the settlement or can become so entitled (otherwise than on the failure of the individual or a member of his family to become entitled).

'*Full-time working director*', in relation to disposals before 16 March 1993 and one or more companies, is a director required to devote substantially the whole of his time to the service of the company or companies in question in a managerial or technical capacity.

'*Full-time working officer or employee*', in relation to disposals after 15 March 1993 and one or more companies, is an officer or employee required to devote substantially the whole of his time (the Revenue suggests at least 75% of the company's full normal working hours where there are other full-time employees; see Revenue Capital Gains Manual CG 63621) to the service of the company or companies in question in a managerial or technical capacity. In *Palmer v Moloney and Shipleys CA, [1999] STC 890*, a case to which the Revenue were not a party, it was held by the CA, reversing the decision of the lower court, that a person who worked for a company for $42\frac{1}{2}$ hours each week qualified as a 'full-time working officer or employee'. The fact that he also spent $7\frac{1}{2}$ hours each week conducting a business as a sole trader was not material. The Revenue had already stated that, pending the final outcome of this case, they will abide by their above-mentioned published guidance (Revenue Tax Bulletin April 1999 p 653).

'*Group of companies*' means a company which has one or more '51% subsidiaries' within *ICTA 1988, s 838(1)* together with those subsidiaries.

'*Holding company*' means a company whose business (disregarding any trade carried on by it) consists wholly or mainly of the holding of shares or securities of one or more companies which are its 51% subsidiaries (within *ICTA 1988, s 838*).

'*Ill-health grounds*'. A person is treated as having retired on ill-health grounds if he has ceased to be engaged in the work previously undertaken, is incapable of engaging in that kind of work by reason of ill-health and is likely to remain permanently so incapable. Prior to 6 April 1996 it was necessary on claim to produce reasonable evidence to that effect on a claim on grounds of ill-health.

Under the rules of self-assessment the Revenue has general powers within *TMA 1970* to enquire into any return, claim or election (see 56 SELF-ASSESSMENT). If an enquiry is made into a taxpayer's claim on the grounds of ill-health, the Revenue has specific power to request that such evidence be produced. In practice, the Board will in all cases require claimants to provide a medical certificate, signed by a qualified medical practitioner. The Board will themselves take advice from the Regional Medical Service of the Department of Health and in some cases a further medical examination by the Regional Medical Officer will be required. The Board will act on the basis of the advice they receive from the Regional Medical Service (Revenue Press Release 16 April 1985). A claim for retirement relief on these grounds must be due to the ill health of the claimant: the ill health of one party cannot force the retirement of another (Revenue Tax Bulletin November 1991 p 5). For a case in which relief was refused, see *Mayes v Woods (Sp C 126), [1997] SSCD 206*.

'*Permitted period*' is a period of one year or such longer period as the Board may, in any particular case, by notice allow.

'*Personal company*', in relation to disposals after 15 March 1993 and an individual, is a company where not less than 5% of the voting rights are 'exercisable' by the individual. '*Exercisable*' means capable of being exercised, whether in fact exercised (*Hepworth v Smith Ch D 1981, 54 TC 396*).

'*Trading company*' and '*trading group*' mean a company or group whose business consists wholly or mainly of the carrying on of a trade or trades, i.e. including every trade, manufacture, adventure or concern in the nature of trade.

[*TCGA 1992, s 163(9), Sch 6 paras 1, 3, 5; FA 1993, s 87, Sch 7 paras 1, 2, Sch 23 Pt III; FA 1996, Sch 20 para 66(2)*].

53.5 **Disposals by individuals on retirement from their own or partnership business or from personal company.** Relief is given where an individual who has attained the age of 50 (55 for disposals before 28 November 1995 and 60 for disposals before 19 March 1991) or has retired below that age on 'ill-health grounds' makes a 'material disposal of business assets'.

A '*material disposal of business assets*' is one of the following.

(*a*) A disposal of the whole or part of a business (including an interest in the assets of a partnership carrying on a business) where throughout a period of at least one year ending with the date of disposal (the '*qualifying period*') the business is owned by

(i) the individual making the disposal; or

(ii) a 'trading company' which is either the individual's 'personal company' ('family company' for disposals before 16 March 1993) or a member of a 'trading group' of which the 'holding company' is that individual's personal company (family company for disposals before 16 March 1993). The individual must be a 'full-time working officer or employee' ('full-time working director' for disposals before 16 March 1993) of that company or, if that company is a member of a 'group of companies' or 'commercial association of companies', of one or more companies which are members of the group or association.

Where the business is carried on by a partnership, it is treated as owned by each partner who is, at that time, a member of the partnership.

[*TCGA 1992, s 163(1)–(3)(8), Sch 6 para 4(1)(2); FA 1993, s 87, Sch 7 paras 1, 2, Sch 23 Pt III; FA 1996, s 176*].

Disposal of 'part of a business', which qualifies for relief as above, must be distinguished from the disposal of assets of the business. In this connection, a number of cases have been heard by the courts, particularly relating to farming. See *McGregor v Adcock Ch D 1977, 51 TC 692* where a farmer sold part of his land for which outline planning permission had been obtained and was refused relief. This decision was followed in *Atkinson v Dancer; Mannion v Johnston Ch D 1988, 61 TC 598,* and see also *Pepper v Daffurn Ch D 1993, 66 TC 68* and *Wase v Bourke Ch D 1995, 68 TC 109*. In *Jarmin v Rawlings Ch D 1994, 67 TC 130*, in which relief was allowed, it was held that the taxpayer had disposed of a dairy farming business, which was 'a separate and distinguishable part' of his business. In *Barrett v Powell Ch D 1998, 70 TC 432*, it was held that a disposal of a tenancy to farm land which the taxpayer then continued to farm under a temporary licence did not qualify for relief; the taxpayer had continued to carry on exactly the same business as before, albeit more precariously. For a discussion of this topic, see Revenue Capital Gains Manual CG 63530–63543.

(*b*) A disposal of one or more assets used for the purposes of a business at the time when the business ceased to be carried on, where throughout a period of at least one year ending with the date of cessation of business (the '*qualifying period*') either the business was owned by the individual making the disposal or by a company where the conditions in (*a*)(ii) above applied. The individual must have attained the age of 50 (55 for disposals before 28 November 1995 and 60 for disposals before 19 March 1991), or retired below that age on 'ill-health grounds', on or before the date of cessation of business and the asset(s) must be disposed of within the '*permitted period*' (defined as a period of one year or such longer period as is allowed in a written notice by the Board) after that date. Where the business is carried on by a partnership, it is treated as owned by each partner who is, at the time, a member of the partnership. [*TCGA 1992, s 163(1)(2)(4)(8), Sch 6 para 4(1)(2); FA 1993, s 87, Sch 7 paras 1, 2, Sch 23 Pt III; FA 1996, s 176*].

Retirement relief was granted on the sale by an individual of land which he had rented to his family company for use for the purposes of its business (which was discontinued at the time of the sale). The CA did not consider it essential that the business for the purposes of which the asset was used had to have been the business of the individual making the disposal as opposed to its being that of a company within (*a*)(ii) above. (*Plumbly & Others (Harbour's Personal Representatives) v Spencer CA 1999, 71 TC 399*).

In practice, the period permitted after cessation will be up to three years provided the asset or, in the case of a company, any chargeable business asset retained by it at the date of cessation, is not used or leased for any purpose beyond the first anniversary of cessation (Revenue Capital Gains Manual CG 63582). See also *Taxation 27 July 1989 p 516* and Revenue Capital Gains Manual CG 63583 *et seq.* for a possible further relaxation in certain cases where assets are retained for reasons beyond the control of the individual concerned. If a business is closed down on a basis intended to be only temporary but that becomes, in the event, permanent, the date, for the purposes of *TCGA 1992, s 163*, when the business ceases to be carried on is the date on which the business is closed down (*Marriott v Lane Ch D 1996, 69 TC 157*).

(*c*) A disposal of shares or securities of a company (including a deemed disposal of an interest in shares under *TCGA 1992, s 122* as a result of a capital distribution (see 58.14 SHARES AND SECURITIES), or a distribution treated as such under ESC C16 (see TOLLEY'S CORPORATION TAX under Distributions) — Revenue Capital Gains Manual CG 63670) where throughout a period of at least one year ending with the 'operative date' (the '*qualifying period*') either

(i) the individual owns the business which, at the date of disposal, is owned by the company, or, if the company is the 'holding company' of a 'trading group', by any member of the group; or

(ii) the company is the individual's 'personal company' ('family company' for disposals before 16 March 1993) and is either a 'trading company' or the 'holding company' of a 'trading group'. The individual must be a 'full-time working officer or employee' ('full-time working director' for disposals before 16 March 1993) of the company or, in the case of a member of a 'group of companies' or 'commercial association of companies', of one or more companies which are members of the group or association.

The '*operative date*' is normally the date of disposal but there are two exceptions.

(A) If within the permitted period (as in (*b*) above) before disposal the company concerned ceased to be either a trading company or a member of a trading group (without becoming the other), and on or before the cessation, the individual making the disposal attained the age of 50 (55 for disposals before 28 November 1995 and 60 for disposals before 19 March 1991) or retired earlier on 'ill-health grounds', then, subject to (B) below, the operative date is the date of cessation. In consequence, the reference in (*c*)(i) above to the date of disposal is to be read as referring to the date of cessation of trading.

(B) If the individual ceased to be a full-time working officer or employee (full-time working director for disposals before 16 March 1993) of the company (or, in the case of a member of a group or commercial association of companies, of one or more companies which are members of the group or association) but remained an officer or employee (a director for disposals before 16 March 1993) of the company concerned (or one or more members of the group or association) and worked an average of at least ten hours per week in a technical or managerial capacity until either the date of disposal or the date of cessation of trading where (A) above applies, the operative date is the date on which he ceased to be a full-time working officer or employee (full-time working director for disposals before 16 March 1993).

Where under *TCGA 1992, s 127* a new holding would be treated as the same asset as a previous holding after a reorganisation under *TCGA 1992, s 126* (including an exchange of shares or securities treated as such a reorganisation under *TCGA 1992, s 135(3)*) the individual may elect by notice in writing on or before the first anniversary of the 31st January next following the year of assessment in which the disposal occurs for *TCGA 1992, s 127* not to apply. Prior to 6 April 1996 the election had to be made within two years of the end of the year of assessment in which the disposal occurred. [*TCGA 1992, s 163(1)(2)(5)–(7), Sch 6 para 1, para 2, para 4(1)(2); FA 1993, s 87, Sch 7 paras 1, 2, Sch 23 Pt III; FA 1996, s 176, Sch 21 para 44(2)*]. For reorganisation and exchanges of shares etc., see 58.5, 58.8 SHARES AND SECURITIES. In the Revenue's opinion an election cannot be made in respect of part only of the shares held before and concerned in the reorganisation (Tolley's Practical Tax 1986 p 166). On a reorganisation of shares into QUALIFYING CORPORATE BONDS (49.3) no such election is available as *TCGA 1992, s 127* is disapplied. However, retirement relief can be taken into account in arriving at the gain otherwise chargeable on the disposal deemed to occur on the reorganisation. Any gain remaining after deduction of retirement relief is deferred under *TCGA 1992, s 116(10)(b)* until disposal of the bonds (Revenue Capital Gains Manual CG 53867–53869).

53.6 **Assets used in an office or employment.** Relief is given where an individual who has attained the age of 50 (55 for disposals before 28 November 1995 and 60 for disposals before 19 March 1991) or has retired below that age on 'ill-health grounds' makes a 'relevant disposal' of the whole or part of the assets provided or held for the purposes of his office or employment.

A disposal is a '*relevant disposal*' if

(*a*) the office or employment was the individual's full-time occupation throughout a period of at least one year ending with the date of disposal (the '*qualifying period*'), or if the office etc. ceased earlier, before the cessation date; and

(*b*) the office or employment was not as officer or employee (as director for disposals before 16 March 1993) of his 'personal company' ('family company' for disposals before 16 March 1993) or a member of a 'trading group' of which the 'holding company' was his personal company (family company for disposals before 16 March 1993) (as this situation is covered by 53.5 above); and

(*c*) where the individual ceased office or employment before the disposal

(i) he either attained 50 (55 for disposals before 28 November 1995 and 60 for disposals before 19 March 1991) on or before the date of cessation or retired on ill-health grounds on that date; and

(ii) the disposal took place within one year of ceasing office or employment (or such longer period as is allowed by the Board; see 53.5(*b*) above).

[*TCGA 1992, s 164(1)(2), Sch 6 para 1, para 4(1)(2); FA 1993, s 87, Sch 7 paras 1, 2, Sch 23 Pt III; FA 1996, s 176*].

53.7 **Associated disposals of assets owned by a partner, or by an officer or employee of a company, and used in the business of the partnership or company.** Where relief is available to partners, or to officers or employees of personal companies (to *directors* of family companies for disposals before 16 March 1993), for a 'material disposal of business assets' (see 53.5 above) consisting of an interest in the assets of a partnership, or of shares etc. in a personal company (family company for disposals before 16 March 1993), relief is also available where the individual concerned makes an 'associated disposal' of assets.

A disposal is an '*associated disposal*' if

(*a*) it takes place as part of a withdrawal of the individual from the business carried on by the partnership or company concerned;

(*b*) the asset was in use for the purposes of the partnership or company business until immediately before the material disposal or, if earlier, the cessation of the business; and

(*c*) the asset has been used for all or part of the period in which it has been owned by the individual for business purposes (including other previous businesses carried on by the individual whether alone or in partnership or by a personal company (family company for disposals before 16 March 1993)).

The '*qualifying period*' in the case of an associated disposal is the same as that for the material disposal of business assets with which it is associated.

[*TCGA 1992, s 164(6)–(8), Sch 6 para 4(1)(2); FA 1993, s 87, Sch 7 paras 1, 2, Sch 23 Pt III*].

See 53.9 below for circumstances, including the charging of rent for the asset, in which only part of the gain on an associated disposal qualifies for relief.

In *Clarke v Mayo Ch D 1994, 66 TC 728*, Evans-Lombe J held that the words 'immediately before . . . the cessation of the business' should not be construed in isolation, but in the context of *TCGA 1992, ss 163, 164* as a whole. The words 'immediately before' could be construed as meaning 'sufficiently proximate in time to the material disposal or cessation so as to justify the conclusion that the transaction formed part of it'.

A withdrawal may be partial and is a disposal of an interest in the partnership, or of shares in the company, concerned (Revenue Helpsheet IR 289 p 2). There is no requirement that a member of a partnership should dispose of the whole of his interest in the partnership (Tolley's Practical Tax 1986 p 40). It is not necessary for the individual to reduce the amount of working time spent on the partnership's or company's business (Revenue Capital Gains Manual CG 63729).

Where the associated disposal takes place before 6 April 2003 and the material disposal on or after that date, the interaction of the above rules and the abolition of retirement relief (see 53.2 above) is such that no retirement relief can be due on either disposal (Revenue Tax Bulletin April 1999 pp 653, 654).

53.8 **Disposal of assets by trustees.** Relief is given where trustees dispose of settled property consisting of shares or securities of a company, or of an asset used or previously used for business purposes, if a beneficiary has an interest in possession (excluding one for a fixed term) in the settled property and certain conditions are met. For consideration of the meaning of 'interest in possession', see 57.7 SETTLEMENTS.

In relation to a disposal of shares or securities of a company (including a deemed disposal of an interest in shares under *TCGA 1992, s 122* as a result of a capital distribution; see 58.14 SHARES AND SECURITIES), the conditions are that

(*a*) the company was the beneficiary's 'personal company' ('family company' for disposals before 16 March 1993) and either a 'trading company' or the 'holding company' of a 'trading group' throughout a period of at least one year (the '*qualifying period*') ending not earlier than one year (or longer if the Board allow; see 53.5(*b*) above) before the date of disposal; and (*b*) the beneficiary was a 'full-time working officer or employee' ('full-time working director' for disposals before 16 March 1993) of the company (or, if the company is a member of a 'group of companies' or 'commercial association of companies', of one or more companies which are members of the group or association) throughout a period of at least one year ending as in (*a*) above; and

(*c*) the beneficiary ceased to be a full-time working officer or employee (full-time working director for disposals before 16 March 1993) on or within one year (longer if the Board allow; see 53.5(*b*) above) before the date of disposal, having attained the age of 50 (55 for disposals before 28 November 1995 and 60 for disposals before 19 March 1991) or retired earlier on 'ill-health grounds'.

Where under *TCGA 1992, s 127* a new holding would be treated as the same asset as a previous holding after a reorganisation under *TCGA 1992, s 126* (including an exchange of shares or securities treated as such a reorganisation under *TCGA 1992, s 135(3)* the trustees and the individual may jointly elect in writing, on or before the first anniversary of 31 January following the year of assessment in which the disposal occurred, for *TCGA 1992, s 127* not to apply. For 1995/96 and earlier years, the time limit was two years after the end of that year of assessment. For reorganisation and exchanges of shares etc., see 58.5, 58.8 SHARES AND SECURITIES. In the Revenue's opinion an election cannot be made in respect of part only of the shares held before and concerned in the reorganisation (Tolley's Practical Tax 1986 p 166).

In relation to a disposal of an asset, the conditions are that

(i) the asset was used for the purposes of a business carried on by the beneficiary throughout a period of at least one year (the '*qualifying period*') ending not earlier than one year (or longer if the Board allow, see 53.5(*b*) above) before the disposal;

(ii) the beneficiary ceased to carry on that business on or within one year (or longer if the Board allow) before the date of disposal; and

(iii) the beneficiary attained the age of 50 (55 for disposals before 28 November 1995 and 60 for disposals before 19 March 1991) or retired earlier on 'ill-health grounds' on or before the date of disposal or, if earlier, the date he ceased to carry on the business.

[*TCGA 1992, s 164(3)–(5), Sch 6 para 1, para 2, para 4(1)(2); FA 1993, s 87, Sch 7 paras 1, 2, Sch 23 Pt III; FA 1996, s 176, Sch 21 para 44*].

53.9 GAINS QUALIFYING FOR RELIEF

Subject to the provisions below relating to trustees' disposals, associated disposals and capital distributions

(*a*) in the case of a qualifying disposal within 53.5–53.8 above, other than one of shares or securities of a company, the gains accruing on the disposal of 'chargeable business assets' comprised in the qualifying disposal are aggregated and only the excess of those gains over 'the amount available for relief' (see 53.10 below) is a chargeable gain [*TCGA 1992, Sch 6 para 6*]; and

(*b*) where the qualifying disposal is of shares or securities of a company, the gains accruing are aggregated, and of the 'appropriate proportion' of the aggregated gains, only the excess of that proportion over 'the amount available for relief' is a chargeable gain (but not so as to affect liability in respect of gains representing the balance of the aggregated gains).

The '*appropriate proportion*' is a proportion given as follows.

(i) *For a trading company which is not a holding company*, the proportion is that which the value of the company's 'chargeable business assets' bears to the value of all its 'chargeable assets' immediately before the end of the qualifying period.

(ii) *For a holding company*, the proportion is that which the value of the trading group's 'chargeable business assets' bears to the value of all the group's 'chargeable assets' immediately before the end of the qualifying period. If a 51% subsidiary of a holding company is not wholly owned, the values of its chargeable assets and chargeable business assets are reduced in proportion to the share capital owned.

See 53.5–53.8 above as appropriate for the qualifying period.

A '*chargeable asset*' is every asset except one where a gain accruing on a disposal immediately before the end of the qualifying period would not be a chargeable gain, but a holding by one member of a trading group of the ordinary share capital of another is not a chargeable asset.

If the company or group has no chargeable assets, the appropriate proportion is the whole. [*TCGA 1992, Sch 6 paras 7, 8*].

Where the qualifying disposal is a disposal which the individual is (or trustees are) treated as making under *TCGA 1992, s 122* (see 58.14 SHARES AND SECURITIES) in consideration of a capital distribution, the recipient of the distribution can elect, by notice in writing on or before the first anniversary of the 31st January next following the end of the year of assessment in which he received the capital distribution for any asset sold not more than six months before the end of the qualifying period to be treated as remaining the property of the company and in use for the purposes for which it was used before the sale. Prior to 6 April 1996 the recipient had to make the election not later than two years after the end of the year of assessment in which he received the capital distribution. The proceeds of disposal are treated as not forming part of the assets of the company. [*TCGA 1992, Sch 6 para 12(5)(6); FA 1996, Sch 21 para 44(4)*].

A '*chargeable business asset*' is an asset which is, or is an interest in, an asset used for the purposes of a trade, profession, vocation, office or employment carried on by the individual or beneficiary concerned, his personal company (family company for disposals before 16 March 1993), a member of a trading group of which the holding company is his personal company (family company for disposals before 16 March 1993) or a partnership of which he is a member. Goodwill is included but not shares or securities or other assets held as investments. An asset is not a chargeable business asset if, on the disposal of it, any gain which might accrue would not be a chargeable gain. [*TCGA 1992, Sch 6 para 12(2)–(4); FA 1993, s 87, Sch 7 paras 1, 2, Sch 23 Pt III*].

In *Durrant v CIR (Sp C 24), [1995] SSCD 145*, it was held that all shares or securities are excluded from being chargeable business assets within *TCGA 1992, Sch 6 para 12(2)*, regardless of whether they are held as investments.

In arriving at the aggregate gains, the normal capital gains tax provisions fixing the amount of chargeable gains apply, and any allowable loss accruing on the qualifying disposal concerned is deducted. The retirement relief provisions do not affect the computation of the amount of any allowable loss. [*TCGA 1992, Sch 6 para 12(1)*].

Example

P Ltd carries on a trade of printing and bookbinding. Its directors include C who owns 10% of the issued share capital and of the voting rights. In December 2000, on reaching the age of 63, C gives his shares to his sister. At the date of transfer, the company's assets are valued as follows

	£	£	Market value £	Cost £
Leasehold printing works			190,000	50,000
Goodwill			60,000	—
Stocks of materials			80,000	75,000
Plant				
Printing presses No 1	8,000			3,000
No 2	8,500			3,500
No 3	6,500	23,000		2,000
Typesetter		10,500		15,000
Binding machine		16,500		12,000
Small tools, type etc.		7,000		10,000
Motor cars		20,000		30,000
Office fixtures and fittings (items under £6,000)		9,000	86,000	15,000
Shares in associated publishing company			60,000	40,000
Cash at bank and in hand			7,500	—
Debtors			11,500	—

The pre-tapered chargeable gain arising on the shares given to C's sister is £75,000.

The value of the company's chargeable assets is as follows

	Business £	Non–business £
Leasehold	190,000	—
Goodwill	60,000	—
Plant (£23,000 + £10,500 + £16,500)	50,000	—
Shares	—	60,000
	£300,000	£60,000

Gain eligible for retirement relief is therefore

$$£75,000 \times \frac{300,000}{300,000 + 60,000} \qquad £62,500$$

Note to the example

(*a*) Chargeable assets are all assets other than those on which any gain accruing on a disposal immediately before the end of the qualifying period would not be a chargeable gain.

Trustees' disposals. Where the disposal is a trustees' disposal under 53.8 above, and at least one beneficiary other than the one carrying on the business etc. (the '*qualifying beneficiary*') also has an interest in possession in the same property at the end of the qualifying period, only the 'relevant proportion' of the gain accruing to the trustees on disposal qualifies for relief, and the remainder is a chargeable gain. The '*relevant proportion*' is the proportion which the qualifying beneficiary's interest in the income from the settled property comprising the shares, securities or asset in question bears to the interests in the income of all the beneficiaries (including the qualifying beneficiary) who then have interests in possession in that part. [*TCGA 1992, Sch 6 para 9*].

Associated disposals. Where the disposal is an associated disposal under 53.7 above, only part of the gain qualifies for relief if (i) the asset was not used for business purposes throughout the individual's period of ownership (*Note.* In the determination of the period of ownership there is no exclusion of any period before 31 March 1982, cf. 55.6 ROLLOVER RELIEF); or (ii) during part of the period of use in a business the individual was not concerned in the carrying on of that business (whether personally, in partnership or as a full-time working officer or employee (full-time working director for disposals before 16 March 1993)); or (iii) rent (including consideration in any form) was paid for use of the asset. The part which qualifies for relief is that which is just and reasonable having regard to the lengths of the periods in question and the extent to which any rent paid was less than the open market rent. [*TCGA 1992, Sch 6 para 10; FA 1996, Sch 20 para 66(4)*]. See Revenue Capital Gains Manual CG 63836 for an example of the Revenue's interpretation of this provision. Note that the CA decision in *Plumbly* (see 53.5(*b*) above) may offer a way around the restriction in (iii) (charging of rent) in a case involving cessation of the business of the company or partnership in which the asset was used.

Capital distributions. Where a material disposal of business assets (see 53.5 above) or a trustees' disposal (see 53.8 above) is a disposal deemed to be made under *TCGA 1992, s 122* in consideration of a capital distribution, the gain on which relief may be given is restricted if the capital distribution consists wholly or partly of chargeable business assets. If the distribution consists wholly of such assets, no relief is available. If the distribution consists partly of chargeable business assets, the aggregated gains are proportionately reduced and the appropriate proportion then applied to the reduced amount. Any question as to whether a capital distribution consists of chargeable business assets is determined by reference to the status of the assets immediately before the end of the qualifying period. [*TCGA 1992, Sch 6 para 11*].

53.10 AMOUNT OF RELIEF

The basic rule. *For disposals after 5 April 1988,* 'the amount available for relief' (or more simply, the amount of relief) is the aggregate of

(*a*) so much of the 'gains qualifying for relief' as does not exceed the 'appropriate percentage' of

£50,000 for disposals after 5 April 2002 and before 6 April 2003;

£100,000 for disposals after 5 April 2001 and before 6 April 2002;

£150,000 for disposals after 5 April 2000 and before 6 April 2001;

£200,000 for disposals after 5 April 1999 and before 6 April 2000;

£250,000 for disposals after 29 November 1993 and before 6 April 1999;

£150,000 for disposals after 18 March 1991 and before 30 November 1993;

£125,000 for disposals after 5 April 1988 and before 19 March 1991;

and

(*b*) one half of any excess of such gains, up to a maximum excess equal to the appropriate percentage of

£150,000 for disposals after 5 April 2002 and before 6 April 2003;

£300,000 for disposals after 5 April 2001 and before 6 April 2002;

£450,000 for disposals after 5 April 2000 and before 6 April 2001;

£600,000 for disposals after 5 April 1999 and before 6 April 2000;

£750,000 for disposals after 29 November 1993 and before 6 April 1999;

£450,000 for disposals after 18 March 1991 and before 30 November 1993;

£375,000 for disposals after 5 April 1988 and before 19 March 1991.

No relief is available for disposals after 5 April 2003 (see 53.2 above).

'*Gains qualifying for relief*' is the aggregate amount of gains described in 53.9 above, after the application of the provisions mentioned there but before deduction of any retirement relief.

The '*appropriate percentage*' is a percentage determined according to the length of the qualifying period, rising arithmetically from 10% (the minimum) where the period is one year to 100% (the maximum) where it is ten years.

For the purposes of the above a trustees' disposal under 53.8 above is regarded as a qualifying disposal by the beneficiary. However, if, on the same day, an individual makes a material disposal of business assets under 53.5 above and is also the beneficiary in relation to a trustees' disposal, the amount available for relief is applied to the former disposal in priority to the latter.

For disposals after 5 April 1998, retirement relief is given in priority to TAPER RELIEF (60), which is thus applied to the balance of the gain after retirement relief. Where there is more than one qualifying gain and they are not wholly covered by retirement relief, that relief is to be applied in the way that then provides the maximum possible benefit from taper relief (Revenue Booklet CGT Reform: The 1998 Finance Act, paras 4.5, 4.6).

For disposals before 6 April 1988, the amount of relief was a percentage of £125,000 (£100,000 before 6 April 1987), determined in the same way as the appropriate percentage described above.

[*TCGA 1992, Sch 6 para 4(3), para 13; FA 1988, s 110(1)(2)(8); FA 1991, s 100(1)(3)(4); FA 1994, s 92; FA 1998, s 140(1)(2)*].

Example

X, who is aged 51, disposes in June 2000 of a business which he has owned for 6 years, and realises gains qualifying for retirement relief amounting to £800,000. His entitlement to relief is calculated as follows.

		£
Appropriate percentage of £150,000: 60% of £150,000		90,000
Excess of gains over £90,000:	£710,000	
Appropriate percentage of £450,000: 60%	£270,000	
Relief is available on £270,000		
Half thereof		135,000
Total relief		£225,000

Aggregation of earlier business periods. The amount available for relief may be increased where the qualifying period appropriate to a qualifying disposal (the '*original* *qualifying period*') would be less than ten years but the individual or beneficiary was 'concerned in the carrying on of another' business ('*the previous business*') in some earlier part (the '*earlier business period*') of the ten-year period up to the end of the original qualifying period. There must be no more than a two-year gap between the end of the earlier business period and the beginning of the original qualifying period. For the purposes of calculating the increase, the previous business is assumed to be the same business as the 'business at retirement', and, in the first instance, any gap between the two businesses is ignored so that the two periods are assumed to be one continuous extended qualifying period. However, this extended qualifying period is not to begin earlier than the beginning of the ten-year period ending at the end of the original qualifying period, and is then to be reduced by the gap between the businesses. Where there is more than one earlier business (and, therefore, more than one earlier business period) the provisions are to be first applied to the latest of the earlier business periods and the original qualifying period, and then to the extended qualifying period so resulting and the next latest of the earlier business periods, and so on.

The reference to a person being '*concerned in the carrying on of another business*' above is a reference to his being so concerned personally or as a member of a partnership or, if the business was owned by a company, then as a 'full-time working officer or employee' ('full-time working director' for disposals before 16 March 1993) of that company or, as the case may be, of any member of the 'group' or 'commercial association of companies' of which it is a member.

The '*business at retirement*' is a reference to the business giving rise to the qualifying disposal being one within 53.5, 53.7 and 53.8 above (i.e. the length of an original qualifying period relating to employee disposals within 53.6 above cannot be the subject of an increase). [*TCGA 1992, Sch 6 para 4(3), para 14; FA 1993, s 87, Sch 7 para 2(1)*].

In strictness, the original qualifying period must be a period of at least one year as in 53.5–53.8 above. However, with effect from 14 April 1994 for all new and still open cases, the Revenue by concession treats as a qualifying disposal a disposal which was not a qualifying disposal by reason only that the original qualifying period was less than one year. Hence any final business period can be aggregated with earlier business periods (presumably subject to the two-year gap limit mentioned above) irrespective of the length of the final business period. The concession does not mean that a final business period of less than one year is treated as a period of one year in calculating the length of the extended qualifying period (Revenue Pamphlet IR 1, D48). With effect to disposals occurring on or after 6 April 1996 ESC D48 is now included in *TCGA 1992, Sch 6 para 14.*

However, although the original qualifying period may be aggregated with previous business periods of any length, the extension will only apply if the total aggregate period exceeds one year. [*TCGA 1992, Sch 6 para 14; FA 1996, Sch 39 para 7*].

There is no specific requirement for there to have been a material disposal of business assets, a trustees' disposal or an associated disposal in connection with the previous business. If a business is owned for some period by a company which is not the individual's 'personal company', the qualifying period cannot be extended by that period. (Revenue Tax Bulletin February 1997 pp 397, 398).

Example

A owned a business for 7 years before disposing of it in 1994 when he was 48 and in good health. After a break of exactly 2 years he buys another business and runs it for 5 years before disposing of it in 2001. The percentage of the maximum relief available on the 2001 disposal is $\frac{8}{10}$ = 80% (and not $\frac{12}{14}$ = 86%).

Relief given on earlier disposals. Where qualifying disposals are made at different times, the relief available on a later disposal is restricted by reference to the relief given on any earlier disposals (including relief given under the provisions of pre-*TCGA 1992* legislation).

Relief on the later disposal is restricted to the excess of

(A) the amount of relief which would otherwise have been available if

(i) the gains qualifying for relief on the disposal were increased by the amount of the 'underlying gains' relieved on earlier disposals, and

(ii) the qualifying period appropriate to this disposal (redetermined as above for aggregation of earlier business periods) were extended by the addition of periods equal to so much (if any) of previous qualifying periods appropriate to earlier disposals not already falling within the qualifying period appropriate to this disposal;

over

(B) the aggregate amount of relief given on all earlier disposals.

The amount of the 'underlying gains' is determined in one of the following ways, according to what disposal(s) occurred.

(I) If the earlier disposal or all of the earlier disposals occurred before 6 April 1988, the amount of the underlying gains is the total relief obtained on that disposal or those disposals.

(II) If there has only been one earlier disposal and it occurred after 5 April 1988, the amount of the underlying gains is the aggregate of the relief obtained by reference to the appropriate percentage of whichever is the appropriate figure of those listed at (*a*) above (under 'The basic rule') and twice the relief obtained by reference to any excess.

(III) In cases not within (I) and (II) above, the amount of the underlying gains is calculated as in (II) above, but on the assumption that

(i) the previous disposal was the only earlier disposal, and

(ii) the totals calculated for (A)(i) and (A)(ii) above on that disposal were the gains qualifying for relief on that disposal, and the qualifying period appropriate to that disposal, respectively.

General. Where earlier disposals took place before 12 April 1978, the reference in (A)(ii) above to the qualifying period appropriate to the later disposal is to be taken as the period of ten years ending with that disposal. [*TCGA 1992, Sch 6 para 4(3), para 15; FA 1988, s 110(3)–(6)(8)*].

Example

P, who was born in 1939, carried on the following businesses, and made gains qualifying for retirement relief on disposals of them at cessation, as follows.

Business A	1.4.82 – 30.6.94	£430,000
Business B	1.4.96 – 30.6.2000	£132,000

His entitlement to retirement relief is calculated as follows.

Business A		
Gains qualifying for relief		£430,000
Qualifying period		10 years
Maximum available for 100% relief:		£
10/10 × £250,000 × 100%		250,000
Maximum available for 50% relief:		
10/10 × £750,000 =	£750,000	
Excess of gains £430,000 – £250,000 =	£180,000	
£180,000 × 50%		90,000
Relief given 1994/95		£340,000
Chargeable gain 1994/95		£90,000
Underlying gains (see (II) above) (£250,000 + (2 × £90,000))		£430,000
Business B		
(1) Before restriction applied:		
Gains qualifying for relief		£132,000
Qualifying period (extended under *TCGA 1992, Sch 6 para 14* as gap between businesses less than 2 years — see above — 10 years (maximum) less 1.75 years from 1.7.94 to 31.3.96)		8.25 years
Maximum available for 100% relief:		£
8.25/10 × £150,000 × 100%		123,750
Maximum available for 50% relief:		
8.25/10 × £450,000 =	£371,250	
Excess of gains £132,000 – 123,750 =	£8,250	
£8,250 × 50%		4,125
Relief due subject to (2) below		£127,875
(2) Applying *TCGA 1992, Sch 6 para 15* restriction:		£
Gains qualifying for relief		132,000
Add underlying gains on earlier disposal		430,000
		£562,000
Qualifying period for later disposal (as above)	8.25 years	
Extended by qualifying period for earlier disposal but up to a maximum of 10 years	1.75 years	10 years

		£
Maximum available for 100% relief:		
10/10 × £150,000 × 100%		150,000
Maximum available for 50% relief: 10/10 × £450,000 =	£450,000	
Excess of gains £562,000 – 150,000 =	£412,000	
£412,000 × 50%		206,000
		356,000
Less relief given on disposal of Business A		340,000
Relief due (as less than £127,875 in (1) above)		£16,000
Chargeable gain 2000/01 (£132,000 – £16,000)		£116,000

For further commentary and examples, see Revenue Capital Gains Manual CG 63880–63888.

Aggregation of spouse's interest in the business. Where an individual makes a material disposal of business assets (within 53.5 above) which, in whole or in part, he acquired either under the will or intestacy of his spouse or by way of lifetime gift from her, he may make a written election, on or before the first anniversary of the 31st January next following the end of the year of assessment in which the material disposal occurs for his qualifying period (which must be at least one year as in 53.5–53.8 above) to be extended by what would have been his spouse's qualifying period if the relevant conditions of ownership etc. had applied to the spouse. Prior to 6 April 1996 the election had to be made within two years after the end of the year of assessment in which the material disposal occurs. The individual and spouse must have been living together at the time of the spouse's death or lifetime gift and the whole of the spouse's interest in the business, assets, shares or securities concerned immediately before the acquisition or, as the case may be, the spouse's death, must be acquired.

Example

R acquired her late husband's 30% shareholding in X Ltd on his death in June 1996. She took over the office he had held for 15 years as a full-time working officer until, at the age of 63, she sold her shares in June 2000 incurring an otherwise chargeable gain of £198,000 (after indexation and before taper relief).

The chargeable gain is calculated as follows	£
Gain eligible for relief	198,000
Maximum available for 100% relief:	
$\frac{4 + 6}{10} \times £150{,}000 \times 100\%$	(150,000)
Maximum available for 50% relief:	
$\frac{4 + 6}{10} \times £600{,}000 = £600{,}000 - £150{,}000 = £450{,}000$	
£198,000 – £150,000 = £48,000 × 50%	(24,000)
Chargeable gain 2000/01 (subject to TAPER RELIEF (60))	£24,000

For disposals after 5 April 1988, where the acquisition was by way of lifetime gift, the amount available for relief is not to exceed the amount that would be available for relief on the assumption that the lifetime transfer had not taken place and the material disposal had been made by the spouse (to whom is attributed anything done by the individual in relation to the business concerned after the lifetime gift). *For disposals before 6 April 1988*, an alternative restriction applied if lower: namely, £125,000 (£100,000 before 6 April 1987) less any relief (including relief under earlier legislation) given on the spouse's own disposals, or on trustees' disposals where the spouse was a beneficiary, up to and including the lifetime transfer. [*TCGA 1992, Sch 6 para 16; FA 1988, s 110(7)(8); FA 1996, Sch 21 para 44(5)*].

For an indication of Revenue practice as to the application of the principles established in decided cases up to and including *Furniss v Dawson* to asset transfers between spouses made for retirement relief purposes, see ICAEW Guidance Note TR 588 25 September 1985.

54 Returns

54.1 SELF-ASSESSMENT

The obligations under self-assessment of individuals and others within the charge to capital gains tax are covered at 54.2–54.7 below. For convenience, these also cover income tax obligations to some extent, but see TOLLEY'S INCOME TAX for full coverage of those. As regards companies, see 54.11 below.

54.2 **Notification of chargeability.** For **1995/96 and subsequent years of assessment**, a person chargeable to income tax or capital gains tax for a year of assessment who has not received a notice under *TMA 1970, s 8* (see 54.9 below for 1995/96 and 54.3 below for later years of assessment) to deliver a return for that year of his total income and chargeable gains must, within **six months** after the end of that year (i.e. by 5 October), notify an officer of the Board that he is so chargeable. The maximum penalty for non-compliance is the amount of tax in which the person is assessed for that year which is not paid on or before 31 January following that year. A person is not required to give notice under these provisions if his total income for the year is fully taxed at source (see TOLLEY'S INCOME TAX for the detailed provisions) *and* he has no chargeable gains (or, in practice, no chargeable gains in excess of the annual exempt amount — see Revenue Booklet SAT 2 (1995), para 2.93).

These provisions also apply with the appropriate modifications to 'relevant trustees' of settlements (see 56.33 SELF-ASSESSMENT).

[*TMA 1970, s 7; FA 1994, s 196, s 199(2), Sch 19 para 1; FA 1995, s 103(1)(2)(7), s 115(1), Sch 21 para 1*].

The trustees of occupational pension schemes which have income or capital gains are also within these provisions (see Revenue Press Release 29 August 1997, Pension Schemes Office Update 30, 5 September 1997 and see generally Revenue Tax Bulletin February 1999 pp 628, 629).

54.3 **Annual tax returns.** For the purposes of establishing the amounts in which a person is chargeable to income tax and capital gains tax for 1996/97 and subsequent years of assessment, an officer of the Board may by notice require that person to deliver a return (i.e. a self-assessment tax return) on or before 31 January following the year of assessment or, if later, within three months beginning with the date of the notice. The return must contain such information and be accompanied by such accounts, statements and documents as may reasonably be required. The return must include a declaration that, to the best of the knowledge of the person making it, it is complete and correct. The information, accounts and statements required by the notice may differ in relation to different periods, or different sources of income, or different descriptions of person. [*TMA 1970, s 8; FA 1994, s 178(1), s 199(2), Sch 26 Pt V; FA 1995, s 103(7), s 104(1)–(3); FA 1996, s 121(1)–(3)(8)*]. Similar provisions apply in relation to returns by trustees. [*TMA 1970, ss 8A, 12; FA 1994, s 178(2), s 199(2), Sch 26 Pt V; FA 1995, s 103(3)(4)(7), s 104(1); FA 1996, s 121(1)–(3)(8)*]. See 56.23 SELF-ASSESSMENT as regards automatic and possible daily penalties for non-compliance (i.e. late returns).

Chargeable gains. Where an individual's chargeable gains for the year (before deducting any losses or taper relief) do not exceed the annual exempt amount (see 2.5 ANNUAL RATES AND EXEMPTIONS) *and* the aggregate amount of the consideration for all disposals of chargeable assets does not exceed *twice* the annual exempt amount, a statement in the self-assessment tax return to that effect complies with the above obligations so far as they relate to chargeable gains (though not so as to prejudice the Revenue's right to more detailed information). [*TCGA 1992, s 3(6)*]. Similar provisions apply as regards certain settlements for the disabled (as in 57.5 SETTLEMENTS), but apply to other settlements (by reference to reduced annual exempt amounts — see 57.4 SETTLEMENTS) only if made before 7 June 1978. [*TCGA 1992, s 3(8), Sch 1 para 1(1), para 2(3)*]. The above-mentioned statement should *not*, however, be made if a net capital loss has been incurred: a claim has to be made for such a loss to be allowable (see 39.3 LOSSES) and this requires full disclosure.

Acquisitions of chargeable assets. The notice under *TMA 1970, s 8* (or *s 8A* for trustees) may also require particulars of chargeable assets acquired in the tax year including the consideration given for them and possibly even details of the person from whom an asset was acquired. [*TMA 1970, s 12(2)(3)(5); CGTA 1979, s 157(2)–(4), Sch 7 para 1(2)(9); ICTA 1988, Sch 29 para 32; FA 1989, s 123(1)(2); FA 1990, s 90(2)(5); TCGA 1992, Sch 10 para 2(1)(3)*]. In practice though, the standard self-assessment tax return does *not* ask for this information.

See 54.7 below and 56.13 SELF-ASSESSMENT for amendments of returns and self-assessments. See 56 SELF-ASSESSMENT for, *inter alia*, record-keeping requirements and enquiries into returns.

54.4 **Form and delivery of returns.** The Board's power to prescribe the form of returns is given by *TMA 1970, s 113(1)*. The basic self-assessment tax return does not include a space to enter details of chargeable gains and allowable losses. These must be entered on supplementary pages, which form part of the return and which may come attached to it if the taxpayer has a history of making taxable gains and/or allowable losses but must otherwise be ordered, along with any required Helpsheets (see 29.4 INLAND REVENUE EXPLANATORY PUBLICATIONS), via the Revenue Orderline on 0645 000404, fax 0645 000604, between 8 a.m. and 10 p.m. seven days a week. If the statement mentioned in 54.3 above under 'Chargeable gains' can be made, it is made in the basic return, and the supplementary pages are not then required. Similarly, if the only gain arises from the disposal of the taxpayer's main residence and it is wholly exempt under the provisions in 48 PRIVATE RESIDENCES, a statement in the basic return to this effect is sufficient. Following submission of the return, the Revenue have the power, under the enquiry provisions at 56.11 SELF-ASSESSMENT, to require full details of gains and losses.

The Revenue do not require detailed calculations or supporting documents to be submitted with the return, although the taxpayer *may* provide these if he feels it necessary in a particular case to indicate how a gain or loss entered on the return is arrived at, bearing in mind the Revenue's 'discovery' powers (see 5.2 ASSESSMENTS). It is necessary in any case to indicate on the return that a valuation (for which see also 54.5 below) or an estimate has been used in calculating a gain or loss, and the return also includes space for additional information to be entered.

A return containing a provisional figure will be accepted provided that the figure is reasonable, taking account of all available information, and is clearly identified as such and that an acceptable explanation is given as to why the final figure is not available, all reasonable steps having been taken to obtain it, and when it is expected to be available (at which time it should be notified without unreasonable delay). Pressures of work and complexity of tax affairs are not regarded as acceptable explanations. If the final figure is not provided by the expected date the Revenue will take appropriate action to obtain it, which may mean opening an enquiry (see 56.11 SELF-ASSESSMENT). See Revenue Tax Return Guide and Revenue Tax Bulletins October 1998 pp 593–596 and December 1999 p 705. Note that a provisional figure is different to an estimate that will not be superseded by a more accurate figure. A return omitting a figure or stating 'to be agreed' will be treated as an incomplete return (Revenue booklet SAT 2 (1995), para 2.53).

Returns (or claims) may, in cases of physical inability to sign, be signed by an attorney acting under a general or enduring power. The attorney must have full knowledge of the taxpayer's affairs and a copy of the original power or a certified copy will need to be provided when the return (or claim) is first made. The attorney will need to be appointed under an enduring power registered with the Court of Protection (except in Scotland, where there is no such registration, and a signature of an attorney or curator bonis will be accepted) where he acts in the case of a mentally incapacitated person, for whom any receiver or committee appointed by the Court may also sign. These criteria apply similarly to any other declaration required for tax purposes. An attorney cannot sign in any case where the taxpayer is physically capable of signing, even if he is unavailable abroad. (Revenue Pamphlet IR 131, SP A13 and Revenue Tax Bulletin February 1993 p 51).

The Revenue has stated its practice concerning the acceptability of facsimile and photocopied tax returns. Whenever such a substitute form is used, it is important to ensure that it bears the correct taxpayer's reference. A facsimile must satisfactorily present to the taxpayer the information which the Board have determined shall be before him when he signs the declaration that the return is correct and complete to the best of his knowledge. It should be readily recognisable as a return when received in the Revenue office, and the entries of taxpayers' details should be distinguishable from the background text. Copies of the return forms for which a facsimile is to be produced together with an information sheet on the production of substitute forms are available from Inland Revenue, Corporate Communications Office, 6th Floor (KB), North West Wing, Bush House, London WC2B 4PP. Approval must be obtained from Inland Revenue, Corporate Communications Office, Room 9/3A, 9th Floor, North West Wing, Bush House, London WC2B 4PP before a facsimile return is used, and the facsimile must bear an agreed unique imprint for identification purposes.

Photocopies must bear the actual, not photocopied, signature of the relevant person. They are acceptable provided that they are identical (except as regards use of colour) to the official form. Where double-sided copies are not available, it is sufficient that all pages are present and attached in the correct order. Although the copying of official forms is, in strictness, a breach of HMSO copyright, action will be taken only where forms are copied on a large scale for commercial gain.

(Revenue Pamphlet IR 131, SP 5/87).

Electronic filing. For one year from April 2000, individual taxpayers who personally file their self-assessment tax return via the internet and pay any tax due electronically will receive a discount of £10 (Revenue Press Release 16 February 2000). For notes on electronic filing and payment, see Revenue Tax Bulletin June 2000 pp 757, 758 and see the Revenue's e-business website at www.inlandrevenue.gov.uk/ebu/info.htm For the pre-existing system of electronic lodgement of returns, normally by agents, see 54.16 below.

54.5 **Post-transaction valuation checks and rulings.** From April 1997 individuals and trustees may submit asset valuations used in their capital gains tax calculations to their Tax Office for checking before they make their returns (**post-transaction valuation checks**). The service is free of charge, but valuations will be considered only *after* the relevant transaction has occurred. Full information about the transactions to which they relate together with any relevant tax computations must be submitted to the Tax Office with the valuations using Form CG34.

If the Revenue agree the valuations they will not be challenged when the return is submitted unless information affecting the valuation was not provided. If the Revenue disagree the valuations they will suggest alternatives. The Revenue should be allowed a minimum of 56 days to agree a valuation or suggest an alternative. The due date for filing the return cannot be deferred.

(Revenue Press Release 4 February 1997).

The costs of obtaining post-transaction valuation checks are not deductible in arriving at the gain (Revenue Capital Gains Manual CG 15261, 16615). The service is extended to companies from January 2000 (see 54.11 below).

On written request to a person's own tax office, and free of charge, the Revenue will also give a ruling (a **post-transaction ruling**) on the application of tax law to a specific transaction. They will deal with such a request only after the transaction has been completed but whether before or (with exceptions) after the self-assessment return has been filed. Rulings can cover matters concerning income tax, corporation tax or capital gains tax. The Revenue will usually consider themselves bound by a post-transaction ruling they have given to a particular person on a particular transaction unless the information provided to them proves to be incomplete or incorrect. A taxpayer is not bound to accept the Revenue's ruling and may choose to treat the transaction differently in his tax return (subject to the Revenue's right to amend on enquiry and the taxpayer's right of appeal). The due date for filing a return cannot be deferred whilst a ruling is awaited. There are copious information requirements. Full details, including circumstances in which the Revenue will not give a ruling and issues they will not rule on, are in Revenue Code of Practice booklet COP 10.

54.6 **Self-assessments.** For 1996/97 and subsequent years of assessment, every return under *TMA 1970, s 8* or *s 8A* (see 54.3 above) must include, subject to the exception below, an assessment (a self-assessment) of the liability, based on the information in the return and taking into account all reliefs, allowances, tax credits, tax at source and tax repayments, of the person making the return to income tax and capital gains tax for the year of assessment. The Revenue's Tax Calculation Guide, which is supplied with the annual tax return, is designed to assist in the calculation of the tax liability, a separate version of the Guide being available for individuals with capital gains.

A person need not comply with this requirement if he makes and delivers his return on or before 30 September following the year of assessment or, if later, within two months beginning with the date of the notice to deliver the return. In such cases, the Revenue will make the assessment. For returns submitted outside these time limits, the Revenue will calculate the tax and make the assessment if the taxpayer fails to do so, but will not guarantee to do so before the due date for payment of tax.

Assessments made as above by an officer of the Board are treated as self-assessments by the person making the return.

[*TMA 1970, s 8, s 8A, s 9(1)–(3); FA 1994, s 179, s 199(2); FA 1995, s 103(7), s 104(4), s 115(2); FA 1996, s 121(1)–(4), s 122(1)*].

See 54.7 below and 56.13 SELF-ASSESSMENT for amendments of returns and self-assessments.

54.7 **Amendments of returns and self-assessments other than where enquiries made.** At any time within nine months beginning with the delivery of a person's return, an officer of the Board may by notice to that person amend his self-assessment to correct ('repair') obvious errors (whether of principle, arithmetical or otherwise).

At any time within twelve months beginning with the filing date (i.e. the date by which the return must be delivered, as in 54.3 above), that person may by notice to an officer of the Board amend his return and self-assessment.

However, no such amendment may be made (by the taxpayer or the Revenue) after an officer of the Board has given notice of intention to enquire into the return (see 56.11 SELF-ASSESSMENT) and before his enquiries are completed. [*TMA 1970, s 9(4)–(6); FA 1994, s 179, s 199(2)*].

The amending of a self-assessment under these provisions does not preclude the Revenue from taking penalty action under *TMA 1970, s 95* (see 56.25 SELF-ASSESSMENT) in relation to the original incorrect figures in cases where the taxpayer has acted fraudulently or negligently (Revenue Tax Bulletin October 1998 p 597).

For amendments to returns and self-assessments following a Revenue enquiry, see 56.13 SELF-ASSESSMENT.

54.8 CAPITAL GAINS TAX BEFORE SELF-ASSESSMENT

Notification of chargeability. A person chargeable to capital gains tax for a year of assessment before 1995/96 who had not received a tax return for completion, was required, within twelve months after the end of that year, to notify the Revenue of his chargeability. This did not apply for years after 1987/88 if all a person's chargeable gains for the year had been assessed. [*TMA 1970, s 7, s 12(1); FA 1988, ss 120–122*]. See 47.1 PENALTIES regarding failure to meet this requirement.

54.9 **Tax returns for 1995/96 and earlier years.** Normally soon after the commencement of each tax year up to and including 1995/96, but sometimes at a later date, return forms are issued to persons considered liable to income tax and/or capital gains tax. In theory, these have to be completed within the time stipulated (30 days) but in practice further time is allowed, but see 54.10 below. Returns must contain such information, and be accompanied by such related accounts and statements, as the inspector requires. [*TMA 1970, s 8, s 8A, s 12(1); FA 1990, s 90*].

The Revenue have issued guidance on the principles adopted in designing tax returns and determining the information which is required in them (Revenue Pamphlet IR 131, SP 4/91).

A taxpayer may use schedules to support a return but must in all cases sign the official declaration. All material in the schedules must be clearly linked to the official return form (Revenue Pamphlet IR 131, SP 5/83).

See 54.4 above for the signing of returns by an attorney in certain cases and for the Revenue's practice as regards facsimile and photocopied returns.

Particulars must also be given, *but only where requested,* of assets acquired, except for

- tangible movable assets (not part of a set, currency, or commodities on a terminal market) acquired for £6,000 or less;
- pool, betting or lottery winnings;
- government non-marketable securities;
- passenger vehicles;
- decorations for valour;
- foreign currency for personal expenditure; and
- assets acquired as trading stock.

[*TMA 1970, s 12(2)(5); FA 1982, s 81(1); FA 1989, s 123*]. For the exemptions available for the above-mentioned assets (other than those acquired as trading stock), see 21 EXEMPTIONS AND RELIEFS.

Where the chargeable gains of an individual, or a settlement for the disabled (see 57.5 SETTLEMENTS), for any year, do not exceed the exempt amount for the year (see 2.5 ANNUAL RATES AND EXEMPTIONS) and the total consideration for the disposal of chargeable assets does not exceed twice the exempt amount, a statement by the taxpayer to this effect is a sufficient return unless the inspector otherwise requires.

Where the 'grouping' anti-avoidance provisions apply to settlements for the disabled, the gains limit is reduced to the greater of ten per cent of the exempt amount for the year and the exempt amount divided by the number of settlements in the group.

In respect of settlements (other than settlements for the disabled) set up before 7 June 1978, the relevant limits are one-half of the exempt amount (gains) and the exempt amount (consideration). For settlements (other than settlements for the disabled) set up after 6 June 1978, these provisions do not apply at all.

[*TCGA 1992, s 3(6)(8), Sch 1 para 1(1), para 2(3)*].

54.10 **Late returns for 1995/96 and earlier years.** Before *TMA 1970, s 88* was amended by *FA 1989* with effect from 27 July 1989 (see 35.8 INTEREST AND SURCHARGES ON UNPAID TAX) the Revenue stated that an interest charge would be considered where, without reasonable excuse or without having been allowed an extension of time, there was a 'substantial delay' in the submission of a return (or where an incomplete return was submitted and there was a substantial delay in providing details required to complete it) if, in consequence, an assessment was made after the normal time in order to make good capital gains tax which turned out to be due. As a separate matter, the Revenue may levy penalties under *TMA 1970, s 93* or *s 94* (see 47.2 PENALTIES) (Revenue Press Release 10 May 1977 later designated as SP A14).

For failures **after 26 July 1989**, the defence of reasonable excuse or extension of time does not apply to *TMA 1970, s 88* interest (see 54.17 below). For failures at any time, the Revenue have stated subsequently that in respect of chargeable gains, a delay is regarded as 'substantial' if the relevant tax return has not been made by the later of the end of the 30-day period immediately following the date on which it is issued and **31 October following the end of the tax year in which the gain arises.** Where it is not possible to submit a return, no interest charge will be raised if the inspector is provided, within such time limits, with sufficient information to enable an adequate estimated assessment to be made, e.g. at least the sale price relating to the disposal of a chargeable asset (Revenue Pamphlet IR 131, SP 6/89).

54.11 CORPORATION TAX RETURNS OF PROFITS

Notification of chargeability. A company chargeable to corporation tax for any accounting period which has neither made a return of its profits for that period nor received a notice requiring such a return (see below) must give notice of its chargeability to the Inspector within 12 months after the end of that accounting period. [*TMA 1970, s 10(1); FA 1988, s 121*]. This requirement remains unaltered under corporation tax self-assessment. [*FA 1998, s 117, Sch 18 para 2, Sch 19 para 1*]. See 47.1 PENALTIES regarding failure to meet the requirement.

Returns under Pay and File. In relation to notices served after 31 December 1993 (and, in practice, relating to accounting periods ending after 30 September 1993; see Revenue Press Release 7 December 1992 regarding Pay and File) and if so required by the inspector, a company must make a return of such information, relevant to its corporation tax liabilities, as is required under the notice. Supporting accounts, statements and reports may also be required, although the accounts required of companies resident in the UK throughout the period to which the return relates ('*the return period*'), and required to prepare accounts under the *Companies Act 1985* (or NI equivalent) for any period consisting of or including the return period, are only those it is so required to prepare. Details of assets acquired on which chargeable gains or allowable losses may arise may also be required under *TMA 1970, s 12(2)(3)* (see 54.3 above).

The return must include a declaration to the effect that, to the best of the knowledge of the person making it, it is correct and complete. *TMA 1970, s 108(1)*, as amended by *FA 1993*, *s 120, Sch 14 para 7*, requires that person to be '*the proper officer of the company*' (i.e. the secretary of a corporate body, except where a liquidator has been appointed when the latter is the proper officer, or the treasurer of a non-corporate body) or, except where a liquidator has been appointed, any authorised person. The return must be made by the later of

(*a*) twelve months after the end of the period to which it relates,

(*b*) twelve months after the end of the period for which the company makes up accounts ('*period of account*') in which falls the last day of the accounting period to which it relates (except that periods of account in excess of 18 months are treated as ending after 18 months for this purpose), and

(*c*) three months after service of the notice requiring the return.

If the period specified by the notice for the making of a return ('*the specified period*') is not an accounting period of the company, but the company is within the charge to corporation tax for some part of the specified period, the notice is to be taken as referring to all company accounting period(s) ending in or at the end of the specified period. If there is no such accounting period, but there is a part of the specified period which does not fall within an accounting period, the notice is to be treated as requiring a return for that part of the period. Otherwise, the notice is of no effect, and the company is not required to make any return pursuant to it. For the determination of a company's accounting period, see TOLLEY'S CORPORATION TAX under Accounting Periods.

Amendments to returns must be in such form, and accompanied by such information etc., as the Board may require.

[*TMA 1970, s 11; F(No 2)A 1987, s 82; FA 1990, s 91; SI 1992 No 3066*].

Useful background information on the making of returns under Pay and File is contained in a Revenue consultative document published on 28 February 1991 and a Revenue Press Release of 7 December 1992. Reference should also be made to Revenue Pamphlets IR 126 and 128 and Revenue Tax Bulletin August 1993 pp 83–85. In addition, three substantive Revenue Statements of Practice have been issued as follows (all dated 8 October 1993).

- Revenue Pamphlet IR 131, SP 9/93 explains that, under Pay and File, an amended corporation tax return for an accounting period may be made by completing and delivering to the inspector an official corporation tax amended return form. Alternatively, a form or letter can be substituted which gives clear and sufficient information about the change, shows the tax effect of the change and includes a declaration that the information is correct and complete.
- Revenue Pamphlet IR 131, SP 10/93 (withdrawn for accounting periods ending on or after 1 July 1999) provides an opportunity for companies to use a simpler procedure under Pay and File for making or revising claims to group relief, and for giving and receiving notices of consent to surrender relief, where a group of companies is dealt with mainly in one tax district.
- Revenue Pamphlet IR 131, SP 11/93 explains the criteria the Board adopts in exercising its power to admit claims to capital allowances or group relief which are made outside the normal time limit.

Returns will also incorporate claims for group relief, capital allowances, payments of tax credits and repayments of income tax deducted from payments received. Such claims are covered in detail in TOLLEY'S CORPORATION TAX under the appropriate subject heading.

See 47.3 PENALTIES regarding non-compliance.

The Revenue will give a post-transaction ruling on corporation tax matters (see 54.5 above) but, in the case of a pre-self-assessment return, will do so only *before* the return is filed.

Corporation tax self-assessment has effect **for accounting periods ending on or after 1 July 1999** (see 56.2 SELF-ASSESSMENT). Subject to the changes in 54.14 below regarding a 'relevant statement' where a company carries on a trade in partnership, the previous requirements and deadlines under Pay and File for a company to make a return of profits remain broadly the same. [*FA 1998, s 117, Sch 18 paras 3–6, 14*]. A return *may* require details of chargeable assets acquired, with certain specified exceptions. [*FA 1998, s 117, Sch 18 para 13*]. Similar self-assessment provisions as in 54.6, 54.7 above apply, except that a company does not have the option of requiring the Revenue to compute the tax liability. [*FA 1998, s 117, Sch 18 paras 7, 8, 15, 16*]. In the absence of a return, the Revenue have power to determine the corporation tax liability. [*FA 1998, s 117, Sch 18 paras 36–40*]. An enquiry regime analogous to that in 56.11–56.13 SELF-ASSESSMENT and a record-keeping requirement as in 56.10 SELF-ASSESSMENT apply to companies. The simplified procedures for group relief, formerly in SP 10/93, are replaced and extended by statutory arrangements under *SI 1999 No 2975*. Corporation tax self-assessment is covered in TOLLEY'S CORPORATION TAX.

From 10 January 2000, the Revenue offer post-transaction (pre-return) valuation checks to companies (in relation to their chargeable gains) as they do to individuals (see 54.5 above). Form CG34 should be sent to the company's tax office together with full information about the transactions to which the valuations relate and any relevant computations. (Revenue Press Release 10 January 2000).

54.12 HOTELS AND BOARDING HOUSES

Certain details of all lodgers and persons resident in any dwelling-house, hostel, hotel, etc. must be given by the proprietor, if required by notice from the inspector. [*TMA 1970, s 14*].

54.13 ISSUING HOUSES, STOCKBROKERS, AUCTIONEERS, NOMINEE SHAREHOLDERS ETC.

Certain details of assets dealt with from issuing houses, members of stock exchanges (but not jobbers or market makers), commodity clearing houses and auctioneers must be given together with a return of the parties to the transaction, if required by notice from the inspector. [*TMA 1970, s 25; FA 1986, s 63, Sch 18 para 8*].

In respect of shares, securities and loan capital registered in the name of a person, that person must, if required by notice from the inspector issued for the purpose of obtaining particulars of chargeable gains, state whether he is the beneficial owner thereof or otherwise provide the name and address of the persons on whose behalf he acts as nominee. [*TMA 1970, s 26*].

54.14 PARTNERSHIPS

Self-assessment. The following provisions apply for 1996/97 and subsequent years of assessment or for company accounting periods ending on or after 1 July 1999 (see 13.2 COMPANIES).

Any partner may be required by notice to complete and deliver a return of the partnership profits together with accounts, statements etc. The return must include the names, addresses and tax references of all persons (including companies) who were partners during the period specified in the notice and such other information as may reasonably be required by the notice, which may include information relating to disposals of partnership property and to acquisitions (see 54.3 above). The general requirements are similar to those for personal returns under *TMA 1970, s 8* (see 54.3 above). The notice will specify the period (the relevant period) to be covered by the return and the date by which the return should be delivered (the filing date). For a partnership including at least one individual, the filing date will be no earlier than 31 January following the year of assessment concerned (normally that in which the relevant period ends). For a partnership including at least one company, the filing date will be no earlier than the first anniversary of the end of the relevant period. In both cases, the filing date will be deferred until, at the earliest, the last day of the three-month period beginning with the date of the notice, if this is a later date than that given above.

Where the partner responsible for dealing with the return ceases to be available, a successor may be nominated for this purpose by a majority of the persons (or their personal representatives) who were partners at any time in the period covered by the return. A nomination (or revocation of a nomination) does not have effect until notified to the Revenue. Failing a nomination, a successor will be determined according to rules on the return form or will be nominated by the Revenue.

[*TMA 1970, s 12AA; FA 1994, s 184, s 199(2)(3); FA 1995, s 103(7), s 104(6), s 115(4); FA 1996, s 121(6)(7), s 123(1)–(4); FA 1998, s 117, Sch 19 para 3*].

See 56.24 SELF-ASSESSMENT re penalties for non-compliance and 56.11 SELF-ASSESSMENT re enquiries into returns.

Every partnership return must include a statement (a partnership statement) showing, in respect of the period covered by the return and each period of account ending within that period,

- the amount of the partnership income or loss from each source,
- the amount of each charge on partnership income,
- the amounts of tax deducted at source from or tax credits on partnership income,
- the amount of consideration for each disposal of partnership property,

and each partner's share of each of those amounts.

Provisions similar to those in 54.7 above apply as regards amendments to partnership statements. Where a partnership statement is so amended, the partners' self-assessments will be amended by the Revenue accordingly, by notice to each partner concerned. [*TMA 1970, s 12AB; FA 1994, s 185, s 199(2); FA 1995, s 103(7), s 104(7)(8); FA 1996, s 123(5)(6); FA 1998, s 117, Sch 19 para 4*].

Where a company carries on a trade etc. in partnership the company tax return (see 54.11 above) for any period must include amounts in respect of the company's share of any income, loss, consideration, tax credit or charge stated in any relevant statement falling to be made by the partnership for a period which includes, or includes any part of, the period in respect of which the return is required. [*FA 1998, s 117, Sch 18 para 12*].

Pre-self-assessment. Under a notice given to the partners of a trading partnership, such person as was identified under rules given with the notice had to complete and deliver a return containing such information, and accompany it with such accounts and statements, as the inspector required as well as the following information.

- The chargeable gains relating to partnership property as if the partnership were itself liable to tax.
- The names and addresses of the other partners.
- The acquisition (including the name of the disposer and the consideration) of all assets as partnership property with the same exceptions as for individuals (see 54.9 above).

The Inspector could, if he thought fit, require a similar return to be made by any partner, any of the partners or all of the partners. [*TMA 1970, s 9, s 12(2)–(4); FA 1990, s 90*]. In practice, a formal return was rarely required, the submission of accounts and tax computations being deemed sufficient.

See, generally, 45 PARTNERSHIPS.

54.15 **EUROPEAN ECONOMIC INTEREST GROUPINGS**

A European Economic Interest Grouping (see 44.15 OVERSEAS MATTERS) registered in the UK or having an establishment there must make and deliver a return (through its manager or the individual representative of its manager) containing such information and accompanied by such accounts and statements as may be required by a notice given by the inspector. In the case of any other grouping, a return is required from any member of it resident in the UK, or, if none is, from any member. [*TMA 1970, s 12A; FA 1990, Sch 11 paras 2, 5; FA 1994, ss 196, 199, Sch 19 para 2*]. See 47.7 PENALTIES, 56.24 SELF-ASSESSMENT regarding non-compliance.

54.16 **ELECTRONIC LODGEMENT OF RETURNS**

Certain returns required to be made to the Board or to an officer of the Board may, subject to the conditions detailed below, be lodged electronically. The provision under which the return is required must be specified for this purpose by Treasury order, which will also appoint a commencement day. For returns under *TMA 1970, s 8, s 8A* and *s 12AA* (see 54.3, 54.14 above), the appointed day is 1 March 1997 (*SI 1997 No 57*), so that returns due from 6 April 1997 under self-assessment are eligible. Any supporting documentation (including accounts, statements or reports) required to be delivered with a return may similarly be lodged electronically if the return is so lodged (or may instead be delivered by the last day for submission of the return).

The normal powers and rights applicable in relation to returns etc. delivered by post are applied to information transmitted electronically. A properly made and authenticated hard copy (see (*c*) below) is treated in any proceedings as if it were the return or other document in question, but if no such copy is shown to have been made, a hard copy certified by an officer of the Board to be a true copy of the information transmitted is so treated instead.

There are four conditions for electronic lodgement.

(*a*) A person seeking approval must be given notice of the grant or refusal of approval, which may be granted for the transmission of information on the person's own behalf or on behalf of another person or persons. Approval may be withdrawn by notice from a given date, and any notice refusing or withdrawing approval must state the grounds. An appeal against refusal or withdrawal must be made within 30 days of such notice having been given, and lies to the Special Commissioners, who may grant approval from a specified date if they consider the refusal or withdrawal to have been unreasonable in all the circumstances.

(*b*) The transmission must comply with any requirements notified by the Board to the person making it, including in particular any relating to the hardware or software to be used.

(*c*) The transmission must signify, in an approved manner, that a hard copy was made under arrangements designed to ensure that the information contained in it is the information in fact transmitted.

(*d*) The information transmitted must be accepted under a procedure selected by the Board for this purpose, which may in particular consist of or include the use of specifically designed software.

As regards (*c*) above, the hard copy must have been authenticated by the person required to make the return:

(i) in the case of a return required by notice, by endorsement with a declaration that it is to the best of his knowledge correct and complete; or

(ii) otherwise by signature.

[*TMA 1970, s 115A, Sch 3A; FA 1995, s 153, Sch 28; FA 1998, s 117, Sch 19 para 43*].

Agents may pre-register for the electronic lodgement service. Copies of an information pack and registration form are available from the Agent Educator in all local tax offices. Revenue Pamphlet IR 131, SP 1/97 describes how the Revenue will operate electronic lodgement and the detailed requirements.

The above provisions are to be repealed from a date (or dates) to be appointed, but only to be replaced by similar rules, with appropriate modifications, under the provisions at 27.9 INLAND REVENUE: ADMINISTRATION. [*FA 1999, s 133(3)(4)*].

54.17 REASONABLE EXCUSE (GENERAL)

It is generally provided for the purposes of *TMA 1970* that a person is deemed not to have failed to do anything required to be done where there was a reasonable excuse for the failure and, if the excuse ceased, provided that the failure was remedied without unreasonable delay after the excuse had ceased. Similarly, a person is deemed not to have failed to do anything required to be done within a limited time if he did it within such further time as the Board, or the Commissioners or officer concerned, may have allowed. [*TMA 1970, s 118(2); F(No 2)A 1987, s 94*]. For failures after 26 July 1989, this provision did not apply for the purposes of *TMA 1970, s 88* — see 35.8 INTEREST AND SURCHARGES ON UNPAID TAX (and see 54.10 above as regards late returns for years before self-assessment applies). [*TMA 1970, s 88(7); FA 1989, s 159(1)(3)(4)*]. Consideration of what constitutes a reasonable excuse was made in *R v Sevenoaks Commrs, ex p. Thorne; Thorne v Sevenoaks Commrs & CIR, Ch D & QB 1989, 62 TC 341* which was concerned with the provision in 35.8 INTEREST AND SURCHARGES ON UNPAID TAX prior to 27 July 1989.

Under self-assessment of income tax and capital gains tax, there are separate 'reasonable excuse' let-outs as regards penalties for late returns (see 56.23 SELF-ASSESSMENT) and surcharges for late payment of tax (see 35.5 INTEREST AND SURCHARGES ON UNPAID TAX).

55 Rollover Relief—Replacement of Business Assets

Cross-references. See 8.12 ASSETS HELD ON 31 MARCH 1982 for 50% relief on rolled over gains relating to an asset acquired before 31 March 1982; 19.27 EMPLOYEE SHARE SCHEMES for application of rollover relief in relation to certain disposals to employee share ownership trusts; 22.2 FURNISHED HOLIDAY ACCOMMODATION for application of rollover relief to such accommodation in the UK; 25 HOLD-OVER RELIEFS generally; 36.11 and 36.12 LAND for rollover relief on compulsory purchase of land and exchanges of joint interests in land (including milk and potato quotas in certain cases) respectively; 43.2 OFFSHORE SETTLEMENTS for disapplication of rollover relief where trustees cease to be UK-resident or liable to UK tax; 44.3, 44.12 and 44.14 OVERSEAS MATTERS for restriction on rollover relief in certain cases; 60.14 TAPER RELIEF.

Sumption: Capital Gains Tax. See A14.01.

See also Tolley's Roll-over, Hold-over and Retirement Reliefs.

55.1 NATURE OF RELIEF

If the consideration which a person carrying on a trade obtains for the disposal of, or of his interest in, assets ('*the old assets*') used, and used only, for the purposes of the trade throughout the 'period of ownership' (which, for disposals after 5 April 1988, excludes any period before 31 March 1982) is applied by him, within a specified period — see below, in acquiring other assets, or an interest in other assets ('*the new assets*') which on the acquisition are taken into use, and used only, for the purposes of the trade, and the old assets and the new assets are within the classes of assets listed in *TCGA 1992, s 155* (see 55.3 below), then the person carrying on the trade is, on making a claim as respects the consideration which has been so applied, treated for the purposes of *TCGA 1992*

(*a*) as if the consideration for the disposal of, or of the interest in, the old assets were (if otherwise of a greater amount or value) of such an amount as would secure that on the disposal neither a gain nor a loss accrues to him, and

(*b*) as if the amount or value of the consideration for the acquisition of, or of the interest in, the new assets were reduced by the excess of the amount or value of the actual consideration for the disposal of, or of the interest in, the old assets over the amount of the consideration which he is treated as receiving under (*a*) above.

The treatment in (*a*) and (*b*) above does not affect the treatment for the purposes of *TCGA 1992* of the other party to the transaction involving the old assets, or of the other party to the transaction involving the new assets. [*TCGA 1992, s 152(1)(9)*].

The relief given under (*a*) and (*b*) above applies in relation to a person who, either successively or at the same time, carries on two or more trades as if both or all of them were a single trade. [*TCGA 1992, s 152(8)*]. For consideration of this provision and activities other than trades, see 55.4 below.

Partial relief is available in certain circumstances. See 55.6 below.

Where (*a*) above applies to exclude a gain which, in consequence of *TCGA 1992, Sch 2* (ASSETS HELD ON 6 APRIL 1965 (7)), is not all chargeable gain, the amount of the reduction to be made under (*b*) above is the amount of the chargeable gain, and not the whole amount of the gain. [*TCGA 1992, s 152(2)*].

The old assets must actually be used for the trade in question, any original intention for such use being ignored. Relief was refused where land was purchased on which it was proposed to build a factory for use in the taxpayer's trade but was sold without the factory being built (*Temperley v Visibell Ltd Ch D 1973, 49 TC 129*). Subject to concessionary treatment as in 55.3 below, the new assets must be taken into trading use immediately on acquisition, and not as soon as reasonably practicable after acquisition, again any original intention to attempt at immediate use being ignored (*Campbell Connelly & Co. Ltd v Barnett CA 1993,66 TC 380*). In this case the taxpayer company (C Ltd) claimed relief in respect of a gain accruing from the sale in 1984 of its trading premises, the sale taking place shortly after C Ltd had become a wholly-owned subsidiary of M Ltd. C Ltd and M Ltd henceforth traded from premises already occupied by M Ltd. In January 1986 C Ltd acquired the freehold interest in a new property but it was not until September 1986 that C Ltd and M Ltd were able to occupy and use it for trading purposes because the property was subject to both a headlease and an underlease to two third parties. Occupation and use was only possible after M Ltd had acquired in September 1986 the underlease for a capital sum. During the period from January 1986 to September 1986 C Ltd received rent from the lessee whilst from September 1986 to November 1987, when the headlease was itself surrendered, M Ltd paid a slightly higher rent to the lessee. Although it had been the intention to acquire the freehold interest in, and vacant possession of, the new property at the same time, relief was refused in relation to C Ltd's claim to roll over the gain into the freehold interest acquisition. It was held that the words 'which on the acquisition are taken into use, and used only for the purposes of the trade' referred to the acquisition of the assets (and *not* to an interest in them) mentioned in the phrase which occurs earlier in *TCGA 1992, s 152(1)* 'If the consideration . . . is applied by him in acquiring other assets'. In addition *TCGA 1992, s 152* only covered one acquisition by one person; it could not be extended to cover two different interests in the same asset being acquired by two different legal persons at different times. *Obiter dicta* of Knox J in the Ch D suggests that the time of acquisition and disposal for the purposes of *TCGA 1992, s 152* is the date of transfer or conveyance, and not the date of the contract (cf. *TCGA 1992, s 28* at 17.2 DISPOSAL).

For convenience, references in the rest of this chapter to the acquisition or disposal of an asset can be taken to include references to the acquisition or disposal of an interest in that asset except where the context requires otherwise.

The Revenue has indicated that in its view the wording of *TCGA 1992, s 152(1)*, which states that 'if the consideration which a person . . . obtains for the disposal of . . . assets . . . is applied by him in acquiring other assets', simply requires the taxpayer to reinvest an amount equal to the proceeds received. It also sees no reason why in principle relief should not be available where the acquisition consideration is satisfied by the issue of shares by a company (Institute of Taxation TIR/11/91, 1991 STI 1097).

In *Watton v Tippett CA 1997, 69 TC 491*, a trader made a part disposal of some business premises and attempted unsuccessfully to roll over the gain against the previous acquisition of the part of those premises still retained. It was held that the premises had been acquired as, and until the part disposal continued to be, a single asset, and that the acquisition cost could not be divided between the part of the premises sold and the part retained and treated as having been given for two separate assets.

The Revenue have confirmed the relief is available where assets are exchanged (CCAB Statement TR 508 9 June 1983). Where land or other assets used for the purposes of a trade carried on in partnership are partitioned by the partners, the asset acquired is treated as a newly acquired asset provided the partnership is dissolved immediately thereafter (Revenue Pamphlet IR 1, D23).

Relief is denied if the acquisition of the new assets was made wholly or partly for the purpose of realising a gain from their subsequent disposal. [*TCGA 1992, s 152(5)*].

Time limit for replacement of assets. The acquisition of the new assets must take place **within one year before, or three years after**, the disposal of the old assets, though the Revenue may allow further time where the trader can show that there was a firm intention to acquire new assets within the time limit but was prevented from doing so by circumstances outside his control (Revenue Tax Bulletin November 1991 p 5 and see Revenue Capital Gains Manual CG 60640). The Revenue seems prepared to extend this treatment even though an asset qualifying for rollover relief is acquired within the statutory time limit but which the taxpayer chooses not to make the subject of a claim (Institute of Taxation TIR/11/91, 1991 STI 1097). It is sufficient if an unconditional contract for acquisition is entered into within the specified periods; but adjustments are made, without time limit, if the contract is not completed. [*TCGA 1992, s 152(3)(4)*]. See also the *obiter dicta* of Knox J in *Campbell Connelly & Co. Ltd v Barnett* above. The non-exercise of the Revenue's statutory discretion to extend the time limit may be challenged by judicial review but cannot be reviewed by the Appeal Commissioners (*Steibelt v Paling Ch D 1999, 71 TC 376*).

Example

L Ltd carries on a vehicle repair business. In December 1998 it sells a workshop for £90,000 net of costs. The workshop had cost £45,000 inclusive in April 1991. A new workshop is purchased for £144,000 (including incidental costs of acquisition) in January 1999 and sold for £168,000 in January 2001.

Indexation factors: April 1991 to December 1998	0.235
January 1999 to January 2001 (estimated)	0.050

L Ltd claims rollover of the chargeable gain.

	£
Allowable cost of original workshop	45,000
Indexation allowance £45,000 × 0.235	10,575
	55,575
Actual disposal consideration	90,000
Chargeable gain rolled over	£34,425
Cost of new workshop	144,000
Deduct amount rolled over	34,425
Deemed allowable cost	£109,575
Disposal consideration, replacement workshop	168,000
Allowable cost	109,575
Unindexed gain	58,425
Indexation allowance £109,575 × 0.050	5,479
Chargeable gain	£52,946

Trade carried on by individual's personal company etc. In relation to a case where

(i) the person disposing of the old assets and acquiring the new assets is an individual, and

(ii) the trade or trades in question are carried on not by that individual but by a company, which, both at the time of disposal and at the time of the acquisition referred to in (i) above, is his 'personal company' ('family company' for disposals before 16 March 1993), within the meaning of *TCGA 1992, Sch 6* (see 53.4 RETIREMENT RELIEF),

any reference in *TCGA 1992, ss 152–156* (see 55.3, 55.4, 55.6 and 55.7 below) to the person carrying on the trade includes a reference to that individual. [*TCGA 1992, s 157; FA 1993, s 87, Sch 7 para 1, Sch 23 Pt III*].

In correspondence the Revenue have expressed the view that *TCGA 1992, s 157* does not extend to the acquisition of a new asset for use by a subsidiary of a personal company (family company for disposals before 16 March 1993) carrying on a trade or trades where the old asset was disposed of by the personal company (family company for disposals before 16 March 1993) (and vice versa). Assets must be disposed of and acquired by the individual for use by the same personal company (family company for disposals before 16 March 1993) (although relief in relation to use by such a company may not be precluded if contemporaneous use is made by one or more subsidiaries of the company) and the provisions of *TCGA 1992, s 175(1)* (see 55.5 below) do not extend to the position of regarding all companies within a group as one taxable entity. The payment of rent to the individual by the company concerned for the use of property will not debar relief under *TCGA 1992, s 157*. In addition, the occupancy test of *TCGA 1992, s 155* for land and buildings (see 55.3 below) may be met by either the individual or the company concerned, so the existence of a lease or tenancy (whether or not with consideration passing), or consideration passing, will not prevent relief under *TCGA 1992, s 157*. The position here should be contrasted with a claim under *TCGA 1992, s 158(1)(c)* by an employee to which Revenue Pamphlet IR 131, SP 5/86 applies (see 55.4 below). It is not possible to 'mix' claims under *TCGA 1992, s 157* and *s 158(1)(c)* (e.g. the disposal of land owned by an individual but occupied and used exclusively for the purposes of a trade carried on by his personal company (family company for disposals before 16 March 1993) cannot be rolled over into his acquisition of land which is to be occupied and used by him exclusively as an employee of the same company). See also Institute of Taxation TIR/11/91, 1991 STI 1097, for confirmation of these points.

It should be noted that *TCGA 1992, s 157* does not require the individual to be a 'full-time working officer or employee' ('full-time working director' for disposals before 16 March 1993) (see 53.4 RETIREMENT RELIEF and 55.4 below).

Partnerships. Relief is available to the owner of assets let to a trading or professional partnership of which he is a member, provided they are used for the purposes of the partnership's trade or profession (Revenue Pamphlet IR 131, SP D11). See also 45.5 PARTNERSHIPS as regards disposals by partners and 45.12 as regards mergers of partnerships and 55.5 below for partnerships involving a member of a group of companies.

Interaction with other provisions. Any provision which fixes the amount of consideration deemed to be given for the acquisition or disposal of assets is applied before operating the relief. [*TCGA 1992, s 152(10)*]. The Revenue has been asked its views on whether relief can be claimed where a gain arises on a simple gift and where an asset is appropriated from 'capital' to 'trading stock' within *TCGA 1992, s 161(1)*. It replied that in its view gifts of assets were within *TCGA 1992, s 152(10)*. Where the other conditions for relief were met, relief will be available based on the amount of the consideration deemed to have been received under other provisions of *TCGA 1992*. It does not, however, regard relief as available where there is a deemed disposal and reacquisition of the same asset (Institute of Taxation TIR/11/91, 1991 STI 1097).

Where the disposal of an asset to a company qualifies for relief both under *TCGA 1992, s 152* and *s 162* (transfer of a business to a company; see 25.10 HOLD-OVER RELIEFS), the Revenue has stated that it will in practice ignore the mandatory nature of the latter relief and allow the former provided qualifying assets are acquired subsequently and within the usual time limits (Institute of Taxation TIR/11/91, 1991 STI 1097). See further, Revenue Capital Gains Manual CG 61560–61562.

For the application of the relief to groups of companies, see 55.5 below. Rollover relief is not available where one company makes a disposal and an associated company makes an acquisition (*Joseph Carter & Sons Ltd v Baird; Wear Ironmongers & Sons Ltd v Baird Ch D 1998, [1999] STC 120*).

For an indication of Revenue practice as to the application of the principles established in decided cases up to and including *Furniss v Dawson* to asset transfers between spouses made for rollover purposes, see ICAEW Guidance Note TR 588, 25 September 1985.

Rollover relief for gains on company shareholdings. The Government is consulting on the possibility of introducing a rollover relief for gains on substantial shareholdings held by companies in trading companies or holding companies of trading groups, with a view to including legislation in Finance Act 2001. It is suggested that shareholdings in excess of 30% might qualify. (Revenue News Release BN2C). The Revenue have published a technical note on these proposals (Revenue Press Release 23 June 2000).

55.2 CLAIMS FOR RELIEF

A claim for rollover relief relates to both a disposal and an acquisition of assets and so cannot be made until both have occurred (but see below re provisional claims under self-assessment).

Form of claim. A claim for relief must be made in writing and must specify:

- the identity of the claimant;
- the assets which have been disposed of;
- the date of disposal of each of those assets;
- the consideration received for the disposal of each of those assets;
- the assets which have been acquired;
- the date of acquisition of each of those assets or the dates on which unconditional contracts for the acquisition of each of those assets were entered into;
- the consideration given for each of those assets; and
- the amount of the consideration received for the disposal of each of the specified assets which has been applied in the acquisition of each replacement asset.

(Revenue Press Release 29 November 1994 and Revenue Helpsheet IR 290).

Before 29 November 1994, it was sufficient to indicate unambiguously to the Inspector that a gain was to be rolled over (Revenue Capital Gains Manual CG 60608).

As regards 1996/97 onwards, Revenue Helpsheet IR 290 (Business Asset Rollover Relief) contains a form on which an individual may make a claim. The completed form can be attached to the Capital Gains supplementary pages of the self-assessment tax return.

Where the disposal is made by one group company and the acquisition made by another (see 55.5 below), a rollover relief claim made on or after 29 November 1994 must be made by both companies. [*TCGA 1992, s 175(2A); FA 1995, s 48(1)(3)(4)*].

Time limits for claims. As no time limit is specified, the general time limits in *TMA 1970, s 43* apply (see 12.5 CLAIMS). For rollover relief purposes, the period of time allowed for the making of a claim (six years for companies and approximately five years ten months for other persons from 1996/97 — previously six years) begins with the *later* of

- the end of the year of assessment or company accounting period in which the disposal takes place, and
- the end of the year of assessment or company accounting period in which the new assets are acquired.

A claim to relief is not prevented by the finality of an assessment on chargeable gains. (Revenue Capital Gains Manual CG 60600).

Provisional claims. It would have been anomalous to require a taxpayer, who intended to roll over gains, to pay the tax on those gains under self-assessment and thus reduce the funds available to invest in the new assets. Provisional rollover relief claims have therefore been made possible for disposals after 5 April 1996 for capital gains tax purposes and in company accounting periods ending on or after 1 July 1999 (the commencement date for corporation tax self-assessment — see 13.2 COMPANIES) as outlined below.

The claimant may make a declaration in his tax return for a tax year or company accounting period in which he has made a disposal of qualifying assets (see 55.3 below) that the whole or a specified part of the consideration will be invested, within the requisite time limits (see 55.1 above), in qualifying assets which on acquisition will be taken into use exclusively for the purposes of the trade. The form in Revenue Helpsheet IR 290 referred to above may be used by an individual for this purpose. As long as the declaration continues to have effect, the same consequences ensue as if both an acquisition and a valid rollover relief claim had been made. The declaration ceases to have effect on the day, and to the extent that, it is withdrawn or is superseded by a valid claim, if either occurs before the 'relevant day'. It otherwise ceases to have effect on the relevant day itself. On its ceasing to have effect, all necessary adjustments will be made to the claimant's tax position, even if they would otherwise be out of time.

The '*relevant day*' means

- in relation to capital gains tax, the third anniversary of 31 January following the tax year of disposal, e.g. 31 January 2003 for disposals in 1998/99; and
- in relation to corporation tax, the fourth anniversary of the last day of the accounting period of disposal.

[*TCGA 1992, s 153A; FA 1996, s 121(8), s 141(2)*].

To the extent that a provisional claim is withdrawn or lapses, interest on unpaid tax is chargeable as if no such claim had been made. There is nothing to prevent a valid claim subsequently being made if new assets are acquired either within the normal time limit or within such further time as may be allowed by the Revenue (see 55.1 above). However, no application for postponement of tax will be allowed (Revenue Capital Gains Manual CG 60707).

As regards disposals in 1995/96 and earlier years for capital gains tax or in company accounting periods ending before 1 July 1999, the Revenue will assess gains at the normal time regardless of the potential for the making of a claim to roll over those gains against assets still to be acquired. It is, however, open to the taxpayer to apply for postponement of tax (see 46.3 PAYMENT OF TAX) and Inspectors are instructed to accept such applications if the taxpayer can demonstrate an intention to acquire a qualifying asset shortly after the normal payable date for the tax and within the normal three-year time limit (see 55.1 above). (Revenue Capital Gains Manual CG 60690, 60691).

55.3 QUALIFYING ASSETS

Subject to the overriding requirement of use for the purposes of a trade as specified in *TCGA 1992, s 152(1)* in 55.1 above, qualifying assets, for the purpose of relief under that provision, are divided into the classes listed below (the Treasury having power to specify additional classes). Both the old and the new assets must fall within these classes though not necessarily within the same class. The classes are as follows.

1. (*a*) Land, buildings (including parts thereof) and any permanent or semi-permanent structures in the nature of buildings, all such assets being occupied (as well as used) only for the purposes of the trade. A lessor of tied premises, within *ICTA 1988, s 98*, is treated as occupying (as well as using) those

premises for the purposes of the trade (to the extent that the conditions of *ICTA 1988, s 98(1)* are met in relation to the premises). See also 55.4 below where the trade involves dealing in or developing land, etc.

(*b*) Fixed plant or machinery (see *Williams v Evans Ch D, 1982, 59 TC 509*, and Tolley's Practical Tax 1983 p 211) which does not form part of a building or of a permanent or semi-permanent structure in the nature of a building.

2. Ships, aircraft and hovercraft.
3. Satellites, space stations and spacecraft (including launch vehicles).
4. Goodwill. See Revenue Capital Gains Manual CG 68000–68976 for consideration of what constitutes goodwill. See also *Kirby v Thorn EMI plc CA 1987, 60 TC 519*.
5. (*a*) 'Milk quotas'; i.e. rights to sell dairy produce without liability to pay milk levy, or to deliver dairy produce without liability to pay a milk levy contribution (see also 6.6 ASSETS).

   (*b*) 'Potato quotas'; i.e. rights to produce potatoes without liability to pay more than the ordinary contribution to the Potato Marketing Board's fund.
6. 'Ewe and suckler cow premium quotas', i.e. rights in respect of any ewes or suckler cows to receive payments by way of any subsidy entitlement to which is determined by reference to limits contained in a European Community instrument.
7. Fish quota, i.e. an allocation of quota to catch fish stocks, which derives from the Total Allowable Catches set in pursuance of specified European Community instruments (see also below). This class qualifies where the old asset is fish quota and the disposal date is after 28 March 1999, where the new asset is fish quota and the acquisition date is after 28 March 1999 and where both old and new assets are fish quota and both disposal and acquisition take place after 28 March 1999. See also below for earlier concessional treatment.
8. (*a*) Syndicate rights of an underwriting member of Lloyd's (see 63.8 UNDERWRITERS AT LLOYD'S) acquired or disposed of after 5 April 1999.

   (*b*) Syndicate rights of an individual (i.e. non-corporate) underwriting member of Lloyd's held through a Members' Agent Pooling Arrangement (MAPA) and treated by *FA 1999, s 82* as a single asset (see 63.9 UNDERWRITERS AT LLOYD'S). Assets under this heading qualify where acquired or disposed of after 5 April 1999: (it is thought that post-5 April 1999 enhancement expenditure must also qualify — by virtue of ESC D22 (see below)).

[*TCGA 1992, s 155, s 156(1)(4); FA 1993, s 86; FA 1998, s 41(2); FA 1999, s 84; SI 1999 No 564*].

As regards disposals and acquisitions thereof before 1 July 1999, except as affects the determination of any Commissioners or the judgement of any court made or given before 14 May 1987, a UK oil licence under *Petroleum Act 1998, Pt I* (or earlier corresponding legislation) or under *Petroleum (Production) Act (Northern Ireland) 1964* was not (and was assumed never to have been) an asset falling within any of the classes above. [*TCGA 1992, s 193; Petroleum Act 1998, Sch 4 para 32; FA 1999, s 103*].

Fish quota (see Class 7 above) are amounts of various types of fish that are allocated by the EU to the UK and sub-allocated to UK fishermen according to rules prescribed by the Fisheries Departments. They are one of a number of items that may be involved in a disposal of a fishing vessel (and may be disposed of separately in certain circumstances). The vessel itself is a qualifying asset for rollover relief. A fishing vessel licence and a 'track record' (being the amount of particular stocks of fish caught in previous years) are separate chargeable assets; each is treated as constituting goodwill and thus eligible for rollover relief in its own right. Fish quota is also a separate chargeable asset but is not regarded as goodwill. However, prior to the addition of fish quota to the above classes of qualifying assets, the Revenue will by concession treat sales of fish quota as qualifying for rollover relief on a similar basis as a licence and track record. (Revenue Press Release 2 March 1999).

Where a building is rebuilt after having been destroyed by fire, gains on other assets may be rolled over into the cost of rebuilding (subject to any claim made under *TCGA 1992, s 23* in respect of insurance proceeds, see 17.8 and 17.9 DISPOSAL and CCAB Statement TR 508 9 June 1983). Capital expenditure to enhance the value of other assets already held is treated for rollover relief purposes as incurred in *acquiring* other assets provided the other assets are used only for the purposes of the trade or, on completion of the enhancement work, the assets are immediately taken into use and used only for the purposes of the trade. An extension to this treatment was announced in a Revenue Press Release of 12 May 1995 so that it is also applied for the purposes of *TCGA 1992, Sch 4* (deferred charges on gains before 31 March 1982; see 8.12 ASSETS HELD ON 31 MARCH 1982) (Revenue Pamphlet IR 1, D22). Similar treatment is given where a *further* interest is acquired in another asset which is already in use for the purposes of the trade (Revenue Pamphlet IR 1, D25). An asset which is repurchased for purely commercial reasons after having been sold as part of a business will be treated as the 'new asset' for the purposes of the relief (Revenue Pamphlet IR 1, D16). (See 3.23 ANTI-AVOIDANCE for the charge arising where concessions involving deferral of gains are abused.)

Where a new asset is not, on acquisition, immediately taken into use for the purposes of a trade it will nevertheless qualify for relief provided

(*a*) the owner proposes to incur capital expenditure for the purpose of enhancing its value;

(*b*) any work arising from such capital expenditure begins as soon as possible after acquisition, and is completed within a reasonable time;

(*c*) on completion of the work the asset is taken into use for the purpose of the trade and for no other purpose; and

(*d*) the asset is not let or used for any non-trading purpose in the period between acquisition and the time it is taken into use for the purposes of the trade.

Where a person acquires land with a building on it, or with the intention to construct a building on it, the land is treated as qualifying for (*a*)–(*d*) above provided that the building itself qualifies for relief whether under (*a*)–(*d*) above or otherwise and provided that the land is not let or used for any non-trading purpose between its acquisition and the time that both it and the building are taken into use for the purposes of the trade (Revenue Pamphlet IR 1, D24). The Revenue have stated that, in some circumstances, relief would not be denied, where the asset is not ready to be taken into use immediately, solely on the grounds that it was not brought into use as soon as acquired, provided that all reasonable steps are taken to make it ready and that it is then brought into use without unnecessary delay (Revenue Tax Bulletin November 1991 p 5). It is not clear to what extent, if any, this last statement extends the scope of ESC D24. It is difficult too, to reconcile both treatments with the Revenue's arguments in the case of *Campbell Connelly & Co Ltd v Barnett CA 1993, 66 TC 380* mentioned at 55.1 above. In *Steibelt v Paling Ch D 1999, 71 TC 376*, Sir Richard Scott V-C commented that on the facts of the case the taxpayer had failed to comply with condition (*b*) above.

Buildings and structures (but not normally including dwelling-houses) provided by a trader for the welfare of employees, though qualifying for industrial building allowances under *CAA 1990, s 18(1)(4)(5)* are technically outside the scope of rollover relief, not being used exclusively for the purposes of the trade. Similar observations can be made in respect of agricultural buildings (which may include dwellings) and agricultural building allowances under *CAA 1990, s 122(1), s 123*. It is understood that the Revenue may not always, in practice, take this point. (In *Anderton v Lamb Ch D 1980, 55 TC 1*, it was held that houses occupied by farm employees were not *occupied for the purposes of the business*, and, therefore, were not qualifying assets. The taxpayer appealed to the CA where the appeal was stayed on agreed terms: see *1982 STI 179*.)

Acquisitions of fixed plant and machinery under hire purchase agreements will qualify for relief as regards the capital element but lease purchase agreements are not considered by the Revenue to be equivalent to the rights which accrue under the former so that acquisitions under the latter will not be eligible for relief (Tolley's Practical Tax 1986 p 136).

Provided relief would be due on the disposal of the underlying land which is the subject of the grant of an option, the Revenue are prepared to ignore the separate disposal treatment of *TCGA 1992, s 144(1)* so that any gain arising on the grant of the option can be the subject of a rollover relief claim. The Revenue point out that relief will only be obtained if the land continues to be occupied and used for the claimant's trade (Revenue Tax Bulletin, February 1992, p 13). Presumably this treatment applies regardless of whether an option is exercised (such an event bringing into play the single transaction treatment of *TCGA 1992, s 144(2)*). The Revenue make no comment whether the cost of the option and the exercise price under it could frank a rollover relief claim where the grantee of an option subsequently exercises it (such an event bringing into play the single transaction treatment of *TCGA 1992, s 144(3)*) and brings the underlying land into trading use and occupation immediately on exercise. Relief would seem to be available on the exercise price but may not be for the option cost. For options generally, see 17.10 DISPOSAL.

Rollover relief is not available to the extent that the new asset is used wholly and exclusively for the purposes of a shipping company's activities within the tonnage tax regime (see 21.15 EXEMPTIONS AND RELIEFS). If a new asset begins to be used for such purposes after rollover relief has been given, the rolled over gain becomes a chargeable gain, which is, however, deferred until the new asset is disposed of. [*FA 2000, Sch 22 para 67*].

55.4 QUALIFYING UNDERTAKINGS

TCGA 1992, ss 152–157 (see 55.1 and 55.3 above and 55.6 and 55.7 below) apply with necessary modifications in relation to the following activities as they apply in relation to a trade.

(*a*) The discharge of the functions of a public authority.

(*b*) The occupation of woodlands where the woodlands are managed by the occupier on a commercial basis and with a view to the realisation of profits.

(*c*) A profession, vocation, office or employment.

(*d*) Such of the activities of a body of persons whose activities are carried on otherwise than for profit and are wholly or mainly directed to the protection or promotion of the interests of its members in the carrying on of their trade or profession as are so directed.

(*e*) The activities of an unincorporated association or other body chargeable to corporation tax, being a body not established for profit whose activities are wholly or mainly carried on otherwise than for profit, but in the case of assets within 1.(*a*) in 55.3 above only if they are both occupied and used by the body, and in the case of other assets only if they are used by the body.

'Trade', 'profession', 'vocation', 'office' and 'employment' have the same meanings as in the *Income Tax Acts* for the purposes of the above and *TCGA 1992, ss 152–157*, but not so as to apply the provisions of the *Income Tax Acts* as to the circumstances in which, on a change in the persons carrying on a trade, a trade is to be regarded as discontinued, or as set up and commenced. These provisions and *TCGA 1992, ss 152–157* are construed as one. [*TCGA 1992, s 158*]. '*Trade*' includes every trade, manufacture, adventure or concern in the nature of trade, but the other expressions are not directly defined. [*ICTA 1988, s 832(1)*].

For disposals after 5 April 1982 commercial letting of 'furnished holiday accommodation' in the UK is treated as a trade for the purposes of the relief. See 22 FURNISHED HOLIDAY ACCOMMODATION.

The Revenue have indicated that both parties to a share farming agreement may be considered to be carrying on a farming business for taxation purposes provided that the landowner takes an active part in the venture, e.g. by concerning himself with details of farming policy, etc. (1992 STI 189 reproducing statement of 19 December 1991 issued by Country Landowners Association).

If land or a building is owned by an employee or office-holder but is made available to the employer for general use in his trade, the employee etc. may nonetheless satisfy the occupation test of *TCGA 1992, s 155* (see 55.3 above at 1.) provided the employer does not make any payment (or give other consideration) for his use of the property nor otherwise occupy it under a lease or tenancy. The qualifying use of assets by an employee etc. for the purposes of *TCGA 1992, s 152* (see 55.1 above) will include any use or operation of those assets by him, in the course of performing the duties of his employment or office, as directed by the employer (Revenue Pamphlet IR 131, SP 5/86). The practice may be applied to all open cases as at 21 August 1986 and may be compared with the relief available under *TCGA 1992, s 157* (see 55.1 above) where the trade is carried on by the individual's 'personal company' ('family company' for disposals before 16 March 1993) although in relation to SP 5/86 consideration passing or the existence of a lease or tenancy would deny relief but would not under *TCGA 1992, s 157*. Provided such factors are absent it is understood that so long as a director is a 'full-time working director' or, presumably for disposals after 15 March 1993, an officer or employee is a 'full-time working officer or employee' (see 53.4 RETIREMENT RELIEF), then he can also qualify as an employee for the purposes of SP 5/86. Where relief under *TCGA 1992, s 157* is unavailable (e.g. where the individual as a partner disposes of an asset which has been used by the partnership and acquires an asset which is to be used by his personal or, as the case may be, family company or, possibly, where different such companies are involved) then, provided the factors mentioned previously are absent, relief may still be claimed (Tolley's Practical Tax 1986 p 183 and subsequent correspondence with the Revenue).

Lessors of tied premises are treated as occupying and using them solely for the purposes of a relevant trade. [*TCGA 1992, s 156(4)*]. Where the trade is one of dealing in or developing land or of providing services for the occupier of land in which the trader has an interest, the trader's disposal of the land does not qualify for relief. However, this does not apply where a profit on the sale of any land held for the purposes of a trade of dealing in or developing land would not form part of the trading profits. [*TCGA 1992, s 156(1)–(3)*]. However, it appears that the Revenue may allow relief on the disposal of a caravan site where the disposer's occupation of that site amounts to the carrying on of a trade, notwithstanding that that trade is one of providing services for the occupier(s). See also 22 FURNISHED HOLIDAY ACCOMMODATION for such accommodation in the UK.

The application of the relief in relation to a person who, either successively or at the same time, carries on two or more trades as if both or all of them were a single trade (see *TCGA 1992, s 152(8)* in 55.1 above) is not further qualified, so that one or all the trades could be situated outside the UK and outside the scope of UK taxation because the taxpayer is neither resident nor ordinarily resident in the UK (see also Tolley's Practical Tax 1981 p 126 but note the restrictions in 43.2 OFFSHORE SETTLEMENTS and 44.3, 44.12 and 44.14

OVERSEAS MATTERS in certain cases and note that 'furnished holiday accommodation' must be in the UK).

Where a trader ceases carrying on one trade and, within three years, commences carrying on another, the Revenue will treat the trades as carried on 'successively'. If the disposal or acquisition takes place in the intervening period, relief will be restricted in respect of the period during which the assets disposed of were not used for trade purposes, and will be conditional on the replacement assets not being used or leased for any purpose prior to commencement of the new trade, and on their being taken into use for the purposes of the new trade on its commencement (Revenue Pamphlet IR 131, SP 8/81). The Revenue generally has no difficulty in regarding a second or subsequent new trade as the successor trade for the purposes of *TCGA 1992, s 152(8)*. This means relief will be available where a gain arises from the old trade and new assets are acquired in the second or subsequent new trade, provided that the other conditions for the relief are met and the gap between the cessation of the old trade and the commencement of the new trade in question is within the limits of SP 8/81 (Institute of Taxation TIR/11/91, 1991 STI 1097). In *Steibelt v Paling Ch D 1999, 71 TC 376*, a nine-year gap between trades meant that they could not be said to be carried on successively.

55.5 **GROUPS OF COMPANIES**

For the purposes of *TCGA 1992, ss 152–158* (see 55.1–55.4 above and 55.6 and 55.7 below) all the trades carried on by members of a group of companies (within 13.11 COMPANIES) are, for the purposes of corporation tax on chargeable gains treated as a single trade (unless, for cases where the acquisition of the new assets was before 29 November 1994, it was a case of one member of the group acquiring the new assets from another or disposing of the old assets to another). Where the disposal or the acquisition, or both, occurs on or after 1 April 2000, the change in the residence requirement as regards groups of companies (see 13.11 COMPANIES) applies in determining whether a company is a member of a group, but the reference above to 'all the trades' does not include any trade carried on by a non-UK resident company otherwise than in the UK through a branch or agency. [*TCGA 1992, s 175(1)(1A); FA 1995, Sch 29 Pt VIII(4); FA 2000, Sch 29 para 10(1)–(3)(7)(8)*].

TCGA 1992, s 154(2) (see 55.7 below) applies where the company making the claim is a member of a group of companies as if all members of the group for the time being carrying on trades within these provisions (see above) were the same person (and, in accordance with *TCGA 1992, s 175(1)* above, as if all those trades were the same trade) and so that the gain accrues to the member of the group holding the asset concerned on the occurrence of the event mentioned in *TCGA 1992, s 154(2)* (i.e. the earlier of the disposal of the depreciating asset, cessation of its trading use or the expiry of ten years from its acquisition). [*TCGA 1992, s 175(3); FA 2000, Sch 29 para 10(6)*].

Acquisitions as a group member by a 'dual resident investing company' within *ICTA 1988, s 404* after 31 March 1987 are excluded from the treatment given by *TCGA 1992, s 175(1)* above. Where either the disposal of the old assets or the acquisition of the new assets (or both such events) occurred after 13 March 1989, then, if either such event occurred before 30 November 1993 (the latter date being the date of the coming into force of *FA 1994, s 249*; companies otherwise regarded as UK resident but under double tax relief arrangements already regarded as non-UK resident to be treated as non-UK resident for *Taxes Acts* purposes after 29 November 1993; see 52.6 RESIDENCE AND DOMICILE), a similar exclusion applied to a company which, though resident in the UK, was regarded as resident elsewhere by virtue of double tax relief arrangements in circumstances such that it would not under those arrangements have been taxable in the UK on any gain arising on a disposal of the new assets immediately after their acquisition. However, the exclusion in the second case did not apply where the acquisition of the new assets was before 20 March 1990 and the disposal of the old assets took place within twelve months beginning with the date of acquisition or such longer period as was allowed in writing by the Board. [*TCGA 1992, s 175(2)(4); FA 1994, s 251(1)(8), Sch 26 Pt VIII*].

In *Campbell Connelly & Co Ltd v Barnett CA 1993, 66 TC 380* (see 55.1 above), an argument that *TCGA 1992, s 175(1)* should be construed such that not only should the trades carried on by members of a group of companies be treated as a single trade and thereby the same trade but that members of a group of companies should be treated as a single person and thereby the same person was rejected. It was pointed out that the wording of *TCGA 1992, s 175(3)* was an instructive contrast to that in *TCGA 1992, s 175(1)*. The words in parentheses at the end of *section 175(1)* 'unless it is a case . . . the old assets to another' were described *obiter* by Knox J in the Ch D as 'an anti-avoidance provision to prevent the shuffling of assets within a group of companies to postpone liability to . . . tax when a member of a group disposes of an asset outside the group'. Subject to this, one interpretation of *section 175(1)* would allow relief to a group member disposing of an asset outside the group at a gain if that member acquired an asset from another group member provided all other conditions for relief are fulfilled. By virtue of *TCGA 1992, s 171(1)* the acquisition cost to the group member would be limited to the cost to the group plus improvement costs, expenses of transfer (but less any reduction in respect of previous rollover relief claims) and any indexation allowance. This interpretation would not allow a claim for relief where one group member disposes of an asset outside the group and another group member acquires an asset from a third group member. In addition to this, the 'normal' use of *section 175(1)* has been accepted as being to frank the disposal of old assets by one group member outside the group by the acquisition of new assets by another group member from outside the group. However, the Inland Revenue indicated that, if necessary, steps would be taken to ensure that the established practice (see below) in relation to rollover relief and groups of companies would continue whatever the outcome of the *Campbell Connelly* case. This practice allowed 'one trading company in a group to obtain rollover relief even though the replacement asset was acquired by another trading member of the same group'. (Revenue Press Release, 15 September 1992).

Provisions were introduced by *FA 1995* to put into effect the long-standing Revenue practice (see below) in order that rollover relief would apply in the following circumstances:

(*a*) where there is a disposal by a member of a group of companies and an acquisition by another member of the same group and both companies claim rollover relief after 28 November 1994 as if they were the same person (giving effect to part of the Revenue's concessionary practice in Revenue Pamphlet IR 131, SP 8/81, see below); or

(*b*) where a non-trading member of a group makes a disposal or acquisition of assets after 28 November 1994 used only for trading purposes by other members of the same group (giving effect to Revenue Pamphlet IR 1, D30 which applied up to that date, see below).

With regard to (*a*) above, this is deemed always to have had effect.

However, rollover relief will not apply where there is an acquisition of new assets after 28 November 1994 by a member of a group from another member of that group resulting from a no gain/no loss disposal (see 8.7 ASSETS HELD ON 31 MARCH 1982 above).

Where the disposal or the acquisition, or both, occurs on or after 1 April 2000, then, in consequence of the change in the residence requirement in 13.11 COMPANIES, the following conditions must be met for (*a*) above to apply:

- *either* the company making the disposal is UK-resident at the time of disposal *or* the assets in question are 'chargeable assets' in relation to that company immediately before that time; *and*

- *either* the acquiring company is UK-resident at the time of acquisition *or* the assets are 'chargeable assets' in relation to that company immediately after that time.

For these purposes, an asset is a '*chargeable asset*' in relation to a company at a particular time if, on a disposal by that company at that time, any gain would be a chargeable gain and would be within the charge to corporation tax by virtue of *TCGA 1992, s 10* (non-UK resident company trading in the UK through a branch or agency — see 44.3 OVERSEAS MATTERS).

[*TCGA 1992, s 175(2A)–(2C); FA 1995, s 48(1)(3)–(5); FA 1996, s 121(8), s 141(3); FA 2000, Sch 29 para 10(4)(5)(7)(8)*].

The remaining part of this section on groups should be read in the light of the *FA 1995* provisions.

The disposing company must be a member of a group at the time of disposal, and the acquiring company must be a member of the same group at the time of acquisition, but the Revenue does not insist that either company be a member of that group at the time of the transaction carried out by the other (Revenue Pamphlet IR 131, SP D19). Where this applies in a case where one member of a group makes the disposal and a second the acquisition, it may happen that the disposal takes place after the first company has ceased to trade, or the acquisition takes place before the second company commences trading. Relief will then be restricted in respect of the period during which the assets disposed of were not used for business purposes, and will be conditional on the replacement assets not being used or leased for any purpose prior to the second company's commencing trading, and being taken into use for the purposes of the trade on its commencement (Revenue Pamphlet IR 131, SP 8/81, and see also 55.4 above). If an asset is sold by a member of a sub-group and a replacement asset is acquired by another member of that sub-group, but in the interval before replacement the sub-group leaves the main group and becomes part of a second main group, the Revenue take the view that rollover relief is not available (CCAB Statement TR 508, 9 June 1983).

Relief is extended to companies which hold assets used for trade purposes by trading companies in the same group. This treatment applies even if the company also holds assets used by non-group members although relief is only available in respect of those assets used by group members (Revenue Pamphlet IR 1, D30 (obsolete from 29 November 1994)).

The Revenue have confirmed that where an asset is transferred to another group company prior to disposal outside the group, entitlement to relief depends on its use during the final period of ownership (CCAB Statement TR 425, 3 April 1981).

If a qualifying unincorporated association uses property owned by a company in which at least 90% of the shares are held by or on behalf of the association or its members, rollover relief can be claimed subject to the usual conditions. (Revenue Pamphlet IR 1, D15). (See 3.23 ANTI-AVOIDANCE for the charge arising where concessions involving deferral of gains are abused.)

See 36.11(*g*) LAND above with regard to rollover relief in cases of compulsory purchase of land.

55.6 PARTIAL RELIEF

A modification of the relief under *TCGA 1992, s 152(1)* (see 55.1 above) is available where not all of the amount or value of the consideration received for the disposal of the old assets is applied in acquiring the new assets. Provided that the part of the disposal consideration *not* applied in acquiring the new assets is less than the amount of the gain (whether all chargeable gain or not; this presumably only applies when *TCGA 1992, Sch 2* is in point for ASSETS HELD ON 6 APRIL 1965 (7)) otherwise accruing on the disposal of the old assets, the person carrying on the trade, on making a claim as respects the consideration applied in acquiring the new assets, is treated for the purposes of *TCGA 1992*

(*a*) as if the gain accruing on the disposal of the old assets were reduced *to* the amount of the said part, and

(*b*) as if the amount or value of the consideration for the acquisition of the new assets were reduced *by* the amount by which the gain is reduced in (*a*) above.

If not all the gain accruing on the disposal of the old assets is a chargeable gain, (*a*) above applies but with a proportionate reduction in the amount of the chargeable gain, and in (*b*) above the reduction in consideration is the amount by which the chargeable gain is proportionately reduced. Neither (*a*) nor (*b*) above affects the treatment for the purposes of *TCGA 1992* of the other party to the transaction involving the old assets, or of the other party to the transaction involving the new assets. *TCGA 1992, s 152(3)–(11)* (see 55.1 above and also see further below) are applied to the above provisions. [*TCGA 1992, s 153*].

If, over the 'period of ownership' (which, for disposals after 5 April 1988, excludes any period before 31 March 1982) or any substantial part of the period of ownership, part of a building or structure is, and part is not, used for the purposes of a trade, *TCGA 1992, s 152* applies as if the part so used, with any land occupied for purposes ancillary to the occupation and use of that part of the building or structure, were a separate asset, and subject to any necessary apportionments of consideration for an acquisition or disposal of the building or structure and other land. [*TCGA 1992, s 152(6)(9)*].

See Revenue Tax Bulletin, October 1994, p 166 for further discussion on partial relief.

If the old assets were not used for the purposes of the trade throughout the 'period of ownership' (which, for disposals after 5 April 1988, excludes any period before 31 March 1982) *TCGA 1992, s 152* applies as if a part of the asset representing its use for the purposes of the trade having regard to the time and extent to which it was, and was not, used for those purposes, were a separate asset which had been wholly used for the purposes of the trade, and this treatment applies in relation to that part subject to any necessary apportionment of consideration for an acquisition or disposal of the asset. [*TCGA 1992, s 152(7)(9)*].

Without prejudice to *TCGA 1992, s 52(4)* (just and reasonable apportionments of consideration and expenditure; see 17.6 DISPOSAL), where consideration is given for the acquisition or disposal of assets some or part of which are assets in relation to which a claim under *TCGA 1992, s 152* applies, and some or part of which are not, the consideration is apportioned in such manner as is just and reasonable. [*TCGA 1992, s 152(11)*].

For disposals before 6 April 1988, periods of ownership before 6 April 1965 were taken into account (whether time apportionment or 6 April 1965 value applied) following *Richart v J Lyons & Co Ltd CA 1989, 62 TC 261*.

Where the taxpayer acquires an undivided share in the new asset which is only partly used for trade purposes, relief is limited to the proportion so used of the individual's undivided share of the asset (*Tod v Mudd Ch D 1986, 60 TC 237*). Vinelott J noted in his judgement that a concession might be in existence as regards *TCGA 1992, s 156(6)(7)(9)(11)* above (although he was not required to consider the point further as it was not argued before him) because those provisions do not seem strictly to prevent relief being denied under *TCGA 1992, s 152(1)* in 55.1 above because the new asset is only partly used for trade purposes. For consideration of the difficulties that arise in such a case, see *Taxation 18 November 1993, p 141*.

Examples

(*a*) In 1993, X purchased a factory for £40,000. It was used and occupied entirely for carrying on his trade until sold for £100,000 in October 2000. In the same month X bought another factory for £120,000 which was immediately used and occupied for carrying on a new trade carried on by him. Assume indexation allowance (computed to April 1998) of £6,000 is available as regards the sale. He claimed rollover relief, computed as follows.

	£
Proceeds of sale of factory 1	100,000
Allowable expenditure on factory 1	40,000
Unindexed gain on sale of factory 1	60,000
Indexation allowance	6,000
Chargeable gain eligible to be rolled over	£54,000
Cost of factory 2	120,000
Rolled-over gain	54,000
Base cost for factory 2 on subsequent disposal	£66,000

Note that a gain does not qualify for taper relief to the extent that it is rolled over. See 60.14 TAPER RELIEF.

(*b*) Facts as in (*a*) above, except factory 2 is bought for £90,000. The part of the £100,000 disposal consideration of factory 1 which is not applied in acquiring factory 2 is £10,000. This is less than the gain otherwise arising on the disposal of factory 1 (£54,000). The gain deemed to arise on the disposal of factory 1 is therefore £10,000 (subject to taper relief). The gain so arising has therefore been reduced by £44,000, with the result that this amount is deducted from the £90,000 consideration given for factory 2, and so producing a base cost of £46,000 on a subsequent disposal.

(*c*) In September 2000, Y purchased a new factory for £100,000, having sold his old one in the same month for £52,000. The original factory had been bought in September 1990 for £20,000 but had only been used for his trade since September 1992. He claimed rollover relief. It is accepted that one-quarter of the new factory is not used for trade purposes. Assume indexation allowance (computed to April 1998) at 26%.

	£
Proceeds of sale of old factory	52,000
Cost of old factory	20,000
Unindexed gain	32,000
Indexation allowance: 26% × £20,000	5,200
Chargeable gain	£26,800

$$\frac{\text{Period of trading use of old asset}}{\text{Period of ownership}} = \frac{8 \text{ years}}{10 \text{ years}}$$

Gain on old asset eligible for relief	
£26,800 × $\frac{8}{10}$	£21,440

	£
Cost of qualifying part of new factory ($\frac{3}{4}$ × £100,000)	75,000
Rolled-over gain	21,440
Base cost of qualifying part of new factory	£53,560

The unrelieved gain of £5,360 (£26,800 – £21,440) is brought into charge on the disposal of the old factory, but can be reduced by TAPER RELIEF (60). The base cost of the non-qualifying part of the new factory, treated as separate, is £25,000.

55.7 WASTING ASSETS

For the purpose of relief under *TCGA 1992, ss 152, 153* (see 55.1 and 55.6 above), if the new asset is at the time of acquisition a WASTING ASSET (66) or will become so within ten years beginning at that time, it is known as a '*depreciating asset*'. In such cases, the gain on the disposal of the old asset is not deducted from the acquisition consideration of the new asset, but held over until ten years after the time of acquisition of the new asset, or until the new asset is disposed of, or until the new asset ceases to be used for the trade, whichever is the sooner, upon which event the held-over gain becomes chargeable to capital gains tax; but the held-over gain is not brought into charge under this provision in consequence of an event after 5 April 1988 if its application would be directly attributable to the disposal of an asset before 1 April 1982. [*TCGA 1992, s 154(1)(2)(7), Sch 4 para 4(5)*].

However, if not later than the time when the held-over gain would be brought into charge a further asset is acquired which is not a depreciating asset, the trader may claim relief under *TCGA 1992, s 152* or *s 153* as if it had been acquired within the time limits of *TCGA 1992, s 152(3)* for the application of the proceeds of the disposal of the old asset, the depreciating asset being effectively disregarded. The trader may claim relief if only part of the proceeds can be treated in this way, the balance remaining held over until crystallisation by virtue of one of the events specified. [*TCGA 1992, s 154(4)–(6)*].

By concession, where a held-over gain would otherwise be brought into charge on a cessation of trading use due to the trader's death, no charge to tax will arise. This concession is stated to apply from 16 December 1993 for both new and open cases so could presumably apply where the case is not final even though death occurred before that date (Revenue Pamphlet IR 1, D45).

A gain which has been held over under *TCGA 1992, s 154* will crystallise on a disposal even where the disposal concerned is within *TCGA 1992, s 162* (hold-over on a transfer of a business to a company; see 25.10 HOLD-OVER RELIEFS) (Tolley's Practical Tax 1985 p 139).

See 60.12 TAPER RELIEF for the application of that relief where a gain is held over under these provisions.

A building constructed on leasehold land where the lease has less than 60 years to run at the time of construction is considered by the Revenue to be a depreciating asset. This is despite the treatment in *TCGA 1992, s 155* (see 55.3 above) which treats land and buildings as separate assets (and contrary to the general rule for land as in 36.2 LAND). If, as contemplated by *TCGA 1992, s 155*, an item of fixed plant or machinery has effectively become a part of a building or structure, it will be so treated for rollover relief purposes, with the result that such assets acquired for installation in a building etc. then held freehold or on a lease with more than 60 years to run will not be treated as depreciating assets. Subject to this, because an item of plant and machinery is always to be treated as being a wasting asset (see 66.1 WASTING ASSETS), it will also be treated as a depreciating asset. Deciding whether an item of fixed plant or machinery has become part of a building etc.

will normally be done by reference to the size and nature of the item in question, how it is attached to the building and whether damage to the fabric of the building would be caused if the item was removed (Revenue Tax Bulletin May 1993 p 73).

Milk quota (see 6.6 ASSETS) is not regarded by the Revenue as a wasting asset (Revenue Capital Gains Manual CG 77940).

Example

In March 1996, a father and son partnership carrying on a car dealing trade sold a freehold showroom for £400,000 realising a chargeable gain (after indexation) of £190,000. On 30 June 1996, the firm purchased for £450,000 the remaining term of a lease due to expire on 30 June 2026 and used the premises as a new showroom. The whole of the gain on the old asset was held over under *TCGA 1992, s 154* on the acquisition of the new asset. In consequence of the father's decision to retire from the business and the resulting need to downsize the operation, the firm assigns the lease for £490,000 on 1 July 2000. The indexation factor for the period June 1996 to April 1998 is 0.063.

The chargeable gains to be apportioned between the two partners for 2000/01 are as follows

	£	£
Proceeds of assignment		490,000
Cost (see note (*a*))	450,000	
Deduct Wasted $\frac{87.330 - 82.496}{87.330} \times$ £450,000	24,909	425,091
Unindexed gain		64,909
Indexation allowance £425,091 × 0.063		26,781
Chargeable gain 2000/01 (see note (*b*))		£38,128
Held-over gain becoming chargeable under *TCGA 1992, s 154(2)(a)*		£190,000

Notes to the example

(*a*) The gain is deferred as opposed to being rolled over and does not reduce the cost of the new asset.

(*b*) Each of the partners will be entitled to taper relief on his share of the gain of £38,128 to the extent that it is not reduced by the offset of capital losses (and the father's share may in any case be covered by retirement relief). Taper relief on the deferred gain operates by reference to the date of disposal and period of ownership of the old asset, and none is due in this case as the disposal was before 6 April 1998. See 60.12 TAPER RELIEF. The deferred gain cannot be covered by RETIREMENT RELIEF (53) as the disposal giving rise to it did not take place on retirement.

56 Self-Assessment

Simon's Direct Tax Service E1.8.

The headings in this chapter are as follows.

56.1 INTRODUCTION

Self-assessment for individuals, partnerships and trustees has effect generally for 1996/97 and subsequent years of assessment, although some aspects of the system came into effect earlier and some in 1997/98. The term 'self-assessment' refers to the system whereby the annual tax return includes a self-assessment of the taxpayer's liability for income tax and capital gains tax. Payment of tax is then due automatically, based on the self-assessment. The main body of legislation introducing self-assessment is contained in *Finance Act 1994*, with further provisions in subsequent Finance Acts. As regards corporation tax self-assessment, see 56.2 below.

Although this work is concerned with capital gains tax, it is felt helpful in many cases to describe the changes brought about by self-assessment not only in relation to that tax but also in relation to income tax. For coverage of the latter in more depth, see TOLLEY'S INCOME TAX under Self-Assessment.

Two detailed Revenue booklets, SAT 1 'The new current year basis of assessment' and SAT 2 'Self Assessment: the legal framework', both guides for Inland Revenue officers and tax practitioners, should have been sent by tax offices to all tax practices with which they dealt in August/September 1995. Further copies are available (price £7.50 and £5.00 respectively) from Inland Revenue Library, Room 28, New Wing, Somerset House, Strand, London WC2R 1LB.

56.1 Self-Assessment

Returns. The return for individuals consists of a basic eight pages to which are attached any supplementary pages relevant to the individual concerned, forming a single 'customised' tax return. The supplementary pages are colour-coded and cover employment, share schemes, self-employment, partnership income, land and property, foreign income, trust income, capital gains and non-residence etc. Each individual should also receive a tax return guide containing explanatory notes relevant to his circumstances. It is the individual's responsibility to obtain any supplementary pages he needs but has not received, which he may do by telephoning a Revenue Orderline, by which means he may also obtain the relevant explanatory notes and/or 'helpsheets' (see 29.4 INLAND REVENUE EXPLANATORY PUBLICATIONS) on specific topics. Each return sent out will be accompanied by a tax calculation guide designed to assist the individual in calculating his tax liability if he chooses to do so. Partnership returns follow a similar pattern.

The first returns affected were those covering the tax year 1996/97, normally sent out by the Revenue in April 1997. Returns must normally be filed by 31 January following the year of assessment (see 56.5 below). Taxpayers who would prefer not to compute their own liabilities do not have to do so providing they file their return early, normally by 30 September following the year of assessment (see 56.6 below). Penalties are imposed for late submission of returns, subject to appeal on the grounds of reasonable excuse (see 56.23 below). There are provisions for making amendments to self-assessments (see 56.7 below). The Revenue are given broadly one year from the filing date to give notice of their intention to enquire into the return (see 56.11 below). A formal procedure is laid down for such enquiries (see 56.11–56.13 below). If they do not give such notice, the return becomes final and conclusive, subject to any 'error or mistake' claim by the taxpayer (see 12.7 CLAIMS) or 'discovery' assessment by the Revenue (see 5.2 ASSESSMENTS). In the event of non-submission of a return, the Revenue are able to make a determination of the tax liability; there is no right of appeal but the determination may be superseded upon submission of the return (see 56.14 below). Capital losses must be quantified on a claim if they are to be allowable (see 56.34 below).

A different style of return has to be filed by partnerships. This must include a statement of the allocation of partnership income between the partners. See 56.8 and 56.9 below.

Payment of tax. Income tax (on all sources of taxable income) for a year of assessment is payable by means of two interim payments of equal amounts, based normally on the liability for the previous year of assessment and due on 31 January in the year of assessment and the following 31 July, and a final balancing payment due on the following 31 January which is also the due date for capital gains tax liability. Taxpayers have the right to reduce their interim payments if they believe their income tax liability will be less than that for the previous year of assessment or to dispense with interim payments if they believe they will have no liability. Interim payments are not in any case required where substantially all of a taxpayer's income is subject to deduction of tax at source, including PAYE, or where the amounts otherwise due are below de minimis limits. See 56.15–56.17 below.

Interest on overdue payments runs from the due date to the date of payment (see 56.19 below). There is also a 5% surcharge on any tax unpaid by 28 February following the year of assessment and a further 5% surcharge on any tax unpaid by the following 31 July, such surcharges being subject to appeal on the grounds of reasonable excuse (see 35.5 INTEREST AND SURCHARGES ON UNPAID TAX). Interest on tax overpaid normally runs from the date of payment to the date of repayment (see 56.20 below); the rate of interest is lower than that on overdue tax.

Miscellaneous. Numerous consequential amendments were made to the taxes management provisions and time limits. There is a statutory requirement for taxpayers to keep records for the purpose of making returns and to preserve such records for specified periods (see 56.10 below).

56.2 CORPORATION TAX SELF-ASSESSMENT

Similarly, there are provisions extending, for company accounting periods ending on or after an appointed day, the principles of self-assessment to the existing Pay and File system for corporation tax payment and returns. The appointed day for corporation tax self-assessment is 1 July 1999. [*SI 1998 No 3173*]. The main body of corporation tax self-assessment provisions is contained in *FA 1998, Sch 18*. Corporation tax self-assessment is covered in TOLLEY'S CORPORATION TAX. See also Revenue booklet 'A Guide to Corporation Tax Self-Assessment — for Tax Practitioners and Inland Revenue Officers (April 1999)'. Except where otherwise stated, the self-assessment provisions in this chapter are those applying other than for the purposes of corporation tax.

56.3 INTERPRETATION OF REFERENCES TO ASSESSMENTS ETC.

Following the introduction of self-assessment, references to a person being assessed to tax, or being charged to tax by an assessment, are to be construed as including a reference to his being so assessed, or being so charged, by a self-assessment under *TMA 1970, s 9* (see 56.6 below) or by a determination under *TMA 1970, s 28C* (see 56.14 below) which has not been superseded by a self-assessment. [*FA 1994, ss 197, 199*].

56.4 NOTICE OF CHARGEABILITY

See 54.2 RETURNS.

56.5 ANNUAL RETURNS OF INCOME AND CHARGEABLE GAINS

For the purposes of establishing the amounts in which a person is chargeable to income tax and capital gains tax for 1996/97 and subsequent years of assessment, an officer of the Board may by notice require that person to deliver a return on or before 31 January following the year of assessment or, if later, within three months beginning with the date of the notice (see also 56.23 below). The return must contain such information and be accompanied by such accounts, statements and documents as may reasonably be required. This will include information relating to disposals on which chargeable gains or allowable losses arise. The return must include a declaration that, to the best of the knowledge of the person making it, it is complete and correct. The information, accounts and statements required by the notice may differ in relation to different periods, or different sources of income, or different descriptions of person. [*TMA 1970, ss 8, 12; FA 1994, s 178(1), s 199(2), Sch 26 Pt V; FA 1995, s 103(7), s 104(1)–(3)*]. Similar provisions apply in relation to returns by trustees. [*TMA 1970, ss 8A, 12; FA 1994, s 178(2), s 199(2), Sch 26 Pt V; FA 1995, s 103(3)(4)(7), s 104(1)*]. See also 54.3 RETURNS.

For 1996/97 and subsequent years of assessment or company accounting periods ending on or after 1 July 1999 (see 56.2 above), minor consequential amendments are made to *TMA 1970, s 12A* (return by European Economic Interest Grouping; see 54.15 RETURNS). [*TMA 1970, s 12A; FA 1994, s 196, s 199(2)(3), Sch 19 para 2*].

Before making their return, taxpayers may ask their Tax Office (on Form CG34) to check their valuation for capital gains tax purposes of an asset they have disposed of (see 54.5 RETURNS). (Revenue Press Release 4 February 1997).

Business accounts are not required with the return except in the case of partnerships with an annual turnover exceeding £15 million. Instead, the return will include a section in which standard accounts information (SAI) *must* be completed as well as space for additional information. See 5.2 ASSESSMENTS re the option of submitting accounts (in addition to completing SAI) to possibly reduce the risk of a discovery assessment. Accounts should otherwise be retained in case of enquiry (see 56.11 below). (Revenue Press Release

31 May 1996, Tax Bulletins June 1996 pp 313–315, June 1997 p 436 and booklet SAT 2(1995), para 2.22). For the transitional year 1996/97, a single set of SAI may, if the taxpayer wishes, be provided covering two or more sets of accounts drawn up for the transitional period, unless a loss was incurred in one or more of the account periods, in which case separate SAI is required for each set of accounts. (Revenue Tax Bulletin December 1996 p 371).

In the case of a person carrying on a profession, trade or business in partnership, a return under *TMA 1970, s 8* must include each amount, which according to any 'relevant statement' is his share of any income, loss, tax, credit or charge for the period covered by the statement. A '*relevant statement*' is a statement falling to be made, as respects the partnership, under *TMA 1970, s 12AB* (see 56.9 below) for a period which includes, or includes any part of, the year of assessment or its basis period. [*TMA 1970, s 8(1B)(1C); FA 1994, s 178(1), s 199(2); FA 1995, s 103(7), s 104(2)*].

A return containing a provisional figure will be accepted provided that the figure is reasonable, taking account of all available information, and is clearly identified as such and that an acceptable explanation is given as to why the final figure is not available, all reasonable steps having been taken to obtain it, and when it is expected to be available (at which time it should be notified without unreasonable delay). Pressures of work and complexity of tax affairs are not regarded as acceptable explanations. If the final figure is not provided by the expected date the Revenue will take appropriate action to obtain it, which may mean opening an enquiry (see 56.11 below). See Revenue Tax Return Guide and Revenue Tax Bulletins October 1998 pp 593–596 and December 1999 p 705. Note that a provisional figure is different to an estimate that will not be superseded by a more accurate figure. A return omitting a figure or stating 'to be agreed' will be treated as an incomplete return (Revenue booklet SAT 2 (1995), para 2.53). See also 56.23 below as regards incomplete returns.

See 56.23 below as regards penalties for non-compliance.

See 54.16 RETURNS re electronic lodgement of returns.

56.6 **SELF-ASSESSMENTS**

For 1996/97 and subsequent years of assessment, every return under *TMA 1970, s 8* or *s 8A* (see 56.5 above) must include, subject to the exception below, an assessment (a self-assessment) of the liability, based on the information in the return and taking into account all reliefs, allowances, tax credits, tax at source and tax repayments, of the person making the return to income tax and capital gains tax for the year of assessment.

A person need not comply with this requirement if he makes and delivers his return on or before 30 September following the year of assessment or, if later, within two months beginning with the date of the notice to deliver the return. In such cases, the Revenue will make the assessment. For returns submitted outside these time limits, the Revenue will calculate the tax and make the assessment if the taxpayer fails to do so, but will not guarantee to do so before the due date for payment of tax.

Assessments made as above by an officer of the Board are treated as self-assessments by the person making the return.

[*TMA 1970, s 8, s 8A, s 9(1)–(3); FA 1994, s 179, s 199(2); FA 1995, s 103(7), s 104(4), s 115(2); FA 1996, s 121(1)–(4), s 122(1)*].

The Revenue need not give notice to deliver a return under 56.5 above, and thus a self-assessment will not be required, in cases where tax deducted under PAYE equates to the individual's total tax liability for the year. The taxpayer may, however, give notice requiring a return to be issued so that he can make a self-assessment (e.g. to initiate the appeals procedure as in 56.28 below), such notice to be given within five years after 31 October following the year of assessment. [*ICTA 1988, s 205; FA 1995, s 111(1)*].

Schedule E taxpayers who wish to have a liability of less than £1,000 coded out through PAYE are advised to comply with the earlier filing date of 30 September following the year whether or not they choose to complete their own self-assessment (Revenue booklet SAT 2 (1995), para 2.37; Revenue Tax Bulletin June 1996 p 315). Coding out of an underpayment will reduce the payments on account (see 56.15 below) due for the next tax year.

56.7 **Amendments of self-assessments other than where enquiries made.** At any time within nine months beginning with the delivery of a person's return, an officer of the Board may by notice to that person amend his self-assessment to correct ('repair') obvious errors (whether of principle, arithmetical or otherwise).

At any time within twelve months beginning with the filing date (i.e. the date by which the return must be delivered, as in 56.5 above), that person may by notice to an officer of the Board amend his self-assessment to give effect to any amendments to his return which he has notified to such an officer.

However, no such amendment of a self-assessment may be made (by the taxpayer or the Revenue) after an officer of the Board has given notice of intention to enquire into the return (see 56.11 below) and before his enquiries are completed. [*TMA 1970, s 9(4)–(6); FA 1994, s 179, s 199(2)*].

The amending of a self-assessment under these provisions does not preclude the Revenue from taking penalty action under *TMA 1970, s 95* (see 56.25 below) in relation to the original incorrect figures in cases where the taxpayer has acted fraudulently or negligently (Revenue Tax Bulletin October 1998 p 597).

See 56.13 below for amendments to self-assessments where the Revenue make enquiries into the return.

56.8 PARTNERSHIP RETURNS

The following provisions apply for 1996/97 and subsequent years of assessment or for company accounting periods ending on or after 1 July 1999 (see 56.2 above).

Any partner may be required by notice to complete and deliver a return of the partnership profits together with accounts, statements, etc. (see also 56.9 below). The return must include the names, residences and tax references of all persons (including companies) who were partners during the period specified in the notice and such other information as may reasonably be required by the notice, which may include information relating to disposals and acquisitions of partnership property — the latter under *TMA 1970, s 12(2)* (see 54.3 RETURNS) or *FA 1998, Sch 18 para 13* (see 54.11 RETURNS). The general requirements are similar to those for personal returns under *TMA 1970, s 8* (see 56.5 above). The notice will specify the period (the relevant period) to be covered by the return and the date by which the return should be delivered (the filing date). For a partnership including at least one individual, the filing date will be no earlier than 31 January following the year of assessment concerned (normally that in which the relevant period ends). For a partnership including at least one company, the filing date will be no earlier than the first anniversary of the end of the relevant period. In both cases, the filing date will be deferred until, at the earliest, the last day of the three-month period beginning with the date of the notice, if this is a later date than that given above.

Where the partner responsible for dealing with the return ceases to be available, a successor may be nominated for this purpose by a majority of the persons (or their personal representatives) who were partners at any time in the period covered by the return. A nomination (or revocation of a nomination) does not have effect until notified to the Revenue. Failing a nomination, a successor will be determined according to rules on the return form or will be nominated by the Revenue.

[*TMA 1970, s 12AA; FA 1994, s 184, s 199(2)(3); FA 1995, s 103(7), s 104(6), s 115(4); FA 1996, s 121(6)(7), s 123(1)–(4); FA 1998, s 117, Sch 19 para 3*].

It will not be possible for individual partners to make, in their personal tax returns, supplementary claims for expenses incurred on the partnership's behalf or capital allowances on personal assets used in the partnership. If not included in the accounts, adjustments for such expenditure etc. must be included in the tax computation forming part of the partnership return (Revenue Booklet SAT 1 (1995), para 5.17).

See 56.24 below as regards penalties for non-compliance.

See Revenue Tax Bulletin April 1996 pp 293–298 for an article explaining the relationship between the 1996/97 partnership assessment and the self-assessment returns issued for that year to partnerships and partners.

56.9 **PARTNERSHIP STATEMENTS**

Subject to the same commencement provisions, every partnership return under 56.8 above must include a statement (a partnership statement) showing, in respect of the period covered by the return and each period of account ending within that period,

(*a*) the amount of the partnership income or loss from each source,

(*b*) the amount of each charge on partnership income,

(*c*) the amounts of tax deducted at source from or tax credits on partnership income,

(*d*) the amount of consideration for each disposal of partnership property,

and each partner's share of each of those amounts.

Provisions similar to those in 56.7 above apply as regards amendments to partnership statements. Where a partnership statement is so amended, the partners' self-assessments will be amended by the Revenue accordingly, by notice to each partner concerned.

[*TMA 1970, s 12AB; FA 1994, s 185, s 199(2); FA 1995, s 103(7), s 104(7)(8); FA 1996, s 123(5)(6); FA 1998, s 117, Sch 19 para 4*].

56.10 **RECORDS**

Subject to the same commencement provisions, any person who may be required (in practice, this would seem to exclude no one) make and deliver a return under 56.5 above (personal, trustee or company return) or 56.8 (partnership returns) for a year of assessment or other period will be statutorily required to keep all necessary records and to preserve them until the end of the 'relevant day'. The '*relevant day*' is normally

(*a*) in the case of a person carrying on a trade (including, for these purposes, any letting of property), profession or business alone or in partnership, the fifth anniversary of 31 January following the year of assessment or, for partnership returns, the sixth anniversary of the end of the period covered by the return; and

(*b*) in any other case, the first anniversary of 31 January following the year of assessment.

Where notice to deliver the return is given before the day in whichever is the applicable of (*a*) and (*b*) above, the '*relevant day*' is the *later* of that day and whichever of the following applies:

(i) where Revenue enquiries are made into the return (or into an amendment of the return), the day on which the enquiries are statutorily treated as completed (see 56.13 below);

(ii) where no such enquiries are made, the day on which the Revenue no longer have power to enquire (see 56.11 below).

Where notice to deliver a return is given *after* the day in whichever is the applicable of (*a*) and (*b*) above, (i) and (ii) above still apply to determine the relevant day but only in relation to such records as the taxpayer has in his possession at the time the notice is given.

In the case of a person within (*a*) above, the records in question include records concerning business receipts and expenditure and, in the case of a trade involving dealing in goods, all sales and purchases of goods. All supporting documents (including accounts, books, deeds, contracts, vouchers and receipts) relating to such items must also be preserved. Generally, copies of documents may be preserved instead of the originals and are admissible in evidence in proceedings before the Commissioners. Exceptions to this are vouchers, certificates etc. which show tax credits or deductions at source of UK or foreign tax, e.g. dividend vouchers, interest vouchers (including those issued by banks and building societies) and evidence of tax deducted from payments to sub-contractors under the Construction Industry Tax Deduction Scheme, which, with effect on or after 29 April 1996, must be preserved in their original form.

The maximum penalty for non-compliance in relation to any year of assessment or accounting period is £3,000. This does not apply to records only required for claims, elections or notices not included in the return, as there are separate record-keeping requirements which apply as in 12.3 CLAIMS.

[*TMA 1970, s 12B; FA 1994, s 196, s 199(2)(3), Sch 19 para 3; FA 1995, s 103(7), s 105; FA 1996, s 124(2)(3); FA 1998, Sch 19 para 6*].

The Revenue have published guidance notes as to the type of records to be kept. The above-mentioned penalty will not be charged for any failure to keep records in accordance with those notes which occurred before 6 April 1996. (Revenue Pamphlet SA/BK3).

No penalty will arise where a person who has not kept the original vouchers can provide other documentary proof of the entry in a return or claim. (See Revenue Press Release 15 February 1996).

For capital gains it is recommended that the following records be kept:

- contracts for the purchase, sale or lease of assets together with related correspondence;
- documentation of assets acquired but not purchased;
- details of assets put into trust;
- copies of valuations used in a computation of chargeable gains or losses;
- bills, invoices or other evidence of payment record such as bank statements and cheque stubs for costs claimed for the purchase, improvement or sale of assets;
- details supporting the proportionate use of an asset for both private and business purposes (e.g. part use of home for business purposes).

Similar record-keeping requirements apply to companies for accounting periods ending on or after the appointed day for corporation tax self-assessment (1 July 1999). A company must preserve its records for six years from the end of its return period. [*FA 1998, s 117, Sch 18 paras 21–23*]. For an article on the record-keeping requirements for corporation tax purposes, see Revenue Tax Bulletin October 1998 pp 587–589.

56.11 ENQUIRIES INTO RETURNS

Power to enquire. An officer of the Board may enquire into a return (or amendment of a return) on the basis of which a person's self-assessment under *TMA 1970, s 9* (personal and trustee's return; see 56.6 above) has been made (or amended by that person), or into any claim or election included in a return (by amendment or otherwise). The officer must give notice in writing of his intention to so enquire, such notice to be 'given' (see below),

(*a*) in the case of a return delivered or amendment made on or before the filing date (i.e. the date on or before which the return must be delivered; see 56.5 above), within twelve months beginning with that date; and

(*b*) otherwise on or before the quarter day (meaning 31 January, 30 April, etc.) next following the first anniversary of the day of delivery or amendment.

A return or amendment cannot be enquired into more than once.

[*TMA 1970, s 9A; FA 1994, s 180, s 199(2); FA 1996, Sch 19 para 2*].

The 'giving' of notice under *TMA 1970, s 9A* is effected not when the notice is issued or posted but at the time it would be received in the ordinary course of post (generally taken to be four working days for second class mail) or, if proved, the time of actual receipt (*Holly and another v Inspector of Taxes 1999 (Sp C 225), [2000] SSCD 50*, and see also *Wing Hung Lai v Bale (Sp C 203), [1999] SSCD 238*). The Revenue now accept this to be the case; for their views on the implications for 1996/97 enquiry notices issued shortly before the 30 January 1999 deadline, see Revenue Special 'Working Together' Tax Bulletin April 2000 p 8.

Provisions similar to those of *TMA 1970, s 9A* apply as regards a partnership return on the basis of which a partnership statement (see 56.9 above) was made and to claims or elections included therein. The notice of intention to enquire may be given to a successor (as defined) of the person who made the return or amendment (see 56.8 above). The giving of such notice is deemed to include the giving of notice under *TMA 1970, s 9A* (see above) (or, where applicable, the equivalent corporation tax provision of *FA 1998, Sch 18 para 24*) to each partner affected. [*TMA 1970, s 12AC, s 118(1)(3); FA 1994, s 186, s 196, s 199(2)(3), Sch 19 para 34, Sch 26 Pt V; FA 1996, s 123(7), Sch 19 para 2; FA 1998, s 117, Sch 19 para 5*].

Conduct of enquiry. A Code of Practice (COP 11 for individuals etc., COP 14 for companies, or in certain simple cases a short, single-page version of whichever is relevant) will be issued at the start of every such enquiry. This sets out the rules under which enquiries are made into returns and explains how taxpayers can expect the Revenue to conduct enquiries. It describes what the Revenue will do when they receive a return and how they will select cases for enquiry, how they will open and carry out enquiries, and what happens if they find something wrong.

The Revenue have also published an Enquiry Handbook as part of their series of internal guidance manuals (see 29.2 INLAND REVENUE EXPLANATORY PUBLICATIONS) and, as an extended introduction to the material on operational aspects of the enquiry regime covered in the manual, a special edition of their Tax Bulletin (Special Edition 2, August 1997). The following points are selected from the Bulletin.

(i) Early submission of a tax return will not increase the likelihood of selection for enquiry.

(ii) The Revenue do not have to give reasons for opening an enquiry — and they *will not do so*.

(iii) Enquiries may be full enquiries or 'aspect enquiries'. An aspect enquiry will fall short of an in-depth examination of the return (though it may develop into one), but will instead concentrate on one or more aspects of it.

(iv) Greater emphasis than before will be placed on examination of underlying records. The Revenue will make an informal request for information before, if necessary, using their powers under *TMA 1970, s 19A* (see 56.12 below)

(v) Where penalties are being sought, the Revenue will aim to conclude the enquiry by means of a contract settlement (as was the case with pre-self-assessment investigations — see 9.9 BACK DUTY) rather than issue a completion notice under *TMA 1970, s 28A* (see 56.13 below).

Where an enquiry remains open beyond the period during which notice of intention to enquire had to be given (see above) and solely because of an unagreed valuation for capital gains tax purposes, the Revenue will not take advantage of the open enquiry to raise further enquiries into matters unrelated to the valuation or the CGT computation except in circumstances where a 'discovery' (see 5.2 ASSESSMENTS) could in any case have been made if the enquiry had been completed (Revenue Pamphlet IR 131, SP 1/99).

From April 1998 onwards, self-employed people whose returns are selected for enquiry will be invited to participate in the Revenue's 'Faster Working' scheme, which involves setting an agreed but flexible timetable for the enquiry. The aim is to complete enquiries within about six months. Participation is voluntary, and either taxpayer or Revenue may pull out of the agreement. The Revenue have published a leaflet — IR 162 'A better approach to local office enquiry work under self-assessment'. (Revenue Press Release 31 March 1998).

See also Revenue Pamphlet IR 160 (Inland Revenue Enquiries under Self-Assessment).

56.12 **Power to call for documents.** At the same time as giving notice under 56.11 above to any person, or subsequently, an officer of the Board may by notice in writing require that person, within a specified period of at least 30 days, to produce to the officer such documents (as are in the person's possession or power) and such accounts or particulars as the officer may reasonably require to check the validity of the return or amendment. Copies of documents may be produced but the officer has power to call for originals, and may himself take copies of, or make extracts from, any document produced. A person is not obliged under these provisions to produce documents, etc. relating to the conduct of any pending appeal by him. There is provision for a person to appeal, within 30 days of the giving of the notice, against any requirement imposed by a notice as above. [*TMA 1970, s 19A; FA 1994, s 187, s 199(2)(3); FA 1996, Sch 22 para 2*]. The minimum 30 days notice required from the Revenue begins with the date of receipt of the *section 19A* notice by the taxpayer (*Self-assessed v Inspector of Taxes (Sp C 207), [1999] SSCD 253*). The Revenue have altered their practice to comply with this ruling, but consider they are entitled still to make use of information previously obtained where insufficient notice was given (Revenue Special 'Working Together' Tax Bulletin April 2000 p 8).

For a case in which the taxpayer failed in an attempt to limit the documentation to be supplied, see *Mother v Inspector of Taxes (Sp C 211), [1999] SSCD 279.*

See 56.26 below as regards penalties for non-compliance.

56.13 **Amendment of self-assessment or partnership statement where enquiries made.** Where notice has been given by an officer of the Board under 56.11 above of an intention to enquire into the taxpayer's return, amendment claim or election the officer's enquiries are treated as completed at such time as he, by notice, informs the taxpayer that he has completed his enquiries and states his conclusions as to the amount of tax which should be contained in the taxpayer's self-assessment and as to any claims or elections into which he has enquired. The taxpayer may before that time apply to the appeal Commissioners concerned for a direction that the officer shall give such notice within a period specified in the direction, such application to be heard and determined in the same way as an appeal against an amendment of self-assessment and the Commissioners to give such a direction unless they are satisfied that the officer has reasonable grounds for not giving such notice.

The taxpayer is given 30 days beginning with the date of completion of the officer's enquiries to amend his self-assessment in accordance with the officer's conclusions. Where the enquiry was into a return rather than an amendment, and the return was made before the expiry of twelve months beginning with the due date for delivery (see 56.5 above), the taxpayer also has this 30-day period to amend his self-assessment in accordance with any amendments to the return which he has notified to the officer. The officer then has a further 30 days in which to amend the self-assessment himself.

If, in the officer's opinion, there is otherwise likely to be a loss of tax to the Crown, the officer may by notice amend the self-assessment before his enquiries are completed.

Similar provisions allow firstly the taxpayer and then the officer to amend or omit, within the same time limits, claims and elections included in the return which do not directly affect the self-assessment, for example a claim to carry forward trading losses, but which the officer thinks should be wholly or partly disallowed, and this is notwithstanding any statutory provision under which the claim or election would otherwise be unamendable or irrevocable.

Where the enquiry is into an amendment by the taxpayer to the return, rather than into the return itself, any amendment by the officer of the self-assessment, whether before or after completion of the enquiry, must be restricted to any deficiency or excess of tax as is attributable to the taxpayer's amendment.

[*TMA 1970, s 28A; FA 1994, s 188, s 199(2)(3); FA 1996, Sch 19 para 2, para 4(1)(2), Sch 22*].

Similar provisions apply in the case of an enquiry into a partnership return etc., taking references above to the self-assessment as references to the partnership statement (see 56.9 above) based on the return. However, there is no provision for the officer to amend the partnership statement before completion of his enquiries. Where a partnership statement is amended under these provisions, the officer will, by notice, make any necessary consequential amendments to the self-assessments of the partners (including company partners). [*TMA 1970, s 28B; FA 1994, s 189, s 199(2)(3); FA 1996, Sch 19 para 2, para 5(1)*].

See 56.28 below for the right of appeal against an amendment by the Revenue to a self-assessment or partnership statement.

56.14 DETERMINATION OF TAX WHERE NO RETURN DELIVERED

Where a notice has been given under *TMA 1970, s 8* or *s 8A* (notice requiring an individual or trustee to deliver a return; see 56.5 above) for 1996/97 and subsequent years of assessment and the return is not delivered by the due date (the filing date), an officer of the Board may make a determination of the amounts of taxable income, capital gains and income tax payable which, to the best of his information and belief, he estimates for the year of assessment. The officer must serve notice of the determination on the person concerned. Tax is payable as if the determination were a self-assessment, with no right of appeal. No determination may be made after the expiry of five years beginning with the filing date.

A determination is automatically superseded by any self-assessment made (whether by the taxpayer or the Revenue), based on information contained in a return. Such self-assessment must be made within the five years beginning with the filing date or, if later, within twelve months beginning with the date of the determination. Any tax payable or repayable as a result of the supersession is deemed to have fallen due for payment or repayment on the normal due date, usually 31 January following the year of assessment (see 56.16 below). Any recovery proceedings commenced before the making of such a self-assessment may be continued in respect of so much of the tax charged by the self-assessment as is due and payable and has not been paid.

[*TMA 1970, s 28C, s 59B(5A); FA 1994, s 190, s 199(2)(3); FA 1996, s 125*].

56.15 INTERIM PAYMENTS OF TAX ON ACCOUNT

For 1997/98 and subsequent years of assessment, where, as regards the year immediately preceding the year of assessment in question,

(*a*) a person is assessed to income tax (including Class 4 national insurance contributions treated as income tax under *Social Security Contributions and Benefits Act 1992, s 16*) under *TMA 1970, s 9* (self-assessment in personal or trustee's return; see 56.6 above),

(*b*) the assessed amount exceeds any income tax deducted at source (including tax deducted under PAYE, taking in any deduction in respect of that year but to be made in a subsequent year but subtracting any amount paid in that year but in respect of a previous year, tax treated as deducted from, or as paid on, any income, and tax credits on dividends), and

(*c*) the said excess (the 'relevant amount') and the proportion which the relevant amount bears to the assessed amount are not less than, respectively, £500 and 20%,

the person must make two interim payments on account of his income tax liability (but not his capital gains tax liability) for the year of assessment in question, each payment being equal to 50% of the relevant amount (see (*c*) above), the first such payment being due on or before 31 January in the year of assessment, the second being due on or before the following 31 July. If the preceding year's self-assessment is made late or is amended, the relevant amount is determined as if the liability as finally agreed had been shown in a timeous self-assessment, with further payments on account then being required as appropriate. If a discovery assessment (see 5.2 ASSESSMENTS) is made for the preceding year each payment on account due is deemed always to have been 50% of the relevant amount plus 50% of the tax charged by the discovery assessment as finally determined.

At any time before 31 January following the year of assessment, the taxpayer may make a claim stating his belief that he will have no liability for the year or that his liability will be fully covered by tax deducted at source, and his grounds for that belief, in which case each of the interim payments is not, and is deemed never to have been, required to be made. Within the same time limit, the taxpayer may make a claim stating his belief that his liability for the year after allowing for tax deducted at source will be a stated amount which is less than the amount otherwise due, and stating his grounds for that belief, in which case each of the interim payments required will be, and deemed always to have been, equal to 50% of the stated amount. Either claim should be made on form SA 303. The maximum penalty for an incorrect statement fraudulently or negligently made in connection with either claim is the amount or additional amount he would have paid on account if he had made a correct statement. Interim payments of tax are subject to the same recovery provisions as any other payments of tax. An officer of the Board may direct, prior to 31 January following the year of assessment, that payments on account are not required. Any payments on account already made will be repaid. [*TMA 1970, s 59A; FA 1994, s 192, s 196, s 199(2), Sch 19 para 45; FA 1995, s 103(7), s 108; FA 1996, s 126(1), Sch 18 para 17(1); SI 1996 No 1654; SI 1997 No 2491*].

See TOLLEY'S INCOME TAX for special transitional arrangements regarding payments on account for 1996/97. For an article on payments on account (including the 1996/97 arrangements), see Revenue Tax Bulletin October 1996 pp 353–356. For an article on Revenue practice on repayment, and allocations and reallocations of overpayments, see Revenue Tax Bulletin June 1999 pp 673, 674.

As an experiment, all self-assessment taxpayers sent a statement of account (see below) in August 1999 and/or December 1999 were given the opportunity to pay their tax by debit card over the telephone (Revenue Press Release 13 August 1999 and Revenue Tax Bulletin December 1999 p 704).

Agents for whom the Revenue holds the taxpayer's authority on form 64–8, for information to be copied, are automatically provided in January and April/early May each year with details (on form SA 327) of their clients' taxpayer statements of account, i.e. advisory statements (on form SA 300) issued to taxpayers notifying them of payments due and outstanding. A customised payslip is attached to the agent statement. A taxpayer may also elect, again using form 64-8, for his statement of account to be sent to his agent instead of to him. Agents registered for electronic lodgement (see 54.16 RETURNS), and authorised to receive copy information, automatically receive electronic copies of statements of account. (Revenue Press Release 12 December 1997 and Revenue Tax Bulletins December 1998 pp 618–620, December 1999 pp 703–705).

Simon's Direct Tax Service. See E1.821.

56.16 FINAL PAYMENT (REPAYMENT) OF TAX

For 1996/97 and subsequent years of assessment, a final payment is due for a year of assessment if a person's combined income tax (including certain Class 4 national insurance contributions treated as income tax as in 56.15 above) and capital gains tax liabilities contained in his self-assessment (see 56.6 above) exceed the aggregate of any payments on account (whether under *TMA 1970, s 59A*, see 56.15 above, or otherwise) and any income tax deducted at source. If the second total exceeds the first, a repayment will be made. Tax deducted at source has the same meaning as in 56.15(*b*) above (but see below as regards partnership income tax for 1996/97).

The due date for payment (or repayment) is 31 January following the year of assessment. The one exception is where the person gave notice of chargeability under *TMA 1970, s 7* (see 54.2 RETURNS) within six months after the end of the year of assessment, but was not given notice under *TMA 1970, s 8* or *s 8A* (personal and trustee's return; see 56.5 above) until after 31 October following the year of assessment; in such case, the due date is the last day of the three months beginning with the date of the said notice. [*TMA 1970, s 59B(1)–(4)(7)(8); FA 1994, s 193, s 196, s 199(2), Sch 19 para 45; FA 1996, s 122(2), s 126(2)*].

As regards partnership businesses commenced (or deemed to commence) before 6 April 1994, each partner's share of income tax assessed on the partnership for 1996/97 is treated for the purposes of determining that partner's final payment or repayment for that year of assessment as if it were tax deducted at source. [*FA 1994, s 198(3); FA 1995, s 116, Sch 21 paras 1, 3*].

ICTA 1988, s 5 (date of payment of income tax) is repealed for 1997/98 and subsequent years of assessment in relation to partnership businesses such as are mentioned in the preceding paragraph, and for 1996/97 and subsequent years of assessment in any other case. For 1996/97 and subsequent years of assessment, the waiting period of one year from the end of the year of assessment before PAYE repaid by the Revenue carries interest is removed. [*ICTA 1988, s 5, s 203(2)(dd); FA 1994, s 199(2), Sch 26 Pt V; FA 1996, Sch 6 para 3*]. *TCGA 1992, s 7* (date of payment of capital gains tax) is repealed for 1996/97 and subsequent years of assessment in order to correspond with the provisions in the preceding paragraphs.

See 56.15 above re notification of taxpayer statement of account details to agents.

56.17 **Due date: Further provisions.** Where a person's self-assessment is amended under the relevant provisions in 56.7, 56.13 or under the partnership 'discovery' provisions (see 5.2 ASSESSMENTS), the due date for the final payment (or repayment) is normally as in 56.16 above but is deferred, as regards any tax payable (or repayable) by virtue of the amendment and subject to the appeal and postponement provisions in 56.28 below, until, if later, 30 days after the date of notice of the amendment (but note that this does not defer the date from which interest accrues on unpaid tax; see 56.19 below).

Where an officer of the Board enquires into the return (see 56.11 above) and a repayment is otherwise due, the repayment is not required to be made until the enquiry is completed (see 56.13 above) although the officer may make a provisional repayment at his discretion. This does not affect the due date of repayment for interest purposes (see 56.20 below).

Subject to the appeal and postponement provisions in 56.28 below, the due date for payment of tax charged by assessment otherwise than by self-assessment under *TMA 1970, s 9* (see 56.6 above), e.g. a discovery assessment under *TMA 1970, s 29* (see 5.2 ASSESSMENTS), is 30 days after the date of the assessment (but see 56.19 below as regards interest on unpaid tax). [*TMA 1970, s 59B(4A)(5)(6); FA 1994, s 193, s 199(2)(3); FA 1995, s 103(7), s 115(6); FA 1996, s 127*].

56.18 SURCHARGES ON UNPAID TAX

See 35.5 INTEREST AND SURCHARGES ON UNPAID TAX.

56.19 INTEREST ON UNPAID TAX

For 1996/97 and subsequent years (1997/98 and subsequent years as regards partnerships whose business commenced before 6 April 1994), interest is chargeable as follows on interim payments (see 56.15 above) and final payments (see 56.16 and 56.17 above) of income tax and capital gains tax which are made late, on tax chargeable on any assessment other than a self-assessment and on tax becoming payable under *TMA 1970, s 55* (payment and postponement of tax pending appeal; see 56.28 below). Interest accrues from the 'relevant date' (even if a non-business day) to the date of payment. For the two interim payments under 56.15 above, the '*relevant dates*' are the due dates, i.e. 31 January in the year of assessment and the following 31 July respectively. In any other case, the '*relevant date*' is 31 January following the year of assessment (with the one exception that where the due date of a final payment is deferred until three months after notice is given to deliver the return (see 56.16 above), the relevant date is identically deferred).

In practice, however, where no statement of account was issued by the Revenue before the end of December 1996, even though the taxpayer had provided all relevant information at the appropriate time, interest on interim tax paid after its due date of 31 January 1997 will run only from 30 days after the date of notification to the taxpayer of the amount due. Confirmation should be sought from the tax office if there is any doubt as to whether the reason for a statement of account not being received in time falls within this practice. (Revenue Press Release 27 January 1997). For subsequent years, where a self-assessment return is submitted by 30 September for calculation by the Revenue of the tax due (see 56.6 above), the relevant date, where it would otherwise have been the following 31 January, is deferred until 30 days after notification of the liability to the taxpayer if this occurs later than 31 December following the tax year (Revenue Self-Assessment Manual — Interest, penalties and surcharge section — para 1.2.1).

There are provisions to remit interest charged on interim payments to the extent that an income tax repayment is found to be due for the year. There are also provisions covering the situation where a taxpayer makes a claim to dispense with or reduce his interim payments (see 56.15 above) and the total income tax liability for the year is found to be such that interim payments should have been made or should have been greater. Interest is chargeable as if each interim payment due had been equal to half the current year's liability or half the previous year's liability, whichever is less.

Interest is also chargeable under these provisions in respect of an income tax or capital gains tax assessment **for 1995/96 or an earlier year which is made after 6 April 1998**, the '*relevant date*' being 31 January following the year of assessment.

[*TMA 1970, s 86; FA 1995, s 110; FA 1996, s 131, Sch 18 para 17(5)*].

Interest is also chargeable on late payment of surcharges (see 35.5 INTEREST AND SURCHARGES ON UNPAID TAX) and penalties (see 56.22 below).

The rate of interest charged on unpaid tax will be in line with the average rate for borrowing. The rate paid on overpaid tax (see 56.20 below) will be in line with the average return on profits. (Revenue booklet SAT 2 (1995), para 3.114). See 35.1 INTEREST AND SURCHARGES ON UNPAID TAX for details of rates.

Where the above provisions of *TMA 1970, s 86* have effect, *TMA 1970, s 88* (interest on tax recovered to make good loss of tax due to taxpayer's fault — see 35.8 INTEREST AND SURCHARGES ON UNPAID TAX) no longer has effect. [*FA 1996, Sch 18 para 4, para 17(3)(4)*].

56.20 INTEREST ON OVERPAID TAX

The provisions of *ICTA 1988, s 824* (see TOLLEY'S INCOME TAX under Interest on Overpaid Tax) are amended for 1996/97 and subsequent years of assessment (for 1997/98 and subsequent years of assessment as regards partnerships whose trades commenced before 6 April 1994). A repayment of income tax (including an amount paid on account as in 56.15 above), or of a surcharge under *TMA 1970, s 59C* (see 35.5 INTEREST AND SURCHARGES ON UNPAID TAX) or of a penalty incurred by an individual under any provision of *TMA 1970* will be increased by an amount (a repayment supplement) equal to interest on the amount repaid for the period (if any) between the 'relevant time' and the date of repayment. The '*relevant time*' is,

(*a*) as regards interim payments (see 56.15 above) and payments of income tax not deducted at source, the date of the payment,

(*b*) as regards income tax deducted at source, 31 January next following the year of assessment for which the tax is deducted, and

(*c*) as regards a penalty or surcharge, the date on which the penalty or surcharge was paid.

Income tax is deducted at source for a year of assessment for these purposes if it is so deducted (or treated as deducted) from any income, or treated as paid on any income, in respect of that year, or if it is a tax credit in respect of that year (but excluding tax deducted under PAYE in respect of previous years). Repayments in respect of income tax for a year of assessment are attributed first to the final payment (see 56.16 above) in respect of income tax for that year, secondly in two equal parts to the interim payments for that year, and finally to income tax deducted at source for that year. Where a payment was made in instalments, any repayment is attributed to later instalments before earlier ones.

Other amendments consequential to the introduction of self-assessment are made to *ICTA 1988, s 824*.

[*ICTA 1988 s 824; FA 1994, s 196, s 199(2)(a), Sch 19 para 41; FA 1997, s 92(1)–(4)(6)*].

The rate of interest paid on overpaid tax will be in line with the average return on profits. The rate charged on unpaid tax (see 56.19 above) will be in line with the average rate for borrowing. (Revenue booklet SAT 2 (1995), para 3.114). See 34.1 INTEREST ON OVERPAID TAX for details for rates.

The provisions of *TCGA 1992, s 283* are amended for 1996/97 and subsequent years of assessment. A repayment of capital gains tax will be increased by an amount (a repayment supplement) equal to interest on the amount repaid for the period (if any) between the 'relevant time' and the date of repayment. The '*relevant time*' is the date on which the tax was paid. [*TCGA 1992, s 283; FA 1994, s 196, s 199(2), Sch 19 para 46, Sch 26 Pt V; FA 1997, s 92(5)(6)*]. See 34.1 INTEREST ON OVERPAID TAX.

56.21 DATE OF PAYMENT BY CHEQUE

For the purposes of *TMA 1970* generally, *ICTA 1988, s 824* and s *826* and *TCGA 1992, s 283* (see 56.20 above) as well as *ICTA 1988, s 825* (repayment supplement in respect of accounting period of a company ended before 1 October 1993; see 34.3 INTEREST ON OVERPAID TAX), where any payment to an officer of the Board or the Board is received by cheque after 5 April 1996 and the cheque is paid on its first presentation to the bank on which it is drawn, the payment is treated as made on the date of receipt of the cheque by the officer or the Board. [*TMA 1970, s 70A; FA 1994, s 196, Sch 19 para 22*].

56.22 PENALTIES

The penalty provisions described below and at 56.23 to 56.26 below apply for 1996/97 and subsequent years of assessment. See also 54.2 RETURNS for the penalty for failing to give notice of chargeability to tax and 56.10 above and 12.3 CLAIMS for penalties for failing to keep and preserve records. Penalties for other returns etc. under *TMA 1970, s 98* (see 47.7 PENALTIES) continue to apply as before, as do the statutory provisions of *TMA 1970, ss 97A, 102, 105* concerning mitigation and limitation of penalties described at 47.10 PENALTIES.

A penalty under 54.2 RETURNS (notice of chargeability), 56.10 above (records), 56.15 above (payments on account), 12.3 CLAIMS (records relating to claims) or any penalty under *TMA 1970, Pt X (ss 93–107)* carries interest, calculated from the due date (broadly, 30 days after issue of a determination of it by an officer of the Board or immediately on determination by appeal Commissioners or judgement of High Court; see 47.9 and 47.10 PENALTIES) to the date of payment. [*TMA 1970, s 103A; FA 1994, s 196, s 199(2)(3), Sch 19 para 33; FA 1995, s 103(7), s 115(8)*]. See 35.1 INTEREST AND SURCHARGES ON UNPAID TAX for rates of interest.

Consequential amendments are made to *TMA 1970, s 100B* (appeals against penalty determinations; see 47.10 PENALTIES) and *Social Security Contributions and Benefits Act 1992, s 16* (Class 4 contributions treated as income tax). In addition, the disapplication of the three-year time limit within which tax-geared penalty proceedings must be commenced from final determination of tax in the case of a deceased person (see 47.13 PENALTIES) is to apply by reference to tax charged in an assessment made later than six years after 31 January next following the chargeable period (previously, after the end of the chargeable period) for which it was charged. [*TMA 1970, s 100B, s 103(2); FA 1994, s 196, s 199(2)(3), Sch 19 paras 31, 32, 45; FA 1995, s 103(7), s 115(7)*].

56.23 **Failure to make timeous return for income tax and capital gains tax.** A person (the taxpayer) who fails to deliver a return when required to do so by notice under *TMA 1970, s 8* or *s 8A* (personal or trustee's return; see 56.5 above) is liable to a penalty of £100 which can be determined by an authorised officer of the Board. For continuing failure, a further penalty of up to £60 per day may be imposed by the appeal Commissioners concerned (but not at any time after the failure has been remedied) on application by an officer of the Board, such daily penalty to start from the day after the taxpayer is notified of the Commissioners' direction (but not for any day for which such a daily penalty has already been imposed). If the failure continues for more than six months beginning with the filing date (i.e. the due date for delivery of the return; see 56.5 above), and no application for a daily penalty was made within those six months, the taxpayer is liable to a further £100 penalty determined as above. If failure continues after the anniversary of the filing date, and there would have been a liability under *TMA 1970, s 59B* (final payment of tax; see 56.16 above), based on a proper return promptly delivered, the taxpayer is liable to a further penalty determined as above of an amount not exceeding that liability. See 56.33 below for trustees.

If the taxpayer proves that his liability under *TMA 1970, s 59B*, based on a proper return promptly delivered, would not have exceeded a particular amount, his liability to penalties other than the daily and tax-geared penalties is reduced to that amount. Thus, a payment on account, made under *TMA 1970, s 59A* or otherwise, which reduces the liability outstanding at 31 January to less than £100 will similarly reduce the total automatic penalties otherwise chargeable (see Revenue Enquiry Handbook para 640).

On an appeal against either of the £100 penalties (reduced where appropriate), the Commissioners may either confirm the penalty or, if it appears to them that *throughout* the period of failure the taxpayer had a reasonable excuse for not delivering the return, set it aside. In practice, the Revenue allow 14 days for the return to be filed after the excuse has ended (Revenue Tax Bulletin April 1998 p 529).

[*TMA 1970, s 93; FA 1994, s 196, s 199(2), Sch 19 para 25*].

The Revenue's intention is to use the sanction of the daily penalty where the tax at risk is substantial and they believe the fixed penalties to be an insufficient deterrent (Revenue booklet SAT 2 (1995), para 2.74).

The Revenue were prepared to exercise some discretion as regards the initial £100 penalty in cases where 1996/97 returns were originally filed by 31 January 1998 but had to be returned to the taxpayer due to some oversight on his part (Revenue Press Release 3 February 1998). A similar concession applies for 1997/98 returns; where the return is delivered on or before 31 January 1999, is found to be incomplete as a result of a genuine oversight and is returned to the taxpayer after 17 January 1999 for completion, the taxpayer is given 14 days to redeliver the return without incurring an automatic penalty. The concession will not be applied if a deliberately incomplete return is filed in order to buy time. (Revenue Tax Bulletin October 1998 pp 593, 594).

See Revenue booklet SA/BK6 'Self-assessment: penalties for late tax returns', and see also Revenue Tax Bulletin April 1998 pp 527–529 for the Revenue's views on what does and does not constitute a 'reasonable excuse'. Where the Revenue stated that they would treat 1996/97 returns hand-delivered before the opening of tax offices on Monday 2 February as timeously delivered, a taxpayer whose return was hand-delivered later that day was held to have had a reasonable excuse throughout the period of default, which consisted solely of Sunday 1 February (*Steeden v Carver (Sp C 212), [1999] SSCD 283*). Following this case, the Revenue announced that 1998/99 returns delivered before 7.30am on Wednesday 2 February 2000 would not incur a late delivery penalty (Revenue Tax Bulletin December 1999 pp 705, 706). The same approach is to be followed as regards the 31 January 2001 deadline for 1999/2000 returns. Note that this does not alter the fact that the period within which the Revenue may give notice of enquiry is itself extended where the return is delivered later than 31 January (see 56.11(*b*) above). In practice, the Revenue will treat a 1998/99 return delivered as above as being within 56.11(*a*) above, but this will not apply for later years' returns. (Revenue Special 'Working Together' Tax Bulletin April 2000 p 8).

56.24 **Failure to make partnership return or return relating to European Economic Interest Grouping.** The same fixed penalties and daily penalties determined and imposed as in *TMA 1970, s 93* (see 56.23 above) apply in the case of failure to submit a partnership return as required by a notice under *TMA 1970, s 12AA* (see 56.8 above). However, there is no tax-geared penalty and no provision for reducing the £100 penalties. Each person who was a partner at any time during the period in respect of which the return was required is separately liable to the fixed and daily penalties. The penalties apply by reference to failure by the representative partner, i.e. the partner required by the notice under *TMA 1970, s 12AA* to deliver the return or his successor (see 56.8 above). Where penalties are imposed on two or more partners, an appeal cannot be made otherwise than by way of composite appeal by the representative partner or his successor. The same reasonable excuse provisions apply as under *TMA 1970, s 93* but by reference to the representative partner (or successor). [*TMA 1970, s 93A; FA 1994, s 196, s 199(2)(3), Sch 19 para 26; FA 1996, s 123(8)–(11)*].

The fixed penalty provided for by *TMA 1970, s 98B* (penalty for failure by European Economic Interest Grouping or member of it to make a return; see 56.5 above) is increased to £300 multiplied by the number of members of the grouping at the time of failure and this can be determined by an authorised officer of the Board. For continuing failure, there is a further daily penalty of up to £60 multiplied by the number of members of the grouping at the end of the day on which the grouping or member is notified of a direction to impose such a penalty by the appeal Commissioners concerned on an application by an officer of the Board, such daily penalty to start from the day after the taxpayer is so notified (but not for any day for which such a daily penalty has already been imposed). Neither the fixed nor the daily penalty can be imposed after the failure is remedied and the aggregate of any fixed and daily penalties cannot exceed £100 if there is no income or chargeable gain to be included in the return. [*TMA 1970, s 98B(1)(2)(2A)(2B)(3)(4); FA 1994, s 196, s 199(2)(3), Sch 19 para 30*].

56.25 **Fraud or negligence.** The provisions of *TMA 1970, s 95* (tax-geared penalty for fraudulently or negligently delivering an incorrect return, accounts etc. for income tax or capital gains tax; see 47.4 PENALTIES) continue to apply, with consequential amendments, under self-assessment. [*TMA 1970, s 95; FA 1994, s 196, s 199(2)(3), Sch 19 para 27, Sch 26 Pt V*].

Similar provisions will apply as regards partnerships. They apply where a partner (the representative partner) delivers an incorrect partnership return (see 56.8 above), or, in connection with such a return, makes an incorrect statement or declaration or submits incorrect accounts, and either he does so fraudulently or negligently or his doing so is attributable to fraudulent or negligent conduct on the part of a 'relevant partner' (i.e. any person who was a partner at any time in the period covered by the return). Each relevant partner is liable to a penalty not exceeding the income tax (or corporation tax) underpaid by him as a result of the incorrectness. Where penalties are imposed on two or more partners, an appeal cannot be made otherwise than by way of composite appeal by the representative partner or his successor (see 56.8 above). [*TMA 1970, s 95A; FA 1994, s 196, s 199(2)(3), Sch 19 para 28; FA 1996, s 123(12)(13)*].

56.26 **Failure to produce documents.** A new penalty applies where a person fails to comply with a notice or requirement under *TMA 1970, s 19A* (notice requiring production of documents, etc. for purpose of Revenue enquiry into a return; see 56.12 above). He is liable to a fixed penalty of £50 determinable by an authorised officer of the Board and, for each day of continuing failure (but not for any day for which such a daily penalty has already been imposed) after the fixed penalty is imposed, a further penalty not exceeding the 'relevant amount'. Neither the fixed nor the daily penalty may be imposed after the failure has been remedied. An officer of the Board may also determine the daily penalty under *TMA 1970, s 100* (see 47.9 PENALTIES), in which case the '*relevant amount*' is £30, or instead may commence proceedings under *TMA 1970, s 100C* (see 47.10 PENALTIES) for determination of the penalty by the appeal Commissioners concerned, in which case the '*relevant amount*' is £150. [*TMA 1970, s 97AA; FA 1994, s 196, s 199(2)(3), Sch 19 para 29; FA 1996, Sch 19 para 3*]. The Revenue decided to discharge any penalty charged after 14 December 1998 following a failure to comply with a *section 19A* notice which was invalid because it required compliance in less than the necessary 30 days from receipt (see 56.12 above) (Revenue Special 'Working Together' Tax Bulletin April 2000 p 8).

56.27 ASSESSMENTS: PROCEDURE AND TIME LIMIT

The procedure for the raising of assessments other than self-assessments is set out in *TMA 1970, s 30A*. All income tax falling to be charged by such an assessment may, even if chargeable under more than one Schedule, be included in one assessment. These provisions apply for 1996/97 and subsequent years of assessment except that, in relation to partnerships whose trades were set up or commenced before 6 April 1994, they apply for 1997/98 and subsequent years of assessment. [*TMA 1970, s 30A; FA 1994, s 196, s 199(2)(3), Sch 19 para 5*].

The normal time limit for the making of an assessment to income tax and capital gains tax for 1996/97 or a subsequent year of assessment is five years after 31 January following the year of assessment to which the assessment relates. The existing normal time limit of six years after the end of the accounting period for the making of a corporation tax assessment continues unchanged under self-assessment for accounting periods ending on or after 1 July 1999 (see 56.2 above). [*TMA 1970, s 34(1); FA 1994, s 196, s 199(2)(3), Sch 19 para 10; FA 1998, s 117, Sch 18 para 46(1), Sch 19 para 17*]. For such chargeable periods, the extended time limit in cases of fraudulent or negligent conduct is twenty years after 31 January next following the year of assessment in the case of an income tax or capital gains tax assessment, and twenty-one years after the end of the accounting period in the case of a corporation tax assessment. Assessments under these extended time limits can be made on partners of the person in default. [*TMA 1970, s 36(1)(2); FA 1994, s 196, s 199(2)(3), Sch 19 para 11; FA 1998, s 117, Sch 18 para 46(2), Sch 19 para 18*]. The latest time for assessing the personal representatives of a deceased person is three years after 31 January following the year of assessment in which death occurred. [*TMA 1970, s 40(1)(2); FA 1994, s 196, s 199(2), Sch 19 para 12*]. (For time limits applying before 1996/97, see 5.5 ASSESSMENTS and 9.4 BACK DUTY.)

56.28 APPEALS

For 1996/97 and subsequent years of assessment or company accounting periods ending on or after 1 July 1999 (see 56.2 above), a right of appeal is conferred by *TMA 1970, s 31* against

(*a*) any assessment other than a self-assessment,

(*b*) an amendment by an officer of the Board of a self-assessment or partnership statement on enquiry into the return on which it is based (see 56.13 above),

(*c*) an amendment of a partnership statement where loss of tax is 'discovered' (see 5.2 ASSESSMENTS), and

(*d*) a disallowance, in whole or in part, of a claim or election included in a return (by amendment or otherwise).

Written notice of appeal must be given within 30 days after the issue of the notice of assessment or amendment. An appeal within (*b*) above against an amendment to a self-assessment cannot be heard and determined before the officer gives notice that he has completed his enquiries, if he has not already done so (see 56.13 above). An appeal within (*b*) to (*d*) above cannot question the exercise by the Revenue of the 'Crown Option' (see 56.13 above). [*TMA 1970, s 31(1)–(3); F(No 2)A 1975, s 67(1); FA 1994, s 196, s 199(2)(3), Sch 19 para 7, Sch 26 Pt V; FA 1996, Sch 19 para 6, Sch 22 para 4*].

Consequential amendments are made to *TMA 1970, s 50* (procedure on appeals heard by Commissioners; see 4.8 APPEALS). The Commissioners are given the power to vary the extent to which a claim or election included in a return is disallowed. [*TMA 1970, s 50(6)–(9); FA 1994, s 196, s 199(2)(3), Sch 19 para 17; FA 1996, Sch 19 para 7*]. Otherwise, the provisions in 4 APPEALS generally continue to apply.

Payment of tax pending appeal. The provisions of *TMA 1970, s 55* (payment and postponement of tax pending appeal; see 46.3 and 46.4 PAYMENT OF TAX) continue to apply in respect of

(i) an assessment other than a self-assessment and

(ii) an amendment by an officer of the Board of a self-assessment on enquiry into the return on which it is based (see 56.13 above).

[*TMA 1970, s 55; FA 1994, s 196, 199(2), Sch 19 para 18; FA 1996, Sch 18 para 1, para 17(1)(2); FA 1998, s 117, Sch 19 para 28*].

See 56.19 above as to the date from which interest on unpaid tax will accrue.

56.29 CLAIMS ETC.

A new formal procedure applies for 1996/97 and subsequent years of assessment as regards the making of claims, elections and notices. See 12.2 CLAIMS.

56.30 JURISDICTION OF COMMISSIONERS

As regards any proceedings relating to 1996/97 or a subsequent year (or for corporation tax any accounting period to which self-assessment applies), certain questions which may be in dispute on appeal (but not necessarily the entire appeal) must be determined by the Special Commissioners. See TOLLEY'S INCOME TAX under Self-Assessment.

An appeal against an assessment made by the Board *must*, as previously, be to the Special Commissioners. [*TMA 1970, s 31(3); FA 1996, Sch 22 para 4*].

Where, on an appeal against an amendment of a self-assessment or partnership statement, the question in dispute concerns a claim made to the Board or made under any one or more specified provisions, the question must be determined by the Special Commissioners. This effectively continues the rules previously in *TMA 1970, Sch 2 paras 2, 3*. The specified provisions cover double taxation relief, management expenses of the owner of mineral rights, exemptions for certain friendly societies, trade unions and employers' associations, and reliefs in respect of royalties, copyright payments, etc. [*TMA 1970, s 46C; FA 1996, Sch 22 para 7*].

Rules for assigning procedures to General Commissioners. Where the General Commissioners have jurisdiction, the rules for prescribing the appropriate division are adapted for self-assessment (see 4.3 APPEALS as regards previous rules and general practice). For proceedings relating to income tax or capital gains tax (except those concerning PAYE or partnerships or where the Board otherwise direct, see below), either the taxpayer or an officer of the Board (whichever commences the proceedings) may elect by notice to the other in writing for the proceedings to be heard in the division situated in either the taxpayer's place of residence, his place of business (as defined) or his place of employment (as defined and regardless of whether the proceedings are in connection with the employment). An officer may make the election if the taxpayer fails to exercise his right to do so when giving notice of appeal or otherwise commencing proceedings or at such later time as the Board allow. The taxpayer's election is irrevocable. Proceedings relating to a partnership to which a partner is a party are brought before the division in the place where the partnership business is, or is mainly, carried on. For proceedings relating to corporation tax (or income tax where a UK resident company is a party), there are rules similar, but suitably modified, to those above for income tax and capital gains tax.

Notwithstanding the above, the Board may direct that specified proceedings be brought before the General Commissioners for a specified division. An officer of the Board must serve on the taxpayer written notice stating the effect of the direction, and the taxpayer may object in writing within 30 days of the notice being served, in which case the direction has no effect. The Board may also give directions for determining the appropriate division, other than in PAYE appeals, where there is no place of residence, business or employment (or corporation tax equivalents) in the UK; procedure is as above except that the taxpayer has no right of objection.

The parties to proceedings may supersede the above rules by coming to an agreement that the proceedings be brought before the General Commissioners for a division specified therein. The rules are also subject to specified provisions involving two or more parties other than the Revenue (which have their own rules), see 4.5 APPEALS.

[*TMA 1970, s 44(1)(2), Sch 3; FA 1988, s 133(2); FA 1996, Sch 22 para 10; Sch 41 Pt V(12)*].

56.31 OVER-REPAYMENTS OF TAX

For 1996/97 and subsequent years of assessment or company accounting periods ending on or after 1 July 1999 (see 56.2 above), *TMA 1970, s 30* (assessments to recover tax over-repaid; see 46.10 PAYMENT OF TAX) continues to apply but subject to the same exceptions (modified as appropriate) as for discovery assessments (see 5.2 ASSESSMENTS). The normal time limit for such an assessment is extended, if necessary, to the later of the end of the chargeable period following that in which the repayment was made and, where relevant, the day on which an officer of the Board's enquiries into a return (or amendment of a return) delivered by the person concerned are treated as completed (see 56.13 above). [*TMA 1970, s 30(1B)(5); FA 1994, s 196, s 199(2)(3), Sch 19 para 4; FA 1998, s 117, Sch 18 paras 52, 53, Sch 19 para 13*].

56.32 COLLECTION AND RECOVERY

For 1996/97 and subsequent years of assessment or company accounting periods ending on or after 1 July 1999 (see 56.2 above), miscellaneous amendments are made to provisions covering the collection and recovery by the Revenue of tax, interest on tax, surcharges and penalties. The limit of £1,000 referred to in 46.7 PAYMENT OF TAX is raised to £2,000. [*TMA 1970, ss 65, 69, 70; FA 1994, s 196, s 199(2)(3), Sch 19 paras 19–21; FA 1998, s 117, Sch 19 paras 30–32*].

56.33 SETTLEMENTS AND TRUSTEES

From 1996/97 new rules take effect for the assessment and collection of tax on trust income and gains where there is more than one trustee. Anything done by a 'relevant trustee' is regarded as done by all the relevant trustees, including the making of returns and self-assessment. Liability for penalties, interest or surcharge may be recovered (but only once) from any one or more of the relevant trustees other than one who was not a relevant trustee at the relevant time (as defined by *TMA 1970, s 107A(3)*). In relation to chargeable gains, the '*relevant trustees*' of a settlement are the persons who are trustees in the tax year in which the gains accrue and any persons who subsequently become trustees. [*TMA 1970, s 7(2)(9), s 8A(1)(5), s 107A, s 118; FA 1995, s 103, Sch 29 Pt VIII(14)*].

For 1996/97 onwards, chargeable gains which accrue to a trustee can be assessed on any relevant trustee (see above), with similar provisions for personal representatives of deceased persons. [*TCGA 1992, s 65(1); FA 1995, s 103(7), s 114*].

Trustees of 'bare' (or 'simple') trusts treated as such for tax purposes are not required to complete self-assessment returns or make payments on account, the beneficiaries under such trusts being liable to give details of the income and gains in their own tax returns. (Revenue Press Release 20 January 1997). The trustees may, *if they wish*, make a self-assessment return of income, and account for basic or lower rate tax thereon. Capital gains and capital losses must *not* be included in any such return, these being the sole responsibility of the beneficiaries. (Revenue Tax Bulletin December 1997 pp 486, 487).

56.34 CAPITAL LOSSES

For 1996/97 and subsequent years for capital gains tax and for accounting periods ending on or after 1 July 1999 (see 56.2 above) for corporation tax, a capital loss is not an allowable loss unless its amount is quantified and notified to the Revenue, such notice being subject to the provisions of *TMA 1970, s 42*, and to the enquiry regime (see 56.11 above), as if it were a claim for relief (see 12 CLAIMS). For capital gains tax purposes, losses must, if possible, be notified on the self-assessment tax return or in an amendment thereto, or failing that may be notified on or before the fifth anniversary of 31 January following the year of assessment in which they arose (regardless of whether they are utilised within that period — there is no time limit on the utilisation of losses brought forward). [*TCGA 1992, s 16(2A); FA 1995, s 103(7), s 113(1)*]. Notice may be given outside the tax return either by making an entry for allowable losses brought forward in a subsequent year's return (within the time limit) and/or by giving the Inspector a separate notice (see Self-Assessment Tax Return Notes on Capital Gains Tax).

Order of set-off. Losses arising to individuals and trustees in the year 1996/97 and subsequent years are to be treated as utilised before losses arising in earlier years. Similarly, losses accruing to companies for accounting periods ending on or after 1 July 1999 (see 56.2 above) will have preference to losses arising in accounting periods ending before that date. [*FA 1995, s 113(2)*].

56.35 UK REPRESENTATIVES OF NON-RESIDENTS

For 1996/97 and subsequent years for capital gains tax and for company accounting periods beginning after 31 March 1996, obligations and liabilities under self-assessment fall upon UK representatives of non-residents carrying on a trade in the UK through a branch or agency. Certain persons are not regarded as UK representatives, in order that certain professional services may be provided without exposing the non-resident client to UK tax. [*FA 1995, ss 126, 127, Sch 23*]. See TOLLEY'S INCOME TAX for the detailed provisions.

57 Settlements

Cross-references. See 2 ANNUAL RATES AND EXEMPTIONS; 5.6 ASSESSMENTS for assessments on trustees; 10 CHARITIES; 11.2 CHILDREN for bare trustees for children; 16 DEATH for provisions relating to death and to personal representatives; 19.25 EMPLOYEE SHARE SCHEMES for certain transfers of shares to employee share ownership trusts; 21.79 EXEMPTIONS AND RELIEFS for settlements for the benefit of employees; 23 GIFTS and 25 HOLD-OVER RELIEFS for disposals not at arm's length and the availability of hold-over reliefs generally; 26.2 INDEXATION for transitional relief for 'indexation losses' in 1993/94 and 1994/95 only in the case of disposals by trustees of settlements made before 30 November 1993; 43 OFFSHORE SETTLEMENTS for overseas resident settlements etc.; 48.6 PRIVATE RESIDENCES for reliefs applicable to trustees; 50.4 and 50.5 REINVESTMENT RELIEF for relief available on disposals by trustees; 53.8 RETIREMENT RELIEF for relief available on disposals by trustees; 54.3, 54.9 RETURNS for returns by trustees; 58.13 SHARES AND SECURITIES for stock dividends received by trustees; 60 TAPER RELIEF; 66.6 WASTING ASSETS for the situation where a disposal of a life interest in settled property gives rise to a chargeable event.

Sumption: Capital Gains Tax. See A6.

The headings in this chapter are as follows.

57.1 RATES OF TAX

For 1998/99 and subsequent years, the rate of capital gains tax applicable to the trustees of any settlement who are liable in respect of disposals of settled property (see 57.2 and 57.3 below) is equivalent to the 'rate applicable to trusts' under *ICTA 1988, s 686* (but subject to the charge on settlors with interests in settlements as in 57.3 below). The rate for 1998/99–2000/01 inclusive is **34%**.

For 1988/89 to 1997/98 inclusive, the rate of capital gains tax applying to the trustees of a settlement (other than an 'accumulation or discretionary settlement') who are similarly liable is equivalent to the basic rate of income tax for the year (but again subject to the charge on settlors with interests in settlements as in 57.3 below). The rate for 1997/98 is 23%, for 1996/97 it is 24% and for 1988/89 to 1995/96 inclusive it is 25%.

For 1988/89 to 1997/98 inclusive, the rate of capital gains tax applying to the trustees of an accumulation or discretionary settlement who are similarly liable is equivalent to the 'rate applicable to trusts' (but again subject to the charge on settlors in 57.3 below). The rate for 1997/98 and 1996/97 is 34% and it is 35% for 1988/89 to 1995/96 inclusive.

An '*accumulation or discretionary settlement*' is, for the above purposes, a trust where

(*a*) all or any part of the income arising to the trustees in the year of assessment is income to which *ICTA 1988, s 686* (income tax rate applicable to discretionary or accumulating trust; prior to 1993/94, liability to income tax at the additional rate) applies, or

(*b*) all the income arising to the trustees in the year is treated as the income of the settlor, but *section 686* would apply to it if it were not so treated, or

(*c*) all the income arising to the trustees in the year is applied in defraying expenses of the trustees in that year, but *section 686* would apply to it if it were not so applied, or

(*d*) no income arises to the trustees in the year, but *section 686* would apply if there were income arising to the trustees and none of it were treated as the income of the settlor or as applied in (*c*) above.

[*TCGA 1992, s 4(1)(1AA), s 5; ICTA 1988, s 1, s 686(1)(1A), s 832(1); FA 1993, s 79, Sch 6 paras 8, 15, 23; FA 1996, Sch 6 paras 27, 28; FA 1998, s 120, Sch 27 Pt III(29); FA 1999, s 26(3)*].

Before 1988/89, gains arising to the trustees of any settlement were charged at the rate of 30%. [*CGTA 1979, s 3; FA 1988, Sch 14 Pt VII*].

57.2 MEANING OF 'SETTLED PROPERTY'

'*Settled property*' means any property held in trust other than property held by 'nominees' or 'bare trustees' (see below). Property held by a trustee or assignee in bankruptcy or under a deed of arrangement (see below) is not settled property. Property under a unit trust scheme (as defined) is also excluded from being settled property. [*TCGA 1992, s 66(4), s 68, s 99*]. See also 64.1 UNIT TRUSTS ETC.

Nominees and bare trustees. Where assets are held by a person

(i) as nominee for another or others, or

(ii) as trustee for a person (or persons) 'absolutely entitled' as against him,

capital gains tax is chargeable as if the assets were held by that other person or persons and such property were not settled property.

A person is '*absolutely entitled*', for these purposes, if he has the exclusive right (subject only to satisfying any outstanding charge, lien or other right of the trustee to resort to the property for the payment of duty, tax, costs or other outgoings) to direct how that asset shall be dealt with, or would have that right but for being an infant or under some other legal disability (e.g. a mentally handicapped person). [*TCGA 1992, s 60*]. The disability must arise from the general law, and not from the wording of the trust deed (see *Tomlinson v Glyn's Exor and Trustee Co Ltd CA 1969, 45 TC 600* where the trustees were held assessable to capital gains tax because the beneficiary's interest was contingent on his attaining majority, and could not be deemed to be vested in him). In *Booth v Ellard CA 1980, 53 TC 393,* several taxpayers by agreement transferred their shares in a company to trustees. The trusts were determinable by a majority of the beneficiaries (who were also the settlors), each beneficiary had a right of pre-emption over the others' shares, and the income was to be distributed in proportion to the number of shares to which each beneficiary was entitled (which corresponded with the number which he had settled). It was held that each beneficiary retained his interest in the same number of shares as he had settled (albeit not the identical shares). Despite the restraints, it was within the beneficiaries' collective power to terminate the trusts, and each beneficiary was therefore absolutely entitled as against the trustees. See also *Jenkins v Brown, Warrington v Brown and related appeals Ch D, [1989] STC 577.*

Kidson v Macdonald Ch D 1973, 49 TC 503 laid down that tenants in common of land held on trust for sale were jointly absolutely entitled. It is not necessary that particular assets to which the beneficiaries are entitled should be identifiable (*Stephenson v Barclays Bank Trust Co Ltd Ch D 1974, 50 TC 374*), but see *Cochrane's Exors v CIR CS 1974, 49 TC 299* (entitlement to residue) and *Crowe v Appleby CA 1975, 51 TC 457*.

Insolvents' assets. Assets held by a trustee or assignee in bankruptcy or under a 'deed of arrangement' are treated as if still owned by the bankrupt or debtor (the trustee's acquisitions from, or disposals to, the bankrupt being disregarded) and as if the trustee's acts in relation to those assets were acts of the bankrupt. But tax on chargeable gains arising from such acts is assessable on, and payable by, the trustee, etc. *'Deed of arrangement'* means a deed to which the *Deeds of Arrangement Act 1914* (or any corresponding Act in Scotland or NI) applies. [*TCGA 1992, s 66(1)(5)*].

When the bankrupt etc. dies, the assets held by the trustee are deemed for the purposes of *TCGA 1992, s 62(1)* (see 16.1 DEATH) to have then been acquired by the trustee as if he were a personal representative. The provisions above do not then apply after death. But if the bankrupt is dead before the trustee is appointed, the provisions above also do not apply, the assets being regarded as held by the deceased's personal representative. [*TCGA 1992, s 66(2)–(4)*].

In re McMeekin QB (NI) 1973, 48 TC 725 it was held that capital gains tax is an administration cost of bankruptcy.

57.3 LIABILITY OF TRUSTEES, SETTLORS AND BENEFICIARIES

Trustees of a settlement are liable to capital gains tax, under provisions relating to the tax generally, on disposals or deemed disposals of settled property (but subject to the charge on settlors with interests in settlements as below). The exempt amount for a year of assessment available to trustees is given in 57.4 and 57.5 below. Trustees are treated as a single and continuing body (distinct from the persons who may from time to time be trustees) which is resident and ordinarily resident in the UK unless the administration of the settlement is ordinarily carried on outside the UK and the trustees or a majority of them for the time being are not resident or not ordinarily resident in the UK. A person carrying on the business of managing settlements (and acting as trustee in the course of that business) is treated as not resident in relation to a settlement if the entire settled property consists of, or is derived from, property provided by a person not at the time (or, in the case of a will trust, at death) domiciled, resident or ordinarily resident in the UK. If, in such a case, the trustees or a majority of them are, or are treated as, not resident in the UK, the administration of the settlement is treated as ordinarily carried on outside the UK. [*TCGA 1992, s 69(1)(2)*].

Special rules apply to overseas resident settlements etc. See 43 OFFSHORE SETTLEMENTS.

Where part of the property comprised in a settlement is vested in one trustee or set of trustees and part in another (and in particular settled land within the meaning of the *Settled Land Act 1925* is vested in the tenant for life and investments representing capital money are vested in the trustees of the settlement), all the trustees are treated as together constituting and, insofar as they act separately, as acting on behalf of a single body of trustees. [*TCGA 1992, s 69(3)*].

The Board may by notice in writing require a person who is a 'party' to a settlement (within *ICTA 1988, s 660G(1)(2)*) to provide within not less than 28 days information it thinks necessary for the purposes of *TCGA 1992*. [*TMA 1970, s 27*].

Charge on settlors with interests in settlements. In certain circumstances gains accruing to trustees in a year after 1987/88 are not chargeable on them, but instead an equal amount of gains (as in (*b*) below) is treated as accruing to the settlor in the year. (See 43

OFFSHORE SETTLEMENTS for interaction between the provisions mentioned therein and those given below.)

The charge on the settlor arises if all of the following conditions are fulfilled.

(*a*) Chargeable gains (including those arising under *TCGA 1992, s 13* as in 44.6 OVERSEAS MATTERS) accrue in a year to the trustees of a settlement from the disposal of any or all of the settled property.

(*b*) The trustees would otherwise, after making deductions for losses (including those taken into account under *TCGA 1992, s 13*) under *TCGA 1992, s 2(2)* (see 39.1 LOSSES) but taking no account of the annual exemption under *TCGA 1992, s 3* (see 57.4 and 57.5 below), be chargeable to tax for the year in respect of those gains.

(*c*) The settlor is, and the trustees are, either resident in the UK during any part of the year or ordinarily resident in the UK during the year.

(*d*) The settlor is alive at the end of the year.

(*e*) At any time during the year the settlor has an interest in the settlement.

(*f*) The settlor is not excepted from the charge as below.

A settlor has an interest in a settlement if

(i) any property which may at any time be comprised in the settlement or any derived property is, or will or may become, payable to or applicable for the benefit of the settlor or his spouse in any circumstances whatsoever, or

(ii) the settlor or his spouse, enjoys a benefit deriving directly or indirectly from any property which is comprised in the settlement or any derived property.

For 1995/96 onwards, references to the spouse of the settlor in (i) and (ii) above do not include a person to whom the settlor is not for the time being married but may marry later, or a spouse from whom the settlor is separated under a court order or similar arrangement that is likely to be permanent, or the widow or widower of the settlor.

A settlor does not have an interest under (i) above if and so long as

(A) none of the property which may at any time be comprised in the settlement and no derived property can become applicable or payable as mentioned in (i) above except in the event of: the bankruptcy of some person who is or may become beneficially entitled to that property or any derived property; any assignment of or charge on that property or any derived property being made or given by some such person; in the case of a marriage settlement, the death of both the parties to the marriage and all or any of the children of the marriage; or the death of a child of the settlor who had become beneficially entitled to the property or any derived property at an age not exceeding 25; or

(B) some person is alive and under the age of 25 during whose life the property or any derived property cannot become applicable or payable as mentioned in (i) above except in the event of that person becoming bankrupt or assigning or charging his interest in that property.

The settlor is excepted from the charge where

(I) he has an interest in a settlement under (i) or (ii) above only because that property is, or will or may become, payable to or applicable for the benefit of his spouse *or* his spouse enjoys a benefit from property, or for both such reasons, and

(II) his spouse dies, or he and his spouse cease to be married, during the year.

For these purposes, derived property means income from that property or any other property directly or indirectly representing proceeds of that property or income therefrom.

For years before 1995/96 the above provisions differed in some degree in their wording. For the previous wording see Tolley's Capital Gains Tax 1994/95 or earlier.

Where the trustees of a maintenance fund for an historic building elect under *ICTA 1988, s 691(2)* that income arising under the settlement or part of the settlement involved is not to be treated as income of the settlor for a year of assessment, no charge arises under these provisions in relation to the settlement or part for the year.

For these provisions a person is a '*settlor*' in relation to a settlement if the settled property consists of or includes property originating from him. Property originates from a settlor where he provides it directly or indirectly for the purposes (see *Countess Fitzwilliam and others v CIR (and related appeals) HL 1993, 67 TC 614*) of the settlement (including property provided by another person under reciprocal arrangements) and where property (or a proper part thereof) represents that property. In general, references to settled property (and to property comprised in a settlement), in relation to a settlor, are references only to property originating from that settlor.

A settlor has a right of recovery against any trustee for the amount of tax he is charged under these provisions. Such amount is identified by treating the gains that are deemed to accrue to him (or, for 1988/89 and 1989/90 only, his wife, if he is chargeable in respect of her gains) as forming the highest part of his chargeable amount for the year. There are provisions for 1988/89 and 1989/90 only to ascertain the amount where tax at a rate equivalent to the higher rate of income tax is charged in respect of gains assessed on a man who is chargeable in respect of his wife's gains and gains under these provisions accrue to either of them.

The inspector may require a settlor, trustee or former trustee to provide him with particulars for the purposes of these provisions. Failure to do so within a specified time (which cannot be less than 28 days) incurs penalties under *TMA 1970, s 98* (see 47.7 PENALTIES).

[*TCGA 1992, s 77, s 78(1)(2), s 79; FA 1988, Sch 10 para 5(3)–(5), Sch 14 Pt VIII; FA 1995, Sch 17 paras 27–29*].

Offset of losses and application of taper relief. The amount treated as accruing to the settlor under the above provisions will be net of TAPER RELIEF (60) where this is available. No further taper relief is available to the settlor. In addition, for 1998/99 and subsequent years of assessment, the settlor's own, untapered, losses, whether of the current year of assessment or brought forward from previous years, cannot be set off against gains treated as accruing to him as above. [*TCGA 1992, s 2(4)(5), s 77(6A); FA 1998, s 121(3)(4), Sch 21 para 2, para 6(1)*].

Collection of unpaid tax from beneficiaries etc. If tax assessed on trustees in respect of a chargeable gain accruing to them is not paid within six months from the date when it becomes payable *and* before or after that date the asset in respect of which the gain accrued, or any part of the proceeds of sale of that asset, is transferred to a person who becomes absolutely entitled to it, or the proceeds etc., that person may be assessed and charged in the name of the trustees within two years from the time when the tax became payable. The tax chargeable is not to exceed the tax chargeable on an amount equal to the chargeable gain and, where only a part of the asset or of the proceeds was transferred, is not to exceed a proportionate part of that amount. [*TCGA 1992, s 69(4)*].

57.4 ANNUAL EXEMPTIONS

An annual exempt amount is allowed to trustees in the same way as it is to individuals, and the same rules apply as to the interaction between this amount, allowable losses and taper relief. See 2.5 ANNUAL RATES AND EXEMPTIONS.

The level and availability of the exemption are subject to conditions. These are given below or, in the case of settlements for the disabled etc., in 57.5 below.

Settlements made before 7 June 1978. For 1980/81 onwards an outright exemption of *one-half* of the full annual exemption for individuals is available to trustees of such settlements. The exemption limits are thus **£3,600** for 2000/01, £3,550 for 1999/2000, £3,400 for 1998/99, £3,250 for 1997/98, £3,150 for 1996/97, £3,000 for 1995/96, £2,900 for 1992/93 to 1994/95 inclusive, £2,750 for 1991/92, £2,500 for 1988/89, 1989/90 and 1990/91, £3,300 for 1987/88, £3,150 for 1986/87, £2,950 for 1985/86 and £2,800 for 1984/85.

Settlements made after 6 June 1978. For 1980/81 and subsequent years of assessment the same exemption is available as for settlements made before 7 June 1978 above with the addition of special provisions for 'groups' of settlements. Where a settlement is one of two or more 'qualifying settlements' comprised in a group, the annual exemption is the amount given by dividing one-half of the full annual exemption for individuals (see above) by the number of settlements in the group. However, there is a minimum exemption per settlement of one-tenth of the full annual exemption for individuals.

A '*qualifying settlement*' is any settlement made after 6 June 1978 and which is not a settlement for the disabled, etc. (see 57.5 below) or an 'excluded settlement' (see below). A '*group*' of settlements constitutes all those qualifying settlements with the same 'settlor'. Where, in consequence of this, a settlement is comprised in two or more groups because that settlement was made by two or more settlors, then, in determining the level of annual exemption available as above, it is deemed to be in the group comprised of the greatest number of settlements.

'*Settlor*' has the meaning given by *ICTA 1988, s 660G(1)(2)* (see 14.7 CONNECTED PERSONS) and includes, in the case of a settlement arising under a will or intestacy, the testator or intestate. Settlements created by a deed of variation within 16.6 DEATH do not 'arise under' a will so that in the Revenue's view the testator is not the settlor of the settlements created (Tolley's Practical Tax 1986 p 48).

'*Excluded settlements*' are any of the following

(i) Settlements, the trustees of which are not for the whole or any part of the year of assessment treated under *TCGA 1992, s 69(1)* (see 57.3 above) as resident and ordinarily resident in the UK.

(ii) Settlements, the property in which is held solely for charitable purposes and cannot become applicable for other purposes. See also 10.1 CHARITIES.

(iii) Settlements, the property in which is held for the purposes of certain retirement benefits and compensation funds which are exempt from a charge on capital gains.

The inspector may, by notice in writing, require any party to a settlement to provide, within a stipulated time (not less than 28 days), such information as the inspector thinks necessary for the application of the above provisions.

[*TCGA 1992, s 3(1)–(5C), Sch 1 para 2; SI 1992 No 626; FA 1993, s 82; FA 1994, s 90; SI 1994 No 3008; FA 1995, Sch 17 para 32; SI 1995 No 3033; SI 1996 No 2957; SI 1998 No 757; FA 1998, s 121(3)(4), Sch 21 para 3; SI 1999 No 591; SI 2000 No 808*].

57.5 **Settlements for the disabled etc.** Subject to the 'grouping' provisions below the same annual exemption as for individuals (e.g. £7,200 for 2000/01) (applied, in general, as for individuals: see 2.5 ANNUAL RATES AND EXEMPTIONS for this and for exemptions for earlier years) is available to trustees of such settlements, provided that, during the whole or part of the year of assessment concerned, the settled property is held on trusts which secure that, during the lifetime of a 'mentally disabled person' or a person in receipt of 'attendance allowance' or of a 'disability living allowance' by virtue of entitlement to the care component at the highest or middle rate,

(*a*) not less than half of the property which is applied, is applied for the benefit of the person concerned, and

(*b*) that person is entitled to not less than half of the income arising from the property, or no such income may be applied for the benefit of any other person.

'*Mentally disabled person*' means a person who, by reason of mental disorder within the meaning of *Mental Health Act 1983*, is incapable of administering his property or managing his affairs.

'*Attendance allowance*' means an allowance under *Social Security Contributions and Benefits Act 1992, s 64* or *Social Security Contributions and Benefits (Northern Ireland) Act 1992, s 64*.

'*Disability living allowance*' means a disability living allowance under *Social Security Contributions and Benefits Act 1992, s 71* or *Social Security Contributions and Benefits (Northern Ireland) Act 1992, s 71*.

For the purposes of (*a*) and (*b*) above, powers of advancement conferred on the trustees under *Trustee Act 1925, s 32* or *Trustee Act (Northern Ireland) 1958, s 33* will not, as such, disqualify the trust from the relief, and requirements that income be applied for qualifying purposes 'during the lifetime' of a person are deemed satisfied if income is applied for such purposes, during a period where it is held for that person on protective trusts, as under *Trustee Act 1925, s 33*.

Groups. For 1981/82 and subsequent years of assessment, where a settlement is one of two or more 'qualifying settlements' made after 9 March 1981 comprised in a 'group', the annual exemption is the full annual exemption for individuals divided by the number of settlements in the 'group'. However, there is a minimum exemption of one-tenth of the full annual exemption.

A '*qualifying settlement*' is any settlement for a disabled person, etc. within the provisions above made after 9 March 1981 and which is not an 'excluded settlement'. A '*group*' of settlements constitutes all those qualifying settlements with the same 'settlor'. Where in consequence of this, a settlement is comprised in two or more groups because that settlement was made by two or more settlors, then, in determining the level of annual exemption available as above, it is deemed to be in the group comprised of the greatest number of settlements.

'*Settlor*' and '*excluded settlement*' are as defined in 57.4 above in relation to other settlements made after 6 June 1978 and there are similar powers to call for information.

[*TCGA 1992, s 3(1)–(5C), Sch 1 para 1; SI 1992 No 626; FA 1993, s 82; FA 1994, s 90; SI 1994 No 3008; SI 1995 No 3033; SI 1996 No 2957; SI 1998 No 757; FA 1998, s 121(3)(4), Sch 21 para 3; SI 1999 No 591; SI 2000 No 808*].

57.6 CREATION OF A SETTLEMENT

A transfer into settlement, whether revocable or irrevocable, is a disposal of the entire property settled even if the transferor is a beneficiary or trustee of the settlement. [*TCGA*

1992, s 70]. The acquisition and disposal are treated as being made at MARKET VALUE (40) subject to the exclusion therein mentioned. HOLD-OVER RELIEFS (25) may be available in respect of chargeable gains that would otherwise arise to the settlor. The settlor of a settlement and the trustees of that settlement are CONNECTED PERSONS (14) and further rules may operate as to valuation and losses (in particular see 3.13 and 3.14 ANTI-AVOIDANCE, 40.1 MARKET VALUE and 39.5 LOSSES).

Example

In December 2000, C transfers to trustees of a settlement for the benefit of his children 10,000 shares in W plc, a quoted company. The value of the gift is £85,000. C bought the shares in 1981 for £20,000 and their value at 31 March 1982 was £35,000. The indexation factor for March 1982 to April 1998 is 1.047.

	£	£
Deemed disposal consideration	85,000	85,000
Cost	20,000	
Market value 31.3.82		35,000
Unindexed gain	65,000	50,000
Indexation allowance £35,000 × 1.047	36,645	36,645
Gain after indexation	£28,355	£13,355
Chargeable gain (subject to TAPER RELIEF (60))		£13,355
Trustees' allowable cost		£85,000

Note to the example

(*a*) If the transfer is a chargeable lifetime transfer for inheritance tax purposes, or would be one but for the annual inheritance tax exemption, C could elect under *TCGA 1992, s 260* to hold the gain over against the trustees' base cost of the shares. The trustees do not join in any such election. This would normally cover only a transfer to a discretionary settlement. Where taper relief is otherwise available, it is the untapered gain that is held over (see 60.13 TAPER RELIEF).

Before 10 March 1981 the legislation used the term 'gift in settlement' rather than 'transfer into settlement'. [*CGTA 1979, s 53*]. For the position regarding the definition of 'gift' in this regard see *Berry v Warnett HL 1982, 55 TC 92*. Here the HL, by a majority, rejected the Crown's contention that 'gift in settlement' should be equated with 'transfer into settlement' but unanimously accepted the Crown's argument that, on a proper construction of the relevant agreement, there had been a disposal of the entirety of the trust fund to the trustee under a bargain other than at arm's length and accordingly MARKET VALUE (40) applied to the disposal. What are now *TCGA 1992, s 70* and *TCGA 1992, ss 71, 72* (see 57.9 and 57.10 below) are special cases of the assumption on which the legislation, in particular *TCGA 1992, s 69(1)(2)* (see 57.3 above) proceeded, namely that tax was chargeable on disposals to trustees.

Exercise of power of appointment or advancement. For the consequences of the exercise of such a power see *Hoare Trustees v Gardner; Hart v Briscoe Ch D 1977, 52 TC 53; Chinn v Collins HL 1980, 54 TC 311; Roome v Edwards HL 1981, 54 TC 359; Eilbeck v Rawling HL 1981, 54 TC 101; Bond v Pickford CA 1983, 57 TC 301; Swires v Renton Ch D 1991, 64 TC 315*. Following the decision in *Bond v Pickford* above, the Board of Inland Revenue issued Pamphlet IR 131, SP 7/84 to set out the Revenue's views on the capital gains tax implications of the exercise of a power of appointment or advancement when continuing trusts are declared. This Statement modified the earlier SP 9/81 which was issued for a similar purpose following the decision in *Roome v Edwards* above and accordingly SP 9/81 was withdrawn from 11 October 1984.

The Board states in SP 7/84 that the judgements in *Roome v Edwards* emphasised that, in deciding whether or not a new settlement has been created by the exercise of a power of appointment or advancement, each case must be considered on its own facts, and by applying established legal doctrine to the facts in a practical and commonsense manner. The Court of Appeal judgements in *Bond v Pickford* explained that the consideration of the facts must include examination of the powers which the trustees purported to exercise, and the determination of the intention of the parties, viewed objectively.

The Board considers it now clear that a deemed disposal under *TCGA 1992, s 71(1)* (see 57.9 below) cannot arise unless the power exercised by the trustees, or the instrument conferring the power, expressly or by necessary implication, confers on the trustees authority to remove assets from the original settlement by subjecting them to trusts of a different settlement. Such powers (which may be powers of advancement or appointment) were referred to by the Court of Appeal in *Bond v Pickford* as 'powers in the wider form'. The Board considers that a deemed disposal will not arise when such powers are exercised and trusts are declared in circumstances such that

(*a*) the appointment is revocable, or

(*b*) the trusts declared of the advanced or appointed funds are not exhaustive so that there exists a possibility at the time when the advancement or appointment is made that the funds covered by it will, on the occasion of some event, cease to be held upon such trusts and once again come to be held upon the original trusts of the settlement.

The Board also considers it unlikely a deemed disposal will occur when trusts are declared following the exercise of such a power if the duties of trusteeship as regards the appointed assets fall to the trustees of the original settlement. This follows from the provision in *TCGA 1992, s 69(1)* that the trustees of a settlement form a single and continuing body (see 57.3 above).

In conclusion the Board accepts that a power of appointment or advancement can be exercised over only a part of settled property and that the foregoing would apply to that part.

See *Begg-McBrearty v Stilwell Ch D 1996, 68 TC 426* for interpretation of *Family Law Reform Act 1969*.

Revenue practice regarding validity of trust deeds for general and tax law purposes. From 6 April 1991 new trust deeds (other than those for special types of trust such as unit trusts, charitable trusts and employee trusts) will not, as previously, be examined individually by the Revenue for their validity under general law as well as tax law. The Revenue will normally rely on the information shown in returns etc. made by the settlors, trustees and beneficiaries and will only seek further information where necessary, and only exceptionally will they ask to see deeds or other documents. Trustees will be asked to supply information about themselves and the settlor and whether the trustees have power to accumulate income or to distribute it at their discretion. This change of practice is for the purposes of income and capital gains tax but the examination of deeds for inheritance tax purposes is unaffected (Revenue Press Release 19 December 1990). It follows that great care should be exercised before executing a trust deed to ensure it is effective for the purposes desired.

57.7 INTERESTS IN SETTLED PROPERTY

Interests in settled property take a variety of forms as outlined below. Their treatment for capital gains tax purposes is given in 57.8 to 57.11 below.

Interests created by or arising under a settlement. These include, in particular, an annuity or life interest (see below), and the reversion to an annuity or life interest, but are otherwise not specifically defined. [*TCGA 1992, s 76*].

Life interests in relation to a settlement. The meaning of 'life interest' includes a right under the settlement to the income of, or the use or occupation of, settled property for the life of a person other than the person entitled to the right, or for lives. [*TCGA 1992, s 72(3)(a)*]. Any right which is contingent on the exercise of the discretion of the trustee or some other person is not a life interest. [*TCGA 1992, s 72(3)(b)*]. The ordinary meaning of 'life interest' (i.e. the right of a person to income etc. during his life) is also accepted as applying. Interests which are not primarily defined by reference to a life are not considered to be life interests, so that a beneficiary with an interest in possession (see below) in settled property which will come to an end on obtaining a specified age does not have a life interest (Revenue Pamphlet IR 1, D43). However, concessional treatment is available for such non-life interests which cease on the death of a beneficiary as in 57.10 and 57.11 below.

An annuity created by the settlement is included as a life interest if

(i) some or all of the settled property is appropriated by the trustees as a fund out of which the annuity is payable and

(ii) there is no right of recourse to settled property not so appropriated or to the income thereof.

While such an annuity is payable, and on the occasion of the death of the annuitant, the appropriated part of the settled property is treated as being settled property under a separate settlement. Annuities, other than those above, are not life interests notwithstanding that they are payable out of, or charged on, settled property or the income thereof. [*TCGA 1992, s 72(3)(c), (4)*]. However, where an annuity which is not a life interest is terminated by the death of the annuitant, certain provisions in 57.10 and 57.11 below apply as on the termination of a life interest by the death of the person entitled thereto.

Life interest in possession in all or part of settled property. The legislation gives no meaning to the term 'life interest in possession' although it seems regard must be made to the meaning of 'life interest' (as above) and to judicial interpretation of the term 'interest in possession'. Such interpretation arose in *Pearson and Others v CIR HL, [1980] STC 318* where the point at issue was the meaning of the term 'interest in possession' as used in certain capital transfer tax legislation dealing with settled property. The majority opinions of the HL indicated the following.

(*a*) There must be a *present right to the present enjoyment* of something for there to be an interest in possession in settled property. So a person with an interest in possession will have an immediate right to trust income as it arises.

(*b*) If the trustees have *any power to withhold income* as it arises there is no interest in possession. There is a distinction between a power to terminate a present right to present enjoyment and a power which prevents a present right of present enjoyment arising. It follows that

  (i) a power to accumulate income is sufficient to prevent a beneficiary from having an interest in possession. The position is the same if there is a trust to accumulate. Whether or not income is in fact accumulated is irrelevant;

  (ii) an overriding power of appointment which could be used to defeat the interest of a beneficiary does not prevent that interest from being in possession if it does not affect the right of the beneficiary to the income which has already arisen;

  (iii) the possibility of future defeasance of an interest does not prevent it from being in possession until the occurrence of the relevant event; and

(iv) a power of revocation does not prevent an interest from being in possession until it is exercised.

(*c*) There is a distinction between trustees' *administrative powers*, such as those to pay duties, taxes etc., and their *dispositive powers* to dispose of the net income of the trust. The existence of the former does not prevent an interest from being in possession. Any interest in possession will be in the net income of the trust after deduction of administrative expenses.

(*d*) The fact that an interest in settled property is not in remainder or reversion or contingent does not automatically make it an interest in possession.

The Revenue had published their views on the meaning of 'interest in possession' prior to the HL decision in *Pearson* above. Their statement, although now withdrawn, is reproduced in Revenue Pamphlet IHT 1 (1991), p 88 and the Revenue regard the views expressed therein as 'not inconsistent' with the opinions given in *Pearson*.

If, in exercise of their powers under the settlement, the trustees grant a beneficiary an exclusive or joint right to occupy a dwelling-house which forms part of the settled property with the intention of providing the beneficiary with a permanent home, the Revenue regard this as creating an interest in possession, even if the right is revocable or for a limited period. A right granted for non-exclusive occupation or for full consideration is not so regarded (Revenue Pamphlet IR 131, SP 10/79). See 48.6 PRIVATE RESIDENCES for the exemption available on the disposal of a dwelling-house which has been occupied in the above circumstances.

57.8 **DISPOSAL OF AN INTEREST IN SETTLED PROPERTY**

Subject to the exclusions below for settlements which are, or have ever been, non-resident settlements, no chargeable gain accrues on the disposal of an interest created by or arising under a settlement (see 57.7 above) if the disposal was made

(*a*) by the person for whose benefit the interest was created by the terms of the settlement; or

(*b*) by any other person except one who acquired, or derives his title from one who acquired, the interest for a consideration in money or money's worth, other than consideration consisting of another interest under the settlement.

Subject to the above, where a person who has acquired an interest in settled property becomes, as the holder of that interest, absolutely entitled (see 57.2 above) as against the trustee to any settled property, he is treated as disposing of the interest in consideration of obtaining the property so received (but without prejudice to any gain accruing to the trustee on the deemed disposal by the trustee under *TCGA 1992, s 71(1)* (see 57.9 below)).

[*TCGA 1992, s 76(1)(2); FA 1998, s 128(1)*].

Where the disposal of a life interest in settled property does give rise to a chargeable event, the interest may be treated as a wasting asset in certain circumstances. See 66.6 WASTING ASSETS.

See 57.12 below for anti-avoidance provisions deeming there to be, in specified circumstances, a disposal of underlying assets at the same time as an actual disposal of an interest in settled property for consideration.

Exclusion for certain non-resident settlements. The exemption above does not apply to disposals of interests in settlements which are, or have ever been, non-resident. See 43.3 OFFSHORE SETTLEMENTS.

57.9 PERSON BECOMING ABSOLUTELY ENTITLED TO SETTLED PROPERTY

General rule. Subject to the exception below, where a person becomes absolutely entitled to any settled property as against the trustee, all the assets forming part of the settled property to which he becomes so entitled are deemed to have been disposed of by the trustee and immediately reacquired by him in the capacity of bare trustee or nominee within *TCGA 1992, s 60(1)* (see 57.2 above) for a consideration equal to the market value of the assets. [*TCGA 1992, s 71(1)*]. See *Figg v Clarke Ch D 1996, 68 TC 645* for interpretation of date of absolute entitlement.

Where an interest in possession in part of settled property terminates (whether voluntarily or involuntarily) and the part can properly be identified with one or more specific assets, or where within a reasonable time, normally three months, of the termination, the trustees appropriate specific assets to give effect to the termination, the Revenue will treat the deemed disposal and reacquisition as applying to those assets, and not to any part of the other assets comprised in the settlement. In particular, agreement will be made of lists of assets properly identifiable with the termination, and any such agreement will be regarded as binding on the Revenue and the trustees (Revenue Pamphlet IR 131, November 1997 Supplement, SP D10).

Any resulting net chargeable gain is assessed on the trustee in the usual way (subject to a claim for HOLD-OVER RELIEFS (25) but note the general relief for gifts in 25.9 was only extant after 5 April 1982 and before 14 March 1989).

Losses. Where, **after 15 June 1999**, a person (the beneficiary) becomes absolutely entitled to any settled property as against the trustee and a loss accrues to the trustee on the resulting deemed disposal under *TCGA 1992, s 71(1)* (see above) of an asset comprised in that property, then, subject to the restrictions below, the loss is treated as a loss accruing to the beneficiary instead of to the trustee. This applies only to the extent that the loss cannot be deducted from gains accruing to the trustee either on the deemed disposal of other assets on that occasion or on disposals made earlier in the same year of assessment, and for this purpose such a loss is treated as deductible in priority to any other allowable losses accruing to the trustee in that year. Where a loss is so treated as accruing to the beneficiary, it is allowable *only* against chargeable gains accruing to him on disposal by him of the same asset, i.e. the asset on the deemed disposal of which the loss occurred, or, where the asset is land, any asset which is 'derived' from it (as defined). The loss can be carried forward to subsequent years of assessment until such time as it has been fully allowed against such gains. Where there is such a gain, the loss in question is treated as deductible in priority to any other allowable losses accruing to the beneficiary in the year of assessment concerned and, where it is brought forward, is deductible as if it were a loss accruing in that year (see 39.1 LOSSES for set-off of losses generally). For a worked example, see Tolley's Tax Computations or Tolley's Capital Gains Tax Workbook.

Where the occasion on which a person became absolutely entitled to any settled property as against the trustee occurred **before 16 June 1999**, *any* allowable loss which had accrued to the trustees in respect of property which was, or was represented by, the property to which the beneficiary became so entitled (including allowable losses on *actual* disposals by the trustees and any such losses brought forward from previous years of assessment) was treated (to the extent that it could not be set against other chargeable gains arising to the trustee in that year of assessment but before that occasion) as an allowable loss accruing to the beneficiary at the time he became entitled. The beneficiary can utilise that loss without restriction.

[*TCGA 1992, s 71(2)–(2D); FA 1999, s 75*].

The position should be contrasted with that of allowable losses made by personal representatives as in 16.7 DEATH.

Where trust losses are transferable to a beneficiary as above, the Revenue do not restrict those losses under *TCGA 1992, s 18(3)* (see 39.5 LOSSES) where the trustees and the person becoming absolutely entitled are CONNECTED PERSONS (14) (Revenue Tax Bulletin February 1993 p. 57).

Miscellaneous. References in the foregoing to the case where a person becomes absolutely entitled to settled property as against the trustee include references to the case where a person would become so entitled but for being an infant or other person under disability. [*TCGA 1992, s 71(3)*].

Where a person disposes of an asset to which he became absolutely entitled as against the trustees of settled property, any incidental expenditure incurred by that person or the trustees in relation to the transfer of the asset to him is allowable as a deduction in the computation of the gain arising on the disposal. [*TCGA 1992, s 64(1)*]. The expenditure incurred by the person concerned, but not that incurred by the trustees, qualifies for indexation allowance (Revenue Capital Gains Manual CG 31192).

Exception where a life interest is terminated by the death of the person entitled thereto. Where, as above, a person becomes absolutely entitled as against the trustee to assets forming part of settled property and that occasion is the termination of a life interest by the death of the person entitled to that interest then, subject to conditions and certain exceptions, *no* chargeable gain arises on the deemed disposal. See 57.11(*a*) below for full details.

57.10 TERMINATION OF LIFE INTEREST IN POSSESSION ON DEATH OF PERSON ENTITLED: ASSETS REMAINING SETTLED PROPERTY

The following provisions apply after 5 April 1982 and are subject to the exception below.

(*a*) Where an interest (a life interest in relation to deaths before 6 April 1996) in possession in all or part (see SP D10 in 57.9 above) of settled property is terminated on the death of the person entitled to it (e.g. a life tenant), the whole or a corresponding part of each of the assets forming part of the settled property and not at that time ceasing to be settled property is deemed to be disposed of and immediately reacquired by the trustee at that time for a consideration equal to the whole or a corresponding part of the market value of the asset. However, any gain arising on such a deemed disposal is not a chargeable gain. [*TCGA 1992, s 72(1); FA 1996, Sch 39 para 5(2)(4)*].

(*b*) The provisions in (*a*) also apply where the person entitled to an interest (a life interest in relation to deaths before 6 April 1996) in possession in all or part of the settled property although the interest does not then terminate. [*TCGA 1992, s 72(2); FA 1996, Sch 39 para 5(2)(4)*]. This situation could occur where the person for whose benefit the interest was created had previously disposed of his interest under 57.8 above to the deceased and was still living at the date of death. The foregoing also contemplates interests created *pur autre vie*, i.e. based on the life of another.

Annuities. For deaths after 5 April 1996 (*a*) and (*b*) above apply on the death of the person entitled to any annuity payable out of, or charged on, settled property or the income of settled property as it applies on the death of a person whose interest in possession in the whole or any part of settled property terminates on his death. Where, in the case of any entitlement to an annuity created by a settlement some of the settled property is appropriated by the trustees as a fund out of which the annuity is payable, and there is no right of recourse to, or to the income of, settled property not so appropriated, then without prejudice to *TCGA 1992, s 72(5)* below, the settled property so appropriated is, while the annuity is payable, and on the occasion of the death of the person entitled to the annuity, treated for the purposes of *TCGA 1992, s 72* as being settled property under a separate settlement. [*TCGA 1992, s 72(3)(4); FA 1996, Sch 39 para 5(3)(4)*]. For deaths before 6 April 1996 broadly similar provisions applied. [*TCGA 1992, s 75; FA 1996, Sch 41 Pt VIII(4)*]. In the case where the annuity is not paid out of specified funds, the Revenue treats the 'corresponding part' (see (*a*) above) of the assets forming the settled property as being given by the proportion which the amount of the annuity bears to the whole of the settlement income arising in the year prior to the date of death.

Part interests and income interests. For the purposes of (*a*) and (*b*) above, an interest (a life interest in relation to deaths before 6 April 1996) which is a right to part of the income of settled property is treated as such an interest in a corresponding part of the settled property. [*TCGA 1992, s 72(1); FA 1996, Sch 39 para 5(2)(4)*].

If there is an interest (a life interest in relation to deaths before 6 April 1996) in income in a part of settled property such that there is no right of recourse to, or to the income from, the remainder of the settled property, then the part of the settled property in which such interest subsists is similarly treated as being settled property under a separate settlement for so long as such an interest subsists. [*TCGA 1992, s 72(5); FA 1996, Sch 39 para 5(2)(4)*].

Interests in possession which are not life interests. For all cases which are settled after 16 February 1993 and relate to deaths before 6 April 1996, the Revenue will extend (subject to *TCGA 1992, s 67* and *s 74* below) concessionally the treatment statutorily afforded by *TCGA 1992, s 72* above regarding life interests to interests in possession which are not life interests. Where the property remains settled property, the concession can be claimed on the subsequent disposal of that property (except where there is a charge on that disposal under *TCGA 1992, s 67* or *s 74* in respect of a held-over gain (see below)) but in cases where there is an amount of outstanding chargeable gain which was held over when the property was transferred to the trustees, that amount must be deducted from the market value of the property at the date of death. If the concession is claimed, it must apply to all of the assets in which the deceased had an interest in possession, other than assets which are covered by agreements made before 17 February 1993 or subject to a charge under *TCGA 1992, s 67* or *s 74*. This concession (ESC D43) is superseded for deaths after 5 April 1996 by amendments made to *TCGA 1992, s 72* above.

Exception where hold-over relief under TCGA 1992, s 165 or s 260 or FA 1980, s 79 claimed previously. In certain circumstances where a claim has been made for hold-over relief in respect of the disposal of an asset to the trustee and, subsequently, the trustee is deemed to dispose of and immediately reacquire the asset so that under *TCGA 1992, s 72* above there would otherwise be no chargeable gain arising, it is specifically provided by *TCGA 1992, s 67* or *s 74* that a chargeable gain, restricted to the amount of the held-over gain, is to accrue to the trustee. See 25.5, 25.8 and 25.9 HOLD-OVER RELIEFS.

57.11 TERMINATION OF LIFE INTEREST ON DEATH OF PERSON ENTITLED: PERSON BECOMING ABSOLUTELY ENTITLED

The following provisions apply after 5 April 1982 and are subject to the exception below.

(*a*) Where, under *TCGA 1992, s 71(1)* in 57.9 above, the assets forming part of any settled property are deemed to be disposed of and reacquired at market value by the trustee on the occasion when a person becomes, or would but for a disability become, absolutely entitled thereto as against the trustee, then, if that occasion is the death of a person entitled to an interest in possession in the settled property (for deaths before 6 April 1996, if that occasion is the termination of a life interest by the death of the person entitled to that interest) (e.g. the death of a life tenant)

(i) no chargeable gain accrues on the deemed disposal; and

(ii) if on the death the property reverts to the disponer (e.g. the original settlor), the disposal and reacquisition by the trustee is treated as taking place on a no gain/no loss basis, and if the acquisition by the trustee was at a time prior to 6 April 1965, the reversion is related back to that date.

(*b*) Where the interest (life interest for deaths before 6 April 1996) is an interest in part (see SP D10 in 57.9 above) only of the settled property to which the person becomes absolutely entitled, (*a*)(i) above does not apply but although a chargeable gain will accordingly arise as under *TCGA 1992, s 71(1)* in 57.9 above it is reduced by a proportion corresponding to that represented by the part in which the interest (life interest for deaths before 6 April 1996) subsisted. Any remaining chargeable gain may be the subject of a claim for one of the HOLD-OVER RELIEFS (25).

[*TCGA 1992, s 73(1)(2); FA 1996, Sch 39 para 6(2)(3)(5)*].

Annuities. For deaths after 5 April 1996 (*a*) and (*b*) above apply on the death of the person entitled to any annuity payable out of, or charged on, settled property or the income of settled property as it applies on the death of a person whose interest in possession in the whole or any part of settled property terminates on his death. Where, in the case of any entitlement to an annuity created by a settlement some of the settled property is appropriated by the trustees as a fund out of which the annuity is payable, and there is no right of recourse to, or to the income of, settled property not so appropriated, then without prejudice to *TCGA 1992, s 72(5)* below, the settled property so appropriated is, while the annuity is payable, and on the occasion of the death of the person entitled to the annuity, treated for the purposes of *TCGA 1992, s 72* as being settled property under a separate settlement. [*TCGA 1992, s 72(3)(4), s 73(3); FA 1996, Sch 39 para 5(3)(4), para 6(4)(5)*]. For deaths before 6 April 1996 broadly similar provisions applied. [*TCGA 1992, s 75; FA 1996, Sch 41 Pt VIII(4)*]. In the case where the annuity is not paid out of specified funds, the Revenue treats the 'proportion corresponding to that represented by the part in which the interest (life interest for deaths before 6 April 1996) subsisted' (see (*b*) above) of the assets forming the settled property as being given by the proportion which the amount of the annuity bears to the whole of the settlement income arising in the year prior to the date of death.

Part interests and income interests. For the purposes of (*a*) and (*b*) above, an interest (a life interest in relation to deaths before 6 April 1996) which is a right to part of the income of settled property is treated as such an interest in a corresponding part of the settled property. [*TCGA 1992, s 72(1), s 73(3); FA 1996, Sch 39 para 5(2)(4), para 6(4)(5)*].

If there is an interest (a life interest in relation to deaths before 6 April 1996) in income in a part of settled property such that there is no right of recourse to, or to the income from, the remainder of the settled property, then the part of the settled property in which such interest subsists is similarly treated as being settled property under a separate settlement for so long as such an interest subsists. [*TCGA 1992, s 72(5), s 73(3); FA 1996, Sch 39 para 5(2)(4), para 6(4)(5)*].

Interests in possession which are not life interests. For all cases which are settled after 16 February 1993 and relate to deaths before 6 April 1996, the Revenue will extend (subject to *TCGA 1992, s 67* and *s 74* below) concessionally the treatment statutorily afforded by *TCGA 1992, s 73* above regarding life interests to interests in possession which are not life interests. If the concession is claimed, it must apply to all of the assets in which the deceased had an interest in possession, other than assets which are covered by agreements made before 17 February 1993 or subject to a charge under *TCGA 1992, s 67* or *s 74*. This concession (ESC D43) is superseded for deaths after 5 April 1996 by amendments made to *TCGA 1992, s 73* above.

Exception where hold-over relief under TCGA 1992, s 165 or s 260 or FA 1980, s 79 claimed previously. In certain circumstances where a claim has been made for hold-over relief in respect of the disposal of an asset to the trustee and, subsequently, the trustee is deemed to dispose of and immediately reacquire the asset so that under *TCGA 1992, s 73* above there would otherwise be no chargeable gain arising, it is specifically provided by *TCGA 1992, s 67* or *s 74* that a chargeable gain, restricted to the amount of the held-over gain, is to accrue to the trustee. See 25.5, 25.8 and 25.9 HOLD-OVER RELIEFS.

57.12 ANTI-AVOIDANCE: DEEMED DISPOSAL OF UNDERLYING ASSETS ON CERTAIN DISPOSALS OF INTERESTS IN SETTLED PROPERTY

Cross-reference. See 57.8 above for the general exemption from CGT on a disposal of an interest in settled property.

Deemed disposal. Where

- a disposal of an 'interest in settled property' is made, or is effectively completed (see below under Time lapse before effective completion), after 20 March 2000,
- the disposal is 'for consideration', and
- specified conditions are present as detailed below (as to UK residence of trustees and settlor and as to settlor interest in the settlement),

the trustees of the settlement are deemed for all CGT purposes to have disposed of and immediately reacquired the underlying assets (see below) at market value. The deemed disposal takes place at the same time as the actual disposal of the interest in settled property. It is regarded as made under a bargain at arm's length (which effectively precludes a claim for the gain to be deferred as in 25.1 or 25.7 HOLD-OVER RELIEFS). [*TCGA 1992, s 76A, Sch 4A paras 1, 4(1)(3), para 9; FA 2000, s 91, Sch 24*]. Where applicable, any gain on the deemed disposal is chargeable on the settlor under the relevant provisions in 57.3 above.

See below for modifications to the above where there is a time lapse before effective completion of the actual disposal.

Where the trust is a maintenance fund for an historic building, the same exception applies as under the charge on settlor rules in 57.3 above. [*TCGA 1992, Sch 4A para 14*].

For these purposes, an '*interest in settled property*' is any interest created by or arising under the settlement. This includes the right to enjoy any benefit arising from the exercise of a discretion or power by the trustees of a settlement or by any person in relation to a settlement. A disposal is '*for consideration*' if actual consideration is given or received by any person for, or in connection with, any transaction by which the disposal is effected. Consideration deemed to have been given under any CGT provision is disregarded for these purposes. Consideration in the form of another interest under the same settlement is also disregarded, as long as that interest has not previously been disposed of by any person for consideration. [*TCGA 1992, Sch 4A paras 2, 3*].

Underlying assets. Where the interest disposed of is in the whole of the settled property, the deemed disposal is of each of the assets comprised in that property. Where the interest disposed of is in a specific fund or other defined part of the settled property, the deemed disposal is of each of the assets comprised in that fund or part. In either case, the deemed disposal is of the whole of each of the assets concerned, unless the interest disposed of is an interest in a specified fraction or amount of the income or capital, in which case the deemed disposal is of a corresponding part of each of the assets concerned. Where part only of an asset is comprised in a specific fund or other defined part of the settled property, that part of the asset is treated as a separate asset for the purposes of these provisions. [*TCGA 1992, Sch 4A para 8*]. See also below under Time lapse before effective completion.

Conditions. All the following conditions must be present for the disposal of underlying assets to be deemed to take place (and see also the modifications below under Time lapse before effective completion).

UK residence of trustees. The trustees must have been either resident in the UK during all or part of the tax year of disposal or ordinarily resident in the UK during that tax year (and, in either case, not regarded under a double tax agreement as resident elsewhere).

UK residence of settlor. In the tax year of disposal or in any of the previous five tax years (not counting years before 1999/2000), a person who is a settlor (defined as in 57.3 above) in relation to the settlement must have been either resident in the UK during all or part of the year or ordinarily resident in the UK during the year.

Settlor interest in the settlement. At some time during the 'relevant period', either

- a person who is a settlor (defined as in 57.3 above) in relation to the settlement must have had an interest in the settlement (for which see 57.3 above), or
- the settlement must have comprised property derived, directly or indirectly, from another settlement in which a settlor had an interest at any time in the relevant period.

The '*relevant period*' is the period beginning two years before the beginning of the tax year of disposal (or beginning on 6 April 1999 if later) and ending with the date of the disposal of the interest in settled property.

Where the settlor dies or the exception from the charge on settlor in 57.3 above on death of spouse or end of marriage would apply, the above condition is treated as not present in the tax year of death or end of marriage.

[*TCGA 1992, Sch 4A para 4(2), paras 5–7, 12*].

Prevention of double charge. Where there would be a deemed disposal as above and the actual disposal of the interest in settled property is not itself exempt by virtue of *TCGA 1992, s 76* (see 57.8 above), the following provisions apply to ensure that there is no double charge or double allowance of a loss.

- If both the deemed disposal and the actual disposal give rise to a chargeable gain (or in the case of the deemed disposal a net chargeable gain by reference to all the assets involved), the lower gain is disregarded.
- If both disposals give rise to an allowable loss (or net allowable loss), the lower loss is disregarded.
- If one disposal gives rise to a (net) chargeable gain and the other a (net) allowable loss, the loss is disregarded.
- If the actual disposal gives rise to neither a chargeable gain nor an allowable loss, any net chargeable gain on the deemed disposal is taken as accruing instead.

[*TCGA 1992, Sch 4A para 10*].

Trustees' right of recovery. Where tax becomes chargeable in respect of a deemed disposal as above and either it is chargeable on the trustees or it is chargeable on the settlor and recovered by him from the trustees as in 57.3 above, the trustees have the right to recover the tax from the person who made the actual disposal (i.e. of an interest in the settlement) giving rise to the deemed disposal. For this purpose, they may require an inspector to certify the gain and the tax paid.

[*TCGA 1992, Sch 4A para 11*].

Time lapse before effective completion. The above provisions are subject to the modifications below where there is a period between the beginning of the disposal of the interest in settled property and the effective completion of that disposal. For these purposes, the disposal begins when a contract is entered into or, where relevant, an option is granted. It is effectively completed when the person acquiring the interest becomes for all practical purposes unconditionally entitled to the whole of the intended subject matter of the disposal.

Where the beginning of the disposal and the effective completion take place in different tax years:

- the deemed disposal is treated as taking place in the tax year of effective completion;
- the conditions as to UK residence of trustees and settlor are treated as present if they are present by reference to either of those tax years or any intervening year;
- the '*relevant period*' for the purpose of the condition as to settlor interest in the settlement is the period beginning two years before the beginning of the first of those tax years (or beginning on 6 April 1999 if later) and ending with the effective completion.

If the identity or value of the underlying assets changes during the period between the beginning of the disposal and its effective completion, an asset is subject to the deemed disposal rules if it was comprised in the settled property (or specific fund or other defined part) at any time during that period, unless it was disposed of (and not reacquired) by the trustees during that period under a bargain at arm's length. The market value of an asset for the purposes of the deemed disposal is its highest market value at any time in that period.

[*TCGA 1992, Sch 4A para 13*].

57.13 ANTI-AVOIDANCE: TRANSFERS OF VALUE BY TRUSTEES LINKED WITH TRUSTEE BORROWING

Deemed disposal. Where

- the trustees of a settlement make a 'transfer of value' after 20 March 2000;
- the transfer is treated as 'linked with trustee borrowing'; and
- it takes place in a tax year in which the settlement is within *TCGA 1992, s 77, s 86* or *s 87* (see below)

the trustees are deemed for all CGT purposes to have disposed of and immediately reacquired the whole or a proportion (see below) of each of the 'chargeable assets' that continue to form part of the settled property immediately after the transfer ('*the remaining chargeable assets*'). The deemed disposal takes place at the time of the transfer of value and is treated as made under a bargain at arm's length and for a consideration equal to the whole or, as the case may be, a proportion of the market value of each asset. Where applicable, gains (less losses) on the deemed disposals are then chargeable on the settlor under *TCGA 1992, s 77* (see 57.3 above) or, in the case of an offshore settlement, on the settlor under *TCGA 1992, s 86* (see 43.4 OFFSHORE SETTLEMENTS) or on beneficiaries receiving capital payments under *TCGA 1992, Sch 4C* (see 43.17 OFFSHORE SETTLEMENTS — note that the normal provisions charging beneficiaries receiving capital payments — *TCGA 1992, ss 87-95*, see 43.13 OFFSHORE SETTLEMENTS — are disapplied).

The significance of the deemed disposal being treated as an arm's length disposal is that the provisions at 25.1 and 25.7 HOLD-OVER RELIEFS are thereby disapplied.

For these purposes, an asset is a '*chargeable asset*' if a gain on a disposal of the asset by the trustees at the time of the transfer of value would be a chargeable gain. A settlement is within *TCGA 1992, s 77* (see 57.3 above) in a tax year if, assuming that there were net chargeable gains (after deducting losses) accruing to the trustees from the disposal of settled property, chargeable gains would be treated as accruing to the settlor in that year under that *section*. A settlement is within *TCGA 1992, s 86* (see 43.4 OFFSHORE SETTLEMENTS) in a tax year if, assuming that there were net gains (after deducting losses) accruing to the trustees from disposals of any of the settled property originating from the settlor, chargeable gains would be treated as accruing to the settlor in that year under that *section*. A settlement is within *TCGA 1992, s 87* (see 43.13 OFFSHORE SETTLEMENTS) in a tax year if, assuming there were 'trust gains for the year' (within the meaning of that *section*) and that beneficiaries of the settlement received capital payments from the trustees in that or an earlier year, chargeable gains would be treated as accruing to the beneficiaries in that year under that *section* or *TCGA 1992, s 89(2)* (see 43.13 OFFSHORE SETTLEMENTS).

[*TCGA 1992, s 76B, Sch 4B paras 1, 3, 10; FA 2000, s 92(1)(2)(5), Sch 25*].

Transfer of value. Trustees of a settlement make a '*transfer of value*' if they

- lend money or any other 'asset' to any person;
- 'transfer an asset' to any person and receive either no consideration or a consideration lower than the market value of the asset transferred; or
- issue a security of any description to any person and receive either no consideration or a consideration lower than the value of the security.

For the purposes of these provisions, an '*asset*' includes money expressed in sterling. References below to the value or market value of such an asset are to its amount. The '*transfer of an asset*' includes anything that is, or is treated as, a disposal of the asset for capital gains tax purposes, or would be if money expressed in sterling were an asset for capital gains tax purposes. Part disposals are not excluded. However, a transfer of an asset does not include a transfer of an asset that is itself created by the part disposal of another asset. For example, the grant of a leasehold interest in freehold land is for these purposes a transfer of the freehold (and not of the leasehold).

The transfer of value is treated as made at the time when the loan is made, the transfer is 'effectively completed' or the security is issued. A transfer is '*effectively completed*' at the point at which the person acquiring the asset becomes for practical purposes unconditionally entitled to the whole of the intended subject matter of the transfer.

The amount of value transferred is taken to be

- in the case of a loan, the market value of the asset;
- in the case of a transfer of an asset:
  - (i) if any part of the value of the asset is 'attributable to trustee borrowing' (see below), the market value of the asset; or
  - (ii) if no part of the value of the asset is attributable to trustee borrowing, the market value of the asset reduced by any consideration received for it; and
- in the case of the issue of a security, the value of the security reduced by any consideration received for it.

For this purpose, the value of an asset is its value immediately before the time the transfer of value is treated as made, unless the asset does not exist before that time in which case its value immediately after that time is taken.

[*TCGA 1992, Sch 4B paras 2, 13*].

Transfer of value linked with trustee borrowing. Trustees of a settlement are treated as borrowing if

- money or any other asset is lent to them; or
- an asset is transferred to them and, in connection with the transfer, the trustees assume a contractual obligation (whether absolute or conditional) to restore or transfer to any person that or any other asset.

References below to a '*loan obligation*' include any such obligation as is mentioned above.

The amount borrowed (the '*proceeds*' of the borrowing) is taken to be

- in the case of a loan, the market value of the asset;
- in the case of a transfer, the market value of the asset reduced by any consideration received for it.

For this purpose, the market value of an asset is its market value immediately before the loan is made, or the transfer is effectively completed (see above under Transfer of value), unless the asset does not exist before that event in which case its market value immediately after that event is taken.

A transfer of value by trustees is treated as '*linked with trustee borrowing*' if at the time of the transfer there is 'outstanding trustee borrowing'. There is '*outstanding trustee borrowing*' at any time to the extent that

- any loan obligation is outstanding, and
- there are proceeds of trustee borrowing that have not been either
  - 'applied for normal trust purposes', or
  - taken into account under these provisions in relation to an earlier transfer of value which was treated as linked with trustee borrowing.

For the purposes of these provisions, the proceeds of trustee borrowing are '*applied for normal trust purposes*' if and only if

(*a*) they are applied by the trustees in making a payment in respect of an 'ordinary trust asset' and the following conditions are met:

   (i) the payment is made under a transaction at arm's length or is not more than the payment that would be made if the transaction were at arm's length;

   (ii) the asset forms part of the settled property immediately after the transfer of value or, if it (or part of it) does not do so, the alternative condition described below is met; and

   (iii) the sum paid is allowable under *TCGA 1992, s 38* (see 17.3 and 17.5 DISPOSAL) as a deduction in computing a gain accruing to the trustees on a disposal of the asset (or would be so allowable were it not for the application of *TCGA 1992, s 17*, see 40.1 MARKET VALUE, or *TCGA 1992, s 39*, see 17.5(*a*) DISPOSAL); or

(*b*) they are applied by the trustees in wholly or partly discharging a loan obligation, and the whole of the proceeds of the borrowing connected with that obligation (or all but an insignificant amount) have been applied by the trustees for normal trust purposes; or

(*c*) they are applied by the trustees in making payments to meet *bona fide* current expenses incurred by them in administering the settlement or any of the settled property.

The following are '*ordinary trust assets*':

(1) shares or securities (the latter as defined in *TCGA 1992, s 132* — see 58.11 SHARES AND SECURITIES);

(2) tangible property, whether movable or immovable, or a lease of such property;

(3) property not within (1) or (2) above which is used for the purposes of a trade, profession or vocation carried on by the trustees or by a beneficiary who has an interest in possession in the settled property; and

(4) any right in or over, or any interest in, property of a description within (2) or (3) above.

The alternative condition mentioned in (*a*)(ii) above in relation to an asset (or part of an asset) which no longer forms part of the settled property is that

- the asset (or part) is treated as having been disposed of by virtue of *TCGA 1992, s 24(1)* (entire loss or destruction of an asset — see 17.7 DISPOSAL), or
- one or more ordinary trust assets which taken together directly or indirectly represent the asset (or part)
  - form part of the settled property immediately after the transfer of value, or
  - are treated as having been disposed of by virtue of *TCGA 1992, s 24(1)*.

Where there has been a part disposal of the asset, the main condition in (*a*)(ii) above and the alternative condition above may be applied in any combination in relation to the subject matter of the part disposal and what remains.

The Treasury has the power to make regulations to add to, amend or repeal any of the provisions defining the circumstances in which the proceeds of trustee borrowing are treated as applied for normal trust purposes.

[*TCGA 1992, Sch 4B paras 4–9*].

Whether deemed disposal is of the whole or a proportion of the assets. If the amount of value transferred

- is less than the amount of outstanding trustee borrowing immediately after the transfer of value, and
- is also less than the 'effective value' of the remaining chargeable assets,

the deemed disposal and reacquisition is of the proportion of each of the remaining chargeable assets given by:

$\frac{VT}{EV}$ where

VT = the amount of value transferred, and

EV = the effective value of the remaining chargeable assets.

If the amount of value transferred

- is not less than the amount of outstanding trustee borrowing immediately after the transfer of value, but
- is less than the effective value of the remaining chargeable assets,

the deemed disposal and reacquisition is of the proportion of each of the remaining chargeable assets given by:

$\frac{TB}{EV}$ where

TB = the amount of outstanding trustee borrowing immediately after the transfer of value, and

EV = the effective value of the remaining chargeable assets.

In any other case the deemed disposal and reacquisition is of the whole of each of the remaining chargeable assets.

The '*effective value*' of the remaining chargeable assets is the aggregate market value of those assets immediately after the transfer of value, reduced by so much of that value as is attributable to trustee borrowing (see below).

[*TCGA 1992, Sch 4B para 11*].

Value attributable to trustee borrowing. The value of any asset is '*attributable to trustee borrowing*' to the extent that

- the trustees have applied the proceeds of trustee borrowing in acquiring or enhancing the value of the asset, or
- the asset represents directly or indirectly an asset whose value was attributable to the trustees having so applied the proceeds of trustee borrowing.

Where the asset itself has been borrowed by trustees, in addition to any extent to which the value of the asset may be attributable to trustee borrowing by virtue of the above, the value of the asset is attributable to trustee borrowing to the extent that the proceeds of that borrowing have not been applied for normal trust purposes (see above).

For these purposes, an amount is treated as applied by the trustees in acquiring or enhancing the value of an asset if it is applied by them wholly and exclusively

- as consideration in money or money's worth for the acquisition of the asset;
- for the purpose of enhancing the value of the asset in a way that is reflected in the state or nature of the asset;
- in establishing, preserving or defending their title to, or to a right over, the asset; or
- where the asset is a holding of shares or securities (the latter as defined in *TCGA 1992, s 132* — see 58.11 SHARES AND SECURITIES) that is treated as a single asset, by way of consideration in money or money's worth for additional shares or securities forming part of the same holding;

at a time when, and to the extent that, there is outstanding trustee borrowing.

[*TCGA 1992, Sch 4B para 12*].

57.14 ANTI-AVOIDANCE: RESTRICTION ON SET-OFF OF SETTLEMENT LOSSES

Cross-reference. See 57.9 above for restrictions on transfer of settlement losses to beneficiary becoming absolutely entitled to settled property.

Where the circumstances set out below apply in relation to a chargeable gain accruing after 20 March 2000 to the trustees of a settlement, no allowable losses accruing to the trustees (whether in the same year of assessment or brought forward from an earlier year) may be set against any part of that gain.

The circumstances are as follows.

- In computing the gain in question, the allowable expenditure would be greater if it were not for a claim having been made for gifts hold-over relief under *TCGA 1992, s 165* or *s 260* (see 25.1, 25.7 HOLD-OVER RELIEFS) in respect of an earlier disposal (not necessarily of the same asset) to the trustees; and

- the person who made that earlier disposal, or a person connected with him (within *TCGA 1992, s 286* — see 14 CONNECTED PERSONS), has at any time acquired an 'interest in the settled property' (defined as in 57.12 above), or entered into an arrangement to acquire such an interest, as a result of which any person has at any time received (or become entitled to receive) any consideration.

[*TCGA 1992, s 79A; FA 2000, s 93*].

57.15 ANTI-AVOIDANCE: ATTRIBUTION TO TRUSTEES OF GAINS OF NON-RESIDENT COMPANIES

The following apply where the trustees of a settlement are participators (within *ICTA 1988, s 417(1)*) in a close company (within *ICTA 1988, ss 414, 415* — broadly a company under the control of five or fewer participators or of directors who are participators, see TOLLEY'S CORPORATION TAX under Close Companies) or in a non-UK resident company which would otherwise be a close company.

Where, by reason of such participation by the trustees, any part of a chargeable gain accruing after 20 March 2000 to a non-UK resident company falls to be attributed to them under *TCGA 1992, s 13* (see 44.6 OVERSEAS MATTERS), nothing in any double tax agreement (see 18.2 DOUBLE TAX RELIEF) is to be taken as averting the tax charge otherwise arising.

Where

(*a*) a chargeable gain accrues after 20 March 2000 to a non-UK resident company which would otherwise be a close company;

(*b*) all or part of the gain is attributed under *TCGA 1992, s 13* to a close company which, by reason of a double tax agreement, is not chargeable to corporation tax on the gain; and

(*c*) had that close company been a non-UK resident company, all or part of the chargeable gain would have been attributed to the trustees by reason of such participation as is mentioned above;

then, for the purposes of the provisions in 44.6 OVERSEAS MATTERS which enable a gain to be attributed through a chain of companies, the company in (*b*) above is treated as a non-UK resident company, with the result that the gain can be attributed to the trustees. This treatment also applies to any other company which, if it were non-UK resident, would have been part of the chain, such that all or part of the gain in question would have been attributed as in (*c*) above.

[*TCGA 1992, s 79B; FA 2000, s 94*].

58 Shares and Securities

Cross-references. See 3 ANTI-AVOIDANCE for certain provisions which apply to share disposals; 4.5 APPEALS for appeals regarding values of unquoted shares; 6.2 ASSETS for location of shares; 7 ASSETS HELD ON 6 APRIL 1965; 8 ASSETS HELD ON 31 MARCH 1982; 13 COMPANIES; 17.10 DISPOSAL for options to acquire shares; 19 EMPLOYEE SHARE SCHEMES; 20 ENTERPRISE INVESTMENT SCHEME (AND BES); 21.5 EXEMPTIONS AND RELIEFS for meaning of 'debt on a security'; 24 GOVERNMENT SECURITIES; 25 HOLD-OVER RELIEFS for relief in respect of gifts of shares in certain cases and transfers to companies in exchange for shares; 38 LOAN RELATIONSHIPS OF COMPANIES; 39 LOSSES for reliefs available for losses arising from certain share disposals and for negligible value claims; 40 MARKET VALUE; 42 MINERAL ROYALTIES for shares in companies deriving their value from exploration etc. rights; 44 OVERSEAS MATTERS for shares in certain overseas resident companies and funds; 49 QUALIFYING CORPORATE BONDS; 50 REINVESTMENT RELIEF, 53 RETIREMENT RELIEF and 55 ROLLOVER RELIEF for relief where shares etc. are held in certain companies; 59 SHARES AND SECURITIES—IDENTIFICATION RULES; 64 UNIT TRUSTS ETC.; 65 VENTURE CAPITAL TRUSTS.

Sumption: Capital Gains Tax. See A12.

The headings in this chapter are as follows.

58.1 INTRODUCTION

See table of headings above for a guide to the subject matter covered in this chapter.

58.2 IDENTIFICATION RULES — DISPOSALS POST-FA 1985

For disposals after 5 April 1985 (31 March 1985 for companies), the identification of 'securities' is governed by the provisions in 59.3–59.5 SHARES AND SECURITIES—IDENTIFICATION RULES.

For the position where quoted and unquoted securities were held on 6 April 1965, see 7.2–7.7 and 7.9–7.12 ASSETS HELD ON 6 APRIL 1965.

Identification rules for disposals of 'relevant securities' are not as above but are as detailed in 59.6 SHARES AND SECURITIES—IDENTIFICATION RULES.

For disposals after 5 April 1998 (other than by companies), the identification rules are as in 59.1, 59.2 SHARES AND SECURITIES—IDENTIFICATION RULES.

58.3 IDENTIFICATION RULES — DISPOSALS POST-FA 1982 AND PRE-FA 1985

For disposals after 5 April 1982 (31 March 1982 for companies) but before 6 April 1985 (1 April 1985 for companies), the identification of 'securities' disposed of was governed by the provisions in 59.7–59.10 SHARES AND SECURITIES—IDENTIFICATION RULES for securities generally.

For the position where quoted and unquoted securities were held on 6 April 1965, see 7.2–7.7 and 7.9–7.12 ASSETS HELD ON 6 APRIL 1965 respectively.

For companies, an alternative method ('parallel pooling') was available to identify 'qualifying securities' which are disposed of after 31 March 1982 and before 1 April 1985 with securities of the same kind acquired previously. See 59.11 SHARES AND SECURITIES—IDENTIFICATION RULES.

58.4 IDENTIFICATION RULES — DISPOSALS PRE-FA 1982

For disposals prior to 6 April 1982 (1 April 1982 for companies), see 59.12 SHARES AND SECURITIES—IDENTIFICATION RULES.

For the position where quoted and unquoted securities were held on 6 April 1965, see 7.2–7.7 and 7.9–7.12 ASSETS HELD ON 6 APRIL 1965 respectively.

58.5 REORGANISATION OF SHARE CAPITAL

A '*reorganisation*' (i.e. a 'reorganisation' or 'reduction' of a company's share capital) does not normally constitute a disposal, the '*original shares*' and the '*new holding*' being treated as acquired at the same date as the original shares, any additional consideration given by the shareholder at the time of reorganisation (e.g. as a subscription for a rights issue: see 58.7 below) being added to the cost of the original holding for the purpose of computing the unindexed (or, before 6 April 1985 (1 April 1985 for companies), the gross gain). See 26.6 INDEXATION for the calculation of indexation allowance in respect of the additional consideration.

For this purpose

(*a*) '*original shares*' means shares held before and concerned in the reorganisation, and

(*b*) '*new holding*' means, in relation to any original shares, the shares in and debentures of the company which, following the reorganisation, represent the original shares and any remaining original shares.

[*TCGA 1992, s 126(1), s 127*].

The surrender, cancellation or alteration of the original holding or the rights attached thereto; and any consideration met out of the assets of the company (e.g. on a bonus issue) or represented by a dividend or other distribution declared but not paid are not regarded as 'additional consideration' for the above purpose. Similarly, in the case of a reorganisation occurring after 9 March 1981, any consideration given, otherwise than by way of a bargain made at arm's length, for part or all of the new holding will be disregarded, to the extent that its amount or value exceeds the amount by which the market value of the new holding, immediately after the reorganisation, exceeds the market value of the original shares immediately before the reorganisation. (See also *CIR v Burmah Oil Co. Ltd HL 1981, 54 TC 200.*) [*TCGA 1992, s 128(1)(2)*].

The Revenue have expressed their views on 'open offers' and 'vendor placings'. An open offer is where a company invites its shareholders to subscribe for shares subject to a minimum entitlement based on their existing holdings, and possibly enabling them to also subscribe for shares which other shareholders do not want. For capital gains tax purposes the Revenue will treat any subscription for shares, which is equal to or less than the shareholder's minimum entitlement, as a share reorganisation. Any shares subscribed for in excess of the minimum entitlement will be treated as a separate acquisition. In addition, a vendor placing is where company shares, which have previously been allotted to a vendor as consideration for an asset disposed of by the vendor to the company, are offered by the company to its existing shareholders on the vendor's behalf. No part of any acquisition by existing shareholders can be treated as a share reorganisation because the shares have already been allotted to the vendor. These treatments usually only become of practical importance where there is a '1982 holding' (see 59.5 SHARES AND SECURITIES—IDENTIFICATION RULES) of shares (Revenue Capital Gains Manual CG 51760–51766).

For the Revenue's views on the treatment of rights to acquire shares in other companies, see Revenue Capital Gains Manual CG 52065–52070.

Where, on a reorganisation, a person receives (or is deemed to receive), or becomes entitled to receive, any consideration, other than the new holding, for the disposal of an interest in the original shares, and in particular

(i) where under *TCGA 1992, s 122* he is to be treated as if he had in consideration of a capital distribution disposed of an interest in the original shares (see 58.14 below and note the procedure where the amount of the capital distribution is small or exceeds the allowable expenditure attaching to the original shares),

(ii) where he receives (or is deemed to receive) consideration from other shareholders in respect of a surrender of rights derived from the original shares,

he is treated as if the new holding resulted from his having for that consideration disposed of an interest (but without prejudice to the original shares and the new holding being treated in accordance with *TCGA 1992, s 127* above as the same asset. [*TCGA 1992, s 128(3)*].

For transactions between companies in the same group, see 13.12 COMPANIES.

Reorganisations covered by the provisions. '*Reorganisation*' for the purposes above includes the making of bonus and rights issues of shares or debentures in proportion to the original holdings, the reduction of share capital and the alteration of rights attaching to the original shares. [*TCGA 1992, s 126(1)(2)*]. See also *Dunstan v Young Austen Young Ltd CA 1988, 61 TC 448.* Unit trusts schemes are treated similarly to companies but see 64.1 UNIT TRUSTS ETC. for the disapplication of the above provisions as regards collective investment schemes entitling participants to exchange rights in one part of a scheme property for rights in another. [*TCGA 1992, s 99*].

'*Reduction*' of share capital for the purposes above does not include the paying off of redeemable share capital, and where shares in a company are redeemed by the company otherwise than by the issue of shares or debentures (with or without other consideration) and otherwise than in a liquidation, the shareholder is treated as disposing of the shares at the time of the redemption. [*TCGA 1992, s 126(3)*].

Alternative rules apply to the reorganisation of share capital involving qualifying corporate bonds. See 49.3 QUALIFYING CORPORATE BONDS.

In certain cases involving RETIREMENT RELIEF (53.5) or, for disposals after 15 March 1993 and before 30 November 1993, REINVESTMENT RELIEF (50.10) an election may be made for the reorganisation to be treated as an actual disposal and reacquisition.

Valuation of different classes of share on subsequent disposal. Where the new holding consists of more than one class of share, security, debenture, etc. none of which is quoted on a recognised stock exchange within three months of the reorganisation, the allowable acquisition cost is arrived at on the basis of the market value of the various classes at the date of a chargeable disposal of the new holding or part thereof. This also applies where consideration, other than the new holding, is received as in *TCGA 1992, s 128(3)* above. [*TCGA 1992, s 128(4), s 129*].

However, in the case of shares and securities any one class or more of which is or are quoted on a recognised stock exchange (within *ICTA 1988, s 841* — see below) in the UK or elsewhere (or, in the case of unit trust rights, of which the prices were published daily by the managers) within three months after the reorganisation takes effect (or such longer time as the Board may allow), the base value is determined *once and for all* by reference to the respective market value, on the first day on which the market values or prices of the shares are quoted or published (whether published before or after the actual reorganisation).The provisions apply, *mutatis mutandis*, to the reorganisation of rights under unit trusts. See 64 UNIT TRUSTS ETC.. A reorganisation which involves the allotment of holdings is deemed to take effect on the day following the day on which the right to renounce any allotment expires. [*TCGA 1992, s 130*].

Under *ICTA 1988, s 841*, the expression '*recognised stock exchange*' means the London Stock Exchange and any overseas stock exchange designated as such by Order of the Board. A list of designated overseas stock exchanges is given in Revenue Tax Bulletin April 1999 p 657. A list of recognised stock exchanges also appears in Simon's Direct Tax Service, Binder 1, p 7521 *et seq*.

For the application of the indexation provisions to holdings of shares arising out of these rules, see 26.6 INDEXATION and 59.4, 59.5, 59.10 SHARES AND SECURITIES—IDENTIFICATION RULES.

Assets held on 6 April 1965. See 7.7 and 7.12 ASSETS HELD ON 6 APRIL 1965 for certain situations that may still arise in relation to reorganisations.

Example

A Ltd, an unquoted company, was incorporated in 1993 with an authorised share capital of £50 million denominated into 500 million Ordinary Shares of 10p each, of which 300 million were issued at par on incorporation. In 1996, the directors decide to reorganise the company's share capital by issuing the balance of the authorised share capital in the form of a bonus issue of 200 million Ordinary Shares of 10p so that two such shares are issued for every three of such shares already held. The 500 million Ordinary Shares of 10p each in issue are then consolidated into 50 million New Ordinary Shares of £1 each. A rights issue is then made on the basis of one 7% Cumulative Preference Share of £1 issued at par for every five New Ordinary Shares of £1 already held.

X was issued 90,000 Ordinary Shares of 10p on incorporation and has held them continually since then. Assuming he takes up the rights issue, his new holding after the reorganisation is as follows.

	No. of shares	*Par value*	*Cost*
			£
Original holding: 10p Ords	90,000	10p	9,000
Bonus issue: 10p Ords	60,000	10p	Nil
	150,000		£9,000
Consolidation: 10p Ords to £1			
New Ords	15,000	£1	9,000
Rights issue: £1 Prefs	3,000	£1	3,000
Cost of complete new holding			£12,000

X disposes of 1,500 £1 Prefs in 2000 when each such share is worth £3 and each £1 New Ord is worth £1.80. The apportionment is as follows

		£
Total value of £1 Prefs: (£3 × 3,000)	=	9,000
Total value of £1 New Ords: (£1.80 × 15,000)	=	27,000
		£36,000
Proportional value of £1 Prefs × original cost		
$\frac{9}{36}$ × £12,000	=	£3,000
Allowable cost of 1,500 £1 Prefs (£3,000 ÷ 2)	=	£1,500

Note. If X later disposes of the remainder (1,500) of the £1 Prefs when their value is £4 each and that of the £1 Ords is £2 each, the calculation will be made as follows

		£
Total value of £1 Prefs: (£4 × 1,500)	=	6,000
Total value of £1 Ords: (£2 × 15,000)	=	30,000
		£36,000
Original cost (as reduced by previous disposal)	=	£10,500
Proportional value of £1 Prefs × original cost		
$\frac{6}{36}$ × £10,500	=	£1,750
Allowable cost of 1,500 £1 Prefs	=	£1,750

58.6 **Bonus issues (aka scrip issues).** These are treated as a reorganisation within 58.5 above, but see 58.13 below for stock dividends.

In practice, where a bonus issue follows a repayment of share capital (e.g. under *ICTA 1988, s 210*), and is treated as income of the recipient, the amount of that income net of basic rate tax is treated as the acquisition cost of the new shares (CCAB Statement June 1968).

Example

X plc, a quoted company, makes a bonus issue in September 2000 of one preference share for every eight ordinary shares held. On first trading after issue, the preference shares were valued at £10 and the ordinary shares at £6.

Mr A had purchased 1,000 ordinary shares in December 1998 for £7,000. After the issue of preference shares, the allowable expenditure on a subsequent disposal of the ordinary and preference shares is computed as follows.

			£
Initial value of preference shares (125 × £10)			1,250
Initial value of ordinary shares (1,000 × £6)			6,000
Total			£7,250

Allowable cost of 1,000 ordinary shares $\frac{6,000}{7,250} \times 7,000 =$ £5,790

Allowable cost of 125 preference shares $\frac{1,250}{7,250} \times 7,000 =$ £1,210

These rules do not apply to loyalty bonus shares issued to subscribers to privatisation issues, for which see 58.17 below.

58.7 **Rights issues.** These are treated as reorganisations within 58.5 above.

Where a person receives or becomes entitled to receive in respect of any shares in or debentures of a company a provisional allotment or shares in or debentures of the company and he disposes of his rights, *TCGA 1992, s 122* applies as if the amount of consideration for the disposal were a capital distribution received by him from the company in respect of the first-mentioned shares or debentures, and as if he had, instead of disposing of the rights, disposed of an interest in those shares or debentures. [*TCGA 1992, s 123*].

See 58.14 below for *TCGA 1992, s 122* and note the procedure where the amount of the capital distribution is small or exceeds the allowable expenditure attaching to the original shares etc.

Example

W plc is a quoted company which in June 1992 made a rights issue of one £1 ordinary share for every eight £1 ordinary shares held, at £1.35 payable on allotment. V, who held 16,000 £1 ordinary shares purchased in May 1984 for £15,000, took up his entitlement in full, and was allotted 2,000 shares. In December 2000, he sells 6,000 of his shares for £12,000.

Indexation factors May 1984 to April 1985	0.065
April 1985 to June 1992	0.470
June 1992 to April 1998	0.167

'Section 104 holding'	Shares	Qualifying expenditure	Indexed pool
		£	£
May 1984 acquisition	16,000	15,000	15,000
Indexed rise: May 1984 – April 1985 £15,000 × 0.065			975
Pool at 6.4.85	16,000	15,000	15,975
Indexed rise: April 1985 – June 1992 £15,975 × 0.470			7,508
June 1992 rights issue	2,000	2,700	2,700
Carried forward	18,000	17,700	26,183

'Section 104 holding'

	Shares	Qualifying expenditure	Indexed pool
		£	£
Brought forward	18,000	17,700	26,183
Indexed rise: June 1992 – April 1998			
£26,183 × 0.167			4,373
			30,556
December 2000 disposal	(6,000)	(5,900)	(10,185)
Pool carried forward	12,000	£11,800	£20,371

Calculation of chargeable gain

	£
Disposal consideration	12,000
Allowable cost $\frac{6,000}{18,000} \times$ £17,700	5,900
Unindexed gain	6,100
Indexation allowance	
$\frac{6,000}{18,000} \times$ £30,556 = £10,185	
£10,185 – £5,900	4,285
Chargeable gain (subject to TAPER RELIEF (60))	£1,815

58.8 **Exchange of securities for those in another company.** (See also 13.7 COMPANIES). The same treatment as under 58.5 above is applied to shares or debentures issued in exchange for the shares or debentures of a company by another company which in consequence of the exchange will hold more than 25% of the 'ordinary share capital' or, in relation to exchanges made after 31 December 1991, more than 50% of the voting power of the first company. Similar treatment applies where the second company issues the shares, etc. in exchange for those of the first company as the result of a general offer made to the shareholders of the first company (or any class of them), provided that the offer was initially made on a condition which, if satisfied, would give the first company control of the second. This covers abortive takeover bids which become unconditional, but which do not succeed. [*TCGA 1992, s 135(1)(3); F(No 2)A 1992, s 35*].

See 64.1 UNIT TRUSTS ETC. for the application of this provision as regards collective investment schemes entitling participants to exchange rights in one part of a scheme for rights in another.

For the tax consequences of a share exchange within a group of companies, see *Westcott v Woolcombers Ltd CA 1987, 60 TC 575* and *NAP Holdings UK Ltd v Whittles HL 1994, 67 TC 166*. See 13.12 COMPANIES for a commentary on the position but note the law was changed for intra-group transactions after 14 March 1988.

'*Ordinary share capital*' means all the issued share capital (by whatever name called) of a company, other than that which produces a fixed rate of dividend and is non-participating. [*ICTA 1988, s 832(1)*].

Incidental costs of acquisition and disposal and warranty payments in respect of contingent liabilities. Any such costs or payments attributable to the new holding of shares or debentures are by concession treated as consideration given for that holding. In the case of warranty payments, relief under this concession and *TCGA 1992, s 49(1)(c)* (see 17.5 DISPOSAL) will in total be restricted to what would have been allowed under *TCGA 1992, s 49(1)(c)* had *TCGA 1992, s 135* not applied (Revenue Pamphlet IR 1, D52).

Anti-avoidance. TCGA 1992, s 135 does not apply unless the exchange is made for bona fide commercial reasons and does not form part of a scheme or arrangements of which the main purpose, or one of the main purposes, is the avoidance of capital gains tax or corporation tax. In such cases, a chargeable disposal is treated as taking place except where a person to whom the new shares are issued owns (or he and persons connected with him together own) less than 5% of, or any class of, the shares or debentures of the acquired company. There are provisions for advance clearance of an exchange by the Revenue. [*TCGA 1992, ss 137, 138*]. For full coverage see 3.16 ANTI-AVOIDANCE.

58.9 **Earn-out rights.** An agreement for the sale of shares in a company may include the right to receive deferred consideration which is itself unascertainable at the time of the agreement, usually because it depends on the future profit performance of the company. Such a right was held to be a separate asset in *Marren v Ingles HL 1980, 54 TC 76* (see 17.7 DISPOSAL). From 26 April 1988, an extra-statutory concession (D27) (see below) provided that, in certain circumstances, this right (known as the 'earn-out right') could itself be treated as a security so that the deferral rules for capital gains on the shares could apply. Finance Act 1997 placed this concession on a statutory footing and elections under those provisions can be made from 26 November 1996, except in settled cases and in those where the concession has already been applied (see below for full commencement rules). Claims to apply the concession cannot be made after 25 November 1996 except under the transitional rules therein for rights acquired before 26 April 1988.

Statutory rules. Where a person ('the seller') transfers securities (i.e. shares or debentures) of a company and, as all or part of the consideration for the transfer, has conferred upon him a right to receive securities ('the new securities') of another company ('the acquiring company'), the value or quantity of which is 'unascertainable' (see below) at that time, such right is known as an '*earn-out right*'. It is a further condition that the terms of the right are such that it cannot be discharged otherwise than by the issue of the new securities. Any right to receive cash and/or an ascertainable amount of securities as part of the total consideration does not fall within these provisions and must be distinguished from the earn-out right.

Election available. Provided that *TCGA 1992, s 135* (exchange of securities — see 58.8 above) would have applied if the earn-out right were an ascertainable amount of securities of the acquiring company, the seller may irrevocably elect, by written notice to an officer of the Board, for the earn-out right to be treated for CGT purposes as if it were itself a security of the acquiring company (so that *section 135* may apply). The election must be made by the first anniversary of 31 January following the tax year in which the earn-out right is conferred, or, where made by a company, within two years after the end of the accounting period in which the right is conferred. Where the election is made, it is then assumed, as regards the seller and any subsequent owner of the earn-out right, that

(*a*) the earn-out right is a security within the definition in *TCGA 1992, s 132* (see 58.11 below);

(*b*) the notional security represented by the earn-out right is not a QUALIFYING CORPORATE BOND (49);

(*c*) all references in *TCGA 1992* to a debenture include references to such a notional security; and

(*d*) the eventual issue of actual securities in pursuance of the earn-out right constitutes a conversion of the right, insofar as it is discharged by the issue, into those securities (see 58.11 below re conversion of securities).

Where an earn-out right is treated as a notional security of a company as above and it is extinguished and replaced with a new right to be issued with securities of the same company, the value or quantity of which is 'unascertainable' (see below) at that time, the person on whom the new right is conferred may make an election in respect of the new right, with the same consequences as above. The time limits for election operate by reference to the tax year or accounting period in which the new right is conferred.

Meaning of 'unascertainable'.

1. The value or quantity of securities to be issued in pursuance of an earn-out right is unascertainable at a particular time if, and only if it is made referable to matters relating to any business or assets of one or more 'relevant companies' and those matters are then uncertain on account of future business or future assets being included in the business or assets to which they relate. A '*relevant company*' is either the acquiring company or the acquired company or any company in the same group of companies as either of those. A group of companies is construed in accordance with 13.11 COMPANIES, and the change in the residence requirement there mentioned applies for these purposes in relation to rights conferred on or after 1 April 2000.
2. The value or quantity of securities to be issued in pursuance of an earn-out right is *not* to be taken as unascertainable merely by reason of any part of the consideration for the transaction being contingent or of any risk of its being irrecoverable. In such cases, *TCGA 1992, s 48* (consideration due after time of disposal — see 17.5 DISPOSAL) applies in computing the gain.
3. The existence of an option to choose between shares in and debentures of the acquiring company does not in itself render unascertainable the value or quantity of such securities. However, neither does such option prevent the above provisions from applying.
4. If the value of securities to be issued in pursuance of an earn-out right is ascertainable and the quantity is to be fixed by reference thereto, or *vice versa*, this does not in itself render the value or quantity unascertainable.

[*TCGA 1992, s 138A; FA 1997, s 89(1); FA 2000, Sch 29 para 22*].

Commencement. The above provisions are deemed always to have had effect. Where the earn-out right was conferred before 26 November 1996, the time limits for election operate as if it had been conferred on that date, *except that* no such election can be made after the final determination of the seller's CGT or corporation tax liability for the actual tax year or company accounting period in which the right was conferred.

Strictly, an election cannot be made until on or after 19 March 1997, being the date of Royal Assent to Finance Act 1997, but a notification given to an officer of the Board before that date either in anticipation of the right to elect or under ESC D27 (see below) counts as a valid and irrevocable election unless the Board otherwise direct. However, a notification under ESC D27 has no such effect in relation to *any disposal before 26 November 1996* (disregarding certain deemed disposals and no gain/no loss transfers) of an asset issued to a person in pursuance of an earn-out right or replacement earn-out right or of a replacement asset.

[*FA 1997, s 89(2)–(8)*].

Previous concessionary treatment. A concessionary treatment (published on 26 April 1988 and available in all cases where liabilities had not then been finally determined) applies **before 26 November 1996** where a takeover, etc. takes the form of an exchange of shares or securities but part of the deal consists of an 'earn-out' element, i.e., of shares or securities issued at some future date, for example if a profit target is met. Where such an agreement creates a right to an unascertainable element (whether or not subject to a maximum) against the purchaser which is acquired by the vendor at the time of disposal and that right falls, under the terms of the agreement, to be satisfied wholly by the issue of shares or debentures, then, notwithstanding a concurrent right to consideration other than in the form of shares or debentures, the Revenue were prepared to treat the right to shares or debentures in the hands of the vendor as a security (within 58.11 below) issued by the purchasing company, provided that

(*a*) the vendor so claims before his liability in respect of the sale of the shares or debentures is finally determined; and

(*b*) as a consequence of its being so treated *TCGA 1992, s 135* would apply to the disposal of the shares or debentures; and

(*c*) any vendor who so claims undertakes to accept this treatment for all capital gains tax purposes.

In determining whether *TCGA 1992, s 135* would apply, regard will be had to the anti-avoidance rules below. If a right falls to be treated as a security and subsequently is satisfied by shares or debentures issued, in accordance with the sale agreement, by the purchasing company to the vendor, the Revenue will treat that issue as a conversion of securities within 58.11 below.

As a transitional measure, where, before 26 April 1988 a right was acquired under which the vendor could receive cash or some other alternative, and a maximum amount for the consideration was specified in the agreement, it will be possible to treat the consideration as if it were ascertainable in that maximum amount even though the cash alternative exists. Subject to a claim by the vendor and to the anti-avoidance rules below, *TCGA 1992, s 135* will therefore be capable of applying to any shares or debentures issued to him by the purchasing company. This concession will also apply where the purchaser is itself subsequently purchased by another company not in the same group, and the vendor's rights against the purchaser are exchanged for similar rights against that other company, or where there is a subsequent variation in the terms of the original sale agreement, provided the conditions in this concession would have been met in either case had the change been part of the original arrangements (Revenue Pamphlet IR 1, D 27).

Notwithstanding the requirement in the concession for the element of deferred consideration to be wholly in 'paper' form, the Revenue are prepared to apply the concession to a separate part of the element of deferred consideration so long as that part is to be satisfied (and can only be satisfied) by the issue of paper without a cash option (Taxation 10 August 1989 p 571).

The above concessionary treatment mitigates the effect of the judgement in *Marren v Ingles HL 1980, 54 TC 76* (see 17.7 DISPOSAL). For the Revenue's views on earn-outs, see Revenue Capital Gains Manual CG 58000–58102.

Example

K owns 10,000 ordinary shares in M Ltd, which he acquired for £12,000 in December 1997. In July 2000, the whole of the issued share capital of M Ltd was acquired by P plc. Under the terms of the takeover, K receives £2 per share plus the right to further consideration up to a maximum of £1.50 per share depending on future profit performance. The initial consideration is receivable in cash, but the deferred consideration is to be satisfied by the issue of shares in P plc. In December 2001, K duly receives 2,000 ordinary shares valued at £6 per share in full settlement of his entitlement. The right to future consideration is valued at £1.40 per share in July 2000. The indexation factor for the period December 1997 to April 1998 is 0.016.

Without an election by K under TCGA 1992, s 138A the position would be

2000/01

	£	£
Disposal proceeds 10,000 × £2	20,000	
Value of rights 10,000 × £1.40	14,000	34,000
Cost	12,000	
Indexation allowance £12,000 × 0.016	192	12,192
Chargeable gain (subject to TAPER RELIEF (60))		£21,808

2001/02

	£
Disposal of rights to deferred consideration:	
Proceeds — 2,000 P plc shares @ £6	12,000
Deemed cost of acquiring rights	14,000
Allowable loss	£2,000
Cost for CGT purposes of 2,000 P plc shares	£12,000

With an election, the position would be

2000/01

	£
Proceeds (cash) (as above)	20,000
Cost $£12,000 \times \dfrac{20,000}{20,000 + 14,000}$	7,059
Unindexed gain	12,941
Indexation allowance £7,059 × 0.016	113
Chargeable gain (subject to TAPER RELIEF (60))	£12,828
Cost of earn-out right for CGT purposes (£12,000 – £7,059)	£4,941

2001/02

The shares in P plc stand in the place of the earn-out right and will be regarded as having been acquired in December 1997 for £4,941. No further gain or loss arises until a disposal of the shares takes place.

An extension to the above concession (announced in a Revenue Press Release of 25 July 1990 and available in all cases where the liability for the relevant chargeable period had not then been finally determined) applies to financial concerns who hold shares or securities as trading stocks rather than as capital assets. (Such concerns cannot benefit from the unextended concession because any profits they make on the disposal of shares would be liable to tax as part of their trading profits rather than as a capital gain.) Where *ICTA 1988, s 473* (conversion etc. of securities held as circulating capital not to be treated as disposal of original holding) does not apply to an exchange of shares only because *TCGA 1992, ss 126–136* would not have applied, then, if the taxpayer so claims, it may apply by concession if *TCGA 1992, ss 126–136* would have applied by virtue of the unextended concession above, if it had been claimed. The vendor must claim the benefit of the extension to the concession before his trading profit or loss for the relevant chargeable period is finally determined, and must agree to accept this treatment for all tax purposes (Revenue Pamphlet IR 1, D27).

58.10 **Schemes of reconstruction or amalgamation involving issue of securities.** Where, under an arrangement entered into for the purposes of such a scheme between a company and its share- or debenture-holders (or any class of them), another company issues shares or debentures to those holders in respect of, or in proportion to (or as nearly as may be in proportion to), their original holdings, which latter are then either 'retained' or cancelled, the new holding is treated as under 58.8 above (without the requirement that the issuing company hold more than 25% of the ordinary share capital, more than 50% of the voting power or have control of the other). [*TCGA 1992, s 135(2)(3), s 136*].

Incidental costs of acquisition and disposal and warranty payments in respect of contingent liabilities. Any such costs or payments attributable to the new holding of shares or debentures are by concession treated as consideration given for that holding. In the case of warranty payments, relief under this concession and *TCGA 1992, s 49(1)(c)* (see 17.5 DISPOSAL) will in total be restricted to what would have been allowed under *TCGA 1992, s 49(1)(c)* had *TCGA 1992, s 136* not applied (Revenue Pamphlet IR 1, D52).

Anti-avoidance. The same anti-avoidance rules apply as in 58.8 above. These rules are fully detailed in 3.16 ANTI-AVOIDANCE.

Example

N Ltd carries on a manufacturing and wholesaling business. In 1993, it was decided that the wholesaling business should be carried on by a separate company. Revenue clearance under *TCGA 1992, s 138* was obtained, and a company, R Ltd, was formed which, in consideration for the transfer to it by N Ltd of the latter's wholesaling undertaking, issued shares to the shareholders of N Ltd. Each holder of ordinary shares in N Ltd received one ordinary share in R Ltd for each N Ltd share he held. W, who purchased his 2,500 N shares for £10,000 in December 1990, received 2,500 R shares. None of the shares involved is quoted. In August 2000, W sells 1,500 of his N shares for £6 each, a total of £9,000, agreed to be their market value. The value of W's remaining N shares is also £6 per share, and the value of his R shares is £4.50 per share. The indexation factor for the period December 1990 to April 1998 is 0.252.

	£
Disposal consideration	9,000
Allowable cost $£10,000 \times \dfrac{9,000}{9,000 + (1,000 \times £6) + (2,500 \times £4.50)}$	3,429
Unindexed gain	5,571
Indexation allowance £3,429 × 0.252	864
Chargeable gain (subject to TAPER RELIEF (60))	£4,707

Note to the example

(*a*) If the original shares had been held on 31 March 1982, the above fraction would be applied to their 31 March 1982 value for the purposes of the re-basing calculation under *TCGA 1992, s 35*.

58.11 **Conversion of securities.** The provisions outlined in 58.5 above apply *mutatis mutandis* to the '*conversion of securities*', which phrase includes

(*a*) a conversion of securities of a company into shares in that company;

(*b*) in relation to any disposal after 25 November 1996 (whenever the conversion itself occurred), a conversion of a security which is not a qualifying corporate bond (QCB) (see 49 QUALIFYING CORPORATE BONDS) into a security of the same company which is a QCB;

(*c*) in relation to any disposal after 25 November 1996 (whenever the conversion itself occurred), a conversion of a QCB into a security of the same company which is not a QCB;

(*d*) a conversion in lieu of redemption at the option of the holder of the securities; and

(*e*) any exchange of securities in pursuance of compulsory purchase powers.

In relation to disposals after 25 November 1996, even where the conversion took place before then, any of the above is a conversion of securities regardless of whether effected by a transaction or occurring as a result of the operation of the terms of any security or debenture.

'*Security*' includes any loan stock or similar security issued by national or local government or public authority in the UK or elsewhere, or by a company, and whether secured or unsecured. Certain company debentures are deemed under *TCGA 1992, s 251* to be securities for the purposes of that section (see 21.5 EXEMPTIONS AND RELIEFS). There are provisions to ensure that (*b*) and (*c*) above operate in relation to such debentures.

[*TCGA 1992, s 132; FA 1997, s 88(1)–(3)(6)*].

A premium in money (in addition to a new holding) on a conversion of securities is treated in virtually identical terms as under *TCGA 1992, s 122* for a capital distribution in 58.14 below. (It would appear that the case of *O'Rourke v Binks CA 1992, 65 TC 165* mentioned therein applies equally to premiums on conversion within this provision as it does to capital distributions within *TCGA 1992, s 122*.) Similar rules as in *section 122* apply if the premium is 'small' (which is as defined in 58.14 below). [*TCGA 1992, s 133; FA 1996, Sch 20 para 53*].

Alternative rules apply to the conversion of securities of a company involving qualifying corporate bonds. See 49.3 QUALIFYING CORPORATE BONDS.

See also 64.1 UNIT TRUSTS ETC. for the disapplication of *TCGA 1992, s 132* as regards collective investment schemes entitling participants to exchange rights in one part of a scheme for rights in another.

Example

N bought £10,000 8% convertible loan stock in S plc, a quoted company, in June 1990. The cost was £9,800. In August 1994, N exercised his right to convert the loan stock into 'B' ordinary shares of the company, on the basis of 50 shares for £100 loan stock, and acquired 5,000 shares. In June 2000, N sells 3,000 of the shares for £5.00 each. The indexation factor for June 1990 to April 1998 is 0.283.

	£
Disposal consideration	15,000
Cost $\frac{3,000}{5,000} \times$ £9,800	5,880
Unindexed gain	9,120
Indexation allowance £5,880 × 0.283	1,664
Chargeable gain (subject to TAPER RELIEF (60))	£7,456

Notes to the example

(*a*) The shares acquired on the conversion in 1994 stand in the shoes of the original loan stock. [*TCGA 1992, s 132*].

(*b*) The loan stock cannot be a corporate bond (and thus cannot be a qualifying corporate bond) as it is convertible into securities other than corporate bonds, i.e. into ordinary shares. [*ICTA 1988, Sch 18 para 1(5); TCGA 1992, s 117(1)*].

Compensation stock. Instead of *TCGA 1992, s 132* above applying, gilt-edged securities issued on the compulsory acquisition after 6 April 1976 of shares or securities are treated as acquired on the date of issue (or, if earlier, of compulsory acquisition) at a cost equal to the value of the shares etc. as determined for the purposes of the exchange, which transaction is treated as not involving any disposal of the shares or securities. The gain that would have accrued had the shares or securities been disposed of at that value at that time is not treated as arising until the gilt-edged securities are disposed of, so that it is added to any actual chargeable gain (or deducted from any actual allowable loss) which may, before 2 July 1986, accrue at that time. However, where the gilt-edged securities received are disposed of after 5 April 1988 no addition or deduction is made under this provision if its application would be directly attributable to the disposal of an asset before 1 April 1982.

Before 2 July 1986 disposals were identified as far as possible with similar securities acquired within the preceding twelve months (otherwise than under the above provisions) and thereafter with securities so acquired, taking earlier issues before later ones. The then rules for identifying gilt-edged securities were disregarded for this latter purpose.

After 1 July 1986 (when disposals of gilt-edged securities are exempt *in all cases*) disposals are, so far as possible, identified with gilts issued under the above provisions rather than with other gilts of the same kind and subject to this, with gilts issued at an earlier time rather than with those issued at a later time.

The deferment of the gain otherwise arising on the issue of the gilt-edged securities is extended to the recipient where their later disposal is within *TCGA 1992, s 58(1)* (spouses), *s 62(4)* (legatee acquiring asset from personal representatives) and *s 171(1)* (groups of companies).

[*TCGA 1992, s 134, Sch 4 para 4(5); CGTA 1979, s 84; FA 1985, s 67(2)(b), Sch 27 Pt VII*].

See 60.12 TAPER RELIEF for the application of that relief to the deferred gain.

Euroconversion of securities. A 'small' cash payment received on a 'euroconversion' of a security, not involving a disposal of the security and therefore not within *TCGA 1992, s 132* (see above), is treated in virtually identical terms as a 'small' capital distribution under *TCGA 1992, s 122* (see 58.14 below). '*Euroconversion*' for these purposes refers to the redenomination into euros of a security expressed in the currency of an EU Member State participating in the European single currency. [*TCGA 1992, s 133A; SI 1998 No 3177, regs 3, 39*].

58.12 **Quoted option granted following reorganisation.** If a quoted option (within *TCGA 1992, s 144(8)*; see 17.10 DISPOSAL) to subscribe for shares in a company (see 17.10 DISPOSAL) is dealt in (on the stock exchange where it is quoted) within three months after (or such longer period after as may be allowed in written notice by the Revenue) a reorganisation, reduction, conversion or amalgamation (within the provisions in 58.5–58.11 above) relating to the company granting the option, then

(*a*) the option is regarded for those provisions as the shares which could be acquired following the reorganisation etc. by exercising the option, and

(*b*) the ordinary market value rules for quoted securities apply (see 40.2 MARKET VALUE).

[*TCGA 1992, s 147*].

58.13 STOCK DIVIDENDS (AKA SCRIP DIVIDENDS).

Individuals. Issues of shares in lieu of dividend on or before 5 April 1975 were treated as bonus issues, and no allowance for capital gains tax purposes was made for the cash dividend forgone. This continues to be the case as regards issues made by a non-UK resident company. Issues made by a UK resident company after 5 April 1975 are subject to income tax (see TOLLEY'S INCOME TAX under Stock Dividends), and the 'appropriate amount in cash' is treated as allowable expenditure for capital gains tax purposes. An issue before 6 April 1998 was then treated as a reorganisation within 58.5 above in respect of which additional consideration was given. [*TCGA 1992, s 141*].

An issue of shares by a UK resident company **after 5 April 1998** in lieu of dividend does not constitute a reorganisation but is treated in the hands of the recipient shareholder as a free-standing acquisition made at the time of the issue for a consideration equal to the 'appropriate amount in cash'. [*TCGA 1992, s 142; FA 1998, s 126*].

The above provisions apply not only where the shares are issued as a consequence of an option to receive additional shares instead of a cash dividend but also where they are issued as a bonus issue in a case where the existing shares carry the right under the original terms of issue (or original terms as extended or varied) to receive bonus share capital of the same or a different class. [*ICTA 1988, s 249(1)(2)*].

The '*appropriate amount in cash*' is

(*a*) where the shares are offered as an alternative to a cash dividend, the amount of that cash dividend;

(*b*) where the shares are offered in a quantity which is determined by, or determines, the amount of a dividend in cash payable in respect of shares in the company of a different class, the amount of that cash dividend;

unless the amount arrived at under (*a*) or (*b*) above is substantially (i.e. 15% or more subject to marginal discretion where this limit is exceeded by one or two percentage points; Revenue Pamphlet IR 131, SP A8) greater or less than the market value of the shares, in which case the latter is substituted. Market value is also used in any other case. [*ICTA 1988, s 251(2)–(4)*]. If two or more persons are entitled to the shares issued, those shares (and the appropriate amount in cash) are apportioned among them by reference to their interests in the shares at the date of issue. [*ICTA 1988, s 249(3)*].

Settlements and personal representatives. The position above applies equally to personal representatives, to trustees of discretionary and accumulation trusts where the dividend would have been chargeable at the rate applicable to trusts if received in cash, and, as regards the position after 5 April 1998, to trustees of interest in possession trusts. [*TCGA 1992, ss 141, 142; ICTA 1988, s 249(4)–(6); FA 1996, Sch 6 para 6; F(No 2)A 1997, Sch 4 para 10; FA 1998, s 126*]. Where, before 6 April 1998, shares were issued in lieu of dividend to trustees of an interest in possession trust where one or more beneficiaries were absolutely entitled as against the trustees (or would have been but for infancy or disability), the issue did not constitute a reorganisation. (The changes made by Finance Act 1998 do not affect that position.) The trustees' acquisition cost of the original shareholding remains unaltered and the beneficiaries are regarded as acquiring the stock dividend shares as at the dividend date for the appropriate amount in cash. However, see SP 4/94 below re enhanced stock dividends.

The beneficiaries of a bare trust are treated in the same way as individuals, the trust being ignored for this purpose (Revenue Capital Gains Manual CG 33811(a)).

In the case of a discretionary or accumulation trust where the dividend would have been chargeable at the rate applicable to trusts if received in cash, the appropriate amount in cash forms part of the trustees' allowable expenditure. Any subsequent distribution of the stock dividend shares to the beneficiaries is a part disposal at market value by the trustees, with the normal identification rules applying (see 59 SHARES AND SECURITIES—IDENTIFICATION RULES).

In the case of an *enhanced stock dividend*, i.e. one which is worth significantly more than the cash dividend forgone, there was some doubt as to whether the position for interest in possession trusts outlined above could apply, the point being that the stock dividend may under trust law be capital rather than income. It is up to the trustees to decide in the light of the trust deed whether the enhanced stock dividend should properly be regarded as income or as capital. The Revenue issued Statement of Practice SP 4/94 (see Revenue Pamphlet IR 131) setting out their views. They are prepared to accept whichever of the three approaches listed below the trustees conclude that they should adopt, provided that their conclusion is supportable on the facts of the case.

- If the trustees treat the dividend as income, the beneficiary is chargeable to income tax under *ICTA 1988, s 249* and is treated as acquiring the shares for the 'appropriate amount in cash'. The issue is not treated as a reorganisation (whether before or on or after 6 April 1998).
- If the trustees treat the dividend as capital, the issue is a reorganisation within *TCGA 1992, s 126* (see 58.5 above) and the trustees are not regarded as having made any payment for the shares.
- If the trustees treat the dividend as capital but pay compensation to a beneficiary in the form of shares for forgoing the cash dividend alternative, the transfer constitutes a part disposal of the new holding.

See Revenue Capital Gains Manual CG 33810–33817 for a full discussion of the above.

Close companies. The appropriate amount in cash relating to shares issued in lieu of a dividend made by a UK resident company to a close company in accounting periods ending before 1 April 1989 was treated as part of its apportionable income for income tax purposes, and any income tax in respect of such income apportioned (but not paid) to a participator can be added to his allowable expenditure, for capital gains tax purposes, on a disposal of shares in the close company. The close company's allowable expenditure in respect of the shares was increased by the appropriate amount in cash. [*CGTA 1979, s 89; TCGA 1992, s 124; ICTA 1988, Sch 19 para 12; FA 1989, Sch 17 Pt V*]. See further in 58.23 below. There is no addition to allowable expenditure of the shares held for later accounting periods or, for any accounting period, where the shares are held by a non-close company.

Example

D holds ordinary 20p shares in PLC, a quoted company. The company operates a scrip dividend policy whereby shareholders are given the option to take dividends in cash or in new fully-paid ordinary 20p shares, the option being exercisable separately in relation to each dividend. D purchased 2,000 shares for £1,500 in March 1980 and a further 3,000 shares for £8,100 in May 1992 and up until the end of 1997 he had always taken cash dividends. In January 1998, he opts for a scrip dividend and receives 25 shares instead of a cash dividend of £100. On 20 April 1998, he purchases a further 1,000 shares for £3,950. In July 1998, he opts for a scrip dividend of 44 shares instead of a cash dividend of £180. He opts for cash dividends thereafter. In May 2000, he sells 2,069 shares for £8,550 (ex div), leaving himself with a holding of 4,000.

In the case of both scrip dividends taken by D, the market value of the new shares is equivalent to the cash dividend forgone. The 'appropriate amount in cash' is thus the amount of that dividend. Relevant indexation factors are as follows.

May 1992 to January 1998	0.145
January 1998 to April 1998	0.019

The gain on the disposal in May 2000 is calculated as follows

(i) Identify 44 shares sold with those received by way of scrip dividend in July 1998 (LIFO)

	£
Proceeds £8,550 × 44/2,069	182
Cost (equal to 'appropriate amount in cash')	180
Chargeable gain	£2

(ii) Identify 1,000 shares sold with those acquired on 20 April 1998

	£
Proceeds £8,550 × 1,000/2,069	4,132
Cost	3,950
Chargeable gain	£182

(iii) Identify remaining 1,025 shares sold with 'section 104 holding' at 5 April 1998

Section 104 holding

	Shares	Qualifying expenditure	Indexed pool
		£	£
May 1992 acquisition	3,000	8,100	8,100
Indexed rise: May 1992 to Jan 1998 £8,100 × 0.145			1,175
	3,000	8,100	9,275
January 1998 scrip dividend 25 × 3,000/5,000	15	60	60
	3,015	8,160	9,335
Indexed rise: Jan 1998 to April 1998 (note (*a*)) £9,335 × 0.019			177
Pool at 5.4.98	3,015	8,160	9,512
May 2000 disposal	(1,025)	(2,775)	(3,234)
Pool carried forward	1,990	£5,385	£6,278

	£
Proceeds £8,550 × 1,025/2,069	4,236
Cost £8,160 × 1,025/3,015	2,775
Unindexed gain	1,461
Indexation allowance £9,512 × 1,025/3,015 = £3,234 £3,234 − £2,775	459
Chargeable gain	£1,002
Total chargeable gain 2000/01 (subject to TAPER RELIEF (60)) (£2 + £182 + £1,002)	£1,186

The remaining holding of 4,000 shares consists of a 'section 104 holding' of 1,990 as illustrated above and a '1982 holding' of 2,010 (which was irrelevant to the May 2000 disposal) consisting of 2,000 purchased in March 1980 and 10 scrip dividend shares acquired in January 1998 and equated with the said purchase.

Note to the example

(*a*) The indexed pool is upgraded as if the entire holding had been disposed of at the end of 5 April 1998 but is not adjusted for any subsequent indexed rise in expenditure (see 59.2 SHARES AND SECURITIES—IDENTIFICATION RULES).

58.14 **CAPITAL DISTRIBUTIONS**

A capital distribution (other than of a new holding within 58.5 above), on liquidation or otherwise (defined as any distribution in money or money's worth by a company to a shareholder, which is not treated as income for tax purposes) is treated as accruing to the shareholder from the disposal of an interest in the shares. [*TCGA 1992, s 122(1)(5)*].

If the amount or value of the capital distribution is 'small' as compared with the value of the shares in respect of which it is made, the capital distribution shall not be treated as a disposal, in which case no immediate capital gains tax liability arises, but the proceeds are deducted from the acquisition cost of the shares on a subsequent disposal. [*TCGA 1992, s 122(2); FA 1996, Sch 20 para 52*]. For this purpose, the Revenue have regarded 'small' as meaning 5% or less (see Revenue Capital Gains Manual CG 57836 and Revenue Tax Bulletin November 1992 p 46). With effect from **24 February 1997**, they additionally regard an amount of £3,000 or less as 'small', regardless of whether or not it would pass the 5% test (Revenue Tax Bulletin February 1997 p 397).

Prior to 6 April 1996 the inspector had specific power (as opposed to general power under self-assessment) to direct that the capital distribution not be treated as a disposal. If the inspector refused such a direction, the taxpayer had right of appeal. [*TCGA 1992, s 122(3) (repealed)*]. Also, if it would be to the taxpayer's advantage for such a direction *not* to be made (for example, where the gain would be covered by the annual exemption), the Revenue would not insist on the application of *section 122(2)* (Revenue Tax Bulletin, November 1992 p 46).

Where the amount or value of the capital distribution exceeds any allowable expenditure on the shares, the taxpayer may elect to have *all* such expenditure set against the distribution with the balance of the distribution being treated as on a part disposal and the expenditure deducted not allowable on that or any subsequent disposal. [*TCGA 1992, s 122(4)*]. In *O'Rourke v Binks CA 1992, 65 TC 165*, it was held that the right to make the election under *TCGA 1992, s 122(4)* was constrained by the requirement of *TCGA 1992, s 122(2)* that the amount or value of the capital distribution be small as compared with the value of the shares in respect of which it was made.

Income tax charges under *ICTA 1988, s 186(3)* (approved profit sharing schemes — see 19.22 EMPLOYEE SHARE SCHEMES) are to be disregarded in determining whether a distribution is a capital distribution. [*TCGA 1992, s 238(2)(b)*].

Example 1

T holds 10,000 ordinary shares in a foreign company M SA. The shares were bought in April 1996 for £80,000. In February 2001, M SA has a capital reconstruction involving the cancellation of one-fifth of the existing ordinary shares in consideration of the repayment of £10 to each shareholder per share cancelled. T's holding is reduced to 8,000 shares, valued at £96,000. The indexation factor for April 1996 to April 1998 is 0.066.

	£
Disposal consideration (2,000 × £10)	20,000
Allowable cost $\dfrac{20{,}000}{20{,}000 + 96{,}000} \times £80{,}000$	13,793
Unindexed gain	6,207
Indexation allowance £13,793 × 0.066	910
Chargeable gain	£5,297
The allowable cost of the remaining shares is £80,000 – £13,793	£66,207

Example 2 (Sale of rights)

X is a shareholder in K Ltd, owning 2,500 £1 ordinary shares which were purchased for £7,000 in October 1996. K Ltd makes a rights issue, but X sells his rights, without taking them up, for £700 in August 2000. The ex-rights value of X's 2,500 shares at the date of sale is £14,500. The indexation factor for the period October 1996 to April 1998 is 0.057.

'Section 104 holding' of K Ltd £1 ordinary shares

	Shares	Qualifying expenditure £	Indexed pool £
October 1996 acquisition	2,500	7,000	7,000
Indexed rise to April 1998 £7,000 × 0.057			399
	2,500	£7,000	£7,399

The Revenue cannot require the capital distribution to be treated as a disposal, as the £700 received for the rights does not exceed 5% of (£700 + £14,500) and in any case does not exceed £3,000. If the transaction is not treated as a disposal, the £700 is deducted from both the acquisition cost of the shares and the indexed pool, leaving balances of, respectively, £6,300 and £6,699. If the transaction is treated as a disposal (possibly because X wishes to utilise part of his annual exemption), the computation is as follows

	£
Disposal proceeds	700
Allowable cost $\dfrac{700}{700 + 14{,}500} \times £7{,}000$	322
Unindexed gain	378
Indexation allowance $£7{,}399 \times \dfrac{700}{700 + 14{,}500} = £341$	
£341 – £322	19
Chargeable gain	£359

The allowable cost of the shares is then reduced to £6,678 (£7,000 – £322) and the indexed pool to £7,058 (£7,399 – £341).

58.15 **Distributions in a liquidation: unquoted shares.** Instead of requiring a strict valuation of unquoted shares for the purposes of the part disposal arising on a distribution, the Revenue are prepared to accept a reasonable estimate of the residual value of the shares if the liquidation is expected to be completed within two years of the first distribution. If the distribution takes longer, the valuations may be reopened. Where time apportionment (see 7.9 *et seq.* ASSETS HELD ON 6 APRIL 1965) applies, the Revenue are prepared to calculate the gain on each distribution by applying the time apportionment fraction as at the date of the first distribution (Revenue Pamphlet IR 131, SP D3).

58.16 **Distributions of assets in specie in a liquidation.** Where a company-owned asset, for example shares in a subsidiary, is distributed by the liquidator in specie to shareholders, *TCGA 1992, s 17* (see 40.1 MARKET VALUE) must be applied in determining the acquisition cost of an asset so received by a shareholder. For this purpose, each distribution to each shareholder is considered in isolation from the others. For example, if an asset is distributed equally to each of five shareholders, the acquisition cost for capital gains tax purposes of the part received by each (and also its disposal value from the point of view of the company) is the value of a 20% share, and not one-fifth of the value of a 100% share which may have produced a different (and almost certainly higher) figure. In a case in which the company is controlled by persons connected with each other, so that each such person is connected with the company (see 14.5 CONNECTED PERSONS), it is understood that the above nevertheless applies and that the Revenue would not normally invoke the linked transactions provisions of *TCGA 1992, s 19* (see 3.14 ANTI-AVOIDANCE) so as to value each distribution as a percentage of the whole.

58.17 **PRIVATISATIONS**

The following is concerned with the privatisations of utilities previously in public ownership, e.g. power, water, telecommunications. For the de-mutualisation of building societies and other mutual organisations, e.g. insurance companies, see 58.26 below.

Payment by instalments. Most privatisation issues required payment of the subscription price by instalments. For the purposes of INDEXATION (26) allowance, the subscriber is deemed to have incurred, *at the time of acquisition of the shares*, relevant allowable expenditure equal to the full amount he is committed to paying (not just the amount of the first instalment). This applies only to privatisation issues — otherwise see 26.7 INDEXATION. If he disposes of the shares before all instalments are paid, the subscriber may choose to include the amount of the unpaid instalments in the cost of acquisition and add that same amount to the disposal proceeds (or, in the case of a non-arm's length disposal, to the MARKET VALUE (40) of the part-paid shares). Where indexation allowance is due, this choice is to his advantage as he thereby receives an allowance on instalments he has not paid. The new owner's allowable expenditure on a subsequent disposal of the shares fully-paid will in any case comprise the actual purchase price (or market value) and the instalments which he has had to pay on the shares. (Revenue Capital Gains Manual CG 50772, 50776, 50777).

Bonus shares. Many privatisations included the option of receiving bonus shares if the subscriber retained his original shares for a specified period. The issue of such bonus shares does not constitute a reorganisation as in 58.6 above. Instead, the subscriber is treated as acquiring the bonus shares at their date of issue at their then market value. (Revenue Capital Gains Manual CG 50773).

Vouchers. A subscriber to a privatisation issue may have been given the option of receiving vouchers which he can set against bills from the privatised company. No tax liability arises on receipt of such vouchers, but the acquisition cost of the shares for CGT purposes must be reduced by the value so received. (Revenue Capital Gains Manual CG 50774).

58.18 COMPANY PURCHASING OWN SHARES

Any consideration given by a company for the redemption, repayment or purchase of its own shares, *except* insofar as it represents repayment of share capital, is normally treated as a distribution, and hence as income in the hands of the recipient (see TOLLEY'S CORPORATION TAX under Distributions). Such payments after 5 April 1982 in respect of shares in certain unquoted trading companies (or holding companies) are *not* treated as distributions, and thus give rise to liability to capital gains tax (or corporation tax on chargeable gains) on the recipient in the normal way. See TOLLEY'S CORPORATION TAX under Company Purchasing Own Shares for detailed conditions. [*ICTA 1988, ss 219–229*].

Where the recipient is a dealer in securities, any payment after 5 April 1982 by a company for the redemption, repayment or purchase of its own shares, or of rights to acquire those shares, is treated as trading income of the recipient. This treatment was extended to cover any distribution made after 25 November 1996 to which *FA 1997, Sch 7* (special treatment for certain distributions) applied. It is further extended by *Finance (No 2) Act 1997* to cover all distributions received by dealers from UK resident companies, and any payment representative of such a distribution, where the distribution or payment is made after 1 July 1997 and the securities in question form part of the dealer's trading stock. [*ICTA 1988, s 95; FA 1997, Sch 7 para 8(1)(3); F(No 2)A 1997, s 24(1)–(9)(15), Sch 8 Pt II(8)*].

In relation to purchases after 19 April 1989, if the purchase of its own shares by a UK resident company gives rise to a distribution, and the shareholder receiving such a distribution is itself a company, the Revenue's practice is to include the distribution in the consideration for the disposal of the shares for the purposes of the charge to corporation tax on chargeable gains. In the Revenue's view the effect of *ICTA 1988, s 208* and *TCGA 1992, s 8(4)* is that the distribution does not suffer a tax charge as income within the terms of *TCGA 1992, s 37(1)* (see 33.1 INTERACTION WITH OTHER TAXES) (Revenue Pamphlet IR 131, SP 4/89).

58.19 ACCRUED INCOME SCHEME

The accrued income scheme provisions of *ICTA 1988, ss 710–728* apply, broadly, to transfers of any government, public authority or company loan stock. (See further 59.6 SHARES AND SECURITIES—IDENTIFICATION RULES.)

The accrued income scheme does not apply for the purposes of corporation tax for accounting periods ending after 31 March 1996 (to which the loan relationship provisions in 38 LOAN RELATIONSHIPS OF COMPANIES apply), except as regards transfers taking place on or before that date, and subject to transitional provisions (see 38.13 LOAN RELATIONSHIPS OF COMPANIES). [*ICTA 1988, s 710(1A); FA 1996, s 104, s 105(1), Sch 14 para 36, Sch 15 para 18*].

For 1996/97 onwards, the accrued income scheme does not apply on a transfer to which *FA 1996, Sch 13* applies (charge to or relief from tax on the profit or loss realised from the discount on a relevant discounted security — see 58.20 below).

For deaths occurring after 5 April 1996 the accrued income scheme no longer applies to the transfer of securities on death to the deceased's personal representatives. [*ICTA 1988, s 710(5)(a), s 721; FA 1996, s 158*].

If a transfer is with accrued interest, the transferor is treated as entitled to the 'accrued amount' for income tax purposes, and the transferee is allowed similar relief for income tax purposes, for the interest period in which the settlement day falls. If the transfer is without accrued interest, the transferor is allowed relief on the 'rebate amount', and the transferee is treated as entitled to the same amount, for the relevant interest period.

Where a transfer within the accrued income provisions also constitutes a disposal for the purposes of *TCGA 1992*, neither *TCGA 1992, s 37* nor *s 39* applies (see 33.1 INTERACTION

WITH OTHER TAXES). Instead, where a transfer is with accrued interest, an amount equal to the accrued amount is excluded for those purposes from the transferor's disposal consideration, and the same amount is excluded from the transferee's allowable expenditure when he makes a subsequent disposal. Where the transfer is without accrued interest, an amount equal to the rebate amount is added for those purposes to the transferor's disposal consideration, and the same amount is added to the transferee's allowable expenditure when he makes a subsequent disposal. Similar rules apply where there is a disposal (e.g. a deemed disposal) for the purposes of *TCGA 1992* without there being a contemporaneous transfer within the scope of the accrued income provisions. Where on a 'conversion' (being one within *TCGA 1992, s 132*; see 58.11 above) or an 'exchange' (being one which is not treated as a disposal: see generally 58.5 above) of securities, a person is treated as entitled to the accrued amount, an equal amount less any consideration received on the conversion or exchange (other than the new holding of securities) is treated for the purposes of *TCGA 1992* as consideration given on the conversion or exchange. Where the consideration received on the conversion or exchange (other than the new holding of securities) equals or exceeds an amount equal to the accrued amount, that consideration is treated for the purposes of *TCGA 1992* as reduced by that amount. If on a conversion or exchange of securities, a rebate amount is allowed for income tax purposes, an amount equal to the rebate amount is treated for the purposes of *TCGA 1992* as consideration received on the conversion or exchange.

Where a transfer of securities is made with the right to receive interest ('unrealised interest') payable on them on an interest payment date falling before the settlement day, neither *TCGA 1992, s 37* nor *s 39* applies. Instead, an amount equal to any such unrealised interest charged to income tax on the transferor is excluded for the purposes of *TCGA 1992* from the transferor's disposal consideration. Where such a transfer is made, an amount equal to the unrealised interest left out of account in charging income tax on the transferee is excluded for those purposes from the transferee's allowable expenditure when he makes a subsequent disposal.

[*TCGA 1992, s 119*].

See TOLLEY'S INCOME TAX under Schedule D, Case VI for full details of the accrued income scheme.

The above procedures will not be required for the purposes of computing a chargeable gain where the security is otherwise exempt. See 24 GOVERNMENT SECURITIES and 49 QUALIFYING CORPORATE BONDS.

58.20 DISCOUNTED SECURITIES AND CONVERTIBLE SECURITIES

Deep discounted securities. For **1995/96 and earlier years** and for company accounting periods ending before **1 April 1996**, the discount element on 'deep discount securities' was brought into charge to income tax or corporation tax (rather than to capital gains tax or corporation tax on chargeable gains) on disposal or redemption. The provisions are replaced, **for 1996/97 onwards**, by the income tax provisions of *FA 1996, Sch 13* (relevant discounted securities — see below), and, for company accounting periods ending **after 31 March 1996,** by the loan relationship provisions outlined in 38 LOAN RELATIONSHIPS OF COMPANIES (and see 38.14 for transitional provisions).

Income and corporation tax legislation relating to deep discount securities was contained in *TCGA 1992, s 118; ICTA 1988, s 57, Sch 4*. For the income tax charge on the holder of the security, see TOLLEY'S INCOME TAX under Interest Receivable and for the relief from corporation tax received by companies issuing such securities, see TOLLEY'S CORPORATION TAX under Profit Computations, and generally see both publications for coverage of the provisions. Broadly, a '*deep discount security*' is a redeemable security issued by a company after 13 March 1984 at a discount exceeding 15% of the amount payable on redemption overall or $\frac{1}{2}$% per annum of that amount for each complete year from issue to redemption. Shares, index-linked securities and share capital within *ICTA 1988, s 209(2)(c)* are excluded. Rules specifically dealing with chargeable gains relating to deep discount securities are given below.

(*a*) *Disposals.* In computing the gain accruing on the disposal of a deep discount security the consideration for the disposal is treated as reduced by the amount which represents the accrued income attributable to the period of ownership and which is charged to income tax under Schedule D, Case III or IV. *TCGA 1992, s 37* (see 33.1 INTERACTION WITH OTHER TAXES) is excluded for this purpose. Where the amount charged to income tax exceeds the disposal consideration, the excess is treated as allowable expenditure within *TCGA 1992, s 38(1)(b)* (see 17.3 DISPOSAL) incurred immediately before disposal (and thus effectively resulting in an additional allowable loss equal to the excess).

(*b*) *Occurrence of disposal.* There is a disposal for the purposes of the income and corporation tax provisions if there would be a disposal for the purposes of *TCGA 1992*. (It would therefore appear that there is a disposal under the income and corporation tax provisions, even when there is only a deemed disposal for the purposes of the charge to tax on chargeable gains.) In addition, death is also an occasion of disposal notwithstanding the general rule given at 16.1 DEATH but this provision appears only to apply for the purposes of assessment to income tax or corporation tax and not for the purposes of the charge to tax on chargeable gains. See also (*f*) below.

(*c*) *Time of disposal.* The time of disposal of a deep discount security for the purposes of income or corporation tax is the contract date but if a contract is conditional, the time of disposal is the time when the condition is satisfied.

(*d*) *'No gain, no loss' disposals.* After a 'no gain, no loss' disposal for the purposes of the charge to tax on chargeable gains of a deep discount security, the allowable expenditure of the acquirer is increased by the amount of accrued income arising in the previous owner's period of ownership.

(*e*) *Identification of securities.* Deep discount securities are identified under the rules applicable to securities generally before 6 April 1985 (1 April 1985 for companies). After 5 April 1985 (31 March 1985 for companies) deep discount securities are designated 'relevant securities' and amended identification rules apply. See 59.6 SHARES AND SECURITIES—IDENTIFICATION RULES. This applies for income and corporation tax purposes as well as for the purposes of the charge to tax on chargeable gains.

(*f*) *Conversion or exchange of securities.* Where on the conversion or exchange of securities (within *TCGA 1992, s 132* or *s 135(3)* (including in the latter case the deemed treatment under *s 136(1)*; see 58.8–58.11 above) any money sum is received (in addition to the new holding) as consideration for the disposal of the deep discount securities, for the purposes of the charge to tax on capital gains, the disposal proceeds are treated as reduced by the amount of accrued income charged to income tax on a disposal deemed to occur for income or corporation tax purposes on the conversion or exchange. Where the accrued income exceeds the proceeds, the excess is treated as allowable expenditure as at (*a*) above.

(*g*) UNDERWRITERS AT LLOYD'S (63) are deemed for the income or corporation tax provisions to dispose of and reacquire securities held in a premiums trust fund at each 31 December date for 1989 and subsequent underwriting years prior to 1994. Such transactions are also treated for the purposes of the charge to tax on chargeable gains as disposals and acquisitions at market value.

[*TCGA 1992, s 118; ICTA 1988, Sch 4; FA 1996, s 105, Sch 14 para 50, Sch 41 Pt V(3)*].

The capital element of a deep discount security can be a qualifying corporate bond and thus totally exempt for the purposes of capital gains tax and corporation tax on chargeable gains. See 49.2 QUALIFYING CORPORATE BONDS.

Where a deep discount security carries interest (in addition to a discount to redemption as above), the accrued income scheme provisions (see above) may apply to a disposal. In addition certain rules relating to indexation allowance and identification applying generally before 6 April 1985 (1 April 1985 for companies) were retained where this would not otherwise be the case, see 59.6 SHARES AND SECURITIES—IDENTIFICATION RULES.

Deep discounted stock and indexed stock not within TCGA 1992, s 118. Companies registered in the UK were permitted to issue deep discounted stock (including zero coupon bonds) after 24 June 1982. However, there was no specific legislation applicable to such issues made before 14 March 1984 (but see below under deep gain securities) but the Revenue indicated their practice in relation to such stocks and also to indexed stock and this practice continued to have relevance where the specific provisions above did not apply. In the Revenue's view the discount on issue of a deep discounted stock was chargeable on redemption as rolled-up interest in the lender's hands and allowable against the borrower's profits for corporation tax purposes. This applied whether or not there had been intermediate transactions. As regards indexed stock issued by companies at a reasonable commercial rate of interest, if the indexed uplift on redemption merely took account of any fall in the real value of the stock, then the lender (provided it was not a bank or financial concern), was liable only to capital gains tax on the uplift. The borrowing company was not able to claim a deduction for the uplift against its corporation tax profits. If, however, the indexing applied to the interest element, and additional sums of interest were rolled up to be paid with the capital on redemption, then both indexed and rolled-up interest was, when paid, given the same tax treatment for borrower and lender as non-indexed interest. (Revenue Press Release 25 June 1982).

Deep gain securities. *FA 1989, s 94, Sch 11* introduced legislation for 'deep gain securities' (see TOLLEY'S INCOME TAX under Interest Receivable). Broadly, a '*deep gain security*' is a security which, at whatever time it was issued and assuming redemption, is redeemable in an amount which exceeds the issue price by more than 15% of that amount or $\frac{1}{2}$% per annum of that amount for each complete year from issue to redemption. Deep discount securities, index-linked securities, shares and (subject to exceptions) gilt-edged securities issued before 14 March 1989 were excluded.

The provisions applied for **1995/96 and earlier years** and for company accounting periods ending before **1 April 1996**. They are replaced, **for 1996/97 onwards**, by the income tax provisions of *FA 1996, Sch 13* (relevant discounted securities — see below), and, for company accounting periods ending **after 31 March 1996**, by the loan relationship provisions outlined in 38 LOAN RELATIONSHIPS OF COMPANIES (and see 38.15 for transitional provisions).

A transfer or redemption of a deep gain security for an amount exceeding the acquisition cost results in an amount equal to the difference (net of transfer costs) being treated as income of the transferor. There are no specific consequential provisions for the purposes of the charge to tax on chargeable gains because, it seems, a deep gain security (or a security falling to be treated as a deep gain security) will be a gilt-edged security (see 24 GOVERNMENT SECURITIES) or, in some cases, a qualifying corporate bond (see 49.2 QUALIFYING CORPORATE BONDS) and thus exempt. If this is not the case it would seem the position is governed by *TCGA 1992, s 37* (see 33.1 INTERACTION WITH OTHER TAXES).

Convertible securities. *FA 1990, s 56, Sch 10* introduced legislation for 'qualifying convertible securities' (see TOLLEY'S INCOME TAX under Interest Receivable). Broadly, a '*qualifying convertible security*' is a quoted redeemable security, other than a share, which is issued by a company after 8 June 1989, which would otherwise be a deep discount or deep gain security (see above) but would not be such a security but for certain provisions as to redemption, and which is convertible into ordinary share capital in the company.

The provisions applied for **1995/96 and earlier years** and for company accounting periods ending before **1 April 1996**. They are replaced, **for 1996/97 onwards**, by the income tax provisions of *FA 1996, Sch 13* (relevant discounted securities — see below), and, for company accounting periods ending **after 31 March 1996**, by the loan relationship provisions outlined in 38 LOAN RELATIONSHIPS OF COMPANIES (and see 38.16 for transitional provisions).

A transfer or redemption of a qualifying convertible security results in a 'chargeable amount' (calculated by reference to the length of ownership and the yield to redemption exclusive of interest) being treated as income of the transferor. There are no specific consequential provisions for capital gains tax and the position seems to be as for deep gain securities above except that, because of the condition that a qualifying convertible security must be convertible into ordinary share capital, such a security cannot be a qualifying corporate bond. Obviously, too, such a security cannot be a gilt-edged security.

Relevant discounted securities. For **1996/97 and subsequent years**, when a person transfers a 'relevant discounted security', or becomes entitled, as holder, to any payment on its redemption, he is chargeable to income tax on the excess (net of incidental costs of acquisition and disposal) of the amount payable on the transfer or redemption over the amount paid for its acquisition. In the event of a loss, a claim may be made for relief against income of the tax year of transfer or redemption. See TOLLEY'S INCOME TAX under Schedule D, Case III for the detailed provisions. The provisions do **not** apply for corporation tax purposes; for company accounting periods ending after 31 March 1996, the loan relationship regime outlined in 38 LOAN RELATIONSHIPS OF COMPANIES is of general application instead.

A '*relevant discounted security*' is, except as excluded below, any security such that the amount payable on redemption (excluding interest) is or might be an amount involving a '*deep gain*', i.e. the issue price is less than the amount payable on redemption by 15% of that amount or, if less, by $\frac{1}{2}$% per annum of that amount (counting months and part months as $\frac{1}{12}$th of a year) to the redemption date. This comparison is made as at the time of issue of the security and assuming redemption in accordance with the terms of issue. 'Redemption' for these purposes referred originally to redemption on maturity or, if the holder of the security could opt for earlier redemption, the earliest occasion on which the holder might require redemption. In relation to any transfer of a security after 14 February 1999 or any occasion after that date on which a holder of a security becomes entitled to payment on redemption, the definition is widened so that one must consider, in addition to redemption on maturity, possible earlier occasions on which a security might be redeemed. The security will be a relevant discounted security if it would be such by reference to at least one such occasion. One need not take into account any occasion on which there may be a redemption other than at the option of the holder *unless* issuer and holder are connected or the obtaining of a tax advantage (as defined) is a main benefit that might be expected to accrue from the redemption provision. Additionally, where the holder has an option entitling him to redeem only on the occurrence of an 'event adversely affecting the holder' (as defined) or of a person's default *and* such entitlement is unlikely, judged at time of issue, to arise, the potential redemption is disregarded.

The following are not relevant discounted securities:

(i) shares in a company;

(ii) gilt-edged securities (other than gilt strips, which are always relevant discounted securities regardless of their issue terms);

(iii) excluded indexed securities (as defined);

(iv) life assurance policies;

(v) capital redemption policies; and

(vi) (with exceptions) securities issued under the same prospectus as other securities issued previously but not themselves relevant discounted securities.

After 14 February 1999, securities within (iii) and (vi) above may, however, be treated as relevant discounted securities in certain circumstances involving their being held by a person connected with the issuer. *ICTA 1988, s 839* applies to determine whether persons are connected for the purposes of these provisions but without taking any account of the security under review or any security issued under the same prospectus.

[*FA 1996, s 102, s 105(1)(b), Sch 13; FA 1999, s 65(1)–(6)(8)*].

For the avoidance of a double charge, i.e. to both income tax and capital gains tax (and double relief for losses), any relevant discounted security, whatever its date of issue, is brought within the definition of a QUALIFYING CORPORATE BOND (49). [*TCGA 1992, s 117(2AA)(8A); FA 1996, s 104, s 105(1), Sch 14 para 61; FA 1999, s 65(11)*]. However, a relevant discounted security does not qualify for the relief at 39.11 LOSSES for irrecoverable pre-17 March 1998 loans on securities.

58.21 DEPOSITARY RECEIPTS

Depositary receipts are used as substitute instruments indicating ownership of shares and securities and designed primarily to enable investors to hold and deal in shares of companies located outside the investor's country. They are issued by a bank or other financial institution (the depositary), with whom the share certificate is deposited. For CGT purposes, the holder of a depositary receipt has two separate chargeable assets, i.e. the depositary receipt itself (being the document evidencing title, and comprising certain rights as against the depositary) and a beneficial interest in the underlying shares. In practice, however, the value of the depositary receipt is likely to relate entirely, or almost entirely, to the underlying shares, and, therefore, no apportionment is usually made, as regards either base cost or consideration received, on a disposal of shares in depositary receipt form. Likewise, there will normally be no chargeable gain or allowable loss on the 'conversion' of a depositary receipt back into shares, even though this does constitute a disposal of the second asset. (Revenue Capital Gains Manual CG 50240–50242). See 6.2 ASSETS as regards location of shares held in depositary receipt form.

58.22 PERSONAL EQUITY PLANS

From 1 January 1987 and before 6 April 1999, a 'qualifying individual' may subscribe a specified maximum to a Personal Equity Plan (PEP) to which no-one else may subscribe. New regulations came into force on 6 April 1989 (the *1989 Regulations* (*SI 1989 No 469*) (subsequently amended)).

No further subscriptions to PEPs can be made after 5 April 1999, but existing PEPs may continue under the same rules as before and independently of individual savings accounts (see 21.27 EXEMPTIONS AND RELIEFS).

A '*qualifying individual*' must be 18 years of age or over, and resident and ordinarily resident in the UK or a non-resident Crown employee serving overseas whose duties are treated as performed in the UK. Subscriptions may be made to only one general plan and one 'single company plan' (see below) in any tax year. From 6 April 1996, a *curator bonis* appointed in Scotland for a qualifying incapacitated individual may subscribe to a plan in his capacity as such, regardless of any subscription he may make in another capacity.

Under the *1989 Regulations*, a maximum of £6,000 may be invested in a personal equity plan in any tax year. For so long as the various conditions continue to be met, dividends and interest on securities are tax-free (and the plan manager may reclaim the related tax credits including, from 21 August 1998, those relating to investors who have ceased to be UK residents since subscribing to the plan). There is no capital gains tax liability (nor is there relief for losses) on the sale of an investment under the plan. All gains arising within the plan are exempt, even where a cash sum equivalent to the amount of the gain is withdrawn. Where plan investments are withdrawn *in specie*, the plan investor is deemed to have made a disposal and reacquisition at market value, thus exempting any gain or loss arising prior to withdrawal. The plan investor is treated as holding securities within the plan in a capacity other than that in which he holds any other securities of the same class so that identification rules and, for acquisitions before 6 April 1998, share pooling rules are applied separately to plan investments. The normal share reorganisation rules are disapplied in respect of plan investments where there is a reorganisation of share capital. There is no deemed disposal when the plan investor transfers shares into a plan (see below under Conditions applicable etc.) and the investor retains his beneficial ownership of plan investments even though legal ownership is held by the manager.

Up to £3,000 per tax year may be invested in a 'single company plan' (often known as a 'corporate PEP') in addition to any investment in a general plan as described above. A '*single company plan*' allows investment only in shares of one designated company. An additional condition imposed is that substantially the whole of the cash subscribed to the plan, or from realisation of plan shares, must be reinvested in plan shares within 42 days, or transferred (with interest) to the investor within 14 days thereafter.

Regulations impose certain requirements as to UK tax representation on European authorised institutions and certain other European plan managers.

Conditions applicable to both 'general' and 'single company' plans. All transactions involving plan investments must be carried out at open market prices, and investments may not be purchased from the plan investor or spouse. Subscription to a plan must be by payment of cash to the plan manager for investment by him, except that

(*a*) qualifying shares allotted under public offers, and

(*b*) (in relation to single company plans, see below) certain shares acquired under employee share schemes,

may be transferred into plans. As regards (*a*) above, the shares must be transferred to the plan within 42 days of allotment, and their cost included within the overall investment limit. This also applies to shares in a building society issued on conversion to plc status and, from 20 March 1997, to shares in a mutual insurer transferring its business to a company limited by shares (see Revenue Tax Bulletins April 1997 p 418 and April 1998 pp 522, 523). No part of the annual subscription limit is used in the case of free shares on building society conversion or other de-mutualisation. The fact that a new issue may take the form of separate offers on slightly different terms (e.g. to employees or customers of the issuing company) does not prevent the shares being eligible for transfer into a plan. (Revenue Press Releases 6 October 1989, 17 October 1990).

Where such would not otherwise be the case, any shares sold during the period allowed for transfer are identified first with shares which are ineligible for transfer so as to ensure that investors are able to transfer the maximum number of shares into a PEP.

No further transfers can be made into a plan after 5 April 1999.

With effect from 23 May 1996, shares acquired in a public offer may not be transferred into a PEP where

(1) the allocation of shares to the investor is connected with the allocation of other classes of shares or securities in the company (or rights to them) or of shares or

securities (or rights to them) in another company (including, from 8 August 1997, shares or rights to shares in an open-ended investment company or sub-fund of an umbrella company and units or rights to units in an authorised unit trust or sub-fund of an umbrella scheme); and

(2) the shares are offered on terms which are significantly more favourable than if they had not been so connected.

Cash held in a plan must be within the overall limit, must be held in sterling and must be invested in a designated account with a deposit taker or building society. Interest is paid gross and will be exempt from tax altogether, so long as it is eventually invested in plan shares, securities or unit trusts. (Revenue Press Release 17 October 1990). If interest etc. exceeding £180 in a year is paid by the plan manager to or for the plan investor in respect of cash held within a plan, the plan manager must account for a sum representing lower rate tax on all such interest payments in the year; the interest payments are for all purposes treated as interest taxable under Schedule D, Case III in the year in which they arise, the lower rate liability of which is satisfied as above. Prior to 6 April 1996 tax was required to be deducted at the basic rate.

General plans. The investments which may be purchased, made or held under a general plan after **7 August 1997** are as follows.

(i) Ordinary shares in UK-incorporated companies (other than investment trusts or OEICs) listed on a recognised stock exchange in an EU Member State (but not the Alternative Investment Market, see Revenue Press Release 20 February 1995).

(ii) 'Qualifying EC shares' (i.e. shares issued by a company incorporated in a Member State other than the UK and listed on a recognised stock exchange in a Member State), provided that they form part of the authorised share capital of the company, carry no fixed, guaranteed or secured redemption rights or preferential rights to dividends or to company property in a liquidation, and are neither shares carrying no right to a profit share other than fixed dividends nor shares carrying no right to fixed dividends but carrying a right of conversion into shares which do carry such a right. The company must not be an open-ended investment company (see 64.4 UNIT TRUSTS ETC.), and must not derive the principal part of its income from shareholdings each of which represents 10% or less of the voting power in the company concerned.

(iii) Shares other than ordinary shares, issued by a company incorporated in a Member State and listed on a recognised stock exchange in a Member State, not being shares in an investment trust, an OEIC or an authorised credit institution (as defined, and including the European equivalent).

(iv) Securities (i.e. any loan stock or similar security, whether secured or unsecured) issued by a company incorporated in the UK, not being securities of an investment trust or an authorised credit institution (as defined), provided that:

(*a*) at the date of issue and throughout the period of the loan they either carry a right to interest at a fixed percentage rate (or a series of consecutive such rates) or carry no right to interest;

(*b*) they are denominated in sterling;

(*c*) judged at the date when first held under the plan, the terms of issue do not require the loan to be repaid or the security to be re-purchased or redeemed, or allow the holder to so require except in circumstances unlikely to occur, within five years;

(*d*) the securities are not deep gain securities within *FA 1989, Sch 11* and do not fall to be treated as such by virtue of *FA 1989, Sch 11 para 21(2), para 22(2), para 22A(2)* or *para 22B(3)*; and

(*e*) at least one of the following conditions is satisfied:

(I) the ordinary shares in the issuing company are listed on a recognised stock exchange in a Member State;

(II) the securities are so listed; or

(III) the issuing company is a 75% subsidiary (within *ICTA 1988, s 838*) of a company whose ordinary shares are so listed.

(v) Units in a securities fund, i.e. an authorised unit trust (AUT) or part of an umbrella scheme (see 64.1 UNIT TRUSTS ETC.), provided that at least 50% in value of the investments held by the fund are either

(I) ordinary shares in UK-incorporated companies (other than investment trusts or OEICs),

(II) qualifying EC shares and shares within (iii) above (or shares which would be such shares if listed on a recognised stock exchange in a Member State),

(III) securities which would be within (iv) above if the condition in (iv)(*c*) required the judgement to be made when they were first acquired by the unit trust, and disregarding the condition in (iv)(*e*),

(IV) shares in (and securities meeting the conditions in (iv)(*a*)–(*d*) above of) an investment trust 50% of the value of the investments of which are within (I) or (II) above, or would be within (III) above if the date in question were that on which the securities were first acquired by the investment trust,

(V) shares in a securities company (see (vii) below) satisfying conditions similar to those in (IV) above, and

(VI) units in a securities fund 50% of the value of the investments of which are shares or securities within (I)–(III) above.

(vi) Units in a fund of funds (i.e. an AUT or part of an umbrella scheme which is categorised as a fund of funds by the Financial Services Authority but which is not permitted to invest in AUTs etc. which are not securities funds — see (v) above — or in open-ended investment companies or parts of umbrella companies which are not securities companies — see (vii) below) where at least 50% in value of the investments held are units in a securities fund or shares in a securities company and where at least 50% in value of the investments of that fund or company meet conditions similar to those in (v)(I)–(III) above.

(vii) Shares in a securities company (i.e. a UK-incorporated open-ended investment company (OEIC) or part of an umbrella company — see 64.4 UNIT TRUSTS ETC.) where at least 50% in value of the investments of the company meet conditions similar to those applicable to units in a securities fund (see (v) above).

(viii) Shares in (and securities meeting the conditions in (iv)(*a*)–(*d*) above of) an investment trust (including a 'split-level' trust, see Revenue Press Release 3 May 1989) 50% of the value of the investments of which meet conditions similar to those applicable to units in a securities fund (see (v) above).

(ix) Subject to an overall limit of one-quarter of the maximum subscription (less any amounts payable for qualifying investment trust shares allotted under public offers, see (*a*) above, and transferred to the plan), investments not within (v)–(viii) above which meet the following conditions:

(A) in the case of units in a securities fund, 50% in value of the investments held by the fund are either ordinary shares in UK-incorporated companies (other than investment trusts or OEICs) or 'other quoted shares' (i.e. shares listed on a recognised stock exchange which satisfy the conditions applicable to qualifying EC shares under (ii) above), or shares/units in securities companies, securities funds or investment trusts at least 50% in value of whose investments are such ordinary or other quoted shares;

(B) in the case of funds of funds, at least 50% in value of the investments held are units in a securities fund or shares in a securities company and where at least 50% in value of the investments of that fund or company are ordinary shares in UK-incorporated companies (other than investment trusts or OEICs) or other quoted shares (as in (A) above);

(C) in the case of investment trusts, at least 50% in value of the investments held by the trust are either ordinary shares in UK-incorporated companies (other than investment trusts or OEICs) or other quoted shares (as in (A) above), or shares/units in securities companies, securities funds or investment trusts at least 50% of the value of whose investments are such ordinary or other quoted shares; and

(D) in the case of securities companies, at least 50% in value of the investments of the company are either ordinary shares in UK-incorporated companies (other than investment trusts or OEICs) or other quoted shares (as in (A) above), or shares/units in securities companies, securities funds or investment trusts at least 50% of the value of whose investments are such ordinary or other quoted shares.

(x) Cash.

An occasional inadvertent fall below the 50% levels referred to in (v)–(ix) above will generally be disregarded, see Revenue Press Release 3 May 1989.

Cash received by the plan manager from dividends, disposals etc. may be reinvested in any qualifying investments within (i)–(ix), and in securities funds, securities companies, funds of funds and investment trusts *not* within (v)–(viii) above, but within (ix) above, provided that the market value of such investments does not immediately thereafter exceed one-quarter of the market value of all plan investments.

Between 6 July 1995 and 7 August 1997 inclusive, the list of general plan qualifying investments differed from that at (i)–(x) above principally in that it did not permit investment in OEICs and did not treat an AUT umbrella scheme sub-fund as an AUT in its own right (see 64.1 UNIT TRUSTS ETC.).

Certain investments held on 5 April 1990 which failed to meet the test for qualification ('non-qualifying investments'), may continue to be held under a plan, provided that

(*a*) the total of such investments made during 1989/90 and held at that date did not exceed £2,400, and

(*b*) apart from the reinvestment of proceeds of sale of non-qualifying investments, the amount invested in non-qualifying investments in 1990/91 did not exceed £900, and

(*c*) after 5 April 1991, the total amount invested in securities companies, securities funds, funds of funds and investment trusts does not exceed one-quarter of the subscription limit.

Single company plans. The investments which may be purchased, made or held under a single company plan are as follows.

(i) Where the company designated for the purposes of the plan is a UK company (other than an investment trust or venture capital trust) quoted on a recognised stock exchange, ordinary shares in the company, and ordinary shares or 'qualifying EC shares' 'representing' those shares.

(ii) Provided that the designated company is not an open-ended investment company (see 64.4 UNIT TRUSTS ETC.), and does not derive the principal part of its income from shareholdings each of which represents 15% or less by value of its investments, 'qualifying EC shares' issued by the company, and 'qualifying EC shares' or ordinary shares 'representing' those shares.

(iii) Investments in units comprising ordinary shares or 'qualifying EC shares' in the designated company which are 'paired' either with ordinary shares in another company meeting the condition in (i) above or with 'qualifying EC shares' in another company meeting the condition in (ii) above.

(iv) Cash.

In addition, the plan investor may subscribe to a plan by transferring to the plan manager shares in the designated company which were appropriated to the plan investor under an approved profit sharing scheme (see 19.22 EMPLOYEE SHARE SCHEMES) or acquired by exercise of options under a SAYE share option scheme (see 19.19 EMPLOYEE SHARE SCHEMES). Shares acquired under SAYE schemes must be transferred within 90 days of exercise of the option, and those appropriated under profit sharing schemes within 90 days of the earlier of the date the plan investor directed the trustees of the scheme to transfer the shares to him and the 'release date' in relation to the shares. The sum of the market value of shares so transferred to a plan and of the cost of any new issue shares so transferred (see conditions applicable etc. above) must, together with any cash subscribed, be within the overall subscription limit for the single company plan.

'*Qualifying EC shares*' are shares issued by a company incorporated in a Member State other than the UK and officially listed on a recognised stock exchange in a Member State. Shares '*represent*' other shares when there is a company reorganisation under which, for capital gains tax purposes, they are (or would but for being plan investments be) equated with the other shares. Shares in two companies are '*paired*' where it is provided in their governing instruments that no share in either company may be acquired otherwise than as part of a unit comprising one share in each company, such units being offered for sale at the same time and at the same price or, where sales are in more than one country, at a broadly equivalent price.

Cash received by the plan manager from dividends, disposals etc. may be reinvested in other shares within (i)–(iii) above. Where the cash arises in respect of shares transferred in from a profit sharing or SAYE share option scheme (see above), it may be reinvested in similar shares even where they are not otherwise qualifying investments.

Pre-1990 plans. Plans under the earlier *1986 Regulations* operated by reference to calendar years rather than tax years. There was an overall limit of £3,000 (£2,400 before 22 April 1988) per year of which the greater of £540 (£420 before 22 April 1988) and one quarter of the plan subscription could be invested in investment trusts and authorised unit trusts.

[*TCGA 1992, ss 151, 287; ICTA 1988, ss 333, 333A, 828; FA 1988, s 116; SI 1989, No 469; FA 1991, s 70; SI 1990, No 678; SI 1991 Nos 733, 2774; SI 1992 No 623; SI 1993 No 756; FA 1993, s 85; FA 1995, s 64; SI 1995 Nos 1539, 3287; SI 1996 Nos 846, 1355; SI 1997 Nos 511, 1716; SI 1998 No 1869*].

General. A list of registered plan managers may be obtained by sending a self-addressed A4 size envelope to (or calling at) Inland Revenue Information Centre, South West Wing,

Bush House, Strand, London WC2B 4RD. The list is updated quarterly. An information pack on personal equity plans is available from the Inland Revenue Library, price £3.50.

The Inland Revenue Financial Intermediaries and Claims Office may be contacted in relation to personal equity plans by telephoning 0151–472 6110 as regards repayments or 0151–472 6157 for technical advice.

See generally Revenue Pamphlet IR 89.

58.23 CLOSE COMPANIES

Income tax which has been charged on a participator as a result of an apportionment under *ICTA 1988, ss 423–430, Sch 19* (broadly only in relation to accounting periods ending before 1 April 1989; see TOLLEY'S CORPORATION TAX under Close Companies) and paid by him in respect of income of a close company which has not subsequently been distributed (including stock dividends; see 58.13 above), may be deducted, pro rata, in computing a gain on the disposal of any of his shares in that company. Apportioned income is treated as the top slice of income and shares are identified on a first in, first out basis. [*TCGA 1992, s 124*].

Tax paid which is referable to gains of a non-resident company charged on a UK participator or shareholder under *TCGA 1992, s 13* (see 44.6 OVERSEAS MATTERS) is similarly deductible. See also 17.4 DISPOSAL for an alternative concessional treatment.

58.24 LIFE ASSURANCE POLICIES

Investments or other assets transferred to a policy holder by an insurance company after 5 April 1967, in accordance with a life assurance policy, are deemed to be transferred at market value. [*TCGA 1992, s 204(3)(4)*].

58.25 STOCK LENDING AND AGREEMENTS FOR SALE AND REPURCHASE OF SECURITIES

The provisions of *TCGA 1992, ss 263B, 263C* come into force on **1 July 1997** (*SI 1997 No 991*) from which date the comparable provisions of *TCGA 1992, s 271(9)* are repealed.

Stock lending arrangements. *Definition.* A '*stock lending arrangement*' is an arrangement between two persons ('the borrower' and 'the lender') under which:

(*a*) the lender transfers 'securities' to the borrower otherwise than by way of sale; and

(*b*) a requirement is imposed on the borrower to transfer those securities back to the lender otherwise than by way of sale.

The disposals and acquisitions made in pursuance of any stock lending arrangement *are disregarded* for the purposes of capital gains tax. [*TCGA 1992, s 263B(1)(2); FA 1997, Sch 10 para 5*].

Disposals by the borrower. If the borrower under any stock lending arrangement disposes of any securities transferred to him under the arrangement such that that disposal is made otherwise than in the discharge of the requirement for the transfer of securities back to the lender, and that requirement, so far as it relates to the securities disposed of, has been or will be discharged by the transfer of securities other than those transferred to the borrower, any question relating to the acquisition of the securities disposed of shall be determined as if the securities disposed of were the securities with which that requirement (so far as relating to the securities disposed of) has been or will be discharged. [*TCGA 1992, s 263B(3); FA 1997, Sch 10 para 5*].

Transfer back to the lender not taking place. The ensuing consequences will occur in the case of any stock lending arrangement, where it becomes apparent, at any time after the making of the transfer by the lender, that the requirement for the borrower to make a transfer back to the lender will not be complied with.

(i) The lender shall be deemed to have made a disposal at that time of the securities transferred to the borrower;

(ii) The borrower shall be deemed to have acquired them at that time; and

(iii) *TCGA 1992, s 263B(3)* (above) shall have effect in relation to any disposal before that time by the borrower of securities transferred to him by the lender as if the securities deemed to have been acquired by the borrower were to be used for discharging a requirement to transfer securities back to the lender.

[*TCGA 1992, s 263B(4); FA 1997, Sch 10 para 5*].

References, in relation to a person to whom securities are transferred, to the transfer of those securities back to another person are to be construed as if the cases where those securities are taken to be transferred back to that other person included any case where securities of the same description as those securities are transferred to that other person either:

(*a*) in accordance with a requirement to transfer securities of the same description; or

(*b*) in exercise of a power to substitute securities of the same description for the securities that are required to be transferred back.

[*TCGA 1992, s 263B(5); FA 1997, Sch 10 para 5*].

Securities shall not be taken to be of the same description as other securities unless they are in the same quantities, give the same rights against the same persons and are of the same type and nominal value as the other securities. '*Securities*' means shares of any company resident in the United Kingdom (*United Kingdom equities*), securities of the government of the United Kingdom, any public or local authority in the United Kingdom or of any company or other body resident in the United Kingdom, but excluding quoted Eurobonds held in a recognised clearing system (*United Kingdom securities*) or shares, stock or other securities issued by a government or public or local authority of a territory outside the United Kingdom or by any other body of persons not resident in the United Kingdom and quoted Eurobonds (within *ICTA 1988, s 124*) held in a recognised clearing system *(overseas securities)*. Reference to '*interest*' includes dividends. [*ICTA 1988, Sch 23A; TCGA 1992, s 263B(6)(7); FA 1997, Sch 10 para 5*].

Provisions to ensure continuity of treatment for stock lending arrangements involving securities redenominated in euros following the introduction on 1 January 1999 of the European single currency in certain EU Member States other than the UK are contained in *SI 1998 No 3177, Regs 20–23.*

Stock lending involving redemption. A transfer back to a person of securities transferred by him shall be taken to include references to the payment to him, in pursuance of an obligation arising on any person's becoming entitled to receive an amount in respect of the redemption of those securities, of an amount equal to the amount of the entitlement. Where, in pursuance of any such obligation, the lender under any stock lending arrangement is paid any amount in respect of the redemption of any securities to which the arrangement relates:

(A) that lender shall be deemed to have disposed, for that amount, of the securities in respect of whose redemption it is paid ('*the relevant lent securities*');

(B) the borrower shall not, in respect of the redemption, be taken to have made any disposal of the relevant lent securities; and

(C) *TCGA 1992, s 263B(3)* (see above) shall have effect in relation to disposals of any of the relevant lent securities made by the borrower before the redemption as if:

(i) the amount paid to the lender were an amount paid for the acquisition of securities, and

(ii) the securities acquired were to be used by the borrower for discharging a requirement under the arrangement to transfer the relevant lent securities back to the lender.

[*TCGA 1992, s 263C; FA 1997, Sch 10 para 5*].

Pre-1 July 1997 provisions. A transfer of securities (including stocks and shares) under either of the following types of arrangement is ignored for the purposes of the charge to tax on capital gains.

(i) Where a person (A) enters into an arrangement under which another person (B) is to transfer securities to A or his nominee, and securities of the same kind and amount are to be transferred by someone to B or his nominee.

(ii) Where, to enable B to make such a transfer to A or his nominee, similar arrangements are made between B or his nominee and another person (C) or his nominee; and where a similar arrangement is entered into after 30 September 1993 as part of a chain of arrangements for overseas securities, all having the effect of enabling B to make the transfer to A or his nominee.

Transfers within (i) or (ii) are also left out of account in computing income for tax purposes of any trade carried on by the transferor or transferee. The Treasury may make regulations by statutory instrument imposing further conditions. Except in so far as those regulations otherwise provide, the above provisions only apply if A enters into the arrangement mentioned in (1) above to enable him to fulfil a contract under which he is required to sell securities. [*TCGA 1992, s 271(9); ICTA 1988, ss 129, 828; FA 1991, s 57; FA 1995, s 84; FA 1997, Sch 10 para 5(2); SI 1989 No 1299; SI 1992 No 572; SI 1993 No 2003; SI 1995 No 1283; SI 1997 No 991*].

Replacement loans. A loan of securities is also left out of account for income and capital gains tax purposes where it is made to enable a borrower to replace an existing loan of such securities rather than to meet a sale, provided the existing loan was within the above provisions (as extended by this concessional treatment if necessary) and the replacement loan would otherwise have been within them but for the requirement that it must be made to enable the transferee to fulfil a contract to sell securities (or to transfer the securities to a third party to enable him to fulfil a contract to sell securities). [*SI 1989 No 1299, Reg 3C; SI 1995 No 3219, Reg 4*]. This applies with effect from 2 January 1996, but previously applied under ESC B36.

Agreements for sale and repurchase of securities. Where *ICTA 1988, s 737A(1)* (treatment of price differential on sale and repurchase of securities as interest payment in certain cases; see TOLLEY'S INCOME TAX under Anti-Avoidance) applies (or would apply were the sale and repurchase price different), the acquisition and disposal by the interim holder, and (except where the repurchaser is or may be different from the original owner) the disposal and acquisition (as repurchaser) by the original owner, are disregarded for capital gains tax purposes. This does not, however, apply

(*a*) where the repurchase price falls to be computed by reference to the provisions of *ICTA 1988, s 737C* ('manufactured' dividends and interest; see TOLLEY'S INCOME TAX under Anti-Avoidance) which are not in force in relation to the securities when the repurchase price becomes due; or (*b*) if the agreement(s) in question are non-arm's length agreements, or if all the benefits or risks arising from fluctuations in the market value of the securities accrue to, or fall on, the interim holder; or

(*c*) in relation to any disposal or acquisition of QUALIFYING CORPORATE BONDS (49) where the securities disposed of by the original owner, or those acquired by him or another person as repurchaser, are not such bonds.

[*TCGA 1992, s 263A; FA 1995, s 80(4)(5)*]. Where *ICTA 1988, s 730A(1)* applies but *TCGA 1992, s 263A* does not, the repurchase price is, as the case may be, either reduced by the excess of that price over the sale price or increased by the excess of the sale price over that price for CGT purposes. [*ICTA 1988, s 730A(2)(4); FA 1995, s 80(1)(5)*].

Provisions to ensure continuity of treatment for stock lending arrangements involving securities redenominated in euros following the introduction on 1 January 1999 of the European single currency in certain EU Member States other than the UK are contained in *SI 1998 No 3177, Regs 20–23*.

58.26 BUILDING SOCIETY AND OTHER DE-MUTUALISATIONS

Statutory rules. The following applies where there is a transfer of the whole of a building society's business to a successor company in accordance with the relevant provisions of the *Building Societies Act 1986*.

Subject to the operation of *TCGA 1992, s 217(1)* (rights to acquire shares in successor company treated as valueless options, see 17.10(*f*) DISPOSAL), shares issued to members by the successor company, or disposed of to members by the society, are regarded as acquired for any new consideration given and as having at the time of acquisition a value equal to such new consideration (if any). Where shares are so issued or disposed of to trustees on terms providing for their transfer to members for no new consideration, and they constitute settled property in the trustees' hands, then

(*a*) they are regarded as acquired by the trustees for no consideration;

(*b*) a member's interest in the shares is regarded as acquired for no consideration and as having no value at the time of acquisition;

(*c*) on the member becoming absolutely entitled to any shares, or where such entitlement would arise but for the member being an infant or otherwise under disability, the shares are treated as disposed of and reacquired by the trustees in a nominee capacity under *TCGA 1992, s 60(1)* and at a no gain/no loss price and *TCGA 1992, s 71* (see 57.9 SETTLEMENTS) does not then apply; and

(*d*) on the member disposing of his interest in the settled property, any gain is a chargeable gain and *TCGA 1992, s 76(1)* (see 57.8 SETTLEMENTS) does not then apply.

Any gain on the disposal by the society of shares in the successor company in connection with the transfer is not a chargeable gain. [*TCGA 1992, s 216(1), s 217(2)–(7)*].

The conferring of any benefit under the above or *TCGA 1992, s 217(1)* on a member of a society in connection with a transfer, or any payment in lieu of such a benefit, or any distribution in pursuance of *Building Societies Act 1986, s 100(2)(b)*, is not regarded as either the making of a distribution for corporation tax purposes or the payment of a dividend by the society. However, any such disregarded benefit etc. may be taken into account as a capital distribution as in 58.14 above. [*FA 1988, Sch 12 para 6*].

Practice. It has become customary for building societies to offer their members cash bonuses or free shares as an inducement towards their voting in favour of de-mutualisation of the society, i.e. a takeover by a limited company or a unilateral conversion from mutual to corporate status. In *Foster v Williams; Horan v Williams (Sp C 113), [1997] SSCD 112*, concerning *cash payments* received by investors on the takeover of Cheltenham and Gloucester Building Society by Lloyds Bank plc in August 1995, a Special Commissioner, allowing the taxpayers' appeals, held that both share account and deposit account investors in the society had made a total disposal of their accounts, for which the consideration consisted of the opening balances on new accounts with the successor company plus the cash bonus payments. No chargeable gain arose on the disposal of a *deposit account*, this being the disposal of a debt (which was not a debt on a security) (see 21.5 EXEMPTIONS AND RELIEFS). On the disposal of a share account, a chargeable gain did arise, and the allowable expenditure was the amount of the closing credit balance on the account on the vesting day (plus INDEXATION (26) allowance, which could therefore reduce or eliminate the gain). The Revenue accepted the decision without further appeal and announced that it would also be applied to cash payments received as a result of the de-mutualisation of other building societies. (Revenue Press Release 27 March 1997 and Revenue Tax Bulletin April 1998 pp 517–523).

Where cash is received by a member on the de-mutualisation of a building society, the resulting gain is not eligible for TAPER RELIEF (see 60.20).

The treatment of *shares* issued to members on the de-mutualisation of a building society is governed by *TCGA 1992, s 217* (see above) and remains unchanged, the member realising no chargeable gain or allowable loss on receipt of the shares but, in the case of free shares, having no acquisition cost (and thus no indexation allowance) in computing the gain on a subsequent disposal. (Revenue Press Releases 21 March 1996, 27 March 1997 and Revenue Tax Bulletin April 1998 pp 517–523).

The Revenue Tax Bulletin article referred to above also comments on a number of specific points, *viz.* the treatment of multiple accounts (a separate calculation is required for each account in the case of cash bonuses; free shares acquired before 6 April 1998 are pooled), free shares sold immediately by successor company on investor's behalf (this is *not* equivalent to a cash bonus), statutory cash bonuses received by members ineligible to vote (treated like any other cash bonus), joint accounts (cash bonus/free shares treated as received/acquired equally between account holders), child, nominee and client accounts (cash bonus/free shares treated as received/acquired wholly by the beneficial owner of the account, i.e. the child etc.), partnership accounts (cash bonus/free shares treated as received/acquired by all the partners in accordance with their partnership sharing ratios), and accounts in the form of permanent interest bearing shares (PIBs) (cash bonuses are free of CGT as a PIB is a QUALIFYING CORPORATE BOND (49)).

There is also a detailed discussion in Tax Bulletin of the position, including that for inheritance tax, where an investor dies before de-mutualisation. Where death occurs after the de-mutualisation is announced and the entitlement to a cash bonus or free shares passes to the personal representatives/beneficiaries, the value of the right to receive the cash bonus or free shares may increase the value at death of a share account for both CGT and inheritance tax purposes (and see *Ward and others (Executors of Cook, deceased) v CIR 1998 (Sp C 175), [1999] SSCD 1*). A Table is provided to assist in valuations. The Bulletin also covers the position of a surviving holder of a joint account.

The CGT treatment of 'windfalls' received on the de-mutualisation of other organisations, e.g. insurance companies, sports clubs, depends on the facts of each particular case. The Tax Bulletin comments on the conversion of Norwich Union (where the position differs according to the date the free shares were unconditionally allotted to policy holders) and the takeover of Scottish Amicable, both in 1997.

(Revenue Tax Bulletin April 1998 pp 517–523).

Example

Mr C Bagger opened a share account with the Toytown Building Society in August 1993. The society was taken over by High Street Bank plc in December 1997 and Mr Bagger received in that month a cash distribution of £13,000 which comprised a fixed payment of £500 and a percentage payment based on the higher of the balances on the account at two stated dates but restricted to 12½% of £100,000. Mr Bagger's passbook showed the following account details.

Date		*Debit*	*Credit*	*Balance*
		£	£	£
4.8.93	Deposit		50,000	50,000
31.3.94	Net interest		1,500	51,500
16.6.94	Deposit		75,000	126,500
31.3.95	Net interest		5,000	131,500
1.5.95	Withdrawal	25,000		106,500
31.3.96	Net interest		4,800	111,300
31.3.97	Net interest		5,300	116,600
1.6.97	Withdrawal	8,000		108,600
12.12.97	Cash bonus on takeover		13,000	121,600
12.12.97	Closing interest		2,800	124,400
12.12.97	Balance transferred to new deposit account at High Street Bank plc	124,400		Nil

Relevant indexation factors are as follows

August 1993 to March 1994	0.008
March 1994 to June 1994	0.015
June 1994 to March 1995	0.019
March 1995 to May 1995	0.014
May 1995 to March 1996	0.013
March 1996 to March 1997	0.026
March 1997 to June 1997	0.014
June 1997 to December 1997	0.016

The chargeable gain on the cash bonus is computed as follows

	Qualifying expenditure	Indexed pool
	£	£
4.8.93 acquisition	50,000	50,000
Indexed rise: August 1993–March 1994		
£50,000 × 0.008		400
31.3.94 acquisition	1,500	1,500
	51,500	51,900
Indexed rise: March 1994–June 1994		
£51,900 × 0.015		779
16.6.94 acquisition	75,000	75,000
	126,500	127,679
Indexed rise: June 1994–March 1995		
£127,679 × 0.019		2,426
31.3.95 acquisition	5,000	5,000
Carried forward	131,500	135,105

	Qualifying expenditure	Indexed pool
	£	£
Brought forward	131,500	135,105
Indexed rise: March 1995–May 1995		
£135,105 × 0.014		1,890
	131,500	136,995
1.5.95 disposal (no gain/no loss)	(25,000)	(26,045)*
	106,500	110,950
Indexed rise: May 1995–March 1996		
£110,950 × 0.013		1,442
31.3.96 acquisition	4,800	4,800
	111,300	117,192
Indexed rise: March 1996–March 1997		
£117,192 × 0.026		3,047
31.3.97 acquisition	5,300	5,300
	116,600	125,539
Indexed rise: March 1997–June 1997		
£125,539 × 0.014		1,758
	116,600	127,297
1.6.97 disposal (no gain/no loss)	(8,000)	(8,734)**
	108,600	118,563
Indexed rise: June 1997–December 1997		
£118,563 × 0.016		1,897
12.12.97 acquisition	2,800	2,800
	111,400	123,260
12.12.97 disposal	(111,400)	(123,260)

$$* \ £136,995 \times \frac{25,000}{131,500} = \quad £26,045$$

$$** \ £127,297 \times \frac{8,000}{116,600} = \quad £8,734$$

	£
Proceeds:	
Cash bonus	13,000
Balance of account	111,400
Total proceeds	124,400
Allowable cost	111,400
Unindexed gain	13,000
Indexation allowance £123,260 – 111,400	11,860
Chargeable gain	£1,140

Note to the example

(*a*) For the purpose of calculating the indexation allowance, each £1 deposited or withdrawn is treated in the same way as an acquisition or disposal of a share in a company.

Mergers of building societies. Cash payments on the merger of two building societies are chargeable to income tax. (Revenue Press Release 21 March 1996).

Cashbacks. Cashbacks paid by banks and building societies as an inducement to purchase goods or services, e.g. to take out a mortgage, are not chargeable to capital gains tax. (Revenue Pamphlet IR 131, SP 4/97). See 21.20 EXEMPTIONS AND RELIEFS.

59 Shares and Securities — Identification Rules

Cross-references. See 26 INDEXATION; 58 SHARES AND SECURITIES; 60 TAPER RELIEF.

Sumption: Capital Gains Tax. See A12.02–14.

59.1 INTRODUCTION

Prior to 6 April 1998, acquisitions by the same person of shares (and securities) of the same class in the same company were pooled and treated as a single asset, each subsequent disposal out of that shareholding being treated as a part disposal of the single asset and the chargeable gain or allowable loss calculated by reference to the average cost (or, where applicable, the average indexed cost) per share of the shares sold. As a consequence of the introduction of TAPER RELIEF (60) for disposals after 5 April 1998 by individuals, trustees and personal representatives, share pooling is abolished for such disposals. A share pool already established at 5 April 1998 continues to be treated as a single asset but acquisitions after that date are not pooled (see 59.2 below). **These changes do not apply for the purposes of corporation tax on chargeable gains**, as regards which share pooling continues after 5 April 1998 as before.

Summary of current identification rules. For capital gains tax purposes (but not corporation tax purposes — see above), disposals after 5 April 1998 are to be identified with acquisitions in the following order.

- acquisitions on the same day as the disposal;
- acquisitions within 30 days after the day of disposal (thus countering 'bed and breakfasting');
- previous acquisitions after 5 April 1998 on a last in/first out (LIFO) basis;
- shares acquired after 5 April 1982 and comprised in the pool at 5 April 1998 (i.e. the 'section 104 holding' in 59.4 below — previously known as the 'new holding');
- shares acquired before 6 April 1982 (the '1982 holding' in 59.5 below);
- shares acquired on or before 6 April 1965 on a LIFO basis;
- if the shares disposed of are still not exhausted, shares acquired subsequent to the disposal (and beyond the above-mentioned 30-day period).

The post-5 April 1998 rules for capital gains tax are covered in detail at 59.2 below. The rules applying at various times previously are similarly covered in the remainder of this chapter, with those applying more recently being considered in priority to earlier rules. The rules at 59.3–59.6 below continue to apply unchanged after 5 April 1998 for the purposes of corporation tax on chargeable gains.

59.2 IDENTIFICATION RULES FOR SHARES AND SECURITIES AFTER 5 APRIL 1998 (OTHER THAN FOR CORPORATION TAX PURPOSES)

See 59.1 above for background and for a **summary** of the capital gains tax identification rules for disposals after 5 April 1998 as detailed below. **The provisions described below do not apply for the purposes of corporation tax on chargeable gains.**

Abolition of pooling and preservation of pools in existence at 5 April 1998. The share pooling rules at 59.3, 59.4 below are disapplied for capital gains tax purposes as regards any shares (or securities) acquired after 5 April 1998. Where, however, shares etc. are actually acquired after that date as a result of a reorganisation (e.g. a scrip or rights issue) but are regarded by virtue of *TCGA 1992, s 127* (see 58.5 SHARES AND SECURITIES) as equating to shares etc. acquired on or before that date and included in the 5 April 1998 single asset pool (the 'section 104 holding' — see below), the newly-acquired shares etc. are themselves added to the pool if they are of the same class as the original shares or form a new single asset pool if they are of a different class (see Revenue Capital Gains Manual CG 50572).

The single asset pool for shares acquired on or after 6 April 1982, previously referred to in the legislation as the 'new holding', is preserved and is renamed, for all purposes, the '*section 104 holding*'. This consists of shares etc. of the same class in the same company acquired by the same person in the same capacity. Such shares etc. are regarded as a single asset growing or diminishing as and when additional shares are acquired and shares are disposed of (see also 59.4 below). However, except as mentioned above as respects reorganisations, the 'section 104 holding' cannot grow for capital gains tax purposes by reference to acquisitions after 5 April 1998. Where appropriate, reference should be made to 59.3 and 59.4 below for the detailed rules on share pooling.

Shares etc. held by a person who acquired them as an employee of the company concerned or of anyone else and on terms which for the time being restrict his right to dispose of them (known as 'clogged shares') are treated as being of a different class as both

- shares etc. held by him in the same company and acquired otherwise than as an employee; and
- shares etc. held by him in the same company which are not, or are no longer, subject to the same restrictions.

Upon the removal of the restrictions, the clogged shares are identified in the same way as any other shares held of the same class in the same company and by reference to their actual acquisition date where this is after 5 April 1998 (Revenue Capital Gains Manual CG 56504).

[*TCGA 1992, s 104; FA 1998, s 123(1)–(6), s 125(3)(4)*].

Application of indexation allowance to section 104 holding. As stated at 26.1 INDEXATION, indexation allowance is frozen for capital gains tax (but not corporation tax) purposes at its April 1998 level and is not available at all in respect of expenditure incurred after 31 March 1998. The indexed pool of expenditure at 5 April 1998 is computed in accordance with the rules in 59.4 below as if the entire holding had been disposed of at the end of that day. Indexation allowance is thus given on the 'section 104 holding' up to and including April 1998. On a disposal after 5 April 1998 of, or out of, the 'section 104 holding' in accordance with the identification rules below, or on any other operative event, the indexed pool continues to be maintained as in 59.4 below and indexation allowance computed accordingly, except that the indexed pool is *not* to be increased by any indexed rise in expenditure after April 1998. [*TCGA 1992, s 110A; FA 1998, s 125(2)(4)(5)*].

Identification rules. The identification rules detailed below apply in relation to disposals after 5 April 1998 for the purposes of capital gains tax. They apply for the purpose of identifying a disposal of shares with an acquisition of shares etc. of the same class made by the person making the disposal and held by him in the same capacity as that in which he makes the disposal. For identification purposes, disposals are considered in the date order in which they take place. These rules override any identification purporting to be made by the disposal itself or by a transfer or delivery giving effect to it. The rules below do not apply to shares to which Enterprise Investment Scheme relief or Venture Capital Trust scheme relief is attributable and shares in respect of which relief has been given (and not withdrawn) under the Business Expansion Scheme. Disposals of such shares retain their own identification rules; see 20.8, 20.10, 20.14 , 20.17 ENTERPRISE INVESTMENT SCHEME (AND BES) and 65.9, 65.10 VENTURE CAPITAL TRUSTS.

The Revenue take the view that shares etc. held in the name of an individual are held in the same capacity as his or her portion of any shares of the same class in the same company which are held in the joint names of that individual and his or her spouse (*Taxation 13 May 1999 p 170*). See 41.1 MARRIED PERSONS re jointly held assets generally.

These identification rules apply not only to shares but to securities of a company, to 'relevant securities' (see 59.6 below) and to any other assets of such nature as to be dealt in without identifying the particular assets disposed of or acquired, e.g. units in a unit trust. Shares and securities are treated as being of the same class only if they are, or would be, so treated by the practice of a recognised stock exchange (as defined by *ICTA 1988, s 841* — see 58.5 SHARES AND SECURITIES). [*TCGA 1992, s 104(3)*].

The rules apply **in the order set out below**, so that each rule is taken into account only to the extent that the shares disposed of are not exhausted by the preceding rule(s).

(1) *Same day rule.* Where two or more acquisitions of shares etc. of a particular class are made on the same day by the same person in the same capacity, they are treated as a single acquisition. The same applies to disposals. A disposal is then identified first and foremost and as far as possible with an acquisition made on the same day.

(2) *30-day rule* (see also below under 'Bed and breakfasting'). If within the period of 30 days after a disposal, the person making it acquires shares of the same class, the disposal is identified with those acquisitions, taken in the order in which they occur within that period.

(3) *LIFO basis.* The disposal is then identified with acquisitions made after 5 April 1998 on a last in/first out (LIFO) basis.

(4) *Share pool at 5 April 1998.* The disposal is then identified with the 'section 104 holding' (if any), i.e. the single asset pool for shares acquired after 5 April 1982 and before 6 April 1998 (see above and 59.4 below). (This is not applicable to disposals of 'relevant securities' (see 59.6 below), which were never included in a 'section 104 holding' and to which the LIFO basis (see (3) above) applies in respect of acquisitions made on or before 5 April 1998 as well as after that date.)

(5) *'1982 holding'.* The disposal is then identified with the '1982 holding' (if any), i.e. the single asset pool for shares held at 5 April 1982 (but treated as having been acquired at 31 March 1982 for these purposes) (see 59.5 below).

(6) *Shares acquired on or before 6 April 1965.* The disposal is then identified on a last in/first out (LIFO) basis with shares held on 6 April 1965 (see 7.4 and 7.11 ASSETS HELD ON 6 APRIL 1965 for quoted and unquoted securities respectively) to the extent, in the case of quoted shares, that these have not, by election, been included in the '1982 holding' (see 59.5(*a*) below).

(7) *Shares acquired subsequent to the disposal.* To the extent, if any, that the rules at (1)–(6) above have not exhausted the shares disposed of, the disposal is finally identified with shares acquired after the disposal (and after the expiry of the 30-day period in (2) above), taken in the order in which such acquisitions occur.

[*TCGA 1992, s 105, s 106A; FA 1998, s 124(1)(2)(7)*].

'Bed and breakfasting' after 16 March 1998. The 30-day rule at (2) above is designed to counter the previously common practice known as 'bed and breakfasting' whereby shares are sold and bought back the next day or very shortly afterwards, the purpose being to realise a gain by reference to historical cost (and upgrade the acquisition cost on a future disposal) or to similarly realise an allowable loss. This particular identification rule also applies for capital gains tax (not corporation tax) purposes to disposals made **after 16 March 1998** and before 6 April 1998. It applies to such disposals in priority to the identification rules in 59.3 below, except for the 'same-day rule' in *TCGA 1992, s 105*, and acquisitions so matched under the 30-day rule do not form part of the 'section 104 holding'. The 30-day rule applies equally to disposals of 'relevant securities' (see 59.6 below). [*FA 1998, s 124(8)(9)*]. 'Bed and breakfasting' remains feasible for couples where the disposal is by one partner and the acquisition is by the other.

It is confirmed by Revenue Capital Gains Manual CG 50566 that a disposal of rights attached to shares (see 58.7 SHARES AND SECURITIES) does not fall to be matched under the 30-day rule with a subsequent acquisition of shares of the same class but with no rights attached. Nor does a disposal of shares fall to be matched with shares of the same class subsequently acquired by a scrip or rights issue (as the reorganisation rules deem such shares to have been acquired at the same time as the original shares to which they attach — see below).

Scrips, rights issues etc. For the purpose of applying the above identification rules, shares and securities acquired as a result of a reorganisation, e.g. a scrip or bonus issue or a rights issue, and treated under *TCGA 1992, s 127* (see 58.5 SHARES AND SECURITIES) as equating to shares already held are regarded as having been acquired at the time the original shares were acquired. Where the original holding comprises a number of acquisitions (counting a 5 April 1998 share pool as a single acquisition), the new holding is apportioned pro rata between them. This does not apply to scrip dividends (aka stock dividends) after 5 April 1998 from a UK resident company; these are treated not as reorganisations but as free-standing acquisitions as at the dividend date (see 58.13 SHARES AND SECURITIES). See also 60.2 TAPER RELIEF.

Example

A has the following acquisitions/disposals of ordinary 25p shares in QED plc. Throughout their period of ownership by A, these shares are non-business assets for the purposes of TAPER RELIEF (60). QED ordinary 25p shares were worth 210p per share at 31 March 1982, and A has not made the universal re-basing election in 8.3 ASSETS HELD ON 31 MARCH 1982. In 2001/02, A made no disposals of chargeable assets other than as shown below.

Date	*No. of shares bought/(sold)*	*Cost/ (proceeds)*
		£
1 May 1980	1,000	2,000
1 October 1983	2,000	4,500
1 December 1996	500	1,800
1 May 1999	(1,000)	(3,900)
25 May 1999	2,000	7,600
	4,500	
2 January 2000	(2,000)	(9,000)
1 July 2001	(2,000)	(12,000)
Remaining holding	500	

Relevant indexation factors are

March 1982 to April 1998	1.047
October 1983 to April 1985	0.097
April 1985 to December 1996	0.629
December 1996 to April 1998	0.053

The disposal on 1 May 1999 is matched with 1,000 of the shares acquired on 25 May 1999 (under the 30-day rule at (2) above). The resulting chargeable gain is as follows.

	£
Proceeds 1.5.99	3,900
Cost (£ 7,600 × 1,000/2,000)	3,800
Chargeable gain (no taper relief due)	£100

The disposal of 2,000 shares on 2 January 2000 is matched firstly with the remaining 1,000 acquired on 25 May 1999 (LIFO — see (3) above), and secondly with 1,000 of the 2,500 forming the 'section 104 holding' (see (4) above) as follows.

	No. of shares	*Qualifying expenditure*	*Indexed pool*
		£	£
Pool at 6.4.85	2,000	4,500	4,500
Indexation allowance to date			
October 1983–April 1985 £4,500 × 0.097			437
	2,000	4,500	4,937
Indexed rise to December 1996:			
April 1985–December 1996 £4,937 × 0.629			3,105
Additional shares 1 December 1996	500	1,800	1,800
	2,500	6,300	9,842
Indexed rise to April 1998:			
December 1996–April 1998 £9,842 × 0.053			522
	2,500	6,300	10,364
Disposal 2.1.2000	(1,000)	(2,520)	(4,146)
Pool carried forward	1,500	£3,780	£6,218

Chargeable gains are as follows.

	£	£
Proceeds 2.1.2000	4,500	4,500
Cost (£ 7,600 × 1,000/2,000)	3,800	
Cost (as above)		2,520
Unindexed gains	700	1,980
Indexation (£4,146 – £2,520)	—	1,626
Chargeable gains	£700	£354

Neither gain qualifies for taper relief. In each case, the shares acquired have been held for less than the requisite three complete years (for non-business asset taper relief) after 5 April 1998.

The disposal of 2,000 shares on 1 July 2001 is matched firstly with the remaining 1,500 in the 'section 104 holding' (see (4) above) and secondly with 500 of the 1,000 shares forming the '1982 holding' (see (5) above).

Chargeable gains are as follows.

	£
Proceeds of 1,500 shares on 1.7.01	9,000
Cost (as per pool above)	3,780
Unindexed gain	5,220
Indexation (£6,218 – £3,780)	2,438
Chargeable gain subject to taper relief	2,782
Taper relief £2,782 × 10% (see below)	278
Chargeable gain	£2,504

	£	£
Proceeds of 500 shares on 1.7.01	3,000	3,000
Cost (£2,000 × 500/1,000)	1,000	
Market value 31.3.82 500 × £2.10		1,050
Unindexed gain	2,000	1,950
Indexation to April 1998:		
£1,050 × 1.047	1,099	1,099
Gain after indexation	£901	£851

	£
Chargeable gain subject to taper relief	851
Taper relief £851 × 10% (see below)	85
Chargeable gain	£766

Taper relief is at 10% as the shares are non-business assets and have been held for three plus one years since 5 April 1998, the one-year addition being by virtue of the fact that both the 'section 104 holding' and the '1982 holding' were acquired before 17 March 1998 (see 60.2 TAPER RELIEF).

59.3 IDENTIFICATION RULES FOR SHARES AND SECURITIES ON OR AFTER THE '1985 DATE' AND (EXCEPT FOR CORPORATION TAX) BEFORE 6 APRIL 1998

For disposals for capital gains tax purposes on or after 6 April 1985 (referred to as the '*1985 date*') and before 6 April 1998 the identification rules for securities are as set out below. These rules also apply for the purposes of corporation tax on chargeable gains, but by reference to a '1985 date' of 1 April 1985; they continue to apply for those purposes to acquisitions and disposals after 5 April 1998.

Special rules apply to the following.

(*a*) Shares to which Enterprise Investment Scheme relief or Venture Capital Trust scheme relief is attributable and shares in respect of which relief has been given (and not withdrawn) under the Business Expansion Scheme. Disposals of such shares retain their own identification rules; see 20.8, 20.10, 20.14, 20.17 ENTERPRISE INVESTMENT SCHEME (AND BES) and 65.9, 65.10 VENTURE CAPITAL TRUSTS.

(*b*) '*Relevant securities*', i.e. securities within the accrued income ('bondwashing') provisions, QUALIFYING CORPORATE BONDS (49), deep discount securities (see 58.20 SHARES AND SECURITIES) and securities which are, or have been, material interests in non-qualifying offshore funds. See 59.6 below for further details.

For shares and securities not falling within (*a*) and (*b*) above and any other assets dealt in without identifying the particular assets disposed of or acquired, then, subject to the rules for

(i) disposals on or before the day of acquisition (see below);

(ii) acquisitions and disposals of securities within a short period by companies (see 13.40 COMPANIES); and

(iii) acquisitions and disposals within a ten day period (see below)

securities disposed of are identified, in order of priority, with

(A) securities acquired on or after the '1982 date' and forming part of a '*section 104 holding*' (see 59.4 below);

(B) securities forming part of a '*1982 holding*' (see 59.5 below); and then

(C) other securities on a 'last in, first out' basis. (Broadly, those held on 6 April 1965, see 7.4 and 7.11 ASSETS HELD ON 6 APRIL 1965 for quoted and unquoted securities respectively.)

Securities held by a person in one capacity cannot be identified with similar securities which he holds or can dispose of only in some other capacity (e.g. as a trustee).

[*TCGA 1992, s 104(1)–(3), s 107(1)(1A)(2)(7)–(9), s 150(5), s 150A(5); FA 1994, s 137, Sch 15 para 30; FA 1998, s 124(3)(7), s 125(3)(4)*].

Disposals and acquisitions on the same day. Securities disposed of on a particular day are matched with securities acquired on the same day by the same person in the same capacity and the pooling rules do not apply for this purpose. Where more securities are disposed of than are acquired, and the excess can neither be identified with previous acquisitions or a 'section 104 holding' (see 59.4 below), that excess is matched with a subsequent acquisition or acquisitions, taking the earliest first. [*TCGA 1992, s 105*].

Acquisitions and disposals within a ten-day period. Subject to the rules for disposals on or before the day of acquisition (see above) if, within a ten-day period, a number of securities are acquired which would otherwise increase or constitute a 'section 104 holding' (see 59.4 below) and subsequently a number of securities are disposed of, which would otherwise decrease or extinguish the same 'section 104 holding', then the securities disposed of are identified with those acquired and are not regarded as forming part of, or constituting, a 'section 104 holding'. If the number of securities acquired exceeds the number disposed of, the excess is regarded as forming part of, or constituting, a 'section 104 holding' and where securities were acquired at different times within the ten-day period, securities disposed of are first identified with those acquired at an earlier time (first in/first out). If the number of securities disposed of exceeds the number acquired, the excess is not identified under this rule. Any securities which are identified under this rule do not qualify for indexation allowance. [*TCGA 1992, s 107(3)–(6)*].

'*Bed and breakfasting*'. The Revenue have stated, in connection with the application of the principles established in decided cases up to and including *Furniss v Dawson*, that the indexation provisions applying on and after the 1985 date are clearly not designed to make bed and breakfast share etc. transactions more difficult as compared to the position before the 1982 date but it will remain necessary to make sure that the transactions involved are effective in (for instance) transferring beneficial ownership of the shares. (ICAEW Guidance Note TR 588, 25 September 1985). **See 59.2 above as regards bed and breakfasting after 16 March 1998.**

59.4 **'Section 104 holdings' of securities acquired on or after the '1982 date'.** Securities acquired on or after 6 April 1982, or, for companies, 1 April 1982 (the '*1982 date*') are pooled. Thus any securities of the same class acquired on or after the '1982 date' and held by the same person in the same capacity immediately before the '1985 date' are pooled as a single asset which grows or diminishes as acquisitions and disposals are made on or after that date. Securities of the same class acquired for the first time on or after the '1985 date' are pooled as a single asset in the same way. This treatment has no effect on any market value that has to be ascertained. Pooling is abolished for capital gains tax purposes (not for those of corporation tax) for acquisitions after 5 April 1998 — see 59.1 above.

Shares and securities of a company are not to be treated as being of the same class unless they are so treated by the practice of the Stock Exchange or would be so treated if dealt with on the Stock Exchange.

The single asset is referred to as the '*section 104 holding*' (previously known as 'the new holding') and the part disposal rules apply on any disposal other than one of the whole holding.

A separate 'section 104 holding' applies in relation to any securities held by a person to whom they were issued as an employee of the company or of any other person on terms which restrict his rights to dispose of them, so long as those terms are in force (known as 'clogged shares'). While such a separate 'section 104 holding' exists the owner of it is treated as holding it in a different capacity to that in which he holds any other securities of the same class. Upon the removal of restrictions, two such separate 'section 104 holdings' merge. If restrictions are removed from only some of the clogged shares, they are transferred from the clogged share pool to the normal share pool at average cost (Revenue Capital Gains Manual CG 56503).

Indexation allowance. On any disposal from a 'section 104 holding' (other than the whole of it) the 'qualifying expenditure' and the 'indexed pool of expenditure' are apportioned between the part disposed of and the remainder in the same proportions as, under the normal capital gains tax rules for part disposals, the relevant allowable expenditure is apportioned (see 17.6 DISPOSAL). The indexation allowance on the disposal is the amount by which the part of the indexed pool of expenditure apportioned to the part disposed of exceeds the equivalent part of the qualifying expenditure. On a disposal of the whole of the 'section 104 holding', the indexation allowance is the amount by which the indexed pool of expenditure at the time of disposal exceeds the qualifying expenditure at that time.

The '*qualifying expenditure*' is, at any time, the amount which would be the aggregate of the 'relevant allowable expenditure' in relation to a disposal of the whole of the holding at that time. See 26.1 INDEXATION for '*relevant allowable expenditure*'.

The '*indexed pool of expenditure*' in the case of a 'section 104 holding' in existence immediately before the '1985 date' comes into existence immediately before that date. It consists of the aggregate of the qualifying expenditure at that time and the indexation allowance which would have been available if all the securities in the holding were disposed of at that time on the assumption that the twelve month qualifying period and restrictions on loss-making disposals (which applied before the '1985 date') had never applied. In the case of any other 'section 104 holding', the indexed pool of expenditure is created at the same time as the holding (or, if earlier, when any of the qualifying expenditure is incurred) and is equal, at that time, to the qualifying expenditure.

Where a disposal on or after 30 November 1993 to a person acquiring or adding to a 'section 104 holding' is treated under any enactment as one on which neither a gain nor a loss accrues to the person making the disposal, *TCGA 1992, s 56(2)* (general treatment on no gain/no loss disposal; see 26.4 INDEXATION) does not apply to the disposal (so that the amount of the consideration on the disposal is not calculated on the assumption that an unindexed gain of an amount equal to the indexation allowance accrues to the person making the disposal). However, an amount equal to the indexation allowance on the disposal is added to the indexed pool of expenditure for the holding acquired or, as the case may be, held by the person to whom the disposal is made, and in such a case where there is an addition to the indexed pool of a 'section 104 holding' already held, the addition is made after any increase required by (*a*) below.

Whenever there is an event, called an '*operative event*', which has the effect of increasing or reducing the qualifying expenditure, a change is made to the indexed pool of expenditure.

(*a*) The indexed pool of expenditure is increased by the 'indexed rise' since the last operative event or, if none, since the pool came into being. This is done before the calculation of the indexation allowance on a disposal.

(*b*) If the operative event increases the qualifying expenditure, the indexed pool of expenditure is increased by the same amount.

(*c*) If there is a disposal resulting in a deduction in the qualifying expenditure, the indexed pool of expenditure is reduced in the same proportion. This is done after the calculation of the indexation allowance on the disposal.

(*d*) If the qualifying expenditure is reduced but there is no disposal, the indexed pool of expenditure is reduced by the same amount.

The '*indexed rise*' is the sum obtained by multiplying the value of the indexed pool of expenditure immediately before the operative event by a figure (expressed as a decimal but with no express requirement as to the number of decimal places to be calculated) calculated by the formula

$$\frac{RE - RL}{RL}, \text{ where}$$

RE = the retail prices index for the month in which the operative event occurs; and

RL = the retail prices index for the month of the immediately preceding operative event or, if none, that in which the indexed pool of expenditure came into being.

If RE is equal to or less than RL, the indexed rise is nil.

See 26.1 INDEXATION for values of the retail price index for March 1982 and subsequent months.

Note. Reorganisations of shares do not normally constitute disposals or acquisitions but they may constitute an operative event as above; e.g. an issue of shares of the same class for payment under a rights issue would be an operative event as the qualifying expenditure is increased, but a bonus issue of shares of the same class would not be. Where the reorganisation involves shares of a different class this automatically gives rise to an operative event as the qualifying expenditure attributable to the 'section 104 holding' consisting of the original class of shares is decreased. An additional 'section 104 holding' is created as only shares of the same class can be pooled in the original 'section 104 holding'. The rules in 58.5 SHARES AND SECURITIES determine the proportions of qualifying expenditure to be attributed to holdings of shares following a reorganisation and these also apply to the indexed pool of expenditure.

Consideration for options. Where an increase in qualifying expenditure under (*b*) above is wholly or partly attributable to the cost of acquiring an option binding the grantor to sell, then the indexed pool of expenditure is additionally increased by a sum obtained by multiplying the consideration for the option by a figure (expressed as a decimal but without any clarification as to the number of decimal places to be calculated) calculated by the formula

$$\frac{RO - RA}{RA}, \text{ where}$$

RO = the retail prices index for the month in which the option is exercised; and

RA = the retail prices index for the month in which the option was acquired, or March 1982 if later.

If RO is equal or less than RA, the indexed rise is nil.

[*TCGA 1992, s 104(1)(3)–(6), s 110, s 114; FA 1994, s 93(6)(11); FA 1998, s 125(1)(3)–(5)*].

The above rules do not apply for capital gains tax purposes where the option, but not the shares, was acquired before 6 April 1998. Indexation allowance to April 1998 on the cost of the option is given under the rules at 26.8 INDEXATION (Revenue Capital Gains Manual CG 50761).

For disposals before 30 November 1993, it was possible in practice not to keep a running total of the amount of qualifying expenditure because the chargeable gain or allowable loss on a disposal was the difference (positive or negative respectively) between the disposal proceeds and the amount by which the indexed pool was reduced. The denial of indexation allowance creating or increasing a loss on a disposal after 29 November 1993 requires the ascertainment of such a running total. It may be possible to arrive at the correct amount if the requisite records have been retained.

Example

At 6 April 1985, B owned 5,000 shares in REG plc purchased at a cost of £7,500 in June 1983. Subsequently B carried out the following transactions in those shares.

Date	*No. of shares bought/(sold)*	*Cost/(proceeds)*
		£
May 1985	1,000	1,250
October 1985	400	500
December 1986	(2,000)	(5,000)
December 1992	(440)	(900)
January 1997	(2,000)	(4,700)

In addition, in January 1994 B acquired from a spouse (i.e. a gain/no loss disposal) 1,000 further such shares which had hitherto comprised the total holding of the spouse and been purchased originally in July 1985 at a cost of £1,500.

Relevant values of the retail prices index are

June 1983	84.84	December 1986	99.62
April 1985	94.78	December 1992	139.2
May 1985	95.21	January 1994	141.3
July 1985	95.23	January 1997	154.4
October 1985	95.59		

	No. of shares	*Qualifying expenditure*	*Indexed pool*
		£	£
Pool at 6.4.85	5,000	7,500	7,500
Indexation allowance			
to initial pool: June 1983–April 1985			
$\dfrac{94.78 - 84.84}{84.84} \times £7{,}500$			878
Carried forward	5,000	7,500	8,378

	No. of shares	Qualifying expenditure	Indexed pool
		£	£
Brought forward May 1985	5,000	7,500	8,378
Indexed rise: April 1985–May 1985			
$\frac{95.21 - 94.78}{94.78} \times £8{,}378$			38
			8,416
Additional shares	1,000	1,250	1,250
	6,000	8,750	9,666
October 1985			
Indexed rise: May 1985–Oct 1985			
$\frac{95.59 - 95.21}{95.21} \times £9{,}666$			39
			9,705
Additional shares	400	500	500
	6,400	9,250	10,205
December 1986			
Indexed rise: Oct 1985–Dec 1986			
$\frac{99.62 - 95.59}{95.59} \times £10{,}205$			430
			10,635
Disposal	(2,000)	(i)(2,891)	(ii)(3,323)
	4,400	6,359	7,312
December 1992			
Indexed rise: Dec 1986–Dec 1992			
$\frac{139.2 - 99.62}{99.62} \times £7{,}312$			2,905
			10,217
Disposal	(440)	(636)	(1,022)
	3,960	5,723	9,195
January 1994			
Indexed rise: Dec 1992–Jan 1994			
$\frac{141.3 - 139.2}{139.2} \times £9{,}195$			139
Additional shares from spouse	1,000	1,500	1,500
Indexation allowance on such shares: Jul 1985–Jan 1994			
$\frac{141.3 - 95.23}{95.23} \times £1{,}500$			725
Carried forward	4,960	7,223	11,559

	No. of shares	Qualifying expenditure	Indexed pool
		£	£
Brought forward	4,960	7,223	11,559
January 1996			
Indexed rise: Jan 1994–Jan 1996			
$\frac{154.4 - 141.3}{141.3} \times £11,559$			1,072
	4,960	7,223	12,631
Disposal	(2,000)	(2,912)	(5,093)
Pool carried forward	2,960	£4,311	£7,538

Computation

		£
Disposal December 1986		
Proceeds		5,000
Cost	(i) 2,891	
Indexation allowance	(iii) 432	
		(ii) 3,323
Chargeable gain		£1,677
Disposal December 1992		
Proceeds		900
Cost	636	
Indexation allowance	386	
		1,022
Allowable loss		£122

Disposal January 1997

Proceeds of £4,700, although greater than the qualifying expenditure attributable to the shares disposed of (£2,912) and so producing an unindexed gain of the excess (£1,788), are less than the indexed pool of expenditure attributable to the shares disposed of (£5,093). The indexation allowance on the disposal of £2,181 (i.e. £5,093 – £2,912) therefore extinguishes the unindexed gain with the result that the disposal is one on which neither a gain nor a loss accrues (see 26.1 INDEXATION).

Note to the example

(*a*) The figure at (i) is given by $\frac{2,000}{6,400} \times £9,250 = \underline{£2,891}$

The figure at (ii) is given by $\frac{2,000}{6,400} \times £10,635 = \underline{£3,323}$

The figure at (iii) is given by the difference between (ii) and (i) i.e. £432.

The corresponding figures for the disposals in December 1992 and January 1997 are arrived at in a similar way.

59.5 **'1982 holding'.** On the introduction of indexation, pools of securities in existence before the '1982 date' continued to be treated as pools which were to be reduced where subsequent disposals were identified with them but which could not grow by acquisitions of additional securities of the same class. There were, however, special rules for adjustments to such pools where the relevant allowable expenditure at the '1982 date' exceeded such expenditure one year previously. All securities acquired between those dates were excluded from the pool in so far as they were not identified with disposals before the '1982 date'. See 59.10 below for full details.

The '1982 holding' comprises the following.

(*a*) Any pooled holding of securities under the above provisions which is retained at the '1985 date'. The pooled holding includes quoted securities held on 6 April 1965 where an election had been made that their actual cost be ignored and computations made by reference to their market value at 6 April 1965 only. A further opportunity is available for an election to be made where the original time limit has expired by extending the time limit so as to apply by reference to the first relevant disposal on or after the '1985 date'. See 7.3 and 7.4 ASSETS HELD ON 6 APRIL 1965.

(*b*) Any securities treated as separate assets under the special rules outlined above which have not been disposed of before the '1985 date'.

The '1982 holding', as determined above, continues, or starts, to be a single asset but one which cannot grow by the acquisition of additional securities of the same class. The relevant allowable expenditure attributable to it for capital gains tax purposes is the aggregate of that for the assets of which it is comprised. The treatment as a single asset as regards reorganisations of shares is believed to follow that in 59.10(*a*) below.

Where securities forming part of a 1982 holding were acquired between 1 and 5 April 1982 inclusive, they are treated for the purposes of re-basing indexation allowance (for disposals before 6 April 1988) under 8.13 ASSETS HELD ON 31 MARCH 1982 as held on 31 March 1982. This treatment also applies for the general re-basing rules of 8 ASSETS HELD ON 31 MARCH 1982.

[*TCGA 1992, s 109*].

59.6 **Relevant securities.** The identification rules in 59.3–59.5 above do not apply to disposals of 'relevant securities' on or after the '1985 date'.

'*Relevant securities*' and their identification rules for such disposals are as follows.

(*a*) *Government securities.* The then identification rules for such securities continued to apply to disposals on or after the '1985 date' and before 2 July 1986. *Disposals after 1 July 1986* are exempt from capital gains tax.

(*b*) *Qualifying corporate bonds.* The then identification rules for such securities continued to apply to disposals on or after the '1985 date' and before 2 July 1986. The rules were those outlined in 59.7–59.9 below subject to additional rules regarding acquisitions and disposals within a short period. Disposals *after 1 July 1986* are exempt from capital gains tax.

(*c*) *Securities within the accrued income ('bondwashing') provisions other than those within (a) or (b) above.* These comprise any loan stock or similar security of any government, public or local authority in the UK or elsewhere or any company or other body other than

(i) shares in a company (except qualifying shares in a building society);

(ii) securities on which the whole of the return is a distribution by virtue of *ICTA 1988, s 209(2)(e)(iv)(v)*;

(iii) national savings and war savings certificates;

(iv) certificates of deposit; and

(v) any security which is redeemable, for which the amount payable on redemption exceeds the issue price and in respect of which no return other than the amount of that excess is payable.

For disposals on or after the '1985 date' and before 28 February 1986, the identification rules in 59.7–59.9 below continue to apply, with the addition of the rule relating to the '1982 holding' under 59.5 above.

For disposals after 27 February 1986, the identification rules in 59.7 and 59.8 (but not 59.9) below apply, with the addition of the rule relating to the '1982 holding' under 59.5 above.

The accrued income scheme has been repealed for corporation tax purposes with effect from 1 April 1996. [*FA 1996, Sch 14 para 36*]. (See 58.19 SHARES AND SECURITIES).

(*d*) *Deep discount securities.* The existing identification rules in 59.7 and 59.8 (but not 59.9) below continued to apply. The legislation relating to deep discount securities has been repealed for 1996/97 onwards and, subject to transitional provisions, for company accounting periods ending after 31 March 1996. See 58.20 SHARES AND SECURITIES.

(*e*) *Non-qualifying offshore funds.* Securities which are, or at any time have been, material interests in a non-qualifying offshore fund continue to be identified under the rules in 59.7 and 59.8 (but not 59.9) below.

Where any of the securities within (*c*) to (*e*) above are disposed of on or after the '1985 date' and within a period of ten days beginning on the day on which the expenditure was incurred, no indexation allowance is due.

[*TCGA 1992, s 54(2), s 108; FA 1996, ss 104, 105, Sch 14 para 59, Sch 41 Pt V(3); FA 1998, s 124(4)(5)(7)*].

'Bed and breakfasting' after 16 March 1998. For capital gains tax (not corporation tax) purposes, the above identification rules for disposals of relevant securities are superseded for disposals after 16 March 1998 and before 6 April 1998 (after which new identification rules apply in any case). See 59.2 above.

59.7 IDENTIFICATION RULES FOR DISPOSALS OF SHARES AND SECURITIES ON OR AFTER THE '1982 DATE' AND BEFORE THE '1985 DATE'

For disposals on or after 6 April 1982 or, for companies, 1 April 1982 (the '*1982 date*') and before 6 April 1985, or, for companies, 1 April 1985 (the '*1985 date*') 'securities' acquired on or after the '1982 date' are not subject to pooling. The identification rules directed how such disposals of securities were to be identified with acquisitions of securities of the same class held by the same person in the same capacity. As adapted by additional provisions, they also applied to disposals from pools of securities acquired before, and held on, the '1982 date'. Where securities were held on 6 April 1965, special rules apply. See 7.4 and 7.11 ASSETS HELD ON 6 APRIL 1965 for quoted and unquoted securities respectively.

The identification rules still apply to disposals of certain 'relevant securities' after the '1985 date'. See 59.6 above.

For companies, an alternative method ('parallel pooling') was available for identifying particular securities disposed of after 31 March 1982 and before 1 April 1985. See 59.11 below.

'*Securities*' meant company shares or securities including qualifying corporate bonds or any other asset (other than gilt-edged securities) of a type to be dealt in without identifying the particular assets disposed of or acquired (i.e. fungible assets).

The general rules were subject to

(i) the special rules for acquisitions and disposals of securities within a short period by companies (see 13.40 COMPANIES),

(ii) special rules for 'contangos' (see 59.8 below), and

(iii) anti-avoidance provisions for married persons and groups of companies (see 59.9 below).

The general rules, in order of priority, were as follows.

(*a*) For identification purposes, disposals were to be taken in chronological order. The identification of securities comprised in an earlier disposal therefore determine (by elimination) which securities could be comprised in a later disposal.

(*b*) Securities disposed of for transfer or delivery on a particular date (e.g. a stock exchange settlement date) or in a particular period (e.g. a stock exchange account) were not to be identified with securities acquired for transfer or delivery on a later date or in a later period. They had to be identified with acquisitions of securities for transfer or delivery on or before that date, or, in or before that period, but, subject to this, they had to be first identified with acquisitions for *transfer or delivery* on or after the contract disposal date. (The 'transfer or delivery', i.e. settlement, date is generally different from the contract date. See also *MacPherson v Hall Ch D 1972, 48 TC 210.*)

(*c*) Disposals were to be identified, on a 'first in, first out' basis, with acquisitions within the twelve months preceding the disposal. Otherwise, disposals were to be identified with acquisitions on a 'last in, first out' basis.

(*d*) Disposals were to be identified with acquisitions at different times on the same day in as nearly as may be equal proportions.

[*FA 1982, s 88(1)–(6)(9); TCGA 1992, s 108(1)–(6)*].

59.8 **Contangos.** Where, under arrangements designed to postpone the transfer or delivery of securities disposed of, a person by a *single bargain* acquired securities for transfer or delivery on a particular date or in a particular period (the 'earlier date' or 'earlier period'), and disposed of them for transfer or delivery on a later date or in a later period, then the disposal and acquisition covered by the single bargain were matched. Any previous disposal which, apart from the above matching provisions, would have been identified with the acquisition under the contango arrangement had to (subject to the general rule that disposals must be taken in chronological sequence) be identified with any 'available securities' acquired for transfer or delivery on the earlier date or in the earlier period. '*Available securities*' were securities which had not been matched under the above 'single bargain' rule, or under the general identification rules, with disposals for transfer or delivery on the earlier date or in the earlier period. Insofar as the previous disposal could not be identified with 'available securities', the disposal was to be treated as being for transfer or delivery on the later date, or in the later period. [*TCGA 1992, s 108(7); FA 1982, s 88(7)*].

59.9 **Inter-spouse and intra-group transfers.** If such a transfer resulted in securities of the same kind transferred to a third party, which would otherwise be 'unindexed', becoming 'indexed', the usual identification was reversed, so that the whole or a corresponding part of the indexed securities transferred to the third party became 'unindexed'. '*Indexed*' securities, for this purpose, were shares acquired or provided more than twelve months before the date of the disposal concerned and the meaning of '*unindexed*' was construed accordingly. Where there were multiple inter-spouse, intra-group, or third party disposals, the reversal of identification was applied to such disposals in chronological sequence. By a process of elimination, the 're-identification' of earlier disposals thus determined how these provisions were to apply to later disposals. [*FA 1982, s 89*].

59.10 **Share pools in existence before the operative date.** The relevant allowable expenditure (see 26.1 INDEXATION) of the holding of shares treated as a single asset ('pool') on 5 April 1982 (31 March 1982 for companies) was deemed the '1982 amount'. The relevant allowable expenditure on 5 April 1981 (31 March 1981 for companies) was deemed the '1981 amount'.

Where the '1982 amount' did not exceed the '1981 amount'

(*a*) The pool (in the legislation termed 'the holding') held immediately before the '1982 date' continued to be treated as a pool, but one which could not grow by the *acquisition* of additional securities of the same class. However, this overrode neither the reorganisation provisions of *TCGA 1992, s 127,* as qualified by the special indexation rules of *TCGA 1992, s 131* concerning reorganisations (see 26.6 INDEXATION), nor the effects of an election under *TCGA 1992, Sch 2 para 4* (see 7.3 ASSETS HELD ON 6 APRIL 1965). Thus the pool could increase by the addition of shares of the same class from bonus and rights issues, from other reorganisations not constituting acquisitions, and from a 6 April 1965 pooling election, but any additional consideration given on a reorganisation was treated, for indexation allowance purposes, as incurred on the *actual* date on which the person concerned gave, or was liable to give, the consideration. Where a reorganisation involved shares of a different class but did not constitute an acquisition it is thought that the relevant allowable expenditure required apportionment as under 58.5 SHARES AND SECURITIES.

(*b*) For indexation allowance purposes, the pool was regarded as having been acquired on 6 April 1981 (1 April 1981 for companies).

(*c*) All relevant allowable expenditure on a disposal out of the pool on or after the '1982 date' and before the '1985 date' was to be regarded for indexation allowance purposes as incurred at such a time that the month which determines RI in the general formula for computing indexation allowance (see 26.1 INDEXATION) is March 1982. Thus the indexation allowance was given for March 1982 onwards (subject to the reorganisation consideration provisions in (*a*) above).

Where the '1982 amount' did exceed the '1981 amount', the rules were modified. Firstly, a separate set of identification rules was applied to all acquisitions and disposals after 5 April 1981 (31 March 1981 for companies) but before the '1982 date', which, apart from these provisions, would have increased or decreased the pool. The separate rules were, in order of priority, as follows.

(i) Disposals of securities were identified in chronological order and the identification of the securities first disposed of accordingly determined the securities which could be comprised in a later disposal.

(ii) Disposals were identified with securities acquired on a later date rather than with securities acquired on an earlier date. The Inland Revenue were prepared to apply the rules to the twelve-month period as a whole (i.e. to the period ending on 5 April 1982 or 31 March 1982) rather than to the period ending with each disposal. As a result it was possible in some cases for a disposal to be identified with a subsequent acquisition and thus give an earlier acquisition date for indexation purposes (Revenue Pamphlet IR 131, SP 3/82).

(iii) Disposals were identified with acquisitions at other times on any one day in as nearly as may be equal proportions.

Only so much of the pool on 5 April 1981 (31 March 1981 for companies) (if any) which was not treated as disposed of before the '1982 date' by the rules in (i)–(iii) above was treated as constituting the pool on the '1982 date'. The pool, as adjusted (if at all) by these provisions, was termed the 'reduced holding', i.e. the reduced pool. All securities acquired after 5 April 1981 (31 March 1981 for companies), but before the '1982 date', were excluded from the pool, insofar as they were not identified under the rules in (i)–(iii) above with disposals before the '1982 date'. The acquisitions excluded from the pool in this manner were treated as separate assets. The rules in (*a*)–(*c*) above applied to the reduced pool but, for the purpose of computing the indexation allowance (if any) on a disposal after the '1982 date' of the reduced pool, or of the excluded acquisitions, the '1982 amount' was apportioned between the reduced pool and the excluded acquisitions pro rata to the number of securities comprised in each of those two categories on the operative date. The apportioned parts of the '1982 amount' were to be regarded for all capital gains tax purposes as the relevant allowable expenditure attributable to the pool, or to the excluded acquisitions, respectively. Such expenditure was deemed, for the purpose of the computing the indexation allowance, to be expenditure falling within *TCGA 1992, s 38(1)(a)* (see 26.1 INDEXATION). [*FA 1982, s 88(8), Sch 13 Pt II*].

59.11 ELECTION FOR 'PARALLEL POOLING' BY COMPANIES FOR DISPOSALS AFTER 31 MARCH 1982 AND BEFORE 1 APRIL 1985

For companies, an alternative method was available, by election, to identify particular shares and securities which were disposed of after 31 March 1982 and before 1 April 1985 with shares etc. of the same kind which had been previously acquired. Following the abolition of the general twelve-month qualifying period for indexation allowance to apply and the general reintroduction of a form of pooling for disposals after 31 March 1985, any 'parallel pooling' election made ceases to apply to such disposals. An opportunity was given to revoke any election previously made, by written notice before 1 April 1987 (or within such longer period as the Board may allow), with the effect that the gains on all disposals which were subject to the election were recomputed under the normal rules in 59.7–59.10 above. If an election was not so revoked, no adjustment was to be made to the gains on disposals which were subject to the election, and further provisions enable the rules given in 59.3–59.6 above to apply to the pooled holding in respect of disposals after 31 March 1985. [*TCGA 1992, s 112; FA 1983, s 34, Sch 6; FA 1985, Sch 19 Pt V; SI 1986 No 387*].

For full coverage of the above, see Tolley's Capital Gains Tax 1986/87.

59.12 IDENTIFICATION RULES — DISPOSALS PRE-FA 1992

Prior to 6 April 1982 (1 April 1982 for companies), any number of 'securities' of the same class acquired after 6 April 1965 and held by one person in one capacity was deemed to form a single asset. A disposal of some of the securities held was treated as a part disposal, the allowable expenditure of the securities disposed of being taken as a proportionate part of the total allowable expenditure of all the securities in the holding, i.e. a 'pooling' treatment applied. The proportion was given by the part disposal fraction, A/(A + B), as in 17.6 DISPOSAL. Securities with restricted rights of disposal (e.g. those issued under a share option scheme) formed a separate pool for as long as the restrictions lasted. The pooling procedure was not to affect the manner in which market value was to be ascertained. [*CGTA 1979, s 65(1)–(3)(5)(6)*].

For the position where quoted and unquoted securities were held on 6 April 1965, see 7.2–7.7 and 7.9–7.12 ASSETS HELD ON 6 APRIL 1965 respectively.

Securities of a particular kind disposed of on a particular day were matched with securities of the same kind acquired on the same day by the same person in the same capacity, and the 'pooling' rules of *CGTA 1979, s 65* above did not apply for this purpose. If more securities were disposed of than acquired on a particular day, and the excess could neither be identified with securities held on or acquired before 6 April 1965, nor be treated as diminishing a holding under *CGTA 1979, s 65* above, that excess was matched pro rata with a subsequent acquisition or acquisitions, taking the earliest first. [*CGTA 1979, s 66(1)(2)*].

'*Securities*' for the above purposes meant shares (which included stock), or securities of a company, or any other assets (except government securities) where they were of a nature to be dealt in without identifying the particular assets disposed of or acquired. Securities were not treated as being of the same kind unless they were treated as being of the same class of any one company by a recognised UK or overseas stock exchange or would have been so treated if dealt with on such a stock exchange. Shares or debentures comprised in any letter of allotment or similar instrument were treated as issued unless the right to the shares or debentures thereby conferred remained provisional until accepted, and there was no acceptance. [*CGTA 1979, s 64, s 65(2)(7), s 66(3)(4)*].

60 Taper Relief

Cross-references. See 17.10 DISPOSAL for taper relief on disposal of asset acquired in pursuance of an option; 19.17 EMPLOYEE SHARE SCHEMES for taper relief on disposal of shares acquired in pursuance of a qualifying option under the enterprise management incentives scheme.

Sumption: Capital Gains Tax. See A4C.

The headings in this chapter are as follows.

60.1 INTRODUCTION

For 1998/99 and subsequent years of assessment, chargeable gains realised by individuals, trustees and personal representatives (but not companies) are reduced (tapered) according to the length of time the asset has been held after 5 April 1998, with greater reductions for 'business assets'. Losses are not reduced as such, but they are set against gains before applying taper relief to the net gain so that the losses are effectively tapered. The provisions are described in detail in this chapter. These provisions start to have effect at the same time as the freezing of indexation allowance at its April 1998 level (see 26.1 INDEXATION), so that taper relief will eventually replace indexation allowance completely.

References are made in this chapter to Capital Gains Tax Reform: The 1998 Finance Act — A Guide for Inland Revenue Officers and Tax Practitioners, a booklet published by the Revenue in November 1998. See 29.1 INLAND REVENUE EXPLANATORY PUBLICATIONS for details.

60.2 TAPER RELIEF

Taper relief applies where for 1998/99 or any subsequent year of assessment a person has an excess of chargeable gains over the aggregate of allowable losses for the year and losses brought forward and the excess is or includes the whole or a part of any chargeable gain that is eligible for the relief. It thus applies *after* the deduction of any INDEXATION (26) allowance available and after any other deductions due, for example RETIREMENT RELIEF (see 53.10), in arriving at the chargeable gain, except that the relief is deducted in priority to the annual exemption (see 2.5 ANNUAL RATES AND EXEMPTIONS). See 60.3 below for the interaction between losses brought forward, the annual exempt amount and taper relief. **Taper relief does not apply at all for the purposes of corporation tax on chargeable gains.**

In computing the extent, if any, to which a gain on a particular disposal is included in the above-mentioned excess of gains over losses, both current year losses and brought forward losses are set against gains in such order as gives the maximum taper relief. See *Example 2* below.

Qualifying holding period. A chargeable gain is eligible for taper relief if at the time of disposal the asset has been held for at least one year in the case of a 'business asset' (see 60.4 below) or at least three years otherwise. For these purposes, only so much of the period for which the asset is held as falls **after 5 April 1998** (called the '*qualifying holding period*') is taken into account.

If the time of acquisition (see below) of an asset fell before 17 March 1998 and either the asset is a non-business asset or it is a business asset disposed of before 6 April 2000, **an additional one year (the 'bonus year') is added**, in arriving at the qualifying holding period, to the actual period for which the asset is held after 5 April 1998. For example, a non-business asset acquired in 1996/97 and disposed of in 2000/01 is treated as having been held for *three* complete years after 5 April 1998. The one-year addition does not apply if there is a period after 5 April 1998 which, under the anti-avoidance rules in 60.17 below, does not count as a period of holding for the purposes of taper relief. See 60.15 below as regards shares. See 20.13 ENTERPRISE INVESTMENT SCHEME (AND BES) for special rules in cases of serial reinvestment in EIS companies.

The period for which an asset is held after 5 April 1998 is expressly defined as the period beginning with the acquisition of the asset by the person making the disposal or 6 April 1998, whichever is the later, and ending with the time of disposal (and see 60.11 below re assets transferred between spouses). Specified CGT provisions which otherwise effectively treat an asset as acquired at a time other than its actual acquisition date are disregarded for this purpose, *viz. TCGA 1992, s 73(1)(b)* (to the extent that it relates the acquisition date back to before 6 April 1965 — see 57.11(*a*)(ii) SETTLEMENTS), *s 239(2)(b)* (settlements for the benefit of employees — see 21.79 EXEMPTIONS AND RELIEFS), *s 257(2)(b)* (gifts to charities — see 10.5 CHARITIES) and *s 259(2)(b)* (housing associations — see 21.44 EXEMPTIONS AND RELIEFS). Where certain anti-avoidance provisions apply (see 60.16, 60.17 below), periods which are thereby treated as not counting for taper relief purposes are left out of account in determining the qualifying holding period.

In the case of shares acquired by way of scrip issue (aka bonus issue) or rights issue or other reorganisation of share capital, such that *TCGA 1992, s 127* treats the new shares as the same asset as the original shares (see 58.5 SHARES AND SECURITIES), taper relief runs from the acquisition date of the original shares (or from 6 April 1998 if later). This does not apply to shares received by way of scrip *dividend* (aka stock dividend) after 5 April 1998, which are treated as a free-standing acquisition as at the dividend date and not as a reorganisation (see 58.13 SHARES AND SECURITIES); the taper period thus begins at the scrip dividend date.

The date of any enhancement expenditure is not relevant for taper relief purposes in that it does not alter the qualifying holding period.

Where an asset was created rather than acquired, for example goodwill, the date of acquisition is the date the asset was created, determined as a question of fact on the basis of the evidence available (Revenue Booklet CGT Reform: The 1998 Finance Act, para 2.15).

Amount of reduction. Chargeable gains are tapered according to the Table below up to a maximum of 75% for 'business assets' (see 60.4 below) and 40% for non-business assets, the maximum reductions applying where the qualifying holding period is at least four years for business assets and ten years for non-business assets. So much of any chargeable gain accruing to any person on disposal of an asset as is not a gain on disposal of a business asset is to be taken to be a gain on disposal of a non-business asset (and see 60.9 below as regards an asset which has been a business asset for part only of its period of ownership and 60.10 below as regards an asset used at the same time for different purposes).

Gains on disposals of **business** assets
after 5 April 2000

No. of whole years in qualifying holding period	Percentage reduction available	Percentage of gain chargeable
0	—	100.0
1	12.5	87.5
2	25.0	75.0
3	50.0	50.0
4 or more	75.0	25.0

Gains on disposals of **business** assets
after 5 April 1998 and before 6 April 2000

No. of whole years in qualifying holding period*	Percentage reduction available	Percentage of gain chargeable
0	—	100.0
1	7.5	92.5
2	15.0	85.0
3	22.5	77.5
4	30.0	70.0
5	37.5	62.5
6	45.0	55.0
7	52.5	47.5
8	60.0	40.0
9	67.5	32.5
10 or more	75.0	25.0

* Including bonus year added for assets held on 17 March 1998 (see main text)

Gains on disposals of **non-business** assets
after 5 April 1998

No. of whole years in qualifying holding period*	Percentage reduction available	Percentage of gain chargeable
0	—	100
1	—	100
2	—	100
3	5	95
4	10	90
5	15	85
6	20	80
7	25	75
8	30	70
9	35	65
10 or more	40	60

* Including bonus year added for assets held on 17 March 1998 (see main text)

The amount on which capital gains tax is to be charged for the tax year, subject to the annual exempt amount and the provisions at 60.3 below re losses brought forward, is the above-mentioned excess of gains over current year and brought forward losses less any available taper relief computed as above by reference to the gains(s) included in that excess.

[*TCGA 1992, s 2A, Sch A1 para 1, para 2(1)(3)(4)(a), (5), para 3(4); FA 1998, s 121, Sch 20; FA 1999, s 72(3); FA 2000, s 66*].

Example 1

Brett acquired an asset in 1996 for £20,000 and sells it in September 2002 for £35,000. He makes no other disposals in 2002/03. At no time after 5 April 1998 was the asset used as a business asset. The indexation factor from date of acquisition to April 1998 is, say, 0.060.

At the time of disposal the asset has been held for four complete years after 5 April 1998. Because it was acquired before 17 March 1998, a further one year is added. Using the Table above, the taper relief for a non-business asset held for five complete years after 5 April 1998 is 15%.

	£
Proceeds	35,000
Less Cost of acquisition	20,000
Unindexed gain	15,000
Indexation to April 1998 £20,000 × 0.060	1,200
Chargeable gain	13,800
Less Taper relief £13,800 × 15%	2,070
Taxable gain subject to annual exemption	£11,730

Example 2

Hannah made four disposals in 2005/06, as follows.

On Asset A, she realised a chargeable gain of £13,000 (after indexation to April 1998). This asset was acquired in 1995 and sold in May 2005 and was a non-business asset throughout its ownership.

On Asset B, she realised a chargeable gain of £2,000. This asset was acquired in December 2002 and sold in October 2005 and was a non-business asset throughout its ownership.

On Asset C, she realised a chargeable gain of £7,500. This asset was acquired in August 2002 and sold in December 2005 and was a business asset throughout its ownership.

On Asset D, she realised an allowable loss of £6,000.

Asset A was held for seven complete years after 5 April 1998 and qualifies for a one-year addition as it was acquired before 17 March 1998. It thus qualifies for 30% taper relief.

Asset B was held for less than the minimum period of ownership necessary for a gain on a non-business asset to qualify for taper relief (three complete years).

Asset C was held for three complete years. It thus qualifies for 50% taper relief.

It is beneficial to offset the loss on Asset D firstly against the gain attracting no taper relief, i.e. the gain on Asset B, with the balance against the gain attracting the lower rate of taper relief, i.e. the gain on Asset A.

	£
Asset A	
Chargeable gain	13,000
Less Allowable loss	4,000
	9,000
Less Taper relief £9,000 × 30%	2,700
Tapered gain	£6,300

	£
Asset B	
Chargeable gain	2,000
Less Allowable loss	2,000

	£
Asset C	
Chargeable gain	7,500
Less Taper relief £7,500 × 50%	3,750
Tapered gain	£3,750
Total taxable gains subject to annual exemption	£10,050

60.3 INTERACTION WITH ANNUAL EXEMPT AMOUNT AND LOSSES BROUGHT FORWARD ETC.

Taper relief is given in priority to deduction of the annual exempt amount (see 2.5 ANNUAL RATES AND EXEMPTIONS), but after deduction of any allowable losses (see 60.2 above).

Where for 1998/99 or any subsequent year of assessment a person's 'adjusted net gains' are equal to or less than the annual exempt amount, any allowable losses brought forward from a previous year or carried back from the year of an individual's death (see 16.5 DEATH) need not be deducted and are thus preserved for further carry-forward (or, if possible, carry-back). Where the 'adjusted net gains' exceed the annual exempt amount, such losses are deducted only to the extent necessary to wipe out the excess. The '*adjusted net gains*' are the chargeable gains for the year *before taper relief* less any allowable losses for the year. (An additional adjustment is necessary if any gains of a settlement fall to be charged on the person concerned as a settlor or any gains of a non-resident settlement fall to be attributed to him as a beneficiary — see 2.5 ANNUAL RATES AND EXEMPTIONS for details of this adjustment.)

[*TCGA 1992, s 3(5)–(5C)(7)(8); FA 1998, s 121(3)(4), Sch 21 para 3*].

It follows that whilst brought-forward or carried-back losses are preserved to the extent that the current year gains are covered by the annual exemption, any taper relief available will then reduce the gains to less than the annual exempt amount so that the taper relief is effectively wasted in this instance.

See the examples at 2.5 ANNUAL RATES AND EXEMPTIONS.

60.4 MEANING OF 'BUSINESS ASSET'

Amendments were made by *FA 2000* to the definition of a 'business asset' for taper relief purposes and these are fully covered below. The amendments have effect for determining the status of an asset at any time after 5 April 2000. They do not affect the status of an asset at any time before 6 April 2000 even if that status falls to be determined as a result of a disposal on or after that date. [*FA 2000, s 67(7)*]. On the disposal of an asset which became a business asset on 6 April 2000 as a result of the changes to the rules, the gain must be apportioned using the normal rules at 60.9 below.

Assets other than shares and securities. For the purposes of taper relief, an asset, other than shares or securities (for which see below) or an interest therein, is a '*business asset*' at any specified time before its disposal if at that time it satisfies whichever is the relevant of the conditions set out below. See below for definitions, except where otherwise stated.

In the case of a disposal by an **individual**, the asset is a business asset at any specified time if at that time it was being used wholly or partly for one or more of the following purposes:

- those of a 'trade' carried on at that time by the individual or by a partnership in which he is a partner;
- those of any trade carried on by a company which is at that time a 'qualifying company' (see 60.5 below) by reference to the individual;
- those of any trade carried on by a company which is at that time a member of a 'trading group' of which the 'holding company' is at that time a qualifying company by reference to the individual;
- where that time is before 6 April 2000, those of any 'qualifying office or employment' to which the individual is at that time required to devote 'substantially the whole of his time' (which the Revenue take to mean at least 75% of normal working hours — see Revenue Booklet CGT Reform: The 1998 Finance Act, para 2.119);
- where that time is before 6 April 2000, those of any office or employment not qualifying as above but with a 'trading company' in relation to which the individual falls to be treated as being, at that time, a 'full-time working officer or employee';
- where that time is after 5 April 2000, those of any office or employment (full-time or otherwise) held by the individual with a person carrying on a trade.

Where the individual acquired the asset as legatee (within *TCGA 1992, s 64* — see 16.9 DEATH), it is taken to be a business asset at any specified time, where such would not otherwise be the case, if at that time it was being held by the deceased's personal representatives and being used for one or more of the purposes specified below for disposals by personal representatives.

The receipt by the owner of rent for the use of an asset by his partnership or qualifying company does not affect its status as a business asset (Revenue Booklet CGT Reform: The 1998 Finance Act, para 2.94).

In the case of a disposal by **trustees of a settlement**, the asset is a business asset at any specified time if at that time it was being used wholly or partly for one or more of the following purposes:

- those of a 'trade' carried on by the trustees;
- those of a trade carried on at that time by an 'eligible beneficiary' (see 60.6 below) or by a partnership in which he is a partner;
- those of any trade carried on by a company which is at that time a 'qualifying company' (see 60.5 below) by reference to *either* the trustees *or* an eligible beneficiary;
- those of any trade carried on by a company which is at that time a member of a 'trading group' of which the 'holding company' is at that time a qualifying company by reference to the trustees *or* an eligible beneficiary;

- where that time is before 6 April 2000, those of any 'qualifying office or employment' to which an eligible beneficiary is at that time required to devote 'substantially the whole of his time' (see above);
- where that time is before 6 April 2000, those of any office or employment not qualifying as above but with a 'trading company' in relation to which an eligible beneficiary falls to be treated as being, at that time, a 'full-time working officer or employee';
- where that time is after 5 April 2000, those of any office or employment (full-time or otherwise) held by an eligible beneficiary with a person carrying on a trade.

In the case of a disposal by the **personal representatives** (PRs) of a deceased individual, the asset is a business asset at any specified time if at that time it was being used wholly or partly for one or more of the following purposes:

- those of a 'trade' carried on by the PRs;
- those of any trade carried on by a company which is at that time a 'qualifying company' (see 60.5 below) by reference to the PRs;
- those of any trade carried on by a company which is at that time a member of a 'trading group' of which the 'holding company' is at that time a qualifying company by reference to the PRs.

Shares, securities or an interest in shares etc. For the purposes of taper relief, an asset consisting of, or of an interest in, any shares in or securities of a company (the relevant company) is a '*business asset*' at any specified time before its disposal if at that time it satisfies whichever is the relevant of the conditions set out below. See below for definitions, except where otherwise stated.

In the case of a disposal by an **individual** or by **trustees**, the asset is a business asset at any specified time if at that time the relevant company is a 'qualifying company' (see 60.5 below) by reference to the individual or, as the case may be, the trustees.

Where the individual acquired the asset as legatee (within *TCGA 1992, s 64* — see 16.9 DEATH), it is taken to be a business asset at any specified time, where such would not otherwise be the case, if at that time

- it was being held by the deceased's personal representatives and
- where that time is before 6 April 2000, the pre-6 April 2000 condition below for disposals by personal representatives is satisfied; or where that time is after 5 April 2000, the relevant company is a 'qualifying company' (see 60.5 below) by reference to the personal representatives.

In the case of a disposal by **personal representatives** (PRs), the asset is a business asset at any specified time before 6 April 2000 if at that time the relevant company is a 'trading company' or the 'holding company' of a 'trading group' and the PRs may exercise at least 25% of the voting rights. The asset is a business asset at any specified time after 5 April 2000 if at that time the relevant company is a 'qualifying company' (see 60.5 below) by reference to the personal representatives.

Definitions. The expressions 'qualifying company' and 'eligible beneficiary' are defined at, respectively, 60.5 and 60.6 below. Otherwise, the definitions below apply for the above purposes.

A '*trade*' means a trade, profession or vocation, as understood for income tax purposes, which is conducted on a commercial basis with a view to realisation of profits. The expression also expressly includes the commercial letting of FURNISHED HOLIDAY ACCOMMODATION (22).

A '*trading group*' means a 'group of companies' the activities of which, taken together, do not to any substantial extent include activities carried on otherwise than in the course of, or for the purposes of, a trade. A '*group of companies*' means a company and its '51% subsidiary(ies)' (within *ICTA 1988, s 838*). A '*holding company*' is a company whose business consists wholly or mainly of the holding of shares in its 51% subsidiary(ies) (and for the purpose of this definition any trade carried on by the holding company itself is disregarded). See 60.5A below for treatment of investments in joint venture companies (as there defined).

'*Qualifying office or employment*' means an 'office' or 'employment' (as those expressions are understood for income tax purposes) with a person who at the time specified is carrying on a trade.

A '*trading company*' is a company which exists wholly for the purpose of carrying on one or more trades, disregarding any purposes capable of having no substantial effect on the extent of the company's activities. (No definition of 'substantial' has yet been provided.) See 60.5A below for treatment of investments in joint venture companies (as there defined).

A '*full-time working officer or employee*', in relation to a company, is an individual who

- is an officer or employee of that company or of that company and any other company(ies) with which it has a 'relevant connection', and
- is required in that capacity to devote 'substantially the whole of his time' to the service of that company or of those companies taken together. The Revenue take this to mean at least 75% of normal working hours — see Revenue Booklet CGT Reform: The 1998 Finance Act, para 2.119.

A company has a '*relevant connection*' with another company at any time when they are both members of the same group of companies (as defined above) or of the same 'commercial association of companies'. The latter expression means a company and such of its associated companies (within *ICTA 1988, s 416*) as carry on businesses which are of such a nature as to be reasonably considered to form a single composite undertaking. See also 60.5A below as regards joint venture companies (as there defined).

[*TCGA 1992, Sch A1 para 4, para 5, para 22(1)(2); FA 1998, s 121(2)(4), Sch 20; FA 2000, s 67(2)(3)(5)*].

60.5 **Meaning of 'qualifying company'**. For the purposes of 60.4 above, a company is a '*qualifying company*' by reference to an **individual** at any time **before 6 April 2000** when

- the company is a 'trading company' or the 'holding company' of a 'trading group' (all expressions as defined in 60.4 above); *and*
- at least 25% of the voting rights are exercisable by that individual;

or at any time when

- the company is a trading company or the holding company of a trading group;
- at least 5% of the voting rights are exercisable by that individual; *and*
- the individual is a 'full-time working officer or employee' (as defined in 60.4 above) of that company or of a company which at that time has a 'relevant connection' (see 60.4 above) with it.

A company is a '*qualifying company*' by reference to an **individual** at any time **after 5 April 2000** when the company is a 'trading company' or the 'holding company' of a 'trading group' (all expressions as defined in 60.4 above) and *one or more* of the following conditions is met:

- the company is 'unlisted' (see below); or
- the individual is an officer or employee (full-time or otherwise) of the company or of a company having a 'relevant connection' (see 60.4 above) with it; or
- at least 5% of the voting rights in the company are exercisable by the individual.

A company is a '*qualifying company*' by reference to the **trustees of a settlement** at any time **before 6 April 2000** when

- the company is a 'trading company' or the 'holding company' of a 'trading group' (all expressions as defined in 60.4 above); *and*
- at least 25% of the voting rights are exercisable by the trustees;

or at any time when

- the company is a trading company or the holding company of a trading group;
- at least 5% of the voting rights are exercisable by the trustees; *and*
- an 'eligible beneficiary' (see 60.6 below) is a 'full-time working officer or employee' (as defined in 60.4 above) of that company or of a company which at that time has a 'relevant connection' (see 60.4 above) with it.

A company is a '*qualifying company*' by reference to the **trustees of a settlement** at any time **after 5 April 2000** when the company is a 'trading company' or the 'holding company' of a 'trading group' (all expressions as defined in 60.4 above) and *one or more* of the following conditions is met:

- the company is 'unlisted' (see below); or
- an 'eligible beneficiary' (see 60.6 below) is an officer or employee (full-time or otherwise) of the company or of a company having a 'relevant connection' (see 60.4 above) with it; or
- at least 5% of the voting rights in the company are exercisable by the trustees.

A company is a '*qualifying company*' by reference to the **personal representatives** (PRs) of a deceased individual at any time **before 6 April 2000** when

- the company is a 'trading company' or the 'holding company' of a 'trading group' (all expressions as defined in 60.4 above); *and*
- at least 25% of the voting rights are exercisable by the PRs.

A company is a '*qualifying company*' by reference to the **personal representatives** (PRs) of a deceased individual at any time **after 5 April 2000** when the company is a 'trading company' or the 'holding company' of a 'trading group' (all expressions as defined in 60.4 above) and *one or both* of the following conditions is met:

- the company is 'unlisted' (see below); or
- at least 5% of the voting rights are exercisable by the PRs.

An '*unlisted*' company is a company none of whose shares are listed on a recognised stock exchange (see 58.5 SHARES AND SECURITIES) and which is not a 51% subsidiary (within *ICTA 1988, s 838*) of a company whose shares (or any class of whose shares) are so listed. Note that shares traded on the Alternative Investment Market (see 40.5 MARKET VALUE) are treated as unlisted for these purposes.

Note that on the disposal of an asset which became a business asset on 6 April 2000 as a result of the changes to the definition of a qualifying company effective from that date, the gain must be apportioned using the normal rules at 60.9 below.

[*TCGA 1992, Sch A1 paras 6, 22(1); FA 1998, s 121(2)(4), Sch 20; FA 2000, s 67(4)(5)(7)*].

60.5A **Joint venture companies (JVCs).** The following has effect for determining whether or not an asset is a business asset at any time after 5 April 2000. It does not affect the status of an asset at any time before 6 April 2000. On the disposal of an asset which became a business asset on 6 April 2000 in consequence of these rules, the gain must be apportioned as in 60.9 below.

For the purposes of these provisions, a company is a '*joint venture company*' if (and *only* if)

- it is a 'trading company' or the 'holding company' of a 'trading group' (all expressions as defined in 60.4 above), *and*
- at least 75% in aggregate of its ordinary share capital (within *ICTA 1988, s 832(1)*) is held by no more than five companies (counting shares held by different members of a 'group of companies', as in 60.4 above, as held by a single company).

The following provisions apply to a company (an '*investing company*') only if

(*a*) it holds more than 30% of the ordinary share capital of a JVC, *or*

(*b*) it is a member of a 'group of companies' (as in 60.4 above) which between them hold more than 30% of the ordinary share capital of a JVC *and* the company itself holds part of that capital.

Where the above conditions are satisfied, the definitions of 'trading group', 'holding company' and 'trading company' in 60.4 above (which are also of application in defining a 'qualifying company' for the purposes of business asset taper relief — see 60.5 above) have effect with the modifications in (1)–(3) below.

(1) In determining whether a group of companies is a '*trading group*', there is disregarded any shareholding in a JVC by any member of the group which is an investing company within (*a*) or (*b*) above. Each such member is regarded as carrying on a share of the JVC's activities proportionate to its percentage shareholding in the JVC. This does not apply if the JVC is itself a member of the group.

(2) In determining whether an investing company within (*a*) or (*b*) above is a '*holding company*', there is disregarded any holding of shares by it in the JVC. It is regarded as carrying on a share of the JVC's activities proportionate to its percentage shareholding in the JVC. This does not apply if the JVC is a 51% subsidiary (within *ICTA 1988, s 838*) of the investing company.

(3) In determining whether an investing company within (*a*) or (*b*) above is a '*trading company*', there is disregarded any holding of shares by it in the JVC. It is regarded as carrying on a share of the JVC's activities proportionate to its percentage shareholding in the JVC. This does not apply if the investing company is a holding company.

Where the JVC is itself the holding company of a trading group, the references in (1), (2) and (3) above to its activities are to the activities of its group.

The following are treated as having a '*relevant connection*' (see 60.4 above) with each other, even if this would not otherwise be the case:

- the investing company within (*a*) or (*b*) above;
- the JVC;
- any company having a 'relevant connection' with the investing company;
- any company having a 'relevant connection' with the JVC by virtue of its being a 51% subsidiary of the JVC or a member of the same commercial association of companies (see 60.4 above).

[*TCGA 1992, Sch A1 paras 22(1)(2), 23(1)–(8)(10); FA 1998, s 121(2)(4), Sch 20; FA 2000, s 67(6)(7)*].

60.6 **Eligible beneficiaries of a settlement.** For the purposes of 60.4 and 60.5 above, an '*eligible beneficiary*', in relation to an asset comprised in a settlement and a specified time, is any individual having at that time a 'relevant interest in possession' under the settlement in either the whole of the settled property or a part which includes that asset. A '*relevant interest in possession*' means any interest in possession in the settlement other than a right to receive an annuity or a 'fixed-term entitlement'. The latter expression means any interest under the settlement which is limited to a fixed term other than a term at the end of which the person concerned will become entitled to the property. The simplest example of an eligible beneficiary is one with a life interest in the whole of the settled property.

Where the settled property originates from more than one settlor, the taper relief provisions have effect, and references to an '*eligible beneficiary*' are to be construed, as if there were a separate and distinct settlement for the property originating from each settlor, and *TCGA 1992, s 79(1)–(5)* (see 57.3 SETTLEMENTS) apply for these purposes.

[*TCGA 1992, Sch A1 paras 7, 20; FA 1998, s 121(2)(4), Sch 20*].

See 57.7 SETTLEMENTS re meaning of 'interest in possession'.

60.7 **Non-qualifying beneficiaries.** A special rule applies where the trustees of a settlement dispose of an asset and that asset's relevant period of ownership (see 60.8 below) is or includes a period (known as a sharing period) throughout which

- the asset is a business asset (see 60.4 above) by reference to one or more eligible beneficiaries (see 60.6 above) and would not otherwise have been so; and
- there is a 'non-qualifying part of the relevant income' or would be if there *were* any relevant income for the period.

The '*non-qualifying part of the relevant income*' for any period is so much of the '*relevant income*', i.e. the income for that period from the part of the settled property comprising the asset disposed of, as is, or would be, income to which no eligible beneficiary has any entitlement or to which a 'non-qualifying eligible beneficiary' has an entitlement. A '*non-qualifying eligible beneficiary*', in relation to any period, is an eligible beneficiary who is not a beneficiary by reference to whom (if he were the only beneficiary) the asset disposed of would be a business asset throughout that period.

Where the above applies, each sharing period is apportioned by reference to the proportion which the non-qualifying part of the relevant income bears, or *would* bear if there were any income, to the relevant income. The resulting part of each sharing period is then deemed to be a period for which the asset was not a business asset (see 60.9 below for ramifications). Where different proportions apply to different parts of a single sharing period, a separate apportionment must be made for each such part.

[*TCGA 1992, Sch A1 para 8; FA 1998, s 121(2)(4), Sch 20*].

For worked examples, see Revenue Booklet CGT Reform: The 1998 Finance Act, paras 2.145, 2.146.

60.8 **RELEVANT PERIOD OF OWNERSHIP**

For the purposes of 60.7 above and 60.9, 60.10 below, an asset's '*relevant period of ownership*' is the period after 5 April 1998 for which the asset has been held at the time of its disposal or, if shorter, the period of ten years ending with that time. Where certain anti-avoidance provisions apply (see 60.16, 60.17 below) or the special rule for serial investors in EIS companies applies (see 20.13 ENTERPRISE INVESTMENT SCHEME (AND BES)), periods which are thereby treated as not counting for taper relief purposes are left out of account in computing the said ten-year period and are treated as not comprised in the relevant period of ownership. [*TCGA 1992, Sch A1 para 2(2)(4)(b); FA 1998, s 121(2)(4), Sch 20; FA 1999, s 72(3)*]. Where a 'bonus year' falls to be added in arriving at the qualifying holding period (see 60.2 above), it is *not* added to the relevant period of ownership.

60.9 ASSETS WHICH ARE BUSINESS ASSETS FOR PART ONLY OF PERIOD OF OWNERSHIP

A chargeable gain on the disposal of an asset is a gain on the disposal of a business asset, and therefore qualifies for the more beneficial taper rates in 60.2 above, if the asset was a business asset (see 60.4 above) *throughout* its relevant period of ownership (see 60.8 above).

If the above is not the case, but the asset has been a business asset for one or more periods comprising part of its relevant period of ownership, part of the gain is taken to be a gain on disposal of a business asset and the remainder taken to be a gain on disposal of a non-business asset, with different rates of taper relief applying accordingly to each part by reference to the qualifying period of holding (see 60.2 above) as if they were two separate gains accruing on separate disposals of separate assets held for the same period of time. The part taken to relate to a business asset is the proportion of the gain which the period(s) comprised in the relevant period of ownership for which the asset was a business asset bears to the whole of the relevant period of ownership. Where appropriate, the provisions at 60.7 above and 60.10 below must be taken into account in ascertaining the numerator of the fraction.

[*TCGA 1992, Sch A1 para 3(1)–(3)(5); FA 1998, s 121(2)(4), Sch 20*].

Example

Penny acquired a freehold property in March 1990 and sold it on 30 September 2007, realising a chargeable gain (after indexation to April 1998) of £95,000. Between March 1990 and September 2001 inclusive, the property was used as business premises and qualifies as a business asset for taper relief purposes. From October 2001 to September 2007 inclusive, it was let to a private tenant and was not a business asset. Penny made no other disposal in 2007/08.

The relevant period of ownership (see 60.8 above) is the $9\frac{1}{2}$ years from 6 April 1998 to 30 September 2007. During that period, the asset was a business asset for $3\frac{1}{2}$ years (April 1998 to September 2001) and a non-business asset for the remaining six years. Therefore, 3.5/9.5 of the gain (£35,000) qualifies for the business assets taper and 6/9.5 of the gain (£60,000) qualifies for the non-business assets taper.

The number of complete years in the qualifying holding period is nine. However, there is a one-year addition in the case of the non-business asset as it was acquired before 17 March 1998.

	Business asset	*Non-business asset*	*Total*
	£	£	£
Chargeable gain	35,000	60,000	95,000
Less Taper relief 75% / 40%	26,250	24,000	50,250
Taxable gain subject to annual exemption	£8,750	£36,000	£44,750

60.10 ASSET USED AT SAME TIME FOR DIFFERENT PURPOSES

An asset's relevant period of ownership (see 60.8 above) may be, or may include, a period (a mixed-use period) throughout which the asset (not being shares or securities or an interest therein) is a business asset by reference to its use for the purposes mentioned in

60.4 above but at the same time is used for other, i.e. non-qualifying, purposes. On the disposal at a gain of such an asset, a fraction of every mixed-use period is taken to be a period throughout which the asset was *not* a business asset (see 60.9 above for the ramifications). The fraction, in relation to any mixed-use period, is that which represents the proportion of non-qualifying use to total use during that period. Where that proportion has been different at different times within a mixed-use period, separate fractions must be applied to separate parts of the mixed-use period. For a worked example, see Revenue Booklet CGT Reform: The 1998 Finance Act, para 2.137.

Where, on a trustees' disposal, both these provisions and those at 60.7 above apply to the whole or any part of a period, the last-mentioned provisions are applied first. These provisions are then applied, to the period(s) for which the asset is taken to have been a business asset, by reference only to the 'relevant part' of any non-qualifying use, being the proportion of that use which is not a use to which a 'non-qualifying part' of any 'relevant income' (see 60.7 above) is attributable. For a worked example, see Revenue Booklet CGT Reform: The 1998 Finance Act, para 2.148. Where different attributions have to be made for different parts of a mixed-use period, separate fractions must be applied to separate parts of the mixed-use period.

[*TCGA 1992, Sch A1 para 9; FA 1998, s 121(2)(4), Sch 20*].

Note that these provisions apply only where there is non-qualifying use. Where part of an asset is a business asset and part is not used at all, for example unoccupied space in a building, there is *prima facie* no restriction of business asset taper relief. For further discussion of this, see *Taxation 17/24 December 1998 p 303*.

60.11 ASSETS TRANSFERRED BETWEEN SPOUSES

On a disposal of an asset acquired from a spouse under the no gain/no loss provisions of *TCGA 1992, s 58* (see 41.3 MARRIED PERSONS), taper relief applies as if the time when the transferee spouse acquired the asset was the time when the transferor spouse acquired it (or is treated as having acquired it, for example where there has been more than one inter-spouse transfer of the same asset). In other words, the combined period of holding of both spouses is taken into account.

As regards assets other than shares and securities, the question of whether the asset was a business asset (see 60.4 above) at any specified time in the combined period of holding is determined by reference to the use to which it was put by the spouse holding it at that time. Thus, if the husband acquires a property on 1 April 1998 and holds it as an investment for four years after 5 April 1998 and then gives it to his wife who uses it in her business for five years before selling it, four-ninths of the gain on the ultimate disposal will attract nine years' taper relief at the non-business asset rate and five-ninths will attract nine years' taper relief at the business asset rate (see the rules at 60.9 above). During that part of the combined period of holding which falls *before* the inter-spouse transfer, the asset is also a business asset at any time if it then qualifies as such by reference to the spouse to whom it is eventually transferred, i.e. where an asset owned by one spouse is used in the other's business.

As regards shares and securities, the question of whether the asset was a business asset at any specified time in the combined period of holding is determined only by reference to the individual making the ultimate disposal. Say husband and wife each own 4% of the voting shares in a quoted trading company (acquired after 5 April 2000) but only the husband is an employee, and that this situation persists for five years at which point the wife gives her shareholding to her husband. After a further one year the husband sells the combined shareholding. The gain will attract six years' taper relief at the business asset rate, as the company has been a qualifying company by reference to the husband (see 60.5 above) throughout those six years. If, on the other hand, only the wife is an employee, only one-sixth of the ultimate gain will qualify for taper relief at the business asset rate. The company is a qualifying company by reference to the husband for only one of the six years; the fact that it is a qualifying company by reference to the wife for five of those years is irrelevant as it is not she who makes the ultimate disposal.

[*TCGA 1992, Sch A1 para 15; FA 1998, s 121(2)(4), Sch 20*].

60.12 POSTPONED GAINS

A special rule applies where a gain would have accrued on an actual or deemed disposal (the 'charged disposal') of an asset at a particular time, but is treated on one or more occasions under any of the CGT provisions listed below as accruing at a later time (whether or not the time of a subsequent disposal) and after 5 April 1998. The said provisions are:

- *TCGA 1992, s 10A* (temporary non-UK residence — see 44.4 OVERSEAS MATTERS);
- *TCGA 1992, s 116(10)* (company reconstruction where new asset is a QUALIFYING CORPORATE BOND — see 49.3);
- *TCGA 1992, s 134* (issue of gilts as compensation for compulsory acquisition of shares or securities — see 58.11 SHARES AND SECURITIES);
- *TCGA 1992, s 154(2)(4)* (ROLLOVER RELIEF into a depreciating asset — see 55.7);
- *TCGA 1992, Sch 5B* (deferral of gains on reinvestment into an EIS company — see 20.9 ENTERPRISE INVESTMENT SCHEME (AND BES)); (but special rules apply in cases of serial reinvestment — see 20.13 ENTERPRISE INVESTMENT SCHEME (AND BES));
- *TCGA 1992, Sch 5C* (deferral of gains on reinvestment into a VCT — see 65.10 VENTURE CAPITAL TRUSTS);
- *FA 1996, Sch 15 para 27* (transitional rules for qualifying indexed securities — see 38.18 LOAN RELATIONSHIPS OF COMPANIES).

Taper relief is applied to the postponed gain only at the time it becomes chargeable but is applied by reference to the time of the charged disposal and the asset which was disposed of, or would have been disposed of, by the charged disposal. Accordingly, the end of the period (if any) after 5 April 1998 for which the asset had been held at the time of the disposal on which the postponed gain accrued is deemed to be the time of the charged disposal.

Where under *TCGA 1992, s 12(1)* (gains charged on REMITTANCE BASIS — see 51.1) or *s 279(2)* (delayed remittances of overseas gains — see 44.5 OVERSEAS MATTERS), a gain is treated as accruing later than it actually accrued, those provisions are ignored for the purposes of taper relief.

[*TCGA 1992, Sch A1 para 16; FA 1998, s 121(2)(4), Sch 20*].

Example

Gordon disposes of shares in A Ltd, his family trading company, in August 2000, realising a chargeable gain (after indexation to April 1998) of £25,000. He had held the shares since 1988 and they qualified as a business asset for the purposes of taper relief. He acquires shares in a Venture Capital Trust in March 2001 for £30,000 and makes a claim for deferral relief under *TCGA 1992, Sch 5C*. He makes no other disposals in 2000/01 and wishes to leave sufficient gains in charge to cover his annual exemption.

The A Ltd shares were held for two complete years after 5 April 1998. The taper is therefore 25%.

	£
Gain before taper relief	25,000
Less Deferred on reinvestment in VCT (optimum amount)	15,400 *
	9,600
Less Taper relief £9,600 × 25%	2,400
Tapered gain covered by annual exemption	£7,200

$$* \text{£}7{,}200 \times \frac{100}{100 - 22.5} = \text{£}9{,}600.\ \text{£}25{,}000 - 9{,}600 = \text{£}15{,}400$$

In June 2007, Gordon sells his VCT shares. The deferred gain becomes chargeable in 2007/08 and is computed as follows.

	£
Deferred gain before taper relief	15,400
Less Taper relief £15,400 × 25%	3,850
Taxable gain subject to annual exemption	£11,550

60.13 HOLD-OVER RELIEF

It is implicit in the legislation that the gain to be held over, where such a claim is made on the transfer of an asset within 25 HOLD-OVER RELIEFS, is the untapered gain; as stated in 60.2 above, taper relief is given only on gains left in charge after all reliefs other than the annual exempt amount have been taken into account.

On the ultimate disposal by the transferee of an asset which he acquired by way of a transfer on which hold-over relief was claimed, only the period for which he personally has held the asset will determine the taper relief available; there is no provision for combining the holding period of transferor and transferee as there is with inter-spouse transfers (see 60.11 above). (Revenue Press Release IR 16, 17 March 1998).

60.14 ROLLOVER RELIEF

Where ROLLOVER RELIEF (55) is claimed on the replacement of a qualifying business asset, taper relief operates on the ultimate disposal of the new asset by reference only to the period for which that asset has been held. (Revenue Press Release IR 16, 17 March 1998). Where the replacement is a wasting asset, so that the gain is postponed rather than rolled over against the cost of the new asset (see 55.7 ROLLOVER RELIEF), the rules at 60.12 above apply on the postponed gain being brought into charge.

It is implicit in the legislation that in the event of a rollover relief claim the gain to be deducted from the cost of the new asset is the *untapered* gain arising on the old asset; as stated in 60.2 above, taper relief is given only on gains left in charge after all reliefs other than the annual exempt amount have been taken into account.

60.15 SHARES AND SECURITIES

In order to apply taper relief, it is clearly necessary to be able to match disposals with acquisitions of shares or securities where more than one acquisition and/or disposal is made of shares etc. of the same class in the same company. Consequently, the 'share pooling rules' which previously operated are abolished for acquisitions after 5 April 1998 and new identification rules introduced in their place. See 59 SHARES AND SECURITIES—IDENTIFICATION RULES.

Shares acquired on or after 17 March 1998 but before 6 April 1998 and added to a 'section 104 holding' (of shares of the same class in the same company) in existence before 17 March 1998 are themselves regarded as acquired before 17 March 1998 and thus may qualify for the 'bonus year' addition in 60.2 above. This follows from the pre-6 April 1998 rules at 59.3, 59.4 SHARES AND SECURITIES—IDENTIFICATION RULES. (Revenue Booklet CGT Reform: The 1998 Finance Act, para 2.18).

60.16 ANTI-AVOIDANCE RULES

Periods of limited exposure to fluctuations in value of an asset. An anti-avoidance rule applies where the period after 5 April 1998 for which an asset has been held includes a period during which the person making the disposal (or a 'relevant predecessor' of his) had limited exposure to fluctuations in the value of the asset. Such a period does not count for the purposes of taper relief and is left out of account in determining the qualifying holding period (see 60.2 above) and treated as not comprised in the relevant period of ownership (see 60.8 above).

The times when a person is taken to have had such limited exposure are all times while he held the asset when a 'transaction' entered into at any time (whether or not after 5 April 1998) by him (or by a 'relevant predecessor' of his) had the effect that, without disposing of the asset, he had relinquished economic ownership of it; in other words that he was neither exposed to any 'substantial' extent to risk of loss from fluctuations in the asset's value nor able to enjoy to any 'substantial' extent any opportunities to benefit from such fluctuations. '*Transaction*' includes any agreement, arrangement or understanding, whether or not legally enforceable, and also includes a series of transactions. The following transactions are excluded from these provisions:

- any policy of insurance against loss and/or damage to the asset, being one which the person concerned might reasonably have been expected to enter into; and
- any transaction having effect in relation to fluctuations only insofar as they result from fluctuations in the value of foreign currencies.

A '*relevant predecessor*' of the person disposing of the asset, or of a relevant predecessor of his, is a person who held that asset at a time falling within the period which is taken to be the period (including for this purpose any time before 6 April 1998) for which the asset has been held at the time of disposal. Typically, it will be the spouse of the person making the disposal.

[*TCGA 1992, Sch A1 para 10, para 22(1); FA 1998, s 121(2)(4), Sch 20*].

For the purposes of the above provisions, '*substantial*' is taken by the Revenue to mean greater than 20%, so that the provisions will apply where a person divests himself of at least 80% of the exposure to fluctuations in value. (Revenue Booklet CGT Reform: The 1998 Finance Act, para 2.54).

Whilst reserving their position on complex or non-commercial arrangements, the Revenue have stated that the above provisions will not be applied where loan notes (other than qualifying corporate bonds) are issued in exchange for shares as part of the normal commercial arrangements on a company takeover (to which *TCGA 1992, s 135* will normally apply — see 58.8 SHARES AND SECURITIES), even if the loan notes are underwritten by third party guarantee as part of those arrangements. (Revenue Booklet CGT Reform: The 1998 Finance Act, para 2.56).

For a brief example of circumstances in which the above provisions would apply, involving put and call options, see Revenue Booklet CGT Reform: The 1998 Finance Act, para 2.57.

60.17 **Close company share ownership: change of activity by the company.** Where there is a disposal of shares in (or securities of) a close company (as defined by *ICTA 1988, ss 414, 415*) and the inclusive period between the 'relevant time' and the time of disposal includes at least one 'relevant change of activity' involving that company, so much of the period after 5 April 1998 for which the shares have been held at the time of disposal as falls before that change, or the latest such change, does not count for the purposes of taper relief. It is left out of account in determining the qualifying holding period (see 60.2 above) and treated as not comprised in the relevant period of ownership (see 60.8 above). Where the shares were acquired before 17 March 1998, the one-year addition in computing the qualifying holding period (see 60.2 above) does not apply. The stated purpose of these provisions is to prevent any increase in taper relief that could otherwise be achieved by transferring to a close company an asset held for a shorter period than the shares in the company, and then selling those shares.

The '*relevant time*' is the beginning of the period after 5 April 1998 for which the shares have been held at the time of their disposal. A '*relevant change of activity*' occurs at either of the times given below.

(1) Where the close company or any of its '51% subsidiaries' begins at any time to carry on a 'trade' and neither it nor any of its 51% subsidiaries was carrying on a trade immediately before that time, there is a relevant change of activity at that time. For this purpose, a company's '*51% subsidiary*' is a company which, under *TCGA 1992, s 170(7)*, is an effective 51% subsidiary of the first company for the purposes of *TCGA 1992, ss 170–181* (see 13.11 COMPANIES and note that the change in the residence requirement therein mentioned has effect for this purpose after 31 March 2000). '*Trade*' is defined as in 60.4 above, but does not include a trade which is merely incidental to any non-trading activities carried on by the company in question or another company in the group.

(2) Where

- at the time of disposal of the shares the close company was carrying on a business of holding or making investments, and
- there has been any occasion falling either within the period of twelve months ending with the disposal or within any period of twelve months ending after the relevant time (see above) when it was not carrying on that business or when the size of that business was small by comparison with its size at the end of that period,

a relevant change of activity is to be taken to have occurred immediately after the latest such occasion before the time of the disposal. For this purpose, the size of a business at any time is determined by reference to aggregate acquisition costs for assets held at that time for the purposes of the business. In determining both whether a company is carrying on a business of holding or making investments and the size of that business, the activities of the company and all its 51% subsidiaries (defined as above) are taken together, but the following activities (of any of those companies) are not to be regarded as included in such a business

- the holding of shares in a 51% subsidiary,
- the making of loans to an 'associated company' or to a participator (as defined by *ICTA 1988, s 417(1)* and whether in the company making the loan or in an associated company), or
- placing money on deposit.

For this purpose, two companies are '*associated companies*' at any time if at that time or at any time in the previous twelve months one has controlled the other or they have been under common control.

[*TCGA 1992, Sch A1 para 11; FA 1998, s 121(2)(4), Sch 20; FA 2000, Sch 29 para 36*].

The acquisition by a company of a shareholding in a 'joint venture company' (see 60.5A above), such that the acquiring company falls within 60.5A(*a*) or (*b*) above, is not to be treated as a relevant change of activity. [*TCGA 1992, Sch A1 para 23(9); FA 2000, s 67(6)*].

For the purposes of (2) above, the mere existence of investments does not necessarily mean that there is a business of making (or presumably of holding) investments. In particular, the Revenue do not regard any of the following activities carried out by a trading company as amounting in themselves to a business of making investments

- investing surplus profits in quoted shares or securities where there is a reasonable possibility of those funds being needed to finance trading requirements, including major expansion,
- letting part of the trading premises,
- letting properties no longer required for the trade and intended to be sold eventually, or
- subletting property where it would be impractical to assign or surrender the lease.

(Revenue Booklet CGT Reform: The 1998 Finance Act, para 2.66).

Close company share ownership: value shifting. Where there is a disposal of shares in (or securities of), or rights over, a close company (as defined by *ICTA 1988, ss 414, 415*) and the inclusive period between the relevant time (defined as above) and the time of disposal includes at least one 'relevant shift of value' involving those shares (or rights), so much of the period after 5 April 1998 for which the shares (or rights) have been held at the time of disposal as falls before that shift, or the latest such shift, does not count for the purposes of taper relief, with the same consequences as above.

A '*relevant shift of value*' involving any shares (or rights) is to be taken to have occurred whenever

- a person having control of the close company exercises his control so that value passed into the shares (or rights) out of a 'relevant holding'; or
- effect was given to any other 'transaction' by virtue of which value passed into the shares (or rights) out of a relevant holding.

A relevant shift of value is disregarded for these purposes if the value passing is insignificant or the shift of value took place at a time when the qualifying holding period (see 60.2 above) for the relevant holding was at least as long as that for the shares (or rights).

A '*relevant holding*', in relation to value passing into shares in (or rights over) a company, is any holding by

- the person who, following the exercise of control or other transaction, held the shares (or rights), or
- any person connected with that person (see 14 CONNECTED PERSONS),

of any shares in (or rights over) the company or in (or over) a company under the control of the same person(s) as that company.

'*Transaction*' includes any agreement, arrangement or understanding, whether or not legally enforceable, and also includes a series of transactions.

[*TCGA 1992, Sch A1 para 12, para 22(1); FA 1998, s 121(2)(4), Sch 20*].

See Revenue Booklet CGT Reform: The 1998 Finance Act, para 2.73 for an example of the application of these provisions.

60.18 **MISCELLANEOUS**

Assets derived from other assets.

Where

- assets have merged,
- an asset has divided or otherwise changed its nature, or
- different rights or interests in or over any asset have been created or extinguished at different times,

and the value of any asset disposed of is thus derived from one or more other assets previously acquired into the same ownership, the asset disposed of is treated for the purposes of taper relief as having been acquired at the earliest time at which any asset from which its value is derived was acquired. For the purpose only of determining whether the asset disposed of was a business asset (see 60.4 above) at a time when another asset from which its value is derived was owned by the person making the disposal, that other asset is deemed to be, or to be comprised in, the asset disposed of.

[*TCGA 1992, Sch A1 para 14; FA 1998, s 121(2)(4), Sch 20*].

For taper relief rules for **options**, see 17.10 DISPOSAL. For rules concerning **Lloyd's ancillary trust funds**, see 63.1 UNDERWRITERS.

60.19 **Property settled by a company.** Where an asset is placed into trust by a company which has an interest in the trust, a gain on a disposal of that asset by the trustees would, in the absence of any special rule, qualify for taper relief, whereas if the asset had been retained by the company it would not so qualify (but would be reduced or extinguished by indexation relief computed beyond April 1998 — see 26.1 INDEXATION). As a compromise, such a disposal is kept within the taper relief provisions but the relief is restricted to the rate applicable to non-business assets.

The detailed rules prevent any part of a gain accruing to trustees on the disposal of an asset from being treated as a gain on disposal of a business asset (see 60.4 above) if the settlor is a company which has an interest in the settlement, i.e. may benefit from it (as defined), at the time of the disposal. The provisions apply equally if an associated company (as defined) may benefit from the trust, but do not apply at all unless the company or an associated company is within the charge to corporation tax on chargeable gains for the accounting period in which the chargeable gain accrues.

[*TCGA 1992, Sch A1 para 17; FA 1998, s 121(2)(4), Sch 20*].

60.20 **Shares acquired in reconstruction of mutual businesses etc.** Where shares are issued to members on the reconstruction of a 'mutual company' and otherwise fall, by virtue of *TCGA 1992, s 136* (see 58.10 SHARES AND SECURITIES), to be treated in the hands of a person to whom they are issued as having been acquired at the same time as the interest for which they are exchanged, the shares are treated for taper relief purposes as having been acquired at the time they were issued to the person concerned and not at any earlier time. A '*mutual company*' means a mutual insurance company (i.e. an insurance company within *Insurance Companies Act 1982, s 96(1)* carrying on a business without having a share capital) or a company of another description carrying on a business on a mutual basis. A similar rule applies where, in consequence of the incorporation of a registered friendly society (see 21.42 EXEMPTIONS AND RELIEFS), a member of the registered society (or branch) becomes a member of the incorporated society (or branch).

[*TCGA 1992, Sch A1 para 18; FA 1998, s 121(2)(4), Sch 20*].

Gains in connection with reorganisations of mutual businesses. A gain is not eligible for taper relief if it accrues on a disposal in connection with a 'relevant reorganisation' or on anything which, in a case in which capital sums are received under or in connection with a relevant reorganisation, falls under *TCGA 1992, s 22* (see 17.7 DISPOSAL) to be treated as a disposal. A '*relevant reorganisation*' means

- any '*scheme of reconstruction or amalgamation*' (as defined by *TCGA 1992, s 136(2)*) applying to a mutual company (defined as above);
- the transfer of the whole of a building society's business to a company (see 58.26 SHARES AND SECURITIES);
- the incorporation of a registered friendly society (see 21.42 EXEMPTIONS AND RELIEFS).

[*TCGA 1992, s 214C; FA 1998, s 121(3)(4), Sch 21 para 7*].

Thus where, for example, a cash bonus is received by a member on the occurrence of any of the above events, no taper relief can be applied to the resulting gain.

60.21 **Apportionments.** Any apportionment needed for the purposes of taper relief is to be made on a 'just and reasonable' basis and on the assumption that amounts accrue evenly over a period. [*TCGA 1992, Sch A1 para 21; FA 1998, s 121(2)(4), Sch 20*].

Provision of assets. References to the acquisition of an asset which was provided, rather than acquired, by the person making the disposal are references to its provision.

Part disposals. In relation to part disposals (see 17.6 DISPOSAL), references to an asset disposed of are to be taken as references to an asset of which there is a part disposal.

[*TCGA 1992, Sch A1 para 22(3)(4); FA 1998, s 121(2)(4), Sch 20*].

61 Time Limits—Fixed Dates

Cross-references. See also 12.5 CLAIMS; 62 TIME LIMITS—MISCELLANEOUS.

Scope of chapter. This chapter lists fixed date time limits (for capital gains tax) falling in the **twelve months to 30 September 2001**. It also notes time limits for corporation tax on chargeable gains where these are dependent upon the company's accounting date (see also TOLLEY'S CORPORATION TAX).

Self-assessment. Under self-assessment from 1996/97 onwards (for capital gains tax), time limits which previously operated by reference to 5 April now operate by reference to 31 January. Generally speaking, deadlines have been brought forward by approximately two months. For example, where action previously had to be taken within two years after the end of a tax year (i.e. where that year was 1995/96 or an earlier year), it must now be taken (where the tax year in question is 1996/97 or a subsequent year) on or before the first anniversary of 31 January following the end of the tax year. Similarly, six-year time limits are reduced to approximately five years ten months (but a six-year limit continues to be relevant where action is to be taken in respect of 1995/96 or an earlier year and no shorter time limit is specified — see 61.6 below). This chapter concentrates on CGT time limits — for other time limits and for key dates under self-assessment, see TOLLEY'S INCOME TAX and TOLLEY'S CORPORATION TAX.

Time limits for companies are generally unaffected by self-assessment.

Exercise of Board's discretion. The legislation dealing with certain claims and elections allows the time limit to be extended at the discretion of the Board of Inland Revenue but where this is not the case the Board may make an extension by exercising its care and management powers as allowed under *TMA 1970, s 1*. Cases in which it would do so are limited but there would be a presumption in favour of admitting a late claim where there had been a relevant error on the part of the Revenue, and the claim is made shortly after the error has been drawn to the taxpayer's attention; where the taxpayer has given clear notice of his intention to claim, but before the time limit expires he has not completed any statutory requirement or specified the claim in sufficient detail; or where the reason for the delay in making the claim was clearly beyond the taxpayer's control (e.g. because he—or in the case of a company the only individual who had the relevant information and experience—was seriously ill and there was no-one else who could reasonably be expected to stand in his shoes). The same stance seems to be taken as regards the withdrawal of elections that are stated to be irrevocable. Claims that have not become final may be withdrawn (even after the time for making a claim has expired), and the same applies to elections that are not irrevocable (Revenue Capital Gains Manual CG 13800–13861).

61.1 TIME LIMITS OF ONE YEAR OR LESS

(*a*) **30 September 2000** for action in respect of **1999/2000**.

Self-assessment. If a taxpayer does not wish to compute his own liability to income tax and/or CGT, he must file his tax return on or before 30 September following the year of assessment to which it relates. See 54.6 RETURNS.

(*b*) **5 October 2000** for action in respect of **1999/2000**.

Chargeability to tax. A person chargeable to CGT for a year of assessment must, unless he has received a tax return for completion, notify the Revenue, within six months after the end of that year, that he is so chargeable. See 54.2 RETURNS.

(*c*) **Nine months from end of company accounting period.**

Payment of tax. Payment of corporation tax in respect of chargeable gains is normally required by the day following the expiry of nine months from the end of the accounting period if interest on unpaid tax is to be avoided. ('Large' companies must pay by instalments for accounting periods ending on or after 1 July 1999.) See 46.2 PAYMENT OF TAX.

(*d*) **31 January 2001** for action in respect of **1999/2000**.

(i) *Returns.* A person other than a company who has received a self-assessment tax return for completion must generally file it on or before 31 January following the year of assessment to which it relates. See 54.3 RETURNS.

(ii) *Payment of tax.* CGT is normally due on or before 31 January following the year of assessment. See 46.1 PAYMENT OF TAX.

(*e*) **5 April 2001** for action in respect of **1999/2000**.

(i) *Claims following late assessments.* A claim (including a supplementary claim) which could not have been allowed but for the making of an assessment to CGT after the year of assessment to which it relates, may be made at any time before the end of the year of assessment following that in which the assessment was made. See 12.5 CLAIMS.

(ii) *Claims following discovery assessments.* Where a discovery assessment not involving fraudulent or negligent conduct is made, a relevant claim, election etc. can be made, revoked or varied within a year of the end of the year of assessment (or company accounting period) in which the assessment was made. See 12.5 CLAIMS.

(iii) *Tax over-repaid.* This (and any associated excess repayment supplement) may be recovered by the end of the year of assessment (or company accounting period) following that in which the repayment was made. See 46.10 PAYMENT OF TAX. This deadline may be extended in the event of a Revenue enquiry into a self-assessment tax return. See 56.31 SELF-ASSESSMENT.

(iv) *Capital payments made by an overseas resident settlement.* Broadly, trustees of overseas resident settlements must distribute capital gains no later than the end of the year of assessment following that in which the gains arose if a supplementary CGT charge under *TCGA 1992, s 91* on UK resident and domiciled beneficiaries is to be avoided. See 43.14 OFFSHORE SETTLEMENTS for the detailed rules, including those for matching capital payments with gains.

(*f*) **Twelve months from end of company accounting period.**

(i) *Chargeability to tax.* A company chargeable to corporation tax for an accounting period must, unless it has received notice to file a return for that period, notify the Revenue, within twelve months after the end of that period, that it is so chargeable. See 54.11 RETURNS.

(ii) *Corporation tax returns.* A company must generally comply with a notice to make a corporation tax return within twelve months of the end of the relevant accounting period or, if later, within three months of service of the notice. See 54.11 RETURNS.

61.2 ONE-YEAR TEN-MONTH (APPROX.) TIME LIMITS (AND EQUIVALENT TWO-YEAR TIME LIMITS FOR COMPANIES)

i.e. for CGT, action in respect of **1998/99** must be taken on or before **31 January 2001** (and for the purposes of corporation tax on chargeable gains, where applicable, action must be taken within two years after the end of the accounting period in question).

(*a*) **Quoted shares and securities held on 6 April 1965**. Election for adoption of 6 April 1965 values for quoted securities (within either of the two categories) that were held on that date, where the first relevant disposal since 19 March 1968 took place during a particular year of assessment (or company accounting period) must be made on or before the first anniversary of 31 January following that year of assessment (or within two years after the end of that accounting period). With respect to disposals after 5 April 1985 (31 March 1985 for companies) the foregoing is to be read as if '5 April 1985' or '31 March 1985' (as relevant) was substituted for '19 March 1968'. See 7.3 ASSETS HELD ON 6 APRIL 1965. An election is only relevant if the rules for ASSETS HELD ON 31 MARCH 1982 (8) do not apply.

(*b*) **Miscellaneous disposals of assets held on 6 April 1965**. Election for adoption of 6 April 1965 value of miscellaneous assets (apart from quoted investments and UK land disposed of for a consideration including development value) disposed of must be made on or before the first anniversary of 31 January following the year of assessment (or within two years after the end of the company accounting period) in which the disposal was made. See 7.10 ASSETS HELD ON 6 APRIL 1965. An election is only relevant if the rules for ASSETS HELD ON 31 MARCH 1982 (8) do not apply.

(*c*) **Assets held on, and gains arising before, 31 March 1982**. The latest time for making an irrevocable election for universal re-basing at 31 March 1982 is the first anniversary of 31 January following the year of assessment (or two years after the end of the company accounting period) in which 'the first relevant disposal' occurs. See 8.3 ASSETS HELD ON 31 MARCH 1982. A claim for 50% relief in taxing deferred charges on gains before 31 March 1982 must be made on or before the first anniversary of 31 January following the year of assessment (or within two years after the end of the company accounting period) in which the disposal or deferred gain in question occurs or accrues. See 8.12 ASSETS HELD ON 31 MARCH 1982.

(*d*) **Loss relief for subscribing individual shareholders.** A claim for a loss arising in a year of assessment on the disposal of qualifying unlisted shares by a subscriber to be set against his income of that year or the preceding year must be made on or before the first anniversary of 31 January following the year of loss. See 39.13 LOSSES.

(*e*) **Furnished holiday accommodation.** A claim for 'averaging' of let periods of holiday accommodation must be made on or before the first anniversary of 31 January following the relevant year of assessment (or within two years after the end of the relevant company accounting period). See 22.1 FURNISHED HOLIDAY ACCOMMODATION.

(*f*) **Retirement relief**. Certain elections must be made on or before the first anniversary of 31 January following the year of assessment in which the disposal occurs. See 53.3, 53.5, 53.8, 53.10 RETIREMENT RELIEF covering, respectively, relief on ill-health grounds, disapplication of normal rules on a reorganisation of share capital, the same disapplication but in the case of a disposal by trustees, and aggregation of a spouse's interest in a business.

(*g*) **Relief for trading losses to be set against chargeable gains of a person other than a company.** A claim to set off a trading loss against chargeable gains of the same or the preceding year of assessment, which can normally be made only in conjunction with a claim under *ICTA 1988, s 380* against income, must be made on or before the first anniversary of 31 January following the year of assessment in which the loss is incurred. See 39.7 LOSSES.

(*h*) **Relief for post-cessation expenditure of a trade to be set against chargeable gains of a person other than a company.** A claim to set off excess post-cessation expenditure of a trade against chargeable gains, which can be made only in conjunction with a claim under *ICTA 1988, s 109A* against income, must be made on or before the first anniversary of 31 January following the year of assessment in which the expenditure is incurred. See 39.7 LOSSES.

(*j*) **Amendment of tax return and self-assessment.** A person other than a company has up to twelve months after the filing date (which itself is normally 31 January following the year of assessment) to notify an amendment to his tax return and self-assessment (other than in a Revenue enquiry case). See 54.7 RETURNS.

(*k*) **Appropriation of asset to trading stock.** An election may be made to treat the transfer as, effectively, taking place at cost instead of market value. See 6.3 ASSETS (and note that for companies, where the accounting period in question ends before 1 July 1999, a six-year time limit applies; thereafter, a two-year time limit applies).

61.3 TWO-YEAR TIME LIMITS

i.e. for CGT, where applicable, action in respect of **1998/99** must be taken by **5 April 2001** (and for the purposes of corporation tax on chargeable gains, action must be taken within two years after the end of the accounting period in question).

(*a*) **Relief for assets of negligible value, loans to traders becoming irrecoverable and loans to traders evidenced by qualifying corporate bonds.** Broadly, a claim to this effect may be made within two years after the end of the year of assessment (or company accounting period) in which the relevant date falls. See 39.9, 39.10, 39.11 LOSSES. (The last-mentioned relief is abolished for loans made after 16 March 1998 — see 39.11 LOSSES.)

(*b*) **Loss relief for subscribing investment companies.** A claim for a loss arising on the sale of qualifying unlisted shares by a subscribing investment company to be set against income (or surplus franked investment income of accounting periods beginning before 2 July 1997) must be made within two years after the end of the accounting period in which the loss arises. See 39.15 LOSSES.

(*c*) **Amendment of company tax return and self-assessment.** A company has up to twelve months after the filing date (which itself is normally twelve months after the end of the relevant accounting period) to notify an amendment to its tax return and self-assessment. [*FA 1998, Sch 18 para 15*].

(*d*) **Groups of companies: pre-entry losses.** Certain elections have to be made within two years of the end of the accounting period in which a loss or gain (as appropriate) is made. See 13.28–13.30 COMPANIES.

61.4 THREE-YEAR TIME LIMITS

i.e. action in respect of **1997/98** must be taken by **5 April 2001**.

Charities. Where property ceases to be held on charitable trusts in circumstances giving rise to a deemed disposal by the trustees, an assessment on the cumulative gains must be made within three years of the end of the tax year in which the cessation occurred. See 10.3 CHARITIES.

61.5 THREE-YEAR TEN-MONTH (APPROX.) TIME LIMITS

i.e. action in respect of **1996/97** must be taken on or before **31 January 2001**.

Deceased persons. Assessments on gains arising or accruing before death must be made on the deceased's personal representatives on or before the third anniversary of 31 January following the year of assessment in which death occurred. Assessments to recoup loss of tax due to the deceased's fraudulent or negligent conduct can be made, on or before that date, for any year of assessment ending not earlier than six years before the death. See 5.5 ASSESSMENTS, 56.27 SELF-ASSESSMENT.

61.6 **SIX-YEAR TIME LIMITS**

i.e. for CGT, where applicable, action in respect of **1994/95** must be taken by **5 April 2001** (and for the purposes of corporation tax on chargeable gains, where applicable, action must be taken within six years after the end of the accounting period in question).

The more important six-year time limits are as follows.

(*a*) **Error or mistake claims.** See 12.7 CLAIMS.

(*b*) **Raising assessments** other than in cases of fraudulent or negligent conduct. See 5.5 ASSESSMENTS.

(*c*) **Claim against double assessment** where the same person has been assessed 'for the same cause' in the same year. See 5.3 ASSESSMENTS.

(*d*) **Relief against double taxation.** See 18 DOUBLE TAX RELIEF.

(*e*) **Relief for unremittable overseas gains.** See 44.5 OVERSEAS MATTERS.

(*f*) **Disposals by way of gift etc. (election for tax to be paid by instalments).** See 46.6 PAYMENT OF TAX.

(*g*) **Capital distributions in respect of shares etc.** Where allowable expenditure on shares etc. is less than the amount of a capital distribution, the taxpayer may make an election to set off all that expenditure against the distribution. See 58.14 SHARES AND SECURITIES.

(*h*) **Extension of private residence exemption to a residence occupied by a dependent relative on or before 5 April 1988.** See 48.7 PRIVATE RESIDENCES.

(*j*) **Small part disposals of land (claim for disposal not to be treated as such).** See 36.8 and 36.10 LAND.

(*k*) **Hold-over relief** for gifts of business assets and assets on which inheritance tax is chargeable etc. See 25.1–25.8 HOLD-OVER RELIEFS.

(*l*) **Rollover relief.** See 55.2 ROLLOVER RELIEF and note that the period for claiming relief starts with the later of the end of the year of assessment or company accounting period in which the disposal takes place and the end of the year of assessment or company accounting period in which the new assets are acquired.

(*m*) **Relief on compulsory acquisition of land.** See 36.11 LAND and note also that proceeds must not be invested in land which would be exempt from CGT under the private residence rules on a disposal of it within six years of acquisition.

(*n*) **Reinvestment relief.** See 50.2 REINVESTMENT RELIEF and note that the period for claiming relief starts with the later of the end of the year of assessment in which the disposal takes place and the end of the year of assessment in which the qualifying investment is acquired.

(*o*) **EIS deferral relief** (for gains otherwise accruing after 28 November 1994). See 20.14 ENTERPRISE INVESTMENT SCHEME (AND BES) and note that the period for claiming relief starts with the later of the end of the year of assessment in which the disposal takes place and the end of the year of assessment in which the qualifying investment (i.e. a subscription for EIS shares) is acquired.

(*p*) **Appropriation of asset to trading stock.** An election may be made to treat the transfer as, effectively, taking place at cost instead of market value. See 6.3 ASSETS (and note that this time limit has been considerably shortened for CGT where the period of account ends in 1996/97 or a subsequent year and for corporation tax where the accounting period ends on or after 1 July 1999).

61.7 OTHER ACTION BEFORE 6 APRIL 2001

Tax-loss selling. Appropriate disposals should be made if it is desired to realise capital losses to set off against chargeable gains in 2000/01. See 26 INDEXATION; 39 LOSSES; 60.2 TAPER RELIEF; and, with regard to companies, 13.40 COMPANIES.

Use of annual exemption. Action should be taken so as to utilise the CGT annual exemption for 2000/01. See 2.5 ANNUAL RATES AND EXEMPTIONS.

'Bed and breakfasting' of shares and securities, i.e. the sale and subsequent repurchase of shares etc. where the seller and buyer are *not* the same person, e.g. disposal by one spouse, repurchase by the other. See 59.2 SHARES AND SECURITIES — IDENTIFICATION RULES.

Disposing of assets prior to tax year of resumed UK-residence. Where an individual plans to resume residence in the UK in 2001/02 following a period of *temporary* non-residence (such that the split year treatment under ESC D2 will not be available for the year of return), any impending disposals need to be made before 6 April 2001 to avoid CGT. Gains on disposals in the tax year of return, whether made before or after the arrival date in the UK, are liable to CGT. See 52.3 RESIDENCE AND DOMICILE. (Note that where the date of *departure* from the UK fell after 16 March 1998, gains accrued during a period of temporary non-UK residence are in any case chargeable on resumption of UK-residence — see 44.4 OVERSEAS MATTERS).

61.8 LLOYD'S UNDERWRITERS

Due to delay in establishing the results from Lloyd's underwriting, the Revenue may, in certain circumstances, extend the time limits for making elections as prescribed otherwise. Some time limits were extended statutorily for years of assessment up to and including 1994/95. See 63.1 and 63.5 UNDERWRITERS AT LLOYD'S, and for full details as regards the years 1992/93 to 1994/95 inclusive, see *SI 1995 No 352, Regs 14, 15.*

62 Time Limits—Miscellaneous

Cross-reference. See 61 TIME LIMITS—FIXED DATES (in particular, the head-note dealing with the Revenue's practice regarding late claims and elections which apply equally here).

Note. Time limits other than by reference to the end of a year of assessment or company accounting period are set out below.

62.1 TIME LIMITS OF ONE YEAR OR LESS

(*a*) **Thirty days**

(i) For appeals against assessments, formal notice of appeal must be lodged within thirty days of the date of issue of the assessment. See 4.4 APPEALS. For postponement of tax, see 35.3 INTEREST AND SURCHARGES ON UNPAID TAX and 46 PAYMENT OF TAX.

(ii) For appeals to the High Court, written notice requiring the Commissioners to state and sign a case must be sent to their Clerk within thirty days of the determination. The case stated must be transmitted to the High Court within thirty days of its receipt. See 4.9 APPEALS.

(iii) Returns of income and chargeable gains for 1995/96 and earlier years ought strictly to be completed within thirty days of issue. See 54.9 RETURNS.

(iv) For 1995/96 and earlier years, capital gains tax generally becomes due and payable thirty days after the issue of the notice of assessment (if later than 1 December following the end of the year of assessment) and interest then begins to run. Interest may run on tax which is yet to be due and payable. See 35.1–35.5 INTEREST AND SURCHARGES ON UNPAID TAX and 46 PAYMENT OF TAX.

(v) A notice specifying the apportionment of a reduction in tax liability involving more than one period or person, in certain discovery cases, must be given within thirty days of the inspector issuing a notice apportioning it. See 12.5 CLAIMS.

(*b*) **Three months**

(i) Appeals against a decision of the Board relating to residence, ordinary residence or domicile. See 52.8 RESIDENCE AND DOMICILE.

(ii) Certain reliefs in relation to a disposal of shares in a 'controlled foreign company' must be claimed within three months of the later of the end of the relevant accounting period and the date that an assessment made on the claimant company in respect of the apportioned profits of the controlled foreign company becomes final and conclusive. See 44.7 OVERSEAS MATTERS.

(iii) Applications for judicial review must be made within three months of the date when the grounds for application arose. See 4.10 APPEALS.

(iv) Certain particulars of a settlement with a foreign element etc. must be supplied within three months of the creation of it. See 43.22 OFFSHORE SETTLEMENTS.

(*c*) **Six months**

In respect of the form of rollover relief available on a disposal of shares to an approved employee share ownership plan or, before 6 April 2001, to an employee share ownership trust, the disposal consideration must be used to acquire replacement assets within six months (or longer period in certain cases) of the disposal. See 19.13, 19.25 EMPLOYEE SHARE SCHEMES.

(*d*) **Twelve months**

(i) To qualify for rollover relief an acquisition must be made twelve months before the associated disposal (or three years after). See 55.1 ROLLOVER RELIEF. This applies also to the general relief for compulsory acquisition of land (see 36.11 LAND).

(ii) Where, within twelve months of receipt, a capital sum, received as compensation is applied in replacing an asset lost or destroyed, a claim may be made for the deemed disposal arising on the loss etc. to be treated as made for a 'no gain, no loss' consideration. See 17.9 DISPOSAL.

(iii) Certain particulars of a settlement with a foreign element etc. must be supplied within twelve months of certain events. See 43.22 OFFSHORE SETTLEMENTS.

(iv) Acquisition of ordinary shares of an approved venture capital trust, against which the deferral of a capital gain can be claimed, must take place within a qualifying period of twelve months before the chargeable event giving rise to the gain and twelve months after the chargeable event. See 65.10 VENTURE CAPITAL TRUSTS.

(v) Acquisition of EIS shares must, for the purpose of EIS capital gains deferral relief, take place within twelve months before the chargeable event giving rise to the gain to be deferred (or three years after). See 20.10 ENTERPRISE INVESTMENT SCHEME (AND BES).

62.2 TWO-YEAR TIME LIMITS

(*a*) **Only or main residence**. The election by individuals with more than one private residence must be made within two years after the acquisition of the second residence. Subsequent notice of variation must be given within two years after the date from which it is to take effect. See 48.5 PRIVATE RESIDENCES.

(*b*) **Family arrangements and disclaimers after death** must be made within two years of the death. An election for a *variation* to have effect must be made within six months of the making of the instrument. See 16.6 DEATH.

(*c*) **Distribution of gains by overseas companies.** Capital gains tax paid by a participator on that part of the gain apportioned to him can be used to offset income or capital gains tax payable in respect of the distribution if the gain is distributed within two years of the time it accrues. See 44.6 OVERSEAS MATTERS.

(*d*) **Unpaid corporation tax.** Where a company fails to pay corporation tax on its chargeable gains within six months of the due date, any of that tax which is recoverable from certain third parties (including members or former group members and shareholders) must be assessed within two years of the due and payable date. See 13.6, 13.7, 13.18 COMPANIES.

(*e*) **Groups of companies.** A group company can be liable for unpaid corporation tax on a chargeable gain arising from the disposal by another group member of an asset owned by the first-mentioned company at any time in the two years preceding the time the gain accrued. See 13.18 COMPANIES.

(*f*) **Know-how.** A joint election for know-how not to be treated as goodwill must be made within two years of the disposal. See 6.4 ASSETS.

(*g*) **Company ceasing to be UK resident etc: postponement of charge on deemed disposal.** Subject to certain conditions an election may be made by the company concerned and the principal company within two years of the cessation of UK residence etc. so that postponement is obtained. If any part of the postponed gain becomes chargeable on the principal company, it and the company concerned can elect within two years of the time the gain becomes chargeable that any unrelieved capital losses of the company be set against the gain. See 44.12 OVERSEAS MATTERS.

(*h*) **Transfer of UK branch or agency of overseas resident company to UK resident company.** Subject to conditions a form of hold-over relief is available on a joint claim within two years after the end of the accounting period of the transferee company in which the transfer was made. See 44.3 OVERSEAS MATTERS.

(*j*) **Employee share ownership plan: rollover relief.** In respect of the form of rollover relief available on a disposal of shares, other than by a company, to an approved employee share ownership trust, the relief must be claimed within the two years beginning with the acquisition of the replacement assets. See 19.14 EMPLOYEE SHARE SCHEMES.

(*k*) **Employee share ownership trust: rollover relief.** In respect of the form of rollover relief available on a disposal of shares before 6 April 2001 to an employee share ownership trust, the relief must be claimed within two years of the acquisition of replacement assets. See 19.25 EMPLOYEE SHARE SCHEMES.

62.3 THREE-YEAR TIME LIMITS

(*a*) **Rollover relief** is only available if the acquisition is made within three years after the disposal (or twelve months before). See 55.1 ROLLOVER RELIEF. This applies also to the general relief for compulsory acquisition of land (see 36.11 LAND).

(*b*) **Reinvestment relief** can be withdrawn if certain events occur within three years of the acquisition of shares whose acquisition value has been reduced by the relief. See 50.1, 50.2, 50.9, 50.11 and 50.13 REINVESTMENT RELIEF.

(*c*) **Acquisition of EIS shares** must, for the purpose of EIS capital gains deferral relief, take place within three years after the chargeable event giving rise to the gain to be deferred (or twelve months before). See 20.10 ENTERPRISE INVESTMENT SCHEME (AND BES).

(*d*) **Company ceasing to be UK resident and non-resident company.** Any tax due by a company ceasing to be UK resident and not paid within six months of becoming payable can, within three years of the amount being determined, be recovered from a person who is, or was in the twelve months before residence ceased, a member of the same group or a controlling director. Similar provisions apply to non-UK resident companies trading in the UK. See 44.13 OVERSEAS MATTERS.

62.4 FIVE-YEAR TIME LIMITS

(*a*) A gain deferred by means of **EIS capital gains deferral relief** becomes chargeable if the investor becomes neither resident nor ordinarily resident in the UK within the five years beginning with the issue of the EIS shares (except in certain cases of temporary working abroad). See 20.10 ENTERPRISE INVESTMENT SCHEME (AND BES).

(*b*) A gain deferred by means of **VCT capital gains deferral relief** becomes chargeable if the investor becomes neither resident nor ordinarily resident in the UK within the five years beginning with his acquisition of the VCT shares (except in certain cases of temporary working abroad). See 65.10 VENTURE CAPITAL TRUSTS.

62.5 SIX-YEAR TIME LIMITS

(*a*) **Intra-group transfers: company ceasing to be a member of a group.** If a company leaves a group within six years of the transfer to it of a capital asset by another member of the group, it will be liable on the market value of the asset at the time of transfer less the 'no gain, no loss' transfer price. See 13.19 COMPANIES. Similar provisions apply where, after 16 March 1998, the company which acquired such an asset becomes an investment trust or venture capital trust. See 13.21, 13.22 COMPANIES.

(*b*) **Company ceasing to be UK resident etc: postponement of charge on deemed disposal.** If within six years after the cessation of residence etc. the company disposes of assets held at that time, the whole or the appropriate part of the postponed gain (insofar as not already so treated) is deemed to accrue to the principal company. See 44.12 OVERSEAS MATTERS.

63 Underwriters at Lloyd's

See also Tolley's Taxation of Lloyd's Underwriters.

63.1 1992/93 AND SUBSEQUENT YEARS

Individual underwriters. For 1992/93 (subject to special transitional provisions which allow for the 'closing' of an underwriting year (i.e. the calendar year) of Lloyd's at the end of the next but one underwriting year) and subsequent years of assessment, the main income tax provisions (*ICTA 1988, ss 450–457*), capital gains tax provisions (*TCGA 1992, ss 206–209*) and various ancillary provisions previously having effect in relation to the taxation of underwriters were repealed and replaced with a new regime of provisions contained in *FA 1993, ss 171–184, Schs 19, 20; FA 1995, s 143*. See TOLLEY'S INCOME TAX under Underwriters for the revised income tax treatment.

Trust funds. For 1992/93 and subsequent years, trust funds held by an underwriting member of Lloyd's are classified as to '*premiums trust funds*' (as referred to in *Insurance Companies Act 1982, s 83*), 'new-style special reserve funds' (see below) and 'ancillary trust funds'. An '*ancillary trust fund*', in relation to the member, does not include his premiums trust fund or new-style special reserve fund but otherwise means any trust fund (including an 'old-style special reserve fund' as below) required or authorised by Lloyd's rules, or required by a members' agent of his or, before 1994/95, the managing agent of a syndicate of which he is a member. Use of an asset as part of an ancillary trust fund does not in itself make the asset a business asset for TAPER RELIEF (60) purposes, but neither does such use prevent the asset from being a business asset; such use is not regarded as non-qualifying use in relation to assets used for more than one purpose at the same time (see 60.10 TAPER RELIEF). [*TCGA 1992, Sch A1 para 19; FA 1998, s 121(2)(4), Sch 20*].

Premiums trust funds. In general terms for 1992/93 and subsequent years, disposals of assets in a Lloyd's member's premiums trust fund are only taken into account for income tax purposes, consideration relating to acquisitions and disposals of those assets being left out of account for CGT purposes. However, because of the special Lloyd's provisions relating to

(*a*) the closing of an underwriting year (above),

(*b*) the allocation of profits arising in one underwriting year over that year and the two previous years,

(*c*) the profits assessed for a year of assessment before 1997/98 being those *arising* in the corresponding underwriting year (an underwriting year and a year of assessment being deemed to correspond to each other if the underwriting year ends in the year of assessment), and

(*d*) the deemed disposal at the end of an underwriting year of assets forming part of a member's premiums trust fund at their value at that time and their deemed reacquisition at the beginning of the next underwriting year at the same value,

this did not apply to acquisitions or disposals made, or deemed to be made, of assets before 1 January 1994. See 63.3 below for the previous treatment of assets in a premiums trust fund.

Basis of assessment of profits. For 1997/98 and subsequent years, the profits charged for a year of assessment are those which are *declared* in the corresponding underwriting year (an underwriting year and a year of assessment being deemed to correspond to each other if the underwriting year ends in the year of assessment). Profits for a particular underwriting year are declared in the underwriting year immediately following the underwriting year in which the particular year is closed. For example, the profits of the underwriting year 1997 are declared in 2000 and taxed in 2000/01, the 1997 year having closed at the end of 1999. This does not apply to ancillary trust funds, for which see below as regards the CGT position.

Gains from ancillary trust funds. For 1992/93 and subsequent years, gains arising from the disposals of assets forming part of an ancillary trust fund are charged in the normal way to CGT (and losses are treated as allowable capital losses) on a fiscal year basis. This represents no change of treatment for practical purposes from that pertaining previously as in 63.2 below.

Entitlement of member. For 1992/93 and subsequent years, a member is treated for CGT purposes as absolutely entitled as against the trustees to the assets forming part of any of his premiums trust funds or ancillary trust funds. From 1994/95, money deposits required to be paid out of a premiums trust fund under overseas regulatory arrangements are still deemed to form part of the fund. Both such funds are therefore not 'settled property' as in 57.2 SETTLEMENTS.

[*ICTA 1988, s 450(6); FA 1993, ss 171, 172, s 174(1), ss 176, 184, Sch 23 Pt III; FA 1994, s 228, Sch 21 para 1(1)(3)(a), paras 2, 3, 8, Sch 26 Pt V; F(No 2)A 1997, s 22(1)(7), s 36, Sch 6 para 20*].

Special reserve funds. The reference above to a '*new-style special reserve fund*' is to the 'new-style' funds authorised by *FA 1993, s 175(1)* to be set up in respect of 1992 and subsequent underwriting years although the capital of '*old-style special reserve funds*' authorised under *ICTA 1988, s 452(1)* for underwriting years prior to 1992 may be transferred to a new style fund within certain time limits, any asset so transferred being deemed for CGT purposes to be disposed of by the member at its market value at the time of transfer. [*FA 1993, s 175(4), Sch 20 para 14(1)*]. As regards a new-style special reserve fund, the member is treated for CGT purposes as absolutely entitled as against the trustees to the assets forming part of his fund but, for 1994/95 and later years, the transfer by the member of an asset to the trustees is a chargeable event for CGT purposes. **Profits and losses arising from assets forming part of the fund are excluded for all CGT (and income tax) purposes.** [*FA 1993, s 175, Sch 20 para 8, para 9(1); FA 1994, s 228, Sch 21 para 13; SI 1999 No 3308, Reg 4*].

On cessation of underwriting, whether on death or otherwise, the amount of a member's new style special reserve fund, so far as not required as cover for cash calls and syndicate losses, must be paid over to him. Where an asset is transferred by the trustees to the member or his personal representatives or assigns on or after 1 January 2000, whether on cessation or otherwise, the asset is treated as acquired by the member etc.,

- in a case where the asset was held by the trustees at the end of the 'penultimate underwriting year', at the end of that year at its market value at that time;
- in a case where it was acquired by the trustees after the end of the 'penultimate underwriting year', at the date on which, and for the consideration for which, it was acquired by the trustees; and
- in a case where it was both acquired by the trustees and transferred to the member etc. before the end of the 'penultimate underwriting year', at the date of transfer at its market value at that time.

Before 1 January 2000, an asset transferred to the member out of the special reserve fund on cessation was treated as acquired by him at its market value as at the end of the 'penultimate underwriting year' and there were no other special rules. The '*penultimate underwriting year*' is the underwriting year corresponding to the year of assessment immediately preceding the member's final year of assessment. [*FA 1993, s 175, Sch 20 para 11(4)(5); FA 1994, s 228, Sch 21 para 15(2)(3); SI 1995 No 353, Reg 8; SI 1999 No 3308, Reg 6(5)*].

Syndicate capacity. From 1995 onwards, members have been able to buy and sell syndicate capacity, i.e. the right to underwrite on a particular syndicate, which is a chargeable asset for CGT purposes. For the CGT consequences, see 63.8 below, and as regards capacity held via a Members' Agent Pooling Arrangement (MAPA), see 63.9 below.

Time limits. Regulations made under *TCGA 1992, s 209(4)* (which allowed the making of regulations to extend certain time limits; see 63.5 below) in force immediately before 6 April 1992 continue in force for 1992/93 and subsequent years and are deemed to have been validly made. The Board have power, for 1992/93 to 1996/97 (both inclusive), to make similar regulations and, for 1992/93 and subsequent years, to make certain other supplementary regulations. [*FA 1993, s 182, s 184(3); FA 1994, s 228, Sch 21 para 7, Sch 26 Pt V; FA 1995, s 83(2)*]. See *SI 1995 Nos 351–353, 1185*.

See *SI 1995 No 352, Regs 14, 15* for extension of time limits (for making elections etc.) for 1992/93 to 1994/95 inclusive. Following the change in the basis of assessment of Lloyd's underwriters for 1997/98 onwards (see above), time limits for 1995/96 and subsequent years are not extended.

Corporate underwriters. For accounting periods ending after 31 December 1993 or, as the case may require, for the underwriting year 1994 and subsequent years, *FA 1994, ss 219–227, 229, 230* (i.e. *FA 1994, Pt IV Ch V* except *s 228* and *Sch 21*) broadly apply the above provisions *mutatis mutandis* to corporate members of Lloyd's except that there is no provision for a corporate member to set up a new-style special reserve fund.

Scottish limited partnerships. Regulations provide for the tax treatment of profits or losses arising to the partners of a Scottish limited partnership from its business as a Lloyd's underwriting member. They apply to accounting periods of such partnerships ending on or after 1 December 1997. See *SI 1997 No 2681*.

63.2 INDIVIDUALS: 1991/92 AND PRIOR YEARS

As indicated in 63.1 above, the provisions below and in 63.3–63.6 below are repealed after 1991/92 (again subject to special transitional provisions which allow for the 'closing' of an underwriting year (i.e. the calendar year) of Lloyd's at the end of the next but one underwriting year).

For 1991/92 and prior years of assessment, an individual underwriting member of Lloyd's is treated for capital gains tax purposes as absolutely entitled as against the trustees to the investments of his '*premiums trust fund*' (as referred to in *Insurance Companies Act 1982, s 83*, his '*old-style special reserve fund*' (as authorised by *ICTA 1988, s 452(1)*) and any other trust fund required or authorised by Lloyd's rules or required by an underwriting agent through whom his business is carried on in whole or part. [*TCGA 1992, s 206(1); FA 1993, Sch 23 Pt III*]. Such funds are therefore not 'settled property' as in 57.2 SETTLEMENTS.

Despite this nominee status for the trustees of a member's premiums trust fund (who may be, and normally is, treated as such a trustee), they are assessed and charged to capital gains tax for years before 1994/95 (see 63.3 below as to the allocation of gains over three underwriting years) as if *TCGA 1992, s 206(1)* above (and *FA 1993, s 174(1)* in 63.1 for years after 1991/92) did not apply. For years after 1987/88 and before 1994/95, such capital gains tax is charged at a rate equivalent to the basic rate of income tax for the year of assessment concerned, an appropriate credit being given of the tax paid if the underwriter is assessed at a higher rate in respect of the same gains. Losses accruing in prior years of assessment are not taken into account in assessing the trustees, and if for that and any other reason the tax paid on behalf of a member under assessments for a year of assessment exceeds the tax for which he is liable, the member can claim (under *TCGA 1992, s 206(4)*) the excess be repaid. [*TCGA 1992, s 206(2)–(5); FA 1993, s 183(7), Sch 23 Pt III*]. Before 1988/89, the rate of tax was 30% and there were no stated circumstances whereby an additional assessment charging a higher rate would have been made. [*CGTA 1979, s 3; FA 1988, s 101, Sch 14 Pt VII*].

It follows that for 1991/92 and prior years of assessment, gains and losses arising from investments in a member's old-style special reserve fund and any other trust fund within *TCGA 1992, s 206(1)* above (other than his premiums trust fund) are assessed and charged personally on him. No special basis of capital gains tax assessment applies.

63.3 **Calculation of gains and losses in premiums trust fund.** For underwriting years before 1994, an allocation is made of the realised and *unrealised* unindexed gains and losses arising from assets forming part of a member's premiums trust fund in the underwriting year (i.e. calendar year). Such gains and losses are arrived at by taking the difference between the valuations at the beginning and at the end of the underwriting year of the assets forming part of the fund, the value at the beginning of the year of assets acquired in the year being taken as their acquisition cost and the value at the end of the year of assets disposed of during the year being taken as their disposal consideration. The allocation (on a percentage basis agreed with the Inland Revenue) is among three underwriting years of account, viz. the calendar year in which the gains and losses arose and the two immediately *preceding* calendar years. (*Note.* An underwriting year of account is kept open for at least two years after the end of that year of account.) Thus, each underwriting year of account will have apportioned to it a fraction of gains and losses arising in that year, and in the two subsequent years. The total of gains so apportioned to a particular underwriting year of account ('syndicate gains') is assessed for the year of assessment in which that year of account ends. The above rules do not apply to GOVERNMENT SECURITIES (24) and QUALIFYING CORPORATE BONDS (49) but apply broadly to deep discount securities (see 58.20 SHARES AND SECURITIES). Securities which have been lent within *TCGA 1992, s 271(9); ICTA 1988, s 129* (see 58.25 SHARES AND SECURITIES) are treated as still held if the lending is still current at the end of the underwriting year of account. [*ICTA 1988, s 450(6); TCGA 1992, s 118(5)(6), s 207; FA 1989, s 91(2), s 96(1)–(4); FA 1993, Sch 23 Pt III*].

It appears that the rules for ASSETS HELD ON 31 MARCH 1982 (8) cannot apply to premiums trust funds for underwriting years before 1994.

For underwriting years before 1994 and after 5 April 1985, the provisions relating to INDEXATION (26) generally after that date apply 'with any necessary modifications' in relation to assets forming part of a premium trust fund as they apply in relation to other assets. Assets within the fund are assumed to be disposed of and immediately reacquired on each 31 December and any indexation allowance computed is allocated on the same basis given above for realised and unrealised unindexed gains and losses. [*TCGA 1992, s 208; FA 1993, Sch 23 Pt III*].

Realised and unrealised unindexed gains and losses in any particular calendar year prior to 1994 in respect of run-off accounts of the premiums trust fund are imputed to the underwriting year of account which closes at the end of that calendar year, i.e. the underwriting account ending two years before the end of the calendar year in which the gain arises. (*Example.* Gains arise in 1991 in respect of the 1985 run-off account. In 1991 the 1989 account closes. The gains in respect of the 1985 run-off account will therefore be attributed to the 1989 account and be assessed for 1989/90.) [*TCGA 1992, s 209(1)(2)(4); FA 1993, s 183(8), Sch 23 Pt III; SI 1974 No 896, Reg 7(1)(b)*].

For the special deduction available on the disposal of foreign securities held in a trust fund established abroad, see 17.4 DISPOSAL.

63.4 **Retirement of underwriter.** Other than on death, retirement of an underwriting member of Lloyd's will normally take place at the end of an underwriting year so his share of syndicate gains for underwriting years prior to 1994 will be treated as in 63.3 above. On death, it is standard practice not to allow a member dying in such an underwriting year to share in the gains or losses of that year unless death occurs on 31 December. In either case, no adjustment is required to the general capital gains tax rules on death (see 16.1 DEATH).

63.5 **Time limits.** For years of assessment prior to 1992/93, due to delay in establishing the results from Lloyd's underwriting, the Revenue may, in certain circumstances, extend the time limits for making elections as prescribed otherwise. In particular, it extends statutorily the time limits under the following heads.

(*a*) **Error or mistake claim** (see 12.7 CLAIMS).

(*b*) **General six-year time limit for making assessments and the time limit for assessments made to make good fraudulent or negligent conduct of taxpayer** (see 5.5 ASSESSMENTS and 9.4 BACK DUTY).

(*c*) **Assessments on personal representatives** (see 5.6 ASSESSMENTS and 9.5 BACK DUTY).

(*d*) **General six-year time limit for making claims** (see 12.5 CLAIMS).

(*e*) **Set-off of trading losses against chargeable gains of a person other than a company** (see 39.7 LOSSES).

In the above cases, the time limit is extended to six years after the end of the year which is the closing year for the underwriting account in relation to the year of assessment i.e., in effect, a further two-year extension. In certain cases such an extension also applies to the making of a claim etc. by the spouse of the underwriting member. [*TCGA 1992, s 209(3)–(6); FA 1993, s 183(8), Sch 23 Pt III; SI 1994 No 728, Reg 3(2), Reg 9*]. See also 63.1 above for the position for 1992/93 onwards.

63.6 **Payment of tax.** For years of assessment prior to 1994/95 the Revenue may make regulations for the assessment and collection of tax charged under *TCGA 1992, s 207* (see 63.3 above) on gains arising from disposals of assets forming part of an underwriting member's premiums trust fund. Such tax is due on or before the fourth anniversary of the beginning of the relevant underwriting year, e.g. capital gains tax payable for the underwriting year 1991 (1 January to 31 December) falls due on 1 January 1995. Tax charged by an assessment made after (or, for the 1986 underwriting year and onwards, within thirty days before) this time limit has expired is due on the day (for the 1986 underwriting year and onwards, thirtieth day) following the date of issue of the assessment. [*TCGA 1992, s 209(1)(2)(4); FA 1993, s 183(8), Sch 23 Pt III; SI 1994 No 728, Reg 4*].

Capital gains tax arising from Lloyd's ancillary trust funds (see 63.1 above) is due at the same time as for non-underwriting investments.

63.7 OVERSEAS RESIDENTS

Where a capital gains tax treatment, rather than an income tax, or corporation tax charging income, treatment (see 63.1 above in relation to the position for 1992/93 and onwards), would apply to assets held as part of an individual underwriter's or corporate underwriter's trust funds, then if the individual or company is neither resident nor, in the case of an individual, ordinarily resident in the UK, he or the company is still liable to capital gains tax or corporation tax on chargeable gains on such assets which are situate in the UK. See 6.2 ASSETS and 44.3 OVERSEAS MATTERS. For this purpose, investments comprised in the Lloyd's American and Canadian Trust Funds are regarded as not situate in the UK. Investments held in the Lloyd's Sterling Trust Fund are situate in the UK, except for non-

UK equities. The double taxation arrangements between the UK and the relevant countries should be consulted, as well as the relevant domestic legislation of the overseas countries concerned. For overseas matters generally and for the determination of residence and domicile, see 44 OVERSEAS MATTERS and 52 RESIDENCE AND DOMICILE.

63.8 TRANSACTIONS IN SYNDICATE CAPACITY

A Lloyd's member can participate in a particular underwriting syndicate only to the extent that he possesses the relevant rights to do so. From the 1995 Account onwards, a member is permitted to realise all or part of his rights in any particular syndicate (his syndicate capacity) by offering them for sale at one of the periodical syndicate capacity auctions or by entering into a bilateral agreement with a purchaser. Each member's right to participate in each syndicate of which he is a member is therefore a marketable asset. Any gain arising on disposal is subject to capital gains tax or corporation tax, as the case may be (other than in exceptional cases where such transactions are sufficiently frequent to constitute a trade of dealing, in which case income tax may apply in the case of an individual). The date of disposal in the case of an auction is normally the day after it takes place. Allowable costs of disposal include tendering and auction expenses. The Revenue do not accept that rights in syndicates had any acquisition value for CGT purposes prior to the 1995 Account. The allowable expenditure on the disposal of rights acquired subsequently by purchase will be their acquisition cost plus any incidental expenditure. As regards a new syndicate set up for the 1996 Account onwards, the allowable expenditure is normally the price paid to the managing agent by the member to join that syndicate. The initial Lloyd's admission fee is also an allowable expense, which may be relieved once the member has resigned.

The Revenue have confirmed that business asset taper relief is available on disposals after 5 April 1998 other than by corporate members. (Lloyd's Market Bulletin TAX/HAB/In/Y2122, 6 September 1999).

'Bespoke' capacity is the term given to rights held by a member in his own name. Bespoke capacity must be kept separate from MAPA (Members' Agent Pooling Arrangement) capacity, for which see 63.9 below.

As regards acquisitions and disposals of syndicate rights after 5 April 1999, such rights are a qualifying asset for the purposes of ROLLOVER RELIEF (55) on replacement of business assets. [*TCGA 1992, s 155; FA 1999, s 84*].

Current Revenue practice is to treat all a member's bespoke capacity in one syndicate as a single asset. Further acquisitions are treated as enhancement expenditure, part disposals are dealt with under the normal rules at 6.6 DISPOSAL, and taper relief is calculated by reference to the date of the initial acquisition. This represents a change of view by the Revenue, who previously considered that acquisitions and disposals of capacity should be treated similarly to those of shares and securities. (Lloyd's Market Bulletin TAX/HAB/In/Y2122, 6 September 1999).

A member's interest in a syndicate (though not his ancillary trust funds — see 63.1 above) is a business asset for the purposes of RETIREMENT RELIEF (53). Where a member disposes of the whole of his syndicate capacity in any one year of account such that he does not underwrite in the following year of account, a 'material disposal of business assets' (see 53.5 RETIREMENT RELIEF) will have taken place. A disposal of part only of a member's syndicate capacity in any one year is regarded by the Revenue as being merely a reduction in the scale of the business, and retirement relief will not be granted. (Lloyd's Market Bulletin TAX/HAB/In/Y2122, 6 September 1999).

Conversion to corporate status. The transfer of syndicate capacity by an individual member to a corporate vehicle, whether by gift or in exchange for shares, is a disposal for CGT purposes. Where the necessary conditions are satisfied, retirement relief and/or the reliefs at 25.1, 25.10 HOLD-OVER RELIEFS are available. (Lloyd's Market Bulletin TAX/HAB/In/Y2122, 6 September 1999).

For more detailed coverage generally, see Tolley's Taxation of Lloyd's Underwriters.

Example

Justin acquires a £1m line on Syndicate X for £60,000 on 30 April 1999. He acquires a further £250,000 line on the same Syndicate for £20,000 on 1 June 2000. The £1.25m line is a single asset for CGT purposes costing £80,000. On 1 May 2002, Justin sells a £500,000 line for £50,000. The remaining £750,000 line is therefore worth £75,000. Incidental costs of acquisition and disposal are ignored for the purposes of this example. Justin makes no other disposals in 2002/03.

	£
Proceeds	50,000
Deduct Cost:	
$£80,000 \times \dfrac{50,000}{50,000 + 75,000} =$	32,000
Untapered gain	18,000
Deduct Taper relief £18,000 @ 50%*	9,000
Chargeable gain (subject to annual exemption)	£9,000

* Business asset held for 3 whole years (30.4.99–1.5.02)

63.9 **Members' Agent Pooling Arrangements.** A Members' Agent Pooling Arrangement (MAPA), in relation to a member, is an arrangement under which

- a 'members' agent' arranges for the member's participation in Lloyd's syndicates,
- the member must participate in each syndicate to which the arrangement relates, and
- the extent of his participation is determined by the members' agent or in accordance with a formula provided for in the arrangement.

A '*members' agent*' is a person registered as such at Lloyd's and acting as such for the member concerned. [*FA 1999, s 83(1)(2)*].

MAPAs have been in existence since 1994 and allow a member access to a wide range of syndicates. It is understood that most individual members underwrite wholly or partly through a MAPA rather than solely through rights (capacity) held directly in individual syndicates. In the absence of special rules, there could be numerous transactions each year which should strictly count as a CGT disposal. For example, whenever a new participant joins a MAPA, the total syndicate rights held in the MAPA have to be re-divided between all participants, so that each existing participant will have disposed of a fraction of his capacity to the new participant. Sales of rights by the MAPA and changes in the syndicates in which it partakes likewise give rise to CGT disposals by its participants. The Revenue and Lloyd's negotiated a practice designed to avoid most of the complexity. For example, where a member transferred capacity into a MAPA (either from his bespoke capacity (see 63.8 above) or from another MAPA), no disposal was deemed to arise on any part of that capacity which was retained within his share of the MAPA capacity (Lloyd's Market Bulletin TAX/HAB/In/Y1082, 4 February 1999). Previous practice was replaced by the statutory provisions in *Finance Act 1999* described below. They do not apply to corporate members of Lloyd's. The provisions do apply, with appropriate modification, to Scottish limited partnerships which are Lloyd's members (see 63.1 above).

The statutory provisions apply where an individual (i.e. non-corporate) Lloyd's member has entered into a MAPA, and apply for the purpose of determining any CGT liabilities of his that may arise from transactions effected in pursuance of the MAPA. They apply in relation to any MAPA entered into on or after 6 April 1999 and also to any MAPA entered into earlier and still in existence on that date (see also below). Under these provisions, the syndicate rights held by the member under the MAPA are treated as a single asset acquired by him at the time of his entering into the MAPA. The member's initial acquisition cost is the amount paid by him on joining the MAPA. Any other amount paid by him under the MAPA is treated as allowable enhancement expenditure on the single asset. A disposal (or, as the case may be, a part disposal) of the single asset occurs *only* when an amount is paid to the member, the disposal proceeds being equal to that amount, or, by virtue of *TCGA 1992, s 24(1)* (see 17.7 DISPOSAL), where the asset is entirely extinguished.

If the MAPA was entered into before 6 April 1999, the time of acquisition is taken to be the earliest time that the member acquired any of the syndicate rights still held by him through the MAPA immediately before 6 April 1999, the initial acquisition cost is the amount paid for such of those rights as were acquired at that earlier time, and the amount paid for any additional rights acquired between that time and 6 April 1999 (and still held) qualifies as enhancement expenditure. The incidental costs of rights acquired before 6 April 1999 (and still held) are taken to be the incidental costs of acquiring the single asset.

References above to the payment of any amount include payments in money's worth, in which case the member's expenditure or disposal proceeds, as the case may be, is equivalent to the market value of the money's worth at the time of payment. This covers, for example, the transfer by a member into a MAPA of syndicate rights which he previously owned directly, and *vice versa*. On the other side of the coin, a transfer of rights by a member into a MAPA constitutes a disposal by him of those rights at market value, and similarly a transfer of rights from a MAPA to a member constitutes an acquisition by him at market value.

[*FA 1999, ss 82, 83*].

Note that where a member has two or more MAPAs, each is treated as a *separate* single asset.

As regards acquisitions and disposals after 5 April 1999 of syndicate rights held through a MAPA and treated as a single asset as above, such rights are a qualifying asset for the purposes of ROLLOVER RELIEF (55) on replacement of business assets. [*TCGA 1992, s 155; FA 1999, s 84*]. It is thought that additions on or after 6 April 1999 to a MAPA held on and before that date (which fall to be treated as expenditure on enhancing the single asset — see above) would qualify for rollover relief by virtue of ESC D22 which allows gains to be rolled over against enhancement expenditure in appropriate circumstances (see 55.3 ROLLOVER RELIEF).

Syndicate capacity, whether held through a MAPA or otherwise, is a business asset for the purposes of TAPER RELIEF (60). The treatment of further acquisitions as enhancement expenditure means that taper relief on a disposal or part disposal falls to be calculated by reference to the date of the initial acquisition. (Lloyd's Market Bulletin TAX/HAB/In/Y2122, 6 September 1999).

64 Unit Trusts, Investment Trusts and Open-Ended Investment Companies

Cross-references. See 7.2 ASSETS HELD ON 6 APRIL 1965 and 40.2 MARKET VALUE for valuation of units in unit trusts; 13.7 and 13.12 COMPANIES for transfers of businesses to, and intra-group disposals of assets by, authorised unit trusts and investment trusts; 26.1 INDEXATION for exclusion of indexation allowance in respect of disposals before 30 November 1993 of certain collective investment schemes; 65.1 VENTURE CAPITAL TRUSTS.

Sumption: Capital Gains Tax. See A11.

64.1 AUTHORISED UNIT TRUSTS

These are 'unit trust schemes' designated by an order of the Department of Trade under *Prevention of Fraud (Investments) Act 1958, s 17* (or NI equivalent) or, after 28 April 1988, designated by an order under *Financial Services Act 1986, s 78*. '*Unit trust scheme*' has the meaning given by *Prevention of Fraud (Investments) Act 1958, s 26(1)*, but after 28 April 1988 this is replaced by that given under *Financial Services Act 1986*, save that the Treasury may after 10 March 1988 by regulation provide for any scheme of a specified description not to be treated as a unit trust scheme for capital gains purposes. [*TCGA 1992, s 99(2)(3); ICTA 1988, s 468(6), s 469(7), s 832; SI 1988 No 266*]. Certain limited partnership schemes and employee profit sharing schemes have been excepted from treatment as unit trust schemes for such purposes.

For capital gains purposes, any unit trust scheme is treated as if the scheme were a company and the rights of the unit holders were shares in the company, and in the case of an authorised unit trust (as defined by *ICTA 1988, s 468(6)*) as if the company were resident and ordinarily resident in the UK. [*TCGA 1992, s 99(1)*]. A unit trust scheme other than an authorised unit trust is not within the charge to corporation tax so that the trustees are assessable to capital gains tax unless there is exemption under 64.3 below (Revenue Capital Gains Manual CG 41351).

Gains realised by authorised unit trusts are not chargeable gains. [*TCGA 1992, s 100(1)*].

Income derived after 26 July 1990 in an accounting period in which a unit trust scheme is an authorised unit trust from transactions relating to futures contracts or options contracts is exempt from income tax under Schedule D, Case I. A contract is included for this purpose notwithstanding that one party to it will not be involved with a transfer of assets other than money. [*ICTA 1988, s 468AA; FA 1990, s 81(1)(5)*]. In effect the legislation now prevents a Schedule D, Case I or Case VI or capital gains tax assessment in respect of such income or gains. See 17.10 and 17.11 DISPOSAL for the Revenue's treatment of options and futures in other cases.

Monthly savings schemes. An individual acquiring units in authorised unit trusts under a monthly savings scheme can opt for a simplified arrangement for computing any chargeable gains arising. To do so, he must make a written request to his tax office no later than the first anniversary of 31 January following the first tax year in which he both disposes of such units and either his *total* gains for the year exceed the annual exemption or his total proceeds exceed twice the exemption or his disposals of other assets result in a net loss. The arrangement must cover all an individual's monthly schemes in the same unit trust. Under the arrangement, the individual will be treated in most cases as having made a single annual investment in the seventh month of the trust's accounting year. This will be made up of savings plus reinvested income less any small withdrawals in the year concerned. Following the freezing of indexation allowance to April 1998 (see 26.1 INDEXATION), the arrangement is withdrawn in all cases where savings commenced after 5 April 1998 and in other cases for acquisitions in any accounting year of a trust ending after 5 April 1999. Where the arrangement is in operation, it has effect in determining the availability or otherwise of the 'bonus year' addition for taper relief purposes (see 60.2 TAPER RELIEF). (Revenue Pamphlet IR 131, SP 2/99). (This Statement of Practice updates SP 2/97 which itself replaced SP 3/89).

Accumulation units. No distributions are made to holders of accumulation units. Instead the net amount that would normally be distributed is automatically reinvested in the fund. No new units are issued but the value of the existing holding of units is increased. Where the notional distribution is subject to income tax in the hands of the unit holder, it is treated as allowable expenditure for CGT purposes. This treatment also applies to both UK resident and non-UK resident trusts. INDEXATION ALLOWANCE (26) is given from the date the unit holder became entitled to the notional distribution. (Revenue Capital Gains Manual CG 57707).

Collective investment schemes. If under a 'collective investment scheme' (within the meaning of *Financial Services Act 1986*) contributions to it and profits arising from it are pooled in relation to separate parts of the property in the scheme and the participants are entitled to exchange rights in one part for rights in another, then for such exchanges after 13 March 1989 *TCGA 1992, s 127* (reorganisation etc. of shares etc.) is not to prevent the exchange constituting a disposal and acquisition for capital gains tax purposes. For this purpose *TCGA 1992, s 127* includes a reference to that provision as applied by *TCGA 1992, s 132* (conversion of securities) but does not include a reference to that provision as applied by *TCGA 1992, s 135* (exchange of securities for those in another company); see 58.5, 58.8 and 58.11 SHARES AND SECURITIES. [*TCGA 1992, s 102*].

From 1 April 1994 (though subject to transitional provisions), each sub-fund of an '**umbrella scheme**' falls to be treated for income tax purposes as being itself an authorised unit trust and the umbrella scheme as a whole falls to be not so treated. An '*umbrella scheme*' is a unit trust scheme covered by an order under *Financial Services Act 1986, s 78* which has arrangements for separate pooling of investors' contributions and the profits or income out of which payments are to be made to them, and under which investors can switch from one sub-fund to another. [*ICTA 1988, s 468(7)–(9); FA 1994, s 113(2)(4)–(11)*]. Consequently, the Revenue view is that, for CGT purposes,

(*a*) each sub-fund of an umbrella scheme falls to be treated as a separate company and the scheme as a whole is transparent; and

(*b*) a unit holder's interest is deemed to be that of a shareholder in a company corresponding to the sub-fund concerned, not in a company corresponding to the whole of the umbrella scheme.

The consequences are that if an individual switches out of a continuing sub-fund into another, there is a disposal for CGT purposes (and *TCGA 1992, s 102* prevents paper for paper rollover treatment under *TCGA 1992, s 127* as applied by *TCGA 1992, s 132* — see above). If, however, one sub-fund disappears on being merged with another, paper for paper rollover treatment is available under *TCGA 1992, s 127* as applied by *TCGA 1992, s 136* — see above (provided the conditions for such treatment are satisfied). *TCGA 1992, s 102* does not prevent paper for paper rollover treatment where an investor switches between income units and accumulation units within the same sub-fund of an authorised unit trust umbrella scheme. (Revenue Tax Bulletin April 1997 pp 419–421).

For exchanges before 14 March 1989 and after 22 July 1987 any question as to whether arrangements of a multi-portfolio collective investment scheme which provided for pooling constituted a single collective investment scheme was determined for capital gains tax purposes without regard to any entitlement of the participants to exchange rights in one part of the property for rights in another. [*TCGA 1992, s 102; F(No 2)A 1987, s 78*]. As regards exchanges before 23 July 1987 the position was governed by *Arbuthnot Financial*

Services Ltd v CIR Ch D, [1985] STC 211 (a stamp duty case in which it was decided that a participant had transferred his units in one fund of a multi-fund unit trust scheme to the managers in consideration for units in another fund of the scheme). See Revenue Tax Bulletin April 1997 pp 419–421 for a summary of the legislative history.

64.2 INVESTMENT TRUSTS

An investment trust is a 'company' fulfilling the following conditions. [*ICTA 1988, s 842; FA 1988, s 117; FA 1990, s 55; FA 1994, ss 146, 170, Sch 17 para 8; FA 1996, s 160, Sch 30 paras 2, 3, Sch 34 para 7*].

(*a*) It is not a close company.

(*b*) It is resident in the UK.

(*c*) Its income consists 'wholly or mainly' of income deriving from shares and securities or, for accounting periods beginning after 29 April 1996, eligible rental income (within *ICTA 1988, s 508A*). In practice, wholly or mainly is taken as 70% or more, although, if the income in an accounting period falls slightly below this figure as a result of the profit on an isolated financial futures or options transaction, the trust may retain its approved status at the Revenue's discretion per Revenue Pamphlet IR 131, SP 14/91.

(*d*) No 'holding' in any one company represents more than 15% of the value of its investments, unless that company is itself an investment trust or would be so but for being unquoted. This requirement is waived in respect of investments which, when acquired, represented no more than 15% of the value of the investments, and in respect of an investment held on 6 April 1965 provided that the holding represented not more than 25% of the overall value of the investments at that date. There is no waiver in either case where there has been an 'addition' to the holding.

(*e*) Its 'ordinary share capital' (and every class thereof, if there is more than one) is listed in the Official List of the Stock Exchange.

(*f*) Its Memorandum or Articles prohibit the distribution by way of dividend of gains arising from the sale of investments.

(*g*) It does not retain more than 15% of its income which is either derived from shares or securities or, for accounting periods beginning after 29 April 1996, consists of eligible rental income as in (*c*) above. However, for accounting periods ending after 25 July 1990, this requirement does not apply if the excess over the 15% limit is less than £10,000 (or proportionately reduced amount if the period is less than twelve months) or the company is required by law to retain an amount of income for the period in excess of the 15% limit and in circumstances such that the aggregate of the excess of the amount of income retained for the period over the amount of income required to be retained for the period and any amount distributed in respect of the period is less than £10,000 (or proportionately reduced amount where the period is less than twelve months).

(*h*) It is approved by the Board.

As regards (*c*) above, units in an authorised unit trust (AUT) (see 64.1 above) or, from 18 July 1997, shares in an open-ended investment company (OEIC) incorporated in the UK (see 64.4 below) are for this purpose treated as shares in a company. Where the condition at (*d*) above is then relevant, it is regarded as being satisfied *provided that* during the period of time in the investment trust's accounting period during which it held investments in an AUT or OEIC, the AUT or OEIC itself satisfied the condition at (*c*) above. This condition will always be regarded as satisfied where the AUT is a 'securities fund' under *Financial Services Act 1986* or the OEIC is a 'securities company' under corresponding regulations.

These practices are modified as necessary to embrace rights in a sub-fund of an umbrella scheme treated as an AUT for tax purposes and shares in an umbrella company which confer rights in a sub-fund treated as an OEIC for tax purposes. (Revenue Pamphlet IR 131, SP 3/97, replacing SP 7/94).

'*Company*' includes any body corporate or unincorporated association, but not a partnership. [*TCGA 1992, s 288(1)*].

'*Shares*' includes stock.

'*Holding*' means the shares or securities of whatever class or classes held in any one company. Where, in connection with a scheme of reconstruction or amalgamation (see 13.7 COMPANIES; 58.8, 58.10 SHARES AND SECURITIES), a company issues shares or securities to persons holding shares or securities in another in respect of and in proportion to (or as nearly as may be in proportion to) such holdings, without the recipients becoming liable for any consideration, the old and the new holdings are treated as the same.

For accounting periods ending after 5 April 1988, if the investing company is a member of a group (i.e. a company and its 51% subsidiaries), money owed to it by another group member is treated as a security and, as such, as part of its holding in that other group member. Holdings in companies which are members of a group (whether or not including the investing company) are treated as holdings in a single company.

An '*addition*' is made to a holding whenever the investing company acquires further shares or securities in any company in which it already has a holding, otherwise than by being allotted them without liability for consideration (e.g. a bonus issue). The holding is deemed to have been acquired at the date of the latest addition.

'*Ordinary share capital*' means all the issued share capital (by whatever name called) of a company, other than that which produces a fixed rate of dividend and is non-participating. [*ICTA 1988, s 832(1)*].

See TOLLEY'S CORPORATION TAX for the definition of a close company.

For the Revenue's views on whether forward currency transactions by investment trusts are on capital or income account and whether such a transaction on income account would breach the test in (*c*) above, see Revenue Pamphlet IR 131, SP 14/91.

See Revenue Pamphlet IR 131, SP 2/99 (as in 64.1 above) re monthly savings schemes, which applies to investment trusts as it does to authorised unit trusts.

Gains realised by investment trusts are not chargeable gains. [*TCGA 1992, s 100(1)*].

See 65.1 VENTURE CAPITAL TRUSTS.

64.3 UNIT TRUSTS FOR EXEMPT UNIT HOLDERS

If, for any reason other than non-residence, none of the holders of units in a unit trust scheme would be liable to capital gains tax (or to corporation tax on chargeable gains) on a disposal of units, gains accruing to the trust itself are not chargeable gains. [*TCGA 1992, s 100(2)*]. This exemption applies whenever the gains accrued, but is of practical importance only in relation to unit trust schemes which have not been designated as in 64.1 above. It is not withdrawn by reason of units being temporarily held by the trust's managers under the ordinary arrangements of the trust for the issue and redemption of units. (Revenue Pamphlet IR 1, D17.)

64.4 OPEN-ENDED INVESTMENT COMPANIES

'Open-ended investment company' (OEIC) means an open-ended investment company within the meaning given by *Financial Services Act 1986, s 75(8)* which is incorporated in the United Kingdom. [*ICTA 1988, s 468(10) treated as inserted by SI 1997 No 1154, Reg 10(4); TCGA 1992, s 99(2)(c) treated as inserted by SI 1997 No 1154, Reg 20*]. It is a form of retail investment fund which can be set up in the UK from 1997. It is similar to an authorised unit trust (AUT) (see 64.1 above) in that the size of the fund and the number of investment units pump up or down according to whether there is a net inflow or outflow of investment, the price per unit is determined according to the value of the investments held by the fund and the fund is regulated by the Securities and Investments Board. An OEIC is, however, constituted as a company, with directors, and issues shares rather than units. The Treasury were given power by *FA 1995, s 152* to make the regulations necessary to establish a tax regime for UK incorporated OEICs (see, in particular, *The Open-ended Investment Companies (Tax) Regulations* (*SI 1997 No 1154*)). The regime is broadly equivalent to that which applies to AUTs and their investors. See TOLLEY'S CORPORATION TAX for information concerning dividend and interest distributions.

OEICs are chargeable to corporation tax at a rate equal to the lower rate of income tax. Gains accruing to an OEIC are not chargeable gains. [*TCGA 1992, s 100(1) as modified by SI 1997 No 1154, Reg 5; SI 1997 No 1715, Reg 4*]. Investors incur chargeable gains and allowable losses in the normal way on disposals of shares. Where shares of a given class consist of both smaller and larger denomination shares, and a person owns both, the shares are treated for CGT purposes as being securities of the same class. [*SI 1997 No 1154, Reg 24*]. The individual sub-funds of an umbrella company are treated as being separate OEICs in their own right and the umbrella company treated as if it were not a company. (An umbrella company is an OEIC whose investments are pooled separately in sub-funds, usually having different investment objectives, and whose shareholders are entitled to exchange their rights in one sub-fund for rights in another.) [*ICTA 1988, s 468(11) treated as inserted by SI 1997 No 1154, Reg 10(4)*].

See Revenue Pamphlet IR 131, SP 2/99 (as in 64.1 above) re monthly savings schemes, which applies to OEICs as it does to AUTs.

AUTs are able to convert to, or merge with, OEICs without the incurring of any significant direct tax charges. [*SI 1997 No 1154, Regs 25–27*]. As far as investors are concerned, the exchange of units in an AUT for shares in an OEIC is subject to the normal rules for reconstructions or amalgamations (see 58.10 SHARES AND SECURITIES) so that the new shares will normally stand in the shoes of the old units and have the same acquisition date and cost for CGT purposes. (Revenue Press Release 7 April 1997, para 6).

64.5 COURT INVESTMENT FUNDS

These are common investment funds established under *Administration of Justice Act 1982, s 42*. The Accountant General is deemed to hold the funds (together with other funds in court) as nominee or bare trustee as in 57.2 SETTLEMENTS. [*TCGA 1992, s 61, s 100(3)*].

Gains realised by court investment funds are not chargeable gains. [*TCGA 1992, s 100(1)*].

64.6 INVESTMENT CLUBS

An investment club is a group of people who join together to invest, primarily in the stock market. Each club will have its own rules, which will, *inter alia*, determine each member's proportionate entitlement to the club's investments, which will change frequently as capital is invested and withdrawn. Members share income, gains and losses according to their entitlement and are personally responsible for declaring the income etc. and personally liable for tax thereon. There are three ways in which members can return their shares of gains (and income) in a particular tax year:

- in accordance with a standard form of agreement (available from the Revenue) whereby the secretary or other responsible officer makes a return of the gains based on less detailed computations than are statutorily required;
- in accordance with a simplified scheme for smaller clubs (see below);
- in accordance with strict statutory requirements, which, in addition to requiring gains (and income) to be returned by individual members, may also involve special returns being made by the treasurer and the person in whose name the club investments are held.

Under the simplified scheme,

- an officer of the club applies on form 185-1 for the club to be included for a particular year;
- all capital gains are apportioned to the members as agreed by them;
- the share of gains to date of a member who leaves partway through the year must either be accepted by him or apportioned between the other members as agreed by them;
- details of transactions, members and their shares of gains and income are included on the form 185-1; and
- upon agreement of the figures, the club gives each member a form 185-2 showing his shares of gains and income, which he then includes in his personal tax return.

An investment club is eligible for the simplified scheme for a particular year if

- it has no more than 20 members at any one time,
- the annual subscription does not exceed £1,000 per member,
- the net gains do not exceed £5,000,
- the average investment per head, based on cost price, does not exceed £5,000, and
- all members agree the division of the capital gains.

(Revenue Capital Gains Manual CG 20600–20650).

64.7 VENTURE CAPITAL TRUSTS

For 1995/96 and subsequent years of assessment, chargeable gains of venture capital trusts are not chargeable gains. See 65.8 VENTURE CAPITAL TRUSTS below.

65 Venture Capital Trusts

Sumption: Capital Gains Tax. See A15A.10.

65.1 From 6 April 1995, the venture capital trust scheme described at 65.2 *et seq.* below was introduced to encourage individuals to invest in unquoted trading companies through such trusts. The provisions dealing with the approval of companies as venture capital trusts, and with the reliefs for investors, were introduced in *FA 1995, ss 70–72, Schs 14–16*. The Treasury has wide powers to make regulations governing all aspects of the reliefs applicable to venture capital trust investments, and for the requirements as regards returns, records and provision of information by the trust. [*FA 1995, s 73*]. See *SI 1995 No 1979*.

See also Revenue Pamphlet IR 169.

65.2 **CONDITIONS FOR APPROVAL** *[ICTA 1988, s 842AA; FA 1995, s 70; FA 1996, Sch 38 para 7; FA 1997, s 75; FA 1998, s 73(1)(6), Sch 27 Pt III(13); FA 1999, s 69(4)(5)]*

A '*venture capital trust*' ('VCT') is a company approved for this purpose by the Board. Close companies (see TOLLEY'S CORPORATION TAX under Close Companies) are excluded. The time from which an approval takes effect is specified in the approval, and may not be earlier than the time the application for approval was made.

Except as detailed further below, approval may not be given unless the Board are satisfied that the following conditions are met.

(*a*) The company's income in its most recent complete accounting period has been derived wholly or mainly from shares or securities, and not more than 15% of its income from shares and securities has been retained.

(*b*) Throughout that period at least 70% by value of the company's investments has been represented by shares or securities in 'qualifying holdings' (see 65.3 below), at least 30% of which (by value) has been represented by holdings of '*eligible shares*', i.e. ordinary shares carrying no present or future preferential right to dividends or to assets on a winding up and no present or future right (before 6 April 1998, present or future preferential right) to redemption. In practice the Revenue will not seek to withdraw approval where the company breaches this requirement inadvertently, so long as the position is corrected, and the Revenue is informed, without delay after discovery (Revenue Press Release 14 September 1995).

(*c*) The company's ordinary shares (or each class thereof) have been listed in the Official List of the Stock Exchange throughout that period.

(*d*) No holding in any company other than a VCT (or a company which could be a VCT but for (*c*) above) has at any time in that period represented more than 15% of the value of the company's investments.

'Securities' for these purposes are deemed to include liabilities in respect of certain loans not repayable within five years, and in relation to which any stocks or securities are not re-purchasable or redeemable within five years of issue. In practice the Revenue will not regard a standard event of default clause in a loan agreement made on normal commercial terms as a provision which would disqualify the loan being a security. A clause in an agreement would not be regarded as standard if it entitled the lender or a third party to exercise any action which would cause the borrower to default (Revenue Pamphlet IR 131, SP 8/95).

As regards the 15% limits in (*a*) and (*d*) above, the provisions which apply to the similar restrictions on investment trusts (see 64.2 UNIT TRUSTS ETC.) apply with appropriate modification.

Where (*a*)–(*d*) above are met, the Board must also be satisfied that they will be met in the accounting period current at the time of application for approval. Where any of (*a*)–(*d*) above are not met, approval may nevertheless be given where the Board are satisfied that:

(i) in the case of (*a*), (*c*) or (*d*), the condition will be met in the accounting period current when the application for approval is made or in the following accounting period;

(ii) in the case of (*b*), the condition will be met in an accounting period beginning no more than three years after the earlier of the time approval is given and the time it takes effect; and

(iii) in any case, that the condition will continue to be fulfilled in accounting periods following that referred to in (i) or (ii).

On a second and subsequent issues by an approved VCT, the requirements of condition (*b*) above do not have to be met, in relation to the money raised by the further issue, in the accounting period of the further issue or any later accounting period ending no more than three years after the making of the further issue.

The value of any investment for the purposes of (*b*) and (*d*) above is the value when the investment was acquired, except that where it is added to by a further holding of an investment of the same description, or a payment is made in discharge of any obligation attached to it which increases its value, it is the value immediately after the most recent such addition or payment.

Share exchanges and conversions. With effect from 16 June 1999, certain transactions in shares held by a VCT are in effect disregarded in considering the value of holdings for the purposes of the 70%, 30% and 15% tests in (*b*) and (*d*) above. The transactions concerned are as follows.

(i) Where, as part of a restructuring, shares or securities in a company are exchanged for corresponding shares and securities in a new holding company. Certain deemed securities (see above) which are not thus acquired by the new company may be disregarded where these provisions would otherwise be prevented from applying.

(ii) Where a VCT exercises conversion rights in respect of certain convertible shares and securities.

In these circumstances, and subject to detailed conditions (see *ICTA 1988, Sch 28B paras 10C, 10D* introduced by *FA 1999, s 69*), the value of the new shares is taken to be the same as the value of the old shares when they were last valued for these purposes.

Approval may be **withdrawn** where there are reasonable grounds for believing that either:

(A) the conditions for approval were not satisfied at the time the approval was given; or

(B) a condition that the Board were satisfied (as above) would be met has not been or will not be met; or

(C) where (ii) above applies, any other conditions prescribed by regulation in relation to the three-year period have not been met; or

(D) in either the most recent complete accounting period or the current one, one of conditions (*a*)–(*d*) above has failed or will fail to be met (unless the failure was allowed for under (i)–(iii) above); or

(E) where, in relation to a second or further issue by an approved VCT, (*b*) above does not have to be met in the period of issue or certain following accounting periods (see above), one of conditions (*a*)–(*d*) above will fail to be met in the first period for which (*b*) above must be met; or

(F) any other conditions prescribed by regulations have not been met in relation to, or to part of, an accounting period for which (*b*) above does not have to be met.

The withdrawal is effective from the time the company is notified of it, except that:

(1) where approval is given under (i)–(iii) above, and is withdrawn before all the conditions in (*a*)–(*d*) above have been satisfied in relation to either a complete twelve-month accounting period or successive complete accounting periods constituting a continuous period of twelve months or more, the approval is deemed never to have been given; and

(2) for the purposes of relief for capital gains accruing to a VCT under *TCGA 1992, s 100* (see 65.8 below), withdrawal may be effective from an earlier date, but not before the start of the accounting period in which the failure occurred (or is expected to occur).

An assessment consequent on the withdrawal of approval may, where otherwise out of time, be made within three years from the time notice of the withdrawal was given.

For the detailed requirements as regards granting, refusal and withdrawal of approval, and appeals procedures, see *SI 1995 No 1979, Pt II*.

Applications for approval should be made to the Financial Intermediaries and Claims Office, St John's House, Merton Road, Bootle, Merseyside L69 9BB.

65.3 **QUALIFYING HOLDINGS** *[ICTA 1988, s 842AA(5AD)(5AE)(13), Sch 28B; FA 1995, Sch 14; FA 1996, s 161(1)(3); FA 1997, Sch 9; F(No 2)A 1997, s 25(2)–(4)(8); FA 1998, s 70(1)(3), s 72, s 73(2)–(6), Sch 12 para 3, para 4, para 5(2)(3), Sch 27 Pt III(13); FA 1999, s 69(2)(3)(5); FA 2000, Sch 18 paras 4–8]*

Shares or securities in a company are comprised in a VCT's '*qualifying holdings*' at any time if they were first issued to the VCT, and have been held by it ever since, and the following conditions are satisfied at that time.

(*a*) The company is an '*unquoted company*' (whether or not UK resident), i.e. none of its shares, stocks, debentures or other securities is

(i) listed on a recognised stock exchange, or a designated exchange outside the UK, or

(ii) dealt in on the Unlisted Securities Market, or outside the UK by such means as may be designated for the purpose by order.

If the company ceases to be an unquoted company at a time when its shares are comprised in the qualifying holdings of the VCT, this condition is treated as continuing to be met, in relation to shares or securities acquired before that time, for the following five years. [*ICTA 1988, Sch 28B para 2; FA 1995, Sch 14 para 2*].

(*b*) Either

(i) the company must exist wholly for the purpose of carrying on one or more 'qualifying trades' (disregarding any purpose having no significant effect on the extent of its activities as a whole). (The case of *Lord v Tustain; Lord v Chapple Ch D 1993, 65 TC 761* concerned the question whether a company exists for the purposes of carrying on a trade), or

(ii) (after 26 November 1996) it must be the 'parent company of a trading group' (previously, its business had to consist entirely in holding shares in or securities of, or making loans to, one or more 'qualifying subsidiaries' (for which see *ICTA 1988, Sch 28B para 10*, as originally introduced by *FA 1995, Sch 14 para 10*), with or without the carrying on of one or more 'qualifying trades').

In addition, the company, or a 'relevant qualifying subsidiary', must, when the shares were issued to the VCT and ever since, have been carrying on a 'qualifying trade' wholly or mainly in the UK, or preparing to carry on such a trade intended to be carried on wholly or mainly in the UK. In the latter case, there is a time limit of two years from the issue of the shares for the trade to be commenced as intended. A '*relevant qualifying subsidiary*' is, broadly, a company which is 90% owned by the company (or by a subsidiary of the company) and which otherwise satisfies the conditions of *ICTA 1988, Sch 28B para 10* (as amended). In considering whether a trade is carried on 'wholly or mainly in the UK', the totality of the trade activities is taken into account. (Revenue Pamphlet IR 131, SP 7/98).

A trade is a '*qualifying trade*' if it does not, or not substantially (see below), consist of any of the activities at (A)–(L) below. 'Research and development' from which it is intended that there will be derived a qualifying trade carried on wholly or mainly in the UK is treated as the carrying on of a qualifying trade. For the purpose of determining whether shares or securities issued after 5 April 2000 are to be regarded as comprised in a VCT's qualifying holdings, '*research and development*' has the meaning given by *ICTA 1988, s 837A* (see TOLLEY'S INCOME TAX). Previously, it meant any activity intended to result in a patentable invention (within *Patents Act 1977*) or in a computer program.

(A) Dealing in land, in commodities or futures or in shares, securities or other financial instruments.

(B) Dealing in goods otherwise than in the case of an 'ordinary' trade of wholesale or retail distribution.

(C) Banking, insurance, money-lending, debt-factoring, hire-purchase financing or other financial activities.

(D) Leasing (including letting ships on charter or other assets on hire) or receiving royalties or licence fees.

(E) Providing legal or accountancy services.

(F) 'Property development' (see below).

(G) Farming or market gardening.

(H) Holding, managing or occupying woodlands, any other forestry activities or timber production.

(J) Operating or managing hotels or comparable establishments (including guest houses, hostels and other establishments whose main purpose is to offer overnight accommodation with or without catering) or property used as such.

(K) Operating or managing nursing homes or residential care homes (both as defined in *ICTA 1988, Sch 28B para 5(1)*) or property used as such.

(L) Providing services or facilities for any trade, profession or vocation within (A)–(K) above and which is carried on by another person (other than a parent company), where one person has a 'controlling interest' in both trades.

Exclusions (F)–(K) (and the reference to those in exclusion (L)) apply for the purpose of determining whether any shares or securities are, as at any time **after 16 March 1998**, to be regarded as comprised in the qualifying holdings of the VCT. However, those exclusions **do not apply** in relation to shares and securities acquired by the VCT by means of the investment of

- money raised by the issue **before 17 March 1998** of shares in or securities of the VCT; or
- money derived from the investment by the VCT of money so raised.

Exclusions (J) and (K) apply only if the person carrying on the activity in question has an estate or interest (e.g. a lease) in the property concerned or occupies that property.

Adventures and concerns in the nature of trade, and trades not carried on commercially and with a view to the realisation of profits, are also excluded.

Activities accounting in aggregate for less than 20% of the trade, judged normally by reference to turnover or capital employed, are not normally regarded as a 'substantial' part of the trade (Revenue Inspector's Manual IM 6997, 7220). As regards (A) above, it is not intended to exclude from relief a building trade in which the builder buys the land on which the building work is to be done and sells it on completion of that work (Revenue Inspector's Manual IM 6998, 7220).

As regards (B) above, a trade of wholesale or retail distribution is a trade consisting of the offer of goods for sale either to persons for resale (or processing and resale) (which resale must be to members of the general public) by them ('*wholesale*') or to the general public ('*retail*') and a trade is not an ordinary wholesale or retail trade if it consists to a substantial extent of dealing in goods collected or held as an investment (or of that and any other activity within (A)–(L) above), and a substantial proportion of such goods is held for a significantly longer period than might reasonably be expected for a vendor trying to dispose of them at market value. Whether such trades are '*ordinary*' is to be judged having regard to the following features, those under (1) supporting the categorisation as 'ordinary', those under (2) being indicative to the contrary.

(1) (*a*) The breaking of bulk.

(*b*) The purchase and sale of goods in different markets.

(*c*) The employment of staff and incurring of trade expenses other than the cost of goods or the remuneration of persons connected (within *ICTA 1988, s 839*) with a company carrying on the trade.

(2) (*a*) The purchase or sale of goods from or to persons connected (within *ICTA 1988, s 839*) with the trader.

(*b*) The matching of purchases with sales.

(*c*) The holding of goods for longer than might normally be expected.

(*d*) The carrying on of the trade at a place not commonly used for wholesale or retail trading.

(*e*) The absence of physical possession of the goods by the trader.

As regards (D) above as it applies for determining whether shares or securities issued before 6 April 2000 are to be regarded as comprised in a VCT's qualifying holdings, the trade of a company engaged in the production of original master films, tapes or discs is not excluded by reason only of the receipt of royalties or licence fees, provided that all royalties and licence fees received by the company are in respect of films, etc. produced by it since the issue of the shares to the VCT or in respect of by-products arising therefrom. The company may also be engaged in the distribution of films produced by it since those shares were issued. Similarly the trade of a company engaged in research and development (as defined) is not excluded by reason only of the receipt of royalties and licence fees attributable to that research and development.

As regards (D) above as it applies for determining whether shares or securities issued after 5 April 2000 are to be regarded as comprised in a VCT's qualifying holdings, a trade is not excluded from being a qualifying trade solely because it consists to a substantial extent in the receiving of royalties or licence fees substantially attributable (in terms of value) to the exploitation of 'relevant intangible assets'. An intangible asset is an asset falling to be treated as such under normal UK accounting practice. A '*relevant intangible asset*' is an asset the whole or greater part of which (in terms of value) has been created by the company carrying on the trade or by a company which throughout the creation of the asset was the 'parent company' of that company or a 'qualifying subsidiary' (within *ICTA 1988, Sch 28B para 10* as modified for this purpose) of that parent company. A '*parent company*' is for these purposes a company with one or more 51% subsidiaries which is not itself a 51% subsidiary. Where the asset is 'intellectual property', it is treated as created by a company only if the right to exploit it vests in that company (alone or with others). The term '*intellectual property*' incorporates patents, trade marks, copyrights, design rights etc. and foreign equivalents.

Also as regards (D) above, a trade carried on by a company will not be excluded by reason only of its consisting of chartering ships, other than oil rigs or ships of a kind primarily used for sport or recreation, provided that

(I) the company beneficially owns all the ships it so lets,

(II) every ship beneficially owned by the company is UK-registered,

(III) the company is solely responsible for arranging the marketing of the services of its ships, and

(IV) in relation to every letting on charter, certain conditions as to length and terms of charter, and the arm's length character of the transaction, are met,

and if any of (I)–(IV) above is not met in relation to certain lettings, only those lettings (together with any other excluded activities) are taken into account in determining whether a substantial part of the trade consists of excluded activities.

'*Property development*' in (F) above means the development of land by a company, which has (or has had at any time) an 'interest in the land' (as defined by *ICTA 1988, Sch 28B para 5(5)(7)*), with the sole or main object of realising a gain from the disposal of an interest in the developed land.

As regards (L) above, a person has a '*controlling interest*' in a trade carried on by a company if he controls the company (within *ICTA 1988, s 416*, see TOLLEY'S CORPORATION TAX under Close Companies, as modified by *ICTA 1988, Sch 28B para 13(2)(3)(5)(6)*); or if the company is close (see TOLLEY'S CORPORATION TAX under Close Companies) and he or an 'associate' (within *ICTA 1988, s 417*, see TOLLEY'S CORPORATION TAX under Close Companies, but excluding a brother or sister) is a director of the company and the beneficial owner of, or able to control, more than 30% of its ordinary share capital; or if at least half of its ordinary share capital is directly or indirectly owned by him. In any other case, it is obtained by his being entitled to at least one-half of the assets used for, or income arising from, the trade.

Rights and powers of 'associates' (as above) are taken into account for these purposes.

Post-26 November 1996 provisions. A company is the '*parent company of a trading group*' if it has one or more subsidiaries, each of which is a 'qualifying subsidiary' (within *ICTA 1988, Sch 28B para 10* as amended by *FA 1997, Sch 9 para 5* and by *FA 1998, s 73(2)*), and if, taking all the activities of the company and its subsidiaries as one business, neither that business nor a substantial part of it consists in either or both of:

(*aa*) activities within (A)–(L) above (but with the same let-outs applying as regards (D)); and

(*bb*) non-trading activities.

Activities are for these purposes disregarded to the extent that they consist in:

(AA) holding shares in or securities of, or making loans to, one or more of the company's subsidiaries; or

(BB) holding and managing property used by the company or any of its subsidiaries for the purposes or either

(i) research and development (as defined — see above) from which it is intended that a qualifying trade to be carried on by the company or any of its subsidiaries will be derived, or

(ii) one or more qualifying trades so carried on.

Activities of a subsidiary are similarly disregarded to the extent that they consist in the making of loans to the company or, where the subsidiary exists wholly for the purpose of carrying on one or more qualifying trades (apart from '*insignificant purposes*', i.e. purposes capable of having no significant effect, other than in relation to incidental matters, on the extent of the subsidiary's activities), of activities carried on in pursuance of those insignificant purposes.

(*c*) The money raised by the issue of shares to the VCT must have been employed wholly for the purposes of, or of preparing for the carrying on of, the qualifying trade (disregarding insignificant amounts used for other purposes), or be intended to be so employed. In the latter case, the money must actually be so employed within twelve months of the later of the issue of the shares to the VCT and the date the qualifying trade was commenced.

After 26 November 1996, where the company is a 'parent company of a trading group' within (*b*)(ii) above, the '*trader company*' (i.e. the company carrying on (or preparing to carry on) the required qualifying trade) must either:

(i) satisfy the requirements in (*b*)(i) above; or

(ii) be a company in relation to which those requirements would be satisfied if activities within (*b*)(AA) and (*b*)(BB) above, or consisting of a subsidiary making loans to its parent, were disregarded; or

(iii) be a 'relevant qualifying subsidiary' which either

(1) exists wholly for the purpose of carrying on activities within (*b*)(BB) above (disregarding purposes capable of having no significant effect (other than in relation to incidental matters) on the extent of its activities), or

(2) has no corporation tax profits and no part of its business consists in the making of investments.

A '*relevant qualifying subsidiary*' is, broadly, a company which is 90% owned by the investee company (or by a subsidiary of that company) and which otherwise satisfies the conditions of *ICTA 1988, Sch 28B para 10* (as amended).

Money whose retention can reasonably be regarded as necessary or advisable for financing current trade requirements is regarded as employed for trade purposes, but by the end of the twelve months funds should no longer be held which are clearly surplus to day-to-day needs. (Revenue Inspector's Manual, IM 7209).

(*d*) The aggregate of money raised from shares issued by the company to the VCT must not have exceeded the 'maximum qualifying investment' of £1 million in the period from six months before the issue in question (or, if earlier, the beginning of the year of assessment of the issue) to the time of the issue in question. Disposals are treated as far as possible as eliminating any such excess. The £1 million limit is proportionately reduced where, at the time of the issue, the qualifying trade is carried on, or to be carried on, in partnership or as a joint venture, and one or more of the other parties is a company.

(*e*) The value of the company's assets as a whole did not exceed £15 million immediately before the issue and did not exceed £16 million immediately afterwards. As regards shares and securities issued by investee companies before 6 April 1998, these limits were £10 million and £11 million respectively. For this purpose, value means the value of the gross assets of the company at a time when it did not have any qualifying subsidiaries (see (*f*) below), or the aggregate value of the gross assets of all the companies in the group where it does have such subsidiaries (but disregarding any rights against, or shares in or securities of, another group member). The value of a company's gross assets at any time is the aggregate of the values of its assets (without any deduction for liabilities) as would be shown in a balance sheet drawn up as at that time. Any advance payment received for the share issue itself is ignored immediately before the issue but the right to the unpaid portion of shares issued partly paid is taken as included in gross assets immediately after the issue. See Revenue Pamphlet IR 131, SP 5/98.

(*f*) The company must not control (within *ICTA 1988, s 416*, see TOLLEY'S CORPORATION TAX under Close Companies, as modified by *ICTA 1988, Sch 28B para 13(2)(3)(5)(6)*, and with or without connected persons) any company other than a qualifying subsidiary, nor must another company (or another company and a person connected with it) control it. The control test disregards all fixed rate preference shares (unless and until they carry voting rights) and loans held by the VCT and by any other investor (Revenue Press Release 4 March 1996). Neither must arrangements be in existence by virtue of which such control could arise. These provisions do not, however, apply to control by a VCT attributable primarily to a change in the value of any shares in or securities of the company. See Revenue Tax Bulletin October 1997 pp 471, 472 for the Revenue's views on the application of the control test where two or more co-investors (including a VCT) invest in a company alongside each other.

(*g*) Where the company is being wound up, none of conditions (*a*)–(*f*) above or (*h*) and (*j*) below are regarded on that account as not being satisfied provided that those conditions would be met apart from the winding up, and that the winding up is for *bona fide* commercial reasons and not part of a scheme or arrangement a main purpose of which is the avoidance of tax. After 20 March 2000, the company does not cease to meet condition (*b*) above by reason of anything done as a consequence of its being in administration or receivership (both as defined), provided everything so done and the making of the relevant order are for *bona fide* commercial (and not tax avoidance) reasons.

(*h*) The holding in question must not include any securities (as defined in 65.2 above) relating to a guaranteed loan. A security relates to a guaranteed loan if there are arrangements entitling the VCT to receive anything (directly or indirectly) from a 'third party' in the event of a failure by any person to comply with the terms of the security or the loan to which it relates. It is immaterial whether or not the arrangements apply in all such cases. '*Third party*' includes any person other than the investee company itself and, if it is a parent company of a trading group (see (*b*) above), its subsidiaries. This condition applies for accounting periods (of the VCT) ending after 1 July 1997, but does not apply in the case of shares or securities acquired by the VCT by means of investing money raised by the issue by it before 2 July 1997 of shares or securities (or money derived from the investment of any such money raised).

(*j*) At least 10% (by value) of the VCT's *total* holding of shares in and securities of the company must consist of 'eligible shares' (as defined in 65.2 (b) above — broadly, ordinary, non-preferential, shares). For this purpose, the value of shares etc. at any time is taken to be their value immediately after the most recent of the events listed below, except that it cannot thereby be taken to be less than the amount of consideration given by the VCT for the shares etc. The said events are as follows.

- The acquisition of the shares etc. by the VCT.
- The acquisition by the VCT (other than by way of bonus issue for no consideration) of any other shares etc. in the same company which are of the same description as those already held.
- The making of any payment in discharge (or part discharge) of any obligation attached to the shares etc. in a case where such discharge increases the value of the shares etc.

This condition applies for accounting periods (of the VCT) ending after 1 July 1997, but, if necessary in order to satisfy the condition, one may disregard shares and securities acquired by the VCT by means of investing money raised by the issue by it before 2 July 1997 of shares or securities (or money derived from the investment of any such money raised).

As regards (*c*) and (*d*) above, where either condition would be met as to only part of the money raised by the issue, and the holding is not otherwise capable of being treated as separate holdings, it is treated as two separate holdings, one from which that part of the money was raised, the other from which the rest was raised, with the value being apportioned accordingly to each holding. In the case of (*c*), this does not require an insignificant amount applied for non-trade purposes to be treated as a separate holding.

As regards (*c*) above, in relation to buy-outs (and in particular management buy-outs), the Revenue will usually accept that where a company is formed to acquire a trade, and the funds raised from the VCT are applied to that purchase, the requirement that the funds be employed for the purposes of the trade is satisfied. Where the company is formed to acquire another company and its trade, or a holding company and its trading subsidiaries, this represents an investment rather than employment for the purposes of the trade. However, the Revenue will usually accept that the requirement is satisfied if the trade of the company, or all the activities of the holding company and its subsidiaries, are hived up to the acquiring company as soon as possible after the acquisition. In the case of a holding company and its subsidiaries, to the extent that the trades are not hived up, the holding cannot be a qualifying holding (Revenue Tax Bulletin August 1995 pp 243, 244).

As regards (*b*)–(*f*) and (*j*) above, with effect from 16 June 1999, certain transactions in shares held by a VCT are in effect disregarded in considering whether the relevant condition is satisfied. The transactions concerned are as follows.

(A) Where, as part of a restructuring, shares or securities in a company are exchanged for corresponding shares and securities in a new holding company. Certain deemed securities (see 65.2 above) which are not thus acquired by the new company may be disregarded where these provisions would otherwise be prevented from applying.

(B) Where a VCT exercises conversion rights in respect of certain convertible shares and securities.

In these circumstances, and subject to detailed conditions (see *ICTA 1988, Sch 28B paras 10C, 10D* introduced by *FA 1999, s 69*), to the extent that the condition was satisfied in relation to the old shares, it will generally be taken to be satisfied in relation to the new shares.

Where, after 20 March 2000 under a company reorganisation etc.,

- a VCT exchanges a qualifying holding for other shares or securities, and
- the exchange is for *bona fide* commercial reasons and not part of a tax avoidance scheme or arrangements,

then under regulations to be made by the Treasury, the new shares or securities may be treated as being qualifying holdings even if some or all of the above requirements are not otherwise satisfied. The regulations may specify the circumstances in which, and conditions subject to which, they apply, which requirements are to be treated as met, and the period for which those requirements are to be so treated; and they may make the necessary administrative provisions. They may also provide for the value of the new holding and of any original shares retained to be taken to be of such amount as to continue to satisfy the requirements at 65.2(*b*) and (*d*) above.

The Treasury have power by order to modify the requirements under (*b*) above as they consider expedient, and to alter the cash limits referred to in (*d*) and (*e*) above.

65.4 INCOME TAX RELIEFS *[ICTA 1988, s 332A, Sch 15B; FA 1995, s 71, Sch 15]*

Relief from income tax is granted for 1995/96 and subsequent years in respect of both investments in VCTs and distributions from such trusts.

65.5 **Relief in respect of investments.** Subject to the conditions described below, an individual may claim relief for a year of assessment for the amount (or aggregate amounts) subscribed by him on his own behalf for 'eligible shares' issued to him in a year of assessment by a VCT (or VCTs) for raising money. There is a limit of **£100,000** on the relief which may be claimed for any year of assessment.

'*Eligible shares*' means new ordinary shares in a VCT which, throughout the three years following issue (five years for shares issued before 6 April 2000), carry no present or future preferential right to dividends or to assets on a winding up and no present or future right (before 6 April 1998, present or future preferential right) to redemption.

Relief is given by a reduction in what would otherwise be the individual's income tax liability for the year of assessment by the lesser of

(i) tax at the lower rate (currently 20%) on the amount(s) subscribed, and

(ii) an amount sufficient to reduce that liability to nil.

In determining what would otherwise be the individual's income tax liability for the year of assessment for this purpose, no account is taken of:

(A) any income tax reduction in respect of enterprise investment scheme investments, personal reliefs (i.e. married couple's allowance, widow's bereavement allowance and additional relief in respect of children), qualifying maintenance payments, interest relief or medical insurance (see TOLLEY'S INCOME TAX under Enterprise Investment Scheme, Allowances and Tax Rates, Married Persons, Interest Relief and Medical Insurance respectively);

(B) any reduction of liability to tax by way of DOUBLE TAX RELIEF (18); or

(C) any basic rate tax on income the tax on which the individual is entitled to charge against any other person or to deduct, retain or satisfy out of any payment.

Where relief is given by repayment of tax more than twelve months after the end of the year of assessment in which the shares were issued, interest under *ICTA 1988, s 824* (see TOLLEY'S INCOME TAX under Interest on Overpaid Tax) is payable.

An individual is **not** entitled to relief where:

(*a*) he was under 18 years of age at the time of issue of the shares;

(*b*) circumstances have arisen which, had the relief already been given, would have resulted in the withdrawal or reduction of the relief (see 65.6 below);

(*c*) the shares were issued or subscribed for other than for *bona fide* commercial purposes or as part of a scheme or arrangement a main purpose of which was the avoidance of tax; or

(*d*) a loan is made to the individual (or to an 'associate' within *ICTA 1988, s 417*, see TOLLEY'S CORPORATION TAX under Close Companies, but excluding a brother or sister) by any person at any time in the period beginning with the incorporation of the VCT (or, if later, two years before the date of issue of the shares) and ending three years after the date of issue of the shares (five years for shares issued before 6 April 2000), and the loan would not have been made, or would not have been made on the same terms, if he had not subscribed, or had not been proposing to subscribe, for the shares. For the Revenue's views on 'loan-linked' investments, see Revenue Pamphlet IR 131, SP 6/98. The granting of credit to, or the assignment of a debt due from, the individual or associate is counted as a loan for these purposes.

[*ICTA 1988, Sch 15B paras 1, 2, 6; FA 1995, Sch 15 paras 1, 2, 6; FA 1998, s 73(1)(6), Sch 27 Pt III(13); FA 2000, Sch 18, para 1(2)(4), para 3*].

An individual subscribing for eligible shares may obtain from the VCT a certificate giving details of the subscription and certifying that certain conditions for relief are satisfied. [*SI 1995 No 1979, Reg 9*].

Example

On 1 August 2000, A Ventura, a 44 year old married man whose salary is £50,000 p.a. from UK employment, subscribes for 50,000 eligible £1 shares issued at par to raise money by VCT plc, an approved venture capital trust. On 1 March 2001 he purchases a further 90,000 £1 shares in VCT plc for £70,000 on the open market. The trust makes no distribution in 2000/01. Mr Ventura's other income for 2000/01 consists of dividends of £14,850 (net).

Mr Ventura's tax computation for 2000/01 is as follows.

	£	£
Earnings from UK employment		50,000
Dividends	14,850	
Add Tax credits	1,650	16,500
Total income		66,500
Deduct personal allowance		4,385
Taxable income		£62,115
Tax payable:		£
1,520 @ 10%		152.00
26,880 @ 22%		5,913.60
17,215 @ 40%		6,886.00
16,500 @ 32.5%		5,362.50
		18,314.10
Deduct Relief in respect of investment in VCT plc:		
Lower of 20% of £50,000 subscribed and £18,314.10		10,000.00
		8,314.10
Deduct Tax credits on dividends		1,650.00
Net tax payable (subject to PAYE deductions from salary)		£6,664.10

65.6 **Withdrawal of relief on investment.** *Disposal of investment.* Where an individual disposes of eligible shares, in respect of which relief has been claimed as under 65.5 above, within three years of their issue (five years for shares issued before 6 April 2000) and other than to a spouse when they are living together (see below), then:

(*a*) if the disposal is otherwise than at arm's length, relief given by reference to those shares is withdrawn;

(*b*) if the disposal is at arm's length, the relief given by reference to those shares is reduced by an amount equivalent to tax at the lower rate (for the year for which relief was given) on the consideration received for the disposal (or withdrawn if the relief exceeds that amount).

Relief is **not** withdrawn where the disposal is by one spouse to the other at a time when they are living together. However, on any subsequent disposal the spouse to whom the shares were transferred is treated as if he or she were the person who subscribed for the shares, as if the shares had been issued to him or her at the time they were issued to the transferor spouse, and as if his or her liability to income tax had been reduced by reference to those shares by the same amount, and for the same year of assessment, as applied on the subscription by the transferor spouse. Any assessment for reducing or withdrawing relief is made on the transferee spouse.

Identification of shares. For the above purposes, disposals of eligible shares in a VCT are identified with those acquired earlier rather than later. As between eligible shares acquired on the same day, shares by reference to which relief has been given are treated as disposed of after any other eligible shares.

Withdrawal of approval. Where approval of a company as a VCT is withdrawn (but not treated as never having been given) (see 65.2 above), relief given by reference to eligible shares in the VCT is withdrawn as if on a non-arm's length disposal immediately before the withdrawal of approval.

Assessments withdrawing or reducing relief, whether because relief is subsequently found not to have been due or under the above provisions, are made under Schedule D, Case VI for the year of assessment for which the relief was given. No such assessment is, however, to be made by reason of an event occurring after the death of the person to whom the shares were issued.

Information. Particulars of all events leading to the reduction or withdrawal of relief must be notified to the inspector by the person to whom the relief was given within 60 days of his coming to know of the event. Where the inspector has reason to believe that a notice so required has not been given, he may require that person to furnish him, within a specified time not being less than 60 days, with such information relating to the event as he may reasonably require. The requirements of secrecy do not prevent the inspector disclosing to a VCT that relief has been given or claimed by reference to a particular number or proportion of its shares. Penalties under *TMA 1970, s 98* apply for failure to comply with these requirements.

[*ICTA 1988, Sch 15B paras 3–5; FA 1995, s 71(3), Sch 15 paras 3–5; FA 2000, Sch 18 para 1(3), para 3*].

Example

On 1 August 2002, A Ventura in the *Example* at 65.5 above, who since 2000/01 has neither acquired nor disposed of any shares in VCT plc, gives 30,000 shares to his son. On 1 March 2003 he disposes of the remaining 110,000 shares for £95,000. The relief given in 65.5 above is withdrawn as follows.

Disposal on 1 August 2002

The shares disposed of are identified with 30,000 of those subscribed for, and, since the disposal was not at arm's length, the relief given on those shares is withdrawn.

	£
Relief withdrawn $\frac{30,000}{50,000} \times$ £10,000 =	6,000

Disposal on 1 March 2003

The balance of £4,000 of the relief originally given was in respect of 20,000 of the shares disposed of. The disposal consideration for those 20,000 shares is

	£
$95,000 \times \frac{20,000}{110,000} =$	17,273

The relief withdrawn is the lesser of the relief originally given and 20% of the consideration received, i.e.

	£
20% of £17,273 = £3,455.	
Relief withdrawn is therefore	3,455
The 2000/01 Schedule D, Case VI assessment is therefore	£9,455

65.7 **Relief on distributions.** A 'relevant distribution' of a VCT to which a 'qualifying investor' is beneficially entitled is not treated as income for income tax purposes, provided, for distributions made before 6 April 1999, that certain conditions are fulfilled as regards the obtaining of an 'enduring declaration' from the investor, and that the VCT claims the related tax credit, which it is required to pass on to the investor. Distributions made after 5 April 1999 remain exempt from income tax but, in line with general tax changes, tax credits are not repayable.

A '*qualifying investor*' is an individual aged 18 or over who is beneficially entitled to the distribution either as the holder of the shares or through a nominee (including the trustees of a bare trust).

A '*relevant distribution*' is a dividend (including a capital dividend) in respect of ordinary shares in a company which is a VCT which were acquired at a time when it was a VCT by the recipient of the dividend, and which were not shares acquired in excess of the 'permitted maximum' for the year of assessment. Shares acquired after 8 March 1999 must also have been acquired for *bona fide* commercial purposes and not as part of a tax avoidance scheme or arrangements. A relevant distribution does not include any dividend paid in respect of profits or gains of any accounting period ending when the company was not a VCT.

Shares are acquired in excess of the '*permitted maximum*' for a year where the aggregate of the market values of ordinary shares acquired in VCTs by the individual or his nominee(s) in that year exceeds £100,000, disregarding shares acquired other than for *bona fide* commercial reasons or as part of a scheme or arrangement a main purpose of which is the avoidance of tax. Shares acquired later in the year are identified as representing the excess before those acquired earlier, and in relation to same-day acquisition of different shares, a proportionate part of each description of share is treated as representing any excess arising on that day. Shares acquired at a time when a company was not a VCT are for these purposes treated as disposed of before other shares in the VCT. Otherwise, disposals are identified with earlier acquisitions before later ones, except that as between shares acquired on the same day, shares acquired in excess of the permitted maximum are treated as disposed of before any other shares. There are provisions for effectively disregarding acquisitions arising out of share exchanges where, for capital gains purposes, the new shares are treated as the same assets as the old.

[*ICTA 1988, Sch 15B paras 7–9; FA 1995, Sch 15 paras 7–9; FA 1999, s 70; SI 1995 No 1979, Reg 10; SI 1999 No 819, Reg 4*].

For the detailed requirements as regards obtaining relief for distributions, including the obtaining of the 'enduring declaration' and the claiming of tax credits, see *SI 1995 No 1979, Pt III Ch II*, repealed with effect from 6 April 1999 by *SI 1999 No 819, Reg 4*.

65.8 **CAPITAL GAINS TAX RELIEFS** *[TCGA 1992, ss 151A, 151B, Sch 5C; FA 1995, s 72, Sch 16]*

From 6 April 1995, the capital gains of a VCT are not chargeable gains. [*TCGA 1992, s 100(1); FA 1995, s 72(2)*]. In addition, for 1995/96 and subsequent years, individual investors in VCTs are entitled to two reliefs:

(*a*) on disposal of VCT shares (see 65.9 below); and

(*b*) by deferral of chargeable gains on re-investment in VCT share issues (see 65.10 below).

Various provisions of *TCGA 1992* which are superseded for these purposes by specific provisions (as below) are disapplied or applied separately to parts of holdings which do not fall within the reliefs.

Withdrawal of approval. Where approval of a company as a VCT is withdrawn (but not treated as never having been given) (see 65.2 above), shares which (apart from the withdrawal) would be eligible for the relief on disposal (see 65.9 below) are treated as disposed of at their market value at the time of the withdrawal. For the purposes of the relief on disposal, the disposal is treated as taking place while the company is still a VCT, but the re-acquisition is treated as taking place immediately after it ceases to be so.

65.9 **Relief on disposal.** A gain or loss accruing to an individual on a 'qualifying disposal' of ordinary shares in a company which was a VCT throughout his period of ownership is not a chargeable gain or an allowable loss. A disposal is a '*qualifying disposal*' if:

(*a*) the individual is 18 years of age or more at the time of the disposal;

(*b*) the shares were not acquired in excess of the 'permitted maximum' for any year of assessment; and

(*c*) the shares were acquired for *bona fide* commercial purposes and not as part of a scheme or arrangement a main purpose of which was the avoidance of tax.

The identification of those shares which were acquired in excess of the '*permitted maximum*' is as under 65.7 above, i.e. where the aggregate of the market values of ordinary shares acquired in VCTs by the individual or his nominee(s) in that year exceeds £100,000, disregarding shares acquired other than for *bona fide* commercial reasons or as part of a scheme or arrangement a main purpose of which is the avoidance of tax. Shares acquired later in the year are identified as representing the excess before those acquired earlier, and in relation to same-day acquisition of different shares, a proportionate part of each description of share is treated as representing any excess arising on that day. Shares acquired at a time when a company was not a VCT are for these purposes treated as disposed of before other shares in the VCT. Otherwise, disposals are identified with earlier acquisitions before later ones, except that as between shares acquired on the same day, shares acquired in excess of the permitted maximum are treated as disposed of before any other shares. See the examples at Revenue Capital Gains Manual CG 57468, 57470.

The normal rules for the pooling of shares and identification of disposals in *TCGA 1992, ss 104, 105, 106A, 107* (see 59.2, 59.3 SHARES AND SECURITIES—IDENTIFICATION RULES) are disapplied in respect of shares which are eligible for the above relief.

There are provisions (see below) for effectively disregarding acquisitions arising out of share exchanges where, for capital gains purposes, the new shares are treated as the same assets as the old.

Where an individual holds ordinary shares in a VCT which fall into more than one of the following groups:

(1) shares eligible for relief on disposal (as above) and by reference to which he has been given or is entitled to claim relief under the provisions in 65.5 above (income tax relief on investments);

(2) shares eligible for relief on disposal but by reference to which he has not been given or will be unable to claim relief under the provisions in 65.5 above;

(3) shares by reference to which he has been given or is entitled to claim relief under the provisions in 65.5 above but which are not eligible for relief on disposal;

(4) shares not within (1)–(3) above,

then, if there is a reorganisation under *TCGA 1992, s 126*, the provisions in *TCGA 1992, s 127* (equation of original shares with new holding) (see 58.5 SHARES AND SECURITIES above) will apply separately to each group of shares (if any) in order that they continue to be kept within their respective groups.

Where an individual holds ordinary shares in a company ('the existing holding') and there is, by virtue of an allotment for payment within *TCGA 1992, s 126(2)(a)* (e.g. a rights issue), a reorganisation affecting the existing holding immediately following which the shares or allotted holding are shares falling within (1)–(3) above, the provisions in *TCGA 1992, ss 127–130* will not apply in relation to that existing holding. The effect is that the rights issue will be treated as an acquisition.

Where holding consists of shares falling within (1) or (2) above and it is exchanged or is deemed to be exchanged for a second holding which does not consist of ordinary shares in a VCT, then the provisions in *TCGA 1992, ss 135, 136* will not apply (see 58.8 and 58.10 SHARES AND SECURITIES above). The effect is that there will be or deemed to be a disposal and acquisition.

[*TCGA 1992, ss 151A, 151B; FA 1995, s 72(3); FA 1998, s 124(6)*].

See 65.8 above as regards relief on withdrawal of approval of the VCT.

Example

On the disposals in the *Example* at 65.6 above, a chargeable gain or allowable loss arises only on the disposal of the shares acquired in excess of the permitted maximum for 2000/01. The shares in VCT plc were acquired in 2000/01 for £120,000, so that there is a £20,000 excess over the permitted maximum. The 50,000 shares first acquired for £50,000 are first identified, so that shares representing the excess are two-sevenths of the 90,000 shares subsequently acquired for £70,000 on 1 March 2001, i.e. 25,714 of those shares. The disposal identified with those shares is a corresponding proportion of the 110,000 shares disposed of for a consideration of £95,000 on 1 March 2003.

Mr Ventura's capital gains tax computation for 2002/03 is as follows.

Disposal consideration for 25,714 shares:

	£
$£95{,}000 \times \frac{25{,}714}{110{,}000} =$	22,207
Deduct Cost:	
$£70{,}000 \times \frac{25{,}714}{90{,}000} =$	20,000
Chargeable gain (subject to taper relief)	£2,207

65.10 **Deferral relief on reinvestment.** *TCGA 1992, Sch 5C* applies where:

(*a*) a chargeable gain accrues to an individual after 5 April 1995

- on the disposal by him of any asset; or
- on the occurrence of a chargeable event under these provisions or the similar provisions governing reinvestment into EIS shares (see 20.10 ENTERPRISE INVESTMENT SCHEME (AND BES));

(*b*) the individual makes a 'qualifying investment'; and

(*c*) the individual is UK resident or ordinarily resident both when the chargeable gain accrues to him and when he makes the 'qualifying investment', and is not, at the latter time, regarded as resident outside the UK for the purposes of any double taxation arrangements the effect of which would be that he would not be liable to tax on a gain arising on a disposal, immediately after their acquisition, of the shares comprising the 'qualifying investment', disregarding the exemption under *TCGA 1992, s 151A(1)* (see 65.9 above).

A '*qualifying investment*' is a subscription for shares in a company which is a VCT, by reference to which income tax investment relief is obtained under 65.5 above, within twelve months (extendible by the Board) before or after the time of the accrual of the chargeable gain in question, and, if before, provided that the shares are still held at that time. The shares are not deemed to be issued by reason only of a letter of allotment.

Broadly, the detailed provisions below allow a claim for the chargeable gain to be rolled over into the VCT shares, and for the gain to become chargeable on certain events in relation to those shares (including, in particular, on their disposal).

Postponement of original gain. Where a chargeable gain would otherwise accrue to an individual ('the investor') and he acquires a qualifying investment, a claim can be made by him to defer the whole or part of that gain against a corresponding amount of his qualifying investment up to the amount of the gain, or for an amount so claimed, whichever is the smaller. The gain eligible for deferral is the gain after all available reliefs (including retirement relief and indexation allowance) other than taper relief (see 60.12 TAPER RELIEF) (Revenue Capital Gains Manual CG 57481). The amount of qualifying investment available for set off is restricted to the amount on which income tax investment relief has been given under 65.5 above (maximum **£100,000** per tax year), less any amount already utilised against other gains. If income tax investment relief is restricted because the investor's income tax liability is insufficient to fully absorb the relief, deferral relief is still available on the full amount of the investment that would otherwise have qualified for the income tax relief. It is, however, necessary for *some* income tax investment relief to have been given; no deferral relief is available if the investor's income tax liability is nil without taking account of income tax investment relief. (Revenue Capital Gains Manual CG 57482).

Subject to what is said at 56.29 SELF-ASSESSMENT re claims being included in a self-assessment tax return if possible, there is no statutory form in which a claim must be made. Deferral cannot be given until income tax relief has been given in respect of the VCT shares, which may not be until after the end of the tax year in which they are issued. (Revenue Capital Gains Manual CG 57507, 57509). The deferral claim must be made by the fifth anniversary of 31 January following the 'relevant tax year' (for 1995/96 and earlier years, within six years after the end of the relevant tax year). The '*relevant tax year*' is the tax year in which the *later* of the following events occurred:

- the gain to be deferred arose;
- the VCT shares were issued.

(Revenue Capital Gains Manual CG 57508).

Chargeable event. The original gain deferred through the making of the above claim will subsequently crystallise if one of the following circumstances arise:

(A) the investor disposes of the shares in his qualifying investment ('the relevant shares') otherwise than under *TCGA 1992, s 58* (an inter-spouse transfer);

(B) the relevant shares are disposed of by the spouse of the investor (otherwise than by a transfer back to him), the spouse having first acquired them from the investor under *TCGA 1992, s 58*;

(C) where shares falling within 65.9 (3) above are exchanged or treated as exchanged for any non-VCT holdings and under *TCGA 1992, s 135* or *TCGA 1992, s 136* (see 58.8 and 58.10 SHARES AND SECURITIES above) there is a requirement (or, but for *TCGA 1992, s 116* (see 49 QUALIFYING CORPORATE BONDS above) there would be a requirement) for those holdings to be regarded as the same assets as those shares;

(D) the investor becomes neither resident nor ordinarily resident in the UK whilst holding the relevant shares and within three years of the making of the qualifying investment (five years as regards shares issued before 6 April 2000);

(E) an individual who acquired the relevant shares through an inter-spouse transfer under *TCGA 1992, s 58* becomes neither resident nor ordinarily resident in the UK whilst holding those shares and within period referred to in (D) above;

(F) the company in which the relevant shares are held has its approval as a VCT withdrawn (in a case in which approval is not treated as never having been given) (see 65.2 above);

(G) the relief given under 65.5 above by reference to relevant shares is withdrawn or reduced in circumstances not falling within (A)–(F) above.

In the case of (D) or (E) above, the original gain will not crystallise where the individual concerned became neither resident nor ordinarily resident in the UK through temporarily working abroad and he again becomes UK resident or ordinarily resident in the UK within three years of that event, without having disposed of any of the relevant shares in the meantime. An assessment will be issued by the Revenue when it is clear that the individual will not regain UK resident status within the three-year period.

There is no crystallisation of the original gain where an event within (A)–(G) above occurs at or after the time of death of the investor or a person to whom the relevant shares were transferred under *TCGA 1992, s 58*.

Without prejudice to the following provisions in a case falling within (F) above, any reference above to a disposal excludes a reference to a disposal deemed to occur on a withdrawal of approval within 65.8 above.

Crystallisation of original gain. Where a chargeable event mentioned in (A)–(G) above relating to relevant shares occurs for the first time in connection with those shares, a chargeable gain is deemed to accrue at that time equal to so much of the expenditure on those shares which was set against the original gain.

Identification of shares. In determining whether any shares to which a chargeable gain relates are shares the expenditure on which has been set against the whole or part of any gain, disposals of shares are identified with those subscribed for earlier rather than later, and as between shares in a company acquired on the same day, those the expenditure on which has been set against a gain are treated as disposed of after any other shares in that company. The normal rules at 59.2 SHARES AND SECURITIES—IDENTIFICATION RULES are disapplied (regardless of whether or not the shares are eligible for CGT relief under 65.9 above). For a practical illustration, see the *Example* below and, for a more complex example, Revenue Capital Gains Manual CG 57501.

Assets. Where at the time of a chargeable event relevant shares are regarded as represented by assets which consist of or include assets other than relevant shares, the expenditure on those shares is apportioned between those assets on a just and reasonable basis. As between different assets regarded as representing the same relevant shares, the identification of those assets will be determined on a similar basis to the identification of shares.

Persons assessable. The chargeable gain is treated as accruing, as the case may be:

(i) to the individual who makes the disposal;

(ii) to the individual who holds the shares in question at the time of the exchange or deemed exchange;

(iii) to the individual who becomes non-UK resident etc.;

(iv) to the individual who holds the shares in question when the withdrawal of the approval takes effect; or

(v) to the individual who holds the shares in question when the circumstances arise in respect of which the relief is withdrawn or reduced.

A chargeable gain is computed separately for the investor without reference to any shares held at the time of the chargeable event by a recipient to the investor from a *TCGA 1992, s 58* transfer).

65.10 Venture Capital Trusts

[*TCGA 1992, Sch 5C; FA 1995, Sch 16; FA 1998, s 124(6); FA 2000, Sch 18 paras 2, 3*].

See 60.12 TAPER RELIEF for the application of that relief to the deferred gain.

Example

The facts are as in the *Example* at 65.5 above except that Mr Ventura sells a painting on 1 November 2000, realising a chargeable gain of £26,200. In addition to the relief against income tax he receives, he also claims deferral of the gain against his subscription for shares in VCT plc up to an amount of £19,000, leaving £7,200 to be covered by his annual exemption.

When the shares in VCT plc are subsequently disposed of in 2002/03 (see *Example* at 65.6 above), the gain of £19,000 deferred on the disposal of the painting crystallises and forms part of his gains for 2002/03 as follows.

1 August 2002 disposal

The 30,000 shares disposed of on 1 August 2002 are initially identified on a first in/first out basis with the 50,000 shares subscribed for on 1 August 2000. Of those 50,000 shares acquired on the same day, deferral relief is attributable to 19,000 shares (acquired for £19,000, the amount of the deferred gain). The disposal is matched firstly with the shares to which no deferral relief is attributable, i.e. 31,000 shares. [*TCGA 1992, Sch 5C para 4(3); FA 1995, Sch 16*]. The disposal therefore includes none of the 19,000 shares to which deferral relief is attributable. See also Revenue Capital Gains Manual CG 57501.

1 March 2003 disposal

This disposal of 110,000 shares is firstly identified on a first in/first out basis with the remaining 20,000 of the shares subscribed for on 1 August 2000. Of those 20,000 shares acquired on the same day, deferral relief is attributable to 19,000 shares. The disposal is matched firstly with the shares to which no deferral relief is attributable, i.e. 1,000 shares, and then with the 19,000 shares to which deferral relief is attributable. The disposal includes all of the 19,000 shares to which deferral relief is attributable. Therefore, the whole of the £19,000 deferred gain is brought into charge on 1 March 2003.

The above interpretation of the rules for identifying disposals of VCT shares to which deferral relief is attributable is the Revenue's interpretation at Capital Gains Manual CG 57501. Where, as in this example, part disposals are involved, they act to the taxpayer's advantage (although in this example both part disposals are in the same tax year in any case). Note the contrast between the application of these rules and those for EIS deferral relief illustrated in the example at 20.10 ENTERPRISE INVESTMENT SCHEME (AND BES).

NB: any taper relief available is disregarded for the purposes of this example, but see 60.12 TAPER RELIEF for a further example.

66 Wasting Assets

Cross-references. See 21.4 EXEMPTIONS AND RELIEFS for tangible movable assets generally and 21.11 for private passenger motor vehicles; 36.13–36.22 LAND for leases of land which are wasting assets; and 55.7 ROLLOVER RELIEF for the relief available where assets are, or will within ten years, become wasting assets.

Sumption: Capital Gains Tax. See A17.04.

66.1 Subject to the following, where an asset disposed of is a 'wasting asset'

(*a*) the original cost, etc. (see 17.3 DISPOSAL) less predictable residual value, is treated as diminishing evenly day by day over the asset's life, and

(*b*) additional expenditure (see 17.3 DISPOSAL) is similarly treated as diminishing evenly over the remaining life of the asset as from the date the expenditure was first reflected in the state or nature of the asset

and only so much of the original cost and additional expenditure as, on the above basis, remains at the date of disposal is then deductible. If additional expenditure under (*b*) above creates or increases a residual value, then the new residual value is taken into account in (*a*) above. [*TCGA 1992, s 46*].

A '*wasting asset*' is an asset with a predictable 'life' not exceeding fifty years and, in relation to tangible movable property, '*life*' means 'useful life', having regard to the purpose for which the tangible assets were acquired or provided by the person making the disposal. However, plant and machinery are always regarded as having a predictable life of less than fifty years and that life is to be based on normal usage. Freehold land is never a wasting asset, whatever its nature and whatever the nature of the building or works on it. The predictable life and predictable residual value, if not immediately ascertainable by the nature of the asset, are to be taken on a disposal as they were known or ascertainable at the time when the asset was acquired by the person making the disposal. [*TCGA 1992, s 44*].

Milk quota (see 6.6 ASSETS) is not regarded by the Revenue as a wasting asset (Revenue Capital Gains Manual CG 77940).

No restriction of allowable expenditure as above occurs where an asset, throughout the ownership of the person making the disposal, is used solely for the purposes of a trade, profession or vocation, and capital allowances have, or could have, been claimed in respect of its cost, or in respect of any enhancement expenditure. This also applies where an asset has otherwise qualified in full for any capital allowances. Where, however, the asset disposed of has been used partly for non-business purposes, or has only partly qualified for capital allowances, the expenditure and consideration are apportioned and the restrictions imposed above applied to that portion of expenditure which has not qualified for capital allowances, or which relates to the period of non-business use. [*TCGA 1992, s 47*].

Tangible movable assets (chattels) which are wasting assets are exempt subject to certain conditions. See 21.4 EXEMPTIONS AND RELIEFS. Chattels such as antique clocks and certain motor vehicles may be 'machinery' and thus exempt subject to those conditions (which broadly correspond to those of *TCGA 1992, s 47* above). See Revenue Tax Bulletin, October 1994, pp 166, 167 for the Revenue's meaning of machinery.

Example

V bought an aircraft on 31 May 1996 at a cost of £90,000 for use in his air charter business. It has been agreed that V's non-business use of the aircraft amounts to one-tenth, on a flying hours basis, and capital allowances and running costs have accordingly been restricted for income tax purposes. On 1 February 2001, V sells the aircraft for £185,000. The aircraft is agreed as having a useful life of 20 years at the date it was acquired. The indexation factor for May 1996 to April 1998 is 0.063.

	£	£
Amount qualifying for capital allowances		
Relevant portion of disposal consideration		
$\frac{9}{10}$ × £185,000		166,500
Relevant portion of acquisition cost $\frac{9}{10}$ × £90,000		81,000
Unindexed gain		85,500
Indexation allowance £81,000 × 0.063		5,103
Chargeable gain (subject to TAPER RELIEF (60))		£80,397
Amount not qualifying for capital allowances		
Relevant portion of disposal consideration		
$\frac{1}{10}$ × £185,000		18,500
Relevant portion of acquisition cost		
$\frac{1}{10}$ × £90,000	9,000	
Deduct wasted £9,000 × $\frac{4\text{y } 8\text{m}}{20\text{y}}$	2,100	6,900
Gain		£11,600

The whole of the £11,600 is exempt.

The total chargeable gain is therefore	£80,397

66.2 OPTIONS AND FUTURES CONTRACTS

Generally speaking, options are treated as wasting assets and are subject to the rules outlined in 66.1 above. However, there are specific statutory exceptions to this and these, together with further rules relating to options generally, are covered in 17.10 DISPOSAL. For employee share options, see 19 EMPLOYEE SHARE SCHEMES. See 21.50 EXEMPTIONS AND RELIEFS and 64.1 UNIT TRUSTS ETC. for options held by pension schemes and authorised unit trusts respectively.

See 17.11 DISPOSAL for certain commodity and financial futures which are excepted from wasting asset treatment.

66.3 LEASES OF PROPERTY OTHER THAN LAND

In accordance with the definition of a wasting asset given in 66.1 above a 'lease of property other than land' may be or become a wasting asset. Such a lease which is a wasting asset is subject to the rules in 66.1 above, and in particular those regarding allowable expenditure. This treatment should be compared with leases of land which are wasting assets where, instead of allowable expenditure being written off at a uniform rate, a special basis is used (see 36.14 LAND). Despite this, the legislation regarding leases of property other than land is mainly by direct reference to that covering leases of land with 'necessary modifications'. [*TCGA 1992, ss 44, 46, 47, 240, Sch 8 para 9(1)*].

A '*lease of property other than land*' means any kind of agreement or arrangement under which payments are made for the use of, or otherwise in respect of, property and '*lessor*', '*lessee*' and '*rent*' are construed accordingly. [*TCGA 1992, Sch 8 para 10(1)(b)*].

Duration of a lease. The duration of a lease is to be decided by reference to the facts known or ascertainable at the time when the lease was acquired or created. In determining the duration, the following provisions apply.

(*a*) Where the terms of the lease include provision for the determination of the lease by notice given by the lessor, the lease is not to be treated as granted for a term longer than one ending at the earliest date on which it could be determined by notice given by the lessor.

(*b*) Where any of the terms of the lease or any other circumstances rendered it unlikely that the lease will continue beyond a date earlier than the expiration of the terms of the lease, the lease is not to be treated as having been granted for a longer term than one ending on that date. This applies in particular where the lease provides for rent to go up after a given date, or for the lessee's obligation to become more onerous after a given date, but includes provision for the determination of the lease on that date, by notice given by the lessee, and those provisions render it unlikely that the lease will continue beyond that date.

(*c*) Where the terms of the lease include provision for the extension of the lease beyond a given date by notice given by the lessee, the duration of the lease applies as if the term of the lease extended for as long as it could be extended by the lessee, but subject to any right of the lessor to determine the lease by notice.

(*d*) In the case of a lease of an asset which itself is a wasting asset and also movable property, the lease is assumed to terminate not later than the end of the life of the wasting asset.

[*TCGA 1992, Sch 8 para 8, para 9(3)*].

66.4 **Premiums for leases.** Where the payment of a 'premium' is required under a lease (or otherwise under the terms subject to which the lease is granted) there is a part disposal of the asset or other interest out of which that lease is granted.

In the part disposal computation (which follows the normal rules in *TCGA 1992, s 42*, see 17.6 DISPOSAL) the property which remains undisposed of includes a right to any rent or other payments (other than a premium) payable under the lease, and that right is valued at the time of the part disposal. [*TCGA 1992, Sch 8 para 2*].

'*Premium*' includes any like sum, whether payable to the intermediate or superior lessor and includes any sum (other than rent) paid on or in connection with the granting of a lease except in so far as the other sufficient consideration for the payment is shown to have been given. Other capital sums payable by a tenant may fall to be treated as premiums (see 36.15 LAND).

Where by reference to any capital sum within the meaning of *ICTA 1988, s 781* (assets leased to traders and others) any amount of that capital sum is charged to income tax then that amount is deducted from the consideration for capital gains tax purposes but not so as to convert a gain into a loss or increase a loss. [*TCGA 1992, Sch 8 para 9(2)*].

66.5 **Sub-leases granted out of short leases.** Where a sub-lease is granted out of a head-lease with less than fifty years to run, the normal part disposal rules do not apply. Instead, subject to below, a proportion of the cost and enhancement expenditure attributable to the lease is apportioned to the part disposed of as follows

$$\frac{P(1)}{P(2)}$$

where

P(1) = the duration of the sub-lease

P(2) = the duration of the lease at the date of acquisition (for apportionment of cost) or the duration of the lease at the date when expenditure is first reflected in the nature of the lease (for apportionment of enhancement expenditure).

If the amount of the premium is less than what would be obtainable by way of premium for the sub-lease if the rent payable under the sub-lease were the same as the rent payable under the lease, the percentage attributable to the sub-lease as calculated above must be multiplied by the premium received over the premium so obtainable before being applied to cost or enhancement expenditure. [*TCGA 1992, Sch 8 para 4(1)(2)*].

Example

P purchases a 40-year lease of a non-wasting asset (other than land) in 1995 for £15,000. In 2000 he grants a sub-lease of the asset to Q for 20 years for a premium of £8,000. Had the rent under head-lease and sub-lease been the same the premium would have been £10,000. The expenditure attributable to the part disposal of the sub-lease is given by

$$£15{,}000 \times \frac{20}{40} \times \frac{8{,}000}{10{,}000} = 0.4 \times £15{,}000 = £6{,}000$$

Where the sub-lease is a sub-lease of part only of the asset comprised in the lease, the cost and enhancement expenditure of the head-lease must be apportioned between the sub-lease and the remainder in proportion to their respective values. [*TCGA 1992, Sch 8 para 4(3)*].

66.6 LIFE INTERESTS

Life interests in settled property within 66.1 above are treated as wasting assets when the expectation of life of the life tenant is 50 years or less. The predictable life of life tenants and annuities is ascertained from actuarial tables which have Revenue approval. [*TCGA 1992, s 44(1)(d)*]. See 57.8 SETTLEMENTS for the disposal of interests in settled property generally.

Example

N is a beneficiary under a settlement. On 30 June 1987, when her actuarially estimated life expectancy was 40 years, she sold her life interest to an unrelated individual, R, for £50,000. N dies on 31 December 2000, and the life interest is extinguished.

R will have an allowable loss for 2000/01 as follows

	£	£
Disposal consideration on death of N		Nil
Allowable cost	50,000	
Deduct wasted		
$\frac{13\text{y } 6\text{m}}{40\text{y}} \times £50{,}000$	16,875	
		33,125
Allowable loss		£33,125

Note to the example

(*a*) The amount of the cost wasted is computed by reference to the predictable life, not the actual life, of the wasting asset.

67 Finance Act 2000—Summary of CGT Provisions

(*Royal Assent 28 July 2000*)

The following is a brief summary of the main provisions of the current Finance Act that are concerned with, or impinge upon, capital gains tax (CGT) and/or corporation tax on chargeable gains. For an exhaustive list of current Finance Act provisions covered in Tolley's Capital Gains Tax, which may also include, for example, taxes management provisions of more general application, see 70 TABLE OF STATUTES.

s 37	**Rates of capital gains tax.** For 2000/01 and subsequent years, the rate of CGT is 10% to the extent, if any, that gains (treated as if they were the top slice of income) fall within the income tax starting rate band (£1,520 for 2000/01). See 2.1 ANNUAL RATES AND EXEMPTIONS.
s 39	**Gift Aid donations by individuals.** Substantive changes are made as regards donations made after 5 April 2000, incorporating covenanted payments due after that date. These include the abolition of the minimum limit per donation and a change enabling the tax treated as deducted at source to be met out of a CGT liability. See 10.7 CHARITIES.
s 47, Sch 8	Subject to Revenue approval on or after Royal Assent (see above), a company may set up an **employee share ownership plan**, which is a tax-advantaged all-employee share plan which may provide free shares, partnership shares, matching shares and/or dividend shares. No chargeable gain (or allowable loss) arises on shares being withdrawn from, or otherwise leaving, the plan at any time. See 19.12 EMPLOYEE SHARE SCHEMES.
s 48, Sch 9	**Transfers to an employee share ownership plan.** A form of CGT rollover relief is available on a disposal of shares, other than by a company, to an approved employee share ownership plan (as above) and the reinvestment of the proceeds into a chargeable asset. See 19.13 EMPLOYEE SHARE SCHEMES.
s 49	**Approved profit sharing schemes** are being phased out following the introduction of employee share ownership plans (see above). No further appropriations of shares may be made after 31 December 2002 and no new schemes will be approved after 5 April 2001. See 19.22 EMPLOYEE SHARE SCHEMES.
s 54	**Transfers to an employee share ownership trust.** The CGT rollover relief previously available for transfers of shares to a qualifying employee share ownership trust is withdrawn for transfers after 5 April 2001. See 19.25 EMPLOYEE SHARE SCHEMES.
s 62, Sch 14	**Enterprise Management Incentives.** With effect on and after Royal Assent (see above), 'small higher risk' trading companies are able to grant tax-advantaged options over shares worth up to £100,000 to each of up to 15 eligible employees. Such shares are normally treated for the purposes of CGT taper relief on disposal as if they had been acquired when the option was granted. See 19.17 EMPLOYEE SHARE SCHEMES.
s 63, Schs 15, 16	**Corporate Venturing Scheme.** For shares issued on or after 1 April 2000 but before 1 April 2010, most trading companies can obtain corporation tax relief at 20% on acquisitions (by cash subscription) of minority shareholdings in 'small higher risk' trading companies. Investing companies are able to defer chargeable gains on disposals of such investments where they make further such investments. An allowable capital loss on the disposal of such an investment can be relieved against income as an alternative to chargeable gains. See 15 CORPORATE VENTURING SCHEME.

s 64, Sch 17 **Enterprise Investment Scheme.** In relation to shares issued after 5 April 2000, the holding period beyond which income tax relief is retained and a CGT exemption obtained on disposal is reduced from five years to (broadly) three years. Corresponding reductions are made within other EIS rules. A number of amendments are made, effective from varying dates, in the definitions of qualifying company, qualifying business activity and qualifying trade. See 20 ENTERPRISE INVESTMENT SCHEME (AND BES).

s 65, Sch 18 **Venture Capital Trusts.** In relation to VCT shares issued after 5 April 2000, the holding period beyond which income tax relief is retained is reduced from five years to three years. Corresponding reductions are made within other VCT rules. A number of amendments are made, effective from varying dates, in the conditions under which a VCT's investment in a company constitutes a qualifying holding. See 65 VENTURE CAPITAL TRUSTS.

s 66 **Taper relief.** For disposals of *business* assets after 5 April 2000, the maximum taper is achieved after holding the asset for four years rather than ten as before. The bonus year addition for assets held at 17 March 1998 is withdrawn for such disposals. See 60.2 TAPER RELIEF.

s 67 **Taper relief.** With effect after 5 April 2000, the definition of a business asset is widened to include all shareholdings in unquoted companies, quoted shares in the taxpayer's employer company and quoted shares held by an outside investor able to exercise at least 5% of the voting rights. Corresponding rules are applied as regards an asset used in a business. Holdings in joint venture companies may qualify for business asset taper relief. See 60.4, 60.5, 60.5A TAPER RELIEF.

s 90 **Business asset hold-over relief** is not available on a transfer of shares or securities after 8 November 1999 to a company. See 25.1 HOLD-OVER RELIEFS.

s 91, Sch 24 **Settlements anti-avoidance: disposal of interest in settled property.** A disposal after 20 March 2000, for consideration, of an interest in a UK settlement in which the settlor has an interest sparks a deemed disposal and reacquisition at market value of the assets to which the interest relates. See 57.12 SETTLEMENTS.

s 92, Schs 25, 26 **Settlements anti-avoidance: transfers of value by trustees linked with trustee borrowing.** Where trustees transfer funds after 20 March 2000 to any person, and any outstanding trustee borrowings have not been used for 'normal trust purposes', the trustees are treated as making a disposal and reacquistion at market value of settlement assets. This applies to UK settlements in which the settlor has an interest and to offshore settlements. There are special provisions to attribute resulting gains to beneficiaries of offshore settlements receiving capital payments. See 57.13 SETTLEMENTS, 43.17–43.19 OFFSHORE SETTLEMENTS.

s 93 **Settlements anti-avoidance: restriction on set-off of trust losses.** Where assets have been transferred into a UK settlement, using gifts hold-over relief, by a person who has at any time acquired (personally or through a connected person) an interest in the settlement for consideration, trust losses cannot be offset against a gain accruing after 20 March 2000 on a disposal of those assets. See 57.14 SETTLEMENTS.

s 94 **Settlements anti-avoidance: attribution to trustees of gains of offshore companies.** Where any part of a gain accruing after 20 March 2000 to an offshore company falls to be attributed under *TCGA 1992, s 13* (see 44.6 OVERSEAS MATTERS) to trustees of a UK settlement, nothing in any double tax agreement is to be taken as averting the tax charge otherwise arising. See 57.15 SETTLEMENTS.

s 95 **Settlements anti-avoidance: disposal of interest in offshore settlement.** On the emigration of a UK settlement after 20 March 2000, the normal uplift in the CGT acquisition cost of a beneficiary's interest is disapplied if the settlement has gains which were realised during an earlier period of non-UK residence and do not fall to be attributed to UK beneficiaries. See 43.3 OFFSHORE SETTLEMENTS.

s 96 **Settlements anti-avoidance: capital payments by trustees to offshore companies.** A change is made to the rules for attributing to beneficiaries capital payments made by an offshore trust to an offshore company controlled by the beneficiaries. For capital payments received after 20 March 2000, the rules cannot be circumvented by including non-residents within the group of persons who control the offshore company. See 43.13 OFFSHORE SETTLEMENTS.

s 101 **Groups of companies.** Two group companies may elect that a disposal by one of them on or after 1 April 2000 to a person outside the group be deemed to have been made by the other and to have been preceded by an intra-group transfer of the asset at no gain/no loss. See 13.13 COMPANIES.

s 102, Sch 29 **Groups of companies.** With effect generally on or after 1 April 2000 (with some exceptions) the condition that members of a CGT group of companies be UK-resident is removed. Individual provisions, for example the facility to transfer assets intra-group at no gain/no loss (see 13.12 COMPANIES), instead now focus on whether assets are within the charge to UK corporation tax. Consequential changes, and effective dates, are dealt with throughout this publication where appropriate. See 13.11 COMPANIES for the principal change.

68 Tax Case Digest

Cases referred to in this chapter are cross-referenced to the relevant paragraph of this edition.

Statutory references marked with an asterisk (*) are to legislation which has replaced that involved in the case summarised.

Aberdeen Construction Group Ltd v CIR 21.5

Loan waiver condition of sale of shares — 'debt on a security'

A company sold its shares in a subsidiary for £250,000, a condition of the sale being that it waived repayment of unsecured loans of £500,000 it had made to the subsidiary. It was assessed on its gain from the sale of the shares with no allowance for the £500,000. The HL rejected the company's contentions that the loan was a 'debt on a security' within *TCGA 1992, s 251(1)** or that *TCGA 1992, s 43** applied, but held that the waiver of the loan was part of the consideration for the £250,000. The appeal was remitted to the Commissioners to make an appropriate apportionment under *TCGA 1992, s 52(4)**. *Aberdeen Construction Group Ltd v CIR HL 1978, 52 TC 281; [1978] STC 127; [1978] 2 WLR 648; [1978] 1 All ER 962.*

Allison v Murray 17.3

Insurance premium paid as part of trust variation

A settlement in Scots form was varied by agreement on 3 March 1965 on terms whereby 60% of the trust fund, less £10,000, became absolutely vested in Mrs M who was required at her own expense to effect a single-premium policy in favour of the trustees against the event of her predeceasing Mrs W. In the event, Mrs W died on 1 March 1966, survived by Mrs M. Mrs M's husband was assessed for 1966–67 on the gain on the sale by the trustees of investments appropriated to Mrs M by reference to their market value at 6 April 1965. The assessment was upheld and a deduction refused for the insurance premium as not falling within *TCGA 1992, s 38(1)(a) or (b)**. Certain other contentions by the husband (who conducted his appeal in person) were rejected. *Allison v Murray Ch D 1975, 51 TC 57; [1975] STC 524; [1975] 1 WLR 1578; [1975] 3 All ER 561.*

Anders Utkilens Rederi AS v OY Lovisa Stevedoring Co AB 17.6

Compromise agreement for sale of defendant's property — whether a part disposal

A Norwegian company obtained judgement against another company for a liquidated sum. The defendant company appealed, but a compromise agreement was reached whereby the defendant's premises, plant and machinery were to be sold and the proceeds divided between the parties. The defendant subsequently went into voluntary liquidation, and the property was sold a year later. The Ch D held that the compromise agreement effected a part disposal of the property by the defendant to the plaintiff, and that each party subsequently disposed of its interest then held to the ultimate purchaser. *Anders Utkilens Rederi AS v OY Lovisa Stevedoring Co AB & Another Ch D 1984, [1985] STC 301; [1985] 2 All ER 669.*

Aspden v Hildesley 14.1, 41.3

Transfer of assets under Court Order on divorce

The taxpayer and his wife had jointly owned certain property, not the private residence of either. They had been separated since 1970 and were divorced by decree nisi on 12 February 1976. The Court Order (by consent) provided, inter alia, for the taxpayer's half share of the property to be transferred to his wife, while she undertook to give an irrevocable order to her personal representatives that, should she die before 10 December 1984 and before her husband, a sum equal to half the equity in the property was to be paid to him out of her estate. The taxpayer was assessed on the footing that he had disposed of his share in the property on 12 February 1976, and that by virtue of *CGTA 1979, s 19(3)(a)** and *TCGA 1992, ss 18, 286** the consideration was to be taken as the market value. The Ch D upheld the assessment, reversing the decision of the Commissioners. On the facts, the taxpayer's interest in the property was transferred at the time of the decree nisi, the consent order being an unconditional contract for the transfer. As the decree was not then absolute, the parties were still married and *CGTA 1979, s 19(3)(a)** applied by virtue of *TCGA 1992, s 18(2)*, s 286(2)*. Aspden v Hildesley Ch D 1981, 55 TC 609; [1982] STC 206; [1982] 1 WLR 264; [1982] 2 All ER 53.* (Note. *CGTA 1979, s 19(3)* was repealed by *FA 1981* and replaced by what is now *TCGA 1992, s 17*.)

Atkinson v Dancer 53.5

Retirement relief

A taxpayer farmed 89 acres and sold nine of them. He was assessed and claimed retirement relief, contending that the sale was a disposal of part of his business. The Ch D, reversing the Commissioners' decision, held that no relief was due, applying *McGregor v Adcock. Atkinson v Dancer Ch D 1988, 61 TC 598; [1988] STC 758.*

Barrett v Powell 53.5

Retirement relief — surrender of agricultural tenancy by farmer — continuation of farming under temporary licence

In March 1990 a tenant farmer received £120,000 from his landlord as compensation for surrendering his agricultural tenancy. He was allowed to continue to farm the land in question, under a temporary licence, until September 1991. The Revenue assessed the compensation to capital gains tax for 1989/90. The farmer appealed, contending that the payment of compensation qualified for retirement relief. The Ch D rejected this contention and upheld the assessment. On the evidence, the payment was made for the disposal of an asset, but was not made for the disposal of the whole or part of the farmer's business, since he had been able to continue farming the land in question for two summers under the temporary licence. *Jarmin v Rawlings* distinguished. *Barrett v Powell Ch D 1998, 70 TC 432; [1998] STC 283.*

Batey v Wakefield 48.1

Bungalow separated from main residence — whether part of dwelling-house

A taxpayer owned a house in Marlborough, built on 1.1 acres of land, but lived with his family in a London flat during the working week, returning to the house at weekends. He had elected under *TCGA 1992, s 222(5)** for the house to be treated as his main residence. Following a number of local burglaries, he had a bungalow built on the land, physically separate from the house and with separate road access. He arranged for the bungalow to be occupied by a farm labourer who acted as caretaker. In 1974 the taxpayer began living in the house on a full-time basis and, no longer needing a caretaker, sold the bungalow with 0.2 acres of land. The Revenue assessed the resulting gain to CGT and he appealed, contending that the bungalow had formed part of his dwelling-house and was exempt under *TCGA 1992, s 222**. The General Commissioners allowed his appeal, finding that the bungalow had been built for the purpose of providing services for the benefit of the main house, and holding that the occupation by the caretaker amounted to occupation by the taxpayer as part of his residence. The CA upheld the Commissioners' decision as one of fact, holding that they were entitled to conclude that the bungalow was part of the taxpayer's residence. *Batey v Wakefield CA 1981, 55 TC 550; [1981] STC 521; [1982] 1 All ER 61.*

(Note. *Dicta* of Fox LJ were subsequently disapproved by the CA in *Lewis v Rook* below.)

Bayley v Rogers 36.14

Sale of new lease — whether a continuation of old lease

A taxpayer's 14-year lease of his business premises expired in December 1974 and, following proceedings under the *Landlord and Tenant Act 1954,* he was granted a new lease. He disposed of the new lease in 1976 and was assessed on the gain on the footing that the new lease was a separate asset from the old. He appealed, contending that the new lease was a continuation of the old and that the straightline basis over the period from 1960 should be used by virtue of *TCGA 1992, Sch 2 para 16**. The Ch D, reversing the Commissioners' decision, held that the two leases were separate assets, and the second lease was not derived from the first within the meaning of *TCGA 1992, s 43*. Bayley v Rogers Ch D 1980, 53 TC 420; [1980] STC 544.*

Baylis v Gregory 3.1, 4.6, 5.1

Avoidance Schemes

The managing director of a company (PGI) controlled the company through his own and trustee shareholdings. Another company, C, entered into negotiations to acquire PGI, and the taxpayer and his associates set up a Manx company to exchange their shares in PGI with shares in the Manx company. However, C ended the negotiations. Nevertheless the share exchange was proceeded with and completed in March 1974. No further steps were taken to sell PGI until May 1975 when a third company, H, became interested in it. Eventually, the Manx company sold the PGI shares to H. The Special Commissioners allowed the taxpayer's appeals and their decision was upheld by the Ch D, the CA, and the HL. The transactions were not a 'pre-ordained series of transactions'. (The case was heard with *Craven v White*, in the CA and HL.) *Baylis v Gregory HL 1988, 62 TC 1; [1988] STC 476; [1988] 3 WLR 423; [1988] 3 All ER 495.*

Begg-McBrearty v Stilwell 57.6

Exercise of power of appointment in favour of grandchildren of settlor — whether grandchildren acquiring an interest in possession at age of 18 or 21

In 1975 the trustees of a settlement made in 1959 exercised their power of appointment in favour of the settlor's three grandchildren, and thereafter held the trust fund contingently for the grandchildren contingently on their reaching the age of 21. The eldest grandchild became 21 in 1990, and thus became absolutely entitled to a one-third share of the settled property. The Revenue issued a 1990-91 assessment on one of the trustees, charging CGT on the deemed disposal to the grandchild in accordance with *TCGA, s 71**. The trustee appealed, contending that the gain should be held over by virtue of *TCGA, s 260(2)(d)**. The Ch D upheld the assessment. The disposal could not be held over under *TCGA, s 260(2)(d)** because the grandchild had become entitled to an interest in possession in her share of the settled property in 1987, when she reached the age of 18. Before the exercise of the power of appointment, the grandchild had had only a revocable interest in the trust property. Her relevant interest arose from the power of appointment. Since this had been exercised in 1975, it fell within the provisions of Family Law Reform Act 1969 (which had reduced the age of majority to 18 with effect from 1 January 1970), even though the original settlement had been made before the date on which that act took effect. *Begg-McBrearty v Stilwell Ch D 1996, 68 TC 426; [1996] STC 413; [1996] 1 WLR 951; [1996] 4 All ER 205.*

Bentley v Pike 17.3

Rate of exchange where gain realised abroad

Under German law, the taxpayer's wife and her sister became equally entitled to real property in Germany under the intestacy of their father, resident and domiciled abroad. The father died on 31 October 1967. Following the issue of the German equivalent of Letters of Administration, the sisters were entered in the German Land Registry in July 1972 as tenants in common of the property. The property was sold in July 1973, the sisters receiving their shares of the net proceeds in Deutschmarks. The Ch D upheld the Commissioners' decision that the taxpayer had been correctly assessed on his wife's gain taken as the difference between the Deutschmark value of her share of the property at her father's death, converted into sterling at the then ruling exchange rate, and the Deutschmarks she received on the sale, converted into sterling at the rate ruling at the date of sale. The taxpayer's contentions that the date of acquisition was the date his wife was entered in the Land Registry, and that the gain was the difference between the two Deutschmark figures converted at the rate at the time of disposal, were rejected. On the evidence, under German law, his wife became absolutely entitled on her father's death. This was the date of acquisition by virtue of *TCGA 1992, s 62(1)(a)**. The unit of account for assessment was sterling and the market value of the deemed acquisition on the death must be arrived at using the exchange rate at the time. *Bentley v Pike Ch D 1981, 53 TC 590; [1981] STC 360.*

Berry v Warnett 57.6

The general treatment of disposals to trustees

In March 1972 the taxpayer transferred shares to a Channel Islands company, G, as bare trustee. On 4 April 1972 he entered into a deed with another Channel Islands company, J, expressed to be a settlement, whereby in consideration of the payment of £14,500 by J to him, he transferred his beneficial interest in the shares to G on trust for himself for life, with remainder to J absolutely. On 6 April 1972 he sold his life interest in the shares to a Bahaman company for £130,753, its market value. His wife made similar arrangements in respect of shares owned by her. He was assessed on the basis that on 4 April 1972 there had been a disposal of the shares, the consideration being taken as their market value under *CGTA 1979, s 19(3)(a)**. He appealed, contending that there had been a disposal only of the reversionary interest on 4 April and that there had been a disposal of the life interest on 6 April, the gain on which was exempt under *TCGA 1992, s 76(1)**. The HL unanimously upheld the assessment. The legislation proceeds on the assumption that tax attaches to disposals in favour of trustees; *TCGA 1992, s 70**, *s 71(1)** and *s 72(1)** are only special cases. There had been a disposal of the shares to G on 4 April, acquired by G otherwise than by an arm's length bargain. *Berry v Warnett HL 1982, 55 TC 92; [1982] STC 396; [1982] 1 WLR 698; [1982] 2 All ER 630.*

Billingham v Cooper; Edwards v Fisher 43.13

Trustees making demand loans to settlor — whether any 'capital payments' within TCGA 1992, s 87(4)

In 1987 a UK resident (C) established a settlement, the trustees of which were resident in Switzerland and the Cayman Islands. The trustees made a number of interest-free loans to C which were repayable on demand. The Revenue issued CGT assessments on the basis that C should be treated as having received capital payments, within *TCGA 1992, s 87(4)*, from the trustees of the settlement, the amount of such payments being the interest that would have been payable had the loans been taken from a commercial lender. C appealed, contending that, while there had been a capital payment when each initial loan was made, there was no further capital payment while that loan remained outstanding. The Ch D rejected this contention, reversing the Special Commissioners' decision, and upheld the assessments. Lloyd J held that, when the trustees made the loans, they conferred a benefit on C by leaving them outstanding for any period. The effect of *TCGA 1992, s 97* was that this was to be treated as a capital payment within *TCGA 1992, s 87(4)*. *Billingham v Cooper; Edwards v Fisher Ch D, [2000] STC 122.*

Bond v Pickford 57.6

Power of Appointment

In 1972 the trustees of a discretionary settlement, which had been established in 1961, executed two deeds to allocate part of the settled property. The allocated funds continued to be held by the trustees of the main settlement and were subject to the administrative powers of that settlement. The trustees were assessed on the basis that there had been a deemed disposal under *TCGA 1992, s 71(1)**. The Special Commissioners allowed their appeal and this decision was upheld by the Ch D and the CA. Applying dicta of Wilberforce J in *Roome v Edwards*, it would not be natural for a person with knowledge of the legal context of 'settlement', and applying that knowledge in a practical and commonsense manner to the facts, to say that separate settlements had been made by the allocations. There is a distinction between powers to alter the trusts of a settlement expressly or by necessary implication authorising the trustees to remove assets altogether from the original settlement (without rendering any person absolutely entitled to them), and powers which do not confer on the trustees such authority. The relevant powers here were of the latter type. *Bond v Pickford CA 1983, 57 TC 301; [1983] STC 517.*

Booth v Ellard 57.2

Shares transferred to trustees under pooling agreement — whether a disposal

Twelve shareholders in a company entered into an agreement under which their shares were transferred to trustees. This was done so that they and their families could retain effective control of the company if its shares were dealt with on the Stock Exchange. The agreement was for 15 years but subject to determination by shareholders who, between them, held a specified proportion of the shares transferred. The broad effect of the agreement was that the shares were pooled. The participants received the trust income proportionate to the shares they transferred and they were able to direct the trustees how to exercise the votes attaching to the shares or decide should there be a rights issue, etc. Provisions ensured that the shares would remain in the family should a participant die or wish to sell. CGT assessments were made on the footing that the agreement was a settlement of the shares. The CA allowed on appeal by one of the shareholders, reversing the decision of the Commissioners. The shareholders collectively had power to end the trust, and although their interests in their shares were subject to restraints, they did not lose their beneficial interests. They were absolutely entitled to their shares as against the trustees, within *TCGA 1992, s 60(1)**; hence the transfer to the trustees was not a chargeable disposal. *Booth v Ellard CA 1980, 53 TC 393; [1980] STC 555; [1980] 1 WLR 1443; [1980] 3 All ER 569.*

Bullivant Holdings Ltd v CIR 40.1

Acquisition of shares — whether TCGA 1992, s 17 applicable*

A company (B) acquired two 25% shareholdings in a publishing company, from different vendors, for a total of £25,000. It subsequently lodged a claim that *TCGA 1992, s 17** should be treated as applying to the acquisitions, so that its acquisition cost should be treated as market value rather than as £25,000. The Revenue rejected the claim and the Special Commissioner dismissed B's appeal. On the evidence, the shares had been acquired at arm's length and the consideration of £25,000 appeared to be 'a full and fair price'.

Accordingly, *TCGA 1992, s 17** did not apply. The Ch D upheld this decision. *Bullivant Holdings Ltd v CIR Ch D 1998, 71 TC 22; [1998] STC 905.*

Burman v Hedges & Butler Ltd 13.19

Avoidance scheme — whether TCGA 1992, s 171 (transfers within a group) applicable*

A company (H) owned the share capital of B Ltd and was itself wholly owned by BC Ltd. BC Ltd agreed, subject to contract, to sell B Ltd to S Ltd, an unconnected company. To avoid the chargeable gain of about £½m which would have arisen on a direct sale, the following scheme was carried out. V Ltd was formed with capital of 76 £1 participating preference shares held by the taxpayer and 24 £1 ordinary shares held by S Ltd. Z Ltd was formed with share capital owned by V Ltd. Z Ltd bought the shares in B Ltd out of a loan to it by S Ltd. V Ltd then went into liquidation, the liquidator transferring its shares in Z Ltd to S Ltd as the ordinary shareholder of V Ltd. H was assessed on the basis that it had sold the shares in B Ltd to S Ltd. The Commissioners discharged the assessment, rejecting the Revenue's contention that V Ltd and Z Ltd had acted throughout as nominees or agents for S Ltd, and holding that the sale from H to Z Ltd was within *TCGA 1992, s 171**. Their decision was upheld by the Ch D. *Burman v Hedges & Butler Ltd Ch D 1978, 52 TC 501; [1979] STC 136; [1979] 1 WLR 160.*

Burman v Westminster Press Ltd 21.4

Wasting assets — whether TCGA 1992, s 45(2)(b) applicable where capital allowances withdrawn*

In 1973 a company (W), which published regional newspapers, agreed to purchase a printing press. The purchase price was paid by instalments beginning in 1973 and ending in 1977. The press was not delivered until 1976, by which time it was surplus to W's requirements. It was never used in W's trade and was kept in storage until 1978 when it was sold to a Dutch company at a profit of more than £650,000. W had been given first-year allowances on the instalments of the purchase price, but these were subsequently withdrawn under *FA 1971, s 41(2)*. The Revenue included the profit on the sale of the press in a CT assessment on W. W appealed, contending that the press was a wasting asset within *TCGA 1992, s 45** and had not qualified in full for a capital allowance within the meaning of *TCGA 1992, s 45(2)(b)**, so that the gain was exempt under *TCGA 1992, s 45(1)**. The Special Commissioner allowed W's appeal and the Ch D upheld this decision. The expenditure on the press had not fulfilled the necessary conditions to attract a capital allowance, so that *TCGA 1992, s 45(2)(b)** did not apply. *Burman v Westminster Press Ltd Ch D 1987, 60 TC 418; [1987] STC 669.*

Campbell Connelly & Co Ltd v Barnett 55.1, 55.3, 55.5

Rollover relief — whether new premises used for trading purposes 'on' acquisition

A music publishing company (C) sold its trading premises in 1984, and moved into the premises of its parent company. In January 1986, it purchased the freehold of another property, but was unable to obtain vacant possession because the property was occupied by lessees. In September 1986, C's parent company purchased the leasehold interest. C then moved into the property and began using it for trading purposes. C claimed rollover relief in respect of the gain on the sale of its previous premises. The Revenue refused to allow relief, considering that the premises had not been taken into trade use 'on the acquisition', as required by *TCGA 1992, s 152(1)**, and that the acquisition into which the gain could have been rolled over was the purchase of the leasehold interest, which had been carried out by the parent and not by C. The General Commissioners dismissed the company's appeal and the Ch D and CA upheld their decision. The premises had not been used for the purposes of C's trade on the acquisition of the freehold, and neither could the acquisitions of the freehold and leasehold interests by different legal persons be regarded as one transaction. Accordingly, relief was not due. *Campbell Connelly & Co Ltd v Barnett CA 1993, 66 TC 380; [1994] STC 50.* (Note. TCGA 1992, s 152 has subsequently been amended by FA 1995, s 48.)

Cann v Woods 39.10

Irrecoverable loans to company — whether TCGA 1992, s 253(12) applicable

In 1988 a wealthy investor (C) purchased a majority shareholding in a company (BG) which had four subsidiaries. The group was suffering financial difficulties. From 1989 to 1992 C made loans of more than £2,000,000 to one of BG's subsidiaries (B). However, B continued to suffer financial problems. In March 1994 BG sold its shareholding in B to another company (GD), and a week later B sold its net assets to GD. GD did not take over B's overdraft or the loans from C. C claimed relief under *TCGA 1992, s 253(3)* for his loans to B. The Revenue rejected the claim, considering that *TCGA 1992, s 253(12)* applied, on the basis that the loans had become irrecoverable as a result of an 'act . . . by the lender', namely the sale of B's shares and assets. C appealed, contending that the loans had become irrecoverable as a result of the commercial situation. The Special Commissioner accepted this contention and allowed the appeal. When C had first invested in B, he believed that it had commercial potential. However, he could not be expected to fund B indefinitely. By February 1994 B had become insolvent and C's loans had become irrecoverable. Such "acts" as took place at the end of March played no part in their becoming irrecoverable at or before the end of February. Accordingly C was entitled to relief. (The Special Commissioner also rejected, as not supported by the evidence, an alternative contention by the Revenue that the loans had not been recoverable when they had been made and thus could not have "become irrecoverable".) *Cann v Woods (Sp C 183), [1999] SSCD 77.*

Capcount Trading v Evans 17.3

Computation of loss on asset purchased and sold in foreign currency

Bentley v Pike (see above) was applied in this subsequent case where a company had made a loss on the disposal of shares in a Canadian company. The shares had been purchased and sold for Canadian dollars, and the Revenue computed the resulting loss by translating the dollar purchase price and the dollar sale price into sterling at the spot rates prevailing at, respectively, the date of purchase and the date of sale, and deducting the sterling equivalent of the sale price from the sterling equivalent of the purchase price. The company appealed, contending that the loss should be computed by deducting the dollar sale price from the dollar cost, and translating the resulting sum into sterling at the spot rate prevailing at the date of disposal. The Special Commissioner rejected this contention and dismissed the company's appeal. The CA upheld the Commissioner's decision. For the purpose of tax on capital gains, foreign currency was not money but was an asset. Therefore, when the company acquired the Canadian shares for Canadian dollars, it gave a consideration in money's worth which fell to be valued in sterling at that time. *Pattison v Marine Midland Ltd* distinguished. *Capcount Trading v Evans CA 1992, 65 TC 545; [1993] STC 11; [1993] All ER 125.*

Caton's Administrators v Couch 17.3

Costs of appealing against valuation of unquoted shares — whether 'incidental costs of disposal'

In a share valuation case, the administrators of a deceased's estate contended that the costs of their appeal qualified as incidental costs of disposal. The Ch D rejected this contention and the CA dismissed the administrators' appeal. Morritt LJ held that, although the costs of an initial valuation were deductible, *TCGA** did not permit a liability to tax to be diminished (or even extinguished) by contesting it. If such expenses were to be treated as deductible, there would be a positive deterrent to reaching a sensible agreement as to the quantum of the liability. Applying *Smith's Potato Estates Ltd v Bolland*, there was a distinction between the costs of producing accounts from which to compute profits and the conduct of a tax controversy with the Revenue. The costs and expenses which a taxpayer might deduct under *TCGA 1992, s 38(2)(b)** were limited to those incurred in complying with the requirements of *TMA 1970, s 12* [and presumably *TMA 1970, s 8* under self-assessment from 1996/97], and did not extend to costs incurred in contesting the tax liability arising from a disposal. *Caton's Administrators v Couch CA 1997, 70 TC 10; [1997] STC 970.*

Chaloner v Pellipar Investments Ltd 17.2

*Development agreement providing for 'money's worth' in the form of site works — whether within TCGA 1992, s 22**

Under a development agreement made in 1987, a company received 'money's worth' in the form of site works. The works were not completed until 1991. The Revenue considered that the effect of *TCGA 1992, s 28** was that the consideration was assessable in the company's accounting period ending June 1988, by reference to the date of the contract. The company appealed, contending that the consideration was a capital sum derived from an asset, within *TCGA 1992, s 22**, so that it was not assessable until the period in which it was received. The Special Commissioner allowed the company's appeal but the Ch D reversed this decision, holding that, since the benefit to the company of the development of the site represented consideration for a lease rather than a licence, it did not fall within *TCGA 1992, s 22(1)(d)*. *Chaloner v Pellipar Investments Ltd Ch D 1996, 68 TC 238; [1996] STC 234.*

Chaney v Watkis 17.3

Deductible money liability replaced by non-monetary obligation — whether money's worth and deductible

The taxpayer had owned a house, occupied by his mother-in-law Mrs W as a protected tenant. He was offered £7,200 for the house subject to the tenancy but refused it. Subsequently he agreed with Mrs W that, if she would vacate the house, he would compensate her by paying her half the difference between the tenanted value and the actual sale price. The house was sold in 1981 for £26,000, but prior to completion he agreed with Mrs W that he would provide her with rent-free accommodation for life if in return she released him from his obligation to pay her £9,400 under their previous agreement. In the event she came to live in an extension to his own residence built for some £25,000. The appeal was against an assessment on the gain from the disposal of the house with no deduction for the £9,400. The Ch D allowed the appeal (reversing the decision of the Commissioners). It was common ground that, had the £9,400 been paid, it would have been deductible under *TCGA 1992, s 38(1)(b)**. The obligation to pay this sum was replaced by an obligation capable of being valued in money terms, despite the domestic nature of the agreement, which, applying *Oram v Johnson*, gave rise to an allowable deduction. The case was remitted to the Commissioners to determine the appeal in accordance with the judgement. *Chaney v Watkis Ch D 1985, 58 TC 707; [1986] STC 89.*

Chinn v Collins 57.6

Whether shares sold held under non-resident settlement

Under a 1960 settlement, shares in L Ltd, a public quoted company, were held on discretionary trusts. A scheme was subsequently carried out to mitigate the incidence of CGT. The existing (resident) trustees were replaced by non-resident trustees and on

28 October 1969 the following transactions were effected. With the settlor's permission, 184,500 of the shares held by the trustees were appointed to each of two brothers, discretionary beneficiaries under the trust, contingently on their surviving three days; each brother assigned his contingent interest to a Jersey company for £352,705; that company contracted to sell each brother 184,500 shares in L Ltd for £355,162 (their then market value), the contract to be completed on 1 November. The brothers survived the three days. The upshot was that they had acquired the shares for their full price, the cost being financed by their disposal of their contingent interests (exempt under *TCGA 1992, s 76(1)**). The brothers were assessed on the basis that *FA 1965, s 42(2)* applied. Their appeals against the assessments were dismissed by the HL. The scheme was an arrangement within the definition of 'settlement' in *FA 1965, s 42(7)*. Although, following *CIR v Plummer*, a settlement must include an element of bounty, there was here an act of bounty in favour of the sons. The settlor's bounty was incomplete when he divested himself of the shares settled. *Chinn v Collins; Chinn v Hochstrasser HL 1980, 54 TC 311; [1981] STC 1; [1981] 2 WLR 14; [1981] 1 All ER 189.*

CIR v Beveridge 7.12

*Share exchange on takeover — application of TCGA 1992, Sch 2 para 19**

In a case in which the issue was the application of *TCGA 1992, Sch 2 para 19**, the relevant shares were originally ordinary shares in S Ltd, a private company, acquired before 6 April 1965, exchanged for ordinary shares in L Ltd in 1967 on a takeover, and disposed of in 1974. There had been a substantial fall in the value of the shares between 1967 and 1974. The assessment was on the basis that *TCGA 1992, Sch 2 para 19(3)** applied. The taxpayer appealed, contending that it did not apply, because the shares in S Ltd were subject to a restriction on transfer to which those in L Ltd were not subject, and consequently not of the same class. The Commissioners allowed his appeal and the CS upheld their decision. The CS also held that *TCGA 1992, Sch 2 para 19(3)** was inapplicable as 'reorganisation of a company's share capital' cannot be construed to cover an amalgamation of two companies. *CIR v Beveridge CS 1979, 53 TC 178; [1979] STC 592.* (Note. See also SP 14/79.)

CIR v Burmah Oil Co 3.1, 58.5

Avoidance Schemes

A company (H), which was a member of a group, was dormant but owned stock with a market value substantially less than its acquisition cost. Its parent company (B) carried out a series of transactions including a capital reorganisation and the loan of £160 million to H via another company in the same group. At the end of these transactions, B held the stock previously held by H, which had been put into liquidation. B claimed that it had made a loss of £160 million on the disposal of its shareholding in H. The HL rejected the claim (reversing the decision of the CS). The whole and only purpose of the scheme had been the avoidance of tax. Applying *WT Ramsay Ltd*, the transactions had 'no commercial purpose apart from the avoidance of a liability to tax', and should be disregarded. *CIR v Burmah Oil Co Ltd HL 1981, 54 TC 200; [1982] STC 30.*

CIR v Chubb's Trustee 17.3

Expenses of terminating trust

Under a marriage settlement, a fund was settled on the wife for life with remainder to the issue of the marriage. The husband had died before the relevant period and the only child was a married daughter with infant children. Arrangements were made under which the trust was terminated and the trust fund vested absolutely in the widow and the daughter. In an appeal against the resultant assessment made under *TCGA 1992, s 71(1)**, the trustee claimed to deduct the cost of legal expenses (including fees to counsel for advice), stamp duty and other expenses as necessarily incurred to bring about the chargeable occasion under *TCGA 1992, s 71(1)**. The Commissioners allowed the deduction and the CS upheld their decision. *CIR v Chubb's Trustee CS 1971, 47 TC 353.*

CIR v Montgomery 17.7

Sale of rights to insurance recoveries

Property was extensively damaged by fire with the result that the owners (trustees of a will trust) became entitled to insurance recoveries of £75,192. The owners assigned their rights under the policies to G in consideration of £75,192 and were assessed on the resultant gain. The taxpayers' contention that there was no chargeable gain was upheld. The £75,192 was derived from the sale of the rights under the policies and no more and *TCGA 1992, s 22** was confined to cases where no asset was acquired by the person paying the capital sum. *CIR v Montgomery Ch D 1974, 49 TC 679; [1975] STC 182; [1975] 1 All ER 664.*

(Note. The law was amended for disposals after 19 December 1974. See now *TCGA 1992, s 225*. *Dicta* of Walton J were disapproved by the HL in *Marren v Ingles*.)

CIR v Richards' Executors 16.8, 17.3

Expenses of obtaining confirmation (probate)

The executors of a deceased person were assessed on their gains from disposals of investments forming part of the estate. On appeal, the Commissioners allowed their claim for the deduction for a proportionate amount of the fees paid to solicitors for valuing the estate, paying the estate duty, obtaining confirmation, etc. and for commission paid to them for their work done in disposing of the investments. The HL upheld this decision. *CIR v Richards' Executors HL 1971, 46 TC 626; [1971] 1 WLR 571; [1971] 1 All ER 785.*

Citibank Investments Ltd v Griffin 17.10

Whether gain from certain transactions in financial options taxable as chargeable gain or as income

The Revenue contended that two options, purchased by the taxpayer company from the same fellow group company, intended to have effect together, and undoubtedly financial options within *TCGA 1992, s 144(8)(c)(i)* when considered separately, should be regarded as a single composite transaction that was not a financial option but a loan, the 'gain' on which should be taxed as income under Schedule D, Case III. The taxpayer company had unused capital losses and had wished to receive funds in the form of capital gains. In allowing the company's appeal, the Special Commissioners held that, even if the options were a single composite transaction (which in their judgement was not the case), to re-characterise them as a loan would be to disregard the legal form and nature of the transactions and to go behind them to some supposed underlying substance. This was not possible in the absence of artificial steps as in *Ramsay* (see 3.1 ANTI-AVOIDANCE). *Citibank Investments Ltd v Griffin (Sp C 228), [2000] SSCD 92.*

Clark (Clark's Executor) v Green & CIR 40.3

*Valuation of unquoted shares — TCGA 1992, s 273(3)**

A taxpayer held a 3.16% shareholding in a substantial unquoted company. She died in September 1987. The company's accounts for the year ending 31 August 1987 (which had not been published at the time of the taxpayer's death) showed pre-tax profits of £2,350,000. In April 1988 all the issued share capital of the company was sold. The Revenue issued a CGT assessment on the basis that the value of the shares at the time of the taxpayer's death was 30p each. (This valuation was computed by applying a gross price/

earnings ratio of 12 to the earnings per share, and discounting it by 65% for unmarketability, leaving a net price/earnings ratio of 4.2.) Her executor appealed, contending that the shares should be valued at 18p each, since the Revenue's valuation took account of unpublished information concerning the company's profits which should have been ignored. The Special Commissioner dismissed the appeal and upheld the Revenue's valuation, holding that the effect of *TCGA 1992, s 273(3)** was that the unpublished information concerning the company's profits should be taken into account, and that the Revenue's valuation had been made on a reasonable basis. The Commissioner observed that *TCGA 1992, s 273** (which derived from *FA 1973, s 51*) had been enacted to overturn the decision in Lynall. Although the shareholding was a small minority holding, the hypothetical purchaser was 'considering an investment of something in the region of £100,000 – £169,000'. The Commissioner also considered that the Revenue's valuation was 'if anything, rather low', and noted that the valuation was significantly less than the valuation of shares in the same company in *Caton's Administrators v Couch (Sp C 6), [1995] SSCD 34*, but observed that 'the difference between the two valuations reflects the difference in the size of the shareholdings which, in turn, reflects the amount of information assumed to be available'. (The valuation in *Caton's Administrators v Couch* was based on the assumption that the prospective purchaser would know that the company's entire share capital was likely to be sold in the near future, which was not the case here since the shareholding here was significantly smaller.) *Clark (Clark's Executor) v Green & CIR (Sp C 5), [1995] SSCD 99.*

Clarke v Mayo 53.7

*Associated disposals — TCGA 1992, s 164(7)**

A company was incorporated in 1954 to take over a retail business which had previously been carried on by a father and son in partnership. The father acquired 50.01% of the company's shares, and the son acquired the remaining 49.99%. In June 1988, when the son was aged 60, contracts were exchanged for the sale of premises which the company occupied (and in which the son had a 25% interest) to an unrelated company. On 25 January 1989 the father died, bequeathing his shareholding to his son. On 31 January 1989 the sale of the property was completed. On 28 February 1989 the company ceased trading. On 28 February 1990 the son transferred his original 49.99% holding in the company's shares to his children. He claimed retirement relief. The inspector rejected the claim, on the grounds that the conditions of *TCGA 1992, s 164(7)(b)** were not satisfied, since the company had ceased to occupy the property four weeks before the date on which the company ceased trading. The Commissioners allowed the son's appeal, holding that the disposal of the shares was a 'material disposal' within *TCGA 1992, s 163(5)**, that the disposal of the property was an 'associated disposal' within *TCGA 1992, s 164(6)**, and that, although the company had ceased to occupy the property four weeks before it ceased trading, the property qualified as having been used by the company 'immediately before' the cessation of the business. The Ch D upheld the Commissioners' decision. Evans-Lombe J held that the words 'immediately before . . . the cessation of the business' should not be construed in isolation, but in the context of *TCGA 1992, ss 163, 164** as a whole. The words 'immediately before' could be construed as meaning 'sufficiently proximate in time to the material disposal or cessation so as to justify the conclusion that the transaction in question formed part of it'. (The Revenue had conceded that the Commissioners were entitled to find that the disposal of the son's interest in the property was an 'associated disposal' within *TCGA 1992, s 164(6)** even though the transfer of his shares in the company did not take place until 56 weeks later.) *Clarke v Mayo Ch D 1994, 66 TC 728; [1994] STC 570.*

Clarke v United Real (Moorgate) Ltd 36.15

Grant of lease of freehold property after development — whether reimbursement of development expenditure a premium within TCGA 1992, Sch 8 para 2(1), para 10(2)

M, a company carrying on property investment and development, agreed in 1978 with contractors for the development of a freehold site it owned. In 1979 it signed an 'agreement for a lease' with another company, N, under which N agreed to reimburse M's expenditure on the development, on completion of which M was to grant N a long lease of the property at a rent below the market value, the formula for which was directly related to N's payments in reimbursement of M's development expenditure. The Ch D, reversing the decision of the Special Commissioner, held that the reimbursement of the expenditure was a premium within *TCGA 1992, Sch 8 para 2(1), para 10(2)**. M's contention that it had been reimbursed the expenditure in its capacity of property developer, and not in its capacity of landlord, was rejected. M developed the site for itself and not for N, which was not a party to the development contracts. *Clarke v United Real (Moorgate) Ltd Ch D 1987, 61 TC 353; [1988] STC 273.*

Cleveleys Investment Trust Co v CIR (No 1) 21.5

Advance for payment of shares — incorporeal rights

C, an investment company, advanced £25,000 to F Ltd, which undertook to reconstruct its share capital, allotting a 51% holding to C. The £25,000 was to be used to acquire the shares. F Ltd accepted a bill of exchange for £25,000 drawn on it by C. F Ltd went into voluntary liquidation before its capital had been reconstructed and the £25,000 was not recovered. The CS held that the advance of £25,000 was part of a composite single transaction conferring incorporeal rights on C — see *TCGA 1992, s 21(1)(a)** — and its loss was an allowable loss. *Cleveleys Investment Trust Co v CIR (No 1) CS 1971, 47 TC 300.*

Cleveleys Investment Trust Co v CIR (No 2) 17.3

Guarantee payment — whether chargeable asset acquired

An investment company guaranteed the bank overdraft of another company and paid £27,351 in pursuance of the guarantee. It contended that in so doing it had acquired the bank's rights as a creditor of the other company, that these rights were an asset for CGT purposes the value of which had become negligible within *TCGA 1992, s 24(2)**, and that accordingly it had an allowable loss of £27,351. The CS rejected this contention. The company's acquisition of the bank's worthless claim was an incident of its discharge of its obligation to the bank. *Cleveleys Investment Trust Co v CIR (No 2) CS 1975, 51 TC 26; [1975] STC 457.*

Coates v Arndale Properties Ltd 3.1, 13.14

Avoidance scheme — whether TCGA 1992, s 173(1) applicable*

Three companies, members of the same group, entered into transactions, not disputed to be genuine, but admittedly to secure expected favourable tax consequences. One company, SPI, had acquired and developed at a cost of £5,313,822 property the market value of which had fallen by March 1973 to £3,100,000. On 30 March 1973 it assigned the property to a property dealing company, A, for a consideration of £3,090,000. On the same day, A assigned the property for £3,100,000 to an investment company, APT. No cash passed, the matter being dealt with by book entries. A then purported to make an election under *TCGA 1992, s 161(3)**; the consequence would be that, by virtue of *TCGA 1992, s 171(1)**, the transfer from SPI to A would give rise to no loss or gain for CGT purposes, and in computing A's Case I profits it could treat the cost of the property as its market value plus the CGT loss which would have accrued under *TCGA 1992, s 161(1)** if the election had not been made. The Revenue assessed A under Case I on the footing that the election was invalid, contending that A had not acquired the property as trading stock within the meaning of *TCGA 1992, s 173(1)**. The HL upheld the assessment, holding that A never did decide to acquire, and never did acquire, the lease as trading stock. The transfer of the lease from SPI to A and from A to APT was procured with the object of obtaining group relief without in fact changing the lease from a capital asset to a trading asset. A lent its name to the transaction but it did not trade and never had any intention of trading with the lease. In these circumstances it was unnecessary to consider the principles enunciated in *CIR v Burmah Oil Co* and *Furniss v Dawson* or the dividend-stripping cases which had been considered in the courts below. *Coates v Arndale Properties Ltd HL 1984, 59 TC 516; [1984] STC 637; [1984] 1 WLR 1328; [1985] 1 All ER 15.*

Cottle v Coldicott 6.6

Sale of milk quota — whether part of cost of land deductible from gain

A farmer owned 56.68 acres of land and was entitled to 120,000 litres of milk quota. In September 1991, he sold 60,000 litres of milk quota to a company. On the same day, but under separate agreements, he granted the company a tenancy of 10.39 acres of his land for a ten-month period, and the company appointed him as its agent to enter into occupation of that part of the land. The land subject to the tenancy was not to be used for milk production, this short-term let being necessary to ensure a permanent and effective transfer of the milk quota, since milk quota could not be used or sold without the land to which it was attached. The Revenue issued a CGT assessment on the gain. The farmer appealed, contending that the sale of the milk quota should be treated as a part disposal of his land, so that part of the acquisition cost of the land should be allowed as a deduction and that on this basis he had made a capital loss rather than a capital gain. The Special Commissioners rejected this contention and rejected the farmer's appeal. The milk quota was a separate asset from the land. Although milk quota corresponded to a holding of land, it did not 'correspond to any particular parcel of land in that holding'. Milk quota did not derive from the occupier's land, but was 'an advantage derived from the context of the common organisation of the market in milk'. Milk quota was a valuable asset, and those holding it had the right (subject to restrictions laid down in EC law) to dispose of it for profit. *Dicta* of the European Court of Justice in *R v Ministry of Agriculture, Fisheries and Food (ex p. Bostock), CJEC [1994] 1 ECR 955* applied. The sale of the milk quota was not a part disposal of the farmer's land within *TCGA 1992, s 21(2)(b)**, and was not a capital sum derived from the land within *TCGA 1992, s 22(1)**. Since the value of the quota did not derive from the holding, *TCGA 1992, s 43** did not apply. *Cottle v Coldicott (Sp C 40), [1995] SSCD 239.*

Craven v White 3.1

Anti-avoidance

Three members of a family owned all the shares in a UK company (Q), which owned a number of shops. From 1973 they conducted negotiations with various other companies with a view to selling Q or merging it with a similar business. In July 1976, at a time when they were negotiating with two unconnected companies, they exchanged their shares for shares in an Isle of Man company (M). Nineteen days later M sold the shares in Q to one of the two companies with which negotiations had been in progress at the time of the share exchange. The sale proceeds were paid by M to the shareholders over a period of five years. The Revenue issued CGT assessments for 1976–77 on the basis that, applying the Ramsay principle, the disposal of the shares to M and their subsequent sale by M should be treated as a single composite transaction and that the transfer of the shares to M was a fiscal nullity. The Special Commissioners reduced the assessments, holding that the transfer could not be treated as a fiscal nullity but that the shareholders were assessable on the amounts they had received from M at the time of receipt. The Revenue's appeals against this decision were dismissed by the Ch D, the CA, and (by a 3–2 majority) the HL. In giving the leading judgement for the majority, Lord Oliver indicated the limitations of the principle adopted in *CIR v Ramsay*, as defined by Lord Brightman in *Furniss v Dawson*. The principle in question — that the Commissioners are not bound to consider individually each step in a composite transaction intended to be carried through as a whole — applied only where there was a 'pre-ordained series of transactions' or 'one single composite transaction' and where steps were inserted which had no commercial purpose apart from the avoidance of a liability to tax. Although the decision in *Furniss v Dawson* extended the *Ramsay* principle, by applying it to a linear transaction as opposed to a circular self-cancelling one, it did no more than apply that principle to different events. It did not lay down any proposition that a transaction entered into with the motive of minimising tax was to be ignored or struck down. In the *Ramsay* case, Lord Wilberforce had emphasised the continuing validity and application of the principle enunciated by Lord Tomlin in *CIR v Duke of Westminster*. Lord Fraser had echoed this view, as had Lord Bridge in *Furniss v Dawson*. (The speech of Lord Roskill in that case, which implied the contrary, did not appear to represent the view of the majority.) The criteria by reference to which the Ramsay principle applied were not logically capable of expansion so as to apply to any similar case except one in which, when the intermediate transaction or transactions took place, the end result which in fact occurred was so certain of fulfilment that it was intellectually and practically possible to conclude that there had indeed taken place one single and indivisible process. For the principle to apply, the intermediate steps had to serve no purpose other than that of saving tax; all stages of the composite transaction had to be pre-ordained with a degree of certainty with the taxpayer having control over the end result at the time when the intermediate steps were taken; and there should be no interruption between the intermediate transaction and the disposal to the ultimate purchaser. In this case, however, the transactions that the Crown sought to reconstruct into a single direct disposal were not contemporaneous. Nor were they pre-ordained since, at the time of the share exchange, it was not certain what the ultimate destination of the property would be. Lord Jauncey considered that 'a step in a linear transaction which has no business purpose apart from the avoidance or deferment of tax liability will be treated as forming part of a pre-ordained series of transactions or of a composite transaction if it was taken at a time when negotiations or arrangements for the carrying through as a continuous process of a subsequent transaction which actually takes place had reached a stage when there was no real likelihood that such subsequent transaction would not take place and if thereafter such negotiations or arrangements were carried through to completion without genuine interruption'. Lord Oliver concurred with this definition. *Craven v White HL 1988, 62 TC 1; [1988] STC 476; [1988] 3 WLR 423; [1988] 3 All ER 495.*

Davenport v Chilver 6.1

*Compensation for confiscation of asset — application of TCGA 1992, s 22(1)**

In 1940 the USSR nationalised private property in Latvia. Following the *Foreign Compensation (USSR) Order 1969 (SI 1969 No 735)*, a woman who was resident in the UK made a claim in respect of such property in Latvia, some of which she had held in her own right and some of which had been held by her mother. In 1972–73 she received a payment in respect of the claim. She appealed against a CGT assessment on the payment. The Ch D held that the compensation for the loss of the assets she had held was within *TCGA 1992, s 22(1)(a)**, and that the compensation for the assets her mother had held was within *TCGA 1992, s 21(a)**. The case was remitted to the Special Commissioner for figures to be determined. *Davenport v Chilver Ch D 1983, 57 TC 661; [1983] STC 426; [1983] 3 WLR 481.*

(Note. See now *TCGA 1992, s 17.*)

Davis v Henderson 17.7

Statutory compensation for disturbance on surrender of agricultural lease

Davis v Powell (see below) was applied in a subsequent case in which a farmer had surrendered an agricultural tenancy to his landlord under an agreement providing for payment of £455,180 as compensation for disturbance under *Agricultural Holdings Act 1986, s 60*, and £520,000 as additional compensation. The Revenue issued an assessment charging CGT on both payments. The farmer appealed, accepting that the £520,000 was chargeable to CGT but contending that the £455,180 was not taxable. The Special Commissioners accepted this contention and allowed the appeal, holding that the payment was statutory compensation under *Agricultural Holdings Act 1986*, and was therefore not taxable. The Commissioners held that 'the notice to quit need not necessarily be the sole or proximate cause of the termination of a tenancy: it may be sufficient for the notice to quit to be one of a number of links in a chain of causal events'. The Revenue's contention that the tenancy had been terminated by agreement was rejected. *Davis v Henderson (Sp C 46), [1995] SSCD 308.*

Davis v Powell 17.7

Statutory compensation for disturbance on surrender of agricultural lease

A farmer surrendered to the Milton Keynes Development Corporation part of land he leased, receiving compensation of £5,971 from the Corporation. Included in this was £591 equal to one year's rent and representing compensation for disturbance under *Agricultural Holdings Act 1948, s 34*. The Ch D held that no gain could be made out of a sum of money given to compensate for loss or expense which was unavoidably incurred after the lease has gone and the £591 was not a capital sum 'derived from' the lease or 'received in return for . . . surrender of rights' (*TCGA 1992, s 22(1)**) and not liable to capital gains tax. (There was no dispute as to the tax treatment of the balance of the £5,971.) *Davis v Powell Ch D 1976, 51 TC 492; [1977] STC 32; [1977] 1 WLR 258; [1977] 1 All ER 471.*

De Rothschild v Lawrenson 43.13

*Interaction of TCGA 1992, s 77 and 87(2)**

In 1989 the trustees of two non-resident settlements, which had been established in 1982 by a UK resident, sold the trust funds and resolved to pay the whole amount realised to the settlor. The Revenue raised an assessment on the settlor under *TCGA 1992, s 87(2)**, charging CGT on the amount on which the trustees would have been chargeable to tax if they had been resident or ordinarily resident in the UK. The settlor appealed, contending that the effect of *TCGA 1992, s 77** was that the gains of the settlements were not to be treated as accruing to the trustees and that the assessment should be reduced to nil. The Special Commissioners dismissed his appeal and the Ch D upheld their decision. *TCGA 1992, s 77** did not apply, since it dealt with cases where trustees were in fact chargeable to tax on realised gains. In a case within *TCGA 1992, s 87(2)**, gains were to be computed on the amount on which the trustees would have been chargeable to tax if they had been resident or ordinarily resident in the UK. That provision did not make the trustees themselves chargeable to tax, and the gains so computed were to be treated as chargeable gains accruing to the beneficiary. *De Rothschild v Lawrenson CA 1995, 67 TC 300; [1995] STC 623.*

Director v Inspector of Taxes 39.9

*Relief under TCGA 1992, s 24(2) (assets of negligible value)**

An individual (D) was allotted 30,000 £1 shares in a company, in consideration of future services to the company. Shortly after being allotted these shares, he was appointed a director of the company. The company's liabilities exceeded its assets, and it subsequently became insolvent. After correspondence, the Revenue accepted for Schedule E purposes that the shares had a nil market value at the time of their allotment. Three years later, D submitted a claim for relief under *TCGA 1992, s 24(2)* in respect of the shares. The Revenue rejected this claim and the Special Commissioner dismissed D's appeal. Under *TCGA 1992, s 17*, the shares were deemed to have been acquired for a consideration equal to their market value, which was clearly nil. Since the shares had a market value of nil when they were acquired, they were not capable of becoming of negligible value, within *section 24(2)*. (The Commissioner observed that D had 'sought both to have his cake and to eat it'.) *Director v Inspector of Taxes (Sp C 161), [1998] SSCD 172.*

Drummond v Austin Brown 17.7

Statutory compensation for disturbance on termination of tenancy of business premises

Davis v Powell was followed in a case in which the taxpayer had for many years carried on practice as a solicitor in premises leased to him by a bank. The bank required the premises for the purposes of its own business and gave him notice under *Part II* of the *Landlord and Tenant Act 1954* that it would oppose a renewal of his lease. He did not oppose the notice and his tenancy was terminated from 1 April 1978. He received compensation of £31,384 under *Landlord and Tenant Act 1954, s 37*. The Revenue assessed him on this sum for 1977–78 on the footing that it was a capital sum derived from an asset within *TCGA 1992, s 22**. His appeal was allowed by the Special Commissioners, and the Ch D and CA upheld their decision. The right to the compensation was a statutory one. There was no entitlement to it under the lease and it was therefore not derived from the lease. Nor was it, as the Revenue contended, for the loss of an asset. The lease had expired, but it was never 'lost'. *Drummond v Austin Brown CA 1984, 58 TC 67; [1984] STC 321; [1984] 3 WLR 381; [1984] 2 All ER 699.*

Dunlop International AG v Pardoe 13.19

*Principal group company becoming non-resident — application of TCGA 1992, s 179**

In May 1978, D, which had been the principal member of a group of companies, became non-resident. The Revenue issued an assessment on the basis that *TCGA 1992, s 179** applied, so that D was deemed to have sold and immediately re-acquired shares in a subsidiary company, which it had acquired from another group member in March 1978. The Special Commissioners upheld the assessment, observing that the change of residence 'was an appropriate point at which to bring to an end the deferral of any gain or loss'. The Ch D and the CA dismissed D's appeal against this decision. Chadwick LJ observed that the object of *section 179** was 'to prevent the transferee company from taking the asset out of the group in circumstances in which the gain will not crystallise on a subsequent disposal — because there will be no subsequent disposal'. *Dunlop International AG v Pardoe CA, [1999] STC 909.*

Dunstan v Young Austen Young Ltd 3.1, 58.5

Whether issue of new shares not acquired at arm's length constituted a capital reorganisation

The taxpayer company (Y) carried on business as a mechanical engineering contractor. In 1977 it acquired for £16,100 the 1,000 issued £1 shares of a company (J) in the same line of business. Shortly afterwards it joined a large group; one of the shares in J was registered in the name of a fellow-subsidiary (T), the remainder being registered in its own name. J was not trading profitably. By March 1979 it had incurred debts of £200,911 to other companies in the group, mainly to Y, and it was decided to sell it. An arm's length purchaser was found, and J issued a further 200,000 £1 shares on 12 June 1979. These were allotted to Y for £200,000 cash, which was promptly repaid to Y to clear its indebtedness.

On 29 June an agreement was completed between Y, T and the purchaser for the sale of the 201,000 shares for £38,000. The appeal was against an assessment for the year to September 1979. The profits were agreed at nil and the substantive issue was whether Y had incurred a capital loss on its disposal of the shares in J and, if so, of what amount. It was common ground that Y acquired the additional 200,000 shares 'otherwise than by a bargain made at arm's length' and by virtue of *CGTA 1979, s 19(3)** the consideration for them should be taken to be their market value, which the Special Commissioner found to be nil 'or so near to it as to make no matter'. However, Y contended that the issue of the further 200,000 shares constituted a reorganisation of J's capital within *TCGA 1992, ss 126, 128**, with the consequence that the new shares would not be treated as a separate acquisition and that the £200,000 would be treated as having been given for the original 1,000 shares, making their cost £216,100 and the loss £178,100. This contention was upheld by the CA, reversing the decision of the Ch D and restoring that of the Special Commissioner. Properly construed, the phrase 'reorganisation of a company's share capital' in *TCGA 1992, s 126** included an increase in a company's share capital and the allotment of the new shares to its parent company for cash. *Dunstan v Young Austen Young Ltd, CA 1988, 61 TC 448; [1989] STC 69.* (Note. *CGTA 1979, s 19(3)* was repealed by *FA 1981*. See now *TCGA 1992, s 128(2)* as regards reorganisations on or after 10 March 1981.)

Durrant v CIR 53.9

Definition of 'chargeable business asset' — TCGA 1992, Sch 6 para 12(2)

An accountant retired from an accountancy partnership. He had held 11.11% of the shares in the partnership's service company, and disposed of these shares on his retirement. He claimed retirement relief, but the Revenue rejected his claim, considering that the shares were not 'chargeable business assets' within *TCGA 1992, Sch 6 para 12(2)**. The Special Commissioner dismissed the accountant's appeal against this decision. *Durrant v CIR (Sp C 24), [1995] SSCD 145.*

Eastham v Leigh London & Provincial Properties Ltd 17.2

Date of acquisition

On 22 June 1962, a company agreed with the owners of land to erect on the land a building to be leased, on completion, to the company for 125 years from 24 June 1962. The building was completed and the lease granted in May 1964. On 28 July 1965, the company disposed of the lease at a large gain which was assessed on the basis that the acquisition and disposal of the lease took place within three years and *FA 1965, s 82(2)(3)* (interim charge of tax) applied. The company contended that the lease was acquired under the 1962 agreement. The Revenue contended that the 1962 agreement comprised two contracts, a building agreement and an agreement for a lease, the latter being a conditional contract within the meaning of *FA 1962, Sch 9 para 1* (compare *TCGA 1992, s 28(2)*), or alternatively, that there was a single but conditional contract. The CA held that the 1962 agreement was a single and absolute contract. *Eastham v Leigh London & Provincial Properties Ltd CA 1971, 46 TC 687; [1971] Ch 871; [1971] 2 All ER 811.*

Edwards v Fisher

See *Billingham v Cooper* above.

Eilbeck v Rawling 3.1, 57.6

Anti-avoidance Scheme of arrangement

A taxpayer made a chargeable gain of £355,094 in 1974–75 as to which there was no dispute. Later in the same year he entered into a chain of transactions with the object of creating a commensurate allowable loss, at a cost to him of only £370 apart from the fees, etc. paid for the scheme, which was an 'off the peg' avoidance device obtained from a Jersey company. The central feature of the scheme involved his acquiring reversionary interests in two trust funds, one held by Jersey trustees and the other by Gibraltar trustees. Under a special power of appointment, the Gibraltar trustees advanced £315,000 to the Jersey trustees to be held on the trusts of the Jersey settlement. The taxpayer then sold both reversionary interests, making a gain on the sale of his interest under the Jersey settlement (claimed to be exempt under *TCGA 1992, s 76(1)**) and a matching loss of £312,470 on the sale of his interest under the Gibraltar settlement (claimed as an allowable loss). The CA refused the claim on the ground, inter alia, that the exercise of the power of appointment did not take the £315,000 outside the Gibraltar settlement; hence the sale of his reversionary interest in the £315,000 was a part sale of his interest under the Gibraltar settlement. The taxpayer appealed to the HL. The appeal was considered with W T Ramsay Ltd, and dismissed for the same general reason that, on the facts, the scheme was to be looked at as a composite transaction under which there was neither gain nor loss apart from the £370. Furthermore, the HL upheld the CA decision that the sale of the reversionary interest in the £315,000 was a sale of part of the taxpayer's reversionary interest in the Gibraltar settlement. *Eilbeck v Rawling HL 1981, 54 TC 101; [1981] STC 174; [1981] 2 WLR 449; [1981] 1 All ER 865.* (Note. The device would also now be caught by the value shifting provisions of *TCGA 1992, s 30.*)

Emmerson v Computer Time International Ltd 17.5

Assignment of lease — whether arrears of rent deductible

A company discontinued its trade and went into voluntary liquidation. It owed rent in respect of its business premises, held under leases with several years to run but which could not be assigned without the landlord's consent. The landlord gave his consent subject to payment of the arrears. The liquidator accordingly sold the leases for £93,135 and paid the landlord the arrears of rent including £6,131 for the period of liquidation after trading had ceased. The company claimed to deduct the £6,131 in arriving at the gain on the disposal of the leases on the ground that it was a payment to enhance the value of the leases or a capital payment for the right to assign them. The CA rejected the claim. The £6,131 was in discharge of the company's obligations under its lease and not within *TCGA 1992, s 38(1)(b)**. Further, even if it were within that provision, deduction would be precluded by *TCGA 1992, s 39(2)**. *Emmerson v Computer Time International Ltd CA 1977, 50 TC 628; [1977] STC 170; [1977] 1 WLR 734; [1977] 2 All ER 545.*

EV Booth (Holdings) Ltd v Buckwell 17.6

Sale of shares accompanied by waiver of debt — amount of consideration

A company entered into an agreement under which it sold shares in a subsidiary for £35,000 and, in addition, accepted £20,969 in full satisfaction of a debt of £55,839 owed to it by the subsidiary. The debt was not a 'debt on a security'. The Ch D held that there were two disposals and that the consideration for the disposal of the shares was the £35,000. *Aberdeen Construction Group Ltd v CIR* distinguished. *EV Booth (Holdings) Ltd v Buckwell Ch D 1980, 53 TC 425; [1980] STC 578.*

Ewart v Taylor 43.20

Year for which gains apportioned to beneficiaries should be assessed

In pursuance of powers under a settlement made on 18 March 1965, the trustees transferred the trust fund in 1969 to the trustees of a Jersey discretionary settlement, set up for the purpose. The 1965 settlement was a UK settlement, the settlor and trustees all being resident in the UK. In 1976 the trustees of the Jersey settlement carried out a series of transactions, designed to distribute the trust property without incurring CGT liability.

In round figures, the trust fund then comprised cash of £534,000 and shares valued at £461,000. The transactions carried out included (in date order) borrowing the requisite money from a Jersey bank; appointing a total of £640,000 absolutely to three beneficiaries, including £314,000 to each of Mrs F and Mrs E, and a further £314,000 to themselves to be held on trusts for the benefit of the issue of Mrs V; and selling the shares at valuation equally to Mrs F and Mrs E. The remaining cash was used or required for expenses and costs. In the period 1969–75 the trustees had realised gains of £379,000 not apportioned to beneficiaries, and the 1976 sale of the shares to Mrs F and Mrs E had resulted in gains of £395,000. All the beneficiaries were resident in the UK. The Revenue made assessments for 1976–77 on the basis that all the gains, including the pre-1976 gains, were assessable on the beneficiaries for that year by virtue of *FA 1965, s 42*. On appeal the Ch D held that under *FA 1965, s 42(2)* the pre-1976 gains were assessable for the years in which they arose. *FA 1965, s 42(3)(b)* did not operate to make them assessable for 1976–77 as the beneficiaries who received the capital payments in 1976 were the beneficiaries among whom the gains were apportionable for the years in which they arose. Applying *Roome v Edwards*, the appointment to Mrs V's children's fund created a separate settlement. It was part of a scheme for the distribution of the trust fund and bringing the Jersey settlement to an end. The result was that the Revenue succeeded as regards the 1976 gains but failed as regards the pre-1976 gains. *Ewart v Taylor and related appeals Ch D 1983, 57 TC 401; [1983] STC 721.*

Fielder v Vedlynn Ltd 40.1

Consideration for sale of companies with tax losses — whether to include sums payable under guarantees by reference to amount of losses

In December 1977 a company (V) sold shares in eight subsidiary companies to an unconnected company (M). The subsidiary companies had incurred capital losses which had not been quantified at the date of the sale. The shares were sold for their market value of £19,529, but under the agreement M provided a guarantee that each of the eight companies should pay V an amount equal to 7.5% of their allowable capital losses. In December 1979 the losses in question were agreed at £19.5 million, and the amounts in question were paid to V by the subsidiaries. The Revenue issued a CGT assessment on V for the period ending 31 December 1977, including the amount received by V from the subsidiaries as part of the consideration for the sale of the shares. V appealed, contending that the consideration should be restricted to the £19,529 which was agreed to be the market value of the companies in December 1977. The Special Commissioner allowed V's appeal and the Ch D upheld this decision. The guarantees were terms of the sale agreements, and no additional monetary value could or should be placed on them. Further, even if they were to be regarded as part of the consideration, they were incapable of valuation within the meaning of *FA 1965, s 22(4). Fielder v Vedlynn Ltd Ch D 1992, 65 TC 145; [1992] STC 553.*

(Note. *FA 1965, s 22(4)* became *CGTA, s 19(3)*, which was repealed by *FA 1981, s 90* with effect from 10 March 1981 and replaced by what is now *TCGA 1992, s 17.*)

Figg v Clarke 57.9

'Absolutely entitled as against the trustee' (TCGA 1992, s 60)
Date on which beneficiaries absolutely entitled

In 1963 the trustees of a settlement made an appointment whereby certain investments and income should be held 'upon trust for such of the children (of the settlor) now living or hereafter to be born . . . as shall attain the age of 21'. In 1964 the settlor was paralysed in an accident, leaving no realistic possibility that he could beget any more children. The settlor's youngest child became 21 in 1976 and the settlor died in 1990. The Special

Commissioner held that the children became absolutely entitled as against the trustees in 1990 (rather than 1976). The Ch D upheld this decision. Blackburne J held that the court could not have regard to the impossibility of a person having children in the future. *Figg v Clarke Ch D 1996, 68 TC 645; [1997] STC 247.*

Floor v Davis 3.4, 14.6

*Arrangements to reduce liability — interpretation of TCGA 1992, s 29(2)**

It had been arranged that, subject to contract, the share capital of a company (IDM) would be sold (at a substantial profit to the shareholders) to another company (KDI). F and his two sons-in-law, who together controlled IDM, carried out a scheme under which the following transactions took place shortly after each other. They transferred their IDM shares to FNW, a company set up for the purpose, for preferred shares in FNW; FNW sold the IDM shares to KDI for cash; a Cayman Islands company, D, acquired a relatively insignificant holding of preferred shares in FNW; following a rights issue open to all preferred shareholders but accepted only by D, D became the sole ordinary shareholder in FNW; FNW went into liquidation and because of the differing rights attached to the two classes of shares, D, as the ordinary shareholder, became entitled to six-sevenths of the assets of FNW. The upshot was that the greater part of the proceeds of sale of the IDM shares reached D. The CA held (Eveleigh LJ dissenting), that F had disposed of his IDM shares to FNW (and not, as contended by the Revenue, to KDI) with the consequence that under *TCGA 1992, s 135** his FNW shares were treated as the IDM shares he originally held. However, the CA unanimously held that value had passed out of the FNW shares within the meaning of *TCGA 1992, s 29(2)** and F was assessable accordingly, on the grounds that (i) 'person' in *TCGA 1992, s 29(2)** includes the plural by virtue of *Interpretation Act 1889, s 1(1)(b)* and the definition of 'control' (see *TCGA 1992, s 288(1)**) and (ii) F and his sons-in-law had exercised their control, notwithstanding that two of them had not voted on the resolution to wind up FNW. The HL rejected F's appeal on this point. (The Revenue's contention that F had disposed of the shares to KDI was therefore not argued in the HL. See now as to this *Furniss v Dawson*, in which the dissenting judgement of Eveleigh LJ, who upheld the Revenue's contention that the shares had been disposed of to KDI, was approved.) *Floor v Davis HL 1979, 52 TC 609; [1979] STC 379; [1979] 2 WLR 830; [1979] 2 All ER 677.* (Notes. (1) The relevant transactions took place in 1969. See now for value-shifting transactions after 13 March 1989, *TCGA 1992, ss 30–34.* (2) The *Interpretation Act 1889* has since been repealed. See now *Interpretation Act 1978, s 6(c).*)

Foster v Williams; Horan v Williams 58.26

Cash bonuses received on takeover of building society

A building society transferred its business to a banking company. Shareholders and depositors were paid lump sums of £500 and percentage bonus payments calculated by reference to the balance on their accounts. Two shareholders appealed against CGT assessments, contending that they had made a complete disposal of their existing assets and that there was no chargeable gain. The Special Commissioner accepted this contention and allowed the appeals in principle, holding that there had been a total disposal of the relevant assets. With regard to the share accounts, the amount of the credit balance on each account was allowable expenditure within *TCGA 1992, s 38.* With regard to the deposit accounts, the effect of *TCGA 1992, s 251* was that there was no chargeable gain. Since payments were made to shareholders and depositors alike, none of the expenditure could be attributed to the shareholders' equity rights. *Foster v Williams; Horan v Williams (Sp C 113), [1997] SSCD 112.*

Fulford-Dobson, ex p., R v Inspector of Taxes 52.3

Gift by wife to husband about to become non-resident — application of ESC D2

On 18 August 1980 an individual (F) entered into a contract of employment in Germany. He was required to begin work on 15 September and he left the UK for this purpose on 29 August 1980. From that date he became resident in Germany, having previously been resident and ordinarily resident in the UK. Acting on professional advice, and admittedly to take advantage of Inland Revenue Extra-Statutory Concession D2, his wife transferred to him on that date a farm which she had inherited in 1977 and had been considering selling in 1980. The farm was in fact sold by auction on 17 September. The Revenue assessed F to CGT for 1980/81 on the gain on the sale. He applied for judicial review to quash the assessment, contending that the Revenue should have applied Inland Revenue Extra-Statutory Concession D2. The QB rejected this contention and dismissed the application, holding that the Revenue had been entitled to refuse to apply the concession. It was clearly stated inside the front cover of Revenue Pamphlet IR1, listing the extra-statutory concessions in operation, that a 'concession will not be given in any case where an attempt is made to use it for tax avoidance'. *R v Inspector of Taxes (ex p. Fulford-Dobson), QB 1987, 60 TC 168; [1987] STC 344; [1987] 3 WLR 277.*

Furniss v Dawson 3.1, 53.10, 59.3

Anti-avoidance

The shareholders in two family companies wished to dispose of their shares, and found an unconnected company (W) willing to acquire the shares at an agreed price. Before disposing of the shares, they exchanged them for shares in a Manx company which in turn sold them to W. The Revenue issued assessments on the basis that the shares should be treated as having been disposed of directly to W, since the interposition of the Manx company had been designed solely to take advantage of the law then in force with regard to company reconstructions and amalgamations. The HL unanimously upheld the assessments (reversing the decision of the CA). Applying *WT Ramsay Ltd*, the transactions should be regarded as a single composite transaction. Lord Bridge of Harwich observed that 'the distinction between form and substance . . . can usefully be drawn in determining the tax consequences of composite transactions'. Lord Brightman held that the *Ramsay* principle applied in cases where there was a 'pre-ordained series of transactions; or . . . one single composite transaction' and steps were 'inserted which have no commercial (business) purpose apart from the avoidance of a liability to tax — not "no business effect". If these two ingredients exist, the inserted steps are to be disregarded for fiscal purposes. The court must look at the end result.' *Furniss v Dawson HL 1984, 55 TC 324; [1984] STC 153; [1984] 2 WLR 226; [1984] 1 All ER 530.* (Notes. (1) See also *TCGA 1992, s 137.* (2) Although the decision was unanimous, there was implicit disagreement as to the continuing validity of the Duke of Westminster principle. Lords Bridge and Scarman indicated that the principle still applied, but Lord Roskill specifically refrained from endorsing the Westminster decision. For subsequent developments, see the judgement of Lord Templeman in *Ensign Tankers (Leasing) Ltd v Stokes*, and that of Lord Keith in *Countess Fitzwilliam v CIR*.)

Garner v Pounds Shipowners & Shipbreakers Ltd (and related appeal) 17.3, 17.5, 17.10

Grant of option to purchase land—treatment of payment for release of restrictive covenants

A company (P) granted an option to purchase freehold land which was subject to certain restrictive covenants. P undertook to use its best endeavours to obtain the release of the covenants but the exercise of the option was not dependent on their release. The purchaser paid £399,750 for the option, this amount being held by P's solicitors as stakeholders pending the release of the covenants. P subsequently paid £90,000 to obtain the release of the covenants. The option was not, in fact, exercised. The Revenue issued an assessment charging tax on the consideration of £399,750 without allowing a deduction for the £90,000. The HL unanimously dismissed P's appeal and upheld the assessment. Lord Jauncey held that 'no payment by the company to a third party can alter the value of the cash sum of £399,750 paid by (the purchaser) in terms of the agreement as a consideration for the disposal, i.e. the grant of the option'. *Randall v Plumb* distinguished. Furthermore, the £90,000 was not allowable expenditure within *TCGA 1992, s 38**. The implementation of the obligation to obtain the release of the covenants was 'not a prerequisite of the option being exercised'. Accordingly, the expenditure was not 'wholly and exclusively incurred by (P) in providing' the option. Additionally, 'the expenditure referred to in *s 38(1)** must be expenditure which is extraneous to the asset rather than part of it'. On a sale of the land itself, there would be strong grounds for claiming the £90,000 as allowable expenditure, as the value of the land would have been enhanced by removal of the restrictive covenants. *Garner v Pounds Shipowners & Shipbreakers Ltd (and related appeal) HL 2000, [2000] STC 420.*

Golding v Kaufman 17.10

Amount received for release of put option

An employee of an investment company owned 25% of the shares of that company. He entered into an agreement with the company under which he could require the company to purchase his shareholding. In 1969 the company paid him £5,000 to relinquish his rights under this agreement. The Revenue included the £5,000 in a CGT assessment on him for 1968–69. He appealed, contending that, by virtue of *FA 1965, Sch 7 para 14(3)*, there had been no disposal of any asset. The Special Commissioners allowed his appeal but the Ch D reversed their decision and restored the assessment. A sum paid to a person who had the right to call on another person to buy property from him (a put option) was a capital sum derived from an asset. *FA 1965, Sch 7 para 14(3)* provided that the exercise of a put option would not be treated as a disposal for the purpose of creating allowable losses, but it did not exempt a gain made from such a transaction. *Golding v Kaufman Ch D 1985, 58 TC 296; [1985] STC 152.*

(Note. *FA 1965, Sch 7 para 14(3)* was modified by *FA 1971*. See now *TCGA 1992, s 144(3)(4)*.)

Goodbrand v Loffland Bros North Sea Inc 17.5

Deferred consideration (TCGA 1992, s 48)
Exchange rate fluctuations — whether TCGA 1992, s 48 applicable*

In 1985 a company (L) sold various assets under a lease-purchase agreement for $38,610,000. The Revenue issued an assessment on the basis that the sterling equivalent of the disposal proceeds, at the then exchange rate, was £33,313,000. As a result of subsequent fluctuations in the exchange rate, L only received £23,853,000. It claimed relief under *TCGA 1992, s 48** for the balance of £9,500,000. The Ch D upheld the Revenue's rejection of the claim, and the CA dismissed the company's appeal, holding that the 'consideration . . . brought into account' was the contractual consideration, rather than its sterling equivalent. The tax computation merely involved a valuation exercise, rather than an actual conversion of dollars into sterling. L had anticipated receiving $38,610,000 and had received that amount. The exchange loss of £9,500,000 was not irrecoverable consideration within the meaning of *TCGA 1992, s 48**. *Goodbrand v Loffland Bros North Sea Inc CA 1998, 71 TC 57; [1998] STC 930.*

Goodwin v Curtis 48.2

Private residence exemption (TCGA 1992, ss 222–225)

Farmhouse inhabited by claimant for only 32 days — whether eligible for relief under TCGA 1992, s 222.*

In 1983 a company had exchanged contracts for the purchase of a farm, which included a nine-bedroomed farmhouse. It agreed that, following completion of the purchase, it would sell the farmhouse to one of its directors (G). The company did not complete the purchase of the farmhouse until 7 March 1985, and the sale to G was completed on 1 April 1985. G, who was in the process of separating from his wife, had already instructed estate agents with regard to the sale of the farmhouse, but moved into it immediately. On 3 April 1985 G completed the purchase of a small cottage, and on 11 April 1985 he advertised the farmhouse for sale. He continued to live in the farmhouse until 3 May 1985, when he completed the sale of the farmhouse and moved into the cottage. He appealed against a CGT assessment, contending that the gain on the sale of the farmhouse was eligible for relief under *TCGA 1992, s 222**. The General Commissioners rejected this contention, finding that G had not intended to occupy the farmhouse as his permanent residence, and holding that the gain did not qualify for relief. The CA upheld their decision. G had only lived in the farmhouse for 32 days, and the Commissioners had been entitled to find that he had not intended to occupy it as his permanent residence. *Dicta* of Viscount Cave in *Levene v CIR* applied. *Goodwin v Curtis CA 1998, 70 TC 478; [1998] STC 475.*

Gordon v CIR 25.10

Whether business transferred as a going concern

A farmer entered into an agreement with his wife to farm an estate in partnership. Five days later the partnership agreed to transfer its business to an unlimited company which the farmer and his wife had formed in the previous month. The Revenue issued a capital gains tax assessment charging tax on the transfer of the business to the company. The farmer appealed, contending that the business had been transferred as a going concern, so that rollover relief was available. The Special Commissioner dismissed his appeal, finding that, although the 'whole assets of the business' had been transferred, the farmer had intended that the company should sell the estate to an outside purchaser, and that the company had not taken over the business until contracts for the sale of the estate had been exchanged. Accordingly, the business had not been transferred as a going concern, since 'its end was too clearly and too closely in sight'. The CS allowed the farmer's appeal against this decision. Although contracts for the sale of the estate to an outside purchaser had been exchanged by the time when the company took over the farming of the estate, no such sale had been agreed at the time when the partnership had agreed to transfer the estate to the company. Accordingly, the company could have continued to operate the business if it had so wished. Furthermore, the company subsequently continued to farm an estate elsewhere, using machinery and cattle transferred to it from the partnership. Lord Hope held that 'a planned move of the entire assets of a business from one place to another is not inconsistent with the continuation of its trade'. On the facts found by the Commissioner, the only reasonable conclusion was that the company had received the whole assets of the business as a going concern. *Robroyston Brickworks Ltd* applied. *Gordon v CIR CS 1991, 64 TC 173; [1991] STC 174.*

Green v CIR 48.1

Whether wing of mansion part of residence — whether TCGA 1992, s 224(2) applicable*

In 1975 a taxpayer sold a mansion house and grounds which he had acquired in 1971. The building comprised a central block with 33 rooms, and two wings connected to it by corridors. Some work of reconstruction and redecoration had been carried out, during which the taxpayer and various members of his family and others had occupied parts of the central block, while a flat had been made in one of the wings for a gardener. The taxpayer claimed that the whole of the gain was within the private residence exemption. The General

Commissioners held that the two wings were not part of the residence and that the gain on their sale was not within the relief. As regards the main block, they applied *TCGA 1992, s 224(2)**, adjusting the relief in respect of a 'change in what is occupied as the individual's residence', and allowed relief on one-third of the gain. The CS held that there was no factual material before the Commissioners which entitled them to adjust the relief under *TCGA 1992, s 224(2)**. Accordingly, the whole of the gain on the sale of the central block and grounds was exempt. Applying *Batey v Wakefield*, whether the wings were part of the residence was a matter of degree for the Commissioners, and their decision was not inconsistent with the evidence. Accordingly, the appeal failed as regards the gain on the sale of the wings. *Green v CIR CS 1982, 56 TC 10; [1982] STC 485.*

Griffin v Craig-Harvey 48.5

Retirement relief

A taxpayer, who owned a house in Stockwell, acquired a house in Winchester on 12 August 1985. On 9 July 1986 he sold his house in Stockwell and bought another house in Clapham. On 21 January 1988 he submitted a notice under *TCGA 1992, s 222(5)** declaring that the house in Winchester should be treated as his main residence. On 26 January 1989 he sold that house, realising a capital gain of around £225,000. The inspector issued a CGT assessment on the basis that $\frac{11}{41.5}$ of the gain was chargeable, considering that the period from August 1985 to June 1986 was not covered by the notice submitted in January 1988, since that notice was for the purpose of determining whether the Winchester house or the Clapham house should be treated as the taxpayer's main residence, and any notice determining whether the Stockwell house or the Winchester house had been the taxpayer's main residence would have had to have been lodged within two years of the taxpayer's acquisition of the Winchester house in August 1985. The taxpayer appealed, contending that the notice should be treated as effective from January 1986, so that only $\frac{5.5}{41.5}$ of the gain was chargeable. The Ch D upheld the assessment (reversing the Special Commissioner's decision). The two-year period of *TCGA 1992, s 222(5)(a)* began to run from the time when it first became necessary to determine which of two specific residences should be treated as a taxpayer's main residence. The taxpayer had made no election covering the period when he owned a house in Stockwell as well as the house in Winchester. The election which he had made in January 1988 was an election between his house in Clapham and the house in Winchester. Since he had not acquired the house in Clapham until July 1986, the notice could not cover any period before that time. (Vinelott J observed that *TCGA 1992, s 222(5)** derived from *FA 1965*, and that during the relevant Parliamentary debates the Financial Secretary had stated that the intention of the clause was so that a taxpayer could 'exercise a choice within two years from the time when he acquires the second house'.) *Griffin v Craig-Harvey Ch D 1993, 66 TC 396; [1994] STC 54.*

Gubay v Kington 52.3

*Gift by resident husband to non-resident wife — application of TCGA 1992, s 58(1)**

The taxpayer's wife took up residence in the Isle of Man on 4 April 1972. The taxpayer remained resident and ordinarily resident in the UK until October 1972, but meanwhile he visited his wife and lived with her in the Isle of Man most weekends. In July 1972 he gave his wife some valuable shares. He appealed against a 1972–73 assessment on him in respect of the resultant gain. The HL allowed his appeal (Lord Scarman dissenting), holding that the combined effect of *ICTA 1988, s 282* and *TCGA 1992, s 58(1)** was that no CGT was payable on the gift of the shares. *Gubay v Kington HL 1984, 57 TC 601; [1984] STC 99; [1984] 1 WLR 163; [1984] 1 All ER 513.*

Hart v Briscoe and Others 57.6

TCGA 1992, s 71(1) — 'absolutely entitled' — whether beneficial entitlement required*

Two cases concerning *TCGA 1992, s 71(1)** were heard together. In *Hart v Briscoe*, trustees, acting under a 1955 settlement, declared that the whole of the settled property should be held on the trusts of a 1972 settlement, made for the purpose by the same settlor with the same trustees. In *Hoare Trustees,* trustees used a power of advancement in a settlement to declare trusts of assets advanced. It was held in both that the 'new' trustees had become absolutely entitled to settled property as against the old. 'Absolutely entitled' in *TCGA 1992, s 71(1)** does not imply beneficial ownership but whether an advancement is a continuance of the existing trust or a new trust is a question of fact and degree. *Hart v Briscoe and Others Ch D 1977, 52 TC 53; [1978] STC 89; [1978] 2 WLR 832; [1978] 1 All ER 791.* (See now *Roome v Edwards* and Revenue Statement of Practice SP 9/81.)

Hatt v Newman 53.4

Retirement relief — sale of let property

A married couple purchased a property in 1967, parts of which they let, furnished, to tenants and other parts of which were used by the husband as a workshop and a store for his business as a haulage contractor which ceased in 1990. The couple sold the property in 1995 and claimed retirement relief. The Revenue rejected the claim and the husband appealed. The Special Commissioner dismissed the appeal, and the Ch D upheld this decision. Applying *Griffiths v Jackson Ch D 1982, 52 TC 583; [1983] STC 184*, the letting of furnished rooms was not a trade. Furthermore, the period between the cessation of the husband's business as a contractor and the disposal of the property exceeded the one-year time limit permitted by *TCGA 1992, s 163, Sch 6* (see 53.5(*b*) RETIREMENT RELIEF). *Hatt v Newman Ch D, [2000] STC 113.* (Notes. (1) The husband appeared in person. (2) The Commissioner and Ch D also upheld the Revenue's contention that, by virtue of *TCGA 1992, s 28*, the disposal took place in 1994/95 when the contract was signed and the condition to which it was subject was fulfilled, rather than in 1995/96 when the contract was completed.)

Hawkings-Byass v Sassen 40.3

Valuation of unquoted shares

In three appeals heard together, members of the same family disposed of shares in an unquoted Cayman Islands company which was the holding company of a trading group concerned principally with the production and sale of sherry. Under the company's Articles of Association, the company could refuse to register the transfer of shares to anyone who was not a member of the two families which had originally formed the company (and the disposals were to members of the other family in question). The valuation of the shares at 31 March 1982 was disputed. The Special Commissioners reviewed the evidence in detail, holding that in the particular circumstances, it was not appropriate to value the shares on an earnings basis or on a dividend basis, but that the company should be valued on an assets basis and on a turnover basis to arrive at a notional quoted value which should be uplifted by a 'control premium' of 30% to arrive at an entirety value of £46,000,000. The shares should then be valued on the basis that the two smaller shareholdings (comprising 11.09% and 9.09% of the total shares respectively) could have been acquired with a bid of two-thirds of their 'entirety value' (i.e. at £256 each) and that, for the largest shareholding (comprising 18.16% of the share capital), a 20% premium should be added to this (arriving at a value of £307 each). *Hawkings-Byass v Sassen (and related appeals) (Sp C 88), [1996] SSCD 319.*

Henderson v Karmel's Executors 40.6

Election for 6 April 1965 valuation — whether land subject to a tenancy

In 1975 a married woman (K) sold land which she had held for many years. From 1961 to 1972 it had been farmed by a company which she controlled, and from then until the sale she had farmed it in partnership. The company had originally paid an annual rental of

£2,000, but this was waived in 1966. The Revenue issued a CGT assessment to the executors of K's husband, charging tax on the disposal. The executors appealed, contending that the land should be valued on the basis of vacant possession of the land at 6 April 1965. The Ch D rejected this contention and upheld the assessment (reversing the decision of the General Commissioners). On the evidence, at 6 April 1965 the land had clearly been subject to a tenancy. *Henderson v Karmel's Executors Ch D 1984, 58 TC 201; [1984] STC 572.*

Hepworth v Smith 53.4

Family company — whether voting rights not exercised are 'exercisable'

In a claim to retirement relief in which the facts are complex, the issue was whether S Ltd was a 'family company' in relation to the claimant. S Ltd had an issued capital of 100 shares of which the taxpayer, his wife and a business associate each held one. The remaining 97 shares were held by B Ltd which had, however, never appointed a representative to exercise its voting rights. The taxpayer contended that, for the purposes of *TCGA 1992, Sch 6 para 1(2)**, S Ltd was a family company, as he held one-third of the voting rights actually exercised. The Ch D, reversing the Commissioners' decision, held that voting rights 'exercisable' were those capable of being exercised. Accordingly, the voting rights of the shares held by B Ltd were 'exercisable' and S Ltd was not a family company. *Hepworth v Smith Ch D 1981, 54 TC 396; [1981] STC 354.*

(Note. *TCGA 1992, s 163, TCGA 1992, Sch 6 para 1(2)* has subsequently been amended by *FA 1993, s 87, Sch 7.* The references in *TCGA 1992, s 163* to a 'family company' have been replaced by references to a 'personal company'.)

Hinchcliffe v Crabtree 7.2, 40.2

Value of quoted shares while secret takeover negotiations in progress

A taxpayer was liable on his gain from the disposal during 1965–66 of certain quoted shares in a manufacturing company of which he was a joint managing director. The question at issue was their market value at 6 April 1965. At that date, takeover negotiations were in progress but had not been made public and the Commissioners accepted evidence that, had they been public, the quoted price at that date would have been substantially higher than the actual quoted price. The HL held that the mere fact that directors of a company possessed information which if made public would affect the quoted prices of its shares was not a special circumstance. (There was no evidence of impropriety in withholding the relevant information.) *Hinchcliffe v Crabtree HL 1971, 47 TC 419; [1972] AC 725; [1971] 3 All ER 967.*

Hirsch v Crowthers Cloth Ltd 33.1

*Machinery and plant — exclusion of amounts taken into account in computing balancing charge — TCGA 1992, s 37**

In 1980 a company sold for £715,967 looms which it had purchased for £545,930. The sale gave rise to a balancing charge under *CAA 1990, s 24**. The company appealed against a CGT assessment on the overall gain of £170,037, contending that, by virtue of *TCGA 1992, s 37(1)**, the acquisition cost of the looms should be excluded from the disposal consideration, since it had been taken into account in computing the balancing charge. The Ch D, reversing the Commissioner's decision, held that the acquisition cost was not to be excluded from the disposal consideration. Although *TCGA 1992, s 37(2)**, which specifically excluded from the scope of *TCGA 1992, s 37(1)** amounts taken into account in making a balancing charge under *CAA 1968*, had subsequently been amended by *FA 1980* to refer also to amounts taken into account under *FA 1971*, this was merely making explicit what was already implicit in *TCGA 1992, s 37(1)**. Where legislation was ambiguously worded, it was necessary to have regard to the context and scheme of the Act under consideration, and to strive to find an interpretation which avoided injustice or absurdity. The words 'taken into account' in *TCGA 1992, s 37(1)** should be read as referring to sums which had to be brought directly into the computation. The purpose of the limitation of the disposal value to the cost of acquisition was to avoid double taxation of any profit on disposal. It would be paradoxical to find that the cost of acquisition was itself to be deducted from the disposal consideration, thereby ensuring that the gain escaped altogether the charge to tax. *Hirsch v Crowthers Cloth Ltd Ch D 1989, 62 TC 759; [1990] STC 174.*

Honour v Norris 48.1

Whether self-contained flat formed part of dwelling-house

The owner of four separate flats, located in separate buildings in the same square within 95 yards of each other, sold one of them, which had been used to provide occasional bedroom accommodation for his children and guests and, on rare occasions, sleeping accommodation for him and his wife. He appealed against an assessment on the gain, claiming relief under *TCGA 1992, s 222**. (The square contained 32 houses, most of which were divided into flats.) The Ch D rejected the claim and upheld the assessment (reversing the decision of the Commissioners). The flat was a separate dwelling-house, which could not be regarded as part of a common entity with the flat in which the owner and his wife lived. The fact that the owner had sometimes used it to accommodate his children or guests did not make it a part of his private residence. *Honour v Norris Ch D 1992, 64 TC 599; [1992] STC 304.*

Innocent v Whaddon Estates Ltd 13.12

*Transfers within a group — construction of TCGA 1992, s 171(2)**

In 1961 the taxpayer company received, on the liquidation of a subsidiary, a capital distribution of shares in a public quoted company which at the time had a market value of 13s 4d each. The value fell to 6s 3d by Budget Day 1965, although this still exceeded their cost to the subsidiary. The company made various sales of the shares and appealed against assessments on the gains arrived at by treating the consideration for the shares as 6s 3d each. The Ch D upheld the assessments, rejecting the company's contention that the cost should be taken as 13s 4d each. The reference in *TCGA 1992, s 171(2)** to *TCGA 1992, s 122** applied to its disposal of its shares in the subsidiary, but not to the shares it acquired on the liquidation. *Innocent v Whaddon Estates Ltd Ch D 1981, 55 TC 476; [1982] STC 115.*

Jarmin v Rawlings 53.5

Retirement relief

A farmer owned 64 acres with a milking parlour and yard, and had a dairy herd of 34 animals. In October 1988 he sold the parlour and yard, and during the next three months he sold 14 of the animals. He transferred most of the remaining animals to a farm three miles away which belonged to his wife. He ceased dairy farming and used his land for rearing and finishing store cattle, although he retained and leased the milk quota, with a view to enhancing the value of the land on an eventual sale. The Revenue issued an assessment charging CGT on the sale of the parlour and yard. He appealed, claiming retirement relief. The Revenue rejected his claim on the grounds that he had only sold assets of his business, rather than a part of his business. The Commissioners allowed his appeal, holding that the dairy farming had been 'a separate and distinguishable part of the taxpayer's business', that he had sold a part of his business and that the sale qualified for retirement relief. The Ch D upheld the Commissioners' decision. Knox J held that the Commissioners were entitled to find that the dairy farming was a separate business from the rearing and finishing of store cattle, and that 'the sale by auction and completion of that sale of the milking parlour and yard, coupled with the cessation at completion of all milking operations for the taxpayer's benefit, amounted to a disposal by him of his dairy farming business'. *Jarmin v Rawlings, Ch D 1994, 67 TC 130; [1994] STC 1005.*

Johnson v Edwards 17.2

*Application of TCGA 1992, s 28(1)**

In a case where the facts were complex, the owner of certain shares agreed on 25 February 1965 to sell them. The date of completion was fixed as 31 January 1970, but in fact completion did not take place until 1971–72. The Revenue assessed the resulting gain in 1971–72 and the taxpayer appealed, contending that, by virtue of *TCGA 1992, s 28(1)**, the date of disposal was 25 February 1965. The Ch D dismissed his appeal, holding that the words 'where an asset is disposed of under a contract' in *TCGA 1992, s 28* apply to a disposal after 5 April 1971 under a contract entered into after that date, but not to a disposal after that date under a contract entered into before that date. *Johnson v Edwards Ch D 1981, 54 TC 488; [1981] STC 660.*

Jones v Wilcock 48.4

Loss on sale of property — whether TCGA, s 224(3) applicable

In 1988 an accountant and his wife purchased a house for more than £120,000. They subsequently incurred considerable expenditure on improvements, but, following a general fall in house prices, sold the house for £97,000 in 1993. The husband had other capital gains in the year of disposal, and claimed that the loss on the house should be set against such gains. The Revenue rejected the claim, on the basis that the house had been the couple's private residence, so that the effect of *TCGA 1992, s 16, s 223(1)* was that the loss was not allowable. The husband appealed, contending that the house had been purchased 'wholly or partly for the purpose of realising a gain', within *TCGA 1992, s 224(3)*, so that *TCGA 1992, s 223* did not apply. The Special Commissioner rejected this contention and dismissed the appeal. On the evidence, the couple's purpose in buying the house was to use it as their home. Their hope that they would be able to make a profit on its eventual sale 'was not a purpose within *TCGA 1992, s 224(3)*'. *Jones v Wilcock (Sp C 92), [1996] SSCD 389.*

Joseph Carter & Sons Ltd v Baird; Wear Ironmongers & Sons Ltd v Baird 55.1

Companies claiming rollover relief in respect of land purchased by associated company

Two associated companies (C and W) disposed of some land in Sunderland. Their controlling director purchased a farm in France, and transferred its ownership to a French company, the shares in which were owned by C and W. C and W claimed rollover relief. The Revenue rejected the claim on the grounds that neither the land in Sunderland, nor the farm in France, had been used for the purpose of the trades of C and W, and that the disposals and acquisition had not been by the same person, as required by *TCGA 1992, s 152**. The Commissioners dismissed the companies' appeals and the Ch D upheld their decision. *Joseph Carter & Sons Ltd v Baird; Wear Ironmongers & Sons Ltd v Baird Ch D 1998, [1999] STC 120.*

Kirby v Thorn EMI plc 6.1, 17.7

Whether consideration for a non-competition covenant a capital sum derived from an asset

A holding company (T) held the shares of M. In December 1977 an elaborate agreement between T, M and an American corporation (G) was completed, under which T procured the sale to G of three subsidiaries of M, engaged mainly in the repairing of electrical motors and generators, with the benefit of a covenant by T under which broadly it undertook that it and its subsidiaries would not engage in a competing business in the UK before 1983. The consideration was $1.73m of which $.575m (then equivalent to £315,934) was apportioned to the covenant. The CA accepted this contention, holding that the sum received in respect of the covenant gave rise to a chargeable gain (reversing the decisions of the Special Commissioners and the Ch D). The Revenue's contention that, by the covenant, T conferred rights on G, and the asset thus created had been disposed of by T to G, was rejected by the Commissioners, the Ch D and the CA. However, an alternative Revenue contention, not advanced in the Ch D, was that if a pre-existing asset was needed for the tax to apply to it, the goodwill of T was such an asset, of which it made a part disposal by the covenant, or from which it derived a capital sum. The CA accepted this contention, holding that the disputed amount was a capital sum derived from T's goodwill. Since the extent and valuation of this goodwill had not been canvassed before the Commissioners, Nicholls LJ considered that the case should be remitted to them, to reconsider the company's appeal in the light of his judgement. (Subsequently the Court agreed that there should be no such remitter and that both the Commissioners' determination and the judgement of the Ch D should be varied in specified terms set out in a schedule of 'terms of compromise'.) *Kirby v Thorn EMI plc CA 1987, 60 TC 519; [1987] STC 621; 1988 STI 90; [1988] 1 WLR 445; [1988] 2 All ER 947.*

Larner v Warrington 4.8

*Assets of negligible value — whether dissipated within TCGA 1992, s 24(1)**

The taxpayer made a substantial gain on the disposal of shares in M Ltd in 1973–74. Shortly after the disposal, he and his wife invested in two companies, the shares in which had become of negligible value by 5 April 1974. He was assessed on his 1973–74 gain in 1978 and appealed against the assessment, claiming relief under *TCGA 1992, s 24(2)** for 1973–74. The General Commissioners heard the appeal in July 1979 and allowed the taxpayer's claim in principle, adjourning the appeal for the value of the shares in M Ltd to be agreed. The appeal was restored for hearing in February 1984. In the interval *Williams v Bullivant* had been decided in the Ch D, and the Commissioners permitted the Revenue to raise the new argument that the notional loss provided for by *TCGA 1992, s 24(2)** took place not earlier than the making of the claim in 1978–79. The Commissioners accepted this, and determined the assessment accordingly. The taxpayer appealed to the Ch D, where he appeared in person and contended that the Commissioners should not have permitted their 1979 decision in his favour to be reopened. Further, since the shares in the companies in which he and his wife had invested had lost their value by April 1974, they had by then been dissipated within *TCGA 1992, s 24(1)**. Both contentions were rejected. There had been no final decision on any matter raised at the July 1979 hearing, as the value of the M Ltd shares was unsettled. The taxpayer had not been prejudiced, for if the final decision had been in his favour, the Revenue could, and no doubt would, have appealed to the Ch D. The relevant assets remained in existence, although they had become valueless, and loss in value as distinct from the loss, destruction, dissipation or extinction of an asset falls under *TCGA 1992, s 24(2)** and not under *TCGA 1992, s 24(1)**. *Larner v Warrington Ch D 1985, 58 TC 557; [1985] STC 442.*

Leedale v Lewis 43.20

Non-resident discretionary trust — whether beneficiaries have 'interests in the settled property'

Capital gains accrued to the non-resident trustees of a discretionary trust. The income was to be accumulated with power to the trustees at their discretion to apply it for the benefit of the settlor's grandchildren and their families. At the expiration of a defined perpetuity period, the trust fund vested equally per stirpes in the issue of the settlor but, in a letter of intent to the trustees, the settlor said they should regard the settlement as 'existing primarily for the grandchildren in equal shares'. At the relevant times there were five grandchildren, all minors and resident in the UK. The gains were apportioned equally to the five under *FA 1965, s 42(2)* and assessed on their fathers (as their guardians). The HL upheld the assessments. In the legislation 'interests in the settled property' has, in the context, a wide meaning and not a narrow technical meaning; accordingly discretionary beneficiaries have 'interests'. Apportionment on a just and reasonable basis is a question of fact and the apportionment here was approved. The question of whether the beneficiaries could recover the tax from the trustees was considered but not formally decided. The majority of the HL reserved decision on this point. Lord Scarman considered that recoupment was permissible, applying *In Re Latham, decd., [1961] 3 All ER 903*, an estate duty case. *Leedale v Lewis HL 1982, 56 TC 501; [1982] STC 835; [1982] 1 WLR 1319; [1982] 3 All ER 808.* (Note. The appeal taken to the HL related to three of the grandchildren. Other related appeals were not taken higher than the CA.)

Leisureking Ltd v Cushing 39.10

Loss relief for payment made under guarantee

In 1985 a company (L), and ten companies in the same group, entered into a composite joint and several guarantee with a bank whereby the liabilities to the bank of each of the companies were guaranteed by all the other ten companies as co-guarantors. In 1988 the bank sought repayment of liabilities incurred by two of the associated companies, which were no longer solvent. L made a payment of £2,115,000 to the bank, and did not seek to recover any contributions from its co-guarantors. L claimed relief for the payment under *TCGA 1992, s 253(4)**. The Revenue considered that the relief should be restricted to take account of the fact that the liability was shared between L and the other companies which had acted as guarantors. The Special Commissioner found on the evidence that only three of the co-guarantors remained solvent at the time when L had made the payment in question, and held that L was entitled to relief in respect of one-third of the payment. The Ch D dismissed L's appeal against this decision. The amount of the relief had to be restricted to take account of potential contributions from the co-guarantors. (Chadwick J also observed that the Commissioner had apparently been wrong to disregard any possibility of recovery from a liquidation of the eight co-guarantors which were no longer solvent, but declined to remit the matter to the Commissioner to reconsider this point, since the Revenue had not appealed against the decision.) *Leisureking Ltd v Cushing Ch D 1992, 65 TC 400; [1993] STC 46.*

Lewis v Rook 48.1

In 1968 a taxpayer purchased a large house, ten acres of land, and two cottages. In 1979 she sold one of the cottages, which was 190 yards from her house and had been occupied by a gardener. The Revenue issued an assessment on the gain and she appealed, contending that *TCGA 1992, s 222** applied. The Commissioners allowed her appeal but the CA reversed this decision and restored the assessment. Applying the non-tax cases of *Methuen Campbell v Walters [1979] 1 QB 525* and *Dyer v Dorset County Council [1989] QB 346*, the true test was whether the cottage was within the curtilage of, and appurtenant to, the main property, so as to be part of the entity which, together with the main property, constituted the dwelling-house occupied by the taxpayer as her main residence. This was not the case here, where the cottage was some way from the main building and separated by a large garden. *Lewis v Rook CA 1992, 64 TC 567, [1992] STC 171; [1992] 1 WLR 662.*

Lewis v Walters 36.14

Whether lease a wasting asset

On the death of their mother in 1982, a brother and sister inherited the freehold interest in a house. The house was subject to a lease, for a term of 99 years from 1904, in favour of their father. He died in 1985 and the brother and sister then acquired the lease as his executors. Neither of them lived in the house, and in 1987 they sold the freehold and leasehold interests to the same purchaser. The Revenue issued a CGT assessment in which the value of the house was apportioned between the leasehold and freehold interests. In the assessment the lease was treated as a wasting asset, so that its value at the date of acquisition was written down in accordance with *TCGA 1992, Sch 8**. The executors appealed, contending that, by virtue of *Leasehold Reform Act 1967*, the lease should not be treated as a wasting asset. Their appeal was dismissed by the General Commissioners and the Ch D. The lease as granted did not contain any express term providing for its extension beyond 2003. The rights conferred by the *Leasehold Reform Act* did not constitute a provision 'for the extension of the lease beyond a given date' within the meaning of *TCGA 1992, Sch 8 para 8(5)**. Furthermore, the executors' father had not given notice of any desire to extend the lease and the executors had no power to extend the lease either in their capacity as executors or as the heirs of his estate. Accordingly, the lease was a wasting asset and the assessment had been computed on the correct basis. *Lewis v Walters Ch D 1992, 64 TC 489; [1992] STC 97.*

Longson v Baker 48.1

Private residence exemption — area required for reasonable enjoyment

An individual (L) separated from his wife in 1990 and moved out of the matrimonial home, which was a farmhouse including stables and 7.56 hectares of land. In 1995 the couple divorced, and L disposed of his beneficial interest in the property to his former wife. The Revenue issued a CGT assessment on the basis that only 1.054 hectares qualified for private residence relief within *TCGA 1992, s 222(3)*. (It was accepted that L was entitled to relief by virtue of ESC D6, although he had not lived in the property since 1990.) L appealed against the assessment, contending that all 7.56 hectares had been 'required for the reasonable enjoyment of the dwelling-house'. The Special Commissioner rejected this contention and dismissed the appeal, holding that 'it cannot be correct that the dwelling-house ... *requires* an area of land amounting to more than 7.56 hectares in order to ensure its reasonable enjoyment as a residence, having regard to its size and character.' While it may have been 'desirable or convenient' for L to have such an area, it was not *required* for the reasonable enjoyment of the dwelling-house. *In Re Newhill Compulsory Purchase Order* applied; *Green v CIR* distinguished. *Longson v Baker (Sp C 238), [2000] SSCD 244.*

In re Lynall 40.3

Value of unquoted shares while public flotation under consideration

In an estate duty case the question at issue was the price which certain unquoted shares 'would fetch if sold in the open market at the time of the death of the deceased'. (*FA 1894, s 7(5)*. Compare *TCGA 1992, s 272(1)*.) At the time of the death, the directors were considering public flotation and favourable confidential reports had been made to them for that purpose by a firm of accountants and a firm of stockbrokers. The HL held, *inter alia*, that although no general rule could be laid down as to the information a hypothetical purchaser in an open market may be deemed to have, the board could not be deemed to disclose confidential information which, if published prematurely, might prejudice the company's interests, including reports on the possibility of a public issue. *In re Lynall HL 1971, 47 TC 375; [1972] AC 680; [1971] 3 All ER 904.*

(Note. See now *FA 1973, s 51*, re-enacted as *TCGA 1992, s 273*, as to disposals after 5 July 1973. The substantive decision here is therefore now of limited application, but the judgements include a useful review of estate duty cases dealing with the valuation of unquoted shares. See also *Battle v CIR* and *CIR v Crossman*, and the 1995 cases of *Caton's Administrators v Couch* and *Clark (Clark's Executor) v CIR*.)

Lyon v Pettigrew 17.2

Consideration for disposal paid in instalments

In 1979–80 a taxi-cab proprietor contracted to sell some of his cabs together with their licences. Under the contract for each, the purchase price was £6,000, payable in instalments of £40 over 150 weeks. The contract provided that the licence would not be transferred until 'payment of all monies hereunder'. The Revenue issued an assessment on the basis that the cabs had been disposed of in 1979–80. The proprietor appealed, contending that the sales had been conditional within *TCGA 1992, s 28(2)**, so that the disposal had not taken place until the date on which the final instalment was paid. The Commissioners allowed his appeal but the Ch D reversed their decision and restored the assessment. By virtue of the *Town Police Clauses Act 1847*, it was not possible to sever the licences from the taxicabs. The contracts as a whole were not conditional, and the full amount of the consideration was chargeable in 1979–80. *Eastham v Leigh London & Provincial Properties Ltd* applied. *Lyon v Pettigrew, Ch D 1985, 58 TC 452; [1985] STC 369.*

McGregor v Adcock 53.5

Sale of part of land by farmer

A taxpayer, aged 70, had farmed 35 acres for over 10 years. He sold some 5 acres for which outline planning permission had been obtained. He was assessed on the large resulting gain and claimed retirement relief. The Ch D, reversing the decision of the Commissioners, held that no relief was due. The only reasonable conclusion on the facts was that there had been a sale of an asset of the business and not of part of the business. *McGregor v Adcock Ch D 1977, 51 TC 692; [1977] STC 206; [1977] 1 WLR 864; [1977] 3 All ER 65.*

MacPherson v Hall 59.7

Identification of shares disposed of

The rules for the identification of securities, etc. disposed of, introduced by *FA 1982, ss 88, 89*, are similar to those which had been in force for Sch D, Case VII (abolished from 6 April 1971). In a Case VII appeal, the taxpayer sold 6,000 shares of a company on the London Stock Exchange on 14 September 1964, the delivery date being 14 October. He had bought 6,000 shares of the same company some months previously and he also bought 6,000 on 11 September, the delivery date for which was 22 September. The Ch D held that under the legislation in force (the wording of *TCGA 1992, s 108(4)(b)* is identical) the shares disposed of should be identified with those acquired on 11 September, resulting in a loss of £20. (It was unsuccessfully contended for the taxpayer that the provision applied only to shares acquired on or after the date of disposal and that the shares sold should have been matched with those first purchased, producing a loss of £3,702.) *MacPherson v Hall Ch D 1972, 48 TC 210.*

Magnavox Electronics Co Ltd (in liquidation) v Hall 3.1

Anti-avoidance

In September 1978 a company (M) exchanged contracts for the sale of a factory to another company (J) for £1,400,000. Completion was arranged for February 1979, but for financial reasons J was unable to complete the purchase, and forfeited its deposit. Meanwhile, M had gone into voluntary liquidation in December 1978. The liquidator did not rescind the contract of sale, but arranged for M to acquire an 'off-the-shelf' company (S), to which it assigned its beneficial interest under the contract on 6 July 1979. Three days later certain variations in the contract were agreed, including a reduction of the purchase price to £1,150,000 and a new completion date of 9 October 1979. On the same day S exchanged contracts with a fourth company (B) for the sale of the factory on terms practically identical with those in the original contract as varied. B duly completed. The Revenue issued an assessment on the basis that the disposal had taken place after M had gone into liquidation. M appealed, contending that the disposal had taken place in September 1978 (so that trading losses of that accounting period could be set against the gain). The Special Commissioners dismissed M's appeal, and the Ch D and CA upheld their decision. The disposal to B was not under the 1978 contract, but under a new contract made in July 1979. Furthermore, the interposition of S was part of an artificial avoidance scheme which could be disregarded, applying *Furniss v Dawson. Magnavox Electronics Co Ltd (in liquidation) v Hall, CA 1986, 59 TC 610; [1986] STC 561.*

Makins v Elson 48.1

Whether caravan a dwelling-house

A taxpayer purchased land on which to build a house on which construction had commenced. Meanwhile, he lived with his family in a wheeled caravan jacked up and resting on bricks on the land, with water, electricity and telephone installed. Before completing the house, he sold the site, with the caravan, and was assessed on the resultant gain. The Ch D held that the caravan was a dwelling-house for the relevant period and that the gain was within the private residence exemption. *Makins v Elson Ch D 1976, 51 TC 437; [1977] STC 46; [1977] 1 WLR 221; [1977] 1 All ER 572.*

Mannion v Johnston 53.5

Retirement relief

A taxpayer who farmed 78 acres sold 17 of them in April 1984 and a further 18 acres in December 1984. He was assessed and claimed retirement relief, contending that the sales were a disposal of part of his business. The Ch D, reversing the Commissioners' decision, held that no relief was due, applying *McGregor v Adcock*. Each of the two dispositions had to be considered separately and the changes caused by each one were merely limited changes of scale. *Mannion v Johnston Ch D 1988, 61 TC 598; [1988] STC 758.*

(Note. The case was heard in the Ch D with *Atkinson v Dancer.*)

Markey v Sanders 48.1

Private residence exemption

In 1951, the taxpayer's mother purchased a small country estate of 4 acres with a main house and outbuildings reached by a 130 metre drive from the main entrance gates. In 1963, this was sold to the taxpayer, who had earlier (in 1956) acquired adjoining land of nearly 9 acres. In 1965, the taxpayer built a three-bedroom bungalow by the entrance gates, with a quarter-acre garden, which was occupied rent-free by a gardener and housekeeper. The bungalow was not separately rated. In September 1980, the whole estate, including the bungalow, was sold to a single purchaser. The issue in the appeal was whether the gain on the sale of the bungalow was within the private residence exemption. Walton J, reversing the Commissioners' decision and applying *Batey v Wakefield* held that it was not. Batey decided that 'residence' need not mean a single building, and a relevant fact there was that the bungalow was 'very closely adjacent' to the main residence. 'Very closely adjacent' is an imprecise test; he preferred to ask whether the relevant group of buildings, looked on as a whole, could be fairly regarded as a single dwelling-house used as the taxpayer's main residence. Here the only reasonable conclusion from the facts was that the bungalow was not part of the taxpayer's residence. *Markey v Sanders Ch D 1987, 60 TC 245; [1987] STC 256; [1987] 1 WLR 864.*

Marren v Ingles 6.1, 17.7, 21.5, 58.9

*Deferred sale consideration — application of TCGA 1992, s 22(1)**

Under an agreement of 15 September 1970, shares in a private company were sold for an immediate payment of £750 per share plus a further amount to be calculated by reference to the quoted price of shares representing them on the first dealing day following a proposed flotation of the company. In the event, the relevant dealing day was 5 December 1972 and the further consideration was agreed at £2,825 per share. It was common ground that, in arriving at the gain on the disposal of the shares, the £750 and the value at 15 September 1970 of the contingent right to further consideration were to be taken into account. A 1972–73 assessment was issued on the basis that the right to receive the further consideration, being a chose in action, was an asset from which a capital sum was derived on 5 December 1972; that there was a deemed disposal under *TCGA 1992, s 22(1)**; and that this right was not a debt within *TCGA 1992, s 251(1)**. The HL upheld the assessment. *Dicta* of Walton J in *CIR v Montgomery* on which the taxpayer relied, were disapproved. *Marren v Ingles HL 1980, 54 TC 76; [1980] STC 500; [1980] 1 WLR 983; [1980] 3 All ER 95.* See now *TCGA 1992, s 138A* at 58.9 SHARES AND SECURITIES.

Marriott v Lane 53.5

Retirement relief

TCGA, s 163(4)(c) — date of cessation of business*

A taxpayer (M) owned land and buildings which were used as an aircraft museum by a company of which he was the controlling director. The museum was closed to the public in October 1988, and in September 1989 the premises were sold to a subsidiary company which had been incorporated to undertake the residential development of the site. The Revenue issued an assessment charging CGT on the disposal, and M appealed, claiming retirement relief. The General Commissioners dismissed the appeal, finding that at the time of the sale, the company had hoped to reopen the museum at different premises, so that the trade had not then ceased and that retirement relief was not therefore due. The Ch D allowed M's appeal, holding that since the museum had never in fact reopened, the fact that the company had originally hoped to reopen it was not conclusive. Accordingly, the business should be treated as having ceased in October 1988, and M qualified for retirement relief under *TCGA 1992, s 163**. *Marriott v Lane Ch D 1996, 69 TC 157; [1996] STC 704; [1996] 1 WLR 111.*

Marshall v Kerr 16.6, 43.13

Whether TCGA 1992, s 62(6) applicable to non-resident settlement established by a UK-resident beneficiary of a non-resident testator*

K's father-in-law (B) died in 1977, resident and ordinarily resident in Jersey. Half of B's personal estate was bequeathed to K's wife, who was a UK resident. By a deed of family arrangement in 1978 she settled her share of the estate on Jersey trustees, to be held on discretionary trusts for herself and her family. The administration of the estate was not completed until 1979 and the assets were at no time vested in K's wife. Between 1981 and 1985 the settlement trustees made capital payments to K's wife. The Revenue issued assessments under *TCGA 1992, ss 87–98**. K appealed, contending that, by virtue of *TCGA 1992, s 62(6)**, B should be deemed to be the settlor of the trusts, so that, since he had been neither resident or ordinarily resident in the UK, there was no CGT liability. The HL upheld the assessments (restoring the decision of the Ch D which had reversed that of the Special Commissioner). The arrangement did not settle any specific assets comprised in the estate, but settled the legatee's half-share in the residuary estate, which had not by then been constituted. The property settled by the legatee constituted a separate chose in action. Where a legatee varied her entitlement under a will by means of a family arrangement, the making of the variation was deemed not to be a disposal in itself. However, *TCGA 1992, s 62(6)** did not have the further effect of treating the assets vested in the legatee as acquired from the deceased at the date of death. Accordingly, the legatee was the settlor of the arrangement for the purposes of *TCGA 1992, s 87**. *Marshall v Kerr HL 1994, 67 TC 56; [1994] STC 638; [1994] 3 WLR 299; [1994] 2 All ER 106.*

Marson v Marriage 17.5, 17.7, 21.5

Deferred sale consideration — whether TCGA 1992, s 48 applicable*

A taxpayer agreed on 31 March 1965 to sell to a development company 47 acres of land with development possibilities. The consideration was £47,040 payable immediately with future payments of £7,500 for each acre developed and provision for compensation to the taxpayer should the land be compulsorily purchased from the company. In the event, the company developed the land in 1975 and paid £348,250 to the taxpayer in settlement of the agreement. He was assessed to CGT for 1975–76 on the basis that the £348,250 was a taxable receipt. The Ch D upheld the assessment, following *Marren v Ingles* and holding that the provision for compensation should the land be compulsorily purchased meant that the future consideration was not ascertainable at 31 March 1965. (The taxpayer had contended that, by virtue of *TCGA 1992, s 48**, the consideration could have been brought into account at that date.) *Marson v Marriage Ch D 1979, 54 TC 59; [1980] STC 177.*

Mashiter v Pearmain 7.8

Land value

A taxpayer sold land in 1976 for consideration exceeding its current use value. The land had been acquired by gift in 1960, and the Revenue issued an assessment computed on the basis that the land should be treated as having been sold on 6 April 1965 and re-acquired at its market value on that date. The taxpayer appealed, contending that the gain should be time-apportioned over the whole period from 1960 to 1976. The CA rejected this contention and upheld the assessment. *Mashiter v Pearmain, CA 1984, 58 TC 334; [1985] STC 165.*

Mayes v Woods 53.4

TCGA, s 163(1)(b) — whether claimant had 'retired on ill-health grounds'.

A greengrocer (M) sold his business and claimed retirement relief on the basis that he had retired on ill-health grounds after suffering chest pains. The Revenue rejected the claim, since a medical report had suggested that the pains were attributable to anxiety or hypertension, rather than to any heart condition. The Special Commissioner reviewed the medical evidence and dismissed M's appeal, finding that M did not satisfy the conditions of *TCGA 1992, s 163(1)(b)** and *Sch 6 para 3(1)**. *Mayes v Woods (Sp C 126), [1997] SSCD 206.*

Moore v Thompson 48.1

Whether a caravan a dwelling house

Makins v Elson was distinguished in a subsequent case where the General Commissioners held that a caravan installed in a small farm while the farmhouse was being renovated was not within the exemption of *TCGA 1992, s 222**, and the Ch D upheld their decision. The caravan was disposed of when the farmhouse was sold. The farmhouse was never occupied by the taxpayer, and the evidence was that she had never used the caravan as a permanent residence. *Moore v Thompson Ch D 1986, 61 TC 15; [1986] STC 170.*

Morgan v Gibson 7.8

Land reflecting development value

In 1948 a taxpayer acquired an interest in land which had an agreed value of £15,545. In 1984 the land was sold to the British Airports Authority for £160,000, with the condition that, should the Authority obtain planning permission within 30 years, a further sum of up to £350,000 would be payable. The Revenue issued an assessment on the basis that the consideration received on disposal included development value and that therefore *TCGA 1992, Sch 2 para 9** applied. The taxpayer appealed, contending that the conditions of *TCGA 1992, Sch 2 para 9(1)(b)** were not satisfied, and that the assessment should be computed on a straight-line apportionment basis. The Ch D rejected this contention and upheld the assessment (reversing the General Commissioners' decision). There was a clear finding of fact that the sale price included an element of 'hope value', which was equivalent to anticipated development value. That being so, the provisions of *TCGA 1992, Sch 2 para 9** had to be applied. *Morgan v Gibson Ch D 1989, 61 TC 654; [1989] STC 568.*

O'Brien v Benson's Hosiery (Holdings) Ltd 6.1

Payment from employee for release from service agreement

A company, on acquiring the shares of another, entered into a seven-year service agreement with B, the sales director of the other company. After two years in which B carried out his duties with conspicuous success, he was released from the agreement on paying £50,000 to the first company, which was assessed on the £50,000 as a chargeable gain. The HL upheld the assessment (reversing the CA decision). The rights, although not assignable, could be turned to account in the hands of the employer and were an asset within the general scheme of the legislation. The concept of market value is introduced for certain purposes; it cannot be deduced from this that all assets within CGT must have a market value. *O'Brien v Benson's Hosiery (Holdings) Ltd HL 1979, 53 TC 241; [1979] STC 735; [1979] 3 WLR 572; [1979] 3 All ER 652.*

O'Rourke v Binks 58.11, 58.14

*Capital distribution — TCGA 1992, s 122**

The taxpayer held a large number of shares in a company (C). The total allowable expenditure on any disposal of those shares was £214,000. Under a merger agreement between C and a public company, he exchanged his shares for 840,000 shares in the public company and 75,000 shares in a subsidiary company (the market value of these being £246,000). The transfer to the taxpayer of the shares in the subsidiary company was treated as a capital distribution and thus as a partial disposal of his shares in C. The Revenue issued a CGT assessment in which the total allowable expenditure was apportioned in accordance with *TCGA 1992, s 42**. The taxpayer appealed, contending that, since the total allowable expenditure was less than the value of the shares in the subsidiary, he was entitled to elect that the amount of the distribution should be reduced by the total allowable expenditure, in accordance with *TCGA 1992, s 122(4)**. The Special Commissioner allowed the appeal but the CA reversed this decision and restored the assessment. The words of *TCGA 1992, s 122(4)** were ambiguous, and in the circumstances the court should give effect to the presumed intention of the legislature by inserting words into the subsection. The taxpayer could not make an election under *TCGA 1992, s 122(4)** unless the distribution was 'small', within *TCGA 1992, s 122(2)**. The capital distribution here (which amounted to

15.58% of the total expenditure) was not small for the purposes of *TCGA 1992, s 122(2)**. *O'Rourke v Binks CA 1992, 65 TC 165; [1992] STC 703.*

Owen v Elliott 48.8

*Private residence partly used as guest house — relief under TCGA 1992, s 223(4)**

A taxpayer and his wife had carried on a private guest house business from premises they owned and lived in. They had occupied different parts of the premises at different times of the year in such a way that every part of the premises had, at some time during their period of ownership, constituted their main residence. When the property was sold it was agreed that one-third of the gain was exempt under *TCGA 1992, s 222** and *s 223(2)**. The taxpayer appealed against an assessment on the gain, contending that further relief was due under *TCGA 1992, s 223(4)**. The CA allowed his appeal (reversing the decision of the Ch D). The phrase 'let by him as residential accommodation' in *TCGA 1992, s 223(4)** did not, directly or by association, mean premises let which were likely to be occupied as a home. It referred to living accommodation as distinct, for example, from office accommodation. The lettings undertaken by the taxpayer were within the words 'residential accommodation'. *Owen v Elliott CA 1990, 63 TC 319; [1990] STC 469; [1990] 3 WLR 133.*

Palmer v Moloney and Shipleys 53.4

Retirement relief — meaning of 'full-time working officer or employee'

A trader (P) was also the majority shareholder in a company, to which he devoted most of his working time. He wished to retire and, on the advice of his accountants, he caused the company to realise the value of his shares by paying an interim dividend. Subsequently he took legal action against the accountants, contending that they had been negligent in that they should have advised him to realise the value of his shares by a capital distribution, so that he could have claimed retirement relief. The CA accepted this contention (by a 2-1 majority, Nourse LJ dissenting) and ordered the accountants to pay P damages. Aldous LJ held that, since P worked for the company for 42>½< hours each week, he qualified as a 'full-time working officer or employee' of the company, within *TCGA 1992, s 163(5)*. The fact that he also worked for a separate business for 7>½< hours each week was not material. *Palmer v Moloney and Shipleys CA, [1999] STC 890.* (NB: For the Revenue's interpretation of the phrase 'full-time working officer or employee', see Revenue Capital Gains Manual CG 63621. For the Revenue's practice following the earlier Ch D decision in favour of the defendants and pending a final outcome to the case, see Revenue Tax Bulletin April 1999 p 653.)

Pepper v Daffurn 53.5

Retirement relief

A farmer had owned 113 acres of land, on which he had reared and grazed cattle, for several years. He gradually ceased to rear cattle, and sold 83 acres in 1986. In 1987 he obtained planning permission in respect of a covered cattle yard comprising 0.6 acres, which he sold in 1988. Thereafter his only activity was cattle grazing. The Revenue issued a CGT assessment on the sale of the cattle yard, and the farmer appealed, contending that he was entitled to retirement relief. The Ch D upheld the assessment (reversing the decision of the General Commissioners). On the evidence, the farmer had changed the nature of his activities from rearing cattle to grazing them in preparation for the sale of the yard. Following this change, the yard was no longer necessary to the farmer's business, so that its sale did not constitute a disposal of a part of that business. *Pepper v Daffurn Ch D 1993, 66 TC 68; [1993] STC 466.*

Plumbly & Others (Harbour's Personal Representatives) v Spencer 53.5

Sale of land leased to family company — whether vendor entitled to retirement relief

In 1988 an individual (H), who was 60 years of age, disposed of 163 acres of land which had been used by a trading company, of which he was a director and shareholder, for the purposes of its business (which was discontinued at the time of the sale). The company, which had paid rent to H for the use of the land, qualified as H's 'family company' under *TCGA 1992, s 163** as then in force. The Revenue issued a CGT assessment, and H's personal representatives appealed, contending that the sale of the land qualified for retirement relief under *TCGA 1992, s 163**. The CA accepted this contention and allowed the appeal, holding that where there was a disposal of assets in a discontinued business, it was not essential that the business must have been the business of the individual making the disposal, and relief could still be claimed where the conditions of *s 163(3)** were satisfied. The CA observed that it would be 'anomalous if (H) had been denied any business relief, after the company had been farming for 40 years, because of his (or his advisers') omission to take one or other of two otherwise fairly pointless steps (that is the transfer of the farming business to (H) personally just before its cessation, or the disposal of his shares in the dormant company)'. *Plumbly & Others (Harbour's Personal Representatives) v Spencer CA 1999, 71 TC 399; [1999] STC 677.* (NB: the references in TCGA 1992, s 163 to a 'family company' have since been replaced by references to a 'personal company'.)

Powlson v Welbeck Securities Ltd 17.2, 17.10

Surrender of an option

In 1961 a company acquired an option to participate in a property development. In 1971 it began proceedings to enforce its option, but these were settled by consent in 1974, the company receiving £2,000,000 in return for agreeing to 'release and abandon' the option. The Revenue assessed the amount as a chargeable gain and the company appealed, contending that, by virtue of *TCGA 1992, s 144(4)**, the surrender of the option did not constitute the disposal of an asset. The CA dismissed the company's appeal, holding that *TCGA 1992, s 144(3)** constituted an exception to the operation of *TCGA 1992, s 24(1)** but did not confer any exemption from the chargeable disposal which arose under *TCGA 1992, s 22(1)** when the company received a capital sum for the surrender of the option. *Powlson v Welbeck Securities Ltd CA 1987, 60 TC 269; [1987] STC 468.*

Prest v Bettinson 10.6

Residuary legatees of estate subject to annuities include charities — whether charitable exemption applies

Under a will the residuary estate was held on the usual trusts for sale and conversion for the benefit of five institutions, equally and absolutely, subject to certain annuities. The income was more than sufficient to cover the annuities and no annuity fund was set up. Assets of the estate were sold, so permitting capital distributions to the residuary legatees, and the gains were assessed on the trustee. Four of the residuary legatees were charities, and the trustee contended that four-fifths of the gains accrued to charities and were exempted by *TCGA 1992, s 256(1)**. The Ch D rejected this contention and upheld the assessment. *Prest v Bettinson Ch D 1980, 53 TC 437; [1980] STC 607.*

Quinn v Cooper 20.17

Indexation allowance — Business Expansion Scheme — TCGA 1992, s 150

An individual (C) had purchased a number of shares which entitled him to relief under the Business Expansion Scheme. He subsequently sold the shares at a loss. The Revenue issued CGT assessments on the basis that the effect of *TCGA 1992, s 150(3)** was that indexation allowance only applied to the sale proceeds of the shares. C appealed, contending that the effect of *TCGA 1992, s 53* and *s 150* was that indexation allowance should be applied to the original purchase price of the shares. The Ch D rejected this contention and upheld the assessments (reversing the decision of the Special Commissioner). Lightman J held that, having regard to the interrelationship of the relevant statutory provisions, indexation should only be applied to the cost as reduced by *section 150(3)*. *Quinn v Cooper Ch D 1998, 71 TC 44; [1998] STC 772.*

W T Ramsay Ltd v CIR 3.1, 21.5

Artificial avoidance scheme — whether a nullity for tax purposes

A company, having made a substantial gain on the sale of a farm, carried out a number of share and loan transactions with the object of creating a large allowable loss at little cost to itself. The loss emerged as one of about £175,000 on shares it subscribed for in a company formed for the scheme, the success of which depended on its establishing that a loan to the same company, sold at a profit of about £173,000, was not a debt on a security within *TCGA 1992, s 251(1)**. The acceptance of the offer of the loan was given orally, but evidenced by a statutory declaration (vide *Statutory Declarations Act 1835*) by a director of the borrowing company. The CA held that the loan, being evidenced by the statutory declaration, which represented a marketable security, was a debt on a security. The scheme therefore failed. The company appealed to the HL, where the appeal was considered with that in *Eilbeck v Rawling* and in both cases the Revenue advanced the new argument that the scheme should be treated as a fiscal nullity producing neither loss nor gain (other than a loss of £370 in *Eilbeck v Rawling*). The HL accepted this approach. Lord Wilberforce held that although the Duke of Westminster principle prevented a court from looking behind a genuine document or transaction to some supposed underlying substance, it did not compel the court to view a document or transaction in blinkers, isolated from its context. A finding that a document or transaction is genuine does not preclude the Commissioners from considering whether, on the facts, what is in issue is a composite transaction or a number of independent transactions. The Commissioners are not 'bound to consider individually each separate step in a composite transaction intended to be carried through as a whole'. The question of whether what is in issue is a composite transaction or a number of independent transactions is a matter of law, reviewable by the courts. Such an approach does not introduce a new principle when dealing with legal avoidance, but applies existing legislation to new and sophisticated legal devices; 'while the techniques of tax avoidance progress, the courts are not obliged to stand still'. Turning to the facts here, it was clear that the scheme was for tax avoidance with no commercial justification, and that it was the intention to proceed through all its stages to completion once set in motion. It would therefore be wrong to consider one step in isolation. The true view was that, regarding the scheme as a whole, there was neither gain nor loss. The company's appeal was dismissed. Furthermore, although this ended the appeal, the CA had been correct in holding that the relevant debt was a 'debt on a security'. *W T Ramsay Ltd v CIR HL 1981, 54 TC 101; [1981] STC 174; [1981] 2 WLR 449; [1981] 1 All ER 865.*

Randall v Plumb 17.10, 36.23

Option payment contingently repayable

The owner of some land granted a gravel company an option to purchase the land for £100,000. He received £25,000 for the option. The agreement included a proviso that he would repay the £25,000 to the company if, after ten years, the company had not obtained planning permission to extract sand and gravel from the land. The Revenue assessed the £25,000 to CGT for the year in which the option was granted. The Ch D allowed his appeal against the assessment, holding that the consideration should not be the full amount of the £25,000, but that the £25,000 should be brought in at a valuation taking the contingency into account. *Randall v Plumb Ch D 1974, 50 TC 392; [1975] STC 191; [1975] 1 All ER 734.*

Rank Xerox Ltd v Lane 4.9, 21.3

*Annual payments under covenant — TCGA 1992, s 237(c)**

R surrendered to X its licence from X to make use of the 'xerographic' process in certain areas in return for a 'royalty' of 5% of certain sales by X in those areas. The relevant agreements to pay the 'royalties' were made under seal. Subsequently, R distributed the 'royalty' rights in specie to its shareholders, who in turn surrendered them to X for a consideration. R was assessed to corporation tax on its gain from the disposal and appealed, contending that the 'royalties' were annual payments due under a covenant within *TCGA 1992, s 237(c)**. The HL rejected this contention and upheld the assessment. 'Covenant' here must be construed in its context and annual payments under a covenant are payments made gratuitously, the promise to pay them being enforceable only because of the form in which it was given, i.e. (in England) given under seal. Here the payments were for consideration and the presence of a seal on the relevant agreement added nothing to the obligation to pay them. *Rank Xerox Ltd v Lane HL 1979, 53 TC 185; [1979] STC 740; [1979] 3 WLR 594; [1979] 3 All ER 657.*

Reed v Nova Securities Ltd 3.1, 13.14

Acquisition 'as trading stock' commercial justification

The taxpayer company (N) had traded in shares and securities since 1955. In March 1973 it was acquired by the well-known Littlewoods group. On 17 August 1973 Littlewoods sold to it shares owned by Littlewoods in, and debts owing to Littlewoods by, certain foreign companies. The sale price for the assets was £30,000, their market value, but their capital gains cost to Littlewoods was nearly £4m. When offering the assets to N, Littlewoods' Board said that about £55,000 would be received in part repayment of the debts and N had received a payment of £35,447 in 1979. They were not part of Littlewoods' trading stock. N purported to make an election under *TCGA 1992, s 161(3)** in respect of the assets acquired, and the issue in the appeal was whether they were trading stock, as defined in *ICTA 1988, s 100(2)** (see *TCGA 1992, s 288**). The General Commissioners found that they were and their decision was upheld by the Ch D and the CA. The HL unanimously upheld the decision as regards the debts but reversed it as regards the shares. The Commissioners had determined the appeal on the basis of an agreed statement of facts, without recourse to oral evidence, and no reasonable body of Commissioners could have concluded that the company had acquired the shares as trading stock; its acquisition of shares that had no value was without commercial justification. *Reed v Nova Securities Ltd HL 1985, 59 TC 516; [1985] STC 124; [1985] 1 WLR 193; [1985] 1 All ER 686.*

Richart v J Lyons & Co Ltd 55.6

Quantum of relief where old asset not always used for business purposes

A company had owned some properties since before 1965, but had ceased to use them for business purposes qualifying for roll over relief before their disposal in 1979 and 1980. The Revenue granted relief under *TCGA 1992, s 152(7)** proportionately restricted on the basis of business and non-business use in the period from the introduction of capital gains tax in 1965 to disposal. The company contended that the whole of its period of ownership should be taken into account in computing the extent to which the properties should be deemed to have been used for business purposes. Its appeal was allowed by the Special Commissioners, whose decision was reversed by the Ch D but restored by the CA. There was no provision in *TCGA 1992, s 152(7)** similar to the provision in *TCGA 1992, s 223(7)**, to provide that the period of ownership for the purposes of the relief should not include any period before 6 April 1965. The company's interpretation was clearly in accordance with the wording of the statute. A second contention by the Revenue, that as two of the properties were to be treated under *TCGA 1992, Sch 2 paras 9, 17** as having been acquired by the taxpayer on 6 April 1965, the period of ownership should run only from that date, was also rejected. *Richart v J Lyons & Co Ltd CA 1989, 62 TC 261; [1989] STC 665.*

Ritchie v McKay 43.20

Treatment of previous losses of trustees

Gains of £3,405 accrued to the trustees of a non-resident settlement in 1975–76, and it was not disputed that these fell to be attributed to the taxpayer's wife by virtue of *CGTA 1979, s 17**. In 1974–75 losses of £41,536 accrued to the trustees, and the taxpayer successfully appealed against the assessment of the £3,405, on the ground that the 1974–75 losses should be set off against the gains. *TCGA 1992, s 2(2)** provides for a deduction of any losses accruing to the trustees in any year of assessment, so far as not already allowed as a deduction. The loss of £41,536 that accrued to the trustees in 1974–75 was not to be deprived in the following year of the status that it enjoyed in 1974–75. *Ritchie v McKay Ch D 1984, 57 TC 719; [1984] STC 422.*

Roome v Edwards 57.6

Exercise of power of appointment or advancement

Under a 1944 marriage settlement (as varied), the trust fund, worth some £912,000, was held on trust for the wife for life with remainder to the husband for life with remainder to two daughters (born in 1948 and 1951) absolutely in equal shares. In March 1972 the beneficiaries assigned their respective interests to two Cayman Islands companies for sums totalling £868,000. The trustees were replaced by Cayman Islands trustees and in 1972–73 one of the companies assigned its interests to the other which, as a consequence, became absolutely entitled to the trust fund as against the trustees. In 1955, pursuant to powers in the 1944 settlement, investments in the fund worth some £13,000 had been appointed in trust for the elder daughter absolutely on attaining 25. There had been no relevant transaction regarding the 1955 fund, which had been administered separately from the 1944 fund and the trustees of which were UK residents. The substantial gain which arose under *TCGA 1992, s 71(1)** as a result of the transactions relating to the 1944 fund was assessed on the trustees of the 1955 fund on the footing that under *TCGA 1992, s 69(3)** the two sets of trustees fell to be treated as a single body of which the UK members could be assessed under *TCGA 1992, s 65(1)**. The HL upheld the assessment, reversing the decisions of the Ch D and CA. Whether a particular set of facts amounts to a settlement should be approached by asking what a person, with knowledge of the legal context of the word under established doctrine and applying this knowledge in a practical and commonsense manner to the facts under examination, would conclude. Here the intention throughout was to treat the 1955 fund as being held on the trusts of the 1944 settlement as added to and varied by the 1955 appointment. Further, the words 'accruing to the trustees of a settlement' in *TCGA 1992, s 65(1)** are to be read in the light of the situation created by *TCGA 1992, s 69(1)(3)**. *TCGA 1992, s 69(3)** is not restricted to cases where property vested in two sets of trustees is held on identical trusts. *Roome and Another v Edwards HL 1981, 54 TC 359; [1981] STC 96; [1981] 2 WLR 268; [1981] 1 All ER 736.* (For the Revenue practice following this decision, see Revenue Pamphlet IR 131, SP 7/84.)

Sansom v Peay 48.6

Occupation of residence under discretionary trust

The trustees of a discretionary trust permitted certain beneficiaries (as they were enabled to do under the trust) to occupy as their residence a house subject to the trust. The house was exchanged and it was held that the resultant gain was exempt under *TCGA 1992, s 225**. The Ch D rejected the Revenue's contention that the beneficiaries were not 'entitled' to occupy the house, because they had no absolute right under the trust. While the beneficiaries were in occupation with the trustees' permission they were entitled to occupy it. *Sansom & Another v Peay Ch D 1976, 52 TC 1; [1976] STC 494; [1976] 1 WLR 1073; [1976] 3 All ER 375.*

Shepherd v Lyntress 3.1

Applicability of Ramsay principle where subsidiary company acquired with accumulated tax losses

A major public company (N) had acquired shares in companies that had appreciated in value. It decided to acquire companies which had accumulated tax losses so that the gains on the holdings could be realised and the accrued losses could be set off against them. Accordingly, in 1979 N acquired the issued share capital of L, a company claiming to have £4m of accumulated tax losses available for set-off. In 1980 N sold part of its holding of appreciated assets to L, and a few days later L realised the gains by disposing of the assets on the Stock Exchange. The Revenue raised assessments on N on the basis that the Ramsay principle applied, and that the sale of the assets by N to L was to be ignored for fiscal purposes, so that the transactions would fall to be treated as disposals on the Stock Exchange by N, and on L on the basis that, again applying the *Ramsay* principle, the losses incurred within the company's former group were not available against gains accruing to a company outside that group. The Special Commissioners reduced the assessment on L, rejecting the Revenue's contention that the accumulated losses were not available for set-off. However, they upheld the assessment on N. Both sides appealed to the Ch D. Vinelott J allowed N's appeal and upheld the Commissioners' decision with regard to the assessment on L. On the facts, the Commissioners were clearly correct in rejecting the Revenue's contention that L's losses were not available for set-off. The real question in the case was whether the Commissioners were justified in concluding that the transfer and sale of the assets were part of a single composite transaction. Following *Craven v White*, this could not be held to be the case here, because no arrangements to sell the shares on the Stock Exchange had been made at the time when they were transferred from N to L. It was therefore impossible to conclude that the transfer of the shares to L, and their subsequent sale by L, was a single composite transaction within the *Ramsay* principle. L had an allowable loss at the time when its share capital was acquired by N. That loss remained an allowable loss after N had acquired L's share capital, and the gains which were realised when the transferred assets were sold on the Stock Exchange were gains realised by L at a time when it was a member of the same group of companies as N. *Shepherd v Lyntress Ltd; News International plc v Shepherd Ch D 1989, 62 TC 495; [1989] STC 617.* (Note. See now *TCGA 1992, Sch 7A*, introduced by *FA 1993, s 88*.)

Smith v Schofield 7.9

Indexation allowance — interaction with time-apportionment

A taxpayer had acquired two chattels in 1952. She sold them in 1987. Her chargeable gain fell to be time-apportioned in accordance with *TCGA 1992, Sch 2 para 16(2)**. The Revenue deducted the indexation allowance from the unindexed gain before time-apportionment. She appealed, contending that the indexation allowance should be deducted only from the amount of the post-1965 gain. The HL rejected this contention and upheld the assessment (reversing the decision of the CA and restoring that of the Ch D). The issue had to be determined by construing the relevant statutory provisions against the underlying philosophy of the legislation, rather than by detailed consideration of hypothetical examples producing apparently anomalous results. The effect of the legislation was that the indexation allowance had to be applied to the gross gain before time-apportionment, and could not be set only against that part of the gain apportioned to the period after 6 April 1965. *Smith v Schofield HL 1993, 65 TC 669; [1993] STC 268; [1993] 1 WLR 398.*

Spectros International plc v Madden 17.1

Consideration for sale of company with substantial debt to bank

A company (S) owned a number of subsidiary companies, one of which operated a liquid chromatography business. Another company (B) wished to purchase this business. S wished to structure the sale in such a way as to minimise its tax liability. In July 1986 one of S's wholly-owned subsidiary companies (H) declared a cash dividend of $20,000,000. It was offered an overdraft facility of this amount by a bank, the overdraft being secured by a deposit of that amount by S (so that, on payment of the dividend, the $20,000,000 effectively travelled in a circle). In September 1986 S sold a number of its subsidiary companies, including H, to B, and agreed not to compete with B in the liquid chromatography business. The agreement provided that B should pay $23,000,000 in total, of which $20,000,000 should be paid to the bank to clear the loan to H, and that $1,000 of the $23,000,000 related to the common stock of H. S appealed against an estimated assessment, contending that the consideration which it had received for the sale of H was only $1,000. The Special Commissioners rejected this contention and dismissed the appeal, holding that the effect of the agreement was that the consideration paid for the common stock of H was $20,001,000, since S 'could and did direct how that sum should be applied'. (The Commissioners noted that neither S nor the Revenue contended that the $20,000,000 should be apportioned between the assets of the liquid chromatography business.) The Ch D upheld the Commissioners' decision. Lightman J observed that, if the parties had intended that the sale of the common stock should be for $1,000, it would have been very simple to say so. Where a holding company sold a solvent subsidiary and the purchaser agreed to discharge a debt owed by that subsidiary, the amount of the debt would not necessarily constitute consideration for the shares in the subsidiary. However, in the case under appeal, the parties had specifically agreed that the amount of the debt should be allocated to the purchase price. Accordingly, on the wording of the specific agreements, the consideration for the common stock was $20,001,000. *Spectros International plc v Madden Ch D 1996, 70 TC 349; [1997] STC 114.*

Stanton v Drayton Commercial Investment Co Ltd 17.3

*Consideration satisfied by issue of shares — definition of 'value' in TCGA 1992, s 38(1)(a)**

In September 1972 a company (D) agreed to acquire investments from an insurance company for £3,937,632, to be paid by means of 2,461,226 shares in D at their issue price of 160p per share. The agreement was conditional on permission being obtained for the shares to be dealt in on the Stock Exchange. The agreement became unconditional on 11 October, when the shares were issued. On 12 October, when they were first quoted on the Stock Exchange, their middle market price was 125p per share. Subsequently D sold some of the investments it had acquired from the insurance company. The Revenue issued an assessment on the gains, in which the cost of the investments was computed on the basis that the shares in D should be valued at 125p each. D appealed, contending that the shares should be valued at 160p each. The CA allowed D's appeal and the HL upheld this decision. There had been an honest arm's length agreement in which the shares had been valued at 160p, and there was no reason for going behind this agreed value. Market value was only relevant where no agreed value was available. *Stanton v Drayton Commercial Investment Co Ltd HL 1982, 55 TC 286; [1982] STC 585; [1982] 3 WLR 214; [1982] 2 All ER 942.*

Steibelt v Paling 55.1, 55.3, 55.4

Rollover relief — extension of three-year time limit for replacing assets; whether trades carried on successively; application of ESC D24

A publican sold his business in October 1986 for approximately £130,000 realising a chargeable gain of approximately £52,000. In February 1988 he purchased a barge for £20,000, which he intended to convert into a wine bar and restaurant. Between December 1989 and November 1994 he incurred enhancement expenditure of approximately £160,000 on the barge. He eventually began to trade from it in August 1995. He claimed rollover relief in respect of the 1986 gain. The Ch D rejected the claim (reversing the General Commissioners' decision). Sir Richard Scott V-C held that whilst the Revenue's decision not to exercise their statutory discretion to extend the three-year time limit laid down by *TCGA 1992, s 152(3)* might be challenged by judicial review, it was not reviewable by the Commissioners. In any case, the two trades, separated by a gap of nine years, could not be said to be carried on 'successively' as required by *TCGA 1992, s 152(8)*. In addition, the terms of ESC D24 (assets not brought immediately into trading use) were not satisfied. *Steibelt v Paling Ch D 1999, 71 TC 376; [1999] STC 594.*

Stephenson v Barclays Bank Trust Co Ltd 57.2

Trust fund subject to annuities — whether beneficiaries absolutely entitled

Under a will, a fund was held in trust for such of the testator's grandchildren who should attain 21 years, subject to the payment of annuities to three daughters during widowhood. There were two grandchildren, both of whom had attained 21 before the relevant year. Under a deed of family arrangement entered into in 1968–69, a fund was appropriated for the annuities and a sum advanced to the grandchildren to purchase further income for the daughters with the intent that the balance of the trust fund, comprising mainly shares, should be transferred forthwith to the grandchildren. The trustees were assessed for 1968–69 on the footing of a notional disposal under *TCGA 1992, s 71(1)**, the grandchildren having become 'absolutely entitled as against' the trustees when the deed of family arrangement was entered into. The assessment was upheld. The trustees' contentions that the annuities were 'outgoings' within *TCGA 1992, s 60(2)** (with the result that the grandchildren became absolutely entitled when the younger attained 21) were rejected. *Kidson v Macdonald* followed as regards the construction of 'jointly' in *TCGA 1992, s 60(1)**. *Stephenson v Barclays Bank Trust Co Ltd Ch D 1974, 50 TC 374; [1975] STC 151; [1975] 1 WLR 882; [1975] 1 All ER 625.*

Strange v Openshaw 17.10

Grant of option to purchase land — whether a part disposal

Four brothers owned some agricultural land and their mother owned some adjoining land. They granted a company an option, exercisable within 10 years, to purchase the land on prescribed terms. (In the event, the option was not exercised.) The company paid £125,000 for the option, and the Revenue issued assessments on the brothers charging CGT on the amount each received. They appealed, contending that, by virtue of *TCGA 1992, s 144(2)**, no assessment should be raised until the option was exercised or abandoned. The Commissioners rejected this contention, holding that there had been a part disposal. Both sides appealed. The Ch D allowed the Revenue's cross-appeal and upheld the assessments, holding that *TCGA 1992, s 144** was not intended to supersede *TCGA 1992, s 21**, but provided how the chargeable gain on the grant of an option was to be computed. Accordingly, the whole amount of the option price, less the costs of granting it, was a chargeable gain under the general provisions of *TCGA 1992, s 144(1)**. The part disposal rules were not applicable to the grant of an option. *Strange v Openshaw (and related appeals) Ch D 1983, 57 TC 544; [1983] STC 416.*

Swires v Renton 57.6

Exercise of power of appointment — whether a deemed disposal

The trustees of a settlement executed a deed of appointment by which the trust fund was divided into two parts. One part of the fund was appointed to the settlor's daughter. The second part was placed on trust, the income to be paid to the daughter for life. It was accepted that the absolute appointment to the daughter gave rise to a deemed disposal of that part of the trust fund under *TCGA 1992, s 71(1)**, and CGT was assessed and paid accordingly. The inspector took the view that there had also been a deemed disposal of the second part of the fund, and issued a further CGT assessment on the grounds that a new and separate settlement of the appointed fund had been created. The principal trustee appealed, contending that the exercise of the power of appointment had not created a new settlement of the fund and had not amounted to a deemed disposal under *TCGA 1992, s 71(1)**. The Special Commissioner allowed the trustee's appeal and the Ch D upheld this decision. On the evidence, the assets of the appointed fund remained subject to the trusts of the original settlement as varied by the deed of appointment, and had not become subject to the trusts of a new settlement. Accordingly, the trustees' exercise of the power of appointment had not amounted to a deemed disposal under *TCGA 1992, s 71(1)**. *Swires v Renton Ch D 1991, 64 TC 315; [1991] STC 490.*

Tarmac Roadstone Holdings Ltd v Williams 21.5

Dollar floating rate notes — whether debts 'on a security'

In July 1986 a US company issued its UK parent company twelve loan notes of $5,000,000 each. The notes could only be transferred with the prior consent of the issuing company, which could be refused without any reason being given, and the issuing company could redeem them at any time. They were redeemed at par in December 1987. Because of the fall in value of the dollar, the UK company made a loss of more than £6,000,000. It claimed that this loss should be allowed against its chargeable gains. The Revenue rejected the claim, considering that the effect of *TCGA 1992, s 251(1)** was that there was no chargeable gain or allowable loss. The company appealed, contending that the loans were debts 'on a security', so that the loss was allowable. The Special Commissioners rejected this contention and dismissed the appeal. The distinguishing feature of a debt on a security was that it is 'in the nature of an investment which can be dealt in as such'. The loan notes in this case were not in the nature of investments, since they could only be transferred with the prior consent of the issuing company and that company could redeem them at any time. *Aberdeen Group Construction Ltd v CIR* and *dicta* in *WT Ramsay Ltd v CIR* applied. *Tarmac Roadstone Holdings Ltd v Williams (Sp C 95), [1996] SSCD 409.*

Taylor Clark International Ltd v Lewis 21.5

Loan to overseas subsidiary secured on property — whether a 'debt on a security'

In 1984 a company gave a promissory note for $15,193,000, repayable on demand, to a US subsidiary. The loan in question was repaid in two stages, in 1986 and 1992. Because of the fall in value of the dollar, the company made a loss on the loan. The company appealed against an assessment for its accounting period ending in 1992, contending that the loan was a 'debt on a security' and that the loss could be set against its chargeable gains. The Special Commissioners dismissed the appeal, holding that the loan was not a 'debt on a security', and the CA upheld their decision. The fact that a debt was secured did not necessarily mean that it qualified as a 'debt on a security'. On the evidence, the debt here was not a marketable security in any realistic sense. *Aberdeen Group Construction Ltd v CIR,* and *dicta* in *WT Ramsay Ltd v CIR*, applied. *Taylor Clark International Ltd v Lewis CA 1998, 71 TC 226; [1998] STC 1259.*

Tesco plc v Crimmin 3.19

*Depreciatory transaction within a group — TCGA 1992, s 176**

On 11 February 1991 S was a subsidiary company of H, which in turn was a subsidiary of T. On 12 February H sold S to T for well below its market value. This sale had the effect of reducing the market value of H from about £2,000,000,000 to about £2,000,000. On 14 February T sold H to an unrelated company for about £40,000,000 (this price reflected ACT prospectively recoverable by the purchaser). Subsequently T appealed against an assessment on chargeable gains, contending that the effect of indexation allowance (based on the value of H at 31 March 1982) was that it had made an allowable loss of some £740,000,000 on the sale of H. (At 31 March 1982 H had had a market value of £1,200,000,000, the indexation allowance on which was £778,000,000, and T contended that this figure should not be affected by the depreciatory transaction.) The Special Commissioners rejected this contention, holding that the loss on the sale of H was eliminated by *TCGA 1992, s 176**. The Ch D upheld this decision and dismissed T's appeal. *TCGA 1992, s 176** had to be applied to the allowable loss after indexation, rather than to the unindexed loss before indexation. The purpose of *section 176** was to negate the use of depreciatory transactions to produce allowable losses. *Tesco plc v Crimmin Ch D 1997, 69 TC 510; [1997] STC 981.*

Thompson v Salah 17.2

Sale coupled with mortgage to purchaser

A taxpayer's wife, having received an offer of £20,000 for land she owned, effected the sale by mortgaging the land to the purchaser for £20,000 and conveying the fee simple the next day in consideration of a release from her obligation to repay the £20,000. The taxpayer was assessed under Sch D, Case VII on the basis that the land had been sold for £20,000. He appealed, contending that the actual conveyance was for the equity of redemption of a nil market value. The Ch D held that the two transactions together constituted a conveyance on sale of the property free of the legal charge. *Thompson v Salah Ch D 1971, 47 TC 559; [1972] 1 All ER 530.*

Tod v Mudd 55.6

Quantum of relief where new asset used partly for business and partly owned by taxpayer as tenant in common

The taxpayer sold a business asset (part of the goodwill of his practice as accountant) for a chargeable gain of £155,688 in April 1982. On 1 June 1982 he and his wife entered into partnership to carry on business as hoteliers at a house being purchased in their joint names. The business was to be carried on in the part of the premises 'attributable to the share provided by' the taxpayer. The total cost of the property with the furniture and fittings and expenses was £209,093, and it was common ground that 75% of this cost (i.e. £156,820) was provided by the taxpayer, and that the premises were used as to 75% for business purposes. The property was transferred to the husband and wife upon trust as to 75% for the taxpayer and 25% for his wife as tenants in common. In an appeal against an assessment on the gain of £155,688 the issue was the taxpayer's entitlement to rollover relief. The Ch D held that since the taxpayer and his wife, as tenants in common, were entitled to an interest in every part of the property, the relief was 75% of the taxpayer's contribution to the cost (i.e. £117,615, being 75% of £156,820) and not £156,820 as contended by the taxpayer. *Tod v Mudd Ch D 1986, 60 TC 237; [1987] STC 141.*

Van Arkadie v Plunket 44.5

Foreign assets — delayed remittances — effect of TCGA 1992, s 279.*

A UK resident (P) owned one-third of the share capital of a Rhodesian company, which would have been a close company if it had been resident in the UK. The company made gains on the sale of assets outside the UK. Under *TCGA 1992, s 13**, part of the gains were treated as accruing to P, although the company did not make any distributions. Regulations imposed by the de facto Rhodesian government (which had made a unilateral declaration of independence from the UK) prohibited the company from paying dividends to shareholders resident in the UK. P claimed relief under *TCGA 1992, s 279**. The Ch D held that the relief was not due (reversing the General Commissioners' decision). *TCGA 1992, s 279** applied only where a gain was represented by money or money's worth in the hands of the taxpayer. P could not receive the money because the company had not made any distributions, so that *TCGA 1992, s 279** did not apply. *Van Arkadie v Plunket Ch D 1982, 56 TC 310; [1983] STC 54.*

Varty v Lynes 48.1

Part of garden retained on sale of house and subsequently sold

A taxpayer owned and occupied a house and garden (of less than one acre). He sold the house and part of the garden in June 1971. In May 1972, he sold at a substantial profit the rest of the garden for which he had meanwhile obtained planning permission. The Ch D upheld an assessment on the gain, rejecting the taxpayer's contention that it was exempted by *TCGA 1992, s 222**. *TCGA 1992, s 222(1)(b)** related only to the actual moment of disposal of the land and *TCGA 1992, s 222(2)** did not extend to a subsequent disposal. *Varty v Lynes Ch D 1976, 51 TC 419; [1976] STC 508; [1976] 1 WLR 1091; [1976] 3 All ER 447.*

Wase v Bourke 53.5

Retirement relief — sale of milk quota following cessation of dairy farming

In March 1988 a dairy farmer sold his entire herd. In February 1989, having reached the age of 60, he sold his milk quota. He appealed against a CGT assessment on the gain, contending that he was entitled to retirement relief on the basis that the sale of the milk quota was 'a disposal of the whole or part of a business'. The Ch D held that retirement relief was not due, since the milk quota was simply an asset and that its disposal was not the disposal of part of a business. The relevant business activity had ceased in March 1988 when the herd was sold. The subsequent disposal of another asset did not amount to the disposal of part of the business. *Atkinson v Dancer* applied; *Jarmin v Rawlings* distinguished. *Wase v Bourke Ch D 1995, 68 TC 109; [1996] STC 18.*

Watton v Tippett 55.1

Rollover relief (TCGA 1992, ss 152–162) — purchase of single property followed by sale of part of property

In 1988 a trader purchased some business premises. In 1989 he sold part of the premises at a profit. The Revenue issued a CGT assessment and he appealed, contending that he was entitled to treat the proceeds of sale as having been used in acquiring the balance of the premises, so that he was entitled to rollover relief under *TCGA 1992, s 152**. The CA rejected this contention and upheld the assessment. The disposal had been a part disposal of the original asset. The consideration which the trader had paid for the premises could not be divided and treated as partly attributable to the part of the premises which he subsequently sold and as partly attributable to the part which he retained. The premises had been acquired 'as a single asset and for an unapportioned consideration', and continued to constitute a single asset until the part disposal. *Watton v Tippett CA 1997, 69 TC 491; [1997] STC 893.*

Whitaker v Cameron 7.10

*Election for 6 April 1965 valuation — construction of TCGA 1992, Sch 2 para 17(1)(2)**

A taxpayer disposed in 1973 of land he had acquired in 1957; his appeal was against an assessment on the gain made on the time apportionment basis. The market value at 6 April 1965 was slightly above the disposal figure, but there had been no timeous application for a 6 April 1965 valuation under *TCGA 1992, Sch 2 para 17(1)**, and an extension of the time limit had been refused. If there had been a timeous application there would have been a no loss/no gain situation as a result of *Sch 2 para 17(2)**, and the taxpayer contended that it was unnecessary to make a 6 April 1965 valuation election where it would produce a no loss/no gain result. The Ch D rejected the contention. The two sub-paragraphs are closely bound up and *Sch 2 para 17(2)** has effect only if there has been an election under *Sch 2 para 17(1)**. *Whitaker v Cameron Ch D 1982, 56 TC 97; [1982] STC 665.*

Whittles v Uniholdings Ltd (No 3) 17.3

Company borrowing US dollars and entering forward contract to purchase sufficient dollars to repay loan — whether transactions to be taxed separately

In May 1982 a company borrowed some US dollars to finance an investment (the rate of interest on the dollar loan being less than the company could have obtained on a sterling loan). It simultaneously entered into a forward contract to purchase sufficient dollars to repay the loan when it matured some ten months later. During the intervening ten months the pound sterling depreciated substantially against the dollar. The Revenue treated the two transactions as separate, with the result that the company had made a loss on the dollar loan which was not allowable for CGT purposes, and had made a chargeable gain on the disposal of its rights under the forward contract. The CA upheld the Revenue's contentions (reversing the decision of the Special Commissioner). Nourse LJ held that the loan and the forward contract had to be considered separately. The fact that the subject matter of the forward contract was currency did not mean that the company had acquired a 'debt' within *TCGA 1992, s 251*. The forward contract was in substance no different from any contract for the sale of real or personal property with a deferred date for completion. In the absence of any specific provision to the contrary, it would be wrong in principle to value the acquisition cost of an asset on any date other than the actual date of acquisition. The cost of acquiring the US dollars had to be valued at May 1982 and their cost to the company was the value of its promise to repay them in March 1983, together with interest during that period. *Whittles v Uniholdings Ltd (No 3) CA, [1996] STC 914.*

Williams v Evans 55.3

Relief claimed on movable machinery

A civil engineering partnership sold some earth-moving vehicles at a profit and reinvested the proceeds in two similar machines. They appealed against a CGT assessment on the gain, claiming roll over relief. The Ch D dismissed their appeals. *TCGA 1992, s 155 (Class 1, Head B)** confined the relief to fixed plant and fixed machinery. The relief did not extend to movable machinery. *Williams v Evans & related appeals Ch D 1982, 59 TC 509; [1982] STC 498; [1982] 1 WLR 972.*

Williams v Merrylees 48.1

Private residence exemption

A taxpayer bought in 1956 a small estate in Sussex comprising a main house with 4 acres of garden and land and a lodge at the entrance of the estate, about 200 metres from the main house. The house became his main residence and the lodge was occupied by Mr and Mrs L whom he employed as caretaker/gardener and domestic help respectively. The house and lodge were rated together. Mrs L died in 1969. In 1976 the taxpayer sold the main house and estate apart from the lodge and a garden of less than an acre, and went to live in Cornwall in a house he had previously bought as a holiday home. He retained the lodge and allowed Mr L to live in it, in case he and his wife did not like their Cornwall house and decided to return to Sussex and live in the lodge. Mr L died in 1979 and the taxpayer then sold the lodge to the purchaser of the main house. The Commissioners held that the gain on the sale of the lodge was within the private residence exemption, finding as a matter of fact that from 1956 to 1976 the lodge had been part of the taxpayer's only or main residence and within the curtilage of the property and appurtenant to the main house. Vinelott J, after reviewing *Batey v Wakefield* and *Markey v Sanders*, considered that the test was whether there is an entity which can be sensibly described as being a dwelling-house although split up into different buildings performing different functions. The propinquity of the buildings is a relevant factor but should not be considered in isolation. Here, after considerable hesitation, he felt that it would be wrong for him to interfere with the Commissioners' decision as one inconsistent with the facts. *Williams v Merrylees Ch D 1987, 60 TC 297; [1987] STC 445; [1987] 1 WLR 1511.*

Willson v Hooker 44.3

*Sale of land — whether UK resident assessable as agent for Isle of Man company — TMA 1970, s 78**

An Isle of Man company realised a gain from the purchase and sale of land in Wales. The Revenue assessed the gain on an individual (W) who was resident in the UK, considering that he was acting as an agent of the company, within *TMA 1970, s 78.* The General Commissioners upheld the assessment and W appealed, contending that he was not assessable because he was not carrying on a 'regular agency', within *TMA 1970, s 82.* The Ch D rejected this contention and dismissed W's appeal, holding on the evidence that W 'was the person through whom all the transactions of (the company) in the United Kingdom were carried out during the relevant period'. *Willson v Hooker Ch D 1995, 67 TC 585; [1995] STC 1142.*

Young v Phillips 6.2

Location of letters of allotment

Two brothers resident and ordinarily resident in the UK, but domiciled in South Africa, owned equally the ordinary shares of three associated UK companies, each with substantial sums to the credit of its profit and loss account. On professional advice, during 1978–79 they implemented a pre-arranged scheme with the aim of 'exporting' the shares outside the UK (and so taking them outside the scope of capital transfer tax) without incurring any CGT liability. In brief, each company created new preferred ordinary shares, ranking pari passu with the existing ordinary shares save for priority in a capital repayment on a winding up; capitalised the amounts credited to profit and loss; appropriated these amounts to the taxpayers and used them in paying up, in full, new preferred ordinary shares issued to them, in respect of which the company issued to them renounceable letters of allotment. Shortly afterwards two Channel Island companies, set up for the purpose, issued to the taxpayers shares at a premium of £1,364,216 and resolved to buy from them (by now directors of the Channel Island companies) their preferred ordinary shares in the UK companies for £1,364,216. The taxpayers then went to Sark with their letters of allotment and the scheme was completed by, inter alia, letters of renunciation in favour of the Channel Island companies. CGT assessments were made on the basis that there had been a disposal of assets situated in the UK. The Special Commissioners dismissed the taxpayers' appeals, and the Ch D upheld their decision. Nicholls J held that there had been a disposal of rights against the UK companies, and that these were situated in the UK irrespective of where the letters of allotment happened to be. Further, even had he held that there had been a disposal of assets outside the UK, *W T Ramsay Ltd* and *Furniss v Dawson*, would have applied, and he would have accepted an alternative Revenue contention that *TCGA 1992, s 29(2)** applied, the relieving provisions of *TCGA 1992, ss 127, 135** being curtailed by *TCGA 1992, s 137(1)** because one of the main purposes of the issuing of the shares in the UK companies was the avoidance of liability to tax. *Young and Another v Phillips Ch D 1984, 58 TC 232; [1984] STC 520.*

Zim Properties Ltd v Proctor 6.1, 17.7

Amount received as part of out-of-court settlement — whether derived from an asset

In July 1973 a company (Z) contracted to sell three properties. The date of completion was fixed for 12 July 1974. However, the sale of the properties was not completed, because the original conveyance to one of them had been lost and Z was unable to provide proof of ownership. The purchaser refused to complete and successfully sued Z for the return of its deposit. Z issued a writ against its solicitors, claiming damages of more than £100,000. Following negotiations, Z agreed to accept payment of £69,000 in two instalments, in settlement of its claim. The Revenue included the amount of the first instalment as a chargeable gain in a CT assessment. Z appealed, contending that the gain was not chargeable since it had not been derived from an asset. The Special Commissioners held that the amount was a capital sum derived from Z's right against its solicitors, and that it was acquired for the purposes of *CGTA 1979, s 19(3)* otherwise than by way of an arm's length agreement, so that its market value was deductible. The Ch D upheld this decision (against which both sides had appealed) and referred the case back to the Commissioners for figures to be agreed. *O'Brien v Benson's Hosiery (Holdings) Ltd* applied. *Zim Properties Ltd v Proctor (and cross-appeal) Ch D 1984, 58 TC 371; [1985] STC 90.*

(Notes. (1) See now ESC D33. (2) *CGTA 1979, s 19(3)* was subsequently repealed; see now *TCGA 1992, s 17.*)

69 Table of Cases

Where the CIR (or, in Scotland, the Lord Advocate) are a party, the case is listed under the name of the other party only. Judicial review cases are listed under the name of the applicant and the person who is the subject of the review but again excluding the CIR etc.

69 Table of Cases

Keren Kayemeth Le Jisroel Ltd *v* CIR HL 1932: 17 TC 27; [1932] AC 650; [1932] All E R 971; 11 ATC 237.	10.2
Kerr, Marshall *v* HL 1994: 67 TC 56; [1994] STC 638; [1994] 3 WLR 299; [1994] 2 All E R 106.	16.6; 43.13; 68
Khan *v* Edwards Ch D 1977: 53 TC 597; [1977] TR 143.	4.8
Kidson *v* Macdonald & Another Ch D 1973: 49 TC 503; [1974] STC 54; [1974] Ch 339; [1974] 1 All E R 849; 52 ATC 318.	57.2
Kime, Coy *v* Ch D 1986: 59 TC 447; [1987] STC 114.	4.8
King *v* Walden; Johnson *v* Walden CA 1995: 68 TC 387; [1996] STC 382.	4.8
Kingston & Elmbridge Commrs, R *v*, ex p. Adams QB 1972: 48 TC 75.	4.5
Kingston Smith, ex p. (R *v* CIR) QB 1996: 70 TC 264.	9.8
Kington, Gubay *v* HL 1984: 57 TC 601; [1984] STC 99; [1984] 1 WLR 163; [1984] 1 All E R 513.	52.3; 68
Kinloch *v* CIR KB 1929: 14 TC 736; 8 ATC 469.	52.4
Kirby *v* Thorn EMI plc CA 1987, 60 TC 519; [1987] STC 621 (and see 1988 STI 90); [1988] 1 WLR 445; [1988] 2 All E R 947.	6.1; 17.7; 55.3; 68
Kirkby *v* Hughes Ch D 1992: 65 TC 532; [1993] STC 76.	36.3
Kirkham *v* Williams CA 1991: 64 TC 253; [1991] STC 342; [1991] 1 WLR 863; [1991] 4 All E R 240.	36.3
Kirklees Metropolitan Borough Council, Pennine Raceway Ltd *v* CA 1988: [1989] STC 122.	17.7
Kissane, ex p., R *v* HMIT QB 1986: [1986] STC 152; [1986] 2 All E R 37.	4.10
Kneen *v* Martin CA 1934: 19 TC 33; [1935] 1 KB 499; [1934] All E R 595; 13 ATC 454.	51.2
Knight, Eke *v* CA 1977: 51 TC 121; [1977] STC 198.	4.8
Knight *v* CIR CA 1974: 49 TC 179; [1974] STC 156; [1974] TR 19; 53 ATC 18.	9.4
Knight, ex p., R *v* Havering Commrs CA 1973: 49 TC 161; [1973] STC 564; [1973] 3 All E R 721.	47.11
Lack *v* Doggett CA 1970: 46 TC 497; [1970] TR 69.	4.9
Lamb, Anderton *v* Ch D 1980: 55 TC 1; [1981] STC 43 (and see 1982 STI 179); [1981] TR 393.	55.3
Lance Webb Estates Ltd *v* Aller Ch D 1954: 35 TC 305.	36.3
Lane, Marriott *v* Ch D 1996: 69 TC 157; [1996] STC 704; [1996] 1 WLR 111.	53.5; 68
Lane, Rank Xerox Ltd *v* HL 1979: 53 TC 185; [1979] STC 740; [1981] AC 629; [1979] 3 WLR 594; [1979] 3 All E R 657.	4.9; 21.3; 68
Lang *v* Rice CA (NI) 1983: 57 TC 80; [1984] STC 172.	17.7
Lansing Bagnall Ltd, ex p., R *v* HMIT and Others CA 1986: 61 TC 112; [1986] STC 453.	4.10
Larner *v* Warrington Ch D 1985: 58 TC 557; [1985] STC 442.	4.8; 68
Last, Turner *v* Ch D 1965: 42 TC 517; [1965] TR 249; 44 ATC 234.	36.3

Roome and Another *v* Edwards 57.6; 68
HL 1981: 54 TC 359; [1981] STC 96; [1982] AC 279; [1981] 2 WLR 268; [1981] 1 All E R 736.

Rose *v* Humbles 4.8
CA 1971: 48 TC 103; [1972] 1 WLR 33; [1972] 1 All E R 314; 50 ATC 373.

Rose, Re, Rose and Others *v* CIR 17.2; 23.1
CA 1952: [1952] Ch 499; [1952] 1 All E R 1217.

Rose Smith & Co Ltd *v* CIR 12.7
KB 1933: 17 TC 586; 12 ATC 59.

Rosette Franks (King St) Ltd *v* Dick 4.8
Ch D 1955: 36 TC 100.

Rossminster Ltd, ex p., R *v* CIR 9.8
HL 1979: 52 TC 160; [1980] STC 42; [1980] 2 WLR 1; [1979] 3 All E R 385; [1979] TR 427.

Rothschild (J) Holdings plc, ex p., R *v* CIR 4.10; 28.1
CA 1987: 61 TC 178; [1987] STC 163.

Rothwell, Fox *v* 4.6
(Sp C 50), [1995] SSCD 336.

Rowe, Gamble *v* 4.8
Ch D 1998: [1998] STC 1247.

Roxburghe's (Duke of) Executors *v* CIR 51.2
CS 1936: 20 TC 711.

Royal Antediluvian Order of Buffaloes *v* Owens 10.2
KB 1927: 13 TC 176; [1928] 1 KB 446; 6 ATC 920.

Royal Choral Society *v* CIR 10.2
CA 1943: 25 TC 263; [1943] 2 All E R 101.

Royal Naval & Royal Marine Officers' Association, CIR *v* 10.2
Ch D 1955: 36 TC 187; [1955] TR 169; 34 ATC 182.

Rushden Heel Co. *v* Keene 4.11
HL 1948: 30 TC 298; [1948] 2 All E R 378; 27 ATC 141.

Ryall, Cardinal Vaughan Memorial School Trustees *v* 10.2
KB 1920; 7 TC 611.

Sainsbury (J) plc *v* O'Connor 13.11
CA 1991: 64 TC 208; [1991] STC 318; [1991] 1 WLR 963.

St Anne Westminster Commrs, Sen *v* 47.11
Ch D 1983: [1983] STC 415.

St Aubyn Estates Ltd *v* Strick 36.3
KB 1932: 17 TC 412; 12 ATC 31.

St Giles & St George Commrs, R *v*, ex p. Hooper 5.2
KB 1915: 7 TC 59.

St Marylebone Commrs ex p. Hay, R *v* 4.8
CA 1983: 57 TC 59; [1983] STC 346.

St Pancras Commrs, R *v*, ex p. Church of Scientology of California 4.5
QB 1973: 50 TC 365; [1973] STC 417.

Salah, Thompson *v* 17.2; 68
Ch D 1971: 47 TC 559; [1972] 1 All E R 530.

Salmon *v* Havering Commrs & CIR 47.11
CA 1968: 45 TC 77.

Salt *v* Young 4.8
(Sp C 205), [1999] SSCD 249.

Sanders, Markey *v* 48.1; 68
Ch D 1987: 60 TC 245; [1987] STC 256; [1987] 1 WLR 864.

Sansom & Another *v* Peay 48.6; 68
Ch D 1976: 52 TC 1; [1976] STC 494; [1976] 1 WLR 1073; [1976] 3 All E R 375; [1976] TR 205.

Sarsfield, Honig and Another *v* 5.5
CA 1986: 59 TC 337; [1986] STC 246.

Sassen, Hawkings-Byass *v* (and related appeals) 40.3; 68
(Sp C 88), [1996] SSCD 319.

Strange *v* Openshaw — 17.10; 68
Ch D 1983: 57 TC 544; [1983] STC 416.

Strick, St Aubyn Estates Ltd *v* — 36.3
KB 1932: 17 TC 412; 12 ATC 31.

Strick *v* Regent Oil Co Ltd — 33.1
HL 1965: 43 TC 1; [1966] AC 295; [1965] 3 WLR 696; [1965] 3 All E R 174; [1965] TR 277; 44 ATC 264.

Stroud Commrs & Morgan, Gibson *v* — 4.6; 4.8
Ch D 1989: 61 TC 645; [1989] STC 421.

Sugarwhite *v* Budd — 36.4
CA 1988: 60 TC 679; [1988] STC 533.

Sulley, Lloyd *v* — 52.3
CES 1884: 2 TC 37.

Sutherland & Partners *v* Barnes and Another — 4.9
CA 1994: 66 TC 663; [1994] STC 387; [1994] 3 WLR 735; [1994] 4 All E R 1.

Swedish Central Railway Co Ltd *v* Thompson — 52.6
HL 1925: 9 TC 342; [1925] AC 495; [1924] All E R 710; 4 ATC 163.

Swires *v* Renton — 57.6; 68
Ch D 1991: 64 TC 315; [1991] STC 490.

T & E Homes Ltd *v* Robinson — 46.4
CA 1979: 52 TC 567; [1979] STC 351; [1979] 1 WLR 452; [1979] 2 All E R 522.

Talib *v* Waterson — 4.8
Ch D 1980: [1980] STC 563; [1980] TR 253.

Tamosius & Partners, ex p. (R *v* CIR) — 9.8
QB 1999: [1999] STC 1077.

Tarmac Roadstone Holdings Ltd *v* Williams — 21.5; 68
(Sp C 95), [1996] SSCD 409.

Tavistock Commrs, R *v*, ex p. Adams (No 1) — 4.8
QB 1969: 46 TC 154.

Tavistock Commrs, R *v*, ex p. Adams (No 2) — 5.1
CA 1971: 48 TC 56.

Tavistock Commrs, R *v*, ex p. Worth & Another — 4.10
QB 1985: 59 TC 116; [1985] STC 564.

Taylor Clark International Ltd *v* Lewis — 21.5; 68
CA 1998: [1998] STC 1259.

Taylor, Ewart *v* — 43.20; 68
Ch D 1983: 57 TC 401; [1983] STC 721.

Taylor, Government of India *v* (re Delhi Electric Supply & Traction Co. Ltd) — 44.16
HL 1955: [1955] AC 491; [1955] 2 WLR 303; [1955] 1 All E R 292; [1955] TR 9; 34 ATC 10.

Taylor, Hurley *v* — 9.2
CA 1998: 71 TC 268; [1999] STC 1.

Taylor *v* Bethnal Green Commrs and CIR — 47.11
Ch D 1976: [1977] STC 44; [1976] TR 289.

Taylor *v* Good — 36.3
CA 1974: 49 TC 277; [1974] STC 148; [1974] 1 WLR 556; [1974] 1 All E R 1137; [1974] TR 15; 53 ATC 14.

Taylor, ex p., R *v* CIR (No 1) — 4.10; 9.8
CA 1988: 62 TC 562; [1988] STC 832; [1989] 1 All E R 906.

Taylor, ex p., R *v* CIR (No 2) — 9.8
CA 1990: 62 TC 578; [1990] STC 379; [1990] 2 All E R 409.

Tebrau (Johore) Rubber Syndicate Ltd *v* Farmer — 36.3
CES 1910: 5 TC 658.

Temperance Council of the Christian Churches of England and Wales, CIR *v* — 10.2
KB 1926: 10 TC 748; 5 ATC 679.

Temperley *v* Visibell Ltd — 55.1
Ch D 1973: 49 TC 129; [1974] STC 64; 52 ATC 308.

Tempest Estates Ltd *v* Walmsley — 36.3
Ch D 1975: 51 TC 305; [1976] STC 10; [1975] TR 275; 54 ATC 313.

70 Table of Statutes

Note. The legislation cited in this publication has been divided into three sections, viz. Miscellaneous Legislation, Main Taxing Acts and Statutory Instruments.

MISCELLANEOUS LEGISLATION
(in alphabetical order)

70 Table of Statutes

STATUTORY INSTRUMENTS

Note. Statutory Instruments (SIs) referred to at 18.2, 18.3 DOUBLE TAX RELIEF are not listed below. Also not listed are those SIs which do no more than confirm indexed rises in tax rates and allowances as announced in the Budget or which alter the rates of interest on overpaid and unpaid tax, though these are referred to in the text where appropriate.

The list below is in date order.

1997	No 57	Electronic Lodgement of Tax Returns Order 1997	54.16
	No 511	Personal Equity Plan (Amendment) Regulations 1997	58.22
	No 991	Finance Act 1997, Schedule 10, (Appointed Day) Order 1997	58.25
	No 1154	Open-ended Investment Companies (Tax) Regulations 1997	64.4
	No 1603	Finance Act 1997, Section 110, (Appointed Day) Order 1997	28.2
	No 1715	Open-ended Investment Companies (Tax) (Amendment) Regulations 1997	64.4
	No 1716	Personal Equity Plan (Amendment No 2) Regulations 1997	58.22
	No 2491	Income Tax (Payments on Account) (Amendment) Regulations 1997	56.15
	No 2681	Lloyd's Underwriters (Scottish Limited Partnerships) (Tax) Regulations 1997	63.1
1998	No 310	Taxes (Interest Rate) (Amendment) Regulations 1998	35.1
	No 311	Finance Act 1989, Section 178(1), (Appointed Day) Order 1998	35.1
	No 1869	Personal Equity Plan (Amendment) Regulations 1998	58.22
	No 1870	Individual Savings Account Regulations 1998	21.27
	No 1871	Individual Savings Account (Insurance Companies) Regulations 1998	21.27
	No 2244	Government of Wales Act 1998 (Commencement No 1) Order 1998	21.44; 21.52
	No 3173	Finance Act 1994, Section 199, (Appointed Day) Order 1998	13.2; 56.2
	No 3174	Individual Savings Account (Amendment) Regulations 1998	21.27
	No 3175	Corporation Tax (Instalment Payments) Regulations 1998	34.3; 35.6; 46.2
	No 3176	Taxes (Interest Rate) (Amendment No 2) Regulations 1998	34.3; 35.6
	No 3177	European Single Currency (Taxes) Regulations 1998	6.1; 13.1; 13.43; 17.10; 21.5; 44.1; 58.11; 58.25
1999	No 527	Social Security Contributions (Transfer of Functions, etc) Act 1999 (Commencement No 1 and Transitional Provisions) Order 1999	28.4
	No 564	Finance Act 1993, Section 86(2), (Fish Quota) Order 1999	55.3
	No 819	Venture Capital Trust (Amendment) Regulations 1999	65.7
	No 1928	Taxes (Interest Rate) (Amendment No 2) Regulations 1999	34.3
	No 1929	Corporation Tax (Instalment Payments) (Amendment) Regulations 1999	46.2
	No 1953	Capital Gains Tax (Definition of Permanent Interest Bearing Share) Regulations 1999	49.2
	No 2975	Corporation Tax (Simplified Arrangements for Group Relief) Regulations 1999	54.11
	No 3292	Special Commissioners (Jurisdiction and Procedure) (Amendment) Regulations 1999	4.8

1999 No 3293	General Commissioners (Jurisdiction and Procedure) (Amendment) Regulations 1999	4.8; 4.9
No 3294	Special Commissioners (Amendment of the Taxes Management Act 1970) Regulations 1999	4.9
No 3308	Lloyd's Underwriters (Special Reserve Funds) Regulations 1999	63.1
2000 No 809	Individual Savings Account (Amendment) Regulations 2000	21.27
No 892	Corporation Tax (Instalment Payments) (Amendment) Regulations 2000	46.2
No 893	Taxes (Interest Rate) (Amendment) Regulations 2000	35.6
No 945	Income Tax (Electronic Communications) Regulations 2000	27.9

71 Index

This index is referenced to the chapter number or to the chapter and paragraph number. The entries printed in bold capitals are main subject headings in the text.

71 Index

71 Index

L

Seize control with

Tolley

Tolley's Taper Relief

***Mike Cochrane**, senior tax partner at Lathams Chartered Accountants*

The changes to business asset taper relief made in this year's Finance Act hold out the prospect of huge benefits for business owners - but the rules contain complex compliance 'traps' that every entrepreneur, tax specialist, accountant and advisor needs to understand.

Allowing up to 75% of the gain on a qualifying business asset to be free of capital gains tax, Taper is one of the most valuable tax reliefs available - but one for which careful, well informed planning is a must.

The first major work on the subject, **Tolley's Taper Relief** incorporates all the major Taper Relief changes in the Finance Act 2000 and explains the complicated and often ambiguous pitfalls in clear terms to avoid misinterpretation.

Tolley's Taper Relief, first edition:

- Brings all the guidance relating to Taper Relief together in a clear and unambiguous format
- Clarifies the complex timing and compliance issues to allow confident tax planning that will secure maximum Taper Relief
- Dispels the myths and misinterpretations surrounding relief on capital gains tax
- Is ideal for accountants in general practice, tax practitioners, business owners and anyone whose work brings them into contact with capital gains tax
- Fully updated for the Finance Act 2000 which has brought substantial improvements to the position of business assets

Product Code: TR01 Price: £44.95 ISBN: 0 7545 1086 7 Publication Date: December 2000

How To Order

To order, please contact Butterworths Tolley Customer Service Dept:
Butterworths Tolley, FREEPOST SEA 4177, Croydon, Surrey CR9 5WZ
Telephone: 020 8662 2000 Fax: 020 8662 2012

Butterworths Tolley

A member of the Reed Elsevier plc group

25 Victoria Street, London SW1H 0EX
VAT number: 730 8595 20
Registered Office Number: 2746621

NB: Your data may be used for direct marketing purposes by selected companies

Butterworths Tax Direct Service is the ultimate on-line service that provides you with instant access to the most authoritative information ... all via the internet.
For more information on all of our products, please visit our website at www.butterworths.com